W0008649

Annals of Communism

THE COMPLETE MAISKY DIARIES

VOLUME 2

THE RIBBENTROP-MOLOTOV PACT AND THE BATTLE OF BRITAIN 1939–1940

EDITED BY GABRIEL GORODETSKY

Translated by Tatiana Sorokina and Oliver Ready

Yale UNIVERSITY PRESS
NEW HAVEN AND LONDON

Published with the permission of the Scheffer-Voskressenski family—Ivan Maisky's heirs. Photographs from Agniya Maisky's album are published with the permission of the Voskressenski family, owners of the copyright and Ivan Maisky's heirs.

Yale University Press books may be purchased in quantity for educational, business, or promotional use. For information, please e-mail sales.press@yale.edu (U.S. office) or sales@yaleup.co.uk (U.K. office).

Set in Minion Pro and ITC Stone Sans type by Newgen.
Printed in the United States of America.

Library of Congress Control Number: 2017942542
ISBN 978-0-300-11782-0 (hardcover : alk. paper)

A catalogue record for this book is available from the British Library.

This paper meets the requirements of ANSI/NISO Z39.48-1992 (Permanence of Paper).

10 9 8 7 6 5 4 3 2 1

Contents

1939

10 January

A new year. What will it bring?

I anticipate a stormy and difficult year, perhaps even a decisive one for our epoch. We shall see…

We celebrated the New Year in Paris. Agniya and I got away for five or six days to have a change of scene. We were sick and tired of our customary London surroundings. We had a good time. Spent much of it wandering around Paris – a wonderful city! What a shame that it is the capital of a country in deep decay. We visited museums, picture galleries and theatres – we saw nearly all the fashionable plays – and, of course, I chatted a lot with S. [Surits] about various political topics.

I returned to London on the 4th, but Agniya is still in Paris. She should be back on the 15th.

51. Before the storm: a break in Paris.

I brought a cold home from Paris. I somehow made it back, but I more or less had to take to my bed on arrival. But even this state has its charms: I'm reading a great deal. I rarely get the chance – the newspapers and the daily hustle and bustle get in the way.

19 January

I congratulate you, Ivan Mikhailovich, on an important birthday: today you are 55 years old!

I've lived more than half a century. And what a time to live! The thread of my life has stretched along the boundary of two great epochs: the end of capitalism and the beginning of socialism.

I've experienced and lived through a lot, thought and felt a great deal during these 55 years. There have been plenty of good things and bad things. But still, when I sum it all up I have to say: 'To life!'

What does the future hold? Who can say?

Looking back now, I can see that my life has included a fair quantity of 'elements of a planned character' in spite of its turbulent current, its numerous jolts and unexpected twists and turns. I was able to set myself definite tasks, sometimes years in advance, and to carry them out. Perseverance and good organization are aspects of my character. And now, when I think of the future, I still cannot get by without some sort of 'plan'.

What does my 'plan' amount to?

Leaving aside unpredictable and unexpected events, which our time has more than enough of, I am mapping out the following tentative 'plan for the end of my life' (the end, after all, is not so far off).

Judging by my current state of health (and leaving aside, once again, unforeseen incidents and circumstances), I can hope to live to about 75. So I have about 20 years at my disposal. I am dividing this period into two more or less equal parts. The next ten years, until I turn 65, can be devoted to active work in the service of the party and the state, that is, in the service of socialism. Considering my experience, knowledge, training and so on, it would be most expedient for me to remain in the sphere of foreign policy. The following ten years, between the ages of 65 and 75, should be devoted to summing up and 'rounding off' my life, and specifically to writing my memoirs, which I may choose to entitle 'The Novel of My Life'. For the events of my life (until now, at least) really have resembled those of a very colourful and entertaining novel. I would feel that I had failed in my duty towards the older and younger generations and to future historians if I died without leaving a 'human document', such as my memoirs would represent. The epoch of which I was a contemporary and in which I played a part has provided an infinite supply of interesting and deeply instructive events, and there are few people who wield a pen with sufficient skill to commit them to paper. This places a very special responsibility on every writer.

Judging by many indications, the second imperialist war may reach its climax within the next ten years, that is, within the remaining period of my full activity. I'll make every effort to facilitate its liquidation with maximum advantage for the cause of socialism. Then (if I stay alive) I will have an even greater store of vivid and rich material for my memoirs.

20 January

I saw Vansittart after a six-week interval. I found him in a state of great anxiety. The situation in Europe, he believes, is exceptionally dangerous: 1939 is going to be a critical year (I heard the same from Cadogan the other day). Hitler and Mussolini are intoxicated by their success. They have lost their equilibrium and are preparing for crazy adventures. Hitler, in particular, is now setting global domination as his goal. Both dictators think that the time is ripe for action: they are gambling on 'defects in armaments' and 'internal discord' in Britain and France, as well as on 'isolationist sentiments' and 'domestic weakness' in the Soviet Union. Growing economic difficulties are also pushing Hitler and Mussolini towards foreign adventures. An explosion is inevitable in the near future, but where? In the west, most likely, but one cannot rule out the east either. If the Spanish government is finally crushed, Mussolini will immediately make heavy demands on France. He will be guaranteed the support of Germany. A decisive moment will then ensue for Britain and France. Vansittart believes that on this occasion the reaction of the two 'democracies' will be sharply negative. If the dictators try to resort to force, war will be a firm possibility. In this connection, Vansittart inquired about our position and asserted that the interests of Britain, France and the USSR are identical and that Hitler's tactics are to crush one country after another, just as an artichoke is eaten one leaf at a time.

I observed that Vansittart was making his points to the wrong party. The USSR has always supported collective security, but what about Britain and France? In the last three years they have systematically undermined the principles of the L[eague] of N[ations]. I fail to see any signs that might indicate a shift in their attitude. On the contrary, there are signs to suggest that they are sinking ever deeper in that swamp.

'What do you mean?' Vansittart asked.

'Take for instance the fuss, kicked up by some groups of British industrialists and evidently supported by the Board of Trade, about the demand for the renunciation of the Anglo-Soviet trade agreement.'

Vansittart, who was clearly not up to date on this matter, asked me to acquaint him with the details. I was only too glad to brief him and pointed out that, given the present alignment of forces, Britain would not be able to obtain a more advantageous agreement under any conditions, even if the current one were renounced. For, in the past five years, the USSR has become considerably stronger and wealthier, and less dependent on imports than it was when the present agreement was signed.

'In February 1934,' I concluded, 'I recommended my government to accept the agreement which was then signed. If I had to conduct trade negotiations again now, I would not consider it possible to recommend signing a similar document. The alignment of forces has changed in our favour and this would have to be reflected in the character of the trade agreement.'

Vansittart was concerned. He thought it absurd to renounce the agreement just because we were buying more re-exports than purely British goods. The political effect of the renunciation would far outweigh its potential economic consequences.

'Renunciation would be most unfortunate,' Vansittart concluded.

And he immediately asked his secretary to summon Collier after lunch so as to discuss the matter with him.

22 January

Saw Attlee. He is in low spirits. Says that the ground is crumbling under Chamberlain, but that Labour is gaining nothing from it. The average voter is perturbed and perplexed; he is unhappy with the government and has no trust in the opposition. If an election were called today, Chamberlain would win again – unconvincingly, perhaps, but he would win.

Attlee's foreign-policy forecast is the following: if Franco wins, Mussolini will immediately make demands on France and Hitler will back him up. How will France respond? It all depends on the nature of the demands. If Mussolini shows relative moderation, France may meekly swallow the pill. But if Mussolini asks too high a price, then… then it is difficult to say what may happen. One cannot rule out the possibility that France will have to put up resistance, and England will support her.

26 January

Barcelona has fallen. The very thought of it makes my heart bleed. Over the past two and a half years, when fate has bound me so closely to the fortunes of Spain, I identified with the heroic struggle of the Spanish Republic. Its victories were my victories, and its defeats my defeats. Strange as it may seem, it's as if we, in the Soviet Union, suddenly rediscovered the Spanish people afresh. Never in the past have the destinies of Spain and Russia intersected. We knew little about this country and her people. We never took an interest in them. It is only now, in the din and thunder of the Spanish war, that we have suddenly come to understand and feel how wonderful, proud and heroic the Spanish nation is and what reserves of revolutionary energy it has accumulated over long years of oppression and suffering…

Barcelona has fallen. I fear that this is the beginning of the end.

Azcárate came to see me today. Despite the tragic events, he has not lost his fortitude and dignity. He has just returned from Geneva (the League of Nations) and Paris. He informed me that yesterday there was a meeting of the Spanish government and the Basque and Catalan presidents in the new temporary 'capital', Figueres, right by the French border. The decision was taken to continue fighting. The mountains of northern Catalonia are better suited for defensive operations. The people in these parts have been distinguished since ancient times for showing greater staunchness and martial spirit than the inhabitants of the Catalan plains. The border between France and Spain is now open. Arms are coming in. In short, the situation is difficult, but not hopeless.

I listened to Azcárate and supported him fiercely. But I couldn't help thinking: will this work?

27 January

I paid a visit to Halifax to discuss the Äland Islands issue.[1] The Finns, backed up by the Swedes, want to fortify the islands. Against whom? The official reply says: against Germany. But, in the first place, even if the Finns wished quite sincerely to remain neutral in the event of war, how could they defend the Äland Islands against occupation by Hitler? Secondly, where are the guarantees that the Finns really will adhere to neutrality? Given the close links that exist between the Finnish militarists and German fascism, there is every reason to fear the opposite. It follows that in both cases the Finns will be serving the German cause by fortifying the Äland Islands. The Germans may even give them money to build the fortifications. In conclusion: we are against the fortification of the Äland Islands and for the preservation of the 1921 convention on their demilitarization.

In light of the fact that the Finns and Swedes recently sent identical notes regarding the fortification of the Äland Islands to all parties to the convention (including Britain) and also to us, I set forth our point of view on the matter to Halifax. This clearly interested him. He summed up our objections in the following way: 'So you are against the fortification of the Äland Islands because you fear they might end up as a gift to Germany, as happened with the Czech Maginot line?'

'Roughly speaking, yes,' I answered.

Halifax promised to take our considerations into account when drawing up Britain's response to the Finno-Swedish démarche, but he would not undertake any firmer commitments. We shall see what happens next. Time is still on our side. The Finns and Swedes want to give us, as a country not party to the convention, the chance to participate in resolving the issue and are putting it on the agenda of the May session of the League's Council.

Then, on his own initiative, Halifax asked me what I thought about the situation in Europe. I answered vaguely: 'A new crisis seems to be approaching.'

Halifax agreed with this, but said that it was not quite clear to him where it would come from and what shape it might take. He wished to know my opinion. I put forward the supposition that this time the storm might start at the Italian end of the Axis. Halifax agreed, but added that he was greatly troubled by the situation in Belgium and the Netherlands. Then he continued: 'Do you think that Mussolini might risk war over his demands on France?'

Halifax finds it improbable that Italy will fight over Tunisia, Djibouti and Corsica. I answered: 'But Mussolini is counting on a bloodless victory over France, of the sort gained by Hitler over Czechoslovakia last year.'

'It's inconceivable!' Halifax exclaimed with uncharacteristic emotion. 'France's attitude to Italy's demands differs from its attitude to the Sudeten problem. Look, through his declaration Mussolini achieved what not a single Frenchman has ever managed to do: he united France as never before. England will certainly support France. A second Munich is impossible.'

To strengthen his case, Halifax referred to yesterday's speeches by Daladier and Bonnet in the Chamber. I smiled and replied: 'We have been through so many disappointments during the past two years that I would not vouch for anything when it comes to the question of how Britain and France might act. Time will tell. As for the speeches made by the French ministers, for now these are only words. As yet, we have seen no deeds. Besides, any statement made by Bonnet is seen…'

Halifax smiled knowingly, nodded, and drawled in a funny way: 'Oh yes, the attitude to Bonnet's speeches is…'

'Somewhat specific,' I finished off, 'especially in Germany and Italy.'

Halifax nodded again. Then he asked what I meant by the 'deeds' which could testify to the genuine impossibility of a second Munich.

'Had France,' I said, 'seriously intended to resist the Italian demands, the first thing it ought to have done straightaway was to alter radically its Spanish policy. From the French point of view, rendering effective assistance to the Spanish Republic would be not only noble, but advantageous as well. It would be "cheaper" to rebuff Italy on Spanish territory with Spanish forces than on French territory with French forces. Meanwhile, the Daladier–Bonnet government clings stubbornly to the old, obsolete phantom: notorious "non-intervention". In this context, my doubts are more than valid. But I am not taking any decisions at the moment. I am prepared to wait dispassionately for further developments.'

Halifax recognized the justice of my scepticism, but assured me once again that this time it would be different from last September.

Then Halifax inquired about the state of our relations with Poland and Germany. He was interested, in particular, in press reports about the forthcoming visit of a German delegation to Moscow for trade negotiations. I confirmed that such a delegation was expected, that the initiative came entirely from the German side, and that in keeping with our general principles we were ready to consider the offers Hitler was planning to make. Halifax asked: 'How would you explain this move by Hitler?'

I replied that to my mind Hitler's motives are clear: Germany's need for raw materials and the deterioration in Anglo-Soviet trade relations as a result of the campaign waged by certain groups for the renunciation of the Anglo-Soviet trade agreement of 1934. Following his trusty nose, Hitler hopes to gain from this 'squabble'.

Halifax was manifestly disturbed and began asking detailed questions about the state of Anglo-Soviet trade and about the campaign against the trade agreement. I provided him with all the essential details.

'And you think that renunciation would have very adverse political consequences?' Halifax asked.

'I have not the slightest doubt.'

'I will speak about this with the trade minister,' concluded Halifax in obvious alarm.

30 January

Saw several 'Soviet Spaniards' on their way home from Catalonia. Some of them stayed in Spain for a year and a half or two years and have an excellent knowledge of the situation there.

Our 'Spaniards' are pessimistic about the fighting prospects in Catalonia. The Republicans have been left with so little territory that the air force has almost no room to manoeuvre. There are no fortified positions in northern Catalonia. It would take at least a month to construct them. In the meantime, Franco continues to attack. Under these circumstances it is very difficult to hold on.

It's most distressing! It seems that my fears may be realized.

The statistics passed on by our comrades are shocking. The ratio of air forces committed to action in recent battles by the Republic and Franco was 1 to 10 (less than 100 Republican aircraft on all fronts and more than 900 on

Franco's side). Moreover, the Republicans have mainly old and battered aircraft, whereas Franco's are brand new. Especially grave is the Republicans' lack of bombers: they have 11 and the insurgents have 300 – roughly 1 to 30! The fighter situation is a bit better: 80 against 600, i.e. about 1 to 8. A similar gap in artillery. Franco can deploy between 50 and 60 pieces per kilometre of the front, against the Republicans' 7–8. The Republicans have a negligible quantity of anti-aircraft weapons. They have few tanks, machine-guns and even rifles.

And yet such furious and stubborn resistance! Truly, the Republicans have added a bright and glorious page to the annals of history. A heroic army! A heroic struggle!

Our comrades believe that the surrender of Barcelona was partly due to an ingrained flaw in the Spanish character: carelessness. The Catalan army did not exceed 150,000 men; if one includes reserves and so on, not more than 200,000 men. Yet the Spanish government did not set about advancing reinforcements from central Spain, where more than 600,000 men are under arms. But this, of course, is only a partial and secondary cause of failure.

3 February

Visited Butler. Total chaos in the corridors of the Foreign Office: filing cabinets, boxes, heaps of files, bundles of documents, etc. Virtually impossible to get through. I asked the attendant what the matter was. It turns out that the Foreign Office is building an anti-gas shelter and the basement has to be temporarily cleared…

Butler was most friendly and enlarged upon the point that A[nglo]-S[oviet] rapprochement is a fundamental guarantee of peace. So far the British government has not paid proper attention to A[nglo]-S[oviet] relations (B[utler] evidently meant the Chamberlain government), but this was not due to any hostility to the USSR. It simply had its hands full. Now, the situation is different. A[nglo]-S[oviet] relations are high on the agenda. In this connection, Butler mentioned that he had familiarized himself with the record of my conversation with Halifax of 27 January and he is of the view that a renunciation of the Anglo-Soviet trade agreement would be entirely unjustified. He will discuss the matter with Stanley…

Excellent! My pressure clearly yields results.

We compared our impressions of Hitler's speech of 30 January. Butler gives it a pessimistic appraisal. Hitler has offered *carte blanche* to Mussolini, who will not be slow to act. Hitler, for his part, will probably take certain steps, too – for instance, in the direction of Holland. In short, a new crisis is in the air. The British, however, are not considering entering into any 'appeasement' talks with Hitler. The return of colonies to Germany is out of the question.

Were the Germans prepared to content themselves with extended access to colonial raw materials, it would be another matter. In that case, the British government would make considerable compromises. But such a solution does not satisfy Hitler. In these circumstances, there is nothing to do but wait. Talks will take place nonetheless between British and German industrialists – without the participation of politicians, but with their blessing – concerning the elimination, or at least the softening, of rivalry on the world market.

[The ill winds of isolation blowing from the Kremlin in the wake of the Munich Agreement, further accentuated by Litvinov's depression, disillusion and exclusion from the formulation of policy – increasingly firmly in the hands of Stalin and Molotov – drove Maisky into reclusiveness. But he was himself partly to blame: in his efforts to keep pace with the Kremlin, he had inflamed suspicions in Moscow by suggesting that Chamberlain was 'deliberately promoting the "Ukrainian direction" of German aggression, in an attempt to prompt Hitler to embark on precisely such a course'.[2] At the same time, Maisky blatantly ignored his instructions to stay out of things, and instead tried to prod the British into action by sounding the alarm. To judge by Butler's record of the meeting, Maisky acknowledged that 'since Munich the Soviet Union had been hesitating before deciding on a policy of complete isolation' and was bound to be discouraged by Chamberlain's continued appeasement, which left no room for 'friendship with Russia'. Maisky was nonetheless faithfully echoing Litvinov's warnings to Seeds that if France and Great Britain were to 'continue to capitulate', the Soviet Union would 'keep aloof all the more readily as their interests were not directly threatened'. No wonder Butler emerged from the meeting convinced that the Russians were 'content to wait' and would 'pursue an isolationist policy'.[3]

And yet Maisky's fervent lobbying revealed an ambiguity which often brought him into conflict with Litvinov, who did not subscribe to his appraisal that the Conservatives were undergoing a 'sobering' process, that 'Chamberlain's road of "appeasement"' could not be pursued indefinitely, and that the moment was approaching 'when one will have to say in all firmness: "So far and no further!"' He remained convinced throughout 1939 that the British and Soviet interests coincided, but he failed to persuade Litvinov. Detesting Maisky's air of superiority, Litvinov reprimanded him: 'I am not claiming that my prognosis is watertight, and surprises are surely possible, but those should be reduced to a minimum.'[4]

Maisky soon reverted to his familiar pattern of seeking to influence the course of Soviet foreign policy by encouraging his interlocutors to usher in ideas which might prompt the Kremlin to alter its policy. Harold Nicolson recorded in his diary how Maisky 'with his little Kalmuk eyes twinkling around the table' argued over lunch that Russia, 'obviously much wounded by Munich', would not embark on any initiative; but if Britain were to make an approach, she would not 'find Russia as aloof or offended as we might have supposed'.[5] Likewise, over tea at the embassy, Maisky told Amery that the exclusion of the Soviet Union from Munich had infuriated the Russians and they were ready 'to break [with the Western powers] altogether'; though 'nothing would induce them to take the initiative in offering cooperation in case of a crisis in the West, the door was still open if the initiative came from our end'.[6] For the moment, Litvinov's scepticism was spot on. Chamberlain boasted to his sister that he would resist the pressure exerted on him by Churchill to 'make a grand alliance against Germany ... Fortunately my nature is as L[loyd] G[eorge] says extremely "obstinate", & I refuse to change.'[7]]

4 February

I learn from a good source that Hitler's general policy amounts to the following:

His long-range objective is to dismember the USSR and set up a number of 'independent' states which would maintain 'friendly' relations with Germany.

However, prior to carrying out 'this large and complicated task', Hitler considers it necessary to secure his rear in the west by obtaining 'real guarantees' from Britain and France that they will not attack him while he is implementing his eastern plans.

What are these 'real guarantees'?

Here they are:

(1) Britain and France should sign an 'air pact' recognizing Germany's absolute air superiority over both of them (at least at a ratio of 2:1).

(2) Britain and France should return former German colonies, which Hitler needs mainly from the strategic point of view.

Hitler evidently has good taste.

6 February

Dr L. Burgin, the minister of transport, spoke about current political issues over lunch at the embassy today. He believes that Hitler's latest speech (30 January) bodes ill, that the support Hitler promised to Italy in his speech is of an unconditional nature, and that the next four or five months will be particularly dangerous.

When I asked Burgin what position the British government might take in such circumstances, he first got on his high horse, as they say, and started impressing on me that anti-German sentiments in the country had never been as strong as they are at the moment, and that any concessions to Germany are out of the question. But these general statements failed to satisfy me and when I asked Burgin to define the situation in more concrete terms it turned out, just as I had expected, that non-territorial concessions to Italy (Djibouti, the Suez Canal, the status of Italians in Tunisia, etc.) were entirely 'discussable', and that sooner or later at least part of Germany's former colonies would have to be returned to it, 'only not Tanganyika or New Guinea'! The 'atmosphere' also needed to be improved. Then everything could be settled to general satisfaction.

And Burgin is one of Chamberlain's closest lieutenants!

There was an awkward incident during lunch. Palmstierna, who was also present at lunch, started speaking all of a sudden about the dominance of Jews in the British press. He evidently did not know that Burgin is a Jew. I hastened to change the subject.

11 February

Azcárate notifies me that the Spanish government has finally settled in Madrid. He thinks that the 'intermezzo', caused by the Spanish army's retreat to France, when the government got scattered for a while and lingered in France as 'exiles', was unreasonably long. The impression was created that the Republic no longer had a government. Franco took full advantage. As did the capitulators in England and France. It has all changed now. Negrín and del Vayo are in Madrid. Some other ministers are there, too. The Spanish government has resumed its activities and embarked on preparations to fight on. It holds solid territory – not Catalan, but real, genuine Spanish – and has a 600,000-strong army, a navy, matériel and gold. The struggle continues. And Azcárate once again feels himself to be the ambassador of the Spanish Republic.

He visited the Foreign Office today. His general impression is that the British government is showing greater diplomatic activity on the Spanish question. It is eager to 'pacify' Spain as soon as possible, but preferably on the basis of an 'English' formula which would give Great Britain a better chance to exert influence on Spain and would raise Chamberlain's stock in his own country. The British government has two cards to play: recognition and money. Azcárate asks himself which would be more advantageous for the Spanish government: to discard outright all mediation or to make the British government understand that it would be prepared to cease hostilities on the basis of Negrín's three points (no reprisals to follow, the withdrawal of foreigners and a plebiscite). He thinks that the second alternative would be the better tactic. He asked my advice. I avoided giving a direct answer, however, and merely recommended that he request Madrid's opinion.

13 February

Samuel Hoare came over for lunch. Unless I am mistaken, it was his first visit to the Soviet embassy. In the short period he headed the Foreign Office he did not manage to visit. Hudson, the vigorous and clever secretary of the Department of Overseas Trade, was also present.

Hoare is full of 'optimism' (recently, he has taken on the role of St George, slaying the dragon of 'defeatism' at every step). Although the next six months may be difficult and complicated, it will not come to war. Hitler and Mussolini have missed the moment for a major initiative against Western countries. Hoare is also convinced that Hitler will not venture to attack the Ukraine, because he does not want to get stuck in a war that can never end. The growth of British and French armaments, Roosevelt's speech on 4 January, and Chamberlain's recent statement promising unconditional assistance to France, have made it clear to Germany and Italy that a second Munich is out of the question. Hitler and Mussolini will not enter a war against Britain and France. The return of their former colonial territories is not a topic for serious discussion. Facilitating their access to raw materials is another matter. Here, if they so wished, certain concessions would be possible. Likewise, France could make some non-territorial concessions to the Italians (Djibouti, the Suez Canal and the status of Italians in Tunisia). Hoare is absolutely certain that Britain and France will succeed in 'buying' Franco. This is the essence of the British government's Spanish policy now. But Hoare does not think that the recognition of Franco could occur unconditionally. In any case, he thinks that even if Franco does win a decisive military victory, a solid and definitively established regime is inconceivable in Spain for at least another five years.

During our conversation, Hoare mentioned that he knew Mussolini personally, having met him during the war, when Mussolini was a corporal in the Italian army and editor of the socialist *Avanti.* At that time, Mussolini adhered to a far-left, anti-war position, and Hoare, as head of British '*intelligence*' in Italy, made efforts to convince him to change his mind and follow a different line.

'I eventually succeeded,' Hoare said modestly.

'And how much did it cost you?' Ewer, who was also sitting at the table, casually asked.

Everyone burst out laughing. Hoare was slightly embarrassed but immediately regained his self-control and answered with a particular smile: 'One doesn't talk about these things, but we all know that propaganda costs money.'

The way Hoare spoke about the USSR was entirely unexpected. He lavished praise on our air force and mocked those who speak of the weakness of the Red Army. He said: 'You are a country which can never be defeated. We, too, are a country which can never be defeated. Both our countries, unlike others, are capable of taking a long-term view when assessing events. It doesn't matter if things go badly for six weeks or six months; ultimately, both you and we will emerge on top.'

He added: 'The crucial thing at present is that both you and we are arming.'

What's more: 'Our enemies are exactly the same.'

Goodness gracious, what a turnabout! I've never heard anything like that from the lips of Samuel Hoare. There must be something behind it. Something is brewing in the political 'atmosphere' here. Hudson was also desperate to tell me something important, but Hoare wouldn't let him get a word in. He merely managed to remark: 'We and you are countries that should be trading with one another on a vast scale. On a much greater scale than we see today.'

Incidentally, it transpired over lunch that Hudson speaks some Russian. In his youth he once served as an attaché at the British embassy in St Petersburg.

14 February

Britain and France desperately want to recognize Franco.[8] At first, for the sake of appearances, they dallied with the idea of laying down some conditions (the withdrawal of foreigners, amnesty for the Republicans, etc.), but having been rebuffed they capitulated, as they always do, and are now ready to recognize Franco unconditionally. Of course, the weightiest and most noble arguments are adduced in justification of this: Franco must be 'torn away' from Germany and Italy, it will be easier to prevent the massacre of the Republicans if British and French ambassadors are in Burgos, etc. All of this [word indecipherable] is sheer hypocrisy which, unfortunately, dupes plenty of fools, including the 'leftists'.

Azcárate saw Cadogan and Vansittart today. On instructions from del Vayo he put to them the following question: the Spanish government can keep up its resistance for a long time yet, but to avoid useless bloodshed it is ready to end the war on the basis of Negrín's three points. It would be excellent if the British government could secure the implementation of these points in exchange for the recognition of Franco. If not, and Franco is recognized regardless, the British government would assume moral responsibility for further bloodshed, reprisals and the massacre of the Republicans. According to Azcárate, his arguments visibly impressed his interlocutors, and Cadogan emphatically advised him to see Halifax. At the same time, Cadogan declared that the recognition of Franco was still an open question, while Vansittart said that the British government is not bringing any pressure to bear upon the French government in this matter, giving them total freedom of action.

Meanwhile Bonnet told Pascua[i] yesterday that he personally would not hasten to recognize Franco, but that London was pressing him. Does Bonnet ever, even occasionally, tell the truth? A matter for the psychologists!

In the evening, Agniya and I went to the Swedish embassy to attend a dinner party given in our honour. Elliot was among the guests. He confirmed that no decision had been taken as yet about the recognition of Franco. I told him what Bonnet had said to Pascua, without mentioning the latter's name. Elliot flared

---

[i] Marcelino Pascua, professor of medicine and a protégé of Negrín; served as Spanish ambassador to Moscow and then to Paris, 1936–39.

up and exclaimed: 'That's going too far! Such things can only harm relations between Britain and France.'

These English are a strange lot: always a decade behind events!

Today I had lunch with Leith-Ross and Waley,[i] two bigwigs from the exchequer. The lunch was arranged by Leith-Ross, and not without purpose. Leith-Ross began the conversation at a high pitch: the international situation is dangerous, a united front of democracies and the USSR is needed, good trade makes a solid foundation for strengthening relations between countries, and therefore – listen up! – the USSR should settle old claims and the debts of the tsarist government. It will not cost much: the English estimate the claims at 250 million pounds, but they will be satisfied with 6 or 7% of that amount, that is, with 14–15 million pounds. Barings Bank in London still keeps as much as 6 million pounds' worth of tsarist gold in its vaults. Why not use this gold to settle the claims, with the Soviet government adding another 8 or 9 million? Then all would be fine. The London money market would open its gates to us, and political relations between London and Moscow would become unusually cordial.

Waley kept nodding his assent.

I laughed and answered that Leith-Ross had approached me with similar words in 1935, and that I had already explained to him then that it would be better not to trouble 'old ghosts' in their graves. Does Leith-Ross think that the situation in 1939 is more favourable for his plans than it was four years ago? No, better to bury the past and think of the future.

Leith-Ross was manifestly disappointed and asked in sincere bewilderment: 'Don't you think that the price of respectability is worth paying?'

A strange lot, the English!

15 February

Shocking reports from France. More than 200,000 Spaniards – old men, women and children – have fled from Catalonia to France, seeking refuge from Franco. Up to 150,000 Republican troops have retreated over the French border. Such events have occurred before in history. In 1870, a 100,000 strong French army, led by General Bourbaki, retreated from the Prussians, crossed the Swiss border, was interned, and returned to France after the peace treaty was signed. The Swiss treated the French well, and this episode helped considerably in consolidating good relations between the two neighbouring countries. The Spanish Republicans had every reason to expect similar treatment in France.

---

[i] Sigismund David Waley, principal assistant secretary to the Treasury, 1931; third secretary, HM Treasury, 1946–47.

Azcárate told me once that when the armies of Modesto[i] and Líster[ii] reached the French border, the two leaders made emotional speeches to their soldiers, telling them that across the border lay France, a country of peace and liberty, where the Republican troops, exhausted by war, would find rest and friendly understanding. Modesto and Líster implored their men to demonstrate exemplary conduct, so as not to stain the good name of the Spanish Republic. The men answered with concerted and resolute pledges...

And now we hear terrible and scandalous news from France. As soon as the Republican troops crossed the French border, they were not only disarmed, as one would expect, but put into concentration camps. The camps are surrounded by black Senegalese soldiers armed with machine-guns. Within the camps, the Republicans have been given nothing but bare ground: no tents, no mattresses, no blankets, no medicine (there are many wounded among them), no food or even water. The men have to sleep in the open on bare ground, lacking those essentials that are usually guaranteed even to criminals. Heroes, whose names history will etch in gold, are being treated worse than thieves and murderers.

It is difficult to imagine anything more vile or cruel, or for that matter more stupid and short-sighted. After all, had the French government so desired, those 150,000 soldiers could have become one of the best armies in France, which is so short of human resources, and the surest defence along the Pyrenean border against Germany and Italy. Or, if the French government had lacked the courage for such a decisive step (cowards are in the ascendancy in the Paris of today!) and had limited itself to affording the Spanish refugees humane treatment, this would have greatly helped promote friendly attitudes towards France on the Iberian Peninsula – an objective that the French government is striving to attain with its humiliating capitulation to the fascist aggressors.

And what do we have now? The French government's treatment of the Spanish refugees will remain an eternal, indelible stain on France's reputation. And this will drastically weaken its international position. Such things cannot be forgotten or forgiven. It is not just a matter of the hundreds of thousands of Spaniards who, seeking friendly help in France but finding barbed wire and Senegalese guards, will turn into bitter enemies of the Third Republic. It is also a matter of the democratic elements in other countries who have observed France's behaviour at this tragic moment and will draw their own conclusions. And when the critical hour arrives for France (and it is not far off), who can say what will happen? Will France find, among the democratic elements, that sympathy, enthusiasm and support which alone can save her from destruction?

---

[i] Juan Modesto, member of the Spanish Communist Party, he commanded Ebro's army in 1938.

[ii] Enrique (Forjan) Líster, member of the Spanish Communist Party and commander of the Republican 5th Army Corps, 1936–38.

I doubt it. But time will tell.

Azcárate affirms that France's policy towards the Spanish refugees is not an accident, nor a product of bureaucratic disorder, but a quite deliberate stratagem: the French government wants to drive the refugees back to Spain, that is, to hand them over to Franco. That is why Franco's agents are allowed to spread propaganda openly among the troops held in the camps. That is why every Republican soldier who agrees to return to Franco is immediately granted good conditions and transferred to another camp for the 'privileged'.

I repeat: what vileness! What utter blindness!

Capitalism is not only decaying, but already beginning to stink.

17 February

Today at long last Cadogan supplied me with an explanation of the strange night raid on the trade mission on 5 February.

Cadogan read me a lengthy 'report' submitted by the chief of the London police, where the latter admits that the raid did take place and that its form and extent were just as I had described them to Cadogan during my first visit to his office on 9 February. According to the chief of police, this is what happened. At about 4.30 a.m., 6 February, the duty policeman checked the 'mark' that he had made on the back door of the trade mission and found something wrong with it. It was obvious that someone had used the door during the night. In accordance with the existing rules, the policeman immediately reported his discovery to Scotland Yard. From there, also in accordance with routine procedure, two cars with police officers and detectives were sent out. Another two or three policemen joined them at the trade mission. Twelve or thirteen men in all. Such considerable forces were employed because the street where the trade mission is located has a bad reputation. It contains many jewellery shops, and there are frequent robberies, break-ins, etc. At first, the police tried to talk to the people located inside the building of the trade mission (with a fat lady in particular– must be Bugacheva, the office cleaner), but since those individuals did not speak English, the police decided not to enter the building, but to search the house from outside. The police officers and detectives climbed over the fence and up the fire escapes onto the roof. Nothing suspicious was found, and at about 5.30 a.m. the police detail retired.

That is how the chief of police presented the facts.

I expressed my doubts about the complete trustworthiness of this story, since the real issue in question relates to the motives for the raid, but since Cadogan apologized for the inconvenience caused to the trade mission I decided not to probe much further into the matter. But I did firmly condemn the actions of the police for infringing the diplomatic immunity of the trade mission. True, the first two floors of the building are not exterritorial, but the four upper floors have diplomatic immunity, while the police used the fire escape to get right up to the roof.

Cadogan then asked: do we find it undesirable for the police to appear in the trade mission under any circumstances? Even in the case of robbery? Or fire? If we did not wish the police to enter the building even in these circumstance, then he would inform the chief of police about it. The latter would hardly object, but would most likely consider himself freed of all responsibility for the protection of the trade mission.

I said I did not agree with Cadogan's point of view. What I meant was that policemen could not enter the embassy building uninvited or, at the very least, without the ambassador's consent, yet the police could still not disclaim responsibility for the embassy's safety. We would like to have the same arrangements for the trade mission. The police cannot enter the building without the consent of the head of the trade mission or of his deputy, but remain responsible for its protection.

Cadogan tried to object, arguing that the ambassador actually lives in the embassy, while there is nobody at the trade mission at night except the watchman. But I couldn't agree with him. So we failed to reach a compromise, each sticking to his guns.

Generally speaking, this whole incident of the raid remains a mystery to me. Who initiated it? Whom did it serve? The British government, and more specifically the Home Office? I doubt it. The British government is currently trying to expand Anglo-Soviet trade. Scotland Yard? Also doubtful. Of course Scotland Yard would like to know what is happening at the trade mission; but had the raid been engineered by them, one can be sure that the police officers and detectives would have found their way into the building. In the end, it was simply ridiculous: they came, nosed around, and scarpered, frightened off by Bugacheva, the office cleaner. What a blow to the prestige of Scotland Yard! Or maybe the raid was the product of excessive zeal on the part of an eager police officer, who, encountering unexpected resistance, did not risk taking more radical steps for fear of a scandal?

We shall see. Meanwhile, we must think about safeguarding the trade mission against the recurrence of similar incidents. The best thing would be to have the head of the trade mission or his deputy living in the building. If necessary, he could give the police access to the building under his supervision. After all, I recall a couple of instances in the life of the embassy when we had to summon the fire brigade after a fire and allow the police inside the embassy building. The same could happen to the trade mission.

18 February

Saw Azcárate. He went to Paris twice this week and met del Vayo and Azaña.[i] Azcárate flatly refutes rumours appearing in the press that Azaña is about to resign and to address the Spanish people with an appeal to end the war. But Azcárate also admitted that del Vayo failed to persuade Azaña to return to Madrid. Using various pretexts, Azaña avoids doing so. Azcárate remarked with sadness that Azaña's conduct is inflicting a heavy blow on the Republic, but that the Republic will maintain its resistance all the same.

Azcárate paid a visit to Halifax on 16 February. Their conversation made it clear to him that the British government no longer supported Negrín's three points. However, Halifax gave him to understand that the British government might be willing to act as an intermediary if the Spanish government agreed to cease hostilities on the condition that repressions would not follow. In the conversation that ensued, the terms were specified as follows: (1) Those who wished to leave the country would be free to do so; (2) Those charged with criminal offences would be tried in ordinary courts; and (3) Franco would leave everyone else in peace.

Azcárate, of course, could not give a definite reply to Halifax there and then. He was in Paris on 17 February and conveyed the content of his conversation with Halifax to del Vayo. The latter was also unable to take an independent decision and asked Madrid. So far, no answer has been received from Negrín. Azcárate was interested in my opinion and said that at this critical moment it was important for the Spanish government to know what the Soviet government thought of the present situation and the conclusions that follow from it.

What could I say in reply?

Azcárate continues to act in as courageous and dignified a manner as before. However, despair must be eating at his soul. The Republic is dying under the assault of fascism and the cowardly panicking of the so-called 'democracies'. His own son, a communist, clenches his weapon in Madrid as I write. But outwardly, Azcárate is his normal calm and unruffled self. He converses, makes his points, calculates his moves with strict discipline, retains a sense of moderation, and even laughs, albeit without mirth. He commands my growing respect.

20 February

We had Halifax, Churchill, Dawson of Penn,[ii] the Rothensteins (father and son), Balutis and some others for dinner, all accompanied by their wives. It was the

---

[i] Manuel Azaña y Diaz, war minister and prime minister of Spain, 1931–33; president of the Spanish Republic, 1936–39.

[ii] Bertrand Dawson (1st Viscount Dawson of Penn), physician to the British royal family.

first time Winston Churchill had crossed the threshold of the Soviet embassy. He had always avoided doing so and we usually met on neutral ground.

Halifax told me, *inter alia*, that following our conversation on 27 January he had made a careful study of Anglo-Soviet trade relations and had reached the conclusion that renunciation of the current trade agreement would be undesirable. However, since the British industrialists have been complaining about a number of difficulties in trade relations between the two countries, the best solution, in his view, would be a visit by a British minister to Moscow in order to try to settle contentious issues through amicable talks. Such a visit, furthermore, could have a certain political effect, which would be particularly desirable in the current situation. Hence Hudson's mission, announced in parliament today.[9]

Azcárate and his wife were also present. Mme Azcárate said to me: 'This will probably be our last official appearance in London. You know, of course, that the British are going to recognize Franco any day now. I am very glad that our last appearance should be at your embassy and at such an important dinner.'

Bidding farewell, Halifax mentioned in passing: 'What a sad figure is Monsieur Azcárate! Such a nice man… And such grave circumstances!'

23 February

Went to see Vansittart to find out something about the subtext of Hudson's mission. Here is what Vansittart had to tell me.

Throughout 1938, he, Vansittart, was greatly concerned about the progressive cooling of Anglo-Soviet relations. Its sad consequences were clearly demonstrated by Munich. That is why Vansittart began, from the end of last year, to impress on members of the British government, Halifax in particular, the urgent need to improve Anglo-Soviet relations. He specifically recommended sending a British minister to Moscow with this end in view. Vansittart hoped that his efforts would lead to a situation where the exchange of ministerial visits between London and Moscow would become as commonplace a phenomenon as, for example, the exchange of similar visits between London and Paris. But all this is just the music of the future. In the meantime, Vansittart thought it very profitable to arrange a trip to Moscow for one member of the government, albeit as a one-off. Alas, his idea initially met with a lukewarm response in the highest circles.

It dawned on Vansittart after our conversation last week that the question of the Anglo-Soviet trade agreement could be a good pretext for putting his long-cherished idea into effect. He suggested to Halifax that Hudson be sent to Moscow ('specifically Hudson,' Vansittart emphasized, 'for I have long known him to be an intelligent, energetic man who shares my views on international issues'). To his considerable surprise, Halifax readily endorsed his idea on this occasion. The British government also approved of Hudson's visit. Vansittart is very happy. Now we just have to ensure that Hudson's visit proves successful!

Referring to my recent conversation with Leith-Ross, I expressed my hope that Hudson would not seek to trouble 'old ghosts' in Moscow. This would doom Hudson's visit to failure. Vansittart promised to keep my comment in mind.

25 February

Azcárate came to see me again, almost straight off the train from Paris. He'd gone there to consult with del Vayo and other members of the Spanish government who'd got stuck in France. Del Vayo left for Madrid after his unsuccessful conference with Azaña, only to receive an instruction from Negrín at Perpignan to turn back and await further directives in Paris.

Azcárate's news is far from comforting: (1) the Republicans are short of weapons and ammunition, and prolonged resistance is unlikely; (2) there is discord in the government coalition: communists are determined to resist, whereas the rightist elements (left-wing Republicans, some socialists and others, not to mention Azaña's group) favour a ceasefire under virtually any conditions. Negrín occupies a middle position between these two poles.

Azcárate himself appears to advocate an end to the fighting, but thinks it necessary to make the most of the Republicans' only remaining trump card – the threat of resistance – in order to bargain with Franco for the best possible conditions. That is why he wants the Spanish government to display the utmost belligerence for the time being.

This morning he met Mounsey[i] and informed him that the Spanish government was ready to end the war on the basis he discussed with Halifax on 16 February. Mounsey responded with a 'spontaneous question': 'Surely you don't expect the British government to make its recognition of Franco conditional on this, do you?' Mounsey made it perfectly clear to Azcárate that the decision to recognize Franco had already been taken and that Britain would announce it next week, probably together with France or soon afterwards. To soften the blow, Mounsey elaborated a lengthy argument (a very fashionable one at present in government circles) to the effect that the British government is hastening to recognize Franco in the interests of the 'Spanish people', with the aim of 'tearing Franco away' from Rome and Berlin and 'preventing the massacre of Republicans' by exerting diplomatic influence through its ambassador

[i] George Mounsey, assistant undersecretary of state, Foreign Office, 1929; secretary, Ministry of Economic Warfare, 1939–40.

in Burgos. English hypocrisy clearly knows no bounds! Unfortunately there are a good many fools (the English left is no exception) who swallow this bait.

27 February

This day will go down in the history of Britain and France as a day of disgrace and folly: London and Paris recognized Franco *de jure*…

It took Britain and France seven years to recognize the Soviet government. And it took them barely seven days to recognize Franco. These facts reflect the true essence of 'capitalist democracies' just as a drop of water reflects the sun.

28 February

Azcárate came to see me at around 6 p.m. Inside he must be deeply perturbed or even shaken, but outwardly he retains his usual restraint and composure.

Yesterday Azcárate received a note from the Foreign Office in which Halifax informed him in refined and courteous language that the British government had taken the decision to recognize Franco, and consequently 'your name can no longer appear on the list of foreign representatives at this court, as a result of which your diplomatic privileges must come to an end'. However, the note mercifully promised to extend Azcárate's personal privileges – tax exemption, in particular – for another three months, so that he could wind up his business without undue haste.

Unwilling to hand over the embassy to Alba[i] in person, Azcárate agreed with the Foreign Office that it would take the building from him and give Alba possession at a later date. This procedure took place today. Before departing, Azcárate summoned all his staff, bade them a warm farewell, and handed over the embassy to Mounsey. Then Azcárate took a car and left for his new apartment, *11, Portland Place*. The entire personnel of the embassy, both diplomatic and clerical, left together with Azcárate. Before vacating the embassy, Azcárate had all the archives, documents and accounts packed and taken out, but left the furniture, carpets, paintings, etc. He reckoned that since this all belonged to the Spanish state, removing this property would have an adverse political effect for the Republicans. On 2 March the Spanish government is going to 'evacuate' its consulate-general in London in the same manner.

Azcárate's future is unclear – and how else could it be in the current circumstances? On Negrín's instructions, he is to remain in London to maintain

[i] Jacobo Fitz-James Stuart (17th duke of Alba), Spanish foreign minister, 1930–31; Spanish ambassador to Great Britain, 1939–45.

contact not only with English, but also with French circles. He will head a small unofficial 'mission'. I asked Azcárate what would happen to Pascua (the Spanish ambassador in Paris), but he had nothing definite to say.

Azcárate described to me his last conversation with Halifax, which occurred on the evening of 26 February, on the eve of Franco's recognition. During their talk, Azcárate gave Halifax a letter in which he had summarized the three points that are currently of greatest concern to the Spanish government:

(1) How does the British government interpret the declaration it has received from Franco concerning the matter of punitive measures? Halifax said the following: the British government interprets the declaration to mean that only persons who committed criminal offences are liable to prosecution and that they ought to be tried according to the law by courts that existed before 16 July 1936. All other citizens should not be submitted to any persecution. (Pious hopes! One cannot but recall Hitler's promises in Munich about Czechoslovakia and what came of them in the end.)

(2) The cessation of hostilities during the negotiations with Burgos concerning the interpretation of the above declaration. Here, Halifax displayed great zeal and asserted that the British government would make every effort to end the war speedily and conclude a truce.

(3) Since even the best of Franco's declarations do not guarantee that punitive measures will not be taken, the only realistic way of preventing the worst excesses after the war would be the evacuation from central Spain of all the most 'compromised' Republicans. Is the British government ready to ensure the unimpeded passage of these people from Spain under the protection of the British navy? Halifax was very vague and evasive on this point. He even came up with the absurd idea of 'agreeing' the lists of the evacuated Republicans with Franco. (Meanwhile, the issue of evacuation becomes increasingly acute. Negrín sent a telegram to Azcárate, after the latter's conversation with Halifax, to the effect that the evacuation could involve as many as 10–20,000 people.)

I fear that little will come either of the projected truce or of the plans for an organized 'evacuation'. Neither the English nor the French are willing to take serious action. Besides, they have already capitulated. After capitulation, one does not discuss conditions.

[Maisky had been absorbed in the activities of the Non-Intervention Committee throughout 1937–39. He appears to have been at odds with Litvinov since its existence, advocating sustained military support for the Republicans, so long as there was no agreement on non-intervention. His fear was that Franco's victory might expose Soviet weakness and bolster appeasement. In early 1938, he even went behind Litvinov's back to approach Voroshilov, and for a while gained Stalin's personal support. But later he was forced to repent for 'this interference in a sphere which is not entirely within my competence'. The activities of the Non-Intervention Committee came to a standstill

52. A terrified Chamberlain, clutching his hat and encouraged by his daughter, enters the lion's den.

following Chamberlain's visit to Rome in November 1938. The Committee was dissolved on 20 April 1939, following British recognition of Franco's government.[10]]

2 March

Yesterday, as today's English papers pompously put it, we had a 'historic reception' at the embassy. In fact, there was nothing special about the reception as such, just the usual evening for 'friends' and 'acquaintances' which we hold every year...

But as for the guest-list... Yes, that was exceptional!

I'll start at the beginning. When, at the end of January, I was sending out invitations for the 1 March reception, I sent cards to all the Cabinet members, as custom dictates. I expected all the ministers to decline politely, or for just two or three of them to accept and then not actually turn up. That's how it has always been.

Imagine my amazement when, on 1 February, I received a long letter from the prime minister's office informing me that Chamberlain would attend the reception, and that his wife, who unfortunately was due to attend a charity ball that evening where she was to meet the duchess of Gloucester,[i] would nevertheless do her best to put in an appearance and would let Mme Maisky know her final answer at a later date. After reading this missive, I said to myself: 'Aha, there is something behind this! Not a single British prime minister (even a Labourite) has ever crossed the threshold of the Soviet embassy during the entire period of Soviet rule, and now look: not only the 'man with the umbrella' himself, but also his spouse, is desperate to attend our reception!' I had guessed correctly. I know from experience that in our 'good' times (1935 and 1936, for instance), 60 to 70 out of 100 invitations tend to be accepted, and in the 'bad' times (such as the beginning of 1938, when I arranged a musical soiree in honour of Prokofiev) – 30 to 40. This time there were very few refusals, no more than 20–25%. What was most important was who accepted the invitation. All the pillars of society: major MPs and businessmen, bankers, lords, diehard Tories, high-born aristocrats, members of government… Well, well, well! Thirteen members of Cabinet, i.e. more than half, promised to come, and most of them did. It's quite unheard of in the six-and-a-bit years of my employment in London. That's what a shift in the international scene means! That's what the growth of Soviet might means!

I nonetheless had my doubts until the very last minute whether or not Chamberlain himself would make an appearance. I rather expected something 'unforeseen' to hold him back at the eleventh hour. Moreover, it was reported in the papers the day before the reception that Mrs Chamberlain had gone down with the flu and had taken to her bed. But I was wrong. On 28 February they phoned me from the prime minister's office to say that Mrs Chamberlain would not be able to attend the reception because of her illness and to inquire, on the PM's behalf, whether he might instead bring along his niece, Miss Cole.[ii] At 10 p.m. on 1 March the tall spare frame of Chamberlain appeared in the embassy doorway, accompanied – a fresh surprise! – not by Miss Cole, but by his daughter.

It's hard to describe the stir created among the guests by the prime minister's appearance. Nobody knew about it in advance, and nobody (of the more than 500 invitees) had expected such a 'daring step' from him. There was a general commotion and agitation. People stopped in the middle of their sentences and rushed childishly to have a look at Chamberlain in the interior of the Soviet embassy. I first led him to the white ballroom and then to my office, where I offered him and his daughter *refreshments*. Chamberlain declined vodka, but had nothing against mulled wine. The office soon filled with people. I tried to

[i] Princess Alice Cristabel, duchess of Gloucester; married Prince Henry, 1st duke of Gloucester, in 1935.

[ii] Valerie Cole.

keep the crowd back, but I didn't always succeed. Standing by the sideboard, the PM and I discussed various topics.

Chamberlain first broached the matter of Hudson's forthcoming trip. Its aim is to settle various trade disagreements and prepare the ground for expanding Anglo-Soviet trade. Unlike Halifax and Vansittart, Chamberlain said not a word about the political aspect of the visit.[11]

I remarked that the British industrialists' complaints about disagreements in Anglo-Soviet trade were unfounded, or at best highly exaggerated. The main difficulty was not increasing our orders for British companies, but finding the companies to take them. For instance, we were unable to place orders amounting to 2.5 million pounds in 1938 and the fulfilment of earlier orders to the amount of 2 million pounds was delayed. English industry is currently overloaded with orders in connection with the British rearmament programme.

Chamberlain grinned and said: 'Yes, you need exactly the same things as we do. But it will not be so forever. The peoples of Europe will not always be thinking only of war and armaments. Besides, the goods we offer are not confined to those you mention. We could also supply you with consumer goods. Why don't you buy them?'

I explained to him that Soviet imports were regulated by a general national economic plan, and that for the moment we could not afford spending our resources on the import of consumer goods.

Chamberlain kept silent for a while and then asked in a very particular way: 'What are you doing with your gold?'

I smiled and said: 'The same everyone else does – we put it aside for a rainy day.'

Chamberlain shrugged his shoulders and observed with obvious irritation: 'At the moment, all anyone can think about is war!' Having calmed down a little, the PM began interrogating me about our relations with Germany and Japan. Was it true that a German trade delegation had come to Moscow? I told him that at the end of January the Germans had indeed intended to send a trade mission to Moscow, but then changed their minds for whatever reason. It was an entirely German initiative, and we were equally unmoved by news both of the visit and its postponement.

Do we fear Japanese aggression? We know from experience, I answered, that Japan is a very restless neighbour, but we are sure that the Japanese will think twice before venturing anything against us: they are well aware of our strength in the Far East.

Chamberlain nodded his assent and added that Japan had got so bogged down in China that it could hardly embark on adventures in other directions.

53. Conversing with 'the revolting but clever little Jew'.

Japan's situation in China reminds Chamberlain more and more of Napoleon's situation in Russia.

I asked the PM what he thought of Europe's immediate prospects.

Chamberlain replied that he remained an 'optimist', despite everything. The general situation is improving. The German and Italian people do not want war. Both Hitler and Mussolini gave Chamberlain their personal assurances that their task was the peaceful development of the resources at their disposal. Chamberlain was left with the definite impression that Hitler and Mussolini are afraid of war.

I smiled and said that I quite agreed with him on one point: Hitler and Mussolini are indeed afraid of any serious war. The danger of the situation, however, lies in the fact that they are firmly convinced that they can gain bloodless victories, victories based on bluffing and on holding their nerve better than other world leaders.

Chamberlain suddenly darkened and seemed to stretch another inch in height. He uttered testily: 'The time of such victories has passed!'

Our conversation moved away from this subject and somehow alighted on Chamberlain's father. The PM instantly brightened up and seemed to become more cordial.

'You know,' he said, 'my father never thought that I would go into politics. When he died (in 1912 [correct date is 1914]), I myself had no idea that I might become a parliamentarian and minister.'

'And how did it happen?' I inquired.

'It happened this way. In 1911, I was elected to the city council of Birmingham. In 1915 and 1916 I was lord mayor of Birmingham. Lloyd George, then prime minister, invited me to take the post of director-general of national service. I agreed and resigned as lord mayor. I soon discovered, however, that Lloyd George was not giving me the support to which I was entitled, so half a year later I resigned.' (Lloyd George, in his turn, once told me that Chamberlain had turned out to be a quite useless director-general.) 'I could not return to my post as lord mayor of Birmingham, as it had been filled. So I had a long think and decided to try my luck at politics. I entered parliament and began to occupy myself with affairs of state. I can say with some justification that I became a politician thanks to Lloyd George.'

Then, with a somewhat spiteful expression and with obvious sarcasm in his voice, Chamberlain added: 'Lloyd George may regret it, but now it's too late!'

There's no love lost between Chamberlain and Lloyd George. None at all!

I asked the PM about his attitude to his father's political legacy. Chamberlain replied: 'In history, one rarely encounters sons who have implemented the political programme of their fathers. But this is exactly what happened in our family. I am happy that it fell to me to carry out the two projects which concerned my father most of all: pensions for the aged and the unification of the Empire through the customs system.'

Having said that, Chamberlain seemed to raise himself up on tiptoes and gaze down on us all with a feeling of benevolent contempt: a giant among pygmies!

I gained the impression from our talk that the PM considers himself a 'man of destiny'! He was born into this world to perform a 'sacred mission'.

A dangerous state of mind.

7 March

Azcárate has just returned from Paris. It's clear that he is highly disturbed and depressed by events, but he carries himself bravely and with dignity.

'Casado's[i] coup d'état is the end of the Republic.' The Junta he has formed is strongly anti-communist. That is why its triumph means capitulation to Franco. Casado himself is an old officer who has always fought against the penetration

[i] Segismundo Casado (López), commander of the Madrid Zone who engineered the coup against Negrín's government and created a loyalist government which sealed the fate of the Spanish Republic.

of 'communist influences' into the army. Besteiro[i] (minister of foreign affairs without credentials) is the most right-wing of the rightist socialists and an old enemy of communism. Carrillo[ii] (minister of the interior) is Caballero's supporter and another enemy of communism. Marín[iii] (minister of finance) is an anarchist who hates communists. The other Junta members, including Miaja,[iv] are political nonentities.

Azcárate holds Azaña chiefly responsible for the latest events. The left-wing Republicans led by Azaña showed their true colours during the Spanish war: they have completely bankrupted themselves.

'Of course,' said Azcárate, 'objective developments meant that the Spanish Republic would have perished anyway, but had Azaña behaved differently its fall could have been marked by pride and dignity and might have served as a source of inspiration for future fighters for the freedom of democratic Spain. But now the Spanish Republic is dying in a state of inglorious chaos and collapse.'

Fine words. They are particularly telling when one considers that Azcárate is himself a former left-wing Republican. What is he now? I don't know. I think he himself has no clear idea as yet. One thing is certain: over the past year his sympathies have shifted more and more towards communism.

8 March[12]

(1) My wife and I had lunch with the Hudsons. We were alone and were therefore able to have a detailed and uninhibited discussion about Hudson's forthcoming visit to Moscow. At first we talked about trifles, such as what Muscovites wear, what the weather is like, what sights should be seen in the city and its environs, etc. (I learned that Hudson's wife is very keen on the arts – especially painting, of the modernist tendency above all – and that she also wishes to visit our schools, rest homes, maternity and infant institutions, and so on.) Our talk gradually moved on to more serious matters.

(2) Hudson directly posed the following question: does 'Moscow' seriously want to talk about a meaningful improvement of relations with Britain? He has heard more than once in London that this is very doubtful. He was told that after Munich, Moscow had decided to retreat into its borders, to break with the West

[i] Julián Besteiro (Fernandez), dean of the Faculty of Humanities of Madrid University, he was the chairman of the Spanish Socialist Workers' Party, 1925–31, and president of the Republican Cortes, 1931–33. Little involved in the Civil War, he put out various abortive peace feelers to Franco. In March 1939 he joined Casado in forming an anti-Negrín National Defence Junta. He was arrested by Franco forces and sentenced to 30 years' imprisonment.

[ii] Santiago Carrillo (Solares), Spanish Republican minister of the interior, 1937–39.

[iii] Manuel González Marín, general secretary of the National Confederation of Labour, Casado's finance minister, following the coup against Negrín.

[iv] José Miaja (Menant), Spanish Republic's minister of war, 1936–39.

and pursue a policy of isolation, and that for this reason it was useless to seek a common language with Moscow. The main objective of Hudson's visit – and this is much more important than the trade talks themselves – is to gauge Moscow's frame of mind in this respect through contact with the leading figures of the Soviet Union. Very much will depend on this because, as Hudson sees it, the next six to twelve months will be crucial in determining British foreign policy for many years, if not for a whole generation. Indeed, he said, a most serious change has occurred in the mood of the country (viz. England, viz. the Conservative Party) in the past two or three months, as I too must have had occasion to observe. We have firmly resolved on preserving our Empire and our position as a great world power. What is needed for this? First, armaments, and here things have taken a turn for the better. As an individual nation, we shall soon be strong as never before in our history. Secondly, to achieve this goal we need to maintain friendly contacts with all the powers that are on the same path at this moment in time. We believe the USSR to be one of these powers. The prejudice against communism that hampered cooperation between our countries has been almost entirely overcome. However, doubts exist in London as to whether or not we desire such cooperation. Hudson's key task is to clarify this point and report to the Cabinet. If we do desire it, Anglo-Soviet political and economic relations could become very close, because the main danger for the British Empire and the Soviet Union comes from the same country, Germany. If we do not desire it, Britain, in order to defend its interests, will have to engage in other international manoeuvres which might not meet with our approval but which Britain will find unavoidable. Hudson is of the view that Britain and the Soviet Union are two countries which complement one another and which, together with France, could establish a genuine guarantee of peace.[13] Hudson leaves for Moscow with his hands untied. The Cabinet has given him no binding instructions. He is prepared to discuss all subjects, whether political or economic. His report to Cabinet (at this point, one could sense a note of 'dizziness with success' in Hudson's words, and of gentle blackmail) will be of decisive significance. His November speeches (Hudson had in mind his attack on Inskip and Hore-Belisha for their poor performance in the rearmament sphere, resulting in Inskip's removal from the Ministry for Coordination of Defence to the Dominions Office, major difficulties for Hore-Belisha, and strict instructions to Anderson[i] to deal with air-raid precautions) were a great success. The country stands by him. He can push whatever he wishes to push through parliament. That is why he attaches great importance to his visit to Moscow and would be very glad if I could tell him, albeit provisionally, what reception he can expect in the USSR.

[i] John Anderson (1st Viscount Waverley), lord privy seal, 1938–39; home secretary and minister of home security, 1939–40; lord president of the council, 1940–43; chancellor of the exchequer, 1943–45.

(3) I told him that he could of course expect a very friendly reception in Moscow and that representatives of the Soviet government would indeed be willing to talk with him about the matters that concerned him. In particular, I told Hudson that if he arrived in Moscow on the morning of 23 March (as he planned to do), he would be able to see Comrade Litvinov and perhaps also Comrade Mikoyan on the same day. Hudson was very pleased. Discussing more general matters touched on by Hudson, I stressed that the USSR has always been an advocate of collective security and the cooperation of all peace-loving powers, and that it was not we who had undermined these principles. Munich, needless to say, could not but cause an adverse reaction in 'Moscow', giving rise to isolationist trends in some sections of Soviet public opinion, but the Soviet government had taken no decisions of this nature and prefers to wait and see, to watch and study the processes currently taking place in the West. If England, as Hudson asserts, wishes to improve Anglo-Soviet relations, so much the better. Hudson can rest assured that the Soviet government is always ready to support any step leading to such an improvement. I deem it my duty, however, to forewarn Hudson that in view of recent experience, 'Moscow' has become distrustful, and that today, as never before, it will judge the seriousness of intentions not by words but by deeds.

(4) Hudson responded to my considerations with fresh statements to the effect that the British government was absolutely sincere in its desire for closer cooperation with the Soviet Union and that further developments would to a large extent depend on our conduct. Further, as if to prove the seriousness of the British government's intentions, he touched on his wishes in the sphere of Anglo-Soviet trade. What do they amount to? The 'maximum programme' amounts to a major increase in the volume of trade. Why can't we double trade turnover in the next five or perhaps ten years? The economic resources and structure of both countries are such that this seems quite possible. The 'minimum programme' amounts to the settling of the problems that have arisen in connection with the current trade agreement – more specifically, stepping up Soviet purchases of goods produced in England. One does not contradict the other. When I asked Hudson how he was going to settle the trade issues that concerned him, he answered that, once again, this would depend to a great extent on us. The Cabinet has given him a free hand here as well. He is under no binding instructions. Hudson will pose the problem of trade expansion and a certain restructuring. He is ready to hear out and discuss with utmost goodwill any proposal of ours or any project that might emerge in the course of joint discussions… At the end, Hudson began to insist anew on the urgency of settling the issue of the structure of Soviet imports from Britain and warned me (with a hint of blackmail once again) that he was a 'tough negotiator', that Britain's economic position in respect to the USSR was much stronger now

than in 1933 and 1934, and that he hoped to persuade us in Moscow to buy not only capital goods, but consumer goods as well. I remarked half-jokingly that we also knew how to bargain and that I looked forward with great interest to the outcome of his talks in Moscow.

(5) Of the other subjects covered during lunch, mention should be made of Hudson's great optimism about the forthcoming Anglo-German business talks. He assured me that the Germans had already realized the weakness of their position, that government subsidies to German exporters would be discontinued, that the Anglo-German cartels would establish an acceptable distribution of markets, and that, in general, peace between British and German industrialists would be concluded on British terms. Hudson, incidentally, was explicit about Britain's continued economic presence in South-East Europe, saying that Britain's economic position in the Balkans and other places would be maintained and strengthened. Somewhat contradicting the first part of our conversation, Hudson contended that in a year's time the military might of Britain and France would reach dimensions enabling the two countries to defend their interests in any part of the world, including the Far East. I tactfully voiced my doubts about that.

(6) In the course of our conversation, Hudson revealed the following information about himself. He is 53; from 1912 to 1914 he was an attaché and secretary at the British embassy in St Petersburg (where he became acquainted with the Russian language); and in 1913, together with the British ambassador, he attended the festivities in Moscow on the occasion of the 300th anniversary of the Romanovs. He spent the war at the front and afterwards returned to the diplomatic service, occupying various posts in Washington, Athens and Paris. His last diplomatic post was as first secretary in Paris. He left the foreign service in 1923 and went into politics. He held the posts of deputy minister of health and of labour, and was also minister of pensions. I should add that Hudson is very rich: his father made a fortune out of soap and left it to his son. At present, Hudson is engaged solely in politics. He is distinguished by his very energetic and independent character, enjoys great influence in the Conservative Party, and is regarded as one of its 'strong' men, with a brilliant career ahead of him. He is somewhat too sure of himself. He has never displayed any marked anti-Soviet tendencies. On the contrary, he stressed with pride that he was the only Tory candidate in 1924 who did not make use of 'the Zinoviev letter' in his election campaign.

[Maisky was far more outspoken in his telegram home, desperately attempting to extricate Moscow from its isolation. He tried to impress on Litvinov that Hudson's task was to establish 'whether or not we seek rapprochement and cooperation with London', and cited the fact that he had been given a free hand to pursue 'not only economic but also political' issues, which could not have happened 'without Chamberlain's sanction'. This was hardly the case. Chamberlain had just referred to Germany in an off-the-record press briefing for the editors of the major newspapers, during which he suggested that 'as a result of the new situation resulting from the Munich Agreement there was good hope of reaching political, economic and military agreements that would bring permanent peace to Europe'.[14] Moreover, the British records reveal that Maisky's unauthorized initiatives in fact encountered a defiant and confident Hudson: 'As he was leaving, Monsieur Maisky said that he was quite convinced that we, the British Empire, were unable to stand up against German aggression, even with the assistance of France, unless we had the collaboration and help of Russia … He insisted on his point of view and I ventured to beg him, if Moscow shared that view, to disabuse their minds.' Hudson was right in doubting whether Maisky 'had any authority from his Government' to encourage the political dialogue. Vansittart was furious, complaining to Halifax that the briefing was 'too heavy-handed to be useful', missing a chance 'to bring the Russians out of their isolationist tendencies'. Maisky continued to woo Litvinov, following meetings with Butler and Beaverbrook, who, he claimed, had confirmed the significance of Hudson's mission and the growing disillusionment with appeasement.[15]]

9 March

Beaverbrook told me that Chamberlain had a talk with Churchill the other day and was forced to admit that the policy of 'appeasement' had failed. Chamberlain will, of course, make every effort to defer conflict and alleviate the tension through various manoeuvres, but the PM can see now that lasting peace and genuine friendship between Britain and Germany are impossible. This, in Beaverbrook's opinion, explains the prime minister's marked turn towards the USSR, which he demonstrated by attending our reception. In this connection, Beaverbrook inundated me with a stream of rather heavy compliments:

'Stay here for another two or three years and you'll be able to reap the rich harvest in the sphere of Anglo-Soviet relations which your work will have prepared over preceding years.'

Beaverbrook also told me that Germanophobia was spreading rapidly among the general public, and that, in the contrary direction, sympathy towards the USSR was clearly on the rise. By way of an example, he cited Rothermere, whose Germanophilia cost the *Daily Mail* more than a third of its readership (1,200,000 instead of the former 1,800,000 or more). Rothermere left the paper and, with his morale shattered and finances battered, set out on a six-month voyage round the world.

Sympathy towards the USSR really is on the increase. Sinclair told me that mention of the USSR and of the urgent need for a joint struggle for peace had been met with stormy applause at every meeting he had spoken at up and down the country.

Butler, who invited Agniya and myself to lunch today, also spoke at length about friendship between our countries and the need to strengthen Anglo-Soviet relations. Butler described the situation as follows: 'The field of relations with the USSR has been neglected until now, but the PM has arrived at the conclusion that we should cultivate this field and see what fruit it will bear.'

[Attached to the entry is a private letter written to Litvinov on 10 March.]

London, 10 March 1939
To People's Commissar Comrade Litvinov

Dear Maksim Maksimovich,
I would like to add a few more thoughts further to the record of my talk with Hudson on 8 March which I am sending with this post.

As you already know from my telegrams, Hudson gave greatest prominence to political matters in our talk, and only secondary importance to matters of trade. I think the reverse will be true in Moscow. Of course, he probably will talk about international political affairs with you, but I find it hard to see what might come of this in concrete terms unless you, on your part, put forward some practical suggestions. Nonetheless, it seems to me that it would be helpful if you had a serious talk with Hudson and, above all, let him know – since he is obviously unsure about this matter – that we do not exclude cooperation with Britain (provided appropriate conditions are observed). This would enable him and like-minded people in the Cabinet and in parliament to counteract the propaganda spread in government circles by elements hostile to us. It would also be very important (although I cannot conceive exactly how this should be done) to make Hudson feel our military might.

On matters of trade, the talks will obviously be more definite and practical. I do have faith in Hudson's sincere desire to expand Anglo-Soviet trade, but we shall probably have to argue a great deal with him about the ways, methods and conditions by which this goal can be accomplished.

He certainly has a tendency to centralize trade with us on the British side, and on this occasion it will probably be more difficult for us to counter this tendency, since we have adopted a clearing system in our latest agreements with Poland and Italy.

Still more manifest is Hudson's sincere wish to modify the structure of Soviet imports from England through an increase in the share of British-made goods, and this point will probably be the main battleground. Hudson will be very persistent in this respect both because of the very strong pressure exerted by business circles on the government and out of purely careerist considerations. Hudson must return from Moscow with some sort of 'achievement' in this area, otherwise his mission will be regarded as a failure. It must be kept in mind that, as I have written to you before, Hudson's visit represents an alternative to the renunciation of the trade agreement, an alternative put forward to the government by the minister of foreign affairs. In general, according to my survey of the situation here, it would be inadvisable to turn down flatly Hudson's solicitations for a change in the structure of Soviet imports from Britain. This could awaken strong feelings in British business and government circles that are undesirable and would merely lead to the deterioration of relations. It would be more productive to find some sort of compromise which would at least go some way to meeting the British wishes. I suppose that such a compromise could be paid for by British credits (providing, of course, that we want credits).

Our current position regarding the purchase of consumer goods abroad, which Hudson will surely raise, is not entirely clear to me. If the newspaper reports concerning our agreement to buy textiles in Poland are true (unfortunately, I have had no information on this matter from the NKID), this would seem to indicate a certain modification of our former practice. Judging by what I hear and see here, I do not exclude the possibility of various credit combinations if we were to agree to buy, say, textiles or footwear in Britain. But this will all become clearer during the talks in Moscow. No matter how the issue of consumer goods is to be settled, I would deem it highly significant if Hudson could bring good news from Moscow for the Scottish herring dealers. As you certainly know, by virtue of a number of circumstances herring is a political commodity in Britain. A hundred thousand pounds spent on herring has a greater political effect than a million pounds spent on capital goods. Herring is an issue on which all parties concur. I am constantly being reminded about this by such various people as Colville, the minister for Scotland, the Tory MP Boothby, the Liberal leader Sinclair, and the Labourite MacLean.[i] If it were possible to come to an agreement on spending a fixed sum of money (say, 200,000–250,000 pounds annually) on herring for several years, this would have a most favourable political effect for us.

I end with a very important question: to what extent does Hudson represent the British government? My impression is that in matters of the economy, he does represent the government and Chamberlain 100%,

---

[i] Neil MacLean, member of the Executive Committee of the Parliamentary Labour Party, 1931–36.

whereas in matters of politics he is hardly a typical representative of the British government, and especially of the views of the prime minister. Rather, Hudson represents those Cabinet members who have little or no faith in the policy of appeasement and the idea of a London–Paris–Moscow axis.

Please keep me informed during Hudson's stay in Moscow.

12 March

Yesterday, Agniya and I visited the Azcárates. They have already left the embassy. They have a *service flat* in a large house near Portland Place. They are lucky: none of their children are currently in Spain. Even the son, who was in Madrid, came to France together with del Vayo. The other son is in Switzerland, while both daughters are in London. The son from Madrid, who has come to visit his father for a few days, furnished me with the following details about the last days, or rather the last hours, of the Negrín government.

The army of Central Spain, in contrast to the Catalan army, was always led by officers of the old Spanish army who sided with the Republicans. Such are Miaja, Casado and Menéndez[i] (head of the Army of the Levante). Barely any of the top positions were taken by commanders from the masses, like Modesto or Líster. The commissars attached to the old officers were often not up to the mark. For instance, the communists Antón[ii] and Hernández[iii] were Miaja's commissars at various times – things went well under them and Miaja stood firm – but there was a rather long period when Miaja's commissar was a socialist from Caballero's faction (I've forgotten his name) and that resulted in a quite different picture. Miaja himself is nothing to write home about. Fate played an unusual trick on him. When Caballero's government abandoned Madrid on 6 November 1936, believing it was no longer possible to save it from Franco's onslaught, someone had to be left behind to hand the city over to the enemy. Miaja was chosen to perform this rather unheroic role. But a miracle happened: Madrid withstood, and Miaja – to his own surprise and that of the government – became a national hero overnight. The government had to take this fact into account and exploit it in the interests of their struggle: his reputation was supported quite deliberately thereafter. This, however, did not make Miaja any more brilliant. Neither did he become a communist, although at one time he did align himself with the Communist Party and it was even rumoured that he

[i] Leopoldo Menéndez López, former officer of the Spanish army who joined the Republicans and rose to the rank of general after excelling in the Battle of Teruel.

[ii] Francisco Antón, Spanish communist and NKVD agent, and lover of 'La Pasionaria'.

[iii] Jesus Hernández, communist minister of education in the Republican government, 1936–38; head of the war commissars in the Central Zone, 1938–39.

had formally joined its ranks. These circumstances explain much of what has happened in the past two to three weeks.

When Negrín and del Vayo flew into Central Spain from France, the army's top brass had already begun to disintegrate. Instead of immediately making their base in Madrid and gathering loyal units (of which there were quite a few) around the government, Negrín began tearing about the country in a frenzy, travelling to one town after another. This had the benefit of raising Republican morale everywhere, but it also had a crucial flaw: the government failed to establish a strong base for itself anywhere. Negrín obviously overestimated his authority and underestimated the imminent danger. An open pro-Franco mutiny broke out in Cartagena, where unrest had long been brewing in the navy. The mutiny was quelled with great difficulty, after which almost the entire navy left for Bizerta.

The critical moment came on 5 March. Negrín, del Vayo and several other members of government were temporarily based in Elda, a small village near Alicante. Why and how Elda had become the 'capital' is unknown to Azcárate's son. On the morning of 5 March, Negrín began summoning the ministers who had remained in Madrid, as well as the top brass – Miaja, who was in Valencia, Casado, who was in Madrid, and chief of staff Matallana,[i] who was with the Army of the Levante – to Elda for a conference. At first, the ministers in Madrid insisted that Negrín and his companions should come to Madrid and hold the conference there. Negrín, however, had already received reports about the perilous situation in the capital and refused to go there, suspecting an ambush. Eventually, all the ministers left in Madrid went to Elda.

The military presented a greater problem. Miaja found various pretexts to put off his journey to Elda till the next day. Casado bluntly stated that the situation in Madrid did not allow him to attend the conference. Matallana alone came to Elda, but he was very agitated and itching to go back to the Army of the Levante. The negotiations with the army leaders lasted throughout 5 March, and at midnight Casado notified Negrín by phone from Madrid that the Negrín government no longer existed and that he, Casado, had taken power into his own hands. Negrín was shaken and at first would not believe it. 'I'm relieving you of your duties!' he shouted down the phone. 'Just you try!' Casado laughed in return. The minister of the interior wrested the receiver from Negrín's hand and tried to persuade Casado not to take the fatal step, but to no avail.

The commander of the Army of the Levante, Menéndez, phoned at about two in the morning. He demanded that Matallana should immediately return, threatening that otherwise he would come right away to Elda with troops to 'liberate' him. The government interpreted this to mean that it was being

[i] General Manuel Matallana (Gómez), republican commander in the Civil War who sided with Casado in March 1939 in an attempt to reach a separate peace with Franco.

threatened with arrest. It was only then that Negrín began to reckon up the forces he could rely on and discovered to his horror that he had a mere 150 guards at his disposal. Matallana was promptly released and allowed to return to his headquarters. Fearing that as soon as Matallana arrived, Menéndez would come to Elda to arrest them, the ministers left the place at once and headed for the nearest airport, where the air force commander (a communist) had promised to have planes ready for them. However, for reasons unknown, not a single plane was to be found at the airport. So Negrín left all the ministers to wait for him there and, accompanied by del Vayo and Azcárate's son, headed for the nearest airport 30 kilometres away, where he hoped to find aircraft.

The road to the other airport passed a village where a meeting was being held of the Central Committee of the Communist Party of Spain, including Pasionaria,[i] Modesto, Líster and others. Azcárate's son asked Negrín to leave him there. But Negrín decided to meet the communists himself. He spoke at the Central Committee meeting, after which there was a long discussion of what was to be done. It was eventually decided that Negrín should make a last attempt to come to terms with Casado. Negrín immediately sent an appeal to Madrid for the popular front not to be split and to unite anew in the struggle against Franco. He then waited for a response from Casado, but none came. News came from the first airport that two planes had landed there. The ministers urged Negrín to go, fearing he might miss the opportunity to fly to France, but Negrín continued to wait for a reply from Madrid. This situation continued until 2 p.m. on 6 March. Still no reply. In the meantime it transpired that the telephone lines connecting the village with the outside world had been cut. To sit still, doing nothing, had become useless and dangerous. So Negrín and del Vayo left for the airport, where they joined other ministers and flew to France. Azcárate's son wanted to stay with the Central Committee, but the CC advised him not to tarry but to go abroad with del Vayo. Which he did.

In the evening of the same day the communist leaders, including Pasionaria, Modesto, Líster and other members of the CC, flew off to France, some of them directly and some via Algeria.

Such are the facts narrated to me by Azcárate's son. I record them, but I admit that much remains unclear to me. In particular, I fail to understand how, at a critical moment, both Negrín and the Central Committee of the Communist Party found themselves as 'refugees', without any armed forces at their disposal, even though, as the events of the last days in Madrid showed, there were many people in the army of the Centre who were ready to die for the cause of the Republic.

Future developments will, I'm sure, solve this riddle.

[i] Isidora Dolores Ibárruri Gómez, known as 'La Pasionaria' (the Passionflower) – was a Republican heroine in the Spanish Civil War.

[In his speech to the 18th Party Congress, on 10 March, Stalin had defended Russia's isolation and urged the party 'to be cautious and not allow Soviet Russia to be drawn into conflicts by warmongers who are accustomed to have others pull the chestnuts out of the fire'. Here Stalin had appropriated the metaphor employed by Maisky a couple of months earlier,[16] warning that Russia would not 'pull the chestnuts from the fire' for France and Britain. Maisky's metaphor had become so fashionable that, as the historian Lukacs shows, it was appropriated by Hitler three weeks later, warning that 'Anyone who declares himself to be ready to pull the chestnuts out of the fire for the Great Powers must be aware that he might burn his fingers in the process.'[17]]

14 March

Saw Vansittart.[18] He began straight away with Hudson's visit and argued at length that it must be used to utmost effect. Will this be done? Do we want this? In particular, are we ready to talk with Hudson about matters of politics as well as of trade? Stalin's and Manuilsky's[i] speeches at the Congress raised doubts in British political circles about the Soviet Union's willingness to cooperate with Western powers. Stalin's speech about the desire of the British ruling class to push Hitler towards the east has been particularly puzzling.

I laughed out loud at this point and interrupted Vansittart: 'Do I need to prove it to you that extremely influential individuals and groups exist in England who are whispering in Hitler's ear that he should mount a campaign against the Ukraine?'

Vansittart immediately weakened and kept silent.

I then put his mind at rest about Hudson. He would certainly be met warmly in Moscow, and Litvinov would of course be glad to talk to him about political matters. But I felt I had to warn Vansittart that Hudson should not expect any political initiatives from us. We would make no proposals. We've had enough experience of that. But if Hudson wished to lead an initiative, we would listen to him willingly and examine his *suggestions* attentively. This seemed to reassure him.[19]

Then Vansittart spoke of the events in Czechoslovakia. They had made a powerful impression in England and driven a nail into the coffin of the Munich policy. The situation must be exploited to the full. The attack on Czechoslovakia indicates that Hitler has turned towards the east. But the west cannot rest easily either. It is essential for the east and the west to join forces to stop Hitler…

Upon leaving, I met Corbin in the reception room. He was in a panic and asked me anxiously what I thought about the events in Central Europe.

---

[i] Dmitrii Zakharovich Manuilsky, general secretary of the Executive Committee of the Comintern, 1931–43.

15 March

I had lunch at Randolph Churchill's. Also present were his father, Lord Dufferin[i] (deputy minister for colonies), the son of Lord Camrose[ii] (publisher of the *Daily Telegraph*), and the American correspondent Roy Howard,[iii] who was granted the celebrated interview with Comrade Stalin in March 1936 which stopped Japanese aggression against the M[ongolian] P[eople's] R[epublic]. We spoke, of course, about the international situation, first and foremost about Czechoslovakia.

Winston Churchill expressed his view that Hitler's move against Czechoslovakia by no means signified a turn towards the east. Before striking a serious blow to the west, Hitler simply had to secure his rear, i.e. liquidate the Czechoslovak army, the Czechoslovak air force, etc. Moreover, Hitler was very keen to reinforce himself with Czechoslovak weapons, ammunition, aircraft and excellent armament factories.

Winston Churchill inquired with great anxiety about the meaning behind Stalin's speech. Was it a refusal to cooperate with the democracies?

I replied that such an interpretation would be incorrect. We have always been and remain advocates of collective retaliation against aggression, but it is essential that the 'democracies' should also be prepared to fight against the aggressors and not just chatter about it.

Churchill attaches great significance to Hudson's visit. This is a manifest sign of change in the sentiments of the ruling circles. Even if Chamberlain conceived Hudson's visit as merely a tactical manoeuvre (I raised this possibility), the logic of events will give it a far more serious tone.

I did not like Roy Howard – too self-assured, too primitive, too 'American'. I had a minor wrangle with him. In a rather arrogant and disparaging manner, Howard began to lecture all of us, particularly the British, about what they must and must not do in the sphere of foreign policy. He gave the impression that we, Americans, could not care less about Europe. Winston Churchill disputed this at length, arguing brilliantly that Britain and France represented the United States' first line of defence, and that if it was broken the Germans would appear in South America and Canada and threaten New York and Washington. But Howard didn't even want to hear about this.

His attitude enraged me, and I moved onto the offensive. I'm very unhappy with the state of affairs in Europe and I frequently and severely criticize British and French policies because they deserve it. But who gave the USA the right

---

[i] Basil Hamilton-Temple-Blackwood (4th marquess of Dufferin and Ava), lord-in-waiting, 1936–37; parliamentary undersecretary of state for the colonies, 1937–40.

[ii] The son was John Seymour Berry (2nd Viscount Camrose).

[iii] Roy Wilson Howard, editor and president of the *New York World-Telegram* and *The Sun*, 1931–60.

to hector us all like this? What is the position of the USA itself? American statesmen deliver fine speeches against Japanese aggression in China, while American industrialists supply Japanese aggressors with guns and aeroplanes. Is this an example of proper conduct? I continued in this vein for quite some time, much to the delight of the British.

Encouraged by my speech, one of them (I think it was Lord Camrose's son) thought it wise to defend Britain's position in the Manchurian issue. Here I had to speak out against the English and I deplored their conduct in 1932, using very strong language. Now it was Howard's turn to rejoice. He clasped my hand and exclaimed: 'You see, we are on the same side of the barricades!'

16 March

Yesterday I gave a speech at a grand dinner of machine-tool builders, attended by more than 600 guests. The speech is cited at great length by today's papers. The *Yorkshire Post* gives the fullest account.

The audience's response to my speech was curious. In general, the people were attentive and sympathetic throughout, but I got the heaviest applause at three particular moments. First, when I said that the Soviet government 'has always been and remains an advocate of universal peace' (moderate cheers), 'but certainly not at any price' (lengthy loud clapping). Second, when I said that 'today no clash of interests exists between the USSR and the British Empire in any part of the world' (loud cheers). Third, when I said at the end that 'in the last resort peace or war in our time depends on the kind of relations which exist between London and Moscow' (a storm of applause).

By contrast, those parts of my speech that concerned economic relations and opportunities for the further development of Anglo-Soviet trade were heard with polite sympathy but without enthusiasm.

Considering that the audience consisted almost entirely of *business men* – industrialists, engineers, bankers, etc. – such a reaction is most significant.

17 March

Aras[i] invited me round at six in the evening to compare views on current events. Simopoulos (the Greek) and Tilea[ii] (the Rumanian) were already there when I arrived. They were all in an agitated state. The Greek was demonstrably alarmed. Tilea was trying to put on a brave face, but I could see that he, too, was not quite himself.

---

[i] Tevfik Rüştü Aras, Turkish ambassador to Great Britain, 1939–42.
[ii] Virgil Viorel Tilea, Rumanian ambassador to London, 1938–40.

Tilea told us that he had just met Halifax. He had handed him an *SOS* on behalf of his government. The Rumanian government wanted to alert the British government to the fact that the complete complacency of the West following Hitler's seizure of Prague had created the impression in Bucharest that Hitler was omnipotent in C[entral] and S[outh]-E[ast] Europe. In the light of this, the Rumanian government must decide on the course of its future conduct. Before making a definitive choice, however, the Rumanian government would like to receive a clear answer from the British government to the following question: can Rumania count on British support in the struggle for its independence and, if she can, what kind of support could Rumania expect from Britain?

To substantiate his démarche, Tilea decided on his own initiative to inform Halifax of the demands made of the Rumanian government by Wohlthat,[i] adviser to Germany's Ministry of Economics, who is presently in Bucharest. In general, these amounted to the demand that Rumania must, in agreement with Germany, gradually dispense with its entire industry, give up trade with all other countries, ship 100% of its exports to Germany, and receive from Germany 100% of its imports.

According to Tilea, this information made a strong impression on Halifax, who promised to reply to the question posed by the Rumanian government in two to three days. Halifax, incidentally, showed interest in the current state of Rumanian–Soviet relations and asked Tilea what the Soviet stand would be in the event of an act of German aggression against Rumania.

Today, Vansittart invited me to the Foreign Office 'for a purely private conversation' and had a talk with me which was anything but private.

The annexation of Czechoslovakia, he said, had made a quite shocking impression on England. The policy of 'appeasement' is dead and will never be resurrected. The rats are already deserting the sinking ship. Just look at Lady Astor: yesterday she demanded in parliament that the prime minister convey to Hitler 'the feeling of outrage felt throughout the country at his actions in C[entral] E[urope]'. Incredible! Look at Beverley Buxton, an orthodox 'appeaser' on the staff of the *Sunday Times* (he runs the '*Men, Women and Memoirs*' section). Two days ago he came out with a speech in London full of indignation against the 'treachery' of Germany. Lastly, just look at the press: even *The Times* has abruptly changed its course. No, the situation today is definitely not the same as it was. There can be no return to the past.

Vansittart spoke with great animation and emotion.

But I was unconvinced. I started expressing my doubts. How many times over the past two years have I heard assurances that the 'situation has changed', that 'Chamberlain has finally understood', that the policy of 'appeasement'

[i] Helmut Wohlthat, director of Göring's Four Year Plan.

54. Robert Hudson, bluffing his way to Moscow.

has come to an end, etc. – but what do we see in reality? Neither Austria, nor Czechoslovakia, nor Spain has had a sobering effect on British policy. I fear the same might happen again. There will be a great hue and cry in England for the next few weeks, both inside and outside parliament, but then feelings will subside, and if Hitler and Mussolini make no new forays, everything will gradually return to its habitual, 'appeasing' routine.

Vansittart would not agree. He began arguing afresh and with even greater excitement that my fears were unfounded. The seizure of Prague does not resemble the seizure of Austria. England really has seen the light. All Vansittart's predictions have come to pass. His time, for which he has been preparing for years, has finally come – the time for setting up a mighty anti-German bloc! But all advocates of resistance to aggression now face a very serious challenge: to exploit to the full the favourable current situation. We must strike while the iron is hot. Hitler will not wait. Where will he throw himself now, after Prague? What's next in line? Memel? Danzig? Rumania? Yugoslavia?… No one can say for sure. But it is absolutely clear that an alliance of Britain, France and the USSR, with the possible participation of Poland, Rumania and Scandinavia, is the only way of stopping German aggression. We must work at frantic speed to achieve this. Beck is coming to London in early April – that's good. Vansittart pins great hopes on Beck's visit, even though he has no illusions about the personal qualities of the Polish foreign minister. Hudson is leaving for Moscow tomorrow, and that is also very good. Everything possible must be done to ensure the success of Hudson's mission. Vansittart is aware that relations between Moscow and Paris have been rather frosty of late – that's bad. Can anything be done to improve Franco-Soviet relations? Could we not take the initiative ourselves in this respect?

I said that, considering the experience of the past year, particularly the September crisis and Munich, the Soviet government would hardly find it possible to take the first step.

Vansittart then displayed interest in our relations with Poland and Rumania. In particular, could Rumania count on our aid if it fell victim to German aggression? In what form?

I conveyed to Vansittart the relevant information, emphasizing the progress made towards the improvement of our relations with Poland and Rumania in the past six months, but I warned him against overestimating the degree of improvement. Concerning aid to Rumania in the event of a German attack, I had nothing concrete to tell him for the time being. I quoted Comrade Stalin's famous statement at the 18th Party Congress about support for the victims of aggression who struggled for their independence, but added that the concrete application of this principle depended on the particular circumstances of each individual case.

Vansittart seemed pleased with my explanations and began insisting once again that all peace-loving powers must urgently *make up their mind*. It is time for Britain, France and the USSR to decide what they are going to do regarding the tripartite bloc. Britain and France must decide now what they would do in the event of German aggression against the Netherlands and Switzerland. The Soviet Union must decide now what it would do in the event of German aggression against Poland and Rumania. The year 1938 was defined by the way Hitler unleashed his blows against a disunited and unprepared Europe. If we wish to avert war, the year 1939 should be marked by the powerful unification of all peace-loving states to repulse the aggressors. The primary prerequisite for this is the formation of a London–Paris–Moscow 'axis'.

I laughed and observed that Vansittart's thoughts struck me as entirely fair, but that he was preaching to the wrong party. He knows better than anyone else that the USSR has always been an advocate of collective resistance against aggressors and of a bloc of peace-loving states in the struggle against international 'gangsters'. But who kept sabotaging the efforts of the USSR? Who systematically inflicted one blow after another on the League of Nations? Who thwarted the creation of a peace front? England and France. Let Vansittart first worry about setting the governments of these two countries on the path of virtue. We won't be the stumbling block.

Vansittart agreed with my reasoning, but added at the end: 'I assure you that from now on we will be singing a different tune.'

'Let's wait and see,' I replied.[20]

19 March

The atmosphere in Europe is becoming increasingly heated. On the evening of 17 March, in a speech in Birmingham, Chamberlain was sharply critical of Germany for its latest actions, but he did not risk drawing all the important logical conclusions. The front pages of yesterday's papers brought sensational news about 'Germany's ultimatum to Rumania', reproducing Tilea's account at Aras's gathering on 17 March. As I have learned, this news was given to the press by Halifax himself on the same evening. The 'German ultimatum' made a deep impression in England and France.

Halifax, however, did not limit himself to publication of the 'ultimatum'. On the same evening of 17 March, Halifax sent out urgent inquiries to Paris, Moscow, Warsaw, Ankara and possibly some other capitals, asking the respective governments what their response would be to German aggression against Rumania.

Seeds presented M.M. [Litvinov] with this inquiry on the morning of 18 March. M.M. inquired in his turn about the British government's position and added that Rumania itself had not sought assistance from us. He nonetheless promised to report Seeds' inquiry to the Soviet government, and the same evening he communicated our proposal to Seeds: to convene immediately a conference of the six powers which were most concerned with the matter (Britain, France, USSR, Poland, Turkey and Rumania), and to discuss measures by which to confront the imminent danger. It would be advisable to hold the conference in Bucharest. But this could be negotiated.

While Seeds was paying his first visit to M.M. in Moscow, here in London I was summoned by Halifax. He first spoke about Hudson (who was about to leave London, at 2 p.m. on 18 March) and asked that he be given a warm welcome. The Cabinet had not given Hudson any strict instructions. He was free to discuss both economic and political issues. His mission was aimed, among other things, at dispelling Moscow's suspicions about the objectives of British policy and, upon returning home, at helping to dispel certain 'misunderstandings' currently circulating in London with regard to the USSR. It would be most important if Hudson could have the opportunity in Moscow to learn a little

55. Maisky bids farewell to Seeds.

about the current state of the Soviet armed forces. In this connection, Halifax began asking me about the Red Army's strength, its armaments, etc. In reply, I supplied the data from Comrade Voroshilov's speech at the 18th Party Congress. One could sense that Halifax had heard an earful of anti-Soviet stories about the 'weakness', 'degeneration', etc. of the Soviet armed forces.

Halifax then moved on to current events. He said that the government had recalled Henderson from Berlin for 'consultation', that Stanley's and Hudson's planned visit to Berlin had been postponed, that payment of British credit worth 10 million to Czechoslovakia was suspended, that the British government was trying to evacuate a certain number of 'refugees' who had got stuck in Prague, and that the Foreign Office had sent a note of protest to Berlin ('which, of course, is absolutely meaningless', Halifax concluded with a weary gesture).

Finally, Halifax informed me about Seeds' démarche in Moscow and persistently asked me what the USSR would do in the event of German aggression against Rumania. Could Rumania expect help from the USSR, and in what way? Arms and ammunition? Or might assistance come in more active forms?

I replied that the general view of the Soviet government had been formulated most recently by Comrade Stalin in his statement at the 18th Party Congress: we advocate assistance to victims of aggression who are fighting for their independence. However, it is difficult to tell in advance how this general principle will be applied in each particular case. That will depend on the specific conditions of every specific case. Halifax seemed satisfied with my answer.

I met Halifax at 12.45. Earlier, at eleven in the morning, I had a conversation with Vansittart, who spoke heatedly and at length about the importance of making Hudson's visit a 'success'. British sentiments are rapidly changing, owing to the latest events. Leadership in foreign policy is returning from *10, Downing Street* to the Foreign Office. Halifax now shares Vansittart's view of things. A successful outcome to Hudson's visit would definitively consolidate the triumph of the new course in British foreign policy, the course Vansittart has been upholding for many years…

At 3 p.m. today I saw Halifax, to inform him of our answer to the British inquiry (although Seeds had certainly notified him about it through his own channels, there was no harm in my repeating it just to make sure) and, most importantly, to find out what the British government thought of it. It was Sunday, but Halifax was in the Foreign Office. Moreover, he had already exchanged opinions with the PM earlier in the morning, concerning our proposal for a six-power conference. Halifax finds the proposal 'premature': if the conference is not prepared properly in advance, it could culminate in failure, with a negative political effect. Besides, we must act quickly, whereas the convening of a conference will take some time. So, instead of a conference, the British government suggests the prompt issuing of a 'declaration of the four' (Britain, France, USSR and Poland) to the effect that the said powers will respond to the threat of aggression by immediately organizing a consultation on measures of resistance. This is the first step. Then, after the four powers sign the declaration, the remaining peace-loving countries will be invited to join, and a conference of the respective countries may be convened, where the methods and forms of fighting aggression will be discussed. Of course, agreement must be reached primarily by the *big boys*, i.e. the 'big four'.

I began to object. I said that the conference could be convened in a few days if there was a desire to do so, that an announcement of the date and venue could be published tomorrow, that this alone would have a far-reaching political effect and that if Britain really *means business*, the risk of the conference failing was very small. But Halifax stuck to his guns. He informed me that the text of the declaration was being worked on. It will be adopted by the Cabinet tomorrow morning and immediately sent to the capitals concerned…

It is clear that Chamberlain does not want a genuine struggle against aggression. He is still working for 'appeasement'.

20 March

Vansittart asked me to come by. I found him in very high spirits. His face was radiant. All his gestures were full of energy and verve.

'Things are going well!' he exclaimed. 'The text of the declaration has already been sent to Paris, Moscow and Warsaw. This is the first step towards the creation of a "great bloc". It does not really matter what exactly is written in the declaration; what is crucial is the mere fact of its birth. It will serve as a crystallization point around which a powerful anti-German coalition will form. Some in the government disagree with it. Some are banking on delays and sabotage. No such luck!'

Vansittart asked me to facilitate a speedy – and favourable – reply from the Soviet government so as to deliver the final blow to the 'appeasers'…[21]

I saw Beaverbrook. He is in a strange mood. He is certain that the policy of 'appeasement' is dead and that the British government will now pursue a policy of resistance to aggressors. Personally, Chamberlain is *not very happy* about it, but the mood in the rank and file of the Conservative Party is such that he cannot act differently. The PM's speech in the Commons on 15 March aroused strong indignation in the party. Had Chamberlain not changed tack in Birmingham on 17 March, he would have lost the premiership.

'The country is saying: Germany – that's our enemy.'

This is why the idea of rapprochement with the USSR is so popular. This is why people in the government are talking about inviting M.M. to London.

'Personally,' Beaverbrook concluded, 'I'm against the policy the Conservative Party is now defending. I'm an isolationist. But if the country wants that policy, I have to take it on board.'

In the evening, first Corbin and then Aras came to visit me. Corbin displayed unexpected revolutionary spirit, saying that he found the text of the declaration too feeble. To his mind, it should have been declared that the powers had already started consultation on measures for repelling aggression, instead of merely stating (as the text of the declaration puts it) that they would hold consultations in the event of a threat of aggression. When I asked how the French government had replied to London's inquiry about the measures to be taken in the event of German aggression against Rumania, Corbin said that Bonnet had stated the necessity of taking 'strong measures'.

'What does that mean exactly?' I asked almost impertinently.

Corbin shook his head and answered with an authoritative air: 'That was not specified!'

So much for the French 'revolutionary spirit'!

Aras informed me that in reply to the English inquiry, Turkey had said that it was prepared to take an active part in any measure which Britain, France, the

USSR and the Balkan Entente[22] deemed necessary in order to save Rumania, but that it would not budge without the USSR. Moreover, Aras told me that the Bulgarian prime minister, Kiosseivanov,[i] who visited Ankara a few days ago, had asked the Turks whether they would agree to support Bulgaria's demand for the return of Dobrudja. The Turks replied that they thought it impossible to support measures directed against a member of the Balkan Entente, but they were ready, together with Rumania and Bulgaria, to study the problem and look for an appropriate solution in the event of Bulgaria joining the Balkan Entente. Kiosseivanov then asked how Turkey would act if, following German aggression against Rumania, Bulgaria occupied Dobrudja by force. To this the Turks apparently replied: 'In such a case, Turkey, in accordance with its commitments to the Little Entente,[23] would immediately act against Bulgaria.'

In spite of this answer, Kiosseivanov, according to Aras, left Ankara with a feeling of deep satisfaction.

22 March

Today we gave our reply to the British: we are prepared to sign their 'declaration of the four' if France and Poland sign it, too. To add weight to the declaration, we propose that it be signed not only by the foreign ministers of the four countries, but also by their premiers.

So, Britain, France and the USSR have given their consent. But what about Poland? Yesterday, at a banquet at the palace in honour of Lebrun,[ii] I questioned Raczyński (the Polish ambassador) about this. He said that he approved of the declaration personally and would willingly sign it, but he wasn't sure that Warsaw shared his attitude. Raczyński is a poor representative of Beck. He is a Westernist and a League of Nations man, and you can hardly use him to judge what the Polish government is thinking. We will see…

At Covent Garden this evening, for an opera in – once again – Lebrun's honour, Aras told me that Bonnet rates the chances of a Franco-Italian 'settlement' as fifty-fifty. I doubt it. In any case, Bonnet is using various unofficial channels (Laval, in particular) to test the ground in Rome for a new act of *appeasement*. The English are egging him on.

At the opera house I also learned the following curious details from Balutis about the talk between the Lithuanian foreign minister, Urbšys,[iii] and Ribbentrop which took place a few days ago. Urbšys was on his way back from Rome, where he had gone to attend the pope's funeral, and had made a stop in Berlin. Ribbentrop told Urbšys in plain words that there was only one 'moot

[i] Georgi Kiosseivanov, Bulgarian prime minister and foreign minister, 1935–40.
[ii] Albert Lebrun, 14th and last president of France's Third Republic, 1932–40.
[iii] Juozas Urbšys, Lithuanian foreign minister, 1938–41.

point' between Germany and Lithuania: Memel. As soon as this was settled, harmony would reign in relations between the two countries. As Ribbentrop sees it, the time has come to 'settle' the problem: Memel must be given back to Germany. Embarrassed, Urbšys said that directly upon his return to Kovno he would report Ribbentrop's point of view to his government and then convey its reply in principle to Ribbentrop. The latter interrupted Urbšys rudely and snapped back: 'I'm interested in Memel, not principles.'

Then, pointing to the telephone on the table, Ribbentrop continued impudently: 'Pick up the receiver, call your prime minister, and we shall settle the Memel problem at once, without further delay.'

Shaken, Urbšys pleaded that he be allowed to discuss the matter with his government on his return to Kovno. In the end, Ribbentrop gave his reluctant consent, but declared: 'I give you two or three days to come to a final decision about Memel. If you fail to do so, we shall have to take other measures.'

Today, Balutis informed Halifax about Urbšys's talk with Ribbentrop. The latter reacted in the following way: England expresses its sympathy for Lithuania, but can do nothing to help.

[There was no ambiguity in the Soviet condemnation of Hitler's annexation of Czechoslovakia on 15 March. Litvinov submitted to Schulenburg 'a sharply worded' message, which was promptly published in the Soviet press. Unexpectedly, Stalin consented to sign the declaration with full pomp and circumstance, regardless of the fact that the Soviet proposal for a six-power conference had been turned down as 'premature'. This acceptance, however, was clearly tactical, probing British reaction to the anticipated Polish refusal to join in. Maisky admitted to Dalton that the object of the Soviet proposal was 'to test British and French intentions of which they were suspicious'.[24] In the meantime, Litvinov, who remained highly sceptical, forbade his diplomats from taking any initiative. 'If Britain and France genuinely change their line,' he instructed them, 'they should either make their views on our former proposals known or else offer their own. The initiative must be left to them.'[25]

The scepticism was well justified. At an ad hoc emergency meeting between Chamberlain, Halifax and a few other ministers at Downing Street that Sunday afternoon, it was agreed that Halifax's idea of consultations between the major powers following the declaration was 'far-reaching and went very far indeed beyond any previous pronouncements'. It was therefore decided to dilute the undertaking by 'laying the chief emphasis on the formal declaration, and dealing in much more general terms with the subsequent consultations'. Seeing which way the wind was blowing, Halifax failed to inform Cabinet that, in his conversation with Maisky, he had already committed Britain to the conference and had even promised a press release to that effect the following day.[26] Maisky, who found it difficult to abide by Litvinov's instructions, continued to use his old method of inciting his interlocutors to come up with ideas which, unbeknownst to the Kremlin, often originated with him. At the same time, even he was forced to admit that the widespread disillusionment with appeasement had only a limited impact for as long as Chamberlain remained 'firmly settled in his saddle'.[27]]

23 March

Today a Labour delegation met Chamberlain and categorically demanded vigorous measures: England should assume definite commitments on the continent, including the eastern part of Europe, and should also support our proposal to convene a 'six-power conference'.

In an obvious effort to chime with the mood of the deputation, the prime minister scolded Hitler, stressed his wish to cooperate with the USSR, complained about Poland, whose attitude to the USSR made it difficult to build a 'peace bloc' in Europe, and ended by stating that the British government was preparing 'serious measures' to fight aggression. The delegation left under the general impression that Chamberlain was scared and had lost all his 'optimism'. But their conclusion must be taken with a large pinch of salt: Labourites are terribly gullible in their dealings with the powers that be.

Later, on meeting Chamberlain in parliament, Attlee and Greenwood asked him bluntly: was the prime minister prepared to undertake firm military commitments in Eastern Europe? The PM replied: 'Yes, I am.'

25 March

Rumania has signed a trade agreement with Germany[28] that differs but slightly from the 'ultimatum' Tilea was talking about a few days ago. Rumania's capitulation has made a very powerful impression on parliament and the press. The newspapers, especially the *Daily Telegraph*, are demanding prompt and forceful measures from the government. In the corridors of the House, there is talk once more of the need for a Cabinet reshuffle. But Chamberlain remains true to himself. My general impression is that the PM still believes in *appeasement* and still hopes to push Hitler toward the Ukraine. But the public's mood is rapidly hardening. England sees again in its mind's eye the phantom of a great power striving for hegemony on the continent. This phantom has awoken past fears and mighty passions in the English soul. Philip II of Spain, Louis XIV, Napoleon I, the kaiser! England has waged stubborn and destructive wars against the 'hegemons' of the past. She has satisfied herself only with their complete annihilation. The same feelings and moods are elicited by the name of Hitler today. Of course, were Hitler to move east, decisive steps against Germany could be postponed. But most Tories are far from convinced about Hitler's 'eastern aspirations'. Very many of them fear the opposite: that Hitler, having secured Balkan and Baltic resources of raw materials and food, and having immobilized Poland by one method or another, will bring his colossal, newly acquired might to bear on France and England. Hence the immense upsurge of anti-German sentiment and the equally immense eagerness to create a united front against aggression. By analogy with the precedents of the past, one would have expected England to take up the fight against Germany, with all the ensuing consequences. But here's the question: to what extent does the 'social factor' (the decay of British capitalism and the English bourgeoisie's fear of revolution) modify the well-known models of centuries past? We will see.

However this may be, we cannot exclude the possibility that Chamberlain – and it has to be Chamberlain – will very soon have to decide whether or not to undertake military commitments in Eastern Europe. And even whether or not to form a close alliance with the USSR.

[On the afternoon of 29 March, barely two hours before entertaining the king and queen to dinner, Chamberlain was alerted by Halifax to intelligence reports from Berlin about an impending German attack on Poland. The two decided 'then & there' to issue a guarantee declaration, promising Poland assistance 'in the event of any action which clearly threatened Polish independence'. The drafting of the impetuous declaration, which was aimed at pacifying public opinion at home while deterring Germany, was deliberately ambiguous. The Germans were expected to infer from the message that the British government was more concerned with Germany resorting to force than with the sanctity of borders. It further implied that activation of the guarantee was conditional on the Poles making conciliatory moves, while it was left to the British to establish whether a threat to Poland existed; meanwhile the issue of military aid was conspicuously absent. To his inner circle, it was clear that Chamberlain was 'unhappy' in his new role as architect of a 'diluted collective security'. 'Munich and the betrayal of the Czechs over again', was Dalton's judgement.[29]

Chamberlain deliberately opted for Poland, rather than Russia, as an ally, against the firm advice of the chiefs of staff. By so doing, he not only pushed the Russians further into isolation, but also inadvertently set the scene for a Soviet–German rapprochement (dictated by the Kremlin's wish to steal a march on Britain).[30] Pondering his diary entries for that period, Cadogan confessed in 1964 that they gave 'the impression of a number of amateurs fumbling about with insoluble problems'. But even then he was entirely dismissive of the Russian alternative.[31]]

29 March

I visited Cadogan.[32]

First of all, I requested an explanation for the strange incident that occurred regarding the communiqué which concluded Hudson's visit to Moscow. The essence of the incident is as follows. On 27 March, Mikoyan and Litvinov on one side and Hudson and Seeds on the other agreed on the text of the communiqué, which was then handed over to TASS. Late in the evening, when TASS had already circulated the communiqué across the Soviet Union, Hudson and Seeds looked for Litvinov and informed him that the Foreign Office was demanding that no mention of politics be made in the communiqué. M.M. replied that it was too late to make any modifications to the communiqué that had already been distributed, but, if the British side so wished, an amended version could be sent abroad. Hudson and Seeds discussed it between themselves and came to the conclusion that such a solution would not be advantageous. So the communiqué remained unchanged. But Seeds and especially Hudson were clearly worried and upset. Having recounted all these circumstances to Cadogan, I asked him: what was I to make of the incident?

Cadogan replied that nothing terrible had happened and that it was senseless to blow the incident out of proportion. It was like this. At about 7.30 p.m. (10.30 Moscow time) on 27 March, the Foreign Office received a telegram from Moscow saying that the communiqué to be issued after the talks touched not only upon trade matters, but also on political ones. The draft communiqué was not, however, attached to the telegram. Cadogan grew anxious. Although Hudson had not been forbidden from discussing political matters, he was not on the staff of the Foreign Office, which had little idea of the nature of the political talks Hudson had pursued in Moscow. Cadogan's first impulse was to request the text of the communiqué from Moscow, but, after a glance at his watch, he realized it was too late for that. So, to avoid any unexpected surprises, Cadogan decided to 'play safe' and sent a directive to Moscow to remove anything political from the communiqué. The directive, it later transpired, arrived too late, and the communiqué was published in its original version. Cadogan does not regret its appearance, for having read the published text he found it quite *all right*. But on the evening of the 27th he did not know that, which is why he acted as he did. And that's the long and the short of it. The significance of the episode should not be exaggerated.

I objected that the incident had produced an unpleasant impression in Moscow. We had no particular desire to include political matters in the communiqué. But since the British press and such persons as Halifax, Vansittart and Hudson himself had constantly been emphasizing the political importance of Hudson's visit, Cadogan's instruction concerning the communiqué struck a dissonant chord. Cadogan was embarrassed, apologized, and assured me that there had been no malicious intent in his actions. Perhaps. Yet there is no doubt that he greatly dislikes Hudson: he spoke about him with obvious annoyance and hidden scorn. Or maybe the whole point is that Hudson is a man promoted, so to speak, by Vansittart? As we know, Cadogan and Vansittart don't get along.

Then the conversation turned to other matters. Cadogan asked me whether I had read yesterday's statement by the PM in parliament. I replied that I had and, moreover, had been greatly surprised by it. Chamberlain said that the British government's intentions 'go significantly farther than mere consultation' and that 'the powers, with which we are in consultation, have been given to understand clearly what actions we are ready to undertake under certain circumstances'. Until now I've had every reason to believe that the Soviet

Union is one of the powers with which Britain is in consultation, but I am as yet aware only of the draft 'declaration of the four' that stipulates 'consultation', and nothing more. Is it any surprise that I was somewhat taken aback yesterday by the prime minister's revelation?

In saying this, I intentionally went a little over the top: I had already gleaned something of the British government's new plans from unofficial sources, but the Foreign Office had not said a word about it to me.

Cadogan was a bit embarrassed and started explaining the current situation. It turns out that 'the declaration of the four' is now in the past. The Poles refused in the most categorical terms, and the Rumanians somewhat less flatly, to join any scheme (whether in the form of a declaration or something else) to which the USSR would be party. Moreover, they made it clear that the 'consultation' specified in the declaration did not suit them at all and that they could enter a peace bloc only if Britain and France undertook firm military commitments. Consequently, intensive consultation had been under way between London and Paris, and also Warsaw, in the last couple of days. The view that has come to dominate British government circles at present is as follows: as an initial stage it is necessary to build a four-power bloc of Britain, France, Poland and Rumania, with the former two committing themselves to armed defence of the latter two in the event of German aggression against them. The USSR remains to one side for the time being, but it will be drawn in at the second stage. As to the forms and nature of cooperation with the USSR, the British government plans to hold special talks with us on this matter.

Listening to Cadogan, I did not hide my deep mistrust. Knowing the English and the traditions of British foreign policy, I could not accept that Chamberlain would make any firm *commitments* in Eastern Europe. Therefore, to clarify the situation fully, I asked Cadogan directly: 'Suppose Germany attacks Poland tomorrow. Will England declare war on Germany if that happens? Will she impose a blockade on the German coasts and bomb German fortifications?'

To my surprise, Cadogan replied: 'Yes, she will declare war, impose a blockade on the coasts, and bomb from the air… Assuming, of course, that the Cabinet accepts the entire plan.'

Cadogan looked at his watch, which showed 1 p.m. and added: 'Maybe the plan has already been adopted. The Cabinet is in session right now.'

I expressed my doubts about this. Cadogan was not quite sure of the Cabinet decision himself. Noticing a smile on my face, Cadogan asked: 'Why are you smirking? Do you not believe me?'

'I'm smirking,' I replied, 'because your new plan, assuming that it is carried out, which I doubt very much, would mean a sort of revolution in traditional British foreign policy, and it is common knowledge that you don't like revolutions here in Great Britain.'

Cadogan shrugged his shoulders and said: 'Yes, of course, that would be a revolution in our foreign policy. That is why it is taking us so long to reach a final decision. But the mood in the country is such that firm guarantees to Poland and Rumania are becoming a real possibility.'[33]

[According to Fitzroy Maclean[i] at the British embassy, Hudson had arrived in Moscow with 'an anodyne message of encouragement' from Halifax and a vague promise of a political deal which served as the basis for the communiqué. A few hours before Hudson's departure from Moscow, a telegram arrived from London instructing the delegation 'to stick to commercial negotiations and in no circumstances to broach any political matters whatever'. Litvinov, who had left for his dacha for the weekend, was hauled back to Moscow. When he heard the news, 'he replied acidly that he had thought he was dealing with a plenipotentiary, but now found that he was a second-rate office boy'. 'A pusher and a crook' was Cadogan's blunt judgement of Hudson.[34] Earlier, Litvinov had convinced Stalin that Hudson had not been authorized to make concrete proposals. 'I think,' he said, 'that we too should not make any concrete proposals or offer a concrete form of cooperation. It will be enough to explain our general stand in the spirit of your report to the Congress.'[35] Litvinov informed Maisky on 28 March that the communiqué contained 'absolutely non-binding formulations', that 'no proposals had been made by either side', and that 'the visit had no political or economic repercussions whatsoever'.[36]]

31 March

Poland is the centre of attention. The German press is waging a rabid campaign against Poland. German troops are concentrated on the Polish border. Hitler is expected to strike any moment now, but in which direction? That is not quite clear as yet. Most probably, Danzig or Silesia. Or maybe in both directions at once.

In view of the current situation, the British diplomatic machinery has been working at a quite uncharacteristically frenzied pace for the last seven or eight days. When it transpired that 'the declaration of the four' was not viable due to Poland's objections, the British government, without breathing a word to us, stepped up its search for other means *to stop aggression*. As usual, the English took the path of creeping empiricism, i.e. the method of the rule of thumb. They decided: since at this precise moment it is Poland that faces acute danger, let's think how to help Poland. And only Poland. Fighting aggression in Europe in general does not interest us. Two days ago already, Cadogan informed me of the direction which the British government's thinking was taking. By the way, no decision was taken in the end at the Cabinet meeting on 29 March. But on

[i] Sir Fitzroy Maclean, member of the British embassy in Moscow; resigned from the Foreign Office in 1939 to join the military, rising from the rank of private to brigadier, to become Churchill's personal representative to Tito in 1943.

the same evening and yesterday, 30 March, there was an almost unbroken flow of meetings of the Cabinet and of its Foreign Policy Committee (Chamberlain, Halifax, Simon, Hoare and two or three more ministers) in attempts to find the best way of helping Poland. It was only today that the results of all this unusual activity on *Downing Street* became known. More on this below.

What needs mentioning now is that Labourites have been in very close contact with the prime minister over the past two days and that yesterday they met him twice. Since the Foreign Office is forever spreading rumours through the press that the British government is *in close touch* with the Soviet government, and since, on the other hand, the Labourites have learned from me that I have not seen Halifax for 12 days (since 19 March) and that almost the same situation obtains with Seeds in Moscow (he last saw M.M. on 22 March, when the latter handed him our reply concerning the 'declaration of the four'), the pressure exerted by Attlee, Greenwood, Dalton and others was all aimed at achieving genuine cooperation between England and the USSR. Late yesterday evening, a Labour deputation consisting of Dalton, Alexander[i] and others had a substantial conversation with Chamberlain on this matter, and the latter assured them that he was all for cooperating with the 'Soviets' right away, but those obnoxious 'Poles' were getting in the way.[37]

Possibly in order to prepare himself with excuses in similar situations, Chamberlain instructed Halifax to meet me. On the 29th, after lunch, I received a call from the Foreign Office asking me to visit Halifax at seven in the evening. I accepted. But at 6 p.m., Halifax's secretary phoned me again to say that, unfortunately, the minister couldn't receive me today and asked me to come at 4 p.m. the following day. Once again I accepted. On 30 March at 3 p.m. there was another call from the Foreign Office: it turned out that the foreign secretary couldn't receive me on this day either and wished to postpone my visit to the following morning at 10.30. I agreed to that as well. On the 31st, at 10 a.m., yet another call came from the FO: Halifax was unable to keep his last promise. He would let me know when he could see me.[38] Finally, at noon on the same day, 31 March, Halifax's secretary asked me to come to the FO at 12.45. Only then did my meeting with Halifax take place.

It began with much bowing and scraping on the part of the foreign secretary. He was terribly sorry that he had had to postpone our meeting again and again, but during the past two days he had been holding endless meetings.

'It is not so easy to edit a document that would mean a revolution in our foreign policy,' Halifax said by way of self-justification.

He then gave me a sheet of paper with the text of the speech the prime minister was to make in parliament at 3 p.m. I quickly skimmed the document.

---

[i] Albert Victor Alexander, Labour's first lord of the Admiralty, 1929–31 and 1940–46.

Halifax watched my face attentively, and when I had finished reading, asked me anxiously what I thought about it. I replied that it was difficult for me to formulate a considered opinion, since I had only just seen the text of the prime minister's statement, but my first reaction was that the document lacked precision. All of the first part repeatedly stressed the importance of 'peaceful means' in the settlement of international conflicts, but there was no clear indication at the end that England was prepared to help Poland with armed support. What effect would this have on Hitler? Would he believe in the seriousness of British intentions? I wasn't sure. Perhaps not.[39]

Halifax started to defend the text of the statement, though it was clear that my words had somewhat confused him. He then asked: 'But generally speaking, the statement is in line with your aims, is it not?'

'Perhaps,' I said, 'but it is not firm and consistent enough.'

Halifax was silent for an instant, before blurting out: 'What would you think if the prime minister told parliament that the Soviet government also approves of his statement?'

And then, after a little hesitation, he added, as if forcing the words out against his will: 'If the prime minister could say this, it would greatly alleviate the situation... This would prevent unnecessary arguments and discord in our midst...'

I immediately realized what was behind it: Chamberlain wanted to use us as a shield against the opposition's attacks. Affecting great surprise, I replied: 'I don't quite understand you, Lord Halifax. You did not consult us while preparing your Polish action. The Soviet government has not seen the present statement. I myself had the opportunity to familiarize myself with it just a few moments ago. How could the prime minister say that the Soviet government approves of his statement under such circumstances? I think it would be rather awkward.'

Halifax was embarrassed and hastened to say: 'You may be right.'

So, misrepresentation did not occur. In part, at least. Having failed to gain my consent, Chamberlain did not of course risk saying what he had wanted to say, but nonetheless, replying to Greenwood's question about the Soviet government's attitude to his statement, the PM announced that this morning the foreign secretary had had a serious conversation on the matter with the Soviet ambassador, and that he [Chamberlain] was positive that the principles of British actions met with understanding and appreciation on the part of the Soviet government.[40]

Mere legalese: empty verbiage, which is impregnable to criticism. At the same time, there is a vague hint at something that nobody knows. This makes it possible to create in the minds of the uninitiated the impression that the Soviet government has given its blessing to the prime minister's statement.

Chamberlain must need us very badly if he has to resort to the type of tricks I observed today…

Another curious detail. The original schedule for today was as follows: the Cabinet was to meet for the final approval of the text of the statement at 10 a.m., and at 11 a.m. the statement was to be read in parliament (since today is Friday, the House of Commons is in session from 11 to 4). However, as a result of yesterday's visit of the Labour delegation to the PM, the schedule was changed slightly: the Cabinet meeting at 10.30, Halifax's meeting with me between 12 and 1 to acquaint me with the text of the statement, and the reading of the statement in parliament at 3. And that's exactly what happened.

[Rather than the Munich Agreement, Stalin's 'chestnuts' speech or the dismissal of Litvinov, the guarantees given to Poland appear to have been the crucial event paving the way to the Ribbentrop–Molotov Pact, and the opening salvo of the Second World War. By guaranteeing Poland, Chamberlain to all intents and purposes abandoned Britain's traditional position as arbiter in the European balance of power, and instead confronted Germany head on. The guarantees had two potential major effects. Beyond redressing the humiliation inflicted on him by Hitler's brazen abrogation of the Munich Agreement, what was uppermost in Chamberlain's mind was the deterrent effect: the guarantees (he hoped) would check Hitler and bring him back to the negotiating table. The second possible repercussion was overlooked by Chamberlain: if Hitler persevered with his territorial claims against Poland, the military axiom of avoiding war on two fronts would make it imperative for the Nazis to seek agreement with the Soviet Union. Consequently, the hitherto inaccessible German option suddenly opened up for the Soviet Union. Conversely, once it did dawn on Chamberlain that the path to a 'second Munich' was not plain sailing and that the possibility of war had become real, he would reluctantly be forced to secure at least a measure of Soviet military commitment, vital for the implementation of the guarantees. In this manner, and without prior design, the Soviet Union now became the pivot of the European balance of power.]

1 April

Yesterday, after the statement had been read in parliament, Chamberlain invited Lloyd George to his office to exchange views on international affairs. An unprecedented event, since Chamberlain and Lloyd George hate each other.

During their conversation, Lloyd George raised the issue, in the sharpest terms, of engaging the USSR in security guarantees in Europe. Chamberlain replied, as always, that he was only too willing to do so, but that Poland and Rumania were making things difficult. Lloyd George then asked: 'But if the question of engaging the USSR is still hanging in the air, how could you risk giving Poland Great Britain's unilateral guarantee? That's damnably dangerous.'

Chamberlain parried Lloyd George's remark by declaring that according to the information available to the government, Hitler would never risk a war on two fronts.

'And where is your second front?' Lloyd George snapped back.

'Poland,' answered Chamberlain.

Lloyd George roared with laughter and started mocking the prime minister: 'Poland! A country with a weak economy and torn by internal strife, a country that has neither aviation nor a properly equipped army… And that's your second front! What nonsense! There cannot be a second front without the USSR. A guarantee to Poland without the USSR is an irresponsible gamble that may end very badly for our country!'

Chamberlain did not have an answer.[41]

6 April

Today I saw Halifax, who briefed me on the results of his talks with Beck. According to Halifax, the three days Beck spent in London have been very profitable. The main achievement is the bilateral agreement on mutual assistance against aggression which the prime minister announced in parliament today. In this way, the unilateral guarantee which Great Britain gave to Poland on 31 March is now transformed into a pact of mutual assistance between the two countries. Only an interim agreement in principle has been concluded for now, but later – the exact date cannot as yet be fixed – the agreement will be formalized as a special treaty.[42] One of the reasons for postponing the signing of the treaty is the need to resolve the matter of the forms and nature of the assistance which the USSR could and would wish to provide in the struggle against aggression. In this connection, Halifax asked me all of a sudden whether the USSR could, if necessary, undertake to supply Poland with arms and ammunition. I replied that I was not in a position to discuss the matter.

Then Halifax brought to my attention the last paragraph in the PM's announcement and interpreted it to mean that the British government wished to retain the possibility of holding talks with the USSR.

In turn, I asked Halifax to clarify the expression 'direct or indirect threat to independence'. What does the word 'indirect' mean? And who is to decide whether there is a threat or not? Each side on its own? Or both sides in joint consultation?

Halifax was unable to give clear-cut answers to my questions. But as far as I could understand him, each side would decide on its own whether there was a threat or not. As for 'indirect' threat, this concept would be subject to 'classification' in further negotiations.

On parting, Halifax expressed the ardent hope that he would be able to get away at Easter to his estate for five days. Just think: he has not been 'home' for a whole six weeks!

Will he leave? I don't know. Dark clouds are gathering on the Albanian horizon.

[Maisky continued cautiously to challenge Moscow's dithering. It was 'extremely important,' he nagged Litvinov, 'to know which direction our work here should take', particularly if the Western powers were to offer a pact of mutual assistance. He was, however, accused of having inadvertently become putty in the hands of Chamberlain and Vansittart. He was called to order and reminded of the Soviet 'present and, possibly, also future restraint in respect of all sorts of English gestures'. To his ambassador in Berlin, Litvinov explained: 'We know full well that it is impossible to restrain and halt aggression in Europe without us, and later our help will be sought, which will cost them dearer, and they will have to recompense us. That is why we remain so placid in the face of the tumult which has erupted around what is referred to as the change in British policy.'[43]

Maisky, though, found it most difficult to follow his own counsel 'to keep quiet, and not show any nervousness or impatience'. In the course of a conversation with Ewer of the *Daily Herald* on 4 April, he claimed to have had 'a brain-wave' which seemed 'spontaneous and his own'. 'Why,' he asked the journalist, 'did not His Majesty's Government invite Litvinov to London?' Maisky offered to convey such an invitation privately to Litvinov. He insisted, though, that in approaching the Foreign Office, Ewer should present the idea 'as entirely his own and not coming from [Maisky] or after discussion with him'. Although the idea that 'a lunch at Windsor to [sic] Litvinov would work wonders' in repairing the wounded Russian *amour propre*, it was hoped that the government would 'not allow Maisky's fictitious grievances and Litvinov's assumed sulks to push us into action against our better judgement'. 'I regard association with the Soviet [sic],' Cadogan sealed the debate in the Foreign Office, echoing Chamberlain, 'as more of a liability than an asset.'[44]

Cautiously steering a course through the rather schizophrenic Soviet policy, Maisky admitted to the Webbs that, like other Soviet diplomats, he had become increasingly isolated, hardly in touch with any of the leaders and 'kept out of the Molotov–Stalin government circles'. He remained sceptical of Chamberlain, 'essentially the same man he used to be', whose new 'gestures' were a reluctant response to the public pressure concealing his cherished hope of 'pushing Hitler in the direction of Soviet Ukraine'. He confided to the Webbs that Moscow 'did *not* trust [Chamberlain] and it was doubtful whether they would join a pact if he remained Premier'. This, however, did not prevent him from trying further to convince Litvinov that the prime minister's position was constantly challenged by the majority of the 'politically minded people' who had 'regretfully' arrived at the conclusion that the 'Western direction' of German aggression was the more likely one.[45]]

11 April

Halifax didn't manage to get away to his estate after all! The Italians attacked Albania on the morning of the 7th, and as of today King Zog[i] is already a refugee in exile.

I visited Halifax at his request.[46] We talked at length about the spread of aggression in Europe and the need to take urgent measures against it. Halifax wanted to know whether we would agree to give Poland a guarantee in the forms that would make Soviet aid acceptable to Warsaw (arms, ammunition, aviation, etc., but not large land forces). I declined to give him a direct answer. Halifax further let me understand that the British government was preparing guarantees for Greece and possibly for Rumania, too. He tried to argue that Britain, like the USSR, was thinking about the organization of security all over Europe, only our methods were different: Britain wants to build security 'from the bottom', laying one brick on another, whereas the USSR wants European security to be built 'from the top' by setting up an all-embracing peace bloc. In Halifax's view, the British path is more practicable.

I objected, arguing that aggression is like water: if you block it in one direction, it finds another. We should not split hairs and set about this like amateurs. We must stop the spread of aggression across Europe right away, and the only way of doing that is to form a 'peace bloc' around 'the big troika': Britain, France and the USSR. Our exchange came to nothing, of course, but I think I managed to put some useful ideas into Halifax's head…[47]

[Litvinov was not impressed by Maisky's telegram, which expanded on the last paragraph of this diary entry. He took the unreserved pledge to Poland to be an 'unfriendly act', which inadvertently strengthened Poland's hand against the Soviet Union. He suspected that Britain sought from Russia 'some sort of binding promise … without entering into any agreement … and without undertaking any commitments'. It was 'intolerable' for the Russians to be in the situation where a man 'is invited to a party and then asked not to come because the other guests do not wish to meet him. We would prefer to be crossed off the guest list altogether.' Litvinov further took a dim view of the line adopted by Maisky in his conversations with Halifax, which could have given the latter the false impression that the Soviet Union opposed 'separate bipartite or tripartite agreements, and in general wanted to gain something from Britain'. He took the unusual step of submitting his response to Stalin for approval, adding that 'Comrade Maisky should be instructed to assume a more reserved attitude in his conversations with representatives of the British government'. Maisky was accordingly reprimanded in harsh terms for indulging in criticism of British politics and for pursuing his own initiatives. He was ordered 'to be guided by our direct instructions rather than by articles from our press'.[48] Seeds, the British ambassador in Moscow, 'emphatically' agreed with Maisky that some way should be found 'to prevail'

[i] Ahmet Muhtar Bey Zog I, king of Albania, 1928–39.

on Poland and Rumania. He issued a prophetic warning that otherwise Russia could 'quite properly be tempted to stand aloof in case of war and confine its advertised support of the victims of aggression to the profitable business of selling supplies to the latter'. He further foresaw the danger of Germany offering the Soviet Union 'Bessarabia and parts of Poland not to mention perhaps Estonia and Latvia'.[49]]

12 April

'Lunch' at Vansittart's: Vansittart, his wife, Agniya and myself, and… Samuel Hoare, without his wife. Taking me aside, Vansittart let me know that Hoare had been 'very reasonable' lately and now shared nearly all Vansittart's views, and that Hoare wanted to talk to me in private in order to find out whether it was possible to speed up Anglo-Soviet negotiations.

Indeed, after 'lunch' Hoare seated himself next to me and began an animated conversation about the necessity of Anglo-Soviet cooperation against Germany. Couldn't we provide Poland with a unilateral guarantee? And the other limitrophe states?

I replied to Hoare in much the same spirit as I did to Halifax yesterday.

14 April

Following instructions from Moscow, I went to see Halifax today. I referred to the interest he displayed in our previous talks about the forms of aid which the USSR could grant Poland and Rumania, and said that the Soviet government was in principle prepared to help Rumania, but that first it wished to hear the opinion of the British about the best way of organizing this assistance.

Halifax was very glad to hear this, but at the same time he was somewhat upset. It transpired that just before my visit he had finished writing instructions to Seeds. He advised Seeds to ask the Soviet government whether it would consent to give unilateral guarantees to Poland and Rumania, similar to the guarantees Britain and France had given to Rumania and Greece, on condition that the USSR would render assistance to Warsaw and Bucharest only at their request and in forms that had been agreed with them. Halifax thought that in this way it would be possible to avoid the difficulties that had sunk 'the declaration of the four'. These instructions were meant to go out to Moscow that night. But what should he do now, on hearing my news? Send the instructions as they were, or not send them at all?

Halifax stopped talking and started thinking it over. At last he said: 'Your communication does not contradict my instructions. Therefore I'll send them as they are and add that I got your communication after the instructions had already been drawn up.'

Halifax expressed his hope that our reply to the British inquiry would come soon, by 17 April if possible. He wanted to know my opinion about the British proposal, but I evaded discussion of this topic.

In reply to my question, Halifax admitted that yesterday's guarantee to Rumania was given mainly at France's insistence. Nobody had expected it so soon.

I left Halifax and, at Vansittart's request, went to see him in his office. Vansittart asserted that 'real consultations' were now beginning between London and Moscow.

On 15 April, referring to my talk with Halifax on 14 April, Seeds posed the following question from the British government to the Soviet government: is the Soviet government willing to make a public statement (perhaps repeating Stalin's recent statement concerning the Soviet Union's support to nation-victims of aggression and referring to the recent statements by the British and French governments) that in the event of an act of aggression against any European neighbour of the Soviet Union, if that country were to put up resistance it could rely on the Soviet Union's assistance, if such were sought, and this assistance would be rendered in a way that would be found most suitable?

Yesterday I was in the House and listened to Chamberlain's speech concerning guarantees to Greece and Rumania…

[Included in the diary is a clipping from *The Times* of 14 April quoting the British government's extension to Greece and Rumania of the guarantees given to Poland.]

The guarantee to Greece was more or less predetermined and surprised nobody, but the guarantee to Rumania was indeed unexpected. Shortly before the session, I asked Tilea how matters stood with the guarantee to Rumania.

'I don't know for sure, but I've heard that the British government has decided to give a guarantee to my country as well today. The French are insisting on it greatly. We'll learn the truth in a few minutes.'

I don't know whether Tilea was telling me the truth or whether he was hiding some information from me, but nevertheless his words struck me as the first faint signal that yesterday the Rumanian issue had perhaps been resolved.

[Halifax proposed that the Soviet government should make a '*unilateral* public declaration *on its own initiative*', to be carefully hedged around by such qualifications as 'that in the event of any aggression against any European neighbour of the Soviet Union *which was resisted* by the country concerned, the assistance of the Soviet Government would be available, *if desired*, and would be afforded in such manner *as would be found most convenient*'. A 'positive declaration' by the Soviet government, Halifax believed, 'would have a *steadying* effect upon the international situation'. This idea of a 'steadying effect' reflected the deterrent element in British policy, which always sought reconciliation.

Litvinov, as Seeds reported home, objected to the fact that a unilateral declaration would bind the Soviet government without binding anyone else. The British ambassador tried in vain to convince him that the British government was already 'committed up to the hilt', and that a unilateral declaration perfectly befitted the position of the Soviet Union as a great power. In Paris, Bonnet proposed to Surits that their two countries should bolster their mutual assistance treaty of 1935. Still attuned to Litvinov's earlier disparaging comments, Surits mocked Bonnet and misrepresented the proposal in his report home.[50]]

15 April

Yesterday, late at night, I received the order to proceed immediately to Moscow for consultations on Anglo-Soviet negotiations. Very good. This will significantly clarify to me the tasks ahead.

Today is Saturday, so it will be impossible to complete all the formalities before Monday, the 17th. I'll leave on the 18th. To save time, I'll fly to Helsinki via Stockholm, and from there I'll take a train for Moscow via Leningrad. I've never flown before. Let's try. It's high time I got used to the most modern means of transport.

16 April

Visited the Hudsons in the country with Agniya. A big, ancient, ice-cold mansion in Kent. Portraits of remote ancestors, the staircase, the fireplaces, the servants in tails and livery. Goodness! Makes one's blood curdle. But the park and the field around the house are magnificent.

By and large, the Hudsons are pleased with their trip to Moscow, especially Mrs Hudson. And so she should be: she received six silver fox furs and two blue Arctic fox furs as a gift from 'Mikoyan's wife'. The hosts in Sweden and Finland made do with 'sweets and flowers'. The comparison is obviously in our favour. To give Mrs Hudson her due, she saw a great deal in Moscow (schools, clubs, museums, etc.), and she was pleasantly impressed by her trip.

Hudson himself is in a more critical mood. The only thing he liked wholeheartedly in Moscow was the theatre. He had seen nothing to compare to it anywhere in the world. But he has reservations about everything else. He does not like the isolation of the British embassy in Moscow. He does not like the status of the British army, navy and air attachés – they are shown nothing and are generally ill-treated. Nor is Hudson entirely satisfied with the trade negotiations: we don't want to buy consumer goods in England!

But Hudson still pins considerable hopes on trade. He envisages future developments as follows. In early June, when he returns from his trip to America, a Soviet delegation headed by Mikoyan (whom he liked very much) should arrive in London. Mikoyan will spend a week or so in Britain, and the

British government will welcome him with great pomp. Then, after Mikoyan's departure, the delegation will get down to practical work.

What ought to be the aim of this work? In Hudson's view, the current interim trade agreement should be replaced with a permanent trade treaty. Old claims could be cancelled by abandoning them on a mutual basis, which would leave 6 million pounds kept with Baring in the hands of the English. The Soviet government could add another 2 million ('Don't count on it!' I butted in) and then everything would be *all right*. The English are determined to raise in a forceful manner questions of arbitration, British tonnage, the expenditure of 50–60% of our takings on British industrial products, the facilitation of English industrialists' visits to Moscow, etc. Hudson is satisfied with Mikoyan's promise to buy yarn and herring in England, but when speaking about this he somehow 'forgot' to mention the condition specified by Mikoyan: long-term and soft credits.

In the final analysis, Hudson's project looks somewhat absurd: talks on a trade treaty are to be conducted in London, but, for some reason, concluded in Moscow! To this end, the English would be prepared to send a special delegation to Moscow.

I was left with the general impression that Hudson has not thought out a plan of action as yet and, most importantly, has not found the time for thorough consultation with his *permanent officials*.

* * *

Far more interesting was my conversation with Elliot, whom I met at Hudson's. He pulled me aside and, strolling with me in the park, disclosed a good deal of intriguing information.

I asked Elliot: 'The British government seems to be changing tack in its foreign policy – is this a serious change or not?'

Elliot firmly assured me that it was most serious. In this connection he cited a relevant fact. Simon's speech, during the parliamentary debates of 13 April, included the following statement: 'Although I cannot say that the USSR has been approached with such a proposal (for a military alliance), the House may rest assured that the government does not have any objections of principle to a proposal of this kind.'

Well, this phrase was not some one-off, uttered by Simon in the heat of argument. This part of his speech was carefully written and edited beforehand by the FO.

Yes, said Elliot, the turn in English policy is serious. The desire to cooperate with the USSR is entirely sincere. As was rightly stated in the communiqué issued four years ago during Eden's visit to Moscow, Britain and the USSR have no conflicting interests in any part of the world. In our days this seems almost miraculous, yet it is undeniably so. At the same time, there exists a common danger and a common desire to support peace. It is on this basis that cooperation between the two countries should develop. The moment has come

56. A caricature by David Low.

to reap the harvest. Elliot fully understands the reasons for our mistrust: the peace bloc against aggression is being created by the same people who have hitherto pursued the policy of 'appeasement'. Our scepticism is justified. But we must have patience. Time will show how serious the British government's intentions are.

Chamberlain? A strange figure! Until now he has placed sincere faith in Hitler, thinking he had only one goal in mind: to unite all Germans within a single state. Prague was a terrible catastrophe for Chamberlain, both politically and psychologically. The PM is certainly undergoing a profound change in his outlook, but this change is not yet complete. Echoes of the past still linger – for instance, in Chamberlain's attitude to Italy. He is grossly disappointed in Hitler, but he still retains some trust in Mussolini. This will eventually pass, too.

Chamberlain understands that cooperation between Britain and the USSR is inevitable. He is moving in this direction, but at a slow and faltering pace. It is not easy for him to make this change. At present, the prime minister has two gnawing doubts: (1) Is the Red Army effective? Like a true merchant he wants to try the goods before he buys them. (2) What are the true intentions of the USSR? Doesn't the USSR plan to cause war in the west, pushing Britain and France into a clash with Germany for its own gain?

I couldn't help laughing. Chamberlain fears that the USSR might push Hitler westward! It's the right equation, but the wrong way round.[51]

[Maisky's dogged determination to open an active dialogue with the British finally resonated with Litvinov, who now urged Stalin to abandon the reactive attitude and 'reveal a number of our preferred options'. He strongly recommended making a proposal to London whereby the unilateral guarantees would be replaced by a full-blown binding triple pact, backed by a simultaneous military agreement. Hoping to maintain control over the conduct of Soviet foreign policy, fast slipping out of his hands, Litvinov attempted in vain to shield Maisky and prevent his recall, arguing that conducting negotiations exclusively through the British ambassador in Moscow was detrimental to Soviet interests. It was vital to monitor public opinion in England and continuously 'influence it'. Were Maisky to leave London, warned Litvinov, the embassy would 'cease to function, for there is no one who could conduct serious diplomatic negotiations or whom the English would take notice of'.

Although Litvinov's proposals were contested and heavily revised by Stalin and Molotov, they were promptly submitted to the British on 17 April.[52] Surits (who had been invited to Moscow as well) did not arrive. Ostensibly this was because the absence of the French ambassador from Moscow might have hindered any progress in the negotiations; but in fact Potemkin, who had served with Surits, had warned him in a handwritten message to be vigilant, as 'the slightest lapse is not only recorded but also provokes a swift and violent reaction'. He advised Surits to remain in Paris and to send Krapivintsev,[i] his counsellor, instead.[53] Indeed, Merekalov, the third ambassador recalled for the meeting, never returned to Berlin and was banished from Narkomindel.]

17 April

The press has already made a first-class sensation out of my trip to Moscow, and today all the papers have been ringing the embassy non-stop to find out the particulars and to learn when I'm leaving and from which station. So far we have managed to keep everything secret.

The day was spent in the usual bustle before any trip. I paid a short call on Cadogan to settle a minor routine matter and to inform him of my departure. I could hardly disappear without warning when difficult diplomatic negotiations were in full swing. Then I attended a bankers' lunch, which was arranged by Brendan Bracken,[ii] editor of *Financial News*, and attended by Anselm Rothschild, the heads of Lloyds Bank, and others. Then I had a talk with our staff.

At around eleven at night, Sir Walter Layton, editor of the *News Chronicle*, suddenly called. He apologized for disturbing me at such a late hour and asked

---

[i] Pavel Nikolaevich Krapivintsev, counsellor to the Soviet mission in France, 1938–34, after which employment with NKID terminated.

[ii] Brendan Rendall Bracken, editor of *The Banker*, chairman of the *Financial News*, and managing director of *The Economist*; parliamentary private secretary to the prime minister, 1940–44; minister of information, 1941–45.

if he could visit right away, as he simply had to see me before my departure. He arrived at 11.30. He immediately directed the conversation to the current state of Anglo-Soviet relations. He insisted that public opinion in England had undergone radical change in the last four or five weeks, that England had taken a new course in earnest and for the long term, and that she sincerely wanted to repel aggression, and to achieve agreement and cooperation with the USSR. It was evident from the tone and nature of Layton's speech that he was paying me this late visit not on his own initiative, but on somebody's instructions... Whose? I can't say with any certainty, but it's possible that he acted on the instructions of the PM, for I know that Layton has access to Chamberlain and that during the September crisis Chamberlain personally 'briefed' Layton more than once.

The British government seems greatly concerned about my being summoned to Moscow and wants to convince me before I leave, and the Soviet government through me, of its sincere wish to work together with us on the establishment of a peace front.

[In the few days left before his departure for Moscow, Maisky toiled day and night to lay his safety net. With the memory of his grim experiences in Moscow in summer 1938 still fresh in his mind, he ensured that the editors of the leading newspapers were familiarized with his itinerary and informed them that they should expect to 'see him again in a few days'. He further deposited with them a long statement condemning the 'spasmodic patch-up scheme' of the guarantees to Poland and the misleading references to 'contacts', 'close touch' and 'consultations' which concealed the absence of 'real collaboration between West and East' in establishing collective security. The statement ended with an ominous warning that while the Soviet Union was in the best position simply 'to watch calmly' the European scene, she was prepared to pursue genuine collaboration, but not 'to be used as a smoke screen for dubious designs ... or pull chestnuts out of the fire for [the French and British] benefit'. Maisky squeezed a succession of dinners, tea parties, press conferences and meetings into two days, in order to generate a positive response to the Soviet proposals. Whistling in the dark, he tried hard to convince the Webbs that he was 'one of the few diplomats who is not on tenterhooks about his own continued future'; but his fear for his life was obvious when he added that he 'envied [them] living among books – he longed for a restful life'. The reason for his recall, he explained to them, was to give Stalin 'an impression of the sentiment in London' which might help to dispel his suspicion that there was 'a nigger in the wood-pile'. He repeated to Moscow a flattering comment made to him by Dalton: 'You will be able to boast, when you get to Moscow, of the resounding success of your diplomatic mission in London.'[54]]

18 April

Yesterday M.M. handed Seeds our reply to the British proposal of 14 April. Here is the essence of our reply.

Following the British inquiry about the Soviet government's readiness to render assistance to our immediate European neighbours in the face of aggression, Moscow received a French proposal to enter into bilateral commitments for mutual military assistance against aggressors. Accepting the French proposal in principle and following its spirit, as well as wishing to lay a firm foundation for relations between the three states, the Soviet government seeks to combine the British and French proposals in the following points offered for consideration by the British and French governments:

(1) The USSR, France and Britain sign an agreement for a term of 5 to 10 years, mutually committing themselves to provide immediate assistance in all forms, including military aid, in the event of aggression in Europe against one of the three contracting states.

(2) The USSR, France and Britain undertake to provide every kind of assistance, including military aid, to the Eastern European states located between the Baltic and Black seas and bordering on the USSR in the event of aggression against these states.

(3) The USSR, France and Britain shall, at the earliest possible date, discuss and establish the forms and extent of military aid to be rendered by each of the said states in compliance with Paras. 1 and 2.

(4) The British government makes it clear that the aid which it promises to Poland stands solely in the event of Germany's aggression.

(5) The Polish–Rumanian military pact is either entirely cancelled or declared valid in the event of any aggression against Poland or Rumania.

(6) The USSR, France and Britain commit themselves, after hostilities commence, not to enter into any separate negotiations or to sign a separate peace treaty with the aggressors.

(7) The joint three-power agreement is to be signed concurrently with the military convention stipulated in Para. 3.

(8) All three powers enter into negotiations with Turkey about a special agreement for mutual assistance.

A step of vast significance! Now the general line is clear.

28 April

The ten days that have passed since my last entry seem almost like a fairy-tale to me now… So, at about a quarter past nine on the morning of 18 April I took the plane from Croydon. I'm proud of myself: I managed to outwit the reporters, and there was not a single representative of the press at the aerodrome! The only people to accompany me were Agniya, Korzh,[i] Popov[ii] and one or two

[i] Mikhail Vasilevich Korzh, first secretary of the Soviet embassy in Great Britain, 1937–42.
[ii] I.S. Popov, second secretary of the Soviet embassy in Great Britain, 1941.

others from the embassy staff. I boarded the plane with my chin held high but, I admit, not without some anxiety in my heart: what if I turned out to be a bad flier after all? The last farewells… The last blown kisses… The last fussing of the service personnel… The propeller starts its noisy whirring, and the huge Douglas, capable of carrying 21 passengers, sets off heavily down the runway… Then it suddenly detaches itself from the ground and begins its climb… A green field, hangars, little houses with red roofs – everything starts to fall away rapidly and unexpectedly… deeper and deeper… And already the plane is at an altitude of 500 metres and, as if straightening out, is heading smoothly and powerfully in a south-easterly direction.

I try to sort out my feelings… Well, everything seems just fine!… No giddiness, no sickness. It's all a bit strange, a bit unusual, but not bad. Just fine. Let's see what happens next. I glue my face to the window and fasten my gaze on the scene opening before me.

The plane is climbing gradually and steadily. The altimeter is already showing 1,500 metres. We're flying over the clouds. Beneath, it seems, is a field of white, curly cotton wool. Farther in the distance there are white cotton cliffs, hills, mountains. They look dense and firm, like snow or ice-floes. The illusion is so great that you feel like jumping out of the plane and walking on the white blanket. Now that would be fun and bracing. Like throwing snowballs in a Siberian glade on a freezing day…

Suddenly, in this endless field of cotton wool I see a black hole: I look into it and somewhere far below is a blue sea all covered with scraps of something white…What could it be? It takes a long while for the penny to drop: why, of course, these are the foamy crests of waves!

Which means we're already flying over the North Sea. Obeying some conditioned reflex, I cast around for cork lifebelts, before I suddenly realize: what's the use of them? If something happens to the plane, cork lifebelts won't help. You'll die while you're still in the air or when the plane hits the surface of the sea. So let's hope the American engines are in good order and let's also rely on good luck.

The plane is flying fairly smoothly and calmly. The two propellers are rotating so fast you can't see them. The engines drone, but the noise is tolerable. One can talk easily in the cabin. The steady drone of the engines reminds me of the sound of the printing-press behind the wall of the proof-reading room where I once worked at the *Saratovsky dnevnik*. On the whole, then, it's *all right*!

Suddenly, the huge steel body of the plane shudders several times. Its long powerful wings bank sharply now left, now right. The shaking is so strong that the passengers jump in their seats and grab feverishly at their seat belts. Thick white fog on both sides of the plane. Nothing to be seen through the windows. We're in the clouds. The pilot gains height again. The pointer on the altimeter is spinning round… Upwards and upwards… Two and a half thousand metres already… The fog has vanished, we're out of the clouds… Above us only the bright but somewhat cold sun and the endless blue sky. Below us once again the mighty fields of white, curly cotton wool, and upon them, like an evil bird of prey, the speeding shadow of our plane, black and shaped like a cross… What beauty!

No, I'm not such a bad flier at all! It's all gone perfectly well so far. I'm either looking out the window or reading Pearl Buck's novel *The Patriot*, which I took for the journey…

Amsterdam. The first stop. I take the cotton plugs out of my ears, step down on the tarmac feeling slightly ecstatic from the discovery that I'm not a bad flier, and send Agniya a telegram: '*Flying well*'. Let her feel happy, too. Then I go to the coffee bar, where I have a talk with the airport manager. It turns out that the daily traffic at Amsterdam airport is 60 planes of all nationalities (English, French, Dutch, German and others). Croydon's traffic is about 100 planes daily. Because of the delay of the Paris plane, which had to struggle with a strong headwind, our plane leaves Amsterdam after not 20 minutes (as scheduled) but 40. It gains altitude fast and is soon gliding quickly over the city. How tiny, toy-like the houses beneath us look now! How narrow are the streets, with little black insects running busily along them! Further on is the port with the toy-like steamers, a blue blanket of seawater, some islands, some canals… The plane climbs higher and higher, and soon we're above the clouds. The same white cotton wool field beneath and the bright shining sun above. I look through the window, listen to the drone of the engines, and think. Then I pick up *The Patriot* and start reading…

I don't know how much time has passed. I glance down. The picture has changed. The plane is flying relatively low, at 500 or 600 metres. A good view of the sea: grey-blue, calm, as if asleep, probably not very deep because here and there the water takes on a yellowish grey colour… Numerous Danish islands – big, medium, small and tiny – are clearly visible. They are all flat, yellow, monotonous, and cultivated to the limit. Every patch of land is used. Everywhere there are tiny houses, fields, railway stations, roads, canals, bays and bridges. Everywhere there are people. And everywhere there are cattle. The basic colour is yellowish green. Quite unlike Holland. There, as you fly in to Amsterdam, you see beneath you a kind of brightly coloured woven carpet, made of fields of flowers – blue, lilac, red, yellow, etc. – which constitute one of the major items of Dutch export. Here, in Denmark, you sense agriculture, cattle, crops, bacon and many other very useful and purely material products.

Copenhagen. A twenty-minute stop. A swarm of reporters and photographers, poisoning my life. Sweden. The plane climbs higher and higher. It turns cold in the cabin. The clouds are beneath us, but the weather is fine and the earth is visible even from a height of three and a half thousand metres. The Swedish land is a great contrast to the Danish. Less cultivation, less human activity, and much more wildness and primitive nature. Mountains, rocks, forests, marshes, lakes. Occasional small towns, occasional cultivated plots with little houses and paths. Well, an emergency landing in Sweden would be no good – almost certain death. The further north, the wilder...

Stockholm. Instead of arriving at four, we arrive at about five. After turning smartly, the plane touches the land lightly and races for a good while along the well-paved but rather dangerous airfield. Dangerous, because there is a high and dark rock standing in its very centre. The plane skirts round it. The rapid change of altitude causes pain in the ears and a rush of blood. But this passes quite quickly. An uncomfortable sensation remains in the ears and the head, but then that also disappears.

A.M. [Kollontay] and the first secretary meet me at the aerodrome. Another swarm of photographers and reporters. We get into a car and drive to the embassy...

I make a telephone call to London to tell Agniya about my safe arrival and my victory over the airways.

* * *

I spent the night in Stockholm and at 9 a.m. on the 19th flew out to Helsingfors. This time the plane was smaller and somewhat simpler, with only 14 passenger seats, and bore the name 'Kalevala'. It belonged to a Finnish air company. We crossed the Baltic Sea with such speed that I barely managed to notice it. We flew over the Äland archipelago as well: from above, the islands looked like flat cakes of grey stone. As if some gigantic hand had splashed cake mixture on the sea surface, the mixture had set and was swimming in the water. It was a fine day. The sun stood high in the sky. We were flying at an altitude of about 400–500 metres above sea level. We made a stop at Abo. No photographers, only reporters. The flight from Abo to Helsingfors takes a little less than an hour. A beautiful panorama opened up of the 'thousand lakes', many of which were still covered with ice. At 11.30 we landed at Helsingfors airport. The whole flight had been a success. Even better than the previous day. I was met by Derevyansky,[i] Yartsev[ii] and others from the embassy and the trade mission.

We drove through the town's familiar streets. Nothing had changed. As if I had left Helsingfors only yesterday, not six years ago. Here was the pale-

[i] Vladimir Konstantinovich Derevyansky, an electrical engineer and devout Bolshevik, he was recruited to the diplomatic service, but after serving as ambassador in Helsinki, 1938–39, and in Latvia, April–October 1940, he sank into oblivion.

[ii] Boris Yartsev, second secretary at the Soviet embassy in Helsinki, serving with his wife as covert agents of the GPU.

pink, five-storey building on the corner. We entered the porch, walked down the corridors and took the elevator to the flat I remembered so well. A few trifling changes had been made, but nothing much on the whole. The same furniture, the same clock melodically striking the hours on the wall, the same arrangement of the rooms, and the same wonderful view of the bay, the sea, and deep-blue Rensher in the distance… Even old Annushka came to see me. She is now a cook in the embassy kitchen.

The hours before evening flew by. Journalists besieged me, of course, eager to find out what 'proposals' I was bringing along with me. I brushed them off with a laugh: 'my pockets are empty'. This only made the reporting brethren even more curious. I didn't pay visits to any of the ministers. Just sent my visiting cards. Then I wandered about the city and bought a few things. I took the train from Helsingfors at 11.20 at night. The train was just the same as before. I slept like a baby and in the morning stepped off in Rajajoki to stretch my legs and have a drink. Here, too, nothing had changed. We crossed the Sestra River… My native land! Beloostrov! I drew a deep breath and listened to my inner voice: yes, the air was different! Strong, bracing, resonant and above all <u>ours</u>!…

I walked along the station with a proprietorial feeling. After all, it was thanks to me that such an imposing, solid stone building appeared here at Beloostrov station! How much blood, how much effort and labour was required to persuade the top railway authorities of the need to construct a decent station building in Beloostrov to replace the shabby, yellow, one-storey wooden barn left over from tsarist days! But the station was not in the best shape. The plaster had peeled off, the doors were cracked in many places, the refreshment bar was empty, and the lavatories were dirty and stinking. I made a mental note of all this and more, put it down in writing and then took the necessary steps in Leningrad and Moscow to bring it to the notice of L.M. Kaganovich[i] himself.

In Leningrad I was met by A.V. Burdukov.[ii] Natasha[iii] had been hospitalized with pneumonia. That was an unpleasant surprise for me. I saw my grandson – a wonderful little boy with blue eyes and fair hair. His favourite amusement is to take a toy and hurl it on the floor. I visited Natasha in the hospital and left for Moscow in the evening.

I spent four days in Moscow (my bosses did not allow me more), which passed like a kind of dream. I stayed in Hotel Moskva. For 47 roubles a day I had a fairly decent room on the third floor with a bathroom, but, alas, the bathtub was in such a state that I had no desire to use it. I saw a great many people,

---

[i] Lazar Moiseevich Kaganovich, a member of Stalin's inner court, he was people's commissar of transport, 1935–44, and of heavy industry, 1937–39; deputy chairman of the Council of People's Commissars, 1938–44 and 1944–47; member of the State Defence Committee, 1942–45.

[ii] Alexei Vasilevich Burdukov, Soviet explorer of Mongolia; member of the Russian Geographical Society from 1927; arrested in 1941, he died in the camps.

[iii] Maisky's daughter.

57. The Chinese ambassador, Guo Taiqi, and his wife acting as 'good neighbours' to Madame Maisky during her husband's temporary absence in Moscow.

attended various meetings concerning Anglo-Franco-Soviet negotiations, dropped in to my apartment, chatted with my relatives, and… failed to visit the theatre even once. There just wasn't enough time.

On 24 April I took the *Krasnaya strela* back to Leningrad and spent half a day there. I visited Natasha in hospital, played with my grandson, and talked with A.V. I also saw some Leningrad officials. At 6.25 p.m. I left for Helsingfors. In Beloostrov I noticed that my conversations in Leningrad and Moscow had already had an effect. The choice of dishes at the refreshment bar was much better now. It turned out that some Leningrad bosses had been here after me and had given the barmaid a dressing-down for complaining to me. Nonetheless, they had advanced her a thousand roubles to buy foodstuffs and even raised her salary. Not bad! The chief of the frontier post told me they were expecting a special commission to come to Beloostrov in a day or two to see what was needed to put the station in order. Well, that's something, too!

After Rajajoki, I slept all the way to Helsingfors. Derevyansky and Yartsev met me at the station again. This time I couldn't avoid meeting the Finnish ministers. Erkko[i] expressly asked me through Derevyansky to pay him a visit,

[i] Juho Eljas Erkko, Finnish foreign minister, 1938–39; ambassador to Sweden, 1939–40.

58. A gloomy Maisky recalled to Moscow, April 1939.

59. A relieved Maisky returns from Moscow, April 1939.

and it would have been inappropriate to decline. So here I was again in the very familiar building of the Foreign Ministry, sitting in the very familiar office of the foreign minister in a very familiar armchair.

Erkko complained about our long silence in reply to the Finnish note concerning the Äland question, lavished assurances of friendly feelings toward the USSR, and hinted that the Finnish government would be ready to give us Lavansaari, Seiskari and other islands (which Shtein had just been negotiating about here, with no success as yet) should we offer more rewarding compensation. Then Erkko started asking me about England's thinking. It so happened that, on the day of my arrival in Helsingfors, the newspapers wrote that Ribbentrop 'could not find time' to receive Nevile Henderson, who had just returned to Berlin.

'What's happened to the notorious pride of the British?' Erkko exclaimed, somewhat puzzled.

Then we talked about the plans for a tripartite pact and I asked Erkko about Finland's attitude to a 'peace front'.

'We would gladly join a "peace front"', said Erkko, 'but where is it, this "peace front"?'

With total frankness, Erkko explained that as long as the said 'peace front' remained nothing but a dream, a project, an unrealized plan, Finland could not take any risks. It cannot disclose its approval of such a 'front' because the Germans move 'fast and decisively'.

At 5.30 I flew out of Helsingfors and at 8 p.m. I was already sitting in A.M. [Kollontay]'s cosy flat in Stockholm. It was a smooth flight, in spite of a very dense fog over the Baltic Sea.

At 9 a.m. on the 27th I left Stockholm and landed safely in Paris at four in the afternoon. There was only one stop in Copenhagen, where I was totally besieged by photographers and reporters, who would later spread absurd canards all over the world. I spent the entire evening talking with Surits. Afterwards we strolled for hours around the old quarters of Paris, and Ya.Z. [Surits] related to me, with love and considerable knowledge, the history of many buildings associated with the events of 1789–93. He spoke engagingly and with real feeling.

Today, at 10.30 a.m., I left Paris by train for Boulogne–Folkestone and arrived in London at about five in the afternoon, without particular incident.

I'm back home. It seems I never left.

* * *

[In a handwritten attachment to the entry of 28 April, unfortunately undated, abbreviated and partly indecipherable, Maisky scribbled a rough outline of what seems to have been Stalin's directives to him while in Moscow.]

(1) A bloc is desirable.

(2) Not less than five years.

- A more precise definition of aggression (not only aggression but a threat of aggression as well).
- Or the En[glish] form[ula] (direct or in[direct] threat to independence + integrity).
- Employing all forces and means.

(3) Aggression as understood by the parties to the agreement (even if the victim did not fight back). The Baltic [states], Rumania.
Status Quo ante
The F[ar] East.
List of countries. Lithuania. Holland. Belgium.
Direct or indirect threat to independence and integrity.

(4) Integral assistance.
Air pact…
Armed forces on foreign territory.
Fleet in the Baltic Sea. F[inland] or [missing text]
(joint action).
Conscription.

(5) Must be ensured that P[oland]–R[umania] are not against…
P[oland] must consent to the participation of [the] S[oviet Union].

(6) Dobrudja…

(7) No separate negotiations once an agreement is reached.

(8) Simultaneous pol[itical] and mil[itary] [agreement].

(9) T. [not clear who] does not lay claim to the defence of P[oland] and Fr[ance].
- Potemkin

(10) Instructions to the press.
Journal de Moscou – a Russian organ.

(11) Personal.

['The unforgettable meeting in Moscow' on 21 April is summed up in the diary in a single, rather muted paragraph. The meeting took place in the early afternoon (a most unusual time for Stalin, who preferred nocturnal sessions) and lasted for more than three and a half hours. Molotov, Mikoyan, Kaganovich and Voroshilov – the entire Politburo *chetverka* in charge of foreign affairs – were present, as were Litvinov and Potemkin. Krapivintsev, the counsellor at the Paris embassy, had a forty-minute meeting with Stalin on his own at noon, during which he undoubtedly conveyed a rather gloomy picture of the total subservience of the French to the British.

At the end of a thorough debriefing on the general mood in Britain, the political perspectives, and the balance between the supporters and opponents of a pact, Maisky was asked to evaluate the prospects for a positive response to the Soviet proposals.[55] His succinct account in his memoirs fails to convey how shocking it was for him to observe for the first time the relationship between Litvinov, Stalin and Molotov – 'strained to the extreme'. When later Beatrice Webb asked Maisky about the encounter with Stalin, she gathered from 'his sullen expression and monosyllabic reply' that he had 'no particular liking for the idolised leader of the masses'.[56] Maisky found the mood in Moscow to be 'disturbingly troubled' by news that Hitler was seriously preparing for war. Stalin, who outwardly looked calm, was 'manifestly dissatisfied with England' for having left the Soviet proposal 'hanging in the air'.[57] Molotov apparently 'turned out violent, colliding with Litvinov incessantly, accusing him of every kind of mortal sin'. The two were to clash again in 1942, in the back of a car during Molotov's visit to Washington, where Litvinov was ambassador. Gromyko,[i] who was also present on that occasion, was struck by Litvinov's continued challenge of 'the official party line'. He maintained that the alternative of negotiations with the West should not have been abandoned.[58]

The prevalent concern, which – judging by his memoirs and diary – Maisky obviously failed to allay, was that 'there might be a plot in London or Paris to involve Moscow in a war and then leave her in the lurch'.[59] Nor does Maisky mention either Molotov's insistence that alternative options, including an improvement in relations with Germany, should be considered, or Litvinov's apparent dramatic offer of resignation, which was rejected (for the moment) by Stalin. Since 1934, Molotov had consistently given collective security a lukewarm reception, and he was behind the various attempts to reopen negotiations with Berlin.[60]

In his memoirs, Maisky's fleeting account of the meeting conceals the fact that once he had acquainted himself with the prevailing mood in the Kremlin, his optimistic outlook on the eve of his departure for Moscow gave way to a 'not very consoling' report. This turned out to be an alarming prognosis of the prospects for negotiations between Germany and the appeasers, and obviously heightened Stalin's obsessive concern about a possible 'Danzig agreement', which would give Germany a free hand in the east. Maisky's report contrasted sharply with Litvinov's refusal to subscribe to the view that England and France were diligently trying to embroil Germany in war with the Soviet Union – a position which contributed to his downfall a fortnight later.[61]

Maisky's survey at the Kremlin was hardly motivated by sincerity (as he claims), but rather by a quite understandable instinct for survival and by opportunism. It had the unintended consequence of compromising Litvinov. When Dalton met Maisky in his study on 7 May, he was careful not to mention Litvinov or to ask whether it was true 'that M. has for some while been undermining him at the Kremlin and that his last visit to Moscow was the final blow'. Dalton was struck by the fact that Molotov's portrait had already replaced Litvinov's, and that when he suggested Molotov had little experience of foreign policy, Maisky dismissed this out of hand, proclaiming that he had 'shrewd practical views of foreign policy'. He insisted that 'always when Soviet Ambassadors abroad went back to Moscow they went to see [Molotov] and had long talks with him'. Dalton concluded: 'I thought: "Yes, you little monkey, and you went and told him that Litvinov was no good."'[62]

Maisky's report certainly encouraged Stalin to probe further into the German option with Merekalov, who was now hastily summoned to the Kremlin for the last hour of the meeting. After the customary exchange of greetings, Stalin asked Merekalov point blank: 'Will the Germans advance on us or won't they?' In his incomplete memoirs, Merekalov

[i] Andrei Andreevich Gromyko, counsellor at the Soviet embassy in the USA, 1939–43, then ambassador, 1943–46.

(like Maisky) misleads his readers into believing that, regardless of what Stalin expected to hear, he took the 'bold step' of telling the *vozhd* that Hitler was bent on attacking the Soviet Union, probably in 1942–43. In reality, still under the impression of a meeting he had had on 17 April with Ernst von Weizsäcker,[i] the German state secretary (who sought to reconcile Moscow), Merekalov actually proceeded to linger on the prospects for at least a short-term rapprochement with Germany, for which – for as long as she was preoccupied with France and Poland – the neutrality of the Soviet Union was indispensable. Merekalov had been personally appointed to Berlin by Stalin as his loyal watchdog a year earlier. A mediocre and unsophisticated diplomat, with rudimentary German, he was no longer allowed to return to Germany, though he was kept under surveillance to make sure he did not 'spill the beans'. Astakhov, his highly competent attaché, who was himself under advanced investigation by the NKVD, was entrusted with the next delicate diplomatic game about to be played. Though Maisky hailed Stalin for his decision to give the negotiations with the West another chance, he was left in no doubt that the talks were 'on probation' and were to be based firmly on the Soviet proposal.[63]

Given the British procrastination, it was clear to Litvinov and Maisky that they were now operating on borrowed time. In a balancing act, Stalin allowed negotiations with the British to continue, despite being aware that the German option had now become viable. The looming danger was clear from Maisky's ominous warning to Lloyd George's son that it was 'vital' to reach an agreement 'before a month was out',[64] as well as from the urgency conveyed in his meeting with Halifax on 29 April.]

29 April

Halifax's invitation to visit came a few hours before I even returned from Moscow. I went to see him today. He first inquired if my trip had been interesting, obviously expecting me to indulge in revelations. I only said 'yes, very interesting', before turning to the question of our 17 April proposals, to which the English had so far not responded at all.

Halifax apologized for the delay, which he attributed to the fact that the British government had been preoccupied with the conscription problem during the last fortnight, but then he set about cautiously criticizing our proposals. True, they were 'very logical and well put together', but great difficulties would arise in their practical implementation. Then he started harping on that old tune of Poland and Rumania.

A few minutes later, however, Halifax started contradicting himself. Speaking about the visit of Gafencu[ii] (the Rumanian foreign minister) he said that, according to Gafencu, Rumania would need Soviet assistance in the event of war, but until that happened Rumania feared that open association

[i] Ernst Freiherr von Weizsäcker served as state secretary at the German Foreign Ministry from 1938 to 1943.

[ii] Grigore Gafencu, Rumanian foreign minister in 1932 and 1939–40; minister to Moscow, 1940–41.

with the USSR might 'provoke' Germany. Rumania wished for the time being to maintain a certain 'balance' between the Soviet Union and Germany. So it seems that Rumanian objections to the inclusion of the USSR in the security guarantee are a matter of tactics, not principle.

Talking about our proposals, Halifax thought it necessary to 'clarify' one 'significant point' concerning the British formula of 14 April. We might have gained the impression that England and France expected Soviet assistance to be given to Poland and Rumania even if England and France were not involved in the war. If that was our impression, then it was based on a complete misunderstanding: what the British government had in mind was Soviet action only if and when Britain and France acted as well. I thanked Halifax for his clarification, but added that it did nothing to address the main cause of our objections to the formula of 14 April.

I asked Halifax about the negotiations between Britain and Turkey. Halifax said they were progressing quite smoothly and that he was expecting an Anglo-Turkish treaty of mutual assistance in respect of the Mediterranean to be concluded before long. A similar Anglo-Turkish treaty concerning the Balkans could be expected in the future. The Turks, however, were constantly stressing their close ties with the USSR, so, Halifax added, 'the outcome of our negotiations with Turkey depends significantly on Turkey's negotiations with you'.

Towards the end, we touched upon Hitler's speech of yesterday.[65] Halifax believes it changes nothing in the present situation. He does not anticipate any new negotiations with Germany in the near future, notwithstanding Hitler's indirect invitation. Halifax was less sure about specifically naval negotiations (the old 'appeaser'!).

With a little embarrassment, Halifax (in response to my question) explained the reasons for the return of the British ambassador to Berlin.

The thing is, you see, that if you are maintaining diplomatic relations with a country, then you need an ambassador there. So Henderson could only be recalled for a short time. Hitler was about to make a speech – what should have been done? If the speech had turned out 'sharp', it would have been awkward for Henderson to return immediately. But his return would also have been awkward if the speech had turned out 'soft', for such a move could well have been interpreted as proof that the British government believed Hitler's promises, when the man should never be trusted. Faced with that dilemma, Halifax decided to cut the knot by sending Henderson back a few days before Hitler delivered the speech. Henderson had only one assignment: to inform the German government of the British government's decision about conscription before it was announced officially in parliament. All other rumours were sheer speculation unworthy of attention.[66]

[Realizing that the Soviet proposals had placed the government in an awkward position, Halifax warned the Cabinet on 19 April that 'it would be necessary to exercise considerable caution' in responding to the Soviet proposals. Particularly, Cadogan conceded, as the British offer to Russia had been made 'in order to placate our left wing ... rather than to obtain any solid military advantage'. The Foreign Policy Committee discussed the 'extremely inconvenient' Soviet proposals that evening, trying to figure out the best ways of preventing the opposition from exploiting a rejection of the offer. It subscribed to Chamberlain's delaying tactics of repeating the original offer of unilateral guarantees, while denying accusations that its policy was motivated by ideological aversion.[67] Maisky gave Halifax more credit, assuming that he made more positive proposals, which, however, were 'tampered with by colleagues'.[68] At the Foreign Office, they did not fail to notice that if 'read between the lines', the real motive for the Cabinet's attitude was 'the desire to secure Russian help and at the same time to leave our hands free to enable Germany to expand eastward at Russian expense'. This was a striking observation, considering the fact that the chief of staff had in the meantime established that Russian help was vital in contending with Germany and had warned of 'the very grave military dangers inherent in the possibility of any agreement between Germany and Russia'.[69]

By 26 April, the French, who had initially considered a positive response to the Soviet proposals, came back with a modified agreement, which confirmed the worst Soviet fears that whenever Britain and France considered it necessary to fight Germany, the Soviet Union would 'automatically be drawn into the war on their side', but if the Soviet Union found itself at war with Germany, the French and the British would not be committed.[70] Yet, clutching at straws, Litvinov, whose days in Narkomindel were now numbered, continued to entertain some hopes that the French draft for the three-power agreement, unsatisfactory as it was, would be approved by the British. In a long letter to Stalin on 28 April, he even dwelt on the positive aspects of the French proposal, and pleaded with him not to turn it down before the final British response was forthcoming.[71]]

30 April

Hore-Belisha, in his role as secretary of state for war, has sent an invitation to Comrade Voroshilov to attend the British manoeuvres which will be held from 19 to 23 September. Today he tried to impress on me how important it was that Comrade Voroshilov actually came. It could have tremendous political significance. Only representatives of 'friendly powers' were invited to attend the manoeuvres. I have my doubts whether K.E. [Voroshilov] will accept the invitation. But he will probably send a military mission.

Hore-Belisha then declared frankly that he would very much like to visit our country – to attend manoeuvres or on some other occasion, or even just like that. I recall Hore-Belisha dropping a hint about his desire to visit the Soviet Union as far back as the summer of 1937, but this time he was much more definite than before.

Well, we will see. If the Anglo-Soviet negotiations end successfully, with the pact being signed, Hore-Belisha will surely come to Moscow. But if not?

Once again, we'll have to wait and see.

1 May

Winston Churchill told me a lot of interesting things about Gafencu's visit to London. Gafencu made an excellent impression here. The Rumanian minister was very outspoken and shared many juicy details from his talks in other capitals.

Gafencu was very pleased with his visit to Ankara. He was also satisfied with his visit to Berlin. Hitler, Göring and others treated him very courteously. They did not intimidate or threaten him, but, on the contrary, were profuse in their expressions of 'love'. Hitler is even said to have told him: Rumania can do without German machines, but Germany cannot do without Rumanian food and raw materials. Hence Hitler's conclusion about the need for Germany to develop 'friendship' with Rumania. Obviously, British guarantees did play a certain role, and Hitler is trying to bring Rumania to heel by offering it the carrot.

Gafencu gave Churchill an account of his conversation with Hitler. Hitler execrated England as the organizer of the policy of 'encirclement'. Gafencu claims to have replied that there was no encirclement of Germany whatsoever and that Germany itself was creating a sort of 'psychological encirclement' through its actions. Hitler then scoffed at the British guarantees to Rumania and insisted that England did not actually wish to implement them and, even if she did, would not be capable of doing so. Gafencu allegedly objected once more, saying that history had showed that England started wars badly but ended them well. Hitler jumped up, stamped his foot angrily and exclaimed: 'In the event of war, my air force will reduce the cities of Great Britain to rubble in 48 hours!'

He suddenly stopped, as if struck by a new thought, and added in a different tone: 'But who'll benefit from it? Only Moscow!'

Churchill talked with Gafencu about the USSR's participation in the security guarantees. Gafencu responded to Churchill in the same way as he had to Halifax. Churchill's general impression is that if a tripartite military alliance were to be formed, Rumania's doubts would largely vanish.

2 May

What is the current situation in England?

Summing up all the material at my disposal, I would describe it as follows.

The attitudes of the broad masses of the population are sharply anti-German everywhere, except for a part of Scotland. Hitler's recent speech did not make much of an impression in the country, even though on the next day some newspapers (e.g. Beaverbrook's) started chattering about the possibility of new negotiations between England and Germany. The need to resist aggression is fast becoming a universal conviction. Hence the country's readiness to accept conscription. Labour's opposition to conscription is insignificant and is already disintegrating. Hence also the colossal popularity of the idea of alliance with the USSR. Every mention of such an alliance is met with a storm of applause at rallies and gatherings all over the country. According to the latest poll by the Public Opinion Office,[72] 87% are in favour of an immediate military alliance with the Soviet Union.

The situation in government is somewhat different. Of course, the public's mood is exerting strong pressure on the government, and the majority of ministers are for resistance to aggression, but the logical conclusions have yet to be drawn. Most important, however, is the fact that Chamberlain, Simon, Kingsley Wood and other 'appeasers' have not yet definitively renounced their Munich policy. They are forced to retreat under pressure from the masses and events, but they do so reluctantly, trying to minimize inevitable concessions and, wherever possible, attempting to return to the methods used in the period of 'appeasement' (e.g. returning Nevile Henderson to Berlin).

The British government's halfway-house policy is more and more obvious. Let me cite three examples.

Reconstruction of the government. This is considered absolutely inevitable now, and even the Beaverbrook press has started a campaign to this effect. But Chamberlain is stubbornly postponing the entry of such figures as Eden, Churchill and others into the Cabinet until the very last moment.

Conscription. This has also been considered absolutely inevitable for the past 4–5 weeks. But Chamberlain also put this off to the last minute, and when he saw that he would have to give in, he still tried to gain some revenge: conscription was applied only to one year group, not the three on which the majority of the Cabinet insisted.

Our proposals. There can be little doubt that the British government will eventually accept them. Its situation is desperate. Yet Chamberlain stubbornly resists and has kept us waiting for the English answer for over two weeks now. Moreover, at first he even tried to hush up the Soviet proposals and conceal them from the public. However, thanks to the supporters of an Anglo-Soviet military alliance in government circles, our proposals were leaked bit by bit to the press, and by the time of my arrival from Moscow their essence had become public knowledge. The opposition started exerting pressure in parliament, and a lively debate got going in the press. So the British government will have to respond to the Soviet proposals one way or another in the very nearest future. It may not wish to accept them immediately, but will have to do so sooner or later.

What is my final conclusion? Here it is. The masses – not only workers but the bourgeoisie as well – are far ahead of their government and demand a tripartite bloc of Britain, France and the USSR. The Cabinet is marking time and digging its heels in, but, urged on by the masses, it is eventually moving forward in the same direction. That is why, leaving insignificant, everyday

60. A caricature by David Low.

details to one side, I am inclined to take an optimistic view of the 'general line' in the development of Anglo-Soviet relations.

[The diary entry conveys Maisky's genuine views. Aware of the rift in Moscow, he couched what turned out to be his last telegram to Litvinov in more cautiously optimistic terms.[73] Ewer of the *Daily Herald* found Maisky on that day in a 'rather truculent mood', admitting the existence of a 'considerable conflict of views' in the Soviet government and appearing most 'anxious' to have the Soviet proposals widely publicized, warning that their rejection might intensify the isolationist tendency.[74] Maisky had goaded the opposition to raise the issue of the negotiations in parliament on 2 May, but Chamberlain was extremely evasive.[75]]

3 May

Attended an Anglo-Chinese dinner where Guo Taiqi, Lord Chatfield[i] and Lord Snell spoke, and where mention of the Soviet ambassador among the guests was greeted with loud and unanimous applause.

When the speeches were coming to an end, Vernon Bartlett came up behind me and hurriedly thrust a piece of paper into my hand. The note read: 'News just in from Moscow that Litvinov has resigned.'

[i] Alfred Ernle Montacute Chatfield (1st Baron Chatfield), admiral, first sea lord, 1933–38, minister for coordination of defence, 1939–40.

4 May

Azcárate visited me today. He now lives in Paris with his entire family, but sometime in the autumn he is going to move to London and spend more time here. At present, Azcárate is chairman of an inter-party or all-party committee of Spanish émigrés, and is responsible for the evacuation of Republicans from France to Mexico. The committee has a large office in Paris and organizes the emigration of those military and civilian elements who have proper political credentials. There are about 30–40,000 such emigrants. The fate of the remaining 300–350,000 who are presently in France is unclear. Some of them will probably settle down in France independently. The greater part will most likely return to Spain when Franco opens the border: there are many ordinary people in this group who fled from Catalonia to France through mass hysteria, but who are not guilty of any crimes, even from the point of view of Franco.

The situation in the concentration camps for the Republican soldiers has improved, although it is still far from decent. The French government's attitude toward Spanish refugees has also changed for the better. Negrín and del Vayo left for the United States, but their intentions are not quite clear yet. Del Vayo is giving lectures, while Negrín will be conducting negotiations with the Mexican government concerning the conditions for the settling of the Republican emigrants. Pascua is also in America now. He was very depressed when he went there, and Azcárate does not know what he is doing now. There was great cause for celebration in Azcárate's family recently: the wife of his eldest son (who on 12 March related the particulars of Negrín's fall to me) managed to flee from Madrid and, after many ordeals, finally reached Paris. The events of recent months first separated them and then reunited them. Telling me of his daughter-in-law's flight from Spain, Azcárate said with a smile: 'This is a quite incredible epic all of its own, which I'll recount to you some other time.' I asked Azcárate whether the Republican soldiers interned in France would fight on the side of France in the event of Italian–German aggression? Azcárate thought for a moment and said: 'I think they would.'

[Litvinov's dismissal on 3 May had colossal repercussions on the international scene and for Maisky personally. A protégé of Litvinov, at a stroke Maisky lost his sanctuary. It is easy to imagine his shock when he read the telegram, unusually signed by Stalin personally, informing him and other key ambassadors of the 'serious conflict' between Litvinov and Molotov 'ensuing from the disloyal attitude of Comrade Litvinov to the Council of Commissars of the USSR'.[76] Considered to be a relic of the past, Maisky was gradually ostracized. He now remained practically the sole genuine exponent of a pact with the West. Despite Molotov's reassurances that the resignation implied no change in Soviet foreign policy, a great deal of anxious speculation circulated in the West, with commentators divided over whether the Soviet Union might wish to ramp up negotiations with Britain or would rather bring about a war, which would induce world revolution.[77] The renowned military analyst Liddell Hart echoed the concern of many in London and Paris that it was only natural for Stalin to suspect that the laggard pace of the British negotiators meant that Chamberlain was 'planning a side-step which would leave Russia to bear the brunt of Hitler's expansionist drive and allow Britain to slide out of the fray'.[78] The recognition that 'the eclipse of the Jew Finkelstein-Wallach[79] was likely to be pleasing to Berlin' led even the Foreign Office to reconsider the proposed British response to the Soviet proposals, the gist of which was common knowledge.[80]

When Litvinov met the British ambassador at Narkomindel early on the morning of 3 May, he was clearly oblivious to what lay in store for him. Seeds, in prophetic mood, had warned Halifax that 'No good purpose would be served here by merely reiterating that His Majesty's Government would lend all support "in their power".'[81] Maisky, too, would claim in retrospect that it was the British failure to pay heed to the Soviet proposals which delivered the 'smashing blow to the policy of effective collective security, and led to the dismissal of Litvinov'. Likewise, Payart, the French chargé d'affaires in Moscow, warned that Halifax's insinuations to Maisky that the British would ignore the Soviet initiative and reiterate their original proposal were responsible for Litvinov's removal, signalling 'a withdrawal into neutrality ... or even an agreement with Germany'.[82]

Pinning the blame for the ousting of Litvinov and the shift towards Germany entirely on British 'appeasement' is, however, becoming an increasingly hard position to sustain. True, even Maisky confided to the Webbs that 'Litvinov felt that the change over from the policy of collective-security ... which he had been authorised to press at Geneva, to a German–Soviet pact, made desirable his retreat from being the Foreign Commissar'.[83] But even Maisky (who, in Moscow in April, had spared no effort to attune himself to the Kremlin's views) continued to maintain that appeasement was being increasingly challenged in Britain. Though the ousting of Litvinov steered Soviet foreign policy in a new direction, the explanation for his dismissal should also be sought elsewhere. Kollontay, who was taken 'totally by surprise' at the 'incomprehensible, inexplicable' coup at such a crucial moment, was forced to admit in her diary that, somewhere in the depths of her consciousness, 'there [had] been a feeling for a long time that Moscow was unhappy with Maksim Maksimovich ... the symptoms were invisible, but they were there'.[84] Ivy Litvinov later reminisced that the 'writing on the wall' had become increasingly 'legible' by the end of 1938, when 'more and more people closely connected with L[itvinov]' had been persecuted, and it was clear to everyone that Zhdanov's criticism of Narkomindel early in 1939 had been targeted at her husband.[85] Maisky told Lord Strabolgi that it was 'only a personal quarrel between Litvinoff and Stalin'.[86] Litvinov himself had complained to the French ambassador in Moscow at the end of 1938: 'How can I conduct foreign policy with the Lubyanka across the way?'[87]

The shift in Soviet policy should be examined within the wider context of the construction of the Stalinist edifice.[88] This process led to the removal from Narkomindel of the cadre of the first generation of Soviet diplomats, most of whom were intellectuals drawn from the revolutionary intelligentsia of the tsarist period. They were rapidly replaced by diplomats who were perhaps inexperienced, but were zealous and educated young Stalinists who could be trusted to follow the Kremlin line, particularly at such a crucial moment. The novices were deliberately denied access to policy-making and their room for manoeuvre was restricted.

The breach was accentuated by the personal antipathy and jealousy that characterized the two types of revolutionary.[89] 'You think we are all fools!' Molotov shouted at Litvinov, as the latter was leaving Stalin's office following his dismissal.[90] It was shrewdly observed by Seeds that Litvinov had 'never been included in the inner councils of the regime, [had] never been a member of the all-powerful Politburo' and headed a commissariat which had 'long held a position of secondary importance'.[91] Molotov continued to bear a grudge against Litvinov well into his retirement. Though giving him his due as a 'first-rate' intelligent person, Molotov accused him of being disloyal. At a meeting of the commissariat in July 1939, Molotov charged Litvinov with failing to toe the party line and with 'clinging to a number of people alien and hostile to the party and to the Soviet state'. The continued presence of independent-minded ambassadors would no longer be tolerated at Stalin's court. Henceforth Maisky would find it extremely hard to abide by Molotov's perception of the ambassador's role, which was 'simply to transmit what they are told to pass on'. A 'centralized diplomacy' guaranteed that 'it was impossible for the ambassador to take any initiative ... it was Stalin, not some diplomat, who played the decisive role in it'.[92] The immediate, visible change was that Stalin tightened his personal grip on foreign affairs, with Molotov acting, in Moscow, as a messenger. As the British ambassador shrewdly observed, Litvinov's dismissal also signalled 'the loss of an admirable technician or perhaps shock-absorber' and his replacement 'with a more truly Bolshevik – as opposed to diplomatic or cosmopolitan – *modus operandi*'.

Reflecting a year later on the Soviet–German pact, Seeds believed that 'personalities' contributed significantly to it. The removal of 'that astute cosmopolitan, M. Litvinov,' he wrote, left Soviet policy in the hands of Stalin and his inner circle, who were 'provincial' and regarded compromise as a 'sign of insincerity'. Churchill regarded Molotov as 'fitted to be the agent and instrument of the policy of an incalculable machine ... the modern conception of a robot'.[93]

What may have further precipitated Litvinov's dismissal (beyond the apparent bankruptcy of collective security) was the verbatim report of the interrogation of Beria's[i] predecessor, Ezhov, conveyed to Stalin by Beria on 27 April. This report would lead to a preliminary investigation by the NKVD into Litvinov's 'high treason', which was dropped later in June. In his report, Ezhov, *inter alia*, recalled how he had unexpectedly found himself spending an evening with Litvinov at a sanatorium in Merano. After dancing a foxtrot, Litvinov teased him: 'Here we are relaxing, going to restaurants, dancing, but if they found out about it in the USSR they'd really kick up a fuss. Nothing particularly terrible is happening here, but, you see, we have no culture, our statesmen have absolutely no culture whatsoever ... If our political leaders established personal relationships with European political figures, a lot of sharp corners in our relations with other countries could be smoothed off.'[94] Litvinov was hardly helped by a letter that his wife had tried to smuggle abroad from Sverdlovsk, through an American architect, revealing her dismay about the purges. The letter found its way to Stalin, who summoned Litvinov and told him his wife 'had nothing to fear – for the time being'.[95]

---

[i] Lavrentii Beria, succeeded Ezhov as head of the NKVD, until his own execution in December 1953, in the wake of Stalin's death, charged with plans to overthrow the communist regime. One of the hidden chapters in Maisky's life had to do with the subversive ties he was compelled to establish with Beria in the latter's purported bid for power.

Maisky's position had become most perilous, as the repressions in Narkomindel continued unabated. Molotov was instructed by Stalin to purge the ministry of the 'semi-party' elements, particularly Jews. Moreover, the NKVD tightened its direct control over embassies, and practically the entire cadre of ministry workers was replaced. Maisky was alienated from those newly arrived diplomats, who were attracted to the more popular and friendly style of Molotov's leadership, which seemed to rejuvenate Narkomindel.[96] However, the acute fear of a 'second Munich' rendered Maisky's continued presence in London indispensable. The astonishingly wide web of contacts he had woven in London made Maisky *l'oeil de Moscou*, charged with detecting any sign of renewed appeasement, which might lead to an Anglo-German agreement.]

6 May

Halifax summoned me and asked straight out: Litvinov has retired – is our old policy still valid? In particular, do our proposals of 17 April remain intact?

The British government has prepared its reply to our proposals, but before sending it to Seeds, Halifax would like to hear my response to his questions.

I laughed and said that I didn't understand his doubts. Of course, both our policy and our proposals remain in force.

Halifax was visibly relieved on hearing my answer.

Then he set out the gist of the British reply. Far from reassuring. The British government does not deem it possible to accept our proposals concerning a tripartite pact because it believes that such a pact would only scare off other powers whose participation in the 'peace front' is very important. This was followed by that old chestnut about Poland and Rumania. Nor are the British willing to give guarantees to the Baltic States because, first, the Baltic States do not want them and, secondly, such guarantees would only provide Hitler with fresh cause to raise the alarm about 'encirclement'. Consequently, the British government decided to forward to us once more its formula of 14 April, after 'clarifying' it in line with the explanation given to me by Halifax during our conversation on 29 April (the British government does not expect us to act unless England and France are active participants).

I expressed great disappointment. It took the British government three weeks to consider our proposals, at the end of which the mountain has given birth to a mouse. Halifax's arguments do not hold water. To the best of my knowledge, his references to public opinion in Poland and Rumania are gross exaggerations. The Baltic States have not yet formed their opinion on guarantees, so Britain and France, should they so wish, could certainly exert a favourable influence on them if necessary. Hitler's cries may safely be ignored, for no matter what the peace-loving powers do, he will carry on yelling about 'encirclement'. It goes without saying that the British government has the right to send whatever formula it wishes to Moscow, but I could tell Halifax in advance that Moscow would reject this formula.[97]

9 May

Yesterday the British government finally gave its reply to our 17 April proposals. An unsatisfactory one.[98] Seeds handed the following formula to Comrade Molotov:

> It is suggested that the Soviet government should make a public declaration on their own initiative in which, after referring to the general statement of policy recently made by Monsieur Stalin, and having regard to statements recently made by His Majesty's Government and the French government accepting new obligations on behalf of certain Eastern European countries the Soviet government would undertake that in the event of Great Britain and France being involved in hostilities in fulfilment of these obligations, the assistance of the Soviet government would be immediately available, if desired, and would be afforded in such manner and on such terms as might be agreed.

A rather long, confusing and clumsy statement, and, above all, even worse than what Halifax told me on 6 May. I went to see him in order to find out the reason for this discrepancy, but the foreign secretary could tell me little beyond the fact that the British formula had not yet been definitively worked out at the time of our conversation. This means that the prime minister must have made changes to the formula prepared by the Foreign Office. I recalled, incidentally, that as I was leaving Halifax's office on 6 May his secretary entered the room and informed him that the PM was expecting him at *10, Downing Street* after my visit.

Later, in the interests of 'clarification', I started criticizing the English formula. I particularly emphasized the absence of reciprocity: we should help England and France if they are drawn into war because of Poland and Rumania, but England and France are not bound to help us if we become involved in a war resulting from aggression against any other East European states.

Halifax first argued at some length that this situation could not arise, as the USSR had not yet given anyone any guarantees; but then he started stressing that the aim of the English formula was to assure us that the British government had no intention of demanding any sacrifices from the Soviet Union before such sacrifices had been made by Western powers. However, if we dislike the British formula, we are welcome to suggest another. He will readily consider our version, provided it takes into account the two elements which the British government deems essential, namely (1) the issue at stake is assistance to Poland and Rumania, and (2) the guarantees will come into force only if both countries put up resistance to aggression.

Halifax further noted that the phrase '*would be immediately available*' was initially followed by '*for Poland and Rumania*', but these words were later removed at the request of the named countries, as they did not want to be mentioned directly in the document. As regards the words '*in such manner and on such terms*', these refer to more specific agreements between the Anglo-French party and us, such as the mutual rejection of separate negotiations, separate peace, etc. But it followed from Halifax's words that all such schemes relate, in his view, to events after the outbreak of hostilities.

In conclusion, Halifax assured me that the British government was eager to negotiate with us as soon as possible and reach an agreement.

I remained cool and critical throughout. Numerous indicators suggest the conclusion that Hitler's speech on 28 April has caused a temporary recurrence of 'appeasement' in government circles. *The Times* wrote the other day that 'one more attempt' should be made to seek reconciliation with Germany, so this must be the view of the prime minister, or at least Sir Horace Wilson. It won't wash! The time for 'appeasement' has come and gone. Whether Chamberlain wants to or not, he will have to make major concessions to our point of view. For such is the logic of the current situation.

[Molotov emphatically rejected the British formula, but he consulted Maisky about a possible response. He was particularly pugnacious because he had learnt from the Polish ambassador earlier in the day that Poland had not raised any objection to the Soviet proposals.[99] Typically, Maisky fawned on the new master, 'the most esteemed Vyacheslav Mikhailovich' and painted a pessimistic picture of Chamberlain's reversion to 'appeasement'. Yet he stubbornly adhered to his belief that public opinion and the intensifying opposition even within bourgeois circles was bound to forestall another 'Munich', and that 'appeasement hardly has any chance of enduring and the logical turn of events should compel England to resist the aggressors'. A day earlier he had cabled to Molotov that although the proposals were 'unacceptable … the English have not yet said their last word'.[100]]

11 May

Yesterday Chamberlain spoke in the House about Anglo-Soviet negotiations and declared, inter alia, that the British government was taking all the necessary measures to dispel the Soviet government's suspicions that Britain and France want to inveigle the USSR into a war with Germany while themselves hiding in the bushes. 'If the Soviet government,' concluded the prime minister, 'still has any doubts on this subject, my noble friend (i.e. Halifax) believes that they can be easily dispelled. In this connection he has invited the Soviet ambassador to inform His Majesty's Government of the specific grounds on which the doubts of his government rest, if they still exist, and the Soviet ambassador has willingly agreed.'

All this is sheer nonsense. Halifax did not ask me anything of the sort during my last conversation with him on 9 May, nor did I agree to anything. However, Chamberlain uttered that phrase for a reason: he was summoning the Soviet government to a 'frank dialogue' about the heart of the matter. That is how I interpreted the PM's speech yesterday. Particularly after the telephone call I received from Strang: half an hour before Chamberlain's speech, Strang called me and said with great emphasis: 'If, in connection with the forthcoming declaration by the prime minister, you should wish to see Lord Halifax, he will be entirely at your disposal.' Strang repeated this two or three times in various combinations.

My assumptions have been fully confirmed today. First, all the morning papers interpret the PM's statement as an invitation to a 'heart-to-heart talk'. *The Times* and the *Manchester Guardian* go so far as to inform the readers about a 'long conversation' between Halifax and myself yesterday following the session in parliament. Needless to say, no conversation occurred.

Secondly, and this is still more important, when I called on Halifax today on another matter (more on this below), his first question was: 'Have you been instructed to communicate anything to me from the Soviet government?'

The foreign secretary was greatly disappointed when he learned that I had brought no news on this subject. Our subsequent conversation actually repeated most of what we had said to each other during our previous meeting on 9 May. I responded to Halifax's arguments and thoughts in the spirit of today's *Izvestiya* editorial, which had been sent to me by cable.

Now about the business that brought me to the Min[istry] of F[oreign Affairs] today. On Monday, 15 May, the Council of the League of Nations will convene, chaired by the USSR. Surits asked Moscow to adjourn the session until 22 May so that Potemkin, who is only today returning to Moscow from his three-week trip around the Balkans and the Near East, could also be present at the session. This certainly makes sense. An adjournment of the Council session, however, requires the unanimous agreement of all its members (and primarily of the great powers). Surits had already gained the consent of the French. I had to obtain the consent of the English.

Halifax opened his diary and started thinking aloud: 'The week beginning 22 May is already very full for me… But… but the decisive consideration here should be the possibility of your government representative coming to Geneva… So, although this is rather difficult for me, I agree to the adjournment.'

Then Halifax asked me who exactly would come from Moscow. C[omrade] Molotov? Or C[omrade] Potemkin?

Out of prudence I did not give a name, merely saying that 'a representative of the Soviet government' would come.

Halifax had obviously made his mind up that C[omrade] Molotov would not go, for he suddenly asked whether C[omrade] Potemkin spoke English. And in general, would Halifax be able to converse in English with the Soviet delegation in Geneva?

I answered half in jest: 'If a common political language is found, linguistic problems will be easily overcome.'

15 May

I have been appointed USSR representative at the forthcoming session of the Council of the League of Nations. Comrade Potemkin is not coming to Geneva. There will be nobody except me in the Soviet delegation. This means, then, that I will also be chairing the Council session.

It's an awkward situation. We asked for the Council session to be adjourned to enable a Soviet delegate from Moscow to come to Geneva. Now, with the session adjourned at our request, nobody from Moscow is actually coming. The English and French will certainly be offended and annoyed, all the more so as Halifax was placing great hopes on the possibility of coming to a final agreement with the Soviet government on the question of 'European security'.

However, the decision of the Soviet government also has its positive side: it prevents the British government from using the excuse of negotiations in Geneva to delay or avoid giving a response to the proposals we made yesterday. There will be no high-up in Geneva to act as judge and jury. In Geneva there will be Maisky, that same Maisky whom Halifax can meet in London any day of the week. What cause can there be for further delays? The answer will have to be given fast and straight.

[The idea that Halifax should proceed to Moscow for 'a straightforward' discussion with Molotov originated with Maisky during a heart-searching conversation with Dalton, who then raised it in parliament on 10 May. Halifax, however, preferred the meeting to take place at the forthcoming session of the Council of the League of Nations in Geneva, to be presided over by the Russians. He looked forward to a conversation with Molotov or Potemkin, 'who could speak with full knowledge of the mind of the Soviet Government'.[101] News of the appointment of Maisky to head the Soviet delegation crossed with a telegram from Maisky urging Molotov to attend the Geneva meeting in view of the drastic shift in British public opinion in favour of an alliance with the Soviet Union. He further advised Molotov to adopt his own method of appealing to the English people over the head of the government.[102]]

16 May

On 14 May in Moscow our reply to the British proposals of 8 May was handed to Seeds. It boils down to the following:

The proposals of the British government of 8 May cannot serve as the basis for organizing a peace front to counter the further expansion of aggression in Europe.

Our reasons:

(1) The British proposals lack the principle of reciprocity with regard to the USSR, thereby placing her in an unequal position. England, France and Poland, on the basis of reciprocity, guarantee each one against direct attack by an aggressor. The English proposals do not provide the USSR with such a guarantee from England and France.

(2) The English proposals provide for guarantees only to Poland and Rumania, while the north-western borders of the USSR (Latvia, Estonia and Finland) are left exposed.

(3) The absence of English and French guarantees in the event of direct attack on the USSR, as well as the exposure of the north-western borders of the USSR, may provoke aggression against the USSR.

In the opinion of the Soviet government, at least three conditions are essential in order for peace-loving states to erect a genuine barrier against the expansion of aggression in Europe:

(1) An effective tripartite pact of mutual assistance between Britain, France and the USSR.

(2) Guarantees on the part of these three great powers to Central and Eastern European states which find themselves threatened by aggression, including Latvia, Estonia and Finland.

(3) The signing of a concrete agreement between Britain, France and the USSR on the forms and scope of assistance to be extended to one another, as well as to the states guaranteed by them. Without this, the mutual assistance pact would risk being stranded in mid-air, as the experience of Czechoslovakia has shown.[103]

Excellent. In particular, our proposals are brief, simple and convincing in their clarity. This will help us a great deal in winning over the public in Britain and France.

[Commenting on the new draft proposal to the Russians, the chiefs of staff embarrassed Chamberlain and Halifax on 16 May by insisting that any arrangement short of a full-blown alliance might have 'serious military repercussions ... of ultimately throwing the USSR into [Germany's] arms'. The Cabinet was split on the issue. While Chamberlain, tacitly backed by Halifax, rejected the idea of a grand alliance, underlining the 'political' aspects which were overlooked by the chiefs of staff, Lord Chatfield, the minister of defence, warned that – 'distasteful' as it was for him personally to contemplate an alliance with the Soviet Union – the chiefs of staff were 'very anxious that Russia should not, in any circumstances, become allied with Germany'. Irritated by Maisky, who was 'working hand in hand' with the opposition, Chamberlain hardly budged from his position, warning that an alliance would increase Britain's 'liabilities' as well as the 'probability of war'. He anticipated 'trouble' from the Russians, who had 'no understanding of other countries' mentality or conditions and no manners'. Halifax, however, wished the Cabinet to reach a decision before his departure for Geneva. It was clear to him that the only choices were for the negotiations to be 'allowed to break down, or a full military alliance with Russia accepted'. This precipitated Vansittart's evening meeting with Maisky, which was aimed at toning down the terms of the proposed agreement.[104]]

17 May

Yesterday the Vansittarts came over for an 'intimate' lunch. We discussed international affairs at length, and above all the Anglo-Soviet negotiations. Vansittart expressed the view that the second point of our most recent proposals (military negotiations) was easy to implement, but that the first (a tripartite mutual assistance pact) and the third (guarantees to Central and Eastern European countries) would be more difficult. I, in turn, made it quite clear to Vansittart that the three points of our proposals were the minimum, and that if the British government was not inclined to accept them, I saw no chance of reaching an agreement at all.[105]

Today, at 12.30 in the afternoon, Vansittart urgently summoned me to the FO. He received me not in his office, but in his secretary's office next door. He apologized, saying that an important meeting was currently under way in his room. Indeed, during my talk with Vansittart, the door to his office opened for a split-second and I caught a glimpse of several Foreign Office officials amid clouds of tobacco smoke.

Vansittart looked highly agitated. He said that yesterday, after our lunch, he had had the chance to speak to Halifax, after which he decided to try 'on his own initiative' to hasten the process of finding a basis for agreement between our governments. To this end, he had drafted a formula, but before sending it to Moscow he wanted to hear what I thought about it. The formula read as follows: as soon as the declaration, stipulated by the British proposal to the USSR of 8 May, is made public, the three great powers shall embark on military negotiations, but only in respect of assistance to Poland and Rumania. Did such a formula have any chance of being favourably received in Moscow? Should it be sent at all?

I replied that there was no need to send the formula worked out by Vansittart to Seeds. It would inevitably be rejected.

Vansittart tried to defend his formula, but I said that there was no use wasting time debating it, since the Soviet government's reaction to the proposal was already perfectly clear to me.

I added that as long as the British government failed to recognize the principle of a tripartite mutual assistance pact, no basis for further negotiations could be found.

Then I left. This evening, at seven o'clock, Vansittart invited me once again to the FO. This time he received me in his own office. He looked even more agitated than in the morning and, handing me a sheet of the bluish paper which is so often used by the FO, he asked me to treat the document he had prepared without prejudice and with an awareness of the responsibility that lay on us all in these critical days. Perhaps the document was not ideal, but it was the most he could get the Cabinet to accept at the moment. Were we to accept it, at least as a starting point for further negotiations, then he hoped he could persuade his government to make further concessions to us. The main thing was that we should not waste time. Alarming information was coming from Danzig. Hitler was planning a new 'sally'. We had to act with the greatest speed and determination.

I skimmed Vansittart's new formula (see attached)[106] and raised my head. Vansittart was looking at me with bated breath, waiting for my response.

I shook my head doubtfully.

'Your new formula,' I said, 'is composed skilfully, but in essence it differs little from what you showed me in the morning. This fact determines my attitude towards it.'

Vansittart started objecting. The new formula effectively gives us a tripartite pact. It will be applicable not only to Poland and Rumania, but also to the Baltic States, for Vansittart is in no doubt that the consultation, stipulated in the third point, will inevitably result in the extension of guarantees to the Baltic States as well. The moment at which military operations commence will be determined jointly by the three governments. What more do we want?

I replied that even if one accepted Vansittart's interpretation, which I did not deem entirely accurate, the tripartite pact he proposed would have as its geographic base only the states that neighbour us, while what we wanted was a pact encompassing the whole of Europe. The pact he proposed completely excluded the instance of a direct attack on our territory. Neither did it resolve the Baltic question categorically and with full clarity.

'So you think that the new formula cannot serve as the basis for agreement?' Vansittart asked

'That's right,' I replied, 'I don't think the Soviet government would accept it.'

But Vansittart insisted on asking me to forward the formula to Moscow and to recommend it to the Soviet government. He also wished to receive our reply as soon as possible, preferably the following day, 18 May.[107]

I promised to inform the Soviet government about his proposal promptly, but refused to recommend it to Moscow. Besides, tomorrow is not a working day in our country, and I am not sure I can get a reply before the 19th.

18 May

Walking in the embassy garden this morning, I pondered Vansittart's move yesterday. I think it can be explained in the following way.

The Soviet government's reply of 14 May put the British government in a tight spot. Our proposals are clear, simple, reasonable and capable of appealing to the consciousness of the *man in the street*. They have already leaked out to the press and, were the Anglo-Soviet argument over the terms and conditions of agreement to be judged by the British public, Chamberlain would most definitely lose.

On the other hand, the British government's commitments towards Poland, Rumania and Greece render a quick deal with the Soviet Union absolutely essential from the British point of view. For, without us, those commitments cannot be made good. What, in fact, can England (or even England and France together) really do for Poland and Rumania if Germany attacks them? Very little. Before the British blockade against Germany could become a serious threat, Poland and Rumania would cease to exist. So British guarantees in the east without an agreement with us will inevitably mean military defeat for Britain, with all the ensuing consequences. That's assuming England honours its word. Should it break its word and avoid giving assistance to Poland and Rumania under some pretext, then it would be signing its own death warrant as a great power. Not only would this entail a catastrophic loss of global credibility – political and economic – but the rapid disintegration of its Empire.

All these considerations – domestic, imperial and international – are undoubtedly occupying the minds of Chamberlain and his ministers. They are especially concerning at the current time, as the House is scheduled to have a debate on foreign policy on 19 May, in which Churchill, Eden, Lloyd George and other 'stars' will speak, and which will essentially boil down to the question: why has a pact with the USSR not been signed yet?[108] Meanwhile, for psychological reasons, the prime minister is still unable to swallow such a pact, since it would throw him into the anti-German camp once and for all, thus putting an end to all projects aimed at reviving '*appeasement*'. That's why Chamberlain keeps bargaining with us like an old gypsy, trying to foist a bad horse on us instead of a good one. It won't work! Yet he still hasn't lost hope…

But why has Vansittart agreed to become Chamberlain's instrument in pushing such a shady deal?

I don't know. Perhaps his true intention is to be back in the mainstream of active politics? Perhaps he thinks that first you have to get in there, no matter how, and then the very logic of things will lead towards an actual agreement?

If Vansittart reasons in this way, he is grossly mistaken. We shall not accept his formula, and this will arm Chamberlain with yet another argument against him.

19 May

To my surprise, the reply from Moscow arrived on the 18th at 5 p.m. I decided, however, not to inform Vansittart about it till the next morning. As I expected, the reply was brief and unambiguous: unacceptable.

I visited Vansittart in his flat today at 10.30 a.m. He did not seem surprised by our reply. It seems that he was fully prepared for it after our conversation in the evening of 17 May. He merely sighed and uttered, as if to himself: 'Well, it can't be helped. Looks like we'll have to get down to work again, and think up something new.'

Corbin called me during the day over the telephone, arguing in detail and at length that Vansittart's formula had to be accepted. In his opinion, the compromise should consist in the fact that we would sacrifice the tripartite pact in exchange for British and French guarantees to the Baltic States. Corbin was greatly disappointed to hear that Moscow had already rejected Vansittart's proposal.

Aras, to whom I paid a visit at 5 p.m., told me that he had just seen Cadogan, to whom he had expressed concern on behalf of the Turkish government regarding the delay in Anglo-Soviet negotiations, as well as the hope that agreement could be achieved promptly. Cadogan assured Aras that the British government was seeking to complete negotiations as quickly as possible and would spare no effort to find a formula which we would deem acceptable.

At 7 p.m. Vansittart asked me to drop by at his flat for a few minutes. When I entered the hall, he rushed to greet me and announced excitedly that he had good news to communicate. The decision had just been taken to ask Seeds to inform the Soviet government that as a result of the recent exchanges (the British proposal of 8 May and our counter-proposal of 14 May, and my talks with Halifax, Vansittart and others) the positions of the parties have been definitively clarified and the existing difficulties accurately identified. The British government would make every effort to overcome these difficulties and hoped to find the appropriate means to do so. However, the new proposals required a special decision by the whole Cabinet and would be adopted at its meeting on 24 May. Following that, the British government would give its official reply to our proposals of 14 May through Seeds (Vansittart had advanced this formula in an unofficial capacity). Until the 24th Halifax and I would be able to keep in touch and exchange views about the negotiations in Geneva.

I remarked that that was all very well, but the most important thing was the nature of the proposals which the British government planned to adopt on the 24th.

Vansittart added still more unofficially that the overall nature of his conversation today with Halifax had given him grounds for optimism. Today's debate in parliament would also have an impact. Vansittart hopes that agreement will be reached next week.

I shook my head doubtfully and, taking my leave, teased Vansittart in a now entirely unofficial manner: 'Admit it, Sir Robert, deep down you are pleased we have taken a firm stand!'

Vansittart burst out laughing and exclaimed: 'Perhaps!'

We parted till the end of the month. Agniya and I are taking the night train to Geneva.

21 May

Here we are in Geneva.

We arrived in Paris yesterday, at 9 a.m., and wandered about the city until evening. Talked a lot with Surits. Did a bit of shopping. I also met Robert Longuet (the son of the late Jean Longuet[i]) and we arranged the transfer to the I[nstitute] of M[arx], E[ngels] and Lenin of various relics and objects that his great-grandfather had left in the family (including two armchairs, in one of which Marx wrote his *Das Kapital*, and Marx's correspondence with the publisher of *Das Kapital*).

It so happened that Halifax and I travelled from Paris to Geneva in the same train and even the same carriage. Photographers at the station made our life hell: they were dying to take a photograph of me next to the British foreign secretary. But I managed to avoid that.

When the train moved off, Halifax met me in the corridor of our carriage and said that he would like to see me in Geneva the following day for a thorough discussion. He promised to call me immediately after our arrival. He has yet to call.

The Paris train gets in to Geneva devilishly early, at 7.13 in the morning. We all crawled out of the carriages sleepy, gloomy and peeved. For some odd reason, Halifax decided to walk from the station to the hotel. It was a grey, drizzly morning, and his long, lean figure striding through Geneva under a black umbrella seemed to have leapt from a cartoon by Low.

* * *

Halifax called, and we met in his hotel at 11.30 a.m. Strang was also present during the conversation, which lasted nearly an hour and a half.

---

[i] Jean Laurent-Frederick Longuet, leader of the French Socialist Party.

Halifax began by asking me to explain our resolute opposition to the British formula of 8 May.

Emphasizing that this was my personal reply, I indicated the reasons underlying our position.

The Soviet Union can pursue one of two courses today:

(1) A policy of isolation and freedom of movement in international affairs. This could ensure its relative security (considering its might, its abundant resources, the size of its population, etc.). I say 'relative' because such a policy would not be able to stave off a world war, with all the ensuing consequences.

(2) A policy aimed at building a peace bloc, primarily with Britain and France, which would impose heavy military obligations on the Soviet Union and limit its freedom of action in international affairs, but which would promise greater security, for by taking this route one could hope to avert a world war.

The USSR prefers the second course and wishes to pursue it. But, naturally enough, it assesses the Anglo-French proposals in the light of the possibilities open to it.

Yes, the Soviet Union is prepared to abandon freedom of action and assume heavy obligations, but only on condition that the British and the French *mean real business*. Otherwise it makes no sense for the USSR to refuse the opportunities offered by the first option.

What do we understand by *real business*?

In the first place, it means the possibility of averting a world war – this is our main goal.

It further means maximum guarantees of security and victory for the USSR should war nevertheless break out.

What is required for these aims to be accomplished?

What is required is a concentration of peace-loving forces so powerful as to make the aggressors lose hope of military success. Such a powerful concentration can only be attained through a tripartite pact, reinforced by a military convention. Therein lies the basis of our proposals. Without a tripartite pact, there can be neither real security nor hope of victory in the event of war. If the Anglo-French side declines the tripartite pact, it will be much more expedient for us to follow the course of isolation and 'relative' security.

Meanwhile, what does the Anglo-French formula offer? Even if we look at the latest 'Vansittart version'?

It does offer a tripartite pact, but on the basis only of Poland and Rumania. Can such a pact prevent war? No, it can't. Can it at least provide a sound guarantee of security for our western borders? No, it can't, since all the Baltic States remain unprotected. What is the point, then, of our accepting the Anglo-French formula? There is none. So we reject it as being deprived of the principles of equality and reciprocity, and as being incapable of preventing war.

Such is our position. I believe I have expounded it with the utmost clarity.

Halifax listened very attentively, interrupting me fairly often to pose a question or request an explanation. At the end, he declared that he now understood our point of view entirely and found much of my argument convincing.

Then I, in turn, asked Halifax why the British government was so opposed to our proposals.

Halifax replied that the British government had two principal motives.

First, the Baltic States, in their fear of Germany, do not want to be guaranteed by a tripartite pact. In the end, one cannot impose guarantees on others by force.

Secondly – and this is far more important – many in Britain think that a tripartite pact may push Hitler to unleash war straight away, and therefore, rather than preventing war, the pact will hasten it. Halifax made a point of emphasizing that this was not his own opinion, but the opinion shared by influential British circles, including some of his colleagues.

I replied that I found both arguments unconvincing. The reluctance of the Balts was being greatly exaggerated (just as the reluctance of Poland and Rumania to form a bloc with the USSR had once been exaggerated). As for the probable effect of the pact on Hitler's conduct, the reverse ought to be the case. The gravest mistake made by certain leading English figures is their complete failure to grasp the psychology of such men as Hitler and Mussolini. These Englishmen perceive them as they would a *business man* from the City or an English *country gentleman*. They could not be any more mistaken! Aggressors have an entirely different mentality! Those who would like to understand the aggressor *mentality* would do better to look to Al Capone as a model. We have experienced this for ourselves in Japan. That experience and our observation of European events have brought us to the firm conclusion that aggressors respect only force! Only force will make them doff their cap! That is why I am absolutely convinced that the creation of a tripartite pact would not only not lead to war, but would make Hitler and Mussolini retreat.

Halifax asked with obvious interest: 'After all, the Japanese seemed to concede to all your demands in the fishery business, didn't they?'

'Yes, they did,' I answered, 'but consider their behaviour: for months they'd been demanding, insisting and threatening, and tormenting Litvinov with endless meetings, but when they finally understood that they couldn't frighten us, they conceded to all our demands at the very last moment, at precisely five minutes to twelve. Five to twelve! The Japanese were playing tough, but our nerves proved stronger than theirs, and as a result we won.'

We then returned to the Anglo-French formula.

'But if,' Halifax continued, 'the Baltics received guarantees like Poland and Rumania, wouldn't that satisfy you? Why would you then need a tripartite mutual assistance pact? Your entire western border would be covered, and the Germans would have no way of attacking you without encroaching on the guaranteed countries on your western border.'

I replied: 'But what if our neighbours fall victim to "indirect" German aggression? What if, using the well-known fascist technique of carrot and stick, Germany provokes internal coups in our limitrophes and sets up its own governments there? Or bribes and threatens the governments that are currently in place? What if these states become German allies, or, at the very least, allow German troops heading for the USSR to pass through their territory? In that case our limitrophes will offer no resistance to German aggression, and your guarantees towards them will remain inactive. What then?'

These arguments set Halifax thinking. They had clearly never entered his mind before, at least not in such a clear and precise form. Eventually he said: 'I understand: You are afraid that at a critical moment your limitrophes might capitulate. Yes, it's a serious consideration.'

Our conversation came to an end. Shaking my hand on parting, Halifax summed up: 'I will think over the content of today's conversation and try to draw the appropriate conclusions in time for the Cabinet's next meeting.'

A strange business! On the day of my departure for Geneva, a Tory MP I know said to me with a wry smile: 'I have nothing to do with diplomacy, and may not understand much about it. Yet it seems strange to me, as an outsider, that in order to have "serious conversations" about the Anglo-Soviet pact, you and Halifax should need to go to Geneva.'

I laughed and readily agreed with him. But here's a curious thing: when talking with me in Geneva, Halifax was far more straightforward, free and human than he is in London. Moreover, we talked for an hour and a half, while in London Halifax never allows ambassadors to stay with him for more than thirty minutes.

How should we understand this? Can it be the effect of Geneva's celebrated atmosphere?

22 May

Today I assumed the chair of the Council of the League of Nations. Simpler than I'd imagined. It's *all right* so far. Nevertheless, today I clashed with Avenol at a special meeting of the Council, for the following reason.

Avenol told the Council about the correspondence that the L[eague] of N[ations] had had with Zog, former king of Albania, and Albanian diplomats. Zog, of course, had protested against Italian aggression and asked for the help of the LN. This correspondence did not give rise to any exchange of views, and Avenol was about to file it when I said, in a brief speech, that we had before us a most serious case, characteristic of the present international situation, and that the LN ought not to ignore Italian aggression against Albania. Considering the significance of the problem arising from this case, I proposed to submit all the relevant documents and materials to the next Assembly of the LN.

Avenol was shocked, and gave a suspicious sniff. He was sitting next to me, and I could sense the slightest movement of his soul and body. The delegates of the other countries kept silent and looked as if something indecent had happened in the conference hall. In the end, Halifax asked what I meant: putting the whole Albanian question on the agenda of the next Assembly, or merely handing over to it the LN correspondence with Zog and others?

I replied that for the time being I meant the latter. The Council should forward all materials to the Assembly, and the Assembly should decide what to do with them.

Halifax said that in that case he had no objections. The other Council members kept dead silent. I gave them no time to come to their senses and, wary of further questions or objections, hastened to announce with a loud voice and resolute air: 'Any comments? Objections?… None! Then the proposal is accepted!'

King Zog will thus come to figure at the Assembly.

I then moved on to the next question. On the eve of the Council session, Beneš sent a telegram from Chicago addressed to the Council chairman, where he protested against the annexation of Czechoslovakia and asked the LN to discuss the situation. Beneš also sent a copy of the telegram to Comrade Molotov.

While Avenol somehow managed to swallow Zog's letter, Beneš's telegram stuck in his craw. He therefore tried to conceal the telegram from the Council, and was helped in this by Sandler (the Swedish foreign minister). It was Sandler who received Beneš's telegram in his capacity as chair of the Council, a post he formally retained until noon today (he chaired the previous Council session in January). Sandler, in agreement with Avenol, decided not to do anything about the telegram, not even to communicate its contents to the Council members. Had Beneš not sent a copy of his telegram to Moscow, the conspiracy of silence organized by Avenol might have succeeded. But I knew about it from Moscow and so, in a private talk with Avenol yesterday, I asked the latter to send a copy to me. I also informed Avenol that I thought it desirable to pass the telegram over to the Assembly. Avenol mumbled something incomprehensible in reply, but he did nevertheless send me a copy.

After settling the question of Zog's letter, I announced, in my capacity as the USSR's representative, that I wished to bring a similar document to the Council's notice. I uttered Beneš's name and was about to read the text of his telegram.

Avenol suddenly turned red as a lobster, blew out his cheeks, and in his fury all but shouted: 'But this runs counter to our constitution!… Beneš's telegram is addressed not to you, but to Mr Sandler as the previous chairman… You can't divulge another person's document… Mr Sandler conceded that there was nothing to be done about it, and you can't change his decision!'

There was a stir in the meeting-room. Everyone sensed a scandal in the air, and knew that something interesting was afoot.

'I have to confess, as a novice, that I do not know the LN regulations backwards,' I replied, 'and if I, as the present chairman, do not have the right to divulge documents received by my predecessor, I would like to ask the latter to do so.'

Saying this, I passed Beneš's telegram to Sandler, who was sitting three seats away from me. Sandler was dying of embarrassment and fended off the telegram as if it were the black death, muttering something about not having instructions from his government. The other Council members sat like lumps of stone, burying their noses in their papers and pretending to be unaware of what was going on.

'If my predecessor,' I went on, 'deems it impossible to read Beneš's telegram, which has great political significance, I will have to do it myself…'

'But you cannot divulge this document without violating League regulations,' Avenol hissed angrily.

'And what solution can you recommend as secretary-general?' I pressed on.

'I don't know,' Avenol hissed again.

'Then I'll have to seek instruction from the Council,' I parried. 'Do the Council members wish to hear Beneš's telegram?'

A tense silence fell. Then, all of a sudden, the booming voice of Jordan (New Zealand) exploded like a bomb: 'I'm a member of the Council and know nothing about Beneš's telegram. It would be interesting to hear it.'

Halifax intervened, declaring in a calm voice: 'Each of us probably has quite a few papers in his pocket that would be interesting to hear, but that is no argument for violating LN procedure.'

Bonnet, who was sitting on my right, hastened to give Halifax his support.

It was clear that they would not allow me to read Beneš's telegram at this session, so I decided to manoeuvre and said in a more conciliatory tone: 'Considering these difficulties of a juridical-procedural nature, I'll not insist on reading Beneš's telegram right now, but after the meeting I will have a special meeting with the secretary-general, and I hope we shall then find ways that accord with regulations to bring the document in question to the Assembly's notice.'

Avenol bristled and parried: 'Our constitution forbids the divulging at Council and Assembly sessions of documents received not from governments but from private persons. We all highly respect Dr Beneš, but at the present time he is a professor at the University of Chicago, not president of the Czechoslovak Republic. Moreover, he was not deprived of his presidency by force, but retired quite voluntarily. Dr Beneš is just a private person now, and the League of Nations cannot consider documents that come from him.'

This enraged me and I replied in a sharper tone: 'Dr Beneš is indeed just a private person from a refined, legalistic point of view, but I think that in matters of this kind it is dangerous to engage in legalistic pedantry. We all know full well the circumstances under which Dr Beneš ceased to be president of the Czechoslovak Republic, and for us, as for the world's public, it is simply not possible for him to be just a private person without the right to speak on behalf of his country. Nevertheless, I repeat once again that I do not insist on the immediate reading of Beneš's telegram and hope to settle this difficulty through talks with the secretary-general.'

No one objected. The Council passed to the next item on the agenda.

After the meeting, I learned that there is a simple way of bypassing the juridical barrier which Avenol referred to: as the USSR representative, I should address a letter to Avenol on behalf of my government, asking him to bring the text of the attached telegram to the notice of the Assembly. Avenol will then be obliged to do so. This is how I shall have to act.

23 May

In my role as Council chairman, I gave a lunch today in Hotel de Bergues for all members of the Council and Secretariat of the League. I'd brought caviar and vodka for this occasion from London. We had traditional Russian hors d'oeuvres, the kulebyaka pie, pickled mushrooms, and other delicacies for which Soviet lunches have long been renowned in Geneva, thanks to M.M. [Litvinov].

During lunch, I spoke a lot with Halifax, who sat on my right as the senior guest. Halifax questioned me about the status of religion in the USSR (he is a very religious man, one of the senior representatives of Anglo-Catholicism). The talk then somehow turned to the fall of the Romanov dynasty, and I related many curious details to Halifax about the last period of tsarist rule in Russia. He displayed great interest in Rasputin[i] and in the correspondence between the tsar and tsarina, published in the early years of the revolution.

We spoke little about current issues. I merely asked Halifax whether he had reached any conclusions, following our talk of 21 May. Halifax didn't give a

[i] Grigorii Efimovich Rasputin, Russian mystic who served as personal and domestic policy adviser to Tsarina Aleksandra Fedorovna; murdered in December 1916, following a monarchist conspiracy suspicious of his intentions.

61. Bonnet and Halifax reluctantly consider a triple alliance in Geneva, May 1939.

straight answer, and asked in return: 'So you are quite sure that a tripartite pact could avert the threat of war?'

'Yes, I am,' I answered.

Halifax had nothing to add, but he gave the impression that he was mentally underscoring some paragraph or other in the speech he'll be giving tomorrow to the Cabinet. He is leaving Geneva today on the night train, he'll be in Paris tomorrow morning at seven, and will fly from there to London at 8.30 a.m. on a plane sent for him from England so that he can attend the Cabinet meeting at eleven. That's what modern transport can do!

Bonnet told me over lunch that after speaking to me, Halifax had reached the definitive conclusion that a tripartite pact was essential, and that he would report to the Cabinet tomorrow along these lines. Bonnet himself is also leaving for Paris tonight in order to exert pressure on London after the governmental meeting 'if need be'. What a hero! What an ardent advocate of the tripartite bloc!

[Halifax had urged the Cabinet to reach a decision before his departure for Geneva, scarcely concealing his 'strongest possible distaste' for an alliance, which would amount to 'acquiescing in Soviet blackmail and bluff' while closing all doors to conciliation with Germany.[109] In Geneva, however, Maisky found Halifax to be more amenable and 'much freer than at the FO'. Expressing his 'personal opinion', he made it plain to Halifax that an alliance was a *sine qua non*, for if Russia 'was to abandon her position of isolation & thus her freedom of action she must be certain that what took its place did not endanger her position'. The only way to prevent the outbreak of war – the main Soviet objective – was through 'a concentration of powerful forces on the side of peace as would crush any hope of victory for the aggressor'. Reporting on his conversation with Maisky, Halifax – oblivious to the more pressing Soviet objective of forestalling Anglo-German collusion – preferred to attribute Soviet rejection of the proposed British guarantees to a fear that they would not cover a German attack on the Soviet Union through a third country.

Maisky tailored his report home to suit the views of Molotov and Stalin, with which he had become acquainted during his latest sojourn in Moscow. The report, based on information he had gleaned from Churchill's circles before his departure for Geneva, maintained that Chamberlain was 'being pushed all the time into a policy which he does not like, and hates abandoning the last bridges which might still enable him to renew his former policy'. It was 'perfectly obvious', Maisky concluded, that the British government was 'avoiding a tripartite pact purely out of a desire not to burn its bridges to Hitler and Mussolini'. He deliberately withheld the information that, notwithstanding Chamberlain's efforts 'to avoid a war alliance', his own sources were convinced that the prime minister would 'have to do what Stalin wants'.[110] Indeed the records describe Maisky emerging from the talks optimistic, convinced that Halifax had appreciated his

62. Maisky, replacing the absent Molotov as chairman of the Council of the League of Nations, at its last meeting before the war, May 1939.

arguments and would make 'a favourable report to the Cabinet'. Journalists expected an agreement to be concluded within a week or two.[111]

In Chamberlain's entourage, however, they were only too familiar with Halifax's tendency to change his tune depending on whom he saw last (not to mention whom he was addressing). Halifax's shift towards the Soviet position occurred after he had conferred with Bonnet and Daladier in Paris on the way to the League meeting. Both stood fast by the Soviet proposal and warned that a failure to reach an imminent agreement might tempt Stalin either to retire into isolation and 'let Europe destroy itself if it would', or (worse still) to reach accommodation with Germany.[112] Chamberlain was indeed disappointed by Halifax's failure to 'shake Maisky' from his demand for an alliance. Yet, guided by domestic considerations, he 'very reluctantly' conceded that it would be most difficult to reject the Soviet proposal. He remained, however, deeply suspicious of Soviet aims. As Maisky had correctly surmised, above all he was concerned lest an alliance 'make any negotiation or discussion with the totalitarians difficult if not impossible'. This indeed figured prominently in Halifax's presentation in Cabinet of the 'pros' and the 'cons' of an alliance. However, it was outweighed by the grim realization that an alliance had become indispensable if Hitler was to be deterred.[113]]

25 May

On instructions from Halifax, Butler met me this morning at the L[eague] of N[ations] and handed me a memorandum, whose essence was the following: His Majesty's Government, having given careful consideration to the matter, is now disposed to agree that effective cooperation against aggression in Europe between the Soviet, French and British governments might be based on a system of mutual guarantees which should be in general conformity with the principles of the League of Nations. The guarantees in question would cover direct attack on any of the three governments by a European state, and also the case where any of the three governments was engaged in hostilities by the attacking state in consequence of aggression upon another European country. The conditions of the last mentioned eventuality would need to be carefully worked out.

The memorandum further informs us that after the Cabinet meeting yesterday, the prime minister made the following statement in the House: I have every reason to hope that as a result of proposals which His Majesty's Government are now in a position to make on the main questions arising, it will be found possible to reach full agreement at an early date. There still remain some further points to be cleared up, but I do not anticipate that these are likely to give rise to any serious difficulty.

The memorandum ended by indicating that in the nearest future the Soviet government would be offered 'a formula that gives expression to the above-mentioned principles'.

'Well, what do you think?' Butler asked me after I had run my eyes over the memorandum.

'It is undoubtedly a step forward,' I answered, 'but I'll withhold my final judgement until I see the promised "formula" in black and white.'

'You are very cautious,' Butler said with a laugh.

'I learned to be so in London,' I responded in the same spirit.

[By Chamberlain's own admission, it is doubtful whether he intended to see the alliance through. Conspiring with Horace Wilson, he came up with 'a most ingenious idea'. Acquiescing on the face of it to the Soviet Union's substantial demands, he would dispense with the term 'alliance' by binding the British obligations to Article XVI of the Covenant of the League. However, he expected this article to be 'amended or repealed' before long, as indeed was openly reported in the press,[114] thus giving the agreement 'a temporary character'.[115] Iverach McDonald, political correspondent of *The Times*, recalled being informed by senior officials of Chamberlain's extreme reluctance to pursue the talks. His chief, Geoffrey Dawson, an intimate friend and co-fellow of Halifax's at All Souls, was convinced that Chamberlain was 'letting the talks trickle on, but he does not think anything much will come of them'.[116] Molotov did not fall into the trap, instead insisting that conclusion of the treaty depended on 'an immediate activation of a pact of mutual assistance'. He accused Chamberlain of adopting a procedure which would ensure the extension of the negotiations 'ad infinitum', rather than 'obtaining concrete results'. Binding the tripartite agreement with the Covenant of the League of Nations naturally intensified the embedded Soviet suspicion that it was to be used either as a card in future negotiations with the Germans, or as an attempt to drive a wedge between Germany and Russia.[117]]

26 May

I've learned that the general secretary of the Rumanian Foreign Ministry arrived in Geneva at the beginning of the week to meet Halifax and Bonnet. The general secretary told them on instructions from Bucharest that Rumania did not particularly fear an attack from Hungary or Bulgaria, or even the two of them combined: Rumania could cope with them on her own. However, should Germany participate in an attack on Rumania, the situation would change drastically. Even the most optimistic forecast of the Rumanian general staff indicates that, without outside help, Rumania could hold out for no more than three weeks. That is why Rumania would be ready in this given case 'to accept the cooperation of the Russian army'.

I'll say! Look at the wording of it: 'to accept the cooperation of the Russian army'!

Be that as it may, the myth about Rumania's non-acceptance of 'cooperation with the USSR', which the British have been peddling for so long, has collapsed for good.

27 May

The Council session is over! But over the last four days I have had to face quite a few difficulties and complications.

At first it looked as though the session could be wrapped up on 24 or 25 May. The various items on the agenda could have been settled in a single meeting. We ended up discussing them over two sessions for no good reason. Of the political issues, two were of greater significance – China and the Äland Islands. Taking past experience into account, I raised the Chinese question at the very first meeting on 22 May. A commission to draft a Chinese resolution was then elected and the resolution was submitted on 24 May, but it was a poor one, because the British and the French refused to agree to the setting up of the coordinating committee which the Chinese insisted on (I supported the Chinese throughout). Nevertheless, one way or another, the Chinese issue was dealt with. Only the Äland question remained, and that's where we got stuck.

The gist of it was as follows. In January, Finland and Sweden requested permission from all members of the 1921 Äland Convention to fortify the southern part of the archipelago. This had received unanimous consent by the time the Council convened. On 21 January, the Finns and the Swedes sent us a note as well, to ask not for our consent to the fortification of the Äland Islands, but only for our support during discussion of the matter at the League of Nations. Prior to the session, the Soviet government had not given the Finns and the Swedes an answer of any kind. The Finns and the Swedes were nevertheless convinced that we would not obstruct their wishes at the Council.

But our position in Geneva has proved quite different. The Soviet government believed, and still believes, the fortification of the archipelago to be a very dubious undertaking, as it carries the great risk that it will be occupied by the Germans in the event of war – with or without the consent of Finland and Sweden. In any case, the Soviet government has not been able to give its blessing to the fortification of the islands while the entire issue remains to be studied fully and while the Finns refuse to provide it with pertinent information about the scale and nature of the intended armaments (some ten days ago the Soviet government addressed the Finish government with a note to this effect, but the latter refused to answer, citing considerations of 'military secrecy'). In the light of the above, the Soviet government asked the Council to postpone discussion of the issue until next time.

The Finns and the Swedes, however, were adamantly opposed to this. When I informed Sandler about our position on 21 May, he flew into a rage and threatened that if the Council did not comply with their wishes, Sweden and Finland would begin to fortify the islands without the Council's permission. Moreover, he hinted that Sweden and Finland might even withdraw from the

League of Nations. The Finnish representative Holsti[i] was less truculent, but his remarks were in the same vein.

The British and the French, bound by prior consent to the fortification and reluctant to quarrel with the Scandinavians, were also against shelving the issue. Avenol, of course, was for Sweden and Finland and against us. The smaller countries (Greece, Bolivia, Belgium, Peru, New Zealand and others) had no desire to interfere in the dispute. China, afraid of treading on the toes of Britain and France, avoided taking sides.

Such were the circumstances in which I began my fight. After conferring with Butler, who had replaced Halifax, and with Charvériat,[ii] who had replaced Bonnet, I proposed a special meeting of the six powers concerned (USSR, Sweden, Finland, Britain, France and Belgium) to try to settle this contentious question. Belgium found itself among the powers concerned purely because its representative, Bourquin,[iii] was due to give a report on the Äland issue. Three special meetings of the six powers were held. In addition, the Äland issue was the subject of a 'special meeting' of all the members of the Council and of a 'special session' of the Council (not to be confused with a 'special meeting' of all Council members). In a word, a great quantity of time and words, and of nerves and passions, was expended on this issue.

First of all, I raised the possibility of postponing discussion of this item on the agenda. This idea was rejected by almost all the other representatives. I then let it be understood that if the issue was to be discussed during the session, I would have to vote down any resolution that might be put to the Council. In order to find a way out of the impasse, the representatives of Britain, France and especially Belgium began to suggest various compromises.

In their address to the League of Nations, the Swedes and the Finns asked the Council to express its 'approval' for their decision to fortify the Äland archipelago. The mediators said that 'approval' should be removed and replaced with 'acknowledgement' of the Swedish–Finnish intention, which would suffice. Sandler and Holsti objected fiercely at first, but eventually they agreed. I stated, however, that 'acknowledgement' was an indirect form of approval, and that I would therefore vote down this resolution as well. We started thrashing the problem out again, and Bourquin suggested that, first, he would not give a 'report' to the Council in the real sense of the word, but would satisfy himself merely with a 'statement of facts', establishing both the Swedish–Finnish and the Soviet positions; and secondly, the Council would not have to vote

[i] Eino Rudolf Woldemar Holsti, Finnish foreign minister, 1919–22 and 1936–38.

[ii] Emile Charvériat, succeeded René Massigli, who was preaching rapprochement with Czechoslovakia and the USSR, as director of the political affairs bureau of the French Foreign Ministry, in 1938.

[iii] Maurice Bourquin, Belgian professor of International Affairs at Geneva University and member of the Belgian delegation to the League of Nations, 1929–39.

'to acknowledge', but that as chairman I alone should announce at the end of the discussion that the Finnish–Swedish message had been acknowledged. To Bourquin's obvious regret, I turned down this scheme as well, on the principle that it was the same, only worse. I, for my part, proposed (twice, in fact) that a vote be held on the following question: 'Do you approve the fortification of the Äland Islands?' My proposal, however, was turned down by the overwhelming majority of delegates at the 'private meeting' of all members.

Since the dispute over the Äland Islands had already been dragging on for three days and most of the delegates were in a hurry to leave, Bourquin, in a state of extreme desperation, eventually proposed the following: he would not make even a 'statement of facts' at the Council, but just present a bulletin about the state of the Äland Islands issue; after hearing the various declarations and speeches of the Council members, no decision would be passed at all, and the chairman would announce that the debates held at the Council would be 'entered in the minutes'. Sandler and Holsti agreed to this, and so did I. Today, at seven in the evening, the last meeting of the 105th Council session was held, devoted entirely to the Äland issue.

Here I must note a rather curious fact. Yesterday, Avenol had a talk with Comrade Sokolin, during which he clearly hinted that since the USSR was a 'party' to the Äland issue, I should not chair the meeting at which it would be discussed. But I turned a deaf ear to these hints. Today, according to information I have received from various sources, Avenol campaigned among the Council members with some success along these lines. But I didn't react to this either. Finally, after lunch, Avenol himself raised the subject with me and cited several precedents in support of his arguments, in particular the case of Beneš, who had declined chairmanship in the dispute between Czechoslovakia and Hungary.

I replied to Avenol: 'Can you show me the article of the Covenant or the regulations which would forbid me to chair the meeting on the Äland issue?'

Somewhat taken aback, Avenol exclaimed: 'No, there is no such article.'

'So you are referring only to old precedents?'

'Yes, to old precedents,' replied Avenol.

'I cannot regard them as binding,' I said, 'and I am prepared to create a new precedent.'

Avenol was beside himself. He puffed out his cheeks, turned red, and exclaimed angrily: 'But what about public opinion? You'll be attacked in the press.'

'Don't worry,' I retorted. 'It won't be the first time I come under fire. I can cope with public opinion.'

Avenol shrugged his shoulders in despair.

So the attempt to unseat me failed. I had firmly decided that I would chair the Äland meeting come rain or shine – not only because I found Avenol's claims senseless, but also because it was important for me to forestall the slightest possibility of the Finns and the Swedes interpreting the examination of the Äland issue by the Council as even the most indirect approval of their intentions. And I managed to get my way.

After Bourquin had read his 'bulletin', after Sandler, Holsti, Charvériat, and others had delivered their statements, and after I had made my statement on behalf of the USSR, in which I stressed the absence of unanimity among Council members, and uttered the words 'the proceedings will be entered in the minutes' – after all this, I loudly added one final sentence: 'This means that the LN Council has taken no decision whatsoever on the issue under discussion.'

The matter was sealed. The Finns and the Swedes had been totally defeated. But then, as soon as the session was closed, Sandler and I shook hands in full view of the whole Council and the audience, as one would do in any good sports club. Like two boxers after a bout.

Sandler was greatly upset. Holsti vanished without even saying good-bye to me.

28 May

It was with great relief that I left Geneva today. I took away with me a vague, unpleasant aftertaste. The weather had been foul throughout. The League of Nations smelled of carrion. But what repelled me most of all about Geneva was the fact that I witnessed at first hand the staggering might of the legal-procedural chicanery which has built its nest in the 'Palace of Nations'. It is the apotheosis of chicanery. An impenetrable web of chicanery. Knots, traps and gaps at every turn. Everything is strictly regulated: every step or action taken by the Assembly, Council or chairman. Even breathing seems to be regulated at the League of Nations. The Secretariat is omnipotent, and Avenol an absolute dictator. He was awfully indignant at my behaviour (and did not conceal this in public). Regulations, traditions and precedents decreed that the chairman should follow the 'advice' of the secretary-general whenever in doubt. It has always been thus. The chairmen usually dance to Avenol's tune like puppets. I took unheard-of liberties: not only did I refuse to be led on his string, but I took issue with him and acted contrary to his advice. He could not forgive me for that. Avenol told everyone that I was too 'independent' a chairman and that it was certainly not possible to call me the '*mouthpiece of the Secretary General*'.

Well, to hell with Avenol! All this is already behind us. I hope I shall never again have to 'grace' the 'Palace of Nations' with my presence.

This morning was exceptionally fine, in stark contrast to the entire preceding week. Bright sunshine, a cloudless sky, the sparkling blue lake. I decided to travel to Paris by car. Agniya was already waiting for me there, having gone by train the previous day. Sokolin accompanied us to Dijon. We went on from there in a group of three: Kozlovsky,[i] Kushelevich and I.

We arrived in Paris at 8 p.m.

Yesterday, 27 May, Seeds presented the following proposals to Comrade Molotov in Moscow. They represent a concrete expression of the 'principles' discussed in the memorandum which Butler gave to me in Geneva on 25 May.

[There follows the text of the British proposals, which were based on Chamberlain's evasive attempt to shift the negotiations to Geneva and conclude an agreement under the umbrella of the League's covenant. Molotov was quick to dismiss the proposals as 'unacceptable'. It was an Anglo-French attempt 'to continue conversations indefinitely and not to bind themselves to any concrete engagement'.[118]]

30 May

In the absence of Halifax and Cadogan, who have left town for Whitsun, Oliphant invited me to see him. He met me somewhat sullenly, with the air of someone who had been unfairly insulted.[119]

He began by reading out to me numerous ciphered messages exchanged over the past four or five days between London and Moscow, i.e. the Foreign Office and Seeds, in which the course of talks between Seeds and Molotov (the 27 May meeting) was set out, as well as Halifax's instructions to Seeds. Having established that the English proposals of 27 May were received very critically by Molotov, Oliphant announced Halifax's great disappointment. Halifax had fully expected us to accept the proposals at once, instead of which Molotov had greeted Seeds with an avalanche of unpleasant comments: that the British government was dragging out the talks, that it did in fact desire effective resistance to aggression, that the League of Nations was included in the British proposals simply for the purpose of creating impediments to a fast reaction to an attack by an aggressor, etc. Seeds and Payart tried to dispel Molotov's suspicions, but had obviously failed.

Oliphant finds all this very distressing. The British government, he says, wishes to reach an agreement as early as possible. In order to overcome the new difficulties, Oliphant sent fresh instructions yesterday to Seeds, which boil down to the following:

(1) In referring to clauses 1 and 2 of Article 16 of the L[eague] of N[ations], the British government had in mind only the principles expressed in them and not the procedure stipulated therein. The reference was dictated mainly by domestic considerations, as well as by the desire to satisfy the smaller nations. The British government does not insist on its wording, however, and is ready to seek some other formula together with us.

---

[i] Yuri M. Kozlovsky, Litvinov's private secretary, removed from this position in 1937.

(2) The British government is prepared to start military talks immediately, so as to resolve our doubts in regard to paragraph 3 of the British proposals.

(3) The British government is ready to offer every assurance to us that paragraph 5 of the British proposals concerns only those countries to which the tripartite alliance will render support.

(4) The British government deems it very important to publish at least a preliminary communiqué about the Anglo-Soviet agreement, as was done in connection with the Polish and Turkish talks.

Having familiarized me with these instructions, Oliphant asked whether they would dispel the doubts of the Soviet government and lead to an early conclusion of the talks.

I replied that I could not give a definite answer to his question. The instructions are certainly intended to dispel some of our doubts, but will they succeed? I am not sure. The Soviet government is used to believing deeds, not words.

Personally, I could only say that, after familiarizing myself with the British proposals, I, too, was disappointed. Following my talk with Halifax in Geneva, I had expected the proposals to be clearer, simpler and more definite. In fact, they contained many ambiguous statements allowing for varied interpretations. Since I was fully aware of the high calibre of the Foreign Office staff, and in particular of those who took part in formulating these proposals, I could hardly attribute the flaws to negligence. Some objective must have been concealed beneath the deficiencies of wording. And this could not but render me, and everyone else on the Soviet side, suspicious. We were conducting negotiations about a document of paramount political and military importance, on which literally millions upon millions of lives would depend – so it was only to be expected that we would carefully weigh every word and clause of the document. Halifax had no reason to be either surprised or disappointed.

In conclusion, I promised Oliphant that I would bring our conversation to the notice of Moscow.

On 2 June, Comrade Molotov handed Seeds the following reply from the USSR to the British proposals of 27 May.

[Included in the diary are Molotov's 'ironclad, well defined commitments', pretty much a repeat of Litvinov's original proposals of 17 April calling for a system of collective guarantees covering the states between the Baltic and the Black Sea and insisting on a simultaneous military agreement to be concluded.[120]

The Kremlin's policy continued to be driven by a deep-seated suspicion of Chamberlain. The Franco-Soviet pact – which, as Molotov explained to Seeds, had 'turned out to be merely a paper delusion' – had taught the Russians the 'absolute necessity' of concluding 'simultaneously, both a political and a military agreement'.[121] In his speech to the Supreme Soviet on 31 May, Molotov found it hard to shake off the suspicion that the 'authoritative representatives' in Britain, who were 'glorifying the success of the ill-fated Munich Agreement', betrayed 'a sincere desire to abandon the policy of non-intervention, the policy of non-resistance to further aggression'. He feared that Britain was trying to divert the aggression and confine it to 'certain areas'. By publicizing in great detail the state of the negotiations, the aim was to exert extraneous pressure on the British government and to put a spoke in the wheels of the anticipated Anglo-German talks. At the same time, the crack opened up by Stalin with his 'chestnuts' speech was further widened when Molotov declared that there was 'no necessity for refusing to have commercial relations with such countries as Germany and Italy'.[122]]

3 June

[Included without a commentary is a satirical verse, 'Decameron', by Don-Aminado (Aminad Shpolyansky), a famous émigré poet, published in the Russian émigré newspaper *Poslednie novosti* on 2 June 1939. The satirist scoffs at the Anglo-Soviet alliance: the 'spousal' ends with the adultery between the 'Russian lady' and Hitler, and the 'English lord' and 'the Italian lady'. The matchmakers Potemkin and Maisky find themselves in prison.]

Decameron
They differed like June and December,
And both had quite high self-regard.
The bride was a Komsomol member,
The groom was an English milord.

This contrast they could not address,
Yet still they decided to wed.
She sported a cotton-print dress
While he wore a tail-coat with velvet.

And so at the registry office,
Performing her citizen's duty,
She offered her husband a kiss
And shone with quite magical beauty.

A telegram came from Kalinin,
And Halifax sent one soon after.
Our couple set out on their journey,
Put one foot in front of the other.

They tried, and they strove, and they suffered.
Out walking in various cemeteries,
They sang of hard labour and workers,
And hoped they could make life more merry.

But soon their neighbours did whisper:
The bloom of their love it is fading,
The lady is visiting Hitler,
The lord his Italian plaything…

The rulers, like angels of Sinai,
Delivered them straight into hell.
The brokers Potemkin and Maisky
Were rapidly sentenced to jail.

D. Aminado [translated by Oliver Ready]

8 June

Halifax invited me to see him today and informed me of the British government's decision to send Strang to Moscow. The motives for the decision are as follows: Seeds has been *out of touch* with the Foreign Office for many months and is poorly informed about the present mood and wishes of the British government. Halifax wanted to summon him to London for instruction, but Seeds went down with the flu. It was therefore decided to send Strang to Moscow to assist and brief Seeds. Besides, the British government finds that the method of exchanging notes which has been practised hitherto leads to misunderstandings and wasted time. Meanwhile, the dangerous international situation renders haste essential. For this reason, the British government would like to have a 'round-table conference' in Moscow. The British representative at the conference will be Seeds, while Strang will prove a good assistant. Out of all this *eloquence*, one thing was clear to me: the Foreign Office considers Seeds poorly qualified for serious negotiations and is sending Strang as reinforcement. Well, let them!

Halifax made three comments concerning the Soviet proposals of 2 June:

(1) The British government acknowledges as entirely rightful our wish to receive a guarantee for our n[orth]-w[estern] border, and is ready to meet us halfway in this respect, but finds it undesirable to name Latvia, Estonia and Finland directly in the agreement (paragraph 1 in the Soviet proposals). These countries do not want a guarantee, and it is undesirable to create the impression that the tripartite bloc is imposing a guarantee upon them.

(2) The British government has grave doubts about paragraph 6 of our proposals (whereby the pact and the military agreement will enter into force simultaneously), as this would entail a major delay in the completion of negotiations. It would be desirable to publish at least a preliminary communiqué as soon as agreement is reached on the essence of the problem.

(3) Paragraph 5 of our proposals (undertakings not to conclude a separate peace, etc.) also raises some doubts. War objectives must be taken into consideration here. But Halifax did not dwell on this point and only said that he thought it would be easy to reach agreement on this matter.

Halifax reckons that Strang will be able to leave for Moscow on 12 or 13 June.

[Ironically, Maisky would henceforth be increasingly removed from the negotiations, warily conducted by Molotov in Moscow at the same time as feelers were put out to Germany. Halifax was reluctant to have the talks in London, as he doubted whether Maisky 'would be given any latitude in negotiating'. Indeed, on the recommendation of Seeds, Maisky was no longer briefed by the Foreign Office about the course of the negotiations.[123] A noticeable dissonance could now be felt. While Maisky evinced confidence in the prospects for concluding an agreement, Molotov remained sceptical and his attitude hardened. Maisky played down the obstacles and was 'inclined to think', as he wrote to Kollontay, that the alliance would be formed 'in the not-too-distant future'. He likewise told Lloyd George's son 'that there was nothing to worry about for ... [the British] Government had been gradually moving towards what the Russians wanted ... He was quite confident ... that agreement would be reached. He said our Government has now come 75% of the way & are bound to come the whole 100%.' He told the Webbs that the agreement would be 'settled and signed this week or next'.[124] It is striking that, at his meeting with Halifax on 8 June, Maisky was still convinced that negotiations were progressing along the right tracks and even spoke in 'warm appreciation' of Strang and his mission. From Paris, the other survivor of Litvinov's protégés, Surits, shared Maisky's optimism, informing Molotov that 'no one here even considers it possible that the talks with us might break down and fail to result in an agreement'.[125]]

11 June

We stayed with the Webbs. I like to visit this serene but thoughtful spot.

A simple but comfortable and cosy country house. Fields, hills and small groves all around. Close by is a small village hotel, once a shady inn which served for centuries as a smugglers' den. There is nothing luxurious, nothing redundant in the house itself, but there are plenty of books, files, manuscripts, various materials and portraits of the intellectual leaders of England of the late-nineteenth and early-twentieth centuries. When you cross the threshold, you can't help but sense, from the atmosphere that pervades the home, that you have stumbled into a hotbed of thought and intellectual inquiry. This wonderful old couple – the best representatives of the nineteenth-century bourgeois intelligentsia – are in their eighties, but they refuse to give in. They read, follow world events, think and write. Beatrice has a particularly bright mind and it seems to me that she has always been the leading force in this rare political, scholarly and literary duumvirate. Returning home from the Webbs, I almost always carry away with me some interesting idea or some curious, if perhaps questionable, generalization.

On this occasion I recall the following observations made by Beatrice.

The first: on Chamberlain's change of policy. There is nothing surprising about this. Chamberlain is a typical English *business man*. The defining feature of a *business man* is his fundamentally opportunistic character. If a *business man* sets himself a definite aim (to conquer the market, to build a factory, to buy a plot of land, etc.) he first resorts to some known method. If experience shows that this method is not leading him to his objective, the *business man* will try another method, even if it flatly contradicts the first. The *business man* will have no psychological difficulties, no qualms of conscience or inner discomfort in making this change. In him it is a natural, organic process. All this applies fully to Chamberlain. His goal is to protect the Empire. At first he tried to achieve this by striking a deal with Hitler and Mussolini against the USSR. It didn't come off. Now he is trying to achieve the same objective by striking a deal with the USSR against Hitler and Mussolini. There is nothing strange or surprising about this: it is the essence of the English *business man*. Beatrice Webb draws the following conclusion from this: Chamberlain's turn is meant most seriously in the given circumstances, but he may retreat or even change his course entirely at any moment, should the circumstances assume a different character.

The second: on the future of the Labour Party. The Labour Party had a good hand after Munich, but played it terribly. If Labour had presented a united front after Munich, it, together with the Liberals and oppositional Conservatives, would be in power today. Chamberlain would have been defeated. But instead, Labour attacked the idea of a united front, expelled Cripps and others, and fell out with the Liberals. In the meantime, Chamberlain changed his foreign policy and left Labour without its trump card. Chamberlain's position is now solid, and Labour should count itself lucky to retain its present standing at the next election. However, a chance may still present itself to Labour in the future. If a tripartite alliance is concluded, the situation in Europe should change drastically. The armaments race may come to an end, and limitations will be imposed instead, perhaps even a reduction. The consequence would probably be wide unemployment and the aggravation of domestic economic problems. The Labour Party would then have a chance of winning at the expense of the Tories.

Beatrice Webb is not right on all points. She misses some important factors in her reasoning. Nonetheless, her arguments are interesting and provide food for+ thought.

12 June

I made the following statement to Halifax today:[126]

> I am instructed by my government to convey to you the following message:
>
> (1) The Soviet government takes note of the decision of the British government to send Mr Strang to Moscow.
>
> (2) In order to avoid any misunderstanding the Soviet government deems it necessary to state that the problem of the three Baltic States is now the problem without satisfactory solution of which our negotiations cannot be brought to a successful conclusion. The security of the NW borders of the USSR by the guaranty of common resistance to a direct or indirect aggression against Estonia, Latvia and Finland on the part of the three contracting parties is indispensable condition of agreement. This opinion of the S[oviet] G[overnment] was fully endorsed only a few days ago by the Supreme Council (Soviet parliament) and is being unanimously supported by the public opinion of the country.
>
> (3) In connection with the question of three Baltic States I have to point out that in the view of the S[oviet] G[overnment] the crux of the problem consists not in the skilful drafting of an ingenious formula which might look admirably on the paper but be of a very little use in practical application. The main thing is to get an agreement on the substance of the problem, i.e. on the common resistance of the three contracting parties to a direct or indirect aggression against Estonia, Latvia and Finland. Given such an agreement it would be not very difficult to find a suitable formula.
>
> (4) With regard to the point 6 of the last Soviet proposals, concerning the simultaneous entry into force of the political and military agreements, I am instructed to say that this question could be settled in the process of negotiations.

...Strang was present during this part of our conversation. Halifax wrote down everything I said. He appeared to be pleased and asked whether an identical statement had been made to the French government in Paris. As I could not give him a definite answer, Halifax said he would himself communicate my *message* to the French.

Halifax made two comments of his own. First, that it is correct that the substance is more important than the formula, but it is still impossible to do without a formula. As for the substance, while the British government recognizes the lawfulness of our wish for a triple guarantee against direct or

63. A caricature by David Low.

indirect aggression in the Baltic States, it wants this right to be exercised in such a way as not to antagonize the Baltic countries. Strang has not been supplied with a rigid 'formula' in this respect, but he and Seeds have been given full authority to find ways of reaching an agreement with the Soviet government on the spot, while taking into account the general British standpoint. Halifax hopes that they will succeed. Secondly, might our doubts about paragraph 6 of the most recent Soviet proposals (whereby the pact and the military convention will enter into force simultaneously) possibly be dispelled if a definite date is set for the opening of military negotiations?

I didn't take Halifax up on these points and merely noted that all these questions would probably come under discussion in Moscow.

Then Strang, who was in a rush to catch his flight, got up and left, and Halifax and I continued our conversation. I asked Halifax how he saw matters developing over the summer. Halifax replied that he expected major problems in July and August, as Hitler would certainly wish to bring trophies with him to Nuremberg. But if the 'peace front' held firm, he would have no trophies. I ventured to suggest that even if a tripartite bloc were organized in the near future, Hitler would undoubtedly attempt to test its solidity in some new European crisis. However, were the Germans to be beaten during this 'test' (if not in the military, then at least in the political sense), it would give Hitler something to think about when drawing up future plans. Halifax agreed with me.

Then I remarked, as if in passing, that I did not quite understand why Halifax had deemed it necessary to deliver Thursday's speech (8 June) at this particular time.[127] It struck me as premature.

Somewhat embarrassed, Halifax defended himself by claiming that his speech was well balanced, that its harsh and soft notes were distributed more or less fairly, and that its main purpose was to counter Goebbels'[i] propaganda about the alleged 'encirclement' of Germany, propaganda which had unfortunately struck a chord in German hearts. There could be no question of returning to appeasement.

I replied that English radio would be a far more effective weapon against Goebbels' propaganda. Halifax agreed and said that as it happened he would be meeting a BBC representative tomorrow to discuss the broadening and deepening of radio propaganda in German.

'In any case,' I concluded, 'your last speech has already given rise to all manner of speculation which it would have been wiser to avoid.'

'I tend to agree,' Halifax responded, 'that it might have been better to postpone my speech till the end of our talks with you. Unfortunately, we English parliamentarians sometimes have to speak not when we find it expedient, but when parliamentary circumstances require.'

Before leaving, I dropped a gentle hint that it would be good for Halifax to visit Moscow and that a warm welcome would be waiting for him there. My hint fell on fertile soil. True, Halifax began making conventional excuses to do with the international situation, which ties him to London, but I could see that he liked my idea. He promised to think it over.

The British were obviously offended by Potemkin's no-show in Geneva. Voroshilov's refusal to come over to attend the British manoeuvres also stung them.[128] Halifax's speech on 8 June was undoubtedly motivated by the desire to shake a fist at us for our unyielding approach in the negotiations. But I still think that, barring extraordinary circumstances, Halifax will go to Moscow.

[Maisky's memoirs, which give a far more detailed (yet highly tendentious) account of the meeting than either his diary or his official report home, reveal his practice of exceeding Molotov's laconic instructions 'to drop a hint' that Halifax would be welcome in Moscow. This is also expanded in his conversation with Eden, on 13 October 1941, revealing that if the Cabinet had endorsed the idea, he would 'have been able to arrange a formal invitation to Halifax from the Soviet Government'. Maisky in fact pleaded with Halifax at length 'that a great deal depends on you personally … If you were to agree immediately, this week or at latest next, to go to Moscow, to carry the negotiations through to the end there and sign the pact, peace in Europe would be preserved.' He

---

[i] Paul Joseph Goebbels, Nazi Reich minister for propaganda and national enlightenment, 1933–45.

would later be 'most anxious' that the circumstances of his confidential pleading with Halifax would not be divulged.[129] Convinced, however, that an agreement was around the corner, Maisky preferred at the time to turn a blind eye to Halifax's diplomatic excuse that although 'nothing would give [him] greater pleasure', he could not absent himself from London. He likewise scoffed at Cripps's proposal to intervene, as he was 'not at all pessimistic' and there was 'no reason to be unduly disturbed'.[130] A couple of days earlier, Chamberlain had dampened Halifax's initial positive response to the suggestion that Churchill or Eden might proceed to Moscow, arguing that 'to send either a Minister or an ex-Minister would be the worst of tactics with a hard bargainer like Molotoff'. His genuine concern, though, was that the opposition, which he knew was constantly plotting with Maisky, might use the mission to topple him.[131]]

16 June

Sir George Paish visited me. He has just returned from Japan, where he spent three weeks studying the state of Japan's economy and finance. He jabbered something absurd along pacifist, free-trade lines about the need to tell Japan that Britain, France, the USSR and the USA were prepared to grant her a 'place in the sun' if she behaved well. He was disappointed when I showed no sympathy with his view.

What Paish told me about Japan's position was much more interesting. Her gold reserves are dwindling. They amounted to 800 million yen a year ago, 500 million as of 1 January 1939, and 300 million as of 1 May. By the end of 1939, only their memory will remain. Meanwhile, Japan has to import great quantities of iron, oil, cotton, etc. Considering the state of Japan's industry, trade and finance, Paish believes that the Japanese economic system will collapse as early as spring 1940. That is why Japan must find a 'solution' to the Chinese war within the next 6–8 months by hook or by crook, or else she is done for.

Would that Paish's calculations prove true! I've heard so many prophecies about an imminent crisis in Japan (as in Germany and Italy), all of which have proved wide of the mark, so I can't help but be sceptical. Yet there must be a genuine *breaking point* somewhere. Are we not approaching it in Japan?

17 June

The talks in Moscow started only on 15 June. It is a real 'round-table conference': Comrades Molotov and Potemkin on the one side, and Seeds, Strang and Naggiar[i] (the French ambassador) on the other. But as yet there is nothing to show for it.

[i] Paul-Émile Naggiar, French ambassador to Yugoslavia and China, 1932–39, and to Moscow, 1939–40.

At the first meeting (15 June), the British and the French set out their views and proposed several possible solutions. Despite the warning I gave on 12 June, their rough drafts were such that TASS published a communiqué in the late afternoon describing them as 'entirely not satisfactory'. The heart of the matter is that the British and the French refuse to satisfy our demands fully concerning guarantees to the Baltic States.

On the 16th another meeting was held, at which C[omrade] Molotov said that, as the talks had shown, the problem of guarantees to small countries from the tripartite bloc was not yet ready to be resolved. Therefore the Soviet government proposed that the problem of guarantees to other countries should be postponed and that for now we should conclude only the tripartite pact between Britain, France and the USSR on mutual assistance in the event of direct aggression against one of these countries.[132]

The British and the French were shocked and wished to consult their capitals. I think ours was the right move to make, and an ingenious one at that. Of course, the solution proposed by C[omrade] Molotov does not suit our partners at all, but we are right in terms of tactics and substance.

22 June

The British and the French pondered this for a whole five days, and only on the 21st was a new 'round-table' meeting held in Moscow.

As was to be expected, the British and the French opted not to discuss our latest proposal (a tripartite pact excluding guarantees to small countries), but to propose a 'new' formula about guarantees. However, as was stated yesterday in a TASS communiqué, the 'new' formula had nothing new in it. Its essence was that while the USSR was supposed to render automatic assistance to Britain and France, should the latter two be drawn into conflict as a result of aggression against a country under their guarantee (Belgium, Greece, Poland, Rumania and Turkey), Britain and France were not obliged to render the same automatic assistance should the USSR be drawn into conflict because of the three Baltic countries (Latvia, Estonia and Finland). Naturally enough, Molotov informed the British and the French today that we found the 'new' formula unacceptable…

In the evening, Agniya and I attended a dinner given in our honour by Sir Roderick Jones (head of Reuters). The guest-list was impressive: Samuel Hoare, Vansittart, McKenna[i] and others, accompanied by their wives. Count von Bernstorff, the former counsellor at the German embassy in London, whom I had encountered here before, in 1932, was also present. The Nazis had subsequently kicked him out of both the embassy and the Foreign Ministry.

[i] Reginald McKenna, chancellor of the exchequer, 1915–16.

Today, Bernstorff is head of a Jewish bank in Berlin, which is becoming more and more 'Aryanized' owing to the 'natural' disappearance of its Jewish owners.

We spoke a lot, of course, about the Anglo-Soviet negotiations, in the course of which Jones' wife confessed that she was against a tripartite pact, while her husband was for it.

Hoare grabbed me after dinner, drew me aside and asked in a state of great agitation: what could be done to bring our negotiations to a prompt and favourable close?

I answered half in jest: 'There is a very simple method: to accept the Soviet proposals.'

Hoare began to complain. The British government has already agreed to almost all of our demands. What was wrong with the last formula? It had everything we insisted on, except for direct mention of the Baltic States. This was out of the question since, if the Baltic States were named, Britain and France would have to add Holland and Switzerland to the list, both of whom, terrified by Germany, would renounce the tripartite bloc's guarantees. Only embarrassment would come of it. Hoare began assuring me with uncharacteristic emotion that the British government really did wish to conclude the talks as soon as possible and to proceed at once with discussing military measures. The British government is prepared to ensure complete equality and reciprocity for the USSR under the pact.

I replied that I was pleased to hear it, but that, alas, the facts did not quite accord with Hoare's words.

'Allow me to cite a minor but very telling calculation,' I continued. 'The Anglo-Soviet negotiations in the full sense of the term (i.e. from 15 April, when the British proposals were presented to us) have been ongoing for 67 days. The Soviet government has spent 16 of these days preparing its replies to various British plans and proposals; the remaining 51 days have been taken up with delays and procrastination on the British side. Who, then, is responsible for the slow pace of the talks?'

Hoare, who'd clearly not been expecting such an incontrovertible argument, was a little confused and mumbled something about being unfamiliar with the figures I had cited. Then he hastened to change horses. Among the Conservatives, he said, there are already many who are opposed to a bloc with the USSR. Until now, they have kept silent and tacitly supported the government. But protracted negotiations that yield no concrete results are grist to the mill of the enemies of an agreement. In the last couple of days, they have been raising their heads above the parapet. If we don't conclude the agreement within a few days, it might be broken off for good. Those who object to the pact may play a fateful role. Hoare finished his tirade with the exclamation: 'It's now or never!'

I laughed and replied that we couldn't be scared so easily. I found it hard to believe in the devil which Hoare had sketched for me. Britain and France need a mutual assistance pact very much. They need it no less, and probably far more, than the USSR.

Hoare stuttered again and beat a retreat. He pressed upon me once more the British government's sincere desire to reach an agreement. The British government bears no grudge against us. It is not going to conclude any kind of agreement with Germany behind our back. Hoare himself has been firmly in favour of an agreement with the USSR ever since the seizure of Prague, and he would consider it the greatest misfortune if mutual suspicion, which cannot be denied and has to be reckoned with, dashes the only hope of averting war.

I shrugged my shoulders and said: 'We want an agreement now, just as we did before. But we want a genuine agreement capable of preventing war, not a *halfway house*. Where we end up depends on you, the English.'

23 June

Halifax invited me over and started complaining bitterly: we were creating unnecessary difficulties, we were absolutely unyielding, we were using the German method of negotiation (offering our price and demanding 100% acceptance), and as a result we were delaying the conclusion of the agreement and dealing a heavy blow to the cause of European peace. Halifax ended his bitter outburst with a direct question: 'Do you or don't you want an agreement?'

I looked at Halifax in astonishment and replied that I did not find it possible even to discuss such a question. The foreign secretary's complaints struck me as entirely unfounded. I supplied Halifax with the same statistics that had produced such a strong impression on Hoare yesterday. The arrow hit the mark this time as well. Halifax became confused and, trying to conceal his feelings, commented with a forced laugh: 'Of course 16 days were enough for you: it doesn't take much time to keep saying "no"!'

'Excuse me, Lord Halifax,' I retorted, 'the Soviet government did not just say "no" to you; it also submitted three detailed drafts of counter-proposals.'

Halifax decided not to continue the argument and moved on to the last two talks (21 and 22 June) with C[omrade] Molotov in Moscow. He confessed that, despite the large quantity of telegrams he had received from Seeds and Strang, he couldn't quite grasp what the problem was. Why weren't we satisfied with the last British formula which, in his view, covers all possible cases of aggression in the Baltic? Why did we insist on naming the three Baltic States in the agreement? Could I not clarify in greater detail the Soviet point of view?

I answered that negotiations were being held in Moscow, and that I was not up to date with their every detail. If Halifax was perplexed or had doubts, the best approach was to seek clarification in Moscow. Halifax obviously did not like my reply, but there was nothing he could do.

I then asked Halifax why he objected so stubbornly to the naming of the Baltic States in the agreement. Halifax referred for the hundredth time to the 'reluctance' of these states to receive guarantees from anyone and, as his trump card, declared that he knew of no precedent in history when guarantees had been imposed on a country that did not request them.

I replied that I was far from convinced about the strength of the Baltic States' 'reluctance'. It was more likely that Latvia, Estonia and Finland did not want to ask for guarantees themselves for various reasons, but would not have anything against guarantees being 'imposed' on them by the powers of the tripartite bloc.

'As for the absence of a corresponding precedent,' I continued, 'I cannot agree with you. First, it is not forbidden to establish new precedents. Secondly, it's not true that there have been no such precedents in history. Please recall the Monroe doctrine. The USA declared unilaterally in 1823 that they would regard any attempt by members of the Holy Alliance to extend "their system" to South America as a threat to their security and welfare. Why can't the three great powers of Europe in 1939 do something similar in respect of the three Baltic States?'

For the English, precedent is everything. My words made a definite impression on Halifax, but first he tried to laugh them off: 'So you would like us to initiate a Monroe doctrine for Europe?'

'Not for Europe,' I replied in the same tone, 'but at least for the Baltics.'

Halifax shrugged his shoulders. Will he draw the appropriate practical conclusions, with all the ensuing consequences, from my appeal to the memory of Monroe? I don't know. At every step of the conversation I could sense Halifax's annoyance and displeasure.[133]

[Maisky's claim in his diary that the triple alliance was a viable alternative to the Ribbentrop–Molotov Pact should be examined against the backdrop of the ongoing German–Soviet negotiations, about which he was not informed. Examination of the protracted Soviet–German negotiations of 1939 casts doubt on the notion that the Ribbentrop–Molotov Pact was signed under duress, in the absence of any alternative, at the twelfth hour. True, on his appointment as foreign minister, Molotov does not seem to have received any explicit instructions to change the course of policy and seek political rapprochement with Germany. For the moment, the alternatives remained a full-fledged agreement with the West or isolation. Both policies had been endorsed by Litvinov. The obvious advantage of isolation for the Soviet Union was its ability to preserve its newly acquired position as holder of the balance of power, by delaying choosing for as long as possible. And yet a retreat into 'isolation' was also a convenient cloak under which alternatives could be cultivated. Alas, the relevant archival material remains under lock and key in Moscow. By the time of Molotov's appointment, the bankruptcy of collective security had been conceded and the new prospects in Germany recognized. Earlier in the year, Litvinov himself had intimated to Nahum Goldman,[i] the Zionist leader, that if he ever read in the newspapers about Litvinov's dismissal 'it would mean a rapprochement between Fascist Germany and the Soviet Union and an approaching war'.[134]

Soviet policies were examined by the 'men of Munich' through an ideologically tinted prism. Likewise, Stalin's decision to consider the German option emerged from an obsessive suspicion that Britain and France were resolved to divert Hitler eastwards. The decision was further sustained by cold calculations concerning the economic and military benefits to be reaped from such an agreement. As early as July 1938, State Secretary Weizsäcker asked Merekalov about Soviet 'concrete plans and offers' for expanding economic collaboration with Germany. The Politburo responded favourably only in December, in the wake of the Munich Agreement. Though the economic negotiations made strides in January 1939, Stalin suspected that Hitler's overtures were mainly aimed at undermining the tripartite negotiations and encouraging the West to extend the scope of the Munich Agreement. He therefore discouraged Schnurre,[ii] the head of the East European economic department of the German Foreign Ministry, from visiting Moscow.

In early May, Hitler issued Operation *Weiss*, the directive for the attack on Poland. Within a week, Stalin was given detailed information about the German designs by military intelligence. The report reinforced Merekalov's assessment that, in the intervening period before he embarked on the offensive, Hitler would seek Soviet neutrality. Stalin was little swayed by the report – 'contradictory and unreliable cypher telegram', he commented. Marking time, he instructed Mikoyan on 12 May to ignore 'the unserious' new German economic proposals. The Kremlin's persistent suspicion of collusion between Britain and Germany is discernible in a twelve-page detailed memorandum (which had hitherto eluded historians) submitted to Molotov on 15 May. Bearing the title 'English diplomacy's dark manoeuvre in August 1914', it sought to demonstrate how the events of that period 'resemble very closely the manoeuvre of May 1939'. While scanning it attentively, Molotov underlined numerous references to the alleged British consent in 1914 to remain neutral and to guarantee France's passivity if Germany diverted the war eastwards. His misgivings and scepticism concerning the 'humiliating' British proposals for a triple alliance were apparent in correspondence with both Maisky and Surits.[135] It seems that the reason the Politburo continued to pursue negotiations was fear of facing Germany in the future, allied to Poland, and with Britain and France neutralized.[136]

Schnurre, however, persevered and informed Astakhov on 15 May that Germany entertained 'no aggressive intentions towards the USSR' and sought measures 'to remove [Soviet] mistrust'. The deep-seated Soviet suspicion that the German overtures were 'a kind of game' aimed at driving a wedge between Moscow and London was reaffirmed during Molotov's meeting with Schulenburg, the German ambassador in Moscow, on 20 May. The way to overcome this mistrust, Molotov asserted, was through the establishment of a proper 'political basis'. Schulenburg picked up the gauntlet,

---

[i] Nahum Goldman, founder, with Stephen S. Wise, of the World Jewish Congress and one of the earliest to warn of the threat posed by Hitler.

[ii] Karl Schnurre, the architect of the economic cooperation established between the Soviet Union and Nazi Germany after the signing of the Ribbentrop–Molotov Pact.

reminding the Russians that the 1926 treaty of neutrality, reaffirmed in 1931, had never been annulled. A week later, Astakhov was reassured by Schnurre, speaking on behalf of Hitler, that Germany harboured no aggressive intentions towards Russia. In a follow-up meeting with Weizsäcker, initiated by Astakhov on 30 May, the state secretary confirmed that ideological differences should not be an obstacle to the normalization of relations. Astakhov further gleaned from a variety of sources that if the Soviet Union were to dissociate itself from England and France, the Germans might be prepared to come to an arrangement concerning 'a division of spheres of influence'.

In early June, as the Soviet draft treaty was being submitted to London, in a rare move Stalin sent Molotov handwritten instructions to find out whether the Germans intended to respond to the Soviet proposals, as he could 'not accept that negotiations were again interrupted unexpectedly by the Germans and for unknown reasons'. Stalin provided guidelines for the negotiations and supplied a list of required commodities, including vital military items, which was obviously aimed at testing German intentions.[137] On 19 June, Stalin received an intelligence report emanating from General Kleist's[i] headquarters that Hitler was determined to solve the Polish question at all costs – even if he risked fighting on two fronts. The report further confirmed the information provided by Merekalov at the crucial Kremlin meeting in April, that Hitler was counting on Moscow to 'conduct negotiations with us, as she had no interest whatsoever in a conflict with Germany, nor was she anxious to be defeated for the sake of England and France'. Hitler, it concluded, now believed that 'a new Rapallo stage should be achieved in German–Russian relations', at least for a limited period of time. The information was confirmed by intercepts of Schulenburg's telegrams to Berlin.[138] Stalin also gleaned from Pŭrvan Draganov, the Bulgarian ambassador in Berlin, that the idea of an agreement advantageous to both sides would be favourably received in the German capital.[139]]

25 June

We visited Beaverbrook at his country house.

Beaverbrook was greatly alarmed, which is quite unlike him. He says that war is inevitable, that it will probably begin in the autumn, and that Danzig must be seen as its likely starting point. Germany has stepped up its war preparations. Ribbentrop is at the height of his influence. He has convinced Hitler that Britain and France will be not drawn into war at any price and that nothing will come of the Anglo-Soviet negotiations. The Germans are behind the blockade of Tianjin. They wish to test the mood of the British via the Far East. Ribbentrop has reached the conclusion that the British are not capable of serious resistance – so, strike while the iron is hot!

Beaverbrook also said that Ribbentrop has sent personal letters to many prominent Englishmen, inviting them to visit Germany and meet the Führer. Beaverbrook himself has received such a letter, but he will not go.

[i] Paul Ewald von Kleist, field marshal, was commander of the First Panzer Group fighting in the Ukraine in 1941 and was charged with the capture of the Baku oil fields in 1942.

28 June

Dalton, Morrison and Citrine met the prime minister today on behalf of Labour's National Council and expressed deep concern about the delays in the Anglo-Soviet talks. They spent a long time proving to Chamberlain that the international situation was very threatening indeed, that the impending war could only be stopped through the signing of a tripartite alliance, and that the pact was therefore urgently required.

The prime minister, following his usual practice when speaking to Labourites, started expanding on the theme of how he, too, wished to conclude the agreement as soon as possible, but observed, as he often does, that the Russians '*are very difficult*' and that Moscow was to be blamed for the delay. The Labourites, however, were expecting this tactic (they were very familiar with the 'calendar' of the negotiations),[140] so Chamberlain's complaints hardly impressed them. In conclusion, the prime minister informed the delegation that new instructions had been sent to Seeds, which 'in essence accept all the Soviet proposals'. Chamberlain assured the delegation that on or before the 30th (Friday), or on 3 July (Monday) at the latest, he would be able to greet parliament with news of the signing of the agreement.

The Labourites left feeling reassured.

I don't like all this one bit. The British government accepts the Soviet proposals 'in essence' – what does this mean? I know from personal experience that the English word 'essence' has a treacherous meaning. Furthermore, why did the prime minister need to assure the delegation so forcefully that agreement was already guaranteed? Might he not have done so in order to increase Labour's disappointment when Chamberlain proves unable to bring them good news either on the 30th [June] or on the 3rd [July], thus making it easier for him to lay the blame for a new delay at the door of the USSR?

We shall see. The prime minister's conversation today with the Labourites looks very much like preliminary indoctrination of the opposition.

29 June

[The diary carries an article by Zhdanov, published in *Pravda* on that day under the title 'The British and French Governments Do Not Want an Equal Agreement with the USSR'. Pointing out that negotiations had reached an impasse, Zhdanov repeated Maisky's now well-worn warning that the Soviet Union would not pull the chestnuts out of the fire for the West. The article was shot through with a lingering suspicion that the Western powers were not really interested in an agreement, but were spreading the word about Soviet obstinacy so as to 'prepare public opinion in their countries for an eventual deal with the aggressors'.[141]]

30 June

[Attached to the diary is a cartoon by David Low.]

1 July

We spent yesterday in Canterbury as guests of the *Dean of Canterbury* (Dr Hewlett Johnson).[i]

His 65 years notwithstanding, the dean recently married a young artist aged 35, his student. True, the dean is still full of life, energy and panache, even though he is nearly bald and the hair that remains (down the sides) is the bright colour of senile silver. But the English take a different view of such things to us Russians. Just the other day, I read in a newspaper that an 89-year-old lord has married a widow of 45. And such an occurrence is no exception.

The deans of English cathedrals don't do too badly! Dr Johnson has a splendid house, servants, a car, a wonderful garden and, of course, a quite 'decent' income. There is a Roman wall in the garden, which is about fifteen hundred years old and along which we walked calmly and comfortably with our hosts. The Romans really knew how to build!

The surroundings of the Dean's residence are steeped in history. The cathedral dates back to the twelfth century and its construction was definitively completed in the fifteenth century. Since then there have been no major changes. The dean's house is nearly 700 years old. It was 'modernized', the dean told me, in the year 1583! With a wide sweep of his arm, the host pointed to a portrait on the wall in the living room – it depicted the notorious sixteenth-century 'modernizer' in the attire and regalia of his time. All the walls in the house are covered with portraits of the dean's predecessors: following established tradition, each new dean adds his portrait to the ancient collection. Dr Johnson has already done his duty: his portrait, done by his own wife, already hangs in the stairway on the second floor. In the garden, we came across a small fountain of unusual design, and I asked the dean whether it had been there a long time. Dr Johnson shrugged his shoulders and replied almost apologetically: 'Oh, no more than two hundred years.'

In spite of all this antiquity, the dean is a perfectly contemporary man. Strolling about the garden we chatted on various philosophical subjects, and the dean confessed to me that the question of the afterlife was unclear to him: maybe it exists, or maybe it doesn't. An equal number of arguments can be adduced for and against, so the dean considers the issue a moot point.

---

[i] Hewlett Johnson, dean of Canterbury, 1931–63.

64. Agniya and Johnson, the 'Red Dean' of Canterbury, sipping tea at the Dorchester Hotel, October 1941.

What he is in no doubt about is that our life on earth must be made better, more beautiful and noble for as many people as possible. Such, in his opinion, is the true essence of true Christianity. This, too, is Dr Johnson's personal aim in life. Seen from that perspective, not only Germany and Italy, but also England and the United States are not Christian countries. In general, the true essence of true Christianity cannot be realized under capitalism. This is possible only under socialism or, still better, under communism. That is why Dr Johnson considers the USSR to be the only truly Christian country in our day. That is why he is so well disposed to the Soviet Union and admires it so much. That is why he makes every effort to disseminate the truth about the USSR among the English masses and, incidentally, devotes so many of his sermons in the cathedral to the USSR. The archbishop of Canterbury has told his dean more than once that he 'speaks too much about Russia', but Dr Johnson sticks to his guns…

Such is the philosophy of the current *Dean of Canterbury*.

Dr Johnson has indeed long been a great friend of the USSR. He spoke in our favour even during difficult times, such as the Metro-Vickers case. He visited the USSR in 1937 and has since made hundreds of enthusiastic speeches about the Soviet Union at hundreds of meetings all over England. He has just finished writing a book about the USSR which is to be published by Gollancz,[i] with illustrations by the dean's wife. Dr Johnson headed a delegation of English clergy to Republican Spain and did much to collect funds and raise the popularity of Republican Spain in England and abroad. The name of the *Dean of Canterbury* was mentioned in Nuremberg, and Goebbels asked indignantly: is there no way of making that dean shut up?

Dr Johnson is certainly a very interesting and typically English figure. Listening to him, you begin to understand better the role of religion in English life, along with such whims of history as, for example, Reverend Stephens, the famous leader of the Chartists.

* * *

Dr Johnson comes from the family of an ordinary Manchester *business man*. As a child, he told me, he lived a comfortable life, but a simple one, without luxury. There were six children in the family. At an early age he was greatly impressed by one Scottish engineer who became a missionary and went to live among black people in Africa. That engineer became for him an object of admiration and imitation. But Johnson's father went broke, and the son had to look for a job in industry. He became a mechanical engineer and worked as such till the age of 27, when he was again carried away by dreams of religious service to others, but in a somewhat different form than before. Working in industry, Johnson encountered the world of workers and was deeply influenced by socialist tendencies. Having made up his mind to become a priest, Johnson was now thinking not so much of black Africans as of English proletarians. He was first appointed to a parish in Manchester – a parish of millionaires, as fate would have it! This gave him the chance to study close-up the opposite stratum of society. At the same time, it caused him many problems, conflicts and struggles. During the term of the first Labour government, Johnson was appointed dean of Manchester Cathedral (deans are appointed by the Crown on the prime minister's recommendation). When the second Labour government came to power, he was appointed dean of Canterbury Cathedral. He has been occupying this post for eight years now. How long will he stay? It's difficult to say. For the dean's position is a *job for life*.[142]

[i] Victor Gollancz, educated at St Paul's and New College, Oxford, he went on to establish a most profitable and successful publishing house bearing his name. His flair for political agitation and publishing found its expression in the promotion of the Left Book Club. A close friend of the Maiskys, he founded (in 1941) and presided over the Anglo-Soviet Public Relations Committee.

2 July

Garvin writes in today's *Observer* in connection with Halifax's speech of 29 June:

> For the whole Defence Front the acid test is Danzig. What is that? Is it a small and local matter as uninstructed error might suppose? Not so. It is the key to issues reaching far and wide; it involves undoubtedly the fate of all Poland and much more, the British Empire not excluded; for it is the touchstone of all our pledges, the criterion of our courage and probity in all respects, the critical point of our entire diplomatic system. Failure and discredit in this connection would disband the Peace Front. The consequence would be British isolation, and not merely that but isolation with ignominy. European surrender would have to be followed by Imperial surrender.

The Gospel truth!

A month and a half ago, I wrote down similar thoughts here about the consequences for England and the British Empire if the British government betrayed its obligations towards Poland and Rumania. Garvin, a most competent man in these matters, has corroborated my thoughts.

4 July

My scepticism concerning the Moscow talks has proved justified.

Indeed, Seeds and others told C[omrade] Molotov on 1 July that they accepted the naming of countries to be guaranteed by the tripartite bloc, but not in the basic agreement itself – only in a secret appendix.

Then two new complications emerged:

(1) The British and the French have demanded that three more countries – Holland, Luxembourg and Switzerland – be added to the list of guaranteed states. Thus, the number of the tripartite bloc's 'children' has grown to eleven at the last minute! True, our partners did mention Holland and Switzerland at the meeting of 21 June, but only now have they raised the matter in all seriousness.

(2) We suggested defining the term 'indirect aggression' and proposed our formula, which the British and the French objected to.

On 3 July C[omrade] Molotov gave our reply to the proposal made by our partners.

We agreed to name the guaranteed countries in an appendix, but expressed our surprise at the fact that, while all previous negotiations had been based on there being only eight 'children', the number had now suddenly leapt to eleven. Being willing to compromise, we were ready to include Holland and Switzerland in the list of guaranteed countries, but on one condition: since their inclusion meant an extension of our obligations, we considered ourselves justified in demanding a corresponding extension of the guarantees of our security, in the form of mutual assistance pacts to be concluded between the Soviet Union on the one side and Turkey and Poland on the other. In addition we proposed, without detriment to the immediacy of aid in the cases stipulated by the pact, to hold a consultation of the 'big three' whenever the probability arose of the obligations of mutual assistance needing to be implemented. We also proposed a regular exchange of information concerning the international situation and an outline of the avenues of mutual diplomatic support in the interests of peace. Finally, we firmly insisted that it was essential to find a satisfactory formula for 'indirect aggression'.

Now it's the turn of the British and the French. Needless to say, a break of several days will ensue.

[Molotov was now more resolute, indicating that the scant hopes still entertained for an agreement were quickly evaporating. He had already told Maisky that the British proposals were 'a repetition of the previous proposal', and had to be 'rejected as unacceptable'.[143] To allay the Soviet fear that the main British object was 'to trap them into commitments and then leave them in the lurch', Halifax swayed the Committee on Foreign Policy on 26 June to accept the Soviet demands to extend guarantees to all the Baltic States. 'We are going to the furthest limit,' observed Cadogan in his diary, 'without any very sure hope – on my part – that the dirty sweeps will respond.' At the other end, Molotov dug in his heels. He referred to the British negotiators as 'crooks and cheats' who were resorting to 'clumsy tricks'. He was now determined to extract a watertight agreement from either the British or the Germans.[144]]

5 July

For the past couple of weeks, a major campaign for an immediate government reshuffle has been waged behind the scenes in parliament. Strange as it may sound, the campaign is being led by none other than the *Cliveden Set*, the Astors, Lothian and Co. Their supporters in the Cabinet are Halifax, Stanley and Kingsley Wood. The 'rebels' plan to remove Runciman, Stanhope and Maugham[i] from the Cabinet and replace them with Churchill, Eden, and Amery or Trenchard.[ii] The *Observer* of 2 July demanded a radical shake-up in government. Still more significantly, the *Daily Telegraph* devoted an editorial (3 July) to the same theme. The demand for a reshuffle is motivated by the worsening international situation in connection with Danzig and Poland in general.

---

[i] Frederic Herbert Maugham (1st Viscount Maugham), lord chancellor of Great Britain, 1938–39.

[ii] Hugh Montague Trenchard (1st Viscount Trenchard), resigned from his post as marshal of the Royal Air Force, which he had founded, in 1928; commissioner of the Metropolitan Police from 1931–35; rejected various offers from Chamberlain and Churchill to resume his military career.

Although events undoubtedly demand a reshaping of government, I remain rather sceptical about the prospects of this campaign (how many have there been now?) despite the 'brilliant' names of its leaders. I've heard so many times that 'it can't go on like this', that 'Chamberlain is skating on thin ice', that a reshuffle is already well under way, that a list of new ministers is being compiled somewhere in some decision-making centre – and yet nothing has changed. Chamberlain doesn't care a straw, and Churchill is still in his favourite corner *below the gangway*. I'm afraid the same will happen this time, too: people will kick up a fuss, talk a lot, get worked up, and the government will remain as it was. I am more and more convinced that the English elite will grant Churchill power only on the day after war is declared. It is not without reason that Mrs Chamberlain told her husband the other day that 'an invitation to Churchill to enter the Cabinet would be tantamount to your political suicide'.

It's a pity, for were Churchill to enter government today, war could still be averted.[145]

6 July

Halifax invited me over.

He began, of course, with complaints about the slow pace of the talks, obviously hinting that we were principally to blame. I parried his objections with little difficulty. Then Halifax told me that he had received a protest from the Finns, who strongly objected to the proposed guarantees from the tripartite bloc; that he could not understand our additional conditions (mutual assistance pacts with Turkey and Poland) in exchange for the guarantees to Switzerland and Holland, since these countries were for Britain and France what the Baltic States were for us; and, finally, that our formula of 'indirect aggression' was too broad and dangerous: it opened the door to interference in the internal affairs of friendly nations. Britain would like to avoid the mere possibility of being accused of anything like that.

I chuckled a little at the Balts' loud claims about not wanting guarantees. Of course, they pretend not to want them from various considerations, but if the guarantees were to be implemented, they would be pleased at heart. Moreover: if and when the tripartite pact becomes a powerful force, the small countries will be queuing up for its guarantees.

In conclusion, Halifax said that the British government wished to make yet another, final attempt to reach agreement with us on the question of guarantees. If this attempt should fail, the British and the French would confine themselves for the present to a simple tripartite mutual assistance pact, effective in the event of direct aggression against one of the signatories.

Halifax is trying to scare us. A simple tripartite pact suits neither Britain nor France. London is bargaining. We shall bargain, too.

7 July

We had an interesting dinner. Beaverbrook was the main guest. Also present were Keynes, Cronin,[i] Korda,[ii] Archibald Sinclair and Harvey[iii], Halifax's private secretary – all accompanied by their wives. Sinclair's wife cast her gaze around the table during dinner and exclaimed: 'What a crowd you've assembled! The most refined intellectual gourmets.'

Lopukhova (Keynes' wife) drank too much and conducted herself far too 'freely'. The rest behaved *all right*.

After dinner I showed my guests *Professor Mamlock*,[146] which greatly impressed them.

Cronin complained – it has almost become his *idée fixe* – that OGIZ [Russian Association of State Book and Journal Publishers] was publishing translations of his books in millions of copies, without paying him a single kopeck.

12 July

Meetings were held again in Moscow on 8 and 9 July, but their details are still a little unclear to me. One thing is certain – three points remain disputed: (1) the 'indirect aggression' formula, (2) guarantees to Holland and Switzerland, and (3) the simultaneous implementation of the pact and the military convention. We strongly insist on the latter point…

Halifax summoned me again today. In the process of 'informing' me about the course of negotiations, he said that, after discussing Seeds' reports on the meetings held on 8 and 9 July, the British government had resolved that for the time being it would not insist on including Switzerland and Holland in the list of guaranteed countries. The British government was prepared to be satisfied with consultation in the event of a threat of aggression against these countries. But as far as 'indirect aggression' was concerned, the British government would adhere to its former formula. Otherwise it 'fears driving the Baltics into the Germans' embrace'. With regard to the simultaneous implementation of the pact and the military convention, the British government would most probably raise no objections. Paris, however, was of a different opinion. Paris was very eager to sign a political pact right now and then immediately to begin military negotiations. Later, Halifax added that the British government did not oppose opening military negotiations immediately. Couldn't the dispute on this matter be resolved by setting dates for both the opening and the closing of military negotiations?

---

[i] Archibald Cronin, Scottish writer, 1896–1981.

[ii] Alexander Korda, Hungarian film producer and director who moved to Britain in 1931 to make films at Denham studios. He moved to Hollywood in 1940.

[iii] Oliver Charles Harvey, personal secretary to Eden and Halifax, 1936–39.

I replied that it was difficult for me to answer his question and that he had better address Moscow on this matter.

In the *Court* this evening, I asked the Polish ambassador Raczyński, who had just returned from Warsaw, about the chances of war and peace. He answered: fifty-fifty. Nevertheless, Raczyński assured me, Warsaw was calm, resolute and prepared to resist. I asked him: 'Who decides when the Polish troops occupy Danzig? Poland? Or England and Poland together?'

I had put the same question to Raczyński about a month ago, and then he replied firmly: 'Poland decides. Britain and France only provide Poland with military aid. True, this was not written down in black and white in the agreement, but it was understood during the negotiations. At any rate, we, the Poles, understand it that way.'

Today Raczyński's reply had a rather different ring. He said that close contact had been established between Warsaw and London, that the two capitals were exchanging information, and that if important events were to occur in Danzig, the Polish government would certainly consult the British government, and they would, of course, find a common language. Raczyński stressed that Poland would avoid taking any 'provocative steps'; in his view, even a note of protest to the Danzig Senate would represent a 'provocation'.

The British have obviously managed to take the Poles in hand over the last four or five weeks. Probably by way of financial negotiations.

13 July

The British government is currently conducting a major campaign: rumours are being spread far and wide in the press, parliament, and public and political circles that the Soviet government is acting stubbornly on trifling matters and thereby deliberately dragging out the negotiations; that it is simply 'playing' and does not actually wish to conclude a pact. As if the Soviet government were flirting with Hitler and were ready to form a bloc with Germany.

The purpose of the campaign is clear. By sabotaging the talks, Chamberlain wants to make a scapegoat of us. We'll do our best to ruin his ploy.

In fairness, however, it must be said that the campaign has had a demoralizing effect even on some of our 'friends' in Labour and left circles. The committee of the Peace and Friendship Congress sent a delegate to me and we arranged an hour-long meeting in the embassy over the next few days, where I'll inform the committee members of how things really stand.

As for Labour, it turns out that Greenwood and Dalton visited Halifax yesterday after me. Halifax put the blame for the delay on us and said that two points of disagreement remained in the negotiations: the indirect aggression formula and the simultaneous implementation of the pact and the military convention. The Labourites recognized our formula of indirect aggression as being too 'dangerous' and supported the British one. As for the second point, they suggested the following solution to Halifax: the pact would be initialled and published, then military negotiations would begin and end on set dates, after which the whole agreement would be signed and ratified.

As we can see, the government campaign has succeeded in demoralizing Greenwood and Dalton.

The naval minister, Stanhope, who sat next to me at the *Pilgrims' Club* dinner on the occasion of Lothian's appointment as British ambassador to Washington, told me among other things that the whole British navy would be mobilized by 1 August. This is being done *to impress* Hitler.

14 July

I had lunch in parliament with Lloyd George and his family (Megan and Gwilym). The old man asked me in detail about the state of the negotiations. I pointed out the delaying tactics employed by Chamberlain and the 'calendar' of the talks. The latter made a strong impression on Lloyd George.

We also talked on general political topics, in the course of which the PM's current manoeuvring became clear to me. It boils down to the following.

Chamberlain has yet to come to terms with the idea of an Anglo-Soviet pact directed against Germany, and he would be happy to use any appropriate pretext to avoid it. He is now preoccupied by the Danzig problem, which may easily set in motion the entire system of British guarantees. Without Soviet assistance, those guarantees cannot be implemented. What if the Danzig problem could be resolved without a fight? Or if its rapid deterioration could at least be postponed? Then the need to conclude a pact with Moscow would no longer be so pressing. Then the prime minister would gain his long-desired 'breathing space', and he would be able to look round, weigh up his chances, judge the circumstances, and perhaps find a way to avoid altogether the pact that he finds so loathsome. Or at least to set it back a few months.

Now Chamberlain is once again engaged in an attempt to resolve the Danzig problem. On the one hand, he is exerting pressure on Warsaw in various ways, in particular through the recent Anglo-Polish financial negotiations, and advising Warsaw to be 'reasonable' on the Danzig issue. On the other hand, through various other means – naval mobilization, air demonstrations in France, 'harsh' speeches by ministers, etc. – Chamberlain is seeking to exert pressure on Germany, suggesting that she, too, should behave 'reasonably' with regard to Danzig. This is how the road is being paved for a new Munich (perhaps a 'little Munich') in its Polish variant. It is, moreover, known that the prime minister is using various unofficial channels to sound out the possibility of attempting a new deal with Germany.

Will he succeed? It remains to be seen. I'm inclined to think he won't. But in any case, these are the plans and ideas that are preoccupying Chamberlain, and even more so Horace Wilson. That is why, by the way, they are being so slow in negotiating. They are still unwilling to take the final step. What if fortune rescues them and they can discard the pact entirely?

On top of that, parliament adjourns on 4 August, and the PM's hands will be untied. It would then be easier, should it prove possible, to break off the talks with Moscow, pinning all the blame, of course, on us.

Such are Chamberlain's calculations and hopes. He won't succeed![147]

15 July

These are the sorts of things that go on in the world, and in England in particular.

[There follows a retraction by the newspaper *Forward* (Glasgow) of a report it published on 8 July 1939, about an interview allegedly given by Maisky to B. Baxter,[i] MP.]

As soon as the original false report appeared in *Forward* (Glasgow), Korzh telegraphed the editor, demanding on my behalf that an apology be placed in the paper's five subsequent issues. The editor groaned, wheezed, tried to weasel his way out of it, and begged for mercy, but I remained adamant. The above apology will be published in five issues of *Forward*.

18 July

Only yesterday did Seeds and Co. deign to pay a visit to C[omrade] Molotov. Thus, the fresh instructions of which Halifax informed me on the 12th travelled for a whole five days from London to the British embassy in Moscow! To judge by our negotiations, British diplomacy must use oxen as its means of transportation.

The ambassadors told C[omrade] Molotov that the Anglo-French side did not insist on including Switzerland and Holland in the list of guaranteed countries. So, one difficulty has been overcome.

On the other hand, no progress has been made on the issue of indirect aggression. On the contrary, all the proposals and modifications put forward by the British and the French looked more like a swindler's tricks and ruses. Our negotiators rejected them in the sharpest possible terms.

---

[i] Sir (Arthur) Beverley Baxter, Canadian-born editor-in-chief and director, *Daily Express*, 1929–33; Conservative MP, 1935–50.

The matter of the simultaneous implementation of the pact and the military convention fared no better. The British and the French proposed first reaching an agreement on the political side, and then moving on to military negotiations. Our position was that there should be one single agreement, divided into a political part and a military part. In addition, we made it absolutely clear that the military part held much more significance than the political one, and that it itself represented politics in distilled form. A pact without the military part would be an empty declaration. On this point, no agreement has been reached.

Indeed, the meeting on 17 July left such an unpleasant aftertaste that our people in Moscow have started wondering whether anything will come of these never-ending talks. Judging by some indicators, one cannot exclude the possibility that they may be broken off in the very near future. For now, let us wait and see.

[At the Cabinet meeting of 19 July, Halifax sided with Chamberlain, preferring 'a breakdown of the negotiations' to acceptance of the Soviet terms.[148] No wonder that, when he visited Maisky that same day, Nicolson found 'a strange collection of leftwing enthusiasts sitting around in the Winter Garden with a huge tea-table spread with delicious cakes and caviar sandwiches, plus a samovar'. Maisky, who was now under 'a definite impression … that the Government did not really want the negotiations to go through' was so desperate to put across the Soviet view that he forgot to offer them any tea, and they all left 'casting regretful glances at the untouched table'.[149]

Having succeeded in warding off the pressure for a treaty with Russia, Chamberlain reverted to attempting to deter Hitler from resorting to force by offering him various economic incentives. A series of intermediaries who had received Halifax's blessing[150] paved the way for a meeting of prominent British industrialists with Göring. Likewise, Rab Butler, Halifax's parliamentary undersecretary of state, was actively engaged in seeking conciliation with Berlin and made a dubious comment about the negotiations with the Russians at a critical stage, which only served to enhance Soviet suspicions.[151]

Meanwhile Horace Wilson and Hudson had – entirely on their own initiative – embarked on dialogue with Helmut Wohlthat, architect of Göring's Four Year Plan. Their plan was to offer Hitler a full-blown economic partnership and recognition of German hegemony over Central and Eastern Europe, in return for Hitler's renunciation of a resort to force as an instrument of international policy. The negotiations with the Russians had hardly regained their momentum when they were interrupted by a distorted press leak, which provoked a rebuttal by Hudson. Although Chamberlain condemned the unauthorized initiative, his fury appears to have been reserved for the liberties taken by Hudson, which had dealt a 'disastrous' blow to a policy he himself subscribed to. Henceforth, he would ensure that negotiations with Germany would be pursued through 'other and discreet channels'.[152]

Though the negotiations never really got anywhere, they did succeed in fuelling Soviet suspicion and may well have contributed to the *volte face* in Maisky's critical assessment of British intentions in the fortnight preceding the conclusion of the Molotov–Ribbentrop Pact. Maisky – who, as the following entry shows, continued to believe in an agreement right up to, and even after, the outbreak of war – was now attuned to Moscow. He saw Chamberlain 'resuscitating his old policy of appeasement' in an attempt to defuse the Danzig problem, which would obviate the need for an early conclusion of the Anglo-Soviet negotiations.[153]]

22 July

Guo Taiqi told me today that the direct cause of the fall of the Chinese dollar [sic] is the *run* on the dollar organized by the Japanese and the depletion of the 10 million 'stabilization fund'. About two weeks ago Guo already warned Halifax that this fund was running out quickly and had to be increased. Halifax promised to *consider* the matter, but nothing has been done so far. Hence the crash of the Shanghai stock exchange.

Guo also asked the British to give the Chinese government a loan of 8 million from its 60 million fund of 'political credits'. This request is also 'under consideration', but there has been no loan as yet.

I get the impression that today, with negotiations with Tokyo on Tianjin having just begun, the British government does not want to give money to China. It does not want to 'annoy' the Japanese by supporting the Chinese dollar. In other words, the British government has already fulfilled one of the most important Japanese demands: to refuse to finance the Chinese currency.

Chamberlain's policy is clearly one of capitulation. He is quite prepared for a Far Eastern Munich.

25 July

Halifax invited me to see him and said that at the last meeting in Moscow, on 23 July, Comrade Molotov had proposed opening military talks immediately, emphasizing again that the Soviet government would not sign the pact without a military convention.[154] Comrade Molotov further let Seeds and Co. understand that, should the question of the military convention be resolved favourably, the remaining political difficulties (indirect aggression) would cease to be insuperable. Since Seeds had not been authorized to decide the matter raised by Comrade Molotov, he appealed to London. Today, the British government took an extraordinarily important decision: it accepted Comrade Molotov's proposal and is prepared to begin military negotiations right away, parallel to the political ones. The pact and the military convention will be signed concurrently. The British and French military missions will leave for Moscow in seven to ten days. The composition of the missions has yet to be decided.

Stating all this, Halifax expressed the hope that since the British government was compromising with us on the question of simultaneous negotiations, the Soviet government would now compromise with the Anglo-French side on the

65. Agniya cherishing the newly arrived ZIS-101, modelled on Buick's limousine of the time.

only remaining point at issue, that of indirect aggression. Halifax thinks that the formula proposed by the British covers instances of indirect aggression similar to the Czechoslovak case. In all other instances, the method of consultation would be applied. Halifax begged us to be satisfied with what has been attained. After all, the British and the French have to satisfy themselves with consultation in the event of a threat of aggression against Holland or Switzerland.

I avoided giving a direct answer and advised Halifax to consult Moscow.

I then asked Halifax how one should understand his and his prime minister's statements yesterday concerning negotiations in Tokyo. The foreign secretary replied that there had been no change in British Far Eastern policy, and that the sole purpose of the statements was to reaffirm the neutral position taken by British concessions in the regions occupied by the Japanese. I asked Halifax whether the British government was going to continue financing the Chinese government, and in particular to support the dollar. I added that this was a *test case* and that the answer to this question would show the world whether a change had occurred in British policy toward China or not.

Halifax even changed countenance. I could hear a note of uncharacteristic excitement in his voice. Yet he was unable to say anything comprehensible. It was quite obvious that the British government was scheming away and that the last thing it wanted to do was to give money to the Chinese, at least at present, for what would the Japanese say if they did?

You can smell a Far Eastern Munich in the offing. If it fails to take place, it will be no thanks to the British.[155]

28 July

Back home at last! We were away for a mere 36 hours, but how many interesting, vivid and unforgettable impressions were amassed in such a short interval!

It all began in a very simple, even prosaic way. About a month ago, the Cardiff branch of the S[ociety for] C[ultural] R[elations with the USSR] invited Agniya and me for *lunch* in Cardiff, to present us with a collection of gramophone records of Welsh folk songs. I accepted the invitation, without attaching any particular significance to my action. Throughout July, my secretary and the Cardiff branch secretary made various arrangements concerning the particulars of our visit, which I did not follow closely. On 26 July, at 3.55 p.m., Agniya and I boarded the train for Cardiff, and events began to unfold…

We were met at the railway station in Cardiff by the local SCR representatives, and also by Mr W.G. Howell,[i] the lord mayor of Cardiff, in full dress and with gold chains around his neck, together with his wife. The lord mayor introduced me to the station master, the chief of police and other city 'notables'. Needless to say, reporters and photographers were present in their droves. We got into the lord mayor's official car and drove to his official residence, where we were to stay throughout our visit to Cardiff. For we were the guests not only of the local SCR, but of the lord mayor himself. On the way there, W.G. Howell remarked, as if in passing: 'Last week the duchess of Kent was our guest.'

I smiled to myself.

When we were driving past the *City Hall* I noticed, with some surprise, a big red hammer-and-sickle flag on top of the building. In answer to my inquiring look, the lord mayor explained that the flag had been hoisted in honour of the Soviet ambassador. Indeed, the red flag fluttered on the mast of the Cardiff City Hall throughout the 24 hours I spent in the city. Nothing like that had ever occurred in the history of Anglo-Soviet relations.

In the evening, the lord mayor gave a grand official reception in our honour at the *City Hall*, at which some 900 people were present – a gaudy mixture of suits, political parties and social groups from this crisis-ridden black-coal region. From dyed-in-the-wool conservatives to communists – such was the range of the political spectrum. The lord mayor and his wife, together with Agniya and me, welcomed the guests. Our hands became swollen from endless handshakes. While the guests were coming in, a young woman in Welsh national costume played folk tunes on the harp. It was a little exotic, but beautiful and pleasant.

The reception began with a concert given by the best Welsh workers' choir – the *Pendyrus Male Choir*. A hundred and fifty singers, of whom 90 turned out to be miners and 60 unemployed. The choir was truly superb. The solo performances were good, but the Welsh folk songs sung in chorus were

[i] William Gough Howell, lord mayor of Cardiff, 1938–39.

best of all. Most remarkably, however, the concert opened with a wonderful rendition of the 'Internationale'. It ended, of course, with '*God Save the King*', but this was mere custom: this was, after all, an official reception given by the official lord mayor in the official *City Hall*.

The concert was followed by *refreshments* and dances. I was interested in the choir. I went to a special hall, where the singers were having a bite to eat after their performance, and asked the conductor to furnish me with details about his organization. It turned out that the choir had emerged in 1926, the year of the memorable miners' strike, and had attracted some 600 singers during the 14 years of its existence. All the choir members are amateurs. They sing in their free time. They are nearly all miners from the Rhondda Valley. I congratulated the choir on its great success. They were flattered, and immediately sang one more beautiful Welsh song for me. All this went on for quite a while, and the lord mayor, who thought it his duty as a courteous host to accompany me, was visibly bored. I had to hurry things along. But the choir was obviously very pleased by the attention shown to them.

Then came the obligatory speeches. The lord mayor welcomed me and expressed the hope that my visit would promote rapprochement and particularly trade between our countries. I responded in the same vein, but in more general terms, without making any commitments.

Early the next morning we began a long and wearying schedule.

First up was the '*Temple of Peace*', the brainchild of Lord Davies,[i] on which he spent about fifty thousand pounds. It's a beautiful building with marble columns, a large hall and dozens of smaller rooms – the headquarters of the local friends of the League of Nations and of societies fighting tuberculosis. A ceremonial meeting was held in the grand hall, where Lord Davies and I made the appropriate speeches. Some 500 people were present. A wonderful children's choir sang a series of pacifist and Welsh folk songs.

Next was a visit to the university. I'd imagined that we would see the building, lecture halls and so on, but much more was in store for us. Agniya and I were met at the entrance by the university senate, headed by the rector, all in formal attire (gowns and caps). We followed the rector into the grand hall, where there was a horseshoe table with space to seat all of us. The rector made a long welcome speech, in which he declared directly and clearly: we need an Anglo-Soviet pact. I had to improvise a very cautious response, in view of the current phase of the negotiations. On the whole, it turned out all right.

Then came the Welsh National Museum. We were taken round by its director and his assistants. I took the opportunity to question one of the experts present about the past inhabitants of Great Britain. I learned that

---

[i] David Davies (1st Baron Davies), founder and trustee of the League of Nations Union.

little is known about the ancient inhabitants of the British Isles, but between 800 and 1000 BC the isles were conquered by the Celts, who arrived from the continent and settled in England, Wales and Scotland. It was those Celts whom the Romans encountered here in the first century BC and called 'Britons'. Later, however, the Celtic-Britons mixed with, and were strongly influenced by, Romans, Norsemen, Anglo-Saxons, etc., as a result of which there emerged the Englishmen of today, with their English language. Wales was far less susceptible to these foreign influences, and here the Celtic race and the Celtic language were preserved in a purer form. That is why the Welsh are so unlike the English. The Bretons in France are also Welshmen, who fled there some 1,500 years ago at the time of the Anglo-Saxon invasion. They still understand each other now, even though their languages have, of course, inevitably diverged over 15 centuries of separate existence. Welshmen also settled in Cornwall. I don't know whether all these historical facts are true (a Welsh national bias cannot be excluded), but they seem credible enough. There is no question that the Welsh are different from the English: lively, talkative, merry, melodious, artistic. Welsh songs rather recall those of the Ukraine…

'Lunch' in the *Dorothy Café*. One hundred and twenty people, including the lord mayor and his wife, Lord Davies and his wife, and other notables. Professor Shakesby, who introduced himself as a pupil of Pavlov, presided. Speeches. The presentation of a collection of gramophone records by the local SCR.

The *Nine Mile Point Colliery*, belonging to Lord Davies. We are welcomed by a huge crowd of miners, women and children. Greetings, friendly cheers, clapping, fists raised in salutation. We put on miner's overalls and pick up miner's lamps. Newspaper photographers snap away. We descend 1,200 feet. Accompanied by the mine director, administrators, and trade union men, we, together with Lord Davies, walk for two hours in the underground galleries, touch the timbering with our own hands, break off pieces of coal, stroke the *pit ponies* (which turn out to be huge horses) and on the whole do everything that should be done on such occasions. Agniya is in high spirits – excited and cheerful. But the mine makes no particular impression on me. It's not the first time I've been underground. Besides, I'm sure that this dry, well-timbered and highly mechanized mine is to some extent a 'model mine' to be shown to 'eminent travellers'.

We climb back up. Inspect the coal washing and the scales for weighing the mine cars. Then we go to clean ourselves. I have a shower in the well-equipped *pithead bath*. Then we drink tea in the pit's office and get ready to return to Cardiff in order to catch the 6.36 train to London.

When suddenly… the lord mayor's secretary, Mr Chamberlain (what a name!), approaches me and, in some embarrassment, informs me that I am invited to visit Tylorstown, which is located 15 miles from the *Nine Mile Point*

66. The Maiskys tour a mineshaft in Wales.

Colliery up the Rhondda Valley. The town's Chamber of Commerce wants to deliver a ceremonial address in my honour. Several thousand people have gathered there, expecting me. As Chamberlain had known nothing about this until now, a visit to Tylorstown had not been included in the schedule. It all happened unexpectedly, impromptu. Could I satisfy their request? True, the weather wasn't so bright (a nasty drizzle had just started falling) but still… What was my decision?

It would have been bad form to refuse. Besides, I was intrigued by the mysterious Tylorstown, which had demonstrated such rare initiative. I replied that I would go to Tylorstown and would return to London later, on the night train.

We set out for Tylorstown, with Chamberlain, Lord and Lady Davies travelling in another car. The road runs through the charming Rhondda Valley, with its soft green hills and sooty mining towns. A slight mist. Drizzling rain falls noiselessly from the sky. The car speeds along like an arrow. Curious heads lean out of the windows of miners' shacks and little houses along the wayside. Greetings and friendly shouts come our way. Hands wave. Fists are raised every now and again in salutation.

Here we are in *Tylorstown*. A typical little mining town. Small houses, a church, pithead buildings, a high hoisting tower with openwork wheels. We are met by a huge crowd of several thousand people – men, women and children. They cry 'Hurray!' and many raise clenched fists. Our car moves with difficulty through the dense crowd toward a small wooden shed standing on the right. It's the local office of the Miners' Federation. A large police detail keeps the crowd back and makes a narrow path for Agniya and me to pass through. We enter a *lodge*, as all the local British mining organizations are called: plain, unpainted wooden walls, plain wooden tables and benches, an iron stove. Looks more like a heated goods van or a repair hut.

Daniel Ashton, president of the Chamber of Commerce, welcomes us, saying that it is a great honour to receive the ambassador of the Soviet Union. He then hands me an extravagant certificate in red morocco, beautifully printed, with fine ornamentation. The certificate states that *Tylorstown* is welcoming a foreign ambassador for the first time. This would be pleasing under any circumstances. But it is triply pleasing to welcome the Soviet ambassador. The Rhondda Valley has always sympathized with the USSR, even when others doubted the success of your cause, but 'what Rhondda thought yesterday all Britain will think tomorrow'. Here, in the Rhondda Valley, many people read Russian writers and follow your achievements with keen interest. The certificate ends with the hope that Agniya and I will stay in England for a long time, and that the Anglo-Soviet pact will soon be concluded.

Then it was the turn of various speakers: the *lodge* secretary, Lord Davies and others. I responded. Then the president stated provocatively that he would be a bad chairman if he failed to give the floor to 'Madam Maisky'. This made me anxious – how would Agniya get out of this tricky situation? She coped perfectly well. She stood up and said with a smile: 'My speech will be very short. In fact, it will consist of one word only, which, moreover, I will probably mispronounce. "Diolch!"' ('Thank you' in Welsh).

An outstanding success. Endless applause.

We left the *lodge*. We were met outside by nearly all the members of yesterday's *Pendyrus Choir*. It turned out that the majority of the choir is recruited from this very region. We bowed to one another like old acquaintances and, overcome with enthusiasm and friendly emotions, they sang to us a farewell song in Welsh under the open sky at the entrance to the *lodge*. The policemen who were keeping the crowd back sang along. We got into the car, moved slowly through the vociferously applauding mass of people, and headed back to Cardiff.

I confess I was truly touched and moved: after all, these were workers and proletarians who were greeting us!

* * *

Sitting in the lord mayor's dining room after supper, shortly before our departure for London, I conversed with Lord Davies.

'What you've told me about the Anglo-Soviet negotiations saddens me greatly,' said Lord Davies. 'When I see what's happening in my country now, when I see Chamberlain and his government meekly making one crucial concession after the other to the aggressor, when I see how this stupid and narrow-minded policy is paving the way to the downfall of our Empire, I can feel my heart breaking. I often ask myself: why was I not killed by a German bullet in France in the last war? That would have been easier.'

Such are the feelings evoked by the current decline of the British bourgeoisie among its most honest and far-sighted representatives!

I remembered that Lloyd George once told me about Lord Davies. In early 1917, the Allies sent an Anglo-French mission headed by Lord Milner[i] to Petrograd to appraise the situation in Russia. The mission spent a couple of weeks in Petrograd, encountered only ministers and high society, and returned to London fully convinced that all the rumours about popular discontent and impending revolution were groundless. Lord Davies, assigned to the mission as young secretary Davies, didn't meet any Russian aristocrats while in Petrograd, but spent a lot of time wandering about the city, visiting workers' districts, and meeting with representatives of the opposition and revolutionary parties. Upon returning home, he told Lloyd George: 'Expect a revolution in the next few weeks.'

He was right.

30 July

In today's *Observer* I found the following report, which seems most relevant to the present situation.

[Maisky includes a cutting of the editorial of the *Observer*, arguing that the opposition leaders do not conceal the fact that the prime minister – the architect of the Munich Agreement – is not a man who could challenge the aggressors. The opposition leaders and dissident ministers are afraid that the parliamentary recess until 3 October will provide the prime minister with an opportunity to weaken the front against the aggressors in some way. The article further reports on the informal talks held by Hudson and Wohlthat.]

4 August

Azcárate arrived from Paris. The Republicans are slowly being transferred to Mexico. One ship, with some two thousand émigrés, has just embarked for

[i] Alfred Milner (1st Viscount Milner), member of the War Cabinet, 1916–18; secretary of state for war, 1918–19; secretary of state for the colonies, 1919–21.

Chile, where the Popular Front government is presently in power (will it last long?).

The French government's attitude to Spanish refugees has improved significantly. The horrors of the 'Spanish camps' are in the past. Some Spaniards are engaged in military construction work, some have been recruited by the French army, and still others are settling down in rural areas near the Italian border. But many thousands, it seems clear, will be repatriated to Spain. According to the agreement between Franco and the French government, which stipulates the return of Spanish gold (about 8 million francs, Franco will also receive up to 50,000 Spanish refugees. The French government has not forced anyone to return home as yet, but what will it do in the future? Nobody knows. The settling of refugees in Scandinavia, and especially in Sweden, is fraught with difficulties. At the beginning of the year, Sandler agreed to accept…100 refugees. But now he refuses to fulfil even that promise. That's typical of him, if one recalls his conduct in Geneva in connection with Beneš's telegram.

There is internal strife and division among the Spanish émigrés in Paris. Upon returning from Mexico, Prieto[i] challenged Negrín as leader of the Spanish émigrés. Resorting to various ploys, he pushed through a decision unfavourable for Negrín in the so-called 'Cortes delegation', a mythical body of 21 men which seeks to arrogate to itself the right to speak on behalf of the former Spanish parliament. But most of the real émigré organizations, such as the party executive committees, the Evacuation Committee, and others, support Negrín.

Well, fights and squabbles among émigrés are almost an iron law of existence.

Azcárate spoke at length about the profound internal disintegration of the French Socialist Party. He did not conceal that he sides with the communists.

The members of the military mission to Moscow – Admiral Drax[ii] (head), Air Marshal Burnett[iii] and Major General Heywood[iv] – came for lunch. The guests were highly reserved in conversation and preferred to discuss such innocuous topics as partridge hunting, the season for which they will clearly have to spend in Moscow.[156]

During lunch, however, I did learn one thing which seriously alarmed me. When I asked Drax, who was sitting on my right, why the delegation was not flying to Moscow by plane to save time, Drax drew in his lips and said: 'You see, there are nearly 20 of us and a lot of luggage… It would be uncomfortable in the plane…'

---

[i] Indalecio Prieto (Tuero), minister of national defence of the Spanish Republic, 1937–38; chairman of the Spanish Socialist Workers' Party, 1937–62.

[ii] Reginald Aylmer Ranfurly Plunkett-Ernle-Erle-Drax, admiral, commander-in-chief at Plymouth, 1935–38.

[iii] Charles Stuart Burnett, air officer commanding Iraq Command, 1933–35; Training Command, 1936–39; inspector-general of the RAF, 1939–40.

[iv] Thomas George Gordon Heywood, major general, Royal Air Force, Aldershot Command, 1936–39.

67. Anglo-French military mission embarking on a freight steamer on the way to Russia.

I can hardly say that I found his response convincing. I continued: 'In that case, why not travel by warship… On a fast cruiser, for example… It would look impressive and it would hasten your arrival in Leningrad.'

Drax sucked his lips again and said, deep in thought: 'But that would mean kicking 20 officers out of their cabins… That would be awkward…'

I couldn't believe my ears. Such tender feelings and such tactful manners!

The admiral hastened to gladden me, though, with the news that the military delegation had chartered a special vessel, *The City of Exeter*, which would take them and the French mission to Leningrad. At this point Korzh intervened in the conversation, remarking pointedly that he had heard from the owner of this ship earlier today that her maximum speed was 13 knots an hour. I cast a look of surprise at Drax and exclaimed: 'Is that possible?'

Drax was embarrassed and mumbled: 'The Board of Trade chartered the ship. I don't know the particulars.'

So, the English and the French military missions are travelling to Moscow by freight steamer! It must be a freighter, to judge by its speed! And this comes at a time in Europe when the ground is beginning to burn beneath our feet! Incredible! Does the British government really want an agreement? I'm becoming more and more convinced that Chamberlain is pursuing his own game regardless: it's not a tripartite pact that he needs, but talks about a pact, as a trump card for cutting a deal with Hitler.

The following information has been obtained from official sources:

Admiral the Hon. Sir Reginald Plunkett-Ernle-Erle-Drax, KCB, DSO, was, until very recently, commander-in-chief at Plymouth. He is said to be a first-class fellow. He is still on the Active List, but at the moment holds no official position.

Air Marshal Sir Charles Burnett, KCB, DSO, is at present inspector-general of the Royal Air Force.

Major General T.G.G. Heywood. In the Army List he is shown as brigadier in charge of the Royal Artillery at Aldershot. He has recently received promotion to major general and now commands the 7th Anti-Aircraft Division.

[Bar the occasional lapse, right up until the very day the Ribbentrop–Molotov Pact was concluded, Maisky maintained that an agreement with the Western powers was inevitable. In his apologetic memoirs, he puts a misleading gloss on the narrative, whereby Halifax's refusal to proceed to Moscow and the bizarre episode of the military mission startled and convinced him that an agreement was doomed. This narrative, meticulously constructed and widely disseminated by Maisky, through Boothby, to justify the pact, was later also adopted by Stalin, who told Beaverbrook in October 1941 that 'Chamberlain and the Conservative Party ... fundamentally disliked and distrusted the Russians.' Halifax's refusal to travel to Moscow and the arrival of the forlorn military mission in Moscow had supposedly left him with no choice but to conclude the Pact. This narrative laid the foundations for the Soviet 'falsifiers of history' mainstream historiography. When Boothby interjected, accusing the Russians of treachery, Maisky replied 'somewhat uneasily' that everyone was 'now playing a cold game of power politics and that it was merely a question of technique'.[157] Maisky's narrative is refuted by the following diary entry – a rare but telling exposition of his inner thoughts at the time. Moreover, visiting the Webbs at their cottage two days later, he nonchalantly dismissed the decision to send the military mission by cargo boat as 'an amusing instance of Chamberlain's subconscious desire to delay and hamper these negotiations – a rather far-fetched indication of his sinister sub-consciousness!' Manifestly 'in good spirits' and 'enjoying [his] sudden popularity with the newspaper world and the public', he was certain that 'Great Britain will be *forced* to come into alliance' with the Soviet Union.[158]]

5 August

Went to *St Pancras* railway station to see off the British and French military missions. Lots of people, reporters, photographers, ladies and young girls. I met

General Doumenc,[i] head of the French mission, and a few of his companions. The heads of the British mission – Admiral Drax (head), Air Marshal Burnett and Major General Heywood – were my guests for lunch yesterday and we greeted one another like old acquaintances.

On my way home, I couldn't help smiling at history's mischievous sense of humour.

In subjective terms, it is difficult to imagine a situation more favourable for an Anglo-German bloc against the USSR and less favourable for an Anglo-Soviet bloc against Germany. Indeed, the spontaneous preferences of the British 'upper ten thousand' most definitely lie with Germany. In his sleep, Chamberlain dreams of a deal with Hitler at the expense of third countries, i.e. ultimately at the expense of the USSR. Even now, the PM still dreams of 'appeasement'. On the other side, in Berlin, Hitler has always advocated a bloc with Britain. He wrote about this fervently back in *Mein Kampf*. Highly influential groups among the German fascists, bankers and industrialists also support closer relations with England. I repeat: the subjective factor is not only 100%, but a full 150% behind an Anglo-German bloc.

And yet, the bloc fails to materialize. Slowly but unstoppably, Anglo-German relations are deteriorating and becoming increasingly strained. Regardless of Chamberlain's many attempts to 'forget', to 'forgive', to 'reconcile', to 'come to terms', something fateful always occurs to widen further the abyss between London and Berlin. Why? Because the vital interests of the two powers – the objective factor – prove diametrically opposed. And this fundamental conflict of interests easily overrides the influence of the subjective factor. Repulsion is stronger than attraction.

The reverse scenario holds for Anglo-Soviet relations. Here the subjective factor is sharply opposed to an Anglo-Soviet bloc. The bourgeoisie and the Court dislike, even loathe, 'Soviet communism'. Chamberlain has always been eager to cut the USSR's throat with a feather. And we, on the Soviet side, have no great liking for the 'upper ten thousand' of Great Britain. The burden of the past, the recent experience of the Soviet period, and ideological practice have all combined to poison our subjective attitude towards the ruling elite in England, and especially the prime minister, with the venom of fully justified suspicion and mistrust. I repeat: the subjective factor in this case is not only 100%, but a full 150% against an Anglo-Soviet bloc.

And yet the bloc is gradually taking shape. When I look back over the seven years of my time in London, the overall picture is very instructive. Slowly but steadily, via zigzags, setbacks and failures, Anglo-Soviet relations are improving.

---

[i] Joseph Édouard Aimé Doumenc, French general in command of the 1st Military Region, 1937–39; member of the Supreme War Council, 1939–42.

From the Metro-Vickers case to the military mission's trip to Moscow! This is the distance we have covered! The abyss between London and Moscow keeps narrowing. Field engineers are successfully fixing beams and rafters to support the bridge over the remaining distance. Why? Because the vital interests of the two powers – the objective factor – coincide. And this fundamental coincidence overrides the influence of the subjective factor. Attraction proves stronger than repulsion.

The military mission's journey to Moscow is a historical landmark. It testifies to the fact that the process of attraction has reached a very high level of development.

But what an irony that it should fall to Chamberlain to build the Anglo-Soviet bloc against Germany!

Yes, mischievous history really does have a vicious sense of humour.

However, everything flows. The balance of forces described above corresponds to the present historical period. The picture would change dramatically if and when the question of a proletarian revolution outside the USSR becomes the order of the day.

[Negotiations with the British and French were now being conducted in parallel to those with the Germans, even if the latter had lost some steam since April. Maisky, like the other Soviet plenipotentiaries, was oblivious to their existence. On 10 July, the Germans acquiesced to the procedure proposed by the Russians to link the economic and political negotiations, eliciting from Stalin an immediate reaction: 'we are ready to move ahead'. Further negotiations, however, stalled until 26 July, when Schnurre informed the Soviet attaché that Ribbentrop had been displaying a personal interest in the improvement of Soviet–German relations.

Given Maisky's warning that the British were still trying to agree terms with the Germans, Stalin was resolved to steal a march before the military negotiations got under way with the democracies. On 2 August, Astakhov was given the green light to meet Ribbentrop. He found the German foreign minister eager to conclude a trade agreement, which might 'signal an improvement in political relations'. Ribbentrop insisted that no conflict existed between the two countries 'from the Black Sea to the Baltic' and that 'all related issues were open for discussion'. Satisfied with 'the leap forward' on the political front, Molotov curiously dismissed as 'inappropriate' a cryptic reference to a possible 'secret protocol'. The Germans, however, pressed on. On 12 August, Astakhov relayed from Berlin that, in anticipation of a conflict with Poland, the Germans were eager to enter economic as well as political negotiations. 'The Germans got really frightened,' recalled Maisky a year later, 'when the Anglo-French Mission arrived in Moscow & strained every nerve to reach an agreement with Russia.'[159]

Hardly had the military talks got under way in Moscow than Schulenburg suggested to Molotov on 15 August that Ribbentrop should come to Russia. The Kremlin, as the historian Geoffrey Roberts aptly put it, 'continued to hedge its bets'. Though welcoming the idea, Molotov, who was always suspicious of behind-the-scenes intrigues, wanted more precise information on the nature of the German proposals. Moreover, he obviously wished to extract the best terms from the Germans while military negotiations with the democracies were on. It was not until 17 August, following the collapse of the forlorn military negotiations, that Molotov raised with Schulenburg the idea of a non-aggression pact and a 'special protocol', addressing the mutual interests of the two countries. The text of such an agreement was ironed out by both sides on 19 August.

Two days later, Hitler addressed Stalin personally, in what was tantamount to an ultimatum, demanding that Ribbentrop be received in Moscow in the next couple of days to sign the agreements. Stalin responded within two hours. The negotiations at the Kremlin were brief. Stalin predicated the signing of the non-aggression pact on an agreement in principle for a secret protocol governing the division of Central and Eastern Europe into 'spheres of influence'. He arranged for the startled Ribbentrop to have a direct phone link to Hitler, who gave his consent on the spot.[160]]

6 August

Elliot lunched with me yesterday. We discussed the negotiations, Anglo-Soviet relations, and international affairs. But above all we discussed the visit to the USSR of a group of British MPs headed by Elliot. Formally they are going to see the agricultural exhibition, but their actual purpose is to meet our leaders. Elliot, in particular, wishes to meet Comrade Stalin and have a talk with him.

I promised to make inquiries. I don't know what Moscow will make of this proposal. I have a feeling that difficulties and obstacles may arise. Especially in fulfilling Elliot's wish to meet Comrade Stalin. We shall see.

11 August

Today I invited Chief of the General Staff Lord Gort,[i] Lord Lloyd, Degville[ii] and others for lunch.

Lloyd spoke at length about his work as chairman of the British Council for cultural relations with foreign countries, and, in particular, about visits made by foreign journalists (Turkish, Rumanian, Spanish, Portuguese, etc.) to England. In this connection, he wished to know whether he might expect a visit by a group of Soviet journalists to England. Remembering that I had yet to receive a reply from Moscow to my inquiry about Elliot's group, I refrained from giving an answer in advance.

Responding to a query of mine, Gort said that although officially, for the general public, the British government does not plan to send a large army to the continent in the event of a new war, the general staff understands perfectly well that this will have to be done and is already making all the necessary

---

[i] John Standish Surtees Vereker (6th Viscount Gort), chief of imperial general staff, 1937–39; in September 1939 became commander-in-chief of the British Expeditionary Force.

[ii] Howard Degville, head of the Empire Parliamentary Association.

preparations, particularly as regards the procurement of weapons, ammunition and equipment. Conscription, according to Gort, will continue. The first year-group to be conscripted will be followed by the second, the third, and so on. He boasted that only 9% of the first levy was found unfit for military service. (NB: I wonder, what were the standards demanded of the recruits?). Gort's estimate of the military potential of Germany is low: the number of her first-line machines does not exceed 3,000, and Germany will not be able to fight for more than one year. Gort was very interested in the prospects of the Moscow military negotiations and declared himself in favour of a tripartite pact.

20 August

We got away for a week and spent it at the Malvern drama festival. Eleven years ago, Barry Jackson, the prominent and wealthy Birmingham patron, and Bernard Shaw decided to put on the first-ever drama festival in England. The chosen venue was Malvern. The festival was held in August and lasted for four weeks. Six plays were shown: five English masterpieces and a new play by Shaw. The festival was well received. Since then it has been held annually. Two years ago, having lost 30 or 40 thousand (the festival did not pay its way), Barry Jackson abandoned the enterprise. He was replaced by a certain Roy Limbert, a theatrical entrepreneur and director. The nature of the festival has also changed somewhat. Limbert stages six new plays and sells the successful ones to London theatres. We saw all six, including Bernard Shaw's *In Good King Charles's Golden Days* and Vansittart's *Dead Heat*.

Apart from going to the theatre, we drove around the wonderful Malvern countryside, scrambled up and down the beautiful but modestly sized mountains which surround it, walked, rested and read. We had been invited to Malvern by Shaw and Vansittart. We met a few diplomats there and others from London 'society'. We were guests at the estate of Sir Sidney Clive, marshal of the diplomatic corps. Most of the talk at the tea table was about the threatening international situation. One of the guests from the City asked me what was to be expected in the upcoming week. Not wanting to embark on a lengthy analysis, I just said: 'I fear that next week will be very difficult.'

I think I was right. But we shall see.

21 August

It seems that our negotiations with the British and the French have collapsed. Already in July there had been a strong desire in Moscow for their termination. Now things have gone from bad to worse. To judge by information received from various sources, the situation is roughly as follows.

When negotiations between the military delegations opened in Moscow on 12 August, the Soviet side inquired about the British and French missions' letters of credentials. It turned out that they had not brought any with them. Naturally, this produced a very bad impression. The Soviet side asked the British and the French to get the required letters from London and Paris. A few days later these were received and presented, but… they turned out to be so general and vague that it became clear to us that London and Paris had no serious intention of concluding an agreement.

Next came the issue of Poland. When the British and the French, having set forth their considerations concerning the assistance they could provide to Poland in case of need, asked the Soviet side what it could do for Poland, Comrade Voroshilov outlined our plan. Since the USSR does not have common borders with Germany, it could of course offer effective aid to Poland, France and Britain only if Poland were to let the Red Army pass through its territory. This is the only way the USSR could engage in combat with Germany. Comrade Voroshilov indicated two possible routes for the Red Army: one army would head to East Prussia through the Wilno and Nowogródek provinces, and the other to Breslau through the Krakow province. The British and the French decided that Warsaw had to be asked about our proposal and initially wanted us to make a corresponding démarche there. We refused categorically. Then the British and the French addressed Warsaw themselves. The Polish government refused categorically to let the Soviet troops pass through its territory and even announced that it did not need any assistance from the USSR. Poland would manage by itself if Britain and France fulfilled their duty. What shocked the Polish most was the prospect of the Red Army marching through Wilno, Piłsudski's[i] birthplace. 'The shade of Piłsudski,' they exclaimed theatrically, 'will rise from his grave if we allow the Russian troops to pass through Wilno.' The French tried to reason with the Poles, while the British remained neutral. In the end, the Poles insisted on having it their own way. The response from Warsaw was conveyed to the Soviet delegation. The latter wanted to know what the British and French thought about the Poles' decision. They shrugged their shoulders and said they were unable to change anything.

The negotiations stalled on this issue. Deadlock had been reached. Indeed, what's the use talking to the British and the French if the Poles refuse categorically to accept the only plan that could save Poland?

Once again it has become clear that London and Paris are not serious about an agreement. Or, perhaps they even incited the Poles to reject our proposal?

Some major decisions, one feels, are in the offing…

* * *

[i] Józef Klemens Piłsudski, Polish prime minister, 1926–28 and 1930; minister for war, 1926–35.

Guo Taiqi told me that after many delays and hesitations, the British government has at last given China a 3 million pound loan for 14 years at 5% interest. They made it a condition, however, that the agreement should be kept secret. This shows how much the British fear the Japanese.

A curious detail. When everything was ready, the head of the Foreign Office's far eastern department called Guo Taiqi and asked him for a letter confirming that the signing of the agreement in China would not be divulged. Guo Taiqi said that he would provide such a letter, provided the Foreign Office asked him about it in writing. The Foreign Office got scared and belted up.

[Although the British government accepted the Soviet wish to embark expeditiously on military negotiations, the delegation was instructed to 'go very slowly with the conversations' and treat the Russians 'with reserve' until a political agreement was reached. Once that hurdle was removed, the delegation was instructed to 'put forward their recommendations for future procedure and ... await authorization from London' before dealing with the core issues. Even then, its members were instructed to avoid tying the hands of the government: the agreement should be confined 'to the broadest possible terms'. On no account were they to consider offering any assistance in exerting pressure on Poland and Rumania to receive Soviet assistance. This nonchalant attitude stemmed from a feeling that no 'rapid or spectacular [German] success' in the campaign was to be expected, and that this was bound to throw Germany into economic chaos. The British had reverted to their initial April stance of expecting from the Russians mostly logistical and 'moral support', which would allow Poland and Rumania 'to maintain a long, solid and durable front'.[161] Doumenc, reported Surits to Molotov, was not pleased with the instructions, which were 'nothing more than general and stereotyped phrases and remarks'. He clearly realized that they were aimed at 'gaining time'. There was something symbolic in 'the old cargo ship ... representative of the old British commercial fleet. Sturdy, somewhat dated, with an entirely Indian crew carrying the testimony of the Empire'. There was ample time during the six-day cruise for daily conferences, but British reticence meant that these led nowhere.[162]

By 16 August the negotiations had reached stalemate, while the German pressure was mounting. Marshal Voroshilov warned that 'a definite' response to the Soviet request to enter Poland 'as soon as possible was of cardinal importance'.[163] On the same day, Molotov insisted, in conversations with the American ambassador, that he attached 'great significance' to the negotiations and was 'counting on their success', so long as they were concluded with 'concrete obligations' for mutual assistance, rather than with 'general declarations'.[164] Doumenc duly alerted his government. He believed the Russians 'clearly expressed the intention not to stand aside ... to act in earnest'. He was impressed by the detailed and 'precise' statement of the Soviet delegation concerning their military resources, and estimated their assistance to be 'considerable ... between 70 and 100 per cent of the forces we would put up'.[165] A partially positive French response was conveyed to Voroshilov on 22 August, together with a draft agreement which declared the 'general objective' of the three powers to form an eastern and western front and to render each other unrestrained assistance. However, the nature of such assistance was left open, to be decided by 'the course of events'. When the two met in the evening, it emerged that Doumenc could neither vouch for the British, nor could he explain the position of either Poland or Rumania. He should perhaps have been more attentive to Voroshilov's insinuation that 'certain political events' could not be excluded. Indeed, the die had been cast. By now the news had been broadcast that Ribbentrop and a retinue of forty people were flying to Moscow the following morning to sign a non-aggression pact.[166]]

22 August

Last night, at around twelve, I got a telephone call from Hillman of the International News Service, who shouted down the phone, in great alarm and agitation, that the following news had just come in from Berlin: Germany and the USSR were signing a non-aggression pact. Ribbentrop would be flying to Moscow for that purpose tomorrow. Was this possible?

Involuntarily, I threw up my hands.

This was quickly followed by calls from various newspapers and agencies. That was just the start of it. Within half an hour taxis lined up in front of the embassy and a few reporters tried to force their way in, demanding a *statement* from me. Needless to say, I avoided speaking to the press. The doorman told the reporters that I was out. They decided to wait until I returned, got into taxis and sat there. A few journalists, however, headed off to Korzh's apartment. The siege of the embassy lasted until two o'clock. Worn out, the journalists left soon after two, satisfied that they wouldn't catch me there.

Since early morning there has been a great commotion, almost panic, in town today. Telephone calls. Visits. Requests to see me. Lloyd George came specially from Churt, and invited me for lunch in his office. The old man is anxious, but he fully understands us. He told me plainly: 'I've been expecting this for a long time. I'm still amazed at your patience. How could you negotiate with <u>this</u> government for so long?'

We had a long talk about the current situation and discussed the position that the old man would take on the issue. Finally, he stated directly: 'While Chamberlain remains in charge, there will be no "peace front". This man will destroy the Empire.'

Later, the duchess of Atholl paid me a visit. Worried and confused. What is this? The complete neutrality of the Soviet Union? A free hand for Germany in Europe? We had a long talk. The duchess left somewhat reassured.

Greenwood and Dalton came to see me in the evening. They are also worried, bewildered and unable to understand anything. Particularly Greenwood. He seems to have quite lost his bearings, and keeps spouting sentimental maxims. I eventually lost my patience and gave him a piece of my mind.

By evening, the morning panic had somewhat subsided. People began saying that in essence nothing catastrophic had occurred, that the military negotiations in Moscow could be continued, and that the tripartite pact could still be concluded, since hitherto Soviet non-aggression pacts had always contained a clause relieving the USSR of the obligation of non-aggression should the other party commit an act of aggression against a third power.

Nonetheless, anxiety still prevails in political circles. It is not for nothing that the Cabinet has decided to convene parliament on the 24th and to hurry the new *Defence of the Realm Act (DORA)* through the House in the space of a single sitting. Simultaneously, the Cabinet has adopted and published a resolution declaring that it will fulfil its commitments towards Poland, no matter what.

[Dalton and Greenwood found Maisky 'as much surprised as we were by the latest turn'. In Stockholm, Kollontay was 'annoyed and irritated' for not having been briefed. She learned of the pact when she went through the newspapers in the embassy the following morning. Litvinov, hidden away in his dacha, 'went almost crazy: "what do they mean? What do they mean? Do they really intend to link up with the Germans?"'[167] For Maisky, as Agniya indiscreetly admitted to Eden over lunch, 'the recent events had been a disappointment'.[168] Out of touch since the negotiations were moved to Moscow in mid-June, Maisky still clung to his belief – even after the pact was signed – that an agreement with the Western powers would be concluded, and he appeared 'apprehensive' about the likelihood that the military mission would be withdrawn from Moscow. 'If you don't hurry up and finish the political and military conversations,' he pleaded with Dalton and Greenwood, 'we shall be neutral if there is a war.' 'Oily old dodger!' was Greenwood's comment as they left the embassy.[169]

After the initial shock, most ministers and Foreign Office officials 'did not regard [the news] too tragically'. It seemed to have come as a relief, 'justifying the suspicion of Russian good faith which some of us had long held & explained all these dilatory negotiations'. Besides, the government was desperately seeking an eleventh-hour agreement with Hitler to avert war, and that would render the Nazi–Soviet pact redundant.[170] Still working towards a positive conclusion of the negotiations, Maisky hastily informed Molotov that 'the panic' which seized the political circles had given way to a more complacent mood which did not exclude the continuation of the talks.

At the same time, he held frenzied talks with members of the government and the opposition to ward off accusations of 'duplicity', in anticipation of the parliamentary debate set for 24 August. He hastily dictated to Lloyd George – who was 'depressed and pessimistic' – a 'defence line', which the 'old fox' did indeed forcefully deliver in parliament, based on a detailed and apologetic narrative of the course of the negotiations.[171] 'If Russia had been on our side,' concluded Lloyd George, 'we should not now be discussing peace negotiations … we should have crushed Hitlerism like an eggshell'.[172]]

23 August

Nevile Henderson has been to Berchtesgaden and handed Hitler a personal letter from Chamberlain, in which the latter brought it to the Führer's notice that, in the event of German aggression against Poland, England would fulfil the pledges she had undertaken. Hitler replied in the sharpest terms that no British letter would stop Germany securing her 'vital interests'.

Ribbentrop has flown in to Moscow surrounded by 32 attendants! That's just like him. I remember that when he was ambassador in Britain, he travelled between London and Berlin accompanied by no fewer than 30–40 adjutants. The negotiations have already begun.

Boothby telephoned. In his private capacity, but on behalf of his friends in the government, he expressed the hope that the following would be made clear to Ribbentrop in Moscow: in the event of war, the USSR would have its hands free. This could save the peace. Several Conservative MPs spoke to me in the same vein today.

The Greek and Danish envoys came by. Both are very worried and frightened. Especially the Dane. He confessed to me directly that he failed to see any way out of the situation except war.

Preparations for an *emergency* are in full swing in the city. Shelters are being dug, piles of sandbags are being heaped up in front of buildings, windows are being blacked out, museums and picture galleries are being emptied, the evacuation of schools, women and children is being organized, and instructions are being given over the radio about what to do with… cats and dogs.

Tension is growing, along with the expectation of something frightful, menacing and unavoidable. Is this serious? Or are these just psychological preparations for a new Munich? We'll see. There's no doubt that Chamberlain would like a second Munich very much. The trouble is that Hitler's appetite is growing fast, which makes a repeat of Munich more difficult.

What if Poland decides to fight? What then? Will Britain and France support her? Who knows? The experience of the past year obliges one to be cautious in making predictions.

Beneš came over for lunch. A short, skinny, sprightly man with bright eyes and greying hair. We conversed tête-à-tête. Beneš thanked me for my action in connection with his telegram to the League of Nations at the Council session in May. Then he familiarized me with his plans.

He is staking everything on war, a great European war in the nearest future. Only such a war can lead to the liberation of Czechoslovakia. Beneš kept asking me what I thought about the likelihood of an imminent war, and noted with satisfaction every remark I made that could be interpreted as suggesting that war would break out in the next few weeks or even days.

In concrete terms, Beneš's thoughts are as follows. If war breaks out in the nearest future, he will form a Czechoslovak government under his premiership and seek recognition from the United States, Britain, France and the Soviet Union. A historical precedent exists: Belgium in the First World

War. Nearly all Belgium's territory was occupied by the enemy, but the Belgian government continued functioning in France and was recognized by the Allies. The Czechoslovak territory is now also occupied by the enemy, but the Czechoslovak government could function in England and be recognized by the said four powers. Beneš already has his 'chancellery' in London: the embryo of the future government.[173]

In the event of war, Czechoslovakia plans to form its national army in France, comprising one or two divisions. It will form part of the French armed forces, but it will retain national command and colours. The army will be recruited from Czechoslovak émigrés, whose total number in all countries reaches 100,000. Presently, up to 2,000 Czechoslovak officers have been enlisted in the French Foreign Legion. In the event of war, they will command the Czechoslovak troops. A Czechoslovak division might also be formed on the eastern front, in Poland, but this is less certain as yet. The French government views Beneš's military plans with sympathy.

In financial terms, the Czechoslovak movement is more or less secure. It is financed by various sources, and particularly generously by American Czechs, but never by foreign powers. Beneš's ties with Czechoslovakia are very tight. He receives complete and reliable information from his country almost daily.

Roosevelt is fully sympathetic towards Beneš's plans. Beneš had a couple of meetings with the president during his visit to America. Beneš told me with obvious satisfaction that Sumner Welles[i] (under secretary of state) had visited him at his place on behalf of the president on the eve of his departure from the United States and told him: 'For me, you are still the president of Czechoslovakia.'

I asked Beneš what the British government thought of his plans.

Beneš replied that he had not yet discussed his plans with the British government and had not had meetings with any of the Cabinet members, but intended to do so very soon. Beneš was interested in the Soviet government's opinion on the same matter. I promised to find this out for him.

Naturally, we also spoke about current events. Beneš seemed somewhat puzzled by the reports in the press concerning Ribbentrop's visit to Moscow to sign a non-aggression pact, but he didn't seem greatly concerned. Beneš told me in this connection that Hilger,[ii] the German embassy counsellor in Moscow, went to Berlin in early August and made a report on the Anglo-Franco-Soviet negotiations to German leaders, mostly the military. It was decided at that meeting that the immediate signing of a non-aggression pact with the USSR was essential in order to counteract Britain and France. Hitler objected at first,

---

[i] Benjamin Sumner Welles, American under secretary of state, 1937–43.

[ii] Gustav Hilger, economic and political expert in the German embassy in Moscow, 1923–41.

but the military succeeded in winning him over by skilfully arguing that a war on two fronts might otherwise arise. The result was Ribbentrop's journey to Moscow.

Hitler's plan is to secure Soviet neutrality, crush Poland in three weeks, and then turn to the west against Britain and France. Italy will probably remain neutral, at least in the first phase of the war. That was the subject of Ciano's recent talks with Ribbentrop in Salzburg and then with Hitler in Berchtesgaden. The Italians don't want to shed blood over Danzig, and a war stemming from a German–Polish dispute would be most unpopular in Italy. Besides, the combat capability of the Italian army is highly questionable. Italy's economic situation is lamentable. She has neither oil, nor iron, nor cotton, nor coal. Should Italy take part in the war, she would be a heavy burden – military and economic – to Germany. That is why, in the end, Hitler did not object to Italy retaining neutrality.

Germany has already mobilized 2 million people. Another million and a half were called to arms three days ago. With such forces Hitler hopes to implement his plan single-handed.

24 August

Yesterday, late at night, the non-aggression pact between the USSR and Germany was signed in Moscow, and today Ribbentrop is flying back. The pact stipulates consultations between the governments on matters of mutual interest, and does not contain an *escape clause*. The duration of the pact is ten years.

Our policy is obviously undergoing a sharp change of direction, the meaning and consequences of which are not yet entirely clear to me. I must wait for further information from Moscow.

In London, there is confusion and indignation. Labourites are especially furious. They accuse us of betraying our principles, rejecting the past, and extending a hand to fascism. Difficulties arose in the 'Anglo-Russian Parliamentary Committee'. Coates[i] rushes like a madman between us and the Labourites and doesn't know what to do.

But there is no need to be embarrassed. One should keep one's self-control and composure. The Labourites will quieten down. 'This too will pass!'

The Conservatives are far calmer.[174] They never seriously believed either in the League of Nations or collective security, and take a much more straightforward view of Europe's return to a policy of 'national interest'. As if they are returning home from a 'Palace of Peace' – a lofty and solemn building, but one which they are not used to and find terribly uncomfortable.

[i] William Coates, Labour MP and secretary of the Anglo-Russian Parliamentary Committee.

26 August

The shock elicited by the Soviet–German pact of non-aggression is gradually subsiding. The Conservatives continue to behave in a very restrained manner, and before the parliamentary session on 24 August, Chamberlain asked Greenwood '*to go slow*' and not to attack the USSR too harshly in connection with the pact. Greenwood and other leading Labourites who spoke during the session did indeed behave quite decently this time. But the *backbenchers* gave vent to their feelings and heaped abuse on the USSR. The foulest speech on the 24th was given by the 'Independent' MP, McGovern,[i] yet it notably failed to draw approval from the House. The *Daily Herald* set new records for vileness. But, as I've said, passions seem to have started cooling off a bit in the last two days, and Labour is slowly coming to its senses. At every step you hear: how could the Soviet Union, a socialist state, enter into an alliance with the 'Nazis'? Aren't they foolish, those Labourites! They don't understand the ABC of Soviet foreign policy. The Liberals understand it better, and not only Lloyd George; men such as Mander also take a quite acceptable position.

Chamberlain certainly knows how to wind Labour round his little finger! He told Greenwood the other day that during the Moscow talks the French had divulged all their military secrets. The British had been more cautious and said very little.

'I tremble when I think of the use the Soviet government might make of the information it obtained!' Chamberlain concluded.

Greenwood is obviously 'trembling' as well! That's something I've learnt today for certain.

A new Munich is looming. Roosevelt, the pope, Leopold of Belgium – all are openly striving for it. Mussolini strives behind the scenes. Chamberlain sleeps and dreams of *appeasement*. Should Hitler show himself to be in the least compliant, the experience of last year may be repeated. But will he? Everything depends on Hitler.

28 August

Here is an account of the course of the Anglo-German talks over the last four days.

In the afternoon of the 25th, Hitler summoned Henderson and talked with him for more than an hour. Hitler declared most resolutely that he must have Danzig and the 'Corridor' immediately. After that he would be willing to discuss at any given conference more general problems, such as those of trade,

[i] John McGovern, Independent Labour Party MP, 1930–47.

colonies and disarmament. Moreover, Hitler let it be understood that Germany would need a loan to convert military industries into civilian ones, and that he does not insist on the compulsory return of all former colonies to Germany, but would be prepared to accept a corresponding equivalent (i.e. compensation at the expense of France, Belgium, Holland and others). But all this could happen only after he got Danzig and the 'Corridor'. No outsiders should interfere in the settling of the problem of Danzig and the 'Corridor'. It was an entirely German affair. Hitler boasted at this point that after the signing of the German–Soviet pact, Poland's position was hopeless and she would not risk going to war. In conclusion, Hitler asked Henderson to proceed to London and personally report their conversation to the British government.

On the morning of the 26th, Henderson flew to London. The Cabinet met in the evening of the 26th, and on the 27th and 28th, and the result was the reply which Henderson brought to Berlin today. The British government had discussed its response with Washington, Paris and Warsaw. The reply boils down to the following: the British government recommends settling the difficulties that have arisen by means of peaceful negotiation between Berlin and Warsaw and, should Hitler accept this, promises to consider at a conference the more general problems which he raised in his talk with Henderson on the 25th. At the same time, the British government firmly declares its intention to fulfil all its obligations to Poland.

Today, at 10.30 p.m., Henderson handed Hitler the British government's reply.

What will be the next step? War or peace?...

29 August

A day of anxiety and suspense.

Hitler has received the British reply and must now decide what to do. Enter into peaceful negotiations with Poland? Deliver an ultimatum to Poland? Simply attack Poland without prior warning? Or resort to diplomatic trickery against Britain and France?

The fates of war and peace are being weighed on unsteady, quivering scales, and who can tell what the next day will bring?

The people have become extraordinarily modest in their demands. Answering my question about the City's response to the latest events, Davidson[i] from the *Economist* said: 'It seems that war will not begin in the next 24 hours – so the City is calmer today than yesterday.'

---

[i] Basil Risbridger Davidson, on the editorial staff of *The Economist*, 1938–39; diplomatic correspondent for *The Star*, 1939.

In the next 24 hours! Now even that is considered a consolation.

Parliament met. Chamberlain made a short announcement, in which he said that nothing had changed since the session of 24 August, and that the threat of war had not diminished. The prime minister further noted the most important events of the last few days, such as Henderson's arrival and the British reply to Hitler's proposal, and once again emphasized that Britain would honour its obligations towards Poland. On the whole, the prime minister's speech sounded quite resolute. Greenwood and Sinclair said a few words pledging the opposition's support for the government. The last speaker was Gallacher. The MPs did not wish to give the floor to him at first, but he overcame their resistance and suggested that through the Speaker, parliament should address other parliaments, particularly the Supreme Soviet of the USSR, which was currently in session in Moscow, and call upon them to join forces in the struggle for peace. The MPs listened calmly to the concluding part of Gallacher's speech. The session, which had lasted not more than 40 minutes, was then closed.

Towards evening, it became known that Hitler had handed Henderson his reply to the British government's statement and that the reply was being conveyed to London 'through the normal diplomatic channels'. What does this mean? It's not the sound of a fist hitting the table. Not an ultimatum to Poland. What is it? Is he putting the brakes on? Unlikely. Hitler has gone too far, especially after his letter to Daladier, and it would be difficult for him to retreat. But perhaps he needs an extra day or two for some reason or other and is therefore delaying the decisive move. They say that some 700,000 tons of German commercial shipping are out at sea, within reach of the British and the French, and Hitler wants to give the ships time to hide in neutral ports or return home. Maybe. We shall see.

Planes are constantly buzzing in the air. At night the searchlights' flashing swords furrow the sky, 'catching' enemy bombers.

In Moscow, a quite different mood clearly reigns: they are not expecting war, and are counting on a new Munich. Here are the facts.

A few days ago I asked NKID whether it was safe to send confidential materials by diplomatic mail, in view of the possible disruption of the railways or even the opening of hostilities between Germany and Poland in the nearest future. I received the reply: send mail in the normal fashion – and in such a tone that Moscow clearly wished to tell me: 'Don't panic!' Nevertheless I did not send confidential materials with the couriers. And I was quite right not to do so. Today I learned that these couriers have got stuck in Berlin.

On 27 August, NKID informed me that I have been appointed head of the Soviet delegation to the League of Nations Assembly scheduled for 11 September. Thanks for the vote of confidence. I doubt, however, whether the Assembly will take place in the present situation.

Today, 29 August, the *Kooperatsiya* set sail from Leningrad with members of the Red Banner Song and Dance Company on board. Tomorrow, the 30th, the *Mariya Ulyanova*[175] should leave with the others. In Southampton, the Company is to board the *Aquitania*, bound for America. I fear, however, that this may not happen: new events may force the Company to return to the USSR.

30 August

Hitler's reply to the British note given to him by Henderson on the evening of the 28th amounts to the following. Hitler declares his desire to live in friendship with Britain and his willingness to respect 'the independence of Poland'. He further agrees to conduct direct negotiations with Poland and asks the British to exercise their influence in Warsaw to ensure the urgent arrival of a 'Polish plenipotentiary' in Berlin, but he insists that Danzig and the 'Corridor' should be given to Germany right away, after which he will negotiate the settlement of economic issues with Warsaw. It appears as though Hitler expects the arrival of a Polish Hácha[i] in Berlin, and that he intends to establish an economic protectorate over Poland. It is also most interesting that Hitler agrees to guarantee the new Polish borders only if the Soviet Union will do the same.

The Cabinet met today and sent a message to Berlin. In its message the British government promises to use its influence in Warsaw to facilitate the opening of direct negotiations between Germany and Poland, but on condition that the status quo is maintained during the negotiations and that both border incidents and the anti-Polish campaign in the German press should cease. As soon as the Polish question is settled, the British government will be ready to take part in discussion of the more general questions which Hitler raised during his meeting with Henderson on 25 August.

A strong smell of Munich in the air. But will Hitler accept the British proposal? Will the Poles accept it? Let's wait and see.

31 August

Another day of tension and suspense. What will Hitler say or do in response to yesterday's communication from the British government?

Various visitors came to see me, talked, asked questions, complained, expressed astonishment. I had to give clarifications and explanations to all of them. This seems to yield some results.

[i] Emil Dominik Hácha, president of Czechoslovakia from 1938 to 1939, he surrendered the rest of Czechoslovakia to Hitler in March 1939.

At about five o'clock, Agniya and I got into a small car and drove around town to see what was going on. It was the end of the working day. The usual hustle and bustle in the streets, on the underground, and on the buses and trams. But no more than usual. All the shops are trading. The cafés are open. The newspaper vendors shout out the headlines. In general, the city looks normal. Only the sandbags under the windows and the yellow signs with arrows pointing to the nearest bomb shelters indicate that England is on the verge of war.

In the evening, Agniya and I went to the Globe to see Oscar Wilde's delicious comedy *The Importance of Being Earnest*. The actors were superb. An image of the 'good old times' – without automobiles, radio, aeroplanes, air raids, Hitlers and Mussolinis – seemed to come alive. People were funny and naive then, to judge by today's standards. We laughed for two hours. That's something to be grateful for.

When we got back from the theatre, the radio brought sensational news: the 16 points which Hitler demands from Poland. The immediate return of Danzig, a plebiscite in the 'Corridor', an international committee made up of Italian, British, French and Soviet representatives, a vote in 1940, and so on and so forth.

What's this? A step back? Slowing down?

I doubt it. It's too late for Hitler to retreat. It's almost certainly a manoeuvre. Is it an attempt to hoodwink the world's public and perhaps the German people as well before a decisive 'leap'?

1 September

Yesterday's doubts have been fully justified. Today, early in the morning, Germany attacked Poland without any prior warning and began bombing Polish cities. The Polish army and air force are putting up strong resistance everywhere.

So, war has begun. A great historical knot has been loosened. The first stone has rolled down the slope. Many more will follow. Today, the world has crossed the threshold of a new epoch. It will emerge from it much changed. The time of great transformations in the life of humankind is nigh. I think I'll live to see them unless, of course, some crazy incident cuts my days short…

Parliament met at six in the evening. As I drove up to Westminster, photographers began snapping away. And why not? What a sensation: the Soviet ambassador at a parliamentary session on the matter of war. And this directly after the signing of the Soviet–German pact!

A nervous and panicky mood reigned in the corridors of parliament. A motley crowd of every age and status had gathered. There were many rather young women and girls, gesticulating frantically and speaking in raised voices.

I walked down the corridors, was saluted in the usual manner by the parliament policemen, and approached the entrance to the diplomatic gallery. It was quite jammed with ambassadors, envoys, high commissioners and other 'notables'. As soon as the door attendant caught sight of me, he pushed back a few 'ministers' to clear a narrow path for me to the staircase. On the way, I greeted the Rumanian, the Dane, the Egyptian, the Finn and a few other diplomats. I immediately sensed the atmosphere: an attitude of restrained hostility, but with a hint of deference.

The same was repeated upstairs, where I squeezed past some *distinguished strangers* and sat down on the front bench next to Guo Taiqi. We greeted each other in a friendly fashion, as we always do. Raczyński, who sat down on the other side of Taiqi, shook my hand and did so, it seemed, with a certain feeling. As for Cartier (the Belgian) and Corbin, who has turned quite grey over these past few weeks, they barely stretched out their hands. I responded by offering just a couple of fingers. Kennedy immediately leapt out of his seat when he saw that we would be neighbours, made a clumsy gesture, and took a seat in the second row (the 'envoys' row'), his great vanity as American ambassador notwithstanding. The events of recent days have certainly affected the mood in diplomatic circles.

I looked down. The small chamber of the Commons was full to bursting with agitated, tense MPs. They were packed in like sardines. The government bench was just the same. All the stars – if there are any – were present: Chamberlain, Simon, Hore-Belisha, Kingsley Wood, Brown,[i] Inskip and the rest. All the opposition 'stars' were also in attendance on the front bench, minus Attlee, who has not yet fully recovered from a recent operation. The atmosphere was heavy, menacing and oppressive. The galleries of the Lords, the press and guests were jam-packed. Near the 'clock', wearing plain grey suits, sat the duke of Gloucester and the duke of Kent. A few MPs were in khaki, among them Captain Macnamara,[ii] who has paid me several visits on Spanish matters. All eyes were trained on me. The mood was the same: restrained hostility, but with a hint of deference. I calmly endured this bombardment of glances. Then I began to make out individual faces. Lady Astor, as is her custom, seemed to be sitting on needles, and looked at me as if she meant to grab me by the hair. Mander, Nicolson and Ellen Wilkinson[iii] looked at me with friendly, sparkling eyes. I had the impression that Eden also cast a quick, and not remotely hostile, glance at me, but I can't say for sure.

---

[i] Ernest Brown, minister of labour, 1935–40; minister of national service, 1939–40; secretary of state for Scotland, 1940–41; minister of health, 1941–43.

[ii] John Macnamara, Conservative MP, 1935–44.

[iii] Ellen Wilkinson, Labour MP nicknamed 'Red Ellen' for her militant and activist role in the trade union movement; parliamentary secretary, Ministry of Home Security, 1940–45.

The speeches were brief and failed completely to rise to the great historical level of the occasion.

Chamberlain, looking terribly depressed and speaking in a quiet, lifeless voice, confessed that 18 months ago (when Eden retired!) he prayed not to have to take upon himself the responsibility for declaring war, but now he fears that he will not be able to avoid it. But the true responsibility for the unleashing of war lies not with the prime minister, but 'on the shoulders of one man – the German Chancellor', who has not hesitated to hurl mankind into the abyss of immense suffering 'to serve his senseless ambitions'. After giving a brief account of the negotiations between London and Berlin over the past few days, Chamberlain declared that today the British and French ambassadors in Germany handed Ribbentrop a note demanding that the German government stop Germany's aggression against Poland and withdraw German troops from her territory. Should this not be done (and the PM, of course, did not expect the demand to be fulfilled), the British and French ambassadors would have to ask for their passports, and Britain and France would come to the aid of Poland using all the means available to them. This would mean war, a long and hard war, but 'it only remains for us to grit our teeth and see it through to the end'.[176] As long as Germany is headed by her present government, there can be no peace in Europe.

Strong and serious words. At times, Chamberlain even tried to bang his fist on the famous 'box' on the Speaker's table. But everything cost him such torment and was expressed with such despair in his eyes, voice and gestures that it was sickening to watch him. And this is the head of the British Empire at the most critical moment in its history! He is not the head of the British Empire, but its grave-digger![177]

Greenwood spoke next. His speech was full of commonplaces and soap-box ranting, but at one point (though he may not have realized it himself) some truly prophetic words slipped out. 'In the course of this struggle,' said Greenwood, 'great and profound economic and social changes will occur, which are difficult to foresee today. But one thing is clear: a new social order will arise from the smouldering ruins of this struggle.'

Correct.

Sinclair followed Greenwood. His speech was even shorter. He said that war had begun not this morning in Poland, but with the occupation of the Rhineland three years ago. Its aim was the domination of Germany in Europe and the whole world. In this war, Germany had had consecutive, albeit temporary, successes in Spain, Austria, Czechoslovakia and, finally, Russia. Sinclair demanded immediate assistance to Poland.

Nobody else spoke. All the speeches took no more than 45 minutes.

The House moved on to discuss bills submitted by the government in connection with the impending war. By 11 p.m., 16 bills had passed all three readings. I, together with other diplomats, left Westminster after Sinclair's speech, that is, after the general part of the session was over.

Leaving parliament, I felt that something of exceptional importance had happened in the world. The first step had been made in the quick march of events which would bring Europe and possibly the whole world to new shores.

Unless an extraordinary miracle happens at the very last moment, Britain will find itself at war with Germany within the next 48 hours.

2 September

In announcing yesterday the British government's demand that Hitler cease hostilities and withdraw German troops from Poland, Chamberlain failed to say how long he was prepared to wait for his demand to be fulfilled or for a reply to his note to arrive. What did the 1 September note mean? Was it an ultimatum or wasn't it? If it was an ultimatum, then why was a final date not indicated? If it wasn't, then why did it contain a demand to withdraw troops and the threat of hostilities being opened?

The explanation is straightforward enough. Even at this very late stage, Chamberlain hoped to escape the trap which he had been preparing for us and into which he had fallen himself. At his instigation, Mussolini has expended a great deal of energy over the past two days in trying to cobble together either a five-power conference or some rotten 'compromise' to prevent war. So Chamberlain wished to buy himself at least two more days, or even just one, for manoeuvring.

This created an atmosphere of distrust and suspicion towards the PM's actions, both in the country and in the House. This mood broke through yesterday evening in the speeches of Greenwood and Sinclair.

At about eight o'clock Chamberlain announced in the House that Henderson had not yet received a reply to his 1 September note from Ribbentrop, that this could perhaps be explained by Mussolini's efforts, mentioned above, and that the British government was consulting with Paris as to how long Britain and France were prepared to wait for Hitler's reply. The prime minister's announcement drew a sharp response from Greenwood. He demanded that the PM give an immediate answer to the question: war or peace? He said that the present tension and uncertainty could not continue any longer, that an act of aggression had been committed 38 hours earlier, that Britain had not yet offered its assistance to Poland, and that the country's interests and honour were at stake.

Sinclair spoke in the same vein.

Chamberlain took the floor for the second time and declared that he would have been *horrified* had anyone thought he could hesitate at such a moment as this. He referred to the need to agree his every move with the French government, which rendered a certain delay inevitable. Lastly, he promised to make a definite and categorical statement in parliament tomorrow.

The denouement is approaching.

* * *

The situation clarified itself late at night. *Chief whip* Margesson brought it to the prime minister's attention that the mood in the Conservative Party was *very ugly* and that if the PM did not declare war on Germany the next day, the Cabinet would undoubtedly collapse. Chamberlain found himself forced to give in. At midnight an emergency Cabinet meeting was held, at which the decision was taken to declare war tomorrow.

3 September

Today, the denouement really did take place.

At 9 a.m. Henderson, acting on instructions from London, handed Ribbentrop the 'final note', in which the British government asked the German government to present by 11 a.m. its final response to the note of 1 September, which contained the demand to withdraw German troops from Polish territory. In addition, the British government warned that if the German government failed to present its reply before eleven o'clock, this would signify the breaking-off of relations and the beginning of war.

It goes without saying that no reply followed from Hitler. As a result, the prime minister went on air at 11.15 a.m. and declared that, as of then, Britain was at war with Germany.

Half an hour later, the air filled with the bellowing sounds of the siren. People scampered off to their houses, the streets emptied, and cars stopped in the road. What was it? A drill? Or a genuine raid by German bombers?

Fifteen minutes of tension and anxiety – then we heard the prolonged siren wail: '*all clear*'! It had been just a drill. There were no enemy planes.

I got to parliament by midday. I was a couple of minutes late because of the alarm.[178] I took the first available seat in the second row. Chamberlain was already speaking. A darkened, emaciated face. A tearful, broken voice. Bitter, despairing gestures. A shattered, washed-up man. However, to do him justice, the prime minister did not hide the fact that catastrophe had befallen him.

'This is a sad day for all of us,' he said, 'and to none is it sadder than to me. Everything that I have worked for, everything that I hoped for, everything that I have believed in during my public life – has crashed into ruins.'

I sat, listened and thought: 'This is the leader of a great Empire on a crucial day of its existence! An old, leaky, faded umbrella! Whom can he save? If Chamberlain remains prime minister for much longer, the Empire is ruined.'

The House was full, but not as crammed as on 1 September. The electricity that so charged the atmosphere two days ago was absent. Everything bore [indecipherable].

Gallacher was last to take the floor. He spoke for just a few minutes: he was for the defeat of the 'Nazi regime', but he was not prepared to break with his 'class comrades in the Soviet Union'.

The entire meeting lasted about 45 minutes.

So, war has begun! How will Britain and the whole world look in a year's or two years' time?...

4 September

The second day of the war!

Yesterday, 200 miles west of the Hebrides islands in the Atlantic Ocean, a submarine sank the British liner *Athenia*, which was heading for Canada. On board there were 1,400 passengers, including more than 300 Americans. Most of them were rescued, but the fate of 200 to 300 is unknown. A good *Auftakt* [prelude] for the start of the war. The Germans are true to themselves. They have learnt nothing since the era of Tirpitz.[i]

On the night of the 3rd, British aeroplanes dropped 6 million leaflets in Western Germany, addressed to the German people. And this evening a British air squadron bombed German warships at Wilhelmshafen, Cuxhafen and Brünsbuttel. The British have sustained losses, but two German ships have been hit.

German troops are advancing fast from East Prussia and Pomerania, from the direction of Breslau. The Germans' first aim is to occupy the Corridor and they seem to be closing in on their objective. The Corridor is so narrow that it is difficult for the Poles to defend it against simultaneous attacks from both sides. The Germans are also putting pressure on Silesia. The Poles are defending themselves, but more feebly than might have been expected. Why? Perhaps they haven't yet taken up their positions?

The French have begun an offensive on the western front. They are approaching the German border and establishing 'contact' with the enemy.

The Yugoslavian envoy Subbotić[ii] dropped in. He told me about the compromise that had been reached in his country between the Serbs and the Croats, and emphasized that Yugoslavia wished to remain neutral whatever the circumstances.

---

[i] Alfred von Tirpitz, commander of the German navy forces, 1914–16.
[ii] Ivan Subbotić, Yugoslav ambassador to Great Britain, 1939–41.

5 September

Chamberlain has carried out a 'reconstruction' of his Cabinet. Everything was done the Chamberlain way, i.e. halfway and with much splitting of hairs. His former Cabinet has swollen a bit in quantity, but has altered little in quality. A few ministers have swapped places. 'Fresh blood' was added in the persons of Churchill (first lord of the Admiralty) and Eden (secretary for the dominions). Gwilym Lloyd George was appointed parliamentary secretary at the Board of Trade.

Next, the 'War Cabinet' was formed, comprising nine members (Chamberlain, Halifax, Simon, Hoare, Chatfield, Hore-Belisha, Kingsley Wood, Churchill and Lord Hankey[i]). Eden has been granted the right of 'access' to the Cabinet. Only three of the nine members of the War Cabinet are without portfolios (Chamberlain, Hoare and Hankey), while in Lloyd George's War Cabinet during the last war, five out of six members did not hold ministerial positions and could devote all their time and efforts to the matter of conducting the war.

If the 'reconstruction' goes no further, Churchill and Eden will find themselves hostages, and Britain will surely lose the war. But I think that the 'reconstruction' cannot end at this point. This is just the beginning. Further steps will follow.

There are neither Labourites nor Liberals in the Cabinet. Chamberlain would not let them into the 'War Cabinet', and Sinclair, Greenwood and others did not want to be held responsible for government policy without being able to influence it.

The situation on the Polish front is not brilliant. The Germans advance, the Poles retreat. True, the press insists that the retreat is being conducted 'as planned', but one can hardly believe this in good conscience.

The British, meanwhile, have won an important victory in South Africa. Hertzog, who stood for South Africa's neutrality in the current war, has retired, and in his place General Smuts is forming a government which will support Britain in the war. The majority of the South African parliament spoke against Hertzog.

7 September

The Germans are having astonishing success in Poland. The Corridor has been occupied, Krakow has fallen, Łódź is under fire, the motorized sections of the German forces are closing in on Warsaw. The Polish government has evacuated and moved to Lublin.

[i] Maurice Pascal Alers Hankey (1st Baron Hankey), minister without portfolio in War Cabinet, 1939–40; chancellor of the duchy of Lancaster, 1940–41; paymaster general, 1941–2.

And all this in the course of a single week!

The weakness of the Poles is quite striking. They are retreating everywhere. Nowhere can they hold out for more than a few hours, or one or two days at most. There have been no major, dogged conflicts. True, the Germans are pressing the Poles with their motorized forces and air force, but still… One can't help thinking of Spain. Franco probably had no less technical superiority over the Republicans, but the Republican armies fought with astonishing stubbornness and true heroism! And what do we see here? Motorization is clearly not the whole story. It would seem that the current Polish state is rotten to the core. So deeply rotten that its army is unable to put up serious resistance to the enemy, even in the cause of the defence of national independence.

Yesterday, the British government granted Poland a loan of 8.5 million pounds. Is it not too late?

A tragicomic incident occurred early on the morning of 5 September. The sirens began blaring at about 6 a.m. and we all jumped out of our beds. Some of our embassy staff ran down to the basement with their families. We waited. All was quiet and normal. The *all clear* signal came after an hour and a half. By then my wife and I had already returned to the bedroom and got into bed. Later it transpired that there had been no air raid. A German reconnaissance plane had approached England's eastern shore. Fighters had rushed to meet it. The German plane turned around and flew away. The fighters headed home. But as they approached their own shores, they were taken for enemy machines and were fired on by anti-aircraft guns. Fortunately, the mistake was promptly discovered, and none of the pilots seem to have been hurt.

Smuts has formed a government, and South Africa has declared war on Germany. Hertzog has decided to assume the role of loyal opposition for the time being. Will this last? We shall see.

[Once again, Maisky's survival was hanging by a thread. The *Daily Herald* suggested that he was being recalled to Moscow to report. Beatrice Webb felt sorry for him, as his friends were bound to 'fall off'. She was wondering whether their forthcoming encounter was 'a farewell visit? I fear so … Poor Maiskys, we shall never see them again … With their friend, Litvinoff, they will disappear, let us hope safely, somewhere in the background of that enormous and enigmatic territory.'[179] In no time, however, Maisky bounced back, hoping that the inclusion in the Cabinet of Eden and Churchill, whom he had been cultivating for years now, would still bring the countries together.[180] 'I earnestly hope,' Churchill wrote for the first time on Admiralty notepaper, 'all will go well between our two countries, and I am sure you will do all in your power to that end.' Maisky was relieved to hear from Boothby that Churchill had indeed told him that 'in those circumstances, it was the way he would expect that particular crocodile to behave'. If there was a change in government, Maisky threw down the gauntlet, 'they might well be prepared to modify their attitude and even … co-operate with us'. 'Winston Churchill,' Maisky told the Webbs, 'would be trusted by the Kremlin.'[181]]

8 September

Just back from the *Kooperatsiya.*[182] It was late in the evening when we drove back. An incredible sight.

The giant city was in pitch darkness. No street lamps (all removed!). No lights in the houses. No sparkling restaurant or café windows. No brightly lit signs or advertisements. Everything had gone dark, as if at the wave of a magic wand. Only the stars shone in the sky, along with the blind winking of the automatic traffic lights. But they, too, were on the wane: instead of the usual bright lights of red, yellow and green, little crosses, pale and slender, hung pensively on the sombre garments of the night.

Gloomy, darkened and lifeless buildings looked like menacing cliffs. The streets between them were black gorges. Cars moved slowly in the thick darkness, like ghostly shadows. Like magic birds with a red eye on their tail. Quiet. Gloomy. Watchful. Fantastical. A scene from Dante's *Inferno...*

That is how London lies low, waiting for the raids of the German bombers.

I visited the *Kooperatsiya* for the following reason. On 29 and 30 August, the Red Banner Song and Dance Ensemble departed from Leningrad on board the *Kooperatsiya* and *Mariya Ulyanova*. Its destination was the fair in New York. In Southampton, the Ensemble was meant to board the *Aquitania*. It was going to give dozens of concerts and performances in America. Everything was ready. The contract had been signed.

Then, suddenly, war broke out! Navigation between England and America was disrupted. German submarines began sinking ships. Moscow decided to bring the Ensemble back home from England. Paris asked for one of our steamers to stop at Le Havre to pick up wives and children of personnel who wanted to be evacuated to the USSR. As a result, it was decided that the *Mariya Ulyanova*, which had come to Southampton directly from Leningrad, would sail to Le Havre, while two hundred Ensemble members would be taken off the ship (for reasons of safety) and bussed to London, where they would board the *Kooperatsiya*, which had brought 20 Ensemble members from Leningrad. And so it was done.

This evening, I visited the *Kooperatsiya* and discussed the international situation with the Ensemble.

9 September

[Enclosed is a newspaper cutting with an article entitled '6000 Spies in Britain. Nearly All Are Under Detention. Scotland Yard's Swoop'.]

Before the war of 1914, Scotland Yard kept a network of German spies in England under surveillance for a long time without arresting them. The Germans were off their guard. The day after war was declared, the entire network was arrested and put in prison. Germany found itself without informers at the time when it needed them most and was forced to create a new network during the war, which was very difficult. Of course, it could never be a patch on the old one.

The British seem to have used the same strategy now. But what a difference in numbers! If memory does not fail me, only 28 people were arrested in 1914, while in 1939 – 6,000. Everything in our time is becoming 'colossal', from ships to spy rings.

12 September

Finally today, at 5 p.m., the *Kooperatsiya* and *Mariya Ulyanova* sailed for Murmansk. What a palaver!

On 5 September, I got a message from Moscow that the Ensemble was to return home. I summoned Prof. Aleksandrov,[i] the Ensemble's director, and Commissar Yurchenko from the *Mariya Ulyanova* in Southampton and informed them of the government's decision. They were very disappointed, but nothing could be done.

Aleksandrov (and Milsky) stayed at the embassy, while Yurchenko went back to the *Mariya Ulyanova*. The first directive said: send the Ensemble to Murmansk. We took the Ensemble off the *Mariya Ulyanova*, brought it to London, and accommodated it temporarily on the *Kooperatsiya*. Meanwhile, the *Mariya Ulyanova* sailed to Le Havre to pick up the women and children waiting in Paris. Having done so, she was meant to return to London. Here, the Ensemble was meant to be divided more or less equally between the two steamers and head off homeward.

But no sooner had the *Mariya Ulyanova* reached Le Havre than we received a new directive: send the Ensemble via Gibraltar. All the plans had to be revised. Now the *Mariya Ulyanova* was to stay in Le Havre and wait for the *Kooperatsiya*. The transfer of passengers would take place not in London, but in Le Havre. The *Kooperatsiya* had to stock up with fuel and provisions in London for the 15–18 day voyage to Odessa.

We had just begun arranging the southern route when a new message came: cancel Gibraltar and send the ships to Murmansk again!

The route had to be remade, the preparations revised, and the plans drawn up from scratch. The *Ulyanova* sails to Gravesend. The *Kooperatsiya* meets her there, and that is where the reloading and transfer of passengers now occurs. We plan the departure from Gravesend for 10 September. On the morning of that

---

[i] Aleksandr Vasilevich Aleksandrov, founder and artistic director of the Red (Soviet) Army Song and Dance Ensemble.

day, the *Kooperatsiya* departs from London Bridge and moors at Gravesend. Alas, owing to unforeseen circumstances, the *Mariya Ulyanova* is nearly 24 hours behind schedule and arrives in Gravesend on the afternoon of the 11th. Then everything begins: the transfer of passengers, various formalities, loading the mail and two tons of gold sent by Mosnarbank [Moscow People's Bank] to Moscow... The crews of the two steamers ask permission to go ashore to spend their foreign currency. The identification marks for Soviet ships that have just been established by the Soviet government need to be painted on the sides and the decks. The pilots need to be spoken to. Additional provisions need to be obtained for the *Kooperatsiya*, to supplement what was given in London. In short, dozens of assignments, formalities, demands and negotiations with the authorities – meaning that the steamers only cast off today at 5 p.m.

A curious detail. In addition to the endless formalities introduced in connection with the war (licences for fuel, provisions, etc.), and in addition to the chilly but polite sabotage on the part of the irritated British authorities, there was one further misfortune. The Hay's Wharf loading company that has worked with us for many years now presented, in a state of panic and vexation, bills which had not been paid by Narkomflot and which dated back to 1936. It called in the law and arrested the *Kooperatsiya*! Curses! We settled this unexpected conflict with the greatest difficulty and freed the *Kooperatsiya*. Korzh had to call the Foreign Office, the Board of Trade, the customs office, the pilotage service, and some other institutions which, though unknown to me, are very important for seamen. He pleaded, insisted, argued and threatened them with 'the Ambassador's intervention'...

In the end, everything was settled. The *Kooperatsiya* and *Mariya Ulyanova* embarked on their long voyage. Both steamers have experienced pilots. The route is the following: through territorial waters from Gravesend to Aberdeen with pilots, and then, without pilots, across the North Sea toward Norwegian shores. To be on the safe side, the *Kooperatsiya* carries the eastern group and the *Mariya Ulyanova* the western group of the Ensemble. The steamers will sail together at a distance of half an hour. If one is unlucky, the other will help.

Bon voyage! Everything humanly possible has been done to guarantee the Ensemble's safe return home. The rest depends on the captains' skill and on luck.

13 September

'Well hello, my neutral!' said Lloyd George with a smile as I shook his hand in Churt today.

The old man wanted very much to see me. I came for *lunch* and we spent two hours in lively conversation.

Naturally, we spoke mostly about the war and related matters. I asked Lloyd George whether Britain would fight in earnest.

'Yes, it will,' Lloyd George replied with a toss of his grey mane. 'Chamberlain, of course, wants peace. He'd be ready to make peace with Hitler tomorrow and pull off a second Munich. But he can't do it. The country is against him.'

I pointed out the absence of military enthusiasm or of a visible patriotic surge such as had occurred at the beginning of the last war, but Lloyd George demurred: 'Yes, that's true. Today, you'll not see that somewhat light-headed military enthusiasm which was so striking in 1914. I remember how easy it was then to arrange a noisy meeting in any village, with patriotic speeches and victorious shouting. You couldn't do that now. But do not delude yourself: there is a *grim determination* in the masses – among workers, farmers, shopkeepers, intellectuals and the "middle class" – to carry the war to the end. A government that decided to ignore this would not last a fortnight.'

To prove his point, Lloyd George told me the story of how war was declared (about which I wrote on 2 and 3 September).

Lloyd George considers the so-called 'reconstruction' of the government carried out by Chamberlain to be a temporary tactic. In the near future, when the war starts in earnest, a quite different government will have to be formed, one truly capable of conducting a war.

I enquired whether the prime minister had offered Lloyd George a Cabinet position. Lloyd George burst out laughing, loudly and infectiously: 'Neville would rather lose the war than let me into his government!'

Lloyd George is absolutely certain that any peace proposals made by Hitler after the Polish campaign will be rejected by London. The war will continue, but what kind of war?

After Poland's defeat, which Lloyd George considers inevitable, the war will essentially take the following forms:

(1) Air warfare.

(2) Limited military operations on the Franco-German border. A breakthrough on the Siegfried Line would be likely to cost 1–2 million lives, which is a risk the French will never take. As for Britain, it will be a long time before it builds a large army for the continent.

(3) The blockade. This should do the main job, namely, strangle Germany's economy, supply of provisions, and so on.

As a result, there will be a revolution in Germany, and this will solve the problem of the war. But before things get to that stage, two or three years may pass.

Then Lloyd George moved on to the USSR.

'Chamberlain's greatest crime,' he exclaimed, 'are the Moscow talks! History will never forgive him! At the root of it, of course, is the prime minister's class hostility to a socialist state. Narrow-minded, stupid hostility. Who is Chamberlain?'

Lloyd George shook his mane again, laughed, and exclaimed: 'He is a manufacturer of iron beds! Yes, iron beds, and not very good beds at that! That is his place in life and that is the range of his vision! And this man currently stands at the head of the British Empire! He will destroy the Empire!'

Lloyd George liked Comrade Molotov's speech,[183] finding it sensible and convincing. Lloyd George understands our policy very well. It was the only way to act. But is the break between Britain and the USSR really final? Couldn't something be done to restore more friendly relations between the two countries?

'In the world of politics,' I replied, 'nothing is final. Everything is in flux. But for the moment, in all honesty, I see little likelihood of our countries drawing closer in the immediate future.'

Lloyd George shook his head and said: 'For the moment, of course, Neville is in power, and there is little chance of a rapprochement. But what if he leaves office? And if a very different government comes to power?'

Lloyd George began talking quickly and fervently about how war in Britain would end with the triumph of socialism. I didn't try to ask him exactly what kind of socialism he meant. That is not so important at this stage of development. What does matter is that a man like Lloyd George sees no way out for Britain but to replace the capitalist system with a socialist one.

14 September

The Swedish ambassador Prytz[i] came over for lunch today. He is greatly concerned by prospects for the near future. The newly established Ministry of Economic Warfare, led by Leith-Ross, poses the matter of neutrality as follows: we guarantee you normal imports of the foreign products you need, as long as you undertake to trade with Germany without exceeding the usual norms. Applied to Sweden, this means that Britain guarantees normal imports of coal, so long as Sweden does not sell more iron ore than before to Germany (7–8 million tons annually, out of the total 11 million tons produced in Sweden). The Swedish government might be ready to go along with the British conditions, but what will Germany say? Moreover, Sweden is prepared to sell ore to Germany for cash only, but Germany does not have any cash. How will Germany react to the refusal to sell on credit? Will she regard it as a *casus belli*?

Prytz further complained of the difficulties which Swedish trade faces in Britain. What will the future bring? How to maintain trade with other countries when the Baltic Sea is blocked by Germany?

---

[i] Björn Prytz, Swedish ambassador to Great Britain, 1938–47.

Before leaving, he told me a very funny story. He has an English *butler*. A quintessential English butler. When sirens began wailing on the morning of 4 September, the *butler* put on his most official uniform, knocked on the door of Prytz's bedroom and said most respectfully: '*May I suggest, Sir, that you retire to the cellar?*'

Following the butler, in his ceremonial dress, Prytz and his wife proceeded to the cellar in their pyjamas, along with all the other members of the *household*, who'd put on whatever attire was at hand. A scene fit for the gods!

After this, there were no alarms for a week. Yesterday morning at tea, the *butler*, addressing Prytz with his usual deference, pronounced: '*The nights are getting monotonous, Sir. Don't you think so?*'

[Prytz forged close relations with Maisky. Beatrice Webb found him to be 'a cold-blooded philosopher, secularist in his outlook on man's relation to the universe' who preferred a Swedish alliance with the Soviet Union rather than with Germany. His attractive young wife, she noted, was 'a great admirer of Maisky and a warm friend of Madame Maisky. When I showed her Lenin's portrait, given me by the Ship's Captain who took us to Russia, she observed that Maisky had the same expression as the great genius who created the Soviet Union.'[184]]

15 September

Chamberlain has not relinquished the idea of a new Munich. The compromise racket continues behind the scenes, with Mussolini and Kennedy, American ambassador in London, playing major roles. The latter is an advocate of '*peace at any price*'. He is terribly afraid of a revolution in Germany and of any revolution as a result of war.

What is behind it?

I've heard the following. The British government no longer has the slightest doubt that Poland is definitively lost. They expect that any day now Hitler will set up a 'puppet government' in Poland which will make peace with him, thereby relieving Britain and France of their obligations of guaranteeing Poland. Then the path to reconciliation with Germany, as well as to the 'settlement' of European issues, will be opened. The Labourites, Liberals and some Conservatives will, of course, be against a new Munich. To sweeten the pill, Chamberlain's group has devised the following plan: to remove Hitler and some of the 'extremists' and make peace with Göring and the Reichswehr generals. The *Daily Telegraph* editorial of 13 September clearly hints at this. There is a further allusion to this in the PM's recent speech in parliament, where he attacked not Germany, not the 'Nazis' and not 'Nazism', but 'Hitler' and 'Hitlerism'.

It is easy enough to say, 'Remove Hitler', but how is this to be done? The *Daily Telegraph* recalls the history of the kaiser's removal in the last war. The same, but different. The kaiser was removed, or removed himself, at the end of the fourth year of the war, when the German Empire had begun cracking at the seams. But Hitler is currently at the zenith of his power and fame. Just try to remove him!

Or are the British considering a terrorist act?…

17 September

Today, at 6 a.m., Potemkin handed a note to the Polish ambassador, Grzybowski,[i] in which the Soviet government declared that since the Polish state has disintegrated and the Polish government has gone into exile, the Soviet–Polish non-aggression pact is null and void. Under these conditions, Poland in general, and especially its eastern part, has become a land where anything can be expected. In its eastern part there live 10–11 million Belorussians and Ukrainians, oppressed by the Polish state and Polish landlords. The conclusion: the Red Army is crossing the Polish border and occupying Western Belorussia and Western Ukraine in order to protect the population's lives and property. At the same time, the Soviet government will undertake all possible measures to rescue the Polish people from the war into which their former leaders have dragged them and to provide them with the opportunity to live and work in peace.

At six o'clock in the morning, the Red Army began its offensive.

At 11.30 a.m., Comrade Molotov came on air with a speech explaining the motives and goals of the government's decision.

All this struck London like a bolt from the blue. True, there has long been talk and suspicion here of a German–Soviet agreement to 'partition Poland', but the crossing of the Polish border by the Red Army has come as a real shock. A shock so great that today in the late afternoon Greenwood issued a 'declaration' sharply attacking the USSR and affirming that Poland must be restored.

What will be the response to our actions in England? Can England declare war on us as an 'aggressor' against Poland, which is under its guarantee? Might England, as a last resort, sever diplomatic relations with us?

I don't think so. Such a policy is clearly beyond Britain's capabilities for now. On the contrary, it will take pains to avoid anything that might further aggravate its current difficult position and facilitate the strengthening of ties between the USSR and Germany. That is why I expect a note of protest, an angry speech in parliament by the prime minister, and campaigns in the press, but nothing more.

---

[i] Wacław Grzybowski, Polish ambassador to the USSR, 1936–39.

19 September

My expectations are beginning to be fulfilled. Yesterday, late in the evening, the British government made a toothless statement, not even a protest, concerning our actions in Poland, and reaffirmed its determination to fight the war to the end. We shall see what Chamberlain says in parliament tomorrow.

Lord Davies came by. We had a long talk about the current situation. Davies takes quite a sensible view of things. When it comes to his aims for the future, however, he still lives in cloud cuckoo land. He brought me a memorandum where he proposes formulating the 'war aims' as the creation of a United States of Europe. He has already handed this memorandum to members of government and is now distributing it among diplomats.

The events of recent weeks have wreaked havoc with people's minds. Gollancz is in despair: in his view, the Soviet–German pact killed off communism. Strachey, in connection with the same pact, came to Harry [Pollitt] with tears in his eyes. Cummings, writing in the *News Chronicle* (19 September), simply cannot make sense of things. Duff Cooper published an article in today's *Evening Standard* about 'Two Breeds of Bolshevism' – communism and fascism. Every day I receive many letters – anonymous and otherwise – which show their authors to be in a quite incredible state of shock. Yes, the general muddle is on a colossal scale. And it is not easy to combat: there's a lack of information and materials for that purpose. Besides, the entire press, especially on the Labour side, is now against us. The *Daily Herald* is the worst of all.

68. Maisky at the home of the socialist publisher Gollancz in better days.

[Attached to the diary is a cutting from the *Daily Telegraph* of 19 September entitled 'Britain Stands by Poland. Pledge Unaffected by New Invasion'.]

20 September

Went to the House. I was the focus of attention, for both the press and MPs.

Chamberlain lacked the guts even to make a sharp statement against the USSR. After setting out the chronological order of events and emphasizing in particular the promise of neutrality we had given to Britain and other countries in our note of 17 September, the PM declared that the Soviet action could not be justified by the arguments adduced by the Soviet government, but that, on the other hand, it was too early to give a final verdict on the motives and consequences of the Russian initiative. That was all. My forecast is confirmed yet again.

Greenwood was also more modest than might have been expected. True, he declared that one more power had committed an act of aggression, but moved on very quickly to other subjects and did not make a second mention of the events of 17 September. Sinclair spoke in a similar vein. Boothby, with whom I talked a few days ago, spoke very well. He warned the MPs against hasty conclusions and argued that the appearance of Soviet troops on the Polish–Rumanian border was a positive event and that the most dangerous thing would be '*to indulge in fits of morality*', something which good Brits are very fond of. He was, of course, referring to Labour. In the following debates there was little of interest.

On leaving the diplomatic gallery, I met Strabolgi. We went to have tea. We had a serious and generally satisfactory conversation about the current situation.

21 September

Will England fight in earnest or not?

What is certain is that current developments in the west are highly suspicious.

The French on the western front are presently occupied not with war, but with *slow motion* military exercise. The British ship troops across the Channel, mass them, organize and train them, but do not even participate in the drills which the French are so keen on. No air warfare as yet. British planes are busy dropping not bombs but toothless leaflets on Germany. Their one raid on Wilhelmshafen and Brünsbuttel, during which two German warships were hit, took place two weeks ago. Since then not a single raid! The Germans are also keeping quiet: no air raids yet on London or Paris. A real war is being waged and a real blockade maintained only at sea, but that is due to the fact that Churchill heads the Admiralty. Even at sea, however, they are fighting with kid gloves: the commanders of German submarines are vying with one another in gallantry, rescuing the crews of the ships they have sunk. English newspapers devote whole columns to glowing accounts of their feats.

No, this is not war! Particularly at a time when the situation in Poland demanded immediate and highly effective aid.

Now that Poland no longer exists, it is entirely reasonable to ask: will England fight in earnest or will she not?

History has played a cruel joke on the elite of the British bourgeoisie. Today, they really do find themselves *between the devil and the deep* [*blue*] *sea*.

If Britain refuses to fight and agrees to a new Munich (Chamberlain's constant dream), the consequences will be not only direct losses in territory, capital and so on, but even greater indirect damage. The blow inflicted on its prestige and position in the world will be so devastating that the Empire will begin to crumble and its remaining 'friends' among neutral countries will turn their backs. Even the blind now realize that a new Munich will not guarantee Britain lasting peace. It will serve only as a prelude to further and more insatiable demands on the part of Hitler. Moreover, there is no doubt that a new Munich would have a psychological effect within the country such as would render renewed mobilization (should this becomes necessary six or twelve months later) simply impossible. Finally, a new Munich would almost certainly bring Chamberlain down, send acute tremors through the Conservative Party, and produce a very different political constellation in the country, which would augur no good to the upper ten thousand. Not to fight, therefore, is very dangerous.

On the other hand, fighting would mean facing the gravest military difficulties, sustaining colossal human and material losses and, in the end, coming round to 'socialism'. The conviction that 'socialism' would be the inevitable result of a major war is now universal – even in bourgeois circles. Of course, everyone has his own idea about what kind of 'socialism' this would be, but all are convinced that there is no getting round it. So, to fight is also very dangerous.

No wonder the bourgeois leaders are in two minds. How will the war problem be resolved? It's too early to say. But the possibility of a serious war cannot be excluded. Yesterday in parliament, Chamberlain stated once again, absolutely categorically, that the government was braced for a war that would last at least three years. This was not his first statement of the kind. If words mean anything, the B[ritish] G[overnment] has committed itself beyond the point of no return. All the more so as the mood among the masses is strongly in favour of war. But do the words of British ministers mean anything?…

22 September

If a 'three-year war' does become fact, then, to judge by the information I have gathered, it will take approximately the following forms:

(1) Fierce air warfare.

(2) Limited military operations ('*military pressure*') on the western front. Military experts estimate that a breakthrough on the Siegfried Line would cost 1–2 million lives. The Allies will not risk it.

(3) A very tight blockade by land and sea, including the introduction of 'rations' for neutral countries. The main hopes are pinned on the blockade, which should strangle Germany and bring about internal convulsions, possibly even a revolution. Hence, incidentally, the anticipation of a long war.

Boothby, quoting Churchill, said that Gamelin shares this conception of the war.

In light of the above, our position acquires immense importance. Will we supply Germany with raw materials and food or not? If we do, in what quantities and on what conditions? These questions concern everybody here. No wonder. The outcome of the blockade and, therefore, of the war depend on the answers to these questions.

Two circumstances are capable of undermining the conception set out above:

(1) Germany moving over to active operations on the western front (including the possible violation of the neutrality of Holland, Belgium and Switzerland). This would be true to Hitler's spirit and would also conform with Germany's direct interests, as she cannot risk a 'three-year war'.

(2) Revolution in Germany. A revolution would alter radically the alignment of forces in Europe and would lead to the quick termination of war.

I visited Beneš at *26, Gwendolen Avenue, Putney*. A quiet street, the quiet, cosy home of an average intellectual, the quiet footsteps of a few servants.

But the spirit of the house is far from quiet.

Beneš, whom I had not seen for a month, told me about his affairs. A special 30,000-strong Czech army, under General Inger, is being formed in France. True, the French government does not want an 'army', but only a 'legion' (Osouský is for it, too), but Beneš is sure he will cope with this obstacle. A Czech military unit is also being formed in England. Here, it probably will be called a 'legion'. Under the command of General Prchal, a Czech 'legion' some 800 strong has been organized in Poland. Beneš did not support this idea. He wanted to bring the legionaries from Poland to France. Everything was ready, but the Poles got in the way at the last minute. Beneš then recommended that Prchal at least station the legion somewhere near the Soviet border, thinking that if the Germans defeated the Poles (as Beneš was sure they would), the

Czech legion would be able to retreat to the Soviet Union. As a result, the legion was stationed in Baranovichi, which has been recently occupied by the Red Army. Beneš asks the Soviet government to take care of the Czech legionaries and consider the expense of their upkeep as a loan granted to Czechoslovakia, which will certainly be restored as a result of the war. It would also be very good if the legionaries could be moved from the USSR to France. I said I would forward his request to Moscow, but I suspect that we, as a neutral country, can hardly undertake the transportation of legionaries to France. But we shall certainly render assistance to the legionaries in the USSR.

Beneš wants the Czech army to be put under the command of a Czech government. What is the attitude of the B[ritish] G[overnment] to the idea of a Czech government? Three days ago, Beneš had his first meeting with Halifax, who told him that the restoration of Czechoslovakia's independence is one of the 'war aims' of the Allies. As for the recognition of a temporary Czechoslovak government, Halifax promised to think it over. The French government holds a similar position.

How does Beneš view the Red Army's entry into Poland? He fully approves. He understands it and agrees entirely with our policy. The USSR could not have acted differently. He asks for one thing only: to make sure the USSR has a common border with Slovakia. This is very important.

'I don't know what government the free Czechoslovakia of the future will have,' said Beneš. 'It makes no odds to me. I'm not against a Soviet government. So long as Czechoslovakia is free and independent. So long as she rids herself of the German yoke.'

As far as 'Ruthenia' (Transcarpathian Ukraine) is concerned, Beneš thinks it should be incorporated into the Ukrainian Soviet Socialist Republic. Even during his time as president of the Czechoslovak Republic, he had envisaged 'Ruthenia' as part of the USSR.

Beneš regrets the recent revolt in Czechoslovakia. It was premature and merely led to heavy casualties. But nothing could be done. The situation was too tense in the localities. When it became known in Czechoslovakia that the Red Army had entered Poland, the revolt flared up spontaneously. But Czechoslovakia will not stop fighting. It has strength in abundance.

Beneš thinks that the war will be a long and serious one. Moreover, he has the impression that in this respect England's attitude is far tougher than that of France.

23 September

Today, quite out of the blue, Halifax invited me over. I hadn't seen him for almost two months, since 25 July. Total chaos reigned in the familiar corridors of the Foreign Office: tables, bookcases, files, boxes, papers – all piled up in complete disorder. They must have been making some additional arrangements in the event of air raids.

My talk with Halifax lasted 20–25 minutes. The atmosphere was tense and unnatural throughout. Halifax spoke slowly and chose his words carefully. He often paused, sighed and stared at the ceiling. He was excruciatingly polite, but I felt all the time that looking at me he was thinking: are you an enemy or not?

In essence, Halifax called me over to probe our mood and intentions. He beat about the bush for a good long while, saying that the international situation had changed beyond recognition in recent weeks, that one had to find one's bearing anew, and that he would be extremely grateful to me and the Soviet government if we could enlighten him as to our views about the present situation and the immediate future.

After these prefatory remarks, Halifax moved on to more practical questions. He was specifically interested in four points:

(1) Does our old position, which was based on the need to fight aggression and provide assistance to victims of aggression and which he had always associated with the USSR (Halifax referred here to Stalin, Litvinov and others), remain in force or does it not?

(2) How do we imagine the future of Poland?

(3) What is our view of the present phase of Anglo-Soviet relations?

(4) What are our trade relations with Germany?

An argument arose between us on these points. For instance, as far as the first point is concerned, I referred Halifax to Comrade Molotov's latest speeches. I myself argued within the framework of these speeches. My reply did not satisfy Halifax. He said that Comrade Molotov's speeches do not give a clear answer to the question he is interested in. As for the third point, I reminded Halifax of our note of 17 September, which defined our relations with Britain as neutral. Halifax received my explanation with the greatest distrust and, after some consideration, asked me to clarify with Moscow whether there is any point in the B[ritish] G[overnment] starting trade negotiations with us such as it currently conducts with other neutral countries, or whether the new character of Soviet–German relations renders such negotiations senseless. I attempted to find out from Halifax what he meant by trade negotiations, but he avoided giving me a direct answer. Finally, as regards the fourth point, I directed Halifax to the Soviet–German trade agreement of 19 August of this year. This did not satisfy Halifax either.

On parting, Halifax asked me to communicate with Moscow and provide him with more exhaustive information on the issues that interested him.

My general impression: the British government is very anxious about our relations with Germany and wishes to glean how far they have advanced. At the same time, it is plainly considering the resumption of contact with us, but hesitates to make a corresponding démarche, not knowing how we would receive it.

* * *

We visited the Webbs. The old couple is alarmed and upset. They are of the view that this will be a war in earnest because the ruling elite understands perfectly well that in essence the question is now 'to be or not to be' for the capitalist system. It also understands that it has succeeded in creating a united national front in the country, crushing the Labourites and even interesting the USA in the ongoing struggle. Such a combination may never be repeated. That is why the ruling clique will be for a 'three-year war'.

[Grim and defiant, Maisky paid a short visit to the Webbs a few hours before meeting Halifax. He felt that 'power politics, pure and simple' were now at work all over the world, 'all idealism has vanished'. Maisky, who had been excluded from the negotiations leading to the Ribbentrop–Molotov Pact, was in no position to establish whether pragmatism or ideology was behind the Kremlin's policies. Halifax found him to be 'ill-informed', 'very embarrassed' and 'unable to answer any questions about the future'. Laurence Collier, head of the northern department of the Foreign Office, believed that he was 'not in M. Stalin's confidence'. Emerging from the meeting, Maisky begged Molotov to 'urgently' send him instructions.[185] In Moscow, though, Dimitrov, president of the Comintern, was discouraged by both Stalin and Zhdanov from entertaining any fancy revolutionary illusions. 'In the First Imperialist War,' he was told, 'the Bolsheviks overestimated the situation. We all rushed ahead and made mistakes! This can be explained, but not excused, by the conditions prevailing then. Today we must not repeat the position held by the Bolsheviks then.'[186] Stalin's assignments to the various communist parties shortly after the outbreak of war stated *a priori* that Russia was 'content being confined to its own *small* Lebensraum'.[187]]

27 September

Today I conveyed to Halifax the following answers given by the Soviet government to the questions raised by Halifax during our conversation of 23 September:

(1) The fundamental principles of Soviet foreign policy remain unalterable. The Soviet–German relations are being governed by (a) the Soviet–German Non-Aggression Pact of 23 August 1939 and (b) the Soviet–German communiqués of 18 and 22 September in connection with the Polish affairs (no contradiction between the USSR and Germany, demarcation line).

(2) The present demarcation line in Poland cannot be considered as the final state frontier between the USSR and Germany. The future of Poland, however, is dependent on so many factors and contradictory forces that it is impossible at present to foresee the final sequel of all that interplay.

(3) The USSR would be prepared to start trade talks if Great Britain really desires such talks, as the USSR takes a neutral attitude with regard to the war in the west now and contemplates maintaining this neutral attitude in the future, but with one important reservation: the USSR contemplates remaining neutral in the future if Great Britain herself by her attitude and behaviour towards the USSR does not compel the Soviet government to interfere in this war.

Halifax was not fully satisfied. He asked whether we intended to form a buffer Polish state, but I was unable to satisfy his curiosity on this score. In addition, he was obviously bewildered by the statement that the USSR would remain neutral only so long as England did not force her to intervene in the war, and asked me anxiously: 'Have we done anything to you?'

I replied that except for various complications in matters of trade (the delay in issuing licences for the goods we had bought, for the orders carried out for us, etc.) we held nothing against England for the moment, but who could vouch for the future? War is war, and in war anything can happen.

With regard to the question of the trade complications, Halifax said that these difficulties would be settled along with other matters during the proposed trade negotiations.

Halifax asked in some detail about the current situation in the Polish areas occupied by the Soviet army. Using the information which I receive every day on Moscow radio, I told him about the temporary administrations being set up in cities and towns, the peasant committees, the opening of schools, factories and shops, etc. Halifax asked how the local population was greeting the Red Army. I replied: 'That depends. Landlords and factory owners are hardly enthusiastic, but peasants, workers and Jews are highly sympathetic.'

I related some facts to illustrate my point.

'So what do you do with the landlords?' asked Halifax.

'Nothing. They have nearly all fled.'

'And what if any of them had remained?'

'That would depend on who that specific landlord was. If he had been responsible for any serious sins in the past, he would have been arrested and put on trial. If he was a good person who hadn't sullied his name in any way in the past, he would have been left alone. I must tell you, though, that there are few decent people to be found among the Polish landlords, if any. The Polish landlord is one of the worst representatives of his class in Europe.'

At Halifax's request, I gave a brief description of Polish landownership and the poverty and exploitation of the Polish, Ukrainian and Belorussian peasantry.

'And what do you do with the landlords' land?'

'It is confiscated without exception and distributed among the peasants.'

Halifax shook his hand and uttered gloomily: '*A grim tale*.'

His landlord's heart couldn't bear it.

I noticed one curious detail. Judging by the nature of the questions he posed to me, it was clear that Halifax wanted to sound me out as to whether we considered the fate of the part of Poland we had occupied to have been definitively resolved, or whether we allowed for the possibility of it changing in the future. When I told him about the distribution of the landlords' land, Halifax sighed heavily and no more questions followed. The answer to the question that concerned him was as plain as daylight.

At the end, Halifax touched upon the first point.

'Still,' he remarked, 'I just can't reconcile the events of recent weeks with the foreign-policy principles proclaimed by Mr Stalin at your last party congress.'

I looked at Halifax with half a smile and replied: 'There's this folk tale we have. A peasant fell ill and took to his bed. While he lay there helpless, one of his neighbours took his horse, another stole his cow, and a third grabbed his plough. When the peasant recovered and went back to work, he saw that he had been robbed. He went to the house of the first neighbour, punched him in the face and took his horse back. Then he came to the second and third neighbours, and got his cow and plough back in the same way. Can the peasant's actions be qualified as "an act of aggression"? No, they can't. He simply retrieved that which his neighbours had illegally appropriated when he was weak.'

'So you think that this Russian tale has relevance to recent events?' Halifax asked.

'Undoubtedly,' I replied, 'with the sole difference that in this case the USSR didn't punch anybody in the face. We did not start a war in Poland to return the regions taken away from us in 1920. But when the Polish state collapsed and the Polish government fled abroad, when Poland became a 'no man's land' under the threat of German occupation of its entire territory, then the USSR intervened and said: that which was illegally taken away from us 20 years ago must now be returned. What objections can there be to our way of acting? None. That is why I dare to assert that there is no contradiction between our principles and our actions in the area of foreign policy.'

Halifax did not reply. I doubt, though, that he entirely agreed with me.

28 September

In the *Daily Sketch* of 25 September, I came across Lady Oxford's[i] sad reflections.

[There follows a cutting entitled 'World I Loved Has Gone'.]

Lady Oxford expressed the thoughts and feelings (especially the feelings) that are plaguing the souls of the 'upper ten thousand' more honestly than any

---

[i] Lady Helen Kelsall Asquith, widow of Lord Asquith.

other representative of her class. They are gripped by a vague, spontaneous terror of the future. Every day they see thousands of small and big examples to convince them that the machinery of capitalist society has entered a state of deep decay. They sense the icy breath of Nemesis. They see a fearsome hand writing on the wall of their cosy, pleasant world: 'Mene, Mene, Tekel, Parsin.'[188] They feel the soil giving way beneath them as they fall into the abyss of a new, unknown and terrible world. The widow of the former prime minister has accurately grasped this present state of 'society', but she understands neither the causes of the phenomenon nor the prospects for capitalism. She will probably understand them soon.

29 September

Another day of excitement and sensations. Journalists have been calling all day on the telephone.

Communications about the outcome of Ribbentrop's visit to Moscow have come in. A friendship and boundary treaty, an exchange of letters concerning the strengthening of trade relations, and a joint declaration about peace in Western Europe. In addition, a Soviet–Estonian pact of mutual assistance.[189]

The British are most concerned about the peace declaration. Glasgow, Gordon-Lennox, Cummings and others pose one and the same question: what is the meaning of the last paragraph of the declaration stipulating 'consultations' on the measures to be taken if Britain and France refuse to cease hostilities. Does it mean that in this case the USSR will provide military aid to Germany against Western powers?

Glasgow was highly agitated when he came to see me and came straight out with it: 'So is it war?'

'War with whom?' I inquired.

'With the USSR!' cried Glasgow.

I laughed out loud and began to ridicule him. He gradually returned to a more normal state. On parting, I recommended that he and Garvin not hasten with their conclusions and await new developments.

Cummings was less bellicose. He merely told me about the mood in the City, the extreme irritation aroused in political circles by the Soviet–German agreements (Labour is especially furious), and a new campaign to change the government.

Gordon-Lennox understands the situation better than anyone. His reasoning is that of a cynical imperialist, and he even told me directly: 'The USSR is playing its cards splendidly.'

I put him right on a number of points, while confirming that Moscow knows how to use a favourable situation in the interests of its general policy of peace.

Yes, there's no doubting that the English are highly irritated. Serves them right. They should have thought about that earlier. Looks like there are difficult days ahead of us. But it's not the first time. We'll stick it out!

[The narrative of the events leading up to the pact, assiduously composed by Maisky and adopted almost verbatim by Stalin, maintained that the Soviet Union was left with no choice but to sign an agreement with Hitler: Russia was in desperate need of a breathing space to prepare for the supposedly inevitable war with Germany.

It comes as a startling revelation, however, that – contrary to the accepted wisdom – Stalin believed he could successfully avoid war altogether. The German–Soviet collaboration was not, therefore, transient and precarious, but appeared to have long-lasting prospects. Stalin was bent on exploiting the new opportunities to redress the grievances which, he felt, had been inflicted on Russia not only at the Versailles peace conference, but also during the nineteenth century – specifically by the humiliating Paris Peace Treaty of 1856 (following the Crimean War) and at the Congress of Berlin (following the Russo-Turkish wars of 1877–78). His gaze, like that of the tsars, was fixed on the Balkans, the littoral of the Black Sea and the Turkish Straits.

Rather than being a manifestation of defeatism, motivated by ideological expectations of the outbreak of revolution, the 'peace campaign' launched by the Comintern on the outbreak of war served more mundane Soviet interests. It was to be instrumental in efforts to bring the war to a rapid conclusion. That was to be followed by a peace conference, probably in 1941–42. The main thrust of Stalin's policies in 1939–41, therefore, was to gather together the best cards he could, ahead of the anticipated peace conference. He expected the conference, which would be attended by a debilitated British Empire, to topple the Versailles Agreement, acknowledge the new Soviet security arrangements in Central and Northern Europe, and extend them to the south.[190]

After a short period of being left in the lurch, Maisky grasped the essence of the new policy, and this would give him a fresh lease of life. The line he consistently pursued, as Vansittart alerted Halifax, was that 'it is time to make peace', as the common foe, Germany, 'has been defeated, thanks to the far-sighted policy of Stalin. If the Western Powers are as resolute in dealing with Hitler as Stalin has been, then Hitler is finished. There is no way out left for Hitler – neither in the East, nor in the West, nor in the Balkans.' It was therefore 'useless to shed more blood, seeing that Hitler is vanquished. Poland was the price that had to be paid to achieve this victory'.[191] He hastened to enlist Lloyd George, whose secretary was horrified to find the Russian ambassador 'absolutely defeatist' seeking 'peace NOW', with a brief along these lines for Lloyd George's speech in parliament. Maisky urged Lloyd George to stress that the Soviet Union's commitment to Germany was limited, and that the trade agreement was not 'because of the blue eyes of Hitler' but because, as a neutral, Russia could trade with both sides. He urged Lloyd George to think twice whether it was in Britain's interest to commit an even 'greater blunder' than the Polish guarantees 'and plunge into a three years' war'. He advocated the convening of a peace conference with Soviet participation, which was bound to culminate in a settlement 'much more durable and stable than Munich'. Speaking in parliament later that day, Lloyd George did indeed champion the peace front, urging the government to treat Russia 'purely as neutrals ... we do not want to multiply our enemies'.[192] Maisky, who had not briefed Moscow about his preliminary talk with Sylvester,[i] reported that although Lloyd George's speech went against the mainstream, it proved 'a great sensation'.[193] In his memoirs, Maisky claims that he 'did not believe in the durability and stability of the agreement with Germany'. He assuredly did not share the views of the Kremlin that Britain would respond favourably to Hitler's peace proposals.[194]]

3 October

Today Chamberlain gave his appraisal in parliament of the German–Soviet agreements. Nothing sensational, just as I'd thought. The PM did not declare war on us. He did not even risk expressing disapproval of the Moscow treaty. He merely emphasized once again that the events of the last week had changed little in the current situation (loud approval from both sides of the House), that Britain and France were not afraid of threats (loud approval), and that Hitler was not to be trusted (thunderous approval). Britain and France would pursue the war until Hitlerism had been crushed. Nevertheless, they were prepared to consider any proposals of peace.

Attlee, who had resumed his duties as the leader of the opposition, supported the prime minister, as did Sinclair. They said not a word about the USSR. Sinclair insisted once again on the proposal he made last week: to hold a closed session of parliament.

Lloyd George spoke next. His speech, as ever, was a model of oratorical mastery. He spoke very cautiously, for the subject was a very hazardous one, and it was as if he was constantly probing the atmosphere in the chamber with invisible hands. Lloyd George's feel for parliament is astonishing. It derives from talent and fifty years' experience. The chamber listened to him tensely, with bated breath, even though he was clearly going against the stream. Only the occasional weak hissing could be heard from the Labour benches, and even these sounds merely accentuated the dense hush which had filled the House.

Lloyd George said that the anticipated peace proposals should be carefully studied and discussed by parliament before the British government responded. Then he said that Hitler was of course not to be trusted, but that if the great neutral powers – the USSR, Italy and the USA – could be involved in resolving the question of peace, a different situation would emerge. The

[i] Albert James Sylvester, Lloyd George's influential private secretary from 1923 until his death in March 1945.

terrible bloodshed that threatened Europe might possibly be avoided. In conclusion, Lloyd George, like Sinclair, demanded a closed session of parliament.

Lloyd George's speech lifted the mood of the House. A significant number of Conservatives obviously sympathized with him, but did not dare to support him openly. The Labourites and Liberals were just as obviously opposed to the speaker. But everybody felt that something important, something big, had happened. The prime minister took the floor once again right after Lloyd George. He ruled out a closed session of parliament (Chamberlain fears that MPs might subject the Cabinet to too much criticism at a closed session and that he would have to resign), but promised not to be too hasty in replying to peace proposals, and even half-promised to give the Houses the chance to have their say.

Duff Cooper and Grenfell attacked Lloyd George sharply and accused him of taking a capitulatory stance. Grenfell also took the opportunity to give the USSR a dressing down, half-turning in my direction. And this man calls himself a socialist!

Eventually I tired of all this dawdling and went to see Lloyd George. He received me in his room in parliament. We drank tea and spoke about the current situation.

'Winston is awfully angry with me,' the old man said with a chuckle. 'Did you see how he was behaving while I was speaking?'

I had seen Churchill turn various shades of red and white during Lloyd George's speech, shake his head in agitation, and generally express his disagreement with the speaker through gestures and glances.

'Winston is insanely determined to fight to the end! He is enraged and thinks of nothing else but how to throttle Germans… But that doesn't bother me. I always say what I think. During the Boer War I was against the war…'

'And almost got killed for it in Birmingham,' I finished.

'Yes, yes, they very nearly got me,' Lloyd George remembered with another chuckle.

Then he summed things up: 'One must have the courage of one's convictions!'

Lloyd George holds that it would be better for Britain to keep out of the war, but doubts that this will be possible. Hitler enrages the English bulldog which, once enraged, becomes dreadfully obstinate.

4 October

Harold Nicolson, who came over for lunch, told me that he was writing a small book on the theme: why is England waging war?

I asked him how he answers this question. Nicolson expressed his point of view concisely, stressing in particular that Europe must at last be freed of the constant fear of aggression and that all its nations should be given the chance to develop peacefully and fruitfully.

'And are you sure,' I asked, 'that the current war will lead to this outcome. Are you sure it won't end in a new Versailles – doubled or even tripled?'

'That's just it,' Nicolson admitted frankly. 'I am not sure. I am greatly troubled. But every effort should be made to prevent a new Versailles.'

He paused, then added: 'I fear victory most of all. Victory will end in Versailles. A *stalemate* would be best of all. Then there would be a chance for a good peace.'

I objected that war can't be measured out in doses like medicine, and that only socialism can provide a serious guarantee for a just peace, at least in the major European countries. Nicolson brightened up and exclaimed: 'I often think exactly the same thing. I have no objections to a socialist Europe.'

6 October

Churchill's secretary called and asked me to come to see him at the Admiralty at 10 p.m.[195] Not exactly the ordinary hour for receiving ambassadors in England, but the present situation is far from ordinary, and the man who invited me is also far from ordinary!

It's dark and misty tonight. The clouds are low and gloomy. It's pitch-dark on the streets. I reached *Horse* [*Guards*] *Parade*, where the Admiralty is located, with some difficulty. We had to stop the car frequently to check our bearings. We eventually arrived. The familiar square seemed quite unfamiliar. The Admiralty building rose darkly out of the swirling fog like a fairy-tale fortress. Not a single light or human being in sight. I knocked and rang at the various doors and gates – silence. Were they all asleep in there? Or had this huge institution, which governed the movement of the British navy all over the globe, twenty-four hours a day, given up the ghost?… I was beginning to lose my patience. At last I saw a pale ray of light in the archway of the gates, and behind it there appeared a sleepy watchman. I explained my business. A few minutes later I was already sitting in the office of the 'First Lord of the Admiralty'.

Churchill greeted me with a welcoming smile. The walls of his office are covered with a collection of the most varied maps of every corner of the world, thickly overlaid with sea routes. A lamp with a broad, dark shade hangs from the ceiling, giving a very pleasant soft light. Churchill nodded to the lamp and, pouring a whisky and soda,[196] said with satisfaction: 'The lamp was here

25 years ago, when I was naval minister for the first time. Then it was removed. Now they've put it up again.'

How very English!

Then Churchill led me over to a wide, folding door in the wall and opened it. In the deep niche I saw a map of Europe with old, faded small flags pinned onto it in various places.

'It's a map of the movements of the German navy in the last war. Every morning, on receiving the naval reconnaissance information, the flags were moved, meaning that we knew the location of each German ship at any given moment. I ordered this map 25 years ago. It's still in good condition. Now we will need it again. We just have to bring the flags up to date.'

I looked at Churchill with a smile and said: 'So, history repeats itself.'

'Yes, it repeats itself, and I'd be only too happy to philosophize about the peculiar romance of my returning to this room after a quarter of a century, were it not for the devilish task at hand of destroying ships and human lives.'

We returned to the present and I asked: 'What do you think about Hitler's peace proposals?'

Churchill sprang to his feet and, quite abruptly, began pacing the room: 'I've just looked them through and haven't had time to exchange views with my colleagues in the Cabinet. Personally, I find them absolutely unacceptable. These are the terms of a conqueror! But we are not yet conquered! No, no, we are not yet conquered!'

Churchill once again set about pacing the room in vexation.

'Some of my Conservative friends,' he continued, 'advise peace. They fear that Germany will turn Bolshevik during the war. But I'm all for war to the end. Hitler must be destroyed. Nazism must be crushed once and for all. Let Germany become Bolshevik. That doesn't scare me. Better communism than Nazism.'

But all this was just an opening flourish. The main story which Churchill wanted to discuss with me so late at night was the state of Anglo-Soviet relations.

Churchill asked me how we define the present state of our relations. I repeated to him what I had told Halifax on 27 September. Churchill listened to me attentively and then spent nearly an hour relating to me the British government's view of Anglo-Soviet relations. The essence of this view is as follows.

Anglo-Soviet relations have always been poisoned by the venom of mutual suspicion, today more than ever before. What are these suspicions? Britain suspects the USSR of having concluded a military alliance with Germany and that it will openly come out, one fine day, on Hitler's side against the Western powers. Churchill himself does not believe this, but many (including some in government circles) do. This circumstance cannot but affect the general tone of Britain's attitude to the USSR. On the other hand, the USSR suspects Britain of pursuing a hostile policy toward the USSR and of various machinations against it in the Baltic, Turkey, the Balkans and elsewhere. This condition cannot but affect the general tone of the Soviet attitude to Britain. Churchill understands why our suspicions are especially acute today. The Anglo-Franco-Soviet pact negotiations were conducted in a repulsive way (I know his view on this matter) and have left bad memories in Moscow's mind. But let the dead bury the dead. The present and the future are more important than the past. And the present and the future are precisely what Churchill wants to talk about.

His starting-point is that the basic interests of Britain and the USSR do not collide anywhere. I know this to have been his view in the past, as it is in the present. It follows that there is no reason why our relations should be poor or unsatisfactory.

In fact, what is the situation right now?

As a result of the events of recent weeks, East and South-East Europe have ended up outside the war zone. Is this a good thing or a bad thing from the point of view of correctly perceived British interests? A good thing. Therefore, the interests of the two parties in this matter coincide sooner than they conflict. We should not take too much to heart the criticism and indignation with which the Soviet–German non-aggression pact and the subsequent moves of the Soviet government have been met in Britain. This was due to their unexpectedness. The initial shock, however, has now passed, and people are beginning to see things in a more accurate perspective.

The Baltic States. The Soviet Union is going to be master of the eastern part of the Baltic Sea. Is this good or bad from the point of view of British interests? It is good. True, some Labour–Liberal sentimentalists shed tears over the 'Russian protectorates' established in Estonia and Latvia, but this should not be taken seriously. In essence, the Soviet government's latest actions in the Baltic correspond to British interests, for they diminish Hitler's potential *Lebensraum*. If the Baltic countries have to lose their independence, it is better for them to be brought into the Soviet state system rather than the German one. Moreover, the inclusion of the Baltic countries in the orbit of the USSR tallies with historical and geographical tendencies and, consequently, favours stabilization and peace in Eastern Europe.

Finally, the Balkans and the Black Sea. Churchill walked up to a big map of Europe and drew a sweeping line which approximately traced the new Soviet–German border and northern Rumania and Yugoslavia. He then exclaimed: 'Germany must not be allowed any further! It is especially important not to let Germany reach the Black Sea.'

He set about arguing, with some feeling, that if Germany were to reach the Danube estuary, it would not only seize the Balkans, but would inevitably extend itself also to Asia Minor, Iran and India. It would want to possess the Ukraine and Baku. Neither Britain nor the USSR can allow this to happen. Here, too, their interests coincide rather than clash. The Soviet government is greatly mistaken if it thinks that Britain is plotting against it in Turkey and the Balkans. Britain is interested in one thing only: not to let Germany reach the Black Sea. Hence its Balkan policy, its friendship with Turkey, and its wish to be able to send its navy through the Straits if need be. But if the Soviet Union, alone or together with Turkey, blocked Germany's access to the Black Sea, Britain might wrap up its Balkan policy and abandon its right of passage through the Straits. Britain has enough cares in other parts of the world.

What conclusion can be drawn from the above?

The conclusion is that today, just as before, the basic interests of Great Britain and the USSR do not collide, but coincide. It means that there is a common basis for good relations between our countries. The British government treats our declaration of neutrality as a positive fact, merely wishing for it to be benevolent neutrality.

I asked whether the Cabinet shared the thoughts which Churchill had just expounded to me. After all, I could hardly forget that only very recently Churchill was fiercely opposed to the British government, and Chamberlain in particular. Churchill replied: 'Naturally enough, the Cabinet is not responsible for every nuance of my statements, but what I told you reflects the views, by and large, of the entire government.'

Churchill asked me what could be done to improve relations between the two countries. Were there no useful steps or measures that I might recommend?

I refrained from offering advice. Churchill himself thought that the best way of alleviating tension would be to expand trade operations. Then, as though summing up his thoughts, he noted with a sly smile: 'Stalin is playing a big game at the moment and is doing so felicitously. He can be satisfied. But I fail to see why we should be dissatisfied.'

We parted 'like friends'. Churchill asked me to keep in close touch and to turn to him without ceremony whenever the need arose. I'll keep this in mind.

Returning home through dark, overcast streets, I couldn't help wondering: why was it Churchill, and not Halifax, who had that very important talk with me?

I can see two explanations: (1) the leading role which Churchill is gaining in the Cabinet and (2) Halifax's extreme annoyance with the USSR ever since the Soviet–German pact, rendering him an unsuitable channel for improving Anglo-Soviet relations. I know that Halifax was very reluctant to invite me to see him on 23 September. Only strong pressure from the Cabinet forced him to do so.

7 October

Elliot came for lunch. We spoke, as he put it, 'over the café table', that is, not like an ambassador and a minister of His Majesty's Government, but like two 'irresponsible students'.

In general, Elliot kept within the bounds of what I heard from Churchill yesterday. He regrets that the temperature of Anglo-Soviet relations has dropped to zero, he sees no serious basis for this, and thinks that urgent measures should be taken to improve our relations. But which?

Elliot is unclear on that score. He acknowledged that there is great confusion in government circles on the question of how to approach the USSR and find a common language with it. The British government does not wish to be rebuffed or affronted. That is why Elliot was asking my advice: what should be done?

I was very restrained on this matter with Elliot, as I had been with Churchill. He appears to have in mind a visit by some prominent Englishmen to Moscow, for he twice asked, half in jest, whether our agricultural exhibition was still open. He was also interested in the question of the possibility of an Anglo-Soviet non-aggression pact. It goes without saying that he also spoke about the expansion of trade.

I have a feeling that the ice in A[nglo]-S[oviet] relations is beginning to melt. Here is yet further proof. Dalton and Noel-Baker visited me on 5 October and stayed for two hours. We had a long and frank conversation, in which I *machte keine Mördergrube aus meinem Herzen* [did not conceal my thoughts]. They left me if not satisfied, then at least with a far better understanding of our position than they had before. At the end of our conversation they insisted that I tell them which measures are needed to improve Anglo-Soviet relations.

I replied: 'First and foremost, do something to stop your Labourites saying and writing stupidities about the USSR.'

My interlocutors laughed, but, it would seem, took my advice to heart.

11 October

There are two breeds of Labourites: 'idealists' and 'realists'. Both, of course, in quotation marks.

Yesterday I had a long conversation with the 'idealists', members of the Anglo-Russian Parliamentary Committee (Neil MacLean, Tom Williams, Tom

Sykes and others), who have experienced considerable emotional turmoil in recent weeks and are full of doubts. Some (like Tom Sykes) have experienced still sharper feelings with regard to Soviet foreign policy. My interlocutors constantly employed such terms and concepts as 'collective security', 'aggression', 'the League of Nations', etc., while quite failing to notice that they are moving in some astral world that has nothing in common with the realities of our days. Proceeding from those habitual but now dead notions, they criticized and failed to understand our actions in the field of foreign policy. We argued at length, and I must say that I found the company of those 'idealists' tedious and dreary.

Today Herbert Morrison, a bright representative of the 'realists' in the Labour movement, came for lunch. He expressed his position on the war in approximately the following way: 'Yes, of course it is an imperialist war in the sense that the fight is between Britain, which is defending its Empire, and Germany, which wishes to profit at the British Empire's expense. I, for one, prefer the British form of imperialism to the German. I prefer our, even imperfect, form of bourgeois democracy to the perfect German fascist form. Therefore, reasoning in terms of the theory of relative evil, I think it necessary to defend the British Empire against Germany. The masses, of course, should be offered this concept in an appropriate, touched-up form.'

Frank and cynical. To tell the truth, though, I prefer 'realists' to 'idealists': things are simpler and clearer with them. Less muddling. You know exactly *where you are.*

12 October

Today in parliament, Chamberlain delivered his long-awaited statement on Hitler's 'peace proposals' (of 6 October). The meaning of the statement is clear: No!

'Hitler's proposals,' the prime minister said, 'are unacceptable in themselves. What's more, we don't believe a single word spoken by this man. If Hitler really wants peace, he must first prove it in deeds, not words. Then we can start talking in earnest. It all depends on Hitler.'[197]

Attlee and Sinclair spoke in the same vein. Lansbury called for peace. Amery and Wedgwood dreamt of a European federation as an outcome of the war, but now called for a resolute continuation of the war. Cripps insisted on the urgent formulation of war aims such as might justify war and inspire the army. At the same time, he hinted that the matter at stake was not the redrawing of the map of Europe, but great social shifts and the rejection of imperialism. What naivety! It's ridiculous to appeal to a tiger in the hope that it parts with its claws and fangs. The general level of debate was not high, and I went to drink tea with Dalton and Philips Price.[i]

So, if Hitler makes no concessions in the next few days and suggests no new, more acceptable conditions of peace – directly or through neutrals (Mussolini, Roosevelt, etc.) – the war will start in earnest.

13 October

The Edens came to us for lunch. There were four of us and we conversed candidly. Eden was in a good mood. He is clearly delighted about returning to the bosom of government. His light grey suit and colourful tie gave him a cheerful, almost vernal appearance. His 'Beatrice', though, was all in black and unusually stern and silent.

We spoke, of course, about the burning issue of the moment – the war. Eden confessed that he was quite *puzzled* by our change of policy. He was in the camp with his battalion when news arrived of Ribbentrop's trip to Moscow. An officer woke him up in his tent at 6 a.m. to inform him. Eden exclaimed 'nonsense!', turned onto his side, and wanted to go back to sleep. So the officer thrust a fresh paper with the news under his nose. That made Eden jump out of bed right away. He was wide awake. And although subsequent events clarified a great deal for Eden, he still hasn't understood everything.

I explained to Eden in a few words the meaning and causes of the Soviet actions, beginning with the Soviet–German non-aggression pact. He listened to me attentively and seemed to display understanding.[198]

Then it was his turn to speak. He believes, just as he did four years ago, that British and Soviet interests do not seriously collide anywhere, on any issue or in any part of the world. What we observe today is a temporary and transient tension. It must be eased. How? Eden, like Churchill and Elliot, began sounding me out: mightn't an authoritative delegation be sent to Moscow? A trade delegation, perhaps? Or a delegation dealing with some other affairs? Or a member of government? What if Seeds were replaced with a more suitable person? Whom would we like: a diplomat, a politician, a public figure, a writer, Bernard Shaw? Mentioning Shaw, Eden openly smiled, but in essence he was dead serious.

Since I didn't know Moscow's feelings on the matter, I preferred to refrain from giving advice.[199]

As far as war is concerned, Eden strongly supported the official point of view. War is inevitable and must be fought to the end.

---

[i] Morgan Philips Price, correspondent of the *Manchester Guardian* in Russia, 1914–18 and of *Daily Herald* in Berlin, 1919–23; Labour MP, 1935–50.

14 October

Chamberlain is definitely beginning to rise in my esteem. In the sphere of foreign policy he was and remains, of course, 'the grave-digger of the Empire', but he is exceptionally skilful in domestic affairs, particularly in his ability to cling onto power and to manipulate British 'public opinion'. Current events in the country give the best possible testimony to this.

Indeed, the true nature of the war becomes clearer with each passing day. It is a purely imperialist war. One imperialist grouping, Britain and France, is defending its great wealth and world standing. Another imperialist power, Germany, is striving to snatch at least a part of Britain and France's possessions and to strengthen its position in the world. And since this struggle is occurring during the decline of the capitalist system, when enthusiasm is a less and less frequent product in the everyday life of bourgeois society, it would seem a very difficult, almost impossible task to form a united national front with which to pursue an imperialist war. Yet, somehow, Chamberlain manages to pull off this trick. For much longer? That's a different question. But for the moment he is succeeding.

How exactly do things stand?

I'll begin with the Conservatives. In this, the most crucial party, there is a certain group (Montagu Norman, some of the City businessmen and others) which fears a proletarian revolution in Germany and therefore wants to stop the war and conclude peace as soon as possible. For now, however, this is a small minority. The overwhelming majority supports 'war to the end'. Why? First, because any Conservative is ready to 'give his life' for the Empire, which not only supplies him with food and drink, but ensures his position as aristocrat among the ruling classes of all other capitalist states. Secondly, because the British bourgeoisie, despite everything, still feels itself to be strong and is convinced (a little presumptuously, perhaps) that, whatever the fate of Germany, Great Britain is not yet threatened by Soviet power. Therefore, they can and must fight. They must not let slip this favourable moment. And the moment, from the point of view of the British ruling class, really is favourable. Germany is weaker than it was in 1914, it is isolated, and it is exhausted physically and economically. England, meanwhile, has managed on this occasion to mobilize the Empire for war (a feat which many had doubted). The events in South Africa were especially indicative. She also succeeded in creating a united national front for the war inside the country. These things don't happen every day. Who knows whether they can be repeated some other time – in 6, 12, 18 months – should the necessity arise? Hence the conclusion: seize the moment, don't let it slip! Chamberlain isn't letting it slip. To buy off the internal opposition in the Tory Party, he brought Churchill and Eden into the government, who, for all the PM's flirting, are playing the parts not of bosses, but hostages.

Next, Labour. A cursory glance at His Majesty's opposition is enough to understand why the British bourgeoisie is not yet afraid of a proletarian revolution in its country. There is a group within Labour as well – quite motley in composition (with, on the one hand, advocates of non-resistance like Lansbury, and, on the other, left socialists like Cripps, Pritt and Ellen Wilkinson) – which opposes the war, but it is small (15 out of 150 at the last meeting of the parliamentary faction) and uncoordinated. The attitude of most Labourites is extremely bellicose, more so even than that of the Tories. This is understandable: the stewards are always more royalist than the king. Their mood can be ascribed to two main factors: (1) the 'imperial' motive also holds sway over the souls of Labour, although this is often bashfully veiled (as in the case of Morrison); and (2) Chamberlain bought off 'His Majesty's opposition' by declaring the fundamental war aim to be the struggle 'against Hitlerism' and for 'freedom and democracy'. The prime minister hypocritically dons the mask of an 'anti-fascist', while the swindlers and simpletons among the Labourites (both exist) fall into raptures and are ready to shed the blood of the masses in this imperialist dogfight.

As a result, even the old opposition, feeble and spineless as it was, has been liquidated. Labour no longer risks attacking the government in parliament. All they dare do is ask dutiful questions and offer deferential advice. Greenwood, a 'persona grata' at *10, Downing Street*, is especially servile, and the PM sends him personal letters (handwritten, not typed) beginning 'Dear Arthur'. The Tory press puffs him up at every opportunity, lavishing compliments on this 'true statesman'. Greenwood takes it all seriously and sees before him a career as prime minister of the National Government which is bound to be formed sooner or later in the course of the war. The situation in the trades unions is no better: under the leadership of Citrine, the governing bodies dance attendance on the government and frustrate the local union's attempts to resist the widespread worsening of labour conditions, which employers excuse on the grounds of 'the necessities of war'. There's no use even discussing the *Daily Herald*, which has broken all records of vileness, especially when it comes to the USSR. The ruling classes of England know exactly how to subordinate the apparatus of the 'workers' movement' to its interests and thereby take the masses with them. Chamberlain has carried off a clever trick that is especially noteworthy: he has kept the Labourites in his pocket, while not including them in his government. They are far more valuable to him in opposition. In this role they can be more effective in pulling the wool over the eyes of the workers.

The Liberals. Old Lloyd George, despite his 76 years, is a real nuisance to the government. He stands for peace, demanding a peace conference now, not after the war. But L-G is in the minority. The majority of the Liberals, headed by

Sinclair, support the government and, above all, the war. But to do them justice, they are more independent than Labour.

So the existence of a united national front is a fact. How strong it is and how long it will survive is difficult to predict. But for the moment it exists and it is led by Chamberlain. This front resolutely advocates 'war to the end'. In such circumstances, one may permit oneself the luxury of fighting for the Empire.

In conclusion, I should note one further characteristic feature. So great is the spiritual influence of the ruling clique here that it has also affected the British Communist Party to a significant extent. Initially, the Communist Party fought 'on two fronts': against German fascism and against the Chamberlain government for its inability to wage an effective struggle against the former. Only in early October did the Communist Party take the right stand: it recognized the war as imperialist and began agitating for peace. This change, however, was not without losses: Pollitt and Campbell[i] resigned from the Politburo.

I recall 1914. Then it was the Independent Labour Party, a strong and influential organization at the time, which opposed the war, albeit on pacifist grounds. Major 'national figures', such as MacDonald, Snowden,[ii] Robert Smillie[iii] and others, were against the war.

The situation today is different. Setting aside the Communist Party (in which disagreements also exist on the issue of war), there are neither influential organizations nor major 'national figures' leading opposition to the war in the rest of the workers' movement. Quite the reverse: Transport House and Parliamentary Labour are passionately belligerent. So far, at any rate. We'll see how things develop.

Indeed, 1939 is not 1914. It is easier for Chamberlain to conduct a war than it was for Asquith.[iv] At the same time, however, it will be far harder for capitalism to survive this current war. I even think that it will fail to do so, at least in Europe.

16 October

Halifax summoned me today and said that the British government would like to improve Anglo-Soviet relations. It is ready to discuss all possible measures with this end in view, but thinks it best to begin with trade (truly: a *nation of*

---

[i] John Ross Campbell, founding member of the British Communist Party and member of the Executive Committee of the Communist Party, 1923–64, and of Communist International, 1925–35.

[ii] Philip Snowden (1st Viscount Snowden), prominent Independent Labour Party leader.

[iii] Robert Smillie, president of the Scottish Miners' Federation, 1894–1918, and of the Miners' Federation of Great Britain, 1912–21; Labour MP for Morpeth, 1923–29.

[iv] Herbert Henry Asquith, prime minister of Great Britain 1908–1916, leader of the Liberal Party.

shopkeepers!). On 27 September, in response to his enquiry, I had informed Halifax that the Soviet government did not object to the opening of trade negotiations.[200] All well and good. Halifax conferred with Stanley and they both arrived at the conclusion that it would be better to talk with me in London first. Should these talks reveal a common platform, then further steps could be taken. Which steps exactly Halifax preferred not to divulge, but I gleaned from some of his hints and remarks that he had in mind a visit to Moscow by a serious British delegation.

I answered that I was, of course, always at his service and that I would communicate his proposal to Moscow.

Halifax then turned to Turkey. The British government fully understands that Turkey should have friendly relations with the USSR, but maintains that the interests of Britain and the USSR do not conflict in that corner of the globe and that Turkey's friendship with the USSR should not therefore hinder Turkey's friendship with Britain. Patently alluding to difficulties in the Soviet–Turkish talks, Halifax added that he would be only too glad to contribute to their successful conclusion.

Sounds a bit suspicious! Time will tell.

Halifax was especially interested in the state of affairs in the Baltic and asked me in detail about our pacts with the Baltic countries, the bases we have acquired, and the motives of our 'expansion' in that region. He mentioned Finland several times, and it was clear that he was greatly concerned about the Soviet–Finnish negotiations, without, however, having decided on a direct démarche on this matter. Eventually, he said by way of a summary: 'Well, perhaps you are right to say that your actions in the Baltics stabilize relations and serve the cause of peace in Eastern Europe.'

Halifax asked for my opinion of the prime minister's speech on 12 October. I made do with empty phrases, then asked: 'What would be the response of the British government if Hitler were to make some new proposals?'

Halifax replied: 'Any new proposal by Hitler would be considered and discussed *on its merits*.'

* * *

Went to see the Webbs yesterday. The old man has made an excellent recovery and looks fine. Better still, he has started speaking quite decently. He said to me proudly: 'Now I can walk for an hour and read a lot. But I can't think and write.'

Can't think and write! How hard it must be for a man who has spent his entire life thinking and writing in the most intensive way!

Bearing in mind, however, that Sidney Webb has turned 81, there can be little cause for complaint about his current condition. Especially since his memory never fails him even now.

Beatrice Webb spoke a great deal about the war. Her forecasts are gloomy. The war will continue. She sees no basis for a peace conference at the present time. This renders immense sacrifices and losses inevitable. There will probably be a revolution in Germany, followed by a civil war. In all likelihood, the USSR will support the revolution, at least by supplying arms, ammunition and so on. Britain, France and the USA will support counter-revolution by the same means. A covert war may occur on German soil between the USSR on the one side and the bourgeois democratic powers on the other. Covert war may easily grow into open conflict. It is difficult to predict how this will all end.

I argued at length with my host and reproached her for her excessive pessimism…

How much snobbery there is even in the best English people! In conversation with the Webbs, I mentioned what Churchill said to me the other day: 'Better communism than Nazism!' Beatrice shrugged her shoulders and noted that such a statement was not typical of the British ruling elite, and I would tend to agree. But then, for some reason, she found it necessary to add: 'Churchill is not a true Englishman, you know. He has negro blood. You can tell even from his appearance.'

Then Beatrice Webb told me a long story about Churchill's mother coming from the South of the USA and there being some negro blood in her family. Her sister looked just like a 'negroid'.

Then I happened to mention the famous African explorer Henry Stanley,[i] who lived in the second half of the last century. Beatrice Webb suddenly became agitated: it transpired that she had known him in her youth. She described Stanley as a rather unpleasant man – and I am quite prepared to believe her – but one thing shocked me. Relating the elderly Stanley's marriage to a beautiful young girl, who was a friend of hers, Beatrice said with a certain distaste: 'At the time everyone was astonished by this match. She came from a very good family, an educated, considerate and beautiful girl, while he was a real upstart, a coarse, uncouth fellow.'

Beatrice appealed to her husband, whose expression and gestures indicated full assent.

The crux of the matter is that Stanley was the son of a small farmer, studied in a school for the poor, served as a ship's boy, experienced the hard life of a worker and clerk in America, and only much later broke through as a journalist. Stanley was a true plebeian, and that matters, even to the Webbs.

[i] Henry Morton Stanley, commanded the search expedition for the missionary David Livingstone, 1871–72, and discovered the source of the Congo River.

17 October

I had a telling conversation today with Butler (parliamentary undersecretary for foreign affairs). We lunched *tête-à-tête* and he spoke very candidly.

First and foremost I was interested in the prospects of Hitler's 'peace offensive'. Butler replied: 'None for the moment. Not because we are against peace – on the contrary, we very much wish to avoid war, and that is why we need a solid and lasting peace and assurance about this peace. We need the assurance that if we conclude peace today, it will not be broken in six months' time. We are ready to pay a high price for a solid and lasting peace of 20–25 years. We would not even refuse Germany substantial colonial concessions. We have a large Empire and we do not need every part of it. Something could be found for the Germans. Not Tanganyika, of course, which could easily be turned into a naval and air base on the Indian Ocean, but perhaps Togo, Cameroon, etc. But we must be guaranteed that if we make concessions now and conclude an agreement, peace and the status quo will be ensured for at least a whole generation. Otherwise it makes no sense.'[201]

'What kind of guarantees do you want?' I asked.

Butler replied: 'Either Germany must have a different government, which we can take at its word, or the peace treaty and its observance must be guaranteed by all the great powers, including the USA and the USSR. The USSR was not admitted to the Munich settlements, and experience shows that such a treaty has no value. Any future decision has to be taken with the participation of the Soviet Union. Since I see no possibility at the present moment of a treaty being concluded that would provide for a solid, lasting peace, we have no way out but war, counting on the superiority of our resources over those of Germany. That is why Hitler's "peace offensive" is to be considered a failure. But that does not of course preclude another "peace offensive" in the future, one which may have much better chance of success. "Peace offensives" will probably arise more than once in the course of the war. One or other will meet with success.'

'But which?' I intervened.

Butler just shrugged his shoulders.

Then the conversation moved on to Anglo-Soviet relations. During the whole period of his employment in the Foreign Office (since Eden's retirement) Butler has upheld the view that no contradictions exist between Britain and the USSR and that rapprochement between them is therefore possible and desirable. Butler was highly critical of the way in which Anglo-Soviet talks on a tripartite pact were conducted. Today, without concealing his regret about the failure of those talks, Butler assured me, like many before him, that the British government wants very much to improve Anglo-Soviet relations, but does not know where to begin. Politics? Trade? Dispatching a member of the Cabinet to Moscow? But who exactly? Could I not make a suggestion? Or perhaps a new ambassador should be appointed to replace Seeds? In short, he covered almost exactly the same ground with me as had Eden, Elliot and Churchill. Butler dropped obvious hints that he would not be at all averse to visiting the USSR himself. As always, I was very circumspect and refrained from giving advice.

As if to prove the sincerity of the British government's desire to improve relations with the USSR, Butler touched upon two questions:

(1) Poland. The British government does not contemplate the restoration of Poland within its former borders. All it aspires to is an ethnographic Poland (resembling the 'Duchy of Warsaw' of Napoleonic times) guaranteed by the USSR, Germany, Britain and France. Nobody in Britain is thinking of returning Western Ukraine and [Western] Belorussia to Poland. Zaleski,[i] who recently visited London, also made no claim on the territories occupied by the Soviet Union, but – oh, these incorrigible Polish gentlemen! – he did demand East Prussia on strategic grounds. Zaleski envisaged the expulsion of Germans from this province of Germany and its colonization by Poles.

(2) Turkey. England considers Soviet–Turkish friendship to be in its own interest and would be prepared to assist in every possible way the conclusion of an agreement between Moscow and Ankara. Butler added that Turkey was in constant contact with London during Saraçoğlu's[ii] stay in Moscow, and the British government sanctioned all those changes in the Anglo-Turkish pact that would follow from the Moscow talks. Thus, the British government did not object to Turkey's non-participation in a war against the Soviet Union under any conditions. It was also prepared to accept the closing of the Straits to warships. She stood only against the division of the Balkans into Soviet and German 'spheres of influence'. On the whole, Butler merely elaborated in greater detail what Halifax told me yesterday. He even admitted that recent weeks have shown how little Britain can do to influence events in Eastern Europe. The British government is prepared to draw from this the necessary practical conclusions.

What Butler told me is very interesting, but needs to be properly digested. Clearly, the British government is greatly concerned about the current situation and would like to set Anglo-Soviet relations straight. But what's behind all this? We must see.

---

[i] Count August Zaleski, Polish foreign minister, 1926–32, and foreign minister in the Polish government in exile, 1939–41.

[ii] Mehmet Şükrü Saraçoğlu, Turkish foreign minister, 1938–42, and prime minister, 1942–46.

19 October

Today I saw Lloyd George for a few minutes. The old man was leaving for Wales, where he is to make a speech on peace at a big rally on the 21st. I caught him at the station. Sitting in his compartment, Lloyd George painted a picture of the present with his usual fervour.

At the moment neither Germany on the one side, nor Britain and France on the other, can make concessions capable of guaranteeing peace. Neither the United States nor the Soviet Union wishes to act as mediator. Mussolini is also silent, and, what's more, he is not sufficiently respectable. In these circumstances, the continuation of war is inevitable. Especially now, after the sinking of the *Royal Oak* at Scapa Flow ('A tidy job!' L-G exclaimed with a mixture of envy and admiration). The British are furious. Their bulldog instincts have been aroused. Today, the mood in the country is less favourable for peace than it was last week, and it is quite possible that the rally on the 21st will be Lloyd George's last opportunity to speak about peace in public.

The old man asked whether a peace initiative could be expected from the Soviet Union.

I answered vaguely, for even though I had some grounds for believing that Moscow is discussing the possibility of our mediation, I had no definite information.

'If only the USSR would act!' L-G exclaimed. 'That would have huge significance.'

Then the old man added with a laugh: 'But of course, if the USSR did want to act, it would have to act not as an "ally" of Germany, but as a genuinely neutral power capable of taking an absolutely independent stand at a peace conference. Otherwise the Soviet proposal would be immediately discredited in the eyes of the British public, and the whole business would collapse.'

21 October

The new Italian ambassador Bastianini[i] paid me his first visit today. A man of average height, with black hair and brown eyes, and lively, impulsive gestures. A true Italian. Not like Grandi, who, whether in appearance, behaviour or manners, did not live up to the classic image of the Italian handed down to us in books and at school.

Bastianini has just arrived from Rome. Showing particular interest, Halifax sent his car to pick him up at Dover – a sign of the times! Bastianini asked me

[i] Giuseppe Bastianini, Italian ambassador to Great Britain, 1939–40.

about the mood in England, especially with regard to the war. I gave him a brief account. Then I asked him about Italy's position, and in particular whether Mussolini was planning to act as mediator.

Bastianini denied this categorically: Mussolini deems the situation unsuitable for mediation. Feelings in Berlin and London are such that agreement between them is hardly possible. Berlin is ranting and raving against London and is openly setting itself the task of crushing Britain. Ribbentrop and others are firmly convinced that they will be able to attain this goal even if it requires a protracted war. At the same time, London continues to declare that it will not agree to any peace without a guarantee by all the great powers of the inviolability of the peace treaty, and there is hardly much chance of such a guarantee today. Why invite obvious failure in such a situation?

I enquired about Italy's position in the present war. Bastianini said some rather interesting things. He told me, for instance, that when Ciano visited Salzburg and Berchtesgaden in August, he tried to persuade the Germans on behalf of Mussolini not to launch a war against Poland, stressing that Britain and France would undoubtedly enter the fray and a dangerous situation would be created. In Mussolini's opinion, the Polish question could be resolved without a war. Ribbentrop poured ridicule on Ciano and told him that the 'democracies' would 'chicken out' at the last moment and betray Poland. Hitler seconded Ribbentrop. Consequently Mussolini stated that in view of this serious divergence of views, he could take no part in the war and would remain neutral. Hitler had to accept this.

* * *

Yesterday my guests for lunch were the minister of supply, Burgin, Leith-Ross (now director-general of the Ministry of Economic Warfare), Ashton-Gwatkin, Hemming, Degwell and others.

Burgin assured me that the British government wished to improve relations with the Soviet Union and, in particular, to increase Anglo-Soviet trade. Leith-Ross enquired with some insistence whether we might be thinking of waging war against Britain and was very pleased to hear from me that we wanted to remain neutral, so long as Britain did not force us to change our stance by its actions. Leith-Ross, like Burgin, said that Britain did not intend to fight us; on the contrary, it intended to restore good relations by any means available. Both Burgin and Leith-Ross asserted that if Roosevelt were to take the lead in mediating, Britain and France would enter into negotiations, but so far Roosevelt had shown no desire to do this.

24 October

A strange war!

It's as if you were on the western front. The bulletins of the French general staff contain phrases such as: 'the night passed uneventfully', 'the day was marked by patrol operations', 'German forces about the size of a single company mounted an offensive', etc. The bulletins of the German general staff are in the same vein.

In the skies, we also see only minor advance guard operations, with no serious consequences. The Germans announced proudly over the radio not long ago that they have shot down 37 French and 12 British planes in the course of almost an entire month. The English, in their turn, boasted some three days ago that of the 30 German machines that recently raided Scotland, 25% were destroyed! What astonishing successes!

The war at sea is a bit more serious. The British blockade is being conducted in earnest, and the Germans feel it. More than 20 submarines have been sunk by the British and the French. One hears that this represents between a quarter and a third of the German submarine fleet. This might be possible, were it not for the fact that the Germans have begun manufacturing submarines as quickly as they produce aircraft. Germany, in turn, has delivered a number of impressive blows to Britain at sea, of which the most painful was, of course, the loss of the *Royal Oak* at Scapa Flow. This was a truly superb strike on the part of Germany and a shameful failure for Britain. Still, even at sea 'real' war has not yet begun.

A strange war! One gains the impression that everything that is being done today is just an opening flourish: the main story is still ahead of us. Sometimes it seems to me that on the European arena, before my very eyes, two prize fighters are circling one another, sizing each other up, sniffing, spitting on their palms, and occasionally giving each other little shoves, as if to test one another's vigilance and readiness for the fight. But the real fight has not yet started. Something is holding them back from delivering the first resolute blow; something restrains their energy, their will, and their muscles…

What?

If one listens to the local 'sages', there is a simple and natural explanation for everything.

The British and the French, they say, are counting on wearing their opponents down. The Allies have time on their side. Their aim, with minimum human losses to themselves, is to impose a long 'siege' on the enemy's fortress by way of a blockade, pressure on the western front, air operations, and the economic and diplomatic encirclement of Germany. Let this siege last one, two, three or more years – the Allies are far richer than Germany in resources and capability, and in the long run they ought to win. That is why the Allies do not want to seize the initiative in any major, sensational operations on the western front or even in the skies. Major air initiatives might shock US 'public opinion', which is always taken into account here. Besides, winter is approaching. The mud and weather conditions make serious operations on the front impossible until spring. All the better. We shall save our strength for March. In the meantime, Germany will become not stronger, but weaker.

On the other hand – the same people say – Germany is slow to pursue the war in earnest, since Hitler fears war, would like to avoid it, and seeks ways and means to conclude peace. On 6 October, Hitler made his peace proposals. They were rejected by Britain and France. He refuses to accept, however, that his 'peace offensive' has failed. Germany has poor resources and difficulties with food supply. Within Germany, Hitler, Ribbentrop and the other adherents of the 'Russian Entente' line are wrestling with the Reichswehr leaders, the landlords of East Prussia, and the big industrialists, who dread 'playing games with Bolshevism'. In the international sphere, Germany is isolated. Japan and Spain have turned their backs on Germany. Italy acts ambivalently. The USSR cares only for its own interests and is not going to make any sacrifices on behalf of Germany. Waging war means certain defeat for Germany, with all the ensuing consequences. Sure enough, Hitler is frantically searching for ways to annul the war through some sort of Anglo-French agreement. Despite disappointments, he still pins his hopes on the 'rotten state of the democracies' and continues to trust his phenomenal 'luck'. That is why he is in no hurry to move onto the attack, all the more so as the approach of winter does indeed render large military operations difficult (although not entirely impossible).

Are these speculations correct?

Yes and no. They are correct in so far as they accurately portray the state of affairs and the alignment of forces on both sides. They are incorrect in so far as they leave out one very important motive, perhaps the crucial, most fundamental one, which paralyses the rivals' will to fight.

This crucial, fundamental motive is a vague, elementary, deep-seated terror felt by the ruling classes on both sides of the front: terror of a proletarian revolution. Wherever I turn here I keep hearing that 'in the final reckoning only Russia stands to gain from the war', or that 'when the Western capitalist countries cut one another's throats, communism will triumph', or else that 'a long war will definitely lead to a revolution in Germany – and what will become of Britain, and of Europe, then?', and so on and so forth. There is no doubt that similar conversations may be heard now among Germany's ruling elite.

It is this fear which keeps the two 'prize fighters' from fully launching themselves on one another. They're scared stiff. What will their fight lead to? The future is fraught with frightening possibilities. A terrifying spectre, the spectre of communism, haunts Europe – in a far more real and direct form than it did at the time of Marx's *Communist Manifesto*. Is there no way of avoiding historical destiny, even if it means crawling on all fours?

There is no shortage of symptoms to indicate that the ruling elites on both sides of the front are trying even now to find a modus for a deal, an agreement.

Will they succeed? I doubt it. The imperialist contradictions within the dying capitalist system are so deep that constructing a bridge between them is difficult even for Chamberlain and Daladier. Barring a truly extraordinary turn of events – some sort of real political 'miracle' – a terrible, bestial, blind slaughter will begin in the very nearest future.

[Although Molotov kept Maisky very much at arm's length, the ambassador continued to seek an improvement in relations through trade negotiations at his meeting with Halifax on 25 October and with Oliver Stanley, president of the Board of Trade. He also exerted indirect pressure on Halifax to replace Seeds in Moscow with an ambassador who enjoyed the confidence of the British government and yet was favourably disposed towards Russia. Aware of the gap between his position and that of Molotov, his correspondence continued to be highly censored. He nonetheless pursued his subversive line, overlooking Molotov's instructions of 11 November to hint to Halifax that, since British policy was not defined by Churchill and Eden and remained hostile, 'the Soviet government does not see at the present time encouraging possibilities' for an improvement in relations.[202] Molotov's reserve betrayed his belief that the British lay behind the Finnish intransigence in the negotiations that were under way. Vansittart – formerly an ally of Maisky's, but now highly critical of him – alerted Halifax that Maisky 'was going beyond his functions as a foreign ambassador'. He had been 'entertaining several members of the Cabinet at different times (and incidentally boasting about it behind their backs), though the gambits that he plays on them are of course very different from his typical moves among the dupes'.[203]]

26 October

In the last few days, the government has emblazoned the entire political front with the slogan '*not to antagonize Russia*', in order 'not to push it into Germany's arms'. Evidently, this has also affected the matter of trade negotiations. A whole month has passed since my talk with Halifax on 27 September without any progress (except for a purely commercial deal between the Ministry of Supply and the trade mission concerning the exchange of 88,000 timber standards for 10,000 tons of rubber and 600 tons of tin). Then yesterday, all of a sudden, things started moving at a speed quite unfamiliar to the English.

First, Halifax invited me over to say that the British government had instructed Stanley to enter into talks with me about the immediate prospects for Anglo-Soviet trade and that Stanley was hoping to see me today. I agreed to the meeting, and Halifax undertook to inform the Minister for Trade. Then Halifax asked me about the incident with the *City of Flint*[204] and about our talks with Finland, expressing the hope that peaceful relations between the Soviet Union and Finland would be maintained. I could hardly illuminate Halifax about the first matter, for my own information about the incident came only from TASS and newspaper reports. As far as the second question was concerned, I did my best to reassure Halifax along the lines of Comrade Kalinin's letter to Roosevelt on the subject. It was clear, however, that Halifax was interested not in Finland itself, but in the effect the Finnish situation could have on Anglo-Soviet relations. That's why Halifax set about assuring me once again that the B[ritish] G[overnment] very much wished to improve or 'at least not to worsen' our trade relations and that the forthcoming trade negotiations would be just the first step in this direction. However, the honourable Lord's assurances were accompanied by such an evident lack of faith in the possibility of anything being achieved that I sniggered and called him an 'incorrigible pessimist'.

Secondly, my meeting with Stanley took place late yesterday evening. Also present was Cripps, who has been displaying great energy behind the scenes with regard to the matter of improving Anglo-Soviet relations. This even led to his recent appointment as legal adviser to the Board of Trade. At Stanley's request, I came to his flat. We talked for about an hour.

Stanley spoke at some length about the British government's desire to maintain or even expand Anglo-Soviet trade and suggested that we begin talks on the plan for next year's trade between our countries. He will present me with a provisional list of the goods Britain would like to buy from us in 1940, and we will prepare the same for the British government – this will allow us to reach agreement on the yearly balance. The trade plan involves many other issues that should also be discussed, such as prices, licences, transport, etc. Stanley thinks that the first, preparatory part of the negotiations should be held in London. If and when it becomes clear that an agreement is likely, Stanley will go to Moscow to 'crown' the whole business. As he can stay in Moscow for only a couple of days, it would be good to do all the drafting and preparatory work in England. I promised Stanley that I would consult with the Soviet government just as soon as he provided me with a plan for British purchases, albeit in the most provisional form, and a rough outline of what Britain could export to the USSR in 1940.

Today Stanley sent me this 'plan', or rather a rough draft. The British government intends to buy goods from us to the value of no less than 12 million pounds (timber and raw materials to a sum of more than 9 million, including petrol and oil to the sum of 1.5 million) and is ready to provide us, 'for the USSR's internal use', with rubber, tin, lead, jute, certain types of copper, etc. Regarding machines, equipment and so on, the draft is highly cautious: the British government is prepared to discuss the matter, but does not promise anything.

I communicated all this to Moscow. We'll be waiting for the response.

Cripps told me that the British government was very keen for Stanley to visit Moscow, but feared that his visit could end in failure, which would be a blow to the Cabinet's prestige. Stanley is also wary of failure, for the effect it would have on his career. So the British government's aim is for the ground to be prepared as thoroughly as possible, so as to be sure of striking lucky. In Cripps's words, 'Stanley does not wish to follow in Saraçoğlu's footsteps.'

[There follows a newspaper cutting dated 27 October 1939 and entitled 'New UK–Russia Trade Moves. Negotiations Opened for Barter Pact'.]

27 October

Yet another year has passed! I've been ambassador in England for seven years now, and how many events, changes and people have I seen in that time!

I've even lived to see the war. What a capricious turn of fate: I was here in London when the first imperialist war began and spent most of it here. Now I'm here again to see the second imperialist war in its European development. In time, a quarter of a century stands between them, but politically and psychologically it's as if they are centuries apart. Like two different epochs in the history of humankind. And all this in the space of one short life!…

28 October

'How old are you, if you may excuse such an indiscreet question?'

'Why indiscreet? I'm 55. And you?'

'Oh, I'm significantly older than you… I'm 57.'

'You surprise me! What does a two-year difference mean for men of our age?'

Horace Wilson (for it was he) shrugged his shoulders and said: 'Perhaps you are right. But that's not the point. The point is that you belong to the same generation as I and must remember the time when only one event happened at any given moment, not a hundred, when one could live, breathe, move without haste, make plans for the future and, most important, *ponder*. Are you familiar with this English word?'

'Yes, I am.'

'Well, I like to *ponder* on life, people and events. But now I have absolutely no opportunity do so. Events are unfolding at such a frenzied, unstoppable pace that one barely has time to breathe. So what chance does one have of controlling events? You can count yourself lucky just to flow with the current and avoid the most overpowering blows coming from right and left.'

I gazed at this unprepossessing, skinny man with his calm, somewhat feline movements, a face both intelligent and sly, the man into whose hands capricious fate had placed the future of the British Empire, and found myself wondering: 'Is this true or not? Is he speaking sincerely or playing some premeditated role?'

We sat down to table and moved on to other topics. The war, of course, immediately became the focus of our attention. I asked Wilson what he thought about the prospects for peace. Once again Wilson shrugged his shoulders and began 'thinking aloud', as he likes to do. He reasoned in approximately the following way: 'In theory, the question of peace can still be raised. For war has not yet begun in earnest. Bombs are not yet falling on London and Berlin. The warring passions of the masses are still dormant; they have not yet reached boiling point. The people are still able to think calmly and to reason. In six or twelve months' time this is likely to be far more difficult. However, when you approach the problem of peace from a practical point of view, you immediately see that it is almost impossible to resolve.'

Wilson took a sip of soda water (he firmly declined the offer of wine) and continued: 'Where can peace come from? There is no chance of us taking the first step, especially after Ribbentrop's speech. That speech, among other things, suggests that Hitler also has no intention of offering the hand of peace. The neutrals are silent and evidently have no wish to interfere. So where can peace come from?'

'But what if one of the neutrals did interfere? Roosevelt, say, or Mussolini? How would Britain respond?'

'Roosevelt will not interfere,' Wilson replied. 'We know that for certain. As for Mussolini… We feel a certain amount of distrust towards Mussolini. Even if he invited us to Milan or Turin tomorrow to meet Hitler, we would of course decline the invitation. We would first need to know why we were being invited and on what basis. And we would need to know what the chances were of reaching an agreement. Otherwise, arranging conferences is senseless. A conference requires careful preparatory work, but there are no signs whatsoever of such work being done. Add to this the fact that we would have to talk with Hitler! We don't believe a single word from this man's mouth!'

'Does it mean,' I asked, 'that the precondition for any talks about peace is the disappearance of Hitler? And even, perhaps, of all his closest associates?'

'Yes, we would like to deal with a different government in Germany,' Wilson answered. 'The disappearance of Hitler alone would be sufficient. I have, as you know, had dealings with Hitler. I looked at him for hours, observed him, weighed him up, and this is my impression: Hitler stands so much taller than his associates and dominates them all to such an extent – just like a mountain over a valley – that if he were to go, the rest would cut each other's throats (they are already at daggers drawn) and would stop disturbing the peace in Europe.

Let the "National Socialist Party" remain, if the Germans so wish, so long as its current leadership disappears. We'll manage to come to terms with everyone else.'

When Wilson spoke of Hitler, I discerned personal hostility, almost hatred, in his tone of voice and in his eyes. Clearly, he is unable to forget how Hitler '*let him down*' with such contempt and cruelty. I've heard that Chamberlain now bears the same personal malice and hatred towards Hitler.

'But since the disappearance of Hitler and others is politically unrealistic at present, then it follows that you consider peace impossible in the next few weeks or even months. Isn't that so?'

'That's probably true,' answered Wilson. 'Besides, I think that the Germans, the German people, must be given a "lesson" in order for them to start thinking and feeling differently. So far they have not had such a "lesson". This is evident from the stories we hear from prisoners of war in our custody. Many of them did not even know right up to the last moment that Britain and France had declared war on Germany. We can give the Germans the "lesson" they need. I am fully confident of our eventual victory.'[205]

I objected that the Germans had already been given a 'lesson' at Versailles, but this failed to secure a lasting peace in Europe. Where is the guarantee that the new peace treaty with which this war, sooner or later, must end, will be better than Versailles? It is far more likely to be even worse, and several times worse at that.

The conversation then turned to the question of how the current war should end. Wilson again began thinking aloud, and his thoughts were most curious.

The future Germany which will emerge from the war should cease to be a unified, centralized Germany, but should turn into a 'free federation' of German states, as was the case in the past. Austria, Bavaria, Württemberg, etc. should become half-independent states within the framework of the federation. Czechoslovakia could also become a member of the German federation, with similar rights to the British dominions. Poland should be restored as an independent state on its ethnographic foundation, without Western Ukraine and Western Belorussia. The German federation might be allowed to establish a condominium with Britain and France in the former German colonies. Disarmament, or at least arms limitation, should then follow. In general, peace and order should be established in Europe, and Germany should be placed in conditions that would prevent her from violating this order.

'We would like,' Wilson concluded, 'for calm to reign at last. For it to be possible to live without mobilization every six months. For these perpetual crises to come to an end. For us to be able to think again about our own affairs, our pleasures, and our holidays.'

The true philosophy of old, rich imperialism, with its surfeit of everything!

Wilson 'complained' that the French were taking a more radical stand than the British, refusing to differentiate between Hitler's regime and the German nation (as the British always do) and cherishing the idea of breaking Germany up into small independent states, disarmed and helpless. These French sentiments exert an inevitable influence on the English. But they are dangerous and could have grave consequences.

I listened to Wilson's 'complaints' and smiled to myself. Was his project of a 'free German federation' so very different from the French idea of partitioning? And won't Wilson – at a certain historical turning point, especially in the heated atmosphere of a real war – change his mind and agree to that very partitioning in the name of solidarity with a 'brave ally' and the greater glory of the policy of 'compromise' which he so loves?

Of course he'll agree to it. It's obvious from the tenor of everything he told me today that in reality he does not visualize any other way of maintaining the present position of British imperialism. He will have to bless partition… provided the Soviet Union allows it.

[Attached is a cutting from the *Evening Standard* of 23 December 1939, corroborating Maisky's impressions. The leader argues that Horace Wilson was the most influential figure in the Cabinet, enjoying Chamberlain's full support, particularly in the conduct of foreign policy. The article also points out Wilson's connections to the City.]

30 October

Agniya and I dined at the Elliots'. White had some trouble finding their house (60, Eaton Square) because of the black-out. It was a very intimate dinner, in daytime attire. Also present, besides the hosts and us, were the husband of Mrs Elliot's sister, the Conservative MP Dugdale[i] (he is one of the party's whips), and Bernays, deputy minister of transport. During dinner, we joked, laughed and told funny stories. Then, when the 'ladies retired', serious conversation began. About the war, of course, or, more precisely, about war and peace.

Elliot is clearly worried about the current situation and the prospects for the future. A former 'Fabian', he has a deeper understanding of many things than his Conservative colleagues. His view boils down to the following: 'Of course it is true that in essence the war is being pursued to secure the position of England and France in the world, is there anything unnatural or unlawful about this? Why should Britain concede its position without a fight to Germany, which, moreover, has supplied record-beating examples of vileness, cruelty, and obscurantism in recent years? Nonetheless, if the English and the French could

[i] Thomas Lionel Dugdale, junior lord of the Treasury, 1937–40; deputy chief government whip, 1941–42.

hold on to their fundamental positions without war, then it would be better to end it. Who needs millions of victims? Who needs terrible destruction and losses? Who needs the extreme animosity that is the inevitable consequence of a long war? Animosity which can easily lead to a new, magnified Versailles? And a new Versailles, in its turn, would mean a new war after a short period of time. All over again. So, if war can be avoided, why not do so? But can it? The British and the French cannot embark on peace negotiations or a peace conference unless certain conditions are met, primarily the restoration of Poland and Czechoslovakia. Not, of course, in their former boundaries. Is Germany ready to make such concessions? Doubtful. For Germany is not yet beaten. So is there any point talking about peace and conferences? Such conversations can only derail the "moral mobilization" of the Western democracies. This "mobilization" was far from easy and cost a great deal of effort, but now it's in full swing. Spoil the mood of today and you might well not be able to recover it next time. Why take the risk if there are no guarantees that negotiations will yield a favourable outcome?'

This has its own 'imperialist' logic. I remember what Elliot told me some three weeks ago: 'Last time, four years of war gave us 20 years of peace and guaranteed our positions in the world. This game is worth the candle.'

Candid and cynical.

Elliot, Bernays and Dugdale all kept asking me what could be done to improve Anglo-Soviet relations. The same old questions: perhaps Seeds should be replaced? Maybe a prominent member of the government should be sent to Moscow? Whom exactly?

I refused to give any advice.

* * *

The English are a cunning lot!

Our note of 25 October concerning contraband flickered on the pages of the press for a single day, then everyone fell silent, as if prompted by a magic wand. Yet the note touches a raw English nerve.

The explanation is simple. First, there is once again no need '*to antagonize Russia*'. Secondly, no one knows what the practical consequences of the note will be. Maybe none at all. Maybe the 'Bolsheviks' just made a 'gesture' to please Hitler – after all, they have to find some way of paying for the real benefits they obtained from the pact with Germany. If they intend to pay with bits of paper, is that any great cause for concern? If the note grows into something more serious, we'll have plenty of time to pick a fight about it. For the moment, we're better off keeping our counsel. There's no great rush.

Such are the thoughts and reasoning of the English, which can be heard at every turn.

Yes, the English are a cunning lot! But all their cunning won't help them find a painless solution for the 'upper ten thousand' of the key problem of the forthcoming epoch: who – whom?[206]

31 October

I arranged a lunch for Hore-Belisha. He was half an hour late (it's said that his pretty driver was to blame) and kept the guests waiting: General Kirke,[i] William Strang, Bernays, the Bulgarian minister Momchilov[ii] and others. It was an awkward situation.

At lunch, the conversation was, of course, mainly about the war. Hore-Belisha, as befits a minister of war, takes a negative view of the idea of peace.

'Peace with Hitler,' he said, 'is impossible. A different government is needed in Germany to make peace. We shall fight until we have such a government. Let it be a government of communists – I believe this may conceivably happen at the end of the first year of the war – we don't care. It'll be easier for us to come to an arrangement with communists than with Hitler.'

I made an attempt to elucidate what exactly Hore-Belisha intended to come to an arrangement with communists about, but he was very evasive and vague. Still, I understood from some of his allusions that the future, post-war Germany should be disarmed and built on the 'federation' principle. In other words, we are dealing once again with the partitioning of Germany.

Hore-Belisha spoke about the war itself with greater interest and greater energy.

'We do not intend to launch large-scale offensive operations,' he said. 'Our tactics are defensive in principle. We would be only too glad for the Germans to begin a broad offensive along the Maginot Line or even across Holland and Belgium, for they would then suffer colossal losses, while British and French losses would be negligible. There are no impregnable military positions in the world. Any position can be taken, if enough lives are expended. Even the Maginot Line can be broken. But, even if the Germans were to carry through such an operation, they would be too exhausted to be able to deliver a decisive blow. The Germans understand this, and that is why I think that, at least until spring, things will be relatively quiet on the western front.'

'In other words,' I remarked, 'you are saying that the Germans will also be waging a war of attrition?'

'No, that's not what I think,' Hore-Belisha retorted. 'Germany cannot risk such a war. It needs a rapid solution, or at least an attempt at one. That is why I fear some kind of mad move on the part of Hitler.'

---

[i] Sir Walter Mervyn St George Kirke, general, director-general of Territorial Army, 1936–39; inspector-general of home defences, 1939; commander-in-chief of home forces, 1939–40.
[ii] Nicola Momchilov, Bulgarian ambassador to London, 1938–41.

'What do you mean?'

'Well, a massive air bombardment of England, for example. Hitler may go for broke and throw all his air force against us at once.'

I inquired about the effectiveness of the air defence. [Hore-]Belisha replied that it was now in good order: 130,000 people, all over England, are involved in it. The country is saturated with anti-aircraft artillery. In London, in particular, any enemy plane would find itself under fire at any given moment from 50 to 100 anti-aircraft guns. On the whole, the British think (based on Scotland's experience) that the enemy loses 25–30% of its machines every raid. The joint Anglo-French air force is presently equal to, or a little weaker than, the German air force, but it will be notably stronger by spring. Irrespective of American deliveries, Anglo-French production is immense (a monthly output of 1,500 machines in England) and is increasing each month.

Hore-Belisha revealed interesting information concerning the war at sea. Before the war began, the Germans had a maximum of 65 submarines (including 30 of the ocean-going type). The British and the French have destroyed at least 22. The Germans are able to manufacture 5–8 submarines monthly, but the main problem is the crews, which require long training and outstanding bravery. Here, the Germans find themselves in a tight spot. The British are fighting the submarines with torpedo boats, light cruisers, and special craft which are halfway between torpedo and mosquito boats. These vessels are cheap and quickly assembled. Hore-Belisha is confident that even though German submarines may inflict certain losses on Britain, they are not able to threaten the country with a serious blockade.

2 November

General Lelong,[i] the French military attaché, came by. He has just returned from Paris, where he conferred with Gamelin. We talked about the Anglo-French war plan. A replica of the conversation with Hore-Belisha: the very same thoughts, almost the same words. The 'Allies' will not launch an offensive, at least not until spring. Let the Germans advance and suffer huge losses. The 'Allies' prefer to save their human resources and stockpile arms and ammunition. If the Germans make a thrust via Holland and Belgium, they will gain nothing because (1) the British and the French are well prepared for such an eventuality and (2) the Germans will in addition have to cope with the Belgian and Dutch armies, which are at least a million strong. Moreover, it is not so easy to occupy Holland. The Dutch will flood some areas, making it very difficult, indeed almost impossible, for a motorized army to move.

[i] General Albert Lelong, French military attaché in London, 1938–50.

Lelong lived in tsarist Russia, he served before the war, in 1914, in a Russian regiment stationed in Suvalki; he was in Russia during the revolution right up until 1918, and he attended manoeuvres in Kiev in 1935. He knows Russian and the old Russian army. I asked him what differences he discerned between the Red Army and the tsarist army. In his opinion, the Red Army is well equipped, far better than the old army. The rank and file are as good as before, but the Red Army soldier is more conscientious and intelligent. The Red Army NCOs are a cut above those in the tsarist army (and this is a quite crucial element in any army). The Red Army officer class is much more serious and diligent than the tsarist one, which did not exert itself much, but it lacks cultural training, particularly in the higher echelons. In Lelong's opinion, staff officers were trained better in the old army than today. However, on the whole the Red Army is a much more powerful instrument than the tsar's army, and is one of the best in the world today. Lelong also noted that the Red Army is more loyal to the regime and enjoys greater popularity among the people.

An interesting comparison. I had the impression that Lelong was speaking quite sincerely.

3 November

The British have paid a high price for their Turkish policy. It turns out that the signing of the pact with Turkey has cost them 60 million pounds (a 15 million gold loan, mostly to stabilize the currency, a loan of 30 million for armaments and equipment now, and a further loan of 15 million in the future).

Why have the British paid the Turks so much?

For three reasons:

(1) The Turkish pact is a trump card for Britain against Italy, because it makes it far harder, if not impossible, for Italy to retreat from the policy of benevolent neutrality towards Britain which it adopted at the beginning of the war. The British have thus settled their cursed Mediterranean problem.

(2) The Turkish pact is also a trump card against the Soviet Union, for it opens up various political and military opportunities for Britain in the Balkans and the Black Sea area, which she can employ against us in certain situations.

(3) Finally, the Turkish pact is a trump card with respect to the whole Muslim world, whose traditional leader Turkey is still considered to be. Turkey was against Britain in the last war, which created many serious problems for the latter in the Near and Middle East. Now Turkey is with Britain, and this ensures the benevolent neutrality towards Britain, and perhaps even the direct assistance, of Egypt, Arabia, Iraq and Indian Muslims. It also serves to protect the road to India and the Suez Canal area.

Enough reasons not to begrudge several score million pounds.

7 November

We celebrated the October anniversary in a war situation.

There was a meeting, which I addressed, and a comradely lunch with toasts in the embassy, followed by dancing, music and entertainments. The organizers' original intention was to show a film after lunch, but the 'masses' protested and insisted on something more cheerful and lively. After two months of war, black-outs and all manner of restrictions, the people were yearning for light, noise, movement, crowds, meetings. So the organizers yielded and cancelled the film; in any case, because of the war we hadn't been able to bring in a new, topical film. Spirits were high, and everybody was satisfied with the celebration, which began at noon and ended at seven – black-out time.

In the morning, I listened to the radio broadcast from Red Square. There was great pride in my heart, but sadness too, because for many years now I have had to celebrate this immense, incomparable anniversary far from my homeland. I hope this is my last October abroad.

9 November

Relations between Rome and Berlin can't be all that brilliant – otherwise how can one explain the behaviour of Bastianini, to whom I paid a return visit today?

First of all, he told me that Mussolini had decided to do nothing in response to Holland and Belgium's offer to mediate on 7 November. The reason? Very simple: London and Paris demand the evacuation of Poland and Czechoslovakia as a precondition for peace talks. This is manifestly unacceptable to Germany. So there is no basis for peace. So there is no point getting involved in a hopeless initiative.

With a sarcastic smile on his face, and the occasional shrug of his shoulders, Bastianini continued: 'If I were in Hitler's shoes, I would declare that in principle I was prepared to restore Poland as a special political entity and withdraw German troops, but I would suggest discussing these matters at a peace conference. Britain and France would not be able to simply say "No!" to this. But Hitler holds a different view. His speech in Munich yesterday showed beyond a shadow of a doubt that there is still no point talking about peace.'

In an irritated, mocking voice, Bastianini concluded: 'Well, he must be in a better position to judge!'

Notable also was the emphasis Bastianini placed on the imminent improvement of Anglo-Italian relations and on the fact that Italy was rapidly arming.

'We can't be certain,' he added, 'that we won't have to fight.'

Against whom? It by no means followed from what Bastianini had been saying that he meant Italy's obligations under the German–Italian treaty. On the other hand, he did not conceal the fact that Mussolini is taking a lively interest in the idea of a Balkan bloc.

A word or two about this Balkan bloc. The idea is being pushed from three directions:

(1) Rumania, Yugoslavia, Hungary, and to a lesser extent Bulgaria and Greece, are toying with the idea of erecting a Balkan bloc to defend their 'neutrality'. They think that Germany and the USSR represent a real danger. Rumania is particularly active in this respect.

(2) Italy wants to take advantage of this 'favourable moment' and, making the most of Germany's engagement in other areas, set up a Balkan bloc under its own leadership. Such a bloc would be directed, of course, against the USSR. It's not for nothing that Italian radio has been sending out propaganda every night recently against 'communism' and threatening Italian intervention in the event of 'Bolshevism' emerging in the Balkans.

(3) Turkey, intoxicated by its recent diplomatic and financial 'victories' (the pact with Britain and France), is also not averse to a Balkan bloc being set up under its own leadership.

Behind all these plans, hopes and schemes stands Britain, which, as ever, is playing a double game. On the one hand, Britain encourages Mussolini's ambitions in the Balkans; on the other, it hints to Turkey that it regards *her* as the natural leader in the Balkans. For now Britain sits on the fence. At a certain moment it will make a choice.

10 November

Cripps came to see me. He was highly agitated and upset: why has Moscow still not given its answer to Stanley's proposals?

Cripps declared, somewhat emotionally, that the purpose of his life at the moment is the improvement of A[nglo]-S[oviet] relations. If our relations are allowed to take their own course, the results could be deplorable. Mutual suspicions, unfortunate incidents, misunderstandings and so on will poison the atmosphere for good. Horace Wilson's intrigues in various parts of the world (Scandinavia, the Balkans and the Far East) will assume gigantic dimensions. Finland is a good example. Wilson and Co. promise 'moral support' to the Finns or, more precisely, they promise 'moral support' to the Scandinavians in the exertion of their 'moral support' to Finland. The Finns, as true provincials in politics, see Britain's 'moral support' as a sheet anchor. Becoming stubborn and uncompromising, they miss out on the opportunity to settle contentious issues with the USSR in good neighbourly fashion. This has a boomerang effect on Anglo-Soviet relations. A gigantic effort should be made to arrest this line of development and to declare: 'Stop!' Eden, Stanley, Elliot, Churchill and others understand this perfectly well. Hence their desire to improve relations with the Soviet Union. Hence, by the way, the idea of trade negotiations. Cripps himself offered his services as legal adviser to the Board of Trade precisely so that he could assist the process more robustly. But Moscow is not responding! Why not?

I objected: 'How long did it take the British government to offer us its trade proposals?'

I reminded Cripps that I presented Halifax with the framework agreement for the trade negotiations on 24 September. Stanley submitted his proposals only on 25 October.

The Soviet government is now conducting more urgent negotiations – with Germany, Finland, etc. Britain's turn will come…

Cripps was greatly discouraged when he left.

13 November

I lunched with Winston Churchill and Brendan Bracken at Bracken's flat in Westminster (*8, Lord North Street*). From the outside, a very plain, small house; on the inside, a superbly furnished modern apartment fit for a representative of the bourgeois intelligentsia.

Churchill arrived slightly late from a meeting of the War Cabinet. He is in fine fettle: fresh, younger, full of energy, a spring in his step. He is pleased with his power, pleased with his ministry, and pleased at the opportunity to bring his strengths to bear on matters of great consequence. Another source of satisfaction, it seems to me, is the awareness and expectation of historical possibilities unveiling themselves before him…

I mentioned Moscow's wish to improve relations with England (such was the latest information I had received). Churchill's face lit up and he exclaimed: 'That's very good! The desire is the main thing. If there's a will, ways and means will also be found.'

Whereupon, right off the bat, Churchill set about expounding his old idea that the real interests of Britain and the USSR do not collide anywhere, and that this makes a solid foundation for good relations between our countries.

I argued that at first sight this might indeed appear to be the case, but why in that case had British diplomacy been systematically working against the USSR over the last two or three months in all parts of the world where, one way or another, our interests coincide – in the Far East, the Near East, the Balkans, Scandinavia and Finland?

'There's nothing to be surprised about,' answered Churchill. 'The drastic turn in your foreign policy at the end of August came as a great shock to us. Subsequently, during the first two months of the war, your position remained unclear to us. Many thought that you had made an alliance with Germany (though I never believed it) and that we would be open enemies in the nearest future. It was only natural in such a situation that old prejudices, fears and suspicions should surface. This inevitably affected our state apparatus. Local bodies and individual officials immersed themselves in anti-Soviet machinations. But that in no way represents the policy of the government.'

I couldn't agree with Churchill and gave him a number of examples to prove that the problem is not the excessive zeal of individual ambassadors or admirals, but the carrying out of specific instructions that emanate from London. Churchill was somewhat perturbed and said: 'I'll make some inquiries, and if what you say is true, I'll try to rectify the situation.'

Then, at Churchill's initiative, the conversation moved on to Finland. Churchill asked me about the details of our negotiations and also about our further intentions. I complained to him once again about the conduct of British diplomats: they incite the Finns to resist, promising them Britain's 'moral support', and the Finns – those true provincials in politics – imagine that this 'moral support' will make the walls of Soviet Jericho fall and stubbornly refuse to recognize our utterly lawful claims. As a result of London's interference, the prospects for an agreement between Moscow and Helsinki are reduced. Why is British diplomacy doing this? I don't know. Perhaps just to spoil things for us, as Britain is unable to offer Finland any real assistance. For as long as London keeps machinating against the USSR in Finland and other parts of the world, it's hardly possible to think about improving relations between our countries.

'My view on the issue you have raised is as follows,' replied Churchill. 'Russia has every reason to be a dominant power in the Baltic, and should be one. Better Russia than Germany. That's in our, British, interests. I don't see why we should put a spoke in your wheel as you build naval and air bases on the Baltic coast. I consider your claims towards Finland to be natural and normal. It's truly ridiculous that Leningrad should find itself in the firing-line of long-range guns on the Finnish border, or that the Finnish isles should block the entrance to the Gulf of Finland. You have every right to demand that the Finns rectify the frontier on the Karelian Isthmus and give you a few isles in the Gulf of Finland. I also see no reason why you should not have a naval base at the entrance to the Gulf. The stronger your position in the Baltic, the better for you and for us, and the worse for Germany. The Finns can bargain and argue about the size of the compensation you are prepared to offer them – that's their proper right – but they cannot refuse you "in principle" one or other base or one or other chunk of border-land.'

And then, pulling on his cigar – we had already finished lunch – Churchill added thoughtfully: 'My sense of history compels me to approach the question of your claims in the Baltics from a different angle as well. Why did Russia lose the Baltics? Because it acted as our ally in the last war and did us a huge service, especially at the beginning of the war. Were it not for Russia, the Battle of the Marne would have ended in our defeat and the entire outcome of the war would probably have been different. That is why I think that Britain and France owe Russia in general a historical debt, whatever Russia that may be – Red or White – and we now have a moral obligation to help Russia strengthen her position on the Baltic Sea.'

'Wonderful!' I rejoined. 'Then the behaviour of the British diplomats in Finland and Scandinavia is all the more disgraceful.'

'I'll deal with this question, too,' Churchill replied. 'Finland should not impede rapprochement between Britain and the USSR, which is my chief political objective.'

Churchill hinted that he would try to arrange things in such a way that British diplomats would 'advise' Finland to settle its affairs with the USSR peacefully. We shall see what the practical results of this hint will be. Churchill added: 'I would hope, however, that the USSR will not resort to force to resolve its dispute with Finland. If the USSR chose to follow such a path, as I'm sure you understand, it would make a most painful impression here in England and would render the improvement of Anglo-Soviet relations impossible for a long period of time.'

I replied to Churchill in the spirit of Comrade Kalinin's letter to Roosevelt and cited some facts relating to Finland from Comrade Molotov's speech of 31 October. At the same time, I added that the Finnish leaders also bear a large share of responsibility for subsequent developments. Much will depend on how sensibly they act.

We turned to the war. Churchill exclaimed: 'Your non-aggression pact with Germany triggered the war, but I bear you no grudge. I'm even glad. For a long time now I've felt that a war with Germany is <u>necessary</u>. Without your pact, we would have hesitated and drawn things out, until we procrastinated to the point when we could no longer win the war. But now we will win it, even though it will cost us dearly.'

Churchill set out his thoughts about the war. Peace is impossible in the near future. In peace time the British often look like pampered, gluttonous sybarites, but in times of war and extremity they turn into vicious bulldogs, trapping their prey in a death grip. The country now finds itself in such a mood. Germany should not be underestimated: she is a serious and dangerous enemy (although Churchill senses that the Germany of 1939 is weaker than the Germany of 1914), but she will be defeated all the same. The British Empire is powerful: it just needs time to mobilize its resources. This time will be found.

I asked Churchill how he visualized post-war Europe. Churchill replied: 'I see it in the form of a reformed League of Nations, which must serve as a real tribunal and have at its disposal a mighty air force. Individual states – members of the League – can retain their own armies, navies and so on, in a reduced size, but not air forces.'

'What about Germany's position after the war?'

'Germany? Germany's position should be on the same basis as that of other states. Germany will become democratic. Plans to partition Germany are absurd.'

Churchill pulled deeply at his cigar and added: 'The future League of Nations cannot confine itself to military and political problems alone. It must take up social problems as well. It must, for example, introduce the six-hour working day in all member states, double wages, and so on. This is quite feasible. All one needs to do is apply science to production and cut profits and dividends.'

All this sounded rather fantastic – not in general, but within the framework of capitalism cloaked in the garb of the League of Nations. While listening to Churchill, however, I couldn't rid myself of the impression that the British ruling class is keeping the card of social demagogy up its sleeve, to be played at an appropriate moment in the course of the war. I can see it now: after 6 or 12 or 18 months of war, when really hard times fall and heroic measures are needed to summon the 'fighting spirit' of the masses, Churchill will become prime minister and call upon England to fight not only against Germany, but also for a six-hour working day and four pounds a week for each citizen.

We shall see.[207]

14 November

Sun Fo came by. I met him for the first time here in the spring of 1938. At the end of May, that same year, I bumped into him quite by chance in a Moscow theatre. Today was our third meeting. He's come to London for a few days 'to sniff the air' and, most importantly, to learn something about British intentions and policies in the Far East. He also wanted to speed up British supplies (in particular, of machine-gun steel) under the three-million loan, but this was a secondary task.

Sun Fo told me a lot of interesting things about China. The Japanese offensive has run out of steam. Tokyo is no longer thinking about new conquests, but about consolidating what it has captured. Within the next few weeks, Japan plans to put Wang Jingwei on the throne and sign a peace treaty with him. The Japanese hope that after this they can withdraw from China at least half of their army, which now numbers nearly a million. But Japan is miscalculating. Jiang Jieshi is building up and training a large army for an offensive. Now that the Japanese attack has petered out, the Chinese mean to begin a general, lengthy and dogged offensive, which can end only in the expulsion of the Japanese from the continent.

Arms are critical, of course. China gets them from two sources: the USA and, in particular, the USSR. We provide China with considerable assistance in arms, ammunition, instructors, etc. The credit agreement concluded this June on the basis of commodity exchange is functioning well. The road through Tianjin is in good condition. Transportation by lorry from the Turksib to Lanzhou takes about three weeks. The air link that is currently being established between Moscow and Chongqing will take five days. There are some problems to do with fuel, but a highly original solution has been found: fuel is delivered to fuelling stations along the Tianjin Road not by lorries, but by camels, which consume no petrol on the way, while goods are carried by truck. What a combination: Noah's ark and aeroplanes!

Incidentally, big oil fields have been found recently in Tianjin and Gansu. Soviet engineers are already developing them in Tianjin and will soon start to do so in Gansu. Oil refineries will then be built. Then the problem of transportation via the Tianjin Road will be resolved for good.

On the whole, Sun Fo is optimistic about the future. Or is he just pretending…?

Sun Fo's London impressions are rather vague. He met Halifax and Churchill. Halifax told him that in connection with the war in Europe, the British government is most eager to normalize its relations with Japan, but does not intend to achieve this 'at China's expense'. Sun Fo, however, takes a very sceptical view of the foreign secretary's statement. Halifax asked him about the state of Chinese–Soviet relations and was pleased to hear from Sun Fo that there had been no changes in this area. Halifax told Sun Fo that the British government wanted to put right its relations with the Soviet Union.

Churchill was more definite. He said: 'We are friends with China. China is a friend of the USSR. All three of us should be friends.'

Churchill interrogated Sun Fo at length about the USSR and spoke of the British government's intention to improving relations with Moscow. Churchill was especially interested in the volume of Soviet economic aid to Germany, and asked whether it was true that the USSR was selling planes and submarines to Germany. Sun Fo apparently replied that the latter was hardly probable and that the quantity of food, raw materials and so on that Germany might get from the USSR was relatively small. Churchill also wished to know the meaning of the new Soviet policy in the Baltics. What is it: defensive measures or the beginning of major imperialist expansion? Sun Fo apparently replied that we are guided by defensive interests. Churchill then said that if that was the case, he would not object to Soviet actions in the Baltics and Finland, for they do not conflict with the interests of Great Britain. Sun Fo, interestingly enough, spoke with Churchill prior to my evening meeting with the latter.

Sun Fo will fly back to China in a few days.

15 November

Beaverbrook lunched with us. I hadn't seen him since that memorable lunch in the embassy in early July. Since then he has managed to make two trips to America and, as ever, was full of news, primarily from overseas. His most interesting revelation was that, in Beaverbrook's words, Roosevelt is quite definite in his support of war and the participation of the USA in the war on the side of the 'Allies', because he believes that 'fascism' must be crushed once and for all. Of course, the isolationist sentiments of the American masses hinder the realization of Roosevelt's intentions, but he will still do everything in his power to help Britain and France win the war. Under certain conditions (if, for instance, the Germans attacked Holland and Belgium) Roosevelt could even draw the United States into the war.

Beaverbrook himself opposes the war.

'I'm an isolationist,' he fretted. 'What concerns me is the fate of the British Empire! I want the Empire to remain intact, but I don't understand why for the sake of this we must wage a three-year war to crush "Hitlerism". To hell with that man Hitler! If the Germans want him, I happily concede them this treasure and make my bow. Poland? Czechoslovakia? What are they to do with us? Cursed be the day when Chamberlain gave our guarantees to Poland! A peace conference must be convened immediately, without any preliminary conditions. Were this to be done, I'd support the move with all the means at my disposal, even if I had *to ruin my papers* to do so.'

According to Beaverbrook, there are two parties in government: the 'war party' led by Churchill (Hore-Belisha, incidentally, belongs to this group), and the 'peace party' led by Chamberlain (which also includes Simon, Hoare and Halifax). The former advocates the defeat of Germany as the premise for peace; the latter is ready to conclude peace at the first opportunity because it fears a revolution in Germany with all the ensuing consequences. For the moment the two parties are acting as one, because no hope for peace has appeared on the horizon so far. But should such a hope emerge, who knows what will happen?

In Beaverbrook's opinion, peace depends first and foremost on the USA and the USSR. He pins little hope on the USA (Roosevelt wants war!), but what about the USSR? Beaverbrook expects a great deal of us. For obvious reasons, however, I was entirely *noncommittal*.

I asked Beaverbrook what would happen if the war dragged on.

Beaverbrook shrugged his shoulders and replied that he had little faith in 'dynamic forms' of war. It is far more likely, he said, that the present situation will last for a good while. It suits the 'Allies'; as for Hitler, he doesn't dare raise a real storm. Germany is in ferment (as witnessed by the recent explosion in Munich), and has encountered serious resistance from the outside for the first time. Hitler is at a loss and doesn't know what to do. He wants peace more than anything, but peace will become impossible if war begins in earnest. It will only need German planes to carry out a couple of bombardments of London for any hope of peace to be nipped in the bud. Hitler understands this, which is why he hesitates to make a decisive move: maybe something will turn up?!...

I was interested to know Beaverbrook's opinion about the future *settlement*, should the war take its course. With a dismissive wave of his hand, Beaverbrook uttered abruptly: 'Nothing good will come of it! Already in 1919 the French were dissatisfied with the Treaty of Versailles. They found it too soft. Clemenceau[i] thought that peace should have been concluded in Berlin. Should the Allies triumph now and enter Germany, I'm convinced that the French would destroy everything there which speaks of culture and civilization.'

'And what would the British do in that case?'

Beaverbrook shrugged his shoulders.

Then we spoke about Anglo-Soviet relations. Beaverbrook would like to see them improved, but reproached us for delaying with our reply to the trade proposals. This makes a bad impression in London. We touched upon the Baltics and Finland. I informed Beaverbrook about the details. He said that personally he couldn't care less about the Baltic Sea – the fate of the British Empire doesn't depend on it. But, he added, the British are 'a strange people' and have 'sentimental feelings toward small democracies'. That is why he 'fears' that if it comes to an 'armed conflict' between the USSR and Finland, this will be an even greater shock to British public opinion than the Soviet–German non-aggression pact.

I rebuked Beaverbrook for his comments and underlined the harmful and dangerous role played by the British press, including his own, with regard to the Finnish question. Beaverbrook tried to defend himself, but without much success.

Beaverbrook is sure that Chamberlain will retire soon for reasons of ill-health. He thinks that either Hoare or Halifax will succeed him. Churchill, apparently, has no chance at all. Even Eden is more likely to become prime minister. We shall see, however, whether Beaverbrook's forecast proves correct, particularly as far as Churchill is concerned. I've noticed that Beaverbrook's

[i] Georges Clemenceau, French prime minister, 1906–09 and 1917–20; minister of war during the First World War; played an instrumental role in the establishment of the Treaty of Versailles.

attitude to Churchill is very changeable: one day he might praise him as Britain's greatest statesman, on another he might call him a 'swindler', 'turncoat' or 'political prostitute'. Today he is madly annoyed with Churchill – isn't that the real reason for his extreme pessimism about Churchill's chances of becoming prime minister?

Time will tell.

[While making his unauthorized overtures to his former allies in Britain, Maisky toiled hard to reconcile Molotov. In a tedious eight-page report, he addressed the crucial issue of whether England was heading towards war or peace. Having been reprimanded in a letter from Molotov of 11 November, Maisky reassured him that the present observations were based only on those politicians who counted. He portrayed Chamberlain as being firmly in the saddle, having successfully created a 'united national front' and having mobilized the Empire. In foreign policy, Chamberlain had been successful in isolating Hitler, now that the 'anti-Comintern pact' had lost its meaning, while the pact with the Turks had reconciled Britain with the Muslim world. On the whole, the position of British foreign policy had been 'significantly enhanced during the first three months of the war'. Contradicting what he entered in his diary, he wrote to Molotov that he believed Chamberlain would 'emerge victorious' over the Churchill group and would seek to end the war through a dignified compromise. In the same breath he warned that Chamberlain's policy remained hostile to the Soviet Union and 'at the end of the day he might somehow succeed in diverting Hitler to the east'.[208]]

16 November

I paid Aras a visit.

He said that in essence the Italians and French have already reached an agreement. The French are ceding Djibouti and the Djibouti–Addis-Ababa railway line to the Italians, as well as shares in the Suez Canal and posts in its administration. The status of Italians in Tunisia will be nearly equivalent to that of the French. In exchange, Italy pledges to remain absolutely neutral for the duration of the war. The signing of the agreement has to be postponed, however, as it would contravene the German–Italian pact, and Mussolini does not desire an open break with the Führer as yet. I'll say! Mussolini is manoeuvring and marking time: maybe he'll be able to raise his price. Besides, he does not want to commit himself too much to one or the other side until he is quite certain of who will come out on top.

Aras believes in the possibility neither of a Balkan bloc in general nor of a Balkan bloc specifically led by Italy. He discounts the former because the Balkan countries are still too much at variance with one another; and as for the idea of Italian leadership, he deems no Balkan bloc to be possible without Turkey, which will never agree to a bloc directed against the USSR. Aras would personally favour a 'genuinely neutral' Balkan bloc which maintains cordial relations with all the great powers (the USSR, Germany, Italy and Britain), but, unfortunately, he sees no likelihood of this being formed in the near future.

Aras does not believe that the war will be fought on a major scale. The Allies are still unwilling. Nor will Hitler agree to it, for he wants peace. War 'in earnest' would kill off that possibility. The two sides will drag this out until spring, especially after Göring's assurance to Hitler that Germany is capable of holding out for at least two years. And in spring – who knows? – the USSR, Turkey and Italy might take it upon themselves to convene an international peace conference, and the war will be ended.

The Turks want peace, or else they will not be able to spend the money they now receive from Britain. For Aras, *der Wunsch ist der Vater des Gedankens* [the wish is the father of thoughts].

18 November

Noticeable changes have occurred over the last two or three weeks in the attitudes of the working masses towards the war.

On the whole 'war enthusiasm' has always been lacking here. Unlike at the beginning of the last war. And yet there has not been any noticeable opposition to the war either. This, again, is in stark contrast to 1914, when the I[ndependent] L[abour] P[arty] (a very serious organization at the time), under the leadership of MacDonald, Snowden, Smillie and others (then major figures in the labour movement), spoke out against the war from the very beginning. Opposition to the 1914 war may have been far removed from Marxist principles, but it played a major role in that period.

Things have turned out differently this time. Even the Communist Party did not immediately find the right line. In the early months of the war, the Communist Party acted under the slogan of war on two fronts, against fascism in Germany and against Chamberlain in Britain, for his failure to organize a real war against German fascism. It was only in early October that the Communist Party recognized this war as an imperialist war and began to advocate the necessity of peace. An anti-war position was still less to be expected from various groups and currents within the Labour Party or from the trades unions. I tell a lie: there was one exception, Lansbury, but he opposed the war as an advocate of non-resistance. It's no wonder in such circumstances that the working masses, disorientated, stunned and shocked by the sudden events, followed Transport House out of habit. The latter not only gave Chamberlain its full support, but turned out to be more royalist than the king in its belligerence ('Down with Hitler! Down with fascism!').

Since late October, however, a certain shift in the mood of the masses has become apparent (the correction of the Communist Party line has played its part here). This immediately affected the 'leaders'. Trades union councils in Glasgow, Edinburgh, Aberdeen, Bradford, Birmingham and other cities moved resolutions protesting against the war and calling for peace. Many local organizations of the Labour Party, together with county and district trades union organizations and others, acted in the same spirit. Out of 160 Labour MPs, only some 15 or so (including 6–7 associates of Lansbury) were against the war in early September. Today they number 40, that is, a quarter of Labour MPs. True, this 40 is a motley group – Lansbury and Co., Maxton and his Independents, lonely Cripps, and others – but still, opposition to the official line of the Labour Party is now fairly solid. Add to this floaters and doubters, who demand that the war aims of the British and the French be published, and it appears that about half of Parliamentary Labour is infected with ideas that Transport House finds undesirable. Moreover, there are many prominent figures in that half: apart from those mentioned above, there are also Shinwell,[i] Ellen Wilkinson, Pritt, Kirkwood,[ii] Neil MacLean, Noel-Baker and others.

A symptom of the current shift is the election of Attlee as leader of Parliamentary Labour for the new session of parliament that is soon to begin. His rival was Greenwood, who stood in for Attlee during the latter's illness over the summer and autumn months, including the moment when war was declared. Greenwood is in Chamberlain's pocket and undoubtedly rendered him good service in the critical days leading up to the war and following its declaration. That is why the government wanted to see Greenwood, not Attlee, as leader of Parliamentary Labour. The bourgeois press campaigned noisily for Greenwood. Nonetheless, it was Attlee who was chosen. One should have no illusions about Attlee, but still, his election in the present situation is a 'sign of the times'.

An interesting situation has also arisen in the Anglo-Russian Parliamentary Committee [ARPC]. Right after the conclusion of the Soviet–German non-aggression pact, and especially following the entry of the Soviet army into Poland, there was great agitation among the members of the Committee. Some even thought of resigning (like Tom Smith). Coates pleaded with them to keep their heads and not rush to conclusions. The members wanted to see me. We had a few meetings. As a result, nobody resigned and the Committee continues its work. They regularly publish important Soviet documents (in particular, speeches by Molotov and Voroshilov). Assuming there are no unexpected changes in the situation, one can count on the ARPC preserving its existence.

[i] Emmanuel Shinwell (Baron Shinwell of Easington), Labour MP, 1922–24, 1928–31, 1935–70; financial secretary to the War Office, 1929–30; minister of fuel and power, 1945–47.
[ii] David Kirkwood, British socialist.

But won't there be changes…? Hard to predict. The times are exceptionally 'dynamic'.

Yes, there are definite shifts in the mood of the masses. But let's not delude ourselves: Transport House has a firm grip on the machinery of the Labour movement and any struggle against it will be far from easy.

20 November

Elliot came for lunch.

We talked mostly about A[nglo]-S[oviet] relations. Elliot welcomes our readiness to seek ways of improving Anglo-Soviet relations. In response to my comment that, in order to ensure the improvement of relations, British diplomats should cease working against the USSR, Elliot said that Soviet accusations are highly exaggerated.

Then Elliot surveyed the global situation, making some observations along the way. In his opinion, British and Soviet interests in the Far East coincide: both sides want to prevent Japan's victory in China. In Turkey, these interests, far from conflicting, are complementary. Britain is desperately keen for Ankara and Moscow to maintain a very close friendship, if only from its own egotistic considerations, namely, that the value of Turkey as an ally would fall steeply if its neighbour were an unfriendly or even simply indifferent USSR. As for Finland, the British government wishes above all for a peaceful settlement of the Soviet–Finnish dispute. Britain has no interests of its own in Finland, and it could hardly help Finland should help be needed (the case with Poland is instructive in this regard), so the British government would very much welcome an agreement between Moscow and Helsinki in the nearest future.

I retorted: 'So what's the matter? Why, in practice, do British diplomats follow the opposite line on the Finnish question?'

Elliot made reference to English public opinion, which is *violently pro-Finnish*, and to the pressure exerted on the government by Labour, which has close ties with the Finnish Social Democrats and Cooperatives (Tanner[i] is the president of the International Cooperative Alliance) and is doing its best to help them.

I replied that I did not find his arguments terribly convincing. I adduced my own, showing that the issue was not just 'public opinion' but also the government.

At this point Elliot decided 'to take the bull by the horns' and stated directly that one should look at the root of the matter. The root of the matter is that Moscow and London are deeply suspicious of each other. The entire atmosphere

[i] Väinö Alfred Tanner, Finnish social-democrat foreign minister, 1939–40.

of A[nglo]-S[oviet] relations is poisoned by this suspicion. As a result, even the most straightforward step taken by one side is immediately interpreted in the most menacing light by the other. Both sides live in an atmosphere of perpetual nightmare and invented fears. If the Soviet and British governments really do want to improve relations, then it is essential, first of all, that they change the current atmosphere. The suspicions and fears that have accumulated must be dispelled. The British government is of the opinion that personal contacts between members of the Soviet and British governments would be the best way of achieving this. Hence the idea of Elliot heading a delegation of ministerial colleagues and noted MPs to travel to the Moscow agricultural exhibition, about which we spoke in August. Unfortunately, the trip never took place. It was already too late. Hence now the idea of trade talks and sending Stanley to Moscow, about which Halifax and Stanley spoke to me a month or so ago. But there has been no response from us to this proposal. A great pity. Some members of the government interpret the delay as the Soviet government's unwillingness to improve relations with Britain. Elliot himself does not think this to be the case, but he does think that unless Anglo-Soviet relations improve in the near future, they will begin to deteriorate. To what end? Elliot sees no good grounds for this deterioration.

I argued that relations between countries are defined not by fine words or personal contacts, but by deeds. The actions of British diplomats speak for themselves.

Then Elliot suddenly uttered out of the blue: 'What is the sense in our disarming ourselves in advance? After all, we haven't had the slightest signal from you to indicate that you really do want to improve relations.'

I parried this lunge.

21 November

Lunched with Beneš.

He recently returned from a trip to Paris and gave me a detailed account of his misadventures. He travelled to Paris to clarify whether a temporary Czechoslovak government could be established. It transpired that there was no chance of this happening because of the position taken by the French government. The French government strongly dislikes Beneš, considering him 'too leftist'. They say on the Quai d'Orsay: 'Beneš is a programme.' A programme, moreover, that is unacceptable to a French government set on a highly reactionary course. Daladier did not want to receive Beneš officially, and Beneš did not want to meet him privately. As a result, the meeting never happened. Beneš saw Reynaud, Mandel, Herriot and others: they paid him private visits.

The specific cause of the French government's hostility is the following. Daladier and other ministers advocate the partitioning of Germany (which Beneš deems nonsensical) and the creation after the war of an Austro-Hungarian monarchy headed by Otto von Habsburg.[i] The monarchy should incorporate Austria, Bavaria, Hungary and Czechoslovakia. With aims such as these, Daladier is clearly not going to find common ground with Beneš.

Beneš says he is treated perfectly well in London, but, as far as the establishment of a Czechoslovak government is concerned, the British government 'displays little activity, despite its general sympathy'. Typically English: the British government plays a double game and refuses to make any commitments.

The question of a Czechoslovak government was raised during Beneš's stay in Paris, but the French government was against 'forcing' the issue and categorically objected to Beneš's possible participation in the government (to say nothing of the premiership). The French government would accept, as a last resort, a Czechoslovak government headed by Osouský, who dances attendance on the French government and directs his efforts against Beneš. No government, however, could be constructed on such a basis.

Then Czech circles in Paris put forward the idea of establishing a temporary 'National Committee', which would have at its disposal the Czechoslovak army currently being formed in France (it now numbers some 5,000). The French government agreed to this, but on condition that the committee did not include Beneš. The Czech army then organized a *revolt*, and the project for a National Committee faded. To rectify the situation, the French government suggested that the Czechoslovak army should be placed under Osouský as the sole representative of Czechoslovakia to be officially recognized by the French government. The army organized a second *revolt*, and declared that it did not want to be subordinated to a single man in general and to Osouský in particular. This led to a strange compromise: a National Committee should be formed, with Beneš as a member, and also Osouský, but Beneš would not be president. And that's exactly what happened. But the National Committee has no official president; the unofficial one, of course, is Beneš.

All these frustrations with the 'democracies' has inevitably pushed Beneš towards the USSR. In the past, he has often told me that Czechoslovakia should maintain close ties with the Soviet Union, but he has never been as definite about it as he was today. He declared that he could not conceive of Czechoslovakia's further historical existence outside an extremely close, inextricable bond with the USSR. He hinted that under certain conditions he could accept a federal link between his country and the Soviet Union. With precisely these considerations

[i] Otto von Habsburg, the last crown prince of Austria-Hungary, 1916–19.

in mind, Beneš deems it absolutely essential for Czechoslovakia and the USSR to share a common border. This can be attained in one of two ways: by ceding the Carpathian Ukraine either to Czechoslovakia or to the USSR. Beneš does not care which of the alternatives is chosen. The only thing that matters to him is the existence of a common border between the two states. Hungary has no right whatsoever to possess the Carpathian Ukraine.

'Bear in mind,' Beneš said in conclusion, 'that if during the war a socialist revolution should occur in Germany, to be followed by a civil war, and if in this civil war the West should support counter-revolutionaries and the East support the revolution, Czechoslovakia will certainly be on the side of the East.'

22 November

Sikorski[i] and Zaleski have left London. Their visit had three main aims:

(1) To enhance the prestige of their so-called government.

(2) To arrange with the British for the provision of essential supplies for the Polish army in France, and to facilitate the formation of a Polish division in Canada.

(3) To obtain a promise from the British government to include in its 'war aims' the restoration of Poland within her pre-war borders.

Everything went more or less *all right* as far as the first point was concerned. Sikorski and Zaleski lunched with the king, dined with the PM and Halifax, and met Churchill, Hore-Belisha and other members of the government. But the English public gave them the cold shoulder. Even the press did not make much of a fuss. Little homage was rendered, and minimum attention paid.

On the second point, the Poles were given all sorts of promises, but only the future will show their real value.

As for the third – and fundamental – point, Sikorski and Zaleski were in for a big disappointment. In reply to their persistent requests for Poland's former frontiers to be recognized, Halifax lectured them at length on the merits of the Curzon Line and generally stuck to the substance of his speech on 26 October in the House of Lords, stressing that now was not the time to fix the borders of the future Poland. Mention of the fact that Daladier had already recognized the pre-war frontiers also made no difference.

In connection with the question of boundaries, the following incident occurred in the Polish embassy during Sikorski's stay in London. Sikorski was

---

[i] Władysław Eugeniusz Sikorski, Polish prime minister, 1922–23, and prime minister of the Polish government in exile and commander-in-chief of the Polish armed forces, 1939–43. Unsubstantiated conspiracy theories claim that Maisky, whose plane happened to be on the tarmac next to Sikorski's at Gibraltar airport in July 1943, was involved in Sikorsky's death, when the plane crashed during take-off.

giving an interview to the press. About a dozen noted diplomatic correspondents were present, as well as Gu Weijun. The interview itself was extremely dull, but it was followed by questions. Gu asked whether the Polish government drew a distinction between German and Soviet actions in respect of Poland. Sikorski answered in the negative. He didn't limit himself to this answer, however, and came right out with it like a soldier: 'Our point of view is supported by both the French and British governments.'

The next day the FO raised hell with Raczyński: what grounds did Sikorski have to make such a statement?

Raczyński was rattled and began denying outright the fact of Sikorski's statement.

27 November

Halifax invited me over to discuss the trade negotiations. He began, however, with Finland.

Expressing his great concern about the aggravation of the Soviet–Finnish conflict, Halifax began interrogating me in detail about the Moscow talks. I told him as much as I knew, stressing the uncompromising and even provocative behaviour of the Finnish government, particularly that of Erkko and Cajander.[i] I also pointed out that the Finns refuse to come to terms with reality and inhabit a world of incomprehensible fantasy. Their strange behaviour cannot be explained merely by their stubbornness and slow-wittedness. I myself lived in Finland for three and a half years. I know the Finnish character and could assure Halifax that, left to their own devices, the Finns would not have behaved as they have during the entire course of negotiations with us. It is quite clear that there is someone behind them, encouraging them and pushing them towards their insane policy. I say 'insane' because, although the USSR would like nothing better than to settle the present dispute in neighbourly fashion, it has to consider its own security interests and those of Leningrad in particular. It is beyond doubt that influence is being exerted on the Finns from abroad.

Halifax interrupted me at this point and asked with an air of angelic innocence: 'And where might those influences come from? America?'

I replied that the USA in general, and Roosevelt in particular, bear some responsibility for the aggravation of the Soviet–Finnish conflict, but there are some countries 'closer to home' whose responsibility is even greater. I named Scandinavia (especially Sweden) and… England. Halifax was evidently shocked at this mention of his motherland. To show straightaway the basis of my accusation, I drew his attention to the behaviour of the British press:

[i] Aimo Kaarlo Cajander, Finnish prime minister, 1937–39.

'Think about it,' I said. 'Throughout the six weeks of our talks with the Finns, I haven't seen a single article in the English press which would support, or at least explain, the position of the Soviet Union and the motives that guide it. Quite the opposite. During this period there have been hundreds of articles in the English press shielding Finland unconditionally and defending its position. Doesn't that say something?'

'But we have freedom of the press…,' Halifax began, dishing up the old English excuse.

'Forgive me, Lord Halifax,' I interrupted him, 'for pointing out that I am quite familiar with your practices. I know the extent of your powers with regard to the press. And I also know, from long experience, that the English press would not have displayed such amazing unanimity on the Finnish issue, over such a long period of time, without being guided by some hidden hand. However, the Soviet government also has other evidence of the regrettable role that Britain has been playing in the Soviet–Finnish conflict, in addition to the conduct of the English press.'

Halifax started objecting. There is no denying that Britain is well disposed to Finland, but it has no serious interests there. All the British government wishes for now is a peaceful settlement of the present dispute. For it would be undesirable to create a new focus of international complications in addition to those that already exist. Halifax has told the Finnish ambassador in London more than once that Finland should not be *unreasonable* in its negotiations with the USSR.

'This, however, was not noticeable during or indeed after the negotiations,' I retorted.

Halifax turned to the incident which occurred yesterday on the Finno-Soviet border and asked whether there might not be some mistake or misunderstanding. He half-suggested getting a mixed Soviet–Finnish commission to investigate.

I replied that the matter was now entirely in the hands of the Soviet government, and that I didn't know what their next step would be.

That was the end of our conversation about Finland. Halifax sighed and moved onto another subject. He took out a sheet from the papers lying in a folder in front of him, looked at it and said in the most innocent, matter-of-fact tone that Citrine and some other trades union leaders had asked him to talk to me about the fate of the Polish trades union leaders who were said to have been arrested in the part of Poland that had passed over to us. Halifax wanted to hand me a list of the said persons, in which the names of Alter,[i] Himelfarb,[ii]

[i] Viktor Alter, Polish trade union leader and a member of the Central Committee of the Bund, 1919–39; arrested and shot in 1941.

[ii] Hershl Himelfarb, a leading figure in the Bund and active trade unionist in Warsaw, 1918–39.

Ehrlich,[i] Mastek[ii] and others caught my eye. But I declined to take the piece of paper and said: 'To tell you the truth, I'm greatly surprised at your démarche. The individuals concerned are former Polish subjects. As far as I know, they have not become British citizens. So what does the British government have to do with them? The British government does not have a *locus standi* here.

Halifax was embarrassed and started defending himself. The British government does indeed lack formal grounds for raising the matter of Polish trades unionists. Halifax merely wanted to carry out Citrine's request. He thought that if we attached importance to the English workers' movement, then…

'But you scarcely attach any importance to it now,' he said, cutting himself short.

I did not object. Halifax put the paper back in the folder, apologized for the misunderstanding, and finally moved on to the main issue – the trade negotiations.

He took the bull by the horns and asked me bluntly: do we want these negotiations or not? Basing itself on my statement of 27 September, the British government had prepared its proposals, which Stanley submitted to me more than a month ago. Halifax has been actively promoting the opening of negotiations in government. He believes it to be the best way to attain a general improvement in Anglo-Soviet relations, which he greatly desires. However, our prolonged silence has begun to make him doubt whether we genuinely wish to negotiate.

I replied that I saw no reason for such doubts and said that the British themselves also seemed to be in no hurry to begin trade negotiations. Besides, one should not forget that trade is bound up with politics. Sometimes politics gets in the way of trade, and sometimes it's the other way round.

Halifax agreed that politics and trade are closely linked, but asked me to make inquiries in Moscow and give him a definite answer. The British government wants to clarify this question. I promised to do so.

At the very end, Halifax raised the question of the behaviour of the Soviet press. I think he meant not so much the press, as Comrade Molotov's speeches, but preferred to lay everything at the door of the press out of diplomatic considerations. Halifax has been keeping a close eye on the Soviet press recently and has established to his regret that its general tone is not merely unfriendly, but openly hostile to Britain. This is most unfortunate, for it hinders the improvement of Anglo-Soviet relations, which he so desires.

I answered that in my opinion the Soviet press has taken a critical position in respect to Britain for two main reasons.

[i] Henryk Ehrlich, leader of the Jewish Workers' Federation in pre-war Poland; arrested and shot in 1941.

[ii] Mieczysław Mastek, member of the Sejm and deputy chairman of the Union of Railroad workers.

First, the Soviet press is simply paying back the British press in its own coin. After all, the latter has been utterly hostile to the USSR in recent months. I have just mentioned Finland as one example, but there are others.

Secondly, our press reflects our public opinion, and our public suspects and feels that British diplomacy is working against us all over the world (I cited the examples I had given earlier in conversations with Churchill, Elliot and others). This elicits an unfriendly attitude on the part of Soviet public opinion towards Britain, an attitude echoed in the press.

My words produced a quite unexpected effect. Halifax – always so pale, unperturbed, almost half-frozen – suddenly turned red, became agitated, all but leapt out of his armchair, and set about heatedly demonstrating that the Soviet government's suspicions were unfounded (I had been speaking about public opinion, not the Soviet government, but Halifax named the latter). Britain has enough troubles as it is. Britain is not scheming against the Soviet Union on the international stage and does not wish to do so. He fails to see why the British government should wish to do so, since there is nowhere that the interests of our countries collide. In the Far East, the British government is merely striving after a certain improvement in relations with Japan ('which the Soviet government is also striving after', added Halifax rather spitefully), but not at the expense of the USSR. In Turkey, the British government is extremely keen to see the strengthening of Soviet–Turkish friendship. In Scandinavia and Finland, the British government is not conducting a policy hostile to the USSR. On the contrary, the British government wishes to improve its relations with the Soviet Union – 'if, of course, the Soviet government desires the same', Halifax sniped again. The proposal for trade talks was a concrete manifestation of this wish. These talks may be stuck at present, but that's not the fault of the British government.

I replied that all this was very well, but if British diplomacy did not change its line, it would be difficult to conceive of a real improvement in relations between the two countries.

Halifax flared up once more and, clearly irritated, set about proving once again that we are in the wrong. Of course the British government is not happy about what happened in Poland, but it would not like to be detained by this episode for too long. Rather, it would like to improve its relations with the USSR as soon as possible. He asks me to explain all this to my government.

As he was seeing me out of his office, Halifax returned once again to the question of Finland. Appealing to me as president of the Council of the L[eague] of N[ations], he asked me to bring all my influence to bear on warding off an acute conflict with Finland.[209] Looking Halifax straight in the face, I replied: 'This will depend not only on us, but also on the conduct of the Fin[nish] G[overnment] and some others!'

Halifax gave an embarrassed laugh.

28 November

[Included is a cutting from the *Evening Standard* with a satirical description of the ceremony to mark the opening of parliament.]

A fine sample of journalism from the paper which some like to call the *Evening Rubbish*.

Agniya and I attended the opening of parliament.

Afterwards I went to lunch with Butler. He received me not at his place (he was afraid I might catch the 'flu from his father, who was ill), but at the home of his *parliamentary secretary*, a beautiful mansion with numerous paintings, luxurious furniture and a handsome dining-room in the style of the Alhambra. The host was absent. We ate alone.[210]

For no less than an hour and a half, Butler, swearing on his honour, deployed every means possible to persuade me that the British government was not engaged in any kind of diplomatic game against the USSR (Butler obviously knew about my conversation yesterday with his boss). Our suspicions about the intentions of the British government are absolutely unfounded. The British policy is not as Machiavellian as some assume it to be. It is simple,

69. Cast out after the Molotov–Ribbentrop Pact, Maisky has to make do with 'Rab' Butler.

and is currently defined by the basic and decisive fact that Britain is at war with Germany. Britain has its hands full. It does not have the slightest desire to aggravate the difficulties ensuing from this war by adding to their number. Britain has no desire to have the USSR, as well as Germany, as its enemy. Hence the sincere desire of the British government to improve Anglo-Soviet relations. All the more so as this is quite possible: the British government believes that the actual interests of Great Britain and the USSR do not clash anywhere. Hence the proposal for trade negotiations, which are important not so much *per se* but as a first step on the way to a general settling of relations. Unfortunately, nothing has been heard from the Soviet government for more than a month in response to the British proposals. A great pity. Halifax is particularly vexed by our silence: he was fighting energetically in government for negotiations to be opened, and now finds himself in a foolish position.

I listened more than I spoke.

Butler then made 'a short tour of the globe' to illustrate the fact that the interests of the two powers do not clash in any place.

He began with Finland. Britain has never induced or encouraged Finland to oppose Soviet proposals. Britain maintains cordial relations with Finland and advised the Finns not to be *unreasonable* (Halifax's words exactly). Unfortunately, the Finns are too 'stubborn and inflexible' and failed to understand the British 'advice', which was of course given 'in a delicate form'. That's the whole trouble.

I mocked Butler – 'in a delicate form', of course.

Then Butler turned to Scandinavia. Britain's interests there are mainly economic. In particular, it imports some of its iron ore from Sweden. However, Britain could not accept the capture of Sweden or Norway by a great power. At first I thought Butler was referring to the German threat to the Scandinavian countries. It turned out he was not! He suspects the USSR of such far-reaching ambitions. Perhaps the USSR would like to have an ice-free port in the Atlantic. Maybe Narvik? Or Bergen? Perhaps the USSR would like to add Swedish iron ore to its riches…

I mocked Butler once again – delicately, of course.

From Scandinavia, Butler moved on to the Balkans. The British policy there consists of fattening up the Balkan states (particularly Turkey, Greece and Rumania) and relieving their markets of a certain quantity of products which Germany needs to wage war (food, oil, etc.). In the field of politics, Britain is taking a restrained, wait-and-see position in the Balkans. The major aim of British policy there is to prevent Germany's access to the Black Sea and to Rumanian oil, and to keep the Balkans from being drawn into the war. Britain is indifferent to the fate of Bessarabia. In Butler's opinion, there are no clashes of interest between Great Britain and the Soviet Union in this part of the world.

The British government is wary about the idea of a Balkan pact. It avoids taking sides between Italy and Turkey. Anglo-Italian relations are improving fast, but still have a long way to go before 'both partners could go off hunting tigers together'. That's why Britain keeps its counsel about Italian aspirations in the Balkans: it does not want to injure its 'friend', Turkey. But it was unclear from Butler's words what the British government's eventual choice would be.

As far as Turkey is concerned, the British government desires above all the resumption of cordial negotiations between Moscow and Ankara.

The Near East? Here Butler surprised me again. He admits, or rather suspects, that the USSR might wish to have a 'warm port' in the Persian Gulf and might even entertain the idea of a 'march on India'. If the USSR does cherish such aspirations, then some complications could arise in its relations with England. But does the USSR have such aspirations?

I mocked Butler for a third time, but now in a far less delicate form.

Finally, the Far East. The British policy in this part of the world boils down to the possible normalization of relations with Japan, without renouncing Jiang Jieshi. This is no easy task, but it does not at any rate contradict Soviet interests. Moreover, the internal situation in Japan is currently very bad today, and Butler reckons that she will need to start retreating before too long.

What conclusion can be deduced from this 'tour of the globe'?

Butler's conclusion is as follows: there is every chance of a serious improvement in A[nglo]-S[oviet] relations. All that is needed is the will. The British government has the will. Does the Soviet government?

I tried to reassure Butler.

29 November

Yesterday evening the Soviet government renounced the Soviet–Finnish non-aggression pact in view of its violation by the hostile actions of Finland. Diplomatic relations with Finland were broken off tonight… At the same time, Molotov has said, in a speech which I heard over the radio, that had Finland been an amicably disposed country, it would have been possible to discuss the issue of the reunification of Soviet Karelia with Finland.

So, the non-aggression pact has been renounced! When I signed it on 21 January 1932 with Yrjö-Koskinen, Finland's foreign minister at the time, it never crossed my mind that the pact would meet such an end.

I vividly recall the various details of that diplomatic event. Almost simultaneously, at the end of 1931, the USSR launched a large-scale 'peaceful offensive', entering into negotiations on non-aggression pacts with France in the west and Poland, Latvia, Estonia and Finland in the east (the non-aggression pact with Lithuania had been signed back in 1926, while we still did not have diplomatic relations with Rumania). The Soviet government had already made an attempt to conclude non-aggression pacts with the limitrophes back in 1927 and 1928, but French opposition put paid to it. In 1931, however, change was afoot in Franco-Soviet relations, and Paris raised the question of such a pact being signed. The negotiations, it must be said, were hard-going, bumpy and subject to interruptions, but they continued all the same. This altered the situation and encouraged one to hope of pacts being concluded with the limitrophes.

Each of the countries with whom we conducted negotiations had its own internal problems, which hampered the progress of the talks. Moreover, each country kept glancing at its neighbour to see how it was going. Was it really going to sign a pact or was it just playing games and manoeuvring? This was an additional and serious obstacle in our path. A diplomatic breakthrough needed to be made somewhere and the first pact concluded. Then the remaining partners would agree more easily.

I managed to make a breakthrough in Finland. On the face of it, the chances of this happening seemed negligible. Finns are extremely sluggish and slow-witted in their actions. They are extremely cautious. And they are extremely hostile to everything 'Russian', especially 'Soviet Russian' – far more hostile than Estonians or Latvians. Finally, they are significantly stronger and more solid as a nation than all the other Baltic countries. Everything seemed to come together to make a breakthrough in Finland utterly unfeasible and improbable.

Yet it was right here that the breakthrough was made! The political situation in Finland had improved considerably by early 1932, as compared with 1931 and especially 1930. It was also a stroke of luck that Yrjö-Koskinen happened to be minister for foreign affairs at the time. In a sense, I was the one who made him foreign minister. It happened like this. Changes in the Cabinet were under way in the spring of 1931, after Svinhufvud[i] was elected president of Finland. The former foreign minister Procopé[ii] retired and, being a 'non-party Swede', decided to leave politics and go into *business*. Svinhufvud was looking for a new foreign minister. Yrjö-Koskinen was one of several candidates. At the end of 1930 he had been sent to Moscow as the Finnish envoy (I pulled strings for him there, too), but now Svinhufvud was recalling him to Helsinki for consultation. Yrjö-Koskinen found himself in a difficult position: on the one hand, he did not want to leave his Moscow post, which he had been seeking for so long; on the other hand, the prospect of becoming foreign minister flattered him. He turned to me for advice: could he not leave Moscow for an extended trip to

[i] Pehr Evind Svinhufvud, Finnish prime minister, 1917–18 and 1930–31; Finnish president, 1931–37.

[ii] Hjalmar Johan Fredrik Procopé, Finnish foreign minister, 1927–31; ambassador to the USA, 1939–44.

Helsinki without abandoning his post as envoy? Would the Soviet government be satisfied if – for several months, a year, or perhaps more – only a chargé d'affaires were present in Moscow? The query did not come out of the blue. A few years earlier, Procopé, then the Finnish envoy in Warsaw, was appointed foreign minister, but tried to keep his post in Poland as well. It didn't work! The Poles waited three or four months and then demanded: either Procopé returns to Warsaw or the Finnish government must appoint a new envoy, because, you see, the prestige of the Polish state cannot permit the lengthy representation of Finland in Warsaw by a chargé d'affaires. Procopé chose the Foreign Ministry and cut his ties with Poland. Yrjö-Koskinen feared we might follow the example of the Poles. That wouldn't have suited him at all. In that case, he'd have preferred to stay in Moscow.

Yrjö-Koskinen had to give his answer to the president in a few hours. I had no time to consult Moscow. So I decided to act at my own risk, guided by common sense. I told Yrjö-Koskinen: accept the foreign minister portfolio; Moscow will not feel 'offended' if a chargé d'affaires occupies the embassy for a year or more. Yrjö-Koskinen thanked me with an ardour out of keeping with his phlegmatic temperament and was appointed foreign minister the next day. Moscow also approved of my action: Yrjö-Koskinen was the best possible Finnish foreign minister in the circumstances of the time. Moreover, purely selfish considerations meant that he had every reason to aim for an improvement in relations between the USSR and Finland.

So now, when a breakthrough was needed on the diplomatic front, Yrjö-Koskinen was just the man. The idea of a non-aggression pact had his full approval. Svinhufvud valued his opinion and had taken him under his wing. Personally, I was on good terms with Koskinen: he never forgot that I had helped him become envoy in Moscow and foreign minister in Helsinki. All this was in our favour. There was just one problem: Yrjö-Koskinen was an incorrigible, beastly drinker. A true Finn. This sometimes put him out of action for several days running. During these bouts his wife would tell everyone, even his close colleagues and friends, that her husband was ill, and she wouldn't let anyone near him, not even his closest colleagues and friends. But I had no time to spare.

In any case, the talks began on or around 7 January 1932. I had been to Moscow for a week and had brought all the necessary materials and instructions. I was in a great hurry, with Yrjö-Koskinen's sluggish temperament uppermost in my mind. We met nearly every day. On the whole, I was making good progress. The military and members of the 'suojeluskunta' [Finnish White Guard fighters during the Russian Civil War] got in the way a bit. Once, Yrjö-Koskinen hit the bottle and the conference was delayed for three days. After that I asked his wife to keep an eye on him and not let him get so drunk. She gave her word and kept it. The talks were concluded in 15 days, and the non-aggression pact was signed on 21 January. The first pact in our 'peace offensive' of 1931–1932. M.M. sent me his congratulations by telegram. The Central Committee was very pleased.

Things got easier after my breakthrough. Pacts were signed with Latvia on 5 February, with Estonia on 4 May, with Poland on 25 July, and finally with France on 29 November. We were victorious along the whole front.

Yrjö-Koskinen was also rewarded: he remained Finland's permanent representative in Moscow for almost nine years. His ambassadorship ended today...

I can't understand the present position of the Finnish government. Of course, the British, French and Scandinavians have all been meddling there, confusing the Finns and drastically exacerbating a conflict which could have been settled in a neighbourly way. Still... don't the Finns understand that, if trouble comes, they can't count on anyone to help them? Who will help them? The Swedes? The British? The Americans? Like hell they will! A racket in the newspapers, moral support, oohing and aahing – yes. Troops, aeroplanes, cannons, guns – no. Butler told me plainly yesterday: 'Should anything happen, we wouldn't be able to send a single warship to Finland.'

What are the Finns counting on? What explanation can be found for their crazy provocations?

[As early as February 1939, Stalin had unsuccessfully sought to persuade Finland to cede territories which he deemed to be essential for the defence of Leningrad, a mere 33 kilometres away from the Finnish border. Haunted by the still vivid memory of Western intervention in that region during the Civil War, Stalin feared that Finland might serve as 'a springboard' for an Anglo-Franco-German attack on the Soviet Union. After subjecting the Baltic States to similar arrangements, negotiations with Finland were resumed in Moscow on 12 October and limped on until 9 November. The Russians demanded that Finland cede a number of islands in the Gulf of Finland, part of the Karelian Isthmus, and a peninsula in the Petsamo district, as well as lease to the Soviet Union part of the Hanko peninsula. In return, the Finns were to receive the large but unpopulated East Karelian territory. The Finns rejected the Soviet offers and the talks broke down. A border incident on 30 November led the Russians to unleash a full-scale war. In the early stages of the 'winter war', the Russians faced unexpectedly stiff resistance, which exposed the fragility of the Red Army in the wake of the purges. Only in March 1940 did the Russians break through the Mannerheim Line and force a peace treaty. The unpopular task of blaming the war on the stubbornness of the Finns, allegedly encouraged by the British, fell to Maisky.[211]]

1 December

So, we too have our own 'war'. Cajander, Tanner and Co. finally brought things to a head. On the morning of 30 November, the Red Army was forced to cross Finland's border and move deep into its territory...

The British have reacted with fury. The press, the radio, the cinema, parliament – everything has been mobilized. Chamberlain, Attlee, Dalton, Mander, Fletcher,[i] Silverman[ii] and others delivered anti-Soviet speeches at yesterday's session in the House of Commons. The newspapers are kicking up a storm. They began, of course, with sensational and heart-rending reports, claiming that the Soviet planes which bombed Helsinki yesterday were specifically targeting the civilian population and that some planes swooped to shoot from machine-guns at women and children running along the roads! An old story! Regrettably, however, it still has its effect on *the man in the street*. I'm taking measures to rebuff such anti-Soviet slander.

The British government's position is to wait and see. It wants to observe which way the wind is blowing. There are no signs of active British intervention in Finnish affairs so far. But I can't say for sure how the British government will act if the events in Finland drag on. I doubt, however, that Chamberlain will give open military assistance to Tanner, Cajander and Co.: he won't want to have the USSR as an enemy in the European war, in addition to Germany.

3 December

Three months of war.

Much has changed in British life over this short period of time. More than a million have been called to arms, with some being deployed on the French front, and the greater part training at home. On the street, on the omnibus, on the underground, in the theatre, at the skating-rink – everywhere there are military uniforms. And not only men's. A great number of women are to be seen in khaki: rugged boots, short skirts and perky caps from which clumps of unruly hair stick out. They are members of the women's Auxiliary Territorial Service. There are relatively few cars on the roads and in the city: petrol is rationed and the rations are far from generous. Sandbags are piled up high in front of buildings, shops, institutions and monuments. The monument at Piccadilly Circus is shielded by an entire pyramid of sandbags. In parks, gardens and on public squares there are gas-proof shelters, bomb shelters and anti-aircraft batteries. The air is filled with hundreds of balloons, their silver scales sparkling in the sun (on the rare occasions when it shines). Strict black-out is enforced in the evenings. It's pitch-black, especially in our Kensington Palace Gardens. It's difficult, dangerous and cheerless to move around after sunset. The theatres and picture-houses are open, but not all of them, and those that are open close early. *Social life* has come to a stand-still: no grand receptions, no banquets,

[i] R.T.H. Fletcher, lieutenant commander, personal parliamentary secretary to the first lord of the Admiralty, 1935–42.

[ii] Samuel Sydney Silverman, Labour MP for Nelson and Colne, 1935–68.

no *diplomatic functions*. Even the lord mayor cancelled his annual banquet scheduled for 9 November. Food prices are rising, while the quantity and choice of products shrink. Rationing is being introduced for butter, bacon and sugar. There are complaints of food shortages in certain regions. A series of restrictions has been imposed on the freedom of movement, the press, correspondence, etc.

Yes, there are many changes. But so far the basic patterns of English life have not been disturbed too much. Parliament functions normally, albeit with a few restrictions. The old party system is also functioning, although an electoral truce has been concluded between the parties for the duration of the war. The old government is also working as before, although it has been somewhat 'freshened up' with the introduction of Churchill and Eden. Chamberlain is stronger than before: all rumours and discussions of his retirement have subsided. 'Public liberties' have not been entirely curtailed in spite of the DSRA [sic – probably Defence of the Realm Act intended]. Even the *Daily Worker* still comes out regularly. The Communist Party remains legal, and people are not yet being thrown into prison for anti-government speeches in Hyde Park. Workers' wages have been raised because of the spiralling prices, but these wage hikes, of course, always lag behind increases in costs. The war has begun to inflame patriotic passions, but these have not yet enslaved the people's minds completely. Sober voices can still be heard, and signs of tolerance can be noted: out of the 13,000 Austro-German refugees who appeared before a specially established tribunal, only 300 to 400 people were interned and the rest were set free (in France all were interned, including such men as Leon Feuchtwanger[i]). On the whole, the customary machinery of British bourgeois power, with its subtle systemic bribing of the working masses, is still in good order, although slight faults are beginning to emerge in individual levers and cogs. London itself has changed little in appearance. It's the same old London – true, it has furrowed its brow, tightened its belt and put on its work clothes for a dirty job, but it's still the familiar London. Even the places of amusement are chock-full, regardless of the darkness and the bleakness of the 'black-out'.

Such is the situation for now. Will it last long?

Hard to say. One thing is certain: the habitual, familiar, age-old mode of life will be eroded more and more with each additional month of war.

5 December

In Terijoki, the People's Government of the Finnish Democratic Republic has been formed. The Soviet government has recognized it and concluded a pact of mutual assistance. The People's Government ceded Hangö to the USSR (for

[i] Lion Jacob Feuchtwanger, German novelist and playwright.

30 years) and a number of islands in the Gulf of Finland, and has agreed to rectify the borders on the Karelian Isthmus and the Rybachi Peninsula. By way of compensation, the Soviet government has given the FDR 70,000 square kilometres of land in the territory of the K[arelian] A[utonomous] R[epublic] and paid out more than 2 million pounds. The First Finnish Corps is being formed in Terijoki. Ratifications are to be exchanged in Helsinki.

The die is cast. Now we have to see it through to the end. Yesterday, on behalf of the reorganized 'government of Finland' headed by Bank of Finland director Ryti[i] (Tanner is his foreign minister), a Swedish messenger in Moscow, Winter, proposed to Comrade Molotov that the negotiations should resume. Comrade Molotov declined the proposal, saying that the Soviet government recognizes only the People's Government in Terijoki. Earlier, on 2 December, Ryti and Tanner had appealed to the League of Nations to demand that the 'Finnish question' be placed before the LN's Council and Assembly. Avenol, of course, leapt at this excellent chance to spite the Soviet Union. He consulted the British and the French, who gave their blessing. As a result, on 3 December the secretariat sent out invitations to all members to come to the Council meeting on the 9th and to the Assembly on 11 December. In his response to Avenol by cable on 4 December, Comrade Molotov said that there were no grounds for raising the 'Finnish question' because the Soviet Union was not in a state of war with Finland, but was merely giving assistance to the People's Government of the FDR, which was pursuing the struggle to purge Finland of Ryti, Tanner and Co. If the LN is nevertheless convened, the USSR will not attend.

In connection with all this kafuffle, the *Star* devoted much space to me personally. First, it published the following leader:

> December 5, 1939
> MR MAISKY STAYS AWAY
> The urbane Mr Maisky is not going to Geneva. He begs to be excused, even though he is the retiring President of the League Council. His coyness is understandable. During the past five years no diplomat has put the case against aggression with greater force than Mr Maisky.
>
> If Mr Maisky went to Geneva now he might find himself disconcerted by echoes of his old speeches. Banquo's ghost, in the shape of the Finnish delegate, might rise up and quote the words Mr Maisky used at Oxford on August 7, 1936: 'The peaceful nations have so far been timid and not coherent enough to effect any real resistance to the few bullies who aimed at the domination of the world… It should take the form of a united front of all peaceful nations against the danger of war and against

[i] Risto Heikki Ryti, Finnish prime minister, 1939–40; Finnish president, 1940–44.

aggression from whatever quarter it might come.' Heard again, after the bombing of Helsinki, those words would have a hollow, mocking ring.

Or the Polish government's representative at Geneva might be tactless enough to quote Mr Maisky's pledge on behalf of the Soviet [sic] when he visited the Temple of Peace at Cardiff in July of this year, 'We have always believed that the principle of peace must if necessary be defended against aggression.'

We wonder if Mr Maisky recalled some of these phrases when he regretted his inability to accept the kind invitation of the League. There is often no critic a man dislikes facing so much as his own former self.

Second, on the previous day, 4 December, the paper's columnist devoted half a column to me and the current situation.

[There follows a cutting from the *Star*, 4 December 1939.]

The *News Chronicle*, which currently finds itself in a paroxysm of anti-Soviet frenzy, also saw fit to mention me.

All these people have not the slightest notion of dialectics!

[There follows a cutting from the *News Chronicle*: an excerpt from the editorial, 4 December 1939.[212]]

8 December

The events in Finland have elicited very strong responses and reverberations all over the world. Here are a few details.

Guo Taiqi visited me two days ago. He was terribly alarmed and upset. What was the matter? It turned out that some Brits (he swore they were not from the Foreign Office) had been persistently whispering in his ear over recent days that the USSR had changed its general political line, that one could not rely on the USSR any longer, and that sooner or later it would turn its back on China to seek an agreement with Japan. Proof of this was the Soviet Union's 'attack' on Finland. Guo Taiqi had come to ask me if there were any grounds for these rumours. Naturally, I did my utmost to reassure him. At the end Guo Taiqi himself began reasoning 'almost like a Marxist' (as he put it). He constructed the following syllogism: 'The policies of the USSR are guided entirely by its own interests. A strong China, capable of withstanding Japan, is a direct Soviet interest. *Ergo*, the USSR cannot leave China to the mercy of fate.'

Guo Taiqi left me with his mind at ease. On parting, he told me that he would do all he could at the League of Nations (where is going as second delegate) to 'alleviate the situation'. I doubt he can do anything tangible as China's situation in the League of Nations will be very delicate this time around, while Gu Weijun (the first delegate) is not a brave fellow and prefers to go AWOL in difficult situations. This has happened more than once in the past – on the Spanish question, for example.

Yesterday, Aras came over. A different circumstance concerns him. The German press and radio have been carrying out a major campaign in recent days to the effect that Berlin and Moscow have a secret agreement to bring about a radical realignment of forces in the world. It is alleged, in accordance with this agreement, that after finishing with Finland, the USSR will turn southward and advance to the Balkans, the Near East and India, and that Germany will give it the requisite support. Yesterday the *Völkischer Beobachter* openly called on the USSR to repeat the conquests of Alexander the Great. In Washington, the German chargé d'affaires gave an interview to the press (see *Washington Times and Herald* of 4 December) in which, appearing to speak on behalf not only of Germany, but also of the USSR, he stated that Bessarabia and control over the Straits would be the Soviet government's next moves after Finland.

All these concoctions had worked Aras up into a state and he spent a long time arguing that Germany wants to 'push' the USSR into Asia, so as to deal a blow to Britain throughout the Near East and India with 'Russian hands', thereby alleviating Germany's position and simplifying its tasks in Europe.

So, once again I had to do the job of reassuring, demonstrating to the Turkish ambassador the absurdity of Germany's calculations – if such calculations actually exist in the minds of Hitler and Ribbentrop.

Aras told me in passing that in October and November he himself had advised Gripenberg[i] on several occasions to lean on the Finnish government and convince it to reach an agreement with the USSR.

'I told him,' Aras exclaimed, 'that if the conflict comes to a head, you will be abandoned! Nobody will help you!'

Gripenberg, according to Aras, agreed entirely, but Helsinki, spurred on by Sweden and others, adhered to a different point of view. As for the British government, Aras says it behaved like Pontius Pilate: it dispensed no advice at all, simply telling the Finns to 'decide for yourselves'. Somehow I find this difficult to believe.

On the whole, it seemed to me that on this occasion Aras had been sent to me by the FO. He told me that the previous day he had seen Butler, who was most unhappy at having to represent the British government in Geneva and who was going to adopt a 'moderate line' there. Before leaving, Aras asked me

[i] George Achates Gripenberg, Finnish envoy to Great Britain, 1933–41.

'between friends' whether there was anything I wished him to pass on to Butler before he left. He was seeing Butler the next day. I said I had no such messages.

Yesterday I also had a visit from Subbotić, the Yugoslav ambassador. He was also alarmed, almost panicking. The German campaign plus Stefanov's[i] article in the recent issue of the *Communist International* (which makes it clear to Rumania that it had better conclude a mutual assistance pact with the USSR according to the example of the Baltic States, and which emphasizes the status of Rumania's 'minorities', including Russians, in Bessarabia) have caused a commotion in the Balkans.

'I fully understand your claims to Bessarabia,' said Subbotić (even though I hadn't said a word about Bessarabia). 'In essence, the Rumanians understand them as well and would probably be prepared to make concessions. But how is this to be done? If Rumania were to agree to return Bessarabia to you, Hungary would immediately raise the question of Transylvania, and Bulgaria that of Dobrudja. What would be left of Rumania then?'

Be that as it may, Subbotić 'understands' that Bessarabia should be returned 'to the bosom' of the USSR. The question is how to do it.

If it is done 'quietly', 'calmly' and 'gradually', no one in the Balkans will even wince. If we decide to resolve the question abruptly and hastily (Subbotić didn't say it, but he was probably thinking about the 'Finnish model'), major complications may arise. Italy will interfere and occupy Saloniki and certain points in Yugoslavia. The Germans, not to be outdone, will follow suit. Turkey will not be able to keep out of it. Britain and France will come to the aid of Italy and Turkey. In short, a large war involving all the great European powers will break out. The Balkan peoples will be the first to suffer…

Subbotić's conclusion could be formulated as follows: 'Take Bessarabia, but do it on the sly, so as not to trigger a war in the Balkans.'

I once again had to allay the ambassador's anxiety. I explained to him that we pursue a policy of peace and that while we care a great deal about strengthening our security, we seek to avoid unnecessary complications.

The NKID press department issued a statement today saying that Stefanov's article does not reflect the point of view of the Soviet government. Excellent!

12 December

The Red Army is advancing relatively slowly in Finland. The nature of the terrain, the climate, the season (short days, low cloud cover, lakes and marshes not yet properly frozen) – everything is against us. In such conditions, the mechanized forces of the Red Army cannot be fully effective. Moreover, the

[i] Boris Stefanov, general secretary of the Rumanian Communist Party, 1936–40.

Karelian Isthmus is strongly fortified by the Finns, who have exploited the numerous rivers, lakes and marshes. All these difficulties will be overcome, of course, but for now what's needed is patience…

The slow development of events in Finland is helping to fan a frenzied anti-Soviet campaign in Britain. The campaign began almost a fortnight ago, and there are no signs of it subsiding. If anything, the tension is growing.

The press is still raging, and the 'left' (*Daily Herald* and *News Chronicle*) turns out to be even worse than the 'right' (*The Times*, *Daily Telegraph*, etc.). All sorts of slanders, lies, and nonsense concerning the USSR are published under foot-long headlines on the front pages of the London papers. The press simply excels itself when it comes to 'the bombing of women and children' and 'the use of gas' by the Red Army. We have already issued official denials, but to no avail.

The radio and the cinema are no better. The other day I even had to submit a protest to the FO about the BBC repeating the slander about the use of gas (despite our refutation).

In parliament, a touching 'united anti-Soviet front' has been formed, ranging from right Conservatives to left Labour. Only the Labourites Pritt, Wedgwood and Neil Maclean, and the Liberal Richard Acland[i] take a friendly stance. The rest of the Labourites and Liberals are experiencing different degrees of anti-Soviet fury. The National Labour Council published a pogrom-like manifesto against the USSR last week.

A most peculiar situation obtains in the institutions of the judiciary: there we now find ourselves systematically losing even those cases which seem to us incontestable.

The British government has clearly decided against shyness. *Gloves off*! Otherwise, this whole frenzied campaign would be inconceivable. Halifax's speech in the House of Lords on 5 December is very indicative in this respect. Similarly indicative is Butler's belligerent activity in Geneva, where he supports the proposal to expel the USSR from the League of Nations. Equally interesting is the fact that the British government has decided to publish a 'White Book' on the summer negotiations in Moscow. The Foreign Office had until now been against publishing it, arguing on more than one occasion that 'it could have an unfavourable effect on Anglo-Soviet relations'. Now this consideration has been dropped. One can easily imagine the content of this 'White Book'! The British government will exploit the opportunity to justify its conduct during the talks and to accuse the USSR. Lies, slander, distortion – everything will be used for this purpose. Not blatant lies, in all probability, but (which is far more dangerous) a crafty mixture of truth and deceit. It would be a good idea

[i] Sir Richard Acland, Liberal MP, 1935–45; with J.B. Priestley founded the Common Wealth Party in 1942.

for us to prepare our own 'White Book' for publication right after the British one. Otherwise the British version will circulate around the world without any resistance from our side.

What will happen next?

The League of Nations will take a decision any day now. The decision is likely to be 'expulsion'. The response of the British government is hard to predict. One thing is clear: it will not give open armed support to Ryti and Co., but will help them politically and diplomatically and supply them with planes, arms, etc.

As for the anti-Soviet campaign, one thing is particularly striking. In the campaigns connected with events in Poland and then in the Baltic, the USSR was accused of 'imperialism'. Now emphasis is placed on 'world revolution' and 'communism'. The question 'who is the No. 1 enemy? – Germany or the USSR?' is the subject of heated discussion in governmental and political circles. The answers vary. No wonder London is abuzz with rumours about new attempts to test the ground for a deal with Hitler. Montagu Norman and Horace Wilson are mentioned in this connection.

The position taken up by the USA will play a major role, as it has always done. Chamberlain and Co. look to the States more than ever before.

However, in spite of the anti-Soviet frenzy dominating the social and political atmosphere in the country, there is no talk here (unlike in France) of severing diplomatic relations with the Soviet Union. The English are cleverer than the French. Moreover, they have already tried it once and do not wish to repeat the unfortunate experience. However, I cannot vouch for the more distant future. Anything may happen in time of war.

Superficially, we are treated here in a perfectly correct manner. But there is an icy emptiness around the embassy and the trade mission, as there always is in the days of large anti-Soviet campaigns. With a few exceptions, all our 'friends', both on the 'right' and on the 'left', dived for cover when the campaign was launched. Well, it's not the first time. They'll come back.

I'm an old bird, and this isn't the first storm I've had to face. As soon as the events in Finland come to an end, it will blow over. The British are past masters at accepting the 'fait accompli'.

14 December

Yesterday, the House of Commons held a closed session, the first in the course of the war. But since nothing is ever secret in this world, especially if the secret is known to 600 people, something of what was going on in the Commons has already leaked out.

The whole meeting was devoted to matters concerning supplies to the armed forces. No other subjects (including the USSR) were discussed. The debate was opened by Greenwood and Sinclair. Burgin, the minister of supply, responded. Attlee and Chamberlain closed the debate. In between, it was almost exclusively *backbenchers* who spoke. An incident occurred at the beginning of the meeting. Quentin Hogg (son of Lord Hailsham), a Conservative, asked whether a closed meeting of the Commons could be held in the presence of the *king's enemy*, an obvious reference to Gallacher. Gallacher picked up the gauntlet and said that unlike some fascist-minded members of the Conservative Party (of which Hogg was one), he never concealed his true convictions, but was fully aware of the responsibilities that ensue for every MP from the fact of a session being held in camera. The vast majority of the audience greeted Gallacher's pronouncement with full approval, and that was the end of the incident (I heard this not from Gallacher).

What of the debate itself?

Greenwood was very weak; he spoke mostly of boots for the army. Sinclair delivered the best speech of the session. Greenwood and Sinclair spoke for 45 minutes each. Attlee was lifeless; nor was Chamberlain at his best. The backbenchers touched upon various subjects. One group criticized the government for the shortage of clothes, boots, uniforms and so on, in the army. Another complained of defects in arms production, the scarcity of machine-guns, 25-pounders, etc. A third group stressed that machine-tools were the problem. A fourth pointed out that the mobilization of industry was fast leading to the liquidation of small and medium firms by large companies (exactly as Marx has it!). In submitting orders and assigning raw materials, manpower, etc., the controllers assigned by the Ministry of Supply to all branches of industry (they are usually big industrialists themselves in the relevant branch) always give preference to powerful concerns over their weaker competitors. As a result, medium and small firms go bust.

All those complaints and accusations were dealt with mostly by Burgin, who spoke for about an hour and a half. His defence was simple: the 'programme' of the ministry was being 'fulfilled and over-fulfilled' – what else do you want? Responding to almost Soviet-like heckles from the floor asking whether the programme did not aim too low and inquiring about the views of the army, Burgin made a casual lawyer's gesture and replied: 'Have you ever seen an army content with its supplies?'

In particular, Burgin rejected categorically Greenwood's accusation that the army was short of boots.

On the whole, MPs were assured that although there were numerous difficulties and defects in military supplies, the apparatus was operating satisfactorily and military production was growing fast.

The atmosphere at the session was very 'bellicose', with Labour being especially keen to demonstrate its loyalty.

15 December

Yesterday the League of Nations expelled the USSR from its ranks.

The session began on 9 December. The Council meeting was chaired by Count de Wiart[i] of Belgium. Holsti's complaint was heard and it was decided to submit the Finnish issue to the Assembly. The Assembly met on Monday 11th, with that same Holsti delivering a sharp philippic against the USSR in which he cited phrases from M.M. Litvinov's earlier speeches in Geneva about Spain. There was virtually no debate in the Assembly. A committee of 13 members (of whom only four maintain diplomatic relations with the USSR) was elected to consider the issue. The committee cabled the USSR and Helsinki to propose that explanations be presented. Butler, who was representing Britain in Geneva this time, suggested that the two sides be given 24 hours to send in their replies. His proposal was accepted. Comrade Molotov responded, of course, by declining the LN's proposal, referring to the reasons presented in his first telegram to the League of Nations (4 December). The committee of 13 then immediately passed a resolution condemning the USSR. The Assembly approved the resolution with ten abstentions. A new Council was elected at the same time. The Portuguese representative proposed a motion to the Assembly to expel the USSR. The proposal was passed on to the Council. The Council carried the expulsion by seven votes, with four abstentions.

Britain and France directed everything in Geneva. The USA backed them up by exerting pressure on the South Americans. A US representative attended the LN meetings as an 'observer'. It is said that Paul-Boncour, who headed the French delegation in Geneva, was personally against the expulsion of the Soviet Union, but it was Daladier who took the decision. As for Butler, he was clearly unhappy with the role assigned to him, but he conscientiously pursued the Cabinet's line. The result: Britain and France have played in Geneva the unenviable role of organizers of a new 'anti-Comintern bloc'. I don't think they will have any more luck in their enterprise than Germany. In the meantime, the sight of 'Western democracies' proudly marching at the head of such truly 'progressive' powers as Portugal, Colombia, Argentina, Egypt and others, against the USSR is capable of cleaning out the brains not only of those on the 'left'. This can already be sensed, for instance, in Vernon Bartlett's reports from Geneva.

Here in London, the response to the LN's decision has so far been muted. Today's papers pushed the expulsion of the USSR to the background. In *The Times* there is not even a leader on this topic. The *Daily Telegraph* and *Daily Herald* keep to the line of Chamberlain's speech yesterday in parliament,

---

[i] Count Henri Victor Carton de Wiart, Belgian prime minister, 1920–21; delegate to the League of Nations, 1928–35 and 1939.

namely, that Britain is at war with Germany and this should not be forgotten. The *News Chronicle* is full of doubts about the 'wisdom' of the decision, and the *Manchester Guardian* criticizes it directly. It is reported from Geneva that yesterday, after the decision was taken, Butler said to a group of journalists that Britain voted for expulsion in the LN because it was a matter of 'principle', but that relations between Britain and the USSR as individual states are quite another matter, and he does not expect any particular changes in this area. In reply to a question asked by one of the journalists, he added that the trade proposals Stanley made to me in October held good. It looks like the British government, after giving 'principles' their due in Geneva, is ready to do business in London.

So, it's all over with the LN! No point crying about it! Perhaps this will even work out in our favour.

When I was leaving Geneva in May, I hoped I would never again have to honour the grand rooms of the Palais des Nations with my presence. Seems that my hope has been fulfilled. At any rate, never again will I have to deal with this League of Nations!

21 December

It seems that the acute anti-Soviet wave is abating somewhat. There are two main reasons:

(1) The firm and decisive stand of the Soviet government has made it absolutely clear to the British government that notwithstanding the clamour made by Mannerheim[i] and Co., the question of Finland is essentially closed. What does the British government, which is hardly in a position to 'save' Finland, have to gain by flailing around with its fists, thereby merely worsening still further its relations with the USSR? Of course, the British government will send arms, aeroplanes, etc. to Finland (albeit in limited quantities), but it is unlikely to wish to ratchet things up to breaking-point.

(2) The Geneva farce of an 'anti-Comintern bloc' has produced a strong impression on many leftists, and they are beginning to scratch their heads.

Moreover, newspapers cannot keep a 'sensation' going for three weeks. They need a new trick.

If nothing unexpected happens, the present wave will gradually subside. It would be a gross mistake, however, to imagine that Anglo-Soviet relations could return even to the level of October–November (a not very satisfactory level at that). On the contrary, my general impression leads me to the conclusion that if no new factors come into play in the nearest future (from the British side, our

[i] Baron Carl Gustaf Emil Mannerheim, commander-in-chief of the Finnish army, 1939–40 and 1941–46; Finnish president, 1944–46.

side, or both), we shall face a period of further deterioration in Anglo-Soviet relations, in which even a rupture is possible.

23 December

I went to see Cadogan in the Foreign Office today. Because of Christmas, the FO is practically deserted. Not a soul in the corridors and offices. Even the attendants are nowhere to be seen. Cadogan alone sits in his room 'on duty', but it is obvious that he has no desire whatsoever to attend to business. Nevertheless, I did manage to make him attend to one unpleasant matter.

On the 20th in the afternoon, at the Chancery Lane underground station, two police agents (having shown their badges) arrested Comrade Doshchenko,[i] director of the engineering department at the trade mission. The agents took Doshchenko by taxi to the trade mission, where a police car was waiting for them, and then drove in the police car to Doshchenko's place. The agents searched his flat, without taking anything, and brought him to Scotland Yard. There he was subjected to a personal search, which also proved fruitless. Doshchenko was then moved to Brixton prison (where M.M. [Litvinov] was interned in 1918) and he is still there now. The police told Doshchenko that orders had come from the Home Office to expel him from England and that he would be kept in prison until then.

As soon as he learned about Doshchenko's arrest, Korzh called Collier and demanded that Zonov[ii] (head of our consulate) be allowed to see Doshchenko. Permission was granted and Zonov visited Doshchenko in prison on 21 December. The conditions (the cell, the food, exercise, etc.) are good. Doshchenko's wife has been permitted to visit him…

I demanded an explanation for Doshchenko's arrest from Cadogan and insisted on his innocence. I also demanded that his case be reviewed. Cadogan said he did not know the details of the case, but he was certain that the Home Office could not expel Doshchenko without good reason. I then demanded that the incriminating materials be presented to me. Cadogan promised to contact the Home Office and inform me afterwards. I asked Cadogan to act promptly, emphasizing that Doshchenko was being kept in prison. Tonight I received a reply from Cadogan: a flat refusal. Cadogan informs me that he made inquiries in the Home Office and received confirmation that Doshchenko has engaged in activities that make him undesirable to His Majesty's Government and that, unfortunately, he is not in a position to share further details with me.

---

[i] Aleksei Aleksandrovich Doshchenko, member of the Soviet trade mission in Great Britain 1939; expelled from the country on charges of espionage activity.

[ii] Vasilii Matveevich Zonov, head of the consular section at the Soviet mission in Great Britain, 1939–41; second secretary at the embassy, 1941–44.

It is the first time an important colleague of ours has been arrested in the seven years of my ambassadorship in London. And it is also a sign of the deterioration in Anglo-Soviet relations about which I wrote a few days ago.

24 December

Although the acute anti-Soviet wave elicited by the events in Finland is gradually subsiding, the general curve of Anglo-Soviet relations is, to judge by all the information at my disposal, falling steeply.

The 'general line' followed by the British government since the outbreak of war has been to 'neutralize' the USSR in order to facilitate the struggle against Germany. The British government's reasoning was simple: better one enemy than two. That is why I heard so many statements in October and November about the desire 'to improve relations', culminating in Stanley's trade proposals.

Now the situation is changing. The British government has practically given up any hope of 'improving relations' (the lack of a reply to Stanley's proposals played a major role here) and is looking for a new direction on the 'Russian question'. Now a 'French concept' (ascribed to Daladier and Gamelin) has emerged, which assumes that it would be dangerous for the Allies to tolerate a situation in which the Soviet Union remained neutral till the end of the war. For this would mean that when the major European capitalist powers have exhausted their resources, the USSR alone would have fresh forces and an intact army. What would then become of Europe and the capitalist system? (By the way, I remember hearing in the spring from someone in Geneva that the Turks, who were insisting at the time to France that a tripartite mutual assistance pact was essential, subscribe to a similar notion.) The USSR, therefore, must be drawn into the war – on the side of the Allies if possible, or on the side of Germany if this is inevitable. The main thing is to 'bleed' the USSR. To support their concept, the French adduce various additional arguments: the war in the west has turned out to be easier than expected; the Red Army, to judge by the Finnish experience, is less formidable than was assumed; and therefore Britain and France could cope with two enemies, all the more so as the USA would definitely render extensive aid in this case, or even enter the war.

Until recently all those French arguments were met with scepticism in London. Now a clear shift can be observed. A majority in government still adheres to the old concept of 'neutrality', but some ministers have begun speaking in the spirit of the French thesis. The more so as it seems that the British government recently received assurances from Washington that the USA would probably enter the war on the side of Britain and France, should the Soviet Union join Germany.

The severance of diplomatic relations between Britain and France on the one hand and the USSR on the other is seen as the first step in drawing the USSR into the war. And then who knows? Perhaps it will be possible *to switch the war* and attack the USSR through a united capitalist bloc, including Germany.

Strange rumours are afloat in this connection about the 'White Book' on the summer talks in Moscow, which the British government is preparing and which should appear in early January. It's said that the advocates of 'neutralizing [the Soviet Union]' want to word it in such a way as not to eliminate the possibility of maintaining relations at their present level or even improving them in future. The advocates of the French thesis, on the contrary, want to edit the 'White Book' in such a way as to guarantee after its publication either a clear severance of relations or, at the very least, the recalling of ambassadors.

At the same time, strange news is arriving from the USSR. The consular department of the British embassy in Moscow has summoned a British representative of an Anglo-American company from Leningrad and suggested that he leave the USSR as soon as possible. The US embassy has advised its citizens in the USSR to leave the USSR before 1 January. It is known that the consular section of the British embassy in Moscow has already made preparations for evacuation via Rumania.

It's obvious that some kind of anti-Soviet brew is currently being cooked up in London, Paris and Washington. Will it come to the boil? Will it lead to the rupture of diplomatic relations or at least to the recalling of ambassadors?

Time will tell.

[Maisky tried to put on a brave face. He lightly dismissed as 'absurd' the expulsion of the Soviet Union from the League of Nations. He did not, however, fool Beatrice Webb, who gathered from his English chauffeur 'that the Ambassador did not even go to his Club – Diplomats Club – in St James Street'. The Maiskys were clearly being ostracized by foes and former friends alike. Cut off from news from Moscow, as he complained in a private letter to Litvinov, Maisky feared that Britain and France 'had become definitely hostile to the USSR and were planning a peace with a defeated Germany and then an anti-communist alliance!' He could only console himself with the thought that the defeat of Germany would spark a revolution there, and that Moscow would be forced to intervene if the West tried to crush it by force.[213] The mask slipped, though, at Christmas, when rumours started circulating of a breakdown in relations and of his recall. He was little encouraged by a rather acrimonious exchange of telegrams with Molotov. Maisky's distress is discernible in his desperate attempts to persuade Molotov that his continued stay in London was indispensable to prevent the outbreak of hostilities.

He persevered with his distinctive *modus operandi* of attributing his own ideas to his interlocutors. On his way to visit Lloyd George on Christmas Eve, Maisky had stopped for tea with the Webbs (who assumed that this was 'a farewell visit'). He told them that he regarded the state of Anglo-Soviet relations as 'serious', and that he expected the publication of a White Book on the 1939 negotiations.[214] It would expose Molotov's duplicity in carrying on military talks with the British, while secretly arranging for the pact with Ribbentrop (and would also expose Maisky's own ploys). This was bound to lead to the severance of relations between the countries and to the granting of assistance to the Finns in their war against Russia. In his telegram to Molotov following dinner at Lloyd George's, Maisky conveyed at length the advice of the trustworthy politician to bring the war in Finland to a swift end, echoing almost verbatim his own exposé to the Webbs a couple of hours earlier.[215]]

25 December

Agniya and I had a proper Christmas Eve yesterday! Straight out of a fairy tale. Yet it was also thoroughly saturated with contemporary reality.

We left London at 3 p.m. to visit the Webbs and then Lloyd George – their *country houses* are not far apart.

The city was under a blanket of dense fog, and our driver White shook his head sceptically when I decided on travelling all the same. The fog outside the city was even thicker. We could barely see two feet ahead of us. We drove slowly, anxiously, hooting all the time. We got lost three times and were forced to drive a fair distance back. We were enveloped in a milky mist, through which our car sailed like some fairy-tale ship on some fairy-tale sea. The fog thinned as we approached the Webbs' place. The visibility improved and we could drive faster, but then we suddenly had to turn off onto a side road: the main road was closed off because of an accident involving some military lorries that had been travelling ahead of us.

It was gone five when we reached the old couple. The long delay had alarmed them and they were even thinking of making inquiries about us at the embassy. As always, we sat down by the blazing fire in their cosy, book-lined *drawing room*, and began to talk. About what? About the war, of course, about prospects for the future and about Anglo-Soviet relations.

The Webbs are in a pessimistic mood. They think we underestimate the capitalist forces, which will cost us dearly. Finland is an illustration of this state of affairs. The Webbs understand and even share the motives that made the USSR take a stand against Mannerheim and Co., but they ask: was it wise at this time to exacerbate the conflict to this extent? They believe that what is happening in Finland is the collision of two systems, socialist and capitalist, albeit, for now, merely in a limited area. That is why Finland has immediately become a focal point for all the world's reactionary forces. Was it profitable for the Soviet Union to trigger such a conflict at this precise moment?

We argued at length and I tried to prove to the Webbs that it's not always possible to choose the time and conditions for an action which, of itself, is entirely necessary. Sometimes one has to strike in a less favourable situation than might be desired. But that's the way it goes. My arguments seemed to shake the Webbs a little, without, I believe, convincing them.

But Finland, from their point of view, is not the only example, nor the most significant. Far more serious are the potential developments in the European theatre of war. If proletarian revolution and civil war break out in Germany, the capitalist governments of Britain and France will certainly come to the aid of the German counter-revolution.

'Will they be able to do it?' I asked. 'Will the "upper ten thousand" in Britain and in France manage to lead their armies, which consist after all of workers and peasants, against a proletarian government in Germany?'

The Webbs are convinced they will. Particularly if the German revolutionary government seeks the help of the Red Army. It won't, of course, be possible to pitch the entire Anglo-French army against the German revolution, but a considerable force could be found for this purpose. It would be difficult to keep even this force in a revolutionary climate for a long time, but it would prove useful for a certain period in suppressing the revolution. Moreover, all German officers would be on the side of the counter-revolution, and this could not but have a negative effect on the combat efficiency of the proletarian legions. On the whole, the Webbs take a grim view of the prospects for a German revolution (even if one assumes our support). Revolution in Britain or even in France, if they are not defeated in the war, is out of the question.

We argued again for some time, but the Webbs stuck to their guns, charging us, Soviet communists, with the accusation that in our ideas and calculations *der Wunsch ist der Vater des Gedankens.*

How do the Webbs themselves see the future?

In an utterly gloomy light. The war will drag on. Europe will be ruined and impoverished. England will enter a period of decline. She will lose a considerable part of her Empire. She will be corroded from within by the two severe diseases of modern capitalism: unemployment and falling birth-rates. The ruling classes will not be able to cope with these illnesses. But nor will the proletariat, headed by Labour-party types, demonstrate the ability and revolutionary energy sufficient to rebuild decaying bourgeois society from top to bottom. The long epoch of Britain's decline, decay and dying will follow: its transformation from a world empire to a second-rate power, as happened to Spain and Holland. The Webbs refuse to hazard a guess as to how the international situation may change during and after the war, claiming not to be 'experts' in this sphere.

I listened to the old couple (Beatrice did most of the speaking, while her husband merely made the odd comment or expressed his assent) and couldn't help thinking that they were actually the mouthpiece of capitalism, which, though old, enfeebled and decaying, is, unfortunately, still far from powerless. I felt that these people, who have devoted their lives to the cause of socialism and have recognized in their old age that 'Soviet communism is the new civilization' destined to replace the capitalist one, themselves adhere to the bedrock of that very capitalism, whether consciously, half-consciously, or even subconsciously. For I had the strong impression that they feared revolution and the inevitable temporary dislocation of their entire, habitual existence – in England, yes, in England, and not in some distant land…

Continuing our debate, we moved to the dining-room for tea with the 'jam' and biscuits I have come to know so well. The Webbs are very concerned about the state of relations between the USSR and Britain. They criticized the government and expressed their fear of a possible rupture of diplomatic relations. This distressed them greatly.

On leaving, I told them half in jest: 'If I happen not to visit your home again, please remember that I spent the best hours of my stay in England here.'

This is true. For the Webbs, despite everything, are the most interesting, the most pleasant and the dearest (in so far as this word is appropriate in this case) of all the people I have met during my ambassadorship in Great Britain…

We are in the car once again. The sky has cleared up. The stars are shining brightly. The fields and trees are covered with thick, white hoar-frost. Magical silvered branches bend down over both sides of the road. The remnants of the recent mist hide, as if ashamed, in groves and copses. The moon comes out, and the whole scene takes on the features of a fairy-tale. Christmas Eve once more! The heart fills with childhood images and reminiscences!…

And here, at long last, is *Churt*, Lloyd George's country estate. We enter the house, take off our coats and are ushered into the warm drawing room. The host meets us at the door. Lloyd George looks wonderful: a fresh haircut, eyes shining like a young man's, bright snow-white hair framing an animated, clever and almost cheerful face. Such handsome old age! Lloyd George, after all, is nearly 77.

Lloyd George's son Gwilym and his wife are also in the room. Gwilym went down with a stomach ulcer last month and he looks very wan and faded.

Cocktails. Radio. Small talk at the fireplace. Dinner.

Lloyd George and I are in constant conversation. To be more exact, he speaks and I ask him occasional questions, explain, even argue and object. The old man sparkles and shines like a precious diamond.

'The war?' he exclaims. 'I expect that in spring, most likely in March, the Germans will try to land us a heavy blow via Belgium. I see no other route for an offensive. If Hitler doesn't do this, then it's clear that the war on the western front will assume the character of more or less permanent *stalemate*. Real war will be waged only at sea and partly in the air, and to an even greater extent in the economic sphere. It will be a war of attrition. Who will win? It's difficult to say. Germany was defeated mostly by hunger in the war of 1914–1918. Today,

Germany is better prepared for war. First, Hitler has stored up big reserves of food for the war (which the kaiser did not have). Second, he has the Soviet and Balkan markets at his disposal. The fate of Germany in this war is in the hands of the Soviet Union. Everything depends on the size of the aid – economic, raw material, food, etc. – which Hitler will be able to get from you. If you set about supporting him in earnest, the war may last five or six years.'

I started objecting and stated that one could hardly imagine so long a war. But the old man wouldn't agree.

'Where peace can come from,' he exclaimed, 'I fail to see. Military sentiments in Britain are now profound and serious. Don't cultivate any illusions on that score. Peace is impossible without restoring Poland and giving at least partial autonomy to Czechoslovakia. Britain committed itself too far. You know my attitude to the Polish guarantee. From the very beginning I considered it madness without a prior agreement with you. Pitt[i] refused to give such a guarantee at the end of the eighteenth century. He understood that Britain was not in a position to send a single battalion to help Poland in case of need. But Chamberlain is not Pitt. That's why he made the Polish guarantee. Let me repeat: it was madness! But Chamberlain's madness has tied Britain and now we can't retreat, although I myself think that Hitler's ultimatum to Poland (the 16 points of 31 August) was an acceptable basis for negotiations. What's more, Winston confessed to me not long ago that he thinks the same. This is all in the past, however. Today, peace without the restoration of Poland is impossible. Will Hitler agree to it? I don't think so. And who could act as mediator? Roosevelt? Stalin? Mussolini? The pope?... Unlikely. Anyway, the position of each of them is such that they could hardly mediate successfully on their own, and on the other hand it is difficult to conceive a sufficiently weighty combination emerging from their midst. No, I don't believe in an early peace, and certainly not while Hitler rules Germany. I also don't believe, unlike some people here in Britain, that the United States may take part in the war. No, the overwhelming mood in the USA today is isolationism and a reluctance to meddle in European quarrels and fights.'

Lloyd George sighed, made a gesture with his pince-nez as only he can do, and suddenly drew an unexpected conclusion: 'I think that the current war is capitalism's last great struggle for survival.'

I asked whether the British masses understood that.

Lloyd George replied: 'I don't think so. At any rate, the greater part of those we call the *man in the street* do not understand it. A doctor I have known since 1914 visited me the other day. I asked him what he thought would be the outcome of this war. The doctor shrugged his shoulders and said: "...in the

[i] William Pitt the Younger, British prime minister, 1783–1801.

end we will win. I don't know how, but *somehow we will win.*' This answer is deeply typical. Such is the conviction of the masses. Why? Because the English have never before been beaten in a big war. They have, of course, had isolated failures, defeats and losses in the course of their history. They've sent their armies to the continent and sometimes not seen them return. Yet the English have never been completely beaten in a big war. Disaster has never come to the gates of their capital city. Their main base has always remained impregnable. Which means that single defeats have never had a fateful significance. They did not turn into a national catastrophe. And, in the end, the English would emerge victorious. So it was in the wars with the Spaniards, the Dutch, the French, Napoleon and the kaiser. This sense of invincibility has entered the flesh and blood of the people. An average Englishman just cannot imagine that his country might have suffered the same fate as France in 1871 or Germany in 1918. It's not by chance that the English have such expressions as "*somehow we will muddle through*" or "*we will blunder through*". No other language uses such expressions. Every Englishman – from worker to lord – is imbued with this spontaneous-subconscious feeling, which is a potent weapon against any anti-war sentiments.'

Our conversation naturally turned to Finland and Anglo-Soviet relations. Lloyd George questioned me closely about the progress of military operations, the climate, terrain and other aspects of the Finnish theatre of war, and then drew his conclusions.

'If I were you,' he says, 'I would conclude the Finnish operations as quickly as possible. I fully understand your motives and objectives. No doubt the USSR has good grounds to take possession of bases, islands, etc. on Finnish territory. But the issue has outgrown these comparatively narrow bounds. On the limited territory of Finland, the clash of two worlds – yours and that of capitalism – is currently under way. In Finland you are facing not only the Finns, but all the other representatives of the capitalist world as well. Every further week of delay in the settlement of the conflict is fraught with the danger of new international complications, the appearance of new "supporters" and new "volunteers", and new attempts at setting up the united anti-communist bloc that failed to materialize in 1918–19. These circumstances should not be underestimated. I remember that at the beginning of the last war Cambon,[i] the French ambassador in London at the time, implored us to send at least one squadron to France "to raise morale". Cambon was a clever man and understood that if you sent a squadron, a division would soon follow. This is exactly what happened. At first we sent six divisions to the continent and thought we would keep to that level till the end of the war. But what actually happened? We had 70 divisions

[i] Pierre Paul Cambon, French diplomat; ambassador to Great Britain, 1898–1920.

in France at the end of the war! The same will happen now in Finland. First Sweden will send 2,000 "volunteers", then the army will follow. Other countries will do the same. Please allow me, an old fellow who knows a few things about international and military affairs, to give you a piece of advice: conclude the operations in Finland as fast as possible, but without resorting to the methods used by the Germans in Poland, as that would only complicate your situation.'

I protested against Lloyd George's suggestion that we might be using 'German methods' of conducting a war. The old man grinned and added, in an accommodating spirit: 'Don't be angry, I didn't mean to offend you. I just know from my own experience that war is war. And the present war is the last big war of the capitalist system for its survival.'

I asked Lloyd George what he thought about the prospects for Anglo-Soviet relations.

'The entire recent behaviour of the British government – its campaign in the press, activity at the League of Nations, and aid to Finland – should logically lead to the severance of relations. I consider this an insane policy and a highly dangerous one for Britain. To provoke the Soviet Union to war (the severance of relations could easily turn out to be a stage on the path to war) would mean the birth of the greatest global catastrophe. For in this case war would not be confined to Europe, but would extend to Asia. It would sweep up India, where the communists are the second force after Gandhi. Imbecilic scribblers are screaming in the papers about the failure of the Red Army in Finland. Downright nonsense! The Soviet Union is a great power. Maybe it is slow to act, maybe it makes mistakes – any great power can afford to make mistakes – but once the USSR gains momentum, it will become something powerful and colossal, akin to the movement of glaciers. In which direction will these "glaciers" drift? Towards warm shores, of course. Those warm shores of which we have plenty and which are far from easy to defend. That is why I consider the British government's policy towards the USSR insane… But then, hasn't this government already done many other things no less insane?'

Lloyd George gave a sardonic grin and added: 'I was talking about this with Winston the other day. He agrees with me. In general, it's hard to spot any sharp anti-Soviet prejudice in him as yet. But Winston is up to his eyes in naval affairs; he enjoys his job very much and devotes little attention to major politics. It's a pity. Chamberlain, Simon, Halifax and Hoare often meet as a foursome, to discuss and decide issues which really ought to be decided on by the War Cabinet as a whole.'

Lloyd George waved his pince-nez around again and continued: 'There is no doubt that not only in France, but also in our governmental circles there are provocateurs who seek the severance of relations with the USSR. But they are still in the minority in Britain. If you don't play into their hands, the situation can still be saved. I think the Soviet government's response to the decision of the League of Nations was very wise. To tell the truth, I had feared the worst. You should continue in the same vein. Don't display nervousness or a hot temper with regard to the forthcoming publication of the "White Book", which contains some digs in your direction. Don't harp on the issue of Anglo-French aid to Finland, considering, among other things, that the actual size of the aid will hardly be great. In general, remain calm and collected. And, above all, get these Finnish operations over with as soon as possible! That's the main thing. A rupture in relations can still be avoided.'

We toasted the incoming year, wishing for 1940 to be better than its predecessor, then returned to the *drawing-room*. We listened to the radio, laughed at the famous Lord Haw-Haw[i] (the English announcer on German radio) who, according to Lloyd George, has of late been all but propagating 'communist propaganda'. We set off home after ten…

And there she was again, Christmas night! Bright stars, the moon, trees in silver, wreaths of mist, the long road, and the light shadows of half-forgotten childhood images and visions bound up with the magic words: Christmas Eve.

P.S. A few more 'morsels' from my conversation with Lloyd George.

> Labour? They are simply Chamberlain's errand-boys. All socialists are like that. I remember meeting German social democrats in 1909. I was preparing a workers' national insurance bill at the time and went to Berlin to study how the workers' insurance system operated in the 'classic country' of national insurance. Bethmann-Hollweg,[ii] who was then chancellor ('*a second-rate man*'), received me cordially. I was offered every opportunity to study the subject. When I had finished seeing ministers, functionaries and all sorts of other officials, I asked Bethmann-Hollweg to let me talk to the leaders of social democracy as well. Bethmann-Hollweg willingly agreed (he knew his social democrats very well!). Our meeting shocked me to the core. I had heard much about German social democrats in England and imagined them as ardent revolutionaries with wide horizons, racing pulses and the most radical plans for social transformation. And whom did I find? Philistines, the most narrow-minded, respectable philistines! They uttered not a word about socialism, revolution or the decisive struggle to abolish the capitalist system! But they were positively passionate, even

[i] Lord Haw-Haw was the nickname of William Joyce, German radio's infamous English radio broadcaster.

[ii] Theobald von Bethmann-Hollweg, German secretary of state for home affairs, 1907–09; chancellor of the German Empire, 1909–17.

> ecstatic, about a wage rise of 1 mark or the reorganization of the national insurance reserve fund. I, a liberal, was much more to the left, much more radical than they. I was deeply disappointed…But then, with the passage of time and long experience, I have come to the firm conclusion that socialists are like that the world over. Such is their nature. To fight, to fight in earnest – this they cannot do. Communists are different. They are made of different stuff. Communists can fight – they sometimes lose, but they also know how to win…

'When I was first appointed minister, one intelligent man told me: "Never forget that there, at the top, friendship does not exist." How right he was! How profoundly right he was! Later, I would learn this for myself.'

31 December

In view of the current situation, we cancelled the New Year's celebrations for the whole colony in the embassy. We decided to greet the New Year individually or in groups at home. Agniya and I did so as if we were in Moscow, at nine o'clock London time. Then we dropped in for a moment at the L.s' [unidentified] upstairs, where a small group of embassy personnel were celebrating with their wives, singing and dancing. After that we drove around the city to see how the English were seeing in the New Year. The streets were shrouded in the usual black-out gloom. The pavements were white with snow: the week has been uncommonly cold and snowy for England. There were people in the streets, but immeasurably fewer than in former years. At Piccadilly, where huge, noisy crowds, singing and dancing, always flood the square on New Year's Eve, there were now only a few sparse, silent groups. At St Paul's Cathedral, where there is always a sea of human beings, shouting, laughing and dancing, there was nobody to be found. It was the same all over. Only Whitechapel was noisier, but perhaps that was due to the character of the locals.

War! Its deadly breath has frozen the New Year celebrations of 1940.

Now, back at home, I sit and ponder: what does tomorrow have in store?[216] What will 1940 bring us? What indeed?

It's hard to guess. But I expect nothing good, whether in general or personal terms.

I recall past New Year's Eves, the first of each decade.

I saw in 1900 at home in Omsk, while still a schoolboy. I was nearly 16. I wrote verses, suffered from *Weltschmerz*, and was making my first shy steps toward revolutionary political consciousness. On the threshold of the new century I was reading Byron's *Cain*, which I thought to be the greatest literary work of the nineteenth century. A whole life lay in front of me.

I saw in 1910 in Munich, in emigration, already a conscious revolutionary, with some experience to my credit: exile, prison and underground activity. A small group of émigré comrades gathered in the artistic-bohemian *Simplicissimus* café of Kathi Kobus, who was very well known in Munich at the time.

I saw in 1920 in Mongolia at A.V. Burdukov's outpost, together with his family and the members of my expedition carrying out an economic survey of Mongolia.

I saw in 1930 as ambassador in Helsinki and celebrated the New Year together with the whole Soviet colony.

And here I am, seeing in the year 1940 in London, in circumstances of war and 'black out', entirely uncertain of the near future – not only of my personal future (what would that matter?), but of the future of Europe and all mankind.

And what does tomorrow have in store? And how many New Years am I still destined to celebrate?

Where and how will I greet the year 1950? That's still conceivable, but the question arises of itself: will I make it?

And 1960? I don't know. Will I make it? And is it worth living till then?

At any rate, one thing is clear: if a sudden revolution doesn't happen in medicine, two decades is the utmost I can count on. The greater part of my life is behind me. Even in the best scenario, only a short period lies ahead. But as yet I have no fear of death, nor sharp regret for the fact that three quarters of my life have already passed.

1940

2 January

A visit from Guo Taiqi, whom I hadn't seen for nearly a month. He's been in Geneva as a sort of semi-official Chinese delegate to the League of Nations Assembly (at any rate, I couldn't find his name in the official list of delegates).

Guo's Geneva impressions contain one point of interest: the major role played by the United States in the expulsion of the Soviet Union. The USA staged the whole comedy with the South American republics and encouraged France every way it could. Bullitt[i] made a special démarche in Paris, after which Daladier called Paul-Boncour (head of the French delegation in Geneva) four times, insisting that extreme measures be taken against the Soviet Union. Paul-Boncour himself was against expulsion. According to Guo, the British took a more passive stance, and Butler initially spoke against expulsion. However, once he had learned of the position taken by the USA, he decided 'not to object'. Or perhaps the British, with their customary dexterity, merely did a better job of simulating passivity?

Guo preferred to keep his counsel about the conduct of China in Geneva, but assured me most emphatically of the strength of China's friendship with the USSR.

But this is all in the past. Today, Guo is concerned by the intensified talk in British political circles about the formation of two large, opposing blocs:

(1) 'totalitarian and continental' – Germany, USSR and Japan.

(2) 'democratic and maritime' – England, France and the USA.

Guo dislikes this talk very much and asked me anxiously what I thought about it. I did my best to reassure him.

3 January

The curve of Anglo-Soviet relations continues to drop.

The 'White Book' about the summer negotiations in Moscow is to be published in a fortnight or less. Rumours keep circulating that it will be prepared

---

[i] William Christian Bullitt, first US ambassador to the USSR, 1933–36; ambassador to France, 1936–40.

in such a way (unless something unexpected happens at the last moment) that it will inevitably result in the severance of diplomatic relations between the two countries, or at least the mutual recall of ambassadors.

The *Daily Worker* raised the alarm back on 27 December, giving the first warning about the danger of a break in relations. On the same day, the Foreign Office refuted the newspaper's report through Reuters and interviews with foreign correspondents.

Nevertheless, yesterday, 2 January, Seeds left Moscow 'on leave'. Before his departure, he visited C[omrades] Potemkin and Molotov for discussions about the state of Anglo-Soviet relations. He was given to understand that the Soviet government harboured no hostile intentions towards England, but was resolutely determined to eliminate the danger to Leningrad presented by hostile, bourgeois Finland. It was also pointed out to Seeds that Britain was continuing to pursue a line hostile to the USSR, in particular in the League of Nations and on the Finnish issue. Seeds asked the Soviet government to make a gesture to signify our desire to maintain normal relations with England, tacitly threatening their further deterioration should such a gesture not be made. Seeds' request was not satisfied, but he nonetheless expressed the hope that Halifax, with whom he was planning to talk in London, would be able to 'come up with something'. Seeds' departure merely confirms the rumours that the publication of the 'White Book' will preclude his continued presence in Moscow. The same rumours say that my stay in London will also become very precarious after the appearance of the Book, although I confess that it is not entirely clear to me how this might happen. Time will tell.

Today's newspapers report that Naggiar, the French ambassador in Moscow, is also soon to depart on 'extended leave'. The Italian ambassador in Moscow Rosso[i] has also received instructions from his government to go 'on leave': this is clearly a response to the recall of our new ambassador in Rome, C[omrade] Gorelkin,[ii] who, on the eve of the presentation of his credentials, was called back to Moscow in protest against the anti-Soviet demonstrations in front of the embassy about the events in Finland.

So, three great powers are recalling their ambassadors from Moscow. This is no coincidence. It is part of the plan presented by Daladier at the last meeting of the Inter-Allied Supreme War Council on 19 December. Daladier argued that the 'Allies' should sever diplomatic relations with the Soviet Union. Chamberlain objected, saying this was still 'premature' and that in any case it would be more advantageous for the break to occur at the initiative of the USSR. It was eventually decided to pursue a wait-and-see policy and to use

---

[i] Augusto Rosso, Italian ambassador in Moscow, 1936–40.

[ii] Nikolai Vasilevich Gorelkin, head of the western department of NKID, 1939; Soviet ambassador in Italy, 1939–41.

various means to provoke Moscow to sever relations: by lending assistance to Finland, by recalling ambassadors, by publishing the 'White Book', and so on. It's possible that poor Doshchenko is also a cog in this general plan.

[A cutting from the *Yorkshire Post*, 2 January 1940, is attached to the diary.]

4 January

On New Year's Eve, Beaverbrook unexpectedly called me to extend his good wishes, and yesterday Agniya and I went to his place for lunch. There were only three of us, so the conversation was quite frank.

Beaverbrook, who has told me before that he sees no sense in the current war, is now most interested in the prospects for peace. He questioned me long and hard about my thoughts on the war, the situation in Germany, Soviet intentions, etc. and then set about expounding his ideas.

Beaverbrook is currently enthused by the Vatican's reconciliation with the Quirinale (the pope's visit to the Italian king,[i] etc.), which, he believes, should greatly raise the prestige of the Italian government everywhere, especially in the United States, through the influence of the Catholic Church. Beaverbrook draws the following conclusions: Mussolini is still perched on the fence, but he already has one leg in the 'Allies'' camp as a result of the reconciliation. And yet, he has not broken with Hitler. Therefore, given Italy's growing international prestige, Rome may become a good channel by which to probe the prospects for peace. The main question is whether Hitler is willing to agree to the conditions which the British government and British public opinion might deem acceptable. Beaverbrook does not have a clear answer to this.

What is the alignment of forces in the British ruling circles? The 'big four' (Chamberlain, Simon, Hoare and Halifax) are ready to conclude peace without crushing Germany, if an acceptable basis is found. Churchill, who relies on the Labour–Liberal sector and certain Conservative circles, believes that, before discussing peace, Germany must be crushed.

What are the prospects? Beaverbrook believes that if Hitler were to agree to the minimal acceptable conditions, including Poland and Czechoslovakia – conditions, in other words, which could be presented to the nation as a fulfilment, albeit not absolute, of the 'war aims' – the 'big four' would immediately conclude a peace. Should Hitler not agree, Churchill will triumph and the war will continue.

Beaverbrook told me that in France and in some British circles the following conclusion is being reached with increasing frequency: since a 'stalemate' has

---

[i] King Victor Emmanuel III of Italy, 1900–46.

occurred on the western front, a more 'mobile' front should be sought to end the war as soon as possible. Previously, before the events in Finland, it was assumed that this second front would be in the Balkans. Now, thoughts have turned to Scandinavia. I asked Beaverbrook: what position would England take should Scandinavia be drawn into the war? Beaverbrook answered without hesitation: 'We would most certainly fight for Scandinavia, especially for Norway.'

Beaverbrook is extremely worried about Anglo-Soviet relations. He himself is definitely against a rupture, and certainly against waging war with the USSR. He thinks therefore that the British can 'applaud Finnish bravery', but should not send arms and ammunition to Finland. Unfortunately, there are notable elements among the general public and in government who favour meddling in Finnish affairs, even at the risk of provoking the USSR to break off relations. Beaverbrook is anxiously awaiting the outcome of the debate on 'the Russian question' in the US Congress. If the USA severs diplomatic relations with the USSR, the British advocates of a 'resolute policy' on the Finnish question will gain the upper hand. But Beaverbrook hopes that the USA will not go so far. He is also consoled by Churchill's support for a 'cautious' line regarding the Soviet Union. This is important because Churchill's influence at the present time is great. As a result, Beaverbrook has not yet lost hope that a rupture in Anglo-Soviet relations may still be avoided, but he deems the situation dangerous.

[Beaverbrook's attitude was an exception. Maisky had become a pariah in London. He found most doors bolted, while his invitations were politely turned down. Formerly a frequent visitor, Harold Nicolson steered clear of the embassy: 'Spending the Christmas holidays here and trying to get through a little work.' Samuel Hoare excused himself, explaining that, since the outbreak of war, the Cabinet was sitting so late that he 'reluctantly had to adopt the practice of not lunching out at all', while Cadogan was 'engaged for lunch on Thursday. As regards Friday – having been on duty here all through the Christmas "holiday", I had arranged to go away on that day for 10 days or so.'[1] Bilainkin, the journalist for whom the doors of the embassy were always open, noted in his diary 'the deep lines' under Maisky's eyes 'when the clamour rose' for a declaration of war against the Soviet Union: 'As I walked away, along the icy cold and ice-covered "Millionaires' Row", I thought of its principal tenant, who had so eagerly striven for success in his mission, had nearly won it in the middle of last year, and then watched triumph being taken from his grasp.'[2]

Maisky barely recovered his social standing after the conclusion of the Winter War. As late as May, an invitation for Eden and his wife to come to lunch at the embassy 'quite privately' drew the lukewarm response 'I will, if I may, let you know later about my wife as she is away in the country at present.'[3] Dalton likewise describes in his diary a luncheon he attended on his own at the embassy, as his wife 'would sooner be found dead than in [Maisky's] Embassy'. He was greeted by Madame Maisky, 'advancing upon me with rather too red lips, says she is so sorry that my wife is in the country. She adds, rather malapropos, "So many people's wives seem to be in the country just now." I say,

"Yes, it is such beautiful weather isn't it."'[4] Relations with the court fared no better. 'The King and Queen at a B.P. [Buckingham Palace] dinner,' Maisky told the Webbs, 'had been markedly rude to them; in spite of the fact that Madame Maisky was *"doyenne"* the Queen had not spoken to her after dinner ... On retiring the King and Queen had passed by Maiskys, without recognition.'[5]]

5 January

A remarkable incident happened today.

Strang dropped in unexpectedly. I hadn't seen him for a long time, since early August, when he had just got back from his unsuccessful visit to Moscow.

I asked him to sit down and offered him a Russian cigarette. Strang took a deep drag before declaring that he had come 'on the instructions of Lord Halifax, but in a private capacity'. In mid-January the 'Blue Book', devoted to the Moscow negotiations on the pact, is to be published (it turns out to be a 'Blue', not a 'White' Book, the difference being that the 'White Book', which has no dust-cover, is usually smaller than the 'Blue Book', which does have one). This Book will contain, among other materials, records of a few conversations which Halifax once had with me. As a point of courtesy and on a private basis, Halifax would like to offer me the opportunity to acquaint myself with the passages that relate to me before the Book is published, should any corrections be required. After all, records of conversations are made after the fact, and one can never be entirely sure of their accuracy. Having said this, Strang took the proofs from his pocket (a sizable parcel) and pushed them towards me, suggesting that he was prepared to leave them for me to peruse and correct as required.

I confess that I was sorely tempted to take the Book into my hands at once. But I immediately checked myself, for the thought suddenly flashed across my mind that 'honourable' Halifax had laid a trap for me. For indeed, had I accepted his 'courteous' suggestion and kept the Book even till tomorrow, this would have given him the opportunity in future to assert that the Soviet government had been informed of the contents of the Book before its publication and that its text had been at least partially agreed upon. In this way, the Soviet government's hands would have been tied in respect of the Book. This had to be prevented at all costs.

So I replied to Strang in the politest of tones that I was grateful to Halifax for his courtesy, but that unfortunately I could not take advantage of it. The publication of the Blue Book had not been agreed with the Soviet government. The latter had not even been informed of the decision to publish the Book. The Book was therefore solely the work of the British government, which was fully responsible for its every line. The Soviet government had nothing to do with the Book. In these circumstances I felt I was unable either to correct the records of my conversations in the Book or even to acquaint myself with its contents prior to publication. Least of all did I want to respond with rudeness to the foreign minister's courtesy, but I hoped he would understand the reasons for my refusal.

And, without a glance at the proofs of the Blue Book, I pushed them nonchalantly back to Strang.

Strang was clearly nonplussed, but assured me that he quite 'understood' me and would convey my exact words to Halifax, who would, of course, also 'understand' everything. Then, returning the proofs of the Book to his pocket, Strang added: 'Lord Halifax thought it his moral duty to make you this offer… Now he may consider his conscience to be clean.'

That's Halifax to a tee! Pritt once told me that, according to Butler, Halifax used to say to the latter at the beginning of each working day: 'Mind, Butler, we mustn't sacrifice a single principle today!'

And, having sent up this 'prayer' to God and put his soul at ease, Halifax would apply himself to the next intrigue being cooked up in the dirty kitchen of British foreign policy.

They are dangerous, these men of God! Halifax has now made two cynical attempts to deceive me: the first on 31 March, in connection with last year's guarantee to Poland, and the second today. He has failed, but I must be vigilant!

Strang also declared during our conversation today that the British government was not planning to break off diplomatic relations with the USSR ('provided, of course, that the Soviet government does not intend to do this', he added rather pointedly) and that Seeds was indeed taking the two months' leave due to him for rest and medical treatment.

7 January

The political atmosphere is abuzz: Hore-Belisha has been 'pushed'. Two days ago Chamberlain summoned the war minister and offered him a new ministerial portfolio – the Board of Trade. Hore-Belisha refused. The PM then rather rudely showed him the door.

What's this all about?

The gist of the matter is as follows.

When Hore-Belisha was appointed war minister in 1937, he invited two 'advisers' to help him: Lord Gort, who was made chief of the imperial general staff, and Liddell-Hart. The triumvirate directed the war office for about a year, and much useful work was done. In particular, progress was made in the mechanization and democratization of the army (NCOs were admitted to the officer corps, soldiers were permitted to eat in the same canteens as officers, etc.). The generals were also rejuvenated (men aged 65–75 were removed).

However, as Liddell-Hart told me back in 1938, Hore-Belisha did not dare go all the way with his reforms and stopped at half-measures. Of particular significance was the fact that, having removed the 'old men', Belisha [sic] failed to take the 'middle-aged' generals (55–65) down from their commanding heights and replace them with 'youth' (40–55), as Liddell-Hart had insisted. 'Teasing the geese' too much, Belisha feared, would damage his career.

Belisha's indecisiveness would come to haunt him. First, it set him against Liddell-Hart, who resigned his post as adviser right before the Munich Conference. As a result, Belisha was left alone in the ministry with Gort. Second, it spoiled Gort. The latter arrived in the ministry as a 'radical' and reformer, and initially he was true to his colours. But once he sensed his position to be fairly secure, and the influence of the conservative 'middle-aged' generals to be fairly stable, he began to change his bearings. He made common cause with the generals, who were particularly unhappy with the democratization of the army and the rejuvenation of the top brass, against Belisha. In the meantime, having learnt about the discord between Belisha and Liddell-Hart, Gort began to scheme against the latter and hastened his resignation. A struggle between Belisha and Gort continued on and off until the beginning of the war. In September, Belisha managed to shake off Gort by sending him to France as commander-in-chief. Gort was peeved with Belisha and waited for a convenient moment to take his revenge. An opportunity soon presented itself. At the end of last year, a group of dominion ministers, headed by Eden, visited the front in France. Some of the ministers, who remembered how fortifications were prepared in the last war, found the present fortifications in the British section of the front to be insufficiently solid. Their impression was quite mistaken: the current fortifications are state of the art, but they look rather different from those of 1914–18 because of the changes in armaments. It was Gort's duty to enlighten the ministers, but he did not do so. Quite the opposite: he did his utmost to cast a shadow on the war minister. The dominion ministers returned to London and started complaining at every opportunity about imaginary faults in the front-line fortifications and about Hore-Belisha himself. The latter wrote a sharp letter to Gort. Soon afterwards, Chamberlain visited the front line, and Gort told him bluntly that the army command could not work with Belisha. The PM reported the matter to the king, who dislikes Belisha for being a parvenu and a Jew. As a result, the war minister was forced to resign.

It's a pity. Belisha is a clever man and, most importantly, he is against a break with the Soviet Union.

Although the press is up in arms, I don't think that the storm will last very long or have any dangerous consequences for the government. The 'cream' of the ruling elite is entirely against Belisha – a plebeian and a Jew – while Belisha is a careerist and he won't want to ruin his future for good. They'll come to an arrangement somehow.

8 January

Although I politely refused Strang's offer to acquaint myself with the text of the 'Blue Book', I came to learn of its contents all the same.

The book comprises 95 separate documents, which fill some 150 pages. There is also an introduction, which summarizes the contents of the documents and the general course of the negotiations about the pact.

Sixty-nine documents are telegrams exchanged between Halifax and Seeds. These mainly cover the history of the negotiations, Seeds' conversations with C[omrade] Molotov, Halifax's talks with me, amendments and counter-amendments to the drafts of the pact, assessments of the situation, the impressions of the foreign secretary and of the British ambassador in Moscow, etc.

Twelve documents are speeches in parliament on the course of the negotiations, by Chamberlain (9), Halifax (2) and Simon (1).

Then there are three versions of the text of the pact, instructions given to Strang on his departure to Moscow, and a memorandum, dated 12 December, summing up the military negotiations in Moscow. For some reason, there are no authentic documents relating to these negotiations in the Book (if one can speak of 'authenticity' at all in this case). Also included is the LN [League of Nations] resolution of 14 December on the expulsion of the USSR.

As far as documents of Soviet origin are concerned, the Book contains a quotation from C[omrade] Stalin's address to the 18th Party Congress, C[omrade] Molotov's speech in the Supreme Soviet on 31 May, C[omrade] Zhdanov's article in *Pravda* on 29 June, and the texts of Soviet treaties with Germany (23 August) and Estonia, with a comment on the latter mentioning that similar treaties were concluded with Latvia and Lithuania.

The structure of the Blue Book is as follows: it opens with a quotation from C[omrade] Stalin's address to the 18th Party Congress, stating that one of the principles of Soviet foreign policy is to help victims of aggression who are struggling for independence. This is followed by the entire history of the negotiations in documents, the break, the USSR's pacts with Germany and Estonia, etc. The Book concludes with the LN's resolution to expel the USSR for its act of aggression against Finland.

It seems that the object of the British government's selection and arrangement of the materials was to create the impression that the summer negotiations collapsed owing to the USSR's 'duplicity'. This is illustrated in two ways: (1) the Soviet government held parallel negotiations throughout the summer with the

British and the French on the one hand, and with the Germans on the other, without really wishing to conclude an agreement with the British and French, but merely manoeuvring so as to lay the blame for the break on the 'Allies'; (2) declaring through C[omrade] Stalin its duty to assist victims of aggression, the Soviet government was itself occupied solely with thoughts of aggression and eventually committed it in Finland. The reader of the Book is therefore meant to draw the conclusion that the Soviet Union is in essence a 'wolf in sheep's clothing' and that the British government was very wise to avoid concluding a pact with such a dangerous partner.

The division of roles between C[omrade] Molotov and me during the negotiations is given as further evidence of Soviet 'duplicity'. In Moscow C[omrade] Molotov was stubbornly sabotaging any progress in negotiations by piling one obstacle on another. Meanwhile I in London was weakening the vigilance of the British government, using nice words to assure its members of the USSR's desire to maintain friendship with Britain, and praising British moves and proposals. And so it went on until the very moment the talks were broken off.

There is no doubt that the materials in the Blue Book have been heavily 'edited'. I have evidence to prove this: there is, for example, no record in the Book of my conversation with Halifax of 12 June, when I hinted to him that a visit by him to Moscow would be highly desirable; second, no more than a quarter of my conversation with him of 23 June is included in the Book.

Let us wait until 15 January, when the Book is to go on sale. That is still a week ahead, and the Book may well be 're-edited' in such a way that only odds and ends will remain of the present version. All the more so as the French are said to be dissatisfied with the British text, finding it too 'vegetarian'.

[The White Book contained 150 pages of documents conveying the official British version of the 1939 triple negotiations. Its publication would surely have exposed Maisky's autonomous initiatives (by revealing discrepancies between his and Halifax's records of the meetings), and his disagreements with Molotov. This was particularly true of the thread running through the long, analytical introduction by the distinguished All Souls' scholar Llewellyn Woodward, who had been entrusted with the editorial work. He particularly dwelt on Maisky's assurance to Cadogan at the end of March that the guarantees to Poland 'would be a revolutionary change in British policy' and 'would increase enormously the confidence of other countries'. Maisky feared that the appearance of the White Book would lead to his recall. Indeed, Seeds had been advised by Cadogan on 22 December 1939 to return home in anticipation of the publication, which might make his continued stay in Moscow 'difficult for a time at least!'[6]

Rumours concerning Maisky's own recall were rife, as Mikhail Korzh, who replaced Kagan as counsellor at the embassy, complained. Someone had noticed, for instance, that vans were loading up what turned out to be large quantities of art exhibits (detained in England since the outbreak of war and now being shipped to Moscow from Liverpool) and jumped to the conclusion that the shipment included the ambassador's personal effects. Maisky, who rarely lost his composure, now seemed despondent. Bilainkin, engaged in writing the ambassador's biography, did not fail to notice that his request for a further interview was met with a nervous response: 'Three weeks these days is a long time ... Who knows?'[7] When Maisky told the Webbs about the incident, he seemed certain that publication would lead to a breach in relations, strongly advocated by the French government. 'The Soviet Embassy in Paris,' he complained, 'was surrounded with secret service men; every member of the staff or person coming or leaving the Soviet Embassy, except the Ambassador himself, was stopped and questioned by the Paris police.'[8]

It is hardly surprising, therefore, that Maisky remained obsessive about the incriminating document. He was, however, saved by the bell. The idea of publishing a White Book invited opposition from the outset, as it exposed not only what was assumed to be Russian treachery, but also the reluctance of Chamberlain to reach an agreement and the conflicting French and British positions. On 6 March, Chamberlain announced in parliament that publication of the White Book was to be dropped.[9] In due course, Maisky succeeded in obtaining a microfilm of the scrapped book, from 'friends of the USSR', most likely through intelligence channels (thereby exceeding his own authority), which he concealed from his superiors. After his return to Moscow, he hid the microfilm ('a small box, the size of a match box' in his own words) in his flat. Indeed, the KGB, overwhelmed by the 80 large bags of documents they collected, failed to spot the microfilm during their search of the flat after his arrest in 1953. He then revealed its existence, of his own free will, most likely fearing that sooner or later it would be recovered and would implicate him even further. The episode was the main reason for his indictment in his trial in 1955. Seeking a full rehabilitation, Maisky went on to make the dubious claim that it was a mere case of negligence and a 'slip' of his memory.[10]]

11 January

Scandinavia is on the agenda.

Scandinavia undoubtedly played a very negative role in the period before the Finnish war. She does the same today. Scandinavia, and Sweden in particular, is not merely pursuing a frenzied anti-Soviet campaign, she is also supplying Finland with arms, ammunition, money and 'volunteers', whose numbers seem to have already reached the size of an entire division.

Scandinavia is now at the centre of true international bedlam.

First, in view of the 'stalemate' on the western front, some influential circles in England and especially in France are looking for a second, more 'mobile' front and find it in Scandinavia. Other, even more influential circles (including most of the British government) fear that Germany itself will seize the initiative and attack Denmark and Sweden in order to secure Swedish ore for itself once and for all. As a result, a week or so ago the British government offered the Swedish government a guarantee against Germany. The Swedish government has not accepted the British guarantee so far, fearing to 'provoke' Hitler, but it is confident that Britain will unconditionally come to its aid in the event of a serious threat to Sweden, whatever its source. Those seeking a 'mobile' front would welcome a German march against Scandinavia, as it would enable them to use Swedish and Norwegian territory immediately for military operations.

Second, Germany is doing its utmost to scare Scandinavia, above all Sweden. In particular, a week or so ago the German press threatened Sweden with all manner of disasters were she to assist Finland. The German envoy or counsellor in Stockholm even warned Sweden, albeit in a fairly mild form, that Berlin would consider Swedish consent to the transit of arms and matériel from the Western countries to Finland as a violation of Sweden's neutrality, with all the ensuing consequences. That transit, however, still continues, and Germany still does nothing. Looks like Germany is toying with Sweden.

Third, the Soviet Union has made it unequivocally clear that it absolutely objects to the aid supplied by Sweden and Norway to Finland. On 5 January our envoys in Stockholm and Oslo even submitted strong notes of protest, to which the Swedes and Norwegians replied yesterday, 10 January, in a rather impudent tone. The TASS communication acknowledges these responses to be 'not entirely satisfactory'. It remains rather unclear what conclusions will be drawn from this appraisal.

The Scandinavians themselves are torn by two conflicting feelings: on the one hand, they want to help Finland; on the other, they are afraid of being drawn into a war, whether with Germany or with the USSR. In this difficult situation, the Scandinavians try to help themselves with various intricate theories and comparisons. Prytz, for one, has been developing the following theory.

Finland should be treated in the same way as Spain was once treated. There were two governments in Spain – the Republican government in Barcelona and Franco's in Burgos – which were waging a civil war. There are two governments in Finland today, in Helsinki and in Terijoki, and they are waging a civil war. The Soviet Union recognized as 'lawful' the Spanish Republican government elected in 1936, and supplied it with arms, ammunition and so on. Germany and Italy recognized as 'lawful' the Franco government, which nobody elected, and supported it in every way. Sweden and other countries recognize as 'lawful' and support the Finnish government in Helsinki, which was elected in 1939, while the Soviet Union recognizes and supports the government which nobody elected. During the Spanish Civil War the USSR on the one side and Germany and Italy on the other maintained 'normal' diplomatic relations, which were only occasionally interrupted by periods of tension, even though they were conducting a covert war against each other on Spanish territory. With the conclusion of events in Spain, this element of conflict in their relations disappeared. It is desirable that the same should happen now in connection with the Finnish events. Each country has the right to support the Finnish government which it likes best, but there is no sense being offended with one another. It would be better to turn a blind eye to what is happening, since the course of the war will put paid to this present controversy one way or another. I don't know whether this 'philosophy' can help the Scandinavians.

Will the British render serious assistance to the Finns?

I doubt it. Of course, they will do something and send something to Finland, but not much. Not only because they are in need themselves, but also and to a greater extent because the British government nurtures no illusions about the final outcome of the struggle and does not wish to supply the Red Army through its feckless stooges, as occurred in the era of the Civil War and intervention.

Establishing a 'mobile' front in Scandinavia is a different matter. It is now thought of as an anti-German front. I don't doubt, however, that the British government or, to be more precise, those elements in the British government that share this notion, always keep in mind the possibility of using a Scandinavian front against the USSR as well. For many, very many people in England nurture a deep suspicion, even conviction, that we have a secret military pact with Germany or, if this alliance does not yet formally exist, that it will do very soon.

And, although the USSR is not tied to Germany by either a military or a political alliance, it is very difficult to persuade people otherwise.

14 January

These last two days I have had interesting conversations with Guo Taiqi and Aras.

Guo Taiqi told me about his recent visit to Halifax (a week or so ago). They talked on various subjects, but Anglo-Soviet relations were the central issue. Halifax told Guo Taiqi that he was against the further deterioration of Anglo-Soviet relations, especially their severance on British initiative, and that he had not lost hope of their possible improvement in the future. In Halifax's view, the world was large enough to allow for the peaceful coexistence of the British Empire and the USSR. The complications that had occurred in relations between the two countries over the last five months contained much that was invented and artificial. Were the two governments to be *on speaking terms*, many mutual suspicions and grievances could be easily dispelled and settled. The conflict over Finland is the focus of attention at present. Yes, the British government deeply regrets that the USSR attacked Finland. The British government lends assistance to Finland in the light of the LN's resolution and in response to British public opinion, but the significance of this episode should not be exaggerated. Finland is a temporary and to large extent incidental conflict in Anglo-Soviet relations. As soon as the Finnish war is terminated, this conflict will also be terminated. For Halifax does not believe that the Soviet Union is planning conquests in respect of Sweden or Norway (though he does believe that Germany has such plans). Such actions would mean a clash with Germany, and also with England, France and perhaps the United States. The Soviet Union will not risk it, especially after its experience in Finland. Halifax also does not believe that friendship between Germany and the USSR will prove long-lasting: there are serious points of conflict between the two countries (Scandinavia and the Balkans). The Soviet government, moreover, will not want to play forever with just the German card in its hand. Considering all this, Halifax thinks that Anglo-Soviet relations can not only be preserved, but even, under certain conditions, improved. This is why he would like to keep all avenues open. But of course, it's a different matter if the Soviet government thinks otherwise and plans to bring relations with England to breaking-point. The British government will accept severance of relations as a fact and draw the appropriate practical conclusions. But Halifax would regret such a course of events.

If Guo Taiqi has related Halifax's words correctly, all this is very *significant*. But has Guo Taiqi been faithful to the truth? I'm afraid there is much subjectivity in his account for, as he told me, China wishes above all to avoid a situation where it would have to choose between the USSR and Western democracies.

70. Maisky in the company of (left to right) the Belgian, Egyptian and Turkish ambassadors in London.

Aras also had a talk recently with Halifax about Anglo-Soviet relations. Halifax told him that he did not desire a worsening of Anglo-Soviet relations and did not intend to break them off, but was prepared for the fact that the Soviet Union might decide to break off relations on its own initiative.

Aras's forecast for the war is as follows. Germany has three alternatives: (1) to attack France through Holland and Belgium in spring; (2) to attack the Balkans and possibly even capture the Straits; and (3) to wage a long war of attrition. Aras thinks that the last alternative is the most probable and that by properly exploiting the resources of the USSR and South-East Europe, Germany could hold out against England and France for many years. But in this case there is also a much better chance of an early peace through mediation, in which, he hopes, Turkey will participate, together with Mussolini and Roosevelt. In our previous talks, Aras named the USSR among possible mediators, but did not do so this time. In his view, a serious 'peace offensive' can be expected this spring or autumn.

Aras is just back from Paris. He wanted to see his 'old friend' Surits[11] there and invited the Turkish ambassador [Aktai[i]] in Paris to come along. The latter, however, was terrified by Aras's invitation. He said that a visit by two Turkish ambassadors to the Soviet ambassador would be regarded by the French as a 'demonstration' and that, as a result, the windows of the Turkish embassy would be shattered. I think that Aras's heart must have sunk as well, as he did not go to see Surits even on his own, although he assured me that he would visit him next time 'without fail'. True heroes!

What a terrible situation the Soviet embassy in France finds itself in!

15 January

Saw Liddell-Hart.

He has left *The Times*, where he was a war correspondent for two years. There was a difference of opinions, which doesn't surprise me in the least. In fact, it's rather strange that L-H could work for this paper at all. L-H is now *freelance*, lives at Elmhirst's in *Dartington Hall* and writes a bit. He suffered a *breakdown* in the summer from working too hard, and has still not fully recovered.

We talked about the war. L-H considers it absolutely 'pointless', not only from a general political perspective, but also from a purely military one. Indeed.

The stalemate on the western front is a brilliant confirmation of L-H's theory about the relative supremacy of the means of defence over the means of offence in contemporary warfare. The Germans will not even be able to

---

[i] Haydar Aktai, Turkish ambassador to Moscow, 1940–43.

force their way through Holland and Belgium. First, these two countries are capable of mounting strong resistance (especially Belgium). Second, England and France will interfere at once if need be. Given Germany's links with the USSR and the Balkans, a blockade cannot be especially effective. British and German air strength is virtually equal (the Germans have more planes, while the British machines are of better quality and have unlimited supplies of petrol at their disposal) – so neither side will be able to gain a serious advantage in the skies. Consequently, nothing will be resolved in the near future. In these circumstances, it would seem that an early peace would be the sole reasonable solution, but… governments are rarely dictated by reason and logic. They never think problems through properly or approach them scientifically, and that is why L-H is very pessimistic about the future.

I asked him what he thought about the chances for a 'second front', perhaps in Scandinavia. L-H is sceptical: the military and political obstacles are too great. But, of course, anything may happen in the course of a war.

18 January

There is reliable information that the Germans are preparing great quantities of a special gas, *calcium arsenide*, which can't be seen or smelled. It can be spread by shells or bombs or even simply scattered like powder. It is extremely noxious. Ordinary protective masks are useless against it. People are poisoned unawares and die in terrible agony within 24 hours. It is thought that the Germans may use 'arsenide gas' during their spring offensive (possibly this is the 'secret weapon' of which Hitler spoke a few months ago). In any case, the British general staff is expecting this offensive.

What a terrible thing! This is how human genius is expended! When will the social system that permits such things be done away with at last?!

19 January

Another year further down the road: today I turned 56.

A year ago to this day, when I was outlining a 'plan' for the remainder of my life, I reckoned that a new imperialist war in Europe would break out within a decade at the most and that after that there would be enough socialist construction in this part of the world to keep me busy till the end of my days. Reality has confirmed my forecast earlier than I could have expected: the imperialist war in Europe broke out less than eight months after I wrote those lines. Well, so much the better. Since the war was clearly inevitable, better that it happen sooner rather than later. I will see more of the epoch of socialist construction in Europe (if, of course, I am fated to live).

One more consideration in this regard. The more powerful technology becomes, the more damage a modern war will cause. That is why a war in 1939 is preferable to a war in 1949.

20 January

Czech sources report:

(1) The Czechoslovak National Committee has been formed. Beneš is its president (the French government has had to retract its objections against him). The committee has been recognized by England and France. On that basis, it receives some funds belonging to the former Czechoslovak state. The Czech army in France already numbers 10,000. It is expected to be increased to two divisions.

(2) Beneš is in a fairly difficult position. His policy up to now has been to steer a course between the British and the French on the one side and the Soviet government on the other. Now, with the Soviet Union having recognized Slovakia and Fierlinger[i] having been deprived of his official status in Moscow, this task has become a great deal more difficult. Beneš is afraid of being 'eaten up' by Britain and France, with the result that the mistakes of 1914–1918 may be repeated. That is why Beneš's mood at present is rather pessimistic.

(3) Germany's current policy is aimed at bringing relations between the USSR and Western democracies to breaking-point. Finland is the means to achieve that. The German government wants to prolong the Finnish war, in the hope of causing a definitive split between the USSR and Western democracies. That is why the German government is not inclined to object to the neutral countries (Sweden, Norway and Italy) lending their support to Mannerheim and Co., and will not prevent them sending arms and volunteers to Finland. The transit of Italian arms to Finland via Germany was effectively agreed between Rome and Berlin. The Germans merely warned the Italians that should this be disclosed, they would have to undertake measures 'to soothe the Russians'. The German government also turns a blind eye to the transit of weapons from Western countries via Scandinavia. What the German government cannot permit is the dispatch of Anglo-French troops via Sweden and Norway, as this could be dangerous for the Germans themselves. Should London and Paris try to follow such a course, Germany would interfere and exploit the opportunity to establish its dominance in Scandinavia (including control over Swedish ore).

(4) In the Balkans, Germany is resisting the formation of a Balkan bloc, as well as the consolidation of British, French and Turkish military positions. This is being done, in particular, by encouraging revisionism in Hungary and

[i] Zdeněk Fierlinger, Czechoslovakian minister to the Soviet Union, 1939–45.

Bulgaria. Germany has now massed 43 divisions in Austria, Czechoslovakia and southern Poland. Evidently, she is prepared to threaten or even fight Rumania, through Hungary.

All this is rather interesting and has the ring of truth. Naturally, however, one needs to make allowances for the nature of the source.

21 January

I've been receiving information in the last few days that a dispute has emerged in Labour circles concerning Finland and the Soviet Union. There was a long and confusing debate on this matter at the meeting of the Executive Committee of Parliamentary Labour on 16 January. In the end, no decision was taken. The general mood among the members of the Executive Committee was that the Finnish conflict should be settled by 'mediation'. What kind of mediation? On whose behalf? Opinions varied. Some wished the Labour Party to assume the role of 'mediator', while others thought that the party should put the question before the British government. Attlee said that a few days before the meeting he had, on his own initiative, raised the subject of 'mediation' with Chamberlain, who had responded with sympathy to his proposals. The members of the Executive Committee showed interest in their leader's communication, but the matter was taken no further. What was quite clear was that all those present were frightened by the prospect of war between England and the USSR.

At about the same time Jordan, high commissioner for New Zealand in London, informed me through a third party that if the Soviet government desired 'mediation' in the Finnish conflict, he was prepared to offer his services. He understood that the USSR could not accept the 'mediation' of a major imperialist power, such as England or the United States, but hoped that it might accept the 'mediation' of small non-imperialist New Zealand, which is ruled by a socialist government. Jordan reminded me of his friendly relations with Soviet representatives in Geneva, where his plebeian openness and backing of the Soviet delegation have indeed upset the British apple-cart on more than one occasion. Naturally, I had to explain to Jordan, through the same third party, the full inappropriateness of his proposal.

Today, meanwhile, Lord Strabolgi arrived unexpectedly, in sports clothes, straight from the skating rink. After emphasizing that he was acting in a private capacity, Lord Strabolgi (formerly Kenworthy) first began asking whether the Soviet government might wish to invite a trade union–Labour delegation like the one which had left for Helsinki on 19 January at the invitation of Finnish trade unions and cooperatives (Citrine, Noel-Baker and Downie[i])? Labour

[i] John Downie, Scottish representative of the cooperative movement.

would like to be entirely 'impartial' and hear out both sides. I expressed my astonishment at his suggestion and made it clear to him that there were no chances whatsoever that it might be accepted.[12]

Strabolgi changed the subject and set about impressing on me that the British government wants to maintain good relations with the USSR, that Finland alone stands in the way, that the Soviet–Finnish conflict could be settled by 'mediation', and that if the matter in question is the replacement of the government in Finland, this too could be discussed, although such a move would, of course, be fairly problematic. I had to disappoint Strabolgi once more and declare quite frankly that it made no sense to speak of 'mediation' in the Soviet–Finnish conflict.

Who stands behind Strabolgi and Jordan?

First and foremost, of course, the Labour Party, but not only. Some hints dropped by Strabolgi suggested that his visit to me had the blessing of the Foreign Office. No wonder! At this very moment, when the situation on the Finnish front is not in our favour, the British government would like to kill two birds with one stone: to reinforce the 'blow to the prestige of the Red Army' and gain a reputation as 'peace-maker'.

As for Jordan, I'm not sure there is anyone behind him. He is a very unusual and original man. A former London policeman, he emigrated to New Zealand many years ago, joined Labour there, made a career for himself, and four years ago, when the Labour government came to power in this dominion, came to London as high commissioner. Jordan, as one would expect of a policeman, is tall, strong and rough-mannered. He looks like a bear and has a gruff voice and red hair. Politically, he is very primitive and direct. He doesn't understand diplomacy and always likes to shoot straight from the hip. He could easily have thought up this scheme all by himself.

23 January

Here is the sensation of the day:

[Attached is the front page of the *News Chronicle* of 23 January 1940 carrying an article entitled: 'Maisky Is Going Back to Moscow'.]

And our response:

[Attached is the front page of *Evening Standard* of 23 January 1940 carrying an article entitled 'M. Maisky Denial. The Soviet Embassy to-day denied to the *Evening Standard* a report that M. Maisky, the Soviet Ambassador, will shortly return to Moscow'.]

25 January

The further we go, the greater the problems.

At first the British government reacted to the Finnish events with a frenzied press and radio campaign, as well as active participation in the expulsion of the USSR from the League of Nations. Next it supplied Mannerheim with weapons and aeroplanes. Now it is ready to send a 'volunteer' corps to Finland, on the Spanish model, supplying a justification for this à la Prytz.

Here are the details. Mannerheim is demanding 40,000 trained volunteers to hold the front. He does not expect all 40,000 to be British, of course, but Great Britain should send its share. It is expected that the British government will send not Brits but Canadians. To start with, they are more accustomed to the Finnish climate. Second, this is more convenient and legal from the political point of view, since there is no conscription in Canada, making it easier to pull off the 'volunteers' trick. It goes without saying that there will be a certain number of Brits among the Canadians. Not for nothing are skiers and men commanding Scandinavian languages being urgently sought in the mobilization effort. France will also send 'volunteers'. The British government would also very much like to recruit some from the USA, but it's hard to say if it will achieve this. But nothing is impossible here. Roosevelt has already let it be known that 'there is no war in Finland' and therefore American subjects would not be forbidden from fighting for Mannerheim. The British plan is to mass a sufficient quantity of 'volunteers' by spring.

The situation is becoming more and more complicated.

* * *

It transpires that the *News Chronicle*, in printing a report about my departure (23 January), fell victim to the machinations of those elements desperate to achieve a severance of relations between the 'Allies' and the USSR. It is they who furnished 'information' about my recall.

26 January

About a month ago (24 December) I established in my diary the state of Anglo-Soviet relations at the time. Today, I can summarize the processes that have unfolded since then. There's nothing to celebrate!

The general curve of Anglo-Soviet relations continues its downward path. If, in the language of statistics, we take the state of Soviet–British relations last May and June to be 100, the figure for October and November would be 50, the end of December 40, and barely 30 today. Two facts supply the best evidence for this: Churchill's speech over the radio on 20 January and Chamberlain's reply to Knox's[i] inquiry about the severance of Anglo-Soviet relations on 24 January. True, once Churchill's speech had been received unfavourably in neutral countries, the British government hastened to dissociate itself from the speaker, saying that Churchill had merely expressed a personal opinion; but this is sheer knavery. I know perfectly well that most of the Cabinet members share Churchill's views.

In brief, the situation is as follows. At the end of December, two tendencies could be discerned in government circles:

(1) The old one (which dated from the very first days of the war) aimed for the isolation of Germany, neutralization of the Soviet Union, and localization of the war, and was considered the shortest and cheapest route to victory. Hence the policy '*not to antagonize Russia*'; indeed, rapprochement with Russia would be even better.

(2) The new tendency (which raised its head only at the beginning of the Finnish war) did not believe in the possibility of neutralizing the USSR, considered the USSR to be a covert ally of Germany, with the potential of becoming an open ally at any moment, and called for an extension of military operations and the drawing into the war of as many neutral countries as possible, regardless of the risk of a clean break or even armed conflict with the USSR.

A month ago the old trend clearly dominated in government circles; the new one was represented by a modest minority. Churchill, for one, adhered to the old tendency. Today the situation is different: the old trend has weakened and the new one has been strengthened. It is difficult to say for sure whether the latter has won over the majority in government as there are many *yes-men* in the Cabinet. One thing is beyond doubt: the new trend may become the prevailing one at any given moment. This is demonstrated in particular by the fact that Churchill now espouses the new tendency. Chamberlain has not yet stated his definitive position, he manoeuvres and waits, but his reply of 24 January shows that he does not exclude the possibility of an Anglo-Soviet split. The British government's intention to send a corps of 'volunteers' to Finland also shows how far these processes have gone.

How to explain all this?

It all boils down to the fact that at the beginning of the current year one thing became completely clear to the British government: with the present alignment of forces (the British and French empires on the one side, and Germany, which has access to Soviet, Balkan and Scandinavian resources and can use Italy as a channel for imports, on the other) the 'Allies' stand a slim chance

---

[i] Sir Alfred Knox, major general, British military attaché in Petrograd during the First World War, where he witnessed the revolution; Conservative MP, 1924–45.

of an early victory and a good chance of a protracted, gruelling war with a doubtful military outcome and the probability of revolutionary reverberations in Europe. The gruelling nature of the war is already making itself felt. War expenses amount to 6 million pounds a day and will certainly increase. Since their chances of concluding an advantageous peace are negligible, the 'Allies' have no way out other than by radically changing the alignment of forces in their favour by drawing as many neutral countries as possible onto their side in the war, particularly Sweden (ore), Rumania (oil) and Italy (transit). Moreover, the expansion of the war sphere promises to open a number of the 'mobile' fronts which are so keenly desired by the British and French general staffs. In view of these circumstances, I do not doubt that, although the British government has found it necessary to disassociate itself from Churchill, the question of involving neutrals in the war will be repeatedly entered in the agenda in the course of the war.

In this connection, the matter of Finland acquires special significance for British ruling circles. By helping Mannerheim, they hope to kill two birds with one stone. First, they hope to raise the spirits of the small neutral countries (the 'Allies' do not leave them to the mercy of fate in their hour of need!) and thus draw them into the war more easily. Second, they hope to prolong the war in Finland, weaken the USSR, tie us hand and foot in the north and thus reduce our freedom of manoeuvre in other directions, and, finally, deprive the Germans of the possibility of getting raw materials, food and so on, from the USSR.

This plan is particularly attractive to the British government for two other reasons. First, having convinced themselves of the 'weakness' of the Red Army, the British ministers think they will need relatively modest forces and means to carry out their plans. Second, since left and right are in agreement on the question of 'aid to Finland', there is no danger of splitting the 'united national front' which is so important to the British government. A touching display of unanimity: royalty – Bourbon, Liechtenstein, and others – joining the Mannerheim army along with the socialists. Attlee and Citrine are hoarse from advocating aid to Finland, the queen donates 50 shirts to the Finns, and the princesses knit warm clothes for 'Finnish children'. An affecting picture! All are suddenly reconciled when the fight against the 'blood-thirsty' Bolsheviks is on the agenda!...

But it is still too early to say whether the British government will succeed in realizing its plan, and to what extent. Any number of obstacles could get in the way: military, international, domestic. The reaction of the neutral countries to Churchill's speech is a useful reminder in this respect.[13] But we must be doubly vigilant. Should the British government fulfil even 60% or 70% of its intentions, the rupture of Anglo-Soviet relations would be most likely inevitable.

[This entry dovetailed with a long letter sent to Molotov on the same day. Convinced that the severance of relations was imminent, Maisky depicted in sombre colours the state of Anglo-Soviet relations which, he warned, posed 'a serious danger' to the Soviet Union. The object of his apocalyptic letter was to impress on Molotov that the sooner the war in Finland was concluded 'in terms favourable to us the better are the chances for Anglo-Soviet relations to survive the present crisis'. It was entirely clear to the Labour leadership that Maisky was left with little choice but to staunchly defend the invasion of Finland, conscious of the danger that it might lead to war and aware that 'he could not say otherwise, would be recalled & liquidated'.[14]]

27 January

Doshchenko left for Moscow today. All our efforts came to nothing. I made a second visit to Cadogan on this matter on 29 December. I tried to prove Doshchenko's innocence and insisted that his case should be reviewed. I demanded evidence of his guilt and remarked that the incident might have an adverse effect on Anglo-Soviet relations. Cadogan replied that at this time of war, every government has to increase its 'vigilance', that the Home Office has compromising evidence against Doshchenko – so there is nothing to be done. He dropped a hint that if we chose to make too much of the incident, it could 'leak' to the press. But he promised to contact the Home Office once more and ask for a more specific statement of the charge.

Cadogan's silence lasted for five days. I then sent him a letter on 3 January, reminding him of his promise. I received his reply on 4 January, in which he informed me that, 'Mr Doshchenko abused the hospitality of this country by seeking to collect confidential information by illegal methods.'

The wording of the charge was so elastic that it merely enhanced my suspicion that the matter lay not with Doshchenko himself, but somewhere else, that it was yet another 'dirty trick' in the attempt to provoke a rupture. It was absolutely clear that it would be impossible to vindicate Doshchenko. In fact, there was the danger that in view of the further deterioration in Anglo-Soviet relations, the Home Office might come out with yet another trick, such as bringing Doshchenko to court. I consulted with Moscow. It was decided to evacuate Doshchenko as soon as possible and submit a note of protest to the Foreign Office after his departure.

Meanwhile, a Home Office representative visited Doshchenko in prison and started asking him how long he intended to remain in prison, whether the Soviet government trusted him fully, and what he was up to in England. The official stressed that he was familiar with all the details of his negotiations with companies, and gave a few examples. Doshchenko says that he succeeded in wriggling out of these questions. There was no transcript of the interrogation. Doshchenko was not made to sign any papers.

It took ten days to obtain the exit visa, tickets, etc. Doshchenko and his wife departed today. He was accompanied to Folkestone by Zonov, Feonov,[i] and… a police inspector. Correct procedure was followed. However, our request for Doshchenko to be released a day or two prior to his departure, in order for him to settle his affairs, was rejected by the Home Office.

29 January

What a journey!

Yesterday, Agniya and I went to see the Webbs after lunch. The weather this January is unusually cold and snowy. As we were leaving, it was getting a little warmer. The snow began to melt and, even on the way to the Webbs, the car was occasionally sliding. We set off back home at about 8.30. It was very dark. A very unpleasant surprise awaited us on the main road: it was just like an ice-rink. Driving was nearly impossible. The car slid from one side of the road to the other. The wheels would not bite. At times the car threatened to turn over. After driving for an hour and a half and covering barely 7–8 miles, we decided to stop somewhere for the night. With the greatest difficulty we reached a tiny roadside *Inn* bearing the resonant name *Red Lion Hotel, Thursley*. Unfortunately the inn was already crammed with fellow travellers stranded like us. Like everywhere now, there were many sailors and soldiers. A room was out of the question. We had to content ourselves with two armchairs at the fire-place in the dining-room and two fascinating novels borrowed from the hosts' library. So Agniya and I spent the whole night reading by the fire. We set out again this morning. It had snowed overnight and our car, which had been parked outside (the inn had no garage), was completely frozen up. White had a big job to start the engine. We saw dozens of fallen trees, torn telegraph wires, and broken-down cars on the way to London. In town we learned that the railway had been disrupted overnight: many trains had got stuck en route, trains from Scotland were running 8–9 hours late, etc.

Well, such a thing has never happened to me before in England!…

Beatrice Webb told me yesterday that in her opinion the capitalist system has only 20–30 years left to live, and no more. Real progress! If the Webbs have arrived at such a conclusion, then God himself has ordered us to set optimistic deadlines. I definitely hope to live to see the triumph of the socialist revolution, at least in Europe.

Brendan Bracken came to lunch today. In spite of his Conservative parliamentary mandate and his proximity to Churchill, he too is unsure about capitalism's future. He expounded his thoughts at length, arguing that the world

---

[i] Nikolai Ivanovich Feonov, member of the Soviet trade delegation in Great Britain, 1938–45.

is heading for the triumph of socialism, even if not exactly the socialism we have in the Soviet Union. Just like Gretchen in *Faust*. Bracken is not opposed to socialism in principle. But he would like it to establish itself in a 'respectable' manner, without smoke and powder, and without financial collapse and economic chaos. In his opinion, the best way to 'bring about socialism' is through the inheritance tax. By raising this tax to 80–90%, all capitalists will be gradually 'expropriated' and socialism will become inevitable.

Bracken revealed to me some interesting facts concerning the financing of the war. The war currently costs England 6 million pounds a day. Together with ordinary, peace-time expenses, the overall British budget is 7.5 million pounds a day. In the last war, England spent 3 million pounds a day on the war, and that was only during the closing stages of the war. The budget will be covered by taxes and loans – approximately 50-50. Income tax is 7.5 shillings per pound in the current budget, and will probably be raised to 8.5 in the pound in the next budget, and then 10. The British government is trying to avoid the spiral effect in the cost of living and salaries. So prices for consumer products will be maintained by the government at a fixed low level (through subsidies to wholesalers). The British government thereby intends to avoid inflation. In addition, very energetic measures are being taken to increase world exports, and notable results ought to be visible in about six months' time. Britain is setting itself the task of seizing German markets in South and Central America.

All this is very interesting, but is it realistic? The future will show.

30 January

I went to see Butler about the release of the Soviet steamer *Selenga*, which has already spent seventeen days in contraband control in Hong Kong. Butler apologized and promised to contact the relevant authorities and inform me of the results.

When we had finished with the *Selenga*, Butler brought up other issues relating to Anglo-Soviet relations. He asked me what I thought about the state of our relations. I shrugged my shoulders and said that he surely knew as much about it as I did. There were no acute, concrete conflicts between us, but…

'You mean to say,' Butler interrupted, 'that the sea is calm, but the water temperature is very low.'

'Yes, you may well be right.'

Butler asked if anything in particular could be done to improve our relations, or at least prevent their further deterioration. I retorted that he was in a better position to know: all our difficulties derive from British policy, and in particular from the British government's desire to interfere in affairs that are of no concern to it.

Butler objected that the government was doing all right, but that 'public opinion' was very worked up and was exerting pressure on the government. I quickly put an end to his wretched arguments, telling him that public opinion is artificially incited by the press, the radio and the cinema – and evidently not without the government's consent. If the British government was really 'all right', it seemed to me, the present temporary difficulties in relations between the two countries might be eliminated by localizing the Finnish question so as not to spoil the entire atmosphere of Anglo-Soviet relations. I resorted to a precedent: our differences on the Spanish question were localized by way of the agreement I concluded with Eden in 1936, which made it possible to maintain Anglo-Soviet relations within the bounds of civility and even friendliness.[15] In addition, of course, it was very important that the British government should avoid any kind of provocative actions towards the USSR.

Butler said he liked the idea of 'localization', but he wasn't sure that the British government could avoid such actions as might seem provocative to us. The most important thing in these difficult circumstances was to keep a *cool head* and have *patience*.

After a moment's pause, Butler continued: 'The main difficulty in Anglo-Soviet relations is that you support our deadly enemy. Many in England are convinced that you have a *cast-iron* agreement with Germany which practically makes you a single bloc.'

Referring to C[omrade] Molotov's speeches, I advised Butler not to heed idle gossip. Butler listened to me with obvious satisfaction, but with little trust. Then he exclaimed: 'If only we knew for sure that your hands really are untied and that you are pursuing your own, independent policy, so much could be different.'

As far as I could understand, he meant that much could be different in England's behaviour on the Finnish question, too.

I laughed and said that the Soviet Union had always pursued and continues to pursue only its own independent policy.

Butler shrugged his shoulders ambiguously. In the end he told me several times that he wanted to maintain close contact with me and that this was especially important at the present time. We arranged to have lunch together.

[Maisky had assured the Webbs that he was complying with the 'orders from Moscow to *stay put*', in a 'jovial defiant manner'.[16] And yet his diary and his report to Molotov deliberately conceal the grave concerns he felt for his own survival and his repeated pleas to Butler 'not to be too spectacular ... and maintain our diplomatic relations'. Moreover, he was apologetic about the Ribbentrop–Molotov Pact, lamenting that 'We lived in a period of change, that anything might happen, that in the jungle the strangest of animals got together – if they felt their joint interests made this advisable.'[17]

Woodward, the editor of the White Paper, was the first to record Maisky's meeting with Butler, in his 1962 official history *British Foreign Policy in the Second World War.* Maisky was furious, and in his memoirs vehemently denied using the jungle metaphor. But according to Alexander, first lord of the Admiralty, the following exchange with Maisky took place a couple of months later: 'I said in a casual way: "We live in strange and rapid times", to which he answered, "Yes, this is the period of the jungle."'[18] And in Bilainkin he confided: 'The world now resembles a jungle and each one of us has to fight for survival ... We must be realistic, treat every problem solely from the aspect of life tomorrow.'[19]

According to Butler, Maisky's despondency also surfaced when he related 'some hair-raising experiences which he had had when in exile in Northern Siberia, especially when on one occasion he had been thrown off a sledge and left in the snow alone for many hours. He sometimes felt as lonely here as he did on that occasion, but he always remembered that his driver and the reindeer had returned to pick him up again. He said wistfully that this weather reminded him of Northern Siberia.'[20]]

31 January

Aras visited me. We spoke on various subjects: the forthcoming Balkan conference, from which Aras expects nothing, the prospects for the war, Mussolini's intentions, Chamberlain's speech today, and many other issues. Of particular interest were Aras's comments on Anglo-Soviet relations.

He believes Anglo-Soviet relations are less strained today than they were three or four weeks ago. Aras is personally conducting 'a struggle in support of the USSR' with the British, emphasizing that an improvement in Anglo-Soviet relations is essential. He claims to have had some successes. I have doubts about them, but he really is trying to do what he can to prevent a rupture. I know this from different, independent sources. His motives are the same as those of Guo Taiqi. Like China, Turkey does not want to find herself in a position which would force her to choose between the USSR and the 'Allies'.

Aras intimated to me that prior to the Finnish events, when the British government counted on the USSR's 'genuine neutrality', it hoped to end the war with Germany in 10–12 months. The British government's calculations have now changed. Now it thinks that the Finnish events have led, or will soon lead, to a rapprochement between the USSR and Germany such as will be practically identical to a 'military alliance'. The war, therefore, will last longer and victory will become harder. For this reason, alongside a massive intensification of the 'Allies'' own efforts, the British government is striving to draw as many neutral countries as possible into the war on its side. Aras gave an example of the 'intensification' of such efforts by the 'Allies': Mandel is organizing a gigantic 'black army' in the colonies, 1.5–2 million strong, which can be transported to France in the course of this year, 1940. How much cheap 'gun fodder' the imperialists have!

* * *

Jouhaux[i] was in London with six other French trade union leaders for the latest meeting of the Anglo-French trade union committee, which was set up at the end of last year with the purpose of strengthening ties between the 'Allies'. The first meeting was held in Paris in December and was attended by representatives of seven British trade unions, headed by Hicks. For the second meeting, the French came to London. The guests were shown factories and plants all over the country and were acquainted with the living conditions and circumstances of the workers. The British were desperate to demonstrate to their French colleagues that they too are 'patriotic' and are also prepared to do anything 'for the war'.

The 'Allies' discussed some practical matters as well. In Paris, in December, the British tried hard, but in vain, to find out from the French exactly how many members there are in the CGT [General Confederation of Labour]. Jouhaux repeatedly ducked the question. Now, in London, he was obliged to reveal the secret. It turns out that the CGT has only 1 million members compared to 2.5 million before the war and 5 million at the beginning of 1937. Such are the catastrophic consequences of the persecution of communists in France. It also transpired that a further drop in the proletariat's standard of living was expected, whether in the form of lower wages or through the introduction of new taxes. And this in addition to the 10-hour working day established (officially!) on 1 January, plus a 15% wage tax! Responding to a question from the British about the position of the trade unions, Jouhaux replied that trade unions cannot protest against the forthcoming decline in the proletariat's living standards because the condition of soldiers and their families is even worse (soldiers' wives have a miserable allowance). There must be 'equality of sacrifice'!

The British were not convinced by Jouhaux's arguments. What's more, they were greatly alarmed, for they fear that the example of France might inspire the British bourgeoisie to follow suit. But that won't happen in England. The British working masses here will fight hard, and men like Citrine, Bevin[ii] and others may find themselves in trouble. That is why the trade union leaders try to take the appropriate 'measures' in advance. On the one hand, they step up the struggle against the 'communist influence' in the trade unions; on the other, they demand that the British government stabilize prices on products of mass consumption. The government meets its 'labour guard' halfway and pays 1 million pounds a week extra to wholesalers to forestall jumps in the cost of food and consumer goods.

---

i Leon Jouhaux, secretary-general of the General Confederation of Labour (CGT), 1909–47.

ii Ernest Bevin, member of General Council of the TUC, 1925–40; minister of labour and national service, 1940–45; fierce opponent of appeasement, as well as of communism; foreign secretary in post-war Labour government.

2 February

Subbotić called in. We discussed Balkan issues.

Subbotić does not expect any sensational decisions at the Balkan Entente conference, which opens in Belgrade today. The reason is very simple. The Entente is flawed: it does not include Bulgaria. Bulgaria would probably join if Rumania ceded Dobrudja. Rumania would probably agree, if the question of Dobrudja were resolved in isolation from all other questions, but Rumania is afraid that as soon as Dobrudja returns to Bulgaria, Hungary will immediately claim Transylvania, and the USSR will claim Bessarabia. That is why Rumania clings to Dobrudja. And that is why Bulgaria remains outside the Balkan Entente. It's a vicious circle.

Subbotić declared in the Foreign Office the other day that the Balkan peoples do not need a 'large Franco-British army' in Syria, and that the greatest wish of the Balkan peoples is for none of the great powers to come to their 'rescue'. Somehow or other, they will look after themselves.

Subbotić also finds that the Balkan countries have become considerably calmer, compared to December, about 'Soviet intentions' in this part of Europe.

* * *

The British government reasons on the assumption that Hitler cannot sit behind the Siegfried Line forever, and that in the spring he must do something, must mount an offensive somewhere. But what and where? The British government can only guess. That is why Ironside[i] has been instructed to prepare for the possibility of a German offensive in spring on three fronts: Holland–Belgium, the Balkans and Scandinavia.

At the same time, the British government has focused its attention on Iceland. It has sent a secret mission there, and is showering it with literature. All this is being done for the following reason. If Germany seizes Denmark, the British government will lay its hands on Iceland, which has great strategic importance for England. If the USSR or Germany or both reach the Norwegian shores of the Atlantic (the British government strongly suspects this might happen), Iceland will serve Great Britain as a good naval and air base against them.

* * *

The 'Blue Book' has not yet come out and nobody knows when it will be released. Some say it will not be published at all, mostly on the insistence of the French government. The latter is said to reason in the following way.

---

[i] William Edmund Ironside, commander-in-chief Allied troops, Arkhangelsk, northern Russia, 1918–19; commanded ISMID Force, 1920; chief of the imperial general staff, 1939–40; commander-in-chief, home forces, 1940.

First, the general problem must be solved: will the 'Allies' maintain diplomatic relations with the USSR or will they not? If they do, releasing the Blue Book may produce an adverse effect on the relations between the 'Allies' and the USSR. If they don't, it will also be undesirable to release the Book, in its present version at least, because it is not provocative enough to trigger a rupture. So, the publication of the Blue Book has come to a standstill and its destiny is unclear.

The British government has started to fret over prices and wages. Chamberlain had a long talk with Attlee a day or two ago and demanded that Labour should not harp on the *standard of life* issue as this 'undermines the country's confidence in the government'. Attlee gave no definite promises, saying that this was a matter for the trade unions. But the latter, when it comes to prices and wages, are afraid to act on their wishes. Their leaders wouldn't be against reaching a compromise with the government, but they fear the masses. They know that even the puniest of trade unionists turns into a lion when his wages are at stake. In this connection, the Labourites and trade unionists scold their French colleagues, who have 'let them down' on the question of prices and wages, as well as on that of war aims. The French socialists are inclining ever more to the route of a 'shattering' peace, with Germany being partitioned and disarmed.

7 February

Umansky[i] visited Cordell Hull the other day on instructions from Moscow. At first Hull was diplomatically indisposed for an entire week (in response to the three-day delay in informing Steinhardt[ii] in Moscow about the American boat *City of Flint*, which the Germans had brought to Murmansk). But then the meeting took place after all.

Umansky protested about a speech by Johnson,[iii] the assistant secretary of war, that was offensive towards the Red Army, and further pointed out that the United States was discriminating against Soviet trade under the guise of a 'moral embargo'.

Hull justified the unfriendly actions against the USSR in terms of US national interests and said that the paths of the USA and the USSR had diverged. Hull behaved correctly. He let it be understood that the United States was not planning to expand its anti-Soviet measures. The question of Finland was not touched upon.

---

[i] Konstantin Aleksandrovich Umansky, a polyglot, he was recruited to head the press and information department of NKID in 1936; rumoured to be associated with the NKVD, he was appointed Soviet ambassador to the United States, 1938–41, and to Mexico, 1941–43, where he died in an air crash.

[ii] Laurence Steinhardt, American ambassador to the Soviet Union, 1939–41.

[iii] Louis Arthur Johnson, assistant secretary of war, 1937–40.

And today there was a noteworthy incident in the US Congress: one of the congressmen tabled an unexpected motion – to remove from the State Department budget the expenses involved in running the American embassy in Moscow. Although the Administration protested against the proposal, it was rejected by a mere three votes (108 to 105).

8 February

The Inter-Allied Supreme War Council met in Paris on 5 February. Both parties were represented by an unusually large number of participants. The Council's communiqué expressed satisfaction with the full unanimity of French and British views. Is it really so?

Some reports suggest not. The French continued to insist on severing relations with the USSR, banning the British Communist Party, and stopping the wage rises under way in England. They argued that this was essential in view of the internal situation in France. But the British adhered to their former position in respect of the USSR (not to break off relations themselves, but to provoke the USSR into doing so) and said that considering their own internal situation, they could not bind themselves by any promises about wages. However, the British government was far more amenable on the matter of the Communist Party.

As far as Finland is concerned, the parties agreed to 'speed up' and 'increase' material aid to Finland and 'stimulate' the 'volunteer' movement.

On the day of the Supreme War Council meeting, the French police arranged a brazen raid on our trade mission. A true *Arcos Raid*,[21] if not worse. Evidently, the French wanted to create a favourable 'atmosphere' in which the decision about breaking off relations with the USSR could be taken, and wished to tie the hands of the British in advance. For now, it seems, they have failed. Surits has sent a protest to the French Ministry of Foreign Affairs.

I've heard that members of the British government have already been sounding out Labour leaders about closing down the Communist Party. As might have been expected, Attlee and Greenwood said there were no obstacles from their side. But the British government has not yet taken decisive measures, as it is evidently uncertain about how the masses would react to such a move. Be that as it may, it would not be a surprise if the Communist Party and its press were banned in the near future. The forces of reaction are advancing rapidly.

9 February

[Enclosed is a newspaper cutting entitled 'The "Little Old Lady" has died. She went to Museum daily for 20 years', by an *Evening Standard* reporter.]

During the years of my emigration, when I used to work as a matter of routine in the Brit[ish] Museum, the following incident occurred.

There was an old French woman, a former governess, who was a regular visitor to the *Reading Room* over many years. She would sit not far away from me and would always be reading or 'mentally experiencing' the scores of various musical works. She always had a hungry look about her, and her clothes were little better than rags; once, the museum administration even denied her admission to the reading room. But the governess's former charge, an important 'lady', intervened on her behalf, and permission to visit the *Reading Room* was restored to her. The old woman spent whole days in the museum, especially in winter, and told people quite openly that this was where she warmed up: she had nothing to heat her dwelling with.

One day I came to the museum and didn't find the French woman in her usual place.

This surprised me. The museum administrators were also taken aback. Two or three days passed, but the old woman still didn't appear. The employees and regulars of the *Reading Room* became very concerned. They started making inquiries.

It transpired that the old woman had died, and one hundred thousand francs (of the pre-war variety!) were found sewn up in her mattress.

10 February

Today, I found the following item in the *Evening Standard*.

[Attached is a cutting entitled 'Closed Down'.]

The effects of the war are beginning to be felt. I heard the other day that Londonderry has also closed up his mansion in London.

This is just the beginning.

11 February

Visited the *Old Wizard* in Churt.[22] It is always pleasant and salutary to talk with him, especially in difficult times. He has an exceptional brain: a sort of clot of high-voltage intellectual energy. He catches your meaning at once and responds with a cascade of brilliant thoughts and comparisons. Yet he also possesses in abundance that supreme wisdom which sees through things, is not distracted by glittering appearances, does not lapse into indignation, does not shout, weep or become agitated, but simply understands and takes everything into account, drawing the appropriate inferences. Whenever you converse with Lloyd George,

71. With Lloyd George, the 'Old Wizard'.

you immediately sense that you are dealing with a man of the highest calibre, a cut above all around him – ministers, parliamentarians and public figures. The difference between Lloyd George and every other contemporary 'leader' is like that between Kreisler[i] and a violinist from a provincial orchestra. One may say without hesitation: he is an astonishing person.

We talked for about three hours today. Leaving my own arguments and considerations to one side, I'll try to convey the gist of what the 'Old Wizard' told me.

'If it comes to war between England and the USSR,' Lloyd George exclaimed, with a toss of his pince-nez, 'this would be the greatest catastrophe. It's terrifying even to contemplate. But one shouldn't close one's eyes to the facts. Anglo-Soviet relations have been deteriorating since the beginning of the Finnish war and are in a precarious state today. The near future holds no hope of improvement. If the Finnish war drags on for another three or four months – you'll hardly be able to occupy the country any sooner – will our relations be able to stand it? Won't they snap?'

[i] Fritz Kreisler, Austrian-born American violinist and composer.

In Lloyd George's opinion, two basic aspects must be taken into account when considering the deterioration in Anglo-Soviet relations, at least as far as the British side is concerned: first, the anti-communist stance of the ruling circles and, second, the admiration of the masses – the *man in the street* – for the strong and stubborn resistance mounted by the Finns. We shouldn't have any illusions: the masses are on the side of Finland. Political experts understand the role that Finland might play in certain circumstances – that of vanguard and springboard in the struggle of the capitalist powers against the USSR. These political experts are capable of appreciating our [i.e. Russian] arguments and possibly even of justifying our actions. But they are the exceptions. The masses do not know or understand any of this. The press, radio and cinema are waging a frenzied anti-Soviet campaign. Not only do they make no attempt to present the *Russian case* with any measure of objectivity, but they spare no effort to stupefy the masses and set them against the USSR. As a result, the *man in the street* perceives what is happening in Finland approximately as follows: huge, 'totalitarian' Soviet Union has attacked small, 'democratic' Finland which, unlike Poland, is putting up a superb fight for its survival. It's clear that all the sympathies of this *man in the street* are with Finland. Labour is playing a critical role here: its stance merely adds fuel to the fire. The ruling circles are skilfully exploiting the situation, fanning the flames of the anti-Soviet campaign. As a result, Anglo-Soviet relations are deteriorating rapidly. It's a threatening outlook. In L-G's opinion, the USSR, against its will and desires, has, by the pure logic of things, neared the edge of the precipice beyond which it will begin to be sucked into a European war. One false move and the fire will spread to the USSR. All the more so as there are enough provocateurs in England, and especially France, advocating rupture and war with the USSR.

Where might one expect the danger to come from most directly? L-G thinks Sweden. The ruling circles in Sweden and Norway have become deeply convinced of late that the USSR has far-reaching imperialist designs and that Finland is just a prelude, following the capture of which Moscow will strike out against Sweden and Norway. Moscow is said to want access to the Atlantic Ocean from Narvik or some other Norwegian port. London and Paris support and exacerbate the Scandinavians' fears as best they can. The broad masses in Sweden and Norway are no less hostile to the USSR than they are in England. Hence the danger that Sweden and Norway may plunge into the Finnish war in fear and despair, thinking it better to fight the 'Russian menace' now, while Finland is still 'alive' and at war with the USSR. Will they take the risk? It's difficult to say, but everything is possible in the present situation. The arrest of communists in Sweden, reported in today's newspapers, is a bad sign. And should Sweden and Norway intervene in the Finnish war, the mood here in England would be such – Lloyd George has no doubts about this – that the British government would be forced to lend them all-out military support. The pressure of public opinion would be so powerful that no Cabinet could withstand it. We should have no illusions on this score either.

Can this looming disaster be prevented? L-G thinks it can. The situation is very serious but not entirely hopeless. Chamberlain, Hoare, Halifax and Kingsley Wood are against the war with the USSR. Simon, as usual, is hedging his bets. This group may indeed be able to withstand French pressure. But the Soviet government must show flexibility as well. First of all, it mustn't yield to provocation. It's very good that the Soviet government responded calmly to the farce in Geneva and to the raid on the trade mission in Paris. And it's very good that the Soviet government did not recall me in response to the departure of Seeds ('a big fool'). Surits mustn't be recalled from Paris. We mustn't protest to the British government about the weapons, aeroplanes and so on that they are sending to Finland. Nothing will come of it except an increase in vexation and anti-Soviet agitation. All the more so as events in Finland have advanced so far that decisions will be made on the battlefield, not in the offices of diplomats. Some positive initiatives would be desirable. First, it would be advisable to assure Sweden and Norway that the USSR is not nurturing any hostile intentions against them. If Sweden remains neutral, Anglo-French aid will necessarily remain quite modest (the British and the French are 'short of weapons themselves', and the number of 'volunteers' will scarcely go beyond a few thousand), for L-G is certain that troops would not be dispatched in such circumstances. Second, it would be good to test the ground for the resumption of trade talks between England and the USSR. This would 'soften' the mood in London.

As usual, Lloyd George made his arguments vividly, rapidly and passionately, scattering them with sparks of humour, images and comparisons. And all that he said deserves close attention.

We spoke on other subjects as well. L-G's verdict on the big war is right on the money: it's a nonsense. It's a nonsense from both the political and the military points of view. The sooner peace is concluded, the better, but will it happen? L-G has grave doubts. He attaches little importance to Sumner Welles' imminent visit to Europe. Little will come of it. Except perhaps harm: Moscow has been excluded from the itinerary of the American traveller. This is fairly significant. Does he not have some anti-Soviet plans? In general terms, Sumner Welles' trip is, without doubt, closely tied to American domestic policy. Roosevelt wants to be a 'peace-maker', he wants to boost his prestige, and wants to decide whether he should put himself up for election.

Among the members of the British government, Chamberlain, Hoare and Halifax are for peace 'at the first opportunity'; Churchill, Kingsley Wood and Stanley are for 'war to the end'. Simon sits on the fence. The first group is supported by most Tories, the second by a Tory minority and the Labour–

Liberal opposition. What does peace 'at the first opportunity' mean? In L-G's opinion, the minimal basis for such a peace is the restoration of at least a puppet Poland, autonomy to Czechoslovakia, and Germany's withdrawal of its demand for the immediate return of its colonies. Peace could be concluded on this basis, even though it would cause a serious split in the country. But would Hitler agree to such conditions? L-G is not sure, but he thinks that Hitler has nothing to gain by dragging the war out for another year or two, because his position would deteriorate: he would lose his present superiority in the air and on land. The British army will be *formidable* in a year's time.

Lloyd George scoffed at the French: some French politicians are convinced that the Ukraine is ripe for an 'uprising'. All that's needed is to send a small French landing force to Odessa. A madman's ravings.

15 February

After a brief interlude, Scandinavia is once again on the agenda.

Since early February, our success on the Finnish front has become quite evident. We are stubbornly battering the Mannerheim Line and gradually breaking through. A little more and the turning point in the war will be a fait accompli. The enemies of the USSR – the friends of Mannerheim, Tanner and Co. – are very worked up: they sense that the end of their adventure is nigh. And they try to mobilize new forces against us while they still have time.

Immense efforts are being made to push Scandinavia, and primarily Sweden, into a direct intervention in Finland. This is being done both inside and outside Sweden. Sandler and his followers are active inside Sweden. Their arguments boil down to the following. The USSR will not be content with swallowing up Finland, but will advance further towards the shores of the Atlantic through Sweden and Norway. Germany will join it. Or vice versa: as soon as the USSR occupies Finland, the Germans will march into Sweden, and the USSR will join Germany. In both cases, Sweden and Norway will, in the very near future, have to fight for their lives against the 'imperialisms' of Germany and the Soviet Union. That is why it is better for Sweden to help Finland openly now, while Finland is still able to fight. All the more so as Sweden and Norway can count on receiving military aid from the 'Allies'. How strong is this tendency? Hard to say. But Prytz, who has just spent a couple of days in Stockholm, assured Halifax the other day that the movement in support of intervention is growing very rapidly in Sweden and that he wouldn't be surprised to find Sweden and the USSR at war within a matter of weeks.

The British and the French are moving in the same direction. Daladier has just summoned Scandinavian representatives and demanded that they should give Finland their entire reserve force, promising to recompense them in full.

The Scandinavians, however, responded very [word missing]. The Second International, and especially the French socialists, are pressing hard along similar lines, even demanding that relations with the USSR be broken off.

The British are acting rather more cautiously. They are swelling the Swedes' and Norwegians' fear of the USSR, attempting to push both countries to intervene directly in Finland. But until this becomes a certainty, they restrict themselves to sending weapons to Helsinki and to organizing 'stimulated voluntary service' (as Beaverbrook put it in our recent conversation). England and France have already sent 300 planes and intend to send some 400 more. They are also sending artillery and anti-aircraft weapons. Sweden, which the British government has promised to compensate fully in kind or in cash, is giving a great deal. Ironside makes the following calculations. The USSR will not accomplish anything decisive before mid-March. Then military operations will get bogged down for a month and a half because of the thaw and the slush. Serious operations will be resumed no earlier than May, and the whole campaign will end, if the USSR is lucky, no earlier than mid-summer. Russian losses will reach nearly half a million. This should weaken the USSR to such a degree that it will hardly be capable of mounting a full-scale attack on Sweden and Norway. I fear that Ironside is mistaken. It's not the first time it's happened to him: the same thing happened in Arkhangelsk 20 years ago. All these calculations are based on the assumption that Sweden and Norway will not interfere directly in the conflict. If they do interfere, then more enticing prospects will open before those who wish to see an expansion of the war. In this scenario, it is clear that Germany will also advance on Scandinavia. Britain's hands will be untied. They will break through to the Baltic and land a 30,000–40,000-strong force in Narvik to capture and hold the region of Kiruna (iron ore).

In our conversation of 10 February, Beaverbrook defined the situation as follows: 'If Sweden and Norway remain neutral, British aid to Finland will most probably not exceed that which the Soviet government gave to the Spanish Republicans. If Sweden and Norway openly intervene, England and France will give them maximum military support.'

That seems about right.

Three days ago, Halifax stated in a confidential talk with several top journalists that the British government does not intend to declare war itself on the USSR, but that, on the other hand, the danger of the USSR declaring war on Britain would not keep the British government from carrying out its plans in respect of Finland.

In other words, the British government plans to assist Mannerheim in so far as it is able to (which depends to a great extent on the position of Sweden and Norway), no matter what the reaction of the USSR might be. I think Halifax overdid it a bit. Well, time will tell.

19 February

Here is Norman Angell's[i] view of the war (he came to lunch with me today).

The present balance of forces is about even. The war is entering its second phase – the fight for the neutrals. Soon there will be no 'free' neutral states in Europe among the small powers. Once they have all been allocated, the balance of forces, in all probability, will nevertheless remain about even. This *stalemate* may become entrenched for several years. Angell thinks, however, that there are limits to how long the human psyche can stand such a state of siege. Something has to snap. He thinks it possible, for instance, that in order to break the *stalemate* the British may one day send their air fleet to bomb Berlin. In his view, the Germans, being accustomed to military and other sorts of discipline, will be able to endure the *boredom* of this war better than the British. Saying this, Angell excluded various contingencies, such as the disappearance of Hitler, some kind of exceptional military invention, revolution, etc.

Time will tell. Human judgements are often very short-sighted. I remember, for instance, that in European socialist circles before 1914, war was widely deemed impossible for two reasons: (1) the psyche of contemporary man was unable to endure the horrors of war and (2) world economies were so intertwined that, should the bonds be broken, global economic catastrophe would ensue, rendering the conduct of war impossible.

But what happened in reality?

21 February

Our undeniable successes at the front (breakthrough in the western section of the Mannerheim Line) have made a powerful, but double-edged impression in Britain.

Our successes have made more reasonable people – among whom should be numbered Chamberlain's group in the government, Beaverbrook, Labourites like Hicks, Tom Williams, Strabolgi and others – more restrained and circumspect on the matter of aid to Finland. They are less inclined than ever to risk the possibility of war with the Soviet Union.

Less reasonable people, including certain ministers who appear to be led by Churchill (though I have no definite information about the latter's stance on the Finnish question), supporters of Hore-Belisha, Liberals headed by Sinclair, and various newspapers – *News Chronicle*, *The Star*, *Sunday Times* and others – draw the reverse conclusion. Sensing Mannerheim to be weakening, they have launched a frenzied campaign in London to provide energetic support to the

[i] Sir Ralph Norman Angell, member of the Council of Royal Institute of International Affairs, 1928–42.

Finns on the broadest scale, *including the sending of troops*, while ignoring the risk of open war with the USSR and the transformation of Scandinavia into a field of battle between the 'Allies' and Germany.

Calmly assessing all these factors, I'm inclined to think that the people in the first group outweigh those in the second group by a significant margin, since England itself is at stake here. There is one complication, though: the majority of the French government supports the line taken by the 'less reasonable'. I've heard that at the meeting of the Supreme War Council on 5 February, the French directly proposed the dispatching of an expeditionary corps to Finland. True, this received a cool response from Chamberlain and Halifax, but still... The French government plus 'activists' in England may lead Chamberlain, step by step, to a point from which it may prove difficult to retreat from direct involvement in the Finnish conflict. The prime minister is a past master at 'gliding', inconspicuously and semi-consciously, into fatal situations. It's enough to recall Munich and the current war. Mightn't something similar happen in this case?

On the whole, the situation has to be recognized as dangerous and fraught with any number of surprises. One might easily be drawn into a major war. The best means of avoiding this danger is speed on the Finnish front. The Anglo-French calculations are based on the assumption that the decisive phase in Finland will not begin until May. If we could upset these calculations and bring the war to an end within a few weeks (or, if not end the war completely, at least deliver a decisive blow to the Finns, after which the hopelessness of their position would be obvious to all), we would exit the danger zone. The British are quick to accept faits accomplis, and they would not risk war with the USSR for the sake of a *lost cause*. But should operations on the Finnish front continue over a long period of time, who knows what this could lead to?

The root of British activism is the widespread conviction that the USSR and Germany are 'allies' – if not yet formally, then in the near future. Hence the tendency to make no distinction between Germany and the USSR and to label both as 'enemies'. This is where explanations must be sought for Churchill's and Hore-Belisha's change of tack. The trade agreement we signed with Germany on 11 February gave new impetus to all those speculations and fears. It's no accident that Butler asked me during our last meeting (he lunched with me on 16 February) whether the USSR and Germany should be viewed as 'allies' following the agreement of 11 February. And it's no accident that Colville declared the USSR to be a 'potential enemy' at a public meeting a few days ago. Not that Colville is a political figure of the first rank, but he is still secretary of state for Scotland. Various statesmen and politicians have displayed similar sentiments recently. I try proving to everybody that talk about a Soviet–German 'alliance' is absurd. But since nobody believes a word anyone says in the world of diplomacy at the moment, I have no illusions about the effectiveness of my refutations on this issue. Moscow ought to have demonstrated this in a more obvious manner.[23]

25 February

I recall a scene I saw once in Mongolia.

A horse slipped off the precipice and tumbled down the side of the mountain towards the abyss. She neighed desperately, turned over several times and managed to stop on a small ledge. Scratched all over, with large bruises and bleeding wounds on her sides, but still in one piece, she was clinging on to the ledge and thrashing her legs about in a feverish attempt to find support. For several minutes she made immense efforts to stand up and remain on the ledge, and there were moments when it seemed that she would succeed. But the ledge was small and uneven, and the horse was huge and ungainly. She was unable to keep her balance, slipped once again and rolled further down the mountain-side. There was another shelf some 100 metres below. Turning somersaults, the horse reached it and came to a stop once again. This second stone shelf was wider than the first, and had the horse been still in one piece, as only a few minutes earlier, she might well have escaped death. But now she had a broken leg and a thick stream of blood gushing from her croup. Yet her survival instinct was still functioning. She was madly scraping her three unhurt legs against the rock face, neighing and swishing her tail. But she lacked the strength to save herself. A few moments later she fell once again and rolled further down, fast and unstoppably. But she was still alive. All beaten up, her legs broken, drenched in blood, the horse fell another 100 metres onto a third small ledge which jutted out whimsically from the cliff face, and made a few weak movements with her head and body to hold on once more. But it was too late. She had no strength left. She slipped off again and careered down the rocky slope into the abyss.

This scene often comes to mind when I think about Anglo-Soviet relations over the last three months.

The curve of our relations has been dropping sharply since the beginning of the Finnish war. It is not a sheer drop, but broken up into stages. The first jump into the precipice was made in Geneva, when the League of Nations, led by the British and the French with the covert assistance of the United States, expelled the USSR for 'aggression'. There were rumours then that England and France would immediately sever diplomatic relations with the Soviet Union. But this didn't happen. On the contrary, Butler declared in the League's lobby that Geneva was one thing and London another. In Geneva, the British were devotees of 'principles' and had to anathematize the USSR 'on grounds of principle'. In London, the British were engaged in *business* and would maintain diplomatic relations with the Soviet 'devil' 'on grounds of expedience'. There followed a relatively calm two-week period in Soviet–British relations.

The next leap down the cliff face happened at the turn of the year: the preparation of the 'Blue Book', the departure of Seeds 'on leave', Doshchenko's arrest, the British embassy in Moscow packing up for evacuation, the rumours spread about my departure from London, and, most importantly, weapons and planes began to be delivered to Finland. This period of agitation lasted until mid-January, when another temporary lull set in. Its outward manifestation was the indefinite deferral of the publication of the Blue Book, which had been scheduled for 15 January.

Two weeks later, and there was a further plunge. Churchill's speech of 20 January, Chamberlain's reply to Knox's query about the severance of Anglo-Soviet relations on 24 January, the British government's decision to provide the Finns not only with weapons but also with 'volunteers', and intense pressure on Sweden and Norway, urging them to support Mannerheim by way of direct armed intervention. This fevered state of affairs lasted until mid-February. The Swedish prime minister, Hansson,[i] put an end to it, declaring on 16 February that Sweden would maintain neutrality in the Finnish war (that same 'neutrality' it had been practising until then). A new temporary lull set in, which continues to this day. It is still unclear how it will be affected by my démarche of 22 February.

Step by step, from one ledge to another. After each fall, Anglo-Soviet relations get back on their feet for an instant and stabilize themselves, but on a lower level every time. The further they fall, the more unstoppable the slide. Will they indeed fall into the abyss of rupture and war? Or will they succeed in getting a firm hold on one of the ledges? Or even, having found it, start climbing back up? Should the Finnish campaign end quickly, Anglo-Soviet relations would correct themselves. If it drags on – who knows? The contest today is between the tempo of the termination of the Finnish war and the tempo of the transformation of the Finnish war into a general capitalist attack on the Soviet Union. Which will win?...

8 March

Well, it looks like our affairs are taking a turn for the better. It seems that we'll make a fool of Ironside for a second time.

---

[i] Per Albin Hansson, leader of the Swedish Social Democrat Party from 1925; prime minister of Sweden, 1932–46.

Yesterday the *News Chronicle* published the first report from Stockholm about the peace negotiations between the USSR and Finland. Sweden is playing the part of mediator. It couldn't have been otherwise after the refusal of the British government. The report caused quite a stir in London.

All the newspapers today are full of the most sensationalist reports on this subject. Leaving aside the absurdities and exaggerations, one thing can be stated for sure: the peace talks are under way. This has been the sole topic of conversation all day long in political and government circles. It's interesting and symptomatic that news of the peace negotiations has been met with obvious displeasure and even irritation among the elite, with Sweden, rather than the USSR, supplying the main target for criticism. Sweden is being accused of all manner of mortal sins: she has 'put pressure' on Finland, she 'toadies' before Germany, she is 'running to seed', she is engrossed in 'manicure culture', etc. It's perfectly clear that Sweden is being intimidated. To what end?

I found the answer in my conversation today with Prytz, who, after a long interval, came over for lunch. It transpires that the Supreme War Council's decision about dispatching an expeditionary corps to Finland was not mere words. My fears have come true: the French government plus British activists succeeded in nudging Chamberlain to the point when the British envoy in Stockholm put the following question to the Swedish government: how would it respond to an Anglo-French request to allow the transit of Allied troops earmarked for Finland through Swedish territory? The Swedish foreign minister, Günther,[i] replied that the Swedish government would regard such a step as a violation of the policy of neutrality, and therefore did not even consider it possible to discuss the question raised by the British envoy. In this way, the 'Allies'' attempt to unleash war in Scandinavia seems to have failed. What is curious, however, is that my démarche was made on 22 February. The British made a démarche in Stockholm in early March, i.e. after the British government had learned of our intention to make peace with the Finns. Only one conclusion can be drawn: not only does the British government not desire an end to the Finnish war but, on the contrary, it makes efforts to prolong and intensify it. True, Prytz makes one qualification: it is not clear to him why the British government tested the ground in Stockholm. Was it seriously considering sending troops to Finland? Or rather was it counting on exploiting the anticipated refusal of the Swedish government as an argument against sending troops to Finland in its negotiations with the French? For the information at Prytz's disposal also suggests that it is the French government which is leading the dance on the question of dispatching an expeditionary corps to Finland. I don't know whether Prytz is right or not about this, but,

[i] Christian Ernst Günther, Swedish minister for foreign affairs, 1939–45.

even taking into account his qualification, we can safely say that the 'Allies' are against putting an end to the Finnish war, that they are attempting to scupper the peace negotiations, and will continue to do so.

Why? The reasons, I believe, are as follows:

(1) The longer the USSR is occupied in the north, the longer the 'Allies' are safe from 'Soviet danger' in the Near East, which is much more important to them than Finland.

(2) The Finnish war is 'weakening' the USSR and reducing its capacity to supply Germany with raw materials and foodstuffs.

(3) For as long as the Finnish war rumbles on, the possibility remains of drawing Scandinavia into a major war and creating a 'mobile' front there against Germany.

(4) A peace agreement, despite and in the face of England's refusal to mediate, would be a heavy blow to the prestige of Great Britain in Scandinavia.

Nonetheless, if Sweden stands firm and the peace negotiations don't drag on too long, the British activists will not be able to do great harm in spite of all their malevolence.

Speed! It is no less important now than it was at the front in February.

11 March

Irritation occasioned by the 'danger' of peace in Finland is growing in government circles. It's hardly surprising. The Finns have sent a delegation to Moscow: Ryti, Paasikivi,[i] Voionmaa[ii] and General Walden.[iii] The negotiators on our side are C[omrades] Molotov, Zhdanov and Vasilevsky[iv] (military). Meetings were held on 8 and 10 March. There are some differences of opinion, but it seems clear that agreement will be achieved. The British government senses this and its fury increases accordingly.

A remarkable scene unfolded in the press department of the Foreign Office today. The French, as is their wont, have been blabbing out the particulars of my démarche of the 22nd. French, Belgian and American journalists already knew about it last week. One American journalist came to see me to check the facts. Seeing that the cat had been let out of the bag (in a rather anti-Soviet manner), I confirmed the whole story, describing matters as they actually stood.

---

[i] Juho Kusti Paasikivi, Finnish minister to Sweden, 1936–39, and to Moscow, 1940–41; prime minister of Finland, 1918 and 1944–46.

[ii] Väinö Voionmaa, a professor of history, he was a member of parliament, a member of the Finnish delegation to the League of Nations and foreign minister in 1938.

[iii] General Rudolf Walden, military representative in the Finnish Cabinet during the Winter War; minister for defence, 1940–44.

[iv] Aleksandr Mikhailovich Vasilevsky, head of operations; deputy chief and then chief of the general staff, 1941–45.

The American speedily telegraphed the story to New York, and, by a peculiar oversight, the censor let it pass. A few hours later, the same report came back to the continent from America. It made a massive splash. The Foreign Office was nonplussed. This morning, items concerning my démarche appeared in the *Yorkshire Post* and *Financial News*. Then the Foreign Office decided to cut the Gordian knot and presented the press with its account of my démarche and the response of the British government. The effect was extraordinary and highly revealing. When the representative of the press department made the statement at the morning *press conference* at the FO, it was as if a bomb had exploded. Moreover, all the neutral journalists (of which there were many at the *press conference*: not only Scandinavians, but also Dutch, Belgians, Swiss, Americans and others) declared with one voice: 'Now we know who wants war and who doesn't want war. Now we can see clearly what the British are playing at.'

The British government, however, continues its game. The papers today try to scare the Swedes and urge the Finns not to agree to the conditions of peace proposed by us, saying that they are 'impossible', 'humiliating', deprive Finland of its 'independence', etc. Furthermore, Chamberlain declared in the House that the British government was ready to help Finland 'by all available means', and Daladier said openly in his speech that since 26 February, 50,000 French soldiers had been waiting to be shipped to Finland. The curtain is being raised ever higher.

According to the press, two conditions are necessary to implement the plans for direct intervention: (1) the Finnish government must make an open appeal for help to England and France, and (2) Sweden and Norway must agree to the passage of the expeditionary corps. The British government calculates that if the peace negotiations fall through, the Finns will make the necessary appeal, while the Swedes and the Norwegians will 'lose heart' and agree to 'cooperate' with the Western powers. And even if they don't agree, they will be forced to. This latter point is not stated overtly, but transparent hints to this effect have been made. I've heard that a specific plan has already been worked out: to land the expeditionary corps in Narvik and make Norway come to terms with it as a fait accompli.

'On paper there had seemed no hitches, Alas! Forgotten were the ditches, which one would have to cross!' That's how things will go with the Anglo-French calculations. For, to judge by the latest news, the peace treaty has already been agreed. Tomorrow it will be signed.

12 March

The new Iranian minister, Moghaddam,[i] has paid me his first visit.

---

[i] Mohammad Ali Moghaddam, Iranian ambassador in London, 1940–41.

A tall, somewhat heavy man of the eastern type. He speaks excellent Russian, having spent many years in the diplomatic service in Russia in the old days. His wife, who is the daughter of the Persian consul-general in Moscow, even studied at a Moscow gymnasium. Moghaddam was court minister to the shah prior to his appointment in London and speaks in ecstatic, lisping tones about his master: how ascetic he is, how hard-working, what an outstanding statesman he is, etc. Moghaddam assured me most emphatically that the shah's one ambition is to stay out of the war and that he will never permit Iran or its territory to be used against the USSR.

I mentioned half in jest that I heard talk of England offering guarantees to Iran. Moghaddam look at me with horror in his eyes, raised his hands and exclaimed: 'British guarantees? God forbid!… After Poland?… Not for the world! Our life is still dear to us!'

What a fine reputation Chamberlain has won for himself!

* * *

Guo told me today that the *Graf Spee*'s scuttling by its own men was easily explained. The crew had revolted and did not want to go out to sea from Montevideo to fight the British ships. Captain Langsdorff[i] reported this to Berlin. Hitler ordered the *Graf Spee* to be sunk. Langsdorff found it impossible to endure this 'disgrace' and, having executed the order, committed suicide.

* * *

Chamberlain told Labourites that he had been forced to decline my démarche of 22 February because of the French government, although he himself was heart and soul for an early Soviet–Finnish peace and wished the Moscow negotiations every success. Pure hypocrisy!

13 March

I barely slept last night. Moscow radio announced in the evening that an important communication would be transmitted after midnight. I immediately understood that this was about the peace treaty with Finland and sat down by the radio to await news. It was a long wait. It was only at 3.30 a.m. Moscow time that the end of the Soviet–Finnish war and the conclusion of peace between the belligerents was finally announced.

Hurrah! I was ready to hurl my hat into the air.

We have emerged from a very great danger. We have preserved the possibility of staying out of an imperialist war. And we have gained what we wanted: Leningrad and our north-western borders are now secure.

---

[i] Hans Wilhelm Langsdorff.

In the afternoon I went to parliament, where Chamberlain was due to make a statement about the conclusion of peace. The diplomatic gallery was practically empty. There were only myself, the Bulgarian and… the duke of Alba (the Spaniard). But the House was packed to the rafters and the air was humming, as before a storm.

Chamberlain made a brief statement consisting of little more than formalities. Attlee and Sinclair said a few words appropriate to the occasion. Sinclair let it be understood that he was not entirely sure whether the British government had fulfilled its 'duty' with regard to Finland. Hore-Belisha made this point far more sharply in his statement, asking the prime minister a few awkward and rather barbed questions. Hore-Belisha, supported by Macmillan and Sinclair, demanded that a closed session of parliament be convened to discuss the government's conduct during the Finnish war. Labour, however, did not second Belisha's demand. In his response Chamberlain did his best to wriggle out of the situation, arguing that the British government had 'fulfilled its duty'. Whether this is true or not is another matter; at any rate, the activists didn't get their way at this session.

But as for parliament … I can't recall seeing it in such a state of excitement and fury. Indeed, the only word to describe the mood of the majority of all the MPs, with only a few exceptions, was <u>fury</u>. Impotent fury, but fury nonetheless – vivid, seething, overflowing fury…

'It's fallen through! What a pity, it's fallen through,' were the words that seemed to hang in the air.

This frenzy was expressed in the House's reactions to the various anti-Soviet volleys by ministers and MPs. When Chamberlain referred to 'aggression' in reference to the Finnish events, the House shook with shouts of approval. When the 'Independent' McGovern[i] took aim at the USSR and C[omrade] Stalin, the hall resounded for an entire minute with deafening yells, *'Hear! Hear!'*

Looking down from the diplomatic gallery, I watched that vile display of angry impotence with a sense of superiority. And at the same time it was clearer to me than ever that peace had been concluded at just the right time.[24]

Newspapers and politicians may carry on fussing about the 'cruelty' of the Soviet–Finnish peace for a few days but, so long as new unexpected factors do not come into play, the frenzied anti-Soviet wave which gathered force at the beginning of the Finnish war will soon ebb. It seems as if Anglo-Soviet relations may succeed in keeping their feet on the current 'ledge'. Their fall has stopped. Will they begin to climb back up?

I can't rule it out. But time will tell.

---

[i] John McGovern, Scottish ILP MP, 1930–59, and chairman of the ILP, 1941–43.

16 March

I visited Lloyd George in Churt. The old man has a cold and is not in the best of health, but he is alive and looking as bright as ever.

He congratulated me on the timely conclusion of peace.

'I won't touch upon the *merits of the case*,' he said. 'I think we might disagree on this point, but I'm very glad about the peace. The danger of war between England and the USSR was quite real. I had much evidence of this in recent weeks, since our last meeting. Had the war dragged on till May, I can assure you that conflict between our countries would have become unavoidable. Not because Chamberlain wanted such a conflict. You know my opinion of Chamberlain, don't you?'

Lloyd George burst into peals of infectious laughter, and I recalled how he used to mock the prime minister in my presence, calling him 'the manufacturer of iron beds'.

'Whatever my opinion of Chamberlain may be,' Lloyd George continued, 'I must say that in this matter he was not seeking war with you. Rather the opposite. The trouble is that Chamberlain never makes a decision about anything. He always goes with the flow, merely permitting himself the odd little splash from time to time. And I am absolutely sure that if the Finnish war had lasted two or three months longer, the prime minister would have slipped into a war with the USSR almost unawares. Thank God the danger has passed! I congratulate you again with all my heart.'

As for the terms of peace, Lloyd George finds them quite normal. He showed me a letter from Liddell-Hart in which the latter says that from the military point of view he finds the terms of peace to be moderate, even soft.

I asked the old man what he thinks about the danger of war between our countries in connection with the situation in the Near East.

Lloyd George replied that much would depend on the USSR's behaviour. For example, if the USSR attempted to solve the question of Bessarabia by force or crossed the Persian border, this would inevitably lead to war in the Near East, which would turn into a world war. But should the USSR *keep quiet*, then Lloyd George fails to see how the British and the French could initiate a war in the Near East. For, in his opinion, the interests of Germany mainly consist in maintaining peace in South-East Europe and exploiting its economic resources. Turkey occupies a 'key' position in this part of the world. Lloyd George is confident that Turkey will not let itself get involved in any anti-Soviet adventures. If the USSR could somehow strengthen its relations with Turkey, the skies in the Near East would be truly cloudless.

Speaking about Bessarabia, Lloyd George remarked in passing: 'I've never sympathized with the annexation of Bessarabia and even warned Brătianu[i]

[i] Ion I.C. Brătianu, foreign minister and prime minister of Rumania intermittently, 1909–27.

against it. But Brătianu was a stubborn, and greedy man. He liked to grab any odds and ends with both hands. The consequence is today's Rumania – an artificial and unviable state, like Poland.'

Then we spoke about the immediate prospects for Anglo-Soviet relations. Lloyd George scolded the British government fiercely for its response to my démarche of 22 February. He said, however, that now, with the end of the Finnish war, the opportunity existed to improve relations between our countries. The resumption of trade negotiations would be the best step.

'As you know very well,' the old man said with a cunning smile, 'every Englishman has a *soft spot* in his heart for trade. Why not take advantage of it?'

Lloyd George also thinks that it would be very useful, in order 'to clear the air', for a Soviet leader to make a public statement to the effect that the USSR has no *sinister intentions* in the Near East. This would be of great comfort to the government and political circles, which are presently discussing in earnest not only the possibility of Soviet expansion in the Balkans, but also of a 'Bolshevik march' on India.

I mocked all these fears, but Lloyd George advised me against underestimating their importance. It even seemed to me that the old man himself is not entirely free of them.

Another detail. In the course of our conversation, L-G asked when I had last seen Halifax. I said I saw him three and a half months ago, on the eve of the Finnish war. Lloyd George raised his hands to the heavens in a comic gesture of despair and exclaimed: 'I say! If I were in Halifax's place, I'd summon you at least twice a week to try to influence you and keep the USSR from getting too close to Germany. Three and a half months! Good heavens!'

A mischievous twinkle sparkled in L-G's eyes, and he said with his infectious laugh: 'I have plum trees in my garden. The short ones yield a lot of fruit. The very tall ones devour a ton of fertilizers but bear no fruit at all. They're absolutely barren. My gardener says about the tall ones: "They're nice to look at, but don't go expecting any fruit from them." The same with Halifax: he is tall and good-looking, but barren as a fig tree.'

The old man roared with laughter once more.

17 March

Our victory in Finland is beginning to make itself felt. Those who hid in the bushes or stood in open opposition to the USSR from the very first weeks of the war are starting to 'return'. The atmosphere around the embassy is still decidedly chilly, but the first warm currents can be felt. As always… As always after an anti-Soviet storm.

The first reports about our peace negotiations with the Finns have already begun to have a 'demoralizing influence' on Labour. To accelerate the process,

I conveyed to Attlee through K.[25] the details of my démarche of 22 February and its results. This has had its effect. Over the last ten days the *Daily Herald* has adopted an unusually 'mild' position in respect of both the negotiations and the conditions of peace. The *Tribune*, which had been pursuing an anti-Soviet line on the Finnish question after Cripps's departure, attacked Halifax the day before yesterday for not exploiting my démarche to improve relations between England and the USSR. Brailsford also emphasizes the British government's refusal to mediate in today's *Reynolds News*.

My conversation with Dalton on 15 March was even more symptomatic. He came for a lunch which I had arranged for Aras and asked afterwards if he could stay on for a private talk. We spoke for about an hour. I understood from the character of our conversation that Dalton was speaking on behalf of the Executive Committee of his party. The essence of Dalton's 'démarche' (for it was a real 'démarche') boiled down to the following.

The USSR, according to the prevailing views in the Labour Party, has indeed committed an act of 'aggression' towards Finland, but there is no point talking about it anymore: the 'Finnish chapter' is closed. Let us accept it as a fact. However, there is a certain nervousness in Labour circles concerning the question: will the USSR allow Finland to develop freely? Will the USSR be satisfied with what it has achieved or will it go further – to Sweden (Kiruna), Norway (Narvik) or Rumania (Bessarabia)? Time will tell. But for the moment Labour would like to conclude its 'quarrel' with the Soviet Union and restore the 'friendly' relations of before. The following action may serve as proof of Labour's sincere intentions. After the parliamentary session of 13 March the Liberals and Hore-Belisha pressed on Labour the need to convene a closed session of parliament. Labour refused, understanding that such a session would be entirely devoted to the Finnish question and attacks on the British government for providing Finland with insufficient aid. The Labour Party, meanwhile, is of the view that at the present time too much should not be made of the 'Finnish question'. One must think about the future, not the past. Consequently, the next session, on 19 March, will be a regular open session and will not be confined to discussion of the Finnish question alone. The House of Commons will discuss various aspects of the conduct of the war. The Labourites themselves are going to speak of Finland as little as possible; they will say just the minimum required to 'observe proprieties'.

Dalton further stated that Labour categorically objects to a war with the USSR wherever that may be – in the north or in the south – and that it wants an improvement in Anglo-Soviet relations and believes that the British government wishes the same.

In response I related to Dalton the particulars of my talks with Butler on the matter of 'mediation' and stressed that the whole episode attests, on the contrary, to the fact that the British government 'does not want' to improve Anglo-Soviet relations. I also expressed my doubts concerning Labour's position on the question of war with the USSR. Its position on the Finnish question hardly points to a desire to prevent at all costs an armed conflict between England and the Soviet Union.

Dalton started protesting. He insisted that the single aim of Labour was 'to kill Hitler' (i.e. the Hitlerite system). To do so, the British and the French should concentrate all their efforts on the struggle with Germany. In fact, Labour would like to be friends with the USSR. Why not resume the Anglo-Soviet trade negotiations that were frozen last year? The USSR, being a neutral country, has every right to trade with both sides. The USSR trades with Germany – why not trade with England, too?

I promised to think it over.

In conclusion, Dalton made a complaint: he had recently been execrated by our press (or on the radio). Why? Wasn't it he who spared no pains in promoting a tripartite pact last year? And now, since the beginning of the Finnish war, wasn't he the only Labour leader who had not spoken out against the USSR?

I tried to set his mind at rest. But his sensitivity to our attacks speaks for itself.

Yes, the atmosphere is getting a little warmer. Here is further proof. Guo Taiqi and I went to see the Webbs today. The old couple were very glad to see us, and I joked that they had representatives of a third of mankind at their table today (China – 450 million, and the USSR – 180 million). On the way, Guo Taiqi told me that he had lunched with Churchill the other day. Churchill told him that war with the USSR had been a real possibility. The danger has now passed and Churchill hopes for an improvement in Anglo-Soviet relations. Most interesting.

18 March

Despite the great air of mystery with which Sumner Welles surrounded his mission to Europe, its character is becoming clear. This is what I have managed to glean about it.

Why indeed did Roosevelt decide to send Welles? Because he lacks reliable information about what is going on in Europe. Kennedy is fanatically '*pro-war*' (he is a typical 'Munich' man), and all the information he sends to Washington is tinted accordingly. Phillips[i] (ambassador to Italy) compromised himself in the president's opinion back in 1938, when he asked Roosevelt for leave on the eve of the Munich Conference, assuring him that all was calm in Europe

[i] William Phillips, American ambassador to Italy, 1936–41.

and that no complications were to be expected in the near future. Since then the president has taken a very sceptical view of Phillips's reports. Finally, the United States has had no ambassador in Germany since the Jewish pogroms in late 1938. So Roosevelt sent Welles to obtain information about the situation in Europe which he could trust.

What task was Welles set? A twofold task. To collect information and to try to find out whether there is any basis for concluding peace in the European war in the near future. Roosevelt is interested in the latter from the point of view of world politics as well as from the point of view of US domestic policy, for he has to decide whether he is going to stand for a third term as president at the elections this year. If peace is possible and near at hand, he will not submit his candidacy; if it is not, he will.

What impressions did Welles gain from his tour of Europe?

(1) Italy. Welles liked Mussolini, who gave him the impression of a man sincerely striving for peace. In Welles' opinion, Roosevelt should 'cooperate' with Mussolini on the issue of 'peace'. Mussolini's price for supporting peace is approximately the following: Djibouti, Italy's representation at the council of the Suez Canal, the settlement of the question of the status of Italians in Tunisia (not Tunisia as such, or, at any rate, not the whole of Tunisia), the internationalization of Gibraltar, and financial aid from the City.

(2) Germany. Contrary to what is written in the newspapers, Hitler was very calm during his meeting with Welles and gave the impression of being a 'moderate' person. Welles left Berlin with the notion that Hitler wants peace and is ready to conclude it on approximately the following conditions: a 'little Poland' is restored on an ethnographic basis, but it should be deprived of any military significance; Bohemia and Moravia should form a single state entity and be dependent to a certain extent on Germany; Germany gets back its former colonies (in this area Hitler concedes the possibility of various compromises); the Western powers allow Germany, without any interference on their part, to form its own 'economic empire' out of Scandinavia, Central and S[outh]-E[astern] Europe on the basis of preferential treatment on the Ottawan model. Hitler also gave Welles to understand that the development of economic relations with the USSR was part of his programme. But Hitler threatened that if peace was not concluded in the near future, he would pursue the war seriously, on the largest scale, and would crush England and France in six months using secret military inventions at his disposal. Of the other German figures, Welles liked Göring best, finding him to be a 'serious and reasonable man'.

(3) France. The French leaders struck Welles as very belligerent, and at the same time greatly worried among themselves about the course and outcome of the war. He liked Reynaud and Mandel most of all. Welles left Paris with the impression that France was not yet ready for peace.

(4) England. In London Welles met the king, Chamberlain, Halifax, Simon, Churchill, Eden, Stanley, Attlee, Greenwood, Sinclair and others. In its list of individuals whom it advised Welles to meet, the FO 'forgot' Lloyd George. Welles corrected the mistake himself. Then the FO assigned him 30 minutes for a talk with Lloyd George. Welles came to see the old man and talked with him for nearly two hours, totally disrupting the official schedule. Welles said afterwards that compared with all the other conversations he had in London, his conversation with Lloyd George was a 'breath of fresh air'. Lloyd George recommended that Roosevelt launch a peace initiative and invite Mussolini and the pope to participate. All the other people Welles met in England largely repeated what they always say about the war. Chamberlain made it clear that he was ready to conclude peace 'at the first opportunity', but on conditions, of course, which Hitler could hardly find acceptable at present. Churchill told the American guest that he did not quite understand why the USA was so anxious about peace. Churchill expressed himself as follows: 'A murder has been committed in a house. Two policemen rush to the house and seize the murderer. At that moment a stranger approaches the policemen and urges them to free the murderer. Why? On what grounds? It's unclear. In any case, if the policemen were to reach the conclusion that the murderer should be freed they would do so themselves, without the interference of a stranger.' On the whole, London also struck Welles as belligerent, but less so than Paris.

What are Welles' definitive conclusions? Even he is probably still unable to say. His tour is not quite over. On his way back from London he met Daladier in Paris and talked with Mussolini once more in Rome, where he also paid a visit to the pope. Mussolini must have informed Welles about Ribbentrop's recent visit to Rome. Welles will be preparing his report and conclusions en route from Genoa to New York. He will refine them in Washington.

Meanwhile I've heard that, upon leaving London, Welles expressed the opinion that: (a) neither side will be able to win, and (b) he can as yet see no basis for peace in the near future.

Conversation with Butler on 18 March 1940

(1) I visited Butler to lodge a protest concerning the detention and shelling of the Soviet vessel *Vladimir Mayakovsky* in the Pacific (near Japan) and to demand its immediate release. I gave Butler details of the ship's cargo (4,655 tons of copper and 216 tons of molybdenum, to a total value of $1,444,000). I warned Butler that the Soviet government reserves the right to claim compensation for losses and damages. Butler already knew about the seizure of the *Vladimir Mayakovsky*. He even said that as soon as he received my request for an urgent meeting, he guessed at once what the matter was and made some inquiries this

morning about the incident. He, Butler, wished to tell me first of all that the vessel had not been 'shelled'. This is what had actually happened. When British warships signalled to the *Mayakovsky* to stop, she did not obey the order. The British warships then fired a warning shot across her bows, in keeping with ordinary maritime laws. Butler further said that the *Mayakovsky* is being sent to Hong Kong for her cargo to be checked, since the Ministry of Economic Warfare harbours serious suspicions that this cargo is intended not for the USSR but for Germany via the USSR. I denied this categorically and stressed that the *Mayakovsky*'s cargo is intended exclusively for our own domestic needs. I insisted once again that the vessel be freed. Butler replied that he would register our protest, our demand to free the vessel, and our position on compensation. He had also taken into account my statement about the cargo being intended solely for Soviet domestic purposes. Butler promised to communicate once more with the appropriate organs (meaning the Ministry of Economic Warfare) and inform me of the results in a few days' time, but avoided giving any binding promises. I then enquired about the *Selenga* and asked how long it would stay in Hong Kong. It was detained more than two months ago and is still unable to leave the port despite my numerous démarches. Butler apologized once again for the delay with the *Selenga* and said that the British government has no objections of its own to freeing the *Selenga*, but since the French government is also involved (the tungsten on board the ship was in transit via Indochina) the British have to coordinate their actions with the French, who are resolutely against releasing the cargo. Butler hopes, however, that the British will settle the matter with the French in the very near future and that the *Selenga* will be freed.

(2) Once we had finished discussing the question of Soviet ships, Butler (as is his wont) seized the opportunity for an exchange of views on some other matters. [Following text omitted as it is a repeat of the above.]

... (4) Having heard Butler out, I asked him a few leading questions in order to find out the reaction of the 'Allies' to the basis for peace set out by Hitler and Mussolini in their conversations with Welles. Butler's feelings could be summed up as follows. Although the British government has quite clearly defined 'military objectives' that are known to all, it does not rule out in advance the possibility of peace. It is prepared to take an *open minded*, unprejudiced approach to any suggested peace conditions. The British government's main concern is security and a stable order in Europe. It is from this point of view that it is ready to consider the peace proposals advanced by Hitler and Mussolini. It was obvious from Butler's remarks that of all the points put forward by Hitler and Mussolini, only one is absolutely unacceptable to the British government: the internationalization of Gibraltar. All others are open for discussion, even if they require considerable adjustments and modifications, which might be made in the process of negotiations.

(5) It goes without saying that in speaking about European affairs we could not avoid touching on the termination of the Finnish war. Butler said that he did not wish to re-open a discussion about the origins of the war or the conditions of the Soviet–Finnish peace; he was simply content to state that a bone of contention had been removed from Anglo-Soviet relations. He expressed the hope that Anglo-Soviet relations could be improved. In this connection, he returned once again to the matter of the detention of Soviet ships in the Pacific and hinted quite transparently that the best way of resolving difficulties of this kind and even of improving Anglo-Soviet relations would be to return to the trade negotiations that had been scheduled for last September/October. Butler also inquired about the rumours of a 'tripartite bloc' of Germany, Italy and the USSR, which Ribbentrop is allegedly trying to create and which is supposedly intended, first and foremost, to regulate the situation in the Balkans. I refuted all these journalistic speculations and reminded Butler of what I had told him about the nature of Soviet–German relations on 22 February. The Soviet Union pursues its own independent foreign policy, and nobody should forget this. At the same time, I drew Butler's attention to the harm done to Anglo-Soviet relations by the sensationalism of the press, as exemplified by the current speculations about a 'tripartite bloc'. Butler agreed with me and promised, on his part, to talk to the diplomatic correspondents of the major newspapers (he named *The Times* and *Daily Herald* in particular) so that they were more reserved and objective in their accounts of everything concerning the Soviet Union. I don't know whether this will bring any tangible results. In conclusion, Butler said that Halifax would gladly see me if I had a question important enough to be discussed with the foreign secretary.

[Ironically, Butler, who would now replace Vansittart as Maisky's 'ally' in the Foreign Office, had been the quintessential appeaser and an arch opponent of a triple alliance prior to the conclusion of the Ribbentrop–Molotov Pact. He remained very much an appeaser after the outbreak of war. He advocated moderation in relation to Russia with the same dogged determination that had characterized his support for appeasement. 'There is a certain noble purity about British policy,' he minuted, 'which tends – provided right is on our side and the human brain dictates the logic of an action – to add one enemy after another to those opposed to us.' His views now paradoxically coincided with the Kremlin's new policy of seeking a peace agreement that would bring the war to an early conclusion and establish a new European order, in which the Soviet Union would share hegemony over Europe with a battered Britain and Germany.

In his report, Butler pointed out that Maisky was eager to leave him with 'the idea that we should satisfy the Germans that we were not interested in the complete destruction of the German people'.[26] Denying the persistent rumours of a German–Soviet military alliance, Maisky reasserted that it was Soviet policy 'to remain, if possible at peace'. The USSR did not 'wish to come under the heel of Germany or to be dragged into further complications with her'. However, he believed it 'might be possible to make a bargain with [Hitler] whereby the German colonies were restored and in return a certain freedom was given to the Poles and the Czechs'.[27]

This short-lived but significant complacency, exposing Stalin's miscalculations, was noted by Beatrice Webb in her frequent meetings with Maisky. On 18 March she found him to be

> quietly self confident. The war would end 'in a draw or in revolution', in Germany or France and even in Great Britain. Without the sacrifice of millions of men ... the Allied forces could not conquer or even invade Germany ... Maisky was, in fact, satisfied with the present situation; he was watching the continued stalemate on the western front, with a smile, at the decrepitude of 'western civilisation'.

He appeared to be 'distinctly anti-British' when the British got bogged down in Norway, apparently 'more amused than offended' by their hostility now that the Soviet Union was again out of the war.[28]]

19 March

I'm just back from Westminster, where parliament was sitting. Dalton was right: the Labourites said little about Finland today, focusing more on other questions related to the conduct of the war. But Finland was on the agenda all the same! Chamberlain spoke almost exclusively of Finland, Sinclair and others spoke about it, too, while Macmillan gave a speech on the subject which, from the government's point of view, was particularly lethal.

The prime minister insisted that his conscience was clean and that the British government had done all it could for Finland. Even a 100,000-strong Anglo-French expeditionary corps had been readied! Norway and Sweden upset the plans by not allowing the corps to cross their territories. As for the United States, they'd better keep silent: they are far from the theatre of military operations and are risking nothing. What moral right do they have to reproach the British?... This volley in the direction of the USA elicited shouts of approval in the Commons. In general, Chamberlain did not conceal his annoyance with the 'neutral countries': they don't want to do anything themselves, but they're quite happy to criticize others! In particular, Sweden and Norway have demonstrated their utter short-sightedness and will be punished for that in the course of subsequent events. Chamberlain hinted fairly clearly that from now on the British government would concern itself less with the principles and customs of 'international law'.

Irritation with the 'neutrals' and the appeal to have done with the 'fig leaf' of 'international law' was echoed in the speeches of Sinclair, Dalton and others.

As for the attacks on the USSR, there were fewer of them than on the 13th, and the reaction of MPs to them was weaker. In general, while on the 13th parliament conveyed a sense of frustrated impotence, today it was in a state of depression and anxiety. The quick successes of the Red Army on the Karelian Isthmus, as well as the position taken by Sweden and Norway, have upset the calculations of Ironside and Co.

* * *

I lunched at Beaverbrook's today. I found him in a state of sheer fury: he is outraged by the '11 points' for peace that have been published in the newspapers. According to Beaverbrook, these points are that very basis upon which Hitler and Mussolini agreed in Brenner.[29]

'This is a conqueror's peace!' Beaverbrook huffed. 'We shall never agree to such conditions!'

Beaverbrook thinks that England could wash its hands of Poland and Czechoslovakia, and it could even sacrifice some of its colonies, but it will never recognize Hitler's right to establish the 'economic empire' in Europe about which he spoke with Sumner Welles and which is outlined in the 11 points.

'You know, I was against war,' Beaverbrook went on. 'I wanted an early peace. But now I'm all for the war! I'm in favour of an intensification of the blockade and of the war in the air! I'm ready myself to be a gunman on a plane piloted by my son!'

Beaverbrook is against all sentimentality in war. International law is irrelevant. An eye for an eye, a tooth for a tooth!

I have never seen Beaverbrook in such belligerent mood.

Beaverbrook is satisfied with the Soviet–Finnish peace: a dangerous moment in Anglo-Soviet relations has receded and a fresh opportunity for their improvement has arisen. He would like to see such an improvement.

23 March

The Finnish war is over and it seems that things have returned to normal. 'Normality', of course, is a highly relative term in this case, considering the severe blockade against Germany, the millions of men stuck fast to the Siegfried and Maginot lines, the black-outs, and the daily toll of torpedoed vessels, but still… Everyone is talking of deadlock at the front, a three-year war, and the slow exhaustion of Germany as the major weapons against 'Hitlerism'. Yes, normality in this strange *Sitzkrieg* has undoubtedly returned.

And yet, I am increasingly gripped by a vague sense of the illusoriness and unreality of everything I see around me.

Parliament sits three times a week… The MPs ask questions, as usual… The ministers read out their answers, as usual… The speaker nods away, as usual, as he sits there in his wig… The departments arrange their *conferences* and do their paperwork, as usual… The newspapers invent sensational stories and spread high-society *gossip*, as usual… Shops sell their goods… Bankers count money and deliver their annual reports… Courting couples hide in the parks… Throngs of children play rowdily in the playgrounds… The taxis line up at the cab-stands… Newsboys, shouting at the tops of their voices, sell the evening papers, as usual…

Everything is as it always is. Everyone lives for today, for the petty interests of the hour, the minute. No one thinks of the future, no one tries to look ahead. One's instinct is to avoid doing so, even if a capricious thought happens to bring one to the verge from which vistas open up into the future. All are especially keen to emphasize that everything is happening in the normal, customary, traditional manner. No novelties. No excesses.

But to me it all seems temporary, unreal, fantastic…

Perhaps I'm wrong, or, at least, not entirely right, but one and the same picture keeps appearing before my mind's eye.

A gigantic wave. It grows, swells, rises higher and higher. Its dark depths conceal powerful turbulence. Immeasurable forces are gathered and concentrated there. Any moment now and the forces will break through in a catastrophic, irrepressible torrent. Yet while the surface of the wave is still relatively smooth and calm, tiny boats full of passengers sail to and fro over this surface in their normal, habitual order, or rather disorder. The boats make intricate patterns as they come together and drift apart, as the passengers shout out to each other, laugh and argue. Gentlemen court ladies, and the ladies flirt and paint their faces. Coloured handkerchiefs flutter, carefree voices are carried on the breeze. Everything seems eternal, normal, immutable, ordinary… No one thinks of the storm that is ready to strike…

And then, a sudden crash and roar!…

The catastrophe arrives.

27 March

[A cutting from *The Times* of 27 March 1940, entitled 'Soviet Union Recalls its Ambassador', is attached to the diary. It obviously alarmed Maisky. It alleged that Surits had sent Stalin a telegram concerning the French position in the Finnish war which had been intercepted by the censor and was regarded by the French government as interference in its domestic affairs. The French government (which had failed to secure

British intervention in the war in Finland and was still intent on bombing the Baku oil fields) declared Surits *persona non grata*. In order to deprive the French of their pretext for severing relations, Molotov (who had always regarded Surits – and Maisky – as accomplices of Litvinov's) reprimanded him and was only too happy to relieve him of his duties as ambassador in France.[30]]

An absolutely idiotic story! I don't know any details about the sending of the telegram (here we never send such things as telegrams *en clair*) but the French are obviously spoiling for a fight. I can't understand their policy. What are they counting on?

I spoke to Surits by telephone today. He is going to leave Paris in a few days. It's not yet been decided who will stay on there. Krapivintsev (counsellor) has been gravely ill with tuberculosis for five months already. He is in a sanatorium and unable to work. Biryukov (first secretary) is in Moscow. A difficult situation.

It was said today in the press department of the Foreign Office that the recall of Surits is a purely French affair, that the British government has absolutely nothing to do with it, and that Anglo-Soviet relations continue as they were. We shall see.

Conversation with Halifax on 27 March 1940

(1) When I received the telegram from Moscow concerning trade negotiations, I was unable to make a corresponding démarche because of the Easter holidays: all officials from the Foreign Office and other departments had left London for the country. I'd been instructed to convey the communication to Butler, but he was away on a ten-day vacation. I therefore decided to approach Halifax direct, all the more so as Halifax had handled all matters relating to the trade talks last autumn. Halifax returned to London on the evening of the 26th and received me on the 27th.

(2) I started by reminding Halifax of the attempt to open trade negotiations during last September/October and of my conversation with Butler on 18 March. I then told him that the Soviet government is ready to open trade negotiations now if the British government genuinely wants this and is minded to seek a satisfactory solution to the problems concerning Soviet–British trade. Naturally, such negotiations can be conducted only in a conducive atmosphere. From this point of view, a most significant step would be for the British government to free the *Selenga* and *Vladimir Mayakovsky* prior to the opening of negotiations and to abstain in future from detaining cargos destined for the USSR. Such an action would produce a good impression in Moscow and would be seen as an indication of Great Britain's readiness to improve trade relations between our countries.

(3) Having heard me out, Halifax replied that he would consult his colleagues in the Cabinet and the Board of Trade, after which he would have something more definite to say. With reference, however, to the question I had raised of the release of Soviet ships, he found it necessary to make some preliminary remarks. He fully understands the inconvenience caused to the USSR by the detention of its ships and cargoes but, on the other hand, the USSR must understand the position of the 'Allies', especially Britain. Britain is fighting for its life with Germany, and the blockade against the latter is one of the key weapons in the war. Therefore, it is vitally important for England to seal all possible channels through which Germany might obtain the means and materials she needs to prosecute the war. It is precisely this point of view which guides the British government in its monitoring of ships sailing to counties adjacent to Germany. The British government makes no exceptions here. The ships of all nations are subject to monitoring, including those of America and Italy, if they follow the routes indicated above. Nothing will change on this score.

(4) I retorted that if England insists on its belligerent rights, the USSR, being neutral, insists on its rights as a neutral state which, as is well known, stipulate the full possibility of free trade with both belligerents. True, the question of the rights of neutrals seems to be 'out of fashion' today (Halifax snickered at this point and interjected, 'That's not our fault'), but any neutral state has the right to defend its position ('If it's a great power,' Halifax interjected again). This is what the USSR is planning to do, and the British government must take that on board. Halifax replied that the interests of belligerent and neutral countries clash on the issue under discussion, and it is obvious that this conflict can be settled only by way of a compromise. Were it possible to find some way of guaranteeing that certain products are imported by the USSR solely for its domestic needs, the British government would prove much more amenable in the matter of the free passage of our ships and cargoes. The British government has already set such precedents. England has concluded a number of 'military trade agreements' with other countries during the war, where a solution to this problem has been found. Similar negotiations are currently under way with other foreign states. I argued that the USSR could not be lumped together with countries with private and capitalist economic systems. In those countries, any individual businessman, guided solely by his private interests, will be ready to re-export any product to Germany for a good price. In this case, the blockading country may perhaps introduce special control measures to prevent 'leakage'. In the USSR, the situation is quite different. We have a monopoly of foreign trade, and in these conditions only the word of the Soviet government can provide a guarantee in the sense meant by Halifax. Unfortunately, I could see that the British government finds such a guarantee unsatisfactory. I, for example, had stated quite officially that the cargoes carried by the *Selenga* and

Vladimir Mayakovsky were destined for the USSR, yet a satisfactory solution to the problem did not follow.

(5) Halifax said that he did, of course, understand the difference between the way trade is organized in the USSR and the way it is done in other countries. The trouble is that relations between the Soviet government and the German government, and their economic relations in particular, are liable to cause the 'Allies' great suspicion concerning the eventual recipient of products imported by the USSR. In this connection Halifax once again raided his memory for all sorts of stories about close cooperation, a 'bloc' and virtually an 'alliance' between Germany and the USSR. I refuted these allegations, ridiculed some of them, and added that the position of the British government struck me as very strange: in the final analysis, the USSR does much less for Germany in the economic field than the USA does for the 'Allies'. Halifax agreed with this but added: 'I think the Germans would be only too glad to bring to a halt our imports from America, if they could.' In the end Halifax repeated that he would report my question to the government and then give me an answer.

(6) Halifax asked me somewhat hesitantly whether I could tell him anything about the general line of Soviet policy today and in the near future. He was interested in Northern Europe and other parts of the world as well. I said I had no instructions from my government to this effect, but I could share my personal considerations with him if he wished me to. I then told him more or less what I told Butler on 22 February. Halifax listened attentively and asked whether the Soviet–Finnish agreement had been ratified. I said it had. Halifax then enquired whether the new Soviet–Finnish borders had been finalized. Not yet, I replied, but a mixed commission was being formed and would get to work soon. Halifax asked how long the commission's work would take. I replied that I did not know for certain, but, providing there was no unexpected delay, I believed the matter could be settled in a relatively short period of time. Halifax then asked whether we anticipated any complications with the final demarcation of borders. I said that I couldn't speak for the Finns, but that the Soviet Union is accustomed to carrying out the agreements it concludes. Halifax then asked with a shade of mistrust in his voice: 'So you don't have any designs on Sweden or Norway?' I suppressed a laugh and replied: 'You may rest assured that we are not aiming for Norway's Atlantic coast.' Next, Halifax wanted to know what lay behind the tumult in the German press about a tripartite bloc (Germany, Italy and the USSR) and its Balkan plans. I advised Halifax to be more sceptical about journalistic sensationalism and referred him to what I told Butler about the nature of Soviet–German relations on 22 February. In turn, I asked Halifax about the Allies' intentions in that part of the globe. For on our side, to put it mildly, there seems to be a lack of clarity in this matter, which does little to improve Anglo-Soviet relations. Halifax avoided the question,

and instead asked me about the current state of our relations with Rumania and Turkey. I replied that our relations with these countries were quite normal. Halifax further enquired whether we intended to resume the talks with Turkey which had been suspended in October. I pleaded ignorance.

[Halifax, who recognized that an operation in Baku 'would almost certainly lead to a definite alliance between Germany and the Soviet Union', instructed the Foreign Office to conduct the negotiations 'with a stiff upper lip', in a manner which would not 'prevent us at a later stage from taking action in the Caucasus, should the Turks agree to co-operate with us there'. Finally, it was only the German attack on France that put a seal on the operation, which might indeed have culminated in Britain finding itself at war with Germany and Russia.[31]]

28 March

The diplomatic correspondent of the *Observer*, G. Glasgow (who suddenly reappeared at the embassy today after a break of nearly four months) set out before me the following outlook for the war.

The war on the western front and at sea is at a *stalemate*. If the situation does not change, the war may last for years without being resolved, while exhausting the belligerent states. It is imperative to effect a drastic change. How? The 'Allies' must switch to 'total war'. What does that mean? It means they must launch a furious offensive in the air and by sea, disregarding the rights of neutral states. The Allies will sink German ships in territorial waters and fly to Germany and the Baltic Sea across neutral territories. If need be, they will use these territories to land or to transport their troops. And if people accuse them of aggression? Let them. It doesn't matter. What matters is to save the Empire; how this is to be done is secondary. Britain has been engaged in aggression for 400 years. It was the world's greatest aggressor in the past. If necessary, England can still provide lessons in aggression such as to turn Hitler green with envy. Such sentiments are on the increase in the country and they will soon be manifest in practice. The French government, Reynaud in particular, takes the same view. As this mood grows, the evaluation of the Soviet Union's conduct in the Finnish conflict is changing.

Of course, Glasgow is a man who gets easily carried away, and not all of his words should be taken at face value, but his reasoning is highly symptomatic.

* * *

Sylvester, Lloyd George's personal secretary, told me the following story.

In 1917 (Sylvester was already working for Lloyd George at that time) Lloyd George appointed Neville Chamberlain as director of the department responsible for conscription. The army needed men badly. Great hopes were pinned on the department. Chamberlain approached the task with the methods and horizons appropriate to a lord mayor of Birmingham, such as he had just been. Chamberlain chose as his *permanent undersecretary* a Birmingham *town clerk*, a certain Smith. Smith was a man of little calibre who had not the slightest idea of London life, the machinery of government, the methods of work essential in wartime, etc. But Chamberlain acted wholly in compliance with the *advice* of his *permanent undersecretary*. It quickly transpired that the department was unable to provide the army with the necessary number of conscripts. Lloyd George was greatly displeased and asked Bonar Law and Austen Chamberlain to exert their influence on Neville Chamberlain. They tried several times, but to no avail. Neville would invariably answer that he should be guided in his job 'by the counsels of Mr Smith'. Lloyd George finally lost his patience and yelled at Neville: '*Get out! Get out you and your Mr Smith!*'

Chamberlain had to leave the department in disgrace. He has not forgotten it to this day. That is why Sylvester thinks it improbable that Lloyd George might enter a Cabinet headed by Chamberlain. Nothing less than absolutely extraordinary circumstances would force Chamberlain to allow this.

* * *

Randolph Churchill is one of those who have recently reappeared on my horizon. His visits used to be a frequent occurrence, and his telephone calls even more so. After the war began, when he became an officer in a tank battalion stationed in the provinces, Randolph would drop by every time he visited London. But after the beginning of the Finnish war he disappeared and I had no news of him for three and a half months. Last week, once peace had been concluded with the Finns, Randolph called on me out of the blue. Just the other day he visited me again, and brought his young wife to me (he married at the very start of the war). This is significant. Even more telling is the change in Randolph's mood: when hostilities began he boasted of an easy victory, but now he displays great anxiety about the course and outcome of the war.

29 March

Everyone is speculating about Hitler's meeting with Mussolini in Brenner. Today Aras pronounced himself convinced that the Balkans were 'carved up' in Brenner: Rumania to Germany, Yugoslavia to Italy. It's possible. But Aras gets carried away all too easily and he is also a great schemer. That is why I always take his judgements with a pinch of salt. It seems to me that the talks in Brennero focused on much more serious matters than the Balkans.

Aras is sceptical about the war. There was a time when he was even predicting an early peace. Today he announced that the chances of war continuing beyond September are even, 50:50. In Aras's opinion, neither side desires war. That is why he believes that peace is not far off. But, should peace fail to arrive, all-out war would ensue, with damaging consequences for neutral states and international law.

The other day Aras saw Halifax, who told him that the Allies would never initiate war in the Balkans themselves. On the other hand, they would respond with force to a German strike. Weygand's[i] army is intended for just that purpose, acting as a strategic reserve in the event of a German attack in the direction of the Balkans.

Aras assured me repeatedly that Turkey would not allow herself or her territory to be used against the USSR. He considers the idea of an air attack on Baku nonsensical. A 'gentlemen's agreement', modelled on the Anglo-Italian agreement of 2 January 1937, should be concluded between Turkey and the USSR.

I asked what Turkey would do in the event of a German attack on the Balkans. Aras replied that Turkey would undoubtedly support the Allies. I then asked: 'Would Turkey allow Allied warships through to the Black Sea?'

Aras avoided the question, arguing that so long as the USSR remained neutral there would be no need for the Allies to sail their warships through the straits. But as for vessels carrying Allied troops bound, for example, for Rumania, Turkey would allow these to pass.

1 April

This is what I've managed to learn about the meeting of the Supreme War Council held on 28 March.

Reynaud pointed out the difficulty of his position and, in order to strengthen his reputation in France, demanded that the war be fought with greater intensity and that the Allies pursue a more 'energetic policy'. As a result, the following measures were taken:

(1) A declaration was published about the joint policies of the Allies not only during the war, but afterwards as well. This is aimed at easing French suspicions about the possibility of a separate deal between the British and the Germans. Rumours to this effect were afloat in France in connection with Sumner Welles' visit.

(2) It was decided to intensify the blockade by toughening up quota restrictions for neutral countries (such restrictions are in principle stipulated in most of the 'military trade agreements' concluded by the British government

---

[i] Maxime Weygand, chief of the general staff and vice president of the Superior War Council of France, 1931–35; commander-in-chief of the Allied forces in France, 1940; Algerian governor-general in French North Africa, 1940–41.

with the neutrals, but in practice they have so far been applied relatively liberally); through more stringent supervision of imports along the routes Holland–Belgium, Spain–Italy and USA–Vladivostok; and by taking more drastic measures to stop Germany importing iron ore from Scandinavia. In the first instance, diplomatic notes are to be sent to Sweden and Norway, after which the territorial waters of Norway are to be mined. In this way the transportation of Swedish ore via Narvik will be terminated. In order to stop or at least obstruct the transportation of ore along the route Lulea–Germany, plans have been drafted to carry out air operations over the Baltic Sea and to send British submarines there.

(3) The decision was taken not to initiate a war in the Near East for now because the conditions there are not yet ripe and because the Allies are not prepared for serious operations in this part of the globe (the Allied forces are inadequate in quantity and quality, the difficulties of transportation are immense, and material and human reserves are lacking). The purpose of the conferences of British and French ambassadors and envoys scheduled for 8 April in the Near East and the Balkans (the decision to hold them was taken before the meeting of the Council) is not only to inform London and Paris about the state of affairs in the corresponding countries, but also to outline plans to 'intensify' Allied activity in this part of the world and to demonstrate to the relevant countries that the British and French governments are determined to pursue an 'energetic' policy. Its main concrete manifestation for the time being will be the launching of an economic offensive in the Balkans.

(4) The 'Russian question' was discussed at length at the Council meeting. Here too Reynaud insisted on 'decisive measures', including the severance of relations with the USSR. He said there was a strong tendency in France (Laval, Bonnet, Flandin and others) advocating a rupture with us and even war. The English spoke out against extreme measures. Halifax reported my démarche of 27 March and suggested opening trade negotiations and 'examining' the possibility of an agreement with the USSR. All the more so as the British government was counting on getting essential products from the USSR (timber in particular). Reynaud was categorically against negotiations. No decision was taken, and further discussions will follow between London and Paris. As a sop to the French, the British handed over to them the *Selenga* and *Vladimir Mayakovsky*. Attlee and Greenwood told Halifax the other day that Labour was unanimously in favour of opening trade negotiations with us. Halifax replied that the question was under discussion. Although the Supreme War Council has not formally forbidden the British from entering into negotiations with the USSR, the British government still has to reckon with the feelings of its 'brave ally'.

2 April

The effect of C[omrade] Molotov's speech at the Supreme Soviet on 29 March will, without doubt, be a positive one.[32] His statement will certainly make life harder for those elements abroad opposed to us, especially in England and France. Beaverbrook is simply delighted. He called me and shouted down the telephone: 'Molotov is for isolation! Wonderful! This conforms with British interests.'

The meaning of Beaverbrook's words is clear. Over the last couple of months the general consensus in England has been that the USSR is an 'ally of Germany'. Even Butler has expressed such fears. In the past few weeks, the press has kicked up a lot of fuss about a 'tripartite totalitarian bloc' (Germany, Italy and the USSR) on the Balkan question. The 'Allied' countries have interpreted C[omrade] Molotov's speech in the following way: no 'alliance' exists between Moscow and Berlin; the USSR maintains its independent policy, and this independent policy is neutrality. What could be better?... The nightmare oppressing the souls of London and Paris is no more.

There are, however, sceptics. Some say: 'Neutrality... hmm... What sort of neutrality? There are many sorts of neutrality.'

These people think it better to wait and see than to start clashing cymbals.

Nonetheless, the fundamental response of public opinion is in our favour. Labour, the Liberals, Beaverbrook, Garvin, Layton – all affirm that the new opportunity should be taken to improve relations with Moscow and forestall the possibility of Moscow 'sliding' towards Germany.

* * *

Subbotić, who has just returned from Belgrade, came over to see me yesterday. He had much of interest to tell.

First of all, Belgrade has finally decided, according to Subbotić, to restore relations with the Soviet Union. The first step will be taken via either London or Ankara. Not only is the government in favour, but also Prince Paul and Maček[i] (leader of the Croats). The reason for the change lies in the dangerous position of Yugoslavia and, in particular, in the suspicious behaviour of Italy. The Yugoslav government found out recently that the organizers of 'communist demonstrations' in various Dalmatian towns have connections with Rome. At the same time, Italian diplomats in Belgrade and other capitals have let it be known 'semi-officially' (but quite plainly) that Italy will not tolerate the emergence of 'communism' in the Adriatic. It all looks like trouble. Yugoslavia has had to reconsider its policy in a hurry and look for new sources of support

[i] Vladko Maček, leader of the Croatian Peasant Party in Yugoslavia, 1928–41; deputy prime minister, 1939–41.

on the international scene. Hence the idea of rapprochement with the USSR. In what form? The Yugoslav government would be prepared to restore diplomatic relations with the Soviet Union, but it is somewhat concerned about how Italy would react to such a step. That is why the Yugoslav government would rather start with a half-measure, the signing of a trade agreement, and then, at the first opportunity, arrange an exchange of envoys.

Second, the internal situation in Yugoslavia has become significantly more stable. The rapprochement between Serbs and Croats is working well. The Croats are unhappy about one issue – the timing of the parliamentary elections – but its significance will not prove especially great. All Yugoslavs, without exception, are united by one and the same passion: to avoid war! This desire is above all internal arguments and disagreements.

I questioned Subbotić about Yugoslavia's relations with Germany and other states. He says that so far Germany has been behaving in an appropriate manner and carrying out the trade agreement with Yugoslavia to the letter, while the German minority in Yugoslavia has been keeping a low profile. Will this last? Who knows?

The economic role of Germany in Yugoslavia is enormous: 60% of Yugoslav foreign trade is with Germany, no more than 12% with France, and only 5% with England. The figures speak for themselves.

Subbotić says that rumours of a tripartite bloc aimed at the Balkans caused great anxiety in Belgrade, but C[omrade] Molotov's speech has dispelled it. Now there is another priority: the improvement of relations between the USSR and Turkey.

4 April

Lloyd George is a truly extraordinary wordsmith! He possesses the rare skill of being able to characterize a man, phenomenon or event with a single word or image, with often lethal consequences for his opponents.

I remember in particular the following episode. In June 1937, Chamberlain, who had just been appointed prime minister and was testing the ground for a long period of 'appeasement', made his first speech in parliament. He spoke of the gathering thunder-clouds, the tense international situation and the need to keep a *cool head* so as not to provoke a catastrophe with an incautious step. The PM employed a metaphor in this connection: he spoke of avalanches of snow in the mountains which had sometimes been caused by movements in the air from a human voice. Chamberlain's speech certainly made an impression in the House, generating a serious and anxious mood.

Lloyd George spoke next. He declared himself profoundly disappointed with the prime minister's speech. The situation is serious indeed, and Lloyd

George sketched a menacing picture of the international situation in a few vivid strokes. But how does Chamberlain propose countering the impending danger?

Lloyd George, standing at the *dispatch box* on the side of the opposition, shrugged his shoulders in bewilderment, jerked his left leg (he was in the habit of doing so when he spoke in parliament), pulled his pince-nez off his nose, waved it about contemptuously, and said in measured tones: 'The prime minister recommends us *to keep a cool head*.'

Then he flashed his pince-nez as if it were a sword pulled from its sheath, cast a scathing look at Chamberlain opposite him, and let fly: '*Any fish can have a cool head!*'

The effect was extraordinary: the House resounded with peals of raucous, irrepressible laughter. Everybody was laughing – on the Labour, Liberal and Tory benches. The impression made by Chamberlain's speech was instantly dispelled. And the 'Old Wizard' shouted in a stentorian voice: 'We need not cool heads but courageous hearts!'

The audience burst into tumultuous applause.

Something similar happened in parliament yesterday. The morning papers announced changes in the government. In fact, the changes amount to an echo of Krylov's[i] fable 'The Quartet'. The only serious change is putting Churchill in charge of the armed forces of Great Britain, although even here Chamberlain tried to put a spoke in his wheel (for instance, by appointing Samuel Hoare as secretary of state for air). This reshuffle actually satisfies nobody and has been criticized quite sharply both in the press and in the corridors of the House. In the evening, agriculture came up for discussion again in parliament. Lloyd George lambasted the government for neglecting this sphere and declared:

[There follows a newspaper cutting entitled 'Mr Lloyd George on "Rabbit Jumps"':

> Mr Lloyd George (Caernarvon, Opp. L.) said that the House ought to have some sort of idea of what the agricultural policy of the country was going to be. (Hear, hear.) There had been too much, in our war preparations, of doing a thing just a little, and then finding that not enough and doing a little more. We had been getting on with what might be called rabbit jumps – (laughter) – a little jump, then a nibble: then another little jump and another nibble. (Laughter.) [underlined by Maisky] In the end we might find ourselves one day in a position with regard to food production when it would not be adequate for the need that would suddenly confront us.]

[i] Ivan Andreevich Krylov, Russian poet and fabulist of the early nineteenth century. The fable produces the comments of a wise nightingale on the unsuccessful efforts of a tricksy monkey, a goat, an ass and a bandy-legged Mishka bear to play a quartet through changes in their seating positions: 'To be a musician, one must have a better ear and more intelligence than any of you. Place yourselves any way you like; it will make no difference. You will never become musicians.'

Another rapier thrust, and a very good one! The '*rabbit jumps*' policy – no one could have made a more exact or more devastating two-word diagnosis of British government policy over recent years, particularly since Chamberlain came to power.

5 April

The Shaws came to lunch with us today. We hadn't seen the old couple for several months. They are still vigorous, especially he, but their health is beginning to fail them. No wonder: he is 83 and she is even older. But Shaw's verve, memory and interest in events are still amazing. There were just the four of us at table (which, we discovered at the end, pleased the old couple). These were the best circumstances for a talk and Shaw plunged into reminiscences of the distant past. He accompanied his vivid account with much gesticulation.

> In the eighties, after we had just set up the Fabian Society, a May Day meeting was arranged in Hyde Park. I was the chairman and the speaker. When the meeting was over I set off across the park through the crowd. Suddenly, I was stopped by a bearded man of medium height in a brown suit. Congratulating me on the successful meeting, he asked: 'Do you know me?' I had the feeling that I had met him before, but could not recall where and when. I responded with the customary banality that his face was very familiar to me but that I couldn't remember the circumstances of our meeting. The bearded man laughed and said in a genial voice: 'No, you don't know me. I'm Friedrich Engels.' So that's what Engels looks like, I thought. I had heard a lot about him, but we had never met. The next May Day I spoke in Hyde Park again. And again Engels came up to me and asked jokingly: 'Well, do you recognize me now?' 'But of course I recognize you! You are the great Engels!' I cheerfully exclaimed and shook his hand firmly.

When asked by Agniya whether he had met Engels in less public circumstances, the old man replied: 'No, we never met privately. In subsequent years I saw Engels a few times at various international congresses, but we were never intimately acquainted. Engels lived a very secluded life at that time, mainly in his study, and had no direct contact with the British workers' movement.'

From Engels the conversation turned to Marx. Shaw had never met Marx. He died before Shaw joined the socialist movement. But he knew Marx's daughter Eleanor, called Tussy in the family.

'She was a striking brunette,' Shaw recounted, 'lively and extremely intelligent. She knew several languages to perfection. Often used to interpret at international conferences and congresses. But she was a very "partial" interpreter: she translated the speeches of "her people" with a brilliance lacking in the original versions (she was a superb speaker herself), but made her "adversaries" seem like fools, which they were not. I noticed this and began insisting on paid and "non-party" translators for our congresses.'

Shaw's face clouded over briefly and he continued in a more subdued tone: 'Eleanor became involved with Aveling.[i] Have you heard the name?'

I nodded.

'I don't know what they had in common. Aveling was a strange man. I have no doubt that he was a convinced socialist and atheist who would go to the scaffold for his convictions, but he was a man of rather low morals in ordinary life.' (A *scoundrel*, Shaw added.)

> A university professor, he coached university entrants, preferring girls (women had just been admitted to study at universities). Aveling usually took payment for 12 lessons in advance, borrowed more money from his students, and gave them one lesson only. When the students lost patience there were scandals, but Aveling never returned their money. Once he came to me and asked me for five pounds. As I knew Aveling well, I refused to lend him so much as a penny. He tried every means of persuading me and finally declared: 'You may be quite sure you'll get my debt back. If you present my receipt to Eleanor two months from now and tell her that I'll end up in prison if she doesn't pay, she'll immediately give you the money.' I was quite disgusted and threw Aveling out of the house.

Shaw paused and then continued:

> Poor Eleanor! She committed suicide. It happened like this. Eleanor and Aveling lived together without ever being wed in church. Aveling had a lawful wife with whom he didn't live, and this made a formal marriage with Eleanor impossible. When Aveling's wife died, her family, who hated Eleanor, did all they could to hurt her even after the wife's death. In the obituary which they published in the newspapers it was mentioned that the deceased was Aveling's lawful wife in order to emphasize Eleanor's unlawful status. Be that as it may, Aveling was now a free man. Eleanor, being a woman of progressive views and noble character, did not insist for a moment on legalizing their long relationship. She was quite happy

[i] Edward Aveling, a prominent 'Darwinist', he was a founder of the Socialist League and the Independent Labour Party.

for them to continue as they were. And do you know what Aveling did? Now that he was free, he deserted Eleanor and married another woman. Eleanor, who had already suffered greatly from Aveling's behaviour in the past, could not endure this final blow and took her own life. When I wrote my play *Doctor's Dilemma*, I used much of what I knew about Aveling's character and escapades.

Shaw paused again before adding:

There was also that wonderful woman, Helene…[i] You know about her, I'm sure. She worked as a sort of maid in Marx's house. It always made me laugh that Marx, who devoted his entire life to the proletariat, actually knew only one proletarian, Helene, whom he didn't even pay!… Yes, Marx's finances were nearly always in an awful state. It was a real tragedy. Marx's wife was at times driven mad with despair. But even though Helene did not receive a salary, she was eventually rewarded: her name is inscribed on Marx's tomb.[33]

Agniya noted that Engels often helped Marx, and that their friendship was something absolutely unique.

'Yes, yes,' said Shaw, 'their friendship was remarkable, which was surprising given that Marx was so difficult to get on with. Now there was a man with a temper!'

Shaw leaned back in his chair and laughed:

I remember one story. Hyndman,[ii] Marx's pupil and admirer, published his first socialist book, *England for All.* It had many borrowings from Marx and no references to him. Marx was furious with Hyndman and made a scene. But Hyndman's wife Matilda told everybody afterwards that the real reason for the quarrel lay elsewhere. Leaving Marx's place, Hyndman put on Marx's hat by mistake, which turned out to be an exact fit. 'You see,' Matilda would say, 'Marx cannot resign himself to the fact that someone may have a head no worse than his own.'

Shaw roared with laughter. 'Hyndman had an interesting life,' he continued.

He and Matilda lived very long and, when Matilda died, Hyndman was already old. Nevertheless, soon after this happened he married a young

[i] Helene 'Lenchen' Demuth.
[ii] Henry Mayers Hyndman.

> woman, Rosalind Travers, who was madly in love with him. Rosalind outlived Hyndman only by a single year. She was beside herself with grief and languished without him. Would you believe it, although she was an atheist, she finally committed suicide hoping to meet her husband 'in heaven'. I don't know why she thought Hyndman had a place reserved for him in heaven. But that's what Rosalind wrote in her final letter.

Shaw glanced at his wife and said half-jokingly: 'Rosalind wrote to me a few times after Hyndman's death. Maybe I was partly responsible for her death. Had I reciprocated her feelings, perhaps she would still be alive now… But my heart was already taken!'

Shaw made a gallant gesture towards his wife.

Then Shaw recalled [a passage is missing].

Shaw then turned to reminiscences of the more recent past.

Shaw visited the USSR with the Astors and Lothian in 1931 and they were received by C[omrade] Stalin. Louis Fischer was their interpreter. M.M. [Litvinov] was also present.

Nancy Astor was, of course, the first to attack C[omrade] Stalin. Lady Astor tried to prove to him that children were brought up in the wrong way in the USSR. She gave an example. She had just visited a kolkhoz school. She didn't like it: the children were dressed too finely and they were too clean. That's unnatural. Children should be dirty – that's how they're meant to be – except at table. And they should be dressed very simply: just a piece of cloth that can be washed and dried in half an hour. Highly agitated, Nancy said to C[omrade] Stalin: 'Send a sensible woman to me in England and I'll teach her how to treat children.'

C[omrade] Stalin smiled and asked her to give him her address. Nancy gave it. Shaw thought this was mere courtesy on C[omrade] Stalin's part, so he was greatly astonished when he later discovered, once he was already back home, that not one but twelve women had visited Lady Astor from the USSR.

Lothian, in his turn, started explaining to C[omrade] Stalin that the British Liberal Party had split in two. The part led by Simon had sided with the Conservatives, while the other part was at the crossroads. In Lothian's view, that second faction, led by Lloyd George, might, after the necessary schooling, become the British party of scientific socialism. He therefore proposed that the S[oviet] G[overnment] invite Lloyd George to visit the USSR.

C[omrade] Stalin was astonished at Lothian's suggestion. There followed a quick exchange of opinions in Russian between C[omrade] Litvinov and C[omrade] Stalin, in which Shaw picked up just one word, 'Wrangel',[i] after which C[omrade] Litvinov replied that, since Lloyd George had been prime

[i] Petr Nikolaevich Wrangel, lieutenant general; commander of the anti-Bolshevik 'white' forces in southern Russia, 1918–20.

minister in the period of intervention, the Soviet government would find it difficult to invite him to the USSR, but that if Lloyd George wanted to make a private visit, he would be assisted in every possible way and acquainted with everything that interested him.

With his natural bent for paradox, Shaw asked: why not arrange a visit to the USSR for Churchill, too?

C[omrade] Stalin laughed and said he would be glad to meet Churchill.

Lord Astor[i] was next. He delivered a conciliatory speech, stating that in general British public opinion was not hostile to the Soviet Union. Lord Astor was in a very radical mood in Moscow. He felt almost as if he were a 'Bolshevik', and wore shirts with short sleeves. He wanted to say something that would please C[omrade] Stalin.

C[omrade] Stalin turned to Shaw and asked him what he thought of Astor's statement. Shaw laughed and said: 'In my country, Ireland – I'm Irish, not English, you know – they still sing a song which Cromwell is alleged to have sung: "*Put your trust in God, But keep your powder dry*." So I'd say: I don't know whether you trust in God – I think not – but I advise you from the bottom of my heart: *Keep your powder dry*!'

Shaw eventually managed to see Krupskaya.[ii] She avoided meeting him at first, but in the end she agreed, and Shaw visited her at the summer house in the country where she was taking a holiday. They spent two hours together, talking in French. From the photographs he had seen, Shaw had expected to meet a plain, if not ugly woman, but he was very pleasantly surprised. He found Nadezhda Krupskaya to be simply *fascinating*. He had never met a woman who had charmed him as quickly as she.

6 April

Another Cabinet reshuffle! Same old, same old. It's been done on the principle of Krylov's 'Quartet'. I can't help quoting that writer of fables: 'My friends, you can change places all you want, But you'll never make musicians.'

Yet, there is one noteworthy thing about the reshuffle, which is significant not so much for the present as for the future: a trend that might have great consequences. I mean the new role of Churchill. He has been appointed president of a committee consisting of the war, naval and air ministers and the chiefs of staff. Churchill is thus theoretically responsible now for the conduct of war. But… Hoare has been made secretary of state for air in the latest *reshuffle*.

---

[i] Lord Waldorf Astor, politician and newspaper proprietor who, with his wife, Nancy Astor, shared a deep reverence for the Empire and for social reform; chairman of the Royal Institute of International Affairs, 1935–49.

[ii] Nadezhda Konstantinovna Krupskaya, Lenin's wife; member of the Collegium of the People's Commissariat for Education, 1917–39.

That is, Chamberlain is putting his own man in the committee to sabotage Churchill's activity. Yet the trend remains, and it will probably manifest itself fully earlier than we expect. In times of war all processes develop at a feverish pace. We shall see.

Churchill is better than Chamberlain from the point of view of Anglo-Soviet relations. True, he attacked communism in his recent speech on the radio (30 March), but this is not very important. Churchill has never been a friend of communism. Besides, his speech was broadcast in the United States and he had to play up to the American audience. What matters most is that Churchill regards Germany as Enemy No. 1, and proceeding from that position he is ready to do anything, even to improve relations with the Soviet Union.[34]

8 April

I would sum up the Allies' intentions concerning a major war in the following way.

The Allies do not intend to launch large-scale military operations this year, provided the Germans do not initiate them themselves and provided the state of the domestic front in England and France does not demand such action. They are not planning major operations either in the west or the east (there are not enough forces, their quality leaves much to be desired, reserves are lacking, and there are many transportation difficulties). Moreover, neither the Balkan countries nor Turkey want to be turned into battlefields. Italy's position is obscure and threatening.

In the meantime the Allies intend to step up the blockade, with no regard for the rights of neutral countries. *Gloves off.* The mining of Norwegian waters announced today is just the beginning. Various measures aimed at stopping the transportation of iron ore from Sweden to Germany are to be expected in the Baltic Sea (air raids, submarine operations, etc.). Also to be expected is stricter supervision of the maritime trade routes Belgium–Holland, Spain–Italy and USA–Vladivostok, and tougher quota restrictions for neutrals' imports.

Yet another measure is the founding of the *English Commercial Corporation*, headed by Lord Swinton with government capital, in order to compete with Germany on neutral markets, above all in the Balkans. Previously the British talked a great deal about this sort of competition, but did little. Now they seem to be getting down to it.

* * *

I saw Colban. The old man is absolutely stunned by the news of the mining of Norwegian waters. He hadn't expected anything of the sort. He says the British government's note, handed to the Norwegian government on 5 April, did not portend such a move. The British government merely outlined its general view of the state of affairs in Scandinavia and stated that England would not be able to remain indifferent should a threat arise to Norway's Atlantic coast from Germany or the USSR. Submitting the note, Halifax tried long and hard to convince Colban that England 'is waging the war of the neutrals', to which Colban allegedly replied that England was in fact fighting for its Empire, and that Norway felt it had nothing bad to fear from the USSR. Saying all this, Colban was preoccupied by just one question: how will Germany respond to the mining of Norwegian territorial waters? But he had nothing lucid to say about this.

[Maisky's standing had hit rock bottom not only in England but – far more alarmingly – also in Moscow. The dismissal of Surits encouraged Molotov to clip Maisky's wings. A series of harsh letters from Fedor Gusev,[i] director of the western department of Narkomindel, severely criticized Maisky's diplomatic work. He was instructed to restrict his encounters to top officials, and to obtain all necessary information from the media. Fulfilment of those instructions would have robbed him of his trump card – his prolific circle of interlocutors. Finding himself up against the wall, Maisky resorted not to his customary survival strategy of intricate manoeuvring and flattery, but rather to confrontation. What follows are some very intriguing excerpts from a nine-page visionary 'lecture' to Gusev on diplomacy in general and on its peculiarities in England. Though an apologia, it was just as much a lament on the vanishing vision of modern diplomacy, of which he was now virtually the sole survivor:

> *(Undated but early April 1940)*
>
> ... The most important and substantive element in the work of every ambassador is the *actual contact* he has with people. It is not sufficient to read the newspapers – that can be done in Moscow. It is not enough to work with books and statistical reports – that, too, can be done in Moscow ... An ambassador without excellent personal contacts is not worthy of the name.
>
> Every country has its peculiarities. The nature and number of the contacts differ in accordance with the varying political, economic and individual conditions of each state. There cannot be a single template in such matters. What is acceptable in Paris may be completely unsuited to Tokyo, and vice versa ... In the case of England, the creation of these vital personal contacts is extremely difficult and requires a great deal of the ambassador's time ...

[i] The archetype of Stalin's and Molotov's new diplomat, Fedor Tarasovich Gusev graduated from the Institute of Soviet Construction and Law and worked in the Economic Planning Commission of the Leningrad region. With the repressions in Narkomindel in full swing, he underwent a crash course in diplomacy. His party loyalty landed him a brilliant career in Narkomindel, where, by 1938, at the age of 35, he had become the director of its West European department. He was appointed the Soviet ambassador in Canada in 1942 before replacing Maisky in London in 1943. Sir Archibald Clark Kerr, the British ambassador in Moscow, characterized him as 'a rude, inexperienced and bad-mannered fellow'.

In order to be *au courant* with what is happening in different areas of English life, it is not enough to know one or two people in each group ... It is quite simply not enough to have contacts with, for example, the secretary for foreign affairs and his deputy, but also one needs to know the head of the northern department of the FO, for the USSR falls within his sphere of competence ... It is necessary to maintain contact with around 15–20 people in the FO alone, and of course our work requires us to have business with other ministries: the Ministry of Trade, of Finance, of the Economy, of Defence and so on.

Or else, to take another example, consider parliament and the political parties. This is an extremely important element of English political life. It is most useful to attend the more important sittings of parliament (which works for about eight months of the year): you get an exceedingly accurate impression of the current mood of the country. But this is not enough. If you wish to be well informed of the different areas of interior and exterior policy, then you need to be in personal contact with a significant number of MPs. Of course, it is inconceivable, as well as unnecessary, to maintain relations with all 615 MPs. But let us say that you do need to know around a hundred MPs from all the different parties.

Here is yet another example: the press. This is an extremely complex and active group, with an immense number of people belonging to it. The people are capricious and don't stand on ceremony. They come to you with all sort of questions, surveys and clarifications – personally, or else by telephone, at any hour of the day or night ... In order to maintain normal contacts with the press, one needs to know about 50 people. I am not going to enumerate the relations one needs to have with the other groups. The preceding examples are sufficient. I will, however, add that, in the English environment, the diplomatic corps plays a comparatively minor role. I have made the calculations and come to the conclusion that, if the ambassador wants to fulfil his duties as they should be fulfilled, then he needs to maintain contact with *at least 500 people* (if we include the representatives of all the groups mentioned above).

Now, as for the nature of these contacts. What does it mean to maintain a contact? Certainly it is not enough to have a nodding acquaintance with a man, and to meet him once or twice a year at some official function or in the corridors of parliament. You will get precisely nothing from such contacts. The sort of contact which can be useful from our point of view must be a much *closer* contact. This means that you must meet the person more or less regularly, invite him to breakfast or dinner, visit him at home, take him to the theatre from time to time, go when necessary to the wedding of his son or his daughter, wish him many happy returns on his birthday, sympathize with him when he is ill. It is only when your acquaintance has come a little closer to you (and Englishmen need to scrutinize someone for quite some time before they count him among their 'friends') that his tongue starts to loosen, and only then may you start to glean things from him, or else start to put the necessary ideas into his head.

... How should an embassy work to maintain contacts? It is normally the case that every English 'circle' of interest to us can be divided into a number of sectors ... and every comrade will be expected to maintain and widen his knowledge of the sector, to meet the relevant people, to have breakfast or dinner with them (in England, all meetings usually take place at table – over breakfast, at tea, at dinner, etc.), to give them the information it is decided to give them, to nudge them in a direction favourable to us. But this work does not have any clear boundaries.

So far as our own London embassy is concerned, the situation over the last year has been as follows: to all intents and purposes all contacts with foreigners have been in the hands of two people, myself and Comrade Korzh. Comrade Popov's poor grasp of the language means that he can be of no use to us. Comrade Zonov has been weighed down with consular work, as well as with the business of the Soviet school in London and the summer camp for the children. Our two interns – Comrades Krainsky[i] and Mikhailov – could not be used for external work, because they are not yet official diplomats. Also, Mikhailov came to London without knowing the language. As a result of this, I repeat that all our contacts have been in the hands of two people – myself and Comrade Korzh. We have had to run like hamsters in a wheel. It has been an advantage that, thanks to my old acquaintances built up in the years of Anglo-Soviet 'friendship', I have been able to behave 'normally' with many people (Lloyd George, Layton, Beaverbrook, Churchill, Eden, Butler, Vansittart and others): it has not been necessary to throw them a breakfast or a luncheon every time I have needed them, and sometimes I could just call them on the phone, or meet them in the corridors of parliament and so on. However, even with these advantages it has sometimes been physically impossible to maintain an active relationship with various individuals with whom we should have kept in contact, and we have had and still have many gaps.

The programme you have set out, if we are to take it seriously (and of course, this is how we should take it), is extremely complex. It will require qualified workers with a great deal of time to devote to this project alone. And whom do we have in the embassy at the moment? Comrade Korzh, whom you wish to control the information gathering, has, as well as a complete lack of time for such work, no experience of literary or scientific research. In the past he was a sailor, then he commanded a charter ship, and for the last two years he has been carrying out current diplomatic duties as a first secretary. The intern Comrade Krainsky has a technical education, was a security officer in Washington for two and a half years and has only just now started embassy work. I have deputed him to watch the English economy. He is a keen worker, but it is a new area for him and he is unaccustomed to it, and it is difficult at the moment for him to orientate himself. The other intern, Comrade Mikhailov, still does not know English and has an incomplete degree from an agricultural academy. Before joining the NKID, he worked at a tractor station, and has never done any sort of either diplomatic or research work. Comrade Mikhailov is also a keen worker, and at the moment he helps Comrade Korzh in the press bureau; but after only four months in England, he is, of course, as yet not particularly comfortable with English, and nor is he at home with the situation here.

---

[i] Anatoly (Ariel) Markovich Krainsky, secretary at the Soviet embassy in Great Britain, 1939–44.

> I will conclude with a couple of words ... In the state of spy mania in which England exists at the moment, we have to be extremely careful with any observations, so as not to give our enemies an excuse for anti-Soviet provocation. On this note, I will bring this letter to an end, and I hope that the department and the embassy will now work more harmoniously together.[35]

The German *Blitzkrieg* in the west, however, would play into Maisky's hands, again rendering him indispensable and ensuring his continued stay in London on his own terms.]

9 April

What a sharp and unexpected turn of events!

Only yesterday the British were planning for a lengthy *Sitz-Krieg* (sic!); today, the Germans have made *Blitz-Krieg* (sic!) the order of the day.

German troops invaded Denmark and Norway this morning. Denmark, it seems, is putting up no resistance and, if German communications are to be believed, the whole country will be occupied within the next 48 hours. Copenhagen is already in German hands. The situation in Norway is more complex. With the help of some trick or other (the nature of which is not yet clear), the Germans managed to land in Oslo. The N[orwegian] G[overnment] evacuated and began to fight back. At the same time the Germans have appeared in Bergen, Trondheim and Narvik. How? That's also still unclear. It seems that treachery on the Norwegian side played a major role here. It's difficult to predict how hostilities will develop, but one thing is clear: the period of sitting and waiting is over. The war has started in earnest.

In parliament the prevailing mood today was one of confusion, anger and chauvinism. All had one and the same question on their minds: where the devil was our navy? How could our navy let the Germans reach not only Oslo, but also Norway's Atlantic ports? However, as soon as Mander set about posing this question to the prime minister, an animal-like roar erupted on all sides of the House against the excessively daring MP. But in the corridors of the House, the navy's miraculous disappearance was the only subject of conversation.

Chamberlain's speech was weak and colourless. He had once again been taken by 'surprise'. Only one thing was clear from the PM's words: the Allies had taken the firm decision to provide Norway with military assistance. The audience met this statement with noisy approval.

Attlee and Sinclair seconded the British government's decision to help. Henderson raised the question of convening the L[eague] of N[ations] in connection with the aggression against Norway, but he met with failure.

So, England and France are coming to Norway's assistance. But the Norwegian government, as Colban told me today, has not yet asked for any help. So what is this: unrequested assistance?

10 April

Saw Aras. He is troubled and agitated. He is sure the Balkans will be next in line after Scandinavia. I asked him: 'Why? … Other directions are also open.'

Aras could not give a clear answer to this question, but continued speaking about the Balkans. By way of evidence, he related that in mid-March the German government had demanded two things from Teleki[i] (the Hungarian prime minister): (1) that the entire Hungarian railway network be put under German administration in the event of war in the Balkans, and (2) that Germany be supplied with a quantity of food exceeding Hungarian food exports to all countries.

Teleki was shocked and replied that the Hungarian government was simply unable to procure so much food from the country. Then the German government declared: if you are unable to do this, allow us to send an unarmed division to Hungary to make requisitions. This really put the wind up Teleki, and as soon as the talks in Brenner were over, he hurried to Rome to seek Mussolini's protection. Mussolini assured Teleki that Italy was a good friend of Hungary, but advised him not to quarrel with Germany. The Germans are currently waging a campaign against Teleki in order to replace him with Csáky[ii] (foreign minister), who suits them better.

Aras is sure that Germany will demand 100% of the Balkan countries' exports of raw materials and food in the nearest future.

11 April

Today Churchill made a speech giving more detailed explanations about the events in Norway. I had never seen him in such a state. He clearly hadn't slept for several nights. He was pale, couldn't find the right words, stumbled and kept getting mixed up. There was not a trace of his usual parliamentary brilliance.

In its essence, his speech was unsatisfactory. Its running thread was a tone of apology. Churchill produced rather lame arguments to explain the German breakthrough: bad weather, the vastness of the sea, the impossibility of controlling it all, and so on. The audience was visibly disappointed with the explanations of the first lord of the Admiralty. The prevailing mood was one of growing irritation and concern for the future.

But Chamberlain, sitting on the front bench next to Churchill, was clearly pleased. No wonder: Churchill's failure is Chamberlain's success.

---

[i] Count Pál Teleki de Szék, a geographer, he was Hungarian prime minister and in charge of foreign affairs, 1920–21 and 1939–41.

[ii] Count István Csáky, Hungarian foreign minister, 1938–41.

12 April

I saw Lloyd George in parliament. This is his assessment of the situation.

The capture of Denmark undoubtedly strengthens Germany. It definitively closes the gateway to the Baltic Sea, providing Germany with a number of naval and air bases on Danish shores and temporarily replenishing German food and oil supplies (Denmark has reserves of up to 250,000 tons of oil). Moreover, Germany has a land border with Denmark which no one can now threaten.

Norway is a different story. It is separated from Germany by the sea, where the Allies dominate. Hitler has only managed to transfer two or three divisions. Sending reinforcements is fraught with difficulties. Norway is poor and can give little to Germany in terms of resources. There are few roads in the country, and the terrain is ill-suited to warfare. The British and the French control Norway's Atlantic coastline and can land large forces there (Lloyd George estimates that their number could potentially reach 500,000). Why, in such circumstances, has Hitler attacked Norway? Isn't this his first *great blunder*?

The attention of the Allies is now focused mainly on Narvik and Kiruna. They don't need to violate Sweden's neutrality to cut off Hitler's access to iron ore. It would be enough to occupy Narvik and linger by the Swedish border, which is just some 50 miles distant from Kiruna. At the first sign of a suspicious move by the Germans, the Allies could occupy Kiruna overnight. And such a suspicious move is inevitable, for how else will Germany be able to reinforce its troops in Norway? The sea is in Allied hands. There remains only Swedish territory, through which troops and weapons may be transported to the north. Should the Germans try to occupy Kiruna themselves, the Allies will move even quicker.

In all probability Scandinavia will be the next and perhaps decisive theatre of war. There is one more alternative: a German attack on Holland and Belgium. Then the west will become the main theatre of war. But if military operations develop in Scandinavia, the Allies will have to come out to the shores of the Baltic, for Sweden will inevitably be drawn into the war. How will this affect Finland? The position of the Soviet Union will become highly delicate as well.

I remarked: 'Even in such conditions we shall make every effort to preserve our neutrality.'

'I don't doubt it,' said Lloyd George. 'The question is, will you be able to preserve it?'

On parting, he added: 'Whatever happens, I hope the course of the war will not force you to leave our country.'

13 April

Great excitement in political circles. A German attack on Holland is expected imminently. The British, French and Belgian military staffs are holding urgent conferences. Contact with Holland is being maintained. One often hears the following opinion. The Germans want to strike in the west in order to divert the Allies' attention from Norway – so be it. That's even better. It is easier for the Allies to wage war in the west than in Scandinavia. Here, they are better prepared.

Until the Dutch situation is clarified, the British government seems disinclined to get involved too deeply in Norway.

Rubinin[i] reports that the Belgians are sceptical about an imminent German offensive. They think the Allies are intentionally exaggerating these fears to make it easier for Belgium to enter the war.

I'm not quite convinced that the Belgians are being sincere. But time will tell.

15 April

Diplomatic relations between the Labour Party and the embassy have been restored.

Our links were practically severed at the beginning of the Finnish campaign. True, I kept in touch with several Labour MPs (Wedgwood, Maclean, Hicks, Pritt, Wilkinson and others) during those months, but these figures were all either marginal or opposed to the Labour leaders. The official leaders of the Labour Party did not visit the embassy and I did not visit them. It was a complete break.

With the end of the Finnish war, Labour's mood started to change. Dalton's conversation with me (15 March) was the first sign. At the beginning of April, Attlee's secretary, Jenkins,[ii] suggested to Coates that it would be desirable to bury the hatchet on the issue of Finland and return to the 'old friendship' between the embassy and the party leadership. I took the position that it was not I who had started the quarrel, but Labour – and Labour should take the first step. I, for my part, was prepared to normalize relations with them. After a week of deliberation between Jenkins and Coates on this matter, Attlee and Greenwood finally paid me a visit today.

We mentioned neither the 'quarrel' nor Finland. Our conversation focused on Anglo-Soviet relations in general and trade negotiations in particular. I informed the Labour leaders about the present state of affairs. They expressed

---

[i] Evgenii Vladimirovich Rubinin, Soviet ambassador to Belgium, 1935–40.

[ii] Arthur Jenkins.

72. Diplomatic relations restored between Attlee and Maisky.

their ardent desire to improve our relations and promised their assistance. Greenwood did most of the talking, constantly addressing Attlee with the words: 'Isn't that so, Clem?'

To which Attlee kept answering: 'Oh yes, absolutely.'

On the whole, I got the impression that Attlee's attitude was more favourable than Greenwood's. Greenwood drank a lot, as is his wont, while Attlee merely sipped his cherry brandy.

And so, diplomatic relations are restored!

Facts are stubborn things, and the power of the USSR is undeniably one of them.

16 April

The former Danish minister in London, Count Ahlefeldt, whose wife used to spread such vile insinuations about Agniya, is back in London. He retired two years or so ago to spend the rest of his days in Madeira (not a bad place!), just like in Nekrasov:[i]

> Under the captivating skies of Sicilia,
> In the fragrant shade of the trees…

But war arrived, and everything was turned upside down. The funds which Ahlefeldt had invested in Danish shipping companies evaporated, especially after the German occupation of Denmark. Ahlefeldt 'went bust' and came to London. He is here with his daughter, without a penny to his name. The

[i] Nikolai Alekseevich Nekrasov, nineteenth-century Russian poet; editor of the literary review *Sovremennik* (*The Contemporary*).

daughter is looking for a job just to feed herself and her father. Ahlfeldt's wife is stuck in Copenhagen. She is ill, in hospital, separated from her family.

They are one of the first victims of the war in London's high society. But not the last!

17 April

A visit out of the blue from Pierre Cot[i] (the former French minister for air). I hadn't seen him for two years. He looked dreadfully thin and pinched. It turns out that he fell very ill at the beginning of the war with acute appendicitis. He only recovered recently and has returned to political life. But he has no official post. 'I prefer to be a deputy,' he added with a certain emphasis.

He is in London on various matters and decided to pay me a visit. The 'Russian question' is clearly in a state of flux in France. In the past, no one wished to listen to people like Cot. Now they listen and scratch their heads. This change of mood leads Cot to wonder whether the time may have come to discuss in earnest the improvement of Franco-Soviet relations. But before speaking about this to Reynaud, Cot wanted to know whether we desire such an improvement. That explains his visit to me.

I replied that the USSR wishes to remain neutral in a big war. All governments should proceed from this premise. However, we certainly do not have the intention of causing a deterioration in our relations with the Allies and, by way of illustration, I divulged to Cot some details concerning the trade negotiations between the USSR and England. It is difficult for me to say how the general line of our foreign policy is refracted in the specific case of France, since Franco-Soviet relations lie outside the sphere of my work. My personal opinion is that the problem of Franco-Soviet relations is far more complicated than the problem of Anglo-Soviet relations. For, even if we can hardly be satisfied with the position of the British government over recent months, it has at least not been arranging raids on the Soviet trade mission in London and has not demanded my withdrawal as a 'persona non grata'.

Cot agreed with me that the policy of the F[rench] G[overnment] had been more aggressive and provocative than the policy of the British government, but reminded me that it was not Reynaud but Daladier who must bear responsibility for the raid on the Soviet trade mission in Paris and the 'Surits case'. True, the 'Surits case' was concluded under Reynaud, but it was initiated by his predecessor, and it was difficult for Reynaud to stop it once he came to

---

[i] Pierre Cot, Radical French MP, 1928–40; minister for air, 1933–34 and 1936–38; minister for trade, 1938–39; in exile in Great Britain, 1940–44.

power, especially in light of the tangled political situation he faced in France during the first days of his premiership.

On the whole, Cot was satisfied with my explanations. Since the USSR is not against improving relations, Cot will raise the matter with Reynaud, whom he knows well, upon his return to Paris. An improvement in our relations was out of the question while Daladier was still premier. The situation has changed. Reynaud is ready to normalize Franco-Soviet relations, but he is afraid of Laval, Flandin and Co. Nonetheless, the question of normalization can now be raised. What is the best way of doing so? Perhaps by starting with trade negotiations here as well? Under this banner, Reynaud would find it easiest to carry the country with him…

I said it was hard for me to give Cot any concrete advice. If the F[rench] G[overnment] really wished to open trade talks, would it not be better for Payart to make inquiries in Moscow?

Cot pondered this a little and said: 'When I get back to Paris, I'll talk to Reynaud, and then it will be easier to decide. Maybe Reynaud will test the ground via Payart, or maybe he would prefer to do so through you. You know, Reynaud is in a delicate position, and it may be more convenient for him not to send an official telegram to Payart through the Foreign Ministry (this could be exploited by Reynaud's enemies), but to carry out initial negotiations through London. But I can't say anything definite for the moment. We shall see.'

We parted.

Obviously, some shifts on the issue of relations with the USSR are occurring in France. Although Cot said that he had visited me in a private capacity, he would have hardly made this move without consulting Reynaud first, or at least others in his circle.

18 April

As far as I can judge from conversations and reports, the British plan of operations in Scandinavia is governed by the following priorities, in order of significance.

First, to consolidate the British position in Narvik and to hover around Kiruna so as to cut off Hitler's access to iron ore at the first opportunity.

Second, to force the Germans out of the ports and the Norwegian coastline in general (Stavanger, Bergen, Trondheim, etc.).

Third, to clear the Germans out of the rest of Norway.

While implementing the plan, of course, as many German war and merchant vessels as possible must be sunk and the transportation of German reinforcements to Norway must be blocked (using mines, aviation, warships, etc.).

The Allies are not yet sending significant forces to Norway. Only one or two divisions are mentioned. The Allies are eager to draw Sweden into the war. This, of course, is a highly appealing prospect, for several reasons. Should Sweden enter the war, Scandinavia would be turned into the main theatre of operations (far away from England and France!), Germany would be exposed to an attack from its poorly protected flank, and the Allies would reach the Baltic and be able to threaten the USSR as well.

But these are just plans. Their realization will take some time. We shall see what happens in reality. I now often recall Tolstoy's lines:

On paper there had seemed no hitches.
Alas! Forgotten were the ditches,
Which one would have to cross!

22 April

Attlee and Greenwood visited me again. They spoke about my meeting with Halifax on 19 April. Greenwood attempted, if not to justify, then at least to explain the conduct of the F[oreign] O[ffice]. I rebuffed him firmly. On the whole, Attlee took my side.

The conversation then turned to international affairs. The two leaders categorically asserted that the Allies would give real assistance to Norway, but that a certain amount of time was needed to gather the forces required in Scandinavia (particularly in Narvik).

Greenwood kept assuring me that the British government is not planning to start a war in the Balkans and that Italy will not risk a military adventure in view of its extreme vulnerability.

I'm not so sure of that.

27 April

Cripps is back from his wanderings in far-off lands. He left London in early December and since then has managed to visit India, China, Japan, the Soviet Union and the United States. Now he is back home, and full of interesting stories. What he told me could be summarized in the following way.

India. The British government's conduct in India is reactionary and short-sighted. Its policy is leading directly to the rise of oppositional and revolutionary movements. India is on the brink of a campaign of 'civil disobedience'. Gandhi undoubtedly remains the most influential of all Indian leaders.

China. Jiang Jieshi has taken a firm stance. There's stalemate at the front. The Japanese are unable to advance, and the Chinese are unable to flush them out of their strongholds because of a shortage of tanks, artillery, planes, etc. The partisan movement is spread wide, but slow to take effect. Jiang Jieshi faces two main dangers. (A) The threat to the Chinese dollar. The stabilization fund has dried up and the dollar may plummet at any moment. Meanwhile, the Chinese dollar is more than just a currency; it is the symbol of China's unity. Thanks to the dollar, the population of the regions 'occupied' by the Japanese can pay taxes and duties to Jiang Jieshi. (B) The aggravation of relations between the Guomindang and the Communist Party. This may lead to open armed conflict. Jiang Jieshi's aides-de-camp bear the brunt of the blame for this (although he himself is quite anti-communist too). According to Cripps's observations, there are many corrupt elements among this group. When he was in the United States, Cripps tried to sound out the possibility of augmenting the stabilization fund. It seems that the Americans may be prepared to go half-and-half with England (up to 15 million pounds is required in total).

Japan. The country's economic situation is difficult but far from catastrophic. Cripps talked with Arita,[i] and his impression is that Japan really fears just one country – the Soviet Union. Arita also outlined provisional conditions of peace with China: (a) recognition of Manzhouguo and the Beijing government; (b) economic preferences for Japan in China; (c) spheres of influence for Japan in some regions, especially those adjoining the USSR; and (d) the conclusion of an anti-Comintern alliance between Japan and China, which is understood as the right to organize a Chinese army under Japanese command against the USSR. Of all these conditions, Arita considers the fourth to be the most important.

USSR. Cripps and his secretary, Geoffrey Wilson,[ii] flew to the USSR from Chongqing. The weather was so bad that they were forced to stay in Kuibyshev for three days. On the way back, after being flown on a Soviet plane to Chinese territory in Tianjin, Cripps had to travel more than two thousand kilometres by car. But it all turned out fine. Cripps liked our pilots and was pleased with the attention accorded to him in the Soviet Union. His conversation with C[omrade] Molotov clarified a great deal for him. Cripps was mostly interested in what had gone wrong in the trade negotiations between England and the USSR last autumn, as well as in the prospects for their resumption. He informed C[omrade] Molotov of his impressions of China and asked him in detail about Soviet policy towards China. Cripps spent merely 36 hours in Moscow before heading back to Chongqing. Cripps spoke highly of Clark Kerr,[iii] the British

[i] Hachiro Arita, intermittent Japanese foreign minister, 1936–40.

[ii] Geoffrey Masterman Wilson, Stafford Cripps's secretary; served in the British embassy in Moscow, and the Russian department of the Foreign Office, 1940–45.

[iii] Archibald Clark Kerr, British ambassador in China, 1938–42, in the USSR, 1942–46, and in the USA, 1946–48.

ambassador in China, whom he found to be a progressive fellow with a friendly attitude towards the USSR.

28 April

Agniya and I had lunch yesterday with Prytz (the Swedish minister). In Prytz's opinion, the position of the Allies in southern Norway is very difficult and their withdrawal cannot be excluded. At any rate, General Dill[i] (deputy chief of the general staff) dropped hints to this effect in his conversation with journalists the other day. The difficulty of the Allied position is due to the fact that the transportation of German reinforcements to Norway continues in spite of their efforts. A quarter of the transport ships are sunk, but the rest arrive in Norway safely. As a result, there are about 4,000 Germans in Narvik, while the Allies have so far landed only a regiment of sappers and the marines. The British hope to defeat the Germans there by starving and exhausting them. They may be mistaken.

Sweden's position, according to Prytz, is difficult in the extreme. The critical moment will arrive when the ice breaks on the Baltic and it becomes possible to transport ore through Lulea. If the Swedes agree to supply Germany with ore, the Allies will most likely attack Kiruna from Narvik. If the Swedes refuse to supply Germany with ore, the Germans will strike from the south. It looks like the only way out for Sweden would be to destroy the iron-ore mines in Kiruna.

Then, as if thinking aloud, Prytz developed the idea that if the USSR could make it clear to Germany and the Allies that they should leave Sweden alone, everything would be settled to the general good.

Prytz spoke with great respect about Al[exandra] Mikh[ailovna Kollontay]. She gained considerable prestige during the negotiations which preceded the signing of the Soviet–Finnish peace treaty. Her position was difficult and delicate, but she emerged with credit.

2 May

During the last two or three days the press has patently been preparing public opinion for the evacuation of Norway. And today Chamberlain declared this plainly in parliament. The PM's speech had an oppressive effect. The MPs were gloomy, and the question of an inevitable government reshuffle was openly discussed in the corridors. Chamberlain is clearly bankrupt. But there were

---

[i] Sir John Greer Dill, field marshal, commander of 1st Army Corps in France, 1939–40; vice-chief of imperial general staff, 1940; aide-de-camp general to the king and chief of imperial general staff, 1940–41.

no debates today. They have been postponed until 7 May, when important developments can be expected.

On 29 April I handed Halifax our reply to the British memorandum of 19 April. Halifax told me that he had to delay his response until he had studied it with the experts. It was already past 6 p.m. when I met Halifax.

On 30 April, at noon, a representative of the Foreign Office press department declared at a press conference that our reply had been deemed 'unsatisfactory' in 'authoritative circles'. This was repeated over the radio a little later. So, in less than twenty-four hours the 'authoritative circles' had succeeded in 'studying' the Soviet reply and pronouncing their verdict!

The Executive Committee of the Labour Party sat on 1 May. Although the Executive Committee members were not in full agreement with all the points of our reply, they found it to be a sufficient basis for negotiations. The Executive Committee also deemed essential the immediate return of a British ambassador to Moscow, although it was strongly against Seeds. They asked Dalton to look into the lists of British diplomats and find a proper man for Moscow. On the same day, Attlee and Greenwood visited the prime minister and demanded the urgent opening of trade negotiations with the Soviet Union and the immediate settlement of the ambassadorial question. Chamberlain mumbled something incoherent in reply.

Today, 2 May, Attlee addressed the prime minister with a *private notice question* concerning trade negotiations with the USSR and mentioned the statement of the 'authoritative circles' on the radio on 30 April. Butler said that the Soviet reply is currently under the *most careful consideration* by the appropriate authorities, and that only his statement should be seen as the correct official response to the Soviet government's memorandum.

Well, we shall see. For myself, I don't expect too much from that *careful consideration.*

Right now in the Foreign Office there are two trends: one for negotiations with us and one against. Someone's hand is constantly sabotaging the improvement of Anglo-Soviet relations.

4 May

Colban paid me a visit. He is upset, shocked, stunned. To top it all, his children – son and daughter – have been left behind in Norway and he has heard nothing from them.

He told me, among other things, that the N[orwegian] G[overnment] did not immediately ask the Allies for help. It hesitated for two or three days and held talks with the Germans. It was only after Germany demanded that Haakon recognize Quisling's[i] government that the N[orwegian] G[overnment], acting through the British minister in Norway, asked England and France for help.

In the first few days, this assistance was promised in the most resolute and definite terms. Chamberlain, Churchill, Halifax and Hoare – Colban had contact with all of them – were lavish with their promises. In particular, they promised very serious aid in Trondheim. But, when the time came to translate promises into action, all manner of 'difficulties' and 'obstacles' suddenly arose.

Colban was not informed about the evacuation of southern Norway. He learnt about it by chance, from one of his acquaintances, on 30 April. Gripped by anxiety, he hurried to Halifax for clarification. Halifax confirmed the fact of the evacuation and tried to throw dust in Colban's eyes with his explanations.

And what's the upshot of it all?

Even Colban, gentle and quiet as a ladybird, is deeply outraged by the conduct of the Allies.

'We've been a pawn in England's hands,' he said bitterly.

Colban did not use the word 'betrayal', but that was the sense of everything he said to me today.

Indeed, the Allies thrust their aid on Norway, drew her into the war by promising support, and then left her at the mercy of fate without even bothering to inform Colban of their decision.

A lesson in brazen cynicism.

7 May

Beaverbrook came for lunch. He is in a resolute and belligerent frame of mind. The Allies will fight to the end! Let it take three, five or seven years – so be it. Both sides will be ruined by the end. Civilization will collapse. So be it. England will not yield! England cannot yield!

Yes, Norway is a failure. But failures occur in every war. He who laughs last, laughs best.

Beaverbrook is in favour of trade negotiations and improved relations with the USSR in general. Now more than ever.

I asked Beaverbrook about the state of the government. Should one expect any changes in this sphere in view of the parliamentary debates that will begin today?

With a dismissive wave of his arms, he asserted with confidence that the government would of course be criticized during the debates, but no serious

---

[i] Vidkun Quisling, founder of the Norwegian Fascist Party, 1933; installed as a Nazi puppet 'minister president' of Norway, 1942–45.

consequences would follow. Chamberlain's position is secure. The Cabinet will be unchanged. He, Beaverbrook, is no supporter of Chamberlain, but he has to acknowledge that the PM is not in danger.

Brendan Bracken spoke to me about this yesterday in equally confident terms. And he, after all, is Churchill's *alter ago*, with an excellent knowledge of all the goings-on in the kitchen of politics.

It's strange. Beaverbrook and Bracken are by all appearances exceptionally well-informed individuals. And yet, I have the feeling that England has approached a crucial boundary; that these debates ought to yield something; that change is in the air…

We'll see.

8 May

My intuition didn't fail me! Following two days of debates, the Chamberlain government has fallen… The government has not yet formally resigned, but this is merely a matter of time, and will happen sooner rather than later. The fatal blow has been struck.

How did it happen?

It happened like this. The MPs spent the weekend in their constituencies, put their ears to the ground, and were back by Tuesday, 7 May, as quite different people from those who had left on the 3rd. For the 'ground' – the country and voting public – is deeply unhappy with the way the war is being conducted, and is agitated and alarmed about the future of England. These feelings found vivid expression in the debates of the past two days, and led to Chamberlain's downfall.

The House presented a very curious spectacle yesterday and today.

Chamberlain, Hoare, Stanley and, last of all, Churchill spoke on behalf of the government. The first three were very weak. Chamberlain's speech was simply rot.[36] Hoare, jerking his leg, related in a thin, sharp voice various trivial details about the raids, landing and take-offs of British aircraft in Norway. Hoare is the air minister, and all these details would be of interest to specialists, who might even find them inspiring. But to devote his whole speech to such things at such a moment (when the fate of the government hung in the balance and the entire conduct of the war was the object of the sharpest criticism) – does this not show him up as a political pygmy? Stanley (the war minister) was a bit better, but only relatively so. Taken together, their speeches, far from raising the reputation of the government, did it significant harm. Churchill's speech made some amends. It was interesting and brilliant, but unconvincing. Churchill tried to defend the government in its Norwegian epic, and a part of his speech was given over to fiery exchanges with the Labourites who were attacking him. Defending Chamberlain is a difficult task, and it brought Churchill no laurels.

The attack on the government was, on the contrary, exceptionally sharp, brilliant, and at times simply devastating. Lloyd George was his inimitable self. When Churchill made an attempt to shield the government, Lloyd George remarked, to the raucous laughter of the Chamber, that Churchill 'must not allow himself to be converted into an air-raid shelter to keep the splinters from hitting his colleagues'.

Turning to Chamberlain, the old man concluded his speech with the words: 'there is nothing which can contribute more to victory in this war than that he should sacrifice the seals of office!'[37] Morrison's attack on the government, and on Chamberlain personally, was astonishingly fierce and ended with a call for the resignation of the prime minister, Simon and Hoare. Duff Cooper spoke brilliantly and was the first among the government's supporters to declare that he would vote against it. His speech made a great impression. Amery also demanded the resignation of the government. Admiral Keyes,[i] who arrived in parliament in full dress uniform with all his decorations, spoke to exceptional effect on behalf of the navy. Keyes is a poor speaker and practically read out his lines. He stumbled, got confused and agitated, and for precisely those reasons produced a very moving speech. Keyes, who distinguished himself in the last war during the raid on Zeebrugge from land and sea, attacked the government for its failure at Trondheim. Keyes is firmly convinced that Trondheim could have been captured. He had proposed leading the operation himself and assuming full responsibility for its outcome, but the government declined his proposal and beat an inglorious retreat from Norway. Keyes' words had the effect of shells fired from 16-inch guns. Almost all MPs present who were connected with military affairs – representatives of the naval, air and land branches – spoke against the government and its conduct of the war. It was very significant.

Yesterday, on the first day of the debates, it was still unclear whether Labour was going to request a vote of no confidence. The Labourites themselves were vacillating. Many were saying that the vote might benefit the government: party discipline would ensure a massive government majority and the effect produced by the debates would thereby suffer. But it became obvious this morning that the storm was reaching a *crescendo*. Not only Labourites and Liberals, but also many, many Tories had reached breaking point. The iron was hot, and Labour declared that it would demand a vote.

Churchill's concluding speech and his fiery exchange with Labour had raised the temperature in the Chamber considerably. The no-confidence vote

---

[i] Roger Keyes, admiral, director of combined operations, 1940–41.

demanded by Labour added more fuel to the fire. When the voting began and the MPs started walking out through two doors, the Chamber buzzed like a disturbed bee-hive. The tension reached its peak when the tellers came in, approached the Speaker's chair, and announced in the dead silence of the House: 'The vote of no confidence is rejected by a majority of 281 to 200.'

Triumphant roars erupted like a storm from the opposition benches. Chamberlain sat in his place, white as chalk. For although the vote of no confidence had been rejected, the government's majority had never fallen so low.[38] Normally the majority commanded by the government reached 200 at least; now it had dropped to 81. Regardless of all the intimidations of Margesson (*chief whip*), more than 80 Conservatives abstained, while 42 voted against the government. And they were some 42! Amery, Duff Cooper, Lady Astor, Boothby, Macmillan, Hore-Belisha, Nicolson and others.

The two-day-long debates ended in Chamberlain's crushing political defeat. I heard the following remark in the lobby: 'Finland finished off Daladier, and Norway finished off Chamberlain.'

I met Lloyd George in the parliament restaurant before the vote. The old man was very excited and in high spirits.

'Well, Chamberlain is done for,' he exclaimed. 'He might hold on for a few weeks… You know, a duck with a broken leg still flutters its wings, but its fate has been decided. The same with Neville.'

He changed the subject abruptly and asked me: 'Where will Hitler go next? What do you think?'

'No one can vouch for Hitler,' I replied, 'but I think the Balkans are the least probable direction for him now.'

'I say the same', Lloyd George responded with feeling. 'Hitler will now attack Holland!'

'Very possibly,' I agreed.

13 May

And so, England is ruled by a new government – the Churchill government!

The duck with a broken leg passed away sooner than Lloyd George predicted. Hitler is to blame for that. But, rather than run ahead of myself, I'll relate the facts as they happened.

The day after the fatal vote, at nine in the morning, Chamberlain summoned Amery and told him that he thought a serious government reshuffle was in order. Measures should be taken, however, to prevent Labour from coming to power. The government must remain in Tory hands. The prime minister went on to offer Amery any portfolio he wanted (except the PM's), including those of chancellor of the exchequer or foreign secretary. He also promised to do the

Conservative 'opposition' a good turn by offering ministerial posts to its more prominent members. Amery, however, categorically refused the offer. He said that it wasn't a question of his portfolio. It was a question of the composition of the government and above all its leadership. Amery though it impossible for Chamberlain to remain prime minister.

Having failed to 'buy' Amery, Chamberlain invited Attlee and Greenwood to see him after lunch and inquired about the possibility of including Labourites in a government headed by himself. The Labour leaders, however, firmly stated that such a move was out of the question. For even if Attlee and Greenwood should agree to work under Chamberlain, they would soon be disavowed at the Labour conference to be held on the 13th in Bournemouth. Chamberlain then asked whether they would join a government headed by a different prime minister? To this, the Labour leaders replied that they would have to consult their colleagues. On parting, the prime minister asked Attlee and Greenwood to give him a definitive answer to two questions, after consulting their colleagues:

(1) Would they agree to serve in a government under Chamberlain?

(2) Would they agree to serve in a government under another prime minister?

Attlee and Greenwood promised to inform Chamberlain of the decision of the Labour organizations the following day.

Later the same day, Chamberlain met Sinclair and talked to him along the same lines. Sinclair proved more amenable and tended towards the opinion that at such a critical moment it would be more expedient not to insist on Chamberlain's resignation. He would be ready to work under Chamberlain should the composition of the government be sufficiently altered. Sinclair even made a statement to this effect in the press on the morning of the 10th.

Wilson and Margesson set their machinery in motion and were preparing to launch a large-scale campaign to 'rescue Chamberlain' by sacrificing some of the most unpopular ministers. But then Hitler unexpectedly intervened and turned everything upside down.

In the night of the 9th to the 10th the Germans attacked Holland and Belgium. This fact had a tremendous effect in England. The temperature immediately shot up. The whole country became tense. Events developed at breakneck speed. Wilson's and Margesson's plans, which required a certain amount of time to be put into practice, fell by the wayside.

It was clear to all that the reconstruction of the government should be carried out immediately and in a far more radical way than conceived before.

On the morning of 10 May, the Labour Executive Committee, excluding Morrison, left for Bournemouth, where Labour delegates had gathered for their annual conference. As head of the London County Council and anti-aircraft defence, Morrison stayed in London, in the event of a German air raid on the capital. The Executive Committee reached Bournemouth in time for lunch, after which they immediately opened the conference in order to work out their answers to Chamberlain's questions. The Executive Committee's mood was fairly well unanimous. They refused categorically to serve under Chamberlain, but agreed to be part of a government under another prime minister, on condition that Labour be 'sufficiently represented' in the key positions. The conference closed at around 4.30 p.m., and it was proposed that Attlee and Greenwood proceed to London at once to negotiate on the basis of the decisions taken at the conference. Attlee and Greenwood were just getting into the car when there was a telephone call and Chamberlain's secretary enquired about Labour's decision. Attlee answered the call and informed him. Then the Labour leaders set off for London. It took them about two and a half hours to get to London, and when they arrived at seven o'clock the Chamberlain government was no longer in existence. In the time they spent travelling, Chamberlain managed to submit his resignation to the king, and the king managed to appoint Churchill as the new prime minister. The decision made by the Executive Committee of the Labour Party left Chamberlain with no choice but to resign the premiership.[39]

Directly upon their arrival in London, Attlee and Greenwood were invited to meet Churchill at the Admiralty. There they conferred with the new prime minister for about two hours. They had no difficulty in agreeing on a common policy. The allocation of portfolios was a trickier matter, but agreement was soon reached on that as well: Attlee and Greenwood became members of the five-member War Cabinet, Alexander was appointed first lord of the Admiralty, and Morrison the minister of supply. Bevin was suggested for minister of labour, and appointed as such two days later. Dalton's candidacy was haggled over for some time, until he was eventually offered the portfolio of minister of economic warfare. On the whole, Labour was satisfied with the quantity and quality of the posts it received.

The hardest thing was to agree with Churchill about Chamberlain. As Attlee and Greenwood travelled from Bournemouth to London, Chamberlain not only resigned but also received a proposal from Churchill to join the new government as a member of the War Cabinet. In doing so, Churchill was guided mainly by consideration of the large group of Chamberlain's supporters among Tory MPs: Chamberlain would be less harmful inside the Cabinet as a 'hostage' than outside as the instigator of all manner of intrigues. Churchill made his offer to Chamberlain. But he did so at his own risk and without informing the Labour leaders in advance. Upon arrival in London, they were confronted with this fait accompli. This led to a heated discussion between Churchill and the Labour leaders. They finally reached a compromise. Chamberlain will remain in the War Cabinet as minister without portfolio, but Churchill will reject the former PM's two demands: Chamberlain will not be appointed chancellor of the exchequer and will not be *leader of the House* (the official representative of the government in the absence of the prime minister). This latter role will be assumed by Attlee.

The Bournemouth conference was told about Labour's entry into the government on the morning of 13 May. It was approved by a majority of 4.5 million votes to 170 thousand. In fact, however, the number of those who opposed joining the government (including the minorities within certain trade unions who cannot express themselves owing to the *block vote* system) stood at about 500,000.

After lunch on the same day, a short closed session of parliament was convened, at which Churchill presented his new government. When Chamberlain entered the hall, most of the Conservatives greeted him with such a storm of fervent applause that it could only be viewed as a demonstration of hostility towards Churchill. This was rendered even more emphatic by the fact that Churchill's entry into the House was met with relatively feeble applause: the opposition is not in the habit of cheering Conservative leaders, and most Tories remained silent. But Churchill didn't seem to mind. Presenting the Cabinet, he uttered only a few, forceful words. He said he could offer his new colleagues nothing but 'blood, toil, tears and sweat'. But he is sure of eventual victory.

This is how a new chapter has opened in the history of this war and in the political history of England.[40]

14 May

A telephone call from Rubinin. Belgian soldiers have surrounded our embassy in Brussels and are not allowing anybody in or out, including Rubinin himself. The excuse: German paratroopers allegedly landed in the embassy's garden (it has a beautiful, big garden). Rubinin invited an officer and two soldiers to walk round the garden and see for themselves that this was pure invention. They walked around the garden and found nobody, yet the siege continues. Rubinin called the nuncio[i] (the doyen), the foreign minister Spaak,[ii] and the premier Pierlot.[iii] all expressed their indignation and promised their cooperation, but nothing has changed. In despair, Rubinin called and asked me to lean on the Belgian government, albeit only through the Belgian ambassador in London. I called Cartier and remarked in passing, in the hope of shaking him up: 'One rather has the impression that the Belgian government has lost its head.'

---

[i] Cardinal Clemente Micara, permanent diplomatic representative of the 'Holy See' in Belgium, 1923–40.

[ii] Paul Henri Charles Spaak, intermittent Belgian foreign minister, 1936–57; prime minister of Belgium, 1938–39 and 1947–50.

[iii] Count Hubert Marie Pierlot, prime minister of Belgium, 1939–45.

My words cut Cartier to the quick. He assured me I was wrong and promised to contact Brussels immediately.

At four o'clock today, the 'siege' was finally lifted.

15 May

Visited Lloyd George in his office in Thames House.

He is greatly alarmed. He thinks Belgium is lost. The Belgians fought poorly in the last war and are fighting equally poorly now. Liddell-Hart, who recently saw the Belgian fortifications on the Albert Canal, assured Lloyd George that they were very solid. They could last for a long time. But the Belgians simply fled. Evidently, there was treason, too. Otherwise it's a mystery why two bridges were left intact, to be safely crossed by German tanks.

However, what happened yesterday at Sedan is much more serious. There were signs of a breakthrough there. If that happens, the situation will become really ominous. Sedan is located at the juncture of the Maginot Line and the lighter fortifications running along the Belgian border towards the sea. After breaking through the French line, the Germans would be able to reach the rear both of the Maginot Line and of the Anglo-French army deployed along the Belgian border. It's terribly dangerous. It could decide the outcome of the war in France. That is why Lloyd George's attention is now fixed on Sedan.

I asked: how can one explain the German success in Holland and Belgium?

'Technology!' exclaimed Lloyd George. 'Technology wins. The Allies had not envisaged such colossal mechanization and were not prepared for it. The Germans have an enormous quantity of tanks. The French staff was quite convinced that the Ardennes were impassable for tanks and lorries. They based their calculations on this assumption. Then the Germans suddenly passed through the Ardennes with heavy tanks and lorries of a special design, of which the French had not the slightest idea! The Germans have armoured trains equipped with 11-inch guns. The Allies have nothing of the sort, or a negligible amount at the most. Suffice it to say that the British have virtually no heavy tanks. The French have them, but the British don't. As for aviation, the Germans have a superiority of 3:1.'

Lloyd George rumpled his snow-white mane with a theatrical gesture and added emphatically: 'Men returning from the front say that our men still haven't seen any German soldiers. They've seen German machines, but not German soldiers. This is entirely different from 1914.'

Flushed with excitement and gesticulating vigorously, Lloyd George continued: 'We, the British and the French, had a fair amount of "junk" among our leaders in the past war. The Germans had, too: the kaiser,[i] Bethmann-Hollweg, many courtiers and even generals, although it should be said that most of the German generals were *first rate*. The situations were more or less the same here and there. It's different today. Germany is undoubtedly led by a remarkable man. He and Mussolini are "revolutionaries" in their own way. They do not abide by traditions or universally acknowledged rules. They have inventive and resourceful minds. They act boldly, decisively, and with lightning speed. And we still have so much "junk" at the top. Even Winston is different from what he was 20 years ago, to say nothing of the others. What's more, we've had Chamberlain up till now. How can our "junk" keep up with Hitler and Mussolini? That is why we encounter a *surprise* at every turn!'

Lloyd George is greatly afraid that Italy will soon come out on the side of Germany. It is also unclear what Spain will do. There is ground to believe that Spain will also join the Axis and demand Gibraltar for itself. On the whole, the prospects are grim.

I asked directly: 'So you think France and England will lose the war?'

Lloyd George waved his hand and said: 'You put the question too brutally. I don't want… I can't answer it.'

He hesitated for an instant, then added: 'The Allies cannot win the war. The most we can think about now is how to hold the Germans back till autumn and then see.'

Can even that be achieved?…

Lloyd George made a vague gesture. I was left with the definite impression that the old man fears that the Allies may be defeated, and especially France. He was silent for a while and then exclaimed bitterly: 'How terribly unfortunate that we failed to conclude a pact with you last year!'

Lloyd George asked me if I had met Churchill since his appointment as prime minister. I said I hadn't. Lloyd George insisted: 'And Winston didn't invite you to see him?'

'No.'

Lloyd George raised his hands in despair: 'Incredible! If I were in Churchill's place, the first thing I would do would be to summon you and have a serious *heart-to-heart talk*.'

Then Lloyd George began to criticize Churchill. Churchill invited him to join the War Cabinet, but Lloyd George declined. He considers the present Cabinet utterly useless and does not wish to bear responsibility for its work. Why have Chamberlain and Halifax been admitted to the War Cabinet? They can do nothing but harm. What kind of a War Cabinet is it? Churchill, Chamberlain,

[i] Kaiser Wilhelm II, last German emperor and king of Prussia, 1888–1918.

Halifax, Attlee and Greenwood. Leaving Churchill aside, what are the rest good for? Chamberlain and Halifax are simply poisonous, and Attlee and Greenwood are nonentities. What can these men bring to the Cabinet? How can they help Churchill?

Lloyd George gave himself over to reminiscence. In his 'War Cabinet' of 1916–18 every member made his contribution to the common cause. Milner, Balfour,[i] Curzon, Henderson, Smuts – they all had their uses, they all had something to offer the PM. And now?... Lloyd George gestured dismissively. Churchill, in conversation with Lloyd George, justified Chamberlain's entry into the War Cabinet by arguing that he would be less harmful inside than outside the Cabinet.

'My reply,' Lloyd George said with a laugh, 'was that if you cannot cope with Chamberlain, how will you defeat Hitler and Mussolini?'

Then, taking a somewhat philosophical tone, the old man continued: 'There's no use hiding the fact: we are governed by a plutocracy. It is absolutely bankrupt. Its unbroken nine-year rule has led to the present catastrophe. All these Chamberlains, Hoares, Simons and Halifaxes – they all deserve the guillotine! And that's what they'd have got if they'd been living at the time of the French Revolution. If members of your government acted as wrongfully as ours, you'd have them "liquidated". And you'd be right to do so. But what do we do? We send Simon to the House of Lords and double his salary!'

Lloyd George paused and continued: 'Yes, our plutocracy is bankrupt. Among the older generation you could still find strong people who made their own way in life and earned their own money. I remember such men; I saw them when I was young. But what good are the plutocrats of today? They are all epigones. They were given everything on a plate. They are not used to struggling and conquering. A real generation of rentiers. Here's an outstanding example for you: Joseph Chamberlain[ii] and his son Neville. Joseph was a big man, and Neville?... Ha ha! A mountain and a mouse!'

As I took my leave Lloyd George said: 'You were very wise to guarantee the Finns fairly mild conditions of peace. This was both noble and far-sighted. I wish you success.'

[Churchill's Machiavellian move was aimed at harnessing Lloyd George's energies by putting him in charge of a Food Council. He assured Halifax, though, that he 'meant to put [Lloyd George] through an inquisition first' to ensure 'that any Peace terms now, or hereafter, offered must not be destructive of our independence'. Lloyd George

---

[i] Arthur James Balfour, first lord of the Admiralty, 1915–16; foreign secretary, 1916–19; president of the Council, 1919–22 and 1925–29.

[ii] Joseph Chamberlain, father of Austen and Neville Chamberlain. Thrice mayor of Birmingham; MP for Birmingham, 1876–85; secretary of state for colonies, 1895–1903.

made his acceptance conditional on the removal of Chamberlain from the Cabinet – which was categorically rejected by Churchill: 'I have received a very great deal of help from Chamberlain; his kindness and courtesy to me in our new relation have touched me. I have joined hands with him, and must act with perfect loyalty.' Sylvester, Lloyd George's secretary, believed the reasons for rejecting the offer were far more mundane: he wanted 'to keep his cake and eat it. He wants a job, but he does not want the bother of it; he does not want it to affect his present mode of life at Churt; and he is frightened to death of the bombs. Added to which he could never sit in an office all day long.' In December, Churchill tried in vain to divert him to the embassy in Washington. Lloyd George produced a letter he had received from Dawson which objected to the appointment, as he was 'not an Ambassador, and had not much patience with people who "dig deeply into the surface" ... in other words, L-G could not stand having to listen to a lot of damn fools talking and having to show some interest in them.' That was only part of the story. When Nancy Astor and her circle of friends wished to vet him as a possible successor to Chamberlain, he cited the example of Clemenceau, who 'had waited until France was in the very gravest danger'. The inference was – as it was observed – that he 'preferred to await his country's summons a little longer, but ... he expected to receive it as the peril grew'. In a moment of truth, Lloyd George told his secretary: 'I am 78 and I want to keep fit because, if these fellows make a mess of it I may be called upon to take over great responsibilities.' Obviously, concluded Sylvester, 'he had in his mind being called in to make a negotiated peace'. Later on, he told his secretary that he would 'wait until Winston is bust'.[41]]

I called on Vansittart. I hadn't seen him for ages, perhaps since Malvern, where we met at the theatre last August, on the eve of the war: his play *Dead Heat* was on. He has not changed much – only the wrinkles on his forehead seem to have deepened and his mood become harsher and more bitter.

I asked him about his new play, which was supposed to have been staged in February (we had tickets), but was for some reason postponed. Agniya even thought it might have been banned by the censors. Vansittart, however, gave me a different explanation. When the play was scheduled for staging, the company began falling ill with the 'flu: first the leading man, then two or three other prominent actors, then five or six less important ones, etc. As a result, the director decided to put everything off until the autumn… 'If plays will be being staged at all in the autumn,' Vansittart added gloomily.

Indeed, things at the front look bad. Vansittart tried to put a brave face on it, but he too demonstrated great anxiety about what is happening in Belgium and Holland. I pointed out the breakthrough at Sedan: nothing major has happened as yet, but it seems that that is the crucial spot, more crucial than the *Low Countries*. Vansittart agreed.

Then we spoke about Anglo-Soviet trade negotiations, or, to be more precise, their absence. I made our point of view absolutely clear to Vansittart: the memorandum of 8 May is absolutely unacceptable to us. If the British government insists on it, nothing will be achieved. Vansittart shrugged his shoulders and expressed his regret at the lack of success in the trade talks.

* * *

I spoke with Beaverbrook over the telephone. He frankly concedes the difficulty of the situation in Belgium. The cause? Germany's supremacy in the air, especially in terms of bombers. The ratio is 4:1 in Germany's favour. Nevertheless, Beaverbrook is firmly resolved to fight to the end. He is also counting on aid from the United States. If not now, then later.

17 May

At last: the forming of the new government is complete. But is it really new?

There are changes, of course, but Chamberlain's defeat has turned out to be significantly less decisive than it initially seemed. Take the War Cabinet, for instance: of its five members, Chamberlain and Halifax represent 'old blood'. Attlee and Greenwood, of course, represent 'fresh blood', but both are minor figures. The only independent figure is Churchill. As a result, unless nothing unexpected happens, the influence of 'old blood' in the War Cabinet should prove very powerful. Moreover, Chamberlain is still the leader of the Conservative Party and Margesson – the party's *chief whip*. Simon may have been shifted to the Lords, but he gets the post of lord chancellor, while Kingsley Wood becomes chancellor of the exchequer. Of Chamberlain's former 'Inner Cabinet', only Hoare remains without a job, but some lofty position will probably be found for him, too, in the near future.

On the other hand, however, a number of key posts in the government (though not in the War Cabinet) have been given to the 'fresh blood': Eden – secretary of state for war, Alexander – first lord of the Admiralty, Sinclair – secretary of state for air, Morrison – minister of supply, Bevin – minister of labour, and Dalton – minister of economic warfare. There is good reason to believe that in contrast to the de jure 'War Cabinet' consisting of the five individuals listed above, a de facto 'War Cabinet' will be created, composed of Churchill plus ministers from the key departments. And this second cabinet will prove far more influential than the first. Time will tell.

In the meantime, Churchill's position is still not very secure. This was vividly demonstrated in parliament on 13 May. Various sources inform me that Chamberlain is currently far more occupied with fighting Churchill than with fighting Hitler. Sounds just like him.

One fact strikes me as especially symptomatic. If one leaves to one side the more or less decorative posts in the de jure War Cabinet, it is Labour that is in charge of the ministries of supply, labour and economic warfare. In other words, the British bourgeoisie has bestowed on Labour the 'honour' of exerting pressure on the proletariat and the neutral states. On the part of the bourgeoisie it's a clever move – but on Labour's?... Labour is performing its historical role.

Lloyd has been appointed secretary of state for the colonies and Amery – secretary of state for India. Two very important posts of our time. What policy will they pursue? Neither has shown himself to be a man of progressive views in this delicate sphere. But this is how Churchill, too, reveals his imperialist colours. Suffice it to recall his 'mutiny' against Hoare's Indian constitution of 1934.

Nevertheless... this is a new government!

The nine-year rule of obtuse, short-sighted Tories such as Chamberlain and Baldwin has come to an end. These men are quite bankrupt, especially in the sphere of foreign and military policy. A coalition of more flexible and far-sighted Conservatives, like Churchill and Eden, has come to power, mixed with Labour and Liberal elements. The 'old blood' will make itself felt for some time yet, but there is much to suggest that we have just seen the back of the first, though not the last, government crisis of the war period.

I think the new government will pursue a more judicious policy towards the USSR, but to what extent? Only the future can tell.

Many in England are asking the question: hasn't the Churchill government come to power too late to save the country? It's a very serious question. But again, only the future will tell.

* * *

All contact with Brussels ceased today. I used to talk with Rubinin over the telephone and exchange occasional telegrams. No longer. The Belgian government has moved to Ostend. The Germans have occupied Brussels.

18 May

Agniya and I travelled out of town to visit friends. We called on Lloyd George.

He is seriously worried. His pessimism has been vindicated. Belgium is lost, and the German breakthrough at Sedan looks more and more ominous. The Germans are using new methods. Dive-bombers are sent out first to clear a path for the tanks, thereby doing the preliminary work that used to be carried out by the artillery. Armoured columns follow, clearing the way for the motorized infantry. Motorized infantry then clears the path for the ordinary infantry. If the tanks or motorized infantry meet an unexpected obstacle, they do not kick against the pricks. They stop for a short while or even retreat, sending the air force ahead of them. After the latter have done their job, the mechanized and motorized divisions resume their advance. Such are the German tactics. The

Allies have almost nothing with which to oppose the Germans, for they have few tanks and are short of aircraft. The quantity of French aircraft is especially feeble, so British planes have to bear the brunt of the burden. That is why Lloyd George has doubts as to whether the Allies will be able to repair the breach.

But if they fail, what then?

Lloyd George remembers that when entering France in the last war, the Germans were in two minds about which direction to take – towards Paris or the Channel ports. In consequence, they ended up neither here nor there and stalled on the Marne. Today, the Germans seem to have a fixed plan: to strike the Channel ports first. They want to cut England off from France and then concentrate all their attention on France: to crush her and force her to sign a separate peace.

'Do you think Germany will manage to achieve this goal?' I asked.

'I can't tell for sure, but I think it quite possible,' Lloyd George answered.

'What would England do if France was taken out?'

'Fight on her own,' Lloyd George exclaimed without the slightest hesitation. 'Fight to the end! We have no choice.'

Then the old man explained his reasoning in greater detail. The British navy is strong enough to protect the country against a serious invasion by German troops. England is facing a greater danger from the air and temporary difficulties are inevitable, but she will fight nonetheless. Together with the dominions and support from the USA, England will be able to hold firm. The war will be long and exhausting, but victory is possible. From this point of view, it is very important to expand agriculture and food production in general inside the country. That is why Lloyd George would be prepared to assume the post of general commissioner for food production with special powers. But he doesn't want to enter the War Cabinet, despite Churchill's continued invitations, so as not to bear responsibility for its policies.

However, in order to wage such a war, England requires an absolutely different government. The plutocracy is bankrupt. The capitalist system is nearing its end. What government will replace the present one? This is not yet entirely clear to Lloyd George, but he thinks it will lean much more to the left than the present one.

To be able to wage such a war, an improvement in relations with the USSR is also required. A meaningful improvement. A genuine improvement!

We drove from Lloyd George to the Webbs. All is well with the old couple, but the growing anxiety can be felt even in this quiet refuge of thought. We spoke, of course, about the war. Without mentioning my conversation with Lloyd George, I asked the Webbs what England would do if France were taken out of the game.

They answered without hesitation: 'Then England would have to fight alone.'

They then produced a precedent (the English cannot manage without their precedents!): the era of the Napoleonic wars. The same response was found then. *Very significant!*

19 May

The German breakthrough at Sedan is expanding.

16 May was a 'black Thursday' for France. Not only did the Germans break through the French lines on the previous day, but panic set in in the French army and the French government.

Complete confusion reigned on the section of the front between Sedan and the Sambre. General Corap,[i] in particular, 'distinguished himself', getting into such a state that he not only fled with his armies, but also 'forgot' to blow up the bridges on the Meuse, which allowed the German tanks to overcome this major obstacle without the slightest difficulty. He was eventually taken captive by the Germans.

Corap was not the only one to panic. The same happened to Gamelin. In total despair, he tried to convince his government that all was lost, that the Germans would reach Paris in a day or two, and that it was necessary to conclude an immediate peace. A significant proportion of the government took fright. Reynaud, who was firmly resolved to continue the war, immediately summoned Churchill from London. On the 16th, the British prime minister arrived in Paris and a meeting of the Supreme War Council was convened. Churchill calmed the French and raised their spirits. The devil, he told them, is not as terrible as he is painted. The German mechanized divisions also consist of human beings. They have to eat, sleep, 'relieve themselves', etc. German tanks also cannot move without petrol. All this gives the Allies the chance to put up resistance and close the breach. Churchill flew back to London on the same day, and two days later Gamelin was replaced by Weygand, while Daladier ceded his post as minister of defence to Reynaud and became foreign minister.

Two diametrically opposed positions have now clashed in France (and in the theatre of the present war in general).

The Allies are staking everything on <u>a long war</u>, a war of attrition, where their immeasurably greater material resources will ensure their eventual victory. That is why they are doing their utmost to hinder the German advance any way they can and drag out the fighting until the autumn or even winter, so as to gain time to mobilize their forces.

---

[i] Andre-Georges Corap, general, commanded the 9th Army, 1939–40.

Germany, on the other hand, is staking everything on a short war, a *Blitzkrieg*, in order to achieve a definitive result this summer, while it still has an advantage over the Allies in terms of aircraft and tanks and while the United States keeps out of the war (the Germans are afraid that America may also declare herself an open enemy after the presidential elections in November).

Two positions, two general ideas. Which will win? Perhaps neither?

Time will tell.

20 May

The Anglo-French bourgeois elite is getting what it deserves.

If one reflects on what has happened in the European arena over the last 20 years, it becomes entirely clear that the main cause of the Allies' current plight is the bourgeois elite's mortal hatred of 'communism'.

This hatred has prevented this elite from establishing any sort of stable, friendly relations with the USSR over these 20 years. There have been ups and downs, but, on the whole, our relations have been unsatisfactory throughout. After all, there are only a few major pieces on the international chessboard, and if a player discards even one of these, for whatever considerations, he considerably weakens his position.

Owing to that very hatred, the ruling elite of England and France systematically supported the Japanese warmongers, Mussolini and Hitler. What's more, it's that same elite which nurtured Hitler – in the hope that one day he would march east and wring the Bolsheviks' necks. But the 'Bolsheviks' proved too strong and too skilful. Hitler headed not east but west. The ruling elite of England and France fell into the same trap they had set for us.

Now they are paying a cruel price for their class narrowness. It's just a pity, however, that the masses in England and France are having to pay this price with them – and perhaps even a higher one.

One more thing. The ruling elite of the 'Western democracies' has not only lost its chance to play the Soviet card and dug its own grave; it also neglected – such is its conceit and arrogance – to take the trouble to put its armaments in order 'just in case'. It did not admit the possibility that its ploy might fail and that Hitler might turn not to the east but to the west.

Yes, the ruling classes of England and France are rotten to the core. How else can one explain their gross blindness, their utter class narrowness, and their complete unpreparedness for war?

We are witnessing the fall of the great capitalist civilization, a fall similar in importance to that of the Roman Empire. Or, perhaps, even more important…

21 May

Aras came by. He is awfully worried about developments at the front. He pins his hopes on the fact that the French army is still in one piece – and that, he thinks, is the main thing. As long as the army still exists and is battle-worthy, the situation can be put to rights. But he also scolded the Allies for the first time in our conversations together: they are always late, they lack a sense of reality, they are bound by dead tradition, and so on.

Aras talked at length about the fact that the Balkans and the Near East can only be saved through friendship with the USSR. He was all but ready to advocate a Soviet 'protectorate' in the Balkans. *Very significant!*

I asked Aras what Turkey's position would be if Italy entered the war. I expected to hear in reply that Turkey would immediately offer armed support to the Allies. In the past, Aras had always said as much. But this time he was far less quick to do so. He did say that Turkey would remain loyal to its obligations, but the nature of Turkey's obligations has suddenly become vague. If Italy's entry into the war extends hostilities to the eastern part of the Mediterranean, then, Aras believes, Turkey would certainly take up arms. But should Italy be involved in the war only in the western part of the Mediterranean – what then? Would Turkey be bound to declare war against Italy immediately, in accordance with its agreements?…

Aras was unclear about this. So too, he said, was Ankara. Also *very significant!*

22 May

Cripps spent the whole evening with me. He told me over dinner that he was making meticulous preparations for his visit to Moscow. He has been to all the ministries concerned: the Foreign Office, the Board of Trade, the Ministry of Economic Warfare, the Ministry of Supply and others; he has collected much material and has received instructions. He told me, among other things, that all notes and memorandums relating to trade negotiations which had been handed to me in the last two months should be considered null and void. The British government wishes to make a fresh start. What is now proposed is the conclusion of a simple barter agreement, with the sole guarantee that the products imported by the USSR from England will not be re-exported to Germany. Cripps will be given authority to discuss all questions, both economic and political, in Moscow.

I expressed my satisfaction with the annulment of the Foreign Office documents and also my scepticism about the prospects for the negotiations: after all, nothing has changed at the FO. I recommended that Cripps ensure the release of the *Selenga* and *Vladimir Mayakovsky* without fail: on the one hand this will make a good impression in Moscow, on the other it will serve as a litmus test to evaluate the attitude of the British government. Cripps promised to do this.

So far there has been no response from Moscow concerning the arrival of Cripps as a *special envoy*. Cripps expressed some anxiety on this score. I tried to reassure him, while cautiously intimating that the reply might indeed not be entirely favourable. I explained that on a personal level the Soviet government was well disposed towards Cripps, as he could see for himself in February (when he flew to Moscow from Chongqing), but when it comes to trade talks the S[oviet] G[overnment] would rather deal with a negotiator who represents the British government. Does Cripps represent the British government?...

There can be only one answer to this question. And Cripps understands this all too well.

23 May

The fog shrouding the operations in Belgium and northern France is gradually beginning to clear. The outline of the main events is taking shape.

The German breakthrough was carried out by 22 divisions, of which 12 were mechanized and 10 motorized. The breakthrough was a bolt from the blue for Gamelin and his staff. First, they thought the Germans had 5–6 mechanized divisions. Secondly, they were convinced that the Ardennes were impassable. That is why there was no second, never mind third, line of defence at the Sedan front. That is why 250,000 of the best French troops had been withdrawn from there and transferred to Belgium without adequate replacement. That is why second-rate troops were stationed in this section when the Germans advanced, while the major reserves were concentrated along the Italian border and the Maginot Line. As a result, the German mechanized units, having broken through, moved on toward the Channel like tourists, meeting no resistance and even fuelling their tanks from French petrol pumps.

The German breakthrough is still relatively narrow (no more than 100 km at the base and much narrower at the head) and has not been consolidated by massed infantry. The breach can be sealed off rather easily, if the Anglo-French forces act quickly. Up to 800,000 Allied troops are stationed north of the breakthrough (about 250,000 British, up to 200,000 French, and more than 400,000 Belgian). The major forces of the French are located southward. Weygand is said to be preparing a crushing blow against the Germans in the next few days.

But will the Allies act quickly and decisively? I don't know. I cannot be certain.

My general impression is that if England and France hold out for 1–2 months, they may avoid defeat and possibly score a moderate victory in the long run. But will they hold out? I don't know. I cannot be certain about that either.

24 May

Events at the front are finding echoes in British domestic politics. There is no panic, but there is very great anxiety. At the same time, the prestige of Chamberlain and Co. is falling steeply. The wave of criticism and indignation against him is visibly mounting, and some (even in Conservative quarters) go so far as to demand: 'Chamberlain should be tried for high treason!'

Knowing the ways of the British, I'm hardly expecting such a radical turn. I'm not even sure Chamberlain will have to leave the government right away. Nonetheless, vexation with the former PM is very intense.

The adoption of a new act by parliament on 22 May is another symptom of the anxiety seizing broad circles of the population. According to the new act, the British government has the right to mobilize and control the nation's property and labour in the interests of the state. On paper, the law is very firm: the government can sequester or even confiscate any enterprise or plot of land, and can send any person to do any job should the interests of the war effort demand it. Somebody here has already spoken of this as 'the introduction of socialism' in England, carried out by peaceful means and within the space of just 2 hours and 43 minutes, the time needed to push the law through all the relevant legislature. See how intelligently they act, these clever Brits! Not like the wild, dishevelled Russians! Attlee, who tabled the motion in parliament, is being feted by many as the 'creator of socialism' in England.

All this, of course, is bourgeois demagogy. First, how will the law be implemented in practice? One need not be a prophet to foresee the actual course of events. Second, even if the law were to be implemented in a more or less serious way, it could create various forms of state capitalism, but not socialism, in England.

In addition to the law concerning the mobilization of property and labour (which only Gallacher and Kirkwood opposed), parliament passed, also unanimously, a law on 'treason', which significantly broadens the powers of the Home Office and effectively abolishes *Habeas Corpus*.

All is clear.

25 May

I went to see Dalton. His ministry is like a fortress: barricades of sandbags at the entrance and men with rifles inside. Dalton welcomed me most cordially. He shook my hand, seated me in the best armchair, and beamed with pleasure.

Dalton is terribly happy to be a minister and to be able to receive me in this capacity.

I spoke to Dalton about the *Selenga* and *Vladimir Mayakovsky*. He said the British government had already decided on their release, but technical execution of the decision would take a little bit more time (the matter must be coordinated with the French). Then I handed him a complaint concerning the arrest in Port Victoria, Canada, of the cargo carried by the Norwegian steamer *Norbryn*, which was bound for Vladivostok. Dalton promised to investigate the case urgently.

We then turned to more general subjects. Dalton shared many interesting details about the change of government. Then he assured me that the new government has drawn a line under the Anglo-Soviet relations of the past and wants to establish genuinely friendly relations with the Soviet Union. In particular, all Halifax's memorandums concerning the trade negotiations will be relegated to the archives. The road ahead is clear. Dalton hopes that Cripps, whom the British government is sending to Moscow, will be able to conclude a trade agreement or at least pave the way for one.

Nice words. We'll see where they take us.

26 May

I heard the following colourful story from a reliable source.

Churchill was appointed prime minister on 10 May. On the morning of 11 May Sir Horace Wilson (now referred to by all and sundry as Sir Horace Quisling), clean-shaven and impeccably dressed as usual, came to 10, Downing Street and, as if nothing had happened, proceeded to his room next to the PM's office (under Chamberlain, Wilson had offices both in the Treasury, where he is permanent undersecretary and *Head of the Civil Service*, and in 10, Downing Street). However, when he opened the door, he found 'German paratroopers' inside, who had descended and occupied his room at night: red-headed Brendan Bracken was sitting at his desk and Randolph Churchill had made himself comfortable on the couch. The two 'paratroopers' looked meaningfully at Wilson, and Wilson looked meaningfully at the 'paratroopers'. Not a single word was uttered. Sir Horace *withdrew*.

Then Wilson was invited to see the new prime minister. Churchill asked him to sit down and said: 'Sir Horace, I've heard you have plenty of work in the Treasury.'

Churchill paused and added even more emphatically: 'Yes, Sir Horace, plenty of work!'

Wilson kept a respectful silence, studying his fingertips.

Churchill sighed and continued with a threatening note in his voice: 'If I learn that you, Sir Horace, are engaged in anything other than Treasury business, ...a different job will be found for you, say, ...as governor of Iceland!'

The audience was over. And Wilson's career as the British prime minister's 'chief adviser' on all matters, particularly matters of foreign policy, was over, too.

Does this signify the end of Wilson's career as a whole? Has he left the historical stage? Who knows?...

28 May

Leopold of Belgium has negotiated a ceasefire with the Germans behind the Allies' backs, and even let the German troops pass through Belgian lines towards the British and the French. The Allies' left flank was thus exposed and they had to regroup speedily and start a full retreat towards Dunkerque. Hopes of closing the German breach, if anyone still entertained them, had to be abandoned. The Allies must concentrate simply on saving their skin. They will do well to withdraw at least part of their troops from Flanders, but even that is far from guaranteed. I heard from many military experts today that the Allied armies have three options:

(1) to evacuate, which in the present conditions means that three-quarters of them are almost sure to die or fall prisoner during the operation;

(2) to fight their way southward and join the main French forces, which is clearly impossible owing to the massive German superiority in numbers and arms;

(3) to fight to the last cartridge, knowing that new supplies are all but inconceivable, and then for those who are left to surrender.

A grim look-out. When you think that there are up to 400–450 thousand Allied forces massed in Flanders!

Dark clouds hung over parliament today. Churchill made a brief statement about the current situation which he concluded with the following words: 'The House must steel itself for grievous and painful news.' A single question was asked over and over again in the lobbies: how could this happen?

Afterwards, I went to see Lloyd George in his office. He was very worked-up and upset. I had never seen him so alarmed.

In Flanders, Lloyd George believes, the Allies are facing a very great disaster. To break through to the south is impossible and to evacuate without incurring colossal casualties and the loss of nearly all military equipment is inconceivable. The Allies have only one port left, Dunkerque, and it is not among the best. The immediate prospects are grim.

What will Hitler do once the battle in Flanders is over?

Lloyd George doubts that his next step will be an attack on England. He cannot do so while leaving a battle-worthy 4 million-strong French army in the rear. It is most likely, therefore, that having completed the operation in Flanders, Hitler will focus his attention on France. He will either force it to sign a separate peace or will march on Paris. An attack on England, furthermore, would require new methods from Hitler. He would need to make certain preparations.

I asked Lloyd George whether Hitler might come out with a proposal now for a general peace.

Lloyd George shook his head. The old man's opinion is that a general peace is impossible at present. For Hitler would undoubtedly propose conditions that would be absolutely unacceptable to England.

'What do you consider to be unacceptable conditions?' I asked. 'Colonies?'

'Oh no,' Lloyd George replied quickly. 'Colonies wouldn't be a cardinal obstacle to peace. We and the French have too many colonies to manage them properly. This has been vividly illustrated by the findings of the royal commission charged with investigating the causes of the recent disorders in Jamaica. No, we could come to an agreement with Hitler about the colonies. The main obstacle is the issue of the navy. Hitler would demand that we surrender our navy. There are some things which the English could never accept. Surrendering our navy is one of them. The English would sooner die than agree to it.'

I asked Lloyd George what he thought about the possibility of a German invasion of England.

The old man lifted his hands and said: 'A fortnight ago I would still have said that it was absolutely impossible. However, Hitler has succeeded in doing so many things which used to be considered impossible, that I refuse to make any forecast concerning an invasion.'

1 June

What is the cause of the Anglo-French defeat in Flanders?

For now, it is the military explanation which is the most obvious: namely, the Germans' massive superiority in aircraft and heavy tanks. Everything else (the wrong deployment of reserves, confusion at the point of breakthrough, etc.), is of secondary importance.

The defeat, however, has not turned into a complete catastrophe, as was feared in London following Belgium's surrender on 28 May. True, the Anglo-French army had to leave all it had on the battlefield – guns, munitions, tanks, etc. – but it seems that the majority of the men will be rescued. Of the 20 divisions (nine of them British) stationed on that front, about 75% have been brought back to England. There are grounds to believe that a further significant number will be successfully evacuated. The Anglo-French troops retreated in very good order and fought back hard and stubbornly. The Germans failed to stage a second Sedan at Dunkerque, as they had hoped. This is surely a great achievement from the purely military point of view, but… wars cannot be won by retreats, no matter how skilfully they are executed.

What will happen next?

Three options are being discussed in London political circles:

(1) Following the operations in Flanders, Hitler, together with Mussolini, may make a new peace proposal. But since, in the current situation, Hitler's conditions are sure to be of a draconian nature, they are not expected to meet with any success in London.

(2) Aware that peace with England and France cannot be achieved, Hitler may attempt to conclude a separate peace with France right after his victory in Flanders.

(3) Finally, Hitler may decide that his most advantageous move would be a direct assault on Paris.

We shall see. One senses that there was a political reason for the defeat, as well as a military one. Indeed, the latter may have been more significant than the former. For the moment, though, I lack sufficient evidence to make a definitive judgement.

4 June

Churchill's speech in parliament today made a powerful and favourable impression on MPs. This is understandable. On 28 May, the prime minister asked his colleagues to steel themselves for grim news from Flanders. Today he confessed that a week ago he had little hope that 30,000–40,000 men would be successfully rescued. Reality proved more merciful. Thanks to a tremendous effort, the valour of the troops, efficient transportation and excellent weather, 80% of the expeditionary corps trapped in Flanders (about 200,000 men) plus more than 100,000 Frenchmen were evacuated – in all, 335,000 men. An undeniable success, and one which supplied Churchill with an appreciative audience.

But that was not all. Everyone was pleased that the prime minister did not try to conceal the gravity of the current situation. He frankly stated that the Allies had sustained 'a colossal military disaster' in Flanders, that the situation at the front was very dangerous, and that, no matter how skilfully the evacuation had been carried out, evacuations do not win wars. At the same time, Churchill firmly declared that the struggle would continue and that England would even fight on her own if she had to!

At this point, I couldn't help recalling Lloyd George and the Webbs.

Anyway, that's the general mood. The events in Flanders came as a sudden and very unpleasant surprise to the British, but as far as I can judge they have not elicited panic or confusion. On the contrary: a wave of cool, stubborn, and truly British fury has evidently been gathering strength. This wave has even swept up groups on the extreme left. The British, by all appearances, will be fighting in earnest.

All this will inevitably lead to certain political consequences. The continued presence of Chamberlain and Co. in the government looks less and less feasible. Especially now that the officers and soldiers returning from Flanders take every opportunity to curse the former government which *let them down* with arms and equipment. Many demand that Chamberlain should be brought to court for high treason! Churchill, of course, will not take that step: he lacks the necessary heroism. But the removal of Chamberlain and Co. from the government at the first available opportunity becomes more and more probable. Each country has its own customs. In old Turkey, the sultans used to send silk laces to ministers due for dismissal. In contemporary Britain, the removal of Chamberlain might possibly be carried out by bestowing on him the title of 'Lord of Birmingham and Munich' upon his resignation 'on grounds of ill health'. It must be 'on grounds of ill health' – that would sound very English. Chamberlain's appearance in the House drew not a single *cheer* today. The audience held an icy silence. When Churchill appeared, he was welcomed with loud (if hardly deafening) cheers, but – which is most significant! – mainly from the opposition benches. 'His people' were largely silent, their eyes lowered. And yet, not a single cheer for Chamberlain! Just remember 13 May! Such a change in three weeks!

Yes, Chamberlain's stock is plummeting. A fresh government reshuffle is in the air. In some influential circles it is even suggested that the government may become utterly leftist, to the point of including such people as Cripps and Pritt.

We shall see. I'm not inclined to believe in rapid change in England and am all too familiar with the British weakness for rotten compromises.

After Churchill's speech I went to drink tea on the parliament terrace, where I met Randolph Churchill and Brendan Bracken. The latter has now become Winston Churchill's private parliamentary secretary. We spoke about the military situation and the immediate prospects. Where will Hitler move next?

Both are convinced that Hitler will attack Paris and try to draw Italy into the war. Britain, they maintain, will be able to help France with air and naval forces and with an army of 15–20 divisions, which, however, Britain is not in a position to send to the front right away. In such conditions, will France be able to hold out under attack? My interlocutors could not be certain.

[The following entries focus on Maisky's role in the appointment of Stafford Cripps as the British ambassador to Moscow. Churchill has often been credited with the appointment. In retrospect, he would regret not realizing sufficiently that 'Soviet Communists hate extreme Left Wing politicians even more than they do Tories or Liberals'.[42] In May, however, the newly elected prime minister was preoccupied with the disasters inflicted on the French army and the British Expeditionary Force in France. Following a familiar pattern, it was Maisky who broached with Butler the idea of conducting negotiations 'by word of mouth and not by notes' and who mentioned *en passant* Cripps's desire to act as a go-between. On 16 May, Butler conveyed the message to Halifax and urged him to 'really move a little more quickly' by appointing Maurice Peterson (who had just been recalled from Madrid to make room for Samuel Hoare) as ambassador to Moscow.[43] That evening, at the instigation of Walter Monckton,[i] the foreign secretary had Cripps to dinner. The odd collusion between Halifax and Cripps dated back to their association with the World Alliance of Christian Churches movement, which had been inspired by Cripps's father, Lord Parmoor. Cripps outlined his views on India and Russia, and offered to proceed to Moscow and exploit the changing circumstances following Hitler's incursion into Holland, Belgium and France and Churchill's appointment as prime minister.[44]

The following morning, Halifax shared the idea with Butler, who enthusiastically endorsed Cripps. Butler suggested that Cripps should be allowed 'latitude to discuss over a reasonably wide field with the Soviet authorities'.[45] Cripps's arch-rival in the Labour Party, Hugh Dalton, now the minister for economic warfare, tried in vain to dissuade Halifax from appointing Cripps. All he could do was to ensure that 'if he goes, he must have a policeman' from the Ministry of Economic Warfare and 'must have very close instruction and no power to make a settlement on his own'.[46] 'After the Cabinet meeting,' Halifax's diary records, 'I talked with [Churchill] in the garden for a few minutes, partly about an idea I had had to send Stafford Cripps on an exploratory mission to Moscow, and partly about future prospects of the war.'[47]

Visiting the Webbs on 20 May, Maisky, oblivious of the turnabout, appeared 'angry and contemptuous of Halifax – "the pious old fool"'.[48] He had been manifestly 'not very well pleased' at Halifax's insistence, at their only meeting since the formation of the new Cabinet, that any trade agreement would have to conform to Allied policy of restricting Soviet exports to Germany of commodities which were vital to the German war effort.[49] Earlier in the day, Maisky had been seen in the corridors of the Foreign Office 'much perturbed' by the news just coming in of the collapse of the French defence and the advance of the Wehrmacht as far as the Channel.[50] He could not know that at that very moment Cadogan was breaking the news to Seeds that he 'would not go back to Moscow but that Sir Stafford Cripps, the extreme Left-Winger MP, is to go there on a Special Mission as with new National Govt (which includes all prominent Labourites) it is hoped that the Kremlin may prove more amenable than it was to me as representing the infamous (!) Chamberlain'.[51]

---

[i] Sir Walter Turner Monckton, an outstanding radical barrister, he was director-general of the Ministry of Information, 1940–41, and later minister of defence under Eden during the 1956 Suez Crisis.

Summoned to Whitehall in the evening, Maisky was therefore pleasantly surprised to find Halifax amenable, 'concerned at the unnecessary misunderstandings which seemed to have developed' and proposing to send Cripps 'to explore' with the Soviet government how to advance the trade talks. Maisky was assured that not only would Cripps be equipped with full authority, but would 'of course enjoy full liberty to explore in discussion any other question which he or the Soviet Government wished to raise'.[52]

Stalin was shaken by the sweeping success of the Wehrmacht's Blitzkrieg in France. He now feared that a special mission by Cripps might provoke Hitler, who would see it as an attempt to cement an alliance between Russia and Britain in an effort to thwart further German expansion. The solution he sought was to ensure that Cripps arrived in Moscow as a normal ambassador, replacing Seeds in a routine diplomatic procedure. Maisky returned to Halifax with Stalin's qualified acceptance on 26 May. 'The Soviet Government agrees to Cripps,' Halifax entered in his diary, 'but wants him to be an Ambassador. I told Maisky we meant to send an Ambassador, and hardly supposed the Soviet Government claimed to choose him for us.' As it turned out, that is precisely what transpired.[53]]

5 June

At last, Cripps's fate has been decided! But what a story it's been!

It all began on 20 May, when Halifax summoned me and said that the Cabinet had decided to send Stafford Cripps to Moscow as *special envoy*. For about a week leading up to this, I heard 'rumours' from all sides that the new government wanted to turn a new leaf in its relations with the Soviet Union. It was being said that the prime minister would invite me for a *heart to heart talk*, that the question of the British ambassador in Moscow would be settled, and that the absurd 'correspondence' concerning trade negotiations would be annulled. Personally, I thought that the question of the British ambassador in Moscow should come first. And when Halifax began speaking to me about improving Anglo-Soviet relations, I expected to hear that either Seeds would be returning to Moscow or that the British government was going to request an agrément for a different ambassador. Halifax's news concerning a *special envoy* greatly disappointed me and I inquired rather coolly about the purpose of this envoy's mission. Halifax sighed, pondered for a moment, and said: '*To explore the possibilities*.'

'*What kind of possibilities?*' I asked.

Halifax replied that he meant the 'possibilities' of a general improvement in Anglo-Soviet relations, in particular the 'possibility' of a trade agreement with the USSR.

I expressed my surprise that even now the British government was planning merely to 'explore possibilities', instead of getting down to practical matters, but promised to convey Halifax's message to Moscow.

As was to be expected, the British scheme did not appeal to Moscow. Indeed, what need have we of some astral *special envoy*, whose obscure mission is *to explore the possibilities*? Moscow, however, took some time over the reply and finally sent it to London on 26 May. The answer was that the Soviet government was prepared to receive Cripps, or any other person authorized by the British government, only not in the capacity of a special envoy, but as an ordinary ambassador accredited on the same basis as I was accredited in London.

Meanwhile, the Foreign Office had been getting impatient. In the week between my meeting with Halifax and the arrival of the reply, Halifax and Butler asked me several times whether there had been a response from the S[oviet] G[overnment] and each time I had to disappoint them. On 24 May, Butler telephoned me and said that notwithstanding the absence of a reply from Moscow, the Foreign Office had decided, after receiving Cripps's consent, to send the latter off on his journey. The international situation, Butler said, was becoming increasingly threatening and travelling between London and Moscow more and more difficult – so why not let Cripps fly to Athens immediately and await his final instructions there. While Cripps was travelling, London and Moscow could discuss his status. What's more, time would be saved: in Athens, Cripps would be halfway to Moscow. I told Butler I would prefer a different procedure: first London and Moscow should agree upon at least the key issues concerning Cripps's visit, and then he could set out, otherwise all sorts of complications and surprises might emerge. Butler, however, stuck to his guns and there was nothing left for me to do but to convey the FO's decision to Moscow. Butler said that Cripps would fly out from England with two travelling companions on 25 May.

I received the aforesaid reply from Moscow on the morning of 26 May and delivered it to Halifax that very evening (even though it was Sunday). The foreign secretary was confused and unpleasantly surprised. He told me that the issue of a British ambassador in Moscow had only just received the attention of the government. Four days earlier, it had been decided to recall Seeds and replace him with someone else. Halifax was just about to inform me of the decision and request agrément for the new ambassador. Unfortunately, not all the procedural details had been arranged, so Halifax would only be able to inform me of the name of the new ambassador in a few days' time. But what should we do with Cripps in the meantime? After all, he had already left and was probably halfway there, perhaps even in Athens.

Halifax sighed again, pondered, and proposed a solution: let Cripps go as a *special envoy*, and in a couple of days the British government would announce the appointment of a new ambassador, who could arrive in Moscow in three or four weeks' time.

I objected, saying that the Soviet government was ready to receive one, not two, representatives, and this sole representative must be the ambassador.

Halifax began fidgeting and tried to convince me that his proposal was highly practical. As a last resort, the British government would be prepared to give Cripps the rank of ambassador for the period of his mission in Moscow, though such a solution did not appeal to Halifax personally: the rank of ambassador is usually given in cases when the *special envoy* intends to stay in the country to which he is sent for a long period of time (like Hoare, who has just been appointed 'ambassador extraordinary and plenipotentiary on a special mission' to Spain), while Cripps's mission was conceived as only a short-term measure.

'Or at least I hope so,' Halifax added.

In conclusion, Halifax asked me whether, regardless of my doubts, I could convey his suggestion to Moscow. I promised to do so.

My meeting with Halifax occurred between six and seven in the evening. At 9 p.m., when I was at home, the telephone suddenly rang and to my very great astonishment I heard the following words: 'Cripps speaking.'

'Where are you calling from?' I asked in bewilderment, thinking that perhaps he was calling from somewhere in France.

I was wrong. Cripps was in England and was calling me from the aerodrome he was meant to have left from the previous day. But for various reasons, the plane was still there and take-off was only expected the next day. On Saturday morning I had been looking for Cripps and rang him at home. Cripps had been informed of my call and now wanted to know what the matter was. I laughed to myself about the coincidence and replied: 'Two hours ago I gave the Soviet government's reply concerning your visit to Halifax. I advise you to get in touch with him before leaving.'

'What is the nature of the response?' Cripps asked.

I briefly related the key points to him. Cripps thanked me and hung up.

An hour had not passed before the telephone rang again. It was Cripps: 'I've just spoken to Halifax. Everything has been arranged. I'll receive the proper appointment. Halifax will summon you to see him on this matter tomorrow.'

'I shall be waiting,' I said. 'I wish you a good journey and a successful trip.'

Cripps thanked me and hung up once more.

The following day, 27 May, I waited in vain for Halifax's invitation. Butler finally called at about seven o'clock in the evening and asked me to come to his apartment right away. I thought he wanted to inform me of Cripps's appointment as ambassador, but that turned out not to be the case. Butler started questioning me once again about the nature of the Soviet government's reply which I had conveyed to Halifax the day before, and tried to clarify whether there was any hope of the Soviet government agreeing to receive not one but two British representatives: the ambassador and the *special envoy*. I left

Butler in no doubt. On parting, Butler told me that the matter of Cripps's status would probably be resolved the following morning.

On Tuesday, 28 May, news of the agreement between Leopold of Belgium and the Germans reached London. The mood in town was one of alarm and vexation. The atmosphere in parliament was highly charged. I met Butler in the lobby after Churchill's speech. He told me that the decision concerning Cripps had indeed been taken and that he would inform me about it officially tomorrow. Now, however, he could tell me unofficially that Cripps had been appointed ambassador.

'Ordinary or "on a special mission"?' I inquired.

'*I'm afraid*, "on a special mission",' Butler replied.

'That's a mistake,' I said. 'It will only cause complications. It would be better to drop "special mission".'

'You think that would be better?' Butler asked.

'I'm absolutely sure of it,' I concluded.

Nonetheless, when the next morning, 29 May, Butler informed me officially that Cripps had been appointed ambassador, it appeared that his rank was that of 'ambassador extraordinary and plenipotentiary on a special mission'. Butler justified this by the fact that according to British law, an MP could not occupy a post whose salary was paid for by the government (the division of legislative and executive power!). Therefore, a member of the House of Commons could not be an ordinary ambassador, but only an ambassador 'on a special mission'. Nor could he receive a salary from the Foreign Office, but must content himself with a 'grant to cover his expenses'. However, such an ambassador should present his credentials on the usual basis, and is in no way tied to the duration of absence from the native country. Butler pointed to historical precedents, the most significant of which were the cases of Goschen,[i] who was appointed ambassador to Turkey in 1880, and Edward Grey,[ii] who travelled to America in his day.

I expressed my regret at the British government not following my advice, but Butler disclosed that the Cabinet had already passed the decision and that the Foreign Office would send instructions to Le Rougetel[iii] (the chargé d'affaires in Moscow) that very day to request agrément for Cripps from the Soviet government.

'True,' Butler added, 'Cripps's appointment has not yet received royal approval, but that is not so important.'

Le Rougetel was received by C[omrade] Molotov on 31 May and requested agrément for Cripps. Surely, C[omrade] Molotov told him that the Soviet

[i] William Edward Goschen.
[ii] Edward Grey, Liberal foreign secretary, 1905–16; ambassador to the USA, 1919–20.
[iii] John Helier Le Rougetel, first secretary at the British embassy in Moscow.

government wanted an ordinary ambassador, not one 'on a special mission', adding that it was ready to receive Cripps or any other person authorized by the British government. C[omrade] Molotov also noted that the British government evidently desired to send a person of leftist leanings to Moscow. The S[oviet] G[overnment], however, thinks that it is not the personal convictions of the ambassador that matter, but the fact that he represents his government. If that condition is satisfied, we are indifferent to the ambassador's party affiliation.

C[omrade] Molotov's reply reached London on the evening of 1 June, and the Cabinet decided at once to satisfy our wishes and appoint Cripps ambassador without a 'special mission'.[54] On the morning of Sunday, 2 June, the deputy head of the northern department, Maclean, invited Korzh to probe the possibility of allowing Postan[i] to join Cripps as commercial adviser to the embassy (Postan, a Russian born in Bessarabia, emigrated in 1919 and is now a British subject and professor of economics at Cambridge). Maclean also informed Korzh that Le Rougetel had been given new instructions to request agrément for Cripps as an ordinary ambassador.

Yesterday, 4 June, Le Rougetel met C[omrade] Molotov once again, having received agrément for Cripps. C[omrade] Molotov mentioned in passing the undesirability of Postan's appointment. C[omrade] Molotov had no objections to Cripps arriving in Moscow prior to the receipt of his credentials from London.

Thus, Cripps's destiny has at last been decided. Excellent. But there is one very curious thing.

The Foreign Office mandarins are furious at Cripps's appointment. First, because he is not one of theirs, and secondly because he is Cripps. Hence all the sabotage. At first this manifested itself in the wish to send Cripps in the capacity of 'special envoy', and then in the raising of various juridical obstacles to his appointment as an ordinary ambassador (the Foreign Office planned to appoint Sir Maurice Peterson, the former ambassador in Madrid, as ambassador in Moscow). The Foreign Office 'experts' undertook an assiduous search for 'precedents', right back to the time of Queen Anne[ii] (mostly on the question of the possibility of an MP being appointed ambassador), and found none. They joyfully informed Halifax and Butler that it couldn't be done. But when the Soviet government stood fast, the British government was finally forced to bestow on Cripps the rank of ambassador on the usual basis and juridical justifications

[i] Michael Postan, born Moisei Efimovich Postan in Bessarabia in 1898, Postan studied at Kiev University, where he was an active member of a Zionist socialist party. He left Russia after the revolution and became a prominent medieval historian in Cambridge, in full denial of his past. He served as an expert on Russia in the Ministry of Economic Warfare during the war.

[ii] Queen Anne of Great Britain, 1702–14.

were immediately found. The same 'experts' soon found a small 'note' in Sir Erskine May's[i] treatise on parliamentary procedure, which states that an MP can be appointed ambassador without losing his parliamentary position. The complex problem was thus resolved. When Butler, in reply to a question in parliament, quoted this 'note', the Chamber burst into laughter.

However, I fear that the sabotaging of Cripps will not stop at that. The Foreign Office machine is too strong, while Butler, who seems to sympathize with Cripps, is not firm or influential enough to restrain the 'experts'.[55]

6 June

Yesterday morning, the Germans launched a massive new offensive on the Somme. Its aim is clear: to attack Paris. Will the French be able to cope with this onslaught?

Only the future can tell, of course, but I must openly admit that the experience of nine months of war inclines one to take a sceptical view of France's prospects. All the more so as the British cannot provide her with effective support. They will assist in the air and at sea, but can offer practically nothing on land, primarily because they left all their military equipment in Flanders, and it will take them at least three months to patch the hole, or even just part of it.

Others share my scepticism. Randolph Churchill and Brendan Bracken, whom I met in parliament the day before yesterday, spoke to me in the same vein. They consoled themselves with the thought that even in the worst scenario the war in France will last two months or so, thus giving England time to prepare to fight on her own, about which the prime minister had spoken on 4 June. As regards France, neither of them was very confident.

Today, Boothby came over for lunch. He also admitted that, while he heartily wishes for France to succeed, he is far from certain, deep inside, that the French will be able to withstand the assault. Moreover, he does not exclude the possibility of a German invasion of the British Isles (according to Boothby, nor does the prime minister). As regards Churchill's assurances about the continuation of the war even in the event of the Germans capturing these islands, Boothby is far from sanguine.

'All that is all very well,' he says. 'The Empire will fight on until it wins! But what kind of Empire? It's quite obvious that if the British Isles fall, the Empire as we know it will cease to exist. What will the new Empire be like? Will there even be one?'

---

[i] Thomas Erskine May, British constitutional theorist.

According to Boothby, opposition to Chamberlain and Co. is mounting. Major changes in the government may be expected in the near future. But how could opposition not be mounting? I asked Boothby (he is now parliamentary secretary to the minister of food) about the country's reserves of the most essential foodstuffs. It turns out that these reserves, while varying greatly according to the individual product, are in the majority of cases insufficient for more than two to four weeks. Even the available wheat supplies will last no longer than two or three months. I was staggered.

'What's Morrison been doing all this time?' I asked (Morrison was the minister until early April).

Boothby shrugged his shoulders. Since being appointed, Boothby has been doing his utmost to establish ample food reserves in the country, but this will take time.

10 June

My scepticism regarding the ability of France to mount successful resistance to Germany is proving warranted. Today is the sixth day of the German offensive on the Somme, and the French army is already retreating, though still in an organized way, while Paris is being evacuated. A few more days and Paris's fate will most likely be decided one way or another, and then… Who knows what will happen then? It's hard to imagine France without Paris, and if Paris falls into German hands will France be able to continue any kind of meaningful struggle? Time will tell.

The situation has been complicated still further by Italy's decision to enter the war on the side of Germany. This means that France will have to wage war on two fronts, in the north and the south. The problems are piling up. How will Spain behave? If Spain also comes out against the Allies, which is quite possible, France will be surrounded.

Yes, the next few weeks will be exceptionally dramatic and will play an enormous role in world history.

* * *

I met Butler today. I raised once again the subject of the *Selenga* and *Vladimir Mayakovsky*. My solution was that we take back the ships minus the cargo confiscated by the French (tungsten, molybdenum, etc.), and receive compensation in cash from the French. Butler jumped at the proposal and promised to get in touch with the French immediately. I fear that the latter have other things on their mind. Nevertheless, I'll try to rescue the ships while a French government still exists capable of sending instructions to Indochina.

Butler is in a gloomy mood. He regards the situation in France as critical (we spoke before Italy's declaration of war). Paris is in jeopardy. If the Germans take Paris, the French could still resist on the Loire, but they would have to abandon the Maginot Line. Reynaud and Weygand would undoubtedly want to fight to the death, but there is also a 'peace party' in France (Laval, Flandin and others). If Italy enters the fray, the situation will become even more daunting. And if Spain joins in, France will be besieged on three sides. A thoroughly bleak look-out. The British help the French all they can, but what can they really do? They have many men, but no weapons. Especially after their losses in Flanders. They are sending their planes to France – as many as they can.

Butler then spoke about what would happen to Europe should Hitler win. He would become the master of Europe. Is that really in the interests of the Soviet Union? After all, the USSR, like everyone else, is interested in maintaining equilibrium in Europe.

I replied that the Soviet Union could take care of itself regardless of the situation in Europe. I added, not very politely, that Butler's arguments were somewhat belated. I nodded towards the room next to his office where the Non-Intervention Committee once held its meetings and said: 'If England and France had taken a different stand then, they wouldn't have found themselves in such a grave position today.'

Butler did not object to this.

* * *

I saw Dalton this morning. He was forthright as usual, full of energy, and chuffed with his ministerial post. I visited him on a 'silly matter': we bought 90–100,000 chests of tea in Hong Kong, and wanted to load them onto a steamer bound for Vladivostok. All of a sudden, the local authorities prohibited loading until they got the go-ahead from London. Dalton shrugged his shoulders, laughed, and said in Russian: '*Chai... Chai...* [Tea... Tea].'

He promised to make enquiries and settle the matter.

Then we discussed other topics. Dalton is glad that the Cripps issue has finally been resolved. He cursed the Foreign Office, whose people are far too bogged down in the routine of diplomatic formalities. Dalton had been constantly advising them to drop this 'nonsense' and simply appoint Cripps ambassador, but they wouldn't listen to him. He's pleased that Cripps is now ambassador and expects him to conclude a *barter trade agreement* before long.

Rumours have been doing the rounds this week that in tomorrow's closed session of parliament the MPs will give Chamberlain and Co. a hiding for their former sins, after which the government will be reshuffled towards the left. Dalton denied these rumours. The Cabinet has decided that in view of the critical situation in France, now is not the right time for a reshuffle. However, much will depend on the behaviour of the House. An interesting detail: Chamberlain, according to Dalton, is now the most 'radical' member of the government as far as the conduct of the war is concerned. Sensing that a storm is on its way, he is covering his tracks.

As regards matters in France, Dalton is also fairly pessimistic, though he is adamant that England will fight alone should the worst come to the worst. He considers an invasion of the British Isles unlikely, and believes that nothing else can break the British people's will to resist. Time must be gained, and then the balance of forces will shift in the Allies' favour. Dalton reckons that by the beginning of 1941 the British and German air forces will be numerically equal, while in terms of combat efficacy the British will catch up even sooner, as their machines and pilots are far superior to those of Germany. According to Dalton, the average ratio of British to German air losses is 1:4. This is difficult to believe, but I have heard it more than once from very well-informed people.

11 June

Aras paid an unexpected visit. He informed me that he had just been to see Halifax at the latter's invitation.

Halifax had immediately asked Aras whether he had received any instructions from Ankara in connection with Italy's entry into the war. Aras said he had not. Halifax then expressed his point of view and made it perfectly clear to Aras that he expected Turkey to declare war on Italy immediately.

Aras replied that he had nothing to say on behalf of the T[urkish] G[overnment] for the moment, but he could share his personal thoughts if Halifax so wished. He then expounded the following view: Turkey will certainly remain loyal to its obligations under the pact, but the factor of expediency must be taken into account when fulfilling these obligations. What does that mean? It means that before taking any decisions on concrete steps, Turkey must consider three points: (1) the importance of safeguarding peace in the Balkans; (2) her friendship with the USSR; and (3) the need to maintain normal relations with Germany. The current direction of Turkish policy will be defined in the light of these considerations.

I asked Aras how Halifax reacted to this. Aras said that he was in complete agreement. Was he really?

Aras then asked Halifax whether arrangements might be put in place for Turkey to spend some of its British credits on the purchase of goods in the USA and the USSR? Halifax promised to clarify this matter in Cabinet.

Then Aras started asking quite insistently whether or not I approved of his reply to Halifax. It was important for him to know this in order to write his report to Ankara.

I replied that his request placed me in a rather awkward position: how could I approve or disapprove of a statement made by the ambassador of another state? All I could do was remind him of the essence of our current policy: to observe neutrality and counteract by all available means the spread of hostilities to new countries and territories, especially neighbouring countries. Aras could draw his own conclusions.

Aras hastened to assure me that he was fully satisfied with my answer and repeated once again that the safety of the Balkans and the Near East depends entirely on close cooperation with the Soviet Union.

So it seems that for the moment Turkey will stay out of the war.

12 June

Events at the front are taking on an ever more ominous hue. Deep pessimism about the immediate prospects reigns in government circles. It's thought that Paris will fall any day now, France will be occupied by the Germans, and the French government will soon move to London. Nonetheless, everybody remains adamant: whatever may happen to France, England is ready to fight on her own.

Italy's entry into the war has not made a particularly strong impression here. There are two reasons for this: first, it was not unexpected, and everyone had already accepted the fact; second, the British have the greatest contempt for the fighting qualities of the Italians (some years ago I heard that Cadogan had called them '*long distance runners*'). I don't know whether this contempt is justified. It could include a big dose of *wishful thinking*. We shall see.

* * *

The more serious the situation becomes, the more intense is the 'psychological assault' against me. Politicians, journalists, public figures – one way or another, they all try to put before me the following questions: Can the Soviet Union really remain indifferent to events in Western Europe? Do the defeat of France and the massively increasing threat to England really leave the USSR unmoved? Does the tremendous strengthening of Germany, and its transformation into the real hegemon of Europe, really not clash with Soviet interests?… Behind these questions lurks another, which is rarely asked openly: Why don't you want to help us? I receive a stream of letters, some signed, some not, in the same vein.

To all these questions, and to all this 'psychological assault', I tend to respond tersely but emphatically: 'Don't worry! The Soviet Union will be able to take care of itself in any situation and under any circumstances.'

14 June

Paris has fallen. German troops are parading down the Champs-Élysées and the Grands Boulevards. Hitler has ordered flags to be hoisted and bells to be rung all over Germany. No wonder! Even Bismarck never saw such a victory in 1871.

The French army has retreated beyond Paris. The army seems to maintain relatively good order and is still battle-worthy, albeit battered and tired. The Germans, too, have apparently sustained great losses, are exhausted and drained. But the victory, of course, will lift their spirits. The French, I was told by Butler yesterday, had only 75 divisions. The Germans moved 100 against them, and now have as many as 120 (20 fresh divisions recently arrived from the Siegfried Line, where Italians replaced them). In addition, the Germans had an enormous advantage over the French in aircraft and tanks. The British aid after the defeat in Flanders amounted to no more than six divisions plus a large quantity of aircraft. Is it any surprise that the Germans captured Paris?

What will happen next?

Reports suggest that a number of ministers inside the French government (eight are mentioned) are in favour of an immediate peace treaty – a general one if possible, or a separate peace if this can't be avoided. So far Reynaud has succeeded in prevailing on them to wait and give him a last chance to get real and meaningful help from the United States and England. Hence his *final appeal* to Roosevelt yesterday. At the meeting of the Supreme War Council held on 11 and 12 June, the British government promised France more active assistance: British troops are now being transported across the Channel in greater numbers. Ten to fifteen divisions are mentioned. Will this really be sufficient to help put France back on her feet?…

Evidently, the English have the following plan: to strengthen the French, prevent a separate peace, and gain time for their own preparations and to obtain equipment from the United States.

The other day I met Middleton in parliament. We discussed current events. Middleton came to the following conclusion: 'The young generation of England, France, Germany and Italy will be annihilated in this war. The young generation of Russia will inherit the whole of Europe.'

Agniya and I went to the Keyneses for lunch two days ago. We found them in a state of extreme pessimism. Lopukhova is utterly lost and stunned, and told Agniya of her feeling that the old world is dying and a new one is being born.

The new world obviously frightens her and she doesn't know what to do. She repeated several times: 'If the British and the French were not ready for war, then why did they declare it?'

Keynes himself tries to behave in a manner befitting an economist and philosopher, but he confessed to taking a very gloomy view of the future. The ruling classes of England have gone to seed. That is now absolutely clear. New forces ought to take their place. Which forces? Keynes does not have a clear answer to that question. But he is convinced that England will fight long and hard, even if she is on her own. Keynes discounts the possibility of a German invasion of the isles.

Butler told me yesterday: 'The war is having a great effect on England's internal condition. Great changes are afoot. I don't think we'll have a revolution, but I think we will see rapid evolution.'

'In what direction?' I asked.

Butler replied: 'Men like Bevin will assume much greater importance in our public and political life.'

So, Butler is putting his stake on Labour's right flank. Maybe he is right. Maybe the next phase of British political development will be marked by the dominant role of men like Citrine, Bevin and Morrison. And then what?

Time will tell.

15 June

According to Czech sources, the main features of Hitler's 'plan for the organization of Europe' allegedly boil down to the following.

Alsace-Lorraine goes to Germany, Savoy and Nice to Italy, and the Pyrenees to Spain. France is disarmed and turns into a de facto German protectorate under an obedient French government. Many German colonists are transferred to France and settled there (including former residents of the Baltic countries). The greater part of the French colonies in Africa are to be divided between Italy and Germany, with Germany, of course, getting the lion's share.

Following its defeat, England also becomes a de facto German protectorate, on approximately the same terms as France. But the British Empire remains intact, with its centre in Canada. It incorporates, as before, Australia, New Zealand, and England's Asian colonies, including India. This is done in order for the USSR not to profit at the expense of British colonies in Asia when the world is 're-partitioned'.

At the end of the war, Germany and Italy will exploit the Balkans together, ousting the USSR. The latter will be left only with Bessarabia.

The same sources say that Hitler forced Mussolini into the war by setting him a dilemma: either Italy enters the war immediately or Berlin would come to an agreement with Moscow on the Balkan question, overlooking the interests of Italy.

* * *

Prytz told me today that at the request of his government he recently suggested the following plan to Halifax: northern Norway would be declared a neutral zone, both belligerents would withdraw their troops from there, and Sweden would send small military units to monitor the process. The Swedish government would be ready to enter into negotiations on this matter with Germany. Halifax's reply was just typical: 'But your proposal is… How can I put it… *very irregular*.'

'But don't you find,' Prytz retorted, 'that the time we live in is also *very irregular*?'

After lengthy persuasion, Halifax agreed to seek the British government's opinion on the matter.

And four days later the British simply cleared out of Narvik, leaving the battlefield to the Germans!

16 June

I visited Lloyd George at Churt. The old man is in a very gloomy mood. He said he had been full of anxiety about the outcome of the war from the very beginning. His forecasts had been far from rosy. However, reality has far exceeded his most pessimistic expectations.

The Germans have completely 'revolutionized' war. The Allies turned out to be unprepared for this new war, in both the military and political spheres. Thanks to their criminal short-sightedness and class limitations, all these Baldwins, Chamberlains, Simons, Halifaxes, Daladiers and Bonnets failed to foresee anything and did nothing to avert the deadly danger.

'They deserve to be punished severely by their peoples. They ought to be *impeached*. Instead, they remain in government! But they will soon be gone.'

France, according to Lloyd George, finds herself in a hopeless situation. She has been comprehensively defeated. Either she will sign a separate peace or she will be entirely occupied by the Germans within a couple of weeks. The French Empire and the French navy may survive, but France will cease to exist as a great European power. The only army on the continent (west of the Vistula) that could confront the German army has been crushed. The balance of power in Europe has altered drastically as a result. Germany becomes the hegemon of Europe.

There is still England. Peace between England and Germany is impossible. The Germans would certainly demand the surrender of the British navy (Hitler recently stressed once again that his aim is the destruction of British sea power), which is out of the question for the British. They would rather die than surrender their fleet. So everything points to war. According to Lloyd George, it will be a very difficult war. He does not even exclude the possibility of a German invasion of the isles, if not by sea, then from the air. Lloyd George proceeds from the following approximations: the Germans have 20,000–25,000 machines (compared with the Allies' 8,000), including 1,000 transport planes capable of carrying up to 50 men each. So the Germans can drop 50,000 men in England in one go. These transport planes will not have far to go – leaving from Boulogne, Calais, Ostend, etc. – so the turn-over will be fast. Even taking into account British resistance and German losses, the Germans can land a 100–150,000-strong army on the British Isles in one day. The transport of heavy tanks, guns and so on may present certain difficulties, but... Hitler has proved more than once that he can achieve the impossible.

Of course, England will put up a fierce fight. But Churchill's predecessors left him an awful legacy: there is an acute shortage of aircraft, tanks, artillery, machine-guns and even rifles. The previous governments had no idea of what contemporary warfare means. Hanging is too good for men like Burgin (ex-minister of supply). Heroic efforts are being made to make up for lost time, but one can't make up for years of neglect overnight. The United States is willing to help England by all available means – in essence they have already entered the war – but the Americans do not have matériel ready in their storehouses either. They need to produce it first, and that takes time. Right now the USA can provide aircraft, tanks and so on in the hundreds, but it's thousands that are needed. The time factor is working against the Allies. That's why Lloyd George looks to the future with great anxiety.

'Do you deem it possible,' I asked him, 'that the British government could be evacuated to Canada?'

'Only as a last resort,' replied Lloyd George, 'but should that happen, it would mean that England had left Europe for good. Of course, many console themselves with the thought that Canada might become the new centre of the British Empire. Maybe. But that would be a very different British Empire!'

The old man waved his hand in displeasure and continued: 'But if France perishes and England is defeated, that would be the end of the "European balance of power" which has been the basis of European politics for centuries and which has guaranteed the more or less independent development of the European nations. What would be left? Omnipotent Germany, drunk on its triumph and victories. And the USSR, one on one with Germany. What does the S[oviet] G[overnment] think about this? Can't anything be done to stop Hitler's march of victory through Europe?'

I replied: 'The Soviet Union will be able to take care of itself under any conditions. You should have no doubt about it.'

Lloyd George shook his finger at me and said: 'Beware before it is too late!'

'What do you mean by that?' I asked. 'After all, we do take precautionary measures.'

'Yes, I can see that,' Lloyd George laughed. 'I fully understand and approve your actions in Lithuania… If you eventually clash with Germany, you'll win. Russia cannot be conquered. But victory will cost you untold effort and blood. The might of the German war machine should not be underestimated.'

We then spoke on other subjects, but the old man kept returning to the role of the USSR in the present events. I gathered from certain of his remarks that he expected the USSR to help England by selling planes and tanks.

17 June

France has capitulated. The F[rench] G[overnment] was in virtually continuous session all day yesterday in Bordeaux. They were discussing Roosevelt's reply to Reynaud's appeal for help, and also the general situation at the front. Judging by the communiqué released during the course of the day, it was obvious that the end was near. Late in the evening Reynaud resigned, whereupon a new government of a rightist-fascist bent, headed by Pétain,[i] was formed (Pétain, Weygand, Darlan,[ii] Chautemps and others). This morning the French government approached the Germans with a proposal for an armistice.

France has capitulated. Why?

Undoubtedly, Germany proved incomparably more powerful than France in terms of army strength, mechanization and aviation. But that is far from all; it may not even be the main thing. I'm growing more and more convinced that France capitulated because of its internal disintegration. The rule of the '200 families' had its effects. It split France, poisoned its political atmosphere, emasculated it militarily, and paved the way for its present defeat. More than that, it introduced elements of decay into the French army and undermined its combat efficiency.[56] For isn't it strange that during all these recent days I have not once heard of French soldiers using hand-grenades against German tanks? And yet such methods are highly effective and were used by our soldiers during the Civil War and by the Republicans in Spain.

What will England do now?

Clearly, she will fight alone. There is nothing else for it. I remember what Randolph Churchill told me a couple of weeks ago: 'Even if the worst comes to the worst, France can survive without its Empire. Her economy is such that

[i] Henri Philippe Pétain, marshal, head of the Vichy government in France, 1940–44.

[ii] Jean François Darlan, French fleet admiral in 1939; vice-president of the Council of Ministers, secretary of state for foreign affairs and the navy, acting secretary of state for war, and minister for national defence, under the Pétain government, 1941–42.

even if she loses her colonies she will be able to fare quite well as a second-rank power, rather like Sweden on a larger scale. England's position is different: if we lose our Empire, we shall become not a second-rank, but a tenth-rank power. We have nothing. We will all die of hunger. So, there is nothing for it but to fight to the end.'

In England, news of France's capitulation was received with dismay and shock. In the street today one could often hear talk of the impossibility of fighting alone. Politicians and journalists sighed voluptuously: 'Ah, if only a revolution would break out in France and the Pétain government could be overthrown!'

Even the Tories have been speaking in a similar vein. No wonder! Some have hinted rather openly that a revolution in France is needed as a bait to draw the USSR into the war. 'Paris is well worth a mass,' said Henry IV. 'The participation of the Soviet Union in the war against Germany is well worth a revolution in France,' say British Tories today. They expect little from the United States. Even if the United States were to enter the war, the effect of this would not be felt in practice for another year. The United States has neither a trained army, nor a sufficient quantity of aircraft, nor ammunition. All this still needs to be created. But time is short.

18 June

Dalton asked me over to the ministry. He requested that we expedite a visa for Gifford, whom he is sending to Moscow as commercial secretary to help Cripps (instead of Postan). He expressed his hope for the quick signing of a simple barter agreement and inquired in this connection whether we could sell a certain amount of weapons and planes to England. I replied that there was not much I could say on this matter. Obviously, the British government will raise this question through Cripps in Moscow. Dalton said his ministry was working on the matter of communication routes with the Soviet Union. Apart from the northern route (via Arkhangelsk and Murmansk), the British also envisage a southern route (via the Persian Gulf and Iran). That's war for you!

We discussed more general subjects as well. On the whole Dalton approves of our actions in the Baltic (just compare that with the response to the Finnish events three or four months ago!). He also asked me about our intentions in respect of Rumania and suggested that once the Soviet Union finds an appropriate moment to act, it should not content itself with Bessarabia alone, but should occupy the entire oil-rich region! What generosity! I responded to Dalton's advice with these words: 'The USSR does not grab foreign lands, even if they are rich in oil.'

* * *

I spent the afternoon in parliament. The dismay and shock of yesterday have passed. Today's speech by Churchill has lifted morale. His firm statement that England, regardless of France's defeat, will fight to the end was met with loud applause from all the benches. The prime minister's arguments about the impossibility of a German invasion of the isles made a great impression. This was the only subject of conversation in the lobbies.

So, first England and France were waging war against Germany; now Germany and Italy are waging war against England. And this war is beginning to escalate. At the same time, the tide of indignation against Chamberlain and Co. is rising. Had it not been for Churchill, who stubbornly defends him, Neville would have been kicked out of government a long time ago. Why did he choose this course? Various explanations are suggested. Some say 'out of gratitude' for the allegedly 'honourable' manner in which Chamberlain ceded to him the post of prime minister. According to others, Churchill thinks Chamberlain will be less harmful within the government than outside it. There's no denying that Chamberlain has a large group of MPs behind him. Inside the Cabinet, Chamberlain is a 'hostage'; outside it, he would start scheming against the prime minister. A third group holds that Churchill's abiding priority is to prevent a split in the Tory Party, which could happen if Chamberlain left the government.

However that may be, Chamberlain and Co. are still in the government. Since many Tories are well aware of the danger of such a situation, a number of Chamberlain's 'friends' have been advising him to 'make a gesture' and resign, but he remains deaf to these exhortations. The political wits have even coined a title for the king to confer upon Chamberlain after he resigns: 'Lord of Birmingham and Munich'.

The end of today's sitting was marked by a rather unusual demonstration. The Labourite John Morgan[i] took the floor and suggested that the House should mark the fact of Cripps's arrival in Moscow and his accession to the post of ambassador. The suggestion was welcomed with cheers from all sides. Furthermore, MPs turned their faces to the diplomatic gallery, where I was sitting in the front row. Morgan then wished Cripps every success in his new job. Friendly approval echoed round the Chamber once more and Churchill, half-rising from the government bench and looking in my direction, waved his hand in salutation. Other ministers followed the PM's example. Evidently, this was a sudden demonstration which had not been prepared in advance, since my presence in the diplomatic gallery at that moment was a matter of sheer

[i] John Morgan, Labour MP for Doncaster, 1938–41.

chance. At the end of Churchill's speech the diplomatic gallery had emptied out. I too went out into the lobbies. After a while I suddenly noticed that the MPs in the crowded lobbies were rushing back to the Chamber. When I asked what was happening, I was told that Lloyd George was speaking. I also rushed back to the diplomatic gallery, but caught only the concluding phrases of the old man's speech. And then there followed the demonstration.

* * *

The Bulgarian minister Momchilov paid me a visit. He is in a very dark mood. He is entirely convinced that now that France has been defeated, events will begin to unfold in the Balkans, for the majority of Hitler's land forces have been freed up. According to Momchilov, events will probably develop as follows. In order to resolve their oil problem once and for all, Germany and Italy will set their sights on Iraq and Iran via Egypt or possibly via the Balkans and Turkey. Even if they choose the first option, Turkey and the Balkan states will not be able to stay out of the war. Momchilov has heard that the Italians have promised to take an active part in military operations in the Iraq–Iran direction, but nowhere else.

23 June[57]

Today it is already clear that the decision of the British government to continue fighting, notwithstanding the capitulation of France, has proved popular among the masses. It has gone down particularly well among the workers. The initial perplexity and confusion have passed. On the contrary, a surge of cold, stubborn, truly British fury is gathering momentum. The English, it seems, will resist to the end.

Such is the general backdrop. Upon it, some very significant patterns can be discerned.

The workers are more determined than anyone. Whether in the industrial north, or among the miners of South Wales, or the iron-workers of London, or the textile workers of Lancashire, the mood is the same: We shan't let Hitler into our country! Down with Hitler! Down with fascism! This mood includes a broad range of variations among the workers: from the brutally jingoist slogan, 'We'll have no peace until we slaughter all the Germans' (the most backward strata) to the newly emerging conception that 'the war, which started out as an imperialist one, has changed against the will of its initiators into a just war of defence!' (the most progressive strata, including a few communists). All anti-war speeches and talks have ceased. The communists, of course, take a rather specific position, but I'm speaking here about the broad working masses.

It is from this point of view that the masses assess people and actions: that which facilitates resistance is popular, that which prevents it is not. Morrison and Bevin are now very popular, as they have boosted military production and expunged the most insolent forms of capitalist influence in their departments. Churchill is popular because the masses see him as the only man who can 'win the war'. In contrast, irritation and indignation against Chamberlain and Co. grow with every passing day. A few days ago, a meeting of 25,000 South Wales miners demanded that Chamberlain be tried for treason! Certain aircraft factories have also witnessed difficulties in connection with the extension of the working week to seven days. The workers said: We are ready to work seven days a week for the defence of the nation, but we don't want to work seven days for this government (on the whole, however, the prolongation of the working day, etc. has met few obstacles). Opposition to Chamberlain is growing, and if Churchill does not relieve his Cabinet of this dangerous burden in time, the whole government may be put in jeopardy.

There is a clear split in the attitudes of the ruling classes. Churchill's group stands for war to the end, for the sake of which it is ready to meet many of the workers' demands in the sphere of domestic and economic policy. Chamberlain's group, on the contrary, is scared stiff about the social and political consequences of the war and is ready to conclude a 'rotten peace' at any given moment, in order to retain its capitalist privileges. They produce a simple argument: better to be 'rich' in a small empire than 'poor' in a big one. This group has not given up hope of diverting Hitler to the east at some point in the war. Naturally, these people are keeping silent. Chamberlain even tries to play the 'extremist' in Cabinet in all that regards the conduct of the war. Nevertheless, Chamberlain's group is a real 'fifth column'. One detail is especially indicative. Chamberlain's circles are now spreading the propaganda that it is not Chamberlain, but Baldwin who is to blame, since he pushed off the throne such a 'good king' as Edward VIII. Yet Edward was known as a fascistic Germanophile. Isn't the 'fifth column' thinking of promoting Edward VIII to the role of British Führer when the moment is right? Time will tell.

So, war to the end. But what is the general strategic plan of the British government? Summing up the information available to me, I can venture the following.

The British government plans to remain on the defensive until about the end of this year: there are not enough men, arms and aircraft. By the beginning of 1941, the British government hopes to have overcome these difficulties, to gain superiority over the Germans in the air, and to move on to the offensive. Until then, England must be turned into an unassailable fortress, capable of repelling every German assault. In addition, it will carry out a rigorous naval blockade of Germany and Italy, which means, in the current situation, a blockade of all Europe. The French navy and French colonies are expected to play a major role in this.

At the root of this strategic plan lie fairly complicated motives. First, the shortage of men and arms, which the British government hopes to eliminate within the next six months with the help of the United States and the Empire. Secondly, an assumption that Germany will exhaust itself (especially in the spheres of oil, war resources, food, etc.). Thirdly, the hope that the international situation will change in favour of England. This envisages, first, the entry of the United States into the war and, secondly, if not the direct participation of the Soviet Union in the war then at least the worsening of its relations with Germany. The latter is reckoned as highly probable, in the event, for instance, of Germany and Italy moving to the Balkans and the Near East 'in search' of Iranian and Iraqi oil.

How realistic is the British government's strategic plan?

The answer to this question depends on the answers to two others. Is Germany capable of starving out England? And is Germany capable of carrying out a serious invasion of England?

The answer to the first question is negative. First, England herself produces up to 50% of the food products she needs. Second, British tonnage amounted to 21 million tons before the war. About 1 million was lost in the course of the war, but was then recovered through the construction of new ships and the seizure of German and Italian vessels. Up to 7 million Dutch, Norwegian and Danish tons have also fallen into England's hands. So the total tonnage at England's disposal amounts to the massive figure of 28 million tons. Even if England loses 2–3 million tons in the next few months as a result of the intensification of the war, this will not be of decisive importance. The Germans, of course, will attack the ports as well. But even if they destroy half the ports, the other half, working day and night (the ports currently work only by day) will still be able to process the cargoes required by the country. All this means that England may have significant difficulties in supplying food and raw materials in the new phase of the war, but it cannot be starved out.

What about an invasion?

Very energetic measures are being taken to repel an invasion. There are 1.25 million troops inside the country (including the best units), and more than 1 million are undergoing training. The eastern and southern coasts have been fortified with artillery batteries, machine-gun nests, etc. Large forces have been concentrated in the coastal areas. Special mechanized units have already been organized, and more will be created. They are stationed at strategically important points and can easily be deployed in any direction. Detachments, anti-aircraft batteries and fighter squadrons have been positioned in the most crucial locations all over the country. Signs and directions have been removed from all roads, and barricades, bastions, fortifications and so on are being constructed. Airfields have been mined and are guarded by strong units. All potential landing sites are being rendered unsuitable for planes. A *Local Defence Volunteers* corps, numbering close to 500,000, has been set up (admittedly, not all have weapons yet). German and Italian residents are being interned, and some are even being sent to Canada. Some repressive measures have also been taken against British fascists (Mosley[i] and others have been arrested). The greater part of the navy is in home waters. The air force is ready to rebuff an invasion. Negotiations are being conducted with Ireland about stationing Canadian and Australian troops there (but not English troops, so as not to irritate the Irish); apparently, they are going well.

Is all that enough to prevent an invasion? On paper it looks sufficient. When you start counting England's defensive advantages, you see that the British are holding a full hand of cards. But will they know how to play them? I don't know. The current war has already brought so many surprises, the Germans have displayed so much skill and invention, and the Allies such helplessness and unpreparedness, that I wouldn't vouch for anything at the present time.

Time will tell.

25 June

The American ambassador Kennedy lunched with me today. He takes a gloomy view of British prospects. He doubts that England will be able to wage a long war single-handedly. He accepts the possibility of a German invasion of the isles. He thinks it utterly inevitable that England will be almost completely destroyed by air raids. Kennedy says the United States will be helping England in every way, with arms, aircraft, etc., over the next few months, but will hardly enter into the war before the presidential election, unless something extraordinary happens, such as the Germans using gas. Kennedy scolded the British government for failing to come to an agreement with the Soviet Union last year and said that the upper classes of British society are '*completely rotten*'. A rather unexpected judgement from a man of his status![58]

* * *

I was in parliament today. Churchill's statement concerning the latest events in France elicited great anxiety about the fate of the French fleet. People could talk about nothing else in the lobbies. In the corridor I bumped into Lady Astor, who started assuring me that communists are to blame for every evil: they're the real 'fifth column' which prevented France from standing its ground! It was both ridiculous and infuriating. Eventually, my patience ran out and I

---

[i] Sir Oswald Mosley, founder in 1932 of the British Union of Fascists and its leader.

said rather impolitely: '*My dear Lady Astor*, if you want to see a genuine "fifth column", just look around you.'

* * *

Saw Alexander, first lord of the Admiralty. I asked him about the chances of a German invasion. Alexander assured me categorically that a major invasion was impossible: the navy would not allow it. Even if Hitler sent a thousand planes to attack at once. Alexander spoke guardedly about the future of the French fleet, but said that even if the entire French fleet in the Mediterranean were to fall into German hands, this would not have a decisive effect: the British would not allow the fleet to pass through Gibraltar and the chances of a German invasion of England would not increase. Is that really so?...

* * *

Clement Davis,[i] an Independent Liberal MP, dropped in. He is in total despair. He says that the ruling classes of England are rotten through and through and compares their present state to that of the French aristocracy on the eve of the Great French Revolution. Hence their criminally short-sighted policy of recent years, which has led to catastrophe. Even now, with the change of government, the situation remains most unsatisfactory. Morrison and Bevin have done a bit to increase production, but they use old methods and operate within the old framework. As a result, there are still many failures and deficiencies. It is even worse with Churchill. He, of course, is full of determination and desire to carry on the war, but in order to save England at this crucial moment it is necessary to mobilize the enthusiasm of the masses. It is necessary to make this war a 'people's war'. That is why Davis launched a campaign for the universal arming of the population two weeks ago. But a different government is needed to awaken the genuine enthusiasm of the people – without Chamberlain, Simon and Co. The masses demand it. A powerful wave of discontent with the present government is rising in the country. But Churchill pays no attention to it and stubbornly protects the men of Munich. Why? Davis thinks he is doing so out of sentimentality: Churchill believes that Chamberlain displayed exceptional 'nobility' in ceding the post of prime minister. Total nonsense! Chamberlain simply had no choice. Protecting the men of Munich may eventually lead to an explosion, to the collapse of the present government and its replacement with another one. Davis envisages a government headed by Lloyd George, in which the old man would enlist bold and energetic 'young men'. But won't this change occur too late for anything to be done?...

---

[i] Clement Edward Davis, supporter of the National Government in the early 1930s, Welsh MP Davis resigned from the Liberal Party in 1939. He subsequently became chairman of the All Party Action Group and later leader of the Liberal Party, 1945–56.

'No matter how the war ends,' said Davis, 'the present rulers of England will be unable to continue ruining it. An entirely new world will emerge after the war. The old world will be razed to the ground.'

It is worth pointing out that Davis is the director of a big capitalist company!

* * *

Garvin came for lunch yesterday. He told me about a conversation he had with Ironside at the beginning of the war. Ironside was *cock sure* at the time. He pictured the war as an extended, calm period of waiting behind the Maginot and Siegfried Lines. The economic blockade was supposed to do the rest. Ironside's attitude towards Hitler was one of the utmost contempt: 'What will some degenerate peasant manage to achieve?'

As for the relative value of the German and Franco-English armies, Ironside expressed himself in the following way: 'We and the French have many old officers who fought in the last war. That is a great advantage. The German army consists of greenhorns who never smelled gunpowder.'

These statements resound with a terrible irony today. Ironside proved a useless chief of staff. What if he proves to be a similarly poor chief of home defence?

27 June

I saw Lloyd George this morning at Thames House. Today he was in a better mood than at our last meeting, on 16 June. He thinks that even though England has lost a great deal in the course of this war, she still has enough cards to play and at least avoid defeat. She just needs to know how to play them. Does she?

That's where Lloyd George's doubts begin. The first condition of a successful game is a good government, a government which can arouse the enthusiasm of the masses, the workers. The workers are the sole hope. The ruling classes are rotten through and through. There is no point in seeking salvation there. There are individual exceptions of course, like Churchill, Eden and others, but the greater part of the ruling classes is rotten to the core. It is essential to kindle the enthusiasm of the broad masses. Is the present government capable of doing that? No, it is not. Is the new government which England needs conceivable?

That question now hinges on Churchill. Is he ready to part with Chamberlain and Co.? Is he ready to bring fresh blood into the government? Is he ready to rely on a coalition of workers, Liberals and those Conservatives who support the prime minister? If he is ready to do this, England still has a chance of winning the war – that is, of avoiding defeat. If he is not ready, the situation may soon become critical. It seems to Lloyd George that Churchill is not yet prepared to take the necessary steps, as he is too scared of splitting the Conservative Party.

I asked Lloyd George whether he thought peace was possible.

The old man answered: 'As you know, I advocated peace at the start of the war. I thought it possible. But then Denmark, Norway, Holland and Belgium were intact and France had not been defeated. At that point we could talk with Germany as equals. Now the situation is different. Today we would be cast in the role of supplicants. Germany would dictate its conditions to us. Its first condition would be the surrender of our navy. The British will never agree to that. They would rather die. In a situation like this, I'm against peace. We shall fight to the end.'

* * *

Bracken came for lunch (incidentally, it is said that he is Churchill's illegitimate son). He was in full agreement with Lloyd George: he argued at length that the ruling classes have degenerated, and that the workers are the only remaining hope. Splendid. But when I asked him for any news about Chamberlain's resignation, his answers became vague and uncertain.

He praised Beaverbrook: in one month he has increased the output of the aircraft industry by 40%. He cleaned the Augean stables in his ministry, sacked quite a few people, and reduced the types of aircraft produced to five models. Bracken pins great hopes on the United States and the Empire. As a result, by November–December England will catch up with Germany in the air and be able to think of offensive operations. But will the Germans allow England that time?

Bracken asserts categorically that a serious German invasion of the isles is impossible. He says that the home defence is led not by Ironside, of whom he has a low opinion, but by Churchill. In fact, this is Churchill's main business today. The prime minister reasons in the following way: the Germans will first launch a campaign of furious air raids to destroy as many factories, ports, railways and other facilities as possible, and then they will make gigantic efforts to land a large army from the air and the sea. They may use gas. Bracken is convinced that England is now prepared to repel a German attempt of this sort.

We shall see. I lack faith in British forethought and efficacy.

28 June

Little by little many, very many people's gazes are turning towards the Soviet Union.

The ill-fated 'Polish government' recently came running to London together with its president. Polish premier Sikorski met Churchill and assured him, first orally and then in writing, that the P[olish] G[overnment] did not wish to impede in any way the improvement of Anglo-Soviet relations. Government circles here interpreted this to mean that the 'P[olish] G[overnment]' is ready to formally relinquish its claims on Western Ukraine and Belorussia. We hardly need this renunciation, if truth be told; but as a symptom of the Polish mood, it is very interesting.

In less official Polish circles the following notion is gaining ground: if the Germans hold Poland, Polish nationality itself will eventually be eliminated. If Poland goes over to the USSR, Polish nationality will survive and even develop. Hence the conclusion: 'Let it be a Soviet Poland, but still Poland!'

An equally radical process is afoot with Czechoslovakia. They have entirely lost faith in the Allies. It was not so long ago that Beneš told me he wanted to balance between the Allies in the west and the USSR in the east. Now Czechoslovakians tends to lean towards the USSR, seeing their salvation in our country. They are also ready to say: 'Let it be a Soviet Czechoslovakia, but still Czechoslovakia!'

Our support is being sought by Yugoslavia, Bulgaria, Greece, Turkey and Sweden. They are all gripped by one desire: to avoid war one way or another! And they all reckon that only the USSR can save them from this ordeal.

* * *

A clean break between England and France. The British ambassador and his entire staff have left France. Corbin has resigned on the basis of his disagreement with Pétain's policy. Counsellor Cambon stays on as chargé d'affaires, but evidently he, too, will follow Corbin very soon. People say – and it is only to be expected – that the entire French embassy in London will soon pack up and go home.

The rupture, however, is not the only issue. The British government clearly wants to go further. First, it aims to use all available means to seize the French fleet, which is dispersed all over the world: part of it is moored in British harbours, other parts are in Alexandria, Martinique, North Africa (Casablanca, Oran and Bizerta) and Toulon. Negotiations are being held with French seamen, who are being tempted, pressed and threatened. It is difficult to say what will come of this, but one thing is clear: the British are desperate not to allow the French fleet to pass into German hands.

Second, the British government is obsessed with plans to form an alternative French government that would be ready to continue the war and that would rely for support on the French Empire, primarily North Africa and Syria. The reports issuing from the French colonies are contradictory. According to some, General Noguès[i] (commander-in chief in North Africa) and General

[i] Charles Auguste Paul Noguès, general, member of Supreme War Council, 1936–39; commander-in-chief of the French troops in North Africa in 1939–40.

Mittelhauser[i] (commander-in-chief in Syria) are against Pétain and in favour of fighting on with the British. Other reports say that they are hesitating and are inclined to follow those in Bordeaux. The latter seems more likely. Duff Cooper told me upon his arrival from Casablanca, where he and General Gort had been sent by the British government, that not only had he failed to win over Noguès, but he had not even been able to see him. Noguès avoided meeting Cooper and Gort, who departed empty-handed. It looks as if the British government's dreams of an alternative government will remain just that – dreams. But it has not yet given up.

'Eminent émigrés' have started arriving in London from France: Pierre Cot, Kerillis,[ii] Pertinax[iii] and others. Blum, Paul-Boncour and even Herriot are said to be here, but I have not managed to verify this. All these people spend their time knocking about at the Savoy. Their condition is one of utter prostration and they argue ceaselessly among themselves on political matters. Hardly first-rate material for an alternative government.

29 June

Yesterday we had Lady V. for lunch, who argued passionately that England was moving rapidly towards a 'revolution'. The aristocracy is bankrupt. The rich are on their uppers and soon there will be no wealthy people left, or only a very few. Life will become simpler and rougher, but more natural and healthier. Lady V. is taking some precautionary measures in anticipation of the changes: she has abandoned her luxurious apartment in London and the whole family now lives in a cottage in *Denham*. They travel in a tiny car. She is teaching her step-daughter cookery, needlework and washing. Lady V.'s husband has stopped 'changing' for dinner. And much else besides.

Of course, there is a great deal of amusing naivety in the deeds and words of Lady V. What is important, however, is that she has a sense, or more precisely a presentiment, of the proximity of the political and social catastrophe towards which England is heading.

Prytz and I sat and talked for three hours in 'Mirabelle' today. We discussed various matters – not only current events. Prytz's general mood is quite remarkable. He thinks that the world is drifting towards catastrophe, recalling in its importance the fall of the Roman Empire. The old order has had its day. The ruling classes of England, France and many other states are rotten and

---

[i] Eugène-Désité-Antoine Mittelhauser, general.

[ii] Henri de Kerillis, formerly editor of *L'Écho de Paris*; director of *L'Époque*; delegate to Chamber of Deputies for the Seine, 1936–45; councillor for the Seine, 1936–45.

[iii] Charles Joseph André Géraud (Pertinax), foreign editor, *L'Echo de* Paris, 1917–38; editor, *L'Europe Nouvelle*, 1938–40.

bankrupt. The Allies are losing the war less because of a shortage of tanks and planes than because of the weakness of their spiritual armour. The Allied armies have no idea for which they would be willing to fight in earnest. For who can be inspired by the idea of 'democracy', as embodied by the regimes of England and France? The German army does have an idea – a stupid, crazy idea, but one which still inspires it. The Allied armies lack such an idea. That's the crucial thing.

And yet Prytz is a major entrepreneur, a capitalist to his bones. He is head of SKF[59] and president of the match conglomerate founded by Kreuger.[i] True, Prytz is a clever and a progressive man, but still…

A sign of the times!

30 June

We spent Sunday in the country with the Azcárates. He has rented a large house with a garden for 50 pounds a year (that's how much large houses cost nowadays!) and moved there with his family. There is great anxiety in the family: their elder son, who was in Paris when the Germans began to advance, is now stuck in France. They have no definite news of him. The son's wife, a young dark-haired, dark-eyed girl from Barcelona is worried sick about it. She is looking after their three-month-old daughter, Carmen.

At the Azcárates, I met Negrín. I hadn't seen him since the autumn of 1937, when we met in Geneva, where he had been sent on an assignment by the Republican government. Regardless of all the tribulations he has endured since that time, Negrín is still Negrín. Tall, massive, confident, with his spectacles and noticeably greying hair, he has held on to his belief in the future. He says, 'Our time will still come' and beseeches fate to let it come soon.

'If only the Spanish Republic could be revived, even if takes two or three years!' he exclaimed.

He asked me to convey a request to the Soviet government: to take all possible steps to prevent the transfer of the Republicans interned in France to Franco.

Negrín said many interesting things about France. He is absolutely confident that the main reason for her collapse lies not in military affairs (although the shortage of tanks and aircraft played its role, too) but in domestic politics. The war was unpopular among the masses from the very beginning. Frequent desertion was observed. Why? Because the masses did not have an idea, a slogan, which would inspire them to fight. That slogan 'defence of democracy' – whose 'democracy'? The 'democracy' of Daladier, Flandin and Laval? – could

---

[i] Ivar Kreuger, Swedish industrialist.

not inspire anybody. What's more, from the very first days of the war, that 'democracy' launched a furious campaign of repressions against communists and 'leftists' in general.

A disastrous role was played by the socialists, the only party besides the communists with a link to the masses. To a man they sided with Daladier. The wing led by Paul Faure[i] (about a third of the party) began to drift directly towards fascism. In spite of all its attempts to dissociate itself from Faure, the wing lead by Blum (about 40% of the party) is not so very different: Blum's main preoccupation was the struggle against the communists. Of all the socialists, only Ziromsky[ii] and (later) Auriol opposed the anti-communist campaign, but they had few supporters. Pierre Cot (from the radicals) also considered it madness to wage war against the communists. As a result of the position taken by the socialists, and the difficulties imposed by persecution on communist propaganda, discord, confusion and dismay infected the masses, including the workers.

This was the atmosphere in which the notorious '200 families' operated. Lebrun, Laval, Flandin, Daladier and others constantly dreamt of an agreement with Hitler, hoping to turn him towards the east. They worked intensively towards this goal, particularly during the Finnish war. The Soviet government displayed remarkable wisdom in choosing the right moment to conclude a peace treaty. Negrín has not the slightest doubt that if the Finnish war had lasted 1–2 months more, France would have made peace with Hitler and come out against the USSR. Thinking of 'peace', the political upper crust was little inclined to concern itself with 'war', with spending big money and effort on fortifications, armaments, etc.

As far as the military leadership is concerned, not only was it entrusted to mediocre men like Gamelin who were bewitched by the 'Maginot Line', but it basically had no wish to put up a real fight. The military leaders panicked after the breakthrough at Sedan. Gamelin and Co. decided that the game was up. The only way out of the situation was to turn the war into a 'people's war', but that was just what Pétain, Weygand and others feared most. Small wonder! In spirit, they were all on the side of the fascists. Negrín himself observed how French officers throughout the war would devour *Grenguar* [untraced – he may be referring to *Gregoire*, though that was not a fascist piece of literature], *Je suis partout* and other publications sustained by German funds. Weygand

[i] Paul Faure, minister of state in Léon Blum's governments, 1936–37 and 1938; supporter of the Munich Agreement and later of Vichy France.

[ii] Jean Ziromsky, a political journalist during the interwar period, Ziromsky advocated a rapprochement between the socialists and communists against the rise of Fascism. He appealed to the Spanish Republicans many times between 1936 and 1939, and took a stand against the ratification of the Munich Agreement. Retiring to his farm in Lot-et-Garonne in October 1940, Ziromsky participated actively in the Resistance.

and Pétain are admirers of Hitler. Particularly Pétain, who, as ambassador to Spain, openly demonstrated his very friendly relations with the German ambassador in Madrid, even during the war. That's why as soon as this top brass had to choose between capitulation and a 'people's war', it chose capitulation. As a result, the French army failed to put up strong resistance anywhere after the breakthrough. Negrín was on the Seine and on the Marne soon after the beginning of the German advance and was greatly surprised not to find any fortifications, or even primitive trenches. Later, he observed the same on the Loire. Paris was handed over not from military considerations, but because the '200 families' were afraid lest a new Commune might arise there…

Bourgeois France is in deep decay. That is the main reason for the defeat.

1 July

My fears that the Foreign Office would sabotage Cripps by all available means are, I regret to say, proving well-founded.

Cripps arrived in Moscow without his credentials for readily comprehensible reasons: after all, he left London while still in the capacity of *special envoy*, and it was only during his journey that he became ambassador. During our discussions about Cripps's status, Butler made casual reference to the credentials: what should be done if Cripps, on being appointed ambassador, proceeded directly from Athens to the USSR? To this I answered just as casually, and with an air of perfect innocence: 'Send the credentials by telegraph.'

I had the impression that my reply struck Butler as something so obvious as to require no further comment. The conversation took place in early June. When the question of Cripps's status was finally resolved, I felt sure that the FO had sent the credentials by telegraph.

What a surprise it was, therefore, to receive on the evening of 15 June (three days after Cripps's arrival in Moscow) a copy of a telegram *telegramen clair* from C[omrade] Molotov to Halifax announcing the decision of the Presidium of the Supreme Soviet to receive Cripps in the capacity of ambassador prior to his presentation of credentials, on condition that the said credentials be presented with all due haste. There had obviously been some kind of hitch. So I phoned Butler the next day to ask what had happened.

It turned out that the credentials had not yet been sent to Cripps. I asked in great astonishment: 'Why not?'

To which Butler replied: 'The Foreign Office experts object to sending credentials by telegraph.'

'So what are you intending to do?' I asked, with still greater amazement.

'We are sending the credentials with Gifford, who has just been appointed the new commercial secretary in Moscow,' was Butler's reply.

'But how and when will Gifford get to Moscow?' I parried. 'You know how difficult it is to get to Moscow now. If Gifford travels via Vladivostok, say, Cripps will be waiting six weeks for his credentials. A fine position for him to be in!'

Butler admitted that the situation really had become a very tricky one, and added rather hesitantly: 'Well, perhaps we'll send the credentials by telegraph after all.'

I thought the matter had been settled. Alas, I was mistaken. Two days later I phoned Butler on another matter and enquired in passing whether the credentials had finally been sent to Cripps.

Butler answered in some embarrassment: 'No, not as yet.'

'But why not?' I yelled down the phone in indignation.

'Our experts,' Butler explained, 'are dead against sending credentials by telegraph… There has been no precedent… Moreover, they find it impossible to telegraph the king's signature.'

I became absolutely furious, and told Butler rather sharply that the situation was becoming quite ridiculous and that the question of credentials had to be settled immediately.

'But what would you advise?' Butler asked helplessly.

'What would I advise?' I retorted. 'Why not do one very simple thing? Why not invite me to the Foreign Office and show me the credentials? I could testify to my government by telegram that the credentials are in order and you could telegraph a copy to Cripps. Then everything would be settled.'

'A brilliant idea!' Butler exclaimed joyfully. 'We'll do as you say.'

That was 18 June. Another two days passed, however, before my suggestion was finally implemented. I was invited to see Butler on the morning of 20 June. He showed me Cripps's authentic credentials, signed by the king, and even gave me a copy (together with a copy of Seeds' letter of recall).

'You know,' Butler complained, 'it was no easy task for me to bully our experts into making a copy of the credentials for you… There has been no precedent!… There are people in the protocol department who haven't changed desks for 40 years. They are steeped in traditions and precedents. It's tough with them.'

'You know,' I replied with some irritation, 'if precedents are revered like this in all your ministries, you will definitely lose the war.'

Butler gave a sour laugh.

That same day I informed NKID that Cripps's credentials had been shown to me, and the FO sent the contents of these credentials to Cripps by telegraph. Just the other day the presentation of credentials to C[omrade] Kalinin was carried out. The Soviet government declared itself 'satisfied' with the telegraph copy. When Gifford reaches Moscow, the telegraph copy will be replaced with the original. Now everything is in order.

FO sabotage is quite something!

2 July

Today I learned many interesting details about the events in Norway from the Norwegian foreign minister, Professor Koht.[i]

According to him, the British government, on its own initiative, declared to the Norwegian government at the very beginning of the war that it would consider any attack by Germany on Norwegian territory as an attack on its own lands. The British government even suggested putting this statement in writing, but Koht declined the offer so as not to create the impression that a military alliance existed between Norway and England.

The Norwegian government received information about German preparations for an attack on Norway more than once during the winter, but no attack followed. Little by little the Norwegian government ceased to believe such rumours. Three days before 9 April the N[orwegian] G[overnment] received fresh reports of a threatened assault but, drawing on past experience, did not treat them seriously. So the German attack struck the N[orwegian] G[overnment] like a bolt from the blue.

The N[orwegian] G[overnment] did not appeal to the Allies for help (Colban's communication that three days after the German invasion began the N[orwegian] G[overnment] appealed to the Allies through the British minister in Oslo proves inaccurate). The Allies themselves 'came to the rescue'. The cooperation between the Norwegians and the British was extremely fragile throughout the campaign. The British thought they knew better than the Norwegians and completely ignored their advice and suggestions. This led to a fundamental mistake. Norway had men but not enough weapons. But rather than immediately sending aircraft and weapons to Norway, the Allies began sending men without planes and virtually without armaments. Moreover, in whatever they did, the Allies were always *too late*. This was shown most vividly at Trondheim. The Norwegian government learned about the Allies' decision to withdraw from southern Norway 24 hours before its implementation. As a result the Norwegian army found itself in an exceptionally difficult situation. Narvik was taken by the Norwegians, French and Poles (some 6,000–7,000 people in total) without the participation of a single Englishman, if we discount the British ships lying at anchor. When the British government decided to evacuate Narvik, the N[orwegian] G[overnment] asked that it be left the British arms and planes. With those resources Norway would have been able to continue the

[i] Professor Halvdan Koht, Norwegian foreign minister, 1935–40.

war. The British government, however, did not agree, under the pretext that it needed all this on other fronts. By an irony of fate, the planes which the British refused to leave to Norway failed to make it home, together with the aircraft carrier *Glorious*, which was sunk by the Germans.

Koht also mentioned the plan for the 'neutralization' of northern Norway (Prytz told me about this not long ago). According to Koht, this project originated not in Norway but in Stockholm, and was advanced by a Swedish friend of Göring's. Koht deduces from this that the Germans would not have been averse to pursuing such a strategy…

The immediate reason for Koht's visit was to clarify the nature of the relations between the N[orwegian] G[overnment] in exile in England and the Soviet government. Koht had taken an interest in this matter while still in northern Norway. The Soviet government answered then that relations remained normal and added (on its own initiative) that it had no claims on Norwegian ports. The N[orwegian] G[overnment] was touched. But how do matters stand now? Koht asked me to make inquiries and inform him of the Soviet government's reply. I said I would do so. Koht also wanted to know whether the Soviet government considered it desirable to restore the independence of Norway after the war. I referred to the general principles of Soviet foreign policy.

The entire N[orwegian] G[overnment] is in London. The British government has offered it the use of a castle some 100 miles away from London, and the ministers will move there imminently. King Haakon is also here, but he will be staying in Buckingham Palace. The N[orwegian] G[overnment]'s finances rest on two foundations: the gold reserves which they managed to bring out of Norway and the income from Norwegian shipping which has been practically nationalized for the duration of the war and which is managed by the *Trade and Shipping Mission* in London (a large institution with about 250 employees). Up to 80% of Norwegian tonnage is presently located outside Norway.

Koht told me, among other things, that Germans are currently conducting a major campaign in Norway against the N[orwegian] G[overnment] and Haakon, demanding that the Storting should renounce the former and dethrone the latter. One hundred of the Storting's 150 members are present in Norway, so a quorum exists. Koht does not exclude the possibility that Germany, by applying pressure in various forms, may force the Storting to make the decision it wants. That would be followed by the formation in Norway of a pseudo-government in German hands. Koht did not say so directly, but he was obviously concerned by the question: How would the Soviet government act in this case? Would it recognize a pseudo-government or not?

I informed Koht that we would be closing our mission in Oslo imminently, leaving only a consulate. This seemed to give him some cheer.

Koht said that eleven years ago, on his way from Oslo to Moscow (then he was just a professor), he paid me a visit in Helsinki. I tried but simply couldn't recall this.

3 July

Today Colban sent me official documents which make it clear that the Presidium of the Storting has appealed to King Haakon to abdicate, but the king refused.

4 July

Churchill's speech in parliament today was a personal triumph and, at the same time, a significant display of patriotism.

Initially, the mood in the House was hard to determine. Churchill's appearance was welcomed with noises that were encouraging without being particularly impressive or unanimous. As usual, most of the cheers came from the opposition benches, while the greater part of the Conservatives held a gloomy silence. This pattern was repeated when Churchill rose to make his speech.

But the longer this brilliant and skilful performance continued, the more it affected the mood of the MPs. Churchill's topic, of course, was a sure winner. He said that the British navy had scored a great success, that the greater part of the French fleet was either in British hands or out of action, and that consequently the chances of a German invasion had fallen steeply… How could the House refrain from rejoicing? How could it fail to greet each rousing sentence of the PM's speech with boisterous applause?

It could not. The House exulted and gave vent to its elation.

Then Churchill spoke about the future. He firmly and categorically refuted all rumours of a possible peace. He vowed to fight to the end. At this point the outburst of patriotism reached its peak, and when Churchill finished his speech and sank into his seat, the whole House, irrespective of party affiliation, jumped to its feet and applauded the prime minister for several minutes – a loud, powerful and unanimous ovation. Sitting on the Treasury bench, the tension draining from his body, Churchill lowered his head and tears ran down his cheeks.

It was a strong, stirring scene. 'At last we have a real leader!' was the cry echoing through the lobbies. Curiously, it was Labour which pronounced these words most often. For the time being, at any rate, talk of a 'rotten peace' can be put to one side.

* * *

Churchill's speech represented, among other things, a reply to last week's peace overtures by Germany and Italy, who conducted their 'soundings' via Madrid. The Spanish foreign minister presented Hoare with 'his' plan for settling the European war (the plan had actually been sent from Rome). It boiled down to the following:

(1) The internationalization of Gibraltar and the Suez Canal and the demilitarization of Malta.

(2) The division of Tunisia between France and Italy.

(3) The restoration to Germany of its former colonies, plus 'something else' (evidently, the Belgian Congo).

(4) The condominium of England, France, Germany and Italy in Iraq, Egypt and Morocco.

(5) Parity between the British and German fleets.

The Cabinet discussed the 'Spanish' plan and rejected it. The main reason? Hitler cannot be trusted.

* * *

Attlee and Greenwood came for dinner yesterday. They spoke of the difficulties with Ireland. The British government is offering De Valera the unification of Northern Ireland and Southern Ireland in exchange for Dublin's aid in the war. De Valera replies that he will readily take Northern Ireland, but wants to remain neutral until an actual attack by the Germans. This is what happened with Norway, Holland and Belgium. It is clear that no agreement can be reached on this basis. So the British government has set about massing troops in Northern Ireland in order that, should the Germans try to land from the air or from the sea, it will immediately occupy all Ireland.

Attlee and Greenwood also confirmed that British air losses are on average three times less than German losses. The reason they gave for this is the superiority of British machines and pilots. The German pilots captured recently are still virtually kids, having barely undergone the minimum period of training. Perhaps this is so, but I find it hard to believe.

[The collapse of France induced a dramatic change in the Soviet attitude to the peace offensive. Complacency gave way to profound concern, leading to the hasty occupation of Bessarabia and the annexation of the Baltic States. Ever since the shift in Soviet policy following the conclusion of the Ribbentrop–Molotov Pact, Maisky had found himself in a perilous state. He was barred from the Kremlin's decision-making process, at the same time as being socially and politically ostracized in Britain. He seldom received a diplomatic bag or newspapers from Moscow.[60] Being of Jewish origin, he could hardly watch with equanimity the blooming romance between Moscow and Berlin. Later on, he was indeed to find himself at the top of Hitler's publicized list of those to be shot after the occupation of England.[61] Maisky certainly reckoned with 'the possibility of a temporary appearance of the Germans in London … I even inquired of Moscow how I should conduct myself if the Germans were to occupy the district in London in which our embassy is situated.' The turn of events, however, meant that the persisting threat of a severance of relations was lifted as 'the prolonged "winter of discontent"' came to an end.[62]

His relief concerning the German threat to the Soviet Union was replaced by a serious worry about the British ability to withstand a German onslaught and the probability of a peace agreement. The 'Red Dean of Canterbury' was quick to detect the change of tone in their 'personal conversations'. The Soviet Union, Maisky appeared eager to impress on him, 'was not anxious for a second Versailles' and was 'still less anxious for a swift triumph of Hitler & Mussolini, who doubtless would look next at the Ukraine & other spots'. Butler, too, found Maisky aware 'of the gravity of the present situation' and intent on convincing him that 'now that the European equilibrium had been considerably upset it was not in the interests of his country or of ours that one Power should gain the complete hegemony of Europe'.[63]

Likewise Bilainkin, almost a member of the household at the embassy, was struck (as he hastily informed Butler) by an 'outstanding sentence' in a conversation with Maisky following the fall of Paris: 'We realise that the position is extremely grave and dangerous to us, just as much…' Maisky described Britain as a 'real Maginot line', having the advantage of 'being a complete line and not one of a small part of the territory'. There was no reason 'why the Germans should not be held if you show enough spirit, in defence'.[64] Speaking to Dalton, he expressed his confidence that Britain would win the war if she held out 'for the next two months', but he feared that during these months the country would be 'in a position of great peril'.[65] His real concern, as he revealed to the Webbs,[66] was that defeat might follow 'a betrayal of the ruling class, somewhat similar to that of Pétain and his group', after which there would be a revolution. The Russian chauffeur told Beatrice Webb's maids that 'the war would be over in two months'.[67]

On 28 June, Alexander, the first lord of the Admiralty who had just come from a meeting with Maisky, alerted Churchill to the Soviet apprehension about a peace agreement modelled on the French surrender. It was most telling that Maisky – who had little patience with Alexander's ironic comment that, until recently, the British communists 'had been leaders of a peace offensive' – insisted that 'the present attitude of the CPGB was to organize resistance against the invader' and reiterated that the situation was 'full of danger'.[68] Briefed by Alexander, Churchill, who had not seen Maisky since taking office, met him on 3 July. The meeting (for which there is no entry in the diary) was, according to Maisky's memoirs, 'brief, but most significant'. It was a relief for him to learn that Churchill 'categorically and forcefully denied rumours on possible peace negotiations' and explained that his present strategy was 'to last out the next three months' before moving on to the offensive.[69] Churchill had been advised by the Foreign Office to avoid any discussion of political value with Maisky, as 'he was not in confidence of his own Government and is therefore useless'. 'You don't doubt Maisky being pro-British, do you?' Randolph Churchill asked Beaverbrook, encouraging him to draw Maisky closer to his circle. 'I don't doubt this at all, Randolph,' replied the press baron, 'but I very much doubt whether Stalin is pro-Maisky.'[70]]

5 July

A visit from Pierre Cot, who has been swept onto British shores by the tide of events. He said that none of the major French politicians have come to London, while such people as Kerillis and Pertinax, who did come to London, quickly evacuated to America. Daladier, Delbos, Campinchi,[i] Mandel and others, 50 in all, departed for North Africa on board a special ship soon after the armistice and are said to be in Casablanca, but Cot does not know the details. He himself is going to settle down in London and set up an unofficial leftist French committee that will publish its newspaper in London and maintain contact with France. Cot may go to the United States to raise money for this enterprise. The attempt to create in England a 'National French Committee' capable of serving as a counterweight to the Pétain government failed: the big names required for this could not be found. As for de Gaulle,[ii] Cot thinks he leans to the right, but is not interested in politics. He is surrounded by mediocrities. Most likely, de Gaulle will form his 'French legion' to fight within the frame of the British army, and that will be the end of it. It is hard to say how many will join this 'legion'. There are at present 30–35,000 French troops in England (the units which did not reach Norway, the rest of the French who were evacuated from Dunkerque, and others). This, it seems clear, is the reservoir from which de Gaulle will draw his 'legionaries'.

Cot told me many interesting things about France. His account fully corroborates what Negrín told me. At the heart of France's crushing defeat lies the internal degeneration of the ruling elite. Cot drew a most vivid picture of this process. He spoke at some length about 'female influences' in politics. Every major French figure has a wife or, more often 'Madame de Pompadour', engaged in politics. In the overwhelming majority of cases these are extremely reactionary politics. One should be thankful, Cot says, if the mistress is stupid, for then she can do less harm. But if she is a clever woman, she presents a very grave danger. Daladier's mistress (Madame Crussol),[iii] for example, isn't the brightest and could be tolerated. But Reynaud's mistress (Madame de Portes)[iv] is very intelligent and witty, and she has played a fateful role in Reynaud's life and in the history of the French government as a whole. Reynaud is not bad in himself. He has good intentions and a good grasp of the situation; but he is not strong enough: he is in the hands of his entourage, in which Madame de Portes plays the leading part. She is an extremely reactionary lady. She is on friendly

[i] César Campinchi, French minister of justice, 1938; minister of the navy, 1937–38 and 1938–40.
[ii] Charles de Gaulle, commander of the French army in exile after the collapse of France; chief of Free French, then president of the French National Committee, 1940–42.
[iii] Marquise Jeanne de Crussol.
[iv] La Comtesse Hélène de Portes.

terms with Madame Bonnet, Madame Aletz and other ladies who not only share utterly retrograde views, but also maintain close ties with the Germans.[71]

By way of illustration, Cot referred to the case of his failed visit to Moscow. When he returned in April from his meeting with me in London, Cot had a serious conversation with Reynaud about relations with the USSR. Reynaud was entirely reasonable. He understood that relations with Moscow should be resumed, and even outlined a few measures in this direction in his conversation with Cot. Cot was pleased. A few days passed, but no practical steps had been taken. Cot visited Reynaud again and was confronted with a completely different scene: the prime minister hummed and hawed, spoke of difficulties and recommended caution. What had happened? Madame de Portes and other persons from Reynaud's retinue had intervened, and the PM's good intentions had faded.

In early May, Germany attacked Holland and Belgium. The situation became critical. Reynaud summoned Cot and announced that he wanted to send him to Moscow as a 'special representative' to restore contact with the Soviet government. Cot said he was ready to go. Negotiations with Moscow were begun through Ivanov.[i] Moscow's position was clear, as it had been regarding Cripps: no 'special representatives' – send us a genuine ambassador. Reynaud was prepared to comply with Moscow's request. But here Madame de Portes, the entourage, and Daladier (the nominal foreign minister) intervened again: they were all against it. Reynaud chickened out. As a result, Cot was pushed aside and Labonne[ii] went to Moscow as ambassador.

Cot takes a quite definite view of France's defeat: the top brass (which is closely linked to the degenerate political elite) simply did not want to fight in earnest. Also, had the war been waged in more or less 'normal forms' – that is, under the protection of the Maginot Line, which exerted an utterly hypnotic influence on France's military minds – Weygand and other generals might have done their job. But when it became clear, after the German breakthrough, that only a 'people's war' could save France, the top brass lost all desire to fight. And that's hardly surprising. Who is Weygand after all? He is essentially a fascist, but a fascist made in France – that is, with a Catholic hue. Many simply call Weygand a traitor. Cot does not rule this out, but he does not have enough evidence to make such an accusation with full conviction. However, even if one assumes only the first charge to be true, that Weygand is a fascist, how could one expect

---

[i] Nikolai Nikolaevich Ivanov, second (then first) secretary to the Soviet mission in France, 1939, acting temporary chargé d'affaires, 1940. Recalled from Paris in December 1940, after warning Moscow of German intentions to invade Russia, accused of undermining German–Soviet rapprochement and banished for five years' imprisonment in Siberia.

[ii] Eirik Labonne, French ambassador to the USSR, 1940–41.

even the slightest enthusiasm for a 'people's war' on his part? The majority of the senior generals are reactionaries too, often fascists or fascist sympathizers. Cot thinks it probable that Weygand was guided by a single 'general idea' after the German breakthrough at Sedan: to stop fighting the Germans and to use the new situation to abolish the Third Republic and establish a fascist regime.

Indeed, after Dunkerque, the French army never fought seriously anywhere. A weak attempt at resistance was made on the Somme, but when that line shook, a systematic retreat began, masked only by feigned counterattacks. Bridges, factories, railways and so on were not blown up. Trenches and fortifications were not constructed even at the most important strategic points (on the Seine, Marne, Loire, etc.). Enormous quantities of arms and munitions, sufficient for the French army to resist for months, were left to the Germans. Nothing was done on the Italian border, although there were excellent opportunities there. Why? Simply because, after the breakthrough, the '200 families' and military leaders had no intention of fighting in earnest. They just manoeuvred, waiting for a good moment to start negotiations with Germany.

Of course, this was an open betrayal of France. The lower ranks – soldiers and junior officers – sensed it, were angry, and protested. Cot himself heard how President Lebrun's son, a young officer, indignantly called the generals 'traitors'. Alas, it was these 'traitors' who had control of the military machine. There was no alternative leadership, and no plans for one. As a result, the indignation and protests of the lower ranks did not assume a constructive form, but were dispersed. Universal chaos, confusion and panic took their place. The consequences of this process are well known.

What next?

In Cot's opinion, France is on the path to becoming completely fascist. Pétain, Laval, Flandin and others are just the first, transitory phase. They will not hang on for long. They are just paving the way for the real fascists, such as Doriot[i] and Marquet,[ii] who will soon take power. The Third Republic is dead. All the old parties, except the communists, are wholly discredited. The masses are in a state of profound disarray and confusion. Naturally, in such a situation the communists' chances increase significantly, but Cot does not think that the Communist Party can become a decisive force in France unless Germany is defeated in the nearest future.

---

[i] Jacques Doriot, expelled from the Communist Party in 1934 for advocating a united front with leftist parties. Became a virulent opponent of the communists and founded the fascist French Popular Party. Snubbed the Vichy government and, backed by the Germans, recruited a French legion to fight Russia.

[ii] Adrien Marquet, former socialist mayor of Bordeaux, he turned fascist and briefly served as the minister of the interior in the Vichy government.

6 July

Paid a visit to Eden at the War Office. I hadn't seen him for some time and I wanted to gauge his mood.

Eden, on the whole, is pleased. He is pleased that, contrary to general expectations, the Germans have not yet attacked England. This has given him time to reorganize the units dispersed during the retreat from Flanders, to arm them, supply them with uniforms and footwear, and deploy them. In the main, this has now been done. The army is ready to meet the enemy, and Eden thinks an invasion will be attempted very soon.

I posed Eden the same question that I put to Churchill a few days ago: what is the *major strategy* of the war, how does the British government understand it?

Eden's answer came down to the following.

The first and most urgent task is to repel any attack on England. Every effort should then be made to achieve superiority over Germany in the air. Eden believes this can be done in approximately six months. At the same time, it is necessary to prepare a large, well-trained and well-equipped army, and also maintain a strict economic blockade of Germany and the countries it has occupied. Later, beginning in the first months or the spring of 1941, the British should move on to the offensive by air and by land. The British offensive ought to be facilitated by the fact that the blockade and its consequences should help undermine Germany from within.

I asked Eden whether he was thinking of concluding a peace agreement in the near future, and, if so, what kind of peace.

Eden categorically rules out the possibility of peace. The war will be fought 'to the end'. The operation with the French fleet has clearly demonstrated England's determination to fight.[72] England's intentions are serious and unshakeable.

7 July

Agniya and I visited the Webbs. As usual, Beatrice expressed a thought worthy of further consideration. Here it is.

England will undoubtedly be able to repulse a German attack on its islands. But it will not be able to win back France, Denmark, Norway, Holland and Belgium from Germany. As a result, a situation might emerge whereby Germany, depending on the European continent it has conquered, will not be able to defeat England, while England, depending on its Empire and possibly part of the French Empire, will not be able to defeat Germany. A *stalemate* will ensue. The Soviet Union and the United States might act as mediators and achieve a decent peace in Europe.

I learned from C. [possibly Cot] the following details of Cripps's conversation with S[talin] in the presence of M[olotov] on 1 July.

Cripps raised four issues on behalf of the British government:

(1) General policy. Germany has seized the greater part of Europe and is about to establish its supremacy in Europe. It is swallowing up one nation after another. This is dangerous for both England and the Soviet Union. Couldn't the two countries establish a common line of defence to restore equilibrium in Europe?

S[talin]'s reply: The Soviet Union is following the development of the European situation with the keenest interest, as it is the key issues of international politics which should be resolved in Europe in the near future as a result of the hostilities. However, the S[oviet] G[overnment] does not see any danger in the hegemony of a single state in Europe, still less in Germany's ambition to absorb other nations. Germany's military successes present no threat to the achievements of the USSR or to the existence of cordial relations between the two said states. These cordial relations are based not on transient, opportunist considerations, but on the vital national interests of both states. As far as the restoration of 'equilibrium' in Europe is concerned, that 'equilibrium' was suffocating not only Germany, but the USSR as well. That is why the Soviet government will do all it can to ensure that the former 'equilibrium' is not restored.

(2) Trade. Regardless of whether or not a common Anglo-Soviet line of defence against Germany is formed, the British government would like to develop trade between the two countries. The only restriction England imposes is that commodities imported from England should not be re-exported to Germany.

S.'s reply: The Soviet Union does not object to trading with England, providing two conditions are met. First, Soviet–German trade relations are our own business and we shall not discuss them with England. Second, some of the nonferrous metals imported from abroad will be re-exported to Germany to meet some of our orders for war material there. If the British government does not accept these conditions, trade will not be possible.

(3) The Balkans. The British government believes that the Soviet Union should assume control of the Balkan countries in order to maintain the status quo in the Balkans.

S.'s reply: It is the opinion of the Soviet government that no single power can claim an exclusive role in the unification and control of the Balkans. The Soviet Union is certainly interested in the Balkans, but it does not claim an exclusive role in this part of the globe.

(4) The Straits. The British government is aware that the Soviet Union is dissatisfied with the situation in the Straits and the Black Sea. It believes that the interests of the Soviet Union in the Straits should be secured.

S.'s reply: The Soviet Union is against Turkey taking unilateral control of the Straits, just as it is against Turkey dictating conditions in the Black Sea. The Turkish government has been informed of the USSR's attitude.

8 July

Now that Cripps is finally settled in Moscow as ambassador of Great Britain, I am trying to recover his true image in my mind. Who is he really? What are his most characteristic features?

It is important to know this. One can then draw the appropriate conclusions about the prospects of Cripps's employment in Moscow.

Cripps is a deeply English type. He was born in 1889, the youngest son of Lord Parmoor, who was a Tory all his life but became a Labour peer in 1924. Lord Parmoor is still alive, but he is very old and has retired from public view.

Nothing in Cripps's childhood and youth foretold that he would become a major politician. On the contrary, his first interest was architecture and construction of every sort. Then, after finishing *public school* at Winchester, he began studying chemistry at London University. Cripps, however, soon dropped chemistry and took up law. He became a lawyer in London in 1913, while in 1914 he found himself in France, working for the Red Cross. A year later, Cripps returned to London and during 1915–17 he was in charge of an explosives factory (studying chemistry had come in handy). He returned to the Bar after the war, and in 1927 was appointed *King's Councillor* [sic]. As a lawyer, his rise to the top was exceptionally fast and, which is most interesting, he earned a good reputation among both the workers and the bourgeoisie. He was particularly popular among the miners, whom he often defended in court. At the same time, as Butler once told me, his son-in-law Courtauld,[i] a leading manufacturer of artificial silk who consulted Cripps on legal matters, considers him one of the most intelligent men in England. As a barrister, Cripps usually earned a great deal: 20–30 thousand pounds a year!

In 1911, at the age of 22, Cripps married the daughter of a naval officer called Swithenbank.[ii] She bore him four children, a son and three daughters. Cripps's wife Isobel is a wealthy lady (her annual income is said to reach 10,000 pounds). So the financial status of the Cripps family is that of the bourgeoisie, perhaps not the upper bourgeoisie by British standards, but quite 'solid' all the same.

Cripps remained outside politics until he was about 40. Only in 1928 did he join this important sphere of British life, and in 1931 he started representing the

[i] Samuel Courtauld.
[ii] Harold William Swithenbank.

Bristol East constituency as an MP for the Labour Party. Cripps was expelled from Labour at the beginning of 1939 for advocating a 'united front', but his constituency remained faithful to him, and he continues to represent Bristol East in the House of Commons.

Cripps is undoubtedly a very intelligent and well-educated man. He is an English intellectual of the left who considers himself a radical socialist, but who has never had anything to do with Marxism. Cripps's socialism is of a particular English breed – a mixture of religion, ethical idealism and the practical demands of the trade unions. Cripps is a republican, which is a rather rare phenomenon in England. In recent years he has spoken out sharply against royal authority, and for a while his name was 'taboo' in Buckingham Palace. Cripps is very emotional, hence his instability and the frequent contradictions in his speeches of different periods. What is especially valuable about Cripps is the fact that he has convictions and is ready to stand up for them. He has proved his honesty and courage in deeds on more than one occasion, especially in connection with the propaganda of a 'united front', for which he had to pay a heavy price.

Despite being, by British standards, a man of the far left, Cripps is deeply religious (not, of course, in a formal, churchly sense). He is a confirmed teetotaller and vegetarian, and even prefers to eat raw rather than boiled vegetables. Yet Cripps is a heavy smoker. He is exceptionally interesting to talk to. He is a fine orator, whose speeches are greatly influenced by the context in which he finds himself. In parliament and in court, Cripps is a model of logical, juridical eloquence. But at mass meetings he is transformed beyond recognition: the sight of a crowd goes to his head and he becomes a tribune of the people. His excited imagination carries him farther and farther afield and he skips his habitual 'buts' and 'ifs', becoming more left-wing than he actually is. That's why he has often found himself in awkward predicaments. Cripps is a very feeble tactician. He does not know how to manoeuvre, how to wait for an advantageous moment, or how to handle people. It was only because of these shortcomings that he was expelled from the Labour Party.

Cripps is a typical political individualist, such as may be found in England fairly often. He is akin to Lloyd George in this sense. Cripps enjoys great popularity in the thinking strata of the proletariat and among more enlightened Conservatives like Churchill, Eden and others. Labour, the Transport House, dislikes him. Butler and, strangely enough, Halifax think highly of him. Perhaps it is religion that unites Halifax and Cripps. It is difficult to foretell Cripps's future, but he will probably play a major role in the political events of the next few years. I've heard it said several times that Cripps is a future 'left-wing' minister of foreign affairs or 'left-wing' prime minister. Even such a man as Lloyd George, upon learning of Cripps's appointment as ambassador to Moscow, told me: 'I almost regret it. We need Cripps here more than in Moscow. He is the only major figure on the opposition bench.'

Cripps's attitude towards the USSR is entirely cordial. I remember the courage and skill with which he defended us on behalf of Labour during the debate on the embargo in connection with the Metro-Vickers case. No doubt, he still has very good intentions in respect of Anglo-Soviet relations. But will he be able to improve these relations significantly? I don't know. All will depend on the policy of the British government, which is much further to the right than Cripps on this matter. If only the British government could reform itself and allow Cripps to genuinely represent it. Will Cripps remain as friendly to the USSR as he has been until now? I don't know that either. We've had quite a few bad experiences on that score. Time will tell.

[A member of a minority left-wing faction in parliament, Cripps now found himself in a crucial role as British ambassador to the sole major power in Europe which still retained its independence, even as he remained an outspoken opponent of the prime minister. Convinced that Russia would eventually find itself at war with Germany, Cripps hoped to lay the foundations for an alliance during the war which could pave the way to a post-war agreement. Hardly had he settled in Moscow than he advocated an agreement with Russia that would recognize part of her acquisitions (mostly in the Baltic States) and lead to the establishment of a south-eastern alliance with Turkey. His detailed plan for post-war reconstruction – a premonition of things to come – contained some very radical thinking: in the wake of the war, which was bound to lead to significant social changes on the home front, Great Britain must, he argued, 'be prepared to regard herself as an outpost' of the United States. Cripps presented his ideas in a letter that he addressed to Halifax and which was shown to Churchill. Churchill attached to the letter a note for circulation to the Cabinet, which he later tore up. Apparently the note ran as follows: 'It seems to me that the ideas set forth by Sir S. Cripps upon the post-war position of the British Empire are far too airy and speculative to be useful at the present moment, when we have to win the war in order to survive. In these circumstances, unless any of my colleagues desire it, it seems hardly necessary to bring this excursion of our Ambassador to the USSR formally before the Cabinet.'[73]

Churchill's own message, which Cripps delivered to Stalin on 1 July (at their only meeting before the German invasion of Russia) was confined to a general declaration of a desire to maintain 'harmonious and mutually beneficial' relations between the two countries, regardless of their 'widely differing systems of political thought'.[74] The concrete proposals which Cripps made to Stalin were aimed at establishing a bulwark against Nazi Germany in the Balkans. The timing, however – just a week after the fall of France – was inauspicious. Stalin feared that Britain, under siege and with no apparent prospect of victory, might try to embroil Russia in a war with Germany. He was as suspicious that Britain might sign a peace agreement with Germany. The 'scramble for the Balkans' that followed best illuminates the nature of Stalin's frame of mind, as well as his *modus operandi* following the Ribbentrop–Molotov Pact.

The annexation of Bessarabia in June 1940 (as stipulated in the Pact) has been perceived by most historians as yet another example of Bolshevik ideological expansionism. But the move was motivated by a need to improve the strategic position of the Soviet Union in the Black Sea area by securing control of the mouth of the Danube. This would bolster Russia's position as a European power and establish a springboard to the Turkish Straits. It mirrored the concessions which were forcibly extracted from Finland after the conclusion of the Winter War of 1939–40 to protect the maritime approaches to Leningrad.

Stalin further sought to achieve the best preconditions for the Soviet Union at the putative peace conference, which he expected to take place in 1941–42. In view of the eventual formation of the Grand Alliance, it is rarely recognized by historians that throughout the 1930s the Russians regarded the Germans and the British with equal suspicion. Well into 1940, British naval dominance of the Mediterranean – taken in conjunction with the legacy of imperial rivalry between England and Russia, the Crimean War, the confrontation of 1877–88, the Balkan wars at the beginning of the twentieth century and British intervention in the Civil War after the Revolution – was perceived by Stalin to be as much of a threat to Russia as German expansion.[75]]

9 July

Met Lloyd George. The old man says that the British government has made good use of the respite, and that the island's defence has been considerably improved. The chances of a German invasion have fallen. Lloyd George fails to see why Hitler is delaying his attack on England. He must have problems of his own.

Nonetheless Lloyd George's mood is far from cheerful.

'All right,' he says, 'so we'll manage to repel the German attack. Then what?… Germany has carved out immense *Lebensraum* for itself from Norway to Spain. Let's face the facts: Spain is also part of that *Lebensraum*. England alone cannot win back the countries occupied by Germany. Nor can England defeat Germany. How? What with? Countries cannot be conquered from the air, and we do not have and will not have an army sufficient for the purpose. An absurd situation results: Germany cannot defeat England and England cannot defeat Germany. What's the solution?'

Lloyd George believes that the only remedy is the close cooperation of England, the United States and the Soviet Union. If this does not happen, Germany will remain master of the continent; peace, progress and indeed any form of tolerable life will become impossible for mankind.

I remarked that I had yet to detect the faintest sign of such a strategy. The relations of England and the USA with the USSR are inadequate even to ensure merely normal contact, to say nothing of 'close cooperation'. Besides, the Soviet Union wants to remain neutral and will be able to take care of itself under any circumstances.

Lloyd George smiled slyly and said: 'Time will tell. What seems impossible today may become possible in three or four months' time. The situation is extremely dynamic.'

The old man developed his thought. It is, of course, impossible to imagine the move he envisages occurring under the present government in London. But that government is not eternal. A change is inevitable, despite Churchill's stubbornness and Labour's spinelessness. There is a swell among the masses, and the government has to be reorganized sooner or later. The crucial thing is to get rid of Chamberlain and Halifax. Yes, yes! Halifax must be removed! In fact, he is much more harmful than Chamberlain. Churchill has once again invited Lloyd George to join the Cabinet, but he refused to sit alongside the 'Men of Munich'. But change is in the air. England is not like France. Of course, she too has her Pétains and Lavals. There are many in the House of Lords and the City who would follow the French right away. But England has her working masses. They are stronger and more influential than in France. So what happened in France will not happen here. There will be a government in London soon which Washington and Moscow can trust. Then Lloyd George's scheme will become possible.

Then the old man described his position on the question of peace. Last October he was in favour of peace, as there was stalemate at the front, France was intact, and Norway, Denmark, Holland and Belgium had not been occupied. The correlation of forces was such that a decent peace was possible, 'without winners or losers'. Now, the situation is entirely different. Now, a decent peace agreement cannot be concluded. The only conceivable peace would amount to England's surrender. The country will not agree to it. And Lloyd George will never advocate such a peace.

In conclusion, Lloyd George spoke of relations between the USSR and Turkey, and in particular about the Straits. He recalled that in the last war an agreement was concluded which handed the Straits to Russia, and added that he considered the present situation with the Straits abnormal. In his opinion, the Straits should belong to the Soviet Union. This is dictated by the USSR's huge interest in the Straits. This development would stabilize the general situation in the Near East, and would place an obstacle to German expansion in that direction.

I responded to Lloyd George's comments by saying that we were not after other people's lands.

10 July

Quite unexpectedly, after a six-week break (I last visited him on 26 May) Halifax invited me round. I arrived at six in the evening.

Halifax began with a semi-apology: he had nothing particular to tell me, but simply wanted to see me and have a chat. We hadn't been in touch for so long, and the times are so complex and unstable.

I bowed to him and replied with a half-smile: 'I'm entirely at your service.'

Halifax moved in his chair, crossed his long thin legs, and said: 'Cripps has had a talk with Mr Stalin. A very useful and interesting one. They spoke quite frankly. I attach great importance to this exchange of opinions. We shall draw the appropriate conclusions.'

As the content of the talk was not known to me, I considered it best to maintain a polite silence and allow the foreign secretary to speak. For several minutes he elaborated in a rather nebulous way on the theme of Cripps's meeting with C[omrade] Stalin, after which he asked me how long I had known Cripps and whether the Soviet government liked the new British ambassador. I replied politely, but in noncommittal fashion.

When this topic was exhausted, Halifax shifted his legs and asked in a somewhat melancholy tone: 'Do you think that the misunderstandings which exist in the relations between our countries can really be dispelled?'

'Yes, of course they can be dispelled,' I replied, 'if the British government takes a new political line. For the problem lies not so much in "misunderstandings" as in concrete actions.'

Halifax paused, as though he were digesting my words, before asking somewhat haltingly: 'So in Moscow they think we were insincere in our negotiations last summer? That we did not actually want to come to an agreement?'

I replied that in his speech of 31 August, C[omrade] Molotov had expressed quite plainly our assessment of the Anglo-French stance at those negotiations. It was riven by internal contradictions. On the one hand, the British and the French feared Germany and wanted an agreement with the USSR. On the other, they feared that such an agreement might excessively strengthen the USSR. The failure of the negotiations was rooted in this contradiction.

Halifax shrugged his shoulders and asked: 'And do you, personally, agree with this analysis?'

'I fully agree with it,' I answered.

Halifax frowned and mentioned the difficulties caused during the negotiations by the formula of 'indirect aggression'. I grinned and inquired: doesn't Halifax now think, after the experience of ten months of war, that we were far more realistic in our appraisal of the methods of the current war than the British and the French? Halifax shrugged his shoulders again and remarked that the British and the French had feared that the formula of 'indirect aggression' might be exploited by the Soviet Union to take actions incompatible with international law in the Baltic States.

'Your error last year,' I objected, 'and the error of your foreign policy in recent years in general, lies in the fact that you have always wanted to insure yourselves against every contingency. This is very difficult, perhaps even impossible. In practice, one always has to take a certain risk to achieve a result.'

'For instance?' Halifax asked with a somewhat twisted smile.

'For instance, if you had made less of a fuss about the intricacies of international law last year, the result of the negotiations would probably have been different… And what is international law anyway?'

Halifax glanced at me with curiosity and asked: 'What is it indeed?'

'It is a set of precedents from the history of the right of might in international relations,' I pronounced, measuring my words.[76]

Halifax nodded and said, with interest suddenly flickering over his features: 'There is much truth in that.'

He paused, his eyes raised to the ceiling, sighed, and asked me a surprising question: 'Do you think that a time will ever come when international matters will cease to be resolved by force?'

His question rather took me aback, but I immediately replied that not only did I think such a time would come, I was firmly convinced of it.

'When?' Halifax persisted.

'I fear that we will diverge in our treatment of this issue,' I replied, 'because the question of wars vanishing from international relations is closely tied to the concept of the *economic man* of which you disapprove.'

I was alluding to the speech Halifax made before Oxford students a few months ago, in which he attacked the concept of the *economic man*.

Halifax smiled and asked me to flesh out my thought a little. I briefly explicated our notion of the causes of war and of the conditions under which they could be eliminated. By way of illustration, I referred to the experience gained by Russia and the USSR in handling ethnic minorities. Halifax listened to me attentively and suddenly said: 'Nevertheless, not everyone in your country agreed with the new regime created by the revolution.'

'Of course they didn't,' I replied. 'It goes without saying that the 130,000 landlords who used to govern Russia did not agree with the new regime. But what of that?'

'Yes, of course,' said Halifax, as if he were apologizing, 'you adhered to the philosophy that the good of the majority justifies the suffering of the few.'

I confirmed that this was so. Halifax then asked whether I believed the landlords in England to be as bad as they were in Russia, and whether they could expect the same fate. I replied that I was insufficiently familiar with the English conditions to take a definite view, but that I felt it was wrong to draw excessively literal parallels. Russia was an agrarian country, so the question of landlords was central to our revolution. England is an industrial country, so here it is not the landlords, but the bankers and industrialists who play the key role. My remark seemed to flatter Halifax and he added with relief: 'Our landlords will be *taxed out of existence*, but I don't think we'll have an agrarian revolution... I'm sure, for instance, that everybody in my village would be sorry if something happened to my family.'

I looked at Halifax and recalled that I had heard the same words from many landlords in Saratov before the 1905 revolution. But in the year of the revolution furious peasants burned down their estates. Does history really repeat itself?

That was the end of our philosophizing. Halifax moved on to current events.[77] First of all, he asked what was happening in those parts of Poland which were transferred to the Soviet Union last year. I answered that they have become an organic part of our country, that elections are being held there, and that they are gradually adapting to the new life. Halifax then asked whether we thought it desirable to restore Poland as an independent state. He cited the opinion of Boheman[i] (a Swedish deputy foreign minister), who told Halifax some time ago that in his view it would be better for the sake of European peace if the Soviet Union and Germany shared a common border, rather than having Poland between them as a buffer state. Such a buffer would represent [illegible] in European politics. I replied that the question of Poland cannot be resolved in abstract terms: it all depends on what kind of Europe we have in mind – a Europe governed by the 'international law' about which we had been speaking, or a Europe in which war would be eliminated once and for all. I added that the current views of my government on the question of Poland were not known to me.

Halifax asked whether the new border between the Soviet Union and Rumania had been definitively fixed. I answered in the affirmative. Halifax inquired, not without suspicion, whether we had any more wishes with regard to the Balkans. He was obviously alluding to today's press report about the Soviet Union's 'ultimatum' to Turkey. I laughed and said: 'Do you remember the little folk tale I told you last September, when the eastern parts of Poland passed over to us?'

'I recall it,' Halifax grinned. 'So now the peasant has recovered all his stolen property?'

'More or less,' I replied in the same tone.

'How do you see it?' Halifax continued. 'Is the population of Bessarabia content with the changes that have befallen it?'

'That depends who you mean,' I answered. 'The Bessarabian landlords, of course, are not best pleased, but the Bessarabian peasants are, just as obviously, quite content. For them, transferral to the USSR signifies national freedom and the improvement of their material well-being.'

---

[i] Erik Carlsson Boheman, Swedish state secretary for foreign affairs, 1938–45, ambassador to the United Kingdom, 1947–48.

I told Halifax that the Soviet government had already passed a resolution to establish the thirteenth Union Republic – that of Moldavia – and that the reforming of Bessarabian agriculture according to the Soviet model had already begun.

'Don't you think,' Halifax continued, 'that the Balkans might be drawn into the war in the near future?'

I expressed my doubts about this. Halifax also admitted that he is not expecting a military conflict in the Balkans at present: Germany and Italy are against it.

Then he asked: 'Imagine that Hitler is run over by a bus tomorrow or that he is forced to quit the stage for some reason or other: would the present German regime be able to hang on? I doubt it. Neither Göring, nor Goebbels nor Hess, nor anyone else would be able to preserve it.'

I objected that this was too simplistic. After the death of Piłsudski, it was widely believed that the regime he had created would collapse in a few months, but in reality this did not happen.

'But the regime of Beck, Edward Śmigły-Rydz[i] and others was rotten through and through,' Halifax retorted with somewhat unexpected fervour. 'The war proved it.'

'I completely agree with you,' I parried. 'The internal regime in Poland was rotten, but it was already rotten under Piłsudski. The decay became more evident under Piłsudski's successors, but they hung on to power for four years and might still be there now were it not for the war.'

My example seemed to impress Halifax and he wanted to say something more when his secretary entered the room and reported that Lord Lloyd (the minister for the colonies) wished to see him urgently. Halifax's face clouded over and he said, rising from his chair: 'We must meet again and have a chat… It is so important to share our thoughts at this time: after all, we are entering a new world.'

We parted.

My conclusions:

(1) In general, Halifax, like many other representatives of the ruling upper crust, is full of dark forebodings and understands that the war will deprive the elite of its privileges. At a certain point, this could push him toward a 'rotten peace' with Hitler.

(2) In particular, as a consequence of the growing swell of opinion against Chamberlain, which this time is also hitting Halifax hard, the latter has to

[i] Edward Śmigły-Rydz, commander-in-chief of the Polish army in 1939; fled to Rumania, September 1939.

manoeuvre, and considers it profitable to demonstrate his contact with the Soviet ambassador. I doubt that this will help him.

11 July

Churchill's speech on 4 July was a great boost to morale in the country and massively enhanced his personal authority. Once the danger of the French fleet passing into German hands had been eliminated, everybody breathed a sigh of relief… including the communists. So what if this required drastic measures? These only raised the prestige of the prime minister, who had not flinched from taking them. Anyone can see that it is now Churchill, not Chamberlain, who rules the country! Such are the sentiments that now dominate the country.

Naturally enough, these circumstances have strengthened the government's position. But the movement against Chamberlain and Co. is growing. A few days ago the powerful National Union of Railwaymen (Marchbank is its general secretary) passed a unanimous resolution demanding Chamberlain's resignation. This made a strong impression on political circles. Similar developments can be observed at present among miners, metalworkers and others. The article by Tucker, leader of the metalworkers, in *Reynolds News* is very symptomatic.

The Tories are divided on Chamberlain. Chamberlain has a definite majority in the Conservative faction elected to parliament back in 1935. But the Tory majority across the country (especially in the army, navy and air force), whose sentiments have changed radically since 1935, is definitely against him. On the other hand, the City, the Court and the party machine are in favour. The result is a very tangled knot. It becomes ever clearer that the top bourgeoisie wants to keep Chamberlain and Co. in government at any cost, as a guarantee that the Cabinet will not dare squeeze the privileges of the capitalist elite too hard in the interests of 'victory over Hitler'. This elite does not fully trust Churchill. It considers him an 'adventurer' and a 'romantic' who can probably win the war but is unfit for the role of Cerberus to guard their bags of gold. A Tory MP clearly defined the position of the party majority at the meeting of the parliamentary Conservatives on 3 June. He said: 'We shall on no account let a "left-wing" government be imposed on us under the pretext of war.'

* * *

Subbotić came to see me. He says that there are two versions of the Soviet position circulating in London.

The first version assumes that the interests of the USSR and Germany are mutually contradictory and that they must collide sooner or later, whatever Berlin's and Moscow's wishes to the contrary. This is the view of the Foreign Office, which formulates its policy accordingly.

The second version assumes that the Soviet Union is now banking on a world revolution and views powerful British capitalism as the main obstacle in the path to such a revolution. Therefore, the USSR aims first and foremost at bringing England to ruin and at destroying the City, after which the road to the revolution will be clear. Hence the Soviet Union's support of Germany and its hostility towards England. This is the view taken by many diplomats.

* * *

Germanophile circles in Norway have demanded the abdication of King Haakon. Haakon refused.

* * *

I saw Aras. He is very alarmed and insists that the Germans are intentionally trying to undermine relations between Turkey and the Soviet Union, spreading all sorts of absurd rumours about Turkey (the 5th and 6th German White Books). Aras thinks that the T[urkish] G[overnment] should make a protest in Berlin and give the necessary clarifications in Moscow.

Regarding the situation following France's defeat, Aras says: if Italy and Germany decide to occupy Syria, Turkey should actively intervene.

* * *

Azcárate told me the following.

Attlee invited Negrín to dinner a few days ago. It was an entirely private affair at Noel-Baker's place. During dinner, Attlee asked Negrín 'in the most cordial fashion'... to leave England. Needless to say, the British government will never expel Negrín from the country! Negrín, it goes without saying, is guaranteed the right to sanctuary in England! If he so wishes, he can stay here as long as he likes! But... the British government would be infinitely obliged were Negrín to go to America 'of his own accord'. His travelling expenses, visa, etc. would be taken care of.[78]

The meaning of this request is clear. The British government is flirting with Franco. Hoare is sending one desperate telegram after another from Madrid; Negrín's stay in London may spoil the mood of the Spanish dictator. Hence Attlee's request to Negrín.

What vileness! What stupidity! Leaving aside considerations of generosity, which seem to be of little concern to the British government, this move is entirely unwise from the purely military and political points of view. It is most probable that despite all Hoare's efforts, Franco will eventually side with Germany and Italy. Then the British government, of course, will try to employ Republican forces against him, and Negrín would prove most useful. It would seem, therefore, that the British government should look after Negrín in case they need him in future. Besides, it could use this very card against Franco. But no! The British government says to Negrín: 'Would you be so kind as to get out!'

And the manner in which it is done! Oh, naturally, we'd never agree to hang you! We are far too pure and noble for that! We wouldn't like to dirty our hands! But if you would be so kind as to hang yourself, we would be so grateful to you, so obliged!

Genuine, well-bred English hypocrisy.

And Attlee's role? Churchill and Halifax don't want to sully themselves, don't you know, so the Labour Party leader willingly does the dirty work for them. European social democracy performs its historical mission.

12 July

Eden and his wife came for lunch with the two of us, Agniya and myself. We were sitting in the winter garden. It was a beautiful day, and Eden was in a good mood. Looking through the garden's open door, he said with a grin: 'One could come to your place just to rest.'

'You are very welcome!' I responded in the same tone.

Eden asked me about our position, and reminisced about the past, his visit to Moscow, and our meetings and conversations during his stint at the Foreign Office. He remarked: 'You know, the hardest thing for me during that time was to convince my friends that Hitler and Mussolini were quite different from British *business men* or *country gentlemen* as regards their psychology, motivations, and modes of action. My friends simply refused to believe me. They thought I was *biased* against the dictators and refused to understand them. I kept saying: "When you converse with the Führer or the Duce, you feel at once that you are dealing with an animal of an entirely different breed from yourself." Some of our statesmen subsequently tried to approach the dictators in the same manner as they would approach *business men*. The results are well known.'

Then we discussed current events. According to Eden, the British government is in a state of great bewilderment. Numerous symptoms and pieces of information clearly foretold the beginning of a German onslaught on England on 6 July. Today is the 12 July, but there has been no attack. Why not? Members of the government are speculating, but are unable to reach any definite conclusion.

I suggested that the attack may have been deferred because of the fate of the French fleet. What if the initial plans for an attack had been based on the assumption that the Germans would have the French fleet in their hands, and now, after the events of 2–3 July, all these plans had to be revised. Such a process requires time.

Eden found my idea most interesting and, on the assumption that it was correct, began to develop it. He said, among other things, that whatever the reasons for the delay may be, the British government was very glad about it. It has more time to prepare. From the sea, England is now fully protected. The situation in the air is more complicated. True, the airfields are properly guarded, but there are too many natural landing strips in the country. An intensive effort is under way to 'spoil' them. All available digging machines in England have been recruited for the task. Teams of volunteers are also helping out. The outskirts of most big cities are already fairly 'spoiled', but two more weeks are needed to complete the destruction of natural landing strips all over the country. It would be good if the Germans gave the British this fortnight.

According to Eden, a large force is being massed in Northern Ireland. Since a joint Anglo-Irish defence of the entire island has not yet been agreed upon with de Valera, the British government has decided to muster a concentrated force in the north which could be deployed in any part of Ireland in case of emergency.

The causes of the France defeat were the last topic of conversation. In general, Eden has a fair grasp of these causes. I asked whether anything similar could happen in England, too.

Eden categorically rejected this possibility.

'Yes,' he said, 'we too have such men as Laval, but they do not play a major role and carry no weight in government. Besides, our army, or at least the greater part of it, has already fought with the Germans and found that "the devil is never so black as he is painted". This is terribly important. On the whole, army morale is high, and I do not expect any unpleasant surprises on this score.'

[Eden was impressed enough by Maisky's analysis of the prospects for a German invasion to send Churchill a personal brief:

> Monsieur Maisky commented several times upon the manifest difficulty which confronted Hitler in any attempt to stage a sea-borne invasion. He seemed to have a surer grasp of this aspect of the problem than I would have expected. In his view a sea-borne offensive could not be expected to achieve anything unless together with an air-borne invasion … Monsieur Maisky admitted that even so he did not see how the problem of communications could be dealt with.[79]

A prominent American journalist observed that 'Maisky, with his practical grasp of day-by-day changes in thought and emotion, his genial but unruffled contemplation of the whole war in all its details, seemed to me one of the most thoroughly competent observers I had the fortune to meet in England.'[80]]

22 July

Nearly a month has passed since the French surrender, and what was already obvious then has now become even clearer. England is resolutely determined to fight Hitler 'to the end' on her own (who will define what 'to the end' means?).

The public mood – one of determination, perseverance and anger – is more robust than a month ago, especially among the working masses. England no longer has any allies to hide behind. No new allies are visible on the horizon and they are unlikely to appear there in the immediate future. England must rely on itself. This has forced the country to wake from its self-induced calm and recognize the menace confronting it. The result has been not panic or dismay, but a readiness to resist, which finds its most vivid and simple expression in the slogan: 'We won't allow Hitler onto our isles!'

The 'appeasers' have fallen silent for the time being – even in the City. In fact, Churchill's prestige has grown immensely, for he now represents the full and definitive embodiment of the notion of resolute struggle against Germany, even though his motives and the motives driving the working masses may differ.

England has made big strides in its military preparations over the past month. Time has not been lost. There are 1.5 million trained and armed troops in the country (and on top of that 1 million in training), 2 million in the 'Home Guard' (volunteers aged between 17 and 65), and more than 600,000 women in auxiliary military organizations. The mediocre and worthless Ironside has been removed, and Alan Brooke[i] has been appointed commander-in-chief. He is reputed to be a capable and lively general. The entire British coastline has been fortified: artillery units, anti-aircraft guns and machine-guns have been placed all over. The airfields have been mined, they are well guarded, and are covered by artillery batteries placed nearby: should they land, the Germans will be smashed to pieces by cannon-fire. Natural landing strips have been systematically 'spoiled' with the help of ditches, beams, barricades and other obstacles. All sign-posts and names have been removed from the main roads, which have been supplied with forts, bastions and obstacles. The cities have been put on a 'war footing'. In particular, official buildings in London have been transformed into small fortresses. Forts have been built near bridges and at strategically important locations. A round metal bastion has been erected by the porch of 10, Downing Street. Rifle barrels, with bayonets fixed to them, stick out of its embrasures. The entrance to the B[oard] of T[rade] is protected with sandbags and machine-guns. The same can be seen at the other ministries. Air-raid shelters are being built on every street and their number is growing by the day. All approaches to England from the sea have been heavily mined. The fleet

[i] Alan Brooke, commander-in-chief, home forces, 1940–41; chief of imperial general staff, 1941–46.

is concentrated in the coastal areas. There can be no doubt: the country has put up its bristles, and a German landing on its shores in the present circumstances would be very arduous indeed. If Hitler really does not have some 'secret' or other, I fail to see how he could manage it, especially when one considers that British air defence has made a big leap forward following the appointment of Beaverbrook as minister of aircraft production.

This is how things stand. In these circumstances it is hard to conceive of the possibility of peace in the near future. Hitler's speech on the 19th, in which he enjoined England 'for the last time' to 'recover its common sense' and conclude peace, produced not the slightest effect here. Earlier still, the Germans and the Italians sent 'peace feelers' via the pope and Franco, but the British government replied with a terse 'No!' On the whole, it is difficult to imagine a 'deal' between England and Germany so long as Churchill remains prime minister. The appeasement outbreak in the Far East (the closure of the Burma–Yunnan road) cannot serve as a precedent for Europe. Churchill told me more than once in years past that he was ready to sacrifice British interests in the Far East temporarily for the sake of the struggle with Germany. He is merely remaining true to his word.

It is, of course, difficult to vouch for the future. It is hard to say what will happen if massive air raids begin, if the tension of waiting drags on and on, if things start going badly in the Empire, or if the British capitalist elite comes face to face with the threat of serious curtailment of its rights and privileges. But for now it is quite obvious that England is not like France. It will put up a tough fight against German invaders.

23 July

Aras came over. He argued at great length that Hitler would not make a move against England because of the many difficulties involved. On the contrary, Hitler's next blow will be directed towards Africa: against Egypt and Sudan via Gibraltar, Spanish Morocco, Algeria, Tunisia and Libya. If he succeeds, he will press on towards Iraq and Iran, ever closer to the oil fields. Aras asserted that good railways and highways exist all along North Africa, and that in 1912 Turkish troops crossed the Libyan Desert. Why should that not be possible now?

'In general, moving towards Africa is far easier than moving towards Britain,' Aras said. 'Why should Hitler inevitably choose the difficult direction?'

There is a certain sense in Aras's reasoning, but he has proved himself such a poor prophet during the course of the war that I am somewhat reluctant to believe him.

* * *

In spite of the efforts taken by the new government, shortcomings and failures are in evidence everywhere. Just a few examples.

Coal. The present annual output is 260 million tons. England's domestic consumption amounts to 200 million tons. The rest was usually exported. Until recently it was thought that in view of the loss of its northern départements France would take 40 million tons a year. But now all export has ceased. Unemployment among the miners is inevitable. Grenfell (the minister in charge of the mining industry) is creating a coal reserve of 20 million tons. He has also appealed to all consumers of coal, advising them to stock up for the winter. But these are mere palliatives. Wait three or four months, and unemployment among miners will once again rise steeply.

Iron. England produced 14 million tons of iron ore in 1937 and imported 7 million tons. England has plentiful supplies of its own ore, which lie close to the surface (2–7 feet), but the metal content is no more than 30%. High-grade ores were imported from Sweden, Spain, Algeria and Morocco. Now all this has stopped or is ceasing. England tries to help itself by increasing its own production, but about two months are needed to rectify the situation. Metal has become the bottleneck industry. England imports high-grade ore, which is also indispensable, from Sierra Leone and Nova Scotia (3–4 million tons). The annual output of the metal industry is about 15 million tons of cast iron.

Machine-tools. The Ministry of Labour conducted a survey recently and established that machine-tools in the *engineering* industry are used on average for only 44 hours a week, even though many factories work two shifts. The reason? The capitalist system with its competition, lack of planning and so on. The clamour about the shortage of machine-tools is just a smokescreen. What is lacking is the organization of production.

Working hours at factories and plants are beginning to be shortened. The Ministry of Labour carried out a survey which revealed that the long working day (12 hours including overtime) and the abolition of Sunday as a day of rest reduces work efficiency. Therefore Bevin (minister of labour) has decided to return to normal weekends and to reduce the working day to 10 hours (including overtime)

Aircraft production is growing fast. Fifteen new aircraft factories should begin production in the period between July and October. When brought to full capacity, their joint monthly output will amount to 1,000 aircraft. The monthly output at present is approximately 2,000 [sic] aircraft.

The production of rifles is currently negligible: no more than 20,000 a month. For now England still survives on rifles imported from the USA. However, within three months it will boost its own production to half a million a month, once new machine-tools are ready to make rifle butts out of a special pulp.

25 July

A crop of amusing anecdotes.

(1) Simopoulos (the Greek envoy) told me the following political *story* the other day. Ciano went to visit God. In paradise, the Italian foreign minister behaved very indecently and freely mocked God, nudged him, and finally dropped him to the ground. Filled with indignation, God summoned St Peter and asked him: 'What is wrong with that impudent young man who treats me so disrespectfully? Can't you do something to mend his ways?'

'All right, I'll have a go,' answered St Peter.

And indeed, Ciano's behaviour changed beyond recognition overnight. He was most attentive towards God, kept bowing to him, and did everything he could to show his respect. God was pleased and turned to St Peter in surprise: 'What have you done with him? He is a changed man.'

'What have I done?' responded St Peter. 'It's very simple. I told Ciano that here in paradise you are the most important photographer.'

(2) Prytz, with whom (together with his wife) we went to visit the Webbs today, described how when he arrived in London as ambassador he decided to make some improvements in the building of his mission. As the building and land had been leased by the Swedish government for 999 years, he had to request permission for the proposed changes from the solicitor of the owner (the duke of Devonshire, if I'm not mistaken). The solicitor answered politely that he had no objections, but added *pro forma* that according to the terms of the contract the owner could demand that the property should be returned to him in its present condition. On reading the solicitor's letter, Prytz laughed and thought: 'Just fancy bothering about what will happen 999 years from now!'

Prytz confirmed his receipt of the solicitor's letter and made the changes he needed to make. As a 'matter of routine', he forwarded his correspondence on this question to Stockholm.

One fine day he received, to his total astonishment, an indignant reprimand from the Foreign Ministry: how dare he assume obligations for 999 years into the future on behalf of the Swedish government, without even obtaining any form of consent from the latter? There was no precedent for this in the entire history of Sweden!

Prytz had thought English formality to be in a class of its own. But even the English had nothing on the Swedes.

(3) And here is one more story Prytz told me. A fortnight before the abdication of Edward VIII in December 1936 he was in London on business (at that time he did not yet hold an official post) and was invited to a lunch arranged by his predecessor, Palmstierna. The lunch turned out to be thoroughly

'political'. The Swedish crown prince[i] was the main guest, but also present were Eden, the archbishop of Canterbury, and other distinguished figures. The issue of Edward's abdication was in the air. Some persons close to the Court were asking the Swedish crown prince to use his influence on Edward to persuade him, in the interests of the 'monarchic idea', to sever all ties with Mrs Simpson[ii] so as to remain on the throne. The crown prince agreed in principle, provided the British government did not object. In fact, it was precisely in order to discover the government's attitude that the lunch had been arranged. But as soon as the guests sat down to table and exchanged initial remarks on the subject in question, it became perfectly clear that there was nothing for the crown prince to do: the English guests immediately let it be understood that they desired Edward's abdication, and did not wish him to remain on the throne. The archbishop of Canterbury was especially categorical. He told Prytz, who was sitting next to him, with a laugh: 'I'm a very small and unknown man in the Empire, but do you think that even I could retain my *job* if I married Mrs Simpson?'

The Swedish prince did not have to save the crown for Edward VIII after all.

26 July

Glasgow (dip[lomatic] corr[espondent] of the *Observer*) surprised me today. Having been a 'pagan' all his life, two years ago he suddenly felt dissatisfied and started 'seeking God'. He met various spiritual luminaries, chatted with them, learned from them, etc., and finally, about a year ago, joined the Roman Catholic Church. Glasgow says he believes in a supernatural God, considers Christ to be the Son of God, and acknowledges life on the other side!

I reminded him of our conversation a few months ago, in which I stressed that every Church always gives its support to reactionary political and social forces. Glasgow agreed that this is so. He declared that he acknowledges all the *rottenness* of the Catholic Church, but... The Church is one thing and Christianity another. He tried to convince me, moreover, that all the most recent popes had been fighting against the 'inequality of property' created by the capitalist system. I grinned and asked him why in that case all the most recent popes had waged such frenzied campaigns against the USSR, a country that had eliminated the inequality of ownership along with the capitalist system in general?

'That,' replied Glasgow, 'is because the Soviet Union is an atheist state.'

I laughed and told him how, in my school years, I embarrassed our priest by asking him point-blank: which is better – faith without deeds or deeds without faith?

[i] Gustaf VI Adolf, Swedish crown prince; married to Lady Louise Mountbatten, sister of Lord Mountbatten and aunt of Prince Philip.
[ii] Bessie Wallis, duchess of Windsor.

'That is a most profound question,' Glasgow responded with animation. 'It is, if you like, the fundamental question of contemporary Christianity.'

Glasgow then set about expounding the thought that in its essence 'Christian faith' not only does not contradict communism, it goes to meet it. And God, it turns out, is leading humanity to communism: capitalism collapsed in Russia and 'in all Europe east of the Rhine' as a result of the last war. Capitalism will collapse throughout the rest of Europe as a result of this war. Both wars have been sent by God: who could doubt the wisdom and goodness of the Lord after that?... Ravings of a madman... But isn't all this characteristic of the spiritual decay of the bourgeois society of our days?

27 July

Dalton lunched with me yesterday. He says the British government sent instructions to Cripps eight days ago, advising him to agree to the conditions put forward by C[omrade] Stalin (in the conversation of 1 July) regarding the principles of the trade agreement. The matter, Dalton said, now lies with you. According to him, Cripps has been pressing on the FO the importance of a more cordial tone in the British press towards the Soviet Union. The FO likes to sabotage Cripps in general, and on this issue in particular, but Cripps's pressure has nonetheless produced some results.

Dalton is very keen to squeeze Germany, and also to spoil our relations with Germany. That's why he once 'recommended' that we occupy not only Bessarabia, but the oil-bearing regions of Rumania as well. Today he 'recommended' that, in one way or another, we secure the nickel deposits in Petsamo for ourselves. I laughed off Dalton's suggestions (as I did when we spoke about Rumania).

Dalton disagrees with the position of the British government concerning the Burma–Yunnan road and the Baltic States. He is inclined to explain the Cabinet's stand on the latter issue in terms of the government's orientation toward the United States. As for the deal with Japan, Dalton believes it would have been better to evacuate Hong Kong than to agree to the closure of the road.

Dalton told me an amusing story about Hoare. Hoare is in a state of permanent panic. He has got the idea into his head that Hitler dreams of capturing him and holding him as a hostage, threatening to lop off his head should circumstances demand it. That's why Hoare has been inundating the British government with desperate telegrams of the 'Munich' type. In particular, Hoare protested against Dalton's intention to make a statement in parliament yesterday, 25 July, about the decision of the British government 'to put Spain on rations'. Dalton has had to postpone this statement until 30 July. Hoare also insisted that Negrín should leave England.

The British government, according to Dalton, wants to settle the question of the Straits; apparently, Cripps has even discussed this issue with the Turkish ambassador in Moscow.

28 July

The meeting of the Labour faction on 24 July was a very stormy one. For the first time since the creation of the new government the question of Labour's general policy in government was raised. Is it the right policy or the wrong one?

The masses took Labour's entry into government to mean the onset of a new era not just in the course of the war, but also in the domestic, and especially economic, life of the country. This impression was reinforced by the very 'resolute' act passed by parliament soon after Churchill came to power, which has given the government the right to requisition the property and labour of any citizen of the state. While dramatic events were unfolding at the front, while France was being crushed, and while English minds were dominated by the expectation of a German invasion 'any day now', the masses were stunned and remained silent. But now all this is in the past, and the daily threat of invasion has abated in view of Germany's month-long passivity. The masses have come to their senses a bit and are beginning to ask: why have no essential changes been made in the economic structure of the country? Why do the capitalist classes still occupy all the commanding heights? And since the masses have failed to receive any satisfactory answers to these questions, their dissatisfaction is growing.

Such is the background to what happened at the Parliamentary Labour Party's meeting on 24 July. A number of speakers (Shinwell, Bevan and others) attacked the leaders sharply along the lines indicated above. Attlee, Greenwood and other ministers defended themselves. The 'opposition', nonetheless, demanded a vote on the question of whether Labour's policy was right or wrong. The leaders won, of course, but a whole third of the faction voted against them, which is highly significant. And while perhaps one shouldn't overestimate the significance of this fact – especially its direct practical significance – it does, as a symptom of a general mood, offer a window onto the future.

31 July

This is what happened yesterday at a secret session of parliament.[81]

The Conservative, Wardlaw-Milne,[i] who has big interests in the Far East, made an attack on the British government in connection with the closure of

[i] Sir John Wardlaw-Milne, a diehard Conservative MP, 1922–45, who attempted to oust Churchill in 1942.

the Burma–Yunnan road. He gave an impassioned speech to the effect that it is impossible to pacify Japan and that any concession to the Japanese will only stoke their appetite in the future. Wardlaw-Milne's speech made such a strong impression on the House that many MPs began demanding an immediate reply from the government, although Noel-Baker was supposed to speak on behalf of Labour after Wardlaw-Milne. As a result, Butler spoke next, and Noel-Baker had to wait his turn.

Butler spoke for about 50 minutes, mostly about Burma. He said that the Japanese navy was strong, while England could not send even a single ship from Europe to the Far East. The British government had consulted with the A[merican] G[overnment] and it had emerged that although the Am. Gov. sympathized with England, it would not be in a position to do anything practical in the event of an armed conflict between Great Britain and Japan. Butler cited a series of coded messages from telegraphic correspondence between London and Washington to corroborate his arguments. Furthermore, Australia insisted strongly on a peaceful settlement of the conflict with Japan because it had sent its troops to Europe and now feels unprotected. Under these circumstances the British government had no choice but to make a concession, even though it was very painful and unpleasant to do so. But the road was not being closed forever, only for three months! Butler had to admit, however, that nobody could foretell how things would stand in three months' time. Responding to reproaches from the opposition that the British government had not consulted the Soviet Union on this matter, Butler said he had informed me of the British government's intentions a day and a half before the prime minister's statement in parliament. In conclusion, Butler announced that the British government's policy in the Far East would remain unchanged: support to China and friendship with Japan. How exactly the British government is planning to square this circle, Butler did not deign to say.

Then Butler touched on Spain and thanked Hoare for his 'work in Madrid', which already appeared to have improved the situation, before adding cautiously that he could not vouch for the future.

He then turned to the USSR. Butler declared on behalf of the British government that England wishes to maintain and develop cordial relations with the Soviet Union and that Cripps has succeeded in establishing useful contacts with members of the Soviet government, but pointed out the difficulties standing in the way: the present disposition of the Soviet Union, says Butler, is akin to that of Peter the Great in its pursuit of purely 'realistic' policies. In particular, the USSR is currently busy swallowing up the Baltic States. The British government does not intend to engage in pettifogging politics, yet it cannot recognize the recent changes in the Baltic. Moreover, considering last year's experience in Poland, the British government has refused to hand over to the Soviet government the Baltic gold held in England, since British citizens have claims towards the USSR relating to the Baltic States. However, the British government does wish to improve Anglo-Soviet relations and hopes that trade negotiations between the two countries will soon be resumed. But one must be careful not to overestimate the benefits of rapprochement with the USSR: the latter is not about to go to war at the moment, whatever happens. All the same, the age-old 'struggle between the Teuton and the Slav' and conflicts between Germany and the Soviet Union are objectively advantageous to England.

After Butler it was at last Noel-Baker's turn to speak, and he sharply attacked the British government for its position on the Burma–Yunnan road, accusing it of pursuing a policy of *appeasement*. At this point Churchill jumped to his feet and exclaimed in indignation: 'How can you hurl such an accusation against a government which has sworn to fight Germany to the end?'

Noel-Baker was exceptionally embarrassed and he hastened to withdraw his accusation. He then demanded energetic measures to improve relations with the Soviet Union. What an about-face! Just recall what he was doing and saying during the Finnish war!

Churchill requested the floor after Noel-Baker. His speech was very effective. The PM took the bull by the horns: 'It has been already said here that the decision to close the Burma–Yunnan road was unpleasant for the government… Unpleasant!… *We simply hate this decision!* But the government had no choice. The present correlation of forces is such that we could not have acted differently.'

Churchill went on to argue that the situation could change in three months, that he pinned great hopes on the United States, and that the time would soon come when England would be able to give China the support it deserves. In the meantime, it is left to the Soviet Union to help China.

In the second part of his speech, Churchill touched on matters of defence and firmly declared that England was readying itself for a possible invasion and had taken big steps in that direction. But the question remained: would Hitler really decide to attempt an invasion? Churchill couldn't be sure.

After the PM's speech, the Chamber emptied.

Pritt took the floor and challenged the government with three questions: (a) Why did the British government not consult with the USSR on the matter of the Burma–Yunnan road? (b) Why has the British government not yet started trade negotiations with the USSR? and (c) Why did the British government recognize the C[zechoslovak] G[overnment], which includes people of reactionary views as well as individuals of dubious reputation?

Next up was Gallacher (he 'caught' the Speaker's eye, as no one else wished to take the floor), who delivered a fiery speech criticizing the British government's position and describing the favourable circumstances of the Soviet masses.

Since Butler, present on the front bench, showed no desire to answer Pritt's and Gallacher's questions, the speaker hurried to close the session.

5 August

A scandal in a noble family!

When France collapsed, General Sikorski was the first Polish notable to flee to England. He met Churchill and declared to him (this was later confirmed in writing) that the 'P[olish] G[overnment]' did not wish to put a spoke in the wheels of rapprochement between England and the Soviet Union. British government circles understood this to represent a renunciation by the 'P[olish] G[overnment]' of Poland's pre-war eastern borders.

Then there appeared in London 'president' Raczkiewicz,[i] foreign minister Zaleski, other ministers, and a large number of Polish landlords who had fled Poland having lost their lands (including in eastern Poland). France's crushing defeat had shaken their belief in the 'might of the Allies' and they had begun to turn towards… Mussolini, as a 'bridge' to Hitler. Hearing of Sikorski's statement to Churchill, the whole gang flew into a rage. They urged Raczkiewicz to dismiss Sikorski. Raczkiewicz agreed and offered the premiership to Zaleski, who now became leader of the 'landlords'. Then the generals, headed by Sosnkowski,[ii] protested, saying that if Sikorski left, they would leave too. Raczkiewicz got cold feet and Sikorski kept his position. However, opposition against him is growing. What's more, Zaleski decided to take revenge. On 29 July, at a Polish function dedicated to the signing of an Anglo-Polish agreement regarding the Polish armed forces, he delivered a long speech in which he declared that, 'Poland is at war with Russia, but she is not at war with Italy, although certain circumstances have forced her to break diplomatic relations with this country!'

It is reported that all is not well in the Polish army evacuated from France. There are two Polish divisions (about 20,000 troops), but there is great agitation among the soldiers, who resent the fascist tendencies of the officers, their anti-Semitism and their beatings.

6 August

Randolph Churchill turned up unexpectedly in his splendid hussar uniform. It turns out that he has been transferred from his tank battalion to the newly formed 'mobile units' [Special Operations Executive], whose task is to 'wage

---

[i] Władysław Raczkiewicz, president of the Polish Republic in exile in London, 1939–47.

[ii] Kazimierz Sosnkowski, general, commander-in-chief of the Polish armed forces from 1943.

partisan warfare' in the event of a German invasion. Randolph said many interesting things.

He says that the military are very put out: they are ready for an invasion, they are desperately eager to give the Germans a 'warm welcome', but the Germans just won't arrive. British air reconnaissance surveys the shores of France, Belgium and Holland every day: not the slightest sign of an imminent invasion. Can Hitler really have abandoned his idea?

Randolph's father sent out a warning over the radio the other day: 'Do not disarm.' The danger of invasion is not over, he said, addressing the public at large. We must remain vigilant. Over the past few days, the newspapers have been following the PM's lead, writing about German preparations for an invasion, the concentration of ships in the Baltic and Norway, etc. But all that, according to Randolph, is mere agitation. Its aim is to counter the August *holiday mood* and complacency in general. In actual fact, W. Churchill has no new signs or evidence of an invasion being prepared. The British government can only speculate: What's up? Why is Hitler moving so slowly? Because he has yet to complete his preparations? Or because he is short of ships? (Randolph mentioned in this connection that British pilots have photographed the *Scharnhorst* and the *Gneisenau* in dry dock, with damage requiring 3–4 months' repairs). Or because Hitler and Mussolini have decided that their next blow will be aimed at Africa, Egypt, etc.? Or because they want to strike simultaneously in different directions – against England, Egypt and Gibraltar?

Nobody really has a clue, but the British government wants to be ready for every eventuality. It is, for example, currently massing forces in the Near East. Australians, incidentally, are being transferred there from England. Why Australians in particular? There are two reasons. First, they are good fighters. Second, no one knows how to deal with them in England: they are just too 'free-spirited'. They disregard discipline, disobey their officers, fail to salute and constantly quarrel with the British soldiers. The war department is only too glad to get them off its hands and is sending them to Egypt and Palestine.

I asked what the British government presumes *the major strategy of the war* to be?

Randolph replied that the immediate objective of the British government is to eliminate the threat of invasion. After which come the following aims: to attain air superiority by the end of this year or the beginning of the following; to form a 3-million-strong land force by spring; and to move onto the offensive in 1941. The blockade, of course, will be stringently enforced. If the war continues for another two years, the British government will have an air fleet of 150–200 thousand machines. Such is the scale according to which the British government conceives the expansion of its military operations. Great hopes are pinned on the United States: it will probably enter the war after the presidential elections. Whatever the circumstances, the USA will provide maximum aid to England in weapons, aeroplanes, etc. No, there is no reason for the British government to be despondent! Things are shaping up in its favour.

We turned to internal affairs. I expressed my doubts about the ability of the British elite to pursue the war 'to the end': for this would raise, in the sharpest terms, the question of the preservation of their present privileges! Are they ready to make such a sacrifice? Hardly. Randolph, however, grinned, and replied with a contemptuous wave of his arm: 'Are they ready? Father will make them do it!...'

And he added with undisguised hostility and irritation: 'My father will find it a particular pleasure to shatter the privileges of our upper crust. Oh yes! He'll gladly disperse that vile, decaying gang!'

What does this mean? Randolph's opinions always reflect those of his father. In which direction is the prime minister prepared to 'liquidate' the privileges of the English upper crust: to the right (towards fascism) or to the left (towards socialism)?

7 August

I saw Attlee in parliament and had a serious talk with him on the Baltic question. Attlee behaved very strangely. At first he cast doubt on the freedom of the peoples of Estonia, Latvia and Lithuania in expressing their will to join the Soviet Union. So I asked him directly: 'Does this mean you don't wish to recognize the changes that have occurred in the Baltic States on considerations of principle?'

Attlee took fright and hastened to answer: 'No, no! You've misunderstood me.'

He then changed tack, arguing that it was not a matter of principle, but of compensation: British citizens had investments in the Baltic States which they will now lose. If the matter of compensation is settled, there will be no complications. I objected, arguing that compensations and recognition of the changes are two quite different things and should not be confused. Moreover, the losses of British citizens are yet to be proved. Here Attlee flew into a rage and set about defending British investments like a lion. He did so far more robustly than Butler or Leith-Ross would have done.

I finally lost my patience and noted rather sharply: 'Since when have you started taking the interests of the City so close to heart?'

Attlee was somewhat embarrassed and replied: 'I'd like to see what you would do in such a situation.'

'Such a situation simply could not befall us,' I parried, before concluding: 'How the British government acts is a matter for you to decide. I, at any rate, have warned you in advance and my conscience is clear. If complications arise, you'll have only yourselves to blame.'

10 August

I had Amery (secretary of state for India), Butler, Boothby and General Spears to lunch today.[82] Amery expressed familiar concerns about Indian affairs, but he made it clear that the Indian viceroy's[i] declaration on 7 August was not the last word. The British government will go further if need be. I even gained the impression that Amery himself would be ready to go further immediately, but the Cabinet won't let him. Butler says Cripps was satisfied with his talk with C[omrade] Molotov on 7 August, and that Cripps is closer to us on the Baltic issue than he is to the British government. Butler also says that the British government is currently discussing that issue and he hopes it will be resolved before long… In what spirit? Butler kept silent about that.

Spears was the most interesting of the company. He was the liaison officer between the B[ritish] E[xpeditionary] F[orce] and the French army throughout the winter and observed many curious things. Boothby asked Spears how he would explain the catastrophe in France?

Spears' answer was very characteristic. The reasons he gave were: the predominance of the 'Maginot psychology' in the French army in general and among the officers in particular; the obsolete nature of military thinking in France; the unsatisfactory performance of the General Staff, and in particular the poor disposition of the French army; the advanced age of the French generals; and the lack of talent in the military leadership. Weygand's reputation, in the opinion of Spears, is greatly inflated. He is in fact a very mediocre general. These, said Spears, were the military causes of the catastrophe. But there were political ones, too. To illustrate the point, Spears referred to Weygand once more. Bolshevism was for him the No.1 enemy. Hitler was always the No. 2 enemy. At the last meeting of the French government before surrender, Weygand insisted on an armistice, arguing that it was the only way to save the army, which was needed to prevent a revolution. The greater part of the French government felt the same.

Spears also related an amusing incident in which he had been involved. It happened on the day when the Germans entered Rouen. The front had essentially already collapsed. The army was in full retreat. France was hurtling towards defeat. It so happened that on that day Spears had to visit Pétain on some business. The old marshal asked him what he thought of the current situation. Spears replied: 'Only a new Jeanne d'Arc could save France.'

[i] Victor Alexander John Hope (2nd marquess of Linlithgow), governor-general and viceroy of India, 1936–43.

'Ah, Jeanne d'Arc,' Pétain echoed with animation. 'Yes, yes, she was an extraordinary woman! I've been fascinated by her all my life.'

Pétain fished out from his drawer the manuscript of a long speech devoted to Joan of Arc, which he had given a few years ago on the occasion of some anniversary, and read it to Spears from beginning to end. Having finished the speech, Pétain launched into a long, general discussion of Joan of Arc. He took thick books down from the bookcase, read out long quotations, commented profusely on the reliability or unreliability of various sources, and offered his judgement. He entertained his guest in this manner for one and a half hours! Then Pétain remembered he had to hurry off somewhere and left, having even forgotten to ask Spears what he'd come to see him about.

And all France thought at that time that the 'old marshal' was stretching every sinew of his mind to lead the army, find a way out of the country's catastrophic situation, and by some great heroic effort 'save the fatherland'...

14 August

Yesterday I attended parliament. The question of India was discussed – one of the most important questions of the war and of the future of the British Empire. What of it? No more than fifty members were present, most of them sat on the opposition benches. The Conservatives' benches were half-empty although Amery (secretary of state for India) is a Tory – as blue as they come! The speeches were grey and boring. The 'stars' kept silent. A cloud of deathly tedium hung over the hall.

But the rare unanimity of persons and parties was striking. All praised with one voice the viceroy's weasel speech of 7 August – Tories, Labour, Liberals and Independents. Vernon Bartlett spoke approvingly, while Eleanor Rathbone[i] expressed her pleasure with her voice and gestures.

A curious incident happened at the meeting of the Labour Executive Committee on 13 August. The meeting was drawing to a close when it dawned on the members of the committee that the question of India would be discussed in parliament the following day. Who should speak? They deliberated for a while, then decided that the first to speak after Amery should be... Lord Winterton (who, as luck would have it, now sits on the opposition front bench next to Shinwell and Wedgwood). Who else? Who else from Labour? Lees-Smith[ii] (the chairman) indecisively surveyed those present. They kept silent until someone suggested: 'Let Ammon[iii] say a few words.'

Ammon is a third-rate *backbencher*, a kind of *Mädchen für alles*.

---

[i] Eleanor Florence Rathbone, critic of appeasement and Independent MP, 1929–46.
[ii] Hastings Bertrand Lees-Smith, chairman of the Parliamentary Labour Party, 1940–41.
[iii] Charles Ammon, Labour MP, 1922–31 and 1935–44.

The decision was made: Ammon would speak.

Pethick-Lawrence then piped up: 'But we need to know what Ammon is planning to say!… What if he decides to support Nehru?'[i]

'Oh no, he won't do that,' came the universal response.

Ammon quite justified the Executive Committee's trust: he did say 'a few words', and foul ones at that.

What a characteristic scene!

15 August

Saw Lloyd George yesterday, who passed on some interesting news: Chamberlain has bowel cancer and although, formally speaking, he remains in the Cabinet, he is to all intents and purposes *done for*. This should have various political repercussions. One is already known: Beaverbrook has been brought into the War Cabinet. Further changes are to be expected. Churchill once again invited Lloyd George to join the War Cabinet (through Beaverbrook), but the old man declined the invitation because he disagrees with the government on two matters: foreign policy and India.

Lloyd George maintains that the main issue in the sphere of foreign policy is the Soviet Union. But the Cabinet is gambling on the United States. That's a mistake. Even if the United States does enter the war, its participation will not have a practical effect for another two to three years, for the USA has neither an army nor an air force. All this still needs to be created. Lloyd George remembers perfectly well how it was with the Americans in the last war. Meanwhile, the role of the Soviet Union already has huge significance today. Even leaving aside the question of the USSR's participation in the war (Lloyd George is well aware of our general stance on this matter), the positions taken by our country have colossal importance in terms of how a satisfactory peace might be arrived at and concluded. Hence the importance of the issue of Anglo-Soviet relations. But what is the British government up to? It's staging an indecent vaudeville show with the Baltic States. This is stupid and dangerous!

The question of India is very serious, too. It is one of the cardinal problems of the war and of the entire future of the British Empire. In Lloyd George's opinion, the British government is treading water. It has plenty to say except the one, crucial word which is called for. A solution to the Indian problem is possible. 'I know Gandhi well,' Lloyd George said. 'I've talked to him a lot. I say!… He is less a "saint" than a clever and skilful politician. The main thing is that he has an excellent sense of how far we can go in making concessions.'

[i] Jawaharlal Nehru, Indian nationalist leader and statesman.

Then, making a cunning face, Lloyd George winked and added meaningfully: 'I'd manage to come to an agreement with him!'

Summing things up, Lloyd George let it be understood quite clearly that he would not enter the government unless he had serious hope for a change of policy in the two directions mentioned.

Then we turned to various other topics. Lloyd George commended C[omrade] Molotov's last speech: 'It is very clever from the point of view of Soviet interests, but unfortunately it promises little from the point of view of British interests. But I understand your irritation. Our Foreign Office has acted with great stupidity with regard to the Baltic States and the Burma–Yunnan road.'

The purport of Germany's recent mass raids on England is not yet clear to Lloyd George. Maybe it is the prelude to an attempted invasion. Or maybe it is the prelude to a more severe blockade of the British Isles. Time will soon tell. At any rate, the morale of the population is still very good, and the scale of destruction suffered by the country is insignificant.

[Cripps, complained Cadogan to Halifax on 17 August, 'argues that we must give everything – recognition [of the Baltic States], gold, ships and trust to the Russians loving us. This is simply silly. Agreed to tell him to sit tight. We will see what we can do here with Maisky. Exactly nil, I should say. However H. proposes to begin by asking Maisky and Madame to dine – and threatens to ask me too! Extraordinary how we go on kidding ourselves. Russian policy will change exactly when and if they think it will suit them. And if they *do* think that, it won't matter whether we've kicked Maisky in the stomach. Contrariwise, we could give Maisky the Garter and it wouldn't make a penn'orth of difference.'[83]]

17 August

The duke of Windsor has arrived with his Mrs Simpson in the Bahamas, where he has been appointed governor. Essentially, of course, this is exile. Why has the former king been treated so harshly?[84]

I've heard from excellent sources that Queen Elizabeth is behind it all. She is 'master' of the house and has the king under her thumb. She is awfully jealous. She has set herself the task of bringing popularity and splendour to the royal family. She sends the king everywhere – to camps, factories, the troops, the front line – so that he should appear everywhere, so that people should see him and grow used to him. She never rests either: bazaars, hospitals, telephone operators, farmers, etc. – she visits them all, gives her blessing, graces with her presence, parades. She even pulled off the following, highly unusual stunt recently. The queen's brother, who serves in M[idle] E[ast] C[command], arranged a private tea party, to which a dozen prominent American journalists were invited. The queen attended the party, too, and for an hour and a half she 'chatted graciously' to the correspondents, together and individually. But not, of course, for the papers. The queen is terribly afraid that the duke of Windsor might return home and 'steal' his brother's popularity, which required so much effort to achieve. That is why the duke of Windsor was exiled to the Bahamas.

18 August

We visited Gollancz at his country home. There we found Guo Taiqi, Strachey, Bevan and his wife, and other guests. We had a long talk, argued heatedly, and exchanged opinions on what lies in store for England.

A great muddle and a great variety of views. There were no two people who would agree with each other.

My thoughts (although I did not voice them fully today) are as follows.

England has enough cards in hand to avoid defeat and successfully extricate itself from the war. But will England be able to play its cards well? That's the crux.

There are four major problems facing England today:

(1) military,

(2) foreign policy,

(3) India,

(4) domestic policy.

Since Churchill came to power, the first problem has been addressed, and, although it is too early to draw a definitive conclusion, seems to be on the path to being resolved. The production of aircraft and weapons has increased sharply, the organization of the army has been expedited, rapid strides have been made in fortifying the island, and the danger of a German invasion has receded. Of course, much remains to be done, but progress is smooth and there are grounds to believe that the problem will eventually be solved. The current British government has been playing this card rather well.

The second problem has not been solved, and it is still not clear how it will be solved. Halifax remains in charge of the FO, whose personnel is still thoroughly imbued with the old Chamberlain spirit. The British government has been playing this card badly, which has particular consequences for relations with the Soviet Union – the key question in the current situation.

The third problem is locked in a stalemate. The viceroy's statement of 7 August and Amery's speech in parliament on 14 August have failed to indicate a way out of the deadlock. Perhaps this will change with time, but up to now the British government has been playing this card badly, too.

The fourth problem has not yet been raised. Essentially, it concerns the very considerable weakening, if not complete elimination, of the domination of the bourgeoisie in England's economic and political machinery and, accordingly, the enhanced influence of working people, above all the proletariat. The British government has been playing this card badly, too.

These are the problems facing England today (when still considered within a capitalist or near-capitalist framework).

Will the Churchill government be able to solve these problems, at least so as to emerge from the war without defeat? For it seems unrealistic to expect such an outcome if these problems are not resolved in a more or less satisfactory manner.

Will it be able to? I don't know. Time will tell.

Of course, everything would change if the possibility of a peace treaty were to emerge within the next few months. But can this happen?

At the moment I can't see such a possibility emerging. The crux of the matter is that the imperialist interests of England and Germany conflict to such an extent that they cannot be reconciled at this stage. Over six years following Hitler's rise to power, desperate attempts were made to find a path of compromise. For three years (1937–39), England was led by a man who was prepared to do whatever was required to come to terms with Germany. In principle, Hitler, too, was always an advocate of an agreement with England against the Soviet Union and France. The 'subjective' factor, on both sides, was expressly in favour of an agreement. Yet an agreement was not reached! Worse still, the matter culminated in war. Why? Because the 'objective' factor – the conflicting imperialist interests of the two states – turned out to be far stronger than the 'subjective' factor: the desire of Chamberlain and Hitler (and the elements they represented) to reach an agreement.

This also applies to the current prospects of peace being concluded in the near future. On what basis could this happen? I still can't see any.

Supposing Hitler were to say: let's divide up the world – I'll have Europe, you'll have the British Empire, and some 'colonial trifles' will go to Germany and Italy. Clearly this is the best that England might expect from Hitler at present. Would an agreement be possible on such a basis?

The young Rothenstein couple paid us a visit a day or two ago. I put that question to him and his reply was: 'No, it would not be possible. And here's why. England's sole advantage over Germany today is its command of the seas. This is what makes it so difficult for Germany to conquer England. Were we to conclude peace now on the basis of Hitler's present conquests, it would mean that, with all the resources and shipyards of Europe at his disposal, he would be able to build a fleet to equal ours in some 5–6 years, and England would become a toy in his hands.'

These words betray the underlying cause of the 'belligerence' currently sweeping both the ruling circles and the population at large, including the workers, although among the latter this cause often appears under the pseudonym, 'the struggle against Nazism'.

That is why I don't see any prospects for an early peace – under the essential condition, of course, that the Soviet Union continues to pursue policies no less wise than it has hitherto. And I'm fully confident it will.

20 August

From a purely oratorical point of view, Churchill was not at his best today, speaking in parliament on matters related to the war and foreign policy. His speech, which lasted for some 50 minutes, was somewhat uneven. There were brilliant and forceful passages that arrested the attention of the House, but there were also moments when the temperature fell and some MPs even started chatting. However, the content of the prime minister's speech was quite coherent. Churchill summed up his government's first three months in office and found them quite satisfactory. Even though the danger of invasion has not yet passed, it recedes with each passing day, while British defence resources are growing at massive speed (especially air defence). Churchill places great hope on 'cooperation' with the United States. The blockade of Europe will be continued relentlessly: provisions for the countries occupied by Germany will not be allowed through from America (Hoover and Co.'s project). The war will be lengthy: preparations must already be made now for an offensive in 1941 and 1942. On the whole, Churchill's entire speech expressed growing confidence in England's fighting efficiency and a belief that the worst had already passed.

The same note of confidence characterized the debates that followed. These were not, on the whole, notable for their brilliance. At our meetings we would say of such a situation: 'all is clear'. That's why the big beasts didn't speak, while the backbenchers dwelt on details. Just one curious fact: Churchill elicited the loudest cheers when he spoke of the British air force and of the refusal to let American provisions through to Europe.

After Churchill's speech I went into the lobbies. I saw many people (Gwilym and Megan Lloyd George, Burgin, Elliot, Leonard,[i] Neil Maclean and others). They all share the same mood of high, new-found confidence, and ecstatic admiration of the British air force. People are literally *crazy* about their pilots. And they all say as one that the German air raids have not done any great damage anywhere. This is partly explained by the fact that the *dummy* system (airfields, factories, etc.) has been widely implemented.

Megan expressed interest in the state of Anglo-Soviet relations. There was nothing I could say to reassure her. She was sorry, scolded Halifax, and gave the

---

[i] William Leonard, Labour MP for Glasgow, 1931–50.

following explanation for the deadlock in relations between our countries: 'I've known Churchill for many years, ever since I was a small girl. He came over for lunch or dinner to our house on countless occasions, discussing various matters with my father... What always appealed to him most was war. He studied the wars of the past and contemplated the wars of the future. He always imagined himself a military leader, destroying armies, sweeping through Europe, overthrowing his enemies or putting them to flight. Military terms were always on his lips, and his head was forever full of military plans and projects. I'm sure that today he is wholly absorbed and intoxicated by the war. He thinks only of that, is interested only in that. Everything else is secondary to Churchill, Foreign Office included. There he's given Halifax the reins... Ah, that man! I think Halifax is now far more dangerous than Chamberlain.'

There is, I sense, much truth in Megan's words.[85]

The other day I saw Little[i] (ex-president of the Engineering Union, he now holds a prominent post in the Ministry of Labour), who told me among other things: 'Churchill says that peace will be agreed in Berlin. He will not settle for less than that. Churchill believes that this time Germany should learn a lesson that will put it off fighting once and for all. This can be done in one way only: by bringing the war onto German territory. So far Germany has waged war mainly on foreign territory (1870 and 1914–18). Let it try fighting at home now. That is why, in Churchill's view, England should move onto the offensive in due course and crush Germany with the weight of metal. British war production must be raised to an unprecedented height.'

This also smacks of truth.

There may come a moment in the course of the war when we find ourselves in sharp conflict with Churchill, as happened in 1920. Time will tell.

22 August

Lunch with Sir Walter Monckton. An idiosyncratic, thoroughly English type. Officially a Tory, but in actual fact an extreme radical to whom even revolutionary ideas are not alien. Legal adviser to the duke of Windsor and a close friend of Cripps. Currently occupies the post of chief censor and thinks about revolution in Europe.

Monckton expressed some very interesting thoughts. In his view, the general military situation in England is now relatively favourable, and Churchill will probably be able to launch a military offensive against Germany as early as

[i] John Carruthers Little, president of the Amalgamated Engineering Union, 1933–39; industrial commissioner, Ministry of Labour and National Service, 1940–45.

next year. But that is not enough. The most England can count on in the purely military sphere is to avoid defeat and agree an *inconclusive peace*, which in essence would amount merely to a more or less durable armistice. The roots and causes of military conflicts in Europe will remain untouched. An offensive is not enough if England wants to really win the war and prevent the emergence of a new armed conflict in the nearest future. What is needed in addition (and perhaps in greater measure) is a political offensive, i.e. changes in the nature of British foreign and domestic politics which could unleash a revolution in Europe, including Germany. Not bad! I only fear that Monckton does not quite perceive what the 'political offensive' he advocates would really entail. And if he were able to perceive this clearly, would he remain faithful to his present aspirations? Who can tell?...

The conversation then turned to Churchill's role in this war. As leader of the military offensive, Monckton said, Churchill is good. But can he become leader of a political offensive as well? Monckton can't yet say, but he doesn't rule out the possibility that Churchill's romantic affection for Empire plus his love of power might make him such a leader. How far would Churchill go in this direction? This is also unclear to Monckton as yet. Churchill would probably be inclined to curtail sharply the privileges of the capitalist upper crust, but would he do so sufficiently *to win the war*? Of course, everything in England will be done the English way. The introduction of a Soviet system may not be necessary here in order to achieve 'victory'. The introduction of a particular, intermediary form of socialism may be enough. Perhaps Churchill will prove capable of 'accepting' or 'creating' such a form: he is, after all, neither a banker nor a businessman – he is not a man of the City. Churchill is a politician and a writer, who makes his living with his pen. He is not as steeped in the capitalist system as, for example, Chamberlain. He does not depend on shares, interest, landed property, etc. He will earn his 'crust' with literary labour whatever the circumstances.[86] Why, then, should he not become the leader of a political offensive? If this happens, England's transition to a new system will proceed more or less peacefully and calmly. But if Churchill were to oppose the transition to a new system, then major domestic complications would be inevitable.

I listened to Monckton and thought to myself: which way will Churchill go? To the left or to the right? Towards socialism or towards fascism? What role is he destined to play in the impending events? In what shades will he be recorded on the pages of history? It is at present difficult to give an answer to these questions. One thing is certain: the following one, two or three years will be an exceptionally interesting period in the history of England and in the life of the prime minister personally.

30 August

A visit from Simopoulos. The Italian press campaign against Greece causes him great anxiety. Yet he doubts that Italy will attack Greece. For what can Italy gain from it? The first consequence of such a step would be for England to occupy Crete (and its magnificent Bay of Suda) and other Greek islands. British warships are already on patrol near Crete. It would mean that British sea and air bases operating against Italy would be transferred from Alexandria to Crete or even Cephalonia. Why would Italy want this?... Simopoulos, therefore, is inclined to think that Mussolini is bluffing and wants to scare Greece in order to get something from it. What exactly? That is not yet clear.

Momchilov came by. He spoke at length about the declining influence of the Italians in Bulgaria, and said that Sofia has decided against raising the matter of Dobrudja now, as it counts on receiving it without a fight and for good at the end of the war. Besides, Bulgaria realizes that Turkey would interfere if this issue were raised in a serious manner. That would lead to an armed conflict, and Bulgaria desires war least of all.

I saw Aras and inquired about Turkey's position with regard to the Italian campaign against Greece. Aras declared that Turkey is obliged to bring its armed forces to Greece's aid in only two circumstances: (1) if Bulgaria attacks Greece (the Balkan Entente) and (2) if a third power threatens the 'maritime boundary' between Greece and Turkey (the mutual assistance pact between Greece and Turkey). The maritime boundary is understood to be the Aegean Sea and its coastline.

I asked what Turkey would do should Italy attempt to seize Saloniki.

Aras started to wriggle. I gleaned from his words that if the Italians had already entered Saloniki, Turkey would have to interfere.

'All right,' I answered, pressing him further, 'and if the Italians were not yet in Saloniki, but had already begun their march on Saloniki from Albania – what would Turkey do then?'

Aras spread his arms and replied that in that case the 'interpretation' of the agreement between Greece and Turkey would be crucial. He went on to admit that this 'interpretation' would wholly depend on the Soviet position.

31 August

We visited the Webbs. Without mentioning Monckton's name, I put to Beatrice Webb the same question which the former had discussed with me (see the entry for 22 August): Are there any grounds to believe that in the course of the war England may be able to switch to a 'political offensive', that is, become a socialist state?

Beatrice considers this impossible. She has various arguments. First, war is an inappropriate time for major social changes. Second, who might carry out such a reconstruction of society? Labour? But the Labour leaders serve capitalism. The very psychology of Transport House precludes it from taking decisive action in any sphere, especially the economic. It lacks the necessary courage, firmness and boldness. The working masses? But they, too, have been excessively corrupted by parliamentarism and trade unionism. They are not revolutionaries, they are gradualists, especially the working aristocracy. A combination of left Conservatives, Liberals of the Lloyd George type, and Labour men like Cripps and Pritt? Beatrice finds it difficult to imagine such a coalition. Even if such a coalition were created, it would be unstable and would hardly be able to carry out serious restructuring within the existing system.

No, talk of a socialist England emerging in the course of the war can be left to one side! So too, then, can talk of 'victory'. Beatrice does not even believe in victory. She thinks that the Germans cannot invade England, while the British for their part cannot drive the Germans out of France, Holland, Belgium and other countries, to say nothing of capturing Berlin. That is why Beatrice foresees a long war of attrition and prolonged mutual destruction from the air. Her sole hope is that the Soviet Union and the United States may perhaps intervene at a certain point in the war and force the belligerents to conclude a 'reasonable peace'. But will this hope come true?

When we went out for a walk, Beatrice told me: 'I'm very glad that in our old age we, my husband and I, came to understand "Soviet communism" and accept it. Had this not happened, we would now be the darkest of pessimists in everything which concerns the future of humankind.'

A valuable confession! And from such a source!

1 September

The Germans have been carrying out mass air raids on England for three weeks now. Three phases may be discerned in the course of this 'invasion' from the air.

(1) 8–18 August. Mass, large-scale daytime raids. Hundreds of planes take part, up to 1,000 daily. That number was recorded on 15 August. The attack is not concentrated on one or several major points, but is spread in short bursts over many localities and cities.

(2) 19–25 August. A lull. Minor daytime raids. Few planes in each raid. Scattered attacks. The Germans seem to be searching for and preparing something new.

(3) 26 August to the present day. Raids by day and by night. The daytime raids bring fewer planes than in the first phase, but they are more concentrated and focused. The Germans mainly target the London–Dover–Portland triangle.

Their main objectives are ports, airfields, industrial facilities and railways – all in this area. They are obviously paving the way for an invasion. The attacks are frequent, several times a day. At night very few machines fly over England, especially over London. But they go round and round in circles for several hours on end and occasionally drop bombs. This is evidently a form of 'psychological attack' against the broad masses of the population. So far the night raids have not made a major impression on the English.

Of course, this is not the end. We'll see what happens next.

[The 'Battle of Britain' was the prelude to Operation *Sealion*, the plan for the invasion of Britain earmarked for mid-September. It was adopted in Berchtesgaden on 31 July by the naval and army chiefs, who, however, had serious reservations over what seemed to be insurmountable obstacles.[87] Greatly impressed by the public spirit and resilience displayed by the residents of London, Maisky had become convinced 'that Great Britain will not be invaded by the German army, and that by next year she will be superior in the air ... the air raids in Great Britain will dwindle, and air raids in Germany and her occupied territories will increase in destruction and effect'. He was further convinced that Britain would preserve its stronghold in the Mediterranean, but he could not see how she could possibly dislodge the Germans from the territories they had gained in Europe.

The two alternatives he saw then were a negotiated peace or for Great Britain to become 'a socialised community, not necessarily on the Soviet model, but practically emancipated from capitalism and landlord control. There could be a real and lasting Soviet and British pact to free Europe from Hitler's dominance.'[88] These views certainly were not in conformity with Stalin's outlook – to which Maisky was not privy – of extending the Ribbentrop–Molotov Pact to cover the Balkans and bring the war to an end, with the Soviet Union and Germany sharing dominance in Europe.[89]]

6 September

Dalton came for lunch. In 'the strictest confidence' he elucidated for me the situation surrounding the Baltic question. This is how things stand.

Since July, the entire British foreign policy has been directed toward supporting Roosevelt's re-election and involving the United States in the war. Every move taken by the British government in the sphere of foreign policy is made with the following thought in mind: what will be the reverberations in the United States? The same is true of the Baltic question: the British government's position depends wholly on that of the A[merican] G[overnment]. Meanwhile, the A[merican] G[overnment] (the English recently did some soundings in Washington) does not intend to recognize the changes which have occurred in the Baltic region and give us the Baltic gold. On the contrary, the US government associates the 'freezing' of the Baltic gold with the freezing of the French, Dutch and Norwegian gold. This makes it difficult for the British government to agree to the 'thawing' of the Baltic gold and to the closure of the Baltic missions in London. Moreover, some British citizens have grievances against the USSR in connection with the events in the Baltic. Hence the vacillating tactics of the FO.

I strongly attacked the British government's conduct, but Dalton spread his arms and said: 'I understand and even sympathize, but you should understand our situation too. America is our priority today.'

So much so that Churchill has basically withdrawn all American affairs from the jurisdiction of the FO and administers them directly.

Dalton expanded the thought that the Soviet Union should seek more friendly contact with the United States. This would facilitate the improvement of Anglo-Soviet relations. Besides, it would lay the foundation for a 'four-power combination': England, the United States, the Soviet Union and China. This would stabilize the situation in the Far East, strengthen China, and prepare the way for a 'reasonable' end to the war. I listened to Dalton, but remained *noncommittal.*

Dalton is awfully pleased with the Anglo-American agreement of 3 September ('bases, destroyers'). There is more to it than destroyers, although they are fairly important by themselves. Dalton says that a *gentleman's agreement* exists between London and Washington concerning the USA's entry into the war after the presidential election. This does not mean, however, that the USA has pledged to send a large army to Europe soon. Actually, England would not want this now anyway. If the United States began forming such an army right away, they would need to arm it before arming anyone else, which would mean a cut in military supplies to England. The USA's entry in the war is understood in London to mean the receipt of credits in America and of the maximum number of weapons. Besides, it would have a tremendous political-psychological impact: Germany would finally understand then that victory is impossible. The end of the war would thereby be hastened.

Dalton is leaving town for two weeks – 'on holiday'.

'But I'll come back instantly if there's an invasion!' he exclaimed, with his customary sweep of the arm.

7 September

A month has passed since the beginning of major air attacks on England. Some conclusions can be drawn.

What was the aim of these attacks, insofar as one may judge by the activities of the German air force and by the official and unofficial statements of the Germans themselves?

Undoubtedly, Hitler's 'general idea' was to pave the way for the invasion of England by means of (1) destroying British air defence (hence the strikes on airfields, aircraft factories, planes, etc., particularly in the London–Dover–Portland triangle); (2) disrupting and dislocating the machinery of the British state and economy; and (3) undermining the population's and government's morale.

Have these goals been attained?

As of today – no.

In fact, the output of aircraft factories has constantly exceeded the losses of the British air force. Almost all the airfields are in working condition, including those in the south-eastern triangle. The losses suffered by the industries, and in particular aviation, are small. Transport is functioning quite well on the whole. Import-exports are maintained on an entirely satisfactory level, and as a result the shops are full of mass-market goods. One can sense no shortage of food in the country (only meat, butter and sugar are rationed, but it is easy to receive in excess of the norm).

The state apparatus is also functioning normally. Of course, there are a fair number of defects, but these are in no way connected with the air raids. No panic may be observed in political quarters. The government stands firm, and it seems to me that Churchill himself even *enjoys the war*. The morale among the wider population remains good, despite the night raids and broken sleep. We shall see what lies ahead.

What is the reason for the manifest German failure?

The strength of British resistance. The German planes have to break through a triple defence wall: anti-aircraft fire, barrage balloons and very effective interceptor fighters (Spitfires and Hurricanes). As a result, the German planes have to fly at high altitude (4–6 thousand metres) and can't remain in the sky for long. They are forced to drop the bombs in haste. Attack dives succeed rarely and only by chance. Consequently the Germans fail to score many hits. Daytime air raids have been particularly unsuccessful, even though the number of fighters covering German bombers was doubled last week. So the Germans are reverting more and more to night raids, which, it seems, will now become a regular occurrence in our life.

8 September

It seems that the Germans themselves have realized the futility of their former tactics, because just yesterday they switched to new techniques of air warfare.

The Germans undertook a massive and intensive air raid of London yesterday afternoon. It was the first raid conducted on such a scale and with such intensity since the beginning of the war. The British were evidently shocked by the surprise attack and responded rather weakly. As a result, the Germans succeeded in setting the dockyards on fire and demolishing many buildings and workers' houses in the East End. The fire is still raging today. I drove around the East End and stood on the hill in Greenwich Park from where I could clearly see columns of fire and clouds of smoke rising from various locations in the port. They say as many as 400 have been killed and 1,500 wounded.

Raids continued throughout the night of the 7th to the 8th. German planes went on pounding the city, taking their bearings from the tongues of fire. The workers' districts – the East End and Kilburn – suffered most of all. Many proletarian shacks have been destroyed. Industrial facilities, power stations, gas plants and so on have escaped serious damage. The Finnish embassy, though, has been wrecked. I don't know whether or not the Germans are targeting military objects; if they are, they are doing a bad job of it. It's hardly surprising: yesterday and today the German planes have been flying at an altitude of about 7 kilometres.

British resistance last night was very feeble. The sky was ablaze with searchlights, but they rarely picked out the enemy planes. The anti-aircraft guns were mostly silent. Strange. The people are greatly alarmed at the absence of any proper retaliation. The government will face serious difficulties if this continues.

9 September

Subbotić visited me a couple of days ago. He arrived in quite a state: he had just received news from Belgrade claiming that the Soviet Union and Germany had reached or were about to reach an agreement about the 'division of spheres of influence' in the Balkans and the Near East. The Balkans would allegedly fall into Germany's 'sphere of influence' and Iran into the Soviet sphere. The question of Turkey remained undecided. If all this was true, was it not possible to arrange for Yugoslavia to be included in the Soviet 'sphere of influence'?

I set about ridiculing Subbotić, saying that one should not believe any old rumour, particularly now. The Soviet Union is not trying to carve out 'spheres of influence'. The Soviet Union pursues a policy of peace, using the means dictated by the given situation, and it takes a negative view of any widening of the current conflict. The Soviet Union has interests in the Balkans, and certainly does not want to see this part of the world ablaze with the flames of war.

Subbotić left somewhat reassured, but not fully convinced.

Today I visited him and managed to dispel his suspicions completely. I assured Subbotić on behalf of the S[oviet] G[overnment] that no agreement exists between the Soviet Union and Germany about the division of 'spheres of influence' in South-East Europe and the Near East, and that the matter has not even been raised in talks between the USSR and Germany.

Subbotić brightened up, shook my hand firmly and said he would wire this exceptionally important news to Belgrade right away. On parting, he said: 'We shall feel ourselves to be, as it were, under the invisible protectorate of the Soviet Union.'

10 September

Today, we made our first acquaintance with the bombs. It was about one in the morning. German planes were constantly buzzing about over our heads. Agniya and I were in the shelter and were about to go to bed. Suddenly the shelter shook from a heavy blow, the lights went out, and there was a terrible crash very close by, in the very building, it seemed, of the embassy itself…

My first thought was that a bomb had fallen on our house.

I grabbed the telephone and asked Krainsky, who was on guard at the entrance, what had happened. Krainsky, his voice shaking, replied that bombs had fallen somewhere nearby. Our building had not been damaged, apart from the knocked-out window panes. He couldn't see much in the dark, but it seemed that the house across the street had been shattered to its foundations and had collapsed.

Agniya and I came up from the shelter to the embassy, walked around the building, and looked into our flat. Everything seemed all right except the panes and electric cable. Feeling a little calmer, we returned to the shelter and lay down to sleep.

At six in the morning, when the *all clear* was sounded, we got up and went out into the street. It was growing light. Pieces of asphalt from the road were

73. Maisky proud of the impregnable shelter built in the grounds of the embassy.

74. Inside the shelter.

scattered over our yard. The Lithuanians' house opposite was in one piece, but it gazed vacantly at us from the cavities of its shattered windows. We learned that three small bombs had been dropped two houses down from us (opposite no. 11). There were shell craters there. People were rummaging about. Workers were hammering away at something. I came closer and picked up a piece of shrapnel. The asphalt was still smouldering.

The house diagonally opposite from us was also intact; only two window panes needed replacing.

We returned to the embassy and went to the flat to catch up on our sleep.

13 September

The seventh day of concentrated air attacks on London.

Once a German, always a German. A German acts according to a meticulous, fixed plan. That's what's happening now. Every day the same pattern is repeated. During the daytime – two, three or four short raids. Each raid generally lasts no more than an hour, sometimes only 15–20 minutes. Mass columns of bombers accompanied by fighters arrive from the French coast. British fighters and anti-aircraft guns usually intercept them at the shore, before they approach London. Only small groups of German planes manage to break through to the capital. British fighters meet them again over London. The contest begins and the raiders either plummet or turn back (anti-aircraft guns operate very rarely during the daytime for fear of harming the population with splinters). These day raids do little to disturb the city's ordinary life, but cost the Germans dear: they lose 60–80 machines a day, and sometimes more, in daytime combat, as against 20–30 British fighters. Pilot losses are even more disproportionate: the English lose single-pilot fighter planes, in which 40% of the pilots manage to save themselves one way or another, while the Germans lose a significant number of bombers with crews of 4–5 men, plus a quantity of fighter planes, some of which carry two men. As a result, the Germans lose 200–300 men in battle daily (for them, every pilot is lost, even if he leaps out of the plane, as he lands in enemy territory), while the English lose 6–7 times fewer.

The night raids begin between 8 and 9 p.m. and usually last until five or six in the morning. German bombers come alone, without a fighter escort, and in smaller numbers than by day – rarely more than 50 or 60. But they cause a lot of damage. Incomparably more than the day raids. Why? Because at night German bombers are masters of the skies: British resistance is negligible during these hours. This is partly due to the fact that fighters are fairly ineffective at night, and partly to the heavy cloud cover over London which often prevents searchlights and anti-aircraft guns being employed. So the German bombers prowl above the city without haste, having a good look before taking aim and dropping their deadly gifts.

It was not until yesterday and the day before that the British tried using anti-aircraft guns on a massive scale. The cannonade was especially furious between the 11th and the 12th. A terrible din filled the air all night long. Thousands of guns shelled a sky divided into squares, confronting the German bombers with a barrage of fire. This seems to have produced a certain effect: German raids over the last two nights have faded a little, in quantity and efficacy. True, not many planes were brought down (only four on the night between the 11th and the 12th), but the powerful anti-aircraft fire forced the German machines to keep to a high altitude and not linger, with obvious consequences.

We pay little attention to air raids by day and try to work as usual. We generally succeed. In the evenings it's a different picture. The whole embassy relocates to the basement and we stay there from the beginning of the first raid until bedtime. If bombs start exploding in very close proximity, we move to the 'shelter'. Agniya and I have a special room down below, where we live like students. At night we sleep in the shelter, which is relatively safe, and hear neither the bombs nor the anti-aircraft batteries. We sleep like soldiers, of course, dressed or half-dressed. The duty officer wakes us at 5 or 6 a.m., once the 'all clear' has sounded, and all of us – sleepy and dishevelled – return home to sleep in our own beds for the remaining three or four hours. That's how we live. It's more or less tolerable (leaving aside the squabbles among the staff over places in the shelter). But can one live like this for long? We'll see.

How London has changed over these past few days! Beyond recognition. Only a week ago everything looked relatively normal. London still resembled itself. And now?

Now the 'front' has come to London. Many streets are closed to traffic. At every step there are wrecked buildings, cracked pavements and broken windows. Most of the theatres and picture houses are closed, and those that are open give only matinee performances. The evening black-out brings pitch darkness. Deserted streets. Omnibuses, trams and taxis caught in a raid stand rooted to the spot. Only the underground functions, along with military machines rushing at full pelt through the city. The anti-aircraft guns roar, while bombs fall silently from the sky. Blazes flare up in one spot after another, and fire engines tear along the streets with a rumble and a rattle…

Yes, little is left of the old, familiar London. Still less will remain with each passing day.

What aim are the Germans pursuing?

They are seeking, it would seem, to pave the way for an invasion by (a) disrupting the means of communication and (b) undermining the morale of the population and the government. Have they attained this aim?

No, not as yet. As far as transport is concerned, the Germans can only boast of very insignificant successes. True, the London dockyards have been partially burned and destroyed, but the London port continues to operate. True, Waterloo station has been closed and the Charing Cross and Victoria stations have been slightly damaged, but the railways still function normally, albeit with a few interruptions (delays, crammed carriages, etc.). All London's bridges are intact. Omnibuses, trams and taxis are in good order, as are the underground and the aerodromes. A remarkable thing: the Germans bomb the most important London stations intensively every night, but without any serious consequences. Industry has sustained some damage (gas plants, power stations, the Woolwich arsenal, the Lipton tea-packing factory, etc.), but none of this is critical. Military production has hardly suffered. Damaged industries are being repaired very quickly.

And how is morale?

In the first 2–3 days of the current assault, the population, particularly in the East End, was confused, alarmed and nervous. What troubled them most was the total impunity experienced by the Germans and the feeble English response to the night raids. Tens of thousands of people were evacuated from the East End to other parts of the city between 7 and 9 September. However, this mood soon passed. Naturally enough, people are still full of concern and uncertainty about what the coming day will bring. Everybody curses and grumbles about the inconveniences caused by the air raids, but there are no signs of defeatist sentiments. On the contrary, feelings of anger and animosity towards Hitler and Germany are on the rise. And when an Englishman is driven to frenzy, he becomes a very dangerous animal.

The government's mood? Oh, quite unshakeable: war 'to the end'! Churchill's speech of 11 September made this quite clear. It's precisely the resolute and definite character of the British government's stance which has done so much to help the masses overcome their initial fright. There is no panic in the country and Churchill intends to fight tooth and nail.

Yet the masses are displeased with the government for the poor quality and quantity of shelters, for the excessively soft treatment of the Germans during the British air attacks on Germany, for the inadequate defence of London, and so on. There is also growing popular discontent towards the rich, who are sitting it out in solid, comfortable shelters, while demands have been voiced to move East End workers to the empty houses of the wealthy in the West End. The *News Chronicle* has already taken up the latter idea, and I would not be at all surprised should the British government decide, for demagogic purposes, to do something (something trifling, of course) in this direction. Meanwhile, outbreaks of anti-Semitism have been reported in the East End.

No, the Germans are still very far from attaining their objective.

How will things develop? Hard to say. The sleep problem begins to acquire a critical importance. People are sleeping badly these days, which is reflected in their mood and their capacity for work. If this problem is not resolved in some way, the further intensification of the air war may have a deleterious effect on the morale of the population.

14 September

Eden lunched with me yesterday.[90] He looks fine: fresh, tanned, full of energy. His mood is confident and resolute. We spoke, of course, about the war.

Eden holds that the next ten days will be decisive: either Hitler will attempt an invasion over this period, or he will have to put it off for a good while, if not indefinitely. After September, there are storms at sea, rain and fog, and the difficulties which the German forces will face on landing will increase considerably. Besides, at least half of the German soldiers will be unfit for action when they reach English shores because of sea sickness (the average German is '*a poor sailor*'). But even if Hitler decides to try his luck and invade, England is ready.

'Many people here,' said Eden, 'hope he does try. They are sure we will manage to beat off the Germans and the war might thus be brought to an early end.'

'And what do you think?' I asked the war secretary.

'I am also convinced we will manage to repel the Germans,' Eden replied, 'but I would prefer to avoid an invasion: it will come at too great a cost to the civilian population.'

'But still, do you think Hitler will decide to invade?' I continued.

Eden thought for a moment and said: 'I think he will. He likes to do what nobody has done before, what everyone considers impossible. An invasion of England?… This hasn't happened for nearly a thousand years. It's a terrible temptation for Hitler. That is why we are prepared.'

According to Eden, 30 well-trained armed divisions represent the core of the island's defence (in all, there are 1,700,000 men under arms in England today, not counting the anti-aircraft defences). There are as many in the reserve, but they are evidently less well trained and armed. The rest are undergoing training.

England has massed and continues to mass large forces in the Near East, where Eden expects major events to unfold in the near future. Egypt is exposed. The situation in Spain, from the English point of view, is a bit better than before.

Eden expressed interest in the condition and prospects of Anglo-Soviet relations. I acquainted him with the recent developments in the Baltic region – he had only a general knowledge of them – and I expressed the opinion that my eight-year experience as ambassador in London has rendered me sceptical about the possibility of a serious improvement in relations between our countries.

'That is sad to hear,' Eden responded. 'Personally, I take the view I took five years ago, when I visited Moscow. I think there are no critical, insurmountable contradictions between England and the Soviet Union in any part of the globe, so relations between our countries can and must be good.'

'Tell me frankly,' I replied, 'do many of your Conservative colleagues think the same?'

Eden admitted that a significant number of people in his party think differently.

'That is the whole problem,' I said. 'That is why I have lost confidence in the possibility of a serious improvement in Anglo-Soviet relations.'

16 September

Nothing much has changed in the air war. The Germans' tactics remain the same. Only there are more raids during the day. Air-raid warnings follow one after the other virtually without interruption. One could say that we have 24-hour raids with relatively short intervals. The Germans exploit the cloudy weather, so typical of England, quite deftly: they hide in the clouds and suddenly appear where nobody expects them. That was how they managed to drop bombs on Buckingham Palace.

In general, however, daytime raids are fairly ineffective: the Spitfires and Hurricanes operate very successfully. At night, the anti-aircraft fire scares the Germans away. It costs a lot, but produces results: the intensity of night raids has decreased, and there are fewer casualties and fires.

The Germans are still having no luck with the major military objects. They are missing even more than before. They try very hard, but all the bridges, railway stations and so on are *intact*. The air supremacy which the Germans require as a precondition for invasion is, if anything, further off now than it was ten days ago.

The morale of the population has improved. First, all are growing accustomed to the situation (as the proverb goes, 'a man is not a pig – he can get used to anything'). Second, everybody is awfully pleased with the anti-aircraft fire.

The Germans have spread the rumour that the king, the government and the diplomatic corps are being evacuated from London. Nonsense!

17 September

I lunched with Alexander. He is evidently very happy in his post as first lord of the Admiralty and willingly discusses naval topics.

Alexander considers the danger of invasion to be real: German preparations 'on the other side of the water' are just too extensive and diverse. The Germans will certainly try to attack from different directions, not only from France and Belgium, but also from Denmark, Norway and Holland. In particular, they are making major preparations on the Norwegian coast, most likely with the intention of striking at Scotland or at least the Orkney Islands. But the British navy is vigilantly following the enemy's every movement in every direction (particularly along the Norway–Scotland route), and it would be difficult for German forces to break through to the British coast. Of course, one cannot rule out the possibility that an isolated unit of Germans troops may make a landing somewhere along the thousand-mile coast, but such a force would be immediately annihilated.

Speaking of the navy's defence measures against invasion, Alexander emphasized with some satisfaction that new warships have begun to come into service, including battleships.

'However,' Alexander noted, 'we may even have too many battleships for this war. The Germans have very few large ships, and our battleships have little to do. To rebuff a German invasion we need not battleships but small vessels of every type – destroyers, submarines, trawlers, etc. We have a good number of these, many hundreds! If the Germans do try to come over, they will pay a cruel price.'

Alexander is terribly pleased to have received 50 destroyers from the United States. This increases the British destroyer fleet by 30%. Alexander hopes that the Anglo-American agreement on the Pacific currently under discussion in Washington will soon become a reality. Then the Americans will have Singapore at their disposal.

Alexander quizzed me in detail about the state of Anglo-Soviet relations. I could say nothing to reassure him. Alexander sighed, shook his head, and promised to speak to the Foreign Office. He also kept sounding me out as to whether grounds for compromise might be found on the Baltic question. I told him very firmly that I consider the proposal put to me by Halifax on 10 September quite unacceptable.

* * *

Butler told Prytz today that the last week has been a 'happy' one for England: great progress has been made in the Washington negotiations.

In response to Prytz's probing, Butler said that England wants to 'shift' some of its burden onto the United States. This concerns the Far East. Once the agreement is concluded, the United States will become the leading power in the Pacific and play the decisive role on issues such as China, Holland, India, Indochina, etc. England will merely second the United States. But this means that England will be able to focus its efforts on Europe, Africa and Asia west of Singapore.

This information is most interesting. One tendency is becoming increasingly manifest: British imperialism is in retreat in America and East Asia, with US imperialism occupying the positions vacated by Britain. Light rear-guard action undertaken by British imperialism (such as the sending of Lord Willingdon's[i] trade mission to South America) does nothing to alter the essence of the matter.

4 October

The British government reshuffle in May was of a fundamental nature: the most dim and reactionary elements of the Conservative Party (the City, the Court, the Church), which had gone bankrupt in the areas of foreign and domestic policy, were replaced by a coalition of more flexible and far-sighted Tories like Churchill and Eden, plus Liberals and Labourites. True, Chamberlain managed to retain a position of some strength inside the 'new government', but it was a 'new government' all the same.

---

[i] Freeman Freeman-Thomas (1st marquess of Willingdon), viceroy and governor-general of India, 1931–36.

The government reshuffle carried out yesterday as a consequence of Chamberlain's resignation 'on grounds of ill health' has nothing fundamental about it. It's just a game of musical chairs – with some very strange results. Anderson, for example, who manifestly failed as home secretary, has now been promoted to the War Cabinet. In general, one can conclude that the political combination found in May still looks durable in October.

What leaps to the eye is the swelling of the War Cabinet: eight members instead of five. This institution is clearly running to seed. In May the ambition was to achieve what Lloyd George had done in the last war: to put in charge a small elite whose members would be free from departmental duties and who could concentrate all their attention on the general problems of the war and the urgent tasks of the moment. Nothing good ever came of it. The May War Cabinet consisted mostly either of nonentities like Attlee and Greenwood or of entirely compromised figures like Chamberlain and Halifax. Churchill was the only exception. The more significant and vibrant individuals were appointed heads of various departments outside the War Cabinet (Eden, Sinclair, Alexander, Bevin, Morrison, Dalton and others). As a result, along with the *de jure* War Cabinet, which usually met three or four times a week for one and a half to two hours, there emerged a far more important *de facto* War Cabinet: Churchill and six or seven prominent ministers directly associated with the conduct of the war. The present reshuffle has finished off the War Cabinet. Now, from being the leading authority responsible for the conduct of the war, it has become merely a board responsible for maintaining the party-political balance in the British parliamentary system. Radical changes may of course occur in this area in the future, but I am speaking only of what is evident today.

Within the War Cabinet we now find the following distribution of forces: a group of Chamberlain men (Halifax, Anderson and Kingsley Wood) are opposed by three Labourites (Bevin, Attlee and Greenwood), with Churchill and Beaverbrook finding themselves in the role of arbitrators. Outside the War Cabinet are Duncan[i] (Ministry of Supply) and Lyttelton[ii] (minister of trade) – experienced men of the City. Together with the Chamberlain 'troika' they will watch out for the interests of the most reactionary elements in the capitalist elite. Far from weakening the position of these elements in the government, the reshuffle has reinforced it. True, Labour's position has, formally speaking, also been strengthened (three members in the War Cabinet), but one must take into

---

[i] Andrew Rae Duncan, MP (National), City of London, 1940–50; president of Board of Trade, 1940 and 1941; minister of supply, 1940–41 and 1942–45.

[ii] Oliver Lyttelton (1st Viscount Chandos), president of Board of Trade, 1940–41; minister of state and member of War Cabinet, 1941–42; minister of production and member of War Cabinet, 1942–45.

account the hare-hearted character of Attlee and Greenwood, and also the fact that Bevin is made of the same stuff as fascist dictators.

For now the war policy of the new government will remain the same: five of its members (Churchill, Beaverbrook and the three Labourites) belong to the 'party of war' and three (Halifax, Anderson and Kingsley Wood) belong to the party of 'peace at the first opportunity'. However, Beaverbrook is changeable and it is difficult to say whether he will maintain his current course for long. Bevin is a strong-willed man and much will also depend on his behaviour, but it is too early to predict his role in the new Cabinet.

The new government's policy towards the USSR will also remain unchanged: the Chamberlain troika plus Bevin (who has long been of a very anti-communist and anti-Soviet mind) will be against us, and Attlee and Greenwood will sit on the fence. Churchill and Beaverbrook will be the ones to decide. I don't expect great things from this combination.

Cripps has been to see C[omrade] Molotov.

Cripps began by informing C[omrade] Molotov about the British government's decision to open the Burma–Yunnan road. This initiative, according to Cripps, should weaken the thrust of Japanese aggression. Cripps also informed C[omrade] Molotov of the British government's attitude towards the recently concluded tripartite pact (Germany–Italy–Japan).

C[omrade] Molotov indicated that the Soviet Union does not take a negative view of the opening of the Burma–Yunnan road, but nor does it overestimate the importance of this fact, since the traffic of goods on that road has never been great.

Then Cripps said roughly the following: the tripartite pact, in the opinion of the British government, is more dangerous to the USSR than to the USA (it caused an upsurge of anti-Japanese feeling in the United States). The British government, counting on US support, will take a firm stance in respect to Japan. The United States has yet to define its position clearly on the Chinese question (owing to the forthcoming presidential election), but it has already granted a 52 million dollar loan to China. The Soviet position will play a massive role in defining that of the USA. For instance, should the Soviet Union conclude a non-aggression pact with Japan, the United States would probably refrain from active measures in the Pacific, even in respect to the Dutch East Indies or British possessions, to say nothing of the USSR. The British government believes that consultation about aid to China between the United States, the Soviet Union and Great Britain would have a strong impact on Japan and other countries. War with China will inevitably weaken Japan and stunt its aggressiveness.

C[omrade] Molotov's reply amounted to the following: the Soviet position in respect to China is known to all and does not require further explanation. It is doubtful whether consultation between the three countries mentioned by

Cripps would be expedient or politically advantageous. The USSR and England and the USSR and the USA have so far failed to reach agreement even on minor questions (not through any fault of the USSR) – so what can be expected from joint consultation on problems of major significance?

As far as the tripartite pact is concerned, the S[oviet] G[overnment] takes the view that the pact does not introduce anything new, but merely formalizes the relations which effectively existed anyway.

Finally, as for the danger of the pact to the Soviet Union, the S[oviet] G[overnment] believes that Germany is currently up to its eyes in Europe and cannot render any real assistance to Japan. Neither can Japan really help Germany.

Cripps argued that consultation on the Chinese question between the USA, the USSR and England might pave the way to a general improvement of relations between these countries.

C[omrade] M[olotov] listened to Cripps's arguments and said that should he have anything more to tell Cripps on the topic of their conversation, he would not fail to do so.

6 October

The air offensive of the last two weeks can be divided into two phases.

The first (21–28 September) was marked by the same intensity as before. The attacks on London were even stepped up. There were several air raids every day. Groups of 150–200 planes crossed the Channel on each occasion, but no more than 10–15 succeeded in breaking through to London. The ratio of fighter escorts to bombers rose, becoming 4:1 in favour of the fighters. The raiders were repelled mostly by Spitfires and Hurricanes, and to a lesser degree by anti-aircraft fire. The material losses from the air raids were not large. It is reported that, having lost many bombers, the Germans started using faster and more manoeuvrable fighters (*Messerschmitt* 109 and 110), but this information needs to be checked.

Much more serious were the night raids in that period – mostly on London, though some provincial centres were attacked, too. These were mass raids, with up to 400 bombers engaged every night. Bombs were dropped chaotically, without military targets being sought. The bombers simply pounded residential homes, shops, cinema houses, and so on. London is a gigantic city (50 km in diameter): wherever you drop a bomb, you'll hit something. The bomb weight kept increasing: 250, 500 and 1,000 kg. There appeared the so-called [word missing in diary], huge mines weighing up to 1.5 tons dropped by parachute. These mines don't go deep into the ground, but their destructive power is immense: they bring down entire blocks. There were many delayed-action bombs, too. I remember paying a return visit to the Siamese minister[i] during this period. He received me in a room with knocked-out windows: a 250 kg bomb had fallen not far from the Siamese mission the previous day. Twice during our conversation we heard the crash of an explosion nearby. These were [word missing].

The second phase (29 September–5 October) was characterized by a decrease in the intensity of attacks both by day and by night. The effectiveness and accuracy of the bombing did not increase. True, the Germans had some successes. They sank a cruiser in Glasgow, hit the aircraft engine factory in Bristol, etc., but the material losses were not significant on the whole. For instance, the aircraft factory in Rochester, about whose alleged destruction the Germans made a great fuss, is intact and continues to operate. All the London bridges are intact, the BBC is intact, and so are nearly all the 'military objects'. One bomb fell on St Pancras Station, where there was at the time a great quantity of explosive material. The English got very lucky on this occasion: the bomb fell at a sufficient distance from the dangerous freight for catastrophic consequences to be avoided.

I do not know how to explain the slackening intensity of the air raids over the last week. Maybe the bad weather and the good defence of the English are responsible. Or maybe it's just a German trick: to lull the enemy before delivering a crushing blow. Some are of the opinion that the German offensive has begun to exhaust itself. We shall see.

Although the two-week air raids have not caused great destruction, they have exerted, and still exert, a considerable influence on London's general condition. The life of the city is undoubtedly thrown into partial disarray by the night raids. The matter of sleep is central to the emerging difficulties. The people do not get enough sleep and their work capacity naturally decreases as a result. The transportation services also suffer from the air raids: the 'tube' from being transformed into shelters, and omnibuses, automobiles, etc. from constant route alterations owing to the temporary closure of streets wrecked by bombs. Hence the confusion, crowds, queues. In the evening the city turns into a desert. The omnibuses, taxis and trams stop. Only the Underground functions, but even then with interruptions. As a result, labour efficiency in London has decreased by approximately a fifth. For instance, the output of the 40 London factories which manufacture aircraft parts has decreased by 18%.

The morale of the population and government remains high. People are growing accustomed to life in shelters, and these have noticeably improved. The appointment of Morrison as home secretary and Wilkinson as his deputy has certainly influenced the mood of the masses.

---

[i] Phra Manuwajwimonnat, Siamese minister in London, 1940–42.

The capitalist firms that sustained damage from the air raids display an exceptional, even animal-like power of survival. Peter Robinson and John Lewis [department stores] were bombed to pieces about three weeks ago. They have already managed to recover and are continuing a lively trade in ladies' articles.

The probability of the German air offensive succeeding diminishes by the day.

9 October

Boothby came for lunch. He is terribly pleased with his job and his post (deputy minister of food).

He told me that from 6 a.m. today he was feeding the 'homeless' in the East End. The Germans dropped an enormous bomb that made a crater about 20–30 feet deep and 100 feet wide. A whole block of workers' houses on *Commercial Road* was demolished. Fortunately, all its residents were spending the night in shelters. When they returned, their houses already lay in ruins: 250 people were left homeless. The first thing to do was to provide them with some sort of food. This should be the business of the borough council, but it is absolutely bankrupt. The Ministry of Food had to help, and Boothby set off for the East End at dawn.

Boothby says he has become enthusiastic about arranging communal kitchens. There are 50 in London already, and a few have been arranged in Birmingham, Manchester, Bristol, Liverpool and other cities. They are needed primarily to feed workers whose families have been evacuated to safe locations. A law will soon be promulgated obliging all factories that employ more than 200 workers to arrange such kitchens. As an advocate of communal kitchens, Boothby is seizing the opportunity to implement his ideas. However, he has to overcome strong opposition on the part of… the workers themselves and especially their wives. The wives stubbornly refuse to admit that communal kitchens might serve food no worse than their own. Their men are also a little suspicious of 'communal lunches'. They are so used to the sandwiches which their wives put in their pockets in the morning. But things are going ahead all the same.

As I listened to Boothby, my mind summoned a scene from the distant past. I happened to spend a fortnight in the so called 'Socialist Camp' near *Great Yarmouth* in the summer of 1913. The camp was at the seaside and any *socialist* or *reformer* could have a proletarian tent and a proletarian meal for a very modest proletarian fee. There were many people there from all over England, mostly skilled workers, clerks, and a few intellectuals from the lower classes. After *tea time*, debates and discussions were held on the most diverse subjects. I remember one of the topics: what will a socialist society look like? The discussion was long and heated. Two Yorkshire miners have stuck in my memory. Socialism had their full approval and they would welcome a socialist society with open arms – under one essential condition: bread must be baked not in big communal bakeries, but by their wives at home. Otherwise the miners would not accept socialism! Not for the world!… The whole debate ended up focusing on the question of baking bread. The passions and excitement aroused by this 'problem' abated only once a compromise had been found, as always tends to happen in England. The debaters agreed that there would be communal bakeries, but people could, if they wished, receive their bread ration in flour, so that wives could bake bread to their husbands' taste in their individual ovens!

I told this amusing story to Boothby. We had a good long laugh at the conservatism of the British worker.

Then we turned to the war. I asked Boothby how he saw the war developing.

Boothby is in a very bellicose mood. In his view, the war will continue until Hitlerism is completely routed.

'Even if takes 10 years of fighting to achieve! Or 40! Peace with Hitler is impossible! I rule out the possibility of England and Germany concluding a peace treaty signed by Hitler in the name of Germany. This cannot happen. If any British government tried to do anything of the kind, it would lead to revolution in the country, for such is the mood of nine out of ten English citizens.'

However, when I began to probe Boothby about how he thought victory against Hitler could be achieved, doubts and uncertainties began to emerge. As far as one could understand, Boothby sees the situation as follows: England will not be invaded. In winter the war will be waged in the Middle East, with its centre in Egypt. For the time being, England will be on the defensive there. The London–Berlin air war will continue, as will the unyielding blockade. When England achieves a decisive advantage in the air, it will go on to the offensive, but it will scarcely do so by land. Boothby does not consider a British march on Berlin possible – unless it is a *victory march*. The main offensive method will be from the air, along with the blockade.

Of course, a ten-year war might bring Germany to its knees, but who is capable of waging a ten-year war? This is not the sixteenth century, nor even the era of Napoleon. Boothby and his ilk neglect the 'human factor', i.e. the psychology of the working masses.

Boothby inquired about the state of Anglo-Soviet relations. I could say nothing in particular to reassure him. He responded by shaking his head, sighing and cursing.

10 October

A reception at the Chinese embassy.

According to Butler, the British government is fast reaching the conclusion that since the questions that C[omrade] Molotov described as 'minor' in his conversation with Cripps cannot be 'put on ice', it would be better to resolve them at once. Cripps is pressing strongly in this direction: he wants to clear the decks for Anglo-Soviet cooperation on more significant matters. We shall see what this means in practice.

Agniya had a go at Butler because of the delay in finding a house outside town for our women and children. He was embarrassed and promised to see to the matter personally.

Colonel Moore,[i] dressed in uniform and ready for battle, described to me the military prospects for the next year: England will attain air supremacy by the end of winter. In April or May it will assume the offensive – not only in the air, but by land as well. By spring, England will have an army of 4 million at its disposal. Germany has an 800-mile coastline plus the coastline of discontented France, Holland, Belgium, etc. The British control the sea. A landing is possible. An invasion can be organized. In addition there is the effect of the blockade. England will be able to claim victory in the autumn of 1941 and conclude an honourable peace.

'Perhaps I am an optimist,' Moore concluded, 'but that's how I see it.'

I expressed my doubts about the accuracy of Moore's calculations, if he is taking only military means of fighting into consideration. I said his notion had a chance of being realized only if England were to embark on a resolute political offensive within the next year, which would concretely mean (1) settling the India problem; (2) internal restructuring tantamount to turning England into a socialist state (I did not, however, use the word 'socialism'); and (3) a radical change in British policy towards the Soviet Union. It is not for me to decide whether England is able to start such a political offensive, but it is clear to me that only such an offensive can bring England a genuine 'victory', one which would not contain the seeds of a new war.

My words greatly impressed Moore. He thought them over and said he agreed with me. But I doubt whether he clearly understood all the *implications* of my idea.

By the way, Moore recently bought a very old bookshop in the centre of London that is associated with Dickens and many other famous writers. He now wants to arrange tea parties there once a week and invite such men as Shaw and Wells to speak.

'Despite the war?' I asked rather sceptically.

'Why should we yield to the war?' Moore responded.

---

[i] John Moore-Brabazon, lieutenant-colonel; responsible for the RFC Photographic Section during the war and the development of aerial photography; MP for Wallasey, 1931–42; minister of transport, 1940–41; minister of aircraft production, 1941–42.

12 October

What a tour that was yesterday!

A bit of history first. During the lunch which the Halifaxes arranged for Agniya and me on 10 September,[91] we spoke at length about air raids and bomb shelters. Some three days earlier, the Germans had launched their air offensive against London. I made a tour of the East End and saw the fires and destruction in the port area. I was struck by the paucity of shelters in this part of London, fewer than in other districts with which I am more familiar. I related this impression during the course of the lunch. About two and a half weeks later, I received a long letter from Halifax where, referring to relevant statistical data, he declared that my impressions were mistaken.[92] In conclusion, he suggested I make a tour of the bomb shelters in the East End. Halifax promised to organize the tour. I decided to accept the invitation and visited the East End yesterday with Agniya.

Our 'guide' was Admiral Evans,[i] who has just been appointed 'dictator' of the London bomb shelters. His chief of staff, Colonel [name missing in diary] accompanied us, as did Ellen Wilkinson, who was appointed deputy home secretary a few days ago and who is (in the words of the gallant Evans) 'the queen of the bomb shelters' in parliament. Ellen was with us only at the beginning of our tour though, for she was urgently needed at her ministry and had to dash off.

Our first visit was to the 'Group 2 HQ' (there are nine groups comprising the 95 boroughs of Greater London). The building of this 'HQ' had been seriously damaged a few days earlier and the staff had moved to poorly lit premises nearby. The head of 'HQ', a gloomy bespectacled gentleman with a hedgehog coiffure, was all but frightened by our arrival: he had not expected such 'eminent guests'. We walked around the premises, inspected the alarm system signalling local bombings, examined a big map of London stuck with coloured pins showing where bombs had fallen (each type of bomb had its own colour), and met local administrators responsible for medical, fire-fighting, transportation, excavation and other services. All these services were concentrated right there, in the headquarters.

Then we drove to inspect the Group 2 district (St Pancras, Kentish Town, etc.). With the district authorities in tow – the gloomy head of 'HQ', the engineer and some others – we became a convoy of three large cars. It was somewhat unpleasant, but it couldn't be helped. The admiral explained that the No. 2 district is one of the best in London. The local authorities have failed to

---

[i] Edward Evans, admiral, naval commander and Antarctic explorer; commander-in-chief, The Nore, 1935–39, he took part in the Norwegian Campaign. Retiring from the navy in 1941, he was appointed London's regional commissioner for civil defence.

rise to the occasion and have coped poorly, if at all, with the task in hand… Nonetheless, he, Admiral Evans, is not ashamed of showing me district No. 2! Let 'Russia' know that the British do not conceal their shortcomings! Democracy reigns in England!

We saw the bomb shelters: the Anderson type, the school type, the trench type, under a clothing store, under a textile factory, in the hotel at Euston Station, at the Carnero cigarette factory, on the streets – small and large, under a bank in the City, in the Borough of Stepney and, finally, in the big railway tunnel at Tilbury.

We were out and about for some four hours, walking, inspecting the shelters, asking questions, exchanging opinions. Summing up my impressions, I must say that all the shelters we saw except one are worthless when it comes to safety. At best they may protect from shrapnel. But they wouldn't save anyone from a direct hit.

The Carnero factory was the only exception. Its owners seem to belong to the category of 'intelligent capitalists'. Evans, who knew the old owner (now deceased), lavished praise on his 'kind heart' and 'noble attitude towards his employees'. The current owners maintain the traditions established by their father. They built a superb bomb shelter for 3,000 people at a depth of 20 feet under the factory building, with a reinforced concrete ceiling, waves of electric light, an excellently equipped medical aid post, powerful air supply pumps, etc.

We chatted with the admiral as we drove from one shelter to another. He turned out to be a very cheerful and talkative man. He looks astonishingly young for his 60 years. Evans told us his story.

'I'm an adventure-seeker by nature!' he exclaimed with a charming laugh. 'Much like our prime minister. Oh, Mr Churchill is a great adventurer! That's why I believe he'll win the war.'

Evans's career bears out his self-portrait. His father was a lawyer. At the age of eight the boy ran away from home, headed for 'the West Indies'. He was caught outside the London suburbs and returned to his parents. He did not calm down, however: he ran away for a second, and then a third time. In the end he was tried for 'vagrancy' and put in a workhouse. Then Evans felt drawn to the sea. He entered nautical school and joined the navy at 18. At the age of 21 he sailed with Scott[i] on board the *Discovery* to the Antarctic, where he spent two years. At 28, he set off with Scott again to the South Pole as his second-in-command. Spent three years on the ice. After Scott's death, Evans led the surviving members of the expedition back to England. He captained a destroyer during the last war. In 1917, the destroyer HMS *Broke*, under the command of

[i] Robert Falcon Scott, British Royal Navy officer and explorer.

75. The Maiskys with Admiral Evans.

Evans, together with another destroyer, the *Swift*, sank six German destroyers. His life became quieter after the war as he rose up the navy. Evans became admiral of the Australian navy (he recalls this with a smile), commanded the British navy in China and in Africa, captained battleship *Repulse*, and finally, three years ago, became… rector of Aberdeen University. The admiral has an endless quantity of medals: his breast is covered with ribbons of different colours. He wields a pen. He is the author of several books – on *sea power* and on Scott's expedition. Writing adventure books for children is his latest hobby. He is married to a Norwegian and has two sons who are also tied to the sea. In general, Admiral Evans cuts an extraordinarily colourful figure. What's more, he is a first-class demagogue, of the classically English variety.

I saw this for myself when we arrived in Tilbury. It was already 6.30 p.m., and a sizeable crowd had gathered in and around the shelter. Anything up to 2,000 people, I would guess. First, Evans brought us to the railway office, where 15 or so officials from Stepney borough had assembled to greet us. They showed the admiral a map of the tunnel and the alterations required to convert it into a shelter. Evans had a look, had a feel, wheezed, and then launched into rapid conversation with the assembled authorities.

'Hm…,' the admiral bellowed, 'will you send me the relevant letter of request tomorrow morning?'

The tall, beefy railway official to whom Evans' question was addressed did not seem too taken with the idea of sending a letter of request, especially in such haste. But the canny admiral glanced at him meaningfully, looked at me, then shifted his eyes back to the railwayman – and the railwayman agreed: after all, it would have been a bit embarrassing to squabble in front of a foreign ambassador. Evans got his way. Then he adroitly turned to another official and added in a rapid patter: 'You guarantee cement for tomorrow, do you not?'

The cement supplier was none too happy either, but what could he do: he also had to agree. The same happened with the suppliers of timber, iron and some other essential *commodities*. Everything was settled in a few minutes. Evans could justly say: '*Veni, vidi, vici.*' My presence helped him greatly. I'm even convinced he brought me there specially to facilitate his victory. A crafty fellow!

Then we went to see the tunnel. By this point the assembled public already knew who had come. They greeted us with loud cheers: 'Hurrah! Long live the Soviet Union!'

Agniya and I were surrounded on all sides. People shook our hands, shouted enthusiastically, punched the air, and embraced us. But the admiral kept his head. He took us by the arm and the three of us, accompanied by a local *warden* and a single policeman, proceeded to the tunnel.

We walked around the shelter for 15–20 minutes. Had a look at the medical aid post, where they asked us to sign the visitors' book. We observed the primitive – very primitive – sleeping arrangements which the East Enders had devised for themselves. The place was crowded and filthy, with wretched bedding on the stone floor, heaps of junk, and hundreds of children of all ages and appearances. The variety of individuals, and the variety of their conditions, was astonishing. I saw emaciated and hungry faces, and next to them red, well-fed physiognomies which belonged, I reckon, to the category of Whitechapel shopkeepers. Tall phlegmatic Englishmen jostled with rowdy Irishmen and nervously mobile Jews. Yes, the whole ethnographic spectrum of the East End was there.

Suddenly the admiral turned to the *warden* accompanying us and exclaimed: 'Gather the people! I want to say a few words to them.'

The *warden* jumped on a platform of sorts and set about shouting at the top of his voice, waving his arms: 'Over here! Over here! Admiral Evans will speak!'

The people quickly hurried over to the platform, onto which the admiral, with a lightness unusual for his age, had also managed to jump. A big, tightly packed, steaming crowd was soon assembled. Men, women and children. Hats, caps and bare heads. About two thousand people. Agniya and I stood at the foot of the platform, trying to keep in the shadows, and waited with curiosity to see what would happen next. Suddenly the admiral bent down towards us and, gesturing emphatically, addressed me: 'And what about you? Over here please! Over here!'

The admiral started tugging me and Agniya onto the platform. Someone helped us from behind and a moment later we were standing side by side with the admiral, who was waving his arms about energetically and shouting to the crowd: 'Come closer! Closer! Don't be shy!'

The people moved closer, bunching up tight. Evans took off his cap, waved it, and exclaimed: 'Our country is the country of *fair play*! Am I right?'

An uncertain rumble passed through the crowd. One could interpret it as a sign of approval or as a mark of disapproval. The admiral continued unabashed: 'A few days ago the king and queen visited you here!'

The same uncertain rumble passed through the crowd, and someone in the back row cried out: 'What about it?'

The admiral went on without batting an eyelid.

'And today,' he shouted with sudden emphasis, 'I've brought you a different guest! I've brought you the Soviet ambassador!'

And with a wide sweep of his arm, Evans gestured towards Agniya and me.

Unrestrained cheering among the crowd. Everyone started shouting: 'Hurrah! Long live the Soviet Union! Long live the Soviet ambassador!'

Then Evans moved on to other topics. He said he sympathized with the people of the East End with all his heart. He couldn't promise them miracles, but he was doing all he could to improve the situation. Half of the tunnel had been freed to turn it into a shelter. It had been cleansed of rubbish and stench. That was progress, but it was just the beginning.

'I'll give you 4,000 beds within the week!' the admiral cried in a stentorian voice. 'Would you like that?'

Needless to say, the crowd welcomed the admiral's announcement with thunderous cheers.

'I'll not stop at that!' roared the admiral. 'Soon each of you will get a special seasonal ticket like this one (he pulled a small piece of green cardboard from his pocket and waved it about in the air)… On the ticket will be written the name of the owner, the name of the shelter, and the number of the bed assigned to him. What do you say, will that be good?'

'Good! Good!' the crowd yelled back.

The admiral continued: 'If there is not enough room for some of you in this shelter, I'll provide you with places in a good shelter in the City of London!'

The crowd roared with delight.

The admiral mopped his forehead, put on his cap, and we all moved to the edge of the platform in order to get down. I already considered myself 'saved': given my delicate diplomatic status, it would have been a bit *embarrassing* for me to speak at this improvised meeting in the East End. So I hastened to get down, when I was suddenly met with deafening cries: '*Maisky! Speech! Speech!*'

Smiling broadly in all directions, I did my best to get out of it, but the shouts grew louder and louder and the people standing in the front rows rushed towards the platform to prevent my descent. The admiral spread out his arms, and giving me a friendly slap on the shoulder exclaimed: 'And really, why not say a couple of words? Speak! You must speak!'

All escape routes had been cut off. Standing on the edge of the platform, I gestured for silence and said: 'On behalf of my wife and myself I thank you kindly, friends, for the cordial welcome which you have given us here today.'

My voice was too weak for the gigantic space, but the crowd responded with frenzied shouts: 'Hurrah! Hurrah!'

'I'm especially touched by this welcome,' I continued, 'because I well understand that your greetings are addressed not so much to me and my wife as to the country I represent.'

The shouts grew even wilder. A section of the crowd started singing the 'Internationale'.

'Let me thank you once more, with all my heart!' I concluded and began getting down from the platform.

A few seconds later and we were all on the ground. The crowd was delirious. A path opened for the three of us – myself, Agniya and the admiral. Agniya and I were once again squeezed on all sides, embraced, and shaken by the hand. An elderly woman with light brown hair and a face webbed with deep wrinkles cried out in Russian: 'Our Russia is still alive!'

Hundreds of people on both sides raised their clenched fists in salutation. The 'Internationale' sounded louder and louder.

'What are they singing?' asked the admiral naively. '"*Red Flag*"?'

'No,' I replied. 'They are singing the "Internationale". It's our Soviet national hymn.'

'Is that right?' The admiral was surprised. 'I had never heard it before.'

We arrived, at last, at our cars and climbed in, to the accompaniment of loud shouts: 'Long live the Soviet Union!'

Once again, the 'Internationale'. Once again, raised fists.

The admiral was somewhat amazed. He had hardly expected the Soviet ambassador to be accorded such a warm welcome. But he lost neither his presence of mind nor his good cheer. We headed off to the embassy for a cup of tea. And on the way I thought: 'This is how the East End greets the Soviet ambassador today. If the war lasts two more years, Piccadilly will greet him in a similar way.'

C[omrade] Vyshinsky[i] summoned Cripps on 9 October to hand him a note of protest against the actions of British authorities in respect of the Baltic ships moored in British ports. The note holds the British government responsible

---

[i] Andrei Yanuarevich Vyshinsky, a former Menshevik, he was prosecutor general of the USSR, 1935–39, in charge of the rigged political trials, most of which ended in death sentences being handed down; deputy chairman of the Council of People's Commissars, 1939–44, and first deputy to people's commissar for foreign affairs, 1940–46; minister for foreign affairs, 1949–53.

for the damage caused by these actions. It further demands the removal of the obstacles preventing the immediate return of the Baltic ships to the Soviet Union, and the release of the gold reserves of the Baltic republics kept in London, at least so as to cover the ongoing expenses of the said ships. The note also stresses the inadmissibility of the arrest of Baltic sailors in Canada (the *Ubari* steamer) and other reprisals committed against them.

Cripps responded with a statement saying that the ships are just one part of the Baltic question, and the British government will hardly agree to consider this matter separately. For his part, Cripps proposes on behalf of the British government to put the entire Baltic question on ice for six months and open trade negotiations in the meantime.

C[omrade] Vyshinsky answered that the Soviet government has no reason to change the point of view which he expounded to Cripps during their previous meeting. The Soviet government is not against trading with England, but it also does not wish to publicize it widely.

Cripps then said that trade deals between the two countries for separate commodities would not produce satisfactory results. They will merely arouse suspicion in England that the USSR is re-exporting to Germany the products it has imported from England. That is no way to improve relations. So Cripps thinks it advisable to open negotiations concerning general commodity exchange between the two countries, if only on a 'narrow base' (he referred to his conversation with C[omrade] Mikoyan on 14 July).

Before parting, Cripps told C[omrade] Vyshinsky that he felt that the conversation had broken the stalemate on the matter of trade negotiations.

C[omrade] Vyshinsky said he thought so, too.

The trade union congress held in Southport from 7 to 10 October has ended. Five million members were represented (a 300,000 increase over the year). A further increase of 500,000 is expected in 1941. In part, this is down to the line taken by Bevin, with his demand that the firms fulfilling government contracts recognize the trade unions.

The mood at the congress was extraordinarily bellicose. Everything proceeded under the banner 'War until Hitlerism is crushed', without further specifications. The following episode serves as a curious illustration of these sentiments. Even before the congress opened, Elvin,[i] on behalf of his union of clerks, tabled a resolution demanding that peace be concluded by way of negotiations and agreement. Sensing the atmosphere at the congress, he withdrew the resolution once the sessions were under way. However, he failed to be re-elected to the General Council and was replaced by a certain O'Brien,[ii] a man of no distinction and a loyal advocate of the 'general line' of the majority.

[i] Herbert Henry Elvin was the general secretary of the TUC in 1938.
[ii] Tom O'Brien, member of the TUC General Council from 1940.

Another symptom of the same mood was the decision to ban the *Daily Worker* correspondent from the congress. Despite strong opposition to this decision on the part of Horner[i] (communist, chairman of the South Wales miners), Wall (secretary of the printers' union) and Hunter (representative of the union of journalists), the congress participants refused to allow the representative of a communist newspaper to attend their meetings.

The trade employees' delegate Berger[ii] put forward a proposal to *refer back* the chapter of a report dealing with the Finnish war and brimming with anti-Soviet insinuations. Berger made a fine speech arguing that the Soviet Union, the only socialist state in the world, was obliged to take measures to safeguard its security at any price. Interestingly, every mention of Soviet successes in Berger's speech was met with loud cheers. Citrine's response, full of anti-Soviet venom, was met with icy silence. But, when it came to the vote, the 'machine' did its job: a 70% majority saw off Berger's proposal.

The dominant figure at the Congress was undoubtedly Bevin. Citrine was pushed to the background and obviously didn't like it. A short while before the congress a minor scandal had occurred between Bevin and Citrine. Bevin had agreed with Churchill that workers who lost their tools as a result of air raids would receive compensation of up to 100 pounds. Unaware of this, Citrine wrote a letter to the Treasury on the same matter and suggested setting a compensation of up to 25 pounds. This led to a real tiff between Bevin and Citrine. It was expected that the issue would be discussed at the congress. But the conflict was quashed behind the scenes.

Bevin engaged in various forms of demagogy at the congress, declaring, for instance, that the Ministry of Labour would get its hands on the Foreign Office and take measures to infuse 'fresh blood' into its ranks. I'd like to see how he does that.

Balkan matters are on the agenda.

Subbotić told me today that the G[erman] G[overnment] has assured Belgrade that its activities in Rumania in no way reflect aggressive intentions towards other Balkan countries, Yugoslavia in particular. The Yugoslav government knows the value of German assurances, of course, but all the same it is, *for the moment*, feeling a little relieved.

Simopoulos, in his turn, tried to show that the Italian press campaign against Greece is nothing but a bluff aimed at undermining the authority of Metaxas[iii] in Greece. Simopoulos does not think it will all end in a real war. I'm not so sure.

[i] Arthur Lewis Horner, president, South Wales miners, 1936–46.
[ii] H. Berger.
[iii] Ioannis Metaxas, prime minister of Greece, 1936–41.

Simopoulos outlined the situation in Bulgaria in the following way: the people are for 'Russia', the top brass for Germany. King Boris[i] manoeuvres between the two poles.

Simopoulos has also gleaned from German sources that the German calculation in September was that a two-week air offensive against London would suffice to bring England to its knees. An invasion would not even be needed. They miscalculated badly.

* * *

Randolph Churchill dropped in. He assured me that *invasion is off*. He outlined the prospects for the winter in the following way: an Anglo-German air war and defensive operations in Egypt. The British government is certain it can repulse the Italians there. By spring 1941, England will achieve air superiority over Germany. It will be followed by British offensives against Germany in the air and against Italy in the air, by land and at sea – in Africa and in Europe. England will not yet be ready for an offensive against Germany by land in 1941. The blockade of Germany, of course, will continue unceasingly and implacably.

I wonder how events will develop in reality.

[In his diary, Bilainkin describes a tour he was given of the £1,500 (approximately £65,000 in today's money) air-raid shelter constructed 'many feet below garden level' at the Soviet embassy (still in *situ* today!):

> The tube, of reinforced concrete, is the size of that in London's underground railways; it is covered by a foot of reinforced concrete, earth, more reinforced concrete, more earth, yet more reinforced concrete and yet much more earth. The whole is well ventilated and has several compartments. One is for the Ambassador and Mme Maisky; here I saw a portable wireless set (house manager promptly obtained Moscow on the short-wave), a house telephone, a central exchange telephone, two forms of lighting, good bedding (tasteful blue satin). Embassy has special plant for cleaning air in shelter; pick-axes are in position, shovels, impressive boxes full of meat in tins, sardines, peaches; also soda water, knives, forks and spoons.[93]

The families and children of the Soviet personnel at the embassy were evacuated in early October to 'a fairly large and comfortable house' in a village near Cheltenham. Agniya categorically refused to leave London. 'Her presence by my side,' recalled Maisky, 'was a serious support for me. And for political reasons it was more to our advantage that the British should see the wife of the Soviet Ambassador "in the front line", not in the rear.' To catch up on their sleep, they tended to spend the weekends out of London at the house of their close friend, Juan Negrín, the former prime minister of the Spanish Republican government.[94] Maisky hinted a couple of times to Molotov that the Germans

---

[i] King Boris III of Bulgaria, 1918–43.

could perhaps be asked to spare the embassy. He was convinced, as he cabled Molotov, that it was no coincidence that the Soviet embassy was particularly targeted by the Germans. He attributed it to Ribbentrop's 'extreme hostility' towards him personally, dating back to the German foreign minister's time as ambassador to London. Being 'a vengeful person', Maisky guessed, he was trying to 'take his revenge' on him from the air. 'It may seem a fantasy,' he concluded, 'but we now live in fantastic times.'[95]]

13 October

There have been no noticeable changes in the character of the air offensive. This past week (6th–12th) was like the previous one. The intensity merely increased a little, roughly reaching the level of the last week of September.

The general picture remained the same. Accuracy was no better. The centre of attention, as before, was London. Liverpool, Birmingham and Manchester were bombed, too, but the strikes were relatively infrequent and weak. The ports in Liverpool and Glasgow are intact. Industry in London and the provinces has suffered little. The Germans have had no luck with 'military targets'. And yet, many households were destroyed, picture theatres, shops, hospitals, etc. The London port has become considerably emptier: because of the air offensive against the capital city, maritime traffic is concentrated to an ever greater extent on the western coast, mostly in Liverpool and Glasgow.

It's now absolutely clear that the Germans have decided to cease using bombers by day: the losses are too great. They are now sending fighters (*Messerschmitt* 109 and 110) instead of bombers during daylight hours. Even though a fighter can carry only 10% of a bomber's load, it is faster and swifter, and it is easier for a fighter to break through to London and escape British interceptors. In consequence, German losses have decreased considerably, but their strike power has been seriously weakened.

20 October

The Germans have finally abandoned the mass bombing of London by day in view of their heavy losses. No more bombers by day. Instead, the capital is bombed by fighters (they break through in small groups), accompanied by fighter escorts (which do not carry bombs) at a proportion of eight escorts per fighter. The fighter-bombers fly at an altitude of 8–9,000 metres. It is difficult to detect them, and still harder to give them chase. The moral and material effect of the day raids is generally negligible.

The night raids (from approximately seven in the evening until six in the morning) are worse. They are executed by bombers without escorts: they are safe at night. The bombers arrive in groups of 200–300 machines. They cause heavy damage but… they barely touch military facilities. These are difficult to hit.

Total daily casualties of up to 600 people, including 200 killed.

To sum up: the Germans are helpless by day, and the British are helpless by night. London generally lives a normal life by day, but turns into a fortress besieged from the air at night.

22 October

On behalf of the British government, Cripps has asked C[omrade] Molotov for an audience on a matter of 'paramount political importance'. C[omrade] Molotov could not receive Cripps, so instead Cripps met C[omrade] Vyshinsky, to whom he submitted a special memorandum. Its concluding part contained three points:

(1) The British government announces its readiness to recognize 'de facto' the changes in the Baltics so as to settle 'de jure' the whole issue later, probably after the war.

(2) The British government declares itself prepared to ensure the participation of the USSR, on an equal basis, in the settlement of European affairs after the war.

(3) The British government promises not to participate in any military actions against the USSR.

C[omrade] Vyshinsky told Cripps that he would report the matter to the Soviet government.

29 October Cripps submitted a note of protest to NKID against the Soviet government's decision to take part in the Danube commission, accusing the USSR of violating neutrality.

2 November C[omrade] Vyshinsky handed Cripps the response of the Soviet government concerning the Danube question, which boiled down to a request to the British government not to meddle in matters which don't concern it.

Then C[omrade] Vyshinsky touched upon several other questions.

(1) Talking with C[omrade] Lozovsky[i] on 23 July, Cripps said that the British government wished the nickel concession in Petsamo to pass into the hands of the Soviet Union or to a joint Soviet–Finnish company and that the British government was even prepared to offer technical assistance in this matter. Meanwhile Paasikivi informed the Soviet government that the British envoy

[i] Solomon Abramovich Lozovsky (Dridzo), a former Menshevik, he was the secretary of the Red International of Labour Unions (Profintern), 1920–37, and deputy Soviet commissar for foreign affairs, 1939–46; a member of the Jewish Anti-Fascist Committee during the war, he was arrested in 1952 during Stalin's anti-Jewish campaign, and executed.

in Helsinki, Vereker, had objected to Cripps's suggestion, calling it 'personal opinion'. How should this be understood?

Cripps replied that this story was the product of a misunderstanding. Three days ago the British government confirmed Cripps's suggestion to C[omrade] Lozovsky by telegram, but with one reservation: the concession should pass over to the USSR or to a Soviet–Finnish company until the end of the war, after which the issue might be reconsidered.

(2) The Soviet government has not received a reply to its note of 9 October concerning the Baltic ships. Neither has Cripps fulfilled his promise to release the Baltic reserves in London to cover the ships' expenses. All this creates a bad impression: there is much talk and desire to improve relations, but no deeds. On the contrary, there are facts testifying to open hostility. One fresh example. A Finnish firm, carrying out Soviet orders, wanted to buy tin in the United States, but the British mission in Helsinki informed this firm that British sea control would not allow the tin, needed to fulfil Soviet contracts, to pass through.

Cripps replied that the incident with the tin was a tragic error which he could easily rectify. The significance of such incidents should not be exaggerated.

C[omrade] Vyshinsky further said that the suggestion made by Cripps on 18 October concerning the signing of a charter deal for requisitioned ships between the Soviet and British governments is unacceptable to us, because the Soviet government cannot, as a general principle, accept the British government's right to requisition Soviet property. C[omrade] Vyshinsky repeated the demand for the removal of obstacles preventing ships from returning to the Soviet Union.

(3) On 26 October, Cripps asked C[omrade] Mikoyan to sell a certain quantity of oil to Greece. In this connection C[omrade] Vyshinsky posed Cripps a question: will the British government agree to allow the passage of 5,000 tons of oil for France through the Mediterranean? Cripps replied that the British government could not agree to this. So C[omrade] Vyshinsky said that the Soviet government could not accept such discrimination. But this was a question for the People's Commissariat for Foreign Trade.

(4) Cripps asked C[omrade] Vyshinsky two questions: (a) What is the USSR's attitude to the war between Italy and Greece? and (b) What does C[omrade] Stalin think of a possible improvement in relations between the USSR and Turkey?

C[omrade] Vyshinsky answered that the Soviet attitude to the war between Italy and Greece follows from the general principles of Soviet foreign policy. As for C[omrade] Stalin's views on the matter which interests Cripps, C[omrade] Vyshinsky cannot say anything on behalf of C[omrade] Stalin without special authorization.

Cripps then inquired about the opinion of the People's Commissariat for Foreign Affairs on this question.

C[omrade] Vyshinsky answered that in its relations with Turkey the USSR abides by the 1925 treaty of non-aggression.

[The British initiative came five days after the invitation for Molotov to meet Hitler in Berlin on 11 November had reached the Kremlin. 'It looks,' Lloyd George wrote to Maisky, 'as if once more we have been too late.'[96]]

2 November

Nearly three months of fierce combat in the air. What are the conclusions and the results?

Let's begin with the protagonists. We have two well-armed, if numerically unequal, parties. This is the first experience so far of large-scale, serious air war.

The Germans' advantages: great numerical superiority (3:1 at the beginning) and the proximity of bases to targets (150–200 km from the airfields in northern France and Belgium to London).

The advantages of the British: better quality of aircraft materials, better petrol quality, a longer period of pilot training, the war is 'at home', which means that the British planes shot down fall on their own territory and nearly half of the pilots save themselves with parachutes.

The large scale of the war is reflected in the fact that many hundreds of planes are engaged in the raids every day. The maximum number of German planes, 1,000, was recorded on 15 August. The raids come in waves, with intervals of several hours. The attacks are not concentrated on one specific city or even a specific part of London. They are of a somewhat superficial, scattered nature. London has been the focus of attack since 7 September. The Germans have been increasingly switching from daytime to night-time sorties. Two to three hundred bombers attack systematically every night from dusk till dawn, but that quantity of machines cannot do serious damage to such a giant metropolis as London.

The efficacy of the German air offensive in respect of military targets is strangely negligible. The damage inflicted on industrial facilities, ports, railways, airfields, etc. does not exceed 5–10% of their capacity countrywide. Human losses are not great: no more than 20,000 killed and 40–50,000 gravely wounded over three months.

The reason for this low efficacy lies in the strength of British resistance. Fighters should be mentioned first. As this three-month experience shows, fighters are the main means of repelling air attacks: 85–90% of crashed German planes were brought down by fighters. Fighters, furthermore, do not allow

German bombers to stay long in the air, forcing them to drop bombs in a rush from high altitude. Fighters also prevent bombers from diving and disrupt the formations of the attack squadrons. British fighters render the Germans powerless in daylight. They tried to change their tactics (at first the bombers were accompanied by an equal number of fighters, then the number of escorting fighters was increased to 8:1, and then fighters accompanied by fighter escorts replaced bombers), but nothing came of it. Following the decision to stop using bombers in daylight, German losses have decreased in the last two weeks (no more than 15–20 planes daily), but the strike power of the attacks has been considerably weakened, since a fighter can carry merely 10% of a bomber's load. On the other hand, the British are powerless at night, when fighters are practically useless. The British have yet to find another means of dealing with night raids (although they are working on this problem intensively). That is why the Germans are increasingly focusing on night raids on London.

The role of anti-aircraft artillery in repelling air attacks proves rather limited. Anti-aircraft guns hit merely 10–15% of all the German planes brought down. However, anti-aircraft defensive fire has two positive effects. First, it forces the Germans to remain at an altitude of 5–7 km, which seriously affects bombing accuracy. Second, it bolsters the morale of the London population.

Barrage balloons play a useful, but auxiliary role. They play on the pilot's mind and make dive bombing still more difficult. The higher the balloons are raised the better. So it is better to fill the balloons with helium rather than with hydrogen.

The defence lines between the coast and London (fighters, anti-aircraft artillery, barrage balloons) are very important. The distance between Dover and London is about 100 km as the crow flies, but thanks to the effective lines of defence no more than 10–15% of German raiders manage to break through to London in daylight hours. These defence lines prove effective (albeit to a far lesser degree) at night as well.

The statistics of British and German losses in air combat published by the British are in general quite realistic. I have had occasion to verify this more than once.

By all appearances, in the second half of September, when the low efficacy of the air offensive from the point of view of an invasion became apparent, the Germans gambled on undermining the population's and government's morale. Curiously, in London, they bombed mainly the city centre (to scare the bourgeoisie) and workers' districts (to spur the masses to protest against the war).

Nonetheless, the experience of these three months shows beyond doubt that, given a firm government, a relatively solid home front, effective resistance to the enemy, and those shelters that have been put up, albeit imperfectly, in London and other cities, it is not enough to launch an air offensive alone, in the forms and dimensions we have observed hitherto (gas has not yet been used), to undermine the morale of the population.

One more conclusion suggests itself: aviation combined with land (especially mechanized) forces is massively powerful. As the experience of Poland and France has shown, this combination can decide a war. Aircraft alone, when unaccompanied by armies on the ground and when met with more or less serious resistance in the air, has relatively limited potential. Aviation alone is not decisive. That is why 'stalemate in the air' has been reached after the three-month air war between England and Germany. Neither party has succeeded in achieving mastery of the skies.

4 November

Conversing with Churchill on 3 July, I asked: what does the *major strategy* of the British government consist of?'

Churchill grinned, shrugged his shoulders, and said: '*Major strategy*? First of all, to survive the next three months, and then we shall see.'

Four months have passed since then. England has not only survived: she is stronger than she was at the time of my talk with the prime minister. German plans for an invasion have fallen through. The famous *Channel* has saved Great Britain once more, as it has on more than one occasion down the ages. Hitler's weakness at sea, together with the failure to secure air supremacy over the Channel, wrecked Germany's only chance of overcoming the resistance supplied by a strip of water 40 kilometres wide. Hitler experienced the same fate as Napoleon 135 years ago: he lost the *Battle of Britain*. It is still too early to review all the consequences of this fact, but they must be serious.

As far as one can judge on the basis of all the information available in London (which tallies well with the facts), Hitler's *major strategy* offered the following picture: a triumphant conclusion of the war before the onset of winter. Hitler was mainly relying on the effect on morale of the French defeat. He was confident that England would cease to resist after the 'French lesson' and would immediately seek a 'compromise'. That's why Mussolini hastened to enter the war in early June: he was firmly convinced that the war would end a few weeks after the capitulation of France. Of course, Hitler had a plan for invasion up his sleeve just in case. However, he counted on the war being over this year whatever the circumstances, and on it ending with Germany's brilliant victory.

All Hitler's plans and hopes came unstuck. England's resistance, which Hitler did not expect, and the increasingly active role of the USA in the war, upset all his calculations. Hitler chose not to risk an open assault on England; it would have been too dangerous. Of course, the decision not to attempt to invade represents, in essence, a failure – Hitler's first serious failure of the war.

But only specialists – strategists and politicians – understand this. For the time being, Hitler may be able to hide his failure from the broad masses, particularly in Germany. But one thing is certain: Hitler's plans for a short, victorious war have been frustrated. Now he has to accept a prolonged war of attrition with all the military and revolutionary dangers that such a war may conceal.

Well, and England? Where does England stand today?

The British government has won the *Battle of Britain*. But that is not enough. Winning one battle does not always mean winning the war. The blow aimed at the heart of the British Empire has been warded off, but… what next? Having lost his *Battle of Britain*, Napoleon marched eastward and soon found consolation in Austerlitz, Jena and Wagram. Won't Hitler do something similar? There are many signs to suggest that Hitler may be turning towards the south and south-east. If he cannot strike at the heart of the British Empire, why not try striking at its most important nerve centres in other parts of the globe? We shall see what successes Hitler will have in this direction, if any.

But for England an extremely difficult situation is now emerging. Its official goal is 'to crush Hitlerism', which amounts to crushing Germany. All, on both right and left, swear to do this. Very well… But how? It is one thing to avoid defeat – England may assume it has achieved this. But winning the war is a very different matter. And it is not clear how this may be achieved in the foreseeable future.

Indeed, how do members of the government and other leaders envisage events unfolding? Summing up what I have heard in recent months from Halifax, Butler, Eden, Dalton, Sinclair, Morrison, Alexander and others, I can sketch the following picture.

The winter period: blockade, London–Berlin air war, combat operations in the Near East (Egypt), and possibly operations in Gibraltar or Western Africa. Simultaneously, a concentrated effort to build up the army, air force and navy. This build-up should reach such dimensions by the summer of 1941 that a 'small offensive' against Italy in Africa and in Europe should be feasible. There is a growing sense in British government circles that Italy is the weak link in the 'Axis' and that England should exploit that link first and foremost. Operations against the Italian navy are possible at any moment, even before the launching of a 'small offensive'.

All this, however, concerns Italy. The strategy against Germany is conceived quite differently in government circles. In 1941, these circles intend to go no further than a major air offensive against Germany, placing great hopes on new machines (the *Sterling* [sic – Stirling] bomber, the modified *Spitfire*, etc.). They are not planning a land offensive against Germany next year. And this is hardly surprising. In 1941, England can count on 4 million soldiers at most, who are not particularly well trained and armed and, moreover, are led by a second-rate general staff. How, then, can one even dream of attacking an 8 million-strong German army of well-trained and well-armed soldiers, commanded by an excellent general staff? Even if the United States were to enter the war within the next few months, it would take no less than two years for serious reinforcements to arrive in Europe to help the British. No wonder, then, that when British leaders are posed the question 'How do you intend to beat Germany?' they usually appeal to the superior material and human resources of the British Empire and promise 'victory' in 1942, 1943 or later.

Their views derive either from misunderstanding or from hypocrisy. A prolonged war of attrition over many years bears huge revolutionary potential – not only for Germany, but also for England and the British Empire. There can be no doubt that the English elite will set about seeking a 'compromise' with 'Hitlerism' long before these possibilities become realities.

That is why it seems to me that the ruling classes here are faced with an acute dilemma: either to find new allies who could help England 'settle' this war by purely military means with their authority and might, or, should this prove impossible, to seek a compromise peace…

The hunt for allies is now on, with the United States to the fore. But in the long run the ruling circles also dream of an alliance with the Soviet Union, in spite of all our refutation, explanation, etc. Should hopes of active support from the United States be frustrated, and should the United States wish to stay above the fray or cut its aid significantly, the issue of a 'deal' with Germany would soon enter the agenda, especially if serious cracks in the social structure of the country started emerging. There are quite a few advocates in England of such a 'deal' with Germany. Now they are lying low, but they are ready to raise their heads and break their silence.

This is what I can see now from my 'London window'.

Much will depend on various other factors that are difficult to take into account at present: on Germany – its military and diplomatic actions and its internal condition; on the sentiments of the broad European masses; and on the activity and consciousness of the proletariat…

Who can foresee all this?[97]

5 November

I saw Lloyd George two days ago. The old man gave the following assessment of the situation.

The 'invasion' failed. However, he does not see how this or that side might 'win'. England and Germany operate in different elements: England does not have an army and Germany does not have a navy. It is like a fight between a shark and a tiger. How can one pin the other to the ground?

The situation would not change radically even if the United States were to enter the war. They would need at least three years to build an army of 3–4 million, to train it, arm it and send it to Europe. But even then, the joint Anglo-American army will number merely 8 million; what's more, the German general staff will be a cut above its British counterpart. England can only crush Germany properly with the aid of the Soviet Union, but the preconditions for this are currently lacking.

Lloyd George believes it highly unlikely that the war will last another three years. He is inclined to think that a situation conducive to a compromise peace will evolve during the winter of 1941/42.

11 November

A huge bomb fell near the trade mission building on the night of the 10th to 11th, causing massive damage. The building still stands, but all the windows are smashed, the inner walls and partitions have collapsed, the furniture is broken, etc. The building has become uninhabitable, and much money and time will be needed to repair it. Our economic planners will have to move. Fortunately, no one was hurt. Everyone was sleeping in the mission's shelter and escaped with nothing worse than a fright.

* * *

I visited Morrison at the Home Office. How dark, dirty and bleak the corridors are in that building! I couldn't help recalling the Police Department of tsarist times.

We spoke first about London anti-aircraft defence and, in particular, shelters. Morrison was guarded and elusive on the topic of 'deep shelters' (in favour of which he himself recently spoke with great enthusiasm from the opposition bench), with words to the effect that he was ready to 'study all practical proposals' in this sphere.

Then he switched to political matters. The threat of an invasion, according to him, has passed. The focus of war shifts to the Near East. To save the world, a united front of England, USA, the USSR and China should be created.

I objected, arguing that it is hardly possible to expect such grandiose combinations at a time when England and the USSR cannot successfully resolve (and through no fault of our own) even the relatively small issue of the Baltic States.

Morrison began explaining to me why there has been no movement on the Baltic issue: 'We would very much like to do something pleasant for you, but we do not want to do something unpleasant for America. And that is understandable. If we do something pleasant for you – we still don't know what we'll get in return. And if we do something pleasant for America – we know very well what we'll get in return. We will get what we most need at this time. So pleasing the USSR conflicts with pleasing the USA, and it is absolutely clear where our choice must lie. Otherwise we would be bad merchants and politicians. I can assure you that the British government is very keen to reach agreement with the Soviet Union, but not at the expense of the United States.'

Straightforward and cynical, as always with Morrison. Still, I prefer his lack of ceremony to the sugary syrup of Attlee and Greenwood.

C[omrade] Vyshinsky received Cripps at the latter's request on 11 November. Cripps was in a very agitated and irritated state of mind.

Cripps began with a statement to the effect that he regards C[omrade] Molotov's refusal to see him on 22 October and receive the British proposals an unfriendly act. The news of C[omrade] Molotov's visit to Berlin (without any response being given to the British proposals) only confirms this. Cripps asks C[omrade] Vyshinsky to answer two questions: (1) Should he understand this as a rejection of the British proposals by the Soviet government? (2) Can he report to the British government that C[omrade] Molotov's visit to Berlin in the current situation indicates the Soviet government's unwillingness to improve relations with England? Cripps finds it useless to make further efforts to improve relations between the two countries and will convey his views concerning Molotov's visit to Berlin to the British government.

C[omrade] Vyshinsky replied that it would be wrong to link C[omrade] Molotov's visit to the Soviet government's attitude to the British proposals of 22 October. These are two different things. The purpose of C[omrade] Molotov's visit is clearly stated in the communiqué published on this matter.

As far as the proposals of 22 October are concerned, C[omrade] Vyshinsky can only express his personal opinion regarding the sentiments they elicit in Soviet government circles. This opinion can be summarized as follows: C[omrade] Vyshinsky fails to understand what England wants from us. The proposals of 22 October give us less than we already have. C[omrade] Vyshinsky wonders how the British government, itself under siege, could have made such proposals at all?

Cripps, speaking more calmly, said that the general basis should be agreed upon first, while individual questions could be discussed later. Cripps was very anxious during the conversation, expressed his indignation, etc., but C[omrade] Vyshinsky put him firmly in his place.

Then Cripps asked whether the rumours were true that the USSR had decided to withdraw from Balkan affairs and was prepared to acknowledge German hegemony in this part of the world.

In reply C[omrade] Vyshinsky referred him to the clarification given in *Krasnaya Zvezda* in connection with Arapetyan's article.

Cripps stated that the quarrel over the Baltic ships could hardly be settled before a general agreement between England and the USSR had been concluded.

C[omrade] Vyshinsky, however, insisted on the satisfaction of the demands set out in the Soviet note of 9 October.

Cripps also declared that the Baltic sailors were not lacking for anything (this is absolutely untrue).

12 November

Subbotić came to see me. He is terribly alarmed and concerned about C[omrade] Molotov's visit to Berlin.

'The Italo-Greek war,' said Subbotić, 'Graziani's plans in Egypt, and British operations in the Mediterranean – all that completely pales in comparison. The outcome of the war, maybe the fate of the world, will be decided at that meeting in Berlin!'

Naturally enough, Subbotić worries most of all about the possible connections between the Berlin meeting and the events in the Balkans, primarily in Yugoslavia and Turkey. He hopes that 'Russia will not forget Yugoslavia', and that the interests of his country will not suffer as a result of the meeting in Berlin. Clearly, C[omrade] Molotov's visit to Berlin has caused great unease in Belgrade.

I told Subbotić that I was not privy to the agenda of the Berlin meeting but, judging by the persons accompanying C[omrade] Molotov, economic issues will be the focus of attention. I could also assure him in advance that the Berlin meeting would not bring about any changes whatsoever to our policy of neutrality.

Then we spoke about events in Greece. In Subbotić's words, the Greeks themselves are greatly amazed at their own heroism. At any rate, this is the impression of Simopoulos and his staff. Despite all the Greek success, however, Subbotić does not believe that the Greeks can hold out for long, unless the British transfer large military resources onto continental Greece. But the British government does not intend to do so. Its policy is confined to occupation of the Greek islands and bases, and to helping Greece with its air force and navy

Subbotić has heard that Eden is back from the Near East in a very optimistic mood. Eden is sure the British will be able to hold on to Egypt.

[Since the fall of France, Hitler had been facing the dilemma of whether to attempt to bring the Ribbentrop–Molotov Pact up to date through arrangements in South-East Europe or, alternatively, to proceed with vigorous preparations for war. The idea of a meeting between Molotov and Hitler originated with von Schulenburg, the German ambassador to Moscow, during a brief visit to Berlin. The realization that Russia had no intention of retreating from the Balkans prompted Schulenburg to seek a four-power pact between Germany, Russia, Italy and Japan, in order to delineate spheres of influence. Hitler's expectations of the meeting did not tally with those of his ambassador: he assumed that, after his general idea for the 'new Europe' was outlined, the negotiations would gradually crystallize into a rigid proposal for delimitation that would exclude Russia from Europe and the Balkans and reflect German military supremacy. He had no intention of accommodating the Russians, beyond forcing Turkey to yield to some guarantees in the Straits and security arrangements in the Baku region. There is little to support the prevailing view that, during his visit to Berlin, Molotov conspired with Hitler to divide up the entire world – and more specifically to carve up the British Empire.

The directive for the talks, dictated to Molotov in Stalin's dacha and taken in longhand, was confined to intrinsic Soviet interests in the Balkans and the Turkish Straits, and was dominated by considerations of security. Foremost were repeated demands for the establishment of Soviet control of the mouth of the Danube and involvement in the decision on the 'fate of Turkey'. Bulgaria, as in the war of 1877–78, was to be 'the main topic of the negotiations' and was expected to fall into the Soviet sphere of influence. In order to mitigate German influence, Stalin sought to include even a battered Britain in a peace conference, which he expected to be promptly convened. Maisky's assertion that Britain could not be written off and might even emerge victorious at the end of a slow and arduous process was of cardinal importance for the objectives sought at the Berlin meeting.[98] A telegram from Stalin caught up with Molotov on the train as he was en route to Berlin. This reaffirmed the instructions not to broach with Germany any issues concerning the British Empire. Indeed, in Berlin Molotov endorsed Maisky's view that it was 'too early to bury England'.[99]

Maisky's firm position following Molotov's talks in Berlin is recorded in Beatrice Webb's diary:

> He is of the same opinion still, that though we shall succeed in the defensive and may control the Mediterranean, we shall not *beat* Germany. The war in the air will drag on, and we may, unless the USA is unlimited in its help, have to accept a patched up peace with Hitler, leaving him still dominant in Europe. Or if Germany gets hopelessly paralyzed by our air attack, there will be an internal revolution (Communist) in both Germany and France, which we shall not be able to put down or control.[100]

No wonder Butler, somewhat misled by Maisky's failure to grasp the premises of Stalin's foreign policy, gained the impression that Soviet policy was 'to await a change in English politics and English political thought, which would result in a Government and a social structure in this country more understandable to the Soviet way of life'. As he assumed that the Soviet leaders were 'bent upon world revolution, and consider England a suitable breeding ground for their ideas', he was in favour of keeping them at arm's length.[101] Cripps was accordingly instructed by Halifax to sit tight, as the Russians seemed to be intent on appeasing Germany, which 'they feel cannot be trifled with', while Britain 'they can ignore and rebuff with impunity'.[102]]

19 November

C[omrade] Vyshinsky received Cripps at the latter's request.

Cripps raised three questions:

(1) Having failed to receive a reply from the Soviet government to its proposal about the chartering of the Baltic ships, the British government will act independently and will, at its own discretion, set the sum of charter money to be deposited in a special account. The fate of this money will be decided later.

(2) The British government would like to know what measures the Soviet government intends to take to repatriate in the USSR the 300 sailors from the Baltic ships who wish to return home. Cripps mentioned the possibility of interning these sailors.

(3) The Finnish government has asked the British government about the latter's opinion concerning the transfer of the Petsamo nickel concessions to the Soviet government. The British government replied that it would not object if two conditions were observed: nickel shall not end up in Germany, and the concession shall be transferred only for the duration of the war.

C[omrade] Vyshinsky's reply boiled down to the following:

(1) The first question. The attitude of the Soviet government to the issue of the ships is well known. The Soviet government does not, as a matter of principle, recognize the British government's right to requisition Soviet property. Consequently, there can be no negotiations on chartering, the cost of chartering, etc.

(2) As for the second question, the Soviet government is certainly concerned about the repatriation of sailors, but does not consider it possible to send a special ship for them from the Soviet Union, as there are enough Soviet ships in British ports. If the British government should try to intern the Baltic sailors, who are Soviet citizens, the S[oviet] G[overnment] would respond in the sharpest manner. Cripps said at this point that he would contact the British government with a view to singling out one of the Baltic ships for the repatriation of its sailors.

(3) The third question. Cripps's present statement regarding the Petsamo concession differs from his previous statement that 'the concession should not fall into German hands'. C[omrade] Vyshinsky promised to report the matter to the Soviet government, but expressed doubt as to whether the conditions set by the British government would be acceptable to us.

In conclusion, C[omrade] Vyshinsky categorically refuted the statement made in the British note of 16 November that the Soviet embassy in London had leaked the proposals of 22 October. Rather, according to information obtained from me, the proposals were made public by the officials of the Foreign Office in London.

Cripps tried to defend himself by referring to the embassy's close connections with the American journalist who published the contents of the British proposals.

But C[omrade] Vyshinsky completely ruled out the possibility that the information had been leaked by the embassy.

Cripps promised to inform the British government about it.

Palewski,[i] former head of Reynaud's Cabinet, came to see me. He told me at length about the degenerate atmosphere in which Reynaud has been living of late and exclaimed in a typically French manner: 'What could be expected of Reynaud when he had a fifth column in his own bed?'

Palewski meant the famous Madame de Portes.

I asked Palewski: What, in his view, lies at the root of the French collapse?

He pondered for a moment and said: 'Hedonism is to be blamed for all that… This generation of Frenchmen was far too fond of pleasure and the good life. They forgot suffering and hated discomfort. That is where it all began.'

I tried, as subtly as I could, to touch upon the social causes of the French catastrophe. Palewski listened attentively, and interrogated me eagerly, but I felt nonetheless that my words failed to reach him.

Palewski praised de Gaulle as an honest and upright soldier. He himself has not joined de Gaulle, however. He renders service to de Gaulle, but does not want to be too closely associated with him.

Palewski recently arrived from Africa and is returning there soon. He promised to call on me should fate bring him back to London.

* * *

Strange but true: the P[olish] G[overnment] is attempting to establish unofficial contact with us through our consulate. Needless to say, I rebuff all such attempts. What is curious is the direction which Polish thinking seems to be taking: they are prepared to 'recognize' Western Ukraine and Western Belorussia as belonging to the USSR, but they want a 'plebiscite' to be carried out in Carpathian Russia after the war.

At the same time, the Polish government has drawn up a map of post-war Poland: it must incorporate not only East Prussia, but also the whole German territory along the Stettin–Bohemia line! What an appetite!

More and more bombs are falling near the embassy, and even on it.

Many explosive and incendiary bombs were dropped in the vicinity of the embassy on the nights of the 14th–15th and 15th–16th. At one point Kensington Gardens looked as if it was brightly illuminated because of the huge

[i] Gaston Palewski, appointed shortly after the meeting with Maisky as director of political affairs of the Free French government.

number of fire bombs dropped on it. There was a big fire at Queen Victoria's Kensington Palace, a five-minute walk from the embassy. Two fire bombs fell on the consulate, but they were quickly extinguished. On the night of the 19th–20th, incendiary and explosive bombs rained down once more in the embassy's neighbourhood. An incendiary bomb fell on our shelter, but it burned out immediately without causing any damage: it left only a small patch of scorched grass. Another incendiary bomb fell near the embassy garage without igniting. In the morning our military people removed the bomb and defused it. Many bombs also fell in the vicinity of the school: glass was smashed and doors torn off their hinges.

Bomb weight is increasing. The bombs dropped on London hitherto have generally weighed 50 or 250 kg. There are none of intermediary size. A small quantity of 500 kg bombs was also dropped. But recently there have appeared many so-called [missing word] that are basically ordinary sea mines weighing up to 1.5 tons. They are dropped by parachute and explode on hitting the surface without entering deep into the ground. Their destructive power is immense. The biggest bombs made craters 15 metres deep. Such bombs even penetrated the Underground, in places where the tunnels lie quite close to the surface. In fact, experts say that only shelters built at a depth of 25 metres are safe.

Kennedy came by to pay a farewell visit. True, formally he is leaving for 'consultations' with Roosevelt, but he did not conceal the fact that he will not be returning.

Needless to say, we spoke about the war and about the prospects for England. Kennedy is still a 'pessimist': of course, the threat of an invasion has passed, but what will happen in Egypt? Judging by the US ambassador's reliable and very accurate information, defeat looms for the English there.

I replied that although I have no grounds to be an Anglophile, in my duties as ambassador I try to be 'objective' and weigh every 'for' and 'against' dispassionately, in order to provide my government with correct information. Taking this approach to the question of war in Egypt, I must repeat what I said about the invasion in June: the British have enough cards in their hands to preserve their position in Egypt and in the Near East in general – everything depends on whether they manage to play their cards well. I can't say whether they will or not, but the conduct of the English when faced with possible invasion inclines me to think they will probably be able to play their cards well in Egypt, too. But time will tell.

I asked Kennedy what he thought about the possibility of the United States entering the war.

Kennedy ducked the question, saying he had not been to his homeland for a long time and was not aware of the sentiments prevailing there. He personally thinks that the United States should not enter the war and that direct US participation in military operations would be less advantageous to the British than US non-interference. Then Kennedy said, as though in self-justification: 'I've never advocated appeasement as a matter of principle. Everything I said could be summed up in the following way: if the British government has succeeded through its policies in dispersing all its friends, both former and potential, then it's senseless for it to risk a war.'

Taking his leave, Kennedy exclaimed with his loud, braying laugh: 'It's easy to be an American ambassador here in England, but devilishly difficult to be a Soviet one! But by God, you cope with your job superbly.'

I thanked Kennedy for his compliment (he likes to shower compliments left, right and centre) but I could not return it even out of courtesy. For although it is indeed easy to be an American ambassador in England, Kennedy has not been up to the job at all. Roosevelt, Churchill and the English political world – all are dissatisfied with him.[103] That is the cause of his dismissal, not his desire to return to his 'business affairs', as he told me today. At the bottom of it all lies the fact that Kennedy is a wealthy, orthodox Irish Catholic who has a mortal terror of revolution and would like to live in harmony with 'fascist dictators'. That explains his dislike of the Soviet Union, his liking of Chamberlain, whom he has always supported, and his fear of a war which may, under certain circumstances, unleash revolutionary potentialities.

C[omrade] Molotov's visit to Berlin has made a big splash in England.

At first, everyone got terribly frightened. The Germans were inflating the importance of the visit and predicting a decision of 'world-historical' significance. They let it be known that an exceptionally significant document was in preparation, and hinted at a 'division of the world' between the 'Axis' and the USSR: Europe would go to Germany, Africa to Italy, China and Eastern Asia to Japan, and India and Iran to the USSR. People in London only half-believed all this, but they got themselves into a state about it all the same. The initial response in political circles was: 'Look where Halifax has led us! Instead of tearing Russia away from Germany, he made Molotov's visit to Berlin possible.'

Rumours of Halifax's imminent dismissal have been doing the rounds again. The *News Chronicle* and the *Daily Herald* published sensational reports to this effect: Halifax would leave the FO within a fortnight. This was officially denied, but rumours and speculations continued. Then Halifax decided to go on the attack.

True, the press was advised *to go slow* on C[omrade] Molotov's visit and not to provoke the Russians, but the FO press department started a rather vigorous *whispering campaign* on the morning of 12 November. The sort of campaign this was can best be judged from what Rigsdale, chief of the press department, told a journalist of my acquaintance: 'Three weeks ago Cripps forwarded to the Soviet government British proposals of "paramount importance" alongside which all the Danube and Baltic issues are mere trifles. However, Molotov would not receive Cripps to accept the proposals and went to Berlin without finding time to give Cripps his reply. Obviously, Molotov was too busy with the German ambassador. Molotov's game-plan is clear: to bring the British proposals to Berlin and show them to Hitler to extract better terms. This whole story definitively clarifies the situation: it is absolutely clear that the Soviet government simply does not want to improve relations, but merely seeks pretexts to maintain relations in their present unsatisfactory condition.'

Naturally enough, the inquisitive journalists wanted to know more about the proposals of 'paramount importance'. Rigsdale and his staff did not need to be asked twice to share a 'state secret'. They willingly spilled it first to the British diplomatic correspondents like McDonald (*The Times*), Werth[i] (*Manchester Guardian*), Ewer (*Daily Herald*), Lennox (*Daily Telegraph*) and others. From the 13th onwards, press department officials started to reveal, little by little, the essence of the proposals to foreign correspondents. C. learned about the proposals from them and from other Foreign Office functionaries (most likely Collier or Maclean in the northern department). C. sent two telegrams on the subject to the United States on the evening of the 13th and the morning of the 14th. The censor, namely Rigsdale, allowed the telegrams through. The Domei agency took up the news in New York and spread it round Japan. On the afternoon of the 15th, the proposals were officially announced at a press conference in the press department and were broadcast by the BBC that same evening.

The purpose of this action was clear: Halifax wanted to shift responsibility for the unsatisfactory state of relations to the Soviet government: 'We are doing all we can to improve relations, but the Soviet government does not reciprocate!'

And by doing so, to divert the danger to himself. Exactly what one could have expected from such a self-seeking foreign secretary.

But since the Soviet government might have taken offence at a unilateral announcement of proposals which had been made to it in confidence, Halifax decided to turn me into the scapegoat.

On the morning of the 16th, Cripps handed the following note to NKID:

> You will undoubtedly learn that this morning the BBC broadcast some information concerning the proposals I handed over to be submitted to the Soviet government on 22 October of this year. The reason for this broadcast is that a US journalist had already obtained full information concerning the proposals. The source of his information was the Soviet embassy in London. The Domei agency went on to publish this

[i] Alexander Werth, an American correspondent.

> information, having received it from the same source. I greatly regret that your embassy in London made the disclosure, one that is undesirable for His Majesty's Government. As you could have judged by the form in which I conveyed the proposals to you, His Majesty's Government was fully aware of the need to preserve confidentiality and avoid the proposals falling into the hands of an unfriendly State.

Cripps was terribly worried about this whole incident. Having fulfilled the British government's assignment, he sent a sharp telegram to the FO protesting against the disclosure of the proposals through the BBC and accusing the FO of sabotaging his efforts in improving Anglo-Soviet relations.

I also received a letter of inquiry from Moscow and explained what had happened in detail. I insisted on sending a note of reply containing the following:

> On 16 November the British ambassador in Moscow handed a note to the NKID informing the Soviet government that the BBC had broadcast some information that morning concerning proposals made to the Soviet government on 22 October. The British ambassador explained the circumstances leading to the disclosure, alleging that a US journalist and the Japanese Domei agency had earlier received full information about the said proposals from the Soviet embassy in London. On behalf of my government I have the honour to state the following: the Soviet government is entirely confident that the Soviet embassy in London did not disclose the British proposals of 22 October. On the contrary, the Soviet government has very serious grounds for believing that the disclosure was made by Foreign Office functionaries in London. In this connection the Soviet government cannot but regret that the British government thought it possible to address the Soviet government with an official note which is founded on unverified information.

Moscow thought this over and decided not to send a note, confining itself to C[omrade] Vyshinsky's oral protest in his conversation with Cripps on 19 November.

But how very nimble is Halifax! Oh, I do dislike these sanctimonious prigs!

* * *

The FO press department uses some interesting methods.

Every day, at 12.30, it holds a press conference. Forty to fifty British and foreign journalists, sometimes more, gather to ask questions (ticklish and delicate questions as often as not) and hear various communications from Rigsdale and his assistants.

Tête-à-tête talks with 'trusted' journalists (MacDonald, Ewer, Bartlett, Gordon-Lennox and others) are held in the afternoon. Here information is disclosed 'off the record'. The 'trusted' journalists also have an opportunity to converse with their 'friends' in the political divisions of the FO, sometimes even with Butler. These journalists are well briefed; sometimes they are even shown foreign ambassadors' coded messages. There have been instances when I learned about Moscow démarches first from British journalists and then from NKID.

Under these conditions, leaks are inevitable even if FO officials have no special interest in a particular 'secret' being divulged. They are all the more probable when there is such an interest.

Leaks also trickle out of various ministerial offices, where members of government receive copies of all the most important talks, documents, etc. which concern the Foreign Office.

30 November

Agniya and I went to the countryside to visit the young Churchill couple.[104] They live in the village of Ickleford, Herts, by the church, in the rectory which has been empty for over half a century. The big house – 15 rooms – is too expensive for the local rector. So the clergymen live in a little cottage nearby, paying a small rent for it. The rectory is rented out to interested parties for 100 pounds a year (the sum has not changed for 50 years – that's British conservatism for you!) and the rector uses the money to cover his current expenses.

Randolph and his wife are awfully proud of their seven-week-old heir, whom they have called Winston.[i] They showed us their treasure: a wonderful boy and, for his age, a very sentient being. He somewhat resembles his grandfather. I liked another of the prime minister's grandsons even more – Julian Sandys,[ii] a red-haired boy of three, vigorous, agile and cheerful. Sandys married the prime minister's daughter and his family shares the house with Randolph and his family. The PM's other daughter, who is unmarried and a film actress, also lives there. On the whole, Ickleford is a 'Churchill commune'. Randolph will soon depart for the Mediterranean. He and his 20-year-old wife were a bit on edge today, maybe because of his forthcoming departure.

Randolph was very talkative. We argued at length about the war prospects. He, of course, could not accept anything other than complete 'victory'. When I asked him 'How?', he started mumbling something incoherent. Randolph's

---

[i] A Conservative MP from 1970 to 1983.

[ii] Edwin Duncan Sandys (Baron Duncan-Sandys), Conservative MP from 1935, was married to Churchill's daughter Diana. Wounded in action in Norway in 1941, he became a junior minister in his father-in-law's Cabinet and in various Conservative Cabinets after the war.

calculations are based on the following: if England delivers a *knock-out* blow to Italy next summer, and the United States enters the war after that, German 'morale' will crack.

'What if it doesn't crack? What then?' I queried. Then, Randolph thinks, the war will continue for one, two, three, even ten years, until the superior British resources and manpower (including the Empire) eventually produce the desired effect. Childish reasoning!

I expounded my thoughts about a 'political offensive' being the sole condition that would permit England 'to win the war'. Randolph brushed aside my arguments, saying: 'There will be no such offensive under the present prime minister! My father is not a socialist.'

I asked why the prime minister had agreed to lead the Conservative Party. His position may constrain him in the domestic and external manoeuvring that is inevitable during a war.

Randolph said his father is not afraid of that eventuality. He is confident that he will be the boss, not a hostage, of the Conservative Party. I have serious doubts on this score as well. Well, we shall see.

We also discussed the gravity of the situation at sea. Randolph did not deny its gravity, but he believes the British government will be able to deal with German submarines within the space of a few months. His arguments are as follows. (1) The shipyards have only just started to supply the small vessels (destroyers and others) which his father commissioned at the beginning of the war, when he was first lord of the Admiralty. Winston's programme was on a major scale and more and more small vessels will be put into service in 1941. (2) There is every reason to expect 50–100 destroyers from the United States. (3) British and US shipyards will be capable of covering the commercial tonnage losses with new construction. (4) The year 1941 will see a great augmentation of the naval air force, which is very important in combating submarines.

There is a good deal of truth in Randolph's arguments, but much will also depend on the intensity of German warfare in the skies and beneath the seas. We shall see.

1 December

In July Attlee, at Halifax's request, made a 'polite' attempt to persuade Negrín into leaving England: this was Hoare trying to please Franco.[105] Negrín took the line: I'm in your hands. If you insist, I have no choice but to leave, but provide me with a visa and passage to the United States. And bear in mind that upon arrival in America I will need to explain to my friends the reasons that forced me out of England. The latter warning scared Attlee and he assured Negrín that the right to sanctuary was unshakable in Great Britain and that he could stay as long as he wished. The FO was less timid and did request an American visa for Negrín. But then came an unexpected hitch: Washington refused Negrín a visa. Matters went no further over the summer. I even thought the British government had finally given up its plan; but I was wrong.

On 8 November, Negrín was invited to see Alexander, first lord of the Admiralty. Halifax was at Alexander's office as well. Alexander spoke first. With tears in his voice he reminisced about the Spanish war. He spoke of his warm feelings towards the Republicans, and recalled the quantity of money and food which the English cooperative movement dispatched to Barcelona. The old man was deeply moved and ready to cover Negrín in kisses.

With the ground thus prepared, Halifax took the floor and got down to business. He explained that the Germans are now waging a furious anti-British campaign in Spain, that they are eager to draw Franco into the war, and that Negrín's presence in England is one of their trump cards. The Germans whisper into Franco's ear that the British are conspiring with Negrín and preparing for the overthrow of Franco and his regime. The conclusion which followed was that, of course, the British government considers the right of sanctuary positively sacred! Naturally, it would never encroach upon Negrín's will! And yet… Couldn't Negrín render the British government a great service? Couldn't he leave England 'of his own free will' – oh, of course, 'entirely of his own his free will'? The British government would be infinitely obliged to him for that.

Negrín replied that, as Halifax must know, he was ready to leave for the States in July, but the US authorities refused him a visa.

Halifax then asked: and what about Negrín leaving for Latin America?

Negrín replied that Latin America did not suit him at the present for various reasons, among which is the following: living in England as an émigré, he can keep silent and refrain from openly discussing current political matters. But if he moves to Latin America, it will be impossible for him to keep silent. He will have to speak and give his assessment of many contemporary events, which might not be favourable to the British government, even though his general position is not to interfere in the war.

This statement confused Halifax and Alexander, and they stopped insisting on Latin America. Halifax suggested instead: 'And why not go, for example, to New Zealand? You could give a series of interesting lectures there.'

Negrín said New Zealand was out of the question: how would he be able to justify to the Spanish people his decision, at this crucial historical juncture, to go ten thousand miles away from his homeland?

Halifax and Alexander did not give up, however, and asked Negrín to reconsider their offers. With that, the audience ended.

On 11 November, Negrín sent a long letter in French to Halifax, in which he explained once again the impossibility of his moving to Latin America or

New Zealand, but added that if the British government was still insisting on his departure, he would ask them to arrange for him to stay in the United States or, as a last resort, Canada.

On 18 November, Halifax sent Negrín a short reply stating that he would bring the content of Negrín's letter to the notice of his colleagues, after which he would meet him again. Such a meeting has not yet taken place.

On the 22nd, Dobbie[i] raised the Negrín issue in the House of Commons, and Strabolgi did the same in the House of Lords. Butler and Halifax were the ones to answer. Both, of course, had to tie themselves in knots arguing that they had nothing to do with it. Halifax even went so far as to assert that no conversation about Negrín's departure had taken place, just a joint discussion about how to counteract German propaganda in Spain.

On 27 November, Dobbie raised the same matter at a meeting of the Labour Parliamentary Group. Attlee, who responded, wriggled like a snake and muddied the issue. Other Labourites spoke, too. Some issued cutting remarks from their seats. It was clear that even this Labour elite was profoundly outraged by the servility of their ministers in this malodorous matter. Attlee and Co. can hardly have failed to understand this. But will they manage to draw the adequate conclusions? May one consider Negrín's continued residence in England secure?

I don't know. That's a question for the future.

2 December

I've received some interesting information about British aircraft production.

	Bombers	Fighters	In total
August	459	549	1767
September	343	480	1440

About 1,700 aircraft in all categories were produced in October. The reduction caused by the air offensive in September was practically eliminated.

The situation in the third week of October was as follows.

New aircraft output	375
Of which	
Bombers (Blenheim, Wellington, Whitley)	49
Fighters (Spitfire, Hurricane)	80
Other bombers and fighters	70

[i] William Dobbie, trade unionist, first Labour lord mayor of York; Labour MP, 1933–50.

Training aircraft	114
Naval aircraft	36
Others	11
Released after repair	92
Placed under repair	146
Repaired	238
New engines	541
Repaired engines	295
New anti-aircraft balloons	289

There were 787 aircraft, including 258 bombers and 262 fighters, at aircraft depots as of 18 October.

11 December

The Germans have changed their tactics once again in the air war.

During the first month of the air offensive (8 August–7 September), the Germans mainly attacked the London–Dover–Portland triangle, paving the way for an invasion. Their plan failed.

During the next two months (after 7 September) they attacked London, striving to undermine the morale of the major centre of the British Empire. That failed, too.

Since 14 November, the Germans have been employing new tactics: they have been executing focused air raids against important industrial centres and ports in the provinces (Coventry, Birmingham, Bristol and Southampton). London is also being bombed, but it is not the main target.

Air raids in this recent phase look more or less the same everywhere.

The Germans attack at night, sending several hundred bombers every time (500 to Coventry; 250 to Southampton two nights running, i.e. once again 500; 300 to Birmingham; and 300 to Bristol). First they drop incendiary bombs. When, as a result, fires illuminate the city, explosive bombs of various calibre are dropped and the so-called *land mines* are parachuted down. Accuracy is rather poor, just as before, because the British anti-aircraft batteries force the German machines to fly very high and retreat quickly. However, the mass dropping of bombs onto relatively small areas creates great damage. The centre of the city is usually bombed, and if industrial and other military targets are located there, they are also damaged, but this occurs by chance rather than design. Plants and factories located on the outskirts usually remain intact.

As for the destructive power of the new type of raids, this proves to be directly proportional to the number of bombers per square metre of the area attacked. Here is an example. Coventry, with a population of 175,000, was attacked by 500 bombers and great destruction was caused. To have an equivalent effect while bombing Birmingham (with a population of more than 1 million), the Germans would have had to send 2,500 bombers, but they engaged 300 machines and the damage was relatively small. In order to turn London into Coventry, then, at least 20,000 bombers would have been needed – an obviously fantastical figure, at least for the current phase of the war. That is why I am relatively calm about London.

The question arises: why don't the Germans throw larger forces into the attack? Why don't they bomb one and the same city systematically night after night with hundreds of planes? Because they don't want to or because they can't?

I have no clear answer to this question as yet.

Neither, it seems, does the British government.

One thing is clear, though: the new type of German air offensive is as incapable of decisively altering the course of the war as the previous one. It does, of course, cause difficulties and complications, but it cannot bring England to its knees. The morale of the population and government remains firm.

It seems to me that the Germans are not setting themselves such a goal at present. They have abandoned the idea of taking the British fortress by storm. They are trying to lay siege to it from the air and from the sea (the sinking of ships has increased sharply of late). Should the Germans manage to weaken England in this way and undermine its morale, they would of course come back to the idea of invading. Will they succeed? I don't think so. Not in the near future at any rate. We shall see.

12 December

I visited Vansittart today. I hadn't seen him for several months and I was struck by his appearance: he looks emaciated, much older, and has become very highly strung. The wrinkles on his face are deeper. His hands tremble. Although he is only 59, he is almost an old man. He has a cold. His wife is losing weight and is confined to her bed. In general, his life has not been a bed of roses recently.[106]

Nonetheless, Vansittart was *in high spirits* today: the British are gaining victories in Egypt. He said that since the beginning of the war he had never been as optimistic about the future as he was today. It was patently obvious from what he said that the British government had definitively decided on its course for 1941: to try to crush Italy.

Vansittart spoke eloquently and at length about the misunderstanding and underestimation of the English character abroad. It has been so since time immemorial. Napoleon, Bismarck, the kaiser, and now Hitler, Ribbentrop and Mussolini – they all were and are grossly mistaken in fancying the English to be a 'nation of shopkeepers', 'degenerate gentlemen', 'depraved plutocrats', etc., who cannot and will not fight whatever the circumstances. A profound mistake. True, in peace time the English like comfort, convenience, sport, travelling. They dislike drills, gaudy uniforms, goose-step and spurs. They give the impression of being a deeply 'civilian', pampered nation. And a little too much fat has grown on their bones in recent decades.

However, if their backs are against the wall and their lives are endangered, if they are irritated or enraged, they change beyond recognition. They become malicious, stubborn, ready to fight like animals and sink their fangs into the enemy. That is why the English, despite entering every war unprepared, with scarce forces and often with poor leaders, never lose wars. This leads Vansittart to the conclusion that England will defeat Germany in 1942 or 1943.

Such is now the typical philosophy of the ruling class, and not of the ruling class alone.

16 December

I visited Lloyd George at his new office (8, Victoria Road) today. It is in fact his old house, where he now works after moving out of his large and stylish office at Thames House, Embankment. It would seem that the economic repercussions of the war have started affecting even the top echelons of the British ruling classes.

I found the old man in a far from brilliant condition, both in body and morale. He coughed and looked pale and sluggish. His outlook for the future lacked confidence and hope.

Despite the victories in Africa, Lloyd George's prognosis for the war remains the same: he cannot see how England could defeat Germany. *Stalemate*, playing out a draw – yes, that's possible and even probable. But victory? No, the old man still cannot discern the necessary preconditions for victory.

'Well, if the Soviet Union entered the war on our side,' exclaimed Lloyd George, 'that would be a different matter! Then we really could beat Germany. But that is out of the question. What's more, our government, even this government, has done everything in its power to alienate Russia. Sheer madness!'

The old man raised his hands in despair.

There was a call from the prime minister's office while I was there: Churchill asked him to be at 10, Downing Street by 1 p.m. The old man was clearly agitated by the call.

Why did Churchill need to see Lloyd George? Does he want to appoint him ambassador to Washington?…

Lloyd George spoke with some contempt about Italy. In his opinion, Mussolini's regime is beginning to *crack*. Mussolini will not be able to recover from his defeats on his own. Will Hitler help him? Lloyd George doubts it. First of all, how? By sending troops to Greece through Yugoslavia and Bulgaria? Or through Turkey to Egypt? That would be dangerous. It could trigger a quarrel between Hitler and the USSR. One also has to take into account Turkish resistance. Second, what for? Lloyd George has an idea: Hitler has been recently thinking about replacing Italy with France in his 'Axis'. This is not impossible. Suppose Hitler says to Pétain: I shan't claim French territories in Europe (except Alsace-Lorraine) and in Africa (except Togo and Cameroon), I shall repatriate 2 million French prisoners, I shall vacate the greater part of occupied France except for the Channel and Atlantic ports, which I need to fight against England, while in exchange you give me a base in Toulon and allow me to use what's left of the French fleet. Could such a scheme not attract Pétain? Of course it could. Lloyd George interprets the fall of Laval and the appointment of Flandin precisely from this point of view: Laval was 'pro-Italian', while Flandin has always been 'pro-German'. Italian stock is falling, while German shares are on the rise. Hence the change 'on the throne'.

We'll see if the old man is right.

I walked home through *Kensington Gardens*. It was damp and slightly foggy. The park was empty. On the shore of the little lake I observed an almost Biblical scene: a young bespectacled soldier in crumpled, filthy uniform was feeding the swans and gulls. He had a big bag under his arm from which he was taking the crumbs and throwing them to the birds. Three big swans climbed out of the water and, gracefully bending their necks, took the crumbs straight from the soldier's palm. Hundreds of gulls surrounded the soldier, crying wildly and violently flapping their wings. They rushed about him as if possessed, plucked pieces of bread out of the air, and landed on his shoulders and arms, even on his head. And he, a puny, clumsy and pensive little soldier, peered through his spectacles with a certain surprise at this kingdom of birds, as if wishing to say: 'Yes, man and nature are one.'

19 December

The situation at sea becomes more and more serious. Here are the most important relevant facts. The pre-war commercial tonnage of the British Empire amounted to 21 million tons, including 18 million in the mother country. England has added some 9 million tons to this since the beginning of the war (the fleets of the Allies – Norway, Holland, Belgium, Greece, etc., captured enemy vessels, purchased and newly built vessels, etc.). In total: 30 million tons or 44% of world tonnage as it stood in the summer of 1939!

The British losses (including Allies) in the naval war were, on average, 63,000 tons a week, i.e. about 4 million tons for the entire period. The losses have increased considerably in the recent three or four months – up to 100,000 tons weekly. Thus, the yearly estimate is about 5 million tons. That is serious! All the more so as the average distance covered by a vessel has increased compared with peace time, while the average speed has decreased. The first is accountable to the fact that, having lost its near European markets as a result of the war, England has to trade with distant countries. Besides, developments in the Mediterranean have rendered the use of the Suez Canal for commercial traffic more problematic, while the route around Africa is 11 days longer than via the Suez Canal. The second follows from the fact that merchant ships now sail in convoy with escorts (40–50 steamships) and have to move at the speed of the slowest vessel in the convoy.

Where should the reasons for the heavy losses sustained by the British commercial fleet be sought? There are actually three main reasons. First and foremost, England has no more than 300 destroyers and other small vessels to protect its commercial sea traffic, compared with the 900 engaged by the Entente (England, France, Russia, Japan and Italy) in the last war. Admittedly, the theatre of this war at present is somewhat smaller than in 1914–18, but still… Second, the war against the commercial fleet nowadays is carried out not only by submarines (as in the last war), but also by aircraft. Third, the Germans use French Atlantic bases (which they did not have in the 1914–18 war), while the British cannot use Irish bases (as they did 25 years ago).

What measures are the English undertaking and planning to combat all this? There are many. I'll list the most important ones:

(1) Frenzied construction of small warships. At the beginning of the war, when still lord of the Admiralty, Churchill laid down a major programme of construction. Up to 100 destroyers are nearing completion, and in 1941 small war vessels will come into service almost in 'conveyor-belt' fashion. Moreover, 40 cruisers are being built, and five King George V class battleships (35,000 tons, 35 knots, 11 guns of 14-inch calibre) will be completed soon. More battleships will enter service in 1941 (one already has). Further down the line, it is expected that the United States will deliver another batch of 'dated' destroyers in 1941 (50–100 are the numbers being bandied about). Other forms of US naval aid are being discussed, such as US convoys to 'neutral' Ireland, the guarding of the western part of the Atlantic by US forces, etc. The quantity of naval aircraft, which are very important in combating German submarines, is also growing rapidly.

(2) The question of using Irish bases is being seriously considered – through an agreement, if possible (such plans rely on the US exerting pressure) or by military occupation if it proves unavoidable.

(3) Large-scale development of commercial shipbuilding in England. One can count on 1.5 million tons a year (the *peak* in 1929 was about that sum).

Shipbuilding in the United States is being promoted in every possible way. Sixty steamers have been commissioned in the USA (10,000 tons each, 10–12 knots) to be delivered in the spring of 1942. But the British government has even more far-reaching plans. It proposes to restore the Hog Island shipyard, where one standard vessel of 5–6 tons was produced daily during the last war. The British government counts on receiving an annual tonnage of up to 3 million from the USA.

(4) Measures have been taken to decrease imports by developing local agricultural production (though their effects will not really be felt in 1941), as well as by rationing more and more foodstuffs and other products.

(5) Great hopes are placed on the defeat of Italy in the near future – then, at any rate, at least half of the fleet engaged in the Mediterranean today could be moved to the Atlantic to combat German submarines.

So what are the prospects?

The situation now is undoubtedly serious. It resembles the situation at the beginning of 1917. However, the British government has enough cards to play. Will it play them well? We shall see. I don't have any great confidence in the abilities of the British to fight successfully on land, but they are past masters of naval warfare.

27 December

During the September air offensive Dutch Queen Wilhelmina[i] was taking refuge quite democratically in the common 'shelter' at Claridge's Hotel, where she lived at that time. She slept together with other people in the shelter (having only one lady-in-waiting), and snored loudly. A lady who had just arrived at Claridge's and did not know the queen by sight came to the shelter for the night. Wilhelmina's snoring disturbed her terribly. When she could not bear it any longer, she snapped at the maid of honour (whom she did not know either): 'Stop her, for goodness sake! It's a sheer disgrace to snore like that!'

The lady-in-waiting told her the name of the snoring old woman. The infuriated lady took fright and ran out.

28 December

The significance of the Irish question is becoming ever more acute.

The Germans operate at sea against British commercial ships from French Atlantic bases. The British government is deprived in this war of the possibility

[i] Helena Pauline Maria Wilhelmina, queen of the Netherlands, 1890–1948, she sought refuge in the United Kingdom following the German occupation of the Netherlands in 1940.

of using Irish bases (Kingstown, Cork and others) to combat German submarines. Chamberlain ceded the bases to the government of Eire in 1938. This creates advantages for Germany and problems for England such as neither had in the last war. The more serious the situation at sea becomes, the more the British dream of using the Irish bases. De Valera is categorically against it: Eire adheres to a policy of neutrality, and there are still German and Italian missions working in Dublin.

Recently, another accusation has been levelled against Eire. The British claim to have proof that German submarines take on fuel in western Irish harbours. This may be a British fib to set the 'mood' prior to a possible occupation of Eire. But there may also be a grain of truth in it: there are elements in Ireland prepared to do anything to spite England. One cannot exclude the possibility that de Valera or his associates may turn a blind eye to suspicious machinations on the part of the German mission in Dublin.

Be that as it may, 'Irish complications' are in the air. There can be little doubt that the British government would occupy Eire, or at least its bases, were it not apprehensive of an adverse response in the United States. But who can tell? Maybe the British government will be able to create circumstances in which the USA would manage to swallow this pill.

29 December

To Churt to see Lloyd George. I found the old man lucid, vigorous and in good spirits. An astonishing individual: after all, he will be 78 in three weeks!

Lloyd George related to me the particulars of Churchill's proposal to appoint him ambassador in Washington. On 16 December, the PM invited him to lunch and made his proposal (I recall how, while I was talking to Lloyd George in his office, Sylvester hurried into the room and whispered to the old man that there had been a call from 10, Downing Street asking him to be there by 1 p.m.).

But Lloyd George refused the offer. Why?

'To start with,' the old man explained, 'an ambassador has no control over the policy he must represent. I don't want to find myself in such a position. That's the main thing. Secondly, the post in Washington would be beyond me, physically speaking. Poor Lothian, during his last visit to London, complained bitterly that he had turned into a talking machine...'

'Even though he liked to speak,' I interjected.

'Yes, despite the fact that he liked to talk,' Lloyd George agreed with a laugh. 'He would begin talking at eight in the morning and stopped only after midnight. Americans are quite unique. They are exceptionally talkative. Before taking any step, they will drown you in a sea of words. And every one of them wants to talk to the ambassador himself. Senator such and such... Banker such and such... Mayor such and such... I know what they're like! Just try not seeing one and you'll have yourself an enemy: "Hm... The ambassador *is too busy? Well! Well!...*" Then you can expect all sorts of unpleasantness. But it's beyond anyone's strength to see them all.'

Lloyd George burst into laughter and added: 'Well, the political result is positive: Eden is in the Foreign Office and Halifax goes to America. Strangely, he did not want to go and Lady Halifax was simply *furious*. The Court did not like it either: Lady Halifax, as I'm sure you know, is one of the queen's ladies-in-waiting. But Churchill dug in and got his way.'

Lloyd George lunched with the prime minister again on 20 December. They discussed matters of war and politics.

I asked Lloyd George about Churchill's present attitude to the Soviet Union. Lloyd George replied that in general the PM is in favour of improving Anglo-Soviet relations and will support Eden in that respect, but he is hardly prepared to go as far as Eden. For Churchill would like to 'win the war' without Soviet aid, so as not to have any obligations towards the Soviet Union. Besides, he counts on receiving active support from the United States.

Then we spoke about the government's situation. Lloyd George says that Churchill's position is very secure, but quite a few of his ministers are 'a disappointment'. Bevin is one of them.

'On the whole,' Lloyd George resumed, 'we have a good old Tory government, even though there are several Labourites in it, who are sometimes more conservative than the Conservatives themselves.'

The old man burst into infectious laughter and added: 'They genuinely believe that they can win the war by military means alone. True capitalist idiocy!'

I asked what Lloyd George himself thought of the war. His reply boiled down to the following: Lloyd George does not believe it possible for England to 'win the war' solely by force of arms. It will take at least two years to arm and train an army of 4 million (the most England can expect). It is a colossal task. To illustrate its grandiosity, Lloyd George gave just one example: in the last war, the English army expended 75 million shells in the Battle of Passchendaele alone!... The United States will hardly enter the war, certainly not in the near future, and if it does, the USA will also have to arm and train its army for a few years. In contrast, Germany has a well-armed and well-trained army of 8 million and, in addition, a general staff which far surpasses that of the British and the Americans. How can one hope of victory through military action alone?

England can achieve a true 'victory' only if the military offensive is backed up by a political offensive and even overshadowed by it at a certain point; that is, if England can, like a snake, cast off its capitalist skin in the course of the war and become an *essentially* socialist state.

I tried to clarify what Lloyd George meant by the little word *essentially*, but it was impossible to get a lucid explanation from him. I don't think I would be the only person to be perplexed by his notion of 'socialism'. Immediately after he made that statement, Lloyd George poured ridicule on the government for its dreams of Mussolini's regime being replaced by that of Grandi. When I asked him what he himself was expecting in the event of Mussolini falling, Lloyd George replied somewhat vaguely: 'A left-wing government of course… Socialists, radicals, communists, left "popolari"…'

Be that as it may, the old man is very sceptical, and not without reason, about the British government's readiness 'to cast off the capitalist skin'. So what can be expected?

Lloyd George thinks Hitler must try, at all costs, to 'resolve' the war in 1941. He will hardly succeed, however, as England has become much stronger in the air and at sea over the last six months and invasion has become a far less realistic proposition. One may expect, therefore, that next year's 'trial of strength' will not prove decisive. In consequence, a situation conducive to the opening of peace negotiations may take shape next autumn or winter. That is when the Soviet Union and the United States could play a major role as mediators and builders of the future world.

'So you really think,' I asked, 'that the war will most probably end in a draw?'

'Looks like it,' was Lloyd George's reply. 'But I think it is premature to start talking about peace today. I refuse categorically to associate my name with the efforts of some "appeasers" who want immediate peace talks. No, it's too early. Germany would charge a price which England would never pay. Germany first needs to be tired out, exhausted, and taken down a peg, then we can talk about peace… But a repeat of Versailles must be avoided at all costs!'

The old man thought for a moment and added: 'If peace is not achieved next winter, then I foresee an endless war of attrition… Yes, an endless war of attrition that will leave nothing of our civilization'.

[Though Maisky did 'not expect miracles', Eden's return to the Foreign Office on Christmas Eve raised new expectations. There was, as he wrote to Eden, 'a lot of debris to be cleared away, and the sooner it is started so much the better'.[107] Shortly after the holidays, Maisky paid a visit to the Foreign Office, to find Eden beaming with excitement. The gloom which had pervaded Halifax's office had been replaced by a bright and orderly atmosphere. Eden projected the image of a triumphant return. He wished to convince Maisky that no major conflict of interest in foreign policy existed between the two countries. The ambassador did not beat about the bush, explaining to Eden that only British recognition of the Soviet absorption of the Baltic States could lead to an improvement in relations. Soon enough it became obvious that the change in scenery did not entail a change in policy. Like those of his predecessor, Eden's interests remained tactical, aimed at detaching Russia from Germany. However, Maisky, who was eager to exploit the change, deviated from the canon, admitting to Eden that Russia certainly did not wish to see Germany emerge as the victorious power in Europe. Soviet foreign policy, he explained succinctly, rested on three principles: 'First, they were concerned with promoting their own national interests. Secondly, his Government wished to remain out of the war. Thirdly, they wished to avoid the extension of the war to any countries neighbouring Russia. In general Soviet policy was not expansionist: the Soviets had already enough territories.'

Maisky certainly did his utmost to convince his superiors at home that the change was significant.[108]]

30 December

Focused air raids have arrived, at last, in London, or more precisely its centre – the City.

On the night of the 29th, between 7 and 10 p.m., about 150 German bombers showered the City with fire bombs. The German planes are said to have dropped tens of thousands of bombs. As the City is empty at night (its daytime population is 500,000, but only 20,000 at night), there were no people there to deal with the bombs. The flames spread to a great many buildings and streets before the fire-fighters arrived. It was a terrible and beautiful spectacle. In the east, half the sky was aglow as we watched from the embassy. The City burned all night and throughout the day today. Even now, the fires have not been completely extinguished.

Usually, a shower of fire bombs is followed by a shower of explosive bombs. This time, however, there were only fire bombs. The English are sure that this was a result of a change in the weather which did not allow the second wave of bombers, carrying the explosive bombs, to take off from their airfields. I don't know if this is true, but it's a fact that there were no explosive bombs yesterday.

But even without them, the destruction in the City is immense. True, the Bank of England and the Stock Exchange have remained intact (how symbolic!), but the famous Guildhall has been reduced to ashes, and nearly a dozen ancient churches (the works of Wren) of great historical and architectural value have been destroyed. Many offices, stores, small shops, etc. are wrecked. All Moorgate Street, where our trade mission was located before 1927, lies in ruins and has been closed. As for 'military targets', only the Central Telegraph, located in the City, has suffered badly, while the Waterloo Bridge has been lightly damaged. Few human casualties.

This time, not only anti-aircraft guns operated on the English side, but also night fighters.

76. In the sanctuary of his private study, still watched over by the *vozhd*.

* * *

I was told the other day that the Germans have special radio stations in Frankfurt on Main and in Brest, which during night raids direct their *beam* at the centre of the city under attack. The *beams* cross directly over the central part of the city. The German bombers equipped with special receivers take their bearings by those beams. When they reach the crossing point, they drop their bombs.

This sounds right. All the recent air raids seem to confirm this explanation. It also explains why it is usually the centre of the city that is hit.

* * *

Sheffield and Manchester were also attacked at night. The results are grave. The central parts of both cities are in ruins. The famous *Free Trade Hall* in Manchester has burned to the ground. Chartists used to gather there in their day and the People's Convention organized by the Communist Party was to be held there on 12 January.

Notes to Volume 2

1939

1. A convention recognizing Finland's sovereignty over the Äland Islands and their demilitarization was signed by members of the League of Nations in 1921. With the Nazi threat looming, the Finnish and Swedish governments approached the Soviet government, as one of the signatories, with a request to sanction a change in the terms of the agreement which would allow a remilitarization of the islands. This is covered in Kollontay, *Diplomaticheskie dnevniki*, II, pp. 481, 490–2.

2. *God Krizisa*, I, nos. 65, 66, 77 & 107. See also Bezymenskii, *Stalin i Gitler*, pp. 149–51.

3. Vansittart papers, VNST 3/2, Seeds to Halifax on meeting Litvinov, 19 Feb. 1939, not mentioned in Litvinov's report in *DVP*, 1939, XXII/1, doc. 103; TNA FO 371 23677 N669 & N1342/57/38; *DVP*, 1939, XXII/1, doc. 128. See also Maisky's concern about isolation in his conversation in the same vein with L. Fischer in *Men and Politics*, pp. 556–7; J. Harvey (ed.), *The Diplomatic Diaries of Oliver Harvey 1937–1940* (London, 1970), pp. 259–60; and Liddell Hart, who gained the impression that Maisky was 'very anxious about the possibility of Stalin turning away from Litvinov's policy of trying to create a common front against Hitler'; *The Liddell Hart Memoirs*, p. 222.

4. *God Krizisa*, I, no. 156, 19 Feb. 1939; see also Roberts, 'The fall of Litvinov', p. 647.

5. Nicolson, *Diaries*, 9 Feb. 1939.

6. Amery papers, diary, AMEL 7/32, 15 Feb. 1939; Amery, *My Political Life*, p. 294.

7. Self, *Chamberlain Diary Letters*, IV, p. 373.

8. Negrín opposed Franco's demand for an unconditional surrender. He sought in vain French mediation in reaching a peace based on three points: (1) inviolability of the principle of Spain's independence, (2) a national referendum to establish the form of government in Spain and (3) guaranteed amnesty to the Republicans; Maisky, *Spanish Notebooks*. On 19 February 1939, Seeds informed Litvinov that Hudson intended to visit Moscow in late March or early April with a view to establishing contact with Soviet leaders and discussing trade opportunities. The Soviet side agreed to see Hudson. On 20 February, Chamberlain announced in the House of Commons that Hudson would visit Warsaw, Helsinki and Moscow. Hudson arrived in Moscow on 23 March 1939 (see *DVP*, 1939, XXII/1, doc. 103; *God Krizisa*, I, no. 157, p. 233).

9. Maisky had spent a whole month meticulously preparing the visit. He hoped to use the conducive atmosphere to exert pressure on Halifax through Churchill and other amenable

members of the opposition. John Rothenstein attests that, after dinner, 'Churchill and Lord Halifax successively withdrew to an adjoining room for the better part of half an hour for private discussion with Maisky … it was impossible to discern what fruits were being yielded by this attempt to bring British leaders into close consultation with the Russians'; Rothenstein, *Brave Day*, p. 31.

10. Maisky, *Who Helped Hitler?*, pp. 91–3.

11. This crucial observation was deliberately left out of Maisky's brisk report to Litvinov. Though boosting the significance of a first visit by a British prime minister to the Soviet embassy, Maisky conceded that it was motivated by 'a desire to somehow placate the Opposition'. Significantly, though, he kept the door open, wondering whether 'even in Chamberlain's own heart there is not a creeping fear lest the insatiability of the aggressors should force England and France to take up arms, and in anticipation of that eventuality it would not be amiss to extend a feeler towards the USSR'; *God Krizisa*, I, nos. 128 and 168, 4 March 1939. Moreover, London was awash with rumours about imminent political negotiations between Germany and the Soviet Union. Litvinov assumed that the gesture of Chamberlain was actually aimed at the Germans, to encourage them to make compromises in their negotiations with the British and forestall any agreement between Britain and the Soviet Union; D.C. Watt, *How War Came: The immediate origins of the Second World War 1938–1939* (London, 1989), p. 209; *DVP*, 1939, XXII/1, doc. 157.

12. The telegram is reproduced in a far more condensed manner in *DVP*, 1939, XXII/1, doc. 126.

13. As concerns this part of Hudson's pronouncement (the significance of his talks in Moscow), Maisky reported to NKID on 8 March 1939 that Hudson's visit 'could play a great role in defining the British foreign policy orientation for the next years. Hudson himself would like it to be along the London–Paris–Moscow line… There are subjective elements in Hudson's pronouncement of course, for he, unlike the premier, disfavours Germany, but he definitely could not have taken up the general line he developed in today's conversation without Chamberlain's sanction'; *DVP*, 1939, XXII/1, doc. 126. One should take Hudson's anti-German sentiments *cum grano salis*, for later on, in the summer of 1939, he was active in pursuing secret negotiations with Helmut Wohlthat, Göring's envoy.

14. Williams, *Nothing So Strange*.

15. *DVP*, 1939, XXII/1, docs. 126 & 128, 8 & 9 March; TNA FO 371 23677 N1389/57/38, 8 March 1939. Carley, *1939*, pp. 95–7, 102–3, is one of the few historians to have traced the discrepancies, but he attributes them to a false reporting by Maisky's interlocutors 'because of Chamberlain's opposition'. He overlooks the fact that the terror at home was increasingly forcing Maisky to deliberately put his own ideas into the mouths of those he spoke to, as the only effective and safe way of introducing a shift in Soviet policy.

16. See diary entry for 11 October 1938.

17. J. Lukacs, *June 1941: Hitler and Stalin* (New Haven, 2006), pp. 51–2.

18. In 1939, as Cadogan explained to Eden years later, Vansittart 'was brought into consultation a good deal on the question of our approach to the Soviet Government, and he was used (I'm not sure why) as a sort of channel to Maisky'; Cadogan papers, ACAD 4/5, 11 Dec. 1961.

19. In his report to Moscow, Maisky stressed the significance attached by Vansittart to Hudson's negotiations in Moscow against the background of the German annexation of the rest of Czechoslovakia on 15 March; *DVP*, 1939, XXII/1, doc. 137.

20. The gap between Litvinov's and Maisky's expectations was widening. Litvinov rightly assumed that Hudson had not been authorized to make any concrete proposals. He discouraged Maisky from making any initiatives, the more so as all the Soviet proposals for collective security had been ignored; *DVP*, 1939, XXII/1, docs. 146 & 155.

21. Vansittart gained the wrong impression that, following the German annexation of Czechoslovakia, Maisky had become concerned that the Germans might after all follow the *Drang nach Osten* and 'sign anything' with the British, 'no matter how definite'; Pimlott, *Political Diary of Hugh Dalton*, pp. 257–8.

22. The alliance of Greece, Rumania, Turkey and Yugoslavia, concluded in 1934.

23. Mutual defence arrangement, signed between Czechoslovakia, Yugoslavia and Rumania as part of the post-First World War arrangements, directed against Austro-German and Hungarian revisionism and attempts to dominate the Danube River basin. It lost its raison d'être after the German occupation of Czechoslovakia.

24. Dalton, *Fateful Years*, p. 232.

25. TNA FO 371 23061 C3683/3356/18, Report of conversations between Seeds and Litvinov, 21 March 1939; *God Krizisa*, I, nos. 206 & 215, 20 & 22 March 1939.

26. TNA FO 371 22967 C3859/15/18, Report of the ministers' meeting. See Maisky's report of the conversation with Halifax in *God Krizisa*, I, no. 202. Also reported at length by Corbin to Paris: 'Il est évident que cette déclaration tentait à certains égards de l'ambassadeur de l'U.R.S.S.' *DDF*, 2 Serie, XV, Doc. 97.

27. *God Krizisa*, I, nos. 194, 197, 198, 204 & 207, exchanges between Litvinov, Maisky and Surits, 18, 19 & 20 March, and Maisky to Litvinov, 22 March; *DVP*, 1939, XXII/2, doc. 16.

28. Signing the agreement on 23 March 1939, Rumania lost her economic sovereignty, ceding control of her economy to Germany and paving the way to her eventual inclusion in the Axis.

29. TNA CAB 23/98 17(39), 31 March 1939; Self, *Chamberlain Diary Letters*, IV, pp. 309–401; Rhodes, *Chips*, p. 193; Dalton, *Fateful Years*, p. 239. On the guarantees, see, A. Prazmowska, *Britain, Poland and the Eastern Front, 1939* (Cambridge, 1987).

30. A sound argument is produced by R. Manne, 'The British decision for alliance with Russia, May 1939', *Journal of Contemporary History 9/3* (1974), pp. 3–17. See also W. Wark, 'Something very stern: British political intelligence, moralism and grand strategy in 1939', *Intelligence and National Security*, 5/1 (1990), pp. 163–4.

31. Cadogan papers, ACAD 4/4, Letter to Colvin, 20 Jan. 1964.

32. Maisky had been trying in vain to meet Halifax. He was finally diverted to Cadogan, whose task was 'to stall him'. Monsieur Maisky, Cadogan concluded the official report, 'as is his wont, accepted very grudgingly my explanations'; Cadogan papers, ACAD 1/8, 23 March 1939; TNA FO 371 23062 C4155/3356/18 & 23681 N1683/92/38, 29 March 1939.

33. Cadogan informed Halifax that Maisky was astonished by the new plan, which, if executed, was tantamount to 'a revolutionary change in British policy' and might have 'far-

reaching results'. Maisky indeed wrote to Litvinov in the same vein on 30 March; TNA FO 371 22968 C4401/15/18, 23062 C4692/3356/18 & 23681 N1721/92/38; and *God Krizisa*, I, no. 243. Maisky's positive response was in brazen defiance of the reserve advocated by Litvinov; A. Resis in 'The fall of Litvinov: Harbinger of the German–Soviet non-aggression pact', *Europe-Asia Studies*, 52/1 (2000), p. 38 is right to be perplexed by the unorthodox line assumed by Maisky.

34. F. Maclean, *Fitzroy Maclean* (London, 1992), pp. 50–1; Cadogan papers, diary, ACAD 1/8, 17 April 1939.

35. *DVP*, 1939, XXII/2, doc. 157.

36. *God Krizisa*, I, nos. 233 & 234.

37. Though prohibited by Moscow from taking any initiative, Maisky was working frenziedly behind the scenes to exert pressure on Chamberlain. On the morning of 30 March, Greenwood had learned of the guarantees from Chamberlain, who was anxious to receive at least tacit Soviet support. Quoting from Cadogan's report on his meeting with Maisky, which was lying on the desk, Chamberlain assured Greenwood that Maisky seemed to be 'satisfied with this formula'. Shortly afterwards, however, as he had suspected, Dalton found the ambassador seriously irritated 'because he was out of touch': he had not met Halifax since 19 March and felt unable to advise his government, which was pressing him for information. Likewise, Beatrice Webb, who visited Maisky at the embassy the following morning as he anxiously waited to be summoned to Whitehall, found him distrustful of the British and the French governments, which he suspected were seeking a pact with Poland 'omitting the Soviet Union and even antagonistic to its interests'. Without delay, Dalton sought a second meeting with Chamberlain late at night. The prime minister, however, was reluctant to bring the Russians in because of the fierce opposition of other countries; Dalton, *Fateful Years*, p. 237–8; Webb, diary, 31 March 1939, p. 6639.

38. Anxious to avoid the meeting, Halifax informed Cabinet that he 'had not been able to see M. Maisky that morning as the Ambassador was not available. He hoped to see him before 3 o'clock. If this was not possible, he intended to send a telephone message to Moscow.' But Maisky, who met Lloyd George's secretary that morning, complained to him that '[Halifax] asked me to come at 10.30 this morning. Half an hour ago he rang up again to say he could not see me now and he would communicate later;' TNA CAB 23/98 17(39), 31 March 1939; Lloyd George papers, LG/G/130, Sylvester to Lloyd George, 31 March 1939.

39. Halifax told Cabinet that his main concern was the impact which consultations with the Russians might have on the Poles. As for Maisky, he expected him to be 'perfectly satisfied' and to say that the Russians 'were willing to help us if they were allowed to do so'; TNA CAB 23/98 17(39), 31 March 1939.

40. Maisky expected the declaration to resuscitate the battered collective security. His reservations reflected the extreme caution he assumed in his communications with Moscow, having been prohibited from making any initiatives. He preferred, therefore, to describe the tough line he had taken with Halifax, discouraging Chamberlain from making any reference to Russia in the anticipated parliamentary debate. However, it emerges from Halifax's report that he had been given the green light by Maisky after offering an assurance

that the guarantees were only an emergency measure and would be followed up by further consultations with the Russians. 'The Ambassador,' Halifax concluded his report, 'finally did not raise objection to a statement being made on the Prime Minister's authority to the effect that His Majesty's Government had reason to suppose that the Soviet Government would not find themselves other than in agreement with our declaration.' Moreover, Maisky emphasized that, if implemented, the policy would dovetail with Stalin's 'chestnuts speech' promising assistance to the victims of aggression, the text of which he promptly sent Halifax once the meeting was over; *God Krizisa*, I, no. 246, Maisky to Litvinov; TNA FO 371 23015 C4528/54/18, Halifax's report, 31 March 1939; RAN f.1702 op.4 d.892 l.3 & d.1290 l.3, exchange between Maisky and Halifax, 31 March and 3 April. Maisky's reserved support is also clear in TNA FO 371 23016, C4575/54/18, Halifax to Seeds, 4 April 1939. Maisky further exerted subtle pressure on Litvinov, seeking permission to maintain more frequent contact with the Foreign Office. To cover his tracks (and in order to vilify the British during the Cold War), in his memoirs Maisky chose to paint a highly dramatic narrative of his gallant stance during the meeting, which he even suggested took place with Chamberlain rather than with Halifax; *VSD*, p. 384 and *Who Helped Hitler?*, pp. 106–8.

41. Chamberlain's circle found Maisky's extra-parliamentary activities during the debate repulsive. 'I saw [Churchill] with Lloyd George, Boothby and Randolph, in a triumphant huddle surrounding Maisky. Maisky, the Ambassador of torture, murder and every crime in the calendar', recorded Sir Henry Channon in his diary; Rhodes, *Chips*, p. 192. Nicolson, who was also present, describes the meeting in detail in Nicolson, *Diaries*, p. 394. Lloyd George's sardonic criticism of Chamberlain was ineffective. 'As … I looked down at his red face and white hair,' Chamberlain reported to his sister, 'all my bitterness seemed to pass away for I despised him and felt myself the better man'; Self, *Chamberlain Diary Letters*, IV, p. 401, 1 April 1939.

42. Chamberlain felt in tune with Beck's views on Europe. 'He was very anxious not to be tied up with Russia … because of the effect on German opinion and policy', he wrote to his sister. 'I confess I very much agree with him for I regard Russia as a very unreliable friend with very little capacity for active assistance but with an enormous irritative power on others'; Self, *Chamberlain Diary Letters*, IV, p. 404, 9 April 1939. The agreement on mutual assistance was only signed on 25 August 1939.

43. AVP RF f.6 op.1 p.5 d.35 ll.76–8, Maisky to Litvinov, 24 March 1939; *SPE*, doc. 210, 4 April 1939; Litvinov to Merekalov, quoted in Dullin, *Men of Influence*, p. 268. As late as 11 April, Surits was instructed, in response to an overture made by Bonnet, to 'sit tight'; Roberts, 'The fall of Litvinov', p. 648.

44. Sylvester papers, diary, A47, conversations with Maisky, 5 April 1939; TNA FO 371 23063 C5430/3356/18.

45. *God Krizisa*, I, no. 257, 9 April 1939; *SPE*, docs. 217 & 218; Webb, diary, 8 April 1939, p. 6640 (emphasis in original).

46. Halifax summoned Maisky to 'keep him in touch', but deliberately concealed from him any details of the agreement being worked out with the Poles; TNA FO 371 23063 C5262/3356/18, 12 April 1939.

47. Evidently not registered with Halifax, who did not feel that 'any great progress' had been made towards solving the real difficulties facing Britain; TNA FO 371 23065 C5068/3356/18.

48. Litvinov to Surits and Maisky, *God Krizisa*, I, nos. 262, 263 & 264, 11 April 1939; *DVP*, 1939, XXII/1, docs. 216 & 217, Litvinov to Stalin and Maisky, 13 April 1939.

49. Vansittart papers, VNST 3/2, Seeds to Halifax, 13 April 1939.

50. The British and Soviet reports are in TNA, FO 371 23063 C5281/3356/18 and *DVP*, 1939, XXII/2, doc. 221; also *DDF*, 2 Serie, XV, Doc. 414, memorandum by Corbin; see also Harvey, *Diplomatic Diaries of Oliver Harvey*, p. 280. Emphasis added.

51. This redeeming picture of Chamberlain is hardly borne out by the prime minister's own admission, in a letter to his sister, 'of being deeply suspicious of [Russia] ... Her efforts are devoted to egging on others but herself promising only vague assistance ... Our problem therefore is to keep Russia in the background without antagonising her'; Self, *Chamberlain Diary Letters*, IV, p. 412, 29 April 1939.

52. *DVP*, 1939, XXII/2, docs. 277 & 283, 15 & 17 April. On Maisky's influence on the shift in Litvinov's attitude, see Resis, 'The fall of Litvinov'; Pons, *The Inevitable War*, ch. 5; Roberts, 'The fall of Litvinov', pp. 648–9.

53. Quoted in Dullin, *Men of Influence*, p. 216.

54. RAN f.1702 op.4 d.1260 & op.3 d.116 l.4, Boothby to Maisky and statement, 16 & 17 April; R.R. James, *Bob Boothby: A portrait* (London, 1991), p. 195; Pimlott, *Political Diary of Hugh Dalton*, pp. 259–60; Webb, diary, 8 April, p. 6640; *Liverpool Post*, 18 April; *New York Times*, 19 April; *The Times*, 19 April 1939.

55. Maisky, *Who Helped Hitler?*, pp. 120–1; A.V. Korotkov and A.A. Chernobaev (eds), 'Posetiteli kabineta Stalina: 1938–1939', *Istoricheskii Arkhiv*, 5–6 (1996); see *SPE*, doc. 249, Maisky's conversation with Surits, and Litvinov to Surits, 23 April 1939.

56. Webb, diary, 12 June 1939, p. 6665.

57. Sheinis, *Litvinov*, p. 294; Kollontay, *Diplomaticheskie dnevniki*, II, pp. 431–2.

58. Gromyko, *Memoirs*, p. 312.

59. Dalton papers, diary, I/20, quoting Maisky from their meeting on 7 May 1939.

60. D. Watson, *Molotov: A biography* (London, 2005), pp. 148–53.

61. On this, see Gromyko, *Pamyatnoe*, II, p. 423.

62. Maisky, *Who Helped Hitler?*, pp. 120–1; Dalton papers, diary, I/20, 7 May 1939. According to Sheinis, *Litvinov*, p. 294, Maisky left for London 'with a sense of dismay at having let Litvinov down', an impression shared by McDonald, *A Man of the Times*, p. 63.

63. Fragments of Merekalov's unpublished memoirs appeared in his 'Missiya polpreda Merekalova', *Voenno-istoricheskii zhurnal*, 12 (2002) and in V.I. Trubnikov, 'Sovetskaya diplomatiya nakanune Velikoi Otechestvennoi voiny: usiliya po protivodeistviyu fashistskoi agressii', *Voenno-istoricheskii zhurnal*, 7 (2001), p. 15. They are confirmed by L. Bezymenskii, 'Dvenadtsat' minut iz zhizni posla Merekalova', *Novoe Vremya*, 7 (1996), pp. 44–5; and L. Bezymenskii, 'Sovetsko-germanskie dogovory 1939g.', *Novaya i noveishaya istoriya*, 3 (1998). On Weizsäcker, see Pons, *The Inevitable War*, p. 164; G. Roberts, 'Infamous encounter? The Merekalov–Weizsäcker meeting of 17 April 1939', *The Historical Journal*, 35/4 (1992).

Petr Stegnii, 'Ivan Maisky's diary on the Molotov–Ribbentrop Pact', *International Affairs*, 6 (2009), is useful. On the drift towards Germany, see V.V. Sokolov, 'Narkomindel Vyacheslav Molotov', *Mezhdunarodnaya zhizn'*, 5 (1991), p. 102–3.

64. This is forcefully argued in I. Fleischhauer, *Der Pakt, Hitler, Stalin und die Initiative der Deutschen Diplomatie 1938–1939* (Berlin, 1990), pp. 154–6; Lloyd George papers, LG/G/30, 17 May 1939.

65. In response to the introduction of conscription in Great Britain, Hitler announced the abrogation of the naval agreement with Britain, concluded on 18 June 1935; claiming Danzig, he also tore up the Polish–German non-aggression pact of 1934.

66. Aware of the deadline he had been set by Stalin, Halifax's response had the effect on Maisky 'of a bucket of cold water'; *Who Helped Hitler?*, p. 123. He pressed Halifax to send a reply to the Soviet government 'in the course of next week'; TNA FO 371 23065 C6338/3356/18.

67. TNA FO 371 22969 C5460/15/18 & 23064 C5747/3356/18, and TNA CAB 27/624, FP(36)43, 19 April 1939.

68. Dalton papers, diary, I/20, 7 May 1939.

69. Carley, *1939*, p. 131; R. Manne, 'The British decision for alliance with Russia', p. 20.

70. *SPE*, docs. 253–6, exchange of telegrams between Litvinov and Surits.

71. *SPE*, doc. 259, Litvinov to Surits; *DVP*, 1939, XXII/1, doc. 259, Litvinov to Stalin.

72. Maisky is referring to the polls conducted by the British Institute of Public Opinion (Gallup).

73. *God Krizisa*, I, no. 316, 3 May 1939.

74. TNA FO 371 23065 C6743/3356/18, 2 May 1939.

75. *Hansard*, HC Deb 2 May 1939, vol. 346, cols 1697–8.

76. *DVP*, 1939, XXII/1, doc. 269.

77. TNA FO 371 23685 N2291/233/38, Phipps to FO, 5 May.

78. Liddell Hart, *The Liddell Hart Memoirs*, p. 241.

79. Litvinov's Jewish name.

80. TNA FO 371 23685 N2293/233/38, minutes, 8 May 1939.

81. TNA FO 371 23065 C6529/3356/18.

82. Dalton papers, II, 5/2, Boothby to Dalton on conversations with Maisky, 18 Sep. 1939; Payart quoted in Carley, *1939*, p. 134.

83. Webb, diary, 15 Oct. 1939, p. 6753.

84. Kollontay, *Diplomaticheskie dnevniki*, II, pp. 432–4.

85. Ivy Litvinov papers, draft memoirs.

86. Dalton papers, II, 3/2, Letter from Strabolgi, 20 Sep. 1939.

87. Quoted by M.J. Carley, 'End of the "low, dishonest decade": Failure of the Anglo-Franco-Soviet alliance in 1939', *Europe-Asia Studies*, 45/2 (1993), p. 315.

88. On the debate concerning the dismissal, see Resis, 'The fall of Litvinov' and Roberts, 'The fall of Litvinov'.

89. Uldricks, 'Impact of the Great Purges', pp. 193–8. See also Kocho-Williams, 'Soviet diplomatic corps'; Dullin, *Men of Influence*, pp. 240–1; Resis, *Molotov Remembers*, pp. 67–9.

90. H.D. Phillips, *Between the Revolution and the West* (Boulder, 1992), p. 166.

91. TNA FO 371 23685 N2547/233/38, 10 May 1939.

92. Resis, *Molotov Remembers,* p. 70; Roshchin, 'People's Commissariat for Foreign Affairs', pp. 111–12.

93. TNA FO 371 23066 C7614/3356/18, private letter by Seeds to L. Oliphant at the FO, 22 May 1939. Seeds quoted also from S. Aster, 'Sir William Seeds: The diplomat as scapegoat?', in B.P. Farrell (ed.), *Leadership and Responsibility in the Second World War* (Montreal, 2004), pp. 146–7; Churchill, *The Gathering Storm*, p. 330.

94. V.N. Khaustov, V.P. Naumov and N.S. Plotnikov (eds), *Lubyanka: Stalin i NKVD-NKGB-GUKR 'Smersh', 1939–1946* (Moscow, 2006), doc. 37. On the NKVD investigations, as well as the transformation of Narkomindel, see the most authoritative and innovative work by S. Dullin, 'Litvinov and the People's Commissariat of Foreign Affairs: the fate of an administration under Stalin, 1930–39', in S. Pons and A. Romano (eds), *Russia in the Age of Wars, 1914–1945* (Milan, 2000) and E. Gnedin, *Vykhod iz labirinta* (Moscow, 1994), pp. 25, 28 and 35.

95. Ivy Litvinov papers, draft memoirs.

96. N.V. Novikov, *Vospominaniya diplomata: Zapiski 1938–1947* (Moscow, 1989), pp. 24–5; Sokolov, 'Narkomindel Vyacheslav Molotov', p. 103; Resis, *Molotov Remembers*, p. 192; Uldricks, 'Impact of the Great Purges', p. 191.

97. Maisky was manifestly disappointed; see his report home in *DVP*, 1939, XXI/1, doc. 281. On the British government's decision to reiterate its position, see Parker, *Chamberlain and Appeasement*, pp. 225–7.

98. Lloyd George, who had lunch with Maisky at the embassy, found him to be 'very depressed, and feared that his country might return to a policy of isolation'; Sylvester papers, diary, A45, 8 May 1939. The successful conclusion of a pact with Britain had become vital for Maisky's own survival after Litvinov's dismissal. He believed that 'the real obstacle' to the acceptance of the Russians remained 'the Umbrella Man', as he expected Halifax to go 'much further than the P.M.'; Dalton papers, diary, I/20, 7 May 1939. Though outwardly Maisky gave the impression of being 'rather truculently pessimistic', he continued to exert pressure on the Foreign Office through sympathetic intermediaries, maintaining that the wide gaps could still be bridged if the British government was prepared 'to go a long way' and conclude a triple alliance; TNA FO 371 23066 C7108/3356/18, telephone conversation with Ewer of the *Daily Herald*, 10 May 1939. Ewer had been exposed in 1929 by MI5 as a Soviet agent working closely with the Soviet embassy. The fact that he retained a prominent position with both the Foreign Office and the Soviet embassy may suggest that he acted as a double agent; TNA KV 2/1016 & 1017.

99. *SPE*, doc. 277.

100. *DVP*, 1939, XXI/1, doc. 290; *God Krizisa*, I, no. 333; TNA FO 371 23066 C7327/3356/18, 10 May 1939; *SPE*, doc. 281.

101. TNA FO 371 23065 C6924 & C6925 & C6743/3356/18, 10 May 1939; *DDF*, 2 Serie, XVI, Doc. 137, Corbin to Bonnet, 11 May 1939.

102. *God Krizisa*, I, no. 347, 15 May 1939; RAN f.1702 op.4 d.1616 l.10, report on conversations with Beaverbrook, 11 May, 1939.

103. The Soviet Union demanded reciprocity, which implied a requirement that the Baltic States be included in the guarantees which would be sustained by an agreement on military assistance; TNA FO 371 23065 C6922/3356/18, 11 May 1939.

104. TNA FO 371 23066 C7268, 7400 & 7401/3356/18, and Halifax's conversation with Corbin in the same vein in TNA FO 371 23066 C7268/3356/18, 17 May 1939; Self, *Chamberlain Diary Letters*, IV, p. 416, 14 May 1939. See also the excellent reconstruction in Manne, 'The British decision for alliance with Russia', pp. 22–4.

105. A rather desperate Maisky deprecated any action which might result in a breakdown of the negotiations; TNA FO 371 23066 C7499/3356/18, 19 May 1939. Maisky assuredly gave Vansittart the impression, as the latter impressed on Cabinet, that he was prepared to drop the issue of guarantees for the Baltic States if military talks commenced promptly; TNA FO 371 23066 C7401/3356/18.

106. Not in the diary but published in *DVP*, 1939, XXII/1, doc. 315.

107. Vansittart reported to Halifax that Maisky's reaction 'had not been too unfriendly' and he had undertaken to submit the formula to Moscow 'forthwith'; TNA EP (36) 48 in FO 371 23066 C7499/3356/18. Maisky continued to exert pressure on Halifax even before he received the Soviet reply, anticipating (as he told the French ambassador in London) that the British proposals would be rejected. He further used informal channels to the Foreign Office to convey the same message, as well as his belief that, unless the British government was prepared to 'climb down' and conclude a triple alliance, there was 'no chance whatever of agreement'; *DDF*, 2 Serie, XVI, Doc. 216; TNA FO 371 23066 C7468/3356/18, phone conversation with Ewer of the *Daily Herald*.

108. Maisky, 'the smirking cat', observed Channon, was 'leaning over the railing of the ambassadorial gallery and sat so sinister and smug (are we to place our honour, our safety in those blood-stained hands?)'. In his speech to the House, Churchill, briefed in detail over the phone by Maisky about the state of the negotiations, reproached Chamberlain with being guided rather by emotion than by state interests, which called for an alliance with Russia; Rhodes, *Chips*, p. 199; Maisky, *Who Helped Hitler?*, pp. 125–6 and letter to *The Times*, 5 Sep. 1969. On the eve of the debate, Maisky dined with Amery and a dozen members of the 'Eden Group' of anti-appeasement backbenchers at the house of General Spears. 'The little man,' wrote Amery in his diary, 'was quite firm on the point that Russia was going to have a black and white alliance or nothing.' Although Amery commented that he now understood 'why our ancestors had considered bear-baiting such good sport,' he found convincing Maisky's argument that instead of facing up to Nazi Germany, the government was 'looking over their shoulder the whole time and hanging on to the carcass of the dead policy of appeasement'; Amery papers, diary, AMEL 7/39.

109. TNA EP (36) 48 in FO 371 23066, C7499/3356/18, 19 May 1939.

110. *God Krizisa*, I, no. 366; TNA FO 371 23066 C7522/3356/18; Harvey, *Diplomatic Diaries of Oliver Harvey*, pp. 37–40; Amery papers, diary, AMEL 7/39, 19 May 1939.

111. *The Times*, 22 May 1939; Bilainkin, 'Mr Maisky sees it through'.

112. TNA FO 371 23066 C7551/3356/18, 21 May 1939; see also a paper by the French chief of staff, in *DDF*, 2 Serie, XVI, Doc. 268, 24 May 1939.

113. TNA FO 371 23066 C7591/3356/18, 22 May 1939; Self, *Chamberlain Diary Letters*, IV, pp. 418–19.

114. See the *New York Times*, 21 May 1939, and *The Times*, 22 May 1939.

115. Self, *Chamberlain Diary Letters*, IV, pp. 418–19, 28 May 1939; S. Aster, *1939: Making of the Second World War* (London, 1973), p. 350. 'Our new obligation,' railed Channon, 'means nothing. A military alliance might have been the signal for an immediate war – "blown the gaff" – but a Geneva alliance is so flimsy, so unrealistic and so impractical that it will only make the Nazis poke fun at us'; Rhodes, *Chips*, p. 201. Even the legal experts who drafted the League's formulae for Chamberlain dismissed it as 'obvious eyewash'; TNA FO 371 23066 C7469 & C7661/3356/18, 25 May 1939. See also Shaw, *The British Political Elite*, pp. 64–6; on Chamberlain's dismissive attitude to the League, see P. Beck 'Searching for peace in Munich, not Geneva: the British government, the League of Nations and the Sudetenland question', in I. Lukes and E. Goldstein (eds), *The Munich Crisis, 1938: Prelude to World War II* (London, 1999).

116. McDonald, *A Man of the Times*, p. 61.

117. *SPE*, doc. 309, Molotov to Maisky, 26 May; TNA FO 371 23066 C7682/3356/18, Seeds to Halifax, 27 May 1939.

118. Neilson, *Britain Soviet Russia and the Collapse of the Versailles Order*, pp. 295–7.

119. In Moscow, Seeds and Payart, too, were taken aback by Molotov's fierce reaction. Seeds tried in vain to convince Molotov that the decision of the British government 'marked a radical turning point in English foreign policy'; *God Krizisa*, I, no. 339.

120. Carley, 'End of the "low, dishonest decade"', p. 322.

121. TNA FO 371 23067 C7937/3356/18, 29 May 1939.

122. *SPE*, doc. 314.

123. TNA FO 371 23067 C8097/3356/18; *DDF*, 2 Serie, XVI, Doc. 422, Naggiar to Bonnet, 14 June 1939.

124. RAN f.1702 op.4 d.111 l.20, 31 May; Lloyd George papers, LG/G/130, Gwilym Lloyd George to his father, 1 June 1939; Webb, diary, 12 June, p. 6665. He gave that same impression to the correspondent of the *New York Times*, 31 May, and as late as 24 June 1939.

125. *SPE*, doc. 332.

126. The text of the statement is in English.

127. Halifax said that if Germany was prepared to discuss 'a real settlement', the British government 'would advocate it' so long as it was achieved through negotiations and without recourse to force; *Hansard*, HL Deb 8 June 1939, vol. 113, col. 361.

128. Maisky was not impressed by Halifax's attempt to puff up Strang, letting him know through Ewer of the *Daily Herald* that Strang was not 'big enough'. He believed that the stiff demands of Molotov were 'an "acid test" of the bona fides' of the British government, which could be restored if Halifax were to proceed to Moscow; TNA FO 371 23068 C8701/3356/18; *DVP*, 1939, XXII/1, docs. 359, 361 & 367, exchanges between Maisky and Molotov, 8, 10 & 12 June 1939.

129. Dalton papers, II, 3/2, letter from Strabolgi, 20 Sep. 1939.

130. RAN f.1702 op.4 d.1401 l.2 & d.973 l.2., 13 &14 July 1939.

131. Maisky, *Who Helped Hitler?*, pp. 140–2; TNA FO 371 23068 C8357/3356/18; Self, *Chamberlain Diary Letters*, IV, pp. 420–1, 10 June 1939. See Maisky's new narrative, in the making, in Stamford papers, diary, 30 April 1940.

132. Molotov disapproved of the 'disadvantageous' agreement: 'It is clear that we shall not go for such a treaty.' *God Krizisa*, II, no. 408. Maisky, though, continued to believe that 'there will be a pact with Moscow which will paralyse Hitler's will to war'; Webb, diary, 18 June 1939, p. 6669.

133. Maisky himself was unsettled by the rigid Soviet stance and embarrassed by Halifax, who reminded him that in Geneva Maisky had assured him that, if his government accepted the principle of a treaty of mutual assistance, 'the rest would be easy'. This, Halifax concluded, 'had certainly not been the case'; see Halifax's report in TNA FO 371 23069 C8979/3356/18. In his memoirs *Who Helped Hitler?*, pp. 149–50 Maisky again constructs an apologetic and anachronistic narrative which misleads his readers to assume that he is actually quoting from his diary.

134. Quoted in Fleischhauer, *Pakt*, 407–8. A succinct but insightful historiographical survey of the issue is in M.J. Carley, 'Soviet foreign policy in the West, 1936–1941: A review article', *Europe-Asia Studies*, 56/7 (2004). See also Carley, 'End of the "low, dishonest decade"'; G. Roberts, 'On Soviet–German relations: The debate continues', *Europe-Asia Studies*, 50/8 (1998); J. Haslam, 'Stalin and the German invasion of Russia 1941: A failure of reasons of state?', *International Affairs*, 76/1 (2000).

135. RGASPI, Molotov papers, f.82 op.2 d.1140 ll.166–8 & 173–84.

136. See Haslam, 'The Soviet Union and the Czechoslovakian crisis of 1938', p. 444.

137. G. Roberts, in 'The Soviet decision for a pact with Nazi Germany', *Soviet Studies*, 44/1 (1992), covers the negotiations well, though mainly from the perspective of the diplomatic exchanges. He attributes the progress that was made entirely to Germany, and dates Stalin's decision to opt for Germany, a reactive policy, to the end of July 1939. It is obvious from the material pieced together here (and Bezymenskii's unique access to the presidential archives) that the courting was mutual and continuous and originated with the dramatic meeting in the Kremlin on 22 April.

138. TsAMO op.9157 d.2 ll.2, 11, 418–31, 447, 453 & 454.

139. Steiner, *The Triumph of the Dark*, p. 892.

140. Dalton was briefed by Maisky, but his intervention with Chamberlain led nowhere. Although the prime minister was aware of the political damage that would ensue from a collapse of the negotiations, he still said 'in his flat, obstinate way, "Well, I don't think that would be the end of the world"'. Chamberlain was sure he had 'succeeded at last in convincing [the delegation] that we had done all we could to get an agreement'; Pimlott, *Political Diary of Hugh Dalton*, pp. 272–8; Self, *Chamberlain Diary Letters*, IV, p. 168, 2 July 1939.

141. *SPE*, doc. 355.

142. Though in a state of despair, Maisky continued to believe in a pact with England. When asked 'point blank' by Johnson whether he expected a pact to be concluded, he 'looked serious and said, "I think not before the war but I think you will after the war"'; TNA FO 800/322, p. 330, Johnson to Halifax, 25 Oct. 1939. Johnson was little deterred by

the Ribbentrop–Molotov Pact, conveying to Maisky 'the deep interest and sympathy and encouragement' with which he was following Soviet policy; RAN f.1702 op.4 d.1337 l.10. See Maisky's sympathetic portrait of Johnson in *VSD*, pp. 206–11.

143. *God Krizisa*, II, no. 340, Molotov to Maisky, 23 June 1939.

144. Carley, *1939*, p. 166; Dilks, *Diaries of Sir Alexander Cadogan*, p. 190; *God Krizisa*, II, nos. 340 & 361, Molotov to Maisky, 3 July 1939; *SPE*, doc. 377.

145. Chamberlain was convinced that the 'drive' to include Churchill in the government was a conspiracy 'in which Mr Maisky has been involved'. He was furious about an article published by the *Daily Mail* on 5 July, following a long talk between its correspondent and Randolph Churchill, who had just met Maisky. The article announced that 'Churchill's early return to the Cabinet … is certain.' In his communications with Moscow, Maisky continued to hope for change. A year later, Maisky explained in the course of a private conversation that the negotiations would have been successful if Churchill had been prime minister; Self, *Chamberlain Diary Letters*, IV, p. 426, 8 July 1939; Gilbert, *The Coming of War*, pp. 1556–7; *DVP*, 1939, XXII/1, fn. 147; Stamford papers, diary, 18 July 1941.

146. The film, directed by Herbert Rappaport, was one of the earliest indictments of the German persecution of Jews. Shot in 1938, the film is now considered to be the first presentation of the holocaust on the screen.

147. See Maisky's alarmist message to Molotov, *God Krizisa*, II, no. 475, 14 July 1939, confirmed by similar impressions from Surits in Paris; *SPE*, doc. 371.

148. Neilson, *Britain, Soviet Russia and the Collapse of the Versailles Order*, p. 309.

149. Nicolson, *Diaries*, 20 July 1939, p. 406. On the perseverance of the 'spirit of Munich', see Kollontay, *Diplomaticheskie dnevniki*, II, pp. 440–1, 20 July 1939.

150. Inskip papers, INKP2, diary, 27 Aug. 1939.

151. Stafford, 'Political autobiography', pp. 903–5; TNA FO 371 23072 C11018/3356/18, Butler's conversations with Maisky, 4 Aug. 1939.

152. Self, *Chamberlain Diary Letters*, IV, pp. 430–1, 23 July 1939. This summary relies also on an excellent and even-handed analysis by S. Newton, *Profits of Peace: The political economy of Anglo-German appeasement* (Oxford, 1996), ch. 5; see also Parker, *Chamberlain and Appeasement*, pp. 269–71; Carley, *1939*, pp. 179f.

153. *God Krizisa*, II, no. 493, 24 July 1939. On the suspicion fuelled by the feelers, see Stamford papers, diary, 30 April 1940.

154. It is doubtful whether the Soviet Union's decision to embark on military talks was a result of Halifax's determination to call its 'bluff'; Neilson, *Britain, Soviet Russia and the Collapse of the Versailles Order*, p. 309. As early as 10 July, General Shaposhnikov, the Soviet chief of staff, submitted to Stalin at his request an outline for a military alliance with England and France. He considered several variants of a possible German offensive and offered a detailed response to them. The document, corrected and approved by Stalin on 19 July, served as the Soviet agenda for the military negotiations; RGASPI, Stalin papers, f.558 op.11 d.220 ll 3–9.

155. Once again, in his memoirs Maisky gives a distorted account of the meeting, claiming (in clairvoyant fashion) that he left Halifax 'with a feeling of great alarm'. Both the full diary

entry and the succinct telegram he sent to Moscow show a guarded optimism. According to Halifax, Maisky thought the arrangement 'was a good one, and that the deterrent value … would be very great and impress the outside world more than any other step could have done'. Moscow, he said, considered that 'real progress had been made … and hoped that we were now approaching the end of our negotiations'. It is true, though, that Halifax did not convey to Maisky any sense of urgency, as he 'did not anticipate any immediate trouble'. *Who Helped Hitler?*, pp. 162–4 and *God Krizisa*, II, no. 500; TNA FO 371 23071 C10456/3356/18.

156. When Drax asked Halifax whether he should attend the luncheon, Halifax replied: 'if you can bear it …' Quoted in Carley, *1939*, p. 186.

157. See Dalton papers, II, 5/2, letter from Boothby, 15 Sep. 1939, and R. Boothby, *Recollections of a Rebel* (London, 1978), pp. 188–93. Stalin's resort to the narrative is in Beaverbrook papers, Balfour diary, 1 Oct. 1941.

158. Webb, diary, 7 Aug. 1939, pp. 6698–700 (emphasis in original).

159. Conversations with Lord Stamford, as described in his diary, 30 April 1940.

160. Bezymenskii, 'Sovetsko-germanskie dogovory 1939 g.'; L. Bezymenskii, 'Al'ternativy 1939 goda: vokrug Sovetsko-germankogo pakta 1939', in *Arkhivy raskryvayut tainy* (Moscow, 1991); Bezymenskii, *Gitler i Stalin pered skhvatkoi*, p. 2009. I further profited from scores of conversations with the late Lev Bezymenskii, whose intimate familiarity with the archival sources and the personae involved was unparalleled. See also V.V. Sokolov, 'Tragicheskaya sud'ba diplomata G.A. Astakhova', *Novaya i noveishaya istoriya*, 1 (1997). A great number of telegrams exchanged between the Soviet embassy in Berlin and Narkomindel have been published in *God Krizisa*. A rare but important source is V.V. Sokolov (ed.), '"Avtobiograficheskie zametki" V. N. Pavlova – perevodchika I. V. Stalina', *Novaya i noveishaya istoriya*, 4 (2000). Also useful was Roberts, 'The Soviet decision for a pact'. Roberts argues, though, that the policy was 'made on the hoof'. It certainly was reactive, as was the policy of all other powers involved. However, as has been shown, it is clear that the German option had been considered a viable alternative since April 1939. For more on the debate, see Roberts, 'On Soviet–German relations', and J. Haslam, 'Soviet–German relations and the origins of the Second World War: The jury is still out', *Journal of Modern History*, 69/4 (1997).

161. The instructions are in TNA FO 371/23072 C10801/3356/18.

162. *SPE*, doc. 398, 4 Aug. 1939 ; F. Delpha, *Les papiers secrets du Général Doumenc, un autre regard sur 1939–1940* (Paris, 1992), pp. 46–56. A lively and insightful description of the mission is in Carley, *1939*, pp. 183–9.

163. The British account is in E.L Woodward and R. Butler (eds), *Documents on British Foreign Policy* (London, 1947–48), Third Series, VII, Appendix II.

164. *SPE*, doc. 427, 16 Aug. 1939.

165. *SPE*, docs. 430 & 431, 17 Aug. 1939 & doc. 435, 20 Aug. 1939.

166. RGASPI, Stalin papers, f.558 op.11 d.220 ll.125–36.

167. Kollontay, *Diplomaticheskie dnevniki*, II, pp. 446–7; Ivy Litvinov papers, draft memoirs.

168. TNA FO 371 23682 N5426/92/38, 13 Oct. 1939.

169. Dalton, *Fateful Years*, pp. 256–7.

170. Dawson papers, diary, Box 43, 22 Aug. 1939; McDonald, *A Man of the Times*, pp. 64–7. The most vivid description of these moves is in the Inskip papers, INSK2, diary, 23–30 Aug. 1939: 'The P.M. is writing a separate letter to Hitler, – the Cabinet were not told this. A long telegram to Kennard at Warsaw … telling him to get the Poles to talk to Germany.' Halifax, who had received information from Dusseldorf 'that the crowd is pulling down Nazi posters' still hoped for an uprising in Germany.

171. *God Krizisa*, II, no. 592; Lloyd George papers, LG/G/130 and Amery papers, diary, AMEL 7/39.

172. Both the dictated notes and the speech are in the Sylvester papers, diary, A45, 24 Aug. 1939.

173. Beneš's misconstrued account in his memoirs of his conversation with Maisky is a reinterpretation of the Munich Agreement in the face of the brewing Cold War and the Soviet occupation of Czechoslovakia, and has misled historians. See I. Lukes, *The Munich Crisis, 1938: Prelude to World War II* (London, 1999), p. 40; J. Barros and R. Gregor, *Double Deception: Stalin, Hitler, and the invasion of Russia* (Chicago, 1995), ch. 1. Beneš's anachronistic impressions were that 'the Soviets want war, they prepared for it conscientiously' and were convinced that 'the time has come for a final struggle between capitalism, fascism and Nazism and that there will be a world revolution which they will trigger' when the rest of the world is exhausted by the war. See E. Beneš, *Memoirs of Dr Eduard Beneš* (London, 1954), pp. 138–9.

174. Even the Webbs were 'dazed … knocked almost senseless!'; it was a 'terrible collapse of good faith and integrity'. However, they conceded that perhaps British 'manners' had been better but the 'morals have been strikingly similar'. Beatrice felt sorry for 'the poor Maiskys and all the Soviet diplomatists … they will be ostracised'; Webb, diary, 25 Sep. 1939, pp. 6711–14.

175. The ship was named after Lenin's sister, Mariya Ilinichna Ulyanova.

176. His actual words were: 'it only remains for us to set our teeth and to enter upon this struggle, which we ourselves earnestly endeavoured to avoid, with determination to see it through to the end'; *Hansard*, HC Deb 1 September 1939, vol. 351, col. 132.

177. In his diary, Sylvester describes how Chamberlain was 'dumbfounded' when Greenwood took the floor to shouts from all sides: 'Speak for England.' Sylvester papers, diary, A45, 2 Sep. 1939.

178. Rhodes, *Chips*, p. 215: 'A little later Maisky dared to appear, and he beamed his Cheshire-cat smile. No wonder. It is the moment he has long intrigued and hoped for.'

179. Webb, diary, 3, 15 & 18 Sep. 1939, pp. 6720 & 6729–31.

180. See correspondence with both in RAN f.1702 op.4 d.1357 l.7 & d.1677 l.4, 7 Sept. 1939.

181. Dalton papers, II, 5/2, letter from Dalton, 15 Sep.; Webb, diary, 2 Oct. 1939, p. 6743.

182. A Soviet ship, carrying a folk dancing group to the United States, which was then stranded in London.

183. In his speech to an extraordinary meeting of the Supreme Soviet, Molotov explained the circumstances which led to the pact with Germany and warned against the 'warmongers

who are accustomed to have other people pull their chestnuts out of the fire'; D.N. Pritt (ed.), *Soviet Peace Policy: Four speeches by V. Molotov* (London, 1941).

184. Webb, diary, 25 July 1940, pp. 6933–5.

185. Webb, diary, 24 Sep. 1939, p. 6739; Dilks, *Diaries of Sir Alexander Cadogan*, p. 219; Pimlott, *Political Diary of Hugh Dalton*, p. 305, 25 Sep.; TNA FO 371 23682 N5426/92/38, 19 Oct. 1939; *DVP*, 1939, XXII/2, doc. 627.

186. Dimitrov's diary, Bulgarian Central National Archives (TsDA MVR).

187. P. Anderson and A.O. Chubaryan (eds), *Komintern i vtoraya mirovaya voina* (Moscow, 1994), I, pp. 122–4.

188. A Hebrew inscription in Aramaic from the Book of Daniel describing Belshazzar's feast. When Belshazzar orders drinks to be served in cups seized from the destroyed Jerusalem temple, a hand appears and writes on the wall: 'God has numbered the days of your kingdom and brought it to an end.'

189. Ribbentrop reached Moscow on 27 September. It was then that the final secret protocols concerning the division of spheres of influence were concluded in seven separate documents, discovered in the archives of Schulenburg by I. Fleischhauer only in 1990.

190. Argued in detail in G. Gorodetsky, *Grand Delusion: Stalin and the German invasion of Russia* (New Haven, 1999).

191. TNA FO 371 23701 N5717/5717/18, 25 Oct. 1939.

192. Sylvester papers, diary, A47, and memorandum on meeting Maisky, 3 Oct. 1939; Lloyd George papers, LG/G/130, 3 Oct. 1939.

193. *DVP*, 1939, XXII/2, doc. 655.

194. Maisky, *Memoirs of a Soviet Ambassador*, p. 35. See his cautious telegram to Molotov, *DVP*, 1939, XXII/2, doc. 679, 12 Oct. 1939.

195. A meeting which was clearly initiated and motivated by Maisky (*Memoirs of a Soviet Ambassador*, p. 32), probably as a result of Churchill's famous radio broadcast on 1 October, in which he described Russia as 'a riddle wrapped in a mystery inside an enigma', but then provided the key of 'Russian national interests' which could not allow Russia to see Germany 'plant herself upon the shores of the Black Sea … That would be contrary to the historic life-interests of Russia.' See M. Kitchen, 'Winston Churchill and the Soviet Union during the Second World War', *The Historical Journal*, 30/2 (1987), p. 415. Censored versions of Maisky's initiatives were only reported to Molotov in part; *DVP*, 1939, XXII/2, doc. 667. The new spate of activities, which again would warrant Maisky's continued stay in England, is attested by a stream of invitations to former allies to visit the embassy, as well as the recruitment of ministers to exert pressure on Halifax. See, for example, RAN f.1702 op.4 d.848 l.2 & d.940 l.10, 7 Oct. 1939, letters to Eden and Butler. By mid-October, Maisky was 'in excellent form; excited over the growing prestige of the USSR as the most powerful and successful world state, in the strange world diplomacy of today' and excited by the 'great change of attitude' towards him, 'far more friendliness on the part of ministers, i.e. Churchill, Eden and Elliott'; Webb, diary, 15 Oct. 1939, p. 6751.

196. When Charles Eade, editor of the *Sunday Dispatch*, met Churchill after Maisky had left, he found him 'wearing a very easy-fitting dinner jacket and walking about in his socks,

having kicked off his shoes. He smoked a big cigar and had a whisky and soda on his desk. He seemed to me to be a little drunk'; Eade papers, Eade 2/1 & 2/2.

197. Chamberlain's precise words were: 'The proposals in the German Chancellor's speech are vague and uncertain and contain no suggestion for righting the wrongs done to Czecho-Slovakia and to Poland… Even if Herr Hitler's proposals were more closely defined and contained suggestions to right these wrongs, it would still be necessary to ask by what practical means the German Government intend to convince the world that aggression will cease and that pledges will be kept. Past experience has shown that no reliance can be placed upon the promises of the present German Government. Accordingly, acts – not words alone –must be forthcoming before we, the British people, and France, our gallant and trusted Ally, would be justified in ceasing to wage war to the utmost of our strength. Only when world confidence is restored will it be possible to find – as we would wish to do with the aid of all who show good will – solutions of those questions which disturb the world'; *Hansard*, HC Deb 12 October 1939, vol. 352, col. 567.

198. Maisky repeated his now familiar apologetic narrative of the events leading up to the pact, suggesting that 'In a world such as this where wild beasts were loose every country had to take certain precautions for its own safety'; TNA FO 371 23682 N5426/92/38.

199. Maisky, who, according to Eden, 'talked almost the whole time', did advise him that the Kremlin would prefer to see someone who enjoyed the British government's confidence, and that it would 'probably always be doubtful of this if they were dealing with a Left Wing politician while the Government of this country was Right Wing'. Seeds' health had been failing for a while, and he was being held – most conveniently – as a scapegoat for the failure of the negotiations with the Russians. Following a Cabinet meeting on 30 September in which his judgements were questioned, Halifax met Dawson tête-à-tête for dinner on 5 October and 'discussed with him possible Labour names to succeed Seeds'; TNA FO 371 23682 N5426/92/38; *DVP*, 1939, XXII/2, doc. 682. The dissonance between the versions has been spotted by Carley, who is correct in attributing it to Maisky's need to save his policy 'and perhaps also his head – since he had to keep the British interested in negotiations'; M.J. Carley, '"A situation of delicacy and danger": Anglo-Soviet relations, August 1939–March 1940', *Contemporary European History*, 8/2 (1999), pp. 184 and 191. See also Dawson papers, diary, Box 43; and Aster, 'Sir William Seeds', pp. 142–5.

200. According to Halifax, it was actually Maisky who initiated the idea of a trade delegation to Moscow; however, in his report home, Maisky (as was his wont) attributed it to Halifax. In fact, Maisky, who had become aware of Cripps's access to Halifax, had raised the idea of such a delegation with him; G. Gorodetsky, *Stafford Cripps' Mission to Moscow, 1940–42* (Oxford, 1984), pp. 12–13.

201. Molotov quizzed Maisky about whether he thought Butler had been hinting at a possible Soviet mediation 'with a view to concluding peace with Germany on particular terms'. Maisky had not gained any such impression, but thought Butler did subscribe to the idea; *DVP*, 1939, XXII/2, docs. 695, 700 & 704. Ironically, Butler, who had been criticized by the Russians for his enthusiastic support of appeasement, would now become the target of Maisky's courtship in the Soviet attempts to create a 'peace offensive'. See, for instance, RAN f.1702 op.4 d.848 l.3, 20 Nov. 1939, letter to Butler.

202. Carley, *1939*, pp. 230–2; see also TNA FO 800/322 pp. 328–9, 20 Oct. 1939, 'The Red Dean' of Canterbury to Halifax.

203. TNA FO 371 23701 N5717/5717/18, 25 Oct. 1939.

204. First American ship to be seized by the German navy on the grounds of contraband. Refused entry into a Norwegian port, it finally berthed in Murmansk.

205. Referring to Halifax's pious image, Bernard Shaw condoned the Russians' peace offensive. He wrote to Maisky: 'The British Empire is the Vicar of God Almighty for the punishment without trial of all foreign sinners.' Together with Beatrice Webb, he buoyed up Maisky, even when his close friends abandoned him following the Soviet invasion of Finland; RAN f.1702 op.4 d.1687 l.71 & d.1184 l.17, 9 Nov. & 7 Dec. 1939; Passfield papers, II/4/l, 49a, Agnes Maisky to Beatrice Webb, 8 Dec. 1939.

206. Lenin's famous slogan *kto kogo?*, a rhetorical question as to who would prevail over whom. This lent itself to the suppression of dissenters and the extermination of opponents.

207. Maisky's detailed report home avoided the important prediction that Churchill would become the next prime minister, as well as his own advocacy of improved relations, which clearly exceeded the mandate he had from Molotov; *DVP*, 1939, XXII/2, docs. 775 & 776.

208. *DVP*, 1939, XXII/2, doc. 806, 23 Nov. 1939.

209. Halifax emerged from the meeting convinced, like Cadogan, that it was 'quite useless talking to Maisky'. The Russians, he complained, were simply 'impossible people' to deal with. In his report home, Maisky, who had gone far beyond what Molotov wished in advancing the trade negotiations, portrayed himself as having been in full command of the conversation, though to Halifax he had seemed evasive and ill at ease. Aware of the likelihood of hostilities in the north, he preferred to water down Halifax's warning; TNA FO 371 N6717/99138 & TNA FO 800/328, Halifax to General Gort, 28 Nov. 1939; *DVP*, 1939, XXII/2, doc. 811.

210. Vansittart had advised ministers to give Maisky 'a rather wide berth … for he derives some illusions from his imaginary successes'. Butler, who regarded Maisky as an 'agreeable scoundrel', politely turned down Maisky's invitations to the embassy and preferred to lunch with him in the privacy of the home of Henry Channon, his parliamentary secretary, so as not 'to be seen with him in public'. The host, on his return, did not forget to 'check up on the snuff-boxes … but did not notice anything missing'. When he finally met Maisky in person, Channon, a notorious right-winger found him 'far better than I had expected … clever, shrewd and humorous … The new order is not so terrible as I feared; one could certainly get on with Bevin and perhaps even with Maisky, too'; TNA FO 371 23701 N5717/5717/18; RAN f.1702 op.4 d.848 l.3; Rhodes, *Chips*, pp. 21 and 261.

211. The best account of the negotiations, seen from the Finnish side, is P. Salmon, 'Great Britain, the Soviet Union and Finland at the beginning of the Second World War', in J. Hiden and T. Lane (eds), *The Baltic and the Outbreak of the Second World War* (Cambridge, 1992); see also H. Shukman and A.O. Chubarian, *Stalin and the Soviet-Finnish War, 1939–1940* (London, 2002).

212. The *News Chronicle* stated that European and American public opinion sympathized with Finland. It was ironical that the Finns appealed to the League of Nations, the president

of which was Maisky, who on behalf of his country had signed the Soviet–Finnish non-aggression pact in 1932.

213. Webb, diary, 1 & 19 Dec. 1939, pp. 6781 & 6790–2; RAN f.1702 op.4 d.143 l.70, Maisky to Litvinov, 14 Dec. 1939. See a letter by Agniya Maisky to Pritt, reproduced in his *The Autobiography of D.N. Pritt* (London, 1965), pp. 213–14.

214. See diary entry for 5 January 1940.

215. *DVP*, 1939, XXII/2, doc. 890; Webb, diary, 24 December, pp. 6794–6. See also Carley, *1939*, pp. 239–40. On British policy towards Russia, see Gorodetsky, *Stafford Cripps' Mission to Moscow*, pp. 15–24.

216. A reference to Lensky's famous verses in Pushkin's *Evgenii Onegin*.

1940

1. RAN f.1702 op.4 d.1495 l.4 d.1657 l.10 & d.1363 l.3, 5 and 8 Jan. 1940.

2. Bilainkin, *Diary of a Diplomatic Correspondent*, 7 Feb. 1940, pp. 9, 21.

3. RAN f.1702 op.4 d.940 l.13 & d.1357 l.10, 3 and 6 May 1940.

4. See for instance a sample of letters from Nicolson, Gwilym Lloyd George and Vernon Bartlett in RAN f.1702 op.4 d.1495 l.5 d.993 l.1 & d.1225 l.5, 12 and 29 March 1940; Pimlott, *Political Diary of Hugh Dalton*, 15 March 1940, pp. 321–2.

5. Webb, diary, 12 April 1940, p. 6863.

6. Quoted in Aster, 'Sir William Seeds', p. 145.

7. Bilainkin, *Diary of a Diplomatic Correspondent*, 16 Jan. and 1 March 1940, pp. 18 and 33, and 'Mr Maisky sees it through', p. 264.

8. Webb, diary, 29 Jan. 1940, p. 6814.

9. *DVP*, 1940, XXIII/1, pp. 53–6; TNA FO 418/86 C3564/23/18; see also Bilainkin, *Diary of a Diplomatic Correspondent*, 16 Jan. 1940, p. 18.

10. The draft White Book, which would have become a Blue Book once published, is in TNA Cab/67/4/7. The text has been published since, with a contextual introduction, by S. Aster and T. Coates, *Dealing with Josef Stalin: The Moscow White Book, 1939* (London, 2009). On the complex nature of the selection and its eventual incorporation in Woodward and Butler, *Documents on British Foreign Policy*, see the fascinating article by U. Bialer, 'Telling the truth to the people: Britain's decision to publish the diplomatic papers of the inter-war period', *The Historical Journal*, 26/2 (1983). On the microfilm episode, see Maisky's letter to the president of the Supreme Military Court, 7 May 1956, and to Khrushchev, 14 July 1960, RAN, f.1702 op.2 d.76 ll.24–8 & op.4 d.275 ll.43–4, respectively.

11. Surits had been the Soviet ambassador in Turkey before taking up the Paris position.

12. The Labour delegation to Finland was headed by Citrine. They visited the front and met Marshal Mannerheim. After their return, Halifax was struck by their belligerent mood 'full of the admirable morale of the Finns … complete contempt for the Russians' and convinced that the Finns 'would hold their own'. Attlee and Greenwood, on the other hand, strongly argued with him against a declaration of war; Halifax papers, diary, A7.8.3, 9 Feb. 1940, and TNA FO 800/281, pp. 369–72, Halifax to Chamberlain, 10 Feb. 1940.

13. In a broadcast speech on 20 January, Churchill suggested that the expansion of hostilities was likely to draw more states into the war. *The Times*, 21 Jan. 1940.

14. *DVP*, 1940, XXIII/1, doc. 27; Stamford papers, diary, 28 Jan. 1940.

15. J. Colville, Churchill's private secretary, furiously jotted down in his diary: 'Maisky has had the impertinence to suggest that we should apply to Finland the same doctrine … to which we adhered in Spain'; J. Colville, *The Fringes of Power: 10 Downing Street diaries 1939–1955* (London, 1985), p. 79.

16. Webb, diary, 29 Jan. 1940, p. 6815.

17. TNA FO 371 24843 N1390/30/38, 30 Jan. 1940.

18. Maisky, *Memoirs of a Soviet Ambassador*, pp. 141–2; Alexander papers, AVAR 5/8, 28 June 1940.

19. Bilainkin, *Diary of a Diplomatic Correspondent*, p. 225, 8 Oct. 1940.

20. TNA FO 371 24843 N1390/30/38. For other discrepancies, see Carley, *1939*, p. 245.

21. A raid on the London offices of the Soviet trade delegation in May 1927 – the pretext for the severance of relations between the two countries; see Gorodetsky, *Precarious Truce*, pp. 221–31.

22. Maisky routinely uses 'Old Wizard' to refer to Lloyd George, rather than the more usual 'Welsh Wizard'.

23. On the turbulent Anglo-Soviet relations during the war and peace negotiations, see Shukman and Chubarian, *Stalin and the Soviet-Finnish War*, and Kollontay, *Diplomaticheskie dnevniki*, II, pp. 482–522. This entry was sparked by Molotov's telegram to Maisky upbraiding the British government for spreading the 'ridiculous and slanderous' rumours about a military alliance between Germany and Russia; *DVP*, 1940, XXIII/1, doc. 49. As was his habit, Maisky had prompted Butler to raise the possibility of British mediation in the negotiations with the Finns. Molotov gave it his full blessing and produced the peace terms, which were however turned down by the Cabinet. It was, as Channon wrote in his diary after meeting Butler, 'A diabolically clever scheme, but Maisky's dove is clearly a vulture.' With a chip on his shoulder since the Munich Agreement, Butler was playing a double game. When a peace agreement was signed with Finland three weeks later, he let it be understood that his 'foresight prevented another Munich, which is what we should have been accused of, had we entertained Maisky's proposals'; *DVP*, 1940, XXIII/1, doc. 50, record of meeting with Butler, 22 Feb.; Butler papers, RAB G11/21, FO's instructions to Butler, 24 Feb.; Rhodes, *Chips*, 22 Feb. and 13 March 1940, pp. 234, 236; *VSD*, pp. 470–2.

24. A feeling shared by Halifax: 'I can't myself resist some feeling of thankfulness at not having got an Expedition bogged where it could not be maintained, and I don't believe anything in the long run would have made much difference. But I certainly shall not say this in public'; Halifax papers, diary, A7.8.3, 13 March 1940. He was surely influenced by Eden's rather cynical (but pragmatic) long letter to him earlier in the month, in which he raised doubt whether it was 'a world-rocking tragedy' for the Allies if 'the Finns go under?'; TNA FO 800/281, 2 March 1940, pp. 394–400.

25. Possibly Korzh, Maisky's counsellor.

26. Maisky had already told Bernard Pares, the outstanding historian of Russia, that his country was 'above all things, against an extension of the war … Russia would prefer a negotiated peace to a vindictive one, which would follow the triumph of either side and would bring more wars'; Pares, *A Wandering Student*, p. 361.

27. TNA FO 418/86 N3485/40/38 and Maisky's version of the conversation is in *DVP*, 1940, XXIII/1, doc. 82, and on Welles in doc. 83. In *Memoirs of a Soviet Ambassador*, p. 55, Maisky completely misleads his readers into assuming that it was Butler who pressed for the peace, while he 'never believed that the German-Soviet pact could be long-lived'.

28. Webb, diary, 18 March and 12 April 1940, pp. 6845, 6863–4.

29. The humiliating peace offer was made by Hitler during his brief meeting with Mussolini in his train carriage at the Brenner Pass on 18 March. Ostensibly the objective of the talk was to cement the Pact of Steel, as Hitler was preparing the ground for his spring offensive and was seeking Italy's entry into the war.

30. *DVP*, 1940, XXIII/1, p. 166.

31. Records of the meeting in TNA FO 371 24839 N3706/5/38, *DVP*, 1940, XXIII/1, doc. 100 and Maisky's draft in RAN f.1702 op.3. d.112 ll.7–11. On Halifax's views, see TNA FO 371 24846 N3698/40/38, 25 March, and 24888 R4467/5/67, record of the meeting of British heads of missions from South-East Europe, 8 April 1940. The most enlightening survey of the episode is in T. Imlay, 'A reassessment of Anglo-French strategy during the phony war, 1939–40', *English Historical Review*, cxix, April (2004), pp. 364–72.

32. Molotov's speech at the Supreme Soviet dealt with Soviet–Finnish relations and the reaction, particularly in France and Great Britain, to the war. It stated the USSR's firm determination to pursue a policy of neutrality and to ensure the restoration and maintenance of world peace, while the country herself prepared economically and militarily for any eventuality. The speech may have been prompted by Maisky, following the advice he had received from Trevelyan that it was 'a matter of quite first-class importance that, as soon as the settlement with Finland has been reached, a full statement should be made to the world by the Soviet government … The more frank and far-reaching that statement the greater would be its value for preventing any later extension of the war into an attack on Russia'; RAN f.1702 op.4 d.1616 l.21, 13 March 1940.

33. It has been rumoured, but never proven, that she bore Marx an illegitimate son, whom Engels chivalrously declared to be his own; S. Padover (ed.), *On Education, Women, and Children* (New York, 1975), p. xxv.

34. Maisky was actively engaged in restoring Churchill's standing in Moscow after his Finnish 'relapse'; *DVP*, 1940, XXIII/1, doc. 110, telegram to Molotov, 5 April 1940.

35. RAN f.1702 op.3 d.278 ll.1–9.

36. Even the sympathetic Dawson described it as 'a lame performance'; Dawson papers, diary, Box 44, 7 May 1940.

37. His precise wording was: 'I say solemnly that the Prime Minister should give an example of sacrifice because there is nothing which can contribute more to victory in this war than that he should sacrifice the seals of office'; *Hansard*, HC Deb 8 May 1940, vol. 360, col. 1283.

38. Kennedy, who sat next to Maisky in the gallery, noted in his diary: 'The Prime Minister looked stunned and while he appeared to carry it off, he looked to me like a definitely beaten man'; Smith, *Hostage to Fortune*, p. 422.

39. According to Halifax, the king told him that he 'had hoped if Neville C. went he would have had to deal with me'. It would have been Chamberlain's choice. Halifax, however,

feared that Churchill, as minister of defence, would be the effective leader, while he, having no access to the House of Commons, would 'become a more or less honorary Prime Minister, living in a kind of twilight just outside the things that really mattered. Winston, with suitable expressions of regard and humility, said he could not but feel the force of what I had said, and the P.M. reluctantly, and Winston evidently with much less reluctance finished by accepting my view'; Halifax papers, diary, A7.8.4, 9 & 11 May 1940.

40. Maisky has more empathy toward Churchill in his memoirs. While recognizing that in Churchill's nature 'there was always something of the actor', he describes how on this occasion 'he was genuinely moved. Even his voice broke from time to time.' As for the drama, visiting Churchill at his 'dugout', Halifax, too, commented that 'he was exactly like a thing on the stage in what I understand nurses are accustomed to call "a romper suit" of Air Force colour Jaeger-like stuff … I asked him if he was going on the stage but he said he always wore this in the morning. It is really almost like Göring'; *The Times*, 14 Jan. 1964, and Halifax papers, diary, A7.8.6, 25 Oct. 1940.

41. Halifax papers, diary, A7.8.4, 6 June, and Sylvester papers, diary, A48, 16, 28 & 29 May and 14 Dec. 1940; see also A. Lentin, *Lloyd George and the Lost Peace: From Versailles to Hitler, 1919–1940* (London, 2001), pp. 74–7.

42. W.S. Churchill, *The Second World War: Their Finest Hour* (London, 1949), p. 118; see Gorodetsky, *Stafford Cripps' Mission to Moscow*.

43. TNA FO 371 24841 N5812/5/38. On the pressure indirectly exerted by Maisky on Moscow to accept Cripps, see his telegram to MID, *DVP*, 1940, XXIII/1, doc. 159, and his own retrospective admission in *Memoirs of a Soviet Ambassador*, p. 137: 'Secretly I was delighted with the selection of Cripps for this purpose … but I gave no sign of this, and maintained an expression of complete diplomatic calm.'

44. Clarke, *The Cripps Version*, p. 184; Halifax papers, diary, A7.8.4, 16 May 1940.

45. TNA FO 371, 24841 NN5812/3/38.

46. Pimlott, B. (ed.), *The Second World War Diary of Hugh Dalton, 1940–45* (London, 1986), p. 10.

47. Halifax papers, diary, A7.8.4, 17 May 1940.

48. Webb, diary, 20 May 1940, p. 6882.

49. RAN f.1702 op.3 d.112 ll.22–5 and Halifax papers, diary, A7.8.4; TNA FO 371 24840 N5524/5/38, 8 May 1940.

50. Rose, *Baffy*, pp. 170–1.

51. Seeds papers, diary, 20 May 1940.

52. TNA FO 371 24847 N5648/40/38. Maisky's more circumscribed report to Moscow is in RAN f.1702 op.3 d.112 ll.26–7; Halifax papers, diary, A7.8.4. Confirmation of Halifax's pivotal role comes in Andrew Roberts, *'The Holy Fox': A biography of Lord Halifax* (London, 1991), p. 254.

53. Halifax papers, diary, A7.8.4, 26 May 1940.

54. Cripps was hardly prepared for the ambassadorship: 'I have no more idea than the man in the moon as to how I shall run the embassy! – which is, I imagine, a large establishment with many servants etc. etc.!! However all these things will no doubt sort themselves out in due course.' Cripps papers, diary, 4 June 1940.

55. Cadogan indeed warned that Cripps had 'not yet won his spurs in diplomacy'. It was assumed in the Foreign Office that Cripps would not remain in Moscow as ambassador 'for more than a brief period'; TNA FO 371 24847 N5689/40/38, 2 June 1940; Thurston, the American chargé d'affaires in the Soviet Union to the Secretary of State, 5 June 1940 in *Foreign Relations of the United States* (hereafter *FRUS*), 1940, I, p. 605. Cripps remained ambassador in Moscow until early 1942.

56. Maisky told Alexander, the new first lord of the Admiralty, that he was convinced that the French collapse 'was not due entirely to force of arms but to the activities of about 200 families … who feared French Communism more than they feared Hitler'; Alexander papers, AVAR 5/8, 28 June 1940.

57. This entry served as a basis for his telegram to NKID, *DVP*, 1940, XXIII/1, doc. 214.

58. Maisky told Bilainkin that 'Kennedy was sceptical about Britain's chances of resisting attacks on the island'. He on the other hand, 'was not pessimistic; everything depends on whether you use your cards, of which you have so many, in the right spirit, with resolution'; Bilainkin, *Diary of a Diplomatic Correspondent*, p.152, 7 July 1940.

59. A leading manufacturer of ball bearings.

60. A description of his position is in Maisky's letter to Kalinin, president of the Supreme Soviet of the Soviet Union, from 6 November; this bears witness to Maisky's increased isolation. The letter is reproduced in A.V. Kvashonkin, *Sovetskoe rukovodstvo: perepiska, 1928–1941* (Moscow, 1999), pp. 416–19.

61. On the list see W. Schellenberg, *Invasion 1940: The Nazi invasion plan for Britain* (London, 2000).

62. TNA FO 418/86 N5788/93/98, 21 June 1940; Maisky, *Memoirs of a Soviet Ambassador*, p. 104.

63. TNA FO 800/322 pp. 338–42, Johnson to Halifax, 13 June 1940, and minutes by Butler.

64. Butler papers, RAB E3/9/74, memo by Bilainkin forwarded to Butler, 17 June 1940.

65. TNA CAB 127/204, 25 May 1940.

66. See diary entry for 7 July 1940.

67. Webb, diary, 8 July 1940, pp. 6912–2.

68. Alexander papers, AVAR 5/8, 28 June 1940, and TNA PREM 3/395/1.

69. Maisky, *Memoirs of a Soviet Ambassador*, pp. 99–100, and report to Molotov in *DVP*, 1940, XXIII/1, doc. 244.

70. TNA PREM 3/395/1, 3 July 1940. Halifax rightly doubted whether Maisky would have received any report about Cripps's meeting with Stalin. Maisky indeed complained to Molotov that he found himself in 'a most awkward situation' when he was asked by Churchill about the meeting, of which he knew nothing; *DVP*, 1940, XXIII/1, doc. 244; *The Times*, 16 Aug. 1967.

71. Daladier and Reynaud were neighbours, and their mistresses were not only acquaintances but also old social rivals; see May, *Strange Victory*, p. 326. Halifax noted in his diary that the French minister, Georges Mandel, had asked George Lloyd, Churchill's special envoy to Paris, whether he could come away to London with him 'but said that he had also

"des bagages," which Campbell interpreted to George to be his mistress. At this George drew the line.' Halifax papers, diary, A7.8.4, 20 June 1940.

72. A reference to Churchill's decision to sink the French fleet, under the command of the Vichy government, at the port of Mers-el-Kebir outside Oran on 3 July.

73. Cripps's views are elaborated in a letter by Monckton to Lady Cripps, Monckton papers, Trustees 03/5, July 1940; Colville, *Fringes of Power*, 10 Aug. 1940, p. 215.

74. TNA FO 371 24844 N5853/30/38, FO to Cripps, 25 June 1940.

75. For a documented survey of Soviet foreign policy during that period, see Gorodetsky, *Grand Delusion*.

76. Halifax elaborated in his diary: 'He amused me by his description of International Law as a combination of legal niceties originating in the will of the strongest Powers: cynical, but not altogether untrue.' Halifax papers, diary, A7.8.4, 10 July 1940.

77. Halifax wrote in his diary: 'With Maisky I had a general talk in order to keep relations warm. He was quite interesting from his beastly Bolshevik point of view about the Russian land system'; Halifax papers, diary, A7.8.4, 10 July 1940.

78. Negrín was refused a visa and was invited to dinner again, this time by Alexander, who asked him quite politely but urgently to quit England. He recommended New Zealand; Webb, diary, 28 Nov. 1940, p. 6998.

79. TNA PREM 3/395/1, 12 July 1940.

80. Sheean, *Between the Thunder and the Sun*, p. 203.

81. Maisky takes particular pleasure in relating the content of the secret session. Sheean, the American journalist who was present at the session, recalled that he saw that 'Maisky and the Duke of Alba, Franco's ambassador, were the only foreign representatives of high rank there. The session was short, for Mr Churchill had decided upon a secret meeting. When he delivered the time-honoured formula for the exclusion of visitors he looked up at the diplomatic gallery and delivered it plain: "I spy strangers." As we walked out, I said to Maisky: "Which is the stranger in this place, you or Alba?" He smiled his inscrutable smile, famous in London (we used to call him Il Giocondo), and said "Who can tell?". And in 1940, indeed, it was not easy to be sure'; Sheean, *Between the Thunder and the Sun*, p. 206.

82. Amery describes in his diary how the 'sight of a sumptuous lunch in a pleasant conservatory overlooking Kensington Gardens prompted Bob [Boothby] to exclaim: "What a relief in these rationing days to share the simple life of the Proletariat"'; Barnes and Nicholson (eds), *The Empire at Bay*, p. 638.

83. Dilks, *Diaries of Sir Alexander Cadogan*, p. 321.

84. Channon, who had been advocating the appointment for two years, saw it in a different light: 'they will adore it, the petty pomp, the pretty Regency Government House, the beach and the bathing; and all the smart Americans will rush to Nassau to play backgammon with Wallis!'; Rhodes, *Chips*, p. 260.

85. Maisky's suspicions of Halifax were hardly warranted. He turned down the Dutch exploratory feelers for a negotiated peace, writing in his diary that 'The more I ponder it, the more convinced I feel that the Germans have got to be more knocked about before they will be in any mood to learn any lesson … to stop on the sort of terms that Hitler would be likely

to contemplate now would definitely look to them as if war did pay not too badly'; Halifax papers, diary, A7.8.5, 19 Aug. 1940.

86. Maisky's erroneous observation indeed proves how successful Churchill was in covering his financial tracks. In *No More Champagne: Churchill and his money* (London, 2015), David Lough exposes the extent to which Churchill relied on shares, interest and insider trading, and describes in great detail the efforts he made to avoid paying income tax on such earnings in order to make his living. He also discloses how Churchill went out of his way to ensure that his haggling with the Inland Revenue would be kept private during his wartime premiership. His talk with Maisky only confirms this. I am most grateful to Mr Christopher Matheson for pointing out the discrepancy to me.

87. A brilliant analysis is in W. Murray, *Strategy for Defeat: The Luftwaffe 1935–1945* (Princeton, 2002). See also R. Overy, *The Battle of Britain: The myth and the reality* (London, 2002).

88. Webb, diary, 31 Aug. 1940, pp. 6954, 6958–9.

89. This argument is developed at length in Gorodetsky, *Grand Delusion.*

90. Maisky was desperately seeking to construct bridges to his former allies within the government. 'As I expect you are having a terribly strenuous time with all this business of war,' he wrote to Eden, 'don't you think it would be a good thing to take a little relaxation by having another "restful" lunch in our winter garden?' RAN f.1702 op.4 d.940 l.16, 4 Sep. 1940.

91. At the luxurious Dorchester Hotel, which they had made their London residence.

92. Halifax's figures proved that in the East End boroughs, where the estimated population was 520,930, there were 328,913 private shelters and 81,821 public ones, while in the West End boroughs, where the estimated population was 462,520, there were 128,744 private shelters and 70,109 public, the comparison being 'definitely favourable towards East London'; RAN f.1702 op.4 d.1290 ll.6–7, 24 Sep. 1940.

93. Bilainkin, *Diary of a Diplomatic Correspondent*, pp. 100–1.

94. Maisky, *Memoirs of a Soviet Ambassador*, pp. 116–18.

95. *DVP*, 1940, XXIII/1, doc. 401, 25 Sep. 1940.

96. Lloyd George papers, LG/G/14/19, 28 Oct. 1940.

97. Maisky's evaluation (based on the diary entry) which he sent to Moscow evidently left a mark on Stalin's directive to Molotov for the negotiations with Hitler in Berlin; *DVP*, 1940, XXIII/2, doc. 479.

98. AVP RF f.06 op.2 p.15 d.157 ll.67–8, 3 Nov. 1940.

99. Presidential Archives, Moscow, copy of handwritten notes by Molotov, 9 Nov.; AVP RF f.059 op.1 p.338 d.2314 l.2, Stalin to Molotov, 11 Nov. 1940. To prevent any misunderstanding, Maisky received a succinct but accurate report from Molotov on what transpired in Berlin, see AVP RF f.059 op.1 p.326 d.2239 ll.112–14, 17 Nov. 1940.

100. Webb, diary, 28 Nov. 1940, p. 6998.

101. TNA FO 371 24848 N7354/40/38, 27 Nov. 1940.

102. TNA FO 800/322, pp. 365–9, Halifax to Cripps, 27 Nov. 1940.

103. Halifax entered in his diary: 'In the afternoon I saw Joe Kennedy, who told me he had decided to chuck up his job the week after next, and seemed in very bad temper with his own Administration. I don't think he is a very good fellow'; Halifax papers, diary, A7.8.6, 10 Oct. 1940.

104. Randolph and Pamela Churchill were divorced in 1945, and she later married Averell Harriman, Roosevelt's personal envoy to Europe and US ambassador to Moscow.

105. On this episode, see D. Smyth, 'The politics of asylum, Juan Negrín in 1940', in R. Langhorne (ed.), *Diplomacy and Intelligence during the Second World War* (Cambridge, 1985).

106. Maisky's unflattering description might have been triggered by a harsh private letter he had received from Vansittart, warning him that 'an increasing number of complaints are being made against your Embassy for offences against the black-out. I am sure that you personally must be unaware of what is going on, but it is evident that a firm hand on your part is required. I hope you will see to this at once.' RAN f.1702 op.4 d.1267 l.12, 27 Nov. 1940.

107. RAN f.1702 op.4 d.940 l.18, Maisky to Eden, 23 Dec. 1940.

108. TNA FO 371 N7548/40/38 and AVP RF f.069 op.24 p.70 d.43 ll.132–7.

Annals of Communism

THE COMPLETE MAISKY DIARIES

VOLUME 3

THE GERMAN INVASION OF RUSSIA AND THE FORGING OF THE GRAND ALLIANCE 1941–1943

EDITED BY GABRIEL GORODETSKY

Translated by Tatiana Sorokina and Oliver Ready

Yale UNIVERSITY PRESS
NEW HAVEN AND LONDON

Published with the permission of the Scheffer-Voskressenski family—Ivan Maisky's heirs.
Photographs from Agniya Maisky's album are published with the permission of the Voskressenski family, owners of the copyright and Ivan Maisky's heirs.

Yale University Press books may be purchased in quantity for educational, business, or promotional use. For information, please e-mail sales.press@yale.edu (U.S. office) or sales@yaleup.co.uk (U.K. office).

Set in Minion Pro and ITC Stone Sans type by Newgen.
Printed in the United States of America.

Library of Congress Control Number: 2017942542
ISBN 978-0-300-11782-0 (hardcover : alk. paper)

A catalogue record for this book is available from the British Library.

This paper meets the requirements of ANSI/NISO Z39.48-1992 (Permanence of Paper).

10 9 8 7 6 5 4 3 2 1

Contents

1941

1 January

The New Year, 1941. What will it bring us?

My hypothetical forecast is the following: This will be the decisive year of the war. Hitler must make a *supreme effort* (most probably in spring or in summer) in order to bring the war to an end this year – in his own favour, of course. It would be catastrophic for him to prolong the war into 1942 and subsequent years, because in that phase of the war time will be on the side of England (and the USA). By the beginning of 1942, British military production will be at its peak, while the US military industry will be entering the phase of full-scale production. Then England and the USA will be capable of simply raining bombs and shells on Germany. By that time, the British Empire will also have sufficiently mobilized its human and material resources. In a word, from 1942 onwards there will be no hope for Germany to tie the war, let alone win it, since the world remains on the plane of 'normal' capitalist relations. That is why Hitler must hurry with his *knockout blow*. He has already had his share of disappointments. There can be little doubt that after losing the Battle of Britain in the autumn of 1940, Hitler's plan was to take advantage of the winter season for a joint onslaught with Mussolini on Egypt, Palestine, Iraq and so on. This would have severed links between India and England, while at the same time solving Germany's oil problem. Italy's defeats in Albania and Africa, plus the Soviet Union's opposition to the German overland march to the Middle East through the Balkans and Turkey, have upset Hitler's plans. Evidently, the winter of 1940/1941 will yield less than he hoped for. So a final, decisive *knockout blow* becomes all the more imperative.

But where? In which direction?

I think it will be directed against England, for a blow in any other direction cannot produce a decisive effect.

In what form?

Most probably, in a combined form – vicious intensification of the sea war, vicious air raids, and vicious attempts at invasion. Hitler will stop at nothing:

gas, germ warfare, a variety of 'secret weapons' (if he really has them) – all will be deployed. So far we have seen hundreds of bombers operating over London and other British cities, and it is quite possible that we shall soon see thousands. For the moment is approaching when Hitler, for all his caution, will have to stake his all and risk coming out with nothing. And he is not the type of man to sell his chance of victory cheaply. That is why all of us living in England must prepare for very hard days. I'm completing the strengthening of our bomb shelters just in time.

The outcome?

At the moment one can only guess. But if we rule out the impact of some entirely new 'secret weapon' (the Germans have yet to reveal any real 'secrets' in this war), then I think Hitler's *knockout blow* will fail. He missed his moment. Immediately after Dunkerque, following the capitulation of France, he still had the chance to make a successful invasion (although even then it would not have been easy). Now England has strengthened and reinforced itself to such an extent – not only militarily, but also in terms of morale – that Hitler, having mastery neither of the sea nor of the air, must be highly uncertain of the success of his *invasion.*[1] His chances are so small that sometimes I think to myself: will he really risk it? Won't the events of autumn 1940 be repeated in 1941? Perhaps Hitler will once again pace the shores of the Channel before retreating with the words: 'The berries are unripe and sour.'

But then I reflect: what else can he do? What choice does he have?

No, a *knockout blow* against England will, by all appearances, be attempted, but it will most probably fail.

What then?

Too early to say. One thing is clear: the failure of a German attempt to invade is not equivalent to an English victory. I mean a <u>victory</u>, not a draw. Victory for England is still a distant prospect – at any rate for the England of Churchill, Simon, Margesson, Attlee and Bevin.

If the trial of strength this spring and summer ends inconclusively, a highly complicated situation will emerge next winter, one which may lead either to a compromise peace or to the unleashing of revolutionary forces.

Time will tell.

9 January

Ellen Wilkinson lunched with us. She is engrossed with her 'shelters' and thinks about them even in her sleep. She has achieved some success. In the public shelters of the Greater London area there are 1,400,000 bunks (for a population of 3 million). About 180,000 people spend their nights in the Underground. In the shelters there is more order, hygiene, etc. There have been no epidemics there: only two cases of diphtheria and three of meningitis. The situation in the provinces varies: there are cities where the shelters are very good (Newcastle) and where they are very bad (Coventry). In a day or two Wilkinson will go to the provinces to deal with this matter. The British government expects colossal air raids in spring (including gas attacks), compared with which all we have seen so far is mere child's play. The shelters must also be ready for this.

Wilkinson's own situation, in terms of day-to-day living, is poor. German bombs destroyed her flat in London; moreover, she lost the greater part of her library. She has no time to visit her cottage in the country. She spends the day at the Home Office and sleeps there in her own office. Her lifestyle is positively spartan.

But the most interesting thing today was Wilkinson's view of the war. In response to my remark that one could not but consider this war an imperialist war, she responded most frankly.

'I'll be *brutally realistic*,' she said with fervour, 'let the war we are waging be a bourgeois war. What of it? It's impossible to choose the conditions for a war. One has to take a war as it is. And I think we ought to win this bourgeois war. For bourgeois England, with all its defects, is still immeasurably better than Nazi Germany. I'd rather die than live under Hitler.'

12 January

Yesterday evening at around 8.30 I was sitting at my typewriter and had just begun the third chapter of my memoirs about emigration. Suddenly I heard the rattle of a machine-gun outside. I raised my head. What was it? A diving German plane?...

At that same moment Agniya ran into the room. She was excited and out of breath, and shouted: 'Bombs! Fire...The street's as light as day!'

Together we ran to the bathroom window. Indeed, all was ablaze outside. Hundreds of bright white fires sparkled under the trees in Kensington Gardens: incendiary bombs. Two fire bombs were also burning in the garden of our Nepalese neighbours. The same in the courtyard of the house adjacent to the Nepalese. As far as we could see, the courtyards of all the houses in Kensington Palace Gardens were lit by the bluish-white flames of burning bombs.

We rushed to another window that overlooked our garden. Several bombs were burning below in various spots near the shelter and near the staircase that descended from the white hall.

I raced downstairs and began mobilizing our people. There were two more bombs outside the front porch, and further bombs by the garage and in the passage between our house and that of our Nepalese neighbours. Fire bombs sparkled opposite in the yard of the Lithuanians and farther along the street.

It was light enough to read a newspaper. But our thoughts were not set on reading.

Our people assembled. Some ran to put out the bombs at the front of the building and others rushed to the garden. I was with the second group. We took sandbags and poured sand over the flames. The bombs were extinguished fairly quickly. I put out one bomb; Agniya came running down to put out another. All our bombs were extinguished in about 15 minutes. Luckily, not a single one fell on the roof.

Others on the street did not fare so well. The roof of No. 21 diagonally opposite us caught fire. Red tongues of flame rose to the sky. But a fire brigade arrived in time to deal with the fire. On the whole, the bombs in Kensington Gardens and other places in our district were dealt with successfully. There were no major fires.

15 January

The 'People's Convention' was held on 12 January after all! Ellen Wilkinson was not deceiving me when she told me over lunch on 9 January that the government had decided not to interfere. There were more than 2,000 delegates (including about a hundred soldiers) representing 1,200,000 people. Passionate speeches, firm resolutions, an animated mood: the Convention was a definite success. It is the first noticeable sign of the wave of mass discontent rising gradually from the proletarian midst. It should not be overestimated, but nor should it be underestimated. It's too early to expect major events on the domestic front in England, but faint subterranean shocks already indicate that processes are under way, that deep social shifts are in the offing.

This is well attested by the conduct of the Church, which in England is very closely tied to the masses and senses its mood quite acutely.

On 13 December, the *Catholic Herald*, the mouthpiece of British Catholics, published an article on the front page under a banner headline: 'If We Don't Ensure Social Justice in National and International Affairs, Communism Will Come'. Sharply attacking the communists and the People's Convention scheduled for 12 January, the paper wrote nonetheless: the meaning of all the Church's statements cited above is patently obvious. The Church senses the first subterranean shocks in the social structure and hastens to pull the wool over the eyes of the masses in advance and (how very English!) to find some rotten compromise through which it might blunt the edges of the rising movement. Moreover, the Church would like to lead this movement in its own way and stop the communists and other left elements from gaining control of it. At the same time, the Church wants to exert a 'moral influence' on diehard elements in the ruling classes who refuse to meet the surging wave halfway. Will the Church's ploy succeed? We shall see.

Secular authorities lag considerably behind the Church. A special committee headed by Attlee has been developing *war aims* for a few months already without making any progress. Why? Because there is disagreement within the committee and the government on a cardinal issue: some, particularly Bevin, insist on including in the *war aims* matters of a social order – otherwise, they say, it will be impossible to restrain the masses for long. Others, such as Beaverbrook and Kingsley Wood, object to this. The result is stalemate.

Be that as it may, the conduct of the Church is very *significant*. It testifies to the fact that the temperature of popular discontent has risen rather high.

17 January

Lunched with H.G. Wells at the embassy. Wells has just returned from spending two months in the United States, where he gave thirteen lectures on topical subjects and met many interesting people. But he did not see Roosevelt. Why not? Wells' own explanations struck me as being rather far-fetched. There's something behind this. Perhaps Roosevelt did not wish to see Wells? I don't know.

What are Wells' impressions of America? In particular, what is the American attitude to the war?

Wells answered as follows:

> To start with, 90% of Americans are *sentimentally* for England and against Germany. Secondly, 100% of Americans are in the grip of 'air terror': the mere thought of air raids causes them to panic. Thirdly, the country is dominated on the whole by the psychology and way of life of peace time. For instance, US automobile plants produced 4 million automobiles (mostly passenger cars) in 1940 and are stirring themselves to the production of aircraft only with the greatest difficulty. US businessmen often prefer a secure 'peaceful market' somewhere in South America, which their British and German rivals have now abandoned, to the insecure (albeit, in the short run, potentially more profitable) 'war market' in England. In Hollywood I saw an amazing procession, so dazzling and so huge that Hitler himself would have been envious, and what was the occasion? Honouring Santa Claus on Christmas Eve!… And yet, emotionally speaking, Hollywood is extremely pro-British and would love to cut Hitler's throat with a feather. Such a discrepancy between emotions and real aid to England can be observed everywhere.

In general, I think that in practice the USA is doing no more than 30% of what it could do for England. The gap, as you can see, is huge.

'And what are the prospects?' I asked.

'Little by little America is nonetheless bestirring itself,' replied Wells, 'and Roosevelt is undoubtedly the mouthpiece of popular sentiments towards the war. In about a year, practical aid from the USA will be in full swing. This will give England such a massive advantage that a German victory will become impossible. But I think Germany has actually lost the war already. I don't believe in the possibility of an *invasion*, and if this is the case, how can Germany beat us?... I am concerned by something else: I fear that in the not too distant future, the USA may be drawn into the war.'

'Why does that worry you?'

'You see,' continued Wells, 'if the USA enters the war, those same capitalist elements who are presently against the transition from peace-time to military production will be obliged to engage in arms manufacture at a frenzied pace and will have purely selfish motives for dragging the war out any way they can. That's the first point. Another thing: if Germany cannot defeat England, then, in all honesty, I also fail to see how England can defeat Germany. The only way for England to win is to get rid of all her Halifaxes, but I don't as yet see how this could be done. Hence the conclusion: in the not-too-distant future, say, in 8–10 months, the war may come to a stalemate. There will be talk of peace negotiations. Should the USA remain outside the war, it would promote peace and, most significantly, would bring an end to the war in such a way as to ensure tranquillity in Europe for many years to come.'

'What do you have in mind?' I inquired.

'I see only one way,' Wells responded eagerly, 'of safeguarding a sustainable peace after the war: a great Air Federation of the three powers, the USA, England and the USSR. These three powers alone should have large air forces and control their use. All the rest ought not to have large air fleets.'

'But what if these three powers fall out? What then?' I asked.

Wells argued that such an eventuality must be ruled out. This is the only hope for mankind. Otherwise the next war will finish it off for good. To fulfil this hope it is imperative to establish friendship between England, the USA and the USSR. In this connection Wells inquired about the state of Anglo-Soviet relations. I informed him about the events of the past 3–4 months, but my words, of course, contained little that was reassuring. Wells became angry and began heaping abuse on 'those Halifaxes of ours' who see no further than their noses. In perfect contradiction to what he had just been saying, Wells now set about assuring me that within a year at most 'Halifaxes' would no longer be in power and England would be ruled by different people, with whom the USSR would be able to establish genuinely cordial relations.

'You know,' my interlocutor added unexpectedly, 'I like Stalin. He's *first class stuff*!'

And, without a pause, following some peculiar logic of his own, he suddenly stated in the most categorical terms: 'Only all of you are so terribly old-fashioned. The *Communist Manifesto* is out of date and you should revise it by adapting it to the new technology and new relations.'

I burst out laughing and said that we were up to the neck in other, more urgent problems, but Wells had warmed to his new theme and kept impressing on me that he, Wells, was a far more advanced and modern man than we, the Bolsheviks.

'What is the general attitude towards the USSR in America?' I asked so as to divert Wells' thoughts to another topic.

'Somewhat better,' he answered, 'but still hostile on the whole. Even the left has not got over Finland and to a certain extent the Baltic. For *Wall Street*, the USSR remains the "communist bogey". Willkie[i] is a fine illustration of this. He is the true voice of *Wall Street*, a hardened capitalist bandit. He is now coming to England – what for? Allegedly to familiarize himself with the situation and to coordinate better the "war efforts" of the two countries. Nonsense! In fact he is coming to see whether England has not become too "Red" or is considering doing so. That's the *Wall Street* spirit for you!'

Wells took a deep breath and added:

> Would you believe it, I had to defend the USSR's position on the Finnish question at one meeting after another. I posed the question in the following way: imagine that *Long Island* were in the hands of a small power hostile to the United State, behind which there stood another hostile power – a great power. Suppose the guns placed by the small power, backed up by the great power, threatened New York from Long Island. What would the government of the United States do? The USA would probably occupy *Long Island* within 24 hours – call it aggression if you like – and you would probably all cheer the US government's actions, wouldn't you?… My arguments usually reached the hearts of the listeners. They began to understand your actions. That's the most important thing. That's how one should talk with an American audience. But your men in America don't know how to do it. I'm sorry to say this,

[i] Wendell Lewis Willkie was the 1940 Republican nominee for president; he favoured a more intense American involvement in the war.

but your propaganda in America is good for nothing. In its unsuitability I can compare it only with English propaganda, but that's the *limit*!

I thanked Wells half-jokingly for his 'propaganda' on behalf of the USSR, and our conversation somehow turned to the Litvinovs. Wells told me a few things about Ivy's family.

It transpires that her grandfather, progenitor of the family, emigrated from Vienna to England after the 1848 revolution. He was a fairly wealthy Jewish *businessman* and fond of gambling on the Stock Exchange. He never struck lucky, and the family of old Low would panic every time he headed off to the City. Then one of the sons would rush to the City, look for his father and try to drag him back home.

Ivy's grandfather had three sons: Sir Sidney Low, who became owner of the *Evening Standard* and the *Pall Mall Gazette*, Sir Maurice Low, who for many years was the correspondent of *The Times* in the United States, and Walter Low, Ivy's father. Rather romantically, Walter married the daughter of an Englishman and an Afghan woman. So there is Jewish, English and Afghan blood mixed in Ivy's veins (knowing this, I am no longer surprised by her temperament and character!). Ivy had an aunt, who hated 'modernism' in women (smoking, *lipstick*, and the like). Ivy's sister is married and lives in Ceylon… She has other relatives, too. What a good theme for a contemporary Rougon-Macquart chronicle!

22 January

Mrs Simopoulos (the English wife of the Greek ambassador) recounted two amusing *stories* at a lunch given by Aras.

The first. Soon after Italy entered the war, Hitler boasted about it in a conversation with an American statesman. The statesman thought for a while and then said: 'Italy was on our side in the last war. It is on yours in this war. That's only *fair*. Providence is just: it does not wish to keep punishing the same party.'

The second. Three weeks have passed since war broke out between Italy and Greece. Hitler calls Rome and asks meaningfully: 'Benito, is that you? What? Are you still at home? I thought you were in Greece already.'

Mussolini retorts: 'Hello! Is that you, Adolf? What?… I can't hear you!… Are you calling from London?'…

* * *

I heard one more anecdote, or more precisely a fact that resembles an anecdote.

Jimmy Thomas[i] liked to speak profusely. Once at a grand dinner, where the prince of Wales and Lord Birkenhead (now deceased) were present, Thomas went on far too long. The prince of Wales was clearly annoyed. Birkenhead, who sat next to him, asked: 'Does Your Highness wish him to conclude?'

'Yes, of course,' answered the prince, 'Shut him up.'

'Right away!'

Birkenhead wrote something on a piece of paper, beckoned a servant and asked him to give it to the speaker without waiting for the end of his speech. Thomas cast a glance at the note and his features instantly took on a peculiar appearance. He blushed, coughed, and was back in his seat within a couple of minutes.

'Whatever did you write?' the prince inquired.

'I wrote: "Jimmy, your trousers are in disarray",' Birkenhead answered with a laugh.

23 January

I had Hicks, Tom Williams, Neil Maclean, Latham,[ii] Dobbie and, of course, Coates for lunch. We spoke about the war, Anglo-Soviet relations, and the food situation. Williams (he is now deputy minister of agriculture) told us that there would be a shortage of four food products during the war: butter, bacon, cheese and fruit (except for oranges – thanks to the Spanish policy of the British government).

During the conversation, I remarked with a laugh that Wendell Willkie was coming to England to see, first and foremost, whether it had become 'too' Red or was in danger of becoming so.

'Oh, Tom,' Hicks exclaimed, addressing Williams and feigning fear, 'it seems that we will have to sink into *obscurity* for the duration!'

One of my guests rejoined: 'Yes, we don't have any sort of socialism here.'

'Ho, ho, ho!' Hicks roared again, before adding in the same tone: 'For as long as we are in power there will be no socialism in England.'

An uneasy silence fell around the table. No wonder: Hicks had inadvertently divulged the truth.

I recalled what Randolph Churchill told me the day before: 'Bevin, of course, has proved himself a *disappointment* in many ways, but my father will not let him leave the government: *he saves us lot of troubles* [sic].'

'What do you mean?' I asked, pretending not to understand.

[i] James Henry Thomas, a trade unionist, he became lord privy seal and minister of employment, 1929–30 and secretary of state for dominion affairs, 1930–35.
[ii] Charles Latham, leader of London County Council, 1940–47.

'Well,' Randolph replied very frankly, 'had it not been for Bevin, we'd have had endless trouble with workers about working conditions, wages, workdays, etc.'

Precisely. Labour is performing its historical mission.

24 January

My first visit today was to Butler, with a protest against the detention near the Falkland Islands of the Greek SS *Karyanthykos* [untraced], which is carrying a cargo of hides for the USSR. Then I visited Dalton on the same matter.

As usually happens, the minister of economic warfare refused to commit himself in any way. He merely promised to investigate the fact that I had reported to him, and then moved on to more general issues.

First, Dalton said that the British government is obliged to treat with suspicion our trade with America, because our neutrality has a certain *bias*: we trade with Germany, but not with England. I replied that the British government's conduct with regard to the Baltic question was not conducive to the creation of a favourable atmosphere for the promotion of trade between our countries.

My reply stung Dalton and he set about proving, with somewhat affected fervour, that reference to the Baltic question is just a pretext. Even if the Baltic issue were to be resolved, the Soviet government would find other pretexts to justify its present attitude towards England. The problem is that the Soviet government does not seek to improve Anglo-Soviet relations. That is why the British government is in no hurry to settle the Baltic question. Naturally, I rebuffed Dalton in the appropriate manner.

Secondly, Dalton attacked me in connection with Cripps's position in Moscow. The Soviet government, you see, 'keeps Cripps at a distance', Molotov does not receive him, everyone else slights him and all but 'humiliates' him. Dalton is most irritated by the fact that Molotov found it impossible to receive Cripps before his visit to Berlin.

I replied to Dalton that the position of an ambassador in the country of his accreditation depends primarily on the character of relations between the governments of the countries concerned (as I know from my own experience). Dalton knows perfectly well that relations between London and Moscow today are far from ideal, through no fault of our own, and this cannot but affect Cripps's position in Moscow and mine in London. In any case, I have not heard of anything that might be interpreted as discrimination against Cripps. As for Cripps's meetings with Comrade Molotov, an important circumstance should not be forgotten: Molotov is first and foremost chairman of the Council of People's Commissars and, secondly, People's Commissar for Foreign Affairs. He has to perform many duties and, naturally enough, cannot receive ambassadors frequently. But Cripps can meet Vyshinsky, first deputy chairman of the People's Commissariat for Foreign Affairs (he is also vice chairman of the Council of People's Commissars), as often as he wishes. However, Cripps rarely visits Vyshinsky. As far as I know, Cripps has not visited the People's Commissariat for Foreign Affairs since 19 November, that is, he has not been there for two months, and he has not asked for a meeting with Vyshinsky. It looks like a boycott. Such behaviour can hardly help the ambassador fulfil his functions. I, for example, have not seen Churchill since 3 July, but I hardly make a fuss about it and I don't declare myself offended.

Dalton was slightly confused by this rebuff and softened his tone. He assured me that he had always been and remains an advocate of good relations between our countries and asked for my assistance in solving Cripps's problem.

27 January

The other day I had the chance to convince myself of Moscow's interest in concluding a Soviet–Turkish pact of mutual assistance. That is why I visited Aras today and in the course of our long talk imparted my personal opinion that, after thorough reflection, I had reached the following conclusion: Aras's idea is interesting, but some details remain unclear to me. Through a series of leading questions, I established the following:

(1) Aras is thinking of a pact that will last ten years at least, and which can be prolonged or renewed.

(2) The pact should be of a 'general character' and be effective with respect to any state. I deliberately listed one state after another – Japan, England, Germany, France, Italy and the United States – and each time Aras confirmed: 'The pact should be effective against this state also.' He merely added that he thought it essential, on concluding the pact, to reassure Iran, Iraq, Afghanistan and so on, that the pact was not directed against them.

(3) According to Aras, Ismet[i] and the Turkish government in general are wholly in favour of such a pact, though he has not specifically asked Ankara about it.

After our talk Aras decided to sound out the Turkish government in a more concrete way. If Ankara's reply is positive, as he fully expects, I could in turn sound out Moscow. Should Moscow take a favourable view, Saraçoğlu would make formal proposals to the Soviet government.

All this is very good, but there's something odd about it. The ground underfoot, it seems, is on fire but Aras is in no hurry to sound out Ankara by

---

[i] Ismet İnönü, prime minister, 1923–24 and 1925–37; president of the Republic of Turkey, 1938–50.

telegraph. Instead, he is sending a letter by special courier. How long will that take?… I tried suggesting to Aras that he should act quickly, but he refused to take my hint. It reminds me of the way Admiral Drax was planning to attend military conferences in Moscow in August 1939. Not serious!

31 January

I visited Dalton today. We keep arguing about the Greek SS *Karyanthykos*, which is carrying a cargo of hides we bought in South America and was detained by the British near the Falkland Islands. The British authorities confiscated half the cargo for some reason, and are prepared to leave the other half alone. It's impossible to understand. Dalton said something about the confiscated part of the hides being sold to us by a person in close contact with the Germans, but this, of course, is complete nonsense.

There's another, more important thing. Dalton told me plainly today that in order to avoid similar problems in future we had better conclude a *wartime trade agreement* with England, like those supposedly concluded with England by all neutral countries.

'What about the United States?' I asked, not without malice.

Dalton had to admit the absence of such a trade agreement with the United States.

I moved onto the offensive, declaring that the Soviet Union would not conclude a wartime trade agreement as a matter of principle: we cannot permit outside control over our foreign policy. Halifax tried to impose such control on us during the trade negotiations last year, and was rebuffed. No further attempts have been made since the present government came to power. Does Dalton really want to take us back to that stage? There's no point.

Dalton was greatly disappointed and began to talk about our imports from the United States: cotton, oil-well drilling machines, etc. The British, you see, suspect that we replace the Soviet-made products we export to Germany with the products we import from the United States. That is why our guarantee that we do not re-export the commodities imported from the USA and other countries to the 'enemy' is insufficient for the British. They want an additional guarantee: that we do not export to the 'enemy' the commodities produced domestically in volumes equivalent to the imported ones, particularly cotton, copper, etc. I dismissed these absurd claims.

Dalton asserted, *inter alia*, that according to our agreement with Germany we are to supply it annually with 90,000 tons of cotton, 960,000 tons of oil, etc.

In conclusion, Dalton complained once again about Cripps not being able to meet Molotov, about Cripps being isolated, etc. This creates ill-feeling in London.

I did not want to go back to this topic and reminded Dalton of our recent conversation on 24 January.[2]

3 February

A few days ago I had an unexpected visitor: the well-known Zionist leader, Dr Weizmann.[i] He is a tall, elderly, elegantly dressed gentleman with a pale yellow tinge to his skin and a large bald patch on his head. His face is very wrinkled and marked by dark blotches of some kind. His nose is aquiline and his speech calm and slow. He speaks excellent Russian, although he left Russia 45 years ago.

Weizmann came to discuss the following matter: at present Palestine has no market for her oranges – would the USSR take them in exchange for furs? It would be easy to sell the furs through Jewish firms in America.

I answered Weizmann by saying that *off hand* I could not say anything definite, but I promised to make enquiries. However, as a preliminary reply, I said that the Palestinian Jews should not place any great hopes on us: we do not, as a rule, import fruit from abroad. I was proved right. Moscow turned down Weizmann's proposal, and I sent him a letter to that effect today.

In the course of the conversation about oranges, Weizmann talked about Palestinian affairs in general. Furthermore, he spoke about the present situation and the prospects for world Jewry. Weizmann takes a very pessimistic view. According to his calculations, there are about 17 million Jews in the world today. Of these, 10–11 million live in comparatively tolerable conditions: at any rate, they are not threatened with physical extermination. These are the Jews who live in the US, the British Empire and the USSR. Weizmann spoke about Soviet Jews in particular: 'I'm not worried about them. They are not under any threat. In twenty or thirty years' time, if the present regime in your country lasts, they will be assimilated.'

'What do you mean, assimilated?' I retorted. 'Surely you know that Jews in the USSR enjoy all the rights of a national minority, like the Armenians, Georgians, Ukrainians and so on?'

'Of course I know that,' Weizmann answered, 'but when I say "assimilated", all I mean is that Soviet Jews will gradually merge with the general current of Russian life, as an inalienable part of it. I may not like this, but I'm ready to accept it: at least Soviet Jews are on firm ground, and their fate does not make me shudder. But I cannot think without horror about the fate of the 6–7 million Jews who live in Central or South-East Europe – in Germany,

[i] Dr Chaim Weizmann, president of the World Zionist Organization and the Jewish Agency for Palestine, 1921–31 and 1935–46; president of the state of Israel, 1949–52.

Austria, Czechoslovakia, the Balkans and especially Poland. What's going to happen to them? Where will they go?'

Weizmann sighed deeply and continued: 'If Germany wins the war they will all simply perish. However, I don't believe that the Germans will win. But even if England wins the war, what will happen then?'

Here he began to set out his fears. The English – and especially their colonial administrators – don't like Jews. This is particularly noticeable in Palestine, which is inhabited by both Jews and Arabs. Here the British 'high commissioners' undoubtedly prefer the Arabs to the Jews. Why? For one very simple reason. An English colonial administrator will usually get his training in British colonies like Nigeria, the Sudan, Rhodesia and so on. These places have a well-defined pattern of rule: a few roads, some courts, a little missionary activity, a little medical care for the population. It's all so simple, so straightforward, so calm. No serious problems, and no complaints on the part of the governed. The English administrator likes this, and gets used to it. But in Palestine?

Growing more animated, Weizmann continued: 'You won't get very far with a programme like that here. Here there are big and complex problems. It's true that the Palestinian Arabs are the kind of guinea pigs the administrator is used to, but the Jews reduce him to despair. They are dissatisfied with everything, they ask questions, they demand answers – and sometimes these answers are not easily supplied. The administrator begins to get angry and to see the Jews as a *nuisance*. But the main thing is that the administrator constantly feels that the Jew is looking at him and thinking to himself: "Are you intelligent? But maybe I'm twice as intelligent as you." This turns the administrator against the Jews for good, and he begins to praise the Arabs. Things are quite different with them: they don't want anything and don't bother anyone.'

And then, taking all these circumstances into account, Weizmann anxiously asks himself: 'What has a British victory to offer the Jews?' The question leads him to some uncomfortable conclusions. For the only 'plan' which Weizmann can think of to save Central European Jewry (and in the first place Polish Jewry) is this: to move a million Arabs now living in Palestine to Iraq, and to settle 4–5 million Jews from Poland and other countries on the land which the Arabs had been occupying. The British are hardly likely to agree to this. And if they don't agree, what will happen?

I expressed some surprise about how Weizmann hoped to settle 5 million Jews on territory occupied by 1 million Arabs.

'Oh, don't worry,' Weizmann burst out laughing. 'The Arab is often called the son of the desert. It would be truer to call him the father of the desert. His laziness and primitivism turn a flourishing garden into a desert. Give me the land occupied by a million Arabs, and I will easily settle five times that number of Jews on it.'

Weizmann shook his head sadly and concluded: 'The only thing is, how do we obtain this land?'

[Virtually no relations had existed between the Jewish Agency and the Soviet Union in the decade preceding the outbreak of war. In autumn 1940, the Jewish Agency for Palestine set up a special committee with the task of dealing with the fate of the Jews from Poland, the Baltic countries and Bessarabia, which had just been absorbed by the Soviet Union. Their attempts to send a special delegation to Moscow proved abortive.[3] It was H.G. Wells who encouraged Weizmann to open up a dialogue with Maisky, which intensified after the invasion of Russia.[4] There are, however, no further entries in Maisky's diary describing his flurry of activity in this sphere. At a second meeting with Maisky in September, Weizmann sought to enlist Soviet support, suggesting that in England 'the Jews are not given any opportunity to express their attitude to the war, and in Palestine the British hinder the formation of Jewish troop units'.[5] A month later, Ben-Gurion[i] himself met Maisky and, like Weizmann before him, tried to win him over by emphasizing that, although Zionism was 'a matter of life and death' for the movement, they were also 'most serious' about their socialist aims, and the proof was the successful construction in Palestine of a 'nucleus of a socialist commonwealth'. But behind the ideological lip service, Ben-Gurion tried to enlist Maisky's support for the Zionist aspiration in Palestine, hailing the role of the Soviet Union, which he expected to be 'at the least one of the three leading powers which would determine the fate of the new world'.[6] Weizmann, too, persevered in his efforts. He continued to address long letters to Maisky, and even extended his efforts to Washington, where, in May 1942, he met Litvinov. His reference to Russia's future role in the region became more open with the 'brilliant successes of the Russians on the battlefield' which 'contribute to lifting the pall of darkness now hanging over a distracted world ... the forces of progress and freedom will then unite in order to undertake the work of reconstruction which will lie before them'.[7] The efforts culminated in Maisky's visit to Palestine on his way back from Russia in 1943.[8]]

5 February

The muddle that rules people's heads today! A storm is raging. The old is crumbling, and part of it has already been overthrown; but the new has not yet emerged – even its contours are not yet clear. The result: extraordinary chaos in the minds of thousands upon thousands of people.

Here is a vivid example. Comert[ii] paid me a visit today. He worked in the League of Nations and headed the press department of the French Ministry of Foreign Affairs. He found refuge in London and is now the editor of the émigré

[i] David Ben-Gurion, chairman of the Jewish Agency Executive in Palestine, 1935–48.
[ii] Pierre Comert was the head of the Information and Press Service of the Ministry of Foreign Affairs, 1933–38.

newspaper *France* (he claims the print-run of his paper is nearly 40,000 copies). We spoke at length about France and the causes of her collapse, about Reynaud, Daladier, Marquise Crussol and Countess de Portes. This is very fashionable today. Everything seemed to be going *all right*, and Comert's analysis coincided in many regards with my thoughts about the roots of the French *debacle*. I asked Comert: 'How do you imagine the future of France after this war? Suppose the Germans evacuate your country tomorrow, willingly or otherwise, what would happen then?'

Comert started thinking aloud. And how strange were his thoughts.

'The Third Republic is dead,' he said. 'Reynaud, Daladier, Laval, Flandin and their like are dead, too. Something new must emerge.'

But as soon as he tried to describe the gist of the new, he exposed incredible confusion in his mind and… intellectual poverty. In Comert's opinion, the curse of pre-war France was total corruption, especially the corruption of officials. This was the source of all the troubles. But, how to explain the corruption? It can be explained by the meagre salaries which the Republic paid its employees, far too small to live on. This made it easy for the 'two hundred families' to bribe the functionaries in one form or another. In the end, the Republic was lost. The situation in France was so bad on the eve of the war that a revolution was needed to clean its Augean stables. This is how Comert sees it.

But then came the war. France suffered defeat, and now a revolution is no longer needed. The war did what a revolution should have done. Comert sees the France of the future as having the same parliament (perhaps with a slight modification of electoral law), the same system of 'democracy' that has just broken down (perhaps with minor amendments and a fresh lick of paint) and, above all, officials well paid by the republic. Should the latter point be implemented, the rest will fall into place. For if government employees get decent salaries, corruption will disappear, along with all the bad things that drove the Third Republic to its grave. The solution, according to Comert, is as simple as that.

Yet Comert, after all, is one of the best representatives of old France: a left radical, an advocate of democracy, and an ardent supporter of the League of Nations!

When Comert left, I reflected at length about France and about what is happening there. A sickening feeling. The people as yet 'keep silent' while a big open wound festers on the prostrate body of the nation, over which crawl nasty black flies: Vichy with its heroes Pétain, Darlan, Weygand, Laval, Flandin, Peyrouton[i] and so on and so forth. How vile! But it will pass.

[i] Marcel Peyrouton, French minister of the interior, 1940–41.

The pinnacle of vileness: Comert related to me the circumstances of Laval's arrest and dismissal in December. Agents of Peyrouton's Ministry of Internal Affairs in Paris tapped Laval's telephone conversation with the Germans. It turns out that all the confiscations, requisitions, etc. made by the Germans in occupied France have been yielding Laval his thirty pieces of silver. Laval was unhappy with his rate, and demanded an increase over the phone. When he was told about this, Pétain was furious and arrested Laval. Later, Abetz[i] rescued him from the 'fires of Gehenna'.

Such Herculean pillars of degradation! This is how the old world dies.

10 February

Aras told me today that he has at last sent a letter to Ankara and is waiting for a reply. He does not exclude the possibility that in order to expedite the process the Turkish government may now sound out Moscow on the mutual assistance pact.

According to Aras (who was informed by Aktai), Schulenburg recently visited Comrade Molotov and explained to him the purpose of the concentration of German troops in Rumania. The reason advanced by Schulenburg was defence of the oil fields. Molotov heard him out coolly and thanked him for his explanation without adding a single comment.

Aras says the Turks proceed from the following calculations:

Germany now has up to 30,000 combat aircraft, including 10,000 first-line machines.

England now has up to 20,000 combat aircraft, including 10,000 first-line machines (some of which are in the Middle East).

Proceeding from these figures, Aras believes that an invasion is hardly likely. More probable is a German offensive in early spring in all directions at once – against England, the Balkans, in Spain and elsewhere. In addition, of course, one may expect an intensification of the submarine war.

11 February

Subbotić came by, extremely troubled by the latest news about increasing German pressure on Bulgaria.

He says the atmosphere in Belgrade is still tranquil. Three days ago he even received from there a reassuring telegram: the German troops were said to have temporarily halted their advance toward Bulgaria's borders. However, he was in the Foreign Office yesterday and the FO confirmed the statement made

[i] Otto Abetz, German ambassador to Paris during the occupation, 1940–44.

by Churchill over the radio on the 9th, concerning the rapid 'infiltration' of Germans into Bulgaria. Subbotić's first move in this difficult situation was to see me and exchange views, as well as to ask me to convey to the Soviet government his fervent hope that the Soviet Union would interfere in Balkan affairs and prevent the capture of the Balkans by Germany. How? In what form? That's up to us. The one important thing at this crucial moment is for the Soviet Union to pronounce its weighty word, which would immediately raise its prestige in the Middle East and in the whole world.

I replied to Subbotić that our political line in respect to the Balkans is well known. I had briefed him on our policy more than once in the past. We don't want the Balkans to be involved in the war, and we don't want the dominance of a single great power in the Balkans. As alarming as the reports from the Balkans may be, one should not draw hasty conclusions. History does not end today.

Subbotić agreed with me, but added sadly: 'Your home is in Moscow, and mine is on the Danube.'

On parting, Subbotić asked once again, in the most insistent manner, for Soviet intervention in favour of Yugoslavia and the Balkans.

14 February

Jacob Epstein[i] has convinced me to permit him to make my bust. I warned the sculptor that the USSR is a country of genuine democracy, so Soviet ambassadors are not able to pay artists of the capitalist world the fees they are accustomed to. Epstein was insistent.

'I'm not asking you to commission your bust,' he said with a perfectly disarming smile. 'It's my initiative, not yours. I just want to have your portrait in my collection. That's all. If you permit me to display it, I'll show it at an exhibition of my work. If not, it will remain in my studio.'

I could find little to say against this and agreed to 'grant' a few sittings to Epstein for him to make my portrait (Epstein calls all his busts 'portraits'). Besides, I was intrigued by the very process by which a major artist works and creates. For whatever one may say, Epstein and Vigeland are the greatest contemporary sculptors.

The second sitting was today. Very interesting. I'm sitting on a soft faded chair placed on a small platform. The sculptor's 'easel' stands in front of me. It is a small table on three legs with a half-metre iron rod in the centre. My

[i] Jacob Epstein, born in New York, studied with Rodin in Paris before settling in London in 1905, establishing himself as a revolutionary and controversial sculptor. Some of his Strand statues were officially and publicly defaced. During the Second World War he carried out several notable portrait commissions, including portraits of Bevin, Churchill and Maisky.

head slowly grows out of the grey clay on the upper end of the rod. Epstein pinches pieces of clay mixed with water in a zinc washtub and rolls them in his palms into thick and thin sausages, from which he moulds my portrait. Much has been done already during two sittings: one can see the contours of my head, face, eyes, moustache and beard… Epstein himself keeps murmuring: 'This is just the beginning… A rough primitive sketch.'

Let's see what happens next. I'll have five or six sittings in all. With such original artists as Epstein, you never know what will come out in the end – you yourself or a monster. We'll see. I'm prepared for the worst.

The set-up is interesting. Epstein has been living for 12 years in a typical English house not far from us: 18, Hyde Park Gate. A long corridor leads from the porch to his studio behind the house. A large, bright room with two enormous windows, one above, the other on the left. Astonishing artistic chaos. Scattered over tables, chairs, benches and the floor are statues, heads, arms, legs and other parts of the human body in clay and plaster of Paris. In the corner stands a blackened and rusted small stove, which burns but doesn't warm. The figure of the sculptor himself moves quickly and deftly amidst the vast chaos. He is dressed in a shabby ginger jacket, over a torn grey shirt. His grey baggy trousers are stained with clay and plaster of Paris.

77. Epstein admiring his bust of Maisky.

Epstein is a quite charming man. He is 60, but his blue eyes have a special sparkle, that of a genius and a child. For some odd reason his face, figure and manners remind me very much of M.M. Litvinov – especially when in the course of his work he sticks out his lips like a child. I told Epstein that he resembles M.M. He was pleased to hear this and said: 'One and the same type, one nation and birthplace: my parents, after all, were Polish Jews.'

When Epstein works, the inspiration is palpable. He steps aside and gazes with absent, wild eyes. He runs to his 'easel' and feverishly flings a clay sausage onto the moist grey mass of clay that will be my head. Or he suddenly drops to his knees and examines the gradually developing oval of the face with a crazed look. Or he throws off his ginger jacket as if he is hot and starts pasting small pieces of moist clay onto the bust.

Yes, he is without doubt an artist, an artist 'by the grace of God'! You see and feel him creating, giving birth, with pain and with joy, to each stroke, each line, and each curve.

I talked a great deal during the first sitting and asked Epstein about his past, his work and his life. He answered about half my questions. Once he noticed this himself and said with his enchanting child's smile: 'Please excuse me… When I'm working, I hear only half of what I'm told.'

[Maisky had attended a private viewing of Epstein's exhibition in October 1940. Epstein's left-wing leanings encouraged Victor Gollancz to arrange for Maisky and his wife to visit the artist's studio. Agniya was particularly struck by Epstein's *Madonna and Child* and suggested that the Russians might be interested in it 'although the title did not accord with the Soviet "Ideology"'.[9] Maisky, who had learnt from Agniya that Epstein had displayed an interest in doing a bust of him, hastened to invite the artist for a luncheon with the Edens at the embassy on 12 February. He was much flattered by the offer, finding the time for the sittings, despite his many commitments.[10] In January 1942, at the zenith of pro-Soviet feelings in Britain, the War Artists' Advisory Committee commissioned a copy of the bust, which was displayed together with a further six portrait-sculptures of prominent war leaders commissioned from Epstein – among them those of Churchill, Bevin and General Wavell. Maisky's modest 'cult of personality' was further boosted when the famous Austrian artist Oskar Kokoschka painted a portrait of him. And when the memoirs of his youth, *Before the Storm*, were published, this could hardly have been observed with equanimity in the Kremlin.[11]]

16 February

For England, the war is becoming ever more expensive. Here are the figures. The British government's general expenditure amounted to 5 million pounds daily in January 1940, 7 million in April, 8 million in July, and 9 million in November. It grew to 12 million pounds daily by February of this year. It has almost doubled, then, in the space of a year.

If we take only the costs of war, this amounted to 4 million pounds daily in January 1940 and reached 10 million pounds this February. So this growth appears to be even greater than that of general expenditure.

How is this gigantic spending reflected in the national budget?

On 31 March 1940, Simon submitted to parliament a national budget totalling 2,667 million pounds, of which 2,000 million was allocated to the war. This quickly turned out to be insufficient, and in July 1940 Kingsley Wood submitted a revised budget totalling 3,467 million pounds, including 2,800 million for war expenses, to the two Houses of Parliament for approval. Soon enough even this proved insufficient, and in February 1941 Kingsley Wood submitted to parliament the third revised budget: 3,967 million pounds, including 3,300 for the war. No further problems are expected before the end of the fiscal year (31 March). Thus, the budget of the first year of this war already requires nearly 4,000 million pounds, i.e. it consumes nearly half the national income (about 8,000 million pounds). The largest budget in the last imperialist war was in 1918 (the last year of the war) and amounted to only 2,500 million.

How is this spending covered?

Last July, parliament adopted a number of measures to increase national revenues. (1) Standard income tax was raised from 7 to 8 shillings per pound, and tax on additional income, above 2,000 pounds, was raised to the maximum rate of 18 shillings per pound. (2) Taxes on beer, tobacco, wine and entertainment were raised, and a new 12% tax on purchases was levied (24% on luxury goods). (3) Property tax was increased by 10% on average (this is a progressive tax; the upper rates for land possessions above 2 million pounds reach 65%). (4) The excess profits tax was raised from 60% to 100% from 1 January 1941.

In addition, a major campaign was launched (led by Sir Robert Kindersley)[i] to sell war savings certificates and similar securities.

These sources are expected to yield up to 1,360 million pounds. In such a way, the budget deficit is reduced to 2,607 million pounds.

How is the budget deficit covered?

Mostly through inflation – by issuing 'Treasury bonds' and various short-term loans. But this cannot last for long. The British government will submit a new budget to parliament in April, and the deficit problem has to be resolved by then one way or another. How? As yet it is difficult to say. There are grounds to assume, however, that the notorious 'Keynes Plan' will be put into operation in one form or another. It is probable that a vigorous struggle will break out among various classes and groups regarding the distribution of the financial burden of the war.

---

[i] Sir Robert Kindersley, a director of the Bank of England, 1914–46.

How typical that, in spite of the high excess profits tax, capitalist companies should make good money from the war. Thus, the 2,261 companies whose reports were published before 31 December 1940 made a profit of 410 million pounds in 1940 in comparison to 376 million in 1939. Likewise, the average dividend of 116 spinning factories over 1940 was 9.56%, compared to 5.93% over 1939. Westminster Bank and Barclay's (two of the 'big five') paid out the same dividends to their shareholders in 1940 as in 1939 (14%, 18%, 12%). Similar facts can be observed in other spheres of the economy.

Why does it happen?

The explanation is very simple. The government now takes 100% of excess profit (compared with just 65% until 1 January 1941), but does not touch 'normal profit'. But what is 'normal profit'? Businessmen usually indicate the highest profit year as the 'standard year', and the exchequer readily accepts this. Thus, the foundations of the capitalist system remain unaffected by the war.

19 February

Visited Aras.

Aras's messenger carrying the letter about the pact was stranded somewhere on the way to Ankara. A quite absurd situation. But Aras is not discouraged. A couple of days ago he received mail from Ankara, in which there was a message from Saraçoğlu: in essence, Aras believes, it provides the answer to the question he put to the Turkish government in his letter.

It turns out that about five weeks ago, Comrade Vinogradov,[i] our ambassador in Ankara, asked the Turkish government on behalf of the Soviet government to confirm the statement made by Aktai in Moscow to the effect that Turkey would not do anything in the Black Sea area or in the Balkans without the consent of the Soviet Union. Saraçoğlu stated in his reply to Comrade Vinogradov:

(1) The Turkish government welcomes the fact that the Soviet government continues to regard the agreement of 1925 as the cornerstone of Soviet–Turkish relations.

(2) The Turkish government is ready to examine in a favourable light any expansion and augmentation of the said agreement on the basis of reciprocity.

Having read the French translation of Saraçoğlu's letter, Aras became very excited and, waving his arms about, began assuring me that the Turkish government is ready to conclude with us a pact of mutual assistance. For the 1925 agreement, together with the three supplementary agreements that exist, represent the utmost of what can be done within the framework of a pact of

[i] Sergei Aleksandrovich Vinogradov, counsellor, then Soviet ambassador in Turkey, 1940–48.

friendship and non-aggression. If the Turkish government now speaks about the expansion and augmentation of the agreement in question, this can mean nothing else but consent to a pact of mutual assistance.

I listened to Aras attentively, but since the circumstances had taken a different turn from what we had envisaged in our previous conversations, I decided not to commit myself. I left the whole matter at the point where, depending on the circumstances, I could either come back to the idea of a mutual assistance pact or forget it and not touch the subject again.

Then Aras told me about the Turkish–Bulgarian declaration. There is nothing new in it, for it ensues from earlier agreements between Turkey and Bulgaria, but it is useful all the same. At any rate, Bulgaria pledges not to attack Greece. Besides, according to Aras's sources, Bulgaria consulted with Germany before signing the declaration, and Germany apparently promised not to move its troops into Bulgaria. The Turks informed the USSR and England about the talks concerning the declaration. The British did not like the declaration, but tried to put a brave face on it. On the whole, Aras believes the declaration to be a compromise deriving from the influences of three powers: Germany, the USSR and England. Momchilov sent a cable to Sofia urging the Bulgarian government to sign similar declarations with Greece and Yugoslavia. Both Athens and Belgrade viewed the idea favourably. Summing up, Aras said he is not pessimistic, as 'it is disadvantageous for Germany to unleash war in the Balkans'. Is that so?

I asked Aras what position Turkey would take if Germany attacked Saloniki.

Aras's speech suddenly lost its clarity and he plunged into lengthy discourse, about how, after all, Turkey is not greatly bothered about who gets their hands on Saloniki. But Western Thrace is another matter! Turkey could not allow Germany to occupy Western Thrace.

Aras, however, soon tried to leave this unpleasant topic behind and said that Hitler was thinking not about the Balkans, but about the west. Aras knows from reliable sources that Hitler has demanded naval and air bases on the Spanish coast from Franco. Hitler is counting on the sea war above all. The Balkans are just a smokescreen.

I expressed some doubts about the validity of this notion, and we had a long argument about it. As I was taking my leave, Aras formulated current Turkish policy, or rather the policy he finds expedient, in the following way: friendship with the Soviet Union, cordial relations with England, and no provocations in relations with Germany.

20 February

About a week ago, Coates came to me with a message: Attlee and Greenwood wanted to see me urgently. We met first on 17 February for a cup of plain tea at

Attlee's office. Greenwood was late, as he usually is, but was present during the important part of the talk.

What was it all about?

The Labour leaders obviously wanted to feel our pulse in connection with the events in the Balkans. Their line of reasoning was roughly the following: Germany is approaching the Black Sea coast. Germany needs oil badly and has to resolve this problem promptly. If Germany gets a firm foothold in the Balkans, it will extend its reach to Turkey. If Turkey falls to Germany, Baku will be endangered. The Soviet national economy is highly mechanized. Oil is its blood. Consequently, a threat to Baku means a threat to our whole economy and to our defence. What do we think about this?

I replied that we understand perfectly well the role and importance of oil in our times and take adequate protective measures. About a year ago, certain European governments showed great interest in the Baku oil, and aeroplanes of 'unknown nationality' even took air photographs of the Baku oil fields, but nothing happened to the Baku oil thanks to the vigilance of our military authorities. Why should we be troubled about the Baku oil now? I see no grounds for that. As for the Balkans, we are closely following the development of events there and, if need be, will certainly take the appropriate steps to protect our interests. In general, it should not be forgotten that the Soviet Union pursues its own independent policy and is able to defend itself under all circumstances.

Attlee and Greenwood were manifestly disappointed.

I, in turn, decided to take their pulse regarding the war prospects in general. To broach the subject, I asked how one should interpret Churchill's rejection of the US army (not only now but in general), contained in his speech broadcast on 9 February. Does this signify a change in the 'general strategy' of the war? For I and many others had the impression that the British government was counting precisely on the arrival of US battalions to help them gain the final 'victory' over Germany.

My question gave rise to a long discussion. The reply the Labour leaders gave me can be roughly summarized in the following way:

(1) No changes have been made to the 'general strategy', but the war experience in Poland, France and Libya has shown that it is not numerical strength but the degree of military mechanization that is decisive in contemporary conditions. Therefore, the British government holds that an army of 3 or 4 million is sufficient to win the war, provided it is a first-class army in terms of training, weapons and mechanization.

(2) On paper, Germany may have an army of 8 million against the English 4 million, but a mere comparison of figures is deceptive. The German forces are scattered all over Europe. In fact, Germany could concentrate no more than half

its forces against England at any given moment. Meanwhile, England will soon be capable of throwing nearly its whole army against Germany (operations in the Middle East will most likely be completed within the next six months).

(3) Furthermore, many important factors are working in England's favour: the growing discontent in the countries occupied by Germany, the blockade, the increasing might of the British air force (the British air force, aided by the USA, will surpass the German air force in 1942), the psychological effect of the United States becoming a de facto ally of England and, finally, the limited German oil resources. The latter is particularly important. Oil is Germany's Achilles' heel. This is where one must strike: the war should be protracted and the Rumanian oil fields bombed. Moreover, the British army is exerting increasing pressure, which will be felt especially strongly from 1942 onwards.

Germany will crack under the impact of all these factors sooner or later – if not in 1941, then in 1942; if not in 1942, then in 1943, etc. England can wait. In the light of the above considerations, it is more important for the British government to have several dozen thousand supplementary American aircraft and tanks than 2 million poorly trained US soldiers in 1942 or 1943.

I objected, saying that Attlee and Greenwood had taken only the enemy's problems into account: what about the problems which England may encounter? Who knows how England will be affected by systematic air raids, a shortage of food and raw materials, etc.? In the final analysis, all will depend on the 'morale' on both sides of the front.

Greenwood interrupted me: 'I bet German morale will crack much earlier than ours,' he exclaimed.

Attlee added: 'We, the British, are a terribly stubborn nation. We were very stubborn in our desire to avoid the war. We will now be awfully stubborn in our desire to fight to the end.'

I summed up: 'Time will tell.'

When the clock struck five, the two ministers rushed to the meeting of the War Cabinet. They said, however, that they had had insufficient time to say all they had wanted to say and that we would need to meet again in the next few days.

Our second meeting took place today in Attlee's office. Greenwood was absent: he had to attend some urgent conference. The two of us, Attlee and I, conversed for some 40 minutes. There was nothing interesting in our conversation. Attlee basically harped on an old theme. I held to my former line. Three of Attlee's statements deserve attention:

(1) The war will probably continue for two more years, but it could possibly end in early 1943 – with British victory, of course.

(2) No preparations for invasion (concentration of ships, barges, etc.) have been spotted on the French coast.

(3) *War aims* must include not only foreign policy, but also social issues, as the former are inseparable from the latter. Attlee did not go into details.

23 February

I chat with Epstein during the sittings. This doesn't distract him; rather, it seems to stimulate him.

Once I asked him why there had been fewer sculptors than painters in the history of art, and whom he admired as the greatest sculptor.

'Why fewer sculptors?' Epstein burst into his infectious laughter. 'It's clear as day. Because it's much easier to be a painter than a sculptor. The work itself is easier and cleaner. You try toiling with clay, stone or metal! It's a far cry from the easel and brush. Every bone aches in the evening. I had pupils who were painters… Nothing came out of it. They'd fumble with clay for a few days and quit: Merci! I'm better off daubing paint on canvas!'

'But you also paint,' I objected. 'What do you consider to be more "your thing": painting or sculpting?'

'Sculpting, of course!' Epstein answered without the slightest hesitation. 'I like real things that I can touch and feel with my hands. A picture will never give you that feeling.'

'What do you prefer in painting: oils or watercolour?' I continued.

'Watercolour. I hate washing oil paints off the brushes.'

I repeated my second question: whom does he consider the greatest sculptor in history?

Epstein thought for a moment and said: 'It's difficult to give a definite answer to your question. I think the ancient Egyptians had wonderful sculptors. Unfortunately, we don't know their names. The one who made the head of an Egyptian queen that's displayed in the Berlin museum was undoubtedly a man of genius. Perhaps he is the greatest sculptor in human history.'

'What about Phidias?'[i] I asked.

'Phidias, of course, was a great sculptor,' Epstein replied. 'But he… But he… How should I put it? He is a bit too sweet for me.'

Then he added emphatically: 'If you want to single out one man as the greatest sculptor, I would name Michelangelo. He is phenomenal! He is for sculpture what Beethoven is for music.'

The conversation turned to music. I asked Epstein to name his favourite composer.

'Beethoven and Bach,' he answered at once. 'I sometimes arrange small concerts at home. My musician friends come and play. Mostly Beethoven. But I like Bach very much as well.'

[i] Phidias, fifth-century BC Greek sculptor, painter and architect.

'What about Tchaikovsky?' I asked, having confessed that although Beethoven was my musical 'idol' too, I liked Tchaikovsky as well. Perhaps because Tchaikovsky is very Russian, our very own composer.

Epstein smiled lightly and said: 'Tchaikovsky is too sweet for me... but I recognize his greatness.'

It was evident that Epstein does not like Tchaikovsky and that he added this last phrase out of courtesy.

Epstein says that music helps him very much in his creative work. Listening to the piano, he always experiences a surge of inspiration. Images and pictures arise in his mind which he then transforms into sculpture. *Adam*, for instance, was inspired by Beethoven's Seventh Symphony (especially its finale).

In literature, by contrast, Epstein has no definite allegiances. He couldn't tell me with any certainty who his favourite writer is, and finally confessed: 'I was very fond of Walt Whitman[i] when I was young. He's a very good poet. He had a great influence on me.'

Nonetheless, Epstein has sculpted quite a lot of heads – or 'portraits', as he calls them – of prominent literary figures: Tagore,[ii] Bernard Shaw, Priestley[iii] and others. His efforts were not always successful. Bernard Shaw's wife did not like her husband's head. Shaw himself thought his 'portrait' a success, but Mrs Shaw declared that if her husband took the portrait, she would leave the house. Under such a threat, Bernard was, of course, forced to capitulate. His portrait remained in Epstein's studio. He showed it to me. I commended the sculptor's work (the bust was made masterfully), but thought to myself that this 'portrait' of Bernard Shaw did not quite catch the man. Something was missing.

'Mrs Shaw very much liked Rodin's[iv] bust of her husband,' Epstein said. He grunted, shrugged his shoulders and added: 'I don't know what she found in it. In my opinion the portrait is no good, although Shaw paid Rodin a heap of money for it. Women always have their fantasies, you know.'

Epstein's impressions of Tagore are interesting. Tagore used to arrive at Epstein's studio escorted by a group of young Hindus, his pupils. He would seat himself on the chair and not utter a word during the sitting. He behaved as if he were a saint. He maintained a meaningful silence and gazed into space with an air of profundity. Tagore's haughty treatment of his 'pupils' bordered on cruelty, while they looked at him in ecstasy, anticipated his every desire, and marvelled at his every gesture. Tagore paid not the slightest attention to them: he did not seem to notice them at all, looked over their heads and gave abrupt orders in a

[i] Walter Whitman, American poet and writer (1819–92).
[ii] Sir Rabindranath Tagore, Calcutta-born poet and educationalist; Nobel Prize for Literature, 1913.
[iii] John Boynton Priestley, English novelist, playwright and broadcaster.
[iv] François Auguste René Rodin, French sculptor (1840–1917).

sharp dictatorial tone. He would, for instance, descend from the studio to the reception room where his pupils were waiting and bark in vexation: 'Taxi!'

The 'pupils' would rush to the door and scatter through the neighbouring streets to hail a car for him.

Once the following incident occurred. It so happened that a small Indian boy was living in Epstein's house at the time when he was doing Tagore's bust. He was the son of Epstein's friend and model (she sat for some of Epstein's best sculptures, such as *Mother and Child*). A brave and progressive woman, she left her husband and went to England despite being a Muslim! Subsequently she returned to India and died in peculiar circumstances. Epstein suspects something tragic. Anyway, that small boy, the son of Epstein's friend, came running cheerfully into the studio one day when Tagore was there. Epstein patted the boy's head and said to his guest: 'Let me introduce a little compatriot.'

Tagore looked at the boy with a kind smile, but then, as if he had suddenly recalled something, asked curtly: 'Is he a Hindu or a Muslim?'

'He is a Muslim,' Epstein replied. 'Does it matter?'

Tagore stiffened. The smile instantly left his face. He turned away and fell into his saintly pose and displayed no further interest in the boy. He simply did not see him. The boy had ceased to exist for him.

Epstein was shocked. Tagore had revealed his true face.

25 February (1)

Attended the reception given by Sklyarov[i] (the military attaché) to celebrate the Red Army anniversary. As far as the number and status of the guests was concerned, the reception was quite a success. Army, navy and air generals and three undersecretaries (Butler, Balfour and Grigg) were present.

During the reception, I spoke with Butler. I demanded the release and repatriation of our sailors from the two requisitioned steamers. Doing so, I made reference to Moscow's wishes. Butler agreed once again to raise the question before the British government, but could not promise a successful outcome. I also informed Butler of the reply concerning access for military attachés (he himself asked me about it). Butler admitted that the British attachés in Moscow have not shown sufficient initiative in asking for access, but that things will be different from now on. Butler is very pleased with Cripps's trip to Ankara to meet Eden. He twice asked me most emphatically to inform Moscow that if the Soviet government wanted to communicate something to Cripps in his absence, this must be done through the British embassy in Moscow, which would be in direct contact with Cripps all the time. The English are a naive lot.

---

[i] Ivan Andreevich Sklyarov, major general, Soviet military attaché in London, 1940–46.

Do they really expect us to show particular interest in the talks between Cripps and Eden in Ankara, given the present state of Anglo-Soviet relations?

I inquired about Churchill's meeting with Shigemitsu (yesterday, 24 February). Butler answered briefly that the peace Matsuoka[i] proposed in his note is out of the question 'until the complete defeat of Hitlerism'.

A propos the PM's meeting with the Japanese ambassador. I heard the following details from other sources. Churchill began by assuring the ambassador that he had displayed full sympathy with Japan throughout his political career and regretted the dissolving of the Anglo-Japanese alliance. An armed conflict with Japan would be a very great disappointment for Churchill, but he ought to warn the Japanese government categorically that peace today is out of the question. England is fighting not for territories, trade advantages, markets, etc., but for the principles of 'democracy'. England shall not bury the hatchet until Hitlerism is wiped off the face of the earth. Churchill got so excited saying this that tears appeared in his eyes. Emotional moments of this kind happen to him every now and again.

25 February (2)

At the reception, Subbotić told me the following concerning Hitler's recent meeting with Cvetković,[ii] the Yugoslavian prime minister.

Hitler, as is his habit, embarked on a pugnacious monologue, in which he stated that he would welcome Yugoslavia's entry into the 'New Europe' and promised in return the free use of Saloniki for trade purposes. However, he did not present a formal invitation to accede to the 'Tripartite Pact'. Cvetković replied that Yugoslavia pursued and hoped to maintain cordial relations with Germany. Hitler objected, however, saying that this was not enough. Yugoslavia had to define its position more clearly. Germany is ready to guarantee Yugoslavia's integrity and inviolability ('whatever happens in the Balkans'), but Yugoslavia should not linger with its decision. Whoever joins the 'New Europe' earlier will gain the utmost. Cvetković said he would 'think over' Hitler's words and left for Belgrade. The Yugoslavian government, according to Subbotić, fully understands that German pressure on Yugoslavia has begun – as yet in a relatively mild form, but what will happen next?

Momchilov, who was also present at the reception, is in a very pessimistic frame of mind. The Germans are sure to enter Bulgaria. They are also sure to occupy Saloniki in order to pound the British from the air along the Saloniki–Dodecanese–Suez line. The British are sure to drop bombs on Rumanian oil

[i] Yosuke Matsuoka, foreign minister of Japan, 1940–41; signed the neutrality agreement with the Russians in Moscow in April 1941.
[ii] Dragiša Cvetković, Yugoslav prime minister, 1939–41.

fields and Bulgarian railways. The USSR, to be sure, will not start quarrelling with Germany over Bulgaria. As a result, Bulgaria will have to foot the bill. Some of the journalists present at the reception were already speculating: what will Momchilov do when the Germans occupy Bulgaria? Will he return to his country or not?

Lord Grigg (undersecretary in the war department) told me: he did not expect an invasion but rather an intensification of the naval and air war. Grigg also said that about two-thirds of the 2 million strong army stationed at home could be considered … in terms of training and weapons, and that serious aid from the United States would start arriving this August or September.

[Shortly after his appointment as foreign secretary, Eden, together with General Dill, left for the Middle East in a last-ditch attempt to reassemble the shattered remnants of the Balkan bloc, comprising Turkey, Greece and Yugoslavia. In Moscow, Cripps was fully aware of the anxiety which seized Stalin when Bulgaria – historically considered to be the pillar of the Russian security system in the Black Sea and the approaches to both the Danube and the Turkish Straits – joined the Axis on 1 March. He was therefore extremely eager for Eden to use the opportunity of his Middle Eastern tour to visit Moscow, 'flatter' the Russians and dispel suspicion. Churchill rejected the idea, stating that he did not trust the Russians as regards Eden's 'personal safety or liberty'.[12] Not so easily dissuaded, Cripps was actually encouraged by the Kremlin to undertake a short sally to Ankara, the result of which was the signing on 9 March of a Soviet–Turkish declaration of mutual non-intervention in the event of war. Eden, however, absorbed in his attempts to forge a Balkan bloc, remained noncommittal in his relations with the Russians.[13]]

27 February

To Subbotić and his wife for lunch with Agniya. Also present were Aras, the Egyptian ambassador, Sargent from the FO and one or two others. Owing to the latest news from the Balkans, the atmosphere at lunch was like at a funeral. The wife of Subbotić remarked, somewhat coquettishly: 'The Balkans are in their death-throes.'

Subbotić himself was gloomy and let it be understood quite clearly that the USSR had failed to live up to the hopes placed in it by the Balkan states.

Aras argued that the Germans will be making a 'very grave mistake' if they cross the Greek border, because then the whole of the Balkans will be ablaze and the war will extend to the Black Sea. The Turks will have to let the British pass through the Straits to deliver a blow to the German left flank. The Turks will also inevitably be drawn into the war. The consequences of all this will be unpleasant for Germany. Future historians may say that Hitler's decision to strike at Saloniki was the fatal step in his career.

After lunch I asked Aras about his last meeting with Churchill (24 February). Aras said the prime minister had no concrete proposals or demands towards

Turkey. He merely informed Aras that Eden was flying to Ankara, where he would raise the question in all seriousness of Turkey's position in the war. Then Churchill assured Aras that the British government had not the slightest desire to open a new front in the Balkans and that if the Balkans did nevertheless become a theatre of war, there would only be Germany to blame. Churchill also expressed the thought that 'Russia's real interests' in this part of the globe lie on the English side. The current Soviet stance can be explained by Russia's desire to avoid a conflict with Germany. This is understandable, but 'Russia will have to change its policy' sooner or later.

I heard from other sources that in his conversation with Aras Churchill was far more insistent in his demands for a 'clarification' of the Turkish position than Aras told me.

2 March (1)

We visited Lloyd George. When his wife died, Agniya and I sent him a warm telegram. He responded recently with a warm and friendly letter. I wrote a few words in reply, asking the old man to tell me when he would feel *fit* enough to see people. Three days ago Lloyd George invited Agniya and me for lunch and today we visited him in Churt.

Lloyd George doesn't look too bad. But some kind of shadow seems to have fallen over his features. On top of that he has a cold: he coughs and blows his nose, pulling a handkerchief from his pocket every other minute. His hands tremble, especially when he pours water into his glass. The irrepressible *Welshman* is growing old. I wonder whether he will hold out much longer…

Lloyd George does not believe in the likelihood of an *invasion*. He waves his hand scornfully and utters with a sneer: 'It's impossible!'

But the situation at sea troubles him. In the 1914–18 war only submarines were engaged against British commercial ships. Now there are aircraft as well. During the last war the Germans operating at sea with bases on the German and Belgian coasts. Today they operate with bases on the Atlantic coast of France. It makes a huge difference. The difficulties of the present situation are all the more evident when one considers that not only the British, but also the French, Italians, Japanese and Russians fought against German submarines in the war of 1914–18.

Lloyd George is rather sceptical about the British statistics of losses. The experience of the last war convinces him that the truth lies somewhere between the German and British communiqués. But even if one fully trusts the British figures, one must still bear in mind that they are incomplete, for these figures refer only to ships sunk, while there are very many damaged ships which often take months to be repaired. The British tonnage loss since the beginning of the war is estimated at approximately 4 million tons. With the addition of the idle damaged ships, the loss amounts to nearly 5 million tons. Moreover, an acute intensification of the German war against British commercial ships is to be expected in 1941. Hitler is evidently wagering on the 'blockade' of England. He understands that any invasion is doomed to fail in the present circumstances, but a 'blockade' – that might even come off! At any rate it should be attempted!

'And, frankly speaking,' Lloyd George concluded, 'I see a serious danger to England here. Perhaps the only serious danger. The Germans cannot beat us from the air. Invasion is out of the question, at least for the foreseeable future.'

I remarked that the commercial tonnage losses were compensated to a certain extent from various sources: the new ships built in England, those being built in the United States, and so on. Hopkins[i] has promised to supply England with new vessels of up to 4 million tons in 1942.

'I don't believe in those promises,' Lloyd George snapped with some irritation. 'They always err on the side of optimism. We'll never get 4 million tons from America next year. It's far from easy to develop a shipbuilding industry in a short period of time. Besides, the Americans are novices in this business. Our shipbuilding industry is more developed, but even we can't cope with such a task. As for British shipyards, they are overloaded with war contracts and commercial ships have to take second place. In 1940 we built only 750,000 tons, while the programme called for 1.25 million.'

I disagreed, saying I was disinclined to be too pessimistic about British prospects in the naval war.

'You see,' I explained, 'it is difficult to defeat a great nation in its own element. Your element is the sea, the German element is land. That's why I don't believe the Germans can beat you at sea. You'll manage somehow. You'll work something out. On the other hand, I doubt your ability to beat Germany on land, for land has been the Germans' element for millennia. And how could it be otherwise? Your army is basically an amateur army. You don't have the skills and traditions of land warfare. You don't have real military science and a good general staff. You only have the experience of colonial wars to fall back on. That does not suit Europe. That is why I regard with scepticism all these cries of "war to the end" or "war till the crushing of Hitlerism". But as for the sea... You'll manage somehow at sea. You'll think of something.'

Lloyd George laughed and looked at me slyly.

'There is much truth in what you say,' he said suddenly. 'Yes, the sea is our home. The sea is in our blood. Take Megan: there is no greater delight for her than the sea. She adores water and swims like a fish. Or Gwilym. He is crazy

---

[i] Harry Lloyd Hopkins, US secretary of commerce, 1938–40; special adviser and personal assistant to Roosevelt throughout the war.

about yachting. The more turbulent the sea, the more he likes it. Yes, we'll manage somehow at sea.'

Lloyd George thought for a moment and continued with animation: 'Look, there is a way out. We have 7 million acres of farmable land in need of drainage. Using this land we could cut food imports by half. What's the problem? The problem is that the land owners have no means to drain the land by themselves. This could be done by the state. It means that 7 million acres of land must be nationalized. This conclusion has been reached by all authoritative British agricultural specialists, irrespective of party affiliation: Liberals, Conservatives, etc. But no! The government does not want to do it. God forbid, it would be so much 'like Russia!' Help! Bolshevism! As a result, our food prospects are worsening with every passing month.'

Lloyd George waved his hand and added: 'Winston is waging a "Tory war". He wants to win without infringing the privileges of the ruling upper crust. This won't do. Something has to be forfeited: either the victory or the privileges. As a matter of fact, it seems to me that the War Cabinet does not have a "general plan" for the conduct of war. I'm sure they have never discussed such a plan seriously. They think the plan is hidden in Winston's head. I doubt it.'

Pausing for a while, the old man concluded: 'Winston has become a hostage of the Conservative Party and swims with the current. I've told you more than once that I see only one way of gaining a real victory over Germany: by drawing the Soviet Union over to our side. But this is just what the British government doesn't want. The government is awfully afraid of the possible effects of such an "alliance" on the internal life of the country. Better to lose the war than to "pave the way for Bolshevism". That's what the wisdom of the Conservatives amounts to, and of Labour – or at least *Transport House*. The interests of the nation clash with class prejudice, and the latter has the upper hand.'

I asked: 'What then? Do you anticipate the defeat of England?'

'No,' Lloyd George answered. 'I don't anticipate that. But I don't believe in victory either. I have a direct question for anyone blathering about ultimate victory: how do you expect to win? Show me clearly, with figures and facts in hand. Nobody has yet given me a satisfactory answer.'

I told Lloyd George about Churchill's demeanour in his recent talk with Shigemitsu. Judging by the prime minister's behaviour, one can hardly expect a compromise peace.

'Tears in his eyes?' Lloyd George smiled. 'Yes, that happens to Winston. He is a very emotional man. So what?… Now he has tears because he wants to crush Hitler. Within a year he may have tears because of the shock of the horrors of the war… Things change.'

Lloyd George suddenly remembered something and burst into peals of laughter.

'If you remember, I twice lunched with Winston in December. His wife was with us at the table. She is a fairly intelligent woman, and above all she has plenty of typically English *common sense*… Winston was being very noisy about fighting to the end. He will not agree to peace until Germany is defeated. He will not sign a treaty with Hitler, etc. I argued with him, saying that the future is a closed book. There may come a time when tactics will need to be revised. One shouldn't tie one's hands for good. Winston, however, continued to growl. Suddenly Mrs Churchill interrupted our conversation and, addressing her husband, said with a smile: "Are we not allowed to change our mind if the moment requires it?" Winston wheezed, but said nothing in reply… Oh, the lady is clever! And Winston listens to her.'

Our conversation shifted to the role of women in politics. Lloyd George said he had been reading [title missing] recently. He liked the first book more than the second, but the second gives a most vivid picture of women's interference in French politics.

'Is there anything similar in England?' I asked. 'I've heard much about the role of such women as Lady Oxford,[i] Lady Londonderry[ii] and Lady Astor in British politics. Is their role comparable, generally speaking, with that of Countess de Portes and Marquise de Crussol?'

The old man pondered, as though recalling his experiences in politics, and replied: 'No, we have never had anything similar to what went on in France, nor do we have it today. The sole comparable case is that of Lady Londonderry and MacDonald. Indeed, Lady Londonderry played a big role in promoting MacDonald to the premiership. But one must give her her due: she did so in masterly fashion, quietly, behind the scenes, without showing herself off or openly interfering in affairs of state. I can't recall any other precedent.'

'What about Lady Astor? Or Lady Oxford?' I prompted Lloyd George.

'Lady Astor?' The old man waved his hand. 'She makes a lot of fuss, but has no influence. Lady Oxford? Oh no! Asquith has never listened to her political judgements.'

Then Lloyd George asked me to tell him about the situation in the Balkans and our attitude to the latest events in this part of the world – in particular, to the entry of German troops into Bulgaria. I briefly described to him our position. Lloyd George shook his grey mane and said: 'What happened in Bulgaria must be unpleasant for you, but, in the final analysis, it is not important enough for you to quarrel with Germany. If the same happens in Yugoslavia, your "vital interests" will not be greatly affected either. And I fear Yugoslavia will follow suit. The Straits are a different matter. You can't yield the Straits! But

[i] Margot Asquith, countess of Oxford and Asquith, was the wife of H.H. Asquith, the British prime minister from 1908–16.

[ii] Edith Vane-Tempest-Stewart, marchioness of Londonderry, was a noted London socialite.

the Germans are well aware of this and I doubt they will dare encroach upon the Straits. Germany cannot afford a quarrel with the Soviet Union.'

I asked Lloyd George whether he thinks the British will try to grab Saloniki before the Germans.

'I can't say,' the old man shrugged his shoulders. 'At least ten or twelve divisions would be needed for the landing. Do we have them? I don't know. You are right to suggest that our army is basically an amateur army. It is difficult to predict what it will do. I am inclined to think that such a landing will not take place: all those who are in a position to make such a decision – Dill, Wavell, Eden – are cautious men averse to risky ventures.'

I felt somewhat sad taking my leave of Lloyd George. His wife has just died. Neither Megan, nor Gwilym, nor any other of his relations lives with him. His home is empty. Two housemaids tend to the old man. And he keeps raising a handkerchief to his face with a trembling hand…

From Lloyd George we drove to the Webbs for tea. A short distance. This old couple looked better than usual. When I told them about Lloyd George's condition, Beatrice said with evident satisfaction: 'He is five years younger than me.'

We discussed current events. What impressed me most was the amazing coincidence of their and Lloyd George's opinions. The Webbs, too, do not believe in the likelihood of an *invasion* and regard the German 'blockade' of England as the main danger. They, too, do not know how England can emerge 'victorious' over Germany, especially after Churchill turned down the American proposal to send troops to England. The Webbs maintain that Germany is unable to defeat England, and England is unable to win the European continent back from Germany. Finally, the Webbs also think that the sole chance for England to 'win' lies in drawing the USSR over to its side, but the British ruling circles will never do so out of fear of Bolshevism. The Webbs are convinced that the British government does not want to improve Anglo-Soviet relations for that very reason. In this situation, they see nothing ahead but a long, hard, exhausting war that will lead Western Europe to attrition and destruction. There is one bright ray in the gloom: the USSR, which even now is moving rapidly towards a mighty economic surge. It's a very good thing that the USSR stays out of the war. It would be still better if it kept out until the war's end. Stalin is a wise leader who knows what he is doing.

I like talking with the Webbs. Clever old people. Wise old people. Besides, they are the ideal embodiment of the 'English spirit'. One can often deduce from their judgements what England will do and how it will behave in a particular situation. A perfect example of this was my conversation with the Webbs last year in mid-May, when the French front started crumbling but there was still no sign of a rout. I asked the old couple what England would do if France was taken out of the game.

Beatrice thought for a moment, as if weighing all possible options on her mental scales, and then answered firmly: 'Of course, England will continue the war alone. We have no other option. What happened during the era of the Napoleonic wars will be repeated.'

Sidney nodded his agreement. The Webbs were proved right.

2 March (2)

And so, Bulgaria has capitulated: yesterday the protocol of Bulgaria's adherence to the Axis was signed, and German troops began marching into Sofia.

A classic example of how an internal contradiction erodes the foreign policy of the whole bourgeois world!

Russophile sentiments are widespread among the Bulgarian population. Traditional Slavophile sentiments blend with the entirely modern sympathy of the poor towards the Soviet system. The national interests of Bulgaria, of course, would have been best served by close ties with the Soviet Union. In early December of last year we proposed a mutual assistance pact to the Bulgarian government, or even just our guarantee. Filov[i] and Co. needed only to say 'yes', and all would have been arranged. But they did not say 'yes'; instead they politely explained that since Bulgaria was not being threatened from any quarter, they found it untimely to discuss a pact or guarantees. The matter of Bulgaria's immediate future was thereby decided. What happened yesterday is the logical outcome of Filov's answer to the offer we made in December.

Why did the Bulgarian government decline the powerful support of the USSR?

The answer is quite clear: because the Bulgarian ruling circles, which consists of representatives of the kulak class and bourgeoisie of the comprador type, reasons according to the principle: better Hitler than Stalin. Under Hitler, they would keep their lands and capital and be permitted to serve as the lackeys of German capitalism; under Stalin, they would be deprived of their lands and capital and thrown into the dustbin of history. The Bulgarian upper crust chose Hitler.

Doesn't the same cardinal contradiction, the contradiction between national-state interests and the class interests of the ruling circles, seep into the foreign policy of other bourgeois countries as well? Didn't the French '200 families' lose the war because they thought: 'better Hitler than Stalin'? Didn't the British ruling elite headed by Baldwin and Chamberlain fail to establish good relations with the Soviet Union and thereby avert the war because it thought: 'better Hitler than Stalin'? Don't the British ruling circles headed

[i] Bogdan Dimitrov Filov, Bulgarian prime minister, 1940–44.

by Churchill sabotage improvements in Anglo-Soviet relations because deep down they think: 'better Hitler than Stalin'?

The fatal and ineradicable contradiction of two worlds. It will make itself felt for the duration of the war. But this circumstance gives hope for the future.

If the last war eventually led to the formation of the Soviet Union even though all the belligerent powers entered into it with no fears of a social order and in full confidence that capitalism would reign forever, then are there not even better grounds for believing that this war, into which the capitalist powers entered with inner trembling before the spectre of impending revolution, might eventually lead to the emergence of several new socialist or near-socialist states? Can it not happen that an armed cataclysm of such grandiose dimensions may pave the way to colossal social shifts in Europe?

Subbotić came by. In a very anxious frame of mind.

'The situation in the Balkans is bad, very bad,' he said, and went on to explain. 'Now that Bulgaria has joined the Axis, Yugoslavia is surrounded on three sides. Hopes for effective Soviet support have proved unwarranted. The Yugoslav government has to manoeuvre to gain time, but this is becoming increasingly difficult with each passing day. Yugoslavia is prepared to trade with Germany and develop economic relations to the maximum (all the more so as the German market is the sole external market for Yugoslavia today), but she does not want to go any further. Does not want to become a member of the 'Axis' or to allow the passage of German troops through her territory against England and Greece. Wants instead to remain absolutely neutral. But Germany demands more. How to behave? What should be done?'

In Belgrade, according to Subbotić, there is great commotion. He is unsure of what is happening there. It has now been eight days since he last had any news from his government. This makes him anxious. Momchilov also did not have any information from Sofia for some ten days before Bulgaria's access to the 'Axis', and then, like a bolt from the blue, came the news that Bulgaria had joined.

What will happen?

I tried to console Subbotić and explain our position to him. I said: 'Just wait! Everything will not be over today!'

The Czechs report:

(1) Although the Germans are creating the impression that they are preparing for an attack on Greece, their major objective is a strike against Turkey in order to proceed further to Syria, Iraq, Iran and Egypt. The Germans are going to concentrate up to 40 divisions in the Balkans for this purpose. Demonstrations of force against the Greeks are possible, so as to compel them to conclude a separate peace with Italy. Yugoslavia will capitulate to the 'Axis' in the nearest future.

(2) Three German divisions are deployed in Tripoli. They got there in the following way: transport ships carrying weapons (and some men) slipped through the Sicilian Straits at night and sailed straight on to Tripoli through Tunisian territorial waters. The French knew about it, but did not warn the British.

(3) There were disagreements about Greece in the Cabinet before the departure of Eden and Dill to the Middle East. Eden was of the opinion that the British were not in a position to help the Greeks effectively on land and therefore recommended not to embark on such assistance so as to avoid the experience of Norway and Dunkerque. Churchill, on the other hand, thought that in this case the British should take the risk: otherwise the prestige of England, particularly among small nations, would be ruined beyond repair. Before taking a firm decision the Cabinet resolved to clarify the situation on the spot and with this object in mind sent Eden and Dill to the Middle East.

(4) In Ankara, Eden and Dill discussed military rather than political issues, with the following outcome. In the event of German aggression, Turkey will defend the Rhodope–Catalca line, and England will render her maximal assistance (10–12 divisions). The British will provide Greece with air support, and operations in North Africa will shift to the defensive.

(5) The disposition of German forces in February: 60 divisions in France, 10 in Holland and Belgium, 6 in Norway, 20 in Central Europe (Czechoslovakia, Austria and Slovakia), 60 in Poland and 40 in the Balkans.

Duff Cooper has had a talk with the most 'trusted' diplomatic correspondents about the situation in the Balkans. The minister of information is in a pessimistic mood.

Yugoslavia? It will most probably follow Bulgaria. Turkey? Turkey will defend itself in the event of German aggression against it. The Turkish position in the event of German aggression against Greece remains uncertain. The formation of a 'Balkan front' against Germany? Very difficult, if it's even possible. First, all Balkan railways are in the hands of Germany, or will soon be so. Second, while in the last war the main German forces were engaged on the western and eastern fronts, today Germany has a huge 'unemployed' army at its disposal and can concentrate any number of troops in the Balkans. England, by contrast, would have great difficulty transporting large army units to the Balkans. Besides, England has to take the situation in Africa into account. Under these circumstances Turkey should play the decisive role in the formation of a 'Balkan front', but Turkey vacillates, reluctant to give a definite 'yes' or 'no'.

Yes, the minister of information is in a gloomy mood. He even left his listeners with the sense that he was preparing them for the imminent capitulation of

Greece. Whether that will happen or not is a different question, but such was the impression made by Duff Cooper's statements.

The minister of information spoke about the Soviet Union as well. In his opinion, the Soviet government wants the 'Axis' to win, but which 'Axis'? An exhausted and weakened 'Axis'. Duff Cooper maintains that Hitler is doing precisely what the Soviet government wants: he is scattering his forces over Europe, thereby paving the way not to his victory, but to exhaustion.

Duff Cooper spoke approvingly of the TASS communiqué of 3 March. In his view, it is bolstering morale in Turkey.

I'm getting information from various sources that Cripps is most unhappy about the current situation, does not see prospects for an improvement in Anglo-Soviet relations, complains of his isolation in Moscow, etc. In his opinion, the reason lies not in the British government's stance, but in the Soviet government's 'fear' of a conflict with Germany. Besides, he suspects that contact between Berlin and Moscow is far closer than many people think.

This is most unpleasant. It looks as though Cripps is turning into our enemy due to his political failures, failures resulting from the British government's reluctance to move towards rapprochement with us. I warned Cripps when he was leaving for Moscow that he might find himself in an awkward position through London's fault. An ambassador, after all, is akin to a travelling salesman. When he sells good commodities, he will be successful even if his personal qualities are quite ordinary. When he sells bad commodities, he is doomed to fail even if his personal qualities are excellent. Cripps has basically had nothing to sell for these past ten months. This is the source of his failure. But instead of directing his anger at his boss, who has not provided him with decent goods, Cripps prefers to curse his buyer, who for very good reasons has no wish to buy rotten stuff. Very short-sighted. But even clever people are often like that.[14]

6 March

More excerpts from my conversations with Epstein.

How does Epstein work? He does everything himself. Not only clay figures, but also sculptures from marble and granite (when he decides to use these materials). He chisels everything out with his own hand. Not all sculptors work like that. Rodin, for instance, whose studio Epstein visited several times, only made statues from clay with his own hands. Then his pupils reproduced it in marble or granite, using the appropriate measuring tools and instruments.

How does Epstein choose his models? His models are either people who commission their 'portraits' or people he seeks out himself. Many celebrities from the worlds of politics, art, literature and business have sat for him. He made the busts of MacDonald, Beaverbrook, Rothermere, Weizmann, Bernard Shaw, and many more. The sessions with Rothermere were amusing. This press baron did not want to waste time. So he did business during the sittings: dictated messages to his secretary, consulted with financial experts, speculated on the stock exchange, etc. Epstein said with a laugh: 'Rothermere made more money during one sitting than I've earned during my whole life.'

As for models of the second group, he looked for them everywhere and sometimes took them straight from the street. There were occasions when he suddenly saw a face that grabbed his imagination in the Underground or in an omnibus. He would immediately ask the person to pose for him. There were complications sometimes, even scandals in the case of women, but Epstein usually got what he wanted. He also searched for his models among outstanding contemporaries. So it was with the Abyssinian emperor, who visited England in 1936. His statue of the Negus (from the waist up) is magnificent. It breathes the tragedy of his life.

Epstein has long contemplated doing a large multi-figure sculpture, 'The Ship of Slaves', and is gathering material for it. I saw many sketches in his studio: heads, busts, figures of the Negro type (including the head of Paul Robeson).[i] Whether Epstein will realize his intention is unclear. He himself is less than definite about it.

I once asked Epstein whether he was a member of the Royal Society of Sculptors. I was certain he was.

'Oh no, no!' Epstein waved his hands. 'How could I be?'

And he told me the following instructive story. About 30 years ago (Epstein is 60), at the beginning of his career, he was commissioned to decorate the Medical Association building in the Strand with figures. He performed the job brilliantly, but caused an awful commotion in the press and in parliament. Why? Simply because the figures were unclothed. There was nothing amoral about them, they were simply nude. The protest campaign was led by the *Society for the Prevention of Vice* whose office, as ill luck would have it, faced the Medical Association building. The bosses of this 'Society' were so furious that they even stuck paper on their windows so as not to see the cursed naked figures. A fierce debate raged in the press. Questions were raised and answered in parliament. Should the figures be removed or not? Since opinions were divided, parliament finally decided to recruit the authority of the archbishop of Canterbury. The archbishop came personally to the Strand to carry out an *inspection*. Fortunately for Epstein, the then archbishop was a reasonable man, and the figures were not removed. But when soon afterwards two of Epstein's colleagues recommended

[i] Paul Leroy Robeson, radical black singer who was awarded the Stalin Peace Prize for his anti-imperialist activities. While in England he prevailed on Maisky to enrol his son in the school for the children of the Soviet diplomatic corps in London.

electing him to the RSS, he was blackballed. Epstein took offence and decided he could live perfectly well without the RSS. He himself has never applied for membership since, and others have not dared raise the matter again.

'The RSS is as nothing compared with those colleagues who, if only they could, would exile me to the farthermost corners of the British Empire!' exclaimed Epstein.

Epstein pays them back in their own coin. When I asked him if there were sculptors in England who deserved notice, he shrugged his shoulders, gave a bitter smile, and said: 'Not that I know of.'

In spite of all his *troubles* and financial difficulties, Epstein the sculptor is a proud man. Once in my presence he lambasted his clients, who understand nothing about art, his colleagues, who envy him, and his critics, who accommodate themselves to the tastes of the crowd. He exclaimed bitterly: 'This damned profession! I'd not advise anybody to become a sculptor!'

I said nothing for a while, but when Epstein had cooled down a little I asked: 'So, if you had to start your life all over again, you wouldn't become a sculptor?'

'Who, me?' Epstein replied in bewilderment. 'Oh, no! Let others find themselves different jobs, but I am a sculptor! And I don't want to be anything else!'

I smiled to myself once more: what a rare fusion of genius and child!

Aras called in. He again spoke at length about the urgent need for a Soviet–Turkish alliance and affirmed that the statement made by Saraçoğlu to Vinogradov in mid-January actually opened the path to an 'alliance'. If I were to tell him that the Soviet government favoured the idea of a mutual assistance pact in principle, he would put the question to Ankara in the clearest possible form. Then practical negotiations concerning the pact could be opened in Ankara or in Moscow, or 'even in London'.

I remained *noncommittal* and left the question open so that I could return to it at any moment or simply 'forget' about it. I merely noted that a pact without corresponding military agreements to sustain the pact is meaningless. Aras fully agreed with this and even set about fervently assuring me that it would not be difficult to conclude military agreements. I reminded Aras of the unsuccessful military negotiations between the USSR, England and France in 1939, but Aras exclaimed with the same fervour that England and France had not displayed a 'sincere desire' to form an 'alliance' during the Moscow negotiations, whereas Turkey today would like such an 'alliance' 'in all sincerity'. Despite all Aras's arguments, I'm not sure he is right. It even seems to me that Aras himself does not quite understand what kind of military agreements are in question here.

Regarding the visit of Eden and Dill to Ankara, Aras says it has not altered one jot the former position of the Turkish government. On the contrary, the English appear to have recognized this position as being quite correct. Its essence consists of the following. Turkey will defend itself resolutely. Its conduct in the event of a German attack on Greece will depend on the circumstances. Turkey will even allow the British to use its territory for military purposes (the newspapers announced this a few days ago), but only if Turkey itself enters the war. A scheme of the Egyptian type is out of the question in Turkey.

As far as the visit of Eden and Dill to Athens is concerned, Aras says the parties reached an agreement: the Greeks will not conclude a separate peace with Italy, and the British will give them their utmost assistance, not only at sea and in the air, but also on land. The latter may occur later, however. The Greeks do not want the British troops to land immediately so as not to 'provoke' Germany, with whom they maintain 'normal' diplomatic relations. This is also the reason why they do not allow the British to bomb the Rumanian oil fields using Greek bases. However, if and when Germany attacks Greece, the British troops will be *welcome*, provided there are no fewer than 10 divisions. If the British government intends to send only 3–4 divisions, it would be better not to send them at all.

I asked Aras how many divisions the British could land in Greece.

'Three to four divisions,' Aras replied.

'And where?' I inquired.

Aras said this would depend on the conduct of Yugoslavia. If Yugoslavia refuses to let German troops march through her territory, the British might well land in Saloniki and try to command the mountain passes between Bulgaria and Greece. If Yugoslavia does let German troops through, it would be difficult to hold out in Saloniki, and the Anglo-Greek front will most probably stretch along the mountain chains of northern Greece, including the famous Pass of Thermopylae.

12 March

I arranged a lunch for Beaverbrook and Alexander, inviting Prytz and his wife, Monckton, Strang, Cunliffe-Owen[i] and others.

Beaverbrook looked quite well, but he was very angry. He barked and fumed his way through lunch. The *troubles* in his ministry must have got to him. Beaverbrook is very optimistic in everything that concerns the air force. He declared that England was approaching parity with Germany in terms of both quantity and quality. England will achieve preponderance at the turn of the year, with a further significant growth in 1942, when American production will be fully developed. Beaverbrook hardly believes in the threat of an invasion, but

[i] Sir Hugo Cunliffe-Owen was chairman of an aircraft construction company bearing his name which produced parts of the Supermarine Spitfires in the Second World War.

he is most anxious about attacks on British commercial shipping. He consoles himself with the hope that the United States will formally enter the war in the near future.

Alexander asserts that the Battle of the Atlantic has already begun. The Admiralty has arrived at such a conclusion on the basis of a number of indicators, including the rate of losses over the last three weeks. Meanwhile, Alexander is confident that his department will manage to prevent an increase in losses in 1941 compared to 1940, and may even be able to achieve a decrease. We shall see.

Monckton told Novikov[i] that Cripps had been in an 'awful' mood before his visit to Ankara. He saw not the slightest grounds for hope. But he cheered up after meeting Eden. He sent Monckton a telegram the other day in which he says, among other things, that Eden will take up the question of Anglo-Soviet relations in all earnestness upon his return to London. We shall see. I'm not too optimistic in this respect.

[On 20 February, Maisky was elected a candidate member of the Central Committee of the CPSU. Trying to boost his rather precarious standing in England, he boasted to Butler about the 'great honour' which was 'a sign of approval of my work in general and here in London in particular'.[15] However, shrewd as he was, he could hardly fail to notice, as did observers in Moscow and abroad, that the full seat on the Central Committee which had become vacant after the expulsion of Litvinov was filled by Dekanozov,[ii] the Soviet ambassador to Berlin and one of the architects of the Ribbentrop–Molotov Pact. Maisky's election to the subsidiary position reflected Stalin's priorities in his efforts to secure at least a semblance of Soviet neutrality in relations with the belligerents.[16] It mirrored Molotov's decision to meet Schulenburg in person and to fob Cripps off with Vyshinsky, his deputy. By early March, Maisky's independence and manoeuvrability had been seriously curtailed by the new counsellor, Novikov, most likely working for the NKVD, who had been ordered to be present at all Maisky's top-level meetings. Maisky introduced Novikov to Butler on 5 March and to Cadogan a couple of days later.[17] Following a meeting with Maisky on 26 March, Butler grumbled that the ambassador was again accompanied by his new counsellor 'who is now always present at his conversations in the Foreign Office'.[18] Maisky brought Novikov along to his meeting with Eden on 16 April. 'He seemed,' observed Eden, 'to be a Kremlin watch-dog upon Maisky.'[19] Even the king was intrigued by the 'watch-dog'.[20] The exceptional practice of being always shadowed by Novikov eventually led to a confrontation with Eden shortly before the German invasion of Russia, but the practice ended with the outbreak of the war in the east.[21]]

---

[i] Kirill Vasilevich Novikov, recruited to NKID in 1937 after pursuing a successful career in the metal industry; counsellor at the Soviet embassy in Great Britain, 1940–42; head of the second European department of NKID, 1942–47; ambassador in India, 1947–53.

[ii] Vladimir Georgievich Dekanozov, deputy people's commissar for foreign affairs, 1939–40, and Soviet ambassador in Berlin, 1940–41. Before embarking on his diplomatic career, Dekanozov was a prominent official in the NKVD. A close associate of Beria, he was arrested with him and shot in December 1953.

13 March

The new US ambassador (John Winant)[i] has paid me his first visit.

The visit was preceded by a minor 'diplomatic incident'.

In the evening of 4 March I received by post a regular notification from Winant in which he informed me that he had presented his credentials to the king and wanted to visit me. The next morning my secretary called the US embassy and offered Winant the choice of two dates, the 6th or the 7th. Winant's secretary promised to reply on the same day, but no reply came until the evening of the 7th. In the evening of 7 March I sent a note to Winant, in response to his notification concerning the presentation of credentials, and mentioned in passing that as he had not been able to visit me on the dates I had proposed because of his numerous *commitments*, I would now be waiting for him to make the next step. My note had the desired effect. He received it on the morning of 10 March, after the weekend, and his secretary called the embassy right away and asked for an appointment that same day.

Winant makes a somewhat strange impression. Tall, dark-haired, with slow, demure manners, a listless, barely audible voice, and a pensive, introspective look, he is the polar opposite of his predecessor, the vociferous, jaunty, loquacious and flighty Joe Kennedy. I had to strain my ears to catch Winant's words.

We talked for about an hour. Winant said he had been eagerly awaiting this visit (something hardly attested by the events that preceded it). We discussed a number of current topics. Recalling our meeting in 1939 in Geneva (where Winant was then director of the International Labour Office). He said: 'You, the Soviet representatives, were most perspicacious. You had already understood where the game between the European powers was headed.'

I thanked Winant for his compliment, but could not return it: as far as I could remember, Winant had not shown great foresight in 1939.

I asked Winant: what are the reasons for the 'defeatist mood' towards England that is so widespread in the USA?

Winant sees two main reasons behind the sharp swings in American attitudes towards the war. First, the American public was not sure whether the Allies were waging the war in earnest. In the epoch of Chamberlain and Daladier, such doubts were entirely legitimate. Second, it is only natural that the American public has wanted and wants its country to keep out of the war. In the past there was a great deal that was unclear in this respect, too. The situation has now changed: Churchill's coming to power has dispelled any doubt Americans might have had, and Roosevelt's formula of the 'arsenal of democracy', backed up by Churchill's statement that there is no need for an

[i] John Gilbert Winant, US ambassador to Britain, 1941–46.

American army in Europe, has softened the fears of the American public on the second point. That is why the 'defeatist mood' in the USA has disappeared for the time being (besides, England has already proved its fighting capability). One can now expect aid to England to get going on the other side of the ocean under the slogan '*full steam ahead*'.

I asked what this meant exactly in regard to the most acute problem of today – commercial shipping.

Winant replied that the USA would not be able to do much in this field this year, but in 1942 it will be in a position to provide England with no less than 3 million tons of newly built ships.

Winant says that Harriman,[i] the 'personal envoy of the president' who has arrived in London, will be on the staff of the US embassy and will act as a high-ranking 'pusher' in all transactions between the USA and England concerning supplies, the delivery of weapons, etc.

15 March

Apparently we are facing a new flare-up of the war, a new battle between two mighty enemies. It is difficult to foresee the outcome of this second 'trial of strength', but it is possible to make an assessment of what the belligerents have at their disposal entering the 1941 'war season'. It is rather tricky to assess Germany's potential from London. But what about England? What will England take into the cruel battles that lie ahead?

I'll try to sum things up.

The navy. The navy has acquired 480 new vessels since the beginning of the war, including two 35,000-ton battleships (a third battleship of the same tonnage will be put into service in May and four more battleships are being constructed), 32 cruisers (of which 12 are heavy cruisers with 8-inch guns), 60 submarines and 140 destroyers and torpedo boats (by 1 July of this year), small-size vessels (corvettes, torpedo boats, mine-sweepers, etc.), plus more than 1,000 mosquito boats. The British government counts on having in the future 10 battleships and torpedo boats monthly. Thus, even considering all previous losses, the British navy is considerably stronger than it was before the war. There is one important shortcoming however: 25–30% of the available vessels are constantly under repair because the shipyards are overloaded and because the ships stay too long in the open sea (in this war the British navy has to do virtually the same job that was done in the last war by the joint navies of England, France, Italy, Russia, Japan and, towards the end, the USA).

[i] William Averell Harriman, President Roosevelt's special representative in Great Britain, with rank of minister, March 1941; US ambassador to the USSR, 1943–46.

The air force. During the past winter, the aviation has made tremendous progress. The monthly production of planes in England now reaches 2,000 aircraft (of which 1,500 are combat aircraft). It is planned to raise the monthly output to 2,500 once some new plants are put into operation towards the end of the year. Up to 600 machines (half of them combat aircraft) and 2,000–2,500 aircraft engines are delivered monthly by the United States. The USA is expected to supply at least 1,000 machines a month by the end of the year. In total, the British air force now has 19–20,000 combat planes, including 11–12,000 first-line planes (of which 6–7,000 are in England, 2,500 in the Middle East, and about 3,000 in the Fleet Air Arm, i.e. throughout the Empire). New, more powerful planes will be put into service this spring: the *Stirling* [sic], *Halifax* and *Manchester* bombers and the *Tornado* and *Whirlwind* fighters. There seems to be no lack of personnel (though I am a little sceptical in this respect). The problem of how to combat night air raids is yet to be resolved.

The army. The army currently numbers 4 million, including 2 million volunteers (aged 17–65) in the *Home Guard* for the special purpose of defending the isles against invasion, and 2 million conscripts in regular service at home and abroad. By and large, the *Home Guard* is well organized and armed. This force is very well suited to its purpose, especially the younger age group. In the regular army there are 50 divisions which may be considered well trained and armed (about 1 million men); the second million requires more training and more arms. The 50 first-line divisions incorporate six mechanized divisions, which are expected to increase to 10 before the end of this year and to 20 by the spring of 1942. To judge by their actions in Libya (where one mechanized division was engaged), the British mechanized troops are of reasonable quality. Military leadership (generals Dill and Brooke) is by all accounts capable and wise, but this still needs to be tested in practice. To the troops stationed at home should be added a further half million – from England, Australia, New Zealand, South Africa, India, etc. – which are fighting or undergoing training in the Middle East, in the dominions, and in India. On the whole, the condition of the army is much better now than a year ago, not to mention the period immediately following Dunkerque.

Commercial shipping. England's pre-war commercial tonnage amounted to 21 million, including 18 million tons at home. About 9 million tons has been added since the beginning of the war (the Allies, purchases, new construction, captures, etc.), giving a total of up to 30 million tons, or 44% of global tonnage as it stood on the eve of the war. About 5 million has been lost, so England now has about 25 million tons. Since losses have been compensated almost exclusively on the side of British tonnage, rather than Allied, the latter's capacity has decreased by only 5% compared with the pre-war period. Yet the English tanker fleet has decreased by about 40%. This is very significant. Even if losses stay on the same level in 1941 (by which I mean 90,000 tons weekly, as happened in the last seven months of 1940, when the Germans started attacking the British commercial vessels in earnest), the loss will be of no less than 4.5 million tons by 1 January 1942. Compensation will be hardly more than 2–2.5 million tons (new vessels built in England and the USA, German and Italian vessels requisitioned in American harbours, etc.). The net loss will be about 2 million tons. And there are grounds to believe that the losses in the coming season will be greater than last year. The tonnage deficit will definitely make itself felt in the winter of 1941–42 in terms of the delivery of supplies, food and so on. Moreover, as a result of the war waged by the Germans against British tonnage, English vessels are forced, as a rule, to take longer routes (e.g. around Africa to Asia) and to sail at a slower pace than usual (big convoys sail at the speed of their slowest vessels, the ships are delayed en route and in ports, etc.). *Shipping* is definitely the weak spot in British armaments this year.

The 'national front' has survived as a united force. The Labourites have been completely absorbed by the Tories and do all their dirty work for them (Bevin and Morrison toil in wholesale in the Ministry of Labour and the Home Office, with Attlee, Greenwood and Alexander executing special orders in retail). This state of affairs, of course, may lead in the future to the explosion of the 'united front' from below, but for the moment it strengthens the position of the ruling classes. For the 'machine' of the Labour Party and the trade unions still keeps a tight grip on the working masses. *Transport House* skilfully exploits in its own interests the workers' anti-fascist sentiments, which are very strong. Pritt told me the other day of his impression that no less than 95% of workers in factories and plants think roughly in the following way: 'First we eliminate Hitler and then we deal with our own lords.' Pritt clearly perceives the weakness of such reasoning, but the masses do not, and they think and act accordingly. Communist influence is very limited, especially after the *Daily Worker* was closed down. There is, of course, dissatisfaction within the wide circles of the proletariat, and it is gradually growing (the 'People's Convention' demonstrated this in January), but it is not yet very acute and does not constitute a serious threat to the ruling upper crust. All is relatively well in the Empire, too. True, Eire retains its neutrality, but Australia, New Zealand, Canada, and even South Africa are being drawn into the war with increasing force. Temporary 'calm' has been restored in India with the help of repressions. It is not stable, but it may well last for the duration of the current 'war season'. So it would seem that no major complications threaten the British government in the immediate future either at home or in the Empire (with the possible exception of India).

<u>Morale</u> among the broad masses of the population is now very strong. The victories in Africa, the insignificant human losses at the front, the respite in the air war over England in the last three or four months, the absence of epidemics,

the tolerable food situation (worse than last year, but by no means catastrophic) and, finally, the government's position – all this and much else creates an atmosphere of great confidence across the nation and a willingness to fight. The USA's open allegiance with England strengthens these feelings still further. The clear position of Churchill and Co. to 'fight to the end' does have an effect on both the state apparatus and the masses. Nothing remains to remind one of the era of Chamberlain, when the air was thick with corrosive rumours, gossip and reports (not always unfounded) about doubts, hesitation and indecision 'at the top'. The future will show how durable the present mood will prove, but today it is universal and, if nothing extraordinary happens, will most likely prevail throughout the current 'war season'.

So England, undoubtedly, is embarking on a new 'trial of strength' much stronger and better equipped than she was last summer. (However, even now England is still not prepared for a large-scale strategic offensive against Germany. England would prefer to remain largely on the defensive this year, but this would not exclude small-scale offensive operations, particularly in isolated theatres of war: in Africa, Sicily, etc.). Eden, it seems to me, was quite frank when he told me in our recent conversation (12 February) that the British government would not like to open a front in the Balkans in 1941 precisely because it is not yet ready to launch serious operations on the European continent. Whether or not the British government will be able to fulfil this wish is another matter entirely, however, for Germany will also have her say.

How do political and party circles here envisage the immediate future?

They are sceptical about the possibility of an imminent attempted invasion, but they can't rule out such an attempt later on, if England is weakened on other fronts and if serious disorders emerge at home.

They consider the German campaign against British commercial shipping to be the gravest danger. The 'Battle of the Atlantic' is commanding everyone's attention. Serious losses and problems are expected, but in their heart of hearts people are confident that even now England will somehow *muddle through.*

Next, they believe that the immediate future may see the launching of large-scale military operations in the Balkans and the Middle East, where Germany will aim for Asia Minor, Iraq, Iran, Egypt, etc. Major developments in the Spanish direction (Gibraltar, Morocco, etc.) are considered less probable.

Finally, people dream of the United States entering the war openly.

That is the general picture insofar as it may be discerned today. Time will show what lies ahead.

In any case, unless numerous signs prove deceptive, the new struggle between the two adversaries will hardly yield an end to the war this year.

24 March

I paid Winant a return visit. The American ambassador has decided to play the democrat: he has abandoned the luxurious house in which the representative of the USA usually resides and has settled in a modest three-room apartment above his office on Grosvenor Square. His wife will arrive soon, but he doesn't intend to change his residence even then. We shall see.

In our conversation, Winant let it be understood that in the near future US supplies may be convoyed by US military vessels (in one form or another). I inquired: 'How would the United States react if the Germans sank such a convoy?'

Winant answered with a timid smile on his lips: 'The answer to your question can be found in the recent past.'

He obviously meant the sinking of the *Lusitania* in the war of 1914–18.

Then Winant started lavishing compliments on me. In our conversation in Geneva in 1939, I had demonstrated outstanding foresight concerning the European situation. Now, in the embassy archives, he has found a record of my conversation with Counsellor Herschel Johnson on 1 March 1938. My

78. Maisky fraternizing with American Ambassador Winant and his wife.

statements of that time have proved most prophetic (I have a poor memory, incidentally, of the conversation with Johnson). Winant concluded half in jest: 'Should you happen to be in a prophetic mood again, please send for me.'

My general impression of Winant is quite clear: he is an advocate of US entry into the war, but is still trying to veil his opinion. Harriman, however, who is busy setting up a special 'department' at the embassy to supervise US supplies to England, is quite brazen in this respect. A few days ago, at a meeting of American journalists, Harriman declared 'off the record' that he hoped to see the United States at war within the next few months.

[Undated – could be any date between 28 and 30 March]

Aras came by. He is very pleased with our communiqué concerning Turkey.

'This is of course less than the alliance I would like,' he said, 'but still, it is an important step forward in the right direction. It is a starting point for a bloc of neutral powers in Eastern Europe and Asia Minor.'

Aras is also very pleased with developments in Yugoslavia. The situation is now very difficult for the Germans. How to advance on Greece? Through the Maritsa valley? This is politically hazardous, as Turkey cannot tolerate the presence of German troops on its Greek border: the entire fortified area at Adrianople would be outflanked. Turkey will have to intervene in the war if the Germans undertake something similar. Through the Struma valley? But here the topographic conditions are adverse in the extreme: a long narrow gorge (about 30 km) between high and steep mountains, through which there runs a rapid, unnavigable river and a single road on which two cars are not always able to pass. Even small forces are sufficient to defend one's positions here with ease. Through the Vardar valley? Yes, topographically this is the easiest way, but following the coup of 27 March in Belgrade, the Germans will not get the Vardar valley without a fight. That is why Aras thinks that Yugoslavia will be drawn into the war; it creates unexpected additional difficulties for Germany.

Germany's situation is further complicated by England's decision to fight in the Balkans in earnest. According to Aras (whose reports must always be treated with a degree of caution), two British divisions are currently stationed in Saloniki.

I enquired about the outcome of Eden's meeting with Saraçoğlu in Cyprus ([date missing] March). Aras assured me that Turkey's stance has not changed one jot and set about asserting, somewhat naively, that Eden was utterly delighted with the results of the meeting. My foot!

A visit from Simopoulos followed. The old man has recovered from the consequences of severe flu, but looks poorly all the same: he is thinner and greyer, and coughs.

Simopoulos considers our communiqué to be of exceptional importance: it signifies a turning point in the situation in the Balkans, perhaps a turning point in the whole war. He is terribly satisfied with events in Yugoslavia. He spoke at length about 'Serbian honesty' and 'Bulgarian perfidy'.

The English, in Simopoulos's opinion, have decided to fight in the Balkans in earnest, but he does not know how many British troops have landed in Greece. He says that the English conceal this even from the Greek government. He believes that the British government has earmarked considerable forces for Greece. Why does he think so? Because during the negotiations in Athens between Eden, Dill and the Greek government, the latter said unequivocally: either serious aid with land forces or no aid at all. A second Norway must be avoided at all costs. Eden and Dill allegedly agreed with this. We shall see.

I tried to discuss the strategic situation in the Balkans with Simopoulos, but to no avail: the old man understands nothing about strategy, mixes up mountains and plains, and doesn't know the difference between a division and a corps. When you ask him anything related to military strategy, he spreads his arms in perplexity and mumbles helplessly: 'You'd better ask my military attaché. I'm clueless in these matters.'

A rum job at a time when diplomacy has become strategy.

31 March

A visit from Harold Nicolson, whom I hadn't seen for ages – since last year, in fact. We chatted about current events, but mostly about the 'general strategy' of the war.

I told Nicolson that I fail to see how the Germans can beat the British or how the British can beat the Germans. Nicolson did not even try to dispute this. He confessed that he himself could not perceive an obvious way for England to emerge victorious over Germany, but added: 'Last summer, after the collapse of France, Churchill said: My belief that we shall win the Battle of Britain rests on faith. I can't prove anything to you. And we won!… The same may happen with our victory over Germany. I confess, however, that I can't prove to you or to myself by way of reasoning or logic that we should achieve victory; nor, more importantly, can I tell you how we can achieve it.'

Then we talked about the problems of 'reconstruction'. I noted that England might achieve victory if it were a socialist England, but that as yet I see no sign of her moving towards such a transformation. Nicolson agreed with me and said what he thought of Churchill: 'He is a fine leader during a war, but I'm far from convinced that he will prove so excellent when the time comes to solve domestic problems.' *Significant!*

* * *

Had tea with Shinwell. He scolded the Labour leaders and asserted, not without reason, that Attlee, Greenwood, Morrison, Bevin and others are a mere appendage to the Tories and, what's more, are perfectly satisfied with their situation. Shinwell expects nothing good from them.

He is greatly concerned about the war on British commercial shipping and the feeble efforts of the Ministry of Shipping (particularly as regards the repair of damaged vessels).

1 April

I saw Alexander today to ask for his assistance in the repatriation of 400 Baltic sailors. I told him the whole scandalous story of this incident from the very beginning. Alexander responded sympathetically and promised to help, after reminding me that since he is not a member of the War Cabinet he is not directly involved in this matter.

Then we talked about the last sea battle of 28 March. Alexander evaluates the situation as follows: at present, the Italian fleet has lost 50% of its combat efficiency. What is the reason for the Italian defeats at sea? Not the vessels (the ships, according to Alexander, are good), but the personnel. Their shooting is inaccurate and they lack skill in manoeuvring. At sea, all this is paramount.

'If the Italian navy,' added Alexander, 'had English crews, our Mediterranean squadron would have ceased to exist long ago.'

He lavished praise on Admiral Andrew Cunningham,[i] commander of the Mediterranean forces, and called him the '*great sea captain*'.

The Italian fleet, according to Alexander, headed out to sea from its own harbours, where it had been hiding until then, to prevent the transfer of British troops to the Balkans, and got itself into a pretty mess. Incidentally, there were 35 German officers among the rescued Italian crews (about 1,000 men). Obviously, the Germans now command the Italian navy.

* * *

I've received the following information:

(1) The actual purpose of Eden's and Dill's second visit to Athens is to try to establish a tripartite defensive bloc of Yugoslavia, Greek and Turkey. I doubt that anything will come of it.

[i] Andrew Browne Cunningham, admiral, lord commissioner of the Admiralty and deputy chief of naval staff, 1938–39; commander-in-chief in the Mediterranean, 1939–42; first sea lord and chief of naval staff, 1943–46.

(2) A Czechoslovak brigade comprising some 4,000 men is setting out for Yugoslavia. A thousand or so more Czechs will join them in Egypt. A Polish brigade is also on its way to Yugoslavia from Palestine.

(3) There are presently some 20,000 Polish troops in England, including 3,000 pilots. The other 17,000 guard the eastern shore of Scotland against invasion. Of these, remarkably enough, some 6,500 are officers!

I saw Beaverbrook in his ministry and asked him to intervene in the case concerning the repatriation of our sailors. I was afforded a magnificent welcome: ten thousand secretaries came to meet me, the minister himself saw me to the lift, and during our conversation he showered me with compliments and promised to raise the question of repatriation at today's session of the War Cabinet. He made it clear that he would insist that my demands be met. *On vivra – verra.*

Beaverbrook stated in passing that the Soviet Union has three 'true friends' in government: he, Eden and Alexander.

Then we spoke about British aviation, and Beaverbrook said that England currently suffers from an overproduction of aircraft: all the depots are crammed and there is nowhere to keep the planes. There is also a shortage of pilots. Production may have to be restrained or even reduced in the next months.

If this is true, it means that the scene has changed beyond recognition since last summer!

On parting I once again asked Beaverbrook to take measures to repatriate our sailors, and added: 'If the Ministry of Shipping is as "effective" in other matters as in the case of our sailors, I'm quite sure you'll lose the war.'

Beaverbrook was simply delighted. He roared with laughter for a long while before eventually exclaiming: '*There is much in what you say!*'

This time Beaverbrook did not poke fun at my *shabby coat*. No wonder! I was wearing a brand-new coat. It seemed to satisfy him.

* * *

Prytz dropped in. He confirmed indirectly what I had just heard from Beaverbrook about overproduction in the British aircraft industry. It turns out that a few days ago a 'high-ranking person' proposed selling two or three hundred British fighters to Sweden in exchange for high-grade steel and the like. Whether this comes off or not is a different matter (transportation is a problem), but it is obvious that the British do indeed now have an abundance of aircraft, particularly fighters.

Prytz said that during the last 5–6 weeks relations between Stockholm and Berlin have been rather tense. The Germans have started violating the Swedish–German agreement on the transit of German troops through Sweden and

Norway: instead of an equal number of troops heading in both directions, they have been sending more troops into Norway than they have been withdrawing. As a result, a concentrated force has been formed in Norway and keeps growing all the time. The Swedish government insists on the observance of the agreement. The Germans respond by delaying coal deliveries and halting the passage of Swedish steamers (one per month) from New York to Göteborg. In addition, the Germans disliked very much the major military exercise recently arranged by the Swedish government. On the whole, the situation is strained. Where will it lead? Prytz is troubled. He fears that after the 'liquidation of the Balkans' Hitler will propose to Sweden and Switzerland to join the 'New Europe' – and then what?

Prytz's news inclines me to take a rather sceptical view of the feasibility of Butler's plan to bring our sailors home on board a 'neutral' Swedish ship. Will this plan fall through as well?

2 April

Today I lunched with Sir Sidney Clive, marshal of the diplomatic corps *in suspense*, in Brook's Club (founded in 1780, Fox's club). From the beginning of the war, Clive was in France with the Red Cross, mostly in Dieppe. He returned to England after the defeat of France, lives in his manor house at Malvern, serves somewhere in the war industry, and has plenty of free time in which to think.

What about? Of course, above all about the war, and even more so about how it might be terminated. Clive has no clear ideas in this respect, but he willingly agreed with the prerequisites which I set out before him (of course, I outlined them in a very *mild* manner). *Significant!*

He inquired rather anxiously whether he could be of any help to the diplomatic corps at present. I replied that there was nothing to worry about on that front, but that if the food situation deteriorated, he could be useful.

I asked Clive: how is the French collapse to be explained? He told me the following story in reply.

Soon after the beginning of the war he happened to talk to a powerful French landowner in Brittany whose son had just joined the army. The landowner gasped and sighed and was full of trepidation about the future of France. Clive inquired about the reasons for this trepidation.

'You see,' the landowner replied, 'when I went to war 25 years ago, it was all very clear-cut. We, the French soldiers of the time, understood perfectly well that defeat would mean the end of France. It had to be avoided at all costs. So that's how we acted. My son reasons differently. He says: if we are defeated, many will suffer and experience all sorts of hardship, but all the same I will stay on my land, or at least on part of my land, and somehow I'll get through it. If we achieve a victory, the Popular Front will be in charge, and they will just cut our throats. That's why I'm greatly concerned about our future.'

3 April

Guo Taiqi came to see me yesterday and announced that he is soon to leave London (in a fortnight or so), as he has been appointed foreign minister of China.

I congratulated him, but he reacted without any great enthusiasm. I asked him why not.

'You see,' he said. 'I'm leaving London with mixed feelings. My appointment is a great honour, of course, but it is a very difficult and complicated task, and I am not certain of being sufficiently equipped to accomplish it.'

Then, adopting a more intimate tone, he continued: 'Here in London, everything is familiar to me. Relations are established. The most difficult time is already in the past. We have achieved victory. We need simply to develop and consolidate our gains. In Chongqing, things are different. I haven't been to China for some 10 years. The situation in Chongqing will be new to me. True, I know almost all the leaders, but I know little about the relationships between the leaders. Neither do I know the people in secondary and tertiary roles. China's international position is also very complicated. I'm a rather lazy person, and I've grown accustomed to a certain level of comfort. How will it be in China?… When the Generalissimo (that's how he calls Jiang Jieshi) proposed the post of foreign minister to me, I hesitated for a long while before replying. Eventually, I took the plunge. The main thing is that I haven't been to China for such a long time. If I miss this chance, I may completely lose touch with my homeland.'

I began to talk about the scale of the job confronting Guo Taiqi and the major opportunities he would have to influence the foreign policy of China in a direction conducive to her victory. Guo Taiqi agreed with me, but added somewhat thoughtfully: 'Yes, that's true, but on the other hand I'll be very cut off from the outside world in Chongqing.'

Guo Taiqi is not taking his family, which is currently in the United States, to Chongqing. Might this not be because he is unsure of how long he will stay there?

Gu Weijun, from Vichy, has been appointed Chinese ambassador to London instead of Guo Taiqi.

4 April

The Czechs report:

(1) Eden can't pull off a tripartite bloc of Yugoslavia, Greece and Turkey because of Turkey's position.

(2) The British have already landed six divisions in Greece, fully armed and equipped, with a large quantity of aircraft. Reinforcements continue to arrive.

(3) A great quantity of troops is passing through Prague in the direction of the Soviet border. There is a Geographical Institute in Prague which passed into German hands long ago. This Institute is now urgently engaged in producing detailed maps of the Ukraine.

* * *

Easterman[i] from the *Daily Herald* came by for a chat about current developments. Among other things, I asked him whether he thought it probable that the British government might be inclined to talk peace next winter should the current 'war season' prove indecisive?

Easterman shook his head and replied: 'No!'

I asked him to elaborate.

'You know,' Easterman replied, 'I'm not wholly English (he is an English Jew) and I take a rather critical view of the English, but I must tell you frankly that I see no prospect of an early end to the war. Why?… Well, simply because the average Englishman cannot even conceive of the possibility of his country being defeated. And by whom? *Bloody foreigners*? No, it's impossible, unthinkable. It's never happened before. It goes against the laws of nature. True, there have been instances when the English lost a battle, but they always won the war. So it was and so it will be. So it must be. That is why, when winter comes, the average Englishman will tell himself: "*Somehow we will muddle through.*"'

Then I had a visit from Glasgow (diplomatic correspondent of the *Observer*), who spoke at length about the general prospects for the war. His reasoning is interesting. This is what it amounts to: England is in a very difficult position. In the last war Germany was actually beaten by hunger, i.e. the blockade. In this war, the blockade is much less effective because Germany has seized nearly the whole European continent and sucks all its juices; and because Japan, Russia, Italy and even the United States are against England in the matter of the blockade. England is unable to beat Germany on dry land. The efficacy of the air war against Germany is nil. So it turns out that England has not got

[i] Alexander Easterman, one of Britain's leading foreign correspondents first for the *Daily Express* and then for the *Daily Herald*. A prominent member of the World Jewish Congress, he drafted in 1943, with the Allied governments, a joint declaration condemning the Nazi holocaust of the Jews.

even a single 'friend' in the world, while Germany has a long list of 'friends'. The countries which still keep out of the war, above all Russia and the USA, are disinclined to change their position as detached observers. It is clear that the situation for England is very difficult, even threatening.

I objected that the USA seemed to have assumed the role of England's ally.

Glasgow gave a disconsolate wave of his arm: 'Idle talk – there's plenty of that. You can't destroy German tanks and submarines with speeches. For now, America simply promises aid in 1942 and the following years. But we need help immediately.'

Glasgow sighed and concluded mournfully: 'America. America won't give us anything for free. Roosevelt's policy is a clever one. The United States will annex England by the end of the war.'

So, England's situation appears hopeless.

'How will it be,' I asked, 'the end of the war?'

'The end of the war?' Glasgow echoed in a different tone. 'We'll win, of course.'

I was dumbfounded and asked in bewilderment: 'But how? In what way? You've just said…'

'Well, what about it?' Glasgow interrupted me. 'The situation is difficult, but we shall win just the same. God will decide. I'm not saying that we, the British, are saints, but the Germans are even worse than we. So God won't forsake us.'

How very English! Every Englishman is instinctively convinced that '*we will muddle through*' and that Providence is of necessity on Great Britain's side.

6 April

Subbotić came by. He is in a gloomy mood. He says that Simović's[i] government is manoeuvring in the hope of somehow avoiding war. That is why the new foreign minister, Ninčić,[ii] summoned the German and Italian ambassadors to tell them that the Yugoslavian government does not renounce the pact concluded by Cvetković's government, but would like to discuss the forms and methods of its application with the German and Italian governments. There has been no reply from the Axis as yet. But Subbotić does not attribute any great significance to that. In his view, the situation is already cut and dried: the new Yugoslavian government cannot agree to let German troops through Yugoslavian territory, while Germany cannot meekly swallow the diplomatic and political affront it has just received – so war, it seems, is inevitable.

---

[i] Dušan Simović, general, led the coup of March 1941 against the Yugoslav government and headed the Yugoslav government in exile from 1941.

[ii] Momčilo Ninčić, foreign minister of Yugoslavia, following the coup against Yugoslavia's access to the Axis in March 1941, held the same post in the émigré government until January 1943.

6 April

Early this morning Germany attacked Yugoslavia and Greece.

Two days ago, Comrade Molotov summoned Schulenburg and, having informed him of the forthcoming signing of a Soviet–Yugoslavian pact of friendship and non-aggression, told the German ambassador that the pact would be concluded in the interests of peace in the Balkans, that peace in the Balkans was in the interests of Germany itself, and that he hoped Germany would observe peace in this part of the world. Schulenburg replied that he had nothing against such a pact between the USSR and Yugoslavia in principle, but found the moment of its conclusion 'unfortunate'.

Today Hitler responded to Comrade Molotov's démarche.

We shall remember this and draw practical conclusions. What conclusions? Time will tell. One thing is clear: through its policy in the Balkans, Germany is taking the fatal action of forcing the USSR to turn its front towards her. This does not mean that the USSR will rush into war against Germany. We shall do our utmost to avoid it. But the USSR is turning its front towards Germany. It cannot afford not to. The USSR cannot resign itself to the presence of German heavy artillery in Constanta and Burgas as a permanent phenomenon – a fact about which the Germans themselves recently boasted over the wireless.

Why has Hitler's policy recently taken such a turn? Is he consciously picking a fight with the USSR? Or does he not see any other way out of the current situation? Hard to say. But it is increasingly clear that we have played our 'German card' and will get little more from it (for as long as Germany remains in Hitler's hands, at any rate). The time draws near when we shall have to look for other cards.

And so the war season of 1941 has opened – nearly a year after the German attack on Norway (on the night of 8–9 April). One can't help but wish to pierce the veil of the near future with one's gaze and imagine how the world will look by autumn.

It's not easy being a prophet in our days, and I don't want to resort to tea leaves. I'll merely note that the beginning of the 1941 war season differs significantly from that of the season of 1940.

In Germany's favour: Germany possessed only Poland beyond its borders at that time, while now all Europe is subject to it in varying degrees, except for England, the USSR and half of the Balkans. Moreover, the prestige of German military might has been firmly established after the experience of Norway, Poland, Holland, Belgium and especially France. On land, Germany is considered 'invincible'.

In England's favour: the German offensive has entirely lost the element of surprise. Churchill has replaced Chamberlain as head of the government.

England has become much stronger in the air and on land during the past year and has defeated Italy in Africa. England has preserved its mastery of the sea. The USA has openly moved into England's camp. Hitler will face not only difficult topographic conditions in the Balkans (this was also the case in Norway), but also the resistance of militant tribes energetically supported by England (which was not the case in Norway).

Yes, there is a difference, but what will be the upshot of the current military season?

The events of the next three or four weeks may give us a clue. All will depend on whether or not the Germans succeed with their Blitzkrieg in the Balkans. Much will become clearer after that.

There is one more factor in the current situation, a factor of great significance – the Soviet Union. The position of the USSR is somewhat different from what it was a year ago, and it may change still further under certain conditions.

[On 25 March the Yugoslavs were forced by Hitler's familiar combination of threats and cajoling to join the Axis. The cards, however, were reshuffled two days later, when a bloodless military coup in Belgrade installed the 17-year-old Prince Peter[i] on the throne. On the night of 4–5 April, the Yugoslavs and the Russians concluded a friendship and non-aggression pact, which in retrospect has been hailed as courageous defiance of Germany. However, Stalin regarded it as a mere demonstration of solidarity with Yugoslavia which, he hoped, would suffice to deter Hitler from attacking her and draw him back to the negotiating table. Hitler, however, reacted swiftly, with a ferocious bombardment of Belgrade and a lightning campaign which brought the whole country under his control within less than a fortnight, followed by a swift occupation of Greece.

The German offensive coincided with an incessant stream of intelligence reports to the Kremlin about the increased German presence on the Soviet border: 37 infantry divisions, three to four tank divisions and two motorized divisions. Forty-three major violations of Soviet air space by German aircraft were registered within a month.[22] The vulnerability and deficiencies of the armed forces' defence were exposed in the January war games; this vulnerability was further enhanced by logistical shortcomings.[23] The games induced Stalin to seek to prolong and extend the scope of the Ribbentrop–Molotov Pact. This led to the hasty conclusion of a neutrality pact with Japan in the Kremlin on 13 April. In hindsight, the agreement seems to have been a tremendous coup, as it removed the threat of a second front in the event of Germany launching an attack on the Soviet Union. However, Stalin's pressing objective (overlooked by historians) was the wish, as he told Matsuoka, the Japanese foreign minister, 'to collaborate extensively with the Tripartite Pact partners'.[24] The overwhelming need to pacify Germany was exemplified by Stalin's unprecedented appearance at the station to see Matsuoka off. There he embraced Schulenburg, who was departing for Berlin for consultations that evening, and impressed on him that: 'We must remain friends and *you must now do everything to that end!*'[25]]

[i] Born in 1923, Peter II ruled through his regent, Prince Paul, from 1934 until 1941, when he was enthroned following a coup d'état.

7 April

I called on Subbotić.

I congratulated him on the pact of friendship and non-aggression between the USSR and Yugoslavia, signed on the night of 5 April. Subbotić was deeply moved: he embraced and kissed me, and there were tears in his eyes.

'The pact,' he exclaimed, 'has saved Yugoslavia's soul. Hardships and suffering may await our people, and the Germans may temporarily seize our country – it doesn't matter. Every Yugoslavian, and every Serbian in particular, will now know: Russia is thinking about us and, sooner or later, will save us. I'm not a communist, but I bow low to Stalin on the occasion of this pact.'

Subbotić saw the Yugoslavian queen yesterday (she lives in England with her two younger sons). She was also deeply affected by the pact between the USSR and Yugoslavia and used the same words: 'I bow low to Stalin on the occasion of this pact.'

Subbotić spoke profusely on this subject, stressing that the most important thing now is to lift the morale of the Yugoslavian people, something which our pact has greatly facilitated. He sees my visit as a further move in this direction. The Yugoslavian people will never forget the USSR's conduct in this critical situation and will draw from it the courage and hope they need for the hard struggle ahead. Despite the tragic circumstances, Subbotić is experiencing a sense of personal satisfaction: he has been working so long for rapprochement between Yugoslavia and the Soviet Union.

We then discussed the British position. It followed from Subbotić's words that here all is not yet clear. He was to meet Churchill today, but the prime minister was held up on business outside the capital and asked Butler to talk to Subbotić. During Subbotić's meeting with Butler in the latter's office, Churchill rang and asked Subbotić to convey his *message* to the Yugoslavian people: from now on Great Britain regards Yugoslavia as its ally; all the British Empire's resources are on Yugoslavia's side; and the struggle will be continued until the aggressor is definitively destroyed.

Subbotić is yet to receive any concrete information about aid. Butler was very evasive about this today, referring the matter to Eden and Dill: being on the scene, they would have a better idea of how to act. Moreover, they had been given broad authority. Butler was also evasive about the quantity of British troops in Greece. True, he hinted that the English plan involved the massing of up to 15 divisions there, but he would not say exactly how many had already assembled. Butler does not attach great importance to the German offensive in Libya, which makes Subbotić think that the British government is going to supply Greece with troops mostly from Africa. Butler is delighted with our pact with Yugoslavia. He congratulated Subbotić and asked him to convey his congratulations to me as well.

Subbotić complained that he was experiencing great difficulties in maintaining contact with his government. The Belgrade radio station was wrecked by the Germans on the first day of their attack. The Yugoslavian government was evacuated from the capital. Where to? Subbotić himself has no idea. The government has a radio station in Ljubljana, but it has a very weak signal and cannot be heard in London. Subbotić receives news from Yugoslavia via Switzerland or North Africa. That is why he is ill-informed about his government's plans. He believes that it will be difficult to defend the flat northern part of the country, but with British assistance a strong front can be created in the mountainous south-western region. For now, however, it is rather risky to speculate about the more distant future. I had the impression that on the whole Subbotić has little faith in the possibility of effective resistance to Germany.

Subbotić told me *en passant* that Simović's government tried to avoid any 'provocations' towards Germany until the very last moment. For instance, it turned down Eden's visit to Belgrade, as proposed by the English. Its dealings with the Anglo-Greek headquarters were conducted through the military attaché in Athens. Only now has the situation changed. But Subbotić does not know how close is the contact between the Yugoslavian general staff and the command of the Anglo-Greek forces. Nor does he know anything about Turkey's position. Butler told him today that the British government has informed the Turkish government of its desire to see Turkey participate in the struggle against Germany alongside Yugoslavia and Greece, but it does not find it possible to go any further lest the Turks suspect that the British government wishes to interfere in Turkish–Soviet relations.

9 April

Subbotić called to give me some very alarming news from the front. The Germans have broken through to Saloniki and Üsküb. The former defence plans are in tatters. New ones have to be improvised in haste. The main reason for the German success, according to Subbotić, is the new tank which can travel over mountains. The Germans employed a large quantity of such tanks and broke through the Yugoslavian lines. The Yugoslavian army doesn't know how to respond to the mountain tanks. It is becoming ever clearer that the Germans plan to deliver a blow in a westward direction, that is, toward Albania. If they succeed in this, Yugoslavia will be cut off completely from Greece and from the English.

* * *

In parliament to hear Churchill's speech. Churchill was evidently in low spirits. No wonder: the Germans occupied Saloniki early this morning. No hint of defeatism, however. On the contrary, he displayed anger and redoubled hatred towards Germany. The House shares this mood, to judge by MPs' remarks and comments during Churchill's speech and by their conversations in the lobbies. The political barometer still clearly indicates: 'Fight!'

On the whole, then, there is no panic, only anxiety.

As far as one can gauge, the initial plan of the British government was as follows: the British and their allies would not make any serious attempt to defend the flat northern part of Yugoslavia, but would establish a strong front along the mountains in western and south-western parts of Yugoslavia and stand their ground against Bulgaria in Greece and southern Serbia. The main blow was to be directed against Albania, in order to force the Italians into the sea as quickly as possible. The role of Yugoslavia itself in this plan was not quite clear: owing to a shortage of time and other reasons, the Yugoslavian military leaders and the command of the Anglo-Greek forces had failed to coordinate a programme for joint action. The roles of the British and the Greeks had been better defined. The British were to provide the second line of defence. Elliot, whom I saw in the lobby today, explained to me that the British did not want to repeat the mistake they made in Belgium last year, when the English and French took responsibility for the first line of defence themselves (i.e. when they occupied advanced positions at the last moment without preliminary preparations and the coordination of defence plans). In Greece the front line would be defended by the Greeks.

But now, after the lightning capture of Saloniki and Üsküb by the Germans, that entire plan is no longer relevant. It needs to be quickly altered. How? Nobody knows; even the war department seems to be at a loss. There was talk in the lobbies today that if Yugoslavia was lost, the British might try to use the Peloponnese as their base and hold the front in northern Greece from there. How serious is this? I don't know. Such a plan hardly strikes me as viable.

English dissatisfaction with Turkey is all too evident. Turkey was openly reprimanded from all sides today. Also evident are the attempts to take our pulse in connection with the new turn of events. Brendan Bracken talked with me on this subject in the lobby today. He said half in jest: 'You'd better remove road signs in the Ukraine double quick.'

Vansittart (I called on him yesterday) spoke in the same vein, predicting an early German attack on the USSR. But Vansittart is a little unstable these days: after his *Black Record*[26] he sees Germans everywhere, even under his bed.

I reply to all our unexpected and unbidden well-wishers that I fail to see any causes that render a clash between Germany and the USSR inevitable; but should such a clash nevertheless occur, the Soviet Union will take care of itself.

[Stalin's desire to seek an agreement with Germany at all costs was strongly motivated by fear that British provocation might entangle Russia in war. Contrary to Churchill's account, the massive concentration of German troops in the east was consistently misinterpreted by British intelligence, too, until just a week before the invasion. It was dismissed as 'a war of nerves' mounted by the Germans to secure positive results in negotiations, which (it was supposed in Britain) must be impending with Russia.[27] Rather than revealing the German intention of attacking Russia, Churchill's famous, albeit cryptic, message to Stalin in early April pointed to a German decision to postpone deployment against the Russians and divert the war to the Balkans. Such a decision, Churchill believed, exposed Germany's weakness and inability to simultaneously prosecute a war against Yugoslavia and Turkey, on the one hand, and Russia on the other. He hoped Stalin would use the lull to align the Soviet Union with Britain in forging a Balkan bloc.[28] The warning had the opposite effect: it fed Stalin's suspicion that the rumours of war were fabricated in London in an attempt to involve Russia in the war. 'Look at that,' Stalin told Zhukov,[i] 'we are being threatened with the Germans, and the Germans with the Soviet Union, and they are playing us off against one another'. His suspicion was reinforced by Cripps's unauthorized threats aimed at drawing the Russians away from Germany, warning them that it was not 'outside the bounds of possibility if the war were protracted for a long period that there might be a temptation for Great Britain (and especially for certain circles in Great Britain) to come to some arrangement to end the war'. This accounts for Eden's failure (at his first meeting with Maisky following his extended Middle Eastern tour) to convince the Soviet ambassador that it was in the interests of the two countries to bury the hatchet and stand up to the 'bad man'.[29] Well attuned to the Kremlin, Maisky attributed the British approaches to an obsession about seeing Germans everywhere, 'even under the bed'. He faithfully informed Moscow of his firm handling of such blunt efforts to involve Russia in war. He reported a well-orchestrated campaign by the British government and the press to 'scare the Soviet Union with Germany'. He was particularly disturbed by Churchill's speeches in parliament on 9 and 27 April, in which he predicted a German attack on Russia.[30]]

10 April

Sylvester called and asked me to visit Lloyd George. The old man had come to London for a day and wanted to talk to me.

When I entered his office, Lloyd George had just come back from lunch with Churchill. He said the prime minister was concerned, perhaps even somewhat *depressed*. The situation in Libya has taken a more serious turn than was initially anticipated. The British relied excessively on the obstacle provided by the Sicilian Channel and exposed Cyrenaica. The Germans, contrary to all expectations, assembled a relatively large force in Tripoli (including, Churchill

[i] Georgii Konstantinovich Zhukov, marshal, as chief of the general staff of the Red Army, he halted the German offensive at the gates of Moscow in December 1941; appointed deputy people's commissar of defence, 1942, and conducted the counteroffensive operations which brought him, at the head of the Red Army, to Berlin; Soviet minister of defence, 1955–57.

maintains, one mechanized brigade… Just a single brigade? Lloyd George has his doubts), and the results are there for all to see: Bengasi has fallen, and there are German tanks on the Egyptian border. The British government, of course, is responding, but does it have time? And can one count on the Sicilian Channel any longer?

The situation in the Balkans is even graver. The swift success of the Germans in the Balkans came as a great surprise to Churchill. The Greeks fought bravely, but what could they do against machines? Moreover, the Germans outflanked them by driving on through Yugoslavia. German and British troops will come into contact in the next few days: what will happen then? The prime minister is somewhat concerned. He does not yet know whether the imperial forces will manage to hold out against German pressure.

The general plan now boils down to the following: to defend the Olympus–Albania line. But will it come off? L-G is not sure. Should it become impossible to hold on in northern Greece, Churchill will try to entrench in the Peloponnese, but will this succeed? Again, L-G has his doubts. The situation in Yugoslavia is equally unclear. The British government is undoubtedly ignorant of what is happening there. Will the Yugoslavians be able to stop the Germans? Will the English be able to supply Yugoslavia, particularly if the Germans enter Albania and cut Yugoslavia off from Greece? L-G is very sceptical about the future of Yugoslavia.

Eden is returning to London today: L-G was informed about this by Churchill. Eden's mission in the Middle East, according to L-G, ended in a complete fiasco. Especially in Turkey. What will he do next? In this connection, the old man asked me what was happening in the sphere of Soviet–British relations. *Nothing doing*, I replied, and told him the unfortunate story of the repatriation of our sailors. L-G raised his hands in despair and exclaimed: 'Sheer madness! After all, the key to all these questions – Turkey, Yugoslavia, Greece – and indeed the key to the entire outcome of the war lies in Moscow!'

The old man fumed and cursed the British ruling circles for being 'blinded by class'. He made no exception even for Churchill. It seems that the prime minister now reasons in the following way: a German attack on the Soviet Union in the very near future is inevitable – because of the Ukraine, because of Baku – and then the USSR will fall like a 'ripe fruit' into Churchill's basket. So is there any point in making efforts to attract the USSR? Is there any point in trying to court it? It will all happen by itself.

L-G does not share this confidence in things taking their own course. He does not believe that Hitler will turn eastward against us. To do so he would have to employ nearly his entire army. What would happen in Western Europe then?…

The old man, nonetheless, thinks that we, too, are in a very difficult position. What if Hitler attacks Turkey? Will the USSR be able to observe German seizure of the Straits with equanimity?

I replied in my usual spirit: namely, we can take care of ourselves. The old man shook his head and answered: 'Don't play with fire! The German army is a terrible machine. Once the Balkan campaign is over, there will be no force left in Europe which could even conceive of opposing Germany on land, except for you. Will Hitler accept such a state of affairs? I doubt it. Hitler, after all, strives for global domination. Moreover, he will be left with an idle army of several million, intoxicated with success and demanding employment. Will Hitler be able to resist the temptation to divert it to the east?'

I took issue with this, pointing out that the Soviet Union has in reserve, as a last resort, a force such as no other state can boast: the social discontent of the lower classes in all capitalist countries. I illustrated my point with the examples of Rumania and Bulgaria. If social discontent is mobilized, organized and supported, it can become a factor of major strategic importance (not to mention its political significance).

Lloyd George listened to me very attentively and exclaimed: 'Pray God that you are right! If your calculations are correct, I've just heard the best news in many a long day... So, there is a way of bringing Hitler to book!'

And the old man once again cursed the British government for its 'Russian policy'.

11 April (1)

I lunched with Dulanty[i] at Scott's. Dulanty told me a curious story about Suñer's[ii] conversation with Donovan,[iii] the American colonel who travelled around Europe as yet another 'special envoy' of Roosevelt. Donovan is Irish and an old and intimate friend of Dulanty.

When Donovan was in Madrid a month ago, he wanted to meet Franco. Suñer did not want them to meet, and made sure that Donovan left without seeing the *caudillo*. He had a rather frank conversation with Suñer instead.

Suñer told Donovan that he was absolutely confident of Germany's eventual victory. In his opinion, Hitler will soon become ruler of the entire European continent west of the USSR. France and Italy will be part of his empire. England will be offered the role of *junior partner* in his scheme. If England refuses, she

---

[i] John Whelan Dulanty, Irish high commissioner, 1930–50.
[ii] Ramón Serrano Suñer, Spanish minister of foreign affairs, 1939–42.
[iii] William Joseph Donovan, major general, US special mission to England and coordinator of information, 1941–42; director of strategic services, US, 1942–45.

will be annihilated by either invasion or blockade. Hitler is not going to wage war against the United States – that would be sheer folly. But having seized Europe, Hitler will launch a violent economic war against the United States. Spain will not be able to keep out of the 'new order' taking shape in Europe and will shortly enter the war on the side of the Axis.

Suñer's views undoubtedly reflect those now prevalent in Berlin.

Dulanty complained of the economic difficulties ensuing from the Irish government's desire to remain neutral at all costs. The British government has stopped supplying Ireland with bread, sugar, tea and petrol. Neither does it want to give Ireland dollars for the purchase of essential food products in the USA. Tension is mounting in Ireland. For instance, if the two Irish ministers who are presently in the United States fail to buy and transport 30,000 tons of wheat in the next few weeks, Ireland will be left without bread in July and August (until the next harvest).

In the course of the conversation, I hinted 'as a matter of personal opinion' at how the problem of the five detained ships might be resolved: the legal case is postponed *for the duration*, and in the meantime the Irish government takes the ships from the Soviet government on time charter. The idea appealed very much to Dulanty and he promised to contact Dublin about it at once. Then he asked: 'And you, perhaps, could sell us the 30,000 tons of wheat?'

I replied that this was not impossible and, if Dulanty wished, I could make further inquiries in Moscow. Dulanty jumped at the offer at first, but then cooled down quickly, as if he'd just remembered something: 'No, better wait before making inquiries… You know our people… They'd say: What? Taking bread from infidels? They may even accuse me of entering into negotiations with a "godless state" without the necessary authority, while the purchase of wheat has been entrusted to ministers in America.'

I did not insist.

The sentiments that reign in Ireland are quite something!… Such is the darkness in which the world still wallows!

11 April (2)

Aras came to see me. In complete panic. He calls what is happening in the Balkans '*terribles evenements*'. The Balkans, in his opinion, are done for. Kemal[i] had always told him that the Balkans could remain independent only by forming an alliance of mutual assistance. Aras has been striving to create such an alliance for many years, but without success ('Bulgaria is to blame!'). And this is what it has led to. Aras feels so miserable on account of the latest events

[i] Mustafa Kemal Atatürk, the founder and president of the Republic of Turkey, 1923–38.

that he has not wanted to see anybody in recent days, neither the English, nor the Balkan ministers. (I think Aras has another, more important motive for avoiding meetings: Turkey's position makes it far from pleasant for him to meet the Yugoslavians, Greeks and English.)

What next? Turkey will not, of course, take action now: the strategic situation is utterly unfavourable, especially after the Germans took Dédéagatch. The British are displeased, but can do nothing about it. The Turks have to mark time, to manoeuvre and, what is most important, to improve their relations with the Soviet Union. Aras spoke of the latter at length and with great insistence. Expressions such as 'you and we', 'we and you' peppered his speech. One's general impression is that the Turks want to find someone to hide behind. It is also unclear how they will behave if the Germans, having completed the Balkan operations, directly raise the question of their joining the 'Axis'.

What are the immediate prospects? Aras thinks that having 'liquidated' the Balkans (of which he seems to have no doubts) the Germans will have the choice of three possible directions: Turkey, the USSR or North Africa (including Gibraltar, French North Africa, etc.). Aras tries to convince himself that North Africa is the most advantageous direction for the Germans and that that's where they will go, but it is evident that he is plagued by doubts, for he told me that in about three months' time Turkey will be faced with a critical juncture.

11 April (3)

Guo Taiqi came by for his farewell visit. In a few days he will be leaving England and heading for his new post in Chongqing via the USA. We shall see what kind of foreign minister he will make.

Guo Taiqi argued at length and with ardour about the need for a united national front with Chinese communists; he promised to cooperate towards this end. He also spoke much about the fact that a genuine and lasting national surge in China is possible only on the basis of sweeping social reforms, particularly regarding the peasantry. He added, somewhat naively, that all Guomindang and Communist Party members are essentially agreed on this point. Disagreements emerge only about the forms and timing of these essential reforms. Just like Goethe's Gretchen.

In the sphere of foreign policy, Guo Taiqi intends to pursue a line of very close friendship with the Soviet Union and very close 'allied' relations with the 'democracies', i.e. England and the United States. I wonder how well these can be combined. We shall see.

This is not the main point, however. What is most important is the extent to which Guo Taiqi's good intentions will be welcome in the atmosphere of Chongqing. And will he be able to demonstrate sufficient will-power and independence to pursue his line should he encounter resistance (as is very likely to happen). Jiang Jieshi, after all, is a strong and authoritarian man. Once more: we shall see.

Guo Taiqi's visit made me somewhat sad. He came to London three months before me, and we have been good colleagues throughout these eight years. We've seen each other often, had long talks, and got used to one another. Relations of trust have been established between us (as far as trust is possible, of course, between a Soviet and a bourgeois diplomat). Guo Taiqi never deceived or misled me. Naturally enough, he didn't tell me everything and preferred to maintain silence on some topics; but when he did tell me something, I knew it to be true. I repaid him in the same coin. We also met several times in Geneva, which he frequently visited as a Chinese delegate. There, too, on the shores of La Léman, we retained a friendly tone in our relations. So many of my memories of diplomatic life here are associated with Guo Taiqi: receptions in the Palace, ministerial dinners, fashionable 'garden parties', political lunches, semi-official 'weekends'...

Eight years of orderly routine and habit – and now Guo Taiqi is leaving London *for good*! His departure serves to remind me of the time that has passed since I first set foot on English soil as *Ambassador*. It also reminds me that nothing lasts for ever and that the time will soon come when I, too, will have to leave London *for good*. Well, I'm always ready. To tell the truth, coming to London in October 1932 I never thought I'd be stuck here for so long. I thought I might remain in London for five years or so, but as for staying longer – it didn't even cross my mind!

Bidding farewell to Guo Taiqi, I made a comment in this spirit. We recalled our 'contemporaries' in the diplomatic corps who arrived in London at about the same time: Hoesch, Grandi, Corbin, Bingham. The twists and turns of fate! 'Some are no more, others are far away'[31]... And now Guo Taiqi is leaving. He grinned and said, with a friendly pat on the shoulder: 'You remain to *hold the fort*!'

13 April

A week has passed since the beginning of the German attack on the Balkans. What are the results?

For the first 3–4 days the German *Blitz* was triumphant. With lightning force, the Germans drove on to Saloniki (bypassing Struma), Üsküb and Monastir, nearly reaching Albania. They unleashed new tanks specially adapted to the mountainous terrain (3–4 tons with one small gun and two machine-guns). They captured Belgrade, Zagreb, Ljubljana and a few towns in the flat northern country. Belgrade was viciously bombed from the air. They set up a 'Croatian state' with Pavelić[i] at its head.

What next? We shall see. During the past three days the Germans came into contact with the major Greek and British forces along the Olympus–Lake Ohrid line. The Yugoslavian army, distraught at the beginning, seems to be recovering from the initial shock and is putting up more effective resistance. The next 8–10 days will be crucial. If the Germans manage to maintain their *Blitz*, they will conquer the Balkans soon and Turkey will be next on the agenda. If, on the contrary, the British, Greeks and Yugoslavians manage to stem the German advance, or at least make it slow and costly, the attack on the Balkans will be the first German failure on land, with all the ensuing consequences.

Events in North Africa will be equally important. The Germans took the whole of Cyrenaica last week and even crossed the Egyptian border. True, only mechanized units operate on the German side so far, repeating Wavell's manoeuvre in the opposite direction, and German victories have not yet been consolidated by infantry. Besides, the Germans, who do not control the sea, face serious problems with supplies. Petrol, for instance, they have to deliver by air. Nonetheless, the British are in a very embarrassing position. The next 8–10 days will be indicative here, too: will the British succeed in thwarting the German advance?

We shall see.

14 April

The communists are going to buy a small provincial newspaper in Wales to transform it into the central party organ instead of the banned *D.W.* The deal has hit a few snags. One is that the present owner insists on handing over to the communists not only the newspaper and the printing-works, but also his sole reporter, who has been on the paper for the last 44 years!

Imagine that: 44 years as the reporter of a small provincial paper! That's the measure of British stability!

Another vivid memory comes to mind.

The year was 1925. I was counsellor in London and head of the embassy's press department. In order to establish closer contacts with the *Manchester Guardian*, I went to Manchester to get acquainted with *C.P. Scott*,[ii] the paper's well-known editor. He received me cordially, introduced me to the editorial

---

[i] Ante Pavelić, the Croatian fascist dictator, placed as the head of the puppet state of Croatia by Hitler, 1941–45.

[ii] Charles Prestwich Scott, editor of the *Manchester Guardian*, 1872–1929, and its proprietor from 1905 until his death in 1932.

staff, showed me how they worked and told me many interesting things about the history of the paper and the city of Manchester. When we concluded the business part of our conversation, concerning Anglo-Soviet relations and other matters, I asked Scott: 'I heard or read somewhere that Marx and Engels once worked for the *Manchester Guardian*. Is it true?'

Scott assumed a serious and thoughtful look. He tossed back his handsome head with its high forehead and thick grey hair (Scott was 75) and seemed to lapse into reminiscence. Then, as if thinking aloud, he said: 'I joined the paper in 1871 and became its editor in 1873...'

He paused for a minute, and it seemed he was trying to pierce the dark veil of the past with his inner eye. Finally, he concluded: 'No, I have no memory of that!'

And in order to remain *on the safe side*, like a true Englishman, he added in an accommodating tone: 'Maybe it happened before my time.'

I was amazed: Scott had been working for the *Manchester Guardian* for 54 years, for 52 of which he was its editor! Such British stability!

But my amazement did not end there. Next day I visited the *Ardwick Cemetery* where, as I knew, the renowned Chartist leader Ernest Jones was buried. The cemetery warden, who resembled a moss-grown old tree, showed me Jones' grave. I stopped and started examining the gravestone, erected by the Trades Union Congress, and read the inscriptions. I was in no hurry. I walked round the grave a few times and saw, to my surprise, that the warden was still there, although I had already given him the customary tip. He, too, was attentively inspecting the gravestone. Suddenly words flew from the warden's lips: 'What a funeral that was! How grand it was! The whole city followed the coffin...'

I looked at the warden in bewilderment. He seemed to be lost in distant memories, and I asked him gently: 'How come you know about Jones' funeral?'

'How?' the warden exclaimed, somewhat offended. 'Well, I was already working in the cemetery then as a young boy.'

I was dumb-struck. According to the inscription, Ernest Jones died in 1869. Now it was 1925. So the warden had been 'on duty' for 56 years! That's British stability!...

But should we really be surprised that the English mentality differs so drastically from our Russian one, and indeed the continental one?

Today I attended a service in the Greek Church on the occasion of the enthronement of the new king of Yugoslavia, Peter II. I was in this church not long ago for Metaxas's funeral service. The diplomatic corps was in attendance, the duke of Gloucester was representing King George, and Cranborne – the British government. The ever-present Monck was there, too. A fair crowd. This time the service was conducted by both Greek and Yugoslavian priests. One of the latter read the prayers and the Scripture in Slavonic and I understood every word. I couldn't help recalling Omsk and the church in our gymnasium.

The press made a big *fuss* of my presence in the church. It's understandable: they want to demonstrate that the USSR is on the side of Yugoslavia, that is, on the side of England, that is, against Germany. They even suggested I was following special instructions from Moscow. Nonsense, of course. I had no instructions whatsoever. I was merely observing the rules for participation in diplomatic ceremonies, wherever they take place.

There was one curious incident. I noticed a young woman fainting during the service and being carried out of the church. I couldn't make out her face as she was standing quite far away from me. In the evening, Andrei brought the following *joke* from Fleet Street: 'Princess *Vsevolod of Russia* fainted at the sight of Maisky!'

Ha-ha-ha!

I exchanged a few words with Aras in church. He was very pleased with Zaslavsky's 'refutation' in *Pravda* yesterday (about the fact that 'it did not occur' to the Soviet government to send a congratulatory telegram to Peter II). Aras says that the German government is ratcheting up the pressure on Yugoslavia and Greece, and that Eden and Dill have flown to Athens again to counteract this. He also says that Belgrade has established close contact with Moscow and Ankara. Its outcome will determine Yugoslavia's policy.

15 April (1)

I've just returned from the grand reception given by Guo Taiqi to bid 'Adieu!' to his numerous friends and acquaintances. There were about 600 guests – ministers, diplomats, journalists, politicians, MPs, businessmen from the City. London has not seen such a big reception for a good long while, perhaps since the beginning of the war. The guests were elated and positively radiant: 'high society' has missed such diplomatic occasions terribly.

In two days' time Guo Taiqi will be flying to America via Lisbon. And here am I, trying to reconstruct his image, to sketch a brief outline of him from our meetings over long years, from conversations, observations and impressions.

There is nothing remarkable about Guo Taiqi's appearance: a short, miniature, almost skinny Chinaman with a round, typically Oriental face, a rather flat nose, and a pair of big horn-rimmed glasses resting on his nose. When he takes off his glasses (which happens from time to time), his eye sockets look terribly small and his face absolutely flat. One cannot guess his age by his appearance: he may be 35 and he may be 60. In fact, he is about 50. Guo Taiqi's movements are even, unhurried and smooth. They reflect his temperament and his nationality. As with many other Chinese people, I was

79. Maisky being introduced to chopsticks, while Lord Cecil resigns himself to using a spoon.

80. Mission accomplished…

always most impressed by a kind of subconscious sense of the venerability of his race, a kind of majestic serenity nurtured by the thousand-year history of his nation. How many times during our conversations did I fly into a rage, become irritated or indignant at one or other action by the British government, one or other machination on the part of Japan? But Guo Taiqi always preserved an imperturbable calmness and merely observed: 'It will pass…', 'It will change…', 'One must not lose one's patience…'

All the time I had the feeling that, gazing at me from the height of the 5,000-year history of his people and smiling to himself like a wise old man before an excited youngster, Guo Taiqi wanted to say: 'Yes, many things have happened in my life… Many things… Good and bad… I used to get excited, too, like this youngster, but not anymore. Life has its own equilibrium. One must learn to wait – and it will come… It will come!'

Indeed, aren't all European nations (even the German, French and English, to say nothing of young Russia) greenhorns compared with the Chinese? The English measure their precedents by the century, while the Chinese measure them by the millennium. A Chinaman, speaking about the most recent events, will let slip: 'There was an incident at the time of the Tang dynasty…'

Or: 'Poet so-and-so said two thousand years ago…'

And so on and so forth.

Guo Taiqi comes from a family of 'Chinese scientists', from the Yangtze valley. He became an orphan at a young age, and ended up in the United States where he studied political science at the University of Pennsylvania. That is why he speaks perfect English with a slight American accent. He then returned to China, where he took an active part in the national revolutionary movement in the ranks of the Guomindang. Fought in the war of 1926/27. He remained with Jiang Jieshi and occupied various posts in the Chinese government. In 1932, he conducted the armistice negotiations with the Japanese in Shanghai. At the end of that year he arrived in London, where he served as a Chinese envoy before becoming ambassador. As a diplomatic representative of China, Guo Taiqi was very active and successful. He had many connections and acquaintances, was well informed, and displayed much common sense in his judgements of people and events. He won himself a good reputation in the Foreign Office and political circles. He maintained friendly relations not only with the right but also with elements on the left. He displayed interest (whether genuine or not I can't say) in the theatre and arts.

Needless to say, Guo Taiqi had his weaknesses, too. He was a sybarite and grew ever more accustomed to the effete bourgeois lifestyle. He had some shady sources of income: I nurture grave suspicions that he exploited his diplomatic status to make some money on the side through contraband. Strange things also went on in his family life. He sought to keep his wife (a fat, uncultured and rather common Chinese woman) at a distance, whether in China or America. Here in London, he always had young and pretty compatriots following him around. But, after all, Guo Taiqi is a bourgeois diplomat, and a Chinese one at that – it would be absurd to apply the standards of communist morals to him.

In the sphere of politics, Guo Taiqi has increasingly fallen under British influence. Now, in the context of the ongoing war, he has become a confirmed supporter of the Anglo-American line. Throughout the eight years of our stay in London, however, he has also tried to strengthen relations with the USSR. He maintained close and cordial relations with me and strove to facilitate improvements in Anglo-Soviet relations to the best of his ability. And when, paying me his farewell visit, he described his line as one of close friendship with the USSR and close friendship with England and the United States, he was undoubtedly being sincere. But is such a line possible? Is it feasible in the current situation?

I don't know. Events will show.

Will Guo Taiqi continue to adhere to this line?

I don't know that either. People often change. Especially in our days.

15 April (2)

Subbotić came to see me. He announced, somewhat excitedly, that he had just received a telegram from Simović in which the prime minister suggested he should keep in very close touch with me. The text of the telegram almost seems to assume the USSR and Yugoslavia to be allies. Subbotić wished to find out whether I had any special messages from Moscow to this effect.

I replied that I had no such messages, but thought that Simović's telegram was the natural outcome of the friendly relations established between our countries.

Subbotić is in a foul mood. There are many reasons for this, but here are the main ones: (1) The situation at the front is bad. The Germans have 2,000 tanks. Yugoslavia is not prepared for such an attack. (2) The situation with the British is unsatisfactory. So far Subbotić has failed to meet Churchill. He has not seen Eden either. He could not even see Butler: 'They've gone away for Easter.' Perhaps, but is this a time for holidays? And what use is that to Yugoslavia? It looks as if the British government does not treat its new ally seriously enough and does not care about its fate. The British government has its hands full in North Africa and Greece. It has no time for Yugoslavia. (3) He has almost no contact with the Yugoslavian government. Where are they? What are they doing? Complete mystery. He gets no instructions from his government. All negotiations concerning aid are conducted, as far as he knows, through the British military attaché in Yugoslavia. But what is the result? That's also unknown. The telegram concerning contact with me is the only one Subbotić has received from home for several days. All his information about the situation in Yugoslavia comes from the English.

I tried to encourage Subbotić, referring, in particular, to our experience of civil war. He listened and often agreed with what I said, but did not believe it.

17 April

Subbotić called on me again.

He saw Butler on the evening of the 15th and Eden on the 16th. He did not meet the prime minister. Subbotić's general impression from the talks is bad. The British government, apparently, either will not or cannot provide effective aid to Yugoslavia. On his own initiative (he still does not have any instructions from his government), Subbotić appealed to Eden with a request for British naval aid to Yugoslavia in the Adriatic. Eden responded warmly and promised all kinds of support, but the Admiralty found thousands of reasons why the aid could not be provided.

The British government, it seems, does not set great hopes on Yugoslavia's continued resistance. Eden spoke with Subbotić about the evacuation of King Peter and the Yugoslavian government. But Subbotić himself has no contact with the latter. All his efforts in this direction have been in vain. Also a bad sign.

Subbotić spoke at length about how the Soviet Union could drastically enhance its prestige among the Yugoslavian people by opening her borders in this difficult moment to Yugoslavian émigrés. For purely objective reasons, only a few Yugoslavians would be able to avail themselves of our hospitality, but the very fact of the borders being opened would have a great impact on morale. Why not do it?

22 April

Visited Aras. Found him somewhat calmer than on 11 April. The reason for this may be a sense of relief: the next item on the German agenda, Aras says, is not Turkey but North Africa. The Germans have even withdrawn the greater part of their troops from the Bulgarian–Turkish border: there are only three divisions left instead of the former eight, and those are stationed at Philippopolis.

Aras assures me that Hitler and Franco have already made a deal: the Spanish government has agreed to join the 'Axis' with all the ensuing consequences. Everything will follow the 'Bulgarian model'. Germany will enter Spain and attack Gibraltar. In anticipation of these events, the Portuguese government is already preparing to evacuate to the Azores. Hitler will advance from Spain to North Africa, subjugate Morocco, Algeria, Tunisia, and later…

Aras spread out his arms in uncertainty, as if to say: 'Later anything is possible.'

Aras says the Germans are now bargaining with Pétain about letting the German troops pass through France as well (the border between occupied France and Spain is too narrow for big formations), and he is sure they will get their way.

The position of Turkey? It's perfectly clear: to stay out of the war at all costs. To hold onto the USSR. 'We'll do as you do', said Aras, repeating this formula several times during our conversation. In Aras's opinion, it is unlikely that Germany will now strike at Turkey or make tough demands of her (such as the transit of troops). What's more likely is that the Germans will try to enfeeble her from within. They may demand that Turkey join the 'New Europe'. What will Turkey do then? Aras does not know. Personally speaking, he would say to the Germans: We'll do as the USSR does. Aras won't venture to say how Ankara might act. I was left with the impression that Turkey's capitulation cannot be ruled out. We shall see.

Aras told me the following about the situation in Greece. The fight is basically over. The English have decided to evacuate Greece. Their objective is to save their forces and weapons, as well as to rescue the maximum quantity of Greek troops (a third to a half of the Greek army, according to their calculations). The Greek government and the king are moving to Crete. The English will also defend the Greek islands. But the focal point of the war now becomes Egypt. And Aras is far from certain that the English will manage to defend it.

23 April

Lunch with Greenwood. Hadn't seen him for about two months.

His mood is so-so. He says Greece will be evacuated, and the British government will try to save as many British and Greek troops and weapons as possible. The defence of the Greek islands will be maintained, in particular of Crete, to where the Greek king has already moved. Egypt is now the centre of attention. Greenwood thinks the British government has a good chance of holding on to it. Two points are unclear: (1) Will Turkey resist or not? and (2) Will Spain join the 'Axis' or not? Personally, Greenwood is doubtful that Turkey will resist and sure that Spain will side with the 'Axis'. If the latter occurs, Hitler will occupy North Africa in one form or another, and Greenwood attaches no significance to the rhetoric of Weygand, Pétain and others. England will then find herself in a very tight corner. Nonetheless, Greenwood is in a bellicose frame of mind and asserts that there will be a radical turn in the war in the autumn of 1942 in England's favour.

I asked how and why such a turn should occur? I fail to envisage a situation in which England could defeat Germany on land.

'No,' Greenwood agreed, 'of course we can't defeat Germany on land, but the blockade and especially the air force will do it.'

That old story! I've heard it so many times.

We spoke little of Anglo-Soviet affairs. Neither I nor Greenwood wanted to discuss the matter. But he did mention at one point that he 'fully understands the policy' of the Soviet government: 'Only a madman could choose to enter the war!' he exclaimed.

Then, touching on the Soviet–Japanese pact, he surprised me by stating that he sees nothing dangerous in it for either England or China.

* * *

Events are developing fast. Yesterday Duff Cooper informed the editors of the major newspapers, for the purposes of their 'orientation', that George of Greece has notified Wavell about the impossibility of further resistance and about his relocation to Crete.

The Portuguese government has sent a considerable military force to the Azores. It is evidently preparing to evacuate there.

24 April

Subbotić visited me.

King Peter and the greater part of the Yugoslavian government are already in Cairo. The rest are in Jerusalem. The gold has been evacuated to a safe place (part of it was taken out earlier to the United States and Egypt). Some air force units are being evacuated from Yugoslavia. Attempts are being made to evacuate warships, too, but it's an uncertain business. Yugoslavian commercial ships, totalling 400,000 tons, have been placed at the disposal of the British government. The resistance has not entirely ended in Yugoslavia. Fighting continues in some places, but it can no longer affect the general course of events. Yugoslavia does not exist any longer, and one has to come to terms with this grave but incontrovertible fact.

Subbotić is now in a position to maintain normal contact with the Yugoslavian government. He also communicates with Gavrilović[i] (the Yugoslavian minister in Moscow). Yesterday, Subbotić went to see Eden, who acquainted him with the statement he was about to make in parliament and even made some

[i] Milovan Gavrilović, Yugoslav ambassador to the USSR, 1940–45. A former leader of the leftist Serbian Agrarian Party, he advocated the creation of a Balkan Union governed by Slavophile ideas.

amendments to the text at Subbotić's request. Eden was most generous and made ample promises for the future, but such promises now leave Subbotić cold. He again insisted on the opening of our border to Yugoslavian refugees and requested that a Soviet envoy remain with the Yugoslavian government in exile. In his view, the latter would be of great political and psychological significance.

Subbotić is very low. One senses as well his vexation with England and his almost panicky *respect* for Germany.

* * *

It turns out that the death of the Greek prime minister, Koryzis,[i] conceals a tragedy. I heard the following story: King George of Greece was informed that some defeatist tendencies could be observed among his top brass, and that some generals wanted an armistice. George summoned his ministers, informed them of this and condemned the defeatists, suggesting that they were to be found among members of the government as well. Such people had to make a choice. That same night Koryzis committed suicide.

26 April

It was only 20 days ago, while noting the beginning of the German attack against Yugoslavia, that I posed the question: will the Germans succeed with their Blitzkrieg in the Balkans?

Today there can be no room for doubts: yes, the German Blitzkrieg was a success. Perhaps even more so than previous ones.

How quickly events unfold in our days! Merely 20 days have passed, and Yugoslavia no longer exists, and within another 2–3 days Greece will be no more. Some 10–12 days are sufficient for 'liquidating' a whole nation, a whole state. That is the meaning of 'mechanized war', as Voznesensky,[ii] chairman of the State Planning Committee, put it at the last party conference.

The capture of Yugoslavia and Greece, i.e. of the whole Balkans (together with the earlier *gleichgeschalteten*[32] of Rumania and Bulgaria) by the Germans poses a whole host of serious problems. The most important of them is: what will be Hitler's next move?

It seems to me that there are two likely alternatives. <u>The first</u>: pressure will begin to be exerted on Turkey, so as to seize her diplomatically or by force, and

[i] Alexandros Koryzis, prime minister of Greece, 1941.
[ii] Nikolai Alekseevich Voznesensky, chairman of the USSR State Planning Commission 1938–41 and 1942–49; deputy chairman of the Soviet Council of Ministers from 1939; arrested 1949, shot 1950 and rehabilitated 1954.

advance through her to Asia Minor and Egypt. The second: Germany will leave Turkey in peace for the time being, draw Spain (even better, Spain and France) into a triple pact, march to Gibraltar, cross the Strait, seize Morocco, Algeria and Tunisia, capture Egypt via North Africa, and press on to Iraq and Iran. The second alternative looks more probable, since there is no danger of serious conflict along this route before the Egyptian frontier. Seen from the German point of view, the first alternative is fraught with a number of dangerous unknowns, relating, first and foremost, to the conduct of the USSR. Well, we shall see. A combination of the two alternatives cannot be excluded: no wonder the Germans have gone to such lengths to occupy the Greek islands in the Aegean. The encirclement of Turkey is beginning, together with her isolation from England and the United States.

Whatever happens, a very dangerous situation is taking shape for England. Her strength lies at sea. On land she cannot dream of matching Germany's might. If England lets the Germans into the African continent or Asia Minor, the Empire will be in shreds. But now it seems that England won't be able to do much about it. If Spain joins the 'Axis' (which, to my mind, is inevitable), then Gibraltar, the sole British naval base in the western Mediterranean, will be 'liquidated' in one way or another (captured or besieged, i.e. no longer capable of serving as a naval base). Then the Germans will be in a position not only to cross the Strait freely, but also to sail almost unhindered in the western part of the Mediterranean and transport troops and supplies from Italy and France directly to Algeria and Tunisia. It will be difficult to effectively control the Mediterranean west of Sicily from Alexandria or even from Crete. How will the British be able to prevent the transfer of large German forces to Africa? How will they be able to organize serious opposition to these forces in Egypt and other parts of the 'black continent'?

I had a long walk with Negrín in the vicinity of Bovingdon. We discussed the current situation. Negrín is in a gloomy frame of mind.

He does not doubt that the Germans will establish a secure route to Africa through Spain for themselves, that they will be able to mass a large force there, capture Egypt and the Suez Channel, march on to the Persian Gulf and even India, and conquer the whole African continent in a relatively short time. Simultaneously, the Japanese will attack Malaya and Dutch India. What will the British do then? Blockade – which even now is not the sharpest of weapons – will then become quite senseless. In fact, the English will be powerless against the Germans on land. The two sides will, at best, become equally effective in the air, or equally ineffective. Acute internal discord and conflict will follow in England (and in the United States). Morale will begin to slide. The Germans will take the opportunity to 'liquidate' England – by force or by the other means which they know only too well. Then Hitler, intoxicated with success, will aim at world domination. Clashes with the USSR and the USA will become inevitable, and Hitler may emerge victorious once again. Japan will turn into a German vassal. The same will happen to any other major state which still happens to be uninvolved in the war at that time. Eventually the swastika will fly over the entire world, with all the ensuing consequences. There will be one *Herrenvolk* of 100 million people; the rest of mankind will become slaves. To stave off any slave revolt, the Germans will mix races and peoples, break families, move Spaniards to China and Chinese to Spain, Frenchmen to India and Indians to France, etc. Amid this ethnographic, political and cultural chaos the Germans will strive to immortalize their mastery of the world.

Such are Negrín's thoughts.

'The dream is terrible, but God is merciful.' Many objections could be raised against Negrín's analysis, but it also contains much that deserves consideration.

One thing is clear: the war is entering a new and exceptionally important phase. The next six months may prove to be a turning point not only in the history of the war, but in the history of mankind as well. We shall see.

29 April

When I talked with Guo a few days ago, I remarked: 'I'm certain of one thing at least: the present "Polish government" will never ride into Warsaw.'

Guo laughed and said: 'As if that's what they want! They live just fine in London.'

Guo furnished me with interesting details about the life and behaviour of members of the 'Polish government' in London. They spend heaps of money. They are puttin' on the Ritz. All of them have cars, secretaries, aides-de-camps, servants or batmen. They drink and eat in the most extravagant London restaurants. They try to make the acquaintance of only the most aristocratic families (without always succeeding). The 'official representatives of Poland', that's to say, squander their money and live fast. And of the 17,000-strong Polish corps defending a section of the Scottish shore against invasion, there are 6,500 officers!

How all this resembles the old Polish szlachta![33] I recall that when Poland sent an embassy to England in the 1670s, it numbered no fewer than 1,600 people! This at a time when Sweden, Germany and other countries would send no more than 70 to 100. The Polish 'Pans', don't you know! They won't be outdone by anyone!

Daudet[i] once wrote about 'Kings in Exile'. Will there be a new Daudet for our times, who will write a novel about governments-in-exile once this war is over? There are more and more of them and they offer good material for a novelist. The 'Polish government' in particular.

---

[i] Alphonse Daudet (1840–97), French novelist.

* * *

Aras came to see me. He is greatly concerned about the occupation of the Aegean islands by Germany and feels relieved at the same time. His concern derives from long-term considerations: from the point of view of Turkey's general interests, this is certainly a very dangerous development. His relief is dictated by immediate realities. Aras explained almost joyously: 'Well, now we are definitely out of the war! Nobody can demand our involvement in the war in view of our current strategic position. In the Mediterranean we are almost entirely cut off from England. The "back door" remains – the way through Basra-Iraq – but it is not exactly reliable.'

And then, as though remembering something, Aras added: 'We shall now fight only in the event of a direct attack.'

Will they? I'm not so sure. For Aras followed the above statement by saying that there was no reason whatsoever for Germany to unleash its forces against Turkey, that Syria (even if it were to fall into German hands) was of no special interest to Turkey, etc.

Then Aras returned once again to the question of relations between Ankara and Moscow, stressing the need for very close ties and hinting that Turkey could only mount effective resistance to Germany if she received the active assistance of the USSR.

On the whole, Aras's mood is defeatist. If he is representing Ankara's attitudes correctly, it won't be difficult for the Germans to lay their hands on Turkey without a war.

Evidently, this is how things stand. It has been reported from Istanbul that a critical attitude towards England and an inclination to reach an agreement with Germany are growing in Turkish ruling circles. Papen[i] will find fertile soil in Ankara when he returns from Berlin. Meanwhile, German representatives in Tehran declare openly that they will now attend to Syria (they promise her 'independence') and will enter Iraq and Iran from there.

It seems that the Middle East will be the theatre of highly significant events in the next couple of months.

30 April

Brendan Bracken came for lunch. I have not seen him for 3–4 months. We had much to talk about. He was here for nearly three hours. Our conversation mostly circled around two issues: Anglo-Soviet relations and the war.

On the first question, we dived deep into the past. Bracken lambasted Baldwin and Chamberlain for their policy toward the USSR, in particular for

[i] Franz von Papen, German ambassador to Turkey, 1939–44.

their conduct during the negotiations about the pact in 1939. I told Bracken that throughout the talks I had the sense that Chamberlain and Halifax did not want the pact.

'Of course they didn't!' Bracken exclaimed.

As proof he adduced a fact which was new to me. It appears that at the end of May, or early June 1939, Eden offered his services to Halifax for the negotiations in Moscow. Halifax, however, declined the offer and sent Strang instead.

I asked Bracken: what may we expect in Anglo-Soviet relations in the near future?

Bracken replied that Eden is undoubtedly striving to improve relations, but Bracken is not sure that he will be successful. Why? For two reasons. (1) Eden is often too cautious: he does not want to take risks and assume responsibility. (2) It is not clear whether the USSR wants an improvement in relations.

I objected to the second point: the USSR was ready to maintain good relations on the basis of reciprocity with all states, be they belligerent or otherwise. Bracken listened to me with great interest and said: 'In Conservative circles one often hears the following argument. If Germany attacks the Soviet Union (as many now believe will happen), the USSR will come to us of its own accord. If Germany does not attack the USSR, it will do nothing for us anyway. So is it worth courting the USSR?'

I burst out laughing and noted that the British government had not even tried to court us, so how can it know what effect its courting might have on the conduct of the Soviet government? Then I strongly condemned the tendency, prevalent in the press and among British politicians, to frighten us with Germany. I mentioned Churchill's recent speeches (9 and 27 April) in this connection, in which he, too, paid his due to this popular craze. I can only regret such speeches. What is their purpose? Why has Churchill suddenly begun taking Soviet interests to heart? We can take care of our interests ourselves, can't we? The Soviet Union needs no outside mentors. The prime minister's remarks sound very infelicitous and even tactless in the current situation. They produce an effect in Moscow quite opposed to the one he intends.

My words seemed to impress Bracken. He even remarked: 'Yes, sometimes it's better not to mention certain things aloud.'

I inquired whether the British government had any exact information about Hitler's intention to attack the USSR, or whether this was all just theoretical speculation based on *wishful thinking*.

Bracken had to admit that the British government has, in essence, no specific information concerning Germany's preparations for an attack. There are only suppositions based on various signs and on conversations between Hitler and trustworthy individuals. As an example of the latter group, Bracken named Cudahy,[i] former US ambassador in Belgium, who as a high-ranking journalist recently visited Berlin and had a long talk with the Führer. Cudahy is a great admirer of Hitler, so his testimony, in Bracken's opinion, deserves special attention. Hitler spoke sharply about the USSR in this conversation, saying that his present policy toward Moscow was just a 'wartime manoeuvre' and that his words in *Mein Kampf* would be realized to the letter. He just needs time. In general, everything written in *Mein Kampf* holds true and will be put into practice sooner or later. One only needs a bit of patience. Then Hitler allegedly added: 'The Soviet–Finnish war taught us a lot. I have no doubt that my armies will cut through Russia like a knife through butter.'

I laughed at Hitler's bragging and repeated my questions to Bracken. Does he know anything more concrete and definite about German preparations for an attack on the Soviet Union? When is the attack to be expected? In what form?

Bracken shrugged his shoulders and said that the British government has no precise information. The attack may be expected this summer or autumn, or maybe next spring.

It was clear that the campaign waged by the British government and the press about the forthcoming German attack on the USSR has no solid foundation whatsoever and follows the model, *Der Wunsch ist der Vater des Gedankens*.[34]

Regarding the prospects of the war, Bracken was more realistic. He remembers that Churchill told him on Christmas Eve: '1941 will be the most difficult year in the war for us, but we shall win nonetheless!' The first half of Churchill's prophecy is coming true. The time will come for the second half, too.

The evacuation from Greece, according to Bracken, will be successfully completed (although the English will have to abandon almost all heavy equipment). The British government has sufficient forces in Libya to defend Egypt and will gradually build them up. I interrupted Bracken and asked: 'Your calculations proceed from the current state of affairs in North Africa, where Germany and Italy have at most six or seven divisions between them. Suppose the Germans reach North Africa through Spain, conquer Morocco, Algeria and Tunisia, immobilize Gibraltar as a naval base in one way or another, thereby attaining almost complete freedom of navigation in the western part of the Mediterranean and, finally, assemble not seven, but 27 or 37 divisions against Egypt – what then? Will England be able to defend Egypt in such conditions?'

Bracken shrugged his shoulders and replied: 'I don't know. It depends on the circumstances.'

---

[i] John Clarence Cudahy, American ambassador to Poland, 1933–37; Ireland 1937–40; Belgium, 1940; and Luxembourg, 1940.

Bracken now outlines the 'general strategy' of the war in the following way: the British government will do its utmost to remain *on the defensive* till the autumn of 1942. Thereafter it will start going over to the offensive. But not on land: Bracken does not think that England can match Germany on land. It will be an air offensive. To corroborate his predictions, Bracken adduced the following calculation.

At the present time, according to information available to the British government, the Germans have 35,000 combat aircraft of all types (of which 5,000 are first-line aircraft – i.e. the Germans have a disproportionate quantity of outdated planes). They produce about 1,500 combat planes every month. In this way, by 1 October 1942 Germany should have 35,000 plus 25,000, minus 8,000 (in losses) – 52,000 aircraft in total.

The English now have 23,000 combat aircraft and produce about 2,000 monthly at home. So by 1 October 1942 they should have 23,000 plus 34,000, minus 8,000 in losses (although Bracken thinks that English losses will be fewer than German ones) – all in all, 49,000. No fewer than 15,000 US and Canadian aircraft should be added to this figure. This means that the English will have 64,000 planes at their disposal as against 52,000 German aircraft. Deliveries from America will increase at a furious pace and reach 5–6,000 aircraft monthly in early 1943. That is why Bracken thinks the war may end in 1943.

There is one weak link in these calculations. Bracken proceeds from the assumption that the German output of combat aircraft will remain at today's level. What if it is raised? For it almost certainly will be raised. Furthermore, what we have observed until now leads one to conclude that an air war cannot bring decisive results on its own. True, only hundreds of planes have been engaged in air raids so far – what will happen with thousands? Nobody can tell for sure. Here we run up against a big X. But let us assume that an air war, in which not hundreds but thousands of bombers are engaged, does bring decisive results. What will it mean? It will mean the barbarous obliteration of German cities and the barbarous obliteration of English cities, a conflict in which England hopes in the end to experience 15% less destruction than Germany. This will be called a 'victory'. A horrific prospect! Will the people really accept this?…

Whose morale will crack first? That is the essential question.

6 May

Stalin has been appointed chairman of the Council of the People's Commissars, Molotov – his deputy and people's commissar for foreign affairs. We return to Lenin's times, when the leader of our party and of the peoples of the USSR held the post of chairman of the Council of People's Commissars.

This is a signal. The threat of war is approaching our frontiers. The time is approaching for major and significant decisions. It is necessary for Stalin himself to be at the helm.

[The looming prospect of war led Stalin to keep his cards even closer to his chest. He resorted to 'divide and rule' tactics, keeping the military ignorant of his political moves. Neither were the diplomats trusted – and particularly not Maisky, whom Molotov, ever since his appointment, had been keeping at arm's length. 'The trouble is,' wrote Cripps in a private letter, 'that Maisky is not really in very close touch with the Government here.' Eden indeed wondered whether 'Maisky is informed of Soviet policy'.[35] Maisky was deliberately kept in the dark about the political initiatives taken by Stalin to avoid war. Left to guess what Stalin's intentions were, his cautious reports sought to conform to what he wrongly assumed to be Stalin's policy. He thus unwittingly contributed to Stalin's fatal misjudgement of German plans on the eve of the war.

Schulenburg, the German ambassador to Moscow returned to Berlin at the end of April, armed with political and military arguments against a military intervention in Russia.[36] He found Hitler, however, fuming about the Soviet pact with Yugoslavia and unable to comprehend 'what kind of devil had possessed' them. Hitler curbed his overzealous ambassador by levelling various accusations against Stalin which would later be employed as pretexts for the attack on Russia.[37] Schulenburg hastened to return to Moscow, resolved to repair the damage. In doing so, he also inadvertently misled Stalin into believing that it was still possible to avert war. His scheme was to prod Stalin to 'involve Hitler in negotiations which would rob him, for the time being, of all pretexts for military actions'. He took the unusual step of prompting three clandestine meetings with Dekanozov, Stalin's ambassador in Berlin (who was on leave), at his own residency and at the guesthouse of the Russian Foreign Ministry – away from potential informers in the embassy – on 5, 9 and 12 May.[38]

Over breakfast on 5 May, Schulenburg attributed the German concentration of troops to the swelling rumours of Soviet mobilization and the inevitability of an armed conflict. Having been provided with little straw to make his bricks, Schulenburg chose to convey to Dekanozov his impression that 'rumours of an imminent war between the Soviet Union and Germany are of explosive nature, and should be suppressed, broken to the bones'. He proposed that the amelioration of relations could best be achieved if the Russians were to advance concrete proposals. This accounts for Stalin's obsessive fear henceforth that an overt and effective deployment of troops on the border might be conceived as provocation in Berlin. Within a day, *Pravda* had published a denial of the allegations that the strong concentrations of military forces on the western border of the Soviet Union signalled a change in relations with Germany.[39] Far more startling was Stalin's assumption of the chairmanship of the Council of People's Commissars the next morning. Schulenburg correctly related the appointment to his own initiative, but he could not inform Berlin of his unauthorized move. He now contemplated a campaign on two fronts. In Moscow he would encourage Stalin to personally approach Hitler; while in his reporting to Berlin he would assume the detached observer's point of view and emphasize the conciliatory Russian attitude, thus preparing the ground for Stalin's approach. These are tactics which were strikingly similar to those used unsuccessfully by Maisky in the negotiations with the West in 1939. Schulenburg prepared Berlin for his next coup by predicting that 'Stalin will use his new position in order to take part personally in the maintenance and development of good relations between the Soviets and Germany.'[40]

Still anticipating a response from Berlin, Schulenburg was invited by Dekanozov for breakfast on 9 May. While the German ambassador appeared impatient and eager to advance his plans, Dekanozov remained cautious, displaying a rather false sense of confidence. To break the ice, Schulenburg urged him that 'as diplomats and politicians, we ought to deal with the arising situation and contemplate which counter measures can be taken'. Dekanozov proposed the publication of a joint German–Soviet communiqué denying the malicious recent rumours that suggested a possible military conflict between the two countries.[41] Schulenburg, however, was anxious to raise the stakes. He encouraged Stalin to address Matsuoka, Mussolini and Hitler with a personal letter assuring them 'that the USSR will conduct in the future a friendly policy towards them'. He expected Hitler to dispatch a courier in a special plane to fetch the letter. Several times during their conversation, Schulenburg stressed the seriousness of the situation, insisting that 'it was necessary to act fast'.[42]

With his initiative gaining momentum, Schulenburg sought an official endorsement from Weizsäcker in the form of a personal greeting to Stalin on his assumption of the premiership.[43] Hitler, however, was furious. 'No diplomacy,' he said, 'would make him change his mind about Russia's attitude.'[44] On 12 May, Dekanozov returned to Schulenburg's apartment for their third breakfast meeting inside a week. This time he seized the initiative at the outset, confirming Stalin's agreement to send the personal letter to Hitler. Stalin urged Schulenburg and Molotov to waste little time and jointly draft the text of the letter.[45] However, shortly before Dekanozov's arrival, Schulenburg had received a laconic message from Weizsäcker that his proposals had not been submitted to Ribbentrop 'because this would not have been a rewarding thing', indicating only too clearly which way the wind was blowing.[46] Schulenburg therefore 'impassively' dampened Dekanozov's enthusiasm by confessing that he had been 'conversing with me privately and made his suggestion on his own initiative without authority', and was 'doubtful whether he was likely to receive any instructions'.

The tenor of the conversation was a strange blend of constant hints about the likelihood of war, equally persuasive attempts to maintain the momentum, and disinformation. All this was to add to the already confused state of mind at the Kremlin. The more so as Schulenburg was eager to salvage his initiative, suggesting that it would have been good if nonetheless Stalin 'were to approach Hitler by letter, on his own initiative and spontaneously'. Baffled, Stalin could easily assume that a cautious policy might still yield an agreement. However it could just as well be a trap set for Russia, whereby a premature approach might be used as a trump card in future negotiations with Britain. Indeed, during the meeting Schulenburg made the entirely speculative assessment that 'in his own opinion the day was not far off when England and Germany were bound to reach agreement and bring the calamity and destruction and bombing of their cities to an end'. This statement was surely scrutinized in the Kremlin in the evening, when news came on Radio Berlin of the flight of Hitler's deputy, Rudolf Hess, to Britain on a self-appointed peace mission.[47] The fact that both Schulenburg and Cripps had been alluding in their conversations in the Kremlin to the possibility of a separate peace alerted Stalin to the need to forestall it by further appeasing Hitler. Schulenburg's activities through winter and spring of 1941, and particularly in the crucial month of May 1941, kept alive in Moscow the hope of a possible diplomatic solution to the conflict and further deflected Stalin from the danger lurking around the corner.[48] The 'appeasement' of Germany and the uncertainty were taking their toll on Maisky, who begged Alexander (the Labourite first lord of the Admiralty, whom he came to see 'as an old friend') to quickly solve the outstanding issues between the two countries. 'He appeared to me,' concluded Alexander, 'to be rather anxious as to his own position … although, of course, he did not say this.'[49]]

7 May

I spent yesterday and today in parliament. Major debates about the course of the war, mostly prompted by the British failures in Greece. Looking down from the diplomatic box at the so-familiar chamber, I unconsciously drew a parallel with similar debates held a year ago (8–9 May) after Norway, which dragged the Chamberlain government to its grave. Drawing this parallel, I asked myself: is it the same as before or not?

No, of course not. There's a big difference.

Then the present war had just begun; now it is in full swing. Then there was confusion, indecision and discord at the highest level; now one senses firmness, unity and clarity about the common goal. There are appeasers in the ruling circles, of course, just like under Chamberlain, but they are not for the time being playing any sort of serious role. The clearly defined motto of the majority led by Churchill is 'Fight!'

Such sentiments found full expression in the two-day debate that concluded today. It's not merely the fact that a vote of confidence in the government was passed by a majority of 447 against 3 that's significant (party discipline certainly played its role here), but the general character of events in the House over these past few days. Typically, all the critics who spoke (Winterton, Shinwell and others) came down on the government not for waging a war, but for waging it with insufficient vigour. The general inference to be drawn from the debate is that the British ruling classes do not want peace, preferring to fight against Germany.

Why?

Because peace today would mean peace on the basis of Germany's present gains. In other words, Germany would come out of the war on the European continent west of the USSR in possession of all the material, technical and other resources of the countries it had occupied or subjugated. This, in turn, would enable Germany, over a period of five years or so, to build a fleet not inferior to that of the English, which would signify the end of the British Empire.

It cannot be ruled out, however, that in spite of the above considerations the ruling classes of England might prefer peace to war at a certain moment, but when? In two cases: (1) if England were to suffer crushing defeats and its position became hopeless or (2) if the soil of society were to catch fire under the feet of the English bourgeoisie at home or in the Empire. Neither case is to be observed at present. That is why the ruling classes of Great Britain can still afford the luxury of continuing the war in order to uphold their position in the world. That is why the political barometer points to 'Fight!' after the two-day debate. The British working class, or the vast majority of it at least, tags after the bourgeoisie – under the influence of traditions, the Church, the press and the radio, the Labour machine, and a dim awareness of its interest in colonial excess profit.

That is the general background, against which the personality of Churchill plays an extremely crucial role. The prime minister was undoubtedly born too late. By nature he is an adventurist on a historical scale, strong-willed and resolute, a romantic of British imperialism and war. Had he lived in previous centuries, he would have been a match for Cortes or Admiral Drake, a conqueror of new lands or a celebrated pirate canonized as [name missing]. It is not without reason that Churchill reveres his ancestor, the duke of Marlborough, who lived at the turn of the seventeenth century and was a brilliant military leader, a political chameleon, and protagonist of the most shameless love affairs. Indeed, the prime minister has dedicated four fat volumes to the career of the duke of Marlborough.

Churchill has told me more than once over the years, and I have no grounds not to believe him, that the British Empire is his alpha and omega. In 1918–20, Churchill organized a crusade against 'Bolshevism', which he considered a major menace to the British Empire at that time. (In 1935–39, Churchill considered 'Hitlerism' the major menace to the British Empire, hence his sharp about-face and his declaration of readiness to join 'Bolshevism' in confronting the new danger. Now Churchill is also waging war for the Empire – he declared passionately yesterday that he would defend the British positions in the Middle East to the last.)

Churchill is just as keen on wars. Megan Lloyd George told me once that ever since childhood she had heard stories about how Churchill, when visiting her father, would always talk about battles, military campaigns and conquests with great enthusiasm and excitement. He always imagined himself in the role of a great military leader who flung armies from one end of Europe to another, conquered kingdoms and won brilliant victories. Today – I know this from the most reliable sources – Churchill is totally engrossed in the war. Fortune has smiled on him at last. He has 'his own' war, a gigantic war in which he, like a fanatical chess player, swears to checkmate Hitler. In this war, Churchill is commander-in-chief, chief of the general staff, and leader of the troops. He won't surrender 'his' war to anyone. And now, when the British bourgeoisie wants to continue the war, Churchill has become its godsend. But he may become an obstacle if and when it desires peace.

All this, however, is just the 'music of the future'. Today Churchill has a massive role to play in England. He is surely 'master' of the country for he is a cut above all other political leaders, except Lloyd George (who is 78!). Moreover, Churchill is a talented writer and orator – extremely important qualities for a major 'historical adventurist' of our days.

Recently Churchill has been cultivating the image of both undisputed 'leader' of the nation and good 'democrat'. He befriends Bevin, who is probably no less militant than he. He extends his 'patronage' to the workers. Together with Bevin, he took a stand against punitive measures in connection with the strike of industrial apprentices. Together with Bevin, he was against open conscription of labour, preferring to do it in a covert form. It is difficult to say how far Churchill's friendship with Bevin will go and what forms it will ultimately assume. It is also hard to say whether Churchill will sustain his present popularity for long. These are all variables. But for the moment, Churchill is unquestionably the premier man in the country.

This has much relevance to Anglo-Soviet relations as well. My general impression is that Eden sincerely wants an improvement in this regard, but cannot do much about it. Talking with me last year, on 27 December, and this year, on 16 April, Eden promised on both occasions to try to resolve the Baltic question, but to no avail. Why?

Eden has two difficulties. The first is Churchill. The prime minister reasons in the following way. If he could count on the immediate entry of the Soviet Union into the war, efforts might be taken to improve relations. Since he cannot count on this, Churchill ceases to care about the Soviet Union and says that the problem of Anglo-Soviet relations does not interest him for now.[50] Also, Churchill suffers from an obsession that a war between Germany and the USSR is inevitable. This being the case, he just has to wait: the USSR will approach England of its own accord as soon as German guns start firing on its borders. No cause for concern. Such reasoning is very strange and nonsensical. But when a social class finds itself on thin ice, even its most intelligent representatives begin to be afflicted by political blindness.

The USA is Eden's second difficulty. Eden tested the ground in Washington after our talk on 16 April, but did not meet with any sympathy for his plan for resolving the Baltic question. The USA, after all, means everything to England today. Eden has not lost hope for a change for the better and is biding his time. We shall see.

For the time being, I can find little cause for optimism with regard to improvements in Anglo-Soviet relations.

9 May

I lunched with Prytz, who is going to fly to Stockholm in a strange and risky way – by British plane across German lines. He wants to 'touch the ground' and familiarize himself with the atmosphere in Sweden. That is what he says, but what he really wants to do, it seems to me, is arrange his private affairs and make sure he is financially secure should anything happen. His wife is flying with him and will stay in Sweden longer, while he plans to return within 3–4 weeks. Will he return? We shall see.

In connection with his departure, Prytz expressed his wish to see Churchill. The prime minister invited him and his wife to lunch (there were half a dozen guests). The situation was ill suited to serious conversation; nonetheless, Prytz was able to glean some interesting things.

Prytz asked Churchill how he envisaged the further development of the war. It would be helpful for the Swedish government to know this. In reply, Churchill told Prytz the following 'fable'.

There lived two frogs – an optimist and a pessimist. One evening they were jumping over some grass and detected the wonderful smell of fresh milk emanating from a nearby dairy. The frogs were tempted and jumped into the dairy through an open window. They miscalculated and flopped directly into a large jar of milk. What to do?… The pessimist looked around and, seeing that the walls of the jar were high and sheer and that it was not possible to climb up, fell into despair. He turned on his back, folded his legs and sank to the bottom. The optimist did not want to perish so disgracefully. He also saw the high and sheer walls, but decided to flounder while he could. All night long he swam, beat the milk energetically with his legs, and displayed varied forms of activity. And?… By the time morning came, the optimistic frog had, quite unawares, churned a big knob of butter out of the milk and thereby saved his life. The same will happen to the British Empire.

Churchill's 'fable' was very good from the literary point of view, but could not, of course, fully satisfy Prytz. However, all his attempts to learn something more definite about the 'general strategy' of the British government in this war were in vain. Prytz even formed the impression that the prime minister did not have a clear idea of the contours of this general strategy and relied more on inspiration and improvisation. I find this quite probable.[51]

In his talk with Prytz, Churchill mentioned, among other things, the impending clash between the USSR and Germany (this is Churchill's recent 'tick'). Prytz expressed his anxiety in this connection, for Sweden would find itself between the devil and the deep blue sea, as both belligerents would want to use its territory for themselves. He then asked if this meant that in the event of conflict with Germany, the USSR would automatically become an ally of England?

Churchill reddened, his eyes became bloodshot, and he cried with fury in his voice: 'To crush Germany I am prepared to enter into an alliance with anyone, even the devil!'[52]

10 May

I went to see Lloyd George in Churt. I wanted to hear the old man's appraisal of the current situation. His son was there for the weekend. We had tea. We sat in the *drawing room*, the big window of which affords a beautiful view over the hills, meadows and woods of southern England; but we were more interested in the planes flying above. With a rumble and a roar, three *Spitfire* followed each other, spun and manoeuvred. The old man's eyes lit up every time he raised his head to the sky.

Lloyd George is in a very gloomy mood. He thinks the most dangerous phase of the war is at hand. All seem to think that Egypt is becoming the focus of events. With a half-smile, the old man exclaimed: 'The war will be decided at the pyramids.'

Is England prepared for this? Lloyd George is unsure. Germany, he believes, can reach Egypt by two different routes: (1) through Spain and North Africa (Algeria and Tunisia), or (2) through Turkey, Syria, Iraq and Palestine.

The first route is long and complex. If he chooses it, Hitler will need at least half a year to assemble a large enough army against Egypt (he will need about a million-strong army because the British already have up to 500,000 troops there and can increase this number significantly in the next couple of months). Supplying and feeding the German army along the Spanish route will be difficult. Hitler will use it if he finds nothing better, but he will first try to secure the more convenient second route. He has already started moving along it: he occupied the Aegean islands along the Turkish coast, fuelled a rebellion in Iraq, and will most probably soon start transferring troops to Syria by air. However, all this is not enough to mount a large-scale campaign. The next step will be a demand for Turkey to allow the transfer of German troops through its territory or at least to allow the delivery of war matériel (as happened with Yugoslavia) along the Smyrna–Aleppo line and then eastward to Baghdad and southward to Palestine. If Turkey permits this, the British position in the Middle East will become critical. The British government might be able to defend Egypt from the west, but it will hardly manage to do so from the east. Should an offensive be mounted simultaneously from the west and from the east (and such is the Germans' usual strategy), the loss of Egypt would be almost inevitable.

If Egypt is lost, Germany will be able to conquer the whole of Africa. This will not satisfy Germany, however, because there is no oil in Africa, and which truly great power can do without oil in our days? There is oil in Asia, and that is why after Egypt (or possibly even earlier) the Germans will move to Iraq, Iran and maybe to India and Burma – all countries rich in oil.

And this is where the USSR steps onto the stage. L-G attaches enormous significance to the fact that Comrade Stalin himself now heads the Council of People's Commissars. This is an obvious symptom of the danger approaching the Soviet borders, and of the fact that in the nearest future (possibly before the end of this month) the Soviet government will have to make decisions of momentous significance. The first of these decisions is whether or not to allow Germany passage to the Middle East. For Turkey will surely ask Moscow's 'advice' when the Germans present their demand to use the Smyrna–Aleppo railway. What will be the response of the Soviet government?

If it says 'Let them pass', the Germans will very quickly appear in Iraq, Iran, Turkey and India. In other words, the Soviet Union will be outflanked, and Baku will be exposed to a German attack. If it says 'Do not let them pass', relations between Germany and the USSR will inevitably cool, leading to possible complications. So the Soviet government will have to make its choice soon.

Personally, Lloyd George is convinced that Hitler will not risk an armed conflict with the Soviet Union now, and therefore the USSR might not let the Germans through to the Middle East. Why should it? From time immemorial, Russia has gravitated toward the 'warm sea'. Previously, the 'warm sea' was the Straits. Now they have seriously lost their former value, but the Persian Gulf?… That is a quite different matter.

I listened to Lloyd George and drew my own conclusions. I asked him: 'Imagine that England loses Egypt and all its positions in the Middle East. Will it continue the war?'

L-G paused and spread out his arms in perplexity.

'That is difficult to say in advance,' he eventually replied.

I repeated the question several times during our conversation in an attempt to get a more definite answer, but L-G kept repeating: 'I don't know. Can't foretell.'

I recalled our conversation from a year ago, when France was still fighting, yet the first signs of impending catastrophe were visible. I asked him then what England would do if France left the battlefield. Lloyd George had answered without the slightest hesitation: 'We shall continue the war alone. We can't do otherwise.'

Today Lloyd George's mood was different. And this is very significant.

The conversation inevitably veered towards Anglo-Soviet relations. I told Lloyd George of my conversation with Eden on 16 April and said that it had not led to anything. The old man was enraged. The British government's policy toward the USSR, he fulminated, is idiotic and fatal for England. Where does it originate? It originates with Churchill. No doubt, Churchill is a major figure, a talented orator and writer. No doubt, he is head and shoulders above the puppets that surround him. But he also has major shortcomings. To start with, he is a poor strategist, both in military affairs and in politics. Regarding military affairs, it is enough to recall the Dardanelles operation in the last war and the Norwegian operation in this war. Yes, yes, the Norwegian operation, as full responsibility for its strategy lies primarily with Churchill. Neither can he boast of strategic perfection in the Greek operation. Regarding politics, it is enough to recall how awkwardly Churchill manoeuvred during the years dominated by Baldwin and Chamberlain, how he always failed not only to win over the majority in the Conservative Party, but even to organize a strong minority faction, in spite of all his talents and his well-grounded position. Lloyd George is worried about Churchill's weakness as a strategist. Another trouble with Churchill is that he always thinks about 'today' and never about 'tomorrow'. Churchill often displays short-sightedness, and this is dangerous, particularly at the present moment.

Second, Churchill is a typical representative of the capitalist world. Lloyd George remembers that before the past war, in the period when Lloyd George introduced laws on the taxation of landlords, Churchill never ceased grumbling at his actions. Lloyd George had to talk with him privately many times in order to persuade him not to interfere in the legislation process. The utmost he was able to achieve was to secure Churchill's neutrality.

'I don't like your land policy,' said Churchill, 'but, very well, I'll not object to it at the Cabinet meeting. I'll keep silent.'

And now Churchill is even staking on the United States. Essentially, he has sold his soul to Wall Street, but, in L-G's opinion, America will not save England. England can win the war only together with the Soviet Union. This was clear to Lloyd George already at the onset of the war, and he is ever more confident of it now. Meanwhile, the British government is doing everything to alienate the Soviet Union and impede cooperation. Staking on the United States only aggravates the situation. What is the United States in the final analysis? It is now the bulwark of capitalism. Capitalism in England is collapsing under the impact of the war. In America, capitalism stands firm. At the end of the war, the United States will annex England along with the British Empire. Anti-Soviet sentiments are even stronger in America than in England. When the British government tries to take a step toward the improvement of relations with the Soviet Union, Washington immediately pours cold water on the initiative.

'Things look bad, very bad,' the old man concluded, and added: 'Churchill invited me to the War Cabinet several times, but I declined his offers because I know that we shall not agree on the main question of this war – "the Russian question". Churchill brushes it aside, but I know that if we don't resolve this problem satisfactorily, we risk defeat.'

About the Dardanelles, incidentally. Lloyd George conveyed some details to me. It was Churchill, then first lord of the Admiralty, who initiated and conducted the operation. Lloyd George was against it, but this matter was beyond his competence, for he was chancellor of the exchequer at that time. Kitchener[i] was against it, too, as was Lord Fisher[ii] in the Admiralty. As always, Asquith went with the flow and followed the leader. Churchill displayed perseverance and resolution. For instance, he forbade Lord Fisher from uttering his opinion in Cabinet, telling him that it was he who represented the Admiralty in Cabinet. Fisher did not dare disobey his chief. A month later, meeting Lloyd George at the door of 10, Downing Street, Fisher told him bitterly that he would probably resign because of that Dardanelles folly. Only then did L-G learn the admiral's genuine opinion of the operation. Kitchener took a strange stand. Churchill asked the war secretary at a meeting whether he could give him enough troops to occupy Gallipoli after the fleet broke through the Dardanelles (Churchill's opinion was that the fleet could force the Straits without the support of the army). Kitchener answered in the affirmative. Churchill was glad and did not bother Kitchener any further. The latter, while not anticipating a successful outcome for the planned operation, did not find it necessary to put up much of a fight: after all, the Admiralty had taken responsibility upon itself. Why should the war secretary be concerned?

Thus, Churchill was provided with the opportunity to pursue his own strategy. The results are well known.

12 May

'What have you done to us?' Subbotić exclaimed on entering my office today.

He raised his hands in despair and started complaining bitterly of the Soviet government's decision (announced on 9 May) to cease recognizing the diplomatic status of the Norwegian, Belgian and Yugoslavian missions in Moscow. This decision is a heavy blow to the morale of the Yugoslavian people during a time of terrible ordeals. It is also a blow to the USSR's prestige among the Slav nations in the Balkans. And why did we feel the need to do this? It was merely five months ago that the pact of friendship and non-aggression between the Soviet Union and Yugoslavia was concluded, and now all that remains of it are scraps of paper. He, Subbotić, has been working for so many years for the rapprochement of Yugoslavia and the USSR. He was so happy when on 5 April

[i] Horatio Herbert Kitchener, secretary of state for war, 1914–16.
[ii] John Arbuthnot Fisher (1st Baron Fisher), first sea lord, 1904–10 and 1914–15.

it became a fait accompli. And now?... Now all is destroyed. All is reduced to dust. He is close to tears over what has happened in the course of the last few days.

My position was far from easy, but all the same I started consoling Subbotić, explaining to him the reasons which led to the decision taken by the Soviet government. I spoke at length, underlying in particular that history does not end today and that in the future the peoples of the USSR would find an opportunity to demonstrate in practice their friendship towards the people of Yugoslavia.

Subbotić listened to me with sceptical impatience and exclaimed in raised tones: 'Why did you feel the need to do it? Rumania... Even trembling Rumania has not severed diplomatic relations with us, but you've gone and done it!... You are simply scared of Germany!'

I intended to make a sharp retort, but looking at Subbotić and seeing that he was beside himself, I restrained myself and replied firmly but calmly: 'Don't say what you yourself don't believe in. If even "trembling Rumania", as you suggest, is not afraid of maintaining diplomatic relations with you, then why should the USSR be afraid of Germany? Your comparison undermines your very argument. It is not the fear of Germany, but very different motives which led the Soviet government to reach its decision.'

I tried once more to explain those reasons to Subbotić.

But he would not calm down. For some reason he suddenly recalled Comrade Plotnikov,[i] our ambassador in Yugoslavia. Subbotić was convinced that Comrade Plotnikov had played a 'sinister role' in the rupture of diplomatic relations with Yugoslavia.

'He was a bad ambassador,' Subbotić said with irritation. 'He did not understand and did not like our people. Everyone in Belgrade felt this.'

I objected that although I was not acquainted with Plotnikov personally, I was sure he had performed his functions as Soviet ambassador with merit.

Subbotić could not agree with me. Then he suddenly seemed to soften and asked my permission to remain in touch with me. I replied that I saw no reason why we shouldn't. We were friends before our countries established diplomatic relations, and we can be friends now, too. Subbotić calmed down a little and said goodbye to me in a more cordial tone.

A grim story!

[The bizarre flight of Rudolf Hess, Hitler's deputy, on a peace mission to Britain on 10 May is vital to any understanding of the Soviet attitude to the approaching conflict. The British archives reveal a clandestine operation by MI6, endorsed by the Foreign Office,

---

[i] V.A. Plotnikov, Soviet ambassador in Yugoslavia, 1940–41.

to use covert channels to pass on disinformation to Moscow in an attempt to discourage Stalin from committing himself further to Germany. Maisky's unenviable task, hardly assisted by the growing rumours of an impending war, was to assess Hess's mission objectively, while remaining attentive to the entrenched concepts prevailing in Moscow. His normally assiduous entries in the diary were suspended for ten days, while his sparse dispatches to Narkomindel stood in sharp contrast to the intensive meetings he held in an attempt to make sense of the affair.[53] At the Foreign Office, Maisky found Butler puzzled and reticent, suggesting that conversations with Hess had 'not yet begun'. His initial brief and noncommittal report was aimed at echoing the expectations in Moscow that 'a very strong anti-Soviet' attitude prevailed in the debriefings.[54] In subsequent meetings Butler developed a hypothesis, deliberately planted on the Russians 'mendaciously', that as a result of a quarrel between Hess and Hitler, 'Hess decided to make his flight to England in the hope that here he would succeed in finding influential circles prepared to make peace with Germany.'[55] By 22 May, Maisky had become convinced that Hess wanted to persuade the British government to join Germany in a crusade to stop the spread of Bolshevism, which was a Devil.[56] He came to believe (as did Stalin) that Hess had either been lured by British intelligence or had come with the full knowledge of the German government, which had been misled by German intelligence into assuming that he would find 'a strong party ready to negotiate with Hitler'. Though convinced that Churchill would not succumb, he failed to advise his government unequivocally what the British response might be.[57]]

22 May

We visited the Webbs. I wanted to drink from the 'fount of wisdom' regarding the British political *mentality* and acquire some notion of what one may expect of England in the near future. I well remember how, in response to my question about a year ago as to what England would do if France were to quit the battlefield, the Webbs answered without the slightest hesitation: 'She will fight alone.'

Events have fully corroborated their prognosis.

Today I asked the Webbs another question: what will England do if she loses Egypt and her positions in the Middle East? Their answer this time was just as categorical: 'England will continue the war, for until this island is conquered by the Germans (and the leaders seem to be sure that invasion is impossible), there is always the hope that the loss of Egypt and so on is temporary – till the end of the war. Besides, Hitler's constant victories irritate and enrage our bourgeoisie. They can't reconcile themselves to his successes. They are stubborn and will do their utmost to beat Germany.'

I was interested to find out whether the attitudes of the British ruling elite are affected by the growing *unrest* in the mother country or in the British Empire. For the unrest will inevitably increase with every passing month of the war. Won't this circumstance make the British bourgeoisie more acquiescent in the matter of peace with Germany? The Webbs gave me a quite definite answer to this question as well: there is no serious *unrest* among the masses at the moment and it is doubtful whether it will manifest itself soon. Of course, the masses are not happy about the bombing, rations and other restrictions brought about by the war, but, in the first place, human losses are 3–4 times less in this war than in the last one. Secondly, the masses earn good money from the war – unemployment has almost vanished, wages have risen and, most importantly, it is not just the worker who works but also his wife and his daughter. Thirdly, 'Transport House' has definitively lost its oppositional spirit: it has associated itself with the ruling classes and has become an integral component of their political machine. One should be under no illusions about that. Fourthly, the masses partly understand and partly sense by instinct that their economic well-being is tightly connected to the preservation of the Empire (England has never had a proletariat in the true sense of this word) and that defeat in this war would signify for them a terrible catastrophe and a hopeless future. All those circumstances find their consummate ideological expression for the masses in the slogan, 'Down with Hitler!' That is why there is little chance of a serious outbreak of *unrest* in England in the immediate future. As far as the Empire is concerned, the situation is less clear (particularly in India). However, the development of dangerous *unrest* in this sphere is neutralized to a certain extent by two factors: the flexibility of the British bourgeoisie, which knows how to make concessions at the right time, and the *natives*' fear of falling under the rule of Hitler with his racist policy. The rule of the British bourgeoisie would strike the *natives* as the lesser evil when compared with Hitler.

The Webbs paint the general prospects for the war in a very gloomy light. It will be a long, exhaustive and destructive war. In the course of it England and the British Empire will become an appendage of the USA. By the end of the war, the United States will become the main stronghold of capitalism. It will be the new centre of the *English-speaking world*. Great Britain will become its European *outpost*. The decline in birth rate, which began before the war, will intensify even further. The population of Great Britain will shrink. London will become empty. The deep decay of the second British Empire will become a fait accompli.

The Webbs say that thoughts of such transformations are already established in the minds of those arriving from across the ocean. They told me the following interesting story.

A nephew of the Webbs' cook, a soldier, arrived in England together with the Canadian Corps. He discovered his aunt, whom he had never seen before, and soon became the object of her adoration and pride. A young, brave and handsome boy! He comes to visit his aunt together with his fellow soldiers. These young soldiers are mostly petty bourgeois or farmers by birth and tend to be progressive in their thinking. There are even socialists among them. The Webbs often meet and talk with these Canadian youths. What do they have to say?

They all say as one that England is, of course, a very pleasant, lovely and picturesque island, but after the war it can no longer remain the centre of the Empire. The centre of the Empire shall move to Montreal or Washington. This is much more expedient geographically, politically and strategically. The Canadians mention Washington because, in their opinion, the United States will inevitably enter the war and as a result, in the course of the war or shortly afterwards, a great empire of English-speaking nations will emerge, led by the United States.

This is most typical!

I started saying that England might emerge from the war strengthened and with enhanced prestige if she turned into a socialist state during or by the end of the war. The Webbs were most sceptical about such a prospect. They fail to see those elements in the country which might make such a 'revolution' here. So, if a 'revolution' must be excluded, what future can be expected for England other than that envisaged by the Webbs?

They advanced another significant argument to reinforce their prognosis. It is quite evident that the British bourgeoisie does not want to be in one bloc with the USSR. They fear such a bloc. 'Transport House', which has never nurtured warm feelings toward the USSR, has now fallen wholly under the anti-Soviet influence of the Tories. But once England declines friendship with the USSR while desiring to continue the war against Germany, she has no way out other than 'to sell herself' to the USA, with all the ensuing consequences.

The old couple say that such prospects scare them. But they don't want to shut their eyes to the bitter truth. This is how it is. As throughout their life, they do not revel in *wishful thinking*, but examine the facts and draw appropriate conclusions.

As usual, it was Beatrice who did most of the talking. Her husband echoed her and made the odd remark. Sidney now speaks with difficulty. Although he regained his speech after his stroke in 1938, he is not the same man as before.

'I can read,' he complained to me today, 'but I can't write much, or think coherently and at length.'

Nor can he speak coherently and at length.

Unlike her husband, Beatrice, despite her 83 years, is full of vital energy – mental and physical. She thinks clearly, speaks much, and writes interestingly. She is writing an extensive introduction to the third edition of their *Soviet Communism* and is preparing it for publication. When we were about to leave, Beatrice recalled that she wanted to give Agniya a bunch of flowers from her garden. Like a young girl, she ran to the gardener's house to give him instructions.

Nonetheless, as we said goodbye, Beatrice said pensively: 'I feel like a *ghost of the past* in today's world.'

Maybe she is right. The Webbs are unquestionably the best representatives of England's past, which is crumbling catastrophically before our eyes.

I'm afraid they won't last long.

25 May

Negrín and I wandered in the neighbourhood of Bovingdon for some two hours today. It was cold and rainy (we have a late and cold spring this year), but that hardly distracted us from a lively discussion of the various topics of the day.

Among other things I told Negrín about my conversation with the Webbs (on 22 May). He started challenging one aspect of their forecast: Negrín, on the basis of the impressions he has formed of the United States, is convinced that if the war should end with the general crisis of capitalism, a proletarian revolution is most likely to take place precisely in the United States. I dissented. We argued at length without reaching agreement.

We then discussed the war prospects, British foreign policy and the position of the Soviet Union. In the course of the conversation I said: 'A future historian may find it highly strange and even tragic that at such a moment two mighty states – the USSR and Great Britain – conducted negotiations concerning the repatriation of 400 sailors for six months and failed to reach an agreement. Even worse is the fact that the issue of the repatriation of 400 sailors was the sole subject of their diplomatic negotiations for those six months. There was nothing else!'

We made a few steps in silence and then I added: 'Actually, there is nothing strange about this. England's foreign policy since the last war (as well as that of the other capitalist countries) has always been characterized by a feral hatred of socialism, of communism, of anything "Red". This hatred blinds the ruling classes of England and makes them pursue a political line that is deeply harmful to their own long-term interests. Hence the policies of Curzon, Baldwin, Chamberlain and Churchill towards the USSR. The servants of the bourgeoisie, like MacDonald, Bevin and others, follow their masters willingly, all the more so as they themselves have little liking for communism and the USSR. There are of course exceptions – Lloyd George, Eden, Cranborne and others – but these are merely the exceptions that prove the rule. In the ninth year of my service in England, I've come to the conclusion that the ruling elites in England and the United States hate us no less than those in Germany or Japan. This explains why the repatriation of 400 Soviet sailors has been the sole subject of Anglo-Soviet diplomatic parley over the last six months.'

'I fully agree with you,' said Negrín. 'I am under no illusions whatsoever concerning the sentiments of the British and American elites towards you. The main question for you, it seems to me, boils down to the following: whose hatred is more dangerous at the present moment? Or, if you prefer, more effective? I have no illusions about that either.'

'Suppose you are right,' I rejoined. 'What of it?... You come to the market to sell your goods. There are several buyers there. Some have more money, some less. Some are handsome, some ugly. You want to sell your goods to those who have more money and are handsome, but they turn up their noses and show you their backs. By contrast, the poorer and uglier ones, whatever their motives might be, make advances to you and offer a good price. What would you do in such a situation?'

'I would sell to the poor and ugly ones,' Negrín answered with a smile, 'entertaining no illusions as to their merits or intentions.'

'Precisely!' I confirmed.

We took another few steps in silence. Then Negrín said: 'All the same, the blindness of the Anglo-American elite amazes me. When your home is on fire, anyone with a bucket of water, no matter what his political convictions are, should be welcome. But they seem to think differently.'

'The reason is,' I concluded, 'that the Anglo-American ruling classes are in an advanced state of decay. As a result, even such men as Churchill and Roosevelt can't understand that the decisive role in this war belongs to the USSR.'

29 May

To *Mansion House* to hear Eden's speech. A strange scene!

I'll start with the surroundings. The City has been smashed to pieces. Whole quarters lie in ruins. There are streets that look like jaws with many teeth ripped out of them. Amidst all this chaos and devastation, the Bank of England, the Stock Exchange and *Mansion House* stand intact – how symbolic! It was in this lord mayor's residence that the meeting was held. At three o'clock hundreds of listeners were seated in dozens of rows of chairs. I have had to go to *Mansion House* on many occasions for banquets. This time I had to go there for a meeting. War!...

Next, the audience. The lord mayor, the City notables, high-ranking officials and ambassadors sit on the platform. Johnson, the US chargé d'affaires, is also there (Winant is on leave): the Americans receive special treatment. Journalists, politicians and businessmen sit in the hall, with the envoys in the first row. Five hundred people in all. Among the diplomats there is a terribly confused and amusing situation. On my right sits Cartier, the Belgian ambassador (the doyen): we ceased being official colleagues three weeks ago. But we exchange greetings as ever, and also a few words. On my left is Raczyński. This is a more complicated matter. We've known each other well for a long time and visited one other, but now 'Poland has declared war on the USSR', so Raczyński sat next to me with his head turned away. He remained in this position throughout the meeting. Although I experience a strong urge to laugh, I too pretend not to notice him. The duke of Alba sits three chairs away from me. He has glanced at me quickly, turned away shyly, and is now examining the handsome ceiling of *Mansion House*. The Estonian Torma (Schmidt),[i] the Latvian Zariņš and the Lithuanian Balutis sit among the envoys opposite me with frozen expressions, pretending not to see me. Again, I have to restrain myself from laughing and assume an air of complete *inscrutability* (as newspapers like to put it). In the same row, somewhat to the right, I can see Subbotić, Colban, Simopoulos and Gripenberg… I couldn't help thinking: 'Yes, it's hard to be a diplomat today!'

Finally, Eden's speech. Foggy and vague. Its central idea was that post-war Europe should not suffer privation. Very well. But how is that to be achieved?… Of course, Eden did not, and could not, give an answer to this essential question. The general impression was of Eden trying to cut iron with a blunt knife.

I repeat: a strange scene! This is how the capitalist world dies.

3 June

Beaverbrook came for lunch (there were three of us: Beaverbrook, I and Agniya). He told us about the present structure of the government. There are three levels: (1) all the ministers, (2) the War Cabinet of nine (Churchill, Beaverbrook, Eden, Bevin, Attlee, Greenwood, Halifax, Anderson and Kingsley Wood), (3) the *Defence Committee* (Churchill, Beaverbrook, Attlee and Eden). The real government is in fact that latter quartet, which meets daily, sometimes twice a day. The War Cabinet does not meet so often and functions poorly. All the other ministers direct their departments and exercise only indirect influence on the general course of policy. Churchill presides over the Defence Committee and deals with military affairs. Attlee is his deputy in the military sphere, Beaverbrook on supply matters, while Eden is responsible for foreign policy. I expressed some surprise that the prime minister's deputy in the military sphere was Attlee. Beaverbrook grinned back and added: 'Oh, there's no danger there: military affairs are dealt with in earnest by Churchill himself.'

[i] August Torma (changed his name from Schmidt in London in 1940). Fought with the British expeditionary forces in northern Russia, 1920; Estonian ambassador in London and representative at the League of Nations, 1934–40.

Beaverbrook said the USSR had three 'friends' in the Defence Committee: Churchill, Eden and himself.

'If that is so,' I asked, 'how can one explain the lack of improvement in relations between our countries?'

Beaverbrook replied that it is the United States that stands in the way. England is now heavily dependent on the USA. The USA is England's only sheet-anchor. And relations between the USA and the USSR are not exactly friendly.

I asked Beaverbrook what he thinks of Hess. Beaverbrook answered without hesitation: 'Oh, Hess, of course, is Hitler's emissary.'

There are many proofs, but Beaverbrook considers two to be the most convincing: an additional fuel tank was attached to Hess's plane, and he flew from Germany to Scotland assisted by a Pelengator.[58] Hess (i.e. Hitler) was counting on British 'Quislings' – the duke of Hamilton,[i] the duke of Buccleuch[ii] and others. It is not without reason that Hess landed near Hamilton's estate. Judging by all the available evidence, Hess expected to spend 2–3 days in England, negotiate with the local 'Quislings' and fly back home. Hess offered England a peace on 'honourable' terms: the British Empire would remain *intact*, the European continent would go to Germany, some colonies in Africa, a non-aggression pact for 25 years. All this was served up with a spicy anti-Soviet sauce in defence of 'civilization against Bolshevist barbarism'. However, the precondition for peace and for an agreement was the removal of Churchill from power. Hess is convinced that as long as Churchill heads the government, there can be no 'friendship' between Germany and England. Beaverbrook remarked sarcastically: 'Hess probably thought that as soon as he presented his plan to the dukes they would run to the king, overthrow Churchill and set up a "reasonable government"... Idiot!'

Hess's gamble on the British 'Quislings' has failed. From being an 'emissary' he has become a 'prisoner of war'. Churchill, according to Beaverbrook, does not fully agree with his theory. However, the PM does not himself have a clear view of the 'Hess incident' and so does not want to speak in parliament on this matter.

Beaverbrook spoke about Hitler's plans. Hitler undoubtedly wants peace. He proposed peace ('on honourable terms') through Sweden right after the collapse of France, he proposed peace through Hess, and is now launching a major 'peace offensive' in the United States – nothing has come or will come of all this! In particular, Roosevelt will not play the role of peace-maker, whatever the Germans may think. The pope, on the other hand, does seem to be seeking

[i] Douglas Douglas-Hamilton (14th duke of Hamilton), Royal Air Force, 1939–45; Conservative MP, 1930–40.

[ii] Walter John Montagu Douglas Scott (8th duke of Buccleuch), a Tory peer.

ways of drawing closer to Hitler. But this will not help him on the question of peace.

Beaverbrook thinks that Hitler's present strategic plan is the following: first, an attack on Egypt and the Suez Channel, then the capture of Gibraltar, and then the liquidation of the British fleet in the Mediterranean.

Will he succeed? Time will tell. The British government, according to Beaverbrook, would have accepted peace with Germany on 'decent terms', but such terms are currently unobtainable. So now it is necessary to fight.

Here Beaverbrook launched a vicious attack on the English: they are carefree and sluggish, underestimate the severity of the situation, do not look ahead, are always late, have grown accustomed to the quiet life and don't want to give up their comforts. They are capable of doing so many stupid things! Examples? There are plenty.

Take, for instance, the loss of Cyrenaica. Why did it happen? Certainly not for the reason assumed by many, that the British government had to remove several divisions from Africa for operations in Greece, but simply because, having reached Bengasi, the Middle East Command became 'dizzy from success'. To such an extent that they sent nearly all their tanks to Cairo! When the Germans launched a sudden attack, there were no tanks in place. They had to be hastily sent back from Egypt. While this was being done, the Germans successfully occupied the whole of Cyrenaica. The British tanks could meet the German forces only on the Egyptian border, which is still the front line today.

Or Crete. Why was Crete lost? Certainly not because the Germans were especially strong or especially capable. It happened for the simple reason that, despite Crete being in British hands for seven months, the Middle East Command did nothing to fortify it. As a result, it fell to the Germans.

The military command in the Middle East? Who are they? Wavell? Just think of the eulogies bestowed on him so recently! And now? *Sic transit gloria mundi.*

On the whole the English, according to Beaverbrook (he himself is a Canadian!), are asleep. They need to be woken up. They need to be struck hard on the head. That, by the way, is why Beaverbrook is conducting such a big campaign in his press about the threat of invasion…

3 June

Together with Novikov, I paid a visit to Leathers,[i] the new minister of war transport, and we seemed to come to an agreement at long last about the repair and adjustment of the SS *Elna* for the repatriation of the Baltic sailors. We shall

---

[i] Frederick James Leathers, minister of war transport, 1941–45.

see. I've already experienced so many disappointments in this affair that I fear to believe anything. Leathers produces a much better impression than Cross, his predecessor. He behaves like a *hard-boiled efficient business man.*

I heard the following colourful story about the appointment of Leathers as minister of war transport. His appointment came as a total surprise to him. He himself confirmed to me in our conversation that he had to accept his post with *24 hours notice*. He has been in coal and transport all his life. I don't know who recommended Leathers to the prime minister as a suitable candidate for leading the War Transport Ministry, but what is certain is that a month ago Churchill summoned him and offered him the newly established post. Leathers' first reaction was negative: he said he had never been engaged in politics before, that he was scared of parliament, which he didn't understand at all, and that he preferred to remain what he had always been, a *business man*.

The prime minister glanced askance at him and said: 'You are afraid of the House of Commons? Hm… I see… But there is a way out: we shall make you a lord.'

'A lord?' echoed Leathers, somewhat perplexed. He had not expected such a turn of events.

Nevertheless, he liked the prime minister's offer and agreed to take the post of minister of war transport.

Coming back to his office, Leathers called his wife: '*Darling*, prepare a bottle of champagne for dinner.'

'What for?' his wife asked in amazement.

'*Darling*, you'll be a baroness tomorrow.'

And that's what happened.

4 June

Shigemitsu arranged a lunch for me. This has never happened before. The Soviet–Japanese pact is obviously having its effect. The other guests were Aras, Monteiro[i] (from Portugal), Nashat-Pasha[ii] (from Egypt), the Thai minister and a certain number of counsellors, including Comrade Novikov. Not a single woman nor a single Englishman.

Aras sat on my right. He has really aged over the past year and looks more and more like an old, exhausted rabbit. In addition, he wears a funny grey pigtail. He is in a state of panic. He prays that fate will spare Turkey disaster over the next two months. Then winter will be on its way… It is difficult to wage war in Anatolia in winter… Turkey will be saved, at least until next spring. He

[i] Armindo Monteiro, Portuguese colonial minister, foreign minister, and ambassador to London until 1943.

[ii] Hassan Nashat-Pasha, Egyptian ambassador to London, 1938–45.

sought my opinion as to whether I deemed it possible that Turkey would not be drawn into the war. How can I make such a prophecy?… My answer was very *noncommittal.*

The general atmosphere at the table was rather funereal. Nashat-Pasha kept saying about war, 'As it was, so it will be.' War will never disappear. It is in humanity's blood. Aras elaborated a strange theory that the victors of wars are not in fact those who win, but those who suffer defeat. He referred to the war of 1914–18 as an example. Someone asked: who was the first inventor of the aeroplane? Shigemitsu, smiling his typically Japanese smile, claimed that the first aeroplane was invented in his country. It appears that a thousand years ago a Japanese saint who lived on the top of a mountain made a flying machine in which he flew from the mountain down to the valley. However, when he was flying over a river in the valley his attention was drawn to two pretty girls washing linen on the river bank. The saint bent over to have a better look, and the machine lost its balance, flipped over, and plunged to the bottom of the river together with the saint. We all laughed. Monteiro recalled Icarus. I spoke of Leonardo da Vinci, the first person who applied himself seriously to the construction of a flying machine.

'Leonardo?' asked Shigemitsu, and then added, 'Ah, that Greek….'

Clearly, the Japanese ambassador is not very well versed in the history of European culture.

'No, he was not a Greek,' Monteiro corrected him. 'He was an Italian artist.'

After lunch Shigemitsu told me that he was going to Tokyo in a few days to consult with his government, and didn't expect to be back soon. My impression is that he might not be back at all. Shigemitsu is one of the few old Japanese diplomats to survive the recent 'purge'. It may be his turn now.

10 June

Less than a month has passed since the last general debate on the war in parliament (6–7 May), and so many changes have already occurred! Time now flies not like an express train, but like a high-speed fighter plane. This was very apparent today, during the parliamentary debate on Crete. Crete is not the main problem, however. Crete is only an excuse, only a vivid symptom of the general disease that is best characterized by the question on everyone's lips, speakers and listeners alike: how long are we going to tolerate defeats from the Germans on land? And what are the causes of our defeats?

It would be wrong to speak of a growing mood in favour of peace. This is not yet the case. Regardless of Crete, the determination to fight, to fight until 'victory', still dominates both government circles and public opinion. But the loss of Crete pained the British more than anything else (perhaps because it happened *on top* of Greece, Cyrenaica and Iraq) and has led them to pose the question: what is going on?

There has not been such a heated debate for a long time – not since Churchill came to power at any rate. During the past year, the House of Commons has turned into an institution which registers, approves and supports the government's decisions. This time it was different. The government was subject to criticism in the House of Commons for the first time this year, and it was not anaemic, official criticism, but real, full-blooded, even passionate criticism, which, of course, does not necessarily make it wholly valid. There was something about the mood that suggested a desire to find a scapegoat for all the recent defeats. And – so typical! – bitter criticism poured in from all directions: Labourites (Bellenger,[i] Griffiths,[ii] Lee-Smith[iii]) competed with Conservatives (Macnamara, Winterton, Beverley Baxter) and National Liberals (Hore-Belisha, Granville[iv]). How may this criticism be summarized?

The attacks targeted the poor coordination between the army and the air force, the absence of a carefully thought-out general plan for the war, the presence of a good number of *duds* in the government, disorder and lack of coordination in industrial mobilization matters, etc. In general, the 'inter-party' attack accused the government of failing to attain a 100% *war effort* in spite of the full authority it enjoys (the act of 22 May 1940). I repeat: for the first time this year the darts of criticism hailed down on the government as a whole, and even on Churchill personally. It was something unprecedented, something new compared with the debates of 6–7 May.

How did the prime minister respond? Very nervously. He was annoyed and irritated, less eloquent than usual, and even made some tactical errors when arguing with his opponents (with Hore-Belisha, in particular). But, on the whole, Churchill rebuffed the attack successfully, although today there was nothing to recall the evening of 7 May, when agitated MPs gave the PM a stormy ovation. Churchill's arguments concerning Crete, however, were entirely unconvincing: the crux of the matter, he said, was that the British had lacked enough anti-aircraft guns to strengthen the Cretan airfields.

Today's debate has left me with a somewhat uncertain impression. Any sensible man would understand the real reason for the British defeats: it is that the British government has no more than 2 million poorly trained and armed soldiers (leaving the Home Guard aside), led by inexperienced officers and commanded by rather thick-headed generals. The British air force, though

---

[i] Frederick John Bellenger, journalist and backbench Labour MP, 1933–68. One of eight Labour MPs to support the no-confidence motion moved by Sir John Wardlaw-Milne in July 1942.

[ii] James Griffiths, Labour MP, 1936–70.

[iii] Hastings Bertrand Lee-Smith, chairman of the Parliamentary Labour Party from 1940–45.

[iv] Edgar Louis Granville, Liberal MP, 1929–51.

not inferior to the German one in quality, lags behind in quantity. With such troops, the British government has to confront a 5–6 million-strong German army, well trained and armed, commanded by excellent generals, and supported by a first-class air force. No wonder the British suffer defeats on land. In fact, considering such conditions, one could say that the British army has not been doing that badly.

None of the critics, however, put the problem in such terms, for this would have led to far-reaching conclusions: either to recognize that the British army is no match for the German army in any conditions and therefore to seek a compromise peace with Hitler, or to acknowledge that England cannot hope for victory without the Red Army, which, in turn, necessitates a complete revision of the 'Russian' (and not only 'Russian') policy of the British government. That is why all critics focused their attacks on various particulars which, though important, could not give a satisfactory answer to the question: what is going on?

The general conclusion: today's debate shows that the government's stock (Churchill's too) has fallen a little, but that the Cabinet is not yet in any serious danger. For deep down everybody understands (without wishing to state openly) the main reason for England's failures, and at the same time everyone understands that the country's position is, despite everything, much stronger and more secure than a year ago. If the prime minister draws the appropriate conclusions from today's debate and throws the *dead wood* out of the government, he will restore his former standing. All the more so as he still has no rivals. But, naturally enough, a lot will depend on developments at the front…

In the corridors of parliament, I met Lloyd George (who did not speak today) and we exchanged a few words concerning the current situation over a cup of tea.

The old man is gloomy and anxious. He, at least, is under no illusions. In view of the present position of the USSR (for which he lays great blame on the British government), Lloyd George excludes the possibility of a British victory. This means that a compromise peace must be sought. On what terms? Lloyd George thinks that peace could be reached if Hitler were to declare himself satisfied with a *Greater Germany*, i.e. incorporating Danzig, Silesia, Austria, Alsace-Lorraine, plus a protectorate over Poland and some other parts of Europe, as well as certain territorial 'modifications' in Belgium and Holland.

I asked Lloyd George what he thought of the peace terms proposed by Hess.

'Absolutely unacceptable,' the old man answered categorically. 'If Hitler decides to insist on these terms, continuation of the war is inevitable.'

As always, Lloyd George enquired about the state of Anglo-Soviet relations. I told him how things stood. He raised his hands in despair and shrugged his shoulders hopelessly.

[Maisky glosses over the most important meeting he had with Eden on 2 June. Eden unveiled to Maisky intelligence reports concerning the German deployment on the Soviet borders, though in order not to compromise the Enigma source he remained somewhat aloof. He even concurred with Maisky that the concentrations might be 'part of a war of nerves' in an attempt to 'force from the Soviet Government concessions'. Eden noted, though, that while Maisky emphatically denied the rumours, it seemed 'that he might be trying to convince himself as he went along'. The British uncertainty was well discerned also in the intelligence passed on to Eden before the meeting. Although he was advised that the deployment pointed 'definitely to final German preparations for an attack on the Soviet Union', this observation was qualified by a reservation 'that it points to a German intention to put such far-reaching demands to Stalin that he will either have to fight or to agree to a "Munich"'. War was therefore likely to be preceded by an ultimatum. As in the case of Churchill's warning in early April, disclosure of the intelligence pursued the aim of encouraging the Russians to resist German pressure by promising British assistance in the event of a German attack.[59] The probability of war was perceived to be so low that Geoffrey Dawson, editor of *The Times*, on being informed of the German deployment, commented that 'no one could really explain it'.[60] In early June, Cripps was unexpectedly rushed back to London for consultations on the German threat that would face the British in the Middle East if the Russians were to conclude a military alliance with Germany. The recall, therefore, was aimed not at laying the foundations for an Anglo-Soviet alliance, but rather at finding ways to discourage the Russians from succumbing to the fanciful German demands concerning the Middle East. The fact that the announcement of his recall was withheld, together with the hints dropped by Cripps during his last meeting with Vyshinsky that if circumstances changed he might not return to his post in Moscow, fuelled a wave of rumours. Maisky went out of his way to establish whether the recall came against the background of Hess's mission and indicated connivance in the German move eastwards.[61] To allay German suspicion, Stalin, briefed by Maisky from London, issued the notorious communiqué of 13 June, dismissing the rumours of an 'early war' as 'clumsy propaganda by forces interested in an extension of the war'.[62]]

10 June

Conversation with Eden

(1) In reply to Eden's question concerning an 'alliance' between Hitler and the USSR, I declared that there has been neither a new agreement nor a dissolution of the old one between us. Powerful impressions and mistrust. Eden says he has information suggesting that the most serious negotiations, on matters of immense importance, are being conducted between Germany and the USSR. I: 'One should not believe every rumour.' Eden: Upon the arrival of Cripps, the further course of Anglo-Soviet relations will be discussed.

(2) Eden: Have I received a reply to his démarche of 2 June concerning the Middle East? No! My personal opinion: considering the present state of relations between England and the USSR, it would be difficult to respond

to this démarche. Eden understood this: he will try to clear a path for the elimination of the controversial issues. I: The door to regulating relations is open. It's the British government's turn. Eden, reverting to the démarche of 2 June, emphasizes its importance and requests that the reply be expedited. Time is running out.

(3) I ask about the fate of Hess. Eden replies that he will have to spend some time in England – until the end of the war. Eden's theory: Hess fled because of a quarrel not with Hitler, but with another dignitary (Ribbentrop or Himmler).[i] All those men are at each other's throats. Cudahy says Göring refused to receive him, having learnt that he had met Ribbentrop and Goebbels.

Talk of peace in the USA–Germany game. Has no effect on Roosevelt. The English will continue 'to the end'. Winant went to Washington not to lay the ground for peace, but to speed up US aid to England.

12 June

Called on Vansittart. Today, on the occasion of the king's birthday, he was given his peerage. He will be 60 next week and he is retiring.

I congratulated Vansittart in a routine manner and then added haltingly: 'To be honest, I don't know whether it's appropriate to congratulate you on your elevation to a peerage. The future is uncertain, and – who knows – might the title become not an *asset but a liability*?'

Vansittart shrugged his shoulders and agreed that the future was indeed impenetrable and that the war would eventually bring about great changes in Europe and in England, in domestic as well as foreign politics.

'Well, this is *Zukunftmusik*,' Vansittart laughed. 'In the meantime, I have secured a platform for my views just in case. I first thought of the House of Commons, but it's too late to embark on a parliamentary career at 60. The House of Lords suits me better. And, of course, my pen remains at my side.'

Vansittart now intends to live in Denham and visit London a few times during the week. He wants to write and to speak. He wants to preserve his name, Vansittart, in his new title.

Parting with Vansittart, I involuntarily cast my gaze over his office, which is so familiar to me. Many reminiscences flashed through my mind. All the emotions, conversations, hopes and disappointments I experienced here!… Especially vivid was the memory of my first sharp clashes with Vansittart at the time of the Metro-Vickers affair. Much water has flowed under the bridges since then! Eight years, no less!

My oh my! I've been too long in England!

---

[i] Heinrich Luitpold Himmler, head of the Gestapo from 1936.

12 June

The press is conducting a vast campaign, focusing on the massing of German troops on the Soviet border and the inevitability of war between the USSR and Germany…

Here is what I have just learnt about the hidden history of this campaign. On 7 June, Churchill summoned the editors of the London newspapers and briefed them on the war situation in the spirit of his speech in parliament on 10 June. The PM's speech gave little cause for cheer. Above all, the listeners couldn't see how and when England might win.

One of the editors asked Churchill a question concerning relations between the British and Soviet governments. Churchill replied that the Soviet government resembles a crocodile, which bites whether you beat it or pat it. The British government, he said, had tried various means of improving relations with the Soviet Union and had sought to influence it, but all to no avail. Eventually, the British government had come to the conclusion that it would be better to let things follow their natural course. A collision between Germany and the USSR is inevitable. The massing of German troops on the Soviet border proceeds apace. One must wait…

Then Churchill upbraided the press for its criticism of the government. The prime minister welcomes healthy criticism, of course, but the scheming against the Cabinet carried out in the newspapers recently is a quite different matter. What followed looked like a scene from *Boris Godunov*.

Churchill announced in an emotional voice that he was not holding on to power, and that if the nation did not approve of his policy, he would resign and leave his place to a better man.

To this the editors cried out that it was not possible to manage without Churchill, that he was the true leader of the nation, and that they were in essence happy with everything. This led to a reconciliation.

After that Churchill gave instructions to Duff Cooper (as well as to the Foreign Office) to go to town on the theme of the inevitability of war between the USSR and Germany.

13 June

Eden telephoned, invited me and asked me to come alone, because Eden would be alone. I answered him that I did not see any reason not to bring Novikov with me. When we were in the reception area, the secretary emerged and stated that it would be better for N. to wait in the reception area. However, I went in to see E. with N. Seeing us together, E. flushed deeply with irritation, which I had never seen in him so far, and shouted: 'I don't want to be rude, but it should be said that today's invitation is for the ambassador alone, not for the ambassador and the counsellor.' I replied that there were no secrets between me and N., and I did not understand why he could not accompany me in the discussions. E. heatedly said that he had no personal animosity toward N., but that he could not set an undesirable precedent; if the Soviet ambassador could arrive with his counsellor, then other ambassadors can do the same. If one can take counsellors, why not take two or three secretaries as well. Then whole delegations will come, not ambassadors. This is inconvenient. Eden has always received ambassadors alone. And he is not about to change his routine. I shrugged my shoulders. N. stayed, but Eden was red-faced and sulky during the whole conversation. An abnormal situation was created. If such a scene is repeated, I will have to bow and go back to the embassy.[63]

(1) Eden informed me on behalf of the prime minister that the concentration of German troops on the Soviet borders has intensified particularly during the past 48 hours. The aim of the concentration: war or a war of nerves? In case it turned out to be war, the British government wished to bring it to the notice of the Soviet government that if Germany attacked, the British government will be prepared to provide assistance using its air force units in the Middle East, to send to Moscow a military mission to share the experiences gained during the war, and to develop economic cooperation in every possible way (through the Persian Gulf and Vladivostok).

(2) I suggested that the proposed measures hinted at a level of friendship between the two countries which presently does not exist.

(3) Even if there was a concentration of troops on the border, I do not believe the Germans will attack the Soviet Union.

(4) I attracted Eden's attention to the press campaign connected with Cripps's return to England. What a pity they were busy speculating.

(5) Asked about Cripps's plans. Eden – he will return within 5–10 days. That is what the plans are right now. I mentioned *The Times's* suggestion to Cripps from 13/6 to remain in England.

[In his memoirs, Maisky overplays his own warnings to Stalin. He has successfully deluded historians into believing that on 10 June he transmitted to Moscow an 'urgent' ciphered telegram with specific intelligence he had obtained from Cadogan. He claims, therefore, that it was with 'extreme amazement' that he reacted to Stalin's response in the form of the communiqué released on the evening of 13 June, denying the rumours of an impending war between Germany and Russia. What he conceals is that the communiqué was in fact a logical culmination of his own appraisals. Fully attuned to the prevailing views in the Kremlin, he attributed the rumours to Churchill and the British government, following Cripps's return to London on 12 June. But in his memoirs he repeats a couple of times that 'the shaft in the direction of Britain with which the Tass communiqué began left no room for doubt that it was the reply to the warning given by Cadogan'.[64] His obsession with the communiqué stands in sharp contrast to the skimpy coverage of the events in the diary leading up to the war. The emphasis conceals the fact that the significant meeting with Cadogan, at which he received the detailed evidence of German troop concentrations, took place not on 10 June, as he claims, but rather on 16 June. 'Maisky at 3,' jotted Cadogan in his diary, 'and I gave him a number of particulars of German concentration on Russian frontier.' Maisky's blatant and misleading falsehood, overlooked by historians so far, was aimed at covering up his own contribution to the self-deception which affected the Kremlin on the eve of war.[65] In private, Maisky admitted shortly after the outbreak of war that he 'never thought Hitler would attack, act of madness'.[66]

At their meeting of 13 June, Maisky warned Eden that 'the type of reports which had appeared yesterday in the press would not be understood in Moscow and would be resented there'. Eden, however, had summoned Maisky to inform him of the increasing flow of reliable intelligence in the previous 48 hours, which now left the Joint Intelligence Committee convinced that Hitler 'has made up his mind to have done with Soviet obstruction and intends to attack her'.[67] The German deployments, he pointed out, 'might be for the purpose of a war of nerves, or they might be for the purpose of an attack on Russia'. However, still under the influence of the press campaign following Cripps's return from Moscow, Maisky paid no heed to Eden's frantic attempts to point out that the information had been obtained from extremely reliable sources. In fact, at a meeting with McDonald of *The Times* on the same day, he deplored the Foreign Office's 'stunt' in the paper and produced extensive arguments against a possible German attack. He dismissed the presence of the 130 German divisions deployed on the border as 'mere embroidery', while the Soviet Union counted on the strength of its military.[68] Burdened nonetheless with the heavy responsibility of weighing the significance of the intelligence, Maisky pressed Eden for specific details 'at an early date, either today or during the week-end'. The urgency of Maisky's request was lost on Eden, who promised to consult Churchill and the general staff before releasing the intelligence.[69]

The decision to part with momentous evidence obtained through Enigma was finally sanctioned by Churchill late on Sunday, 15 June. It included a map that depicted in minute detail the deployment of the German forces on the border, with a sarcastic comment that comparison of it with Maisky's remarks to Eden during their interview makes 'very funny' reading. As Maisky was away for the weekend, the transfer of the information was delayed until the next morning.[70] Maisky was astounded when he was subjected to Cadogan's detached and monotonous recital of 'precise and concrete' evidence. What disturbed him was not so much the realization, subsequently so graphically depicted in his memoirs, that 'this avalanche, breathing fire and death, was at any moment to descend' upon Russia, but rather the content of his previous misleading communications, which had led to the publication of the communiqué denying rumours of war. He hastened, therefore, to cable Moscow, reversing his earlier assessments.[71] Indeed, when Cripps dined with Maisky on 18 June, he formed the distinct impression that Maisky 'seemed much less confident that there would not be a war' than he had been at their meeting a few days earlier. He noticed that their conversation had brought about 'a complete deflation of the Soviet Ambassador who now seemed very depressed'.[72] The same impression was gained by Geoffrey Dawson, who found Maisky suddenly convinced of a German invasion.[73]]

18 June

A week after his arrival in London, Cripps and his wife visited Agniya and me. We lunched together at the embassy.

What mood are the Crippses in?

Lady Cripps is in reasonable spirits. She said frankly that she had been in Moscow [word missing] and that her liking for the Soviet Union, far from weakening, had grown. She has only one grudge against us: not long before her departure from Moscow, their Soviet driver was sentenced to three years' imprisonment for a minor *accident*, despite the driver having 11 years of irreproachable service behind him and despite him not being at fault for the accident. He was definitely a victim of 'politics', since he worked for the British ambassador. I vigorously rebutted Lady Cripps's interpretation, but it proved impossible to convince her.

With Cripps himself, the situation is far more serious. As far as I could understand from our conversation, his general opinion is that improvements in Anglo-Soviet relations are altogether impossible because the Soviet Union, apprehensive of any complications with Germany, does not desire such improvements. Cripps is not inclined to blame us for that. He understands our position: we simply do not want – after the defeat of France – to bear the full brunt of the German army. But why do we repeat over and over again that it is the Baltic question that makes improvement of relations impossible?

Keeping the primary reason for the difficulties of Anglo-Soviet relations in mind, Cripps has tried throughout the last year to approach the thorny problem from the point of view of a change in the general balance of power on the world stage. That is why he suggested from the outset to conclude a general political agreement between England and the Soviet Union that would lead to such a change (particularly with the assistance of the United States), and then to resolve other contentious matters. However, the Soviet government did not follow this path for the reason mentioned above.

Proofs? There are plenty, but Cripps will limit himself to just three. (1) The proposals of 22 October 1940 undoubtedly provided a basis for a desirable agreement between our countries. The Soviet government said they were insufficient to serve as a basis. Let's assume this was so. But then why did the Soviet government not advance any counter-proposals? Why did it not propose amendments to Cripps's proposals? Nothing of the sort happened. Cripps did not even get a reply to his proposals. (2) Trade negotiations with Mikoyan. There was a moment when the negotiations were proceeding quite smoothly and the outlines of an agreement seemed to be taking shape. Mikoyan asked Cripps to finalize the British proposals. Cripps sent him a detailed letter, but did not even receive confirmation that his letter had been delivered to

Mikoyan. It would seem that this fact aggrieved Cripps more than the failure of the trade negotiations. How very English: such impoliteness! (3) When Cripps once complained about the differences in the Soviet government's attitude to Germany and England, Molotov told him that the USSR had a non-aggression pact and trade agreements with Germany. Cripps then said: 'England is also prepared to conclude a non-aggression pact and trade agreements with you.' Molotov immediately shifted the conversation to another topic. Yes, it is absolutely clear to Cripps: the USSR does not want to improve its relations with England out of fear of complicating its relations with Germany.

I asked Cripps: 'What do you actually want? To draw the Soviet Union into the war on the British side?'

Cripps replied: 'No, I don't want that. I accept as a fact your desire to stay out of the war. More than that, I quite understand it. All I want is for your "neutrality" in respect of England to be at least 75% as friendly as your "neutrality" in respect of Germany.'

We argued at length on this issue, but Cripps stuck to his guns.

The conversation then turned to short-term prospects. Cripps is absolutely convinced of the inevitability of a German attack on us and is certain this will happen very soon.[74]

81. Cripps on his way to warn Maisky of the impending invasion of Russia, 18 June 1941.

'If this does not happen before the middle of July,' he noted, 'I'll be greatly surprised.'

Cripps added that, according to the British government's information, Hitler has amassed 147 divisions on the Soviet borders.

I set about disproving this. The point of my objection was that, to my mind, Hitler is not yet ready for suicide. A campaign against the Soviet Union is, after all, tantamount to suicide. That is why it is difficult for me to believe in a German attack on the Soviet Union, especially in the next few days. It is difficult to deny the concentration of German troops on our borders, but I deem this more likely to be one of Hitler's moves in the 'war of nerves'. I cannot rule out the possibility that Hitler may start making demands to us concerning supplies and trade. Politicians seek to create a suitable psychological atmosphere to lend extra weight to their demands. But war? An invasion? An attack?... I can't believe it! It would be madness.

One more thing. Before preying on his victim Hitler always tries to encircle him, isolate him and undermine him from the inside. He acted in this way even in respect to small countries – Norway, Holland, Belgium and Yugoslavia. Preparations of this kind are all the more necessary in respect to the Soviet Union. But no such preparations are to be observed. Sweden and Turkey are neutral. The Middle East is outside German influence. Japan concluded a pact of neutrality with us as recently as April. So there is no encirclement. No isolation. And, needless to say, there is no strong 'fifth column' in the Soviet Union. Given these conditions, will Germany risk an attack on the USSR? Such a step seems improbable.

Cripps would not agree with me. He adduced the following arguments. Hitler cannot plunge into a final and decisive battle against England until the potential threat to Germany from the east has been eliminated. This must be done this year. For the Red Army is a serious force. It will be too late to attack the USSR in 1942, because all the defects exposed by the Finnish campaign will have been rectified by then. The Red Army will be too strong, while the strength of the Reichswehr is more to likely to start diminishing. Today, after eight campaigns (Austria, Czechoslovakia, Poland, Norway, France, Holland, Belgium and the Balkans), the Reichswehr is at its zenith. Army morale is exceptionally high and vast experience has been accumulated. True, the USSR has more men and machines, but the Germans are better at organizing than the Russians. Cripps, comparing the two sides objectively, finds it difficult to foretell the outcome of Germany's clash with the USSR. One thing is clear, however: Hitler's chances of success are much higher now than they will be in a year's time. That is why Cripps is so sure that Hitler will strike. Moreover, Cripps possesses absolutely reliable information that this is just what Hitler is planning. If he manages to defeat the Soviet Union, he will then bring all

Germany's might down on England. Cripps has spoken to some members of the British government who think that before attacking the USSR Hitler will present us with an ultimatum. Cripps does not agree. Hitler will attack us without prior warning because he is interested not so much in getting food, raw materials, etc. from the USSR, as in the destruction of the country and the elimination of the Red Army.

We had a long argument. Cripps stuck to his line.

I asked Cripps when he was going to return to Moscow. He shrugged his shoulders and said this depended on many circumstances. He started elaborating. First, he mentioned the TASS communiqué of 13 June which, in Cripps's view, was issued to please Schulenburg. Its meaning is clear: the Soviet government lets it be known that Cripps is no longer a 'persona grata' and had better leave Moscow. I objected, assuring Cripps that the Soviet government has a high opinion of him personally and that all his difficulties in the USSR have stemmed from the policy of the British government. Cripps, however, did not agree with this and by way of proof cited a telegram he received today from Moscow which says that the Moscow diplomatic corps considers the communiqué to be a 'polite hint' on the part of the Soviet government aimed at showing Cripps the door. Cripps kept returning over and over again to Schulenburg as the cause of all his troubles in Moscow. It was obvious that Schulenburg vexes Cripps greatly.

I could no longer restrain myself and exclaimed: 'Schulenburg has positively bewitched you. This only goes to show how frightened the British are of Hitler.'

Cripps was somewhat embarrassed and switched to a more general theme. The communiqué of 13 June was only the first point. There was a 'second', more important one: the Soviet government's unwillingness to improve its relations with England for the aforesaid reasons. This is manifest in every quarter. Here, Cripps gave vent to his grievances. He was fully 'isolated' from Soviet life in Moscow, he was refused additional accommodation for his staff, he was cold-shouldered at every turn (Molotov, for instance, would not meet him before he left for London). He did not dare to invite members of the Soviet government to the embassy for fear they would decline his invitation: after all, any refusal of this sort would acquire political significance in the eyes of Moscow's diplomatic corps, Schulenburg in particular (again Schulenburg!).

No, Cripps is not planning to return to Moscow soon! What for? Of course, if war breaks out, that's a different matter. He could be of use in Moscow then. But now… now he can wait.

After Cripps left, I fell to pondering: 'Is Cripps right? Will Hitler really attack us?'

I did not reach any certain conclusion. It seemed improbable to me that Hitler could attack, knowing our might and our determination to resist. But does he know of them?...[75]

21 June (Bovingdon)

The Morning

A wonderful summer's day. Bright sun. Hot. Only three or four days since the change in the weather: it had been incredibly cold until the middle of June. Today we wore light suits and cycled. I'm making remarkable progress in this art.

Then I lay on the grass, resting my head on my hands, and gazed into the deep blue skies. I lay and wondered: 'Will there really be war?'

In the past 2–3 weeks the atmosphere in London has been thick with anticipation of a German attack on the Soviet Union. The press writes about it, it is discussed in the corridors of parliament, Churchill has spoken about it in public more than once, offering us the British government's assistance, and Cripps told me about it with absolute confidence just three days ago...

Could this be artificially inflated English speculation? Maybe it's just *wishful thinking* on the part of the British? One more attempt to spoil our relations with Germany and draw us into the war on their side?

82. A weekend at the country house of the exiled Spanish prime minister, Negrín.

To tell the truth, I am disinclined to believe that Hitler will attack us. Fighting Russia has always been hard. Invasions have always ended in sorrow for their initiators. It is enough to recall the Poles (during the Time of Troubles), Charles XII, Napoleon and the kaiser in 1918. The diesel motor has, of course, introduced great changes in the methods and possibilities of the art of war, but still… Russian geography remains the same. Besides, and this is particularly important, we have a mighty army; we have tanks, aeroplanes and anti-aircraft guns. We have the same tools of war as Germany; France, for example, did not have them. We have deep internal unity, as France did not have. We have firm and wise leadership, as France did not have. We shall be able to stand up for ourselves. Will Hitler risk attacking us under these conditions? It would be tantamount to suicide…

Or perhaps Hitler's condition is so critical that there is nothing he can do but go for broke?

Who can tell?

The Evening

After lunch, I was hastily summoned to London at Cripps's request. He came to see me at 4.30 p.m.

He again spoke of the inevitability of a German attack on the USSR. Very soon.

'To tell the truth,' he said, 'I expected the attack to occur this "weekend" – tomorrow, the 22nd – but Hitler has evidently delayed it till next Sunday, the 29th.'

I asked: 'Why till "Sunday" exactly?'

'Because Hitler,' replied Cripps, 'generally likes to attack his victims on Sundays. After all, it gives him a small advantage: the enemy is somewhat less prepared on Sundays than usual.'

Being convinced of the inevitability of war between the USSR and Germany, Cripps has already undertaken some preliminary measures. He has arranged with the British government for a military and economic mission to be sent to Moscow immediately following the outbreak of hostilities. The men have already been selected ('Serious men, who will be able to take decisions on the spot!') and the means of transportation provided for. Not a moment will be lost. But Cripps wanted to know what attitude the Soviet government would take towards such plans. Would the Soviet government find it possible to cooperate with England in the event of a German invasion? Or would it prefer to act quite independently?

I could not give Cripps a definite answer and promised to liaise with Moscow at once.

On parting, Cripps said: 'I am now off to the country. I need to have some rest before things get going.'

Towards eight in the evening I returned to Bovingdon. Negrín and I walked together around the garden for a long while, discussing the situation. Negrín, like Cripps, is also almost certain that war between Germany and the USSR is at hand.

Later I kept turning over in my head all the arguments for and against an imminent attack. It seemed improbable – not in general, but right now. Nonetheless, a puzzling question haunted me: 'Will there really be war?'

By the time I went to bed I had almost convinced myself that Hitler was not bluffing this time, but intended a serious invasion. Still, I did not want to believe it.

22 June

War!

I was woken at 8 a.m. by a telephone call from the embassy. In a breathless, agitated voice, Novikov informed me that Hitler had declared war on the USSR and that German troops had crossed our border at 4 a.m.

I woke up Agniya. There was, of course, no question of going back to sleep. We dressed quickly and went down to hear the nine o'clock news on English radio. Novikov had called for the second time a few minutes earlier: Eden wished to see me at 11.30.

We had a hasty breakfast, listened to the nine o'clock news, which added nothing to what we already knew, and set off for London. In the embassy we encountered a crowd of people, noise, commotion and general excitement. It resembled a disturbed beehive.

When I was getting into the car, to drive to Eden's office, I was told that Comrade Molotov would be going on the air at 11.30. I asked Eden to postpone our meeting by half an hour so that I could listen to the people's commissar. Eden willingly agreed. Sitting next to the radio, pencil in hand, I listened to what Comrade Molotov had to say and took down a few notes.

I arrived at the Foreign Office at midday. I was led into Eden's office. This was without doubt a major, serious and historic moment. One might have been forgiven for thinking, had one closed one's eyes, that everything should be somehow unusual, solemn and majestic at such a moment. The reality was otherwise. Eden rose from his armchair as usual, and with an affable expression took a few steps towards me. He was wearing a plain grey suit, a plain soft tie, and his left hand had been hastily bound with a white rag of some sort. He must have cut his palm with something. The rag kept sliding off, and Eden kept adjusting it while we talked. Eden's countenance, his suit, his tie and

83. Maisky informed of the war through Molotov's radio speech.

especially that white piece of cloth entirely removed from our meeting any trace of the 'historic'. That modest dose of solemnity which I felt in my heart on crossing the threshold of Eden's office quite evaporated at the sight of that rag. Everything became rather simple, ordinary and prosaic. This impression was further enhanced when Eden began our conversation by asking me in the most humdrum fashion about the events at the front and the content of Comrade Molotov's speech. This 'humdrum' tone was sustained for our entire meeting. I couldn't help but recall the sitting of parliament on 3 September 1939, when Chamberlain informed the House about the outbreak of the war. At the time that sitting also struck me as being too simple and ordinary, lacking the appropriate 'historical solemnity'. In real life, it seems, everything is far more straightforward than it is in novels and history books.

I'll not dwell on the content of my talk with Eden here (I have attached it).

At 9 p.m. I listened to Churchill's broadcast with bated breath. A forceful speech! A fine performance! The prime minister had to play it safe, of course, in all that concerned communism – whether for the sake of America or his own party. But these are mere details. On the whole, Churchill's speech was bellicose and resolute: no compromises or agreements! War to the bitter end! Precisely what is most needed today.

At the same time, the response came through from Moscow to the question posed by Cripps yesterday: the Soviet government is prepared to cooperate with England and has no objection to the arrival of British missions in the USSR.

I called Eden and asked him to communicate to Churchill my complete satisfaction with his speech. I also agreed to meet Eden the next morning.

So, it's war! Is Hitler really seeking his own death?

We did not want war; we did not want it at all. We did all we could to avoid it. But now that German fascism has imposed war on us, we shall give no quarter. We shall fight hard, resolutely and stubbornly to the end, as befits Bolsheviks. Against German fascism first of all; later, we will see.

[Well into the morning of 22 June, Stalin did not exclude the possibility that Russia was being intimidated into political submission by the Germans. As Molotov confessed to Cripps a week after the outbreak of war, the Kremlin had not anticipated that war 'would come without any discussion or ultimatum'.[76] Stalin's miscalculation hinged on the belief that Hitler would attack only if he succeeded in reaching a peace agreement with Britain. When war broke out, recalled Litvinov, 'all believed that the British fleet was steaming up the North Sea for joint attack with Hitler on Leningrad and Kronstadt'.[77] This explains the ominous silence and confusion which engulfed Maisky in the early days of the war. It is indeed most revealing that when Maisky met Eden on the day of the invasion, he was entirely haunted by the likelihood of an imminent Anglo-German peace: 'could the Soviet Government be assured that our war effort would not slacken?' Maisky urged Churchill to dispel the rumours of peace (which had been so prominent since Hess's arrival in Britain) in his radio speech to the nation which was scheduled for the evening.[78]

Britain was no better prepared for the new reality of an alliance of sorts. The Ribbentrop–Molotov Pact had entrenched a fatalistic political concept, meticulously cultivated at the Foreign Office, that the Soviet Union was 'a potential enemy rather than a potential ally'.[79] Contrary to common belief, British intelligence did not perceive even the likelihood of a German–Soviet confrontation until mid-June 1941. Once war became almost a certainty (a mere week before the German attack) the chiefs of staff evaluated that the Wehrmacht would cut through Russia 'like a hot knife through butter' within 3–6 weeks, leading to the capture of Moscow. The British government's gloomy prognosis of Soviet prospects, which at best afforded Britain a breathing space and allowed her to pursue the peripheral strategy, did not encompass a full-blooded alliance, but rather, as Eden put it, 'a rapprochement of some sort ... automatically forced upon us'.[80]

Churchill's famous speech of 22 June addressed varying quarters and brilliantly concealed his determination to avoid major commitments. Some, like Amery, saw it as 'almost a caricature of his own most florid style'.[81] Churchill had readily acceded to a request by both the chiefs of staff and the Foreign Office not to refer to the Russians as 'allies'.[82] His firm verbal support for Russia reinforced his grip in the domestic domain – weakened as a result of the chain of military fiascos in North Africa, Greece and Crete against the background of the heavy German bombing of Britain. For the moment, the

Russians were satisfied with the denial of any connivance in the German attack and with a public undertaking to pursue the war right to the end.[83]

Churchill's genuine objective was to avoid a revision of his grand strategy, which might affect the Middle Eastern arena. While drafting the speech, he hastened to issue directives on assistance to Russia, which allowed for supplies and military operations, so long as they did not interfere with British deployment in other theatres or endanger British operations in planning or execution.[84] The inherent reluctance to form an alliance was perhaps justified by the expectations of an imminent Soviet collapse. The military mission to Moscow, headed by General Noel Mason-MacFarlane,[i] was specifically instructed by Dill, the chief of staff, not to enter into any 'political commitment' or take any independent decision on assistance and supplies. Collaboration was confined to forming 'centres of improvised resistance further east' once Moscow fell, as a means of extending the breathing space before Hitler resumed his attack on the British Isles.[85] Contrary to Churchill's claims, Stalin realized that the Red Army would have to bear the full brunt of the actual fighting, due to the frailty of British infantry, and therefore did not initially press for a second front. The Soviet military mission focused its efforts in London and Washington on obtaining supplies, in view of the competition for American resources. They further pressed the British to establish a convoy system via the North Sea route to Russia.[86] The idea of 'the second front' was first raised by Beaverbrook at his meeting with Maisky on 27 June. To an extent, Maisky was reverting to his old tactics of inducing his interlocutors to adopt his own ideas as theirs. Maisky referred to Beaverbrook's proposals when he met Eden on 7 July, fully aware of British constraints but nonetheless 'chiefly interested in some action which would impress his Government with our determination to help the Soviet Union at this time'.[87] Such a commitment, if taken, would, of course, have bolstered his precarious position in Moscow.

The idleness which had marked Maisky's life since the outbreak of war changed dramatically overnight. As an ambassador of the only country among the Allies that was actively fighting the Germans, he was overwhelmed with work. As Agniya wrote to Beatrice Webb:

> My husband is negotiating now with half-a-dozen Governments simultaneously ... and he is most of all afraid that one day he will make the wrong Treaty with the wrong Government! The Military Mission and all sort of things military and naval are coming very much into the picture in my husband's work. Sometimes I think that he is getting more like an Admiral, a General and an Air Marshal, all in one person – in fact, like the whole General Staff itself!

Maisky himself wrote to Litvinov that since the outbreak of war he had been daunted by the colossal work at the embassy: 'Little time is left for sleep. And "weekends" are out of the question.'[88]

---

[i] Sir Frank Noel Mason-MacFarlane, lieutenant general, military attaché in Budapest, Vienna and Bern, 1931–34; Berlin and Copenhagen, 1937–39; head of the British military mission to Moscow, 1941–42.

Inevitably his diary entries become more sporadic and at times abbreviated. For the sake of clarity and ease of reading, the text is produced here in full. As Maisky started seeing Eden on almost a daily basis to deal with various aspects of the war, he described in the diary only his more significant meetings. This is even more conspicuous in 1942 and 1943, his last two years in London. Nevertheless, the diary continues to pursue the narrative of the Grand Alliance at its incipience and provides invaluable insights into the growing mistrust between the Allies.]

27 June

The fifth day of the war. One may draw the following conclusions about the English situation in general:

(1) The first round of political support for the war, if we are talking about Great Britain and the British Empire, has been won. Hitler's calculation was quite clear: to strike to the east, to revive his glory as 'saviour of European civilization from Bolshevik barbarism', to cause a split in the public opinion of the 'democracies' and to secure either a favourable peace with them or, at the very least, their effective withdrawal from the war until he has finished dealing with the Bolsheviks. So far, this plan has entirely failed. Neither England nor the United States swallowed Hitler's bait. I have already had occasion to speak about the causes of British belligerence. Far from diminishing the effects of these causes, Hitler's attack on the USSR has enhanced them, for as a result the 'united front' in the country (and with it the social foundation of the bourgeoisie) has been reinforced, and real opportunities for victory over Germany have opened up. The United States have followed England in this instance.

(2) Against this background, Churchill has played an extremely prominent and positive role. His fable about the optimistic frog has proved unexpectedly prescient. Without a moment's hesitation, he brought all his influence and eloquence to bear on the situation. Not only was the prime minister's radio broadcast on 22 June remarkable for its form and inner force: it also presented the case for fighting to the last and offering maximum aid to the USSR with the utmost clarity and implacability. Eden told me that our conversation on the morning of the 22nd had its effect on Churchill's speech. Eden conveyed my requests to Churchill, and Churchill made some amendments to his speech (it should be added that Eden, Beaverbrook and Winant contributed their 'advice' during the preparation of the text). It was critically important for the prime minister to deliver an immediate blow with his bludgeon before anyone could come to their senses. This set the tone at once – both here and in America. Winant told me frankly that without Churchill's speech Washington would not have taken the position formulated by Sumner Welles on the evening of the

23rd as quickly and as definitely as it did. The same goes for England, as many have testified. Had Churchill dithered with his speech and delayed it for 2–3 days, they say, the anti-Soviet elements in the country would have sown a good deal of confusion in the minds of the public. But the prime minister acted with lightning speed – and salvaged the situation. He was greatly assisted behind the scenes by Eden and Beaverbrook, as well as Winant. What were the Labour ministers doing at that critical moment? They said nothing, and some even engaged in sabotage.

(3) So, the first round has been won. England is with us. Hitler's hopes for a separate peace with the 'democracies' have so far failed. All this is good. But some grey areas remain. First, what will England's aid consist of? And will it really be serious? I'm not sure. In particular, it's unclear to me whether the English are bombing northern Germany to the maximum of their capabilities. Second, *bewilderment* is still palpable in the minds of the public. Psychologically, this is quite understandable. Only recently 'Russia' was considered a covert ally of Germany, all but an enemy. And suddenly, within 24 hours, it has become a friend! This transition was too abrupt, and the British *mentality* has yet to adjust to the new state of affairs. This, by the way, was very noticeable at the sitting of parliament on the 24th, when Eden spoke about the German attack on the USSR. His speech was not bad on the whole, but the response was more reserved than might have been expected. Another example was the big lunch (some 400 guests) on the 25th in honour of Fraser,[i] the prime minister of New Zealand. After the chairman Lord Nathan[ii] proposed a toast to the 'success of Russia' and I answered with a few words of gratitude, the response of the audience was cooler than the circumstances warranted. I hope the mood of the English will settle and that the current *bewilderment* will pass.

(4) Thirdly and lastly, great scepticism concerning the Red Army's efficacy may be observed in all quarters. People in the War Ministry believe that our resistance will last no more than 4–6 weeks. One and the same question is discussed in the lobbies of parliament: will the Red Army be able to stand up against the Reichswehr? The *News Chronicle*'s editorial of the 25th contains the words: 'if a miracle happens and the Red Army's resistance lasts till autumn, then…' etc.; 'if, on the contrary, the Red Army collapses in a few weeks (a possibility which must be taken seriously), then…', etc. In all the conversations I have had during these past five days with people of diverse ranks, positions and political sympathies (including workers' deputations), the tune is always the same: 'will the Red Army resist?' Long years of anti-Soviet propaganda have

[i] Peter Fraser, prime minister of New Zealand, 1940–49; minister of external affairs and minister of island territories, 1943–49.

[ii] Harry Louis Nathan, colonel, Labour MP, 1937–40; parliamentary undersecretary of state for war, 1945–46.

clearly left their mark, as has the hypnotic effect of the military might which Germany has exhibited so brilliantly over the course of the war. Developments at the front will play a decisive role in influencing British sentiments in this sphere.

29 June

The first week of the war is over. I am generally satisfied with its results.

True, we have lost some territory in Lithuania and Western Belorussia (Kovno, Grodno, Vilnius and Brest-Litovsk, if we are to believe the Germans), but this is not so important. The territory occupied by the Germans has neither natural borders nor, most probably, any serious fortifications, as we gained it less than two years ago. Meanwhile, the Germans have not managed to pierce the front line anywhere and, most importantly, it has become absolutely clear that the Red Army is capable of measuring swords with the Reichswehr. Not that I doubted this before, but the past week has been a good test of my a priori opinion.

The first week has even surpassed my expectations. I quite anticipated that in the first days we would face failures and partial defeats. I was prepared for this on two accounts. First, the Germans, being the attacking force, could be expected to possess the advantage of surprise, of choosing the points of attack, and of massing their best forces at these points. Second, the Germans are, of course, better at organizing than we. German plans are always worked out in the minutest detail, and the preparation for their execution is usually 100%. Only once everything is in place is the signal to attack given. Our plans and our preparations are rarely anywhere near as complete. There is too much of 'that'll do' and 'hit or miss' about our work. Besides, it always takes us some time to get moving. That's why the Germans were likely to be in the ascendancy for the first week or two. Only later, in the event of things not going so well for us, would we put our shoulder to the wheel and switch to a furious, shock-brigade pace of activity.

Events so far have proved more favourable than I had expected. We shall see what the second week brings. For there is no doubt that the events of the past week were just the first trial of strength: the Germans have yet to call on their main resources.

3 July

Stalin's speech has had a good effect, making a major impression in the press (particularly the *Evening Standard*) and in parliament. Three points have been noted: (1) the speech testifies to an unshakeable determination to continue to the end, (2) and also to the resilience of the Soviet regime, otherwise Stalin would not have spoken so openly about the gravity of the situation. (3) The declaration that only now are the main forces of the Red Army beginning to enter the fray instils a certain optimism.

[Maisky was very quick off the mark, fighting fit after his long diplomatic seclusion and alienation from the Kremlin, which had lasted since the signing of the Ribbentrop–Molotov Pact. Not only did he regain confidence – enough to shake Novikov off his tail even at his first meeting with Eden – but he also managed to convey the sense that his implicit critical attitude towards association with the Germans had been borne out. 'As you know from my preceding communications,' he reminded Molotov, rather embellishing his stance on the eve of the war, 'I regarded the British will to war as fairly strong and did not anticipate an Anglo-German deal in the foreseeable future.' The 'expeditiousness and decisiveness' with which the British government had acted, he added smugly, 'came to me as a pleasant surprise'. He further hailed Churchill, Eden and Beaverbrook, the 'troika of friends of Russia', whom he had cultivated over the years, for the 'firm and favourable position they have adopted towards us'. As usual, this was coupled with the cautious reservation that he was 'far from thinking that all difficulties in the way of Soviet–British cooperation have been eliminated or that its success is now a foregone conclusion'. For the time being, however, the new circumstances rendered his continued presence in London unassailable and indispensable.[89]]

6 July (Bovingdon)

The second week of the war has ended. I feel somewhat relieved. Of course, it is a great pity that our best forces, our young generation, perish in their thousands on the battlefields, that a sea of blood waters our Soviet land. But on the other hand, it has been proved not only in our patriotically motivated imagination, but also in deeds, that the Red Army can measure up to the Reichswehr, that it can withstand the crushing onslaught of the mechanized German Attila. I was sure of that before as well, but observing how often *wishful thinking* distorted the English perspective, I sometimes asked myself: wasn't I also exhibiting certain elements of *wishful thinking* in respect of the Red Army?

Now my doubts have been dispelled. True, we have suffered great losses in men, tanks, planes and territories. In the second week of the war, the Germans crossed the Western Dvina, reached Ostrov, crossed the Prut, entered Bessarabia, advanced towards Berezina and the region of Novograd-Volynsk, but this is not what matters. What matters is that nowhere did the Germans succeed in seriously breaking through our lines and crushing the Red Army's resistance. Our navy is still intact and sturdy, although it gradually moves to the east; our army is strong and battle-worthy; our reserves of tanks and aircrafts are not running low. As in the past, we stand like a solid,

84. Stalin watching over a gloomy Maisky and his first secretary discussing the state of the war.

invincible wall, defending our homeland against the attack of the mechanized Attila.

For the Germans, on the other hand, the situation is becoming increasingly complicated. They are sustaining enormous casualties (700,000 killed and wounded over the first two weeks of the war); 6–7 mechanized divisions are wrecked; no fewer than 200 planes have been destroyed; their lines of communication are getting longer and less easy to operate; partisan warfare and sabotage in the occupied areas make their life ever more intolerable. A large number of indicators suggest that the first wave of the German attack, launched on 22 June, is petering out, not only before reaching Moscow and Kiev, but even without having brought all the Germans up to the old Soviet borders (1939).

It would be the height of stupidity, of course, to think that the spearhead of the German attack has already been broken. Nothing of the kind. The first wave is exhausted, but it will be followed by a second, and the second may be followed by a third. Hitler will stop at nothing to break through: he may use gas or perhaps something even worse. And it would be frivolity of the most unforgivable kind to crow about an easy victory in advance. The enemy is strong, crafty and dangerous. Great sacrifices and efforts will be required on our side before we crush German fascism. It cannot be ruled out that the loss of significant territories, cities and industrial areas may still await us.

It is already quite clear, however, that this is a case of diamond cut diamond. For the first time Hitler has encountered an army that measures up to his own in terms of arms, methods of warfare and tactical techniques, and that surpasses his army in strength and morale. Moreover, Hitler has for the first time come up against a country that is monolithic within and whose leadership far surpasses his own in firmness, wisdom and confidence. The speech by Comrade Stalin, which I heard on the radio in the small hours of the morning of 3 July, is a document of the greatest historical significance. Its basic idea can be simply formulated: a patriotic war to the end! Until victory! No wavering! No compromises! Not a pound of bread, not a litre of petrol to the enemy!

It's amusing to hear complaints on the German radio that we are not 'playing by the rules' of warfare: German tank columns break through our lines, but our armies do not admit that they are encircled and continue to fight stubbornly against the enemy's main forces. A territory is occupied by German troops, but we do not lay down arms: we mount partisan operations, organize sabotage, and, when retreating, destroy everything that might be of use to the enemy. How very 'unorthodox'! And how unpleasant for the German command! They've seen nothing yet. This is just the beginning.

Yes, there is no doubt we will win. The question is only when and at what price?

[Despite the critical situation at the front, the Russians were adamant from the outset that the war aims, the post-war settlement and the strategic priorities needed to be defined. The Anglo-Soviet agreement, signed on 12 July, was of a purely allusive nature, pledging assistance 'without defining quantity and quality'; but most telling from the Soviet point of view was a mutual undertaking not to conclude a separate peace.[90] The wish to regulate political relations clearly preceded thoughts of concrete military collaboration, let alone of a second front. As early as 27 June, at their first meeting since Cripps's return to Moscow, Molotov pressed the need to establish a 'wide political base for cooperation'.[91] At his meeting with Eden on 30 June, Maisky sought as well to broaden the political and military scope of the cooperation.[92] In private, the Webbs gleaned from Maisky that he was sceptical about the willingness of the British to come to a definite understanding on a new international order.[93]

The Soviet military mission, headed by General Golikov,[i] arrived in London in the second week of July. He was, observed Cadogan, 'quite a live little man. The rest all looked like private detectives.' Golikov relayed Stalin's directives (which again leave one in little doubt as to his priorities): a division of labour was clearly envisaged in Moscow,

[i] Filipp Ivanovich Golikov, from July 1940 deputy chief of the general staff, head of the GRU (Soviet military intelligence); head of the military mission to the United Kingdom and Washington, 1941.

85. Maisky with the Russian military mission, General Golikov and Admiral Kharlamov, watched over by the ubiquitous Novikov.

under which the economic onus would fall on the Americans, while the transport of supplies, and military coordination in general, would be worked out in London. The 'French operation' and an offensive in the Balkans were assigned a 'marginal role in terms of both time and investments involved'. 'We're *not* going to do anything – much. This is pretty hopeless,' was Cadogan's judgement.[94] The members of the mission recalled that when they met Margesson, the minister of defence, he 'did not shake hands with us. Nor did he offer us a seat. Throughout our nearly 20-minute-long talk he remained standing, and there was nothing else left for us to do but to follow his example.'[95] General Dill regarded the association with the Russians mostly as a liability. Britain, he warned, was 'being manoeuvred into a false position': 'It is the Russians who are asking for assistance: we are not … All our forces are now being devoted to the accomplishment of a definite strategy for winning the war *without* having allowed for Russian aid.' The feigned cordiality in the negotiations with the Soviet military mission in July was intended 'to encourage' them and conceal the fact that Britain was 'not allied with Russia' and did 'not entirely trust that country'.[96] No wonder Eden was worried 'at the lack of support of the Chiefs of Staff and even of the PM who, for all his brave words, is reluctant to agree to raids'.[97] Having obtained Beaverbrook's support, Maisky continued to press for implementation of a French operation. He certainly had a receptive ear in Moscow. In a message to Churchill of 18 July, for the first time Stalin raised the second front issue, which would dominate relations between the countries with, as Churchill argued in his memoirs, 'monotonous disregard … for physical facts'.[98]]

12 July

Negotiations with the Yugoslavians about a pact. Simović and Ninčić accept our text and are glad we don't insist on a 'National Yugoslavian Committee'.

13 July (Bovingdon)

The third week of the war is over. I feel even calmer. Of course, there are many, very many hardships ahead: the loss of people and possibly territories, the suffering and deprivation of the civil population, the bombing of cities and the burning of villages. But it is even more evident today than a week ago that the Red Army is a worthy adversary of the Reichswehr, that it has withstood the first terrible strike by the German hordes, and that it is capable of withstanding further blows. Then, in due course, when the enemy's strength begins to wane, it will move on to the offensive.

All last week was spent treading water along the same front line (Ostrov, Polotsk, Lepel, Borisov, Bobruisk, Novograd-Volynsk, Chernovtsy, Prut). It was absolutely clear that the energy of the first German attack had exhausted itself, and that some kind of temporary equilibrium was establishing itself on the front line. Only a temporary equilibrium, of course, for there is no doubt that the first attack will be followed by another, which will probably be even fiercer.

But the second attack will lack the element of surprise which played a significant role in the first days of the war (when several hundred planes, incidentally, were destroyed by the Germans right on the airfields), and, on the other hand, the Red Army will meet the second attack being both battle-hardened and better organized. The latter is evident from the creation of three fronts the day before yesterday: north-western (Finland and the Baltics) commanded by Voroshilov, western (north of the Pripet marshes) commanded by Timoshenko[i] and south-western (south of the Pripet marshes plus Bessarabia) commanded by Budenny.[ii] Comrade Stalin will be commander-in-chief – 'de facto', if not 'de jure'. I accept the possibility that more territories may be lost during the second attack, but I am sure that the Germans will fail to defeat the Red Army.

Today, at 2 p.m., a momentous statement was broadcast over the radio in London and in Moscow: an agreement about a military alliance was signed

---

[i] Semen Konstantinovich Timoshenko, marshal of the Soviet Union, people's commissar for defence, May 1940 to July 1941; deputy people's commissar for defence July–September 1941; commander of the Stalingrad front, July 1942, and of the north-western front, October 1942 to March 1943.

[ii] Semen Budenny, marshal, a former tsarist cavalry officer, his association with Stalin during the Civil War saved his life when the purges racked the top brass of the Red Army. Commander-in-chief of the Russian army in the Ukraine and Bessarabia at the outbreak of the war; removed from his command after the disastrous defeats inflicted on his troops in summer 1941.

yesterday evening in Moscow between the USSR and England. The parties undertake to assist one another in every way during the war and to conclude neither a separate armistice nor a separate peace.

Very good!

I remember that about two years ago, when the Anglo-French military delegation went to Moscow to negotiate a mutual assistance pact, I wrote in my diary that the logic of things, despite the subjective aspirations of the two sides, was driving the USSR and England to form a bloc against Germany. Such was the international situation. I made the reservation, though, that the two countries might cease to share common interests and that their paths might diverge, if and when questions surrounding the final division between capitalism and socialism became the order of the day. After I wrote these lines in my diary, many events occurred which seemed to refute my theory entirely: the non-aggression pact with Germany, rapprochement with Berlin along economic and political lines, confrontation with England during the Soviet–Finnish war, and the cold, hostile relations between London and Moscow in the course of last year... More than once during this period I asked myself the question: did I make a wrong prognosis? Was the theory recorded in my diary in August 1939 correct? Shouldn't I amend it?

But an inner voice kept repeating: no, you were not wrong! Your theory is correct! And I did not make any amendments. Now life has proved me right: the USSR and England are allies. They have joined forces to wage a deadly struggle against Germany.

Both countries can say: 'Our paths have converged.' But nothing is forever. The 'paths' can diverge... Under a variety of circumstances. Especially if and when the problem of capitalism and socialism is placed on the agenda in one form or another.

Cripps must be triumphant! His life's dream (since the war broke out, at least) has been fulfilled. What's more, the success is his. This massively strengthens his position. He will return to England as a hero, to the great displeasure and embarrassment of such men as Citrine, Bevin and Attlee, who sent him to Moscow last year, hoping to get rid of a restless and dangerous rival, and who did so much in the past year to prevent Cripps from achieving even a crumb of success in the matter of improving Anglo-Soviet relations. The Labour elite already senses danger in the air and wants to parry it in advance in a typically English manner. *Transport House* invites Cripps to return to the bosom of the party. We'll see how Cripps responds...

Someone else is triumphant today – Eden. Since 1935, when he visited Moscow, he has been an advocate of maximal rapprochement with the USSR. He has never vacillated in this direction, even at the lowest moments in Anglo-Soviet relations. His dream has also come true. He, too, considers himself victorious. His star now shines brightly in the political sky. As he told me of the impending signing of the alliance treaty the day before yesterday, Eden was terribly excited and agitated. We spoke about negotiations with the Poles, Czechs and Yugoslavs, about exerting pressure on Iran, where too many German 'experts' and 'tourists' had gathered, and about the situation in Syria. Eden joked: 'My head is spinning from all these talks and agreements… I'm afraid to get things mixed up and *to make wrong treaty with wrong man*.'

Then, assuming a more serious tone, Eden added with palpable emotion: 'I hope that in 48 hours at most we shall be allies. This is what I have been striving to achieve for so many years!'

The world is in the grip of the most severe contradictions. Today brought a vivid illustration of this fact.

Ever since the USSR entered the war, a tragicomic *controversy* has flared up in England. The BBC introduced the following practice last year: the national anthems of all the Allies are played on Sundays before the nine o'clock news broadcast. Naturally, after 22 June, the question arose: should the 'Internationale' be played over the wireless or not? The answer would seem obvious: it should. But do, please, remember: the 'Internationale' is not only the national anthem of the USSR, but is also the militant song of the international proletariat, and in particular of the British Communist Party. The hair of thousands of British Blimps stands on end when they hear it. It came to blows – in the press, in parliament, in society. Strabolgi raised the matter in the House of Lords and received a quite absurd answer from his party colleague, Lord Snell, who spoke on behalf of the government. Silverman raised the same question in the House of Commons. The government gave the same stupid answer: the USSR is not an 'ally' in the generally accepted meaning of the word. This caused a minor row in the Chamber.

Lady Cripps called on us at ten in the evening. She told us about the row over the 'Internationale' and asked, at Butler's request and 'in complete confidentiality', whether the 'Internationale' was our sole national anthem. I explained that it was. Duff Cooper rang me up on 11 July and asked whether we might be able to find some other Soviet or Russian song to replace it. He, for instance, had heard an orchestra playing 'Kutuzov's March'[99] after Molotov's speech on 22 June – couldn't that be substituted for the 'Internationale'? Needless to say, I categorically opposed the idea. On the 12th, I visited Duff Cooper to discuss how 'cultural rapprochement' between our countries could be achieved. Duff Cooper asked once again: could we not replace the 'Internationale' with something else? I once again expressed my categorical disagreement. I learnt from my conversation with Duff Cooper that Churchill himself is behind all this. He declares: I am ready to do anything for Russia, but I will not allow the communists to make political capital from the 'Internationale'. A strange man!… In the end, Cooper said that the following solution had been found: national anthems would be played for the last time on Sunday the 13th. They would then be cancelled. Instead of anthems, national music of all the Allies would be played in turn on Sundays. I shrugged my shoulders and remarked that the BBC's programming was an internal matter for England, but that I was nonetheless surprised by the reason which led to the proposed change.

The conclusion of a military alliance between the USSR and Great Britain was announced today at two o'clock. I was waiting with curiosity to hear what the BBC would offer at 8.45 in the evening. And? The first item in the programme of national anthems was… a very beautiful but little-known Soviet song. There was no 'Internationale'. After that song, all the other national anthems were played one after another.

I was vexed and amused at the same time. I was vexed because, despite my repeated warning, Duff Cooper did replace the 'Internationale' with another tune. It would have been better if the BBC had played nothing Soviet at all. It looked especially *odd* on the day of the announcement of an alliance between our countries. I was amused because the fear of playing the 'Internationale' vividly demonstrated England's internal weakness. We would not be afraid to play '*God Save the King*' in similar circumstances. The USSR and England represent two different civilizations, and this small but highly characteristic episode shows quite clearly that English civilization is tottering.

We were at the dinner table when the BBC demonstrated the British government's cowardice and foolishness. Agniya got terribly worked up, while being cross with me for being calm and finding it all amusing (I was mocking the British government). She exclaimed: 'I see we have spent these nine years in England for nothing!'

Unable to contain herself, she leapt to her feet and ran out of the room in tears. It took me some time to calm her down. Agniya's reaction produced quite an impression on our guests (the Negríns, Blume,[i] Casares,[ii] Noel-Baker and the Shinwells)… Maybe it will have good political consequences.

[Regardless of the ironic tone in the diary, Maisky was himself on tenterhooks. The Labourite Noel-Baker, who had spent a whole day with the Maiskys and was a witness to the events, sent Eden a six-page remonstration, describing how Maisky 'could not get the question of the anthem out of his head, and he kept coming back and back to it. He was so anxious not to miss the playing of the anthems in the evening that he turned the wireless on at 8.30 and carried it into the dining-room with him. When, in the end,

---

[i] Isabelle Blume-Grégoire, elected to the Chamber of Representatives in 1936, she was one of the first female parliamentarians of the Belgian Labour Party. Head of the welfare service of the Ministry of Work and Marine in London from January 1941 until September 1944.

[ii] Santiago Casares Quiroga, last Spanish prime minister before the Civil War, May to July 1936, who resigned his post having failed to confront Franco's uprising, finding refuge in London.

the "Military March" was played, his mortification was more than apparent.' Following Agniya's tantrum, Maisky asked Noel-Baker to take a walk with him, during which he said that the issue was of paramount importance, as it would 'inevitably produce a painful impression in Moscow'.[100]]

20 July[101]

Yesterday morning I received Stalin's 'personal message' to Churchill with a request to translate it into English and hand it over at once. It was Saturday. I met Eden in the morning, on matters concerning Iran, and asked him to arrange an appointment for me with the prime minister. Eden asked me in confidence whether he should be present when I handed over the 'message'. I replied that the 'message' dealt with military-strategic issues. Eden exclaimed: 'If so, the business can be handled without me.'

Evidently Eden did not, for some reason, wish to be present when the 'message' was handed over. Perhaps because he had already made his plans for the 'weekend' and thought it a pity to cancel them.

At around one o'clock Eden called me from the Foreign Office and said that Churchill would receive me at five in the afternoon, but asked me to come to Chequers, where he was spending the 'weekend'. Having completed the translation of the message and typed it up (to maintain secrecy I did it all myself) I took off to the countryside. The weather was capricious, with rain giving way to bright sunshine. Teterev, who had not been to Chequers before, lost his way and took the wrong turn. When we finally reached the PM's country residence, it was already nearly 5.30. It was embarrassing, but nothing could be done.

A young secretary met me at the door and led me to the prime minister.

'They are having tea,' he uttered on the way.

Dark halls, old paintings, strange staircases… How it should be in a respectful, solid English house several centuries old. Not that I know how old Chequers is. Maybe it is relatively young – by English standards, of course.[102]

Eventually, the secretary flung a door wide open and I found myself in a large lit room in the shape of an extended rectangle. It was noisy and full of life. Mrs Churchill sat at the table and poured the tea. There were several young people of both sexes at the table and near it. General Ismay[i] sat to one side, by a window. Everyone was talking, laughing, exchanging remarks. The air was filled with chatter. Churchill, dressed in strange grey-blue overalls and a belt (a cross between a bricklayer's work clothes and an outfit suitable for a bomb-shelter), was sitting in the other corner of the room and playing *Halma* with some pretty young girl. He gave my hand a friendly shake and replied good-

[i] Hastings Ismay, general, military adviser to Churchill and deputy secretary (military) to the War Cabinet 1940–45.

humouredly to my apologies for being late: 'That's all right. Have a cup of tea while I finish the game.'

Mrs Churchill sat me next to her very hospitably, while Randolph's red-haired wife set about offering me biscuits. I drank two cups. Ate a few biscuits. Randolph was mentioned. His wife complained that she had little hope of seeing him soon. She said proudly that 'baby Winston' had started to walk.

Finally the prime minister ended the game, stood up, nodded to the guests and led me downstairs to a somewhat large and dreary *drawing room*. We sat on a sofa at the fireplace and I presented Churchill with Stalin's 'personal message'. The prime minister started reading it slowly, attentively, now and then consulting a geographical map which was close at hand. He was evidently pleased – pleased at the very fact of having receiving a 'personal message' – and did not try to conceal it. When Churchill came to the paragraph where Stalin said that the position of our army would now be immeasurably worse if it had had to begin its defence at the old borders of the USSR and not the new ones, he stopped and exclaimed: 'Quite right! I've always understood and sought to justify the policy of "limited expansion" which Stalin has pursued in the last two years.'

When the prime minister finished reading the message, I asked him what he thought of it. Churchill replied that first he had to consult C[hiefs] of S[taff]. He could make just a few preliminary comments. He likes the idea of a northern front in Norway. This can be done. He is prepared to go for it. He is also prepared to send a light division there at the appropriate moment, although it would be not Norwegian (there is no such division), but mixed. Yes, the plan of launching an offensive in northern Norway so as to gradually move down to the south of Scandinavia is most attractive. Such an operation could strengthen the position of Sweden considerably. As if to prove his point, Churchill picked up the telephone and asked to speak to Admiral Pound,[i] chief of the naval staff. He began asking him about the preparations for Admiral Vian's[ii] naval operation and the aircraft carrier operation in the area of Petsamo – they are scheduled for the end of the month. He pressed Pound to act fast and gave him orders in a sharp, somewhat irritated tone.

But on the matter of a second front in France, Churchill immediately took a negative stand. This cannot be done. It's risky. It will end in disaster for England, bringing no benefits at all. All the prime minister's arguments are expounded in detail in his reply to Stalin's 'personal message'. To vindicate his

---

[i] Sir (Alfred) Dudley Pound, admiral of the fleet, 1939; first sea lord and chief of naval staff, 1939–43.

[ii] Sir Philip Louis Vian, as a captain, led the attack on the battleship *Bismarck*, May 1941; promoted to rear-admiral and sent to Russia for naval cooperation in the evacuation of Russians from Spitzbergen, July 1941.

position, Churchill appealed to Ismay, who had just entered the room where we were talking. Ismay fully backed the PM. I realized that for the time being it would be impossible to change Churchill's mind on this matter. He had already formed a quite definite view of it. Perhaps in order to soften the impression made by his refusal, the prime minister began to talk about an air offensive against Germany from the west.

'We shall bomb Germany mercilessly,' he exclaimed emphatically. 'Day after day, week after week, month after month! We will keep expanding our raids and increasing the strength of our strikes. In the end we will overwhelm Germany with bombs. We will break the morale of the population.'

Then Churchill suddenly shifted to Iran, repeating everything I had heard from Eden this morning, but in a sharper and more resolute form.

'The shah must not be allowed to pursue *monkey tricks*,' the prime minister uttered heatedly. 'Persia must be with us! The shah must choose one way or the other.'

Churchill added that if the shah persisted, a military occupation of Persia by Anglo-Soviet forces would be necessary. He hinted, moreover, that the Persian operation, along with Norway, could also be a sort of 'second front'.

Since it was clear that there could be no talk of a landing operation on the other side of the Channel for now, I turned to questions of supplies, emphasizing their importance. In particular, I focused on the Air Ministry's refusal to supply planes to us (we had requested 3,000 fighters and 3,000 bombers) and asked in this connection whether some of the machines could be delivered to us by air from the Middle East. Churchill avoided answering my question directly. He promised to examine the issue without committing himself to anything.

I showed my impatience. Churchill betrayed his anxiety and set about assuring me most emphatically of his sincere desire to provide the USSR with maximum assistance; at the same time, he did not want to place us under any dangerous illusions.

'Today, our possibilities are limited,' the prime minister said. 'We do not know how to fight. We have neither the traditions nor the appropriate education. Ours is an army of amateurs. But we are firmly set on getting rid of Hitler. And we shall get rid of him!'

Then Churchill started asserting that victory was possible only with the active participation of the United States in the war, noting that on questions of supply, the USSR should count first and foremost on the USA. He promised to facilitate our access to the American armaments market, if necessary.

Then our conversation turned to military operations. Churchill expressed his admiration for the Red Army. He confessed he had expected far worse, especially when taking into account the fact that Germany was the attacking party.

'I feared that by now a part of your armies would have been smashed and the Germans would have captured 1–1.5 million of your men. Nothing of the sort has occurred. Even if the Germans have captured 300–400,000, as they claim, that's nothing considering the scope and intensity of the operations. It merely goes to show that the Red Army is fighting well and remains intact. That is what matters. The loss of territories is of secondary importance.'

Churchill added that over the last couple of days he had feared *disaster* near Smolensk, but there too the Soviet military command managed to avoid the traps set for them. They passed with flying colours. On the whole, Churchill has always had a high opinion of the military capabilities of the USSR. The experience of the war fully bears out his a priori forecast.

I asked Churchill what he thought of Japan's position. The prime minister answered that, judging by the information at his disposal, Tokyo was preparing a 'leap' to the south, in the direction of Indochina. Churchill does not think that Japan will risk attacking us, provided our Far Eastern army remains in place.

When our conversation was coming to an end, Hopkins, who was spending the 'weekend' at Chequers as the prime minister's guest, entered the room. We greeted each other, but talked little. I asked Hopkins about certain American supplies with which we had encountered difficulties. He promised to make inquiries and inform me of the results. It's strange, but Hopkins reminds me – in his countenance, manners and dress – of a Zemstvo statistician of olden times.

Churchill and I parted warmly and amicably. As I was leaving, I heard his secretary summoning chiefs of staff for a conference that evening. Churchill promised to dispatch an urgent reply to Stalin through Cripps, and to send me a copy.

Admiral Pound called on me at 11 p.m. today and did indeed present me with a copy of the PM's reply. In it I found everything I had heard from his lips yesterday. In general, it gives little cause for comfort. No second front in France for now. The entire burden of fighting against the German war machine rests on our shoulders. But at least the PM's stance is now clear to me. That is important. Illusions must be avoided! *Wishful thinking* is worst of all.

[Eden and Beaverbrook challenged Churchill's Russian policy. Beaverbrook fancied that the Ministry of Supply gave him a rare opportunity of appearing in public, and especially in the Labour movement, as the architect of assistance to Russia.[103] It was he who had raised the possibility of raids in France at his meeting with Maisky on 27 June, and in a telephone conversation on 1 July he told him: 'It is tanks I am going after. That is what I am going to try – that is the great idea.'[104] Eden had often wished to shake off his image as Churchill's pampered heir. His earlier attempts to assert his independence led nowhere. His extraordinary zeal at the War Office and direct involvement in the successful campaign against the Italians in the Western Desert induced Churchill to transfer him, under duress, to the Foreign Office in December 1940.[105] The German invasion of Russia afforded Eden, reputed to be held in high esteem by the Russians, an opportunity to improve his political standing. Apprehensive lest Eden commit Britain too far, Churchill, who had hitherto shown only a marginal interest in Russia, drove him off the scene and resorted to direct correspondence with Stalin. In private, Eden expressed repugnance at Churchill's 'sentimental and florid' telegrams, which were bound to lead Stalin to the correct conclusion that 'guff no substitute for guns'. He expressed doubts as to whether Churchill's verbal commitments would convince Stalin 'unless they were accompanied by definite promises of military assistance'.[106] Surveying the political scene, Maisky told Harold Nicolson that Eden was 'the best of the lot and really understood that our fate was tied up with that of the USSR. Beaverbrook also took that point of view. Winston, although sympathetic and possessing no reactionary prejudices, was dominated by the idea that the war would last six or seven years ... I went away feeling sad, and liking Maisky more than ever.'[107]]

29 July

So, Harry Hopkins is in Moscow! What a remarkable story this has turned out to be.

On 25 July, I met Hopkins at the American embassy. Winant was present. Molotov had asked me to discuss with Hopkins the possibility of providing us with a range of matériel and fighters which the Americans had sent to the Middle East for the English. My talk on this subject with the president's 'personal emissary' brought little success. Hopkins replied that, first, it was down to the English to dispose of the materials supplied to them, and it would be improper for the Americans to interfere; secondly, the 700 fighters of the *Tomahawk* class, which we would like to get from Cairo, were not in fact in Cairo. The British have already given us 200 of them (in fact, some of them are in England, and some in the US Atlantic ports), 150 are in Egypt and the other 350 are being shipped from America to the Middle East. True, Hopkins assured me that Roosevelt was ready to provide the USSR with every kind of support in the struggle against Hitler, but warned me at the same time against cultivating any illusions regarding the speed and scope of American armaments aid. The US war industry has only now begun to expand, and the production of aircraft, for instance, will become serious only in the middle of 1942 (merely 1,600 machines of all types will be produced this July) and reach a real high level only in early 1943. Hopkins thinks therefore that two programmes should be set up: (1) a programme of immediate aid to the USSR and (2) a programme of aid for the future, say, for the next two years. Work on both must start right away.

Once this topic was exhausted, Hopkins suddenly asked: what could be done to bring Roosevelt and Stalin closer?

I did not understand Hopkins right away. He then started explaining that Stalin was little more than a name to Roosevelt. The abstract head, perhaps, of the Soviet government. There is nothing concrete, material or personal in Roosevelt's perception of Stalin. Roosevelt has no notion of Stalin as a personality, a human being. What are his tastes, views, habits and sentiments? Can he be trusted or can't he? Stalin, for his part, probably has no clear idea of the American president's personality and character either. This is very bad. The USA and the USSR now have to cooperate in the struggle against Hitler. Roosevelt is the leader of the USA, and Stalin the leader of the USSR. The two men should know each other well and understand each other. Only then will cooperation proceed in a smooth and cordial fashion. But how can this be done? Hopkins openly admitted that he lacked a ready answer to this question.

I agreed with Hopkins that it would be a very good thing to make Stalin and Roosevelt better acquainted, but how? Theoretically, there are three methods for such an 'acquaintance': (1) meeting in person; (2) exchanging personal messages; and (3) sending personal representatives to each other. The first method was obviously impossible at this time – Hopkins fully agreed about that. So what was left: personal messages? Sending personal representatives?

Hopkins thought and said: 'There is much that is right in what you say, but I am not in a position to provide a clear answer right away. I need to think it over.'

It was evident that Hopkins was very preoccupied by the matter of 'acquaintance' between Roosevelt and Stalin, and that he had been doing some serious thinking. Winant kept mostly silent during our conversation, but he, too, seemed to be interested in the question over which Hopkins had been racking his brains.

Then we parted, and other affairs, especially the Polish negotiations, quickly dislodged the memory of this meeting from my mind.

On the 27th, I was in Bovingdon. At around ten in the evening a telephone call came from the embassy and I was informed that Winant wanted to see me urgently on important business. I set off to town straightaway. When I entered the embassy building it was ten past eleven. Winant was sitting in my office and talking with Novikov. It turned out that Winant had brought along the passports of Hopkins and his two assistants. He asked me to put visas on their passports immediately, as the three of them were leaving for the USSR in half an hour. I did not understand what he was talking about. But Winant exclaimed impatiently: 'I'll explain everything to you afterwards. For now just give me the visas. The train departs for Scotland at 11.40. Hopkins is already at the station. I must give him the passports with the visas before the train departs.'

That's easy to say: give me the visas! All the stamps and seals were at the consulate. Driving to the consulate would take a quarter of an hour, and there would probably be no one there anyway at such a late hour. What to do?

I adjusted quickly, in the Bolshevik style. After all, Hopkins' visit to Moscow could not be delayed on account of a few paragraphs in the consular instructions! I took Hopkins' passport and wrote on a blank leaf by hand: 'I request that Mr Harry Hopkins be allowed through without inspection of his luggage. Ambassador of the USSR to Great Britain I. Maisky. 27 July 1941.' Then I called Lepekhin and attached our seal. I did the same with the other two passports. I expect the head of the NKID consular department to faint when he sees 'my visa'. Such a visa, I imagine, has never been recorded in the annals of our diplomacy. But why worry? Even Peter the Great used to say: 'The law itself can be changed if the need requires it.' Here the 'need' was unquestionable.

Winant took the passports and left. He came back at midnight.

'I only just made it,' he exclaimed on entering my office. 'The train was already moving.'

He then told me what had happened. It turns out that after their talk with me on 25 July, Hopkins and Winant gave much thought to how to improve relations between the USA and the USSR and between Roosevelt and Stalin in particular, and finally arrived at the conclusion that in the present conditions a visit by Hopkins to Moscow would be the most expedient step. They asked Roosevelt. The reply came this afternoon: the president agrees. And Hopkins set off this very evening.

I called Agniya and introduced her to Winant. The three of us stayed up until half past one, talked a lot, and drank to victory over Hitler. Winant is straightforward, natural and humane – a complete contrast to Kennedy. He is well disposed towards the USSR and sincerely wishes to help us.

And now Hopkins is in Moscow! I'm very glad. This will yield benefit. Hopkins makes a good impression – he is unaffected, democratic and full of energy. In his countenance and manners he resembles a Zemstvo statistician of the old times. He has arrived to meet Stalin as Roosevelt's personal representative. Comrade Stalin, of course, will know how to receive him in the appropriate way.

[Harry Hopkins, Roosevelt's powerful close adviser, left Churchill in no doubt that the president attached supreme significance to the breathing space achieved through the war in the east, was unhappy about the heavy burden that the campaign in North Africa imposed on the United States, and favoured a redistribution of resources.[108] Hopkins' arrival in Moscow as Churchill's envoy made it possible for Cripps to intervene and persuade Hopkins that the *sine qua non* for an alliance was immediate military cooperation, sustained by long-term political agreements. He proposed a conference, at which the United States, the Soviet Union and Britain would 'fully and jointly explore the relative interests of each front'. The assistance to Russia was to be granted not as 'merely sparing to a partner or ally what we feel we can spare out rather as the point upon which we should concentrate all our efforts'. Cripps even provided Hopkins with a draft telegram to Stalin, which Churchill was forced reluctantly to adopt at his first summit meeting with Roosevelt at Placentia Bay a fortnight later.[109] As Maisky reported to Moscow, Churchill's attempts to postpone the proposed summit in Moscow met with strong opposition from both Hopkins and Beaverbrook.[110]]

30 July

Today at long last we signed the Soviet–Polish treaty! I can barely believe it.

Novikov, Korzh, Zinchenko,[i] Zonov and I arrived in the Foreign Office at 4.15 this afternoon. The rain was pouring down, dull grey clouds scuttled over the sky. We entered the reception room. I started telling our young men that meetings on 'non-intervention' in Spain had once been held in this room. Before I had finished my story Sikorski appeared in his general's uniform, accompanied by the chairman of the Polish Sejm and also some ministers: Kot[ii] (home affairs), Stronski[iii] (propaganda) and someone else whose name I don't remember. We introduced ourselves and shook hands. Then Eden's secretary came and ushered us into the foreign secretary's office.

Eden met us at the door. He was smiling, and it was obvious that he was very pleased. There were film cameras in the room and thick cables on the floor. Some people were walking to and fro – they turned out to be cinema men and photographers. Also present were Cadogan, Richard Law (he has just replaced Butler as parliamentary undersecretary of state for foreign affairs) and, of course, the ubiquitous Strang, carrying a heap of papers and documents.

The routine of introductions and handshakes was repeated. When this was over, Eden glanced at his watch and said rapidly: 'The prime minister has not yet come…'

Then, as if to apologize, he added: 'You know, the prime minister likes to take an hour's nap after lunch. Such is his habit. He will be here any moment.'

Then Eden laid his hand on Sikorski's shoulder, led him aside and whispered a few words to the Polish prime minister. After that he came to me, laid his hand on my shoulder in similar fashion, and said in a subdued voice and with slight embarrassment: 'Please forgive my foolish question. During the signing at the table, I'll sit in the middle… Do you mind the general sitting to the right of me, and you on the left? He is the prime minister, after all…'

I laughed heartily and replied: 'No, I don't mind. It's not the place that makes the man…'

Eden sighed with relief and added cheerfully: 'Thank you so much.'

Still no Churchill. Those present wandered about Eden's room rather aimlessly. Strang and Novikov fussed around the table where the signing was

---

[i] Konstantin Emelianovich Zinchenko, from 1940 to 1942 second, then first, secretary at the Soviet embassy in Great Britain; central organ of NKID in Moscow, 1942–44.

[ii] Stanisław Kot, minister of internal affairs of the Polish government in exile, 1939–41; ambassador to the Soviet Union, 1941–42.

[iii] Stanisław Stronski, deputy prime minister of the Polish government in exile, 1939–43.

86. Sikorski and Maisky signing the Soviet–Polish treaty.

to take place. This table, which was long and covered with a cloth, stood to one side, to the right of the table at which Eden usually received his guests, along the wall displaying Pitt's bust.[111]

Sikorski addressed me in French. He was delighted that we were signing the treaty. He came to the conclusion long ago that Poland could not balance between its neighbours in the west and in the east for ever. It had to choose: either with Germany against Russia, or with Russia against Germany. Sikorski himself has always thought that Poland must be with Russia against Germany. He began to pursue this line back in 1925, when he was minister for military affairs. Unfortunately, other currents came to prevail in Polish politics, and their results are manifest today. Sikorski felt a sense of deep satisfaction at the thought of signing a treaty which, he hoped, would prove a turning point in the history of Poland and relations between Poland and Russia.

Sikorski further announced that he had decided to appoint General Anders,[i] whom we are currently holding prisoner, as commander of the Polish army in the USSR, and Kot, his minister of internal affairs and a radical leader of the

[i] Władysław Anders, Polish army general who commanded the Polish armed forces in Russia, 1941–42.

Peasant Party, as ambassador to Moscow. Sikorski beckoned Kot and started talking to him about his future work in the USSR. The general mentioned, by and by, that one of Kot's tasks would be to set up a committee in Moscow to aid Polish citizens who were to receive amnesty under the treaty. Kot, for his part, said that first of all he intended to dispatch two or three men to Moscow, his future assistants in the embassy, while he himself would depart later (in a couple of weeks or so). Kot complained of his poor health and, in this connection, expressed his anxiety about the future.

Suddenly, it was as if a gust of wind had swept through the room. Everyone fell silent and turned their gaze to the door: the prime minister had appeared in the doorway. Eden's warning proved apposite. Churchill really had just got out of bed. This could be seen from his sagging face, his red, somewhat watery eyes, and his generally sleepy appearance. Dressed in a black coat and striped trousers, broad-shouldered, thickset, his head obstinately lowered – a real English bulldog – the prime minister inspected the scene with a furtive smile. Eden hurried to greet him and led him into the middle of the room. Sikorski introduced his 'retinue' to Churchill, and I introduced mine.[112]

We then got down to business. It was already half past four. We took our seats at the table for the signing of the treaty. Eden sat in the middle and Churchill on his left. I sat further to the left at the corner, while Sikorski took his seat to the right of Eden. The Polish Pan had schemed in vain, for fate had tricked him: he may have sat to the right of Eden, but I sat next to Churchill. I smiled to myself. Sikorski's secretary passed him the texts to be signed; Novikov did the same for me.

The camera-men got to work, and the photographers started clicking. The press was not admitted – I don't know why (all *managements* [sic] were in the hands of the Foreign Office). A shame. From the point of view of Allied propaganda, it would have been advantageous to make a fuss over the act of signing. The FO, it seems, has not yet mastered the art of propaganda.

While Sikorski and I were signing (it was necessary to sign six times: the treaty, two protocols, and their copies), Churchill sat grinning and smoking his customary cigar. Every now and then he exchanged a few remarks with me. He repeated once again: 'Night and day I'm thinking about the best ways of helping you!'

The PM had already told me this twice: at the reception in the Palace on 16 July, and afterwards in Chequers on the 19th. Also: 'Things are going well at the front. You are fighting magnificently.'

Also: 'The rubber I promised you is being loaded in England and will be shipped to Arkhangelsk within days.'

Finally: 'Hopkins has arrived safely in Moscow. I'm very glad he is there. I hope he will be able to see Stalin often. That can only be of benefit.'

87. No love lost: Maisky and General Władysław Sikorski, after the ceremony.

At last, the signing procedure is complete. Eden rises, and, looking at a piece of paper, utters congratulations, prepared in advance, to both parties. The camera-men and photographers are clicking fast.

Relieved, I assume that the ceremony is *fini*. But no! What's that?

Sikorski rises from his seat and strikes the pose of the orator. Is he going to make a speech? But we had agreed to do without speeches! And yet! Sikorski delivers a political speech. He speaks in Polish and his secretary translates his words into English. I have to speak, too. Counting on our agreement, I have not prepared anything. I have to speak off the cuff. Fortunately, I consulted with Moscow in advance about the general direction of a speech, should it be required. My impromptu turns out all right. Better than I expected. Churchill rises to his feet after me and also says a few bracing words. Bracing words addressed to the Germans. How he hates Hitler! I do not envy the 'Führer' if he loses the war.

At last, it's over. We shake hands and say goodbye to one another. The camera-men want to film Sikorski and me shaking hands. We do as they ask. On parting, Churchill says to me: 'I'm ready to help you however I can. If you have any thoughts on this score, come and see me. We'll have a talk.'

I thank him and promise to take advantage of his invitation.

Eden stops me and Sikorski: he may make a statement on the treaty in parliament now – if so, perhaps we could be present. We remain in Eden's office while he embarks on negotiations with parliament over the phone. He asks for the order of the day to be disrupted and to be given 15 or 20 minutes to make the statement. Alas! Today is the *Scottish day*, and the stingy Scotsmen flatly refuse to lose a quarter of an hour from the time allotted to them. Eden strives in vain to persuade someone over the phone. With disappointment etched on his face, Eden turns to Sikorski and me – nothing doing. He explains the situation and asks us to come at twelve o'clock tomorrow, when he will make a statement on the Soviet–Polish treaty in the House.

We say goodbye to Eden. I linger for a minute and ask what will happen in parliament tomorrow. He understands me and replies with a smile: 'Don't you worry, I'll keep my word.'

I head home. It's still raining, but the weather is clearing up a little. I have barely crossed the threshold of the embassy building when Iris runs out towards me and informs me: 'Eden's secretary has just called. Eden will speak today after all. If you want to listen to him, you must go to parliament right away.'

I fetch Agniya and we rush to the House of Commons. Race along the corridors and into our seats. Too late! Eden has already finished speaking. Questions and answers follow. I catch McEwen's[i] question and Eden's answer. OK! Eden has kept his word. Everything is all right.

The Soviet–Polish treaty has come into force. What will it bring now and in the future? Is it a turning point or isn't it?

Time will tell.

[Maisky had informed Eden on 4 July that the Soviet government favoured the establishment of an independent national Polish state, the boundaries of which would 'correspond with ethnographical Poland'. Sikorski, however, insisted on Soviet recognition of Polish sovereignty and the legitimacy of his government, and preferred not to discuss frontiers at present. After considerable haggling, a compromise was arranged through Eden. It led to a first meeting between Maisky and Sikorski on 5 July, on the 'neutral territory' of Cadogan's office. Sikorski was only prepared to sign an agreement once Russia repudiated her 1939 agreement with Germany. On taking his leave, Sikorski told Maisky: 'You ought never to have made agreement with Germany in 1939, and we should have been fighting side by side all this time.' Maisky, according to Cadogan, 'took it very well, laughed and said "All that is past history."' Eden brokered the agreement, which was signed on 30 July. The Russians dropped for the moment their demand for a future 'ethnic' Poland, while the Poles gave up their demands for Soviet recognition of the pre-war borders.[113] The Russians further agreed to release their Polish prisoners of war and to arm them. However, the secret massacre of Polish officers

[i] John McEwen, junior member in Churchill's Cabinet and a Conservative MP.

at Katyn meant that there was a huge discrepancy in the estimates of the number of POWs, and this remained a serious bone of contention.[114]]

31 July

I'll summarize some details of the Polish negotiations after the meeting with Eden (11 July) where I formulated 'four points' as the basis for a Soviet–Polish agreement.

Needless to say, those Poles, in spite of their apparent acquiescence with me at that meeting, did not content themselves with my proposals, but began 'improving' them. These 'improvers' do more harm than good! They always confuse and complicate matters.

To begin with, they suggested 'improvements' to the four main points:

(1) It was stated in my first point that the 1939 Soviet–German agreements 'with regard to Poland' were considered null and void. This was not enough for the Poles. They tried to push through, in various guises, an at least indirect recognition on our part of the 1921 borders. Naturally enough, we categorically objected against this intention and although we finally accepted the formula 'the treaty... concerning the territorial changes in Poland', we did not accept even the vaguest recognition of the old borders.

(2) It was stated in my fourth point that the USSR gives its consent to the formation of a Polish army on its territory. The Poles started 'improving' here as well. They refused to accept the appointment of the army commander by the Polish government in agreement with the Soviet government. They also wanted to limit the subordination of the Polish army to the Soviet supreme military command only to those hostilities that took place on the territory of the USSR. This would mean that as soon as the Red Army and the Polish army crossed the Soviet borders during a counteroffensive (and Sikorski was inclined to interpret the Soviet borders along the lines of the Riga treaty of 1921), the Polish army would cease to fall under our command. Finally, the Poles demanded the conclusion of a special convention concerning the command, organization and engagement of the Polish Army. There was a long tussle over this point, and the Poles finally agreed to appoint the commander with the Soviet government's approval, and removed the clause concerning the subordination of the Polish army to our command only on the territory of the USSR. We, for our part, agreed to conclude a military convention regulating all matters related to the existence of the Polish army.

(3) The third point, which my scheme did not contain, but which caused a great dispute, was the question of releasing Polish prisoners held in the USSR (not only prisoners of war but also civilians). Here we met the wishes of the Poles and promised to declare an amnesty after the resumption of our diplomatic relations.

(4) Finally, the fourth point, which also caused controversy, albeit of a less serious kind, was the wish of the Poles (particularly of Zaleski, who lost his estate in that part of Poland which was claimed by us) to guarantee consideration in future of material claims – public and private. We agreed in the end, but proposed that this point be entered in a secret protocol, as was then done. Initially we proposed inserting the words 'reciprocal claims' into the protocol. The Poles objected furiously. Then Eden suggested a compromise, 'various material claims', which we accepted, because this formula makes it possible for us, too, to present counterclaims to the Poles so as to settle scores both old and new.

The disputes on the 'improvements' dragged on for three weeks. There were some dramatic moments. When the Poles persevered in their desire to push through indirect recognition of the 1921 borders, for example, I became angry and asked Eden on July [date missing] to tell Sikorski that if he dug his heels in, I would inform the Soviet government that it was useless continuing negotiations and I would recommend a return to the idea of a Polish National Committee, which we had abandoned in view of the Poles' opposition. My threat had its effect, and Article 1 of the treaty was passed in a version we could accept. Likewise, when towards the end of the negotiations Sikorski excelled himself in devising more and more amendments to Article 4 (the army) and the protocols, Moscow could not stand it any longer and declared: if the Poles do not accept the wordings that have already been agreed, they may go to the devil. We can do without them. This also had its effect and Sikorski immediately withdrew his amendments.

Eden certainly played a major role in the negotiations. I incline to the view that we could hardly have come to an understanding with the Poles without him, or, even if we had finally reached an agreement, it would have happened much later. Eden tried to hold the middle ground, but sometimes he veered off course and became excessively attentive to the wishes and demands of the Poles. He likes Sikorski very much (as do all the leading English politicians, for that matter), and this was reflected in the negotiations. But Eden must nonetheless be thanked.

A strange thing happened just before the signing. On 25 July, I told Eden of Moscow's refusal to make further concessions (the Poles could 'go to the devil' if they didn't like it). On 26 July, Eden told me the Poles were ready to accept the previously agreed text. The signing of the treaty was scheduled for Monday the 28th. On the morning of the 27th, Novikov, Strang and 'Count Mniszek', the Polish representative, finalized the text. All of a sudden, in the afternoon of the 27th, a telegram came from Cripps in which he reported that he had seen Stalin and Molotov the day before and agreed with them a text of the Polish treaty, which slightly differed from the text that had been drawn up with such difficulty in London. The most important difference consisted in the fact that a complete amnesty for all imprisoned Poles had been promised to Cripps in Moscow, while we in London had agreed only that 'all practical questions relating to the release of Polish citizens imprisoned on the territory of the USSR will be considered favourably following the resumption of diplomatic relations'. Besides, according to the Moscow text, the protocol about the prisoners was to be made public, while earlier Moscow had insisted on its secrecy and it had been very hard for me to get Moscow's consent to make a muffled allusion to the forthcoming revision of prisoners' cases in the communiqué the Foreign Office was to issue in connection with the signing of the treaty. Likewise, in the second protocol (about claims), the word 'reciprocal' had been removed, although Moscow had stubbornly insisted on it earlier. On the other hand, the Moscow text restored the clear statement that the Polish army commander was to be appointed by agreement with the Soviet government, while in the text agreed in London this condition had been removed in view of Sikorski's promise to include it in the text of the future military convention.

I was in a fix. The Foreign Office also found itself in a state of confusion. Cadogan summoned me urgently from Bovingdon (Eden was out of town) and asked whether I had confirmation of Cripps's communication from Moscow. I did not, so I hastily called Moscow to ask if Cripps's communication was accurate. When, on returning to the embassy, I was composing my ciphered message, Eden called from the country and asked me not to object to the new version, which looked better to him. He promised, by way of compensation, to somewhat modify the text of his note to Sikorski in terms more favourable for us. I replied that I did not intend to object; I was simply asking what to do.

At three in the afternoon on the 28th, I received a reply from Moscow which threw me into great confusion. Yes, Cripps's communication was accurate, and I should bring the newly agreed text to Eden's notice. Nevertheless, the Soviet government liked my 'London' text more than the 'Moscow' one. After chewing this over, I finally decided to confirm the authenticity of the 'Moscow' text to Eden. My chief consideration was this: since we had agreed to an amnesty for the Poles, we should at least make political capital from this in England, America and Poland. So it was precisely the effective word 'amnesty' that should be used, while the relevant protocol should be made public. I saw Eden at about 3.30 p.m. and informed him about the telegram I had received. Eden informed Sikorski about the new 'Moscow' text immediately. They both grabbed at it with both hands. In conversation with Eden, Sikorski said he was greatly moved by the Soviet government's magnanimity and was now 100% ready to cooperate. Eden called me at about 10 p.m. He related Sikorski's words to me and thanked the Soviet government and me once again for our good intentions and wise statesmanship. At about one o'clock another telegram arrived, which said that

Molotov had seen Cripps on the 28th and told him that the Soviet government preferred the 'London' text *after all*. Cripps had not objected and promised to telegraph Eden about it immediately. It was apparent from the telegram that in fact Moscow wanted very much to conclude the treaty on the basis of the 'London' text. I replied rightaway that now it was too late and explained in detail what had happened during the day of 28 July. I emphasized that I considered it politically advantageous to publish the protocol on the amnesty for the prisoners.

On the 29th I met Eden at a lunch at the *Foreign Press Association*, where he was making a speech. I told Eden about my nocturnal telegram. It turned out that Eden had already received a ciphered message from Cripps in the morning, in which Cripps gave him an account of his talk with Molotov.

'He did not object to keeping the London text!' Eden exclaimed, referring to Cripps, with half-feigned irritation. 'No wonder! He has no idea of the difficulties involved in these negotiations. I've wired Cripps to say it's too late to change anything.'

Late at night on the 29th I received Moscow's authorization to sign the 'Moscow text'. That is how the 'Moscow text' became the text of the treaty. However, it's still not quite clear to me what happened in Moscow on the evening of the 25th and why Comrades Stalin and Molotov agreed with Cripps on the 'Moscow text'. I was placed in a difficult position during my talk with Eden. As soon as I made an attempt to defend the 'London text', Eden immediately took refuge behind the authority of Stalin. What could I say to this?

The speeches at the signing of the treaty were also a strange story. Telling me of his conversation with Sikorski on the evening of the 28th, Eden said, among other things, that Sikorski wanted to make a speech at the signing, adding that the Foreign Office would send it to me the following day so that I could familiarize myself with its content. But in the afternoon of the 29th I got a letter signed by Strang which informed me that Sikorski had decided, on second thoughts, not to make a speech. I, of course, had no objections, and although, just to be on the safe side, I had telegraphed the theses of what I was going to say to Moscow late at night on the 28th, I now relaxed and did not prepare a speech. I was unsure, however, of what would actually happen. Doubts crept in during a lunch for the foreign press on the 29th, when towards the end, quite contrary to the programme, the general suddenly asked for the floor and made a speech in which he foretold the conclusion of a Soviet–Polish treaty. I gained the impression that Sikorski 'loves to talk'. Having my doubts, I called Strang on the morning of the 30th and asked him once more: would Sikorski be speaking at the signing or not? His reply was: no, Sikorski would not make a speech! On the basis of this reply I prepared nothing in advance.[115] But in the end the general could not contain himself and spoke all the same! A real chatterbox!

I kept my head, though, and said a few words off the cuff in keeping with my theses (which, by the way, had been approved by Moscow).

One more detail. So as to compensate Sikorski somewhat for our refusal to recognize even obliquely the 1921 borders, Eden had promised, upon the signing of the treaty, a note from the British government in which the latter would declare that it did not recognize the territorial changes that had taken place in Poland in the course of the war. This, of course, did not mean a recognition of the 1921 borders, and Eden told Sikorski in no uncertain terms during the negotiations that recognition of the old borders by the British government was out of the question. Nonetheless, I insisted that Eden should make a clear-cut statement of non-recognition. At first I suggested to Eden that a corresponding sentence should be included in his note, but Sikorski bristled and Eden capitulated. Then I suggested including such a sentence in the text of Eden's parliamentary speech on the Soviet–Polish treaty. Eden sent me the text of his speech on the afternoon of the 29th. I read it and returned it to him with my draft amendment. However, on the morning of the 30th, the day of the signing, Eden phoned me and said he could not accept my amendment as the text of his speech had already been approved by Cabinet and any change would require fresh approval from the Cabinet, not to mention more lengthy talks with Sikorski. Eden could not agree to this. I then proposed the following solution. Let some MP ask Eden after his speech if the treaty implies a guarantee of the old Polish borders, to which Eden will give a clear answer: 'No!' Eden accepted this proposal and even promised to ensure that such a question would be asked. Indeed, McEwen, a Conservative, asked the question I needed, and Eden gave him the reply I was after. Now the Poles will not be able to claim under any circumstances in the future that England guaranteed the 1921 borders, even indirectly. That's useful. The question of Poland will be one of the most complicated and difficult issues in establishing the post-war order in Europe, and it is better to be well prepared on this matter.

3 August

Hopkins' visit to Moscow has evidently been a success. We will, of course, only be able to judge its outcome later (how will the American deliveries go?), but the situation at present seems satisfactory.

Hopkins met Comrade Stalin twice, on 30 and 31 July. Their talks were long and detailed. Hopkins stated on behalf of Roosevelt that the United States would provide all manner of aid to us without concluding a special agreement. Comrade Stalin thanked Hopkins for his statement and then set out to him the list of our requirements (mostly heavy machine-guns and small anti-aircraft guns). Comrade Stalin also asked that the $500 million loan granted to us by the

US government be expedited. This would also serve to demonstrate openly the existence of the bloc of the United States, the Soviet Union and Great Britain. Hopkins agreed to this and promised to telegraph Roosevelt promptly in the same vein. Comrade Stalin also gave Hopkins firm assurance that our victory is inevitable and that Hitler and his gang must be removed from power, because they lack 'gentlemanliness' and violate all agreements. The observance of such agreements is especially important in view of the existence of different systems of government in different countries.

Comrade Stalin made a very strong impression on Hopkins. Winant, who saw Hopkins on his return to Scotland (Hopkins departed for America without coming to London), told me that Roosevelt's *special envoy* left Moscow having drawn the following conclusions. Comrade Stalin has an exceptionally clear mind and is most realistic. He knows what he wants and is a true master of the situation. He knows the front like the palm of his hand. He is wholly confident of victory. Stalin does not ask for the impossible, and he did not lose heart when Hopkins told him that there was not much the USA could give the USSR at the present moment. On the contrary, he began calmly discussing with Hopkins a programme for the future and various possibilities for supplying the USSR by the spring of 1942. This gave Hopkins the impression that the Red Army has a sufficiently solid base of its own and that in general the USSR is a trustworthy partner with whom the USA can do business.

88. The Grand Alliance forged over lunch in the conservatory at Maisky's residence in Kensington Palace Gardens.

Together with Steinhardt, Hopkins also went to see Molotov (31 July). Hopkins put two questions to Molotov:

(1) What would the Soviet government like the US government to do in respect of Japan? Molotov answered that it might be useful if the US government made clear to Japan its negative attitude to Japan's advance not only in the southern, but also in the northern direction.

(2) What effect will the Soviet–German war have on relations between the USSR and China? Molotov replied that the Soviet government has an understanding with Jiang Jieshi, but owing to the current situation the Soviet government lacks the means of providing China with much help. It would be good if the United States could increase its aid to China.

Hopkins' reaction to Comrade Molotov's explanations was not very well defined. He merely remarked that the USA does not like sending notes of disapproval to Japan concerning the latter's actions. Such notes bear little fruit.

Hopkins' general impression of the USSR is that all, from top to bottom, are fully resolved to annihilate German fascism and are fully confident of victory.

5 August

Relations between the USSR and Norway were normalized today.

On 10 May, the Soviet government asked the Norwegians to close their mission in Moscow. At the beginning of the war, the Soviet government decided to restore normal relations with the Norwegian government. The latter also gave us to understand, through Eden, that they would like to adjust relations. I opened the talks through Colban. On 24 July, I visited Lie,[i] the Norwegian foreign minister, who was once a communist, lived in the *Lux* in 1921/22, and is now a member of the Norwegian Labour Party.

At first I thought about concluding the same treaty with the Norwegians as with Czechoslovakia, and even gave a draft of it to Colban. But Lie said the Norwegian government would not want such a pact at the present time (in view of its difficult relations with the Finns and the Swedes) and proposed that we confine ourselves to a simple exchange of envoys plus a tripartite Anglo-Soviet–Norwegian agreement concerning Spitsbergen. Lie suggested framing the normalization of relations in the form of an exchange of letters about the reciprocal appointment of envoys. Lie also said that the Norwegian government would be happy to see Agniya as the Soviet government's envoy in Norway. I stared at him in astonishment and asked: 'But why specifically my wife?'

---

[i] Trygve Halvdan Lie, foreign minister of the Norwegian government in exile, 1940–41.

Lie then explained that Norwegians nurtured the fondest memory of Kollontay's work in Norway and consequently were of the mind that the role of envoy in Norway would be well suited to a Russian woman. Moreover, Lie sees that my wife understands the spirit of the Norwegian people: she likes Vigeland very much. Here I recalled that three months ago, at a dinner given by Admiral Evans (he is married to a Norwegian), Lie was seated next to Agniya and they had an extensive conversation about Norwegian literature and art. After this conversation Lie exclaimed: 'If only your wife were the envoy in Norway!'

At the time I took this to be a joke. Now I saw that it was all much more serious. I tried to introduce a note of levity into our conversation, but Lie continued treating it with true Scandinavian gravity. In general, he is as Scandinavian as they come: tall, quite heavy and phlegmatic, though his hair is not blond but brown.

Lie admitted by the by that he was against us during the Finnish war, but now he had to concede that the 'statesmen in the Kremlin' saw farther than he. Well, better late than never!

Lie expressed his ardent hope that Soviet troops would enter northern Norway in the near future and told me in this connection that the Norwegians have 27,000 merchant seamen, 3,000 in the navy, 1,500 pilots (some are being trained in Canada, some work in Iceland), and up to 1,500 men in the army (currently training in Scotland).

Moscow agreed to Lie's proposals, and today Lie and I exchanged letters about the envoy swap. The exchange took place in my office in the embassy. Afterwards we drank to friendship between the Soviet and Norwegian peoples and to our common victory.

7 August

Three weeks ago, Spaak asked me informally, through Isabelle Blume, whether the Soviet government would agree to normalize relations with Belgium following the shutting down in early May of the Belgian mission in Moscow (together with the Norwegian one) on the initiative of the Soviet government. I made the necessary inquiries and replied through Isabelle Blume that the Soviet government was ready to exchange envoys with the Belgians. Blume informed Spaak at my request that if he addressed me officially, I had the authority to settle questions relating to the normalization of Soviet–Belgian relations.

Two weeks passed. Spaak kept silent and so did I. Blume told me that Spaak was still 'pondering' the best way to resolve the matter (I think he was simultaneously seeking the Vatican's blessing for such a step). Spaak was of the view (as Blume told me) that since the Belgian mission in Moscow had been closed at the Soviet government's initiative, the Soviet government should now take the first step. I, however, failed to see any grounds for this and patiently waited for Spaak to conclude his 'pondering'. Finally the Belgian foreign minister decided to ask Eden to act as intermediary.

Today, at 11 a.m., Spaak and I met in Eden's office. It wasn't difficult to come to an agreement. At first I proposed to Spaak that we exchange letters, as Lie and I had done two days before, but for some reason Spaak was evidently against this. I did not insist. Spaak proposed a simpler method: simply to release a short communiqué in which it would be said that today, 7 August, he and I had met in Eden's office and agreed on the exchange of diplomatic representatives. I did not object. So that's what was done. The text of the communiqué was produced there and then.

Right now the Belgians are appointing a chargé d'affaires for us (some counsellor who is presently in California). Spaak told me he would need some time to find a suitable envoy. Perhaps. My impression, however, is that Spaak will be in no particular hurry to appoint an envoy (have the talks with the Vatican not been conclusive?). But this does not matter. It is safe to say that starting today relations between the USSR and Belgium have returned to normal.

10 August (Bovingdon)

Seven weeks of war.

The future is hidden, of course, but some very important things are clear even now. The main thing is that the Red Army has held firm against the Reichswehr [sic]. The Hitlerite war machine proved unable to overrun, overthrow and grind down the Red Army as it had done to all other armies, including the French. It was unable to do so in the first 2–3 weeks of the war, when it had every advantage on its side. It has even less chance of achieving such an outcome now. If this is so, Hitler's Germany is effectively beaten, although the realization of this defeat might still take some time and cost us considerable sacrifice in human lives, arms and territories. How to reduce the losses, and bring them down to the absolutely inevitable minimum? That is the task. To accomplish it we need the full assistance of England and the USA. Do we have it? Not yet. Will we have it? I don't know. My mood on this score is rather sceptical.

Let's start with the USA. I read Brailsford's report from Washington in the current issue of the *New Statesman* (8 August). What does it say? It says that actually the United States continues to live almost entirely in a peace-time atmosphere. The war and the war effort hardly make themselves felt as yet despite the *Lease and Lend Bill* and all Roosevelt's speeches. Brailsford reports that car sales increased in the USA by 35% in the first six months of this year, compared to the first half of 1940, refrigerator sales by 42%, and sales of electric ovens by 51%! Military production in the USA currently amounts to not more than 15% of total production. The remaining 85% relates to peace-time industries. And any attempt to curtail peace-time industries in the interests of military production is met with bayonets – not only by the manufacturers, but also by the public at large. Things are especially bad with aluminium. Is it possible, in such circumstances, to count on fully-fledged aid from the USA in the upcoming months, or even in the upcoming year?

Things are no better in England. True, everyone, beginning with Churchill, keeps saying that they are ready to give us the most active assistance. But how is this aid realized in practice?

The idea of a second front in the west, which Comrade Stalin proposed to Churchill, has been rejected in view of the difficulties involved in its attainment. The idea of a joint front in the north has been accepted in principle, but its implementation is going on so slowly and sparingly that our navy and army men are falling into despair. Air attacks on Germany from the west are carried out, but, first, they cannot have a strong impact on the withdrawal of forces from the eastern front and, second, they too are somewhat anaemic. Even in the sphere of supplies, the English try to limit themselves to the absolute minimum. They don't want to grant us sufficient loans, and they don't want to provide us with the weapons we need most badly (small-calibre anti-aircraft guns, fighters, etc.). I wrested 200 American *Tomahawks* from them with the greatest difficulty – now they can't forget about it and boast about it as a symbol of their generosity at every opportunity, suitable or otherwise. They all say: we ourselves don't have them! It's a lame excuse as often as not. The point of the matter is that (a) the British, following their long tradition, want to shift the main burden of the war onto us and to keep out of things whenever possible, and (b) members of the government, including Churchill, still keep to the course of that 'defensive strategy' which they have pursued for the last year and which was quite natural and reasonable before we entered the war, but became an anachronism after 22 June.

As a result, a mood of *complacency* is widespread in the country, infecting the workers as well to a certain extent. On 2 August, a *Bank Holiday*, there were huge crowds of people at the railway stations bound for the *country*, just as in peace time. More than 300 extra trains left London, carrying 'holiday-makers'. Does one need any further proof of widespread complacency?

That is why I do not expect full-fledged aid from England in the near future either, with the possible exception of the Middle East. In the main we must rely on ourselves.

11 August

I've learned some strange things about the Belgian government. Spaak has a wife in Brussels, and Gutt[i] (finance minister) has a family there. Not because the war separated them by chance – oh no! Spaak's wife and Gutt's wife would come to visit them when the Belgian government was still in the territory of unoccupied France, but they did not join their husbands when they left for England, and returned to Belgium instead. So, the Germans hold hostages for Spaak and Gutt, that is, for half of the Belgian government (there are four members in the Belgian government). It is obvious how this must affect the conduct of the two ministers and the whole government. Moreover, the two ministers regularly correspond with their wives via the Vatican diplomatic mail. Both wives write to their husbands regularly, asking them to be cautious, moderate, etc. To judge by many signs, Spaak's wife is the go-between between her husband and the king of Belgium, Leopold. And, perhaps, an indirect link between her husband and the Germans?…

Highly dangerous sentiments are to be observed in Belgian governmental and military circles in England. It is said that the government and the army will return to Belgium right after the end of the war and, before the people recover their senses, will swiftly establish a military dictatorship headed by Leopold. I don't know whether such a venture will succeed, but these sentiments serve as a good reminder of the complex problems we shall encounter the day after Hitler has been eliminated.

16 August

Agniya and I visited Lloyd George in Churt. We had lunch together.

Autumn is already in the air at Lloyd George's manor. Grey skies. Rain. The first touch of yellow on the trees. The wind rustles the branches and tears off leaves. There is a sense of emptiness in the house. Some rooms are closed and are evidently not in use. Even the presence of Mrs Stevenson,[ii] the secretary (and probably not only a secretary), who takes care of the old man and his domestic affairs, does not bring warmth and cosiness to a house grown cold. Or perhaps the approaching end is casting its icy shadow?…

I'm not sure. Lloyd George still looks well, although it is noticeable that he has aged greatly and let himself go over the past year, especially since the death of his wife. But only in relative terms. Only in comparison with how he looked two or three years ago, when he was already 75.

---

[i] Camille Gutt, Belgian minister of finance, 1939; minister of finance in the Belgian government in exile, 1939–45, minister for national defence, 1940–42, and economic affairs, 1940–45.

[ii] Frances Stevenson, private secretary to Lloyd George, 1913–43, became his second wife in 1943.

We talked a lot – about the war, the government and future prospects. Lloyd George is full of admiration for our resistance. He is proud to see that the Red Army and the whole of the USSR have entirely justified the predictions he made a long time ago in his talks with the leading British politicians.

'I told Chamberlain in early 1939: sign a treaty with the USSR, and you can put your mind at rest. There won't be a war, but if war does still break out, the USSR will deliver a tremendous blow to Germany. But no! That idiot, that manufacturer of iron beds was set dead against it. He shrugged his shoulders and scoffed: "The Russian army? It will collapse at Hitler's first attack." To think that such people stood at the head of an empire!'

Lloyd George berated Churchill in the fiercest terms. He was indignant that the British government is not providing the USSR with any real aid. How come? The greatest battle in the current war is being fought, the greatest battle in history, the battle on which the outcome of the war depends – and what is England doing? Nothing. The current raids on Germany don't count as 'doing'. They say it's impossible to establish a second front in France. They say such an attempt will end in failure. I'm not so sure, but suppose it will. It doesn't matter! Samsonov's[i] campaign in the past war ended at Tannenberg, but it did its job: Paris was saved and the war was eventually won. Even if England were now to lose 100,000–150,000 men in France, this would only do for the eastern front what the Russians did for the western front in that war.

The old man was also angry about the prime minister setting off to meet Roosevelt at such a critical moment in the war, abandoning the helm for a whole fortnight, and in addition taking Dill, Pound and other army and navy chiefs with him. The result? A toothless declaration which leaves one neither hot nor cold. Declarations were made during the last war – did anything come of them?

Lloyd George asked me about the assistance we receive from the British and American governments in terms of supplies. I had nothing reassuring to tell him. The old man once again displayed the greatest vexation and cursed the ministers for their narrow-mindedness. Today everything – the fate of the war, the fate of Europe, the fate of the British Empire – is decided on the eastern front, yet they haggle over every plane, every engine! Incredible!

I observed that, according to the impressions I have formed, Eden understands the significance of events in the east better than the other members of the government. Lloyd George agreed with me and mentioned that a recent conversation with Eden had led him to believe that Eden supports the idea of

---

[i] Aleksandr Samsonov, a tsarist general who fought in the Russo-Turkish War and was commander of the forlorn invasion of Prussia; responsible for the disaster at the Battle of Tannenberg, he committed suicide rather than face the tsar.

a second front. As for Churchill, the old man is extremely hard on him. I asked Lloyd George why he refuses to enter the government.

'I would have entered a small authoritative war cabinet,' the old man replied, 'in which all matters were collectively discussed and decided upon. But I would never agree to put my signature under the prime minister's decisions, which he discusses with nobody and merely imposes on the Cabinet. I'm against such a dictatorship. And that is the kind of dictator Churchill is. He does and decides everything by himself. Other members of the government are simply rubber stamps.'

According to Lloyd George, behind Churchill there stands Professor Lindemann.[i] Churchill listens to him and takes his advice on board. This is a real '...'[116] The ministers are just pawns in the prime minister's hands.

Our conversation shifted to the impact of our resistance against Germany.

'Believe me,' Lloyd George exclaimed, 'your resistance has been the very greatest surprise to many people, far too many people...'

'And an unpleasant one to some,' I added with a laugh.

'Yes, yes,' Lloyd George gurgled back, 'most unpleasant to some... Not only among the Conservatives, but among Labour as well.'

'And no wonder!' I guffawed. 'I've heard that the most unhappy man in England today is Citrine.'

'Just think!' Lloyd George exclaimed. 'The magnificent resistance of the USSR is vivid proof of the vitality of your system. A war like this is a severe examination for any regime, for its politics, economy, transport, and for the population's morale. Russia has passed the test with flying colours. Communism will benefit everywhere. How could one expect people from "..."[117] to be pleased about that?'

17 August (Bovingdon)

The eighth week of the war has come to an end. We can be satisfied with the results. True, the Germans have made progress in southern Ukraine recently, and the Berlin radio has made one hell of a racket about the 'destruction' of 25 divisions of Budenny's army. But Lozovsky was right in stating that it was Goebbels who 'destroyed' Budenny, not the Reichswehr.

In fact, the current events on the Ukrainian front have occurred on other fronts more than once in the past. The initiative is still in German hands. They attack. They choose the moment and the spot for a fresh attempt at a 'break-through'. And, of course, they choose the weakest point in the long front line and

[i] Frederick Alexander Lindemann, personal assistant to Churchill at the Admiralty, 1939; scientific adviser to the Cabinet and paymaster general, 1942–45; privy counsellor, 1943.

the most inconvenient moment. Naturally, they have some success in the first days of their attack. Then we bring up reinforcements to the vulnerable point, mount a counterattack and plug the gap. The 'breakthrough' fails. A decisive victory slips from German hands. I think we shall lose some territories in the Ukraine now as well, but we will keep a strong front and a battle-worthy army. But we must avoid the surrender of very important regions! Fingers crossed.

Two elements have played and continue to play a major role in Hitler's calculations for victory:

(1) The speed of the operations and

(2) Their decisiveness.

So far we have succeeded in parrying both. The *Blitzkrieg* has clearly failed. Eight weeks have already passed since the beginning of the war, but there is no victory on the horizon. We have also prevented the Germans from encircling us or destroying our army's major formations. In general, we have avoided a 'decisive' battle in which the chances would have been on the German side. Instead, we have gradually retreated, fighting, counterattacking, and inflicting colossal losses on Hitler. Another 6–8 weeks of the same tactics and – assuming we hold on to the areas of paramount industrial and military importance – victory will be ours (even if not right away).

24 August

Inter-Allied Conference

The full text of the note/invitation has not yet been received in Moscow. No time left to discuss the agenda, etc. (the conference is scheduled for the 27th). We'll not be able to participate. We can't just accede to the Churchill–Roosevelt declaration: it was prepared and published without regard for our opinion and information, although we bear the whole brunt of the war. We do not object to the principles of the declaration, but we would like more decisive demands to be made of Hitlerite Germany. We are irritated by the attempt to transform the USSR into a cost-free adjunct to the other powers. The British government should be told as much.

26 August

Conversation with Eden

Eden asked me about the mood in the USSR.

I replied in my private capacity (not on behalf of the government).

Britain's conduct arouses growing bewilderment and disappointment among the broad Soviet masses. We've been waging a terrible struggle against the most powerful war machine in history for ten weeks. Alone! The people and the army are fighting bravely, but the losses are huge: 700,000 people, 5,500 tanks, 4,500 planes, 1,500 guns, as well as territories, some of which are valuable and important.

And what has England been doing all this time? Our proposal – a second front in the west – was declined in July.

I don't want to discuss the reasons. Supplies? Should be easier, one would have thought, if England is not fighting… Transfer to the active sections of the front… Thanks for the 200 Tomahawks, but what is that compared to our losses? We asked for large bombs; the Air Ministry agreed after prolonged talks and gave us… six bombs! They say: we help with our air offensive against Germany. Something is happening, sure. Thanks. But… it's not enough to pinch the rabid beast's tail; it must be hit round the head with a club! The British bombers haven't forced the Germans to withdraw a single squadron from the east… Much enthusiasm, *admiration*, etc. It's pleasant, but platonic. I often think: 'I'd swap the admiration for more fighter planes!' No wonder the Soviet citizen feels disappointed and bewildered. As the ambassador, who is… etc. I deem it necessary to warn Eden about such sentiments.

Strong impression on Eden. A *half-hearted* defence (he himself an advocate of a second front): England is not prepared for invasion, USA lingers with supplies. Britain pursues an air offensive, cooperation of Britain and USSR in Iran. Good prospects in the Middle East. Forthcoming operations in Libya.

I replied: Iran and Libya are secondary tasks.[118] The main one: how to beat Germany?

What is Britain's overall strategy? Churchill told me in early July 1940: 'My overall strategy is to live through the next three months.' Eden told me then, when he was secretary for war, that Britain must be turned into an unassailable fortress, it must manoeuvre, build up forces, etc. In theory: building up forces in the winter of 1940/41, general advance in 1942/43, dominated by growth of air fleet supremacy with the aid of USA. It was unclear to me how Britain could win (not how it could avoid defeat). While Britain fought alone, there was no other way out… But now? The war situation has been revolutionized since 22 June. Britain has acquired a mighty continental ally in the east. What effect has the change had on British overall strategy? Has it had any? How does Britain plan to defeat Germany now? Explain this to me.

Eden's answers confused and weak (Libya, Turkey, air aid to USSR in the area of Black Sea in future, etc.). My impression Eden promised to talk with Churchill about the whole range of matters. General impression: Eden does not have an overall strategy. Does Churchill? I doubt it.

In conclusion Eden thanked me for my words. It is very important for him to know the true sentiments in the USSR. He wants rapprochement. 'Believe me, the prime minister and I want to assist the USSR in every possible way, although it is not always easy to do so for various reasons. But the desire is there. We are not responsible for the policies of previous governments.'

I said: 'If the British government really wants to improve relations, here is some good advice: don't make important declarations (*deus ex machina*) in the middle of the Atlantic Ocean. It's not about the content (that's OK), but the way they originate. The impression has been created that Britain and the USA imagine themselves lords and masters, judging the rest of the sinful world, including the USSR. You can't forge friendship on such a basis.'

Eden embarrassed. The allusion to Roosevelt – that's his initiative. Churchill didn't even know about the declaration when he set off.[119]

27 August

Hugessen[i] saw İnönü. Talked about British supplies to Turkey. İnönü is displeased with Britain and the USA in this respect. İnönü has doubts about the continued resistance of the Red Army until winter. But he added 'you will win'. He doesn't understand the need for Anglo-Soviet military action in Iran. Turkey is satisfied with the Anglo-Soviet declarations (10 and 25/8).

28 August

Moscow Conference

Beaverbrook back from America. Utterly displeased with US sluggishness. To the question, when is he going to Moscow for a conference, he replied: '*This afternoon!*' Americans delaying. Hopkins would be the best US representative. Will he go? Health. Problems with *Lease and Lend Bill*. Preliminary calculations of American capabilities. Beaverbrook spoke of the USSR with remarkable enthusiasm: 'You are a great nation! You are a real nation! Where would Britain be today without Russia? You ought to have the widest support from our side. Personally, I'm willing to do all I can.' What is the practical value of these declarations? *On verra*.

30 August

My initiative struck home. My conversation with Eden on the 26th made an impression in Moscow. The response from D.I.[120] started with the words: 'Your conversation with Eden on strategy fully reflects the mood of the Soviet people.

[i] Sir Hughe Montgomery Knatchbull-Hugessen, British ambassador to Turkey, 1939–44.

I am glad you caught that mood so well.' There then follow considerations of a political nature. Hitler's aim is to beat his enemies one by one, the Russians today, the British tomorrow. The passivity of the British government at present plays straight into Hitler's hands. True, the British applaud us and hurl verbal abuse at the latter. But, in practice, this doesn't change a thing. Do the British understand this? Of course they understand. So what do they want? Evidently, they want to see us weakened. If so, we must be very wary in our dealings with them.

D.I. gave me some information about the situation at the front. Lately, the situation in the Ukraine and near Leningrad has worsened. The reason: the Germans have transferred 30 more divisions from the west. If we include the 20 Finnish and 22 Rumanian divisions, we now face close to 300 divisions. The Germans consider the threat in the west to be a bluff, so they are quite happy to remove from there every half-decent unit. Where does the Germans' confidence come from?... Unless the English rouse themselves very soon, our situation will become critical. Will the British gain from this? No, I think they will lose.

D.I.'s conclusions are very gloomy: if a second front is not established in Europe within 3–4 weeks, we and our allies may lose everything. It's sad, but it may become a reality.

Having received such a message, I paced my room back and forth for a long time and pondered. D.I., of course, knows the situation better, but I nonetheless find it difficult to believe that we may suffer defeat. I have been firmly convinced of our ultimate victory since the very beginning of the war. For me, it was only the cost of victory that was uncertain. I still stick by my conviction. But D.I.'s words attest to the fact that the situation has become extremely strained. Efforts must be made to relieve the tension, or at least to exploit it in order to 'rouse' the English. Reckoning more on the latter, I immediately replied in that spirit.

I explained that if the situation was so serious, one more attempt should be made to urge the British government to open a second front in France or in the Balkans. At the same time I added: I don't want to create any groundless illusions. At such a moment as now, you need more than ever to know the facts as they stand. So let me tell you in advance that, to judge by my own impressions, the atmosphere in governmental quarters (but not among the masses) is hardly in favour of a second front. This was confirmed, in particular, by my conversation with the prime minister at lunch on 29 August. A complicated knot of motives underlies such attitudes: the hypnotic effect of Germany's invincibility on land; the growing *complacency* caused by our powerful resistance (many say: the Russians are fighting well, so we can mark time and steadily fulfil our plans for a decisive offensive in 1942 or 1943); the desire to weaken the USSR (a significant wing of the Conservatives definitely has such a wish);[121] the ill-preparedness of the British for large-scale landing operations; and the fear of a new Dunkerque (which might undermine the government's position from the inside and damage its prestige in the USA). This is an analysis of the afore-stated mood, not its justification. Proceeding from the given situation, it seems to me that we stand a better chance of 'rousing' the British in the area of supplies.

Nevertheless, considering the menace to the USSR, the question of a second front could be put before the British government once more. Churchill and others must understand at long last that if the USSR leaves the stage, the British Empire is finished. And, even if our second attempt on the issue of a second front ends in failure, we shall nonetheless be vindicated before our own people and before history: we have done everything possible to open the eyes of the British to the impending danger and to prevent the worst. However, we must also consider the other side of the coin: if the British do not open a second front and we reveal to them the critical nature of our situation, this may have an adverse impact on issues of supply. The British may decide: since it is useless helping the Russians, we'd better keep the available tanks and planes for ourselves. All the pluses and minuses of the démarche which I am proposing must be weighed. If it is undertaken, two forms are possible: (1) a personal message from Stalin to Churchill, and (2) an extensive conversation between me and Churchill about the current situation. To my mind, the first form would be better and more effective.

31 August

Religion

Attended public prayers – a demonstration in honour of the Red Army in Feltham (London suburbs). Ten thousand people in the park – mostly workers from the nearby aircraft factory and their families. The priest sang a few psalms. The crowd joined in. A short sermon calling for support for the Red Army and the USSR. Applause. All this took about half an hour. Then the chairman of the local trade union council opened the meeting. Speeches about the heroism of the USSR, the people and the army. One speaker: it is thanks to the *purges* of 1936–38 that there are no longer any Quislings in the USSR. I spoke (symbol: explosion of Dneproges).[122] Applause at the mention of Stalin, the '*Internationale*' and '*God Save the King*'. Two flags above the platform. Dozens of trade union flags (incl. one of Soviet railway workers, a gift to a Feltham workers' delegation in previous years). Prior to the prayers, I met local Home Guard (workers). Children showered us with flowers. Warm and friendly welcome. Typical of the mood in the masses. My speech quoted on the wireless at nine o'clock.

7 September

Novikov attended a service in St Phil. church in South London. In memory of Red Army men fallen in battle. Prayer for Stalin, Soviet government, ambassador in London and his staff. Singing of the '*Internationale*'. Prayer for the king and Churchill, '*God Save the King*'. Father Roberts argued in his sermon that the Soviet economic system is a Christian system. Novikov shook hands with 600 people. Shouts of 'Long live the USSR', 'Red Front'. Collection of donations for Soviet and English Red Cross.

2 September[123]

Moscow Conference

A talk with Beaverbrook and Winant about hastening the conference. They'd like to – the Americans drag their feet. Winant has already sent four telegrams to USA, but to no avail. Mood slump in America (stupid, but a fact). Harriman is coming to London at the end of September. Following a telephone talk with Harriman, Beaverbrook doesn't count on any hurrying up. Regrets the fact. His press wages a campaign for immediate aid. How to travel: a cruiser or the *Catalina*?

4 September

Vyshinsky handed Cripps a copy of Stalin's message to Churchill. Cripps came back to Vyshinsky an hour and a half later and said that having read the message he had decided to fly to Britain with MacFarlane immediately in order to ensure the implementation of the measures indicated in Stalin's message (later London forbade Cripps to leave Moscow).

[Cripps received Stalin's message to Churchill on 4 September. 'It is such a grave document,' he wrote in his diary,

> that it leaves me completely *bouleversé*. The last three weeks have obviously played havoc with the Russian forces and what is worse with their manufacturing capacity. Unless we can do something most immediately and effectively to help them the game is up at any rate for a long time if not *all together*. They will not be able to hold out for the winter. This is the moment that I had always feared and the more so as I saw that we were in fact doing nothing to help to relieve the pressure. If now Russia collapses we shall be left without the possibility of victory … I took the decision to return at once to London and to take the General Mason-MacFarlane with me. Then I went and saw Vyshinsky again and told him of my decision but that I must see Stalin before I went and that the General must

see Marshal Shaposhnikov.[i] Later he rang up and said that Stalin would see me and would let me know the exact time today.

Churchill was determined to deter Cripps from carrying out a *fait accompli*, instructing the Air Ministry that 'the Catalina due to return from Archangel ... should not leave without further instructions, because I did not want it to bring the Ambassador home'.[124] However, no longer able to ignore Cripps's challenge, Churchill addressed him personally with a lengthy recitation of the arguments against direct assistance to the Russians and ridiculing his call for a superhuman effort, which he took to mean 'an effort rising superior to space, time and geography'.[125] The letter heralded a long and acrimonious correspondence between the two, culminating in Cripps's bid for power after his return from Moscow.[126]

Churchill's estrangement from Cripps on the eve of the Moscow conference coincided with a growing crisis on the Russian front. On 8–9 September, the Germans resumed their thrust on the outskirts of Leningrad. In the critical situation which ensued, General Zhukov was rushed to Leningrad on 13 September to replace Voroshilov and ordered that the city must be held at all costs. Meanwhile, much against the opinion of his generals, Hitler had decided on 21 August to halt the advance on Moscow, while making a dash southwards and maintaining the siege of Leningrad. After a fierce but swift armoured battle, Guderian[ii] succeeded on 7 September in ripping apart the Russian defences of the Bryansk and south-eastern fronts. On 11 September, the legendary General Budenny found himself trapped in the Kiev salient; his request to withdraw saw him immediately relieved of command and Marshal Timoshenko appointed in his place. A few days later, Guderian and Field Marshal Ewald von Kleist linked in a pincer movement some 100 miles east of Kiev, trapping Timoshenko's troops. Shaposhnikov cabled the general staff on that day: 'This is the beginning as you know of catastrophe – a matter of a couple of days.' Kiev indeed fell on 18 September, and the bulk of the Soviet army on that front was either annihilated or captured. The situation on the southern front seemed just as bleak, with the German forces encircling Odessa and threatening the Crimea.[127]]

4 September

My proposal has been accepted. This morning I received the text of Stalin's personal message to the prime minister. Firm, clear and ruthless words. No illusions, no sweeteners. The facts as they stand. The threats as they loom. A remarkable document.[128]

I came to Cadogan's office at about 4 p.m. to discuss the Iranian affair. I informed him that I must hand Stalin's personal message to Churchill and asked to arrange a meeting with the prime minister in the evening, if possible,

[i] Boris Mikhailovich Shaposhnikov, chief of the general staff, and deputy people's commissar for defence, 1941–43.

[ii] Heinz Guderian, colonel general, architect of the German armoured corps' doctrine and victory in the west and in the early stages of the campaign in Russia. A critic of the conduct of the war in the east, he was dismissed by Hitler in the winter of 1941 but reinstated in command in 1943.

or tomorrow morning. Cadogan called Churchill's secretary right away, and the latter promised to find out with all haste and report instantly. She warned, though, that it would be impossible to see the prime minister in the morning, as he would be leaving London early for an important *engagement of long standing*.

I also asked Cadogan that Eden be present at my meeting with the prime minister.

'I'm very sorry,' I added, 'that it is necessary to disturb the foreign minister's rest, but the matter is quite serious and I think he will bear no hard feelings towards me on this score'...

Eden had left a few days earlier for a week in the country, for his *holidays*.

Cadogan thought he would get a reply from the prime minister's secretary while we were discussing Iranian affairs, but the response was somehow delayed. I decided to go home and asked Cadogan to inform me by phone about the time and place of my meeting with the PM. The telephone rang as soon as I got back to the embassy. Cadogan said the PM would receive me at ten o'clock in the evening at 10, Downing Street and that Eden would be present at the meeting.

I left home a quarter of an hour before the appointed time. The moon shone brightly. Fantastically shaped clouds raced from west to east. When they blotted the moon and their edges were touched with red and black, the whole picture appeared gloomy and ominous. As if the world was on the eve of its destruction. I drove along the familiar streets and thought: 'A few more minutes, and an important, perhaps decisive historical moment, fraught with the gravest consequences, will be upon us. Will I rise to the occasion? Do I possess sufficient strength, energy, cunning, agility and wit to play my role with maximum success for the USSR and for all mankind?'...

I entered the hall of the famous house in a heightened mood, filled with a kind of resonant, inner tension. Prosaic life immediately brought me down to earth with a crash. The porter, a most ordinary English porter in livery, bowed low and took my hat. Another porter, indistinguishable from the first, led me through a poorly lit corridor along which dashed young men and girls, probably the prime minister's secretaries and typists. This entire, ordinary routine, so familiar to me from the experience of many years, felt like a tub of cold water poured over my soul.

I was then ushered into the PM's office, or, to be more precise, the government's meeting room. Churchill, wearing a dinner jacket and with the habitual cigar between his teeth, was sitting halfway down a long table covered with a green cloth, amid a long row of empty chairs. Eden, dressed in a dark-grey suit of light material, sat near the PM. Churchill looked at me distrustfully, puffed at his cigar and growled like a bulldog: 'Bearing good news?'

'I fear not,' I replied, handing the prime minister the envelope with Stalin's message.

He took out the letter, put on his glasses and began to read it carefully. Having read a page, he would hand it over to Eden. I sat beside the prime minister, keeping silent and observing his expression. When Churchill finished reading, it was clear that Stalin's message had made a powerful impression on him.

I began to speak:

> So now, Mr Churchill, you and the British government know the real state of affairs. We have withstood the terrible assault of the German war machine on our own for 11 weeks now. The Germans have massed up to 300 divisions on our front. Nobody helps us in this struggle. The situation has become difficult and menacing. It is still not too late to change it. But to do so it is essential to carry out quickly and resolutely what Stalin writes about. If the right measures are not taken immediately, the moment may be lost. The greatest responsibility towards your country and the whole world now falls on the British government and on you personally, Mr Churchill. It is either or. Either you take firm and decisive steps to provide the USSR with the help it needs – then the war will be won, Hitlerism will be crushed, and the opportunity for free and progressive development will open before mankind. Or, if you don't provide us with the aid we need, the USSR will face the risk of defeat with all the ensuing consequences. Just think about those consequences! Should Hitler win his 'Russian campaign', not only will fascist Germany become the legislator of the world, and not only will the USSR suffer heavily, but the British Empire, too, will be doomed to ruin. For who then will prevent Hitler from marching on India, Egypt? Who will prevent Germany and Japan from meeting somewhere near Singapore? I'm not fond of lofty words and high-flown phrases, but my conscience obliges me to say that our meeting today, this conversation between three men at 10, Downing Street in the evening of 4 September 1941, has the very greatest significance. Who knows how future generations will regard it? Who knows whether it may not become a turning point in world history, a turning point in one direction or another? Everything depends on the position that the British government and, in particular, you, Mr Churchill, now take.

While I spoke, the prime minister sucked on his cigar and listened, merely responding to my words every now and again with gestures or facial expressions, while Eden pored over Stalin's message and made some notes in the margins.

Then Churchill started responding. Yes, he is well aware of the fact that we have been fighting alone for 11 weeks. He fully understands the difficulties and the dangers of our position. He is perfectly aware of the catastrophic consequences that would follow from our defeat. Of course, in this case India would be temporarily lost to England… Temporarily, because even then the remaining members of the British Empire would continue fighting for 10, 20 or however many years, until victory was secured. But what is to be done?

'I have no doubt,' Churchill exclaimed, 'that Hitler still wishes to pursue his old policy of beating his enemies one by one… I would be ready to sacrifice 50,000 English lives if in so doing I could draw even just 20 German divisions from your front!'

Unfortunately, England currently lacks the strength to establish a second front in France. Here, Churchill repeated everything he had told me on this matter in July and which he had then set out in his reply to Stalin's July message.

'The Channel, which prevents Germany from jumping over into England,' the prime minister added, 'likewise prevents England from jumping over into occupied France.'

Churchill considers a second front in the Balkans to be impossible at present. The British lack the necessary troops, aircrafts and tonnage.

'Just think,' Churchill exclaimed, 'it took us a full seven weeks to transfer 3–4 divisions from Egypt to Greece in the spring. And this on the basis of Greece being not a hostile, but a friendly country! No, no! We can't walk into certain defeat either in France or in the Balkans!'

I replied: 'Sometimes defeat is no less important than victory. Recall the last war. When General Samsonov entered East Prussia, he, too, was not yet ready for such an operation. He also risked defeat. Moreover, he actually suffered defeat and committed suicide. But this defeat saved Paris. This defeat rescued the war for the allies.'[129]

My remark made a strong impression on Churchill. His *historic sense* (which is strong) was aroused. It was clear that this reminder had disrupted his train of thought. But he soon recovered and went on defending his point of view. As if seeking justification, he proposed that I should meet the chiefs of staff tomorrow and see for myself by talking to them that the opening of a second front is impossible.

'We, the British, are poor allies on land,' Churchill openly admitted. 'Could it be otherwise? We are strong at sea, we are not bad in the air, but on land… We have neither the traditions, nor the experience, nor the taste for it. Our army is still weak and insufficiently trained. It needs experience and time. Give it 4–5 years and it can become a serious force!'

I couldn't help thinking: 'Is Churchill seriously thinking in terms of a five-year war?'

Clearly, a second front in the west or in the Balkans was out of the question for now. So I tried to approach the same problem from another angle: how could the German pressure on our front be alleviated?

'If you do not deem it possible,' I said, 'to get 20 or 30 German divisions off our back by opening a second front, perhaps you could at least help us relieve the pressure exerted by 20 Finnish divisions? Couldn't you use your influence and that of America to facilitate Finland's withdrawal from the war? As far as I know, a major internal conflict on this matter is under way in Finland itself at the present time.'

Churchill liked this idea very much. His face seemed to light up. Turning to Eden, he exclaimed emphatically: 'Do whatever you can, without fail! Use every means possible, even if it means declaring war on Finland. Appeal to Washington.'

Eden promised to do this the very next day.

Seeing that there was no point arguing any further on the question of a second front, I fell back on my 'second line', putting special emphasis on matters of military supplies. Here the PM was far more amenable, as I had expected. He promised to consider Stalin's request concerning tanks and planes with the utmost goodwill and then to give a definite answer.

'Only don't expect too much from us!' Churchill warned. 'We, too, are short of arms. More than a million British soldiers are still unarmed.'

Like a schoolboy boasting of how skilfully he has tricked his classmate, Churchill told me with a twinkle in his eye how, at the Atlantic conference, he had managed to wangle 150,000 rifles out of Roosevelt – 150,000! So these are the kind of figures we have to argue about today. As for tanks, 500 a month is out of the question. The entire output of tanks in England does not reach this number!

'I don't want to mislead you,' Churchill concluded. 'I'll be frank. We'll not be able to provide you with any essential aid before the winter, either by creating a second front or through abundant supplies. All we are capable of sending you at present – tanks, planes, etc. – are trifles compared with your needs. This is painful for me to say, but the truth must come first. The future is a different matter. In 1942, the situation will change. Both we and the Americans will be able to give you a lot in 1942. But for now...'

And Churchill concluded with half a smile: 'Only God, in whom you don't believe, can help you in the next 6–7 weeks. Besides, even if we sent tanks and planes to you now, they would not arrive before winter.'

'Suppose that is so,' I objected, 'but if we knew for sure that certain quantities of arms would be arriving from England, we could dispose of our reserves more freely now.'

'That is a serious point,' Churchill responded. 'I'll try to do all that is humanly possible to satisfy Stalin's request for arms.'

The prime minister warned me against placing excessive hopes on the United States. They're forever letting you down. They're always slow to do what they promise. The British have yet to receive all the arms they ordered in America for cash at the beginning of the war. Neither have they got anything yet under *Lease and Lend*. A serious influx of arms from America can be expected only in the second half of 1942.

Here I turned to another question that has long been weighing heavy on my heart. 'The USSR and England,' I said, 'are allies. They are waging a common war against a common enemy. This, one might have thought, would assume the existence of a joint strategic plan for the war (if only in its basic outline). Do they have such a plan? No, they don't. We don't know how the British intend to defeat Hitler, and the British don't know how we envisage doing the same. There are no military negotiations between the chiefs of staff. Nor even so much as a suggestion of serious military cooperation. This is not normal. Couldn't the parameters of the forthcoming Moscow conference be extended to discuss not only matters relating to supplies, but also those relating to a common strategy?'

Churchill agreed with me in principle, albeit without much enthusiasm. He declared that he was ready to develop a general strategic plan together with us.

I asked how the prime minister perceives the further course and outcome of the war.

Churchill's reply boils down to the following.

Until 22 June he was confident of England's ultimate victory, but could not say how and when this would happen. He simply believed in the resilience of the British nation, and counted on the gradual effect of the blockade, the attainment of air supremacy with the help of the USA, and the growth of internal difficulties in Germany. Subconsciously he also relied on the 'good luck' which has fallen England's way over the entire course of her history (here I recalled the fable of the two frogs which Churchill recounted to Prytz).

'But I must confess,' Churchill added, 'that the paths leading to victory were not clear to me at the time.'

The situation changed drastically after 22 June. Now the paths leading to victory are clearly visible, but the prospects, nevertheless, are far from rosy. The war will be long. Hard, exhausting.

I interrupted Churchill at this point and asked: 'All this is as you say, but tell me, do you have a war plan, or at least a draft of a plan, for at least 1942?'

'My plans for 1942 are very modest,' Churchill replied. 'Here they are: to keep a firm hold of the mother country and not permit an invasion, to hold the Nile valley and the Middle East, to win back Libya (and take Tripoli, if we can), to secure supplies to the USSR via Iran and other routes, to draw Turkey onto our side, to bomb Germany incessantly, and to conduct a relentless submarine war. For the rest: to prepare the army, strengthen the air force, develop arms production, reinforce the Middle East. I plan to have 750,000 troops in that part of the world by the end of this year (there are about 600,000 now), and about a million by the spring of 1942.'

What Churchill was saying, essentially, was that 1942 should be merely a 'preparatory' year. No major landing operations. No attempts to bring the war to a conclusion. Then 1943 may be the decisive year, when England, aided by the USA, will raise the number of its tanks to 20,000. However, this, too, is merely hypothetical. One cannot exclude the possibility that the denouement may have to be postponed until 1944.

'I see a striking analogy,' said the prime minister, 'between our time and the time of Napoleon. The war, if you recall, lasted a long time, and for many years we suffered one failure after another. But how did it all end for Napoleon? It ended with Saint Helena. The same will happen to Hitler. Only Saint Helena is too good a place for him.'

Churchill spat these words out with true disgust, almost fury. One could sense the extraordinary hatred that seethes in his soul towards Hitler… and towards Germany.

It was a quarter to twelve when I left the prime minister. We had talked for nearly two hours. The moon had set, and the London streets, plunged into 'black-out', were filled with an ominous silence. Summing things up, I wondered: 'What will the result of it all be?'

[Maisky deliberately concealed in both his report to Moscow and the diary that Churchill, sensing the 'underlying air of menace' in Maisky's appeal, was enraged, telling him that 'Whatever happens and whatever you do, you of all people have no right to make reproaches to us', having collaborated with the Germans before the war. Maisky and his staff at the embassy were desperate to dispel Stalin's suspicion about Churchill's objective and to convince him that, though dead set against a second front, the British prime minister was genuinely prepared to sacrifice for Russia a significant portion of the supplies coming from the United States.[130]]

5 September

Today at 11 a.m. the meeting proposed by Churchill with the chiefs of staff took place in Eden's office. It was chaired by Eden. Present were Admiral Pound, General Dill, Air Marshal Portal[i] and 2–3 other military men. On our side there was myself and Kharlamov,[ii] with Baranov acting as the admiral's interpreter. It lasted about two hours. We discussed the feasibility or otherwise

[i] Charles Portal, chief of the air staff, 1940–45.

[ii] Nikolai Mikhailovich Kharlamov, admiral, from June 1941, naval attaché and head of the Soviet military mission in Great Britain; deputy chief of the general staff of the navy from 1944.

of a second front in France from a purely strategic point of view. I was greatly disappointed – not by the fact that the chiefs of staff deemed such an operation impossible (everything had prepared me for this), but by the poverty and triteness of their arguments. Absolutely nothing new, nothing more convincing than what I had heard a dozen times before from others, beginning with the prime minister and ending with ordinary journalists. One could sense that the chiefs of staff are simply hypnotized by the might of the German war machine and wholly deprived of initiative and boldness. Dill made the best impression on me and Pound the worse. Eden merely presided and barely expressed his views. We finished just before 'lunch'. The verdict of the chiefs of staff is that a second front is impossible, either in France or in the Balkans.[131] They said little about the Balkans in this regard, assuming the matter to be self-evident. Pound said: we don't have the tonnage, the navy cannot undertake the operation – and that was enough. What's more, the Germans have left 26 divisions in France and 1,100 first-line aircraft (including 800 fighters). Hence the conclusion: a landing operation in France is impossible.

When the military conference ended, I remained behind with Eden for a short while. He told me that Churchill had cancelled the trip to the country which he had planned for today and was spending the whole morning working on his reply to Comrade Stalin. The reply would most likely be ready by the evening, and I would receive a copy.

I asked Eden: 'As I understand it, the British government is considering expanding its aid to us in the way of supplies. On what basis will this be done? For cash? On credit?'

My question took Eden unawares and he said he would ask the prime minister. I added: 'Since you are going to talk with Churchill on this matter, couldn't you raise the question of the supplies being granted to us on the basis of *Lease and Lend*? In other words, couldn't England and the USSR establish the same relations in this sphere as have been established between the USA and England? It strikes me as only logical and natural to approach the issue in this way.'

Eden livened up and said he agreed with me. It was evident that he liked my idea. He promised to mention my proposal during his talk with the prime minister.

At six o'clock I was expected to make a short speech at the civil funeral ceremony for Tagore. As I left, I took the precaution of telling people at the embassy that they should immediately come and find me at the ceremony if anything happened. It was just as well I did.

The ceremony took place in *Caxton Hall*. About a thousand people attended. All shades of left-leaning, literary, artistic and political circles were represented. The faces of Indian men and women stood out like bright spots. The mood was

89. Maisky conferring with the clandestine opposition, Lloyd George and Anthony Eden.

elevated, solemn. My appearance on the platform was greeted with tumultuous applause. Negrín sat behind me and Agniya to my right.

The chairman made an opening speech and then asked me when I would like to speak. Considering the possible contingencies, I asked to be given the floor first. This proved very wise. I had barely finished speaking when a message from the embassy was handed to me: Churchill asked me to come immediately to *10, Downing Street*. I had to make my apologies to the chairman and the gathering and leave.

I sat for some ten minutes in the prime minister's reception room. Eden put his head round the door at one point and said: 'Sorry for the delay. The reply is being typed up.'

Then he added with a half-apologetic smile: 'We couldn't satisfy you fully, but we did what we could… You'll see for yourself.'

Eden left and I began speculating what the British concessions might be.

Eventually, they ushered me in. The same long room with a table covered by a green cloth. Churchill and Eden sat at the table, with a bottle of whisky on the table and some soda water. The prime minister, with his customary cigar between his teeth, made a cordial gesture inviting me to sit down and poured out a whisky and soda. Then he grinned and said: 'The text of the message will be brought in a minute… In the meantime I'd like to touch upon another matter.'

It transpired that Churchill had seen Lloyd George just the other day. The old man criticized Churchill's policy toward the USSR and mentioned in passing that the British government was not even supplying us properly: it was sending planes without machine-gun belts (this actually happened, and I once told Lloyd George about it). Churchill became more and more furious with every word. I don't know what happened between the former and the present prime minster, but Churchill is under the impression that I complained about the British government to Lloyd George. This stung him to the quick.

'If you're unhappy about something,' the PM said, 'come to me, to Eden, or to Max (Beaverbrook), and we shall try to do what we can. But why appeal to the opposition?… After all, Lloyd George represents the opposition to the government. It is more advantageous for you to work with the government. The opposition now is nothing…'[132]

Churchill sniffed, shrugged his shoulders and said with a superior smile: 'There is no opposition!… Should it come to a vote, no more than 20 MPs would vote against me.'

One could detect in the PM's tone both contempt for the opposition and sensitivity to its criticism.

I also shrugged my shoulders and replied that I understood Churchill's feelings, but could not give up meeting and talking with my old friends in political and social circles. The prime minister did not object. He even considered my reasoning to be 'fair', but I could see that he was unhappy all the same. What can I do!…

Experience has taught me that an ambassador in England must have good contacts in both governmental and oppositional quarters and, depending on the situation, press this or that button. I don't plan to depart from this rule, even if it means displeasing Churchill. The future is uncertain, and – who knows? – perhaps we and the Churchill government will, at some point, have to go our separate ways.

Eventually, they brought in a copy of the PM's reply to Comrade Stalin. Churchill handed the document over to me and said with a slightly conceited grin: 'This is what we can do now. I think it will be of some help to you after all.'

I quickly glanced through the reply. I found my proposals reflected in it: the agreement in principle to discuss joint war plans and the agreement to apply the lend-lease principle in the sphere of supplies. This was pleasing. What was not pleasing was the categorical rejection of a second front. I was also interested by the paragraph in the reply where Churchill expressed his opinion that the German onslaught on the USSR appeared to have already passed its zenith. I asked the PM: on what grounds was this conclusion based?

'On the general impression derived from all the secret and non-secret information which passes through my hands,' replied Churchill.

Is his impression correct? It would be good if it were. But is it? I'm afraid to believe it.

In the evening, I was pacing my office once more from one corner to the other and thinking: 'What's the outcome? Has a clear-cut and definite decision been taken about the future? Was my meeting with Churchill yesterday a turning point in world history? And, if so, in which direction?'

I could not find a fully satisfactory answer to these questions. Things turned out differently from how I had expected. There was no great, decisive 'either/or'. Instead, we had a kind of compromise. Who knows what it will lead to. My sense of logic was offended. But am I right to be dissatisfied? Some practical things have been achieved… Or perhaps the English, who call themselves an 'illogical people', who do not like logic and do not believe in it, are right after all?

15 September

A new message from Comrade Stalin to Churchill, in reply to Churchill's message to Comrade Stalin of 5 September, arrived today.[133] Its main point: if the British government considers a second front in the west impossible, let it send 25–30 divisions to the USSR to fight against the Germans side by side with our soldiers.

I asked for Eden to be present at the meeting. This was agreed, and my meeting with the prime minister was fixed for 6.30 this evening. That suited me well, as I was scheduled to meet the American delegation to the Moscow conference headed by Harriman at about 4 p.m. in Hendon, together with Umansky, who has arrived from the USA. There was plenty of time.

Suddenly, everything changed. Churchill moved our meeting forward to 4.30. I wondered: should I go to Hendon? Finally I decided to go nonetheless and as a result was a couple of minutes late for the meeting with the prime minister. In Hendon I saw Eden, who, together with Beaverbrook, had also come to greet Harriman. Eden knew nothing about the change in the PM's plans. When I told him about it, he rushed to the telephone to check his schedule. It turned out that Eden had an engagement at 4.30 which he could not think of cancelling at this stage. As a result, Eden was not present at the meeting and my conversation with the prime minister was conducted *tête-à-tête*.

Having read Comrade Stalin's message, Churchill began 'thinking aloud'. His 'thoughts' boiled down to the following.

In principle, Churchill would be willing to carry out Stalin's request and send British troops to the USSR. He would even consider it a matter of honour to do so. But he must discuss this question in advance with his colleagues and advisers.

The prime minister envisages two difficulties in fulfilling Comrade Stalin's request. The first: from where should he draw the troops for such an expedition? The British have about 600,000 troops in the Middle East and hope to bring their number to 750,000 by Christmas. Churchill had already told me about this. The number of trained and armed troops at home does not exceed 1 million (excluding the Home Guard, anti-aircraft defence, coastal defence, etc.). An offensive in Libya is currently being prepared. Is it possible under these circumstances to allocate serious forces for an expeditionary corps in the USSR? Of course, 25–30 divisions are out of the question – that is beyond England's capability today – but can anything *substantial* still be found to send to the USSR? Churchill was uncertain.

I objected, saying that this problem did not strike me as quite so intractable. It was unclear to me why the British government should keep such a large force in the Middle East. Part of the force for an expeditionary corps, it seemed to me, could be taken from the Middle East, and the other part from England. After all, with the Germans being engaged up to their eyes in the east, the danger of invasion to England has receded. The first part of the troops could be brought to the USSR through Iran, and the second through Arkhangelsk.

The prime minister agreed that the danger of invasion is in fact unreal today, but… An offensive in Libya is in prospect… The troops stationed in the Middle East consist mostly of divisions sent by the dominions, and if they were to be dispatched to the USSR delicate talks with the dominion governments would be inevitable… All this makes the problem more complicated.

Lack of tonnage complicates things still further. Things are so bad with shipping that the British government cannot send more than 40–50,000 men each month to the Middle East, and even that only thanks to the covert assistance of the United States. What a joke: everything has to be sent around South Africa! From the point of view of shipping, the transportation of troops to the USSR through Arkhangelsk would be more convenient: the distance is shorter. But there is a catch, too: British soldiers are not accustomed to the cold climate. It would be better if they were to fight somewhere in the south – in the Ukraine, near the Black Sea, etc. Churchill would willingly send British forces by sea through the Straits, but the Turks would not allow it. At this point, Churchill remarked in passing that Turkey is extremely important and that British and Soviet diplomats must set themselves the task of drawing Turkey onto our side. 'We mustn't skimp on it,' the prime minister added with a smile.

Returning to the question of an expeditionary corps for the USSR, Churchill started complaining about the poor means of transportation in Iran. He then asked: could the troops brought in through Arkhangelsk be sent to the Ukraine? I replied that I saw no obstacles to this. Churchill then put the question: wouldn't it be better to launch a landing operation in Norway and thereby rescue Sweden for the Allies as well? I disagreed, saying that we shouldn't scatter our forces, and that if Stalin is asking for troops to be sent to the USSR, he obviously knows what he is doing.

Then I asked: may I assume that the British government agrees in principle to meet Stalin's request? If that is the case, practical military negotiations could be opened in Moscow or in London without delay. The prime minister avoided a direct response to my question and only repeated that he would urgently discuss this question with his advisers and would notify me promptly. This sounds suspicious to me. The 'advisers' (I immediately imagined the faces of Pound, Dill and Portal) will, of course, be against Comrade Stalin's suggestion or, even if they don't say so openly, will raise a barbed-wire fence of unfeasible conditions around its implementation – will Churchill be able to stand his ground? I fear that little will come of it all. But we shall see.

Churchill summed up the situation in the following way: 'I repeat what I told you at our last meeting: I don't want to mislead you. Even if the British government decides to send an expeditionary force to you, it will not arrive before winter. I am afraid the next six weeks will be a hard time for you, but I won't be able to help you with anything substantial in this period. This is sad, but, unfortunately, that's how it is.'

The prime minister glanced through Comrade Stalin's message once again and added with a contented smile:[134] 'It is very good that Mr Stalin has at last come to believe in our good intentions vis-à-vis the USSR. Yes, we want your victory, for it will be our victory, too. And I'm prepared to do all I can for your victory. The trouble is that there is a limit to what I can do. Please understand this!'

And then, after a moment's thought, Churchill added: 'I believe in our cooperation. I believe Mr Stalin. I believe for two reasons. First, because our interests coincide: we face mortal peril from one and the same enemy. Second, because I know that so far the Soviet government has always kept its word.'

I supported the prime minister on both accounts.

Churchill also touched upon that part of Comrade Stalin's message where he speaks about Cripps's memo of 12 September. He, Churchill, fully agrees with Stalin that Germany should compensate the USSR for the damage it has inflicted (in particular, for the ships the Soviet government was forced to blow up in Leningrad), and it goes without saying that at the end of the war the USSR will have prior claim for the replacement of its losses, provided that any German military vessels remain at that stage. Nevertheless, the PM would consider it a question of honour for England also to support us in the matter of compensation, even at the expense of British military vessels, because the sacrifice we would have made in Leningrad would be a sacrifice made on behalf of the common cause.

Churchill is concerned about the Germans' advance toward Kiev, but he thinks Kiev can hold out even if it is 'cut off'. It's an outdated point of view that a city must surrender if the enemy envelops it. Take Tobruk. Take Odessa. Churchill speaks warmly and at length about Odessa, calling it a Tobruk on a colossally magnified scale.

On parting, I asked Churchill to hurry in dispatching the British and American delegations to Moscow. He promised to do so. He also promised, before the delegations leave, to settle the question of the 'American quota' in the delivery amounts agreed upon with us 10 days ago.

I spent about an hour with Churchill. When I came out of his room I found nearly all the members of the Cabinet waiting in the reception room: Anderson, Attlee, Kingsley Wood and others. They all greeted my appearance with laughter and a sigh of relief: it turned out that my talk with Churchill had delayed the War Cabinet meeting for nearly half an hour!

15 September

Umansky and I went to see Beaverbrook. Beaverbrook's intentions: minimum talks in London, 3–4 days, and off they go. What about the Americans? Umansky made it clear to Beaverbrook that the Americans tend to take their time and 'study'. – Then at four we met Harriman and Co. at the airport. Saw Eden, Beaverbrook and Winant there. At 6 p.m. a War Cabinet meeting with the American delegation. The Americans are unhappy about the *rush*.

18 September

Inter-Allied Conference

(1) A visit from Bracken: how to soothe American Catholics? Allow in Catholic missionaries. My refusal. Maybe a Polish bishop can visit the Polish army in the USSR? More *publicity* for religious life in the USSR. A job for Bartlett. (2) The US government recently urged the British government to secure 'concessions' in religious affairs in the USSR. Winant had a conversation with Umansky about it yesterday.

20 September

Finland

Sargent handed Novikov the British government note, which is addressed to Finland through the Norwegian government. – My telephone conversation with Sargent (Eden is in Scotland inspecting the Poles): to cut out the last phrase in the note and publish it. To defer the presentation of the note till Eden's return on 22nd. My letter to Eden in this spirit, as I'm leaving for Birmingham on 22nd. Communication from Eden on 23 September: he agrees with me, but the note had been already presented. – An abrupt statement over the wireless. – My question: what's to be done if Finland doesn't reply or gives an unsatisfactory reply? Must wait 2–3 days and declare war. Eden agrees.

22 September

Visit to Birmingham

At the factories. Rallies.

From platform in front of the tanks. 'Stalin' is the first to roll out.

The crowd's mood like at our meetings in the years of the revolution.

Shop stewards' meeting – all promise '*not to let us down*'.

Crafty Beaverbrook. He organized everything, including *shop stewards*' meeting. He's not afraid.

90. Maisky thanking workers for 'Stalin', the first tank destined for the Russian front.

Is it worth helping increase production in England? On condition that a firm percentage goes our way.

My *broadcast* on 27 Sept.

'Russian tank week' brought a 20% rise in production.[135]

23 September

Eden – reply to my talk on the 19th.[136] My arguments were put before the Defence Committee and discussed, as a result, in Churchill's letter to Stalin, which Beaverbrook brought, it is said that General Ismay is authorized to discuss joint strategy questions, including the transfer of British troops to USSR. Prime minister is now more in favour of this. It will not interfere with the Libyan campaign. Different kinds of troops. Lyttelton agrees with this. Wavell, who has been in London, will go to Tiflis for negotiations. – My question concerning Margesson's article in the *Star* – Eden dismisses its significance.

Moscow Conference

Eden said on 24 September at the Inter-Allied Conference that the Moscow conference should end in approximately 7–10 days. Everything is well prepared. Such is Churchill's line – Beaverbrook also told me before leaving that he hoped to complete the main job in a few days ('it is necessary to act, not investigate'). 'I admire the Russians' bravery and resilience. They are a true people. You told me on the first day of the war: *We will fight like devils.* I went to the PM and said: "Maisky says the Russians will fight *like devils*. We must help them!" It turned out like you said.'[137]

24 September

Directions from Moscow on the resolution concerning food supplies after the war came too late. Spoke with Eden about the internationalization of the Central Bureau. Eden thought changes not possible (he agreed with USA – no time to exchange communications). I entered my amendment to Art. 6.

* * *

Arranged to meet Eden on 17 Sept. – first item: my declaration, second: Atlantic declaration, third: food.

26 September

De Gaulle

Exchange of letters with de Gaulle. In conversation de Gaulle's made *anti-British* statements – they are never prepared for war, always improvise, always late, etc. 'That's the English for you' (shrugging his shoulders). The English won't manage a second front in France now, they can send troops to the USSR, but not many.

* * *

De Gaulle's position, according to Eden and others:

De Gaulle – against Syria's independence, friction with the British in the Middle East. – de Gaulle's anti-English interview in American press ('letting the USA use our colonies without demanding destroyers', etc.) – de Gaulle's circle: openly fascist and anti-British. – Squabble among de Gaulle's supporters. De Gaulle and Muselier[i] in FO, 1.5 hours in two offices. Eden and Alexander the go-betweens. – Churchill refused to see de Gaulle for 10–15 days after his arrival in London. Finally received him. Upbraiding de Gaulle for his anti-British sentiments and inability to unite people. – As a result the National Committee was set up on 26/9. – Eden is not confident about its future. *Give them a chance* – recognition of 'NC' out of the question. – 'If any change in relations with de Gaulle is possible, then only a row, but this is undesirable.' – Eden approves of our exchange and considers the letters a success.[138]

10 October

Simopoulos called on me. Informed me that the Greek king and the Greek government would like to make a gesture of goodwill and compassion for the USSR at this crucial moment and ask all Greek subjects on our territory to arm themselves and defend the Soviet Union. Of course, the practical significance of such a move would be negligible, as the Greeks understand full well, but nonetheless the forming of even a small Greek unit fighting side by side with the Red Army would have a certain moral and political value. How would the Soviet government respond to this intention on the part of the Greek leaders? I promised to make inquiries and give him an answer.

Then we spoke about other affairs. Simopoulos finds himself in a strange and awkward position. His king and his government are in London. This

[i] Émile Henry Muselier, admiral, commander of the Free French Naval Forces during the Second World War.

creates a strange situation for him as ambassador. Apart from anything else, it upsets his usual routine. The king lives in *Claridge's*. The prime minister Tsouderos[i] is at the *Dorchester*. Various 'young men' are flooding the mission and the consulate. 'Flooding' is only the half of it: they treat the mission and the consulate like their own homes. Doors are always banging, telephones ringing and people running about. Poor Simopoulos is quite crushed. His 'madam' is in a panic. The government is in search of premises. Seems they have found some. If that's so, Simopoulos hopes to get rid of the 'young men' and the unnecessary telephone calls. But is that so? Simopoulos doesn't know for sure. The search has been continuing for a while, yet has yielded no results. He is afraid to believe that his happiness is at hand.

We recalled Subbotić. He found himself in a similar situation to Simopoulos, only it was a few months earlier (the Yugoslavian government arrived in London in June). Subbotić could not take it and has now received a post in Washington as the representative of the Yugoslavian Red Cross. Not so long ago, Subbotić and his wife came to us to say goodbye. Over tea Subbotić slapped my knee and exclaimed: 'Lately, I honestly can no longer say who I am: an ambassador or a *butler*?'

One would have to flee from such a life, and not only to Washington.

Simopoulos thinks that Subbotić retired for two reasons: (1) he was 'ousted' because he had been too closely connected with Prince Paul in the past and (2) he insisted strictly on following protocol, which led to inevitable clashes with members of the government.

'Who cares about protocol today?' exclaimed Simopoulos with a wave of his hand. 'Now's the time for war, not protocol!'

Goodness, what progress! The war is, at least, gradually putting the brains of the narrow-minded to rights.

This same Simopoulos expounded to Agniya his view as to 'what should be done with the Germans' after victory. They will need to be 'sterilized', and it is Jewish doctors who should be entrusted with the operation.

Similar thoughts were recently aired by the wife of Colban, the Norwegian, in a conversation with Bogomolov.[ii]

That is how the solution of the 'German problem' after the war presents itself to the enraged, narrow-minded European.

---

[i] Emmanouil Tsouderos, succeeded Alexandros Koryzis as prime minister of Greece in April 1941, then leader of the Greek government in exile in London and Cairo until 1944.

[ii] Aleksandr Efremovich Bogomolov, general secretary and head of the first western department of the USSR People's Commissariat for Foreign Affairs, 1939–40; counsellor to the mission then Soviet ambassador in France, 1940–41; Soviet ambassador to the Allied governments in London, 1941–43; Soviet ambassador representative to the French National Liberation Committee, 1943–44; Soviet ambassador in France, 1944–50.

The following should be added in this connection. The Poles and the Czechs demanded in their declaration at the Inter-Allied Conference on 24 September that the Germans be deprived of the 'means with which they might be able to commit new acts of aggression'. I asked Raczyński how he interpreted this formula. Raczyński answered: 'The German military industry must be destroyed.'

This evening Bogomolov informed me that Sikorski has decided to go to Moscow immediately. Why? Because the Polish army is not yet ready to take an active part in the crucial battles now under way on the eastern front. That general thinks that he should at least be present in Moscow in order to emphasize his allied sentiments at such a difficult moment for the USSR.

Daudet once wrote the novel *Les rois en exil*. A new Daudet is badly needed today to collect material in London for a future novel, *Governments in Exile*!

[On 29 September, a day before the Germans launched their decisive offensive on Moscow, Beaverbrook and Averell Harriman, Roosevelt's coordinator of American supply to Britain, arrived in Moscow. Cripps had envisaged himself as the architect of the Grand Alliance, embarking on a frank strategic dialogue 'to match the requirements and available supplies upon the basis of the strategic needs of each country'.[139] Maisky was indeed led to believe by Eden that General Ismay would be empowered to discuss the transfer of British troops to the eastern front.[140] Beaverbrook, however, was barred by Churchill from conducting any political or strategic talks. Determined nonetheless to profit from the tremendous popular support for Russia at home and to enhance his political standing in London, he opted to set out an extensive supply programme. He staged the conference as a 'Christmas Party', at which the United States and Britain were 'presenting poor Russia with gifts'.[141] He hoped thereby to divert Stalin from the more contentious issues of the 'second front' and post-war arrangements. The conference thus extended 'lend-lease' to Russia, but swept under the carpet the controversial issues which were to resurface throughout the war, particularly at the Tehran and Yalta summit conferences. Maisky's scheme of facilitating the visit of Hopkins and then Harriman to Moscow paid off when Harriman returned, giving Maisky the impression 'of a man who is convinced that serious aid must be given to the Soviet Union'. Beaverbrook's report of the conference, however, was biased, described by Harriman in a telegram to Roosevelt as 'sunshine after the storm', deliberately glossing over the dissensions which were soon to surface.[142]

So as not to spoil the 'festivities' in Moscow, Beaverbrook had deliberately kept Cripps away from most of his meetings in the Kremlin, cunningly telling him that they also discussed him, and that Stalin 'was very complimentary'.[143] Quite a bit of gossip was exchanged between Stalin and Beaverbrook, and this allows a rare glimpse into Stalin's personal attitude to Maisky. Beaverbrook apparently extolled the virtues of Maisky as an ambassador, complaining only that he 'came on too strong at times'. Stalin seemed particularly worried about Maisky's habit of lecturing the British 'on matters of Communist doctrine'. Having no remorse over forfeiting Cripps, Beaverbrook incited Stalin: 'What about our fellow?' Beaverbrook asked, 'barely concealing his personal distaste for Cripps'. Stalin simply shrugged his shoulders: 'Oh, he's all right.' 'The modified acceptance of Cripps,' Beaverbrook reported to Churchill, had led him to observe that there was nothing wrong with Cripps, but that he was a bore. '"In that respect," asked Stalin, "is he comparable to Maisky?" I answered, "No, to Madame Maisky." Stalin liked the joke immensely.'[144] Back from Moscow, Beaverbrook invited the Maiskys to spend the weekend with him at Cherkley. After offering Agniya an apple from a crate of apples and lemons given to him by 'Uncle Joe', he turned to her husband: '"Maisky, you told Stalin that I was a quarrelsome fellow." Maisky, instead of saying, "Well, I have to tell Stalin the truth," or something of this sort, blushed from the back of his head right over all his face. Obviously the story was true; Max had been told by Stalin! Maisky seemed depressed, perhaps not unnaturally.'[145]]

12 October (Bovingdon)

A hard week! These last seven days form a gloomy chain in my memory. In his last speech, Hitler was not only apologetic and bragging [sic]. He was also advertising the huge offensive against Moscow. The greatest offensive in this war. And indeed, in the course of the first 6–7 days, he really did achieve major successes: Timoshenko's army was forced to make a 70–80 kilometre retreat, Orel was captured by the Germans, the fighting goes on at Vyazma and Bryansk, and in the south Berdyansk and Mariupol have been captured. True, in the last 3–4 days we have managed to slow the speed of the German drive in the centre significantly, but it has not yet been stopped. Our further retreat 'to new positions' has been announced today. Will we manage to hold on to the new positions? Will we manage to halt the enemy's advance? Will we manage to hold Moscow?

Some inner feeling tells me that we shall be able to hold Moscow, albeit by dint of great effort and immense losses. But inner feelings are a poor guarantee. Time will tell. My expectations with regard to the south are far gloomier. Will we hold the Donbass? I don't know. Some feebleness can be sensed in our resistance on the Ukrainian front. Perhaps it is the strategic weakness of this front, deriving from its geography (the plain steppe and the absence of natural boundaries), or the defective command, or the character of the Ukrainians. The reason are unclear, but the bitter fact remains. Will we be able to stop the Germans west of Donbass? Time will tell.

A hard week! The next one will yield something. It may prove decisive. Either the Germans will break through to Moscow in the next seven days and smash our armies – then we will have lost this year's campaign and the revival of our resistance will become a long and laborious process fraught with all kinds of danger, or we will further slow the tempo of the German advance or even bring it to a halt entirely – and then we shall actually have won this year's campaign and during the winter we will be able to develop and strengthen not only our defence, but also our offensive capabilities. Yes, the next week will yield something! We shall live from one day to the next, from one communiqué to the next. Hitler will surely throw all he has into the battle. He will go for broke. I won't be surprised if he uses gas...

The events on our front elicit a complex reaction in England.

First, rapidly rising alarm in all walks of life, from Churchill to the common worker. The mood of the masses has undergone three main phases over the 16 weeks of the war in the east. The first phase, covering the initial stages of the war (roughly until the middle of July) was marked by extreme pessimism in respect of Soviet chances. It was expected that the Red Army would be beaten in 3–4 weeks and that the USSR would be out of the war. The War Ministry, as is well known, subscribed to this view. The second phase, covering approximately the next two months (from mid-July to mid-September), was marked, on the contrary, by excessive optimism. It was thought that the Red Army had 'unexpectedly' emerged as a formidable force, that all Hitler's plans had been overturned, that the Germans would inevitably get stuck 'in Russia' or even beaten, and that the winter of 1941/42 would complete their rout. The case of Napoleon was endlessly cited in this connection. It seemed that the British should just sit and wait, provide us with some weapons and supplies, make plans for a 'general offensive' in 1943 and hope that these plans would never have to be implemented. Everything would be done for them by 'those brave Russians' and 'that freezing Russian winter'. The mood in the country became more and more 'peaceful', all the more so as the air raids on England practically ceased with the beginning of military operations in the east. Two curious facts testified to the vigorous growth of such a mood: the mass return of 'evacuated' families to London and the colossal exodus from London during the Bank Holiday weekend at the beginning of August. According to the newspapers, as many people were leaving London as in peace time and the railways had to provide the public with 300 additional trains.

The third phase, beginning approximately in the middle of September (and especially since the fall of Kiev), is marked by growing disappointment and anxiety. Disappointment at the inability to bring the war to a convenient conclusion, without huge and arduous efforts on the part of England itself, and anxiety about the course of events in the east and the course and outcome of the whole war. These feelings have intensified during the past week. Thursday, 9 October, was the worst day. The newspapers came out with panicky headlines. The whole Soviet front, it seemed, was collapsing like a pack of cards. A wave of pessimism rose high in social circles. Rumours (surely emanating from German sources) were abroad in the city that 'Russia' had actually withdrawn from the war and that negotiations between Berlin and Moscow on an armistice were already in progress. Many could find only one, rather dubious, consolation:

'How lucky that Hitler's diabolic machine, the entire might of which we've only seen now, fell not on us but on Russia!'

Beneath this lay the thought: if it had fallen on England first, then she would have been done for a long time ago, but now, after Hitler's machine had taken a good few blows in the USSR, England might somehow survive. But this thought lurked somewhere at the back of the brain. Anxiety and pessimism dominated. The last three days have brought news of a certain slowdown in the German advance and of enhanced Soviet resistance. This has somewhat improved the atmosphere; but only a little. The general mood remains tense, uneasy and primed for a tragic outcome.

That is one facet of the English reaction. There is another, running in parallel to the first. I mean the colossal growth of goodwill and compassion towards the USSR, especially (but not solely) among the lower classes. Since 22 June, the wave of friendly feelings towards us has been consistently rising. In the press, at meetings, in workshops, at factories, at home, and in pubs – the democratic layers of the population everywhere express their admiration for the heroism of the Red Army and the Soviet people. I've been quite inundated with letters and resolutions of solidarity from numerous meetings, trade unions, labour organizations, cooperative societies, sports clubs, etc. I receive as many as a hundred such documents daily (and I should reply to all of them). Financial donations pour in from all sides as well – from individuals, workers' organizations, all sorts of societies, schools, research institutions, even children. The other day, for instance, I received a touching letter written in an unsteady child's hand with a good many grammar mistakes – five little boys aged between 6 and 10 were sending me 10 shillings they had collected for the 'tank fund'. Another case: a young girl sent me the 5 shillings her parents had given her for her tenth birthday...

Everything 'Russian' is in vogue today: Russian songs, Russian music, Russian films, and books about the USSR: 75,000 copies of a booklet of Stalin's and Molotov's speeches on the war, published by Coates, sold out instantly. An unprecedented event in the annals of the ARPC.[146] Our bulletin *Soviet War News* is selling like hot cakes (we began with 2,000 copies, and have raised it to 10,000); the print-run increases daily. One hundred thousand copies of Polyakov's[147] *Diary* have been printed and it looks as if that number will have to be doubled. Lawrence and Wishart have published graphs of the USSR: 25,000 copies have been sold in three days and a second edition is in press. It's the same with everything.

Goodwill towards us has grown particularly strongly over the last 2–3 weeks. 'The Russian Tank Week' organized by Beaverbrook prior to his departure for Moscow was a brilliant success. The mayor of Kensington arranged a special reception for Agniya and me: some 500 guests attended, including many diplomats, political and public figures, the clergy, and all sorts of aristocrats. Sir William Davison[i] himself (MP for Kensington), the bane of our life for so many years with his demands about the Lena Goldfields, shook my hand warmly and showered me with friendly sentiments. My speech at the American Chamber of Commerce on 23 September was a great success, and all the London papers dedicated editorials to it. The same with our declaration at the Inter-Allied Conference on 24 September. Stalin's appearance on the screen always elicits stormy applause. A film devoted to the USSR in which I say a few words brings in excellent donations to the Soviet Red Cross. Ten thousand pounds has been collected in London in a week; the provinces will give even more. On 10 October I was invited as a guest of honour to the Livery Club, the City's holy of holies: they gave me a real ovation. The Athenaeum and the St James's Club have elected me their honorary member.[148] My greetings to the large international youth demonstration in the Albert Hall on 11 October were met with loud applause, while the welcomes given by the king, Churchill, Beneš, the archbishop of York[ii] and others were met with deathly silence. Shvetsov, who spoke on behalf of Soviet youth, received a stormy ovation. Grand demonstrations of sympathy and goodwill for the USSR were arranged in Glasgow and London (St Pancras) on 5 October. I could provide many similar examples.

Yes, the wave of friendly feelings toward our country stands high at present. Above all, of course, amidst the democratic strata, their strength decreasing as one goes up the social ladder. To be fair, it must be said that there are many people also among intellectuals and the middle and even upper bourgeoisie who are suddenly inflamed with goodwill towards us (but for how long?). Even the archbishop of Canterbury has begun to express sympathy for us. Even Bevin came up to me at yesterday's youth demonstration, shook my hand and expressed his admiration for our *stand*. People's feelings change, of course, and perhaps little will remain of the current wave in a month or two. But presently – I repeat – the wave is high and strong. This is making life difficult for Agniya and me: everywhere we are greeted with cheers, everyone wants to photograph and film us and have our autographs. We are always receiving invitations to open something, to make speeches on this or that occasion…

Along with this goodwill and sympathy, a disturbing question sounds louder and louder among the broad masses: 'Has England done everything it can to help the USSR?'

And many, not without foundation, find this to be far from the case. In connection with this, the question of a second front has become the focal point of acrimonious debate among the masses. The Sunday newspapers devote a

[i] William Henry Davison, Unionist MP, 1918–45.
[ii] William Temple, archbishop of York, 1929–42; archbishop of Canterbury, 1942–44.

great deal of space to the question, discussing it in one form or another. The temperature is clearly rising.

Will the campaign for a second front bring practical consequences?

I doubt it – at least as far as the immediate future is concerned. True, there are advocates of armed support to the USSR in the British government (Beaverbrook, Eden and others), but there are opponents as well (Margesson, Halifax, Moore-Brabazon, Samuel Hoare and others). The opponents represent what's left of the *Chamberlain gang*. Halifax has demonstrated recently how far they are prepared to go: his speech in Washington, in which he announced to the whole world that the British government is not intending to undertake an invasion of the continent at the present time, represents, in essence, an act of state treason. Yet he is a member of the War Cabinet!

Worse still, Churchill himself is against a second front in Europe. Why? He set out his reasons to me more than once, and to Comrade Stalin in his personal messages. Is that the whole point? I don't think so. It seems to me that Churchill is simply afraid of the might of the German war machine and, besides, he listens too much to his 'military advisers', particularly Admiral Pound.

Can pressure from below change the government's line? I don't know. For now it does not seem so.

13 October

When we had finished with business (a tripartite treaty of alliance between the USSR, England and Iran),[149] Eden suddenly stretched out in his armchair and asked in a homely kind of way: 'A whisky and soda?'

'I won't say no,' I replied.

It was about eight in the evening. Eden's office was only dimly lit. The atmosphere lent itself to intimacy and heart-to-heart conversation.[150]

Eden took two bottles from a handsome cabinet by the window and put them on his desk. I filled two glasses with the classic English mixture. Eden moved his armchair closer to the fireplace and said: 'Yes, it's a terrible time we are living through! The whole world is in a state of chaos and war.'

He thought for a moment and added: 'We have our share of the blame, too… I mean my country… Our policy has not always been wise or successful.'

I took a sip of whisky and soda and replied: 'Yes, I agree. There are two men who bear especially great responsibility for what is happening today. I am convinced that history will judge them harshly.'

'Who are they?' Eden asked with obvious interest.

'Baldwin and Chamberlain.'

I paused and added: 'To my mind, they bear even more responsibility than Hitler. For they nurtured Hitler with their policy.'

Eden thought for a moment and said: 'Perhaps you are right, with just one reservation: less Baldwin than Chamberlain. I knew both well. The difference between them was this: Baldwin understood and acknowledged that Hitler was not a man with whom things might be settled amicably, but he was too apathetic and lazy to draw the appropriate, practical conclusions. Chamberlain, on the contrary, was firmly convinced that it was possible to come to an agreement with Hitler, and that only people like me could not and did not want to do so. That is why he decided to take foreign policy into his own hands.'

'Let it be so,' I responded, 'but those two men do bear the main responsibility for this war.'

I took another sip of whisky and soda and added: 'Such a pity that our negotiations in 1939 about an alliance collapsed! Things would look very different today had they been successful. There would probably be no war.'

'And you think agreement was possible?' Eden asked a little doubtfully.

It seemed to me, though, that Eden did not really have any doubts on the matter: he merely wished to hear me confirm his own thoughts.

'Of course it was possible,' I replied with conviction.

'I also think so,' Eden confessed. 'Do you know what I did during the talks?... When I learned that Halifax was going to send Strang to Moscow, I came to him and said: "Don't do it! No good will come of such a move!" I must confess I was indignant. Why? After Chamberlain and Halifax had been to Rome, after the prime minister and the foreign secretary – both! – had "gone to Canossa", to send Strang to Moscow after all that... It would be tantamount to an insult! I understood all this, I understood what feelings such a decision might raise in Moscow, and I wanted to prevent the negotiations collapsing. So I asked Halifax not to send Strang but to go himself. Halifax objected, saying he could not go, he was very busy, etc. Then I proposed myself as a *special envoy* to conduct negotiations. I told Halifax this would be better and that, as far as I could judge, Moscow's attitude to me was not unfavourable – so let me test myself in this exceptionally important matter! Halifax promised to think it over. A few days later he told me it would be difficult to implement my plan. I understood what the matter was: Chamberlain, of course, was against my going to Moscow. Strang went in my place.'

'So you think it was all Chamberlain's doing?' I asked Eden, before continuing: 'I think a great deal of the blame should be shared by Halifax, too. I'll tell you why.[151] On 12 June 1939, on the very day of Strang's departure for Moscow, I visited Halifax and, after we had dealt with various routine matters, I asked him here in this room: "Lord Halifax, don't you think the difficulties with the negotiations might be eased considerably should you yourself go to Moscow? I have serious grounds to suggest that the Soviet government would welcome your visit to us." True, I did not tell Halifax at the time that I had instructions from Moscow to say what I said, but that was not required. If an ambassador of a foreign state makes a statement such as mine, what minister of foreign affairs would not understand that there must be a good reason behind it?'

'Did you really say all this to Halifax?' Eden exclaimed in great agitation.

'Yes, of course I did,' I replied, 'and with great emphasis at that. To misunderstand me would have been impossible.'

'I never heard that story,' Eden went on. 'And how did Halifax react to your statement?'

'Halifax replied that my idea was very interesting and he would *bear it in mind*. That was all. Halifax never returned to the question. So Halifax's visit to Moscow never happened. I consider 12 June, when I suggested to Halifax that he visit Moscow, to be the turning point in the entire history of the negotiations. Or, to be more precise, not 12 June, but the following few days. I understood, of course, that Halifax could not take such a decision at his own peril. I expected, therefore, that he would raise this question at a Cabinet meeting and give me the answer in two or three days in approximately this vein: your idea is interesting, I've thought it over and arrived at the conclusion that it should perhaps be implemented, but will your government give its consent?... Then I would have been able to arrange a formal invitation to Halifax from the Soviet government. It would not have been a problem that Strang had gone first. It was always possible to say that Strang had been sent to put the final touches to the text of the agreement and that within a couple of weeks the foreign secretary would come to sign it. But Halifax "forgot" about my proposal. What impression could this produce in Moscow? Only one: that the British government did not want to conclude a pact. And such a conclusion was quite correct.'

Eden was highly agitated. He took a few quick gulps of whisky and soda and exclaimed: 'What a tragedy! What a tragedy!'

I went on: 'This is the reason why I'm inclined to add a third name, that of Lord Halifax, to those whom, as is my strong conviction, history will condemn most severely.'

Eden did not protest. We each drank another gulp of whisky and soda. I moved my armchair closer to the fireplace and said: 'Over all these twenty-something years British policy toward the USSR has been imbued with a deep internal contradiction. The state interests of Great Britain urgently called for rapprochement and cooperation with the USSR, but the class feelings and prejudices of the greater part of the ruling elite hindered this throughout. The result has been a zigzagging course, where attempts at improving relations have alternated with conflicts and friction. Your statesmen and politicians, furthermore, have always been of two types: the first group embodies first and foremost the state interests of Great Britain, while the second embodies primarily the class feelings and prejudices of the ruling elite.'

I glanced at Eden with a smile and added: 'You, for one, embody state interests above all; that is why we can work together.'

Eden grinned and replied: 'There is much truth in what you say. But then in the Soviet Union you, too, have different people. People who, being guided by interests of state, are prepared to make a compromise with the *wicked capitalists*, and people who object to it.'

'Let's assume that this is the case,' I rejoined, 'but the difference is that the Soviet government has never pursued and does not pursue *Gefühlspolitik*. The Soviet government is utterly realistic in its foreign policy. When state interests and feelings collide, state interests always win.'

'You are right about that,' admitted Eden. 'You are more realistic than us.'

'And now,' I continued, 'your state interests are more than ever bound up with Soviet victory. If the Soviet Union is defeated, the British Empire will come to an end. For who will then deter Hitler from marching on to India, Egypt and Africa?… If the Soviet army fails to stop him, will the 750,000 British troops stationed in the Middle East be able to stop him? The very idea is absurd.'

Eden nodded his head and said: 'I quite understand.'

At this moment, the telephone on Eden's table rang. It was his wife. She was calling from the 'foreign secretary's private residence' where Eden presently lives, and asked what he was doing. Having heard that I was with Eden and that the official part of my visit was over, Beatrice invited both of us upstairs (the 'private residence' is two storeys above the foreign secretary's office). There we met the famous author of light comedies Noël Coward,[i] who has just staged his new work, […].[152] Eden's wife was dressed in a short crimson dress and looked very striking. I had not seen her for a long time, since for the past year she has been driving up and down the country with her military *Canteen* and appears in London quite rarely.

We talked about the stage, literature and art. It was a pleasant break from war and politics. I posed the question: whom did they consider to be the greatest playwright, the greatest novelist and the greatest poet of all time and all nations?

All agreed on the playwright: Shakespeare. And on the novelist: Leo Tolstoy. But opinions about the poet differed. Coward said he held Shakespeare to be the greatest playwright and also the greatest poet (I disagreed with him). Eden, after a moment's hesitation, named Dante. Eden's wife refused to commit herself at all. My preference went to Goethe. This was met with objections from Eden and Coward. They do not like Goethe. I replied that I do not like Goethe all that much myself, and that my favourite German poet is Heine; but, without fear or favour, I must name Goethe as the greatest (albeit not the most loved)

---

[i] Sir Noël Coward, popular playwright and producer of a series of wartime films.

of the poets I know. We argued for a good while, without finding anyone whom we could all consider to be the greatest poet of all time and all nations.

Curiously, the same thing happened when I put the same question to Priestley and Winant when we once had lunch together in the Pen Club. Both named Shakespeare as the greatest playwright and Tolstoy as the greatest novelist, but they did not have a definite opinion about the greatest poet.

Our conversation turned of its own accord to *War and Peace*. Here there was complete unanimity. Eden, his wife and Coward – they all had been rereading the famous novel recently and their impressions were still vivid. The general feeling was expressed by Beatrice. 'I've never read anything as great or as wonderful,' she exclaimed. 'Tolstoy has no poorly drawn characters. They are all fine and alive. And what scope: from a duchess to an ordinary peasant – he understands them all superbly, feels and depicts them in such a way that you see and hear them. And how timely this novel is!'

Suddenly the doorbell rang and Eden's secretary entered the room. He brought some urgent papers. Our literary conversation was interrupted.

I said my goodbyes and left.

[Operation *Typhoon*, which the Germans launched on 2 October 1941, led to the capture of Orel in the south and Torzhok in the north, and finally to the annihilation of the forces trapped in the pocket of Vyazma. The reserve forces on the Mozhaisk defence line proved no match for the sweeping German armoured divisions. On 13 October, Kaluga fell on the southern flank, and two days later Kalinin, a key town on the approaches to Moscow. The Moscow defence zone was now, in places, only 60 miles from the capital. Anti-tank ditches were frenziedly dug by battalions of recruited civilians, while barricades and road blocks were built and tank traps set in the main city streets leading to the Kremlin. Discipline and morale sank low in Moscow, and what had been, until that point, a trickle of civilians fleeing from the capital turned into swarms of refugees. The rapidly deteriorating situation led to a hasty evacuation of various ministries and the diplomatic corps from Moscow to Kuibyshev, a small city on the Volga, where Maisky had spent a couple of years of his childhood. Its population was to double in the next couple of days – from half a million to a million.[153]]

19 October

We didn't go to Bovingdon this weekend. Agniya is making a speech today at a meeting about Red Cross aid to the USSR. I stay in town and think.

One more week has passed. It has not proved to be decisive. But the situation has not improved; if anything, it has deteriorated. True, the resistance of our armies is somewhat stronger, but the Germans keep moving ever closer to Moscow. Reports came in yesterday that we have recaptured Orel and Kalinin from the Germans. If we've beaten them off decisively, then that's a significant success. But is that the case? Regrettably, everything in this war so far has gone otherwise: the Germans have tended to capture our cities and territories decisively, and we've then repelled them at certain points for a short while. This pattern has reflected the general trend of the war at a certain stage of its development. How will it go now? We shall see, but frankly speaking I am quite prepared for reports to arrive in the next couple of days saying that both Orel and Kalinin have once again been seized by the Germans.

In the south we have evacuated Odessa. This did not come as a surprise to me. Beaverbrook told me that Stalin was weighing up the possibility of abandoning Odessa if the Crimea needed strengthening. Evidently, this moment has arrived. One feels sorry for Odessa, but it can't be helped.

However, I consider the main deterioration of our position to lie not so much in events at the front as in events in international politics. The Konoe[i] Cabinet has resigned and has been replaced by the Cabinet of General Tōjō,[ii] a notorious militarist and a friend of Germany. So a strike from the Far East is to be expected. True, it seems a bit late now to launch a large-scale campaign in Manchuria, but who knows? I myself, only a month ago, scoffed at the faith placed by amateur strategists in *General Winter*. Of course, for Japan this winter still bears the 'general's stripes', but we can't be fully confident about Japan's behaviour.

I saw Eden several times on the 16th and 17th and enquired about the possibility of England and the USA 'warning' Japan that any attempt to attack the USSR would mean war between Japan and the *English speaking democracies*. Eden sent a telegraphic message to this effect to Washington and spoke with Winant. I have no idea what the outcome will be, but I am not very optimistic.[154] In his talks with me, Eden kept emphasizing that America should play first fiddle in this matter, but America… America is near-sighted and fears war more than anything else. Well, we shall see.

In the course of the last week another important event happened: the Soviet government moved from Moscow to Kuibyshev. This event is both positive and negative at the same time. Positive as an indicator of firm belief in final victory and negative as an indicator of the fact that Moscow is in great danger. No official statement concerning this change has been made yet, and on the whole the situation looks somewhat confused and unclear.

The first hints of the possible evacuation of the Soviet government from Moscow appeared in British newspapers on the morning of the 16th. After lunch on that day, Eden read to me a telegram from Cripps, in which the latter said that at 4 p.m. on the 15th he had been summoned to see Molotov, who

---

[i] Fumimaro Konoe, Japanese prime minister, 1937–39, 1940–41.

[ii] Hideki Tōjō, general, Japanese minister of war, 1940–44 and prime minister, 1941–44.

told the British ambassador about the evacuation of the Soviet government and the diplomatic corps to Kuibyshev. At approximately the same time, a telegram arrived through trade-mission channels saying that all communications with NKVT [People's Commissariat for Foreign Trade] should be addressed from now on to Vneshtorg, Ulyanovsk. On the morning of the 17th, I received a telegram from Molotov in Moscow in which he informed me that on the night of 15–16 October most of the government departments and the diplomatic corps had left for Kuibyshev, but he himself was remaining in Moscow. Molotov also promised that an official statement about the evacuation of the Soviet government would 'probably' appear on the 17th. However, no such statement has yet been made. In the last two days I have not received any telegrams, either from Moscow or from Kuibyshev. The trade mission has not had any telegrams since the 16th.

What is happening? Most likely, the top leadership is being transferred from Moscow to Kuibyshev, and our communications with the government are temporarily interrupted. This, of course, will not last long.[155]

20 October

Agniya and I saw *Sorochintsy Fair*[156] at the *Savoy* theatre. The play is performed by a company of Whites under the direction of 'the King of the Black Exchange' – a certain Pomeroy, a clever Jew from Kharkov. All the revenue from the show goes to the Red Cross for the needs of the USSR. We were given seats in a special box. With us in the box were Churchill's wife, and Baron Iliffe[i] and his wife. '*God Save the King*' and the 'Internationale' were played before the beginning of the performance. All stood. Mrs Churchill was standing, too, even though it was her husband who forbade the 'Internationale' from being played over the radio together with the other anthems of the Allies. The audience clapped the prime minister's spouse, but Agniya and I received even more applause. How this war has jumbled things up! The Soviet ambassador attends a performance by a White company, the White company gathers money for the Red Army, and the wife of the British prime minister blesses this undertaking.

From the artistic point of view, the performance was average, but the British seemed to like it. So much the better. Mrs Churchill repeated several times: '*How fascinating!*'

We had tea during the interval, and Mrs Churchill disclosed a few interesting details about her husband's way of life. Before the war, in peace time, he used to go to bed at midnight and get up at eight. But now there's no chance for

[i] Edward Mauger Iliffe (1st Baron Iliffe), newspaper and periodical proprietor; Conservative MP, 1923–29.

him to sleep his usual eight hours. He almost always goes to bed at two or three in the morning and has to get up at eight, as before. Which means no more than 5–6 hours of sleep. It's not enough. The prime minister makes up for it after lunch: he undresses, lies down in bed in complete darkness, and sleeps for an hour or an hour and a half. Experience has shown that this short daytime rest gives him a lot of strength, and he values it highly. If Churchill does not have any meetings or more or less official engagements in the morning, he stays in bed until lunch, summons his secretary and works with him.

22 October

More reassuring news has been coming from the Moscow front during the last five days. German pressure has somewhat weakened. We are now executing successful counterattacks. Both Orel and Kalinin, which we recaptured at the end of the past week, remain in our hands. The German attempts at an offensive in the areas of Mozhaisk and Malo-Yaroslavets have been repelled with significant losses for the enemy.

What's this? The collapse of the gigantic offensive announced by Hitler three weeks ago? Or just a temporary pause brought about by the need to bring up reserves and arrange transport facilities in the newly captured places?

Once bitten, twice shy. I am therefore rather inclined to accept the second explanation, despite the onset of late autumn with its rains, dirt, snow and cold. We shall see.

I do not like the situation in the south. The Germans have taken Taganrog and battles are raging in the region of Stalino (Yuzovka). The entire Donbass is under direct threat, and then you're already in the pre-Caucasus. A certain lethargy can still be felt in the defence of the southern front. What is it? A weakness of leadership? A shortage of forces? Or the Ukrainian character? The war there is again approaching Russian regions. A *stiffening*, one feels, must begin soon. Time, once again, will tell.

I had a serious talk with Eden today – about activities in the occupied countries. We divided the countries into three categories: (1) 'soft' – France, Belgium, Holland, Denmark – where it is still too early to speak of insurgent warfare at this stage and where attention should be focused on propaganda, sabotage and individual terrorist acts; (2) 'hard' – the Balkans, and primarily Yugoslavia, where insurgent warfare is already under way. The struggle should be fully supported with weapons, supplies, leadership, etc.; and (3) 'moderate' – Czechoslovakia and Norway – where there is no open insurgent movement as yet, but all the prerequisites are in place for its early emergence. Here, clearly, all measures must be taken to form the cadres for such a movement, to prepare it to act at the appropriate moment, etc.

I laid special emphasis on the Balkans. There are some 150,000 partisans in Yugoslavia already, scattered in groups throughout the country. In Montenegro they even have control over part of the coast. Should these flames be fanned (and the quantity of weapons and so on required for this is, in absolute terms, very modest), then it will be easy to kindle fires in Albania, Greece, Bulgaria and Rumania as well. From there the flames would sweep over the whole of the Balkans. Since partisan warfare is in the blood of the Balkan peoples, why not use this in the struggle against Germany? Something like a 'second front' could very well be established there towards spring, thereby also facilitating the landing of the Allied forces. In short, the prospects are good. The situation must be exploited.

'I am a former partisan myself,' I concluded with a grin, 'and my nose tells me that the Balkans can be set ablaze.'

Eden liked my idea. He remarked that the British had already made some investigations in this area, but so far only on a very small scale. He will try to get things moving. Eden promised to talk to Churchill and then return to the question I had raised.

Well, let's see what will come of it. I'm afraid the British government might get scared: partisan warfare is so 'unorthodox'!

23 October

Today I spent half the day in parliament. The course of the war was discussed. There were comparatively few people present, but passions ran high.

It was Noel-Baker who started it all. Fairly cautious yet firm, he expressed the concern and dissatisfaction of the broad masses with the British government's inertia in providing active military assistance to the USSR. He demanded that a large British army be sent to the Ukraine. That set the tone. Those speaking after Noel-Baker argued about the same matter – some attacked the government, others defended it. The attack was stronger and more effective than the defence. The government bench (on which I saw Eden, Alexander, Grigg, Grenfell, Greenwood, T. Johnstone[i] and others) showed some signs of nervousness.

Aneurin Bevan was particularly harsh, delivering a truly belligerent speech in which, inter alia, he attacked Halifax for the public statement he made in America that an 'invasion of the continent' was now impossible because of the lack of shipping and arms. Bevan called Halifax's conduct 'all but high treason' (particularly so because he said all that just as Hitler was preparing his full-scale offensive against Moscow). Addressing the government, Bevan shouted several times: 'If you can't change your policy, then step down!'[157]

---

[i] Harcourt Johnstone, Liberal politician, appointed by Churchill in 1940 as secretary to the Department of Overseas Trade, although he was not an MP.

91. Maisky pampered by his left-wing friends, Bevan (seated on the ground to his right) and Gollancz (wearing a hat).

It all had a powerful effect: such words had not been heard in the Commons since the time of the crisis which brought about Chamberlain's resignation in May 1940.

Then it was Gallacher's turn, who had been given the floor only after exchanging a few harsh words with the Speaker. But his speech was as ineffective as always. No, parliament does not suit him. He is a typical man of the masses.

Eden had to reply to the critics. I didn't envy him his situation. Eden was in agreement with much of what the critics said, but he had to defend the official point of view of the British government. He was trying to reconcile them all and smooth things over. He repeatedly swore that the government was doing all it could to provide maximum assistance to the USSR and fiercely rejected Bevan's accusations that the British government was withholding aid from the USSR because of class prejudices. Alas, on this occasion Eden was unable to calm the raging passions and after he took his seat Bevan demanded that he denounce Halifax's statement, which Eden had preferred not to mention in his speech. Eden had to wriggle his way out, and did so rather awkwardly. But he said nothing either to defend or excuse Halifax.

This failed to satisfy the opposition. Clement Davis jumped to his feet and demanded he be given the floor. He spoke even more sharply than Bevan. He attacked the government furiously and eventually framed the question as follows: either a restructuring of policy or a restructuring of the government.

That marked the end of the debates. They made a decent impression on me. Such stinging and passionate words against the government have not been heard in the House for a long time. True, so far they are being uttered by inveterate 'critics' and cheered only by members of the 'unofficial opposition' (although today's cheers emanated from a significantly broader base), but still… I do know the House of Commons a bit. Today I sensed a 'mood' in it that I have not observed for a good while. The very fact that both Bevan and Davis dared call – without protests from the others! – for the resignation of the Churchill government, or at least its serious restructuring, is highly *significant*.

I lunched in the Commons with the family of Lloyd George (father, son and daughter). This became a kind of 'sensation': all heads in the restaurant kept turning in the direction of our table. H. Morrison came up to us, nodded at me and said with an ironic smile: 'Well, well… A new member of the family?'

I answered in the same tone: 'Why not, it's not a bad family!'…

The Conservatives don't like my friendship with Lloyd George. That's understandable. And that is exactly why (regardless of any other considerations) it should be sustained.[158]

The old man is in a pessimistic mood. Evidently, he does not have much faith in our chances of holding out. He scolds Churchill and the government.

As I was leaving parliament, some young man in soldier's uniform approached me and said with pain in his voice: 'Mr Maisky, I would just like to tell you I'm ashamed of my country, of its conduct at this time.'

I gave the youth a firm handshake.

24 October[159]

Further symptoms of 'popularity'.

The Times editor wants to get acquainted with me – Mrs Churchill is in charge of the Aid to Russia Fund. – Agniya and I are photographed, cheered, asked to act as patrons, etc. Vanity of vanities… We wriggle out, but…[160]

Second front? Mass movement in favour, but the government… Sitting of parliament 23 Oct. Strong feeling against Churchill. For the first time. Bevan demands resignation of the government. Tories keep silent. Confusion on the Treasury bench (Eden, Alexander, Johnstone and others). Bevan's demand would have been met with scornful laughter two months earlier, but now… Churchill's 'Russian policy' at the bottom. A soldier came up to me as I was on my way out and said: 'Mr Maisky, I just want to tell you that I am ashamed of my country.'

Practical results concerning the second front? I doubt it. (1) There is no alternative prime minister even from our point of view. (2) The governmental

92. Maisky addressing the British people from his cosy study at the embassy.

'machine' is strong and crafty. I suspect one of the objectives of the Libyan campaign is to divert the attention of the masses from the second front.

The position of the British government? Eden, Beaverbrook, Cranborne and others are for the second front, immediate military aid, even if it entails risk. The Chamberlain crew (Margesson, Moore-Brabazon and others) want to wait and see, build up forces, etc. Sinclair, Attlee, Alexander and others are neither fish nor fowl. Churchill hesitates with the final word. The reason for such a position by the British government? Doesn't want the weakening of the USSR – too dangerous. But fear of the German war machine is revealed especially clearly in the 'Russian campaign'.

Conclusion: no hope for second front. The chances for a BEF [British expeditionary force] in the USSR increase.

26 October

We are still holding the positions set up near Moscow at the end of last week. Half of Kalinin is in our hands, half in the Germans', and the fighting continues in the streets. It is unclear who is holding Orel, but the Germans have not had any visible successes there during the last 8–9 days. Mozhaisk and Malo-Yaroslavets are again being mentioned in the communiqués as sites of particularly fierce fighting. Can it be said that the German offensive against Moscow has petered out? I don't know. I am inclined to think not. More likely, the Germans are bringing up fresh forces and will then launch one more attempt to capture our capital. I hope they fail.

Everything is quiet around Leningrad.

But things are bad in the south. The Germans have taken Stalino, they are approaching Rostov and most probably have occupied Kharkov. Thus, the whole of the Ukraine is lost. The Caucasus is in imminent danger. All this is very alarming. If we were to lose the Caucasus, I don't know how, without oil, we could continue to fight effectively. Moreover, the links with the outside world through Iran would be severed. The Germans must be stopped at all costs! I hope we succeed. I expect much from Timoshenko, appointed just two days ago as commander of the southern front. Budenny's task now is to form new armies. Evidently, commanding the Ukrainian front was too much for him. It is not entirely clear why Voroshilov has also been assigned to assume Budenny's task. He did not seem to have any particular drawbacks.

We visited the Webbs yesterday. I listened closely and received answers to the following questions:

(1) I asked: Is any kind of agreement between England and Hitlerite Germany conceivable?

The Webbs' answer: No, it's absolutely inconceivable. Not only because Churchill will never agree to it (the ruling class could replace the prime minister if need be), but also because the majority of the ruling class understands perfectly well that the British Empire and Hitlerite Germany cannot co-exist.

(2) My question: What lies behind the British government's reluctance to provide immediate military assistance to the USSR in the west or on our own territory? Is it not that the British ruling class wishes to see the USSR weakened?

The Webbs' answer: What the British ruling class would like more than anything is for the USSR and Hitlerite Germany to destroy one another. But it certainly does not want Hitler to crush the USSR. Because in such an event Hitler would bring all his might down on the British Empire. Since the Soviet Union now finds itself in a grave situation, and there is the danger of German victory in the east, the British government simply cannot desire the further weakening of the USSR. On the contrary, it desires the strengthening of the Soviet Union. If the British government is nevertheless reluctant to provide immediate military assistance to the USSR, then there are other reasons for this. The Webbs cannot formulate these reasons explicitly, but they think that the core of the matter is most probably the British government's awareness of its military inferiority as compared with Germany.

(3) My question: In the country the masses' demands for a second front, etc. are growing – will these demands exert any influence on the policy of the British government?

The Webbs' answer: It's doubtful. Many are dissatisfied with the 'Russian policy' of the British government; yet no sound and well-grounded proposals can be expected from the crowd. The government has all the advantages in this respect.

27 October

Nine years in England as ambassador.

How time flies! How much water under the bridge! An infinite quantity!...

Arriving here, I was psychologically prepared for a stint of five years or so. I reckoned that since I'd worked a little more than three years in Finland, I'd have to spend five years in England. Just five years. Now the second five-year period of my stay in London is coming to an end, and I'm still here. I keep imagining my dear, beloved country. Who knows, maybe the tenth anniversary will have to be celebrated on this island as well. In better circumstances, I hope, than the ninth.

30 October

Lord Cecil dropped in (despite his 77 years, he prefers walking to driving). He has aged. Even more hunched. Doesn't hear well. Uses a hearing aid for conversations. But his head is quite clear and his thinking is sharp and quick. What does Cecil think about? The same as always: how to arrange the life of humankind in such a way that wars end and peace reigns on earth.

I asked Cecil how he imagined the world of the future and the political structure of Europe after the war.

He was very glad to hear my question and started to expound his thoughts in detail.

There are now three main trends in British political circles concerning the future of Europe and the world:

(1) The supporters of Anglo-American *understanding*. These two powers (which may be joined, of course, by some others) will regulate all international affairs and, in effect, impose their will. Here an important, if not central, role is played by the group led by Simon, who, despite having little influence at present, can, Cecil thinks, regain it if the situation changes.

(2) The supporters of a so-called *Federal Union* who conceive the Europe of the future as a federation of states with a certain amount of internal autonomy but subject to a single central authority – a federal parliament, a federal government, etc.

(3) The supporters of a middle line between these two extremes, who believe in the inevitable emergence of a powerful international organization which will exert a very strong influence on relations between states and will guard against possible acts of aggression.

'I, personally, do not agree either with the first or the second group,' Cecil told me. 'The supporters of "*Understanding*" do not take into account the USSR, without which no peace in Europe is possible, thus rendering the organization of the world after the war vague and ineffective. The USA will hardly be willing to take upon itself any obligations with regard to the maintenance of European peace. For words and declarations alone will not suffice any longer. All must be ready to take up arms against an aggressor *at short notice*. Will the USA be willing to do this? I doubt it. The result will be permanent uncertainty as to how the USA will act in the event of an act of aggression in Europe. This uncertainty will keep corroding the very foundation of European peace. Finally, within 5–6 years, relations between England and the USA may sour, mutual estrangement will follow and any chance of maintaining peace with the help of Anglo-American 'understanding' will turn to dust. No, this concept leads nowhere.'

Nor is Cecil fond of the idea of a *Federal Union*. He deems it utopian. Neither England, nor the USSR, nor any other big state will ever agree to surrender their sovereignty to an extent that could render a real European federation feasible in the near future.

Cecil has reached the conclusion that, in the final analysis, the third way is the best. But what kind of an international organization should be set up? Should it resemble the old League of Nations?... Of course not. But how exactly should it differ from the Geneva of old? And how should it resemble it? For not everything about the old League was bad. It had its good aspects, too. How to separate the wheat from the chaff? What are the moulds into which the future organization guaranteeing European peace should be poured? Cecil does not have very clear answers to these questions as yet, although he has been thinking hard about all of them.

I started asking leading questions and finally it emerged that Cecil conceived the future international organization in two concentric circles, so to speak.

The first, wider, circle will cover all or almost all European states (maybe non-European countries as well). It will be a sort of renewed League of Nations and will regulate various economic, political and other international issues, including boundaries, between various states. The obligations of the countries of the first circle will be comparatively light and will not include joint armed struggle against an aggressor.

The second, narrower circle inside the first will cover only those countries which have committed themselves to immediate armed resistance against any aggressor.

When I tried to find out which powers Cecil regarded as possible members of the second circle, he confessed after a few equivocal utterances: 'After victory over Germany there will remain only two powers in Europe which are really worth something – you and us. So peace-keeping shall mainly fall to England and the USSR, with friendly support from the USA.'

So, in essence Cecil considers the solution to lie in an Anglo-Soviet military-political alliance which will maintain peace in Europe (possibly in Asia, too – in cooperation with China) in the name of the new League of Nations. Hence the exceptional importance of consolidating the most cordial relations between the USSR and Great Britain.

I asked Cecil: 'Suppose England and the Soviet Union split – what then?'

Cecil shrugged his shoulders and answered hesitantly: 'I don't know… Then everything will be lost.'

In view of Cecil's general position, I related to him the history of the question of a second front and of the sending of an expeditionary corps to the USSR.

'What do you think,' I asked, 'can this history facilitate the strengthening of cooperation between the two countries, so important not only during the war but after victory as well?'

Cecil was very upset. He said he could not pass judgement without knowing all the facts, but I saw that my information had made a considerable impression on him.

We then spoke about the fate of Germany. In Cecil's opinion, Germany must be totally disarmed, but breaking it up into parts would not be expedient. He also thinks that Germany must compensate (in one form or another) for the damage done by it to the occupied countries. Such is Cecil's general reasoning, but some particulars are still unclear to him.

'I don't go as far as Vansittart,' he remarked, 'but I still acknowledge that the German nation is poisoned with the venom of militarism and the theory of world domination to a far greater extent than all other nations. A lot of time will be needed to remove this poison from her consciousness.'

Cecil enquired about our views on matters of peace and the future arrangement of Europe. I referred him to the declaration I made at the Inter-Allied Conference on 24 September. Our basic principles remain the same: self-determination of nations and collective security. We shall construct our policy on these principles. The exact forms of their application are presently hard to define. It goes without saying that Germany must compensate in one form or another for the damage done by its actions to other nations.

Cecil was satisfied with my answer and said: 'It will not be difficult for us to reach an understanding.'

I listened to Cecil, thinking to myself that the capitalist world has definitively decayed. Cecil is a vivid example. Personally, he is a fine and noble man. He really is 'the conscience of the British nation', as he is often called. But how utterly feeble are his ideas about war and peace!

But I did not consider this a good moment to expound my view of how to do away with war. I'll tell him some other time.[161]

Pipinelli, the Greek minister, asked Vyshinsky the other day about the Soviet government's thoughts regarding the future of the Balkan and Central European countries that were drawn into the war on the side of the 'Axis'.

Vyshinsky answered that after getting rid of the governments that dragged them into the war, the peoples of these countries will decide their fate for themselves. The fate of the peoples that had not managed to get rid of such governments would have to be decided by the victorious democratic countries.

2 November (Bovingdon)

One more week of the war has passed. The nineteenth week. The situation is still grave. All is quiet on the Murmansk–Finnish front. There is little activity around Leningrad too, although we keep counterattacking and seem to improve our position. But fierce fighting continues on the Moscow front, where the Germans have advanced further toward Volokolamsk and Tula during the past week. We are holding our old positions fast along the Kalinin, Mozhaisk and Malo-Yaroslavets lines. The main question is: has the German offensive against Moscow petered out or not? Should the German successes along the Orel–Tula line be viewed as purely local achievements or as the beginning of a new general attack on Moscow?

I don't know. But I rather tend to think that the Germans have not yet abandoned their plan of capturing Moscow. Therefore, a new and desperate attempt is to be expected from Hitler – perhaps even with the use of gas. Such an attempt will almost certainly find support in the German military: the forests and the fields are now devilishly nasty, and the German soldiers might regard Moscow as something like 'the promised land', or at least a decent winter shelter. Hitler is undoubtedly staking on that.

Things are still bad in the south. Having broken through at Perekop, the Germans reached the Crimea three days ago. Sevastopol is now in danger. The Germans might also force a crossing over the Kerch Strait and gain the rear at Rostov. Kharkov has been evacuated. Stalino, Makeevka and Kramatorsk are also lost. The Germans reached the Donets, but seemed to be stopped at the approach to Rostov. There are signs that Rostov will defend as fiercely as Moscow and Leningrad. But who can vouch for anything in this war?… The Caucasus must be defended at all costs! Otherwise our position may become absolutely critical.

Yes, the picture is far from rosy. But we must not lose heart. Our army is intact, our government is intact, and the unity of nation is firm. The party and Stalin lead us. All the elements are in place for eventual victory. All we need is courage, endurance and patience.

3 November

The city is awash with rumours about the 'restructuring' of the government and above all the possible resignation of Beaverbrook.

It all started on 29 October with the appearance of more or less similar information in a number of newspapers (*Daily Telegraph*, *News Chronicle*, *The Times* and others, but not Beaverbrook's) that Beaverbrook had a serious case of asthma, that he was not feeling well, and that the possibility of his resignation could not be excluded. This information worried me. Beaverbrook's resignation at present would be most inconvenient for us! I visited Eden that same morning and at the end of our conversation asked him what was behind the above-mentioned information. Eden shrugged his shoulders and said he knew nothing about it. He was inclined, however, to assume that Beaverbrook was in one of his moods, which usually coincide with bad attacks of asthma. I did not hide from Eden my own view on the matter of the minister of supply's resignation.

The same day, after *lunch*, I paid a visit to Beaverbrook and asked him right away: 'What does this mean?'

Beaverbrook was in a bad mood. On hearing my question, his face turned sallow and he suddenly banged the table viciously with his fist.

'I will not resign if the Cabinet says I ought not to!'

He turned towards me sharply and shouted: 'The *public* will not let me resign!'

Later in the conversation it became clear to me that while Beaverbrook was still on excellent terms with Churchill, he had been at loggerheads with a number of other ministers recently. Beaverbrook would not reveal their names, but remarked: 'Right now I'm on bad terms with Eden.'

'Why?' I asked in surprise.

'Why?' Beaverbrook repeated my question and replied: '*He hasn't got the guts!* He often deserts me in my hour of need.'

From everything Beaverbrook said it became clear to me that he was not contemplating resigning, that he himself had initiated the above-mentioned newspaper articles and that he wanted to play the part of Boris Godunov[i] in

---

[i] Boris Godunov, the Russian tsar, 1585–1605; subject of Mussorgsky's opera based on Pushkin's play.

order to strengthen his position *vis-à-vis* his colleagues in Cabinet. So I did my best to convince Beaverbrook that his resignation would have the direst consequences for England and Anglo-Soviet relations, especially now, right after the Moscow conference. It would be interpreted in the USSR as the abandonment or, at the very least, the weakening of the policy of cooperation between our two countries that alone could lead to victory. In saying that, I was of course aware that I was putting a trump card in Beaverbrook's hands, but I had nothing against this. On the contrary, I had privately decided to do all I could to support Beaverbrook, for at the present time we couldn't have a better minister of supply. Beaverbrook was very glad. My words were a balm to his soul.

From Beaverbrook I went to a reception given by Aras to mark the anniversary of the Turkish Republic, and met Eden there.

'Have you seen Beaverbrook?' Eden asked me, pulling me aside.

'Yes, I saw him and we had a talk,' I replied. 'I think his resignation can be prevented. It would be good if you and Churchill persuaded Beaverbrook that he should remain in this post.'

'I will talk with the prime minister about it today,' Eden reacted quickly.

I thought to myself: 'Very good. Boris Godunov will get what he needs.'

The next day Eden confirmed that he had visited Beaverbrook on the evening of the 29th on Churchill's instructions and that their conversation had left him with the impression that Beaverbrook would not resign.

Meanwhile I started making inquiries through other channels. I found out that lately Beaverbrook had had a number of sharp disagreements with his colleagues in Cabinet on the matters of assistance to the USSR and the expansion of the war industry. He had a quarrel with Sinclair (Beaverbrook dislikes him altogether) because of the 200 (American) *Air-Cobra* fighters which he had borrowed from the Air Ministry for delivery to us in December. Then there was a quarrel with Moore-Brabazon (minister of aircraft production) about aluminium supplies to the USSR. There was also a row with Bevin because Beaverbrook wanted to appeal to the *shop stewards* for the purpose of boosting military production. Beaverbrook also quarrelled with a number of his colleagues because of his support for active military assistance to the Soviet Union in the west (for instance, in the form of a large raid on the Brittany peninsula where two German battleships were sheltering). One must add to all this Beaverbrook's difficult nature, as well as his marked aversion to red tape.

'I can't stand committees,' Beaverbrook told me once. 'I always decide everything myself.'

Eventually the atmosphere around Beaverbrook in the Cabinet became such that he had to contemplate the methods of Boris Godunov. My impression, however, is that the 'crisis' has passed and that my 'intervention' played a significant role in this happening.

[Beaverbrook concealed from Maisky that the reason for the crisis was in fact his mishandling of the Moscow talks and his intrigues against Cripps, which had just come to light through a series of private letters addressed to Eden by the ambassador from Kuibyshev.[162] Beaverbrook's partial and tendentious reports misled the Cabinet into assuming that Stalin had indeed accepted supply as a substitute for proper political and strategic collaboration.[163] The pause allowed Churchill to pursue unhindered his preparations for the long-overdue offensive in the Western Desert. By mid-October, however, Churchill encountered a fierce debate in the Cabinet, prompted by unprecedentedly harsh criticism from Cripps. Cripps urged the dispatch of a high-level mission to Moscow to conclude military and political agreements. In the meantime, he called for the deployment of a force – even a limited one – on the Russian front, warning that: 'We seem to be trying to carry on two relatively unrelated wars to the great benefit of Hitler instead of a single war upon the basis of a combined plan. It appears that we are treating the Soviet Government without trust and as inferiors rather than as trusted allies.'[164]

Eden, too, was concerned by Churchill's 'very evident signs of anti-Bolshevik sentiments'.[165] Nonetheless, the Defence Committee – formed by Churchill to ensure his undisputed control of the war – and General Dill, the chief of staff, gave a positive hearing to Cripps's proposals to assign a force to prevent German troops from pouring into the Middle East through the back door, following the anticipated collapse of the Russian front.[166] Although outwardly Churchill acquiesced with the majority, he took steps to re-establish his authority. His personal instructions to Cripps unequivocally reiterated his intention not to alter British strategy, as 'We shall presently be fighting ourselves as the result of long-prepared plans.' To stifle Cripps's influence at home, he was kept in enforced exile in Kuibyshev, on the dubious pretext that it was his 'duty to remain with these people in their ordeal'. Cripps's appeal for a force was reinforced by a veiled threat: 'I hope I shall never be called upon to argue the case in public.'[167] In Cabinet, Churchill exploited Cripps's criticism to the utmost in order to undermine Beaverbrook's position by blaming him, rather cynically, for the poor state of Anglo-Soviet relations.[168] Above all, Churchill was bent on preventing the dispatch of even a single division to the Russian front. He now secured the overdue resignation of General Dill and the appointment as chief of staff of his own trusted adviser, General Alan Brooke.[169] By late November, Churchill's efforts bore fruit, when the reorganized chiefs of staff recognized that, 'since assistance to Russia raised very delicate political issues, the final decision must rest entirely with the Prime Minister'.[170]]

9 November (Bovingdon)

One more week. The twentieth week of war.

The situation seems to be somewhat better. True, the Germans have captured the greater part of the Crimea and are approaching Sevastopol and

Kerch, but they have not had any success in the past week either at Rostov or in the Donetsk basin. On the contrary, it seems that our defence in these regions is becoming stronger and stronger. Evidently, Timoshenko is gradually wresting the initiative. The main thing, however, is that the Germans have been stopped on the Moscow front. For a while or forever? I don't know. In any case, not only have they not made any progress during the last week, they have even lost a bit of ground. It looks as if the German offensive on this front is running out of steam – particularly with the advent of winter. Still: once bitten, twice shy. I am afraid to draw any conclusions. I'm inclined to think that the Germans will try to come up with something else to surprise us with. For their situation becomes increasingly difficult. Five weeks have passed since Hitler's boastful declarations (3 October), yet Moscow stands firm and, what's more, gives as good as she gets.

The past week brought me two joyful events. The first – the main one – was Stalin's speech on the occasion of the 24th anniversary. It was awfully pleasant that on the evening of 6 November Stalin spoke at a ceremonial public meeting in the Bolshoi Theatre, and that on the morning of 7 November there was a splendid military parade on Red Square, which was made so much more brilliant by Stalin's short second speech. It is said that Hitler had reckoned on reviewing his troops on Red Square on 7 November. He couldn't do it if he tried! What is not hearsay but a fact is that on the evening of 6 November more than 500 German planes tried to bomb Moscow, but couldn't break through our air defences. How fine it is that Stalin decided to hold the public meeting in the Bolshoi and the military parade on Red Square as usual this year! It is a gesture of strength and confidence, a gesture of contempt for the enemy.

Stalin's speeches, on the whole, have had a 'good press' in England, even though he politely scolded the British government for its refusal to open a second front. Simultaneously with Stalin, on 6 November, Roosevelt delivered a most 'belligerent' speech (by American standards). Thus, fists were shaken at Hitler from both east and west.

The second joyful event, albeit on a much smaller scale, was the appointment of Litvinov as ambassador to the USA. My telegram sent 10 days ago, stressing the necessity of immediately sending an ambassador to Washington, obviously played its part in hastening the resolution of this matter. Umansky has been appointed director of TASS (a very good appointment for him). M.M. will surely be in the right place in America. Today more than ever before, we need a reliable, strong and influential figure there. Who knows, maybe I'll be lucky enough to see M.M. soon? His route to America lies through London both politically and geographically – more so politically, of course. Well, I'll try to arrange something in this respect. On the evening of 6 November, when the news about M.M.'s appointment became known, I got a call from Winant. He expressed his delight and asked me to convey his congratulations to Litvinov and to arrange a meeting should he happen to stop in London on the way to America.

Our colony celebrated the 24th anniversary by reading Stalin's speech, which Izvekova managed to copy down from the radio. I had been thinking of making a speech, but decided that our comrades needed Stalin's speech much more than my personal considerations. I read the speech aloud myself and added a coda on the topic of a second front.

So, we have entered into the 25th year of our Republic. Let it be the year in which we see, if not full victory, then at least a decisive *turning of the tide* in the course of the war!

[It was Cripps who started the ball rolling towards the appointment of Litvinov as ambassador in Washington. In late July, following a meeting with Stalin, Cripps was rushed to the Kremlin's luxurious shelter during an air raid. He was surprised to find Litvinov there rather 'shabby and unlike his old self'. In October, Cripps succeeded in convincing Molotov that Litvinov should take part in the conference with Beaverbrook.[171] Meanwhile Harriman had clearly signalled to Stalin that Umansky was *persona non grata* in Washington. A month later the Russians informed the Americans of their decision to appoint Litvinov as ambassador to the United States. Cripps was more justified than Maisky in claiming that he was responsible for putting Litvinov 'right back on the political map'.[172]]

11 November

It seems that we've come to the first crisis in relations between the 'allies'!

Today I handed the prime minister Stalin's reply to his message of 4 November. Churchill received me in his office in parliament. Eden was also present at my request. We had come together from the Foreign Office, where I had had a preliminary talk with Eden on various issues of the day. When we entered the prime minister's office, Churchill stood up to greet us and, shaking my hand, said with a friendly smile: '*Let us have a good talk.*'

We sat down at the long table covered in green cloth at which Cabinet meetings are usually held, and I handed Churchill the package I had brought with me. He took out the letter and began reading. I observed his facial expression: it became increasingly dark. Churchill reached the last line and passed the document to Eden in silence. Then, also in silence, he jumped up from his chair and quickly paced the room a couple of times. It was difficult to recognize the prime minister: his face was as white as chalk and he was breathing heavily. He was obviously enraged. Finally, having gained a measure of control over himself, Churchill uttered: '*Grave message!*'[173]

And added icily: 'I don't want to answer this message now! I have to consult my colleagues.'

It was said in such a tone that I thought it better to rise and take my leave. But Eden held me back and I remained.

Churchill did not maintain his outward restraint for long. He again paced the room a couple of times, getting more and more worked up. Eventually, he could keep silent no longer: 'So, Stalin wants to know our post-war plans? We do have such plans – the *Atlantic Charter*! What else can be said at the present moment?'

I objected that the *Atlantic Charter* was too general a document and that within its framework (for we also recognize the *Atlantic Charter*) a number of points could be usefully clarified. Just one example: about three weeks ago Eden, referring to the question Stalin had asked Beaverbrook during the Moscow conference, told me that the British government would like to build post-war relations between England and the USSR on the basis of friendly cooperation. Couldn't this matter be profitably solved within the framework of an agreement about the post-war plans of both powers?

'It's true that I spoke with you about it,' Eden commented, 'but I asked Mr Stalin to express his own thoughts on this matter.'

'I am inclined to interpret point (a) of Stalin's wishes,' I countered, 'as a reply to the message you conveyed to me.'

Eden smiled sceptically.

Churchill suddenly flared up again and exclaimed: 'If you want to turn England into a communist state in your post-war plans, you should know you'll never succeed!'

'What makes you think so!' I protested with a suppressed laugh. 'Stalin's last speech should have quite reassured you in this respect.'

The prime minister again took Stalin's message in his hands and glanced at the second sheet. It was as if he had been scorched.

'Hm!' Churchill cried out in fury. 'I send two of my chief commanders to him but he can't find the time to see them unless they are authorized to conclude those agreements…'

And the PM poked his finger in vexation at the passage where Stalin mentions the absence of agreements between England and the Soviet Union on mutual military assistance and post-war plans.

'No, I am not going to propose any more military negotiations!' continued Churchill in the same tone. 'Enough!'

The prime minister rapidly paced his office once more and added: 'And why was it necessary for Stalin to assume such a tone in our correspondence? I am not going to stand for it. I could well say things, too! Who will profit from it? Neither we, nor you – only Hitler!'

I remarked that I could see no grounds for such *excitement*. What Stalin is now suggesting is essentially what I discussed with Churchill more than two months ago – a joint strategic plan for the conduct of the war. Is that so unreasonable?

'What strategic plan can there be today?' Churchill exclaimed with irritation. 'We are still on the defensive, you are still on the defensive, and the initiative is still in Hitler's hands… What joint strategic plan can there be under such circumstances? Only to hold out until the moment arrives when we can snatch the initiative from our enemy's hands – that is our plan!'

'I agree that for the moment both you and we have to think about defence,' I interjected, 'but even defence requires a plan. What will we do in 1942, for instance – you and us? Wouldn't it be a good idea to agree on that?'

Churchill made a vague gesture in reply. Turning to Eden, he asked: 'How did it happen that information about the talks on declaring war on Finland has appeared in the press?'

Eden shrugged his shoulders and said that the *publicity* had begun in America. I objected that the first report appeared in *The Times*.

'In *The Times*?' bellowed Churchill in a sudden access of anger. 'First the diplomatic correspondent's report, then the editorial… Yes, yes, *The Times* took a stand against the government!'

It was obvious that the prime minister was taking the stance of *The Times* very much to heart and that in general he was extremely sensitive to any criticism of his government.

'We have nothing in common with these publications!' he exclaimed with irritation. 'They were made specially against us… *To force the hand of the government*… This will not succeed! I also have an opinion of my own! And anyone who thinks that *public clamour* can influence my policy is gravely mistaken. I am not going to commit stupidities just because somebody demands it. We do not have sufficient troops today to help you in any serious way…'

It was obvious that Churchill's thoughts had returned to the question of mutual military assistance between the Allies and a second front.

I asked how matters stood with regard to the possible declaration of war against Finland and other countries.

Churchill answered heatedly that he thought such a declaration would be a mistake, that Sweden objected to it strongly, that Norway was not pleased about it, that the opposition in Finland against the continuation of war was growing, and so on. By way of proof, the PM read me a long telegram from the British ambassador in Stockholm in which the latter described the attitude of the Swedish public to the possibility of England declaring war on Finland.

I replied that this was not very convincing. People have been talking about Finland's anti-war sentiments for a long time, but Finland keeps fighting all the same. In my opinion, Finland has gone beyond the point of no return. Adequate conclusions should be drawn. I am also surprised by the following fact: the British government reckons with Sweden, with Norway, with the USA, and even with Finland itself, but not with the USSR! After all the *publicity* given to this matter, the situation has become really 'intolerable' and must be resolved at once.

Churchill flared up again as if he had touched white-hot iron, and shouted bitterly: 'It was me who acted without hesitation on 22 June and offered you my hand, although only a few weeks earlier I had had no idea what you would do! Perhaps you were going to go with Germany?... Who needs all these disputes and disagreements?... After all, we are fighting for our lives and will keep on fighting for our lives whatever happens!'

'We're fighting for our lives too,' I replied. 'And not badly at that.'

'You're fighting superbly!' exclaimed Churchill with passion.

He thought for a minute, glanced at Eden, who had kept silent throughout, and finally added: 'Right now I don't wish to respond to Stalin... I might say a lot of undesirable things in the heat of the moment... I'll consult our people, calm down, and then write... You will be duly informed.'

'Whether or not you like Stalin's message,' I remarked in conclusion, 'there's little sense in excessive *excitement*. One must keep a sober and cool head. We have a common cause and a common struggle. If I can help in building bridges, I am entirely at your service.'

We bid farewell and I left. There was a large group of MPs from different parties in the lobbies. They all greeted me warmly. Sir Percy Harris[i] (the Liberal whip) exclaimed with laughter: 'It's nice to see you looking so *happy*.'

'Happy?' I responded, 'That's a misunderstanding. *I'm confident but not happy*.'

They all laughed.

We shall see what the outcome of today's meeting will be. In theory, it could be both good and bad. Time will tell.

12 November

Beaverbrook called me today on the phone and blurted out in his typical style: 'Maisky! What a disgrace! We must find a way of clearing up this *mess*! Come over, we'll have a talk.'

When I entered Beaverbrook's office I found Bennett (former prime minister of Canada) sitting there. He gave me a firm handshake and expressed his great

[i] Percy Harris, Liberal MP, 1922–45; deputy leader of the Liberal Party, 1940–45.

admiration for the Red Army and the resistance of the Soviet people. He then left and Beaverbrook and I remained alone.

'What has made Stalin so angry?' Beaverbrook asked straight off. 'Finland?'

'And why do you think he is angry?' I replied, repeating his question.

'Well, you tell me!' Beaverbrook exclaimed. 'I know what he's like! I can see he's angry, that he's peeved with us… Is it because of Finland?'[174]

I answered that the British government's behaviour on the question of Finland and other German vassals could hardly put Stalin in a good mood. Neither could he be cheered by the evasive behaviour of the British government in the matter of sending an expeditionary corps. Stalin is a true realist. He does not care much for words and understands only deeds. And what were the deeds of the British government in both cases?

'Yes, but when it comes to supplies,' Beaverbrook protested, 'we are doing so much right now. I'm prepared to do anything to fulfil my promises. You'll receive everything. If you have complaints or requests regarding supplies, don't hesitate to come straight to me. Tell Stalin to wire me directly. I chair the committee for supplies to the USSR. I'll not feel offended by anything. I have a thick skin… Stalin is my friend. I'll do anything for him. Have you read my Manchester speech?'

I confirmed that I had read it and that I found it very good.

'But of course!' Beaverbrook brightened up, pleasantly flattered by my words. 'I've provided such a good advertisement for Stalin, haven't I!… Ha-ha-ha!'

And Beaverbrook burst into satisfied laughter. Then he became more serious and added: 'We shouldn't upset our prime minister with complaints about broken aircraft or missing ammunition! He takes it too much to heart! Let Stalin wire me directly. I'll sweep away with an iron broom all those saboteurs who fail to pack our cargos in the proper way.'

Beaverbrook paused for a moment.

'Having said that,' he continued expressively, 'we must do all we can to settle this disagreement between the heads of our governments!… Stalin's letter is, after all, rather *harsh*… This must be admitted. Churchill is awfully touchy and stubborn. How can we smooth things over?'

Beaverbrook cast me an inquiring look.

I answered that, in my view, it was not so difficult to settle the matter. First of all, we must remove the problem of Finland, Rumania and Hungary…

'Do you still want us to declare war on them?' Beaverbrook interrupted me.

I confirmed that we did. Then I asked him what it was that he found unacceptable about Stalin's proposals concerning agreement on post-war matters and strategy. Both these proposals seemed quite natural and reasonable to me. Beaverbrook objected: 'The problem is that Stalin wants negotiations of both questions to be conducted by the generals… What sort of post-war problems can generals discuss? This is not their sphere. Here, people say: if Stalin wants it done this way, it means he doesn't want negotiations at all.'

I laughed and said that this was a false conclusion. Of course, the generals are not best placed to discuss matters concerning the post-war reconstruction of Europe, but why couldn't politicians and diplomats discuss them here in London, or in Moscow?

Beaverbrook jumped at the idea and exclaimed: 'I'll definitely support the holding of such negotiations in London.'

'As for military negotiations,' I went on, 'you really ought to *make up your mind*. If you want to send an expeditionary corps to the USSR – very well. Then it makes sense for the generals to go to Moscow. But if you still don't know yourselves whether you want to take such a step or not, then Stalin is absolutely right: there is no point in the generals wasting their time and that of Stalin.'

Beaverbrook shook his head and answered that he himself was in favour of sending an expeditionary corps and that he would do his best to persuade the prime minister of the need to take a final decision on this matter.

I stood up to take my leave. Beaverbrook saw me to the lift and, shaking my hand, said: 'All this was *off the record*, of course. I trust you and share my thoughts and feelings with you. But nobody should know about it.'

I swore complete secrecy.

At seven in the evening I was in Eden's office at his request. The foreign minister obviously felt ill at ease and, having invited me to sit down, said he wanted to make the following official statement to me:[175] 'Mr Stalin's message is being considered by the Cabinet. At the present moment I am not in a position to respond to it, as it raises such serious questions. However, I can't conceal from you the fact that the prime minister as well as the members of the Cabinet were surprised and put out by the tone and content of the message.'

Eden delivered the statement aloud, while glancing at a piece of paper in front of him. I asked Eden to repeat it and wrote it down word for word.

'That is all I can tell you officially for now,' he added.

This was said in such a way for me to understand: 'And now, if you are inclined to speak unofficially, I'm at your service.'[176]

I responded to Eden's unspoken invitation, and we embarked on a lengthy discussion about Anglo-Soviet relations, in which I maintained approximately the same position as I did in my recent conversation with Beaverbrook. Eden acknowledged that there was nothing unacceptable or unreasonable in Stalin's proposals as such. He merely expressed some doubts as to the possibility of saying anything specific at the present time on the question of the organization of the world after the war. Eden, however, had no objection to this matter being discussed – not by generals, of course, but by politicians and diplomats. Eden also said that Beaverbrook had helped him a great deal in dealing with the situation that had arisen, but kept emphasizing the touchiness and stubbornness of the prime minister. It was obvious – and Eden did not try to conceal it – that he was very upset by the incident and that he felt very troubled by Stalin's mistrust of the Churchill government. 'I understand perfectly well that your government could not trust the Chamberlain government, but it seems that it hasn't changed its attitude even towards the Churchill government. That is what's *distressing*.'

I protested that this was not so. However, we cannot help noting the fact that Chamberlain's supporters are very well represented in the present government as well, and that they are backed by very influential elements. Eden denied the significance of Chamberlain's supporters in the Churchill government, but I could not fully agree with him. On parting, Eden said: 'Please help me patch up this unpleasant incident. I, for my part, will do all I can to achieve this.'

I answered: 'You may be sure of my goodwill.'

Citrine dropped in. He told me a lot about his trip to Moscow and Kuibyshev. Most of it is set out in his articles for the *Daily Herald*. Citrine has a special type of mind: it registers what he sees like a photosensitive plate. Citrine's head is always full of facts, figures and details. When Citrine is writing or telling a story, he likes to reproduce all these details. Which often turns him into a bore. When it comes to generalizations, concepts or big ideas, Citrine is rather weak. He is a true 'secretary' by nature and seems to have found his place in life.

Among other things, Citrine told me that upon returning from the Soviet Union he had a conversation with Churchill about active military assistance to the USSR – the result of his meeting with Molotov in Kuibyshev. The PM showed Citrine the instructions given to General Ismay when he and Beaverbrook were leaving for Moscow. They said that, if we so wished, the British government could send 6–8 divisions to the USSR, in which case the supply of arms, etc. would have to be reduced due to transport difficulties. The Soviet government was being offered a choice.[177] Churchill told Citrine that for reasons which he had not quite understood, General Ismay's meeting with our military men had not taken place. Moreover, Beaverbrook was under the impression that the Soviet government was very interested in supplies, but showed little enthusiasm about a British expeditionary corps being sent to the USSR.

So, the British conceive of a corps of 6–8 divisions (at least to begin with)!… I was not so mistaken when I informed Moscow that the 25–30 divisions which Stalin wanted were out of the question at present, but that something in the region of 10 divisions was feasible.

14 November

Simović sent Čubrilović to me, together with Dr Sekulić,[i] who has just arrived from Yugoslavia. Simović is making an appeal to Comrade Stalin. Disagreements and even internal conflict are to be observed among the Yugoslavian insurgents. There are two main groups: 'partisans' and 'chetniks'. The former are led by communists (although far from all its members are communists) and prefer offensive tactics – they attack the Germans themselves. The latter are led by 'farmers' and officers of the former Yugoslavian army, and they prefer defensive tactics: they sit tight in the mountains and fight only if the Germans attack first. There is no accord between these two main groups. They do not help each other. There were even open clashes between them recently. Simović wants to ask Stalin to take measures in order to unite all Yugoslavian insurgents, especially the 'partisans', under the slogan of a united front. I promised to communicate the Yugoslavian prime minister's request to Moscow.

Čubrilović told me a funny story. Peter, the young Yugoslavian king (he is 18 years old), studies at Cambridge. He has acquainted himself with the leftists and was even elected chairman of the students' communist club (there is no communist club in Cambridge as far as I know; perhaps there is a workers' club or a socialist club in which communists play the leading role). Peter told his mother about this. She gasped and sighed, but Peter brushed her disapproval aside and exclaimed: 'You're an old woman, you don't understand! One must learn how to be a modern king.'

16 November

Another week has passed!

The situation on our front has improved. The Germans have failed to break through to Moscow. It looks like they'll never be able to break through – this year at any rate. Leningrad holds firm. The situation in the Donetsk basin is better. The resistance there, particularly at Rostov, is increasingly *stiff*. Things are worst in the Crimea. The Germans are trying to break through to Kerch and to cross the Kerch Strait in order to gain the rear of Rostov and thereby threaten the Caucasus. Whether they will be able to or not is another matter. I think Timoshenko will make his presence felt in due course. Overall, one senses that the coming winter is gradually freezing the blood of the German army, making it less mobile, less energetic, less dangerous. This doesn't mean, of course, that combat operations will cease entirely in the coming months. But their scale and intensity will decline for sure. One also feels that our resistance all along the

[i] Dr Miloš Sekulić, prominent member of the Yugoslav government in exile in London.

front is becoming more confident, more resolute and more effective. The Red Army has learnt much during these months of war; it has gained experience; it has found and continues to find ever more successful methods of fighting the 'panzer divisions' and other novelties of the German military technology. The Germans, on the other hand, display increasing exhaustion in resources and strategy. Besides, their morale ought to gradually fall, both at the front and at home, for it is clear that there is no end in sight. True, Hitler has had victories – many victories, major victories – but he has not achieved that single decisive victory which would bring the war to a happy conclusion. Therein lies his tragedy. Therein lies the guarantee of his downfall and our triumph. Had I not been taught by the bitter experience of the past, I would be prepared to say that Germany has already passed the zenith of its war efforts and capabilities, while ours is still far off. Hence, the future seems clear. However, in view of the events of the past 27 months, I prefer to be cautious and will only say: 'Time will tell.'

[On 24 November, German troops occupied Klin, a key point on the north-western approaches to Moscow. Four days later, the Germans advanced further, to a distance of only 20 miles from the Kremlin. Meanwhile Panzer Commander General Guderian was meticulously executing a pincer move on a wide front in the south, pressing on to Kashira, beyond which there was not a single Soviet formation to prevent the capture of Moscow. The final German thrust was attempted on 1 December by Field Marshal von Kluge[i] along the Minsk–Moscow highway in fierce winter conditions. The next day, however, Zhukov made his bid and successfully drove the Germans back to positions they had occupied a few days earlier. Taking advantage of the parrying of the German offensive, Zhukov mounted a counter-strike on 5 December in temperatures that dipped to –30°C. By 9 December, the Germans had been driven back to positions they held before the major assault, after which they were subjected to continued harassment in their rear and a second counteroffensive at the end of the month.[178] The Russians delayed announcing the successful repulse of German forces until the day after Eden's arrival in Moscow.]

23 November (Bovingdon)

The situation is worse at the front once again. The Germans have mounted a new offensive near Moscow and Rostov. According to the radio and the press, as well as our reports, they massed their forces, brought up fresh reserves and attacked. True, their pressure does not seem to be as strong as in early October,

---

[i] Günther von Kluge, field marshal, succeeded as the commander of the Fourth Army in the battles of Poland and France, but was forced to retreat in December 1941 from the outskirts of Moscow; later excelled as commander of the central front and finally commander-in-chief of the west.

but still... Great difficulties in Tula... Fierce fighting at Klin, probably meaning the loss of Kalinin... Fighting on the streets of Rostov...

Where do the Germans get all their reserves and reinforcements from? Where do all these never-ending panzer divisions come from? When will they reach the bottom of the barrel?

What we need is patience and self-control. Our day shall come! The Germans are so stretched out, their forces so dispersed and so deep into our country, that when the *turning of the tide* begins they will simply be unable to run away. Their destruction will be terrible. All the more so as the population of the occupied areas will simply cut their throats.

Last week (18 November) the British finally started their long-awaited offensive in Libya. Eden claims that they have great superiority over the Germans and Italians there in both land and air forces, not to mention the fleet. In particular, the correlation of mechanized troops is 3:2 or perhaps even 2:1 in favour of the British. According to the information of the British government, there are two German and one Italian mechanized divisions in Libya, i.e. only 800–900 tanks (Germany's African divisions are somewhat weaker than the European ones). So the British must have something like 1,600–1,800 tanks or 4–5 mechanized divisions there.

Eden is in an optimistic mood. If the British manage a successful *Blitzkrieg* in Libya, it may have serious consequences for the general course of the war, because this time they will surely not stop at Bengasi but will go on to Tripoli and possibly even Tunisia. This would be of immense importance for North Africa, would ease the shipping situation in the Mediterranean and would open routes for attacking Sicily, Sardinia and Italy. A second front in Europe could be opened before spring. But can the British launch a *Blitzkrieg*? I am not sure. Well, we'll see.

30 November

We have not gone to Bovingdon. Much to do in London.

Developments on the front are taking a turn for the better. Hitler continues to tread water near Moscow. Suffers massive losses. The general impression is that the Germans are not strong enough to break through to Moscow. All the better. We continue our counterattack near Leningrad. We've had no great successes there, but the Germans are apparently *on the defensive*. Even this is not bad for the present. The best news, however, has come from the south of all places. Timoshenko unexpectedly attacked the Germans in Rostov, dislodged them from there with heavy losses and is now driving them west along the northern shore of the Sea of Azov. General von Kleist's army has been fully

93. Maisky and Eden on board HMS *Kent* on the way to Murmansk.

destroyed. That's a big fish we've caught. It's our first major offensive success. The first but not the last.

What's this? *Turning of the tide?* I don't know. I'm afraid to believe it. Maybe it's just a serious success of local significance. But one thing is clear: the threat to the Caucasus has been seriously reduced and perhaps (as subsequent events will show) even eliminated. One other thing seems indubitable to me: the Germans have neared the limit of their force and capabilities. This does not necessarily mean the beginning of their collapse across the board – oh, no! Fierce fighting and many hardships still lie ahead of us. And yet… And yet, the first ray of light has broken through the heavy dark clouds.

I am going to Moscow. To accompany Eden and take part in the negotiations! Hurrah!

[There are no further entries in the diary for 1941. Maisky, who was actively involved (at Eden's request) in the preparatory stages of the conference in London,[179] joined the foreign secretary on his trip to Moscow during 7–30 December. Never sure as to what was in store, he made sure he took along 'considerable quantity of Dunhills best' for Stalin.[180] On the whole, Eden shared Molotov's hopes of concluding the conference with two agreements, one defining the common strategy and relationship during the war, and the other the nature and borders of Europe in the aftermath of the war (though he did not wish the second to be specific and detailed).[181] At Eden's instigation, the Foreign Office embarked on the drafting of the so-called 'Volga Charter', to be incorporated into the 'Atlantic Charter', recognizing the Soviet demand for a buffer zone in the Baltic and East Poland. This, they insisted, did not reflect expansionist ambitions, but was a 'legitimate security claim'. Once again, Churchill considered only the tactical and propaganda value of the visit. To prevent undesirable commitments, he timed the visit for after the launch of the offensive in Libya. This offensive, he knew, would stifle any debate on strategic priorities and would enable Eden to claim that Britain had indeed opened a second front.[182]

Bypassing Eden, Churchill adhered to his strategy. He now corresponded directly with Stalin, leaving him in no doubt as to the limits imposed on Eden. Stalin was presented with a Hobson's choice between supplies and troops, and was informed that a discussion of political issues would be deferred until the end of the war.[183] Thus Eden's mission, like Beaverbrook's, was doomed before he set foot on Soviet soil. His attempts to back out proved unsuccessful. He was forced to regard the visit as 'exploratory talks', and to fall back on the need to consult Washington, in order to 'stall upon Russian proposals that had awkward features'.[184] He was deprived of yet another crucial card when an additional consignment to Russia of 500 tanks and 100 fighters was postponed, pending the cessation of hostilities in the Western Desert.[185]

Eden's visit in early December was overshadowed by two major events. On his way to Russia he was informed of the attack on Pearl Harbor. A day before the attack, Churchill still appeared conciliatory and flexible in his farewell talk with Maisky, embarking in detail on his vision for a post-war Europe in which the Soviet Union was assigned a prominent role.[186] Churchill's hasty departure for Washington a day after the attack, accompanied by all his chiefs of staff, and the discussion on common strategy at the White House stood in sharp contrast to the perfunctory treatment of Russia. The breathing space gained through the German engagement in Russia lost much of its significance. Eden was prohibited at the last moment from promising even symbolic

94. Arriving in Moscow with Eden.

95. Trailing Eden back from Moscow, December 1941.

assistance, beyond the supply protocol which was indispensable for at least the partial success of his mission. Curiously, the two active British fronts now coincided with British imperial interests in the Middle and Far East, while collaboration on the battlefield in Europe seemed remoter than ever.

The second event that overshadowed Eden's visit was the impressive Soviet counteroffensive at the gates of Moscow. While the Russians gained in confidence, Eden lost a great deal of his bargaining power. In his memoirs, he concocted a success story out of the negotiations that resembled Beaverbrook's of a few months previously.[187] Indeed, the similarities between the two missions are striking, although Eden's closing meetings were stormier. As anticipated, Eden was confronted with the issues of frontiers and strategic collaboration. The initial cordial atmosphere, again coloured by Soviet expectations, soon gave way to frustration and conflict. The intensive negotiations reached deadlock, but a final noncommittal joint declaration and an ostentatious farewell reception at the Kremlin served Stalin as a morale booster at home and a display of unity vis-à-vis the Germans.[188]]

* * *

[The following letter was never sent to Stalin. It was aimed, in case the boat taking Eden and himself to Russia was sunk, at ensuring that the diary would be preserved and eventually published. By admitting to its existence, it was also a measure to protect Agniya in case his papers were confiscated after his death.]

London, 6 December 1941
To Comrade STALIN

Dear Iosif Vissarionovich,

Tomorrow, I am leaving for the USSR together with Eden. As sea voyages are a rather risky business nowadays, I'm writing this letter to you just in case.

In the attached portfolio there is the diary which I have kept – albeit not very regularly – for the last seven years. From the literary point of view, the diary does of course need significant editing, because I wrote it in varied circumstances and almost always in a hurry. Yet, from the historical point of view, it is undoubtedly of some interest. I have, after all, spent these seven years at the major observation post of world politics, with the opportunity to enter into dealings with the major political figures of England and other countries. I am sending my diary to you. Do with it as you see fit. It is hardly possible to publish it right now, even in part and even with a commentary: we are still too close to the events described here, and most of the characters who feature on its pages are still alive. But in the more distant future my diary, or at least its most interesting passages, could perhaps be published. Whether published or not, however, the diary is worth saving: it could be of use to a future historian of our epoch. Apart from the diary, there are various fragmentary notes in envelopes, which I usually entered into the diary at a later point.

I have one more request. In the winter of 1939/40 I wrote reminiscences of my childhood and early youth (before entering university) and sent the manuscript to Comrade Kalinin, who wanted to publish them in Moscow on the very eve of the war. I don't know how things stand now. I would be most grateful to you if you could give instructions to publish these reminiscences when the possibility arises. My wife would willingly take upon herself all the direct work involved in preparing them for publication.

With Comradely regards,
/I. Maisky/

1942

[There are barely any entries following Maisky's return from Moscow. This can be attributed only in part to a severe bout of recurring malaria and the immense burden of work he was subjected to. Not unlike in 1939, the main reasons for the protracted periods of silence were his qualms about the Kremlin's policies.[1] The diary only alludes to the dramatic soul searching going on in Moscow in the first quarter of 1942.

Eden, who, contrary to his public image, often displayed an astonishing weakness under pressure, had left Stalin with the impression that he could sway the Cabinet to sign the agreements drafted in Moscow. Maisky was much encouraged, as he disclosed to the American ambassador, by Eden's favourable response to Stalin's demands and the foreign secretary's conviction that the British government would 'raise no difficulties'. Shortly after their return from Moscow, Maisky implored Eden to recommend to Churchill (who was still in Washington) that he should endorse the agreement concerning Russia's western borders. Churchill, however, responded with an indignant and stiff telegram instructing Eden to inform Stalin that post-war arrangements would have to be left for the peace conference.[2]

Once again mutual suspicion and mistrust afflicted the budding alliance. Maisky's ideologically tinted observation was that the British fear of communism and the thought that the Russians might reach Berlin could impede a post-war agreement and might even lead the 'ruling class to seek a separate peace with the German generals and business men'.[3] He was right, in so far as apprehension of 'Soviet treachery' continued to dominate the attitude of British officialdom towards the Soviet Union. Paradoxically, such emotions now dictated the need for an agreement to be concluded swiftly, before the Soviet Union could finish creating 'a series of autonomous Soviet Socialist Republics in different parts of Germany', thus achieving 'not only its ideological objective but also giving practical effect to Stalin's avowed policy of "breaking up" Germany'. A German–Soviet agreement could therefore never be ruled out, allowing Stalin to achieve what he had always hoped to achieve, and which the war had 'hitherto denied to him, namely, that Germany and the Western Democracies should exhaust themselves in an inconclusive struggle to the ultimate benefit of the Soviet Government'.[4]

Eden accordingly continued to argue forcefully in Cabinet that, in the absence of an agreement which would define the nature of the alliance, there would be 'no counterweight to Russia in Europe' after the war, rendering her position 'unassailable'.[5] Churchill was manifestly enraged over not having been consulted: would it not have been 'wise for you to discuss the matter with me first?', he reproached Eden, as the latter retracted his paper for amendments.[6] The watered-down memorandum was finally discussed in Cabinet on 5 and 6 February. Only Beaverbrook spoke strongly in favour of acceding to Stalin's demands, describing the Baltic States as 'the Ireland of Russia'. Russia, he reminded his colleagues, 'had contributed far more to the war effort than the United States to whom we had made such frequent concessions'. He called for swift action, and threatened to appeal to public opinion, so that 'people may settle the deliberation on our behalf'. Tamed by Churchill, Eden sought compromise, but to no avail. The prime minister, whose gaze was fixed on the United States, insisted that Stalin's demands 'should be settled at the Peace Conference', and duly convinced Cabinet to pass them on to the American president without any comments and recommendations.[7]

The implied subservient British attitude was evident in a somewhat sulky personal letter from Eden to the American ambassador, reassuring him that Britain had not entered into any agreements or commitments of which the United States had not been informed, and that it would 'always be careful' to keep the Americans informed of any commitments which might affect the eventual terms of the peace.[8] Constrained by Churchill, there was little Eden could do to mollify Maisky, who was increasingly worried about the effect the prolonged absence of any response to Stalin's demands was having on Moscow. He knew better than to accept Eden's feeble excuses that the Soviet demands were 'not put in an unfavourable light' to the Americans.[9] Eden, nonetheless, resented Roosevelt for hijacking his own initiative: as it was 'with His Majesty's Government and not with the United States Government that M. Stalin wishes to conclude a treaty … it would seem inappropriate to him that we should not be party to these exchanges'. Maisky could not resist the temptation of again pushing through his own initiatives. He shared with Eden a serious concern that the procedure adopted in consulting the Americans was bound to lead to procrastination and allow the effect of the foreign secretary's own visit to dissipate. He therefore defied instructions from Moscow to keep a low profile,[10] and 'pleaded once more earnestly' with Eden (after learning that Welles had disclosed to Litvinov Roosevelt's wish to bypass the British and open direct dialogue with Stalin) that he should not suspend his response to Moscow for long. The two now conspired to launch tripartite conversations in London, leading to 'close co-operation, both for the conduct of the war and in the period after the war'.[11] In a private letter, Maisky expressed to Kollontay his guarded optimism, and concluded with a cryptic comment that while he could not tell 'how complicated the situation will become in the future … perhaps fate is heading to some sort of a new crossroads'.[12]]

31 January[13]

Three-day parliamentary debate (27–28/1) on government policy. Vote of confidence: 464 to 1, with 27 abstentions. A smart move by Churchill: show your confidence! 'The 1922 Committee' wants debates without votes ('to poison the atmosphere', to undermine Churchill's prestige). The figures are a bit artificial. But Churchill's position is secure. The air has been cleared to some extent. Yet the ship of state does not find itself in calm waters.

The reasons: (1) situation at the front. Imminent threat of losing Singapore and Dutch Indies, invasion of Australia and India. Turning point in the Pacific no earlier than the end of 1942. Libya – Rommel[i] not destroyed, but advancing. Even if the English allow Rommel no farther than Bengasi (or even throw him out of there), Tripoli can't be taken… The enemy holds Tripoli, the Mediterranean is closed, French North Africa follows the lead of Vichy, second front in Europe *unthinkable*. Life for the government won't be easy. (2) Production: 30% of resources are not used. According to Shvernik[ii] and others. In essence: private ownership, poor organization, multiple authorities squabbling with each other, bureaucracy. Production is organized worse than under Lloyd George. Churchill's personality: politician, orator, writer(?), historian, …, but not an economist, not an economic planner. Rooted in the landed aristocracy. Poor links with the City (unlike Chamberlain). Churchill doesn't understand and doesn't like economics. He brushes production problems aside, delegates them. A minister of food is required, but so far Churchill resists. Made vague concessions at the end of the debate. The likely outcome? A fight. (3) The reconstruction of the government: 100 members, 37 ministers. War Cabinet of 10. Declarations have been made (Churchill's speech). Churchill against, but conceded. Australia, New Zealand will send; Canada, South Africa not yet. The party balance in the government. No way to wage a 'total' war. An efficient centre is called for. High time. A struggle ahead. (4) India. War at the gates of India. British government's position …. Churchill's personality gets in the way (the 'revolt' of 1934 against 'revolutionary' Baldwin). Will Churchill shift? Who knows. Doubtful. *Troubles*.

Conclusion: government will have to contend with stormy weather in near future; many of the present ministers will be thrown overboard, but Churchill will stay. The bourgeois elite does not like or trust him, but can't do without him while war with Germany is still on. No other figure on the British political horizon of Churchill's quality and popularity.

5 February

Harriman.

Lunched tête-à-tête.

Moscow negotiations – difficulty – 'not a diplomat', etc.

Question of religion in USA.

Roosevelt's programme will be implemented with a 3-month delay.

Moscow protocol – 4–6 weeks late.

---

[i] Erwin Rommel, German field marshal nicknamed 'Desert Fox' by the British for his leadership of German and Italian forces in the North African campaign, 1940–43.

[ii] Nikolai Mikhailovich Shvernik, a leading Soviet trade unionist and economist; architect of the 'scorched earth' strategy which led to the evacuation of Soviet industry to the east following the German invasion of Russia.

... 50 ships for USSR.
Distribution of American products.
Hopkins committee – Britain and USA.
USSR? No. Reasons:
(a) No *intimacy* of intelligence.
(b) Specifications (military mission)
Litvinov – OK

Harriman's plan – meeting of Roosevelt and Stalin in Iceland or in the vicinity of the Bering Strait.

Reply to Harriman.

According to my information the Soviet government finds it very desirable that a meeting between Stalin and Roosevelt should take place. However, it should be taken into account that a very tense struggle is continuing on the Soviet–German front. Mr S., who is responsible for the conduct of the military operations, cannot leave the USSR at such a time. Wouldn't regions of Arkhangelsk or Astrakhan do?[14]

The Soviet government and Mr S. personally express their conviction that relations between the USSR and the USA, which entered upon a period of steady improvement and which are being strengthened on the basis of the struggle against common foe, will show further improvement. The Soviet government will do its best in this direction.

London, 27 February 1942[15]
Dear Maksim Maksimovich [Litvinov],

I deem it necessary to bring the following to your attention: On 2 February Harriman arrived in London from America, he called me on the 4th and invited me to lunch with him on the 5th. We lunched, just the two of us, in Harriman's hotel room. First we discussed various topics, but then Harriman asked whether it would be possible to arrange a meeting between Roosevelt and Stalin. Harriman believes that there is a great deal of distrust between the USA and the USSR, as well as between the USSR and England. The best way of eliminating it would be a personal meeting between Roosevelt and Stalin. Harriman knows that Roosevelt would be eager to meet, but how about Stalin? Harriman suggested either Iceland or the area around the Bering Strait as the location for the meeting, stressing that it makes no odds to Roosevelt whose territory is chosen for the meeting.

After hearing Harriman out, I began by asking whether there had been any conversations on this matter with you in Washington. For the matter in question lies entirely within your competence. Harriman replied that he did not know whether there had been any talks with you on this topic, and conceded that there may not have been, for the whole question was still too 'raw' for the US government to consider it possible to sound out the Soviet ambassador officially or even semi-officially. I gained the impression from what Harriman told me that the possibility of a meeting between Roosevelt and Stalin is being discussed not in the State Department, but among people in the president's circle such as Hopkins, Harriman and others, and that they probably thought it more convenient and less binding to probe our intentions on this issue through London rather than Washington and via the Harriman–Maisky route rather than the Hull–Litvinov one. It's not for nothing that Harriman stressed several times during lunch that he was 'not a diplomat, but a businessman' and that he was not associated with the State Department.

I reported our conversation to Moscow and received a reply eight days later stating that the Soviet government deemed the meeting desirable; but since Stalin could not leave the USSR because of the tense situation at the front, Arkhangelsk or Astrakhan were proposed as the site of the meeting. I informed Harriman of this. Our second conversation took place after the *Scharnhorst* and the *Gneisenau* had broken through the Channel. Harriman reacted to my message by declaring that due to the increased danger in the North Atlantic he now thought it unwise to arrange the meeting in Iceland or near Arkhangelsk. As for the Caspian Sea, it was too far away – the president would not be able to leave the USA for such a long period at present. So according to Harriman there was only one place left – the Bering Strait. For Roosevelt, at least, that would be the most convenient location. I expressed doubts about the possibility of a meeting in a region so distant from Moscow (indeed today I received confirmation from Moscow that the Bering Strait was unacceptable). Harriman recognized the validity of my doubts. He nonetheless wished to continue exploring, in an unofficial manner, various avenues for a meeting between Roosevelt and Stalin. He added that since the practical possibility of a meeting had not yet taken shape, the best way of handling the matter was through an unofficial exchange of opinions. For the failure of this project, even if caused by purely geographical problems, might leave an unpleasant taste.

This is how things stand at present. I wished to inform you about the afore-said in a purely personal manner because the matter lies within your competence and I was involved in it quite against my will and desires. It goes without saying that I'll hand the matter over to Washington at the first opportunity.

I press your hand warmly,
I. Maisky
P.S. I am typing myself, as I often do.

[For three key players – Halifax and Litvinov in Washington, and Maisky in London – the situation was alarmingly reminiscent of 1939. All three were virtually 'in exile', little trusted by their own governments. Halifax, atoning for mistakes he might have committed on the eve of war, was most eager to forestall a separate Soviet–German peace and to foster the alliance. Litvinov strove for the same goal, but shared Stalin's and Molotov's distrust of the British, who had let him down in Munich and during the negotiations for a triple alliance. Maisky and Litvinov, arguably the most effective advocates of their country's interests, continued to be deadly rivals of Molotov. Apart from Kollontay, they were the only active survivors of the old school of Soviet diplomacy. Litvinov, markedly outspoken and independent, continued to be at daggers drawn with Molotov and was increasingly subject to harassment. For a short while, Maisky – as always, cautious and subservient (though in a subversive way) – was left to his own devices. At times, as his letter to Litvinov indicates, he was placed in a most embarrassing personal situation, such as when he was used as a go-between with the Americans, behind Litvinov's back.]

15 February

What is England's reaction to the military successes of the USSR in the last 10 weeks?

On the whole everyone is pleased. Particularly against the backdrop of the failures in Libya, Malaya, etc. How pleasant it is to have good news, at least from one front – the front of fronts! It is gradually sinking in: it's on our front that the fate of the war will be decided, and from there that salvation will come. The prestige of the Red Army is growing. Rapturous admiration. The myth of German 'invincibility' has been destroyed. We'll crush the German army soon. The question is asked half in jest, half in earnest: 'Couldn't we borrow a couple of your generals?' Cripps has raised the prestige of the 'young' Soviet generals. Gratitude to us for the absence of air raids for nine months. Invasion – paled. The USSR is most popular. So long as I'm not strangled by friendly embraces. A hundred invitations in January!

Analysis. The masses are pleased and have no reservations. The ruling class have a few. Two souls in the breast of the English ruling class: Churchill's and Chamberlain's. Churchill's position: Germany encroached upon the Empire and Britain's global positions. She must be crushed. The Russians are beating Germany and will possibly destroy her. Good. The Russians will do the dirty work and once the show is over the English will march ceremoniously into

Berlin having suffered no great losses. At the peace conference, England, together with the USA, will provide a 'healthy counterweight' to the Moscow Bolsheviks. Everything is in our interests. We will gain a cheap victory. Just let the Russians do their job. Chamberlain's position: What if the Russians reach Berlin alone? If they become too strong? If the Red Army becomes master of the continent? The Bolshevization of Europe? An enforced 'Soviet peace'? Who will be able to stop them?...

The Churchill group (Eden, Beaverbrook, Bracken, Cranborne and others) hates Germany with a passion and is ready to join forces with the Bolsheviks in order to crush her. The Chamberlain group (Margesson, Anderson, K. Wood and others) hates communism with a passion and is prepared to reach a compromise with Germany (the German generals and landlords in particular) in order to avoid this danger. Labour's position is undefined (spineless, hates communism).

For as long as our successes remain reasonably modest, the reserves of the ruling class will keep silent. But what if the Red Army starts approaching Berlin? And on their own to boot? A nightmare! Cold sweat!

And such a situation is possible: 1942, 1943. If our calculations prove justified (there are good grounds for them), the Red Army might reach Berlin alone, before England and the USA. To avoid this, the English might race to open a 'second front' at the end of this year. Can they do it? I doubt it. The sabotaging of our supplies is conceivable in order to put off a 'decision' till 1943, when Britain and the USA will be better prepared.

Which soul has the advantage? If a proletarian revolution happens in Germany, the Chamberlain faction will triumph. If not, Churchill will remain on top till the end of the war. The reasons: (a) The British masses hate fascism. This is Churchill's chief support. (b) The loss of occupied Malaysia, Singapore (things are bad), and probably the Dutch Indies – 'the pledge that Britain will stand firm in the struggle against Germany'. (c) The desire to strike a balance between the USSR and the USA so as to avoid the 'annexation' of the British Empire by the United States. American talk before 22 June 1941 about the post-war reorganization of the 'English-speaking world'. Washington as the centre and England the European outpost. Now, perpetual 'balancing' is a possibility. Theory: England as 'a bridge' between capitalist USA and socialist USSR. (Bracken).

Conclusion: Excluding a 'proletarian revolution', England will stick with us till the end. And after the war? Gallup in *News Chronicle*: 86% would like to cooperate with the USSR after the war, 53% are sure this will happen. Reflects the apprehension of the masses that after the war the English and American bourgeoisie might wish to oppose themselves to the USSR. But until then – *OK*.

18 February

The political atmosphere has remained tense and uneasy. I was in parliament on the 17th. Churchill spoke about the fall of Singapore. He did not look well, was irritated, easily offended and obstinate. The MPs were caustic and sniffy. They gave Churchill a bad reception and a bad sending-off. I've never seen anything like it. Sharp questions made the PM angry. One episode: an MP demanded that a judge be appointed chairman of the committee investigating the issue of the *Scharnhorst* and the *Gneisenau*. Churchill jumped to his feet and replied irritably that the work and composition of the committee was a secret matter. Protests. A verbal skirmish. Oppressive atmosphere. Churchill yielded: it turned out that the chairman had already been appointed – Judge Bucknill[i]... So what was the problem? Churchill's nervousness. After Churchill's performance it became clear: a general debate could not be avoided. But when? Churchill dug his heels in again. It was decided: next week. My general impression: a crisis is brewing.

From parliament I went to see Beaverbrook on supply matters. Beaverbrook was irritated and alarmed. Unhappy with the post of 'food minister': 'As Beaverbrook, I can do something, as food minister – nothing.' Hardly surprising. We talked about the breakthrough by the German vessels. My diagnosis: 'flagrant incompetence or treason'. Beaverbrook rejected 'treason'. I said: one or the other. General political topics. Evident that Beaverbrook expects a crisis soon.

Highly probable. The general situation is clear. The role of Churchill personally: he makes it ever more difficult even for his friends to support his government. 'I answer for everything!' This means that one can't criticize the ministers, generals, etc., although no shortage of fools, mediocrities and potential representatives of the 'fifth column' have gathered under his protective umbrella. 'The War Cabinet is good, no changes are called for!' (high time for a War Cabinet of the Lloyd George type). Criticism is growing as a result. Parliament, the press, the masses. The role of defeats. Yesterday's session has shown: the wave of discontent is high. If Churchill continues to be stubborn, he may be engulfed. But I think Churchill will yield: he will make a compromise.

Who could succeed Churchill if he resigned? Two names are widely touted: Eden and Cripps. Eden has been touted for some time. Cripps's star has risen meteorically of late (particularly after his speeches over the wireless and in Bristol). The reasons: the common man is convinced that Cripps 'brings luck' ('Russia has entered the war'), that he is 'fresh' and 'outside the parties' (the people are sick and tired of parties), progressive, clever, a good orator and, most importantly, has bet on the right horse – the USSR. The symptoms: Cripps

---

[i] Sir Alfred Townsend Bucknill was an English judge and a privy counsellor specializing in maritime law.

received 3,000 letters of sympathy after his radio speech. On the morning of the 18th, Cripps spoke at a private meeting of MPs about Eden's proposals concerning the USSR. Only 20 MPs remained at the official session; Cripps had 400. Cripps got an ovation (from members of all parties). Will Cripps's popularity last? Doubtful. As for now, if not PM, he'll become a member of the War Cabinet at the earliest reshuffle.

Personally, I'm for Churchill as PM. He is reliable: against Germany. Strong-willed: he rules on his own. Neither Cripps nor Eden is strong enough. Churchill has his feet firmly on the ground. Seems to be ready to compromise. Churchill told me that he had an eight-hour talk about India with Cripps last week. Churchill accepts: the legislative assembly of the provinces will elect delegations which together will form an all-India consultative parliament. After the war it becomes the constituent assembly. The British government undertakes in advance to accept the constitution that the assembly will devise. The viceroy's council will turn into an all-India government. India is being mobilized for war on this basis. It is possible that after yesterday's sitting of the House, Churchill will make concessions both on the question of the government and on the question of the military command. The need for this becomes ever more obvious. When I was leaving parliament yesterday, an MP I know stopped me in the lobby and asked: 'What could lead to an outburst of enthusiasm in England today?' – 'What indeed?' – 'If Marshal Timoshenko were to be appointed commander-in-chief of the British army!'

20 February

(1) Government reshuffle sooner than…

Churchill has agreed to a compromise on the matter of the Cabinet… Remained…

Skilful tactician.

A sharp attack in the forthcoming debates … But…

Response in the press: a step forward, but…

First … India. Subsequent reshuffle of the government. Production … Changes ahead.

(2) Details.

By the evening of 18th and on 19th: symptoms of restructuring.

Beaverbrook's visit – what's got into him?

Agitated. 'More than before'.

… Wearing the robe. Line in favour of the USSR.

King's … lit up…

'*Old tough guy*' is still useful.

The same in England …

Eden – 10.30 – what's it all about?
Beaverbrook? *Supply?*
My proposal …
K. Wood, Margesson, Cranborne.

Beaverbrook's misfortunes: (1) military staffs (he managed their resources); (2) industrialists (did not make it up with Beaverbrook and Bevin's *shop stewards*). (3) Two souls: Chamberlain and Churchill supporters among the ruling classes – the reconstruction strengthened the latter group.

On the whole, reshuffle is a plus. Beaverbrook – minus. Will Cripps replace him?

Cripps played a good hand. Became member of the War Cabinet and 'leader of the House of Commons' (a good post for him + *lime light*). Has ironic satisfaction of leading the Labour Party (together with the others) which expelled him three years ago. A man without a party is the leader of the House of Commons (under Lloyd George there was Bonar Law). Cripps's story over the last couple of years is an English political fairy tale. His strong position is all thanks to the reflected light of the USSR's power and the Red Army's heroism.

[Cripps's reception by the public after his return from Moscow was reminiscent of Churchill's 'finest hour' a year earlier. Eden did not even exclude the possibility of serving as minister of war in a Cabinet led by Cripps.[16] It was reckoned in political circles that 'each week his stature will grow' while Churchill's might 'correspondingly sink'. All that was needed was for Cripps 'to make a first-class speech in the House giving a lead to the nation and things political might then begin to take some shape'.[17] Cripps's vow not to serve in a Cabinet alongside Beaverbrook eventually forced the resignation of the latter. It was widely assumed, as Winant informed Washington, that Cripps's entry into the War Cabinet signalled the 'intensification of efforts for closer relations with Russia'.[18] No wonder Maisky was quick to congratulate Cripps on his appointment to the War Cabinet – something he hoped would 'augur well for the conduct of the war in general and for relations between the Soviet and Great Britain in particular'. He expected Cripps's 'knowledge' of Russia and 'understanding of foreign affairs' to facilitate the settlement of the outstanding problems while 'laying the foundations for closer collaboration after the war'.[19] But Beaverbrook was right in claiming that Cripps was 'playing the Russians up while in reality *he* was the only genuine supporter of Russia in Cabinet', and that his own resignation meant 'trouble for the Russians'.[20] Churchill fell back on his abundant political experience to sustain his authority. He neutralized Cripps by including him in the War Cabinet and appointing him Leader of the House. This role, as Churchill must have known, did not suit Cripps's spartan, righteous and ascetic personality: it was a time-consuming task and it alienated him from his potential supporters. When discussions on Russia gathered momentum in March, Cripps was entrusted with a protracted and forlorn mission to India – 'a masterly stroke' by Churchill which 'had shown him up'.[21] In such circumstances, Cripps's continued presence in the Cabinet with little to show for it gradually gnawed away at his credibility. He was the obvious loser when forced to resign his seat in the War Cabinet at the end of the year, following victory at El Alamein.[22]]

25 February

Positive changes in the government (Margesson, Moore-Brabazon and Moyne[i] removed and replaced by Grigg, Llewellin[ii] and Cranborne). Strengthening of the Churchill wing. The disappearance of Greenwood together with his ministry is understandable: Churchill had to balance dismissals among the Tories, too. Greenwood was an obvious candidate: weak and a drunkard. The abolition of the Ministry of Reconstruction is yet further proof of Churchill's lack of interest in the future. He says: my task is to win the war; let someone else clear up the mess once it's over.

Grigg – a new precedent, treated with suspicion by parliament: a civil servant turned minister. Grigg used to work for the finance department (in India in particular), and was appointed undersecretary for war in 1939. He is tough, resolute and a good organizer. What sort of war minister is he? Time will tell.

Results: Chamberl. … in the gov. less decisive; more for struggle. But half-heartedly. The reaction of the country and parliament: 'Give him a chance!' Churchill was more composed and assured in the Commons on the 24th than on the 17th, and the MPs more satisfied and obedient. Content, but waiting. Loud applause at the mention of the Red Army, China's joining the Pacific War Council, and Cripps's appointment to the War Cabinet.

Churchill defended himself in the Commons (military failures and so on). Not a word about India. The air has not yet been cleared. Further complications are likely, especially due to the unsatisfactory situation at the fronts.

26 February

Eden.

I pose the question of additional supplies in March–April to those stipulated by the Moscow protocol: the spring offensive and the danger for lines of communication (ships breaking through). Eden promises to do all he can.

Eden says he handed Winant, who flew off today, a memorandum for Roosevelt in the spirit of my conversation with Winant (although we hadn't

---

[i] Walter Edward Guinness (1st Baron Moyne), secretary of state for the colonies, 1941–42; leader of the House of Lords, 1941–42; deputy minister of state, Cairo, 1942–44.

[ii] John Jestyn Llewellin, parliamentary secretary, Ministry of War Transport, 1941–42; president of the Board of Trade, 1942; minister of aircraft production, February–November 1942.

agreed on this). Eden is all for speeding up the signing of the treaties. Gives it a month. I said: if he doesn't sign it very soon, the effect of Eden's visit to Moscow will evaporate.

Eden is satisfied with the restructuring of the government: it has become more amicable and competent. Great hopes for Cripps. His first speech in parliament was a success.

I voice my impression: the country and the parliament are ready to give the government 'a chance', but without much enthusiasm. Eden agrees.

28 February

At Beaverbrook's in *Cherkley*. Dinner. Harriman and his daughter. Mrs R. Churchill, M. Foot[i] and others.

Before dinner – in the billiard room… Portrait of Stalin between those of Roosevelt and the king on *mantelpiece.*

Agitated. He wants Stalin to know the truth.[23]

Note of resignation. Reasons (15 Feb.).

Period of 25 Jan. – 25 Feb. 1942.

Minister of food – many obligations without rights.

Duncan against Beaverbrook's direct contacts with the *controllers.*

(Churchill first against, then for).

Alexander – *Shipbuilding* (minister of shipbuilding).

Chief of staff.

Bevin – labour. [indecipherable] (fight because of shop stewards).

Churchill's position – wavers, squabbling with Beaverbrook.

Beaverbrook against Cripps as *Leader of the H.*

(Eden)

Against Attlee as ….

(Clashes with A.)

Not 'the Russian question' at bottom.

Afraid of becoming a *scapegoat.*

When re-entering the gov.

Future prime minister?

For Russia! Always!

In the Atlantic (American and British military gave you three weeks!). – Promise of aid to the USSR.

Conference in Moscow.

Meeting their commitments – (December and January!).

Now – questions in the House of Lords. The press.

[i] Michael Foot, assistant editor, *Tribune,* 1937–38; acting editor, *Evening Standard*, 1942; Labour MP, 1945–55 and 1960–92.

96. The Maiskys charmed by Averell Harriman and his daughter Kathleen.

2 March

Beaverbrook.

Came in the evening.

Utmost support to the USSR. It's easier outside than inside the government. Stalin will see this. If there's anything Stalin wants, Beaverbrook is always at his disposal…

Concentrating on supplies… Second front.

Concept: England could not win until the USSR entered the war. Even with the USA. It can after the USSR entered, but the USSR will play the major role. England and the USA – not armies, generals, etc. Hence – assistance to the USSR in every way possible. 'Our hope'.

Unprecedented popularity of the USSR in England (unlike France in 1914–18). Stalin's prestige is very high…

Understands Stalin's resentment: 'I'm fighting alone' (order 23 Feb.).

Military situation in the Pacific – Dutch Indies lost. The Japanese will go on … to India, not to Australia.

[Roaming around his Savoy suite in his 'pyjamas and a Jaeger dressing-jacket … surrounded by Secretaries and valets', Beaverbrook told Bruce Lockhart that he was 'keen to put his Russian deal over in Washington. His real job was to "sell" an

Anglo-American-Russian agreement to Roosevelt.'[24] En route to the United States, he reaffirmed his personal loyalty to Churchill – but not before waving at him his own programme for assistance to Russia, which could hardly have pleased the prime minister. It called for recognition of the 1941 Russian frontiers, an increase in supplies, and an expedition into Europe.[25] Eden and his entourage did not take Beaverbrook's self-engineered invitation to the White House seriously. They doubted whether he 'cuts much ice' with either Roosevelt or Stalin, 'who know their own gangsters'.[26] Halifax did not fail to warn Hopkins that the visit was bound to 'create difficulties with other responsible people', and was assured that the Americans 'never intended for Max to come ... and if there was any idea of him settling down here to tell everyone how to do their job, that would be in his view pretty disastrous'. He was neither helped by the fact that Winant had incited Roosevelt against him, dwelling on how he had 'so harried' Churchill since his return from Washington.[27]]

3 March

At Eden's house in the country. 1 March. Conversation about a 'bloc of eight states'. Eden is against it; has given appropriate instructions to Strang and Makins.[i] Eden holds that federations of states should be rational and established with the support of the great powers, not against them.

Sikorski suggested Spaak go to America and make a statement about the war, its objectives, etc. Spaak consulted with Eden. The latter dissuaded him. Who needs another declaration? The crucial thing is not declarations, but the struggle against Hitler. Now Spaak won't go. The trouble is that all these statesmen in exile have nothing to do, but they still want to be in the *limelight*. That's why they fuss and fume. Strang and Makins must have had a hand in it somehow.

4 March

Cripps.

Cripps dined at mine.

Cripps is trying hard to conclude arrangements for the treaty. The Cabinet has accepted the 1941 borders, albeit without much enthusiasm. Eden and Cripps in favour, Attlee and Bevin sabotage, Churchill agrees unenthusiastically. Churchill's mood can be explained by his desire for close military cooperation with the USSR, but he is not sure this will be achieved even after signing the treaty. What a fine thing it would be for us to show that this is possible! My dispute with Cripps. Cripps's grievances (the story of the northern operations which was discussed in Moscow, Evstigneev, difficulties between MacFarlane and our general staff, etc.). In the end Cripps acknowledged that the British military mission is not living in such bad conditions.

---

[i] Roger Mellor Makins, served on staff of resident minister in West Africa, 1942; counsellor, 1942.

'Unfortunately, about a year ago, when England was fighting alone and wanted to involve the USA in the war, the British government promised the Americans not to recognize changes in the European borders without prior consultation. England became wholly dependent on the Americans. It's awkward, but what can be done?' The Americans are in no hurry (the proposal for the treaty was sent three weeks ago). Cripps's plan to send Eden to the USA failed. Internal crisis. They sent Winant.

Churchill will make a statement on India next week. Cripps considers the planned referendum a major step forward. Hopes for a good reception in India (not sure). Asks for sympathetic treatment from the Soviet press and radio.

5 March

Eden and Cripps.

Military situation: (1) Libya. The English have good defensive positions and hope to hold them. They have 600 tanks and 800 more have been shipped. Superiority in the air and in artillery. Rommel has 600 tanks. The Germans have the upper hand in armoured fire power and tactics. English objective – to take Bengasi (important to relieve the situation in Malta and disrupt communications between Italy and Tripoli). We'll see what happens. England found a good commander there – Ritchie[i] (40 years old). Eden is glad we sent a military mission to Libya. (2) Far East. Dutch Indies are considered lost. Now it's Burma's turn. The British government will be defending her, but not sure of holding her. Unlikely the Japanese will proceed to Australia. Japan may strike at India, but it's a big country and the Japanese may well get stuck. Moreover, next week Churchill will make an important statement on India in parliament, which will radically change the situation. The British government thinks that after Burma the Japanese will hardly be willing to extend their lines of communication further. The balance of power at sea will begin to change in favour of the Anglo-American navy in May–June (the ships damaged in Pearl Harbor will be repaired, supplemented by new ones).

6 March

Moore-Brabazon, the dismissed minister of aircraft production, visited me to 'explain himself and clear up the misunderstandings that have arisen between us'. I told him I knew of no 'misunderstandings' but was ready to listen to him.

[i] Sir Neil Methuen Ritchie, general, replaced General Cunningham as the commander of the British Eighth Army in the North African campaign; dismissed by Churchill in June 1942, after the defeats by Rommel.

M-B feels outraged. He has been slandered. Last August he had to speak unexpectedly, without any preparations, at a lunch chaired by A. Simon in Manchester. About 100 people were present. He said: there was a time when many in England were saying: 'Let the Germans and the Russians cut each other throats, that will help us.' The Russians were saying at that time: 'Let the British and the Germans cut each other throats, that will help us.' But everything changed on 22 June. The Russians are now our allies and our friends, etc.

What happened then? Blackburn (of the Manchester mechanics' union) sent a protest to Simon, in which he blamed M-B for allegedly saying: 'Let the Germans and the Russians cut each other's throats, while we, the British, wait until they all get weak before establishing our rule in Europe.' Blackburn relayed the same to Jack Tanner[i] and the latter made it public at the Trades Union Congress in Edinburgh in September. M-B has had no peace since then. His name has been associated everywhere with the enemies of the USSR and he's been hounded at meetings and in the press. And now Churchill has been forced to *drop* him. Out of concern for his good name, M-B came to assure me that Blackburn had slandered him. He was the opponent of Munich, Baldwin and Chamberlain. He has always been a friend of the USSR, especially now. He did all he could to supply us with aircraft. He asked me to restore his reputation in left circles. I made do with some noncommittal phrases.

How typical this incident is! A symptom of the strengthening of leftist sentiments in the country and our growing prestige.

10 March

Since 20 February the Majlis has been discussing the structure of the Iranian government. On 23 February all the ministers resigned. Foroughi[ii] formed a new Cabinet. The Majlis approved it by a small majority on 2 March. Within a few hours Foroughi resigned. The shah entrusted Soheili[iii] with forming a new government. Soheili eventually did so, and the Majlis approved it by a huge majority.

Two new candidates for the premiership have emerged: Qavām Saltaneh[iv] (an English agent who plays at being a democrat) and Tadayon[v] (a reactionary Muslim and enemy of the USSR). Tadayon is under the patronage of Bullard.[vi]

[i] Jack Tanner, president of the Amalgamated Engineering Union, 1939–54.

[ii] Mohammad Ali Khan Foroughi, Iranian prime minister, 1925–26, 1933–35 and 1941–42.

[iii] Ali Soheili, Iranian prime minister March–August 1942 and 1943–44, ambassador in Britain 1953.

[iv] Ahmad Qavām os-Saltaneh, served five times as Iranian prime minister between 1922 and 1952.

[v] Mohammad Tadayon was the Iranian minister of education during the war.

[vi] Sir Reader Bullard, British ambassador to Tehran, 1939–46.

Without consulting Smirnov,[i] Bullard expressed to the Persians his wish to see Tadayon as head of the Iranian government. He then informed Smirnov, leaving it to him to advise the Persians about his own wishes. We supported Forughi, and then, when he resigned, gave our backing to Soheili.

Smirnov saw the shah, at the latter's invitation, on 7 March. The shah informed him that Soheili would be forming the Cabinet, that the Majlis supported him, and that Soheili's Cabinet would most probably hold out. The shah said that in its foreign policy the new government would take a more explicitly friendly line towards the USSR. The shah would give instructions to this effect to Soheili. The shah said that Iranian troops should be kept in various places to maintain order. Smirnov replied that we were ready to discuss bringing a Persian garrison into the area where our troops are deployed.[28]

[It had become 'daily clearer' to Eden that full strategic talks with Stalin were indispensable, but that unless the frontier issue was cleared out of the way, Stalin would 'neither talk nor listen'. On 7 March, he persuaded a reluctant Churchill that 'the only way of tilting the American scale' was through a personal message to Roosevelt. Churchill's real motive for making the approach was his desire to recruit Russia against Japan in the Far East.[29] He was also under considerable pressure at home. The treaty was, as Cripps put it, the 'acid test' and a small price to pay for continued Soviet resistance.[30] The Foreign Office espoused the views of Bruce Lockhart, an old Russia hand, who observed the 'discomfort' in the United States and Russia over the absence of British support, and the resurgence of old suspicions that Britain wished to see Russia 'bleed White'. 'If we go on dallying with Russia,' he argued, 'we shall lose her.' The Soviet government had to be 'treated as a Great Power ... If it is patronised, it will not only resent such treatment, but will out do us in bad behaviour.' Perhaps even more powerful was the negative argument that only an immediate intervention on the continent would secure a sufficiently strong presence of Anglo-American forces to 'hinder any possible expansionist plans of the Soviet Government'.[31]

'The increasing gravity of the war,' Churchill cabled to Roosevelt, 'has led me to feel that the principles of the Atlantic Charter ought not to be construed so as to deny Russia the frontiers she occupied when Germany attacked her ... I hope therefore that you will be able to give us a free hand to sign the treaty which Stalin desires as soon as possible. Everything portends an immense renewal of the German invasion of Russia in the spring and there is very little we can do to help the only country that is heavily engaged with the German armies.' Halifax was dumbfounded by Churchill's 'sharp change of front on Russia', given that he had been calling Eden 'every name from a dog to a pig for suggesting composition with Stalin'. It is hardly surprising that Halifax found Roosevelt to be 'very sticky', preaching 'general morality' and referring to hostile public opinion. And yet he was convinced that if he had a chance to meet Stalin he could settle the issue 'in five minutes'.[32] In view of the obvious disagreements with Washington, Churchill, too, suggested to Maisky that he would like to 'meet Stalin at somewhere like Baku'.[33]

---

[i] Andrei Andreevich Smirnov, Soviet ambassador in Iran, 1942–43.

After Halifax had officially submitted Stalin's demands, he encountered a defiant Welles, who was committed to a new world order based 'on principle – if it was not again to crash'. He was little moved by Halifax's contention that President Wilson's[i] ideas of 'self-determination ... had not stood up against the stress of power politics', and that if Russia were to be kept in the Allied camp in the war, Stalin's 'exaggerated claims or suspicions' had to be urgently dispelled. To stall the British initiative, Welles prevailed on Roosevelt to 'stick to the Atlantic Charter', convincing him that he was better positioned than the British to reach an agreement with Stalin.[34]

Roosevelt dismissed Churchill's approach in a paternalistic way, 'without too much gravity, saying what Churchill needed was a pat on the back'. The chiefs of staff and Roosevelt's close advisers, who were summoned for consultations at the White House, were quick to recognize that the gist of the prime minister's long message was: 'we would be unable to get our victory in '43 but would have to wait till '44'. They were most critical of the suspension, which was bound to lead to 'further dispersion and plugging up all leaks'. Of the various alternatives, the president now seemed 'strongly and favourably impressed' by the orthodox line of sending an overwhelming force to the British Isles and 'giving Hitler two fronts to fight on if it could be done in time while the Russians were still in'.[35] Eisenhower,[ii] who had been assigned by Marshall[iii] to examine the war plans to defeat Japan and Germany, reinforced Stimson's[iv] views. Standing up in front of the secretary of war's large map of the world, he drew a 'sharp line' around the 'no go' areas, namely Australia and the Mediterranean, which he defined as 'a secondary theatre'. He considered the task of keeping Russia at war to be 'of primary importance for, if she [went] out of the war, he could see nothing better than a stalemate for us'.[36] The demarcation of spheres of activity assigned the Pacific theatre to the Americans and the Mediterranean to the British. The European and Atlantic areas were reinstated as the theatres in which 'the major effort against Germany would be made' and jointly entrusted to the British and Americans. Roosevelt also left Churchill in no doubt that he was 'more and more interested in the establishment of this new front this summer, certainly for air and raids'.[37] He was convinced, as he intimated to his Treasury secretary, that the only reason the Americans were in better standing with the Soviet Union was that they had kept their promises, while the British had let the Russians down. 'Nothing,' he said, 'would be worse than to have the Russians collapse ... I would rather lose New Zealand, Australia or anything else than have the Russians collapse.' In short, Roosevelt later scribbled on a paper: 'Russian resistance counts most today.'[38]

Litvinov was summoned to the White House on 12 March and was bluntly told by the president that, as 'it was difficult to do business with the English and the Foreign Office', he preferred to discuss the Baltic issue directly with him. Roosevelt was cunningly accommodating towards the Russians, recognizing in principle their claim to the region

[i] Thomas Woodrow Wilson, an academic who became president of the United States, 1913–1921, and who introduced the 21 principles upon which the League of Nations was founded.

[ii] Dwight David Eisenhower, general, sent to England as commander of European theatre of operations in March 1942; commander-in-chief Allied forces in North Africa, November, 1942–44; supreme commander, Allied Expeditionary Force in Western Europe, 1944–45.

[iii] George Catlett Marshall, chief of staff of the United States Army, 1939–45; secretary of state, 1947–49.

[iv] Henry Stimson, US secretary of war, 1929–33 and then throughout the Second World War, despite being 72 at the time of his appointment.

which had been torn from Russia after the First World War. However, faced with hostile public opinion at home, he wished to defer discussion to the peace conference. This was counterbalanced by a revelation of the pressure he was exerting on the British to open a second front. Reporting home, the ambassador grudgingly complained that he could have demolished Roosevelt's arguments concerning the treaty had he not been aware that Molotov was 'no longer interested in an agreement with England'.[39] Within a couple of days, Roosevelt introduced a coup in relations with Russia. While appearing to woo Churchill, he mercilessly hammered home the repercussions of the military disasters on Churchill's political standing, in order to justify his independent approach to the Russians: 'I know you will not mind my being brutally frank when I tell you that I think I can personally handle Stalin better than either your Foreign Office or my State Department. Stalin hates the guts of all your top people. He thinks he likes me better, and I hope he will continue to do so.'

To leave Churchill in no doubt about his intentions of assuming command in the military sphere, too, he promised to send him within days 'a more definite plan for a joint attack in Europe itself'.[40]

Churchill's position, as Beaverbrook observed, had become 'very weak', while cooperation with the Americans was crumbling, as evinced by Roosevelt's 'very disappointing' response to Churchill's telegram. Rather than acquiesce to the British suggestion that the political agreement would eliminate the 'danger of Russia's going out of the war', Roosevelt announced that he would 'have a word with Litvinoff and put things right'. The British, it was lamented in the Foreign Office, had been 'snubbed and, more or less, told we know nothing about Russia'.[41]]

10 March

A second English front in Europe is needed by the time all offensives are launched – or the only chance to win the war may be lost.

Roosevelt summoned Litvinov and spoke about the Baltics. He agrees in essence, but is against any open or secret agreement because of public opinion. R. said bluntly that if the British government were to conclude a secret agreement in secret from him, he would not object. – Moscow had informed L. earlier that it was no longer interested in an agreement.

Willkie is for the second front and activity. Success of L.'s speech.

11 March

Beav.

In the *Savoy* – Garvin with Beav. – Garv. left the room … waited till we finished our conversation (40–45 min).

(1) 'Things are better'. Churchill sends a *message* to Stalin. A good one. The first paragraph – telegram … recognition of '41 borders. Saw Churchill's telegram to Roosevelt. *OK*.

The crucial thing – Churchill is prime minister, mutual understanding and trust between Churchill and Stalin.

(2) Supplies. Letters and talks with Eden. Fulfil and exceed the protocol. 500 extra planes! – 50% increase in supplies from 1 June 1942 and 100% from 1 Jan. 1943. Promised by Beaverbrook. On the basis of British government 'guidelines' to Moscow conference … promised Stalin. *Committed.* Harriman the same. – I: is it true? My conversation with H…. – Telephone conversation between B. and H. in my presence. – H. accepts! – I: could it be documented? – B.: I'll announce it in the House of Lords tomorrow!

(3) B.'s disagreements with the government: (a) declaration of war on Finland, Rumania and Hungary – promise must be kept … USSR. Stalin's message. – Draft of Churchill's reply. – Attlee and Bev. oppose. – *Delay.* (b) Second front – B. has long been for it (memo to Cabinet in late summer). (c) 1941 borders – must be recognized. Attlee. 10/20 Jan. threatened to resign on account of the Baltics.

12 March

Eden handed me a copy of Churchill's message to Stalin of 9 March.

My questions: (1) When did Ch. send the telegram to Roosevelt and what reaction? Telegram sent 7 March. No reaction so far. Halifax communicated today that R. wants to talk with Litvinov on this matter. Halifax protested in conversation with Sumner Welles, but R.'s decision is firm. Eden reminded me that he is also against R.'s intervening in our talks on the treaties. (2) What is meant by 'other means' to alleviate USSR's situation (item 3 of the message)? Eden replied that in the first place – air offensive and raids. I asked: And in the second? Could it be a second front?… Eden neither rejected nor supported a second front.[42] The situation has changed. 'Wavering in the enemy's ranks.' I pressed on. Spoke in earnest about a second front. Recalled last year's arguments. Added a new one: an attack-minded spirit must be inculcated in the army (a burning issue now in both the War Ministry and the War Cabinet). Easiest to do this on the battlefield. The second front – a school. My argument hit home. Eden started talking about the army's morale. It suffers from inactivity. If this summer goes like the last one, who knows what will happen. Loss of morale. Promised to talk it over with Ch.

13 March

Eden.

The British government has accepted the 1941 borders. Approached Washington on the 10th. The question was formulated in such a way as to get a positive reply if possible, i.e. no objections on the part of the USA. Winant supports the British government but he doesn't know whether he expresses the opinion of the US government: he hasn't been to the USA for a long time; going in a few days. Promises cooperation.

Talked about the military situation. Eden is depressed by the events in the Far East. The loss of Singapore will be a heavy blow. The Singapore garrison was ordered to fight to the last. Not to retreat. Evacuation impossible. The British government will do its utmost to hold Dutch Indies, but will they succeed? I'm not sure.

The 'Pacific War Council' has been set up in London, although Australia wanted it in Washington. (Britain, Australia, New Zealand, Holland, but not the USA and China.) The military staffs are beneath it. Wavell commands military operations. In Washington a 'war committee' chaired by Roosevelt and including Dill. Tasks of the committee unclear. So too relations between London and Washington on this matter. Muddle and confusion so far.

[The failure to set up a common strategic and political platform presented the Russians with a serious dilemma as to how best to confront the looming German spring offensive. Maisky knew that the disasters inflicted on Britain in the Far East had raised doubts in Stalin's mind about the value of British assistance, 'sincerity, and determination to fight the war to a finish'. While the British 'clearly had an instinct for sea warfare', they 'did not seem to understand war on land'. Although he claimed to know better, Maisky dropped ominous hints that 'some, like Stalin, have never been out of Russia and find us more difficult to understand'. Stalin would tend to assume that 'we've passed the buck to Roosevelt and are hedging'.[43] This could prove disastrous, as Stalin expected 1942 to be the decisive year of the war and the one in which the Germans could be crushed, were Britain to embark on 'a big enterprise' in Italy or the Balkans – let alone a cross-channel attack. Maisky strove hard to eliminate the apparent discrepancy in the timetable, conscious that 'the British did not really want to win victory in 1942' and were preparing for victory in 1943.[44]

The growing disillusionment in Moscow was confirmed by Molotov's startling strict instructions to Litvinov to avoid raising the second front issue – instructions which the ambassador fiercely disputed. Now that the Americans were at war, he expected them to defend the British Isles, 'if not to get engaged in a direct landing in the continent'. Though promising to abide by the directive, in private conversations with prominent politicians and diplomats he argued fervently in favour of a second front. He did not hide from Molotov his intention of arguing in public that the idleness of the Allied armies was inadmissible, just when the destiny of the entire campaign was at stake.[45] Much irritated, Molotov dug in his heels. He deplored Churchill's numerous recent speeches in which he had dismissed the Russian initiative while 'paying no heed to the idea of a second front'.[46] When Litvinov persevered, speaking to foreign journalists in New York, he was roundly reprimanded by Moscow and again reminded that 'the Soviet Government was not at present pressing the Allies to open a second front'. He was castigated besides for warning the Americans that if they failed to mount an offensive against Hitler in the spring, they might 'find it too late to do so later'; by doing so, he presented the Soviet Union in a bad light, as 'unduly nervous and wrong'.[47] A few days later, he was further instructed to 'follow rigorously' Molotov's similar directives concerning the contemplated political agreement, and to confine his activities to ensuring the smooth flow of American supplies.[48] Litvinov was but little moved. He told Admiral Standley,[i] the newly appointed ambassador to Moscow, that although he 'was not empowered by his Government to press for a two front war, and did not believe that his Government was pressing the British for the establishment of a second front at this time, he was doing so in a personal capacity since he was convinced of the wisdom of such action'.[49] The following day, he triumphantly informed Narkomindel that, judging by the press, the call for a second front to be opened was 'falling on fertile ground'.[50]

The puzzling shift in the Soviet position has been either overlooked or misconstrued by Western scholars, who have often attributed the rumours of a separate peace to Stalin's attempts to scare and 'blackmail' the Western powers into further commitment. It is hardly surprising that the topic has been censored in Russian historiography.[51] The major driving force in the West to harness the Russians to the Allied camp was, as in 1939, fear of a German–Soviet reconciliation. The Soviet Union harboured similar suspicions of a possible Anglo-German separate peace. This explains why the proposed draft treaty between the Soviet Union and Great Britain included an undertaking by both sides 'not to enter into negotiations with the Hitlerite Government or any other Government of Germany that does not clearly renounce all aggressive intentions, and not to negotiate or conclude except by mutual consent any armistice or peace treaty with Germany'.[52]

The suspicion at the Foreign Office was enhanced by information from reliable sources that Stalin was deliberately raising artificial grievances against Britain to prevent Anglo-Russian relations from becoming genuinely cordial. It was even suggested that Maisky's complaints that Britain was 'not in earnest' were a component of a deliberate campaign to set the scene for a break with the Allies. Such suggestions seemed to be sustained by Stalin's order of the day to the Red Army on 23 February which implied that, once the country was liberated, the Soviet Union would be ready to make peace with the German people. It was also reported from Moscow that a general, speaking at the Palace of Culture on Red Army Day, had disclosed that two peace overtures had been made by the Germans.[53] Moreover, while anti-Nazi propaganda in the Soviet press subsided, trusted Swedish informers confirmed that Schulenburg had been summoned to confer with Hitler at Berchtesgaden on 4 March.[54] American intelligence, which was shared with the Kremlin, suggested that Hitler's main objective was 'to make peace with Stalin, if possible, on the basis of the present occupancy and possession of the Ukraine'. Only if he failed to conclude peace was Hitler expected to push on either to Moscow or to the Caucasus.[55]

It is indeed conceivable, and there are indications that, in desperation, Stalin resorted to the same tactics he had employed in the spring of 1939 and considered an approach to the Germans through Beria. The essence of this would have been cessation

---

[i] William Harrison Standley, admiral, chief of naval operations, 1933–37; US ambassador to the Soviet Union, 1941–43.

of hostilities with Germany by May 1942, coupled with the bait that Russia might join the war against the West by the end of 1943. The reward for the Russians would have been the reinstatement of the territorial arrangements of the Ribbentrop–Molotov Pact, supplemented by the allocation of spheres of influence in the Balkans, and most likely even in Greece, literally re-establishing the revered frontiers of the San Stefano Agreement, reached in the wake of the Russo-Turkish war of 1878.[56] This would explain the nervousness of both Litvinov and Maisky, and the cryptic comments in the diary (as well as the prolonged silences).

Such a probability is corroborated by an intriguing set of instructions from Molotov to Litvinov which disclosed the state of mind in the Kremlin:

> As is well known, the negotiations with Eden have failed to bring about the conclusion of the two agreements elaborated by us and the English. The proceedings did not go beyond verbal exchanges. Before departing from Moscow, Eden promised to promptly consult the government and the dominions, as well as the USA, about the issues which had been raised. Stalin declared, in his turn, that considering the failure to reach an agreement on the proposal made by our side (borders of 1941 for the USSR, etc.), it is assumed that the two parties were in no way bound by any obligations emanating from these negotiations. Therefore we regard the Moscow negotiations merely as precursory talks on various topics which are of interest to both countries. Since then negotiations between us and the British on this issue have not resumed, and at present we ourselves are not interested in continuing the Moscow negotiations. Whatever, we do not now consider it expedient to seize the initiative in this matter – we do not consider it expedient to rush the British. We particularly would not wish at present to see the United States meddling in this matter ...[57]

Maisky's optimism, as well as his survival instinct, impelled him, just as it had in 1939, to assume that the forging of the alliance was a foregone conclusion. He assured Kollontay that, after all the delays and complications, the agreements on military mutual aid during the war and cooperation on post-war reconstruction 'appear to be nearing completion'. Likewise, he believed in his power to sway the public mood in favour of a second front – a mood which was fast developing 'not just among the public at large ... but also in government circles'.[58]]

13 March (2)

Bruce,[i] Australia's high commissioner, came and asked whether I had received a reply to his request about the establishing of diplomatic relations with Australia. I said: not yet.

Bruce expounded the Australian point of view: Australia is a profoundly democratic country, far more so than England. The Australians are British,

---

[i] Stanley Melbourne Bruce, Australian high commissioner in London, 1933–45.

but they are dissatisfied with England in the military, economic and social spheres… England is too conservative and inert, and too aristocratic. England takes little interest in post-war reconstruction and dreams of the return of the old world. But the world will be different (e.g. India and Dutch Indies will cease to exist as colonies). Economic problems will play a decisive role. The USSR will be more important than Britain and the USA in solving them. Australia would like to be in close contact with the USSR, all the more so as both are Pacific countries. Bruce would like to maintain close contact with me.

Bruce doesn't count on effective aid from England. He counts on the USA (aircraft and troops). The USA cannot permit itself to lose Australia, the only base in the south-eastern part of the Pacific.

14 March

The Iranian envoy Taqizadeh[i] paid me his first visit.

Half-diplomat, half-scholar. Professorial manners combined with the cunning of a Persian bazaar. In 1922–23 concluded trade agreements in Moscow. Envoy in London in 1929–30, then in Paris. Resigned, scholarly research on the history of Persia, Islam, the calendar, etc. Published books in Engl. and Pers. Last few years in England. Appointed envoy three months ago. Regrets having to tear himself away from research.

Taqizadeh disapproves of the Anglo-Soviet occupation of Iran. He said 'there has been no German threat to Iran whatsoever'. The reason for the Anglo-Soviet actions: the desire to secure transit through Iran.

Having the impression that Taqizadeh was inclined to believe in and spread false rumours about the behaviour of our troops in Iran, etc., I started poking fun at such stories and said that if the Iranian government had any complaints, it should address the Soviet government directly (bypassing third powers) in Tehran or Kuibyshev.

Taqizadeh understood what I meant (I didn't name him directly) and agreed that I had indicated the correct course of action, but noted that there are 'restless elements' in Iran who initially thought that the Soviet authorities would support them, but are now convinced that this is not the case. Very well. Only the Soviet government should not seek to defend its every last agent in Iran, no matter whether he is right or not.

I explained to Taqizadeh that the Soviet government is guided by the principle of justice and has no expansionist tendencies. Iran has nothing to fear. Taqizadeh thanked me for the clarification, said he would 'clear the air', and promised to remain in close contact with me.

[i] Hassan Taqizadeh, Iranian ambassador in London, 1929–30 and 1941–47.

16 March

On Saturday, the 14th, I received Comrade Stalin's message to Churchill. I called the Foreign Office at once and asked for an appointment with the prime minister on Monday the 16th. Within an hour the FO called to inform me that Churchill would see me on Monday at 5 p.m. Yesterday, Sunday, I received another call from the FO to inform me of a change of plan: the prime minister would not be able to see me at five o'clock on Monday and instead invited me to come to lunch at Chequers that same day. I agreed.

So today, at around one o'clock, I arrived at Chequers. Eden, whom I had asked to be present during my conversation with Churchill, appeared a few minutes later. Upon entering the room where I sat waiting, Eden took me aside and said anxiously: 'I've just received a telegram from Washington that conveys the essence of Roosevelt's statement to Litvinov… A very unpleasant statement. We must discuss it.'

That very moment the prime minister's adjutant arrived and called us into the dining-room. It was, in fact, not exactly a dining-room, but a small corner room on the first floor with a very private feel to it. A small table was set for the three of us: Churchill, Eden and me. The PM, dressed in his habitual *siren-suit*, greeted me in jovial, friendly fashion and apologized for his domestic appearance. Having undergone a minor operation today, he had been unable to return to the city and was obliged to receive me at home.

When we sat down at the table, I handed Churchill the message from Comrade Stalin. He quickly read it through and was evidently satisfied. Then it was Eden's turn to read the message. At first our conversation revolved around the latest war news. Then Eden touched upon the question of the treaties. He spoke once again about the telegram from Washington and expressed his fear that the attitude of the USA could complicate the situation.

'This does not mean, of course, that we will not sign the treaties with you,' Eden added, 'but you must understand how important it would be to have America on our side.'

Churchill intervened and defined his position: 'I have, since the very beginning, been reluctant to recognize the 1941 borders, but, as Stalin was so insistent, I eventually agreed to do so… Maybe it's a prejudice, but I'm a great believer in the principle of the free self-determination of nations which was also included in the *Atlantic Charter*, while here…'

'But a broad democratic plebiscite was held in the Baltics,' I interrupted, understanding full well what Churchill was driving at.

Churchill grinned slyly and rejoined: 'Yes, of course there was a plebiscite, but all the same…'

He concluded his phrase with a vague gesture.

'Frankly speaking,' I retorted, 'I don't quite understand the position of the British government on this issue. As far as I know, the British government undertook to "consult" the USA, and I stress "consult", on issues relating to European borders, not to seek the USA's permission. As I understand it, "consultation" has already taken place. You made a démarche in Washington which showed there to be a marked difference of opinion between the American and the British governments. Very well. What next? I think you should have told the Americans: "We have informed you of our intention to recognize the Soviet borders of 1941. You don't like it, but we maintain that the move is in the interests of our victory over the common enemy. We are taking this step in the hope that you will come to understand and appreciate the correctness of our policy." Our treaties should have been signed right after such a statement was made. In general, the British government should appeal to its "American uncle" a little less often, and think a bit more about the independence of its policy.'

Churchill and Eden heard me out, but would not commit themselves to anything right away. Churchill merely said: 'Talk with Eden and find an acceptable solution.'

So it was decided: tomorrow, the 17th, I am to meet Eden and discuss the current situation.

Then I mentioned Comrade Stalin's message and drew Churchill's attention to the paragraph where Comrade Stalin expresses his confidence that 1942 will be the decisive year. I asked Churchill: what were his thoughts on the subject?

Churchill's countenance darkened immediately. He shrugged his shoulders and uttered with slight irritation: 'I don't see how 1942 can become the decisive year.'

I was about to protest, but Churchill cut me short with a sharp question: 'Tell me, how do you feel yourselves to be today – stronger or weaker than in 1941?'

'Stronger, of course,' I answered without hesitation.

'Well I feel weaker,' Churchill retorted.

And then he added by way of clarification: 'Last year we had to fight against two major powers, this year – against three.'

'But now,' I responded, 'you have two mighty allies.'

Churchill, however, would not agree with me and started raising additional domestic problems, such as India, the press, parliament, production…

So then I decided to take the bull by the horns and said to Churchill:

> I don't know how you see it, but I think we face a very menacing situation. A crucial moment in the course of the war really is approaching. It's 'either/or'. How do things stand? Germany is preparing an enormous offensive this spring. She is staking everything on this year. If we succeed

> in defeating the German offensive this spring, then in essence we will have won the war. The backbone of Hitler's war machine would be broken this year. It would only remain for us to finish off the crazed beast. With Germany defeated, everything else would be relatively easy. Now, suppose we fail to defeat Germany's spring offensive. Suppose the Red Army is forced to retreat again, that we begin to lose territories once more, that the Germans break through to the Caucasus – what then? For Hitler will not stop in the Caucasus if that happens. He will go further – to Iran, Turkey, Egypt, India. He will link hands with Japan somewhere in the Indian Ocean and stretch out his arms towards Africa. Germany's problems with oil, raw materials and food will be resolved. The British Empire will collapse, while the USSR will lose exceptionally important territories. The USSR, of course, would continue fighting even under such conditions. Let's assume that Britain and the USA would also continue fighting. But what would be our chances of victory? And when?… That is the choice before us! It's now or never!

Churchill, who had been listening to me with a frowning countenance and his head bent to one side, suddenly straightened up with a jerk and exclaimed in great agitation: 'We would rather die than reconcile ourselves to such a situation!'

Eden added: 'I quite agree with the ambassador. The question is exactly that: now or never!'

I continued:

> The Red Army has certainly become stronger compared to last year, and the German army has weakened. Of course we shall fight savagely this year. But who can vouch for the future? Who knows whether Hitler has some new military inventions at his disposal. Some new gas which no one knows about… And even if we lay aside the possibility of a 'secret' weapon, Hitler receives active support (even if not always voluntary) from his allies – all those Rumanians, Hungarians, Finns, Slovaks, etc. Meanwhile, the USSR continues to endure the entire, gigantic onslaught of Hitler's war machine all alone. It is hard for us. The degree of danger is greatly increasing. Yet, Britain and the USA are still deliberating, sizing things up, thinking things over, and are simply unable to decide which is the crucial year: 1942 or 1943? The situation is quite intolerable. The differing 'war schedules' of the USSR, on the one side, and Britain and the USA, on the other, represent the gravest flaw of the Allied strategy. It must be eliminated. Britain and the USA must also place their stake on 1942. This is the year when they must throw into battle all their forces

> and resources, irrespective of the degree of their preparedness. They must deal with any lack of discipline in the rear. If this is not done, a very dangerous situation will emerge: the 'Axis' will be fighting with both hands, while the Allies will use only one. Such a situation cannot be permitted!

Once again Eden was in total agreement.

Churchill sat sunk in thought. Finally, he raised his head and said: 'Perhaps you are right. All the information I have at my disposal testifies that the Germans are preparing an attack in the east. Countless trains are heading east, carrying men and weapons. Anti-aircraft batteries, removed from the centre of Germany, are being sent to the east in order to protect the railways in Poland and the occupied part of Russia. Yes, you will have to withstand a terrible blow this spring. We must help you in every way possible. Do all we can.'

It was clear, however, that arriving at this conclusion had not been easy for Churchill.

Having thus gained victory over Churchill on this matter of principle, I shifted our conversation onto more practical ground. I said that since the USSR would have to engage once again in a life-and-death battle with Germany in the spring, it was very important for the Soviet government to know in advance what aid it could count on receiving from England during these critical days.

There followed a long, animated, at times even heated, exchange of opinions, the results of which may be summarized as follows:

(1) The British government guarantees the fulfilment of the Moscow protocol. The British will take the necessary measures to guard the convoys against *Tirpitz*, etc. In this connection the monthly number of convoys may have to be reduced to two beginning from April (three are scheduled for March), but we will not lose out: all the convoys will be larger than the present ones. Churchill promised to consider exceeding the requirements of the Moscow protocol in March and April. Responding to my question as to whether the British government recognized Beaverbrook's oral promise to Stalin to increase supplies by 50% from 1 July, Churchill replied, a little uncertainly, that it did. I felt at once that all was not yet clear on this point.

(2) The British government also guarantees to maximize the air offensive against western Germany and the occupied countries. The aim of the offensive is to draw at least half of the German air force to the west. The offensive should strike not only military facilities (experience shows precise targeting to be virtually impossible), but civilian districts as well. The pilots' previous restrictions have been lifted: the German population will suffer and that's that. It can't be helped. What's more, this will affect the population's morale. Essen was 'Coventrified' the other day. Other German cities will share the same fate.

(3) The British government guarantees that if the Germans use gas on the eastern front, it will use gas against the Germans in its air raids. There are huge gas stocks in Britain. Should Stalin desire, one could issue a public warning beforehand (Churchill will send a telegram to this effect to Stalin).

(4) The British government guarantees that it will carry out raids on a broad scale against the shores of the occupied countries (France, Belgium, Norway, etc.).

(5) The British government will discuss the question of transferring part of the air force from Libya to the USSR, provided offensive operations are not resumed in Libya (Cripps and Nye[i] will examine the situation in Libya on the way to India and send their report to London).

(6) The British government expects to draw the Japanese to the south, as it plans to resume its offensive in the Pacific against the islands of the Dutch Indies within the next 3–6 months. Besides, Burma and Australia will be defended energetically (Australia and New Zealand will be defended mostly by the USA), as will Ceylon. The latter is being reinforced and its garrison is being strengthened. Churchill hopes that it will be possible to detain the Japanese in Burma: the British are sending reinforcement units and aircraft there and have even assigned the command to General Alexander,[ii] one of their best. Bad roads and long distances work against the Japanese. Should Burma be lost, however, it is not yet known where the Japanese would go – to China or to India. Churchill disclosed the following data concerning the disposition of Japanese forces: 20 divisions in Manchuria, 14 in China, 29 in south-eastern Asia and 9 in Japan – 72 divisions in all. It would seem to follow from this (if the figures are accurate) that the Japanese do not intend to attack the USSR just yet.

(7) Finally, Churchill said he was now studying the question of a second front in Europe. It was clear from this that Eden had already spoken with the PM on this matter, following my conversation with him on 12 March. I tried to develop the matter further and pushed the argument in favour of a second front which had worked so well on Eden (the need to train the British army in an attack-minded spirit). Churchill responded to my argument no less positively than Eden. He even remarked that technically it would be easier to open a second front now, as compared to last year, because the English are currently in possession of a large number of vessels fit for landing operations. Nonetheless, the prime minister resolutely avoided making any specific promises. I noticed just one change: last year, I seemed to run into a brick wall every time I raised

---

[i] Sir Archibald Edward Nye, lieutenant general, vice chief of the imperial general staff during the Second World War.

[ii] Harold George Alexander (1st Earl Alexander of Tunis), general, was appointed commander-in-chief of the Allied forces in Burma in March 1942, and in August was appointed as commander-in-chief of the Middle East, overseeing the successful campaigns at El Alamein and in Tunisia.

97. Churchill and Eden feeling at home at Maisky's residence.

the question of a second front in conversation with Churchill. There was no such wall now. I felt he was ready to discuss this question in earnest and, moreover, with the intention of doing something, if, according to his calculations, he deemed it feasible.

Considering the outcome of this part of our conversation, I felt that something had been achieved. Not everything I had wanted – far from it – but something nonetheless.

As ever, our conversation was by no means systematic. Parts of it were entire and complete, but there were others where we jumped from one topic to another. I'll cite the more noteworthy instances.

India. I mentioned this problem in passing. Churchill responded with considerable anger and irritation.

'Cripps won't be able to do anything there,' he uttered curtly. 'The Indians won't agree between themselves… From the military point of view it is not so important. From the military point of view, the Caspian–Levantine front is far more important than India. Politics and emotions are another matter. We shall see.'

Churchill made an abrupt gesture with his hand and continued: 'In general, the Indians are not a historic nation. Who has not conquered them? Whoever came to India from the north became her master. Throughout their history the Indians have barely ever enjoyed true independence. Look at the Indian villages: each stands on a hill. Where did the hill come from? Each village has been building its mud huts for centuries, for millennia. Every year the rainy season washes the huts away. The old ones are replaced by new ones from the same earth. In turn they too are washed away. And thus from one generation to another. As a result, the hills have grown higher and higher. What kind of people is it that has not been able to invent something better over the course of millennia?'...

Churchill took a sip of wine and continued with still more irritation:

> I'm prepared to leave India this very moment. We won't be living there in any case. But what would happen then? You might think: liberty, prosperity, the development of culture and science... How wrong you would be! If we leave, fighting will break out everywhere, there'll be a civil war. Eventually, the Muslims will become masters, because they are warriors while the Indians are windbags. Yes, windbags! Oh, of course, when it comes to fine speeches, skilfully balanced resolutions, and legalistic castles in the air, the Indians are real experts! They're in their element! But when it comes to business, when something must be decided on quickly, implemented, executed – here the Indians say 'pass'. Here they immediately reveal their internal flabbiness. Flabbiness is an awful thing. We, the English, showed this flabbiness all too often before and during the war. So did the Americans. I believe that responsibility for this war lies not only with the Germans, but with us as well. Two things brought us to the present catastrophe: Hitler's criminality and the flabbiness of the English and the Americans. But the Indians are even worse than we are when it comes to flabbiness. That's why I believe that the withdrawal of the English from India will not do her any good.

Churchill took another sip from his glass and, eyes sparkling, concluded his speech: 'I don't care what happens in India now... Committees, councils, whatever... We are leaving in any case. But then why on earth should we shed our blood? Let the Indians defend themselves!'

It was obvious that Churchill was annoyed, that the mere thought of India affects him like the touch of red-hot iron. It was clear that he had made some of his comments in the heat of the moment. Yet still, how typical were the prime minister's statements concerning a matter of the greatest historical significance!

Churchill's attitude to Iran is absolutely different. Already last August, when our troops and English troops were entering Iran, the prime minister spoke to me with great enthusiasm about the improvements he was going to make on the trans-Iranian railway, about how many locomotives and carriages he would send there, and how this neglected railway line would turn into a first-class communications route between Britain and the USSR during and after the war.

Today he returned to this topic once more. During lunch, his secretary brought him a thick folder of documents. Churchill looked at it with satisfaction, put it beside his plate, nodded to the secretary, and said: 'Yes, yes, this is precisely the material I want to discuss with the ambassador today.'

Churchill opened the folder and, looking at the long columns of tables, began to inform me in detail about everything that had been done on the trans-Iranian railway over the last seven months, how many locomotives and carriages had been delivered, how the route's capacity had increased, etc. All this was important and interesting, of course, but compared to the Indian problem the trans-Iranian route was a mere trifle. Meanwhile, the prime minister spoke of it with gusto, even delight, chewing over every figure and emphasizing every success. I listened to him and couldn't help thinking: 'Of course, Churchill is a considerable man and a major statesman. And yes, he is 67 years old. But nonetheless, something of the small boy lives on in him: Iran is a toy he likes, while India is a toy he dislikes.'

The PM spoke of Beaverbrook and Cripps with great sympathy and respect. According to him, Beaverbrook's resignation was a big blow to the Cabinet and to him personally. But Churchill still hopes that 'Max' will return to the

98. Lord Woolton, minister of food (on the right), presenting his ministry's contribution to the work of the Russian Red Cross, January 1943.

government. He is also thinking of sending Beaverbrook on some kind of official mission to Moscow. Evidently, Churchill is still impressed by Beaverbrook's 'friendship' with Comrade Stalin.

As for Cripps, the PM said he is awaiting his return from India with impatience. Cripps is badly needed here in Britain, and Churchill consented to the trip only because Cripps himself wanted to go.

Churchill spoke about the Red Army with admiration, saying that good-will towards the USSR had grown immensely in England, along with its prestige. He added with a laugh: 'Just imagine! My own wife is completely Sovietized… All she ever talks about is the Soviet Red Cross, the Soviet army, and the wife of the Soviet ambassador, with whom she corresponds, speaks over the telephone and appears at demonstrations!'

He added with a sly sparkle in his eye: 'Couldn't you elect her to one of your Soviets? She surely deserves it.'

The USA. Churchill asks us not to underestimate her significance and role. True, the Americans talk too much and do too little. True, they are devilishly bad at keeping their promises for supplies. Yet, they are a tremendous power, and they are capable of learning. By way of illustration, Churchill recalled the history of the Civil War in America, when the armies on both sides resembled disorganized rabbles in the first year of the war, yet attained a high degree of perfection by the third.

I replied that we fully understand the significance and role of the USA in this war, but the thought of the Americans having a perfect army in 1945 hardly suits us.

During today's conversation with the prime minister, I was struck by one feature which I had not observed before: Churchill is in a 'twilight mood'. He even let slip the remark: 'I'm not long for this world… I'll be ashes soon…'

The same note sounded in a number of other statements. But every time Germany was mentioned Churchill flared up and his eyes flashed with sparks of fury. My general impression is that Churchill has an acute sense of being on the wane and is harnessing his remaining strength and energy in pursuit of one fundamental and all-exclusive goal – to win the war. He looks and thinks no further than that.

Seeing me out on to the porch, Eden quickly whispered into my ear: 'You managed to get a lot out of the prime minister today. He was in a good mood. He is being needlessly irritated – parliament's criticisms and the suspicions of the press exasperate him… Meanwhile, you can see that much is being prepared, though it's too early to speak about it openly… You have many friends here… If you could do something to ease the PM's situation, we'd all gain from it.'

Returning from Chequers I thought: 'How times change!… Moore-Brabazon came to me not long ago to defend himself and to ask for my assistance in restoring his reputation. Now Eden asks me to prop up the prime minister's slightly shaky position… All this reflects one basic fact: the might of the USSR, which has now become evident to the whole world.'

[In his memoirs Maisky, recognizing in retrospect that most of the promises made to him by Churchill had not been fulfilled and that he had exceeded the instructions he had been given, prefers to gloss briefly over the meeting. He dwells instead on Churchill's undertaking to use gas against the German civilian population if the Germans used it on the front. This Maisky presents as his 'greatest achievement … which saved mankind from the additional horror of gas warfare'.[59] In his response to Stalin, Churchill also preferred to confine himself to this issue. Maisky was just as economical in his report to Moscow, considering the initiatives he had taken in trying to galvanize Churchill into action. He dwelt mostly on his attempts to put across Stalin's view that 1942 was 'the decisive year' of the war, and juxtaposed this with Churchill's verbal support, accompanied by a promise to launch the offensive in Libya which Maisky dismissed as a 'small second front'.[60]]

17 March

Eden.

We conferred on the treaties. Halifax has sent the record of Roosevelt's statement to Litvinov; it had been passed on to him by Sumner Welles for his information. The statement is long (two single-spaced pages). Main points: in view of prevalent American public opinion Roosevelt was 'alarmed' to learn about Anglo-Soviet negotiations concerning the 1941 borders, he would like to study the matter more intensively, could in no way approve a secret treaty, and could not now sign any treaty concerning future borders. However, Roosevelt understands that the USSR needs a border which would guarantee it against a new German attack in some 10–15 years. Roosevelt is 100% committed to helping us obtain such a border, but after the war. Referred to the Atlantic Charter (Germany's unilateral disarmament), but stresses that mutual trust between the USSR and the USA is of paramount importance. Hopes to receive a reply from Stalin. Halifax did not disclose the details of the talk between Roosevelt and Litvinov.

Eden asked: what should be done now? In spite of the USA pouring cold water on them, the treaties must be signed quickly. It was obvious, however, that Halifax's telegram had upset him. I set about reassuring him. The British government must be courageous. Roosevelt's statement is more of an insurance policy than a protest. He is shooting at non-existent targets. Nobody is speaking about a secret treaty, and nobody is inviting him to sign anything. Besides, to all intents and purposes he acknowledges the correctness of our demands. Eden calmed down a bit and cheered up.

99. The 'conspirators', Eden and Maisky.

After our discussion Eden reached the following conclusion: let Stalin reply (the statement is addressed to him), then Eden will reply in the same spirit. Then we shall get down to drafting the treaties. Stalin's reply, according to Eden, should be based on the following ideas: there is no question of a secret treaty, no one has invited the USA to sign; the security requirements of the USSR call for a recognition of the 1941 borders now in order to establish trust between England and the USSR.

I'm asking Moscow to send me a copy of the reply to Roosevelt and details of the talk between Roosevelt and Litvinov.

[Maisky was anxious to prevent the political talks from stalling. Eden gained the impression that the ambassador did not share Halifax's gloomy reports of the meeting (read out to him word for word) and 'resolved not to take a tragic view of the President's attitude'. Eden concealed in his own report of the conversations that, despite the 'cold shower' from Washington, the two had conspired over how to pursue the political negotiations. The scheme was for Stalin to assure Roosevelt that the treaty would have no secret clauses and that, while his tacit support was welcome, he was not required to be a signatory. Stalin was to insist, though, that for the sake of 'establishing mutual trust and steadfast cooperation among the Allies it was essential to recognize the borders now and not after the war'.[61] A few days later, when no response had been forthcoming, Eden pressed Maisky to seek a Soviet initiative, as he badly needed an excuse to pursue the matter from London.[62] Maisky was 'extremely disappointed' to find out that in the meantime the number of convoys had been reduced, just when the looming renewed offensive rendered a 'plentiful and constant flow of arms ... an important contributory factor' to Soviet success on the battlefield. The more so as he had been promised by Churchill at their latest meeting that he would make sure supplies to Russia went 'ahead of schedule'.[63]]

19 March

Called on Beaverbrook at the Savoy. Found Harriman and his daughter there. Beaverbrook asked me to send Stalin a telegram he gave me. I promised to do so. This had been agreed with Eden (I had a telephone call from the latter).

On parting, Beaverbrook emphasized that one must stake on 1942, not on 1943. Every kind of assistance should now be given to the USSR. Beaverbrook champions the idea of a second front in governmental circles. Being a free agent, he has greater possibilities than before. I set about thanking him for the line he had taken. Beaverbrook brushed my thanks aside, saying: 'I'm doing all this not because I love the USSR, but because I love the British Empire. But one can't love the British Empire today without staking on the USSR.'

Beaverbrook's Telegram to Stalin (19 March 1942)

> This morning I'm leaving for Washington to discuss the 1941 (Soviet) borders with the president. The talks shall be secret, but I'll possibly need to communicate with you through Litvinov. Please instruct Maisky to inform Litvinov about my plans. These are known only to the prime minister and Eden.
> Cherkley, Leatherhead, Surrey.

20 March

A visit from a Labour delegation (Seymour Cocks,[i] Bellenger, Ridley[ii] and Beaumont[iii]) representing the majority of Parliamentary Labour, which is deeply worried. Things are going badly. England is suffering defeats. The strategy of the British government is bankrupt. The spectre of a lost war looms on the horizon. The country must wake up, realign and mobilize itself, move on to the offensive, and above all establish a close friendship with the USSR. Otherwise Britain

[i] Frederick Seymour Cocks, Labour MP, 1929–53.
[ii] George Ridley, Labour MP and member of the Labour Party Executive (vice-chairman, 1942), 1936–44.
[iii] Hubert Beaumont, captain, Labour MP, 1939–48, parliamentary private secretary in Ministry of Agriculture, 1940–45.

faces destruction. But the government dithers, vacillates, shows no fighting spirit, energy, decisiveness. The Labourites put questions to their ministers, but they (Attlee in particular) dodge them. The majority of Parliamentary Labour decided to send a delegation to me to learn the truth. I complied with their request and pointed out the importance of a second front. My guests fully agreed with me. They promised to besiege their ministers immediately. One of the delegates exclaimed: 'Ah, if only your generals could come to Britain to train our army in the methods of modern warfare!'

Lord Mottistone came to see me. A diehard retired general who held high posts in the past (including secretary of state for war in 1914). Seventy-four years old. An anti-Soviet hero who supported the 'Zinoviev letter' campaign. The purpose of his visit: M. is indignant at the Home Office's instructions recommending that the population 'remain in place' and 'keep calm' in the event of an invasion (the men in uniform will fight). He says the instructions have been written by English quislings. M. is going to raise the question in the House of Lords and protest to the prime minister. He would like to know what our 'instructions' would be for such an event. I gave him Stalin's speeches. He promised to quote them. M. fully shares our view of 1942 and is for a second front. In conclusion, he exclaimed: 'Really, you Bolsheviks are magnificent! You are fighting superbly! You've saved us and civilization. Just to think that I once opposed you!'

I asked him with a smile: 'Maybe you recognize now that there is something healthy about our system?'

'Of course I recognize it. I'm a soldier. If you've created an army like that then there must be something healthy about your system.'

21 March

De Gaulle's future.

There was a fight between de Gaulle and Muselier a fortnight ago. They had not been getting on for some time. Eden and Alexander patched things up between them last September–October. It worked to some extent, but not for long.

De G. sent M. to take St Pierre and Miquelon (Newfoundland). During the operation, he sent instructions to M. which he claimed to have agreed with Ch., but which in fact he had not. M.'s chief of staff in London got to know Ch.'s real instructions and wired them secretly to M., but he was too late. The admiral had already undertaken some acts of which he disapproved and which had brought him into conflict with the Admiralty. Back in England, M. demanded an explanation from de G. A fierce argument followed. M. left de G.'s National Committee. After that de G. dismissed him from his post of fleet commander.

Many sailors left with M. Several of de G.'s ships could not go to sea because of absent or disorganized command. De G. gathered his naval officers in the navy club and demanded an oath of allegiance. M. came too and spoke against de G. There was a scandal, both left the club, the officers almost came to blows. The Admiralty knew nothing about it. When they learned about it, they took M.'s side and asked Eden to make de G. reinstate M. as commander of de G.'s fleet. Aware of the relationship between the two, Eden refused to impose M. on the general, but invited de G. for a talk.

De G. demanded as a precondition that Eden recognize M.'s dismissal. Eden said he wouldn't. So de G. said he wouldn't go to see Eden.

De G. stuck to his position for a few days. Eventually went to see Eden. A long and heated conversation. One moment they both jumped up, stood opposite one another like fighting cocks, and started shouting. De G. drew himself up to his full height and exclaimed, while beating his breast: 'I'm Joan of Arc! You can burn me at the stake like the English once burned Joan of Arc, but you can't make me change my views!' De G. demanded that M. be locked up in a fortress. Eden refused. The British government decided to seize the fleet from de G. and subordinate it fully to the Admiralty. Eden thinks this is not enough: de G's entourage must be purged. He asked me to help him. Wanted to send Peek (the liaison officer between FO and de G.) to me for a talk.

I didn't object as I was in agreement with Eden. It's high time to carry out a purge. De G.'s milieu are all Cagulards[64] and rascals. There are almost bound to be German agents among them. De G. himself understands nothing about politics, sympathizes with fascism of the Italian type, and doesn't know how to lead (he argues with everyone). He is not leadership material. This makes his entourage all the more important. There's work to be done.[65]

23 March

I informed Eden that in fact the Soviet government has decided not to respond to Roosevelt's statement to Litvinov, regarding it merely as information, but only to instruct M.M. Litvinov to tell the president that the Soviet government has taken his statement into consideration. Eden was dumbfounded. I reassured him: we have no obligations in relations to the USA, and have requested nothing from Roosevelt. In such circumstances, our conduct is quite normal. Eden calmed down a little, and eventually declared that since we have given our response to Roosevelt, it was now the turn of the English. In the course of the next 2–3 days he would inform me of the British government's decision.

Eden expressed his great satisfaction with Clark Kerr's first conversation with Molotov.

[Again Molotov appeared to be far from keen to pursue the negotiations. He was puzzled, as he informed his ambassador in London, by Eden's approach. The Soviet Union had not approached Roosevelt with any demands; his conversation with Litvinov had been purely informative, concerning the response to the British consultations, and did not therefore require any intervention on behalf of Stalin.

Like Maisky in London, Litvinov was baffled by the 'incomprehensible' policy pursued by the Kremlin. Expecting Russia to face a 'mighty' United States and a 'weakened and shattered' British Empire at the peace conference, he failed to see the wisdom of pressing the British to sign an agreement against the will of Roosevelt, who was bound to be insulted.[66] Seriously disturbed, Maisky urged Eden to 'make it plain' to the Americans that 'in the interests of the Allied war effort we considered that we should now conclude our treaty with Russia'.[67] It is worth noting, therefore, that rather than specifically demanding a second front at this stage, Moscow was eager for the Allies to put the eastern front at the top of Allied strategy. 'There is no time,' said Maisky, as he pinned the Order of Lenin on British pilots who had flown in Russia, 'to wait until the last button is sewn on the uniform of the last soldier.' The Allies, he claimed, echoing the Americans, were already overstretched and failed to see that in Russia they had the one front where Hitler could be beaten in 1942.[68] Meanwhile Soviet efforts focused on diverting supply from the peripheral theatres to the Soviet front.[69]]

24 March

Clark Kerr's first visit to Molotov.

Clark Kerr expressed his regret at leaving China and said he was proud of being posted to the USSR.

Molotov remarked that Cripps's work in the USSR had made a good impression on us and hoped Clark Kerr would be as successful. – We consider 1942 to be the decisive year in the struggle against Germany. Germany is preparing a spring offensive. We are doing all we can to obstruct the organization of the offensive. Soviet troops are incessantly attacking along the entire front, so as not to give a respite to the Germans anywhere, to frustrate the German offensive plans. If Britain and the USA do the same where they can land blows on the Hitlerites, the aim of reaching a turning point in 1942 will be achieved. – But this means mobilizing all forces. Only under such circumstances will the main aggressor, Hitlerite Germany, get what it deserves. – Molotov hopes that Clark Kerr, while understanding English interests, will also understand the interests of the USSR. Squabbles may occur, but the essential interests of the two countries now coincide to such a degree that this has a decisive significance.

Clark Kerr agreed. Counts on Molotov's support. Will make every effort. There are suspicions and misunderstandings, but they can easily be overcome. Churchill and Eden have an interest in post-war problems being resolved by the 'big three'. The British government is ready to second Soviet proposals on this matter wherever possible.

Clark Kerr delivered Churchill's message of 20 March to Stalin.

1 April

Crisis of the Empire.

Became particularly acute since the Japanese attacks: Malaya and Singapore are lost. Burma is soon to be lost. Australia and New Zealand placed under US military protectorate. India is 'leaving' the British Empire (Churchill admitted as much in our conversation of 15 March 1942). South Africa cold-shoulders England, many pro-Germans there. German and Italian missions still present in Ireland. Channel of German espionage. Canada is loyal, but did not wish to be addressed as a dominion in her agreement with us on the establishment of consular relations. US influence in Canada growing. USA ousting Britain from its commanding economic heights in North and South America. The British government was forced to cede a number of important military bases in North and Central America to the USA. The loss of Singapore posed the question starkly: how strong is British rule in other colonies?

What is the meaning of all this? The disintegration of the British Empire? Premature. We face a 'crisis'. It can end in disintegration or transformation. This depends on a number of conditions, primarily on the behaviour of the British ruling class. It still has cards in hand, but will it be able to play them well? We shall see. If it restructures in time, there will be transformation. If not, there will be disintegration.

What does transformation mean? The bottom line of conversations, readings, etc.: (1) The dominions become independent states after the war, but a military-political alliance of these states with a mother country is established. (2) India becomes independent de jure or de facto, but the British government concludes economic and military agreements with it (modelled on the example of Egypt). (3) The rest of the Empire (mostly Africa): reforms, involvement of the population to a greater or lesser extent in various forms and relations of self-government. This is how transformation is seen by such men as Eden and Beaverbrook, Attlee, Greenwood, Sinclair and Lloyd George. Should transformation occur, the ruling class would still be left with something, even if a large chunk of the British Empire is lost.

The likelihood of transformation being implemented? It's difficult to say, but the signs are that routes for transformation are being sought. Chamberlain was the Empire's grave-digger, but Chamberlainian influence in the government is declining (especially in the wake of the February reshuffle), while the Churchillian wing grows more powerful. Churchill himself is not fit to be the leader of a transformation (old, stuck in the old imperial tradition), but he gives Eden, Cranborne and others their head. Cranborne is the secretary for the colonies. Symptomatic. Cripps's visit to India. Discussion of colonial reform in official quarters. The trend is clear. Is the tempo sufficient? Facts will provide the answer.

5 April (Bovingdon, Easter)

Post-war reconstruction. There is probably no other slogan which could be more popular in England today. The practical results? Zilch. What I have in mind, of course, is not reconstruction itself, which can be embarked upon in earnest only once the war has ended, but the studying of problems and the drawing up of plans for this reconstruction.

What is the matter?

It is often suggested that the problem lies with Greenwood, who was entrusted with matters of post-war reconstruction in the War Cabinet, but is a weakling and a drunkard. It is suggested even more frequently that Churchill is not interested in post-war problems. He says: 'My job is to win the war. Someone else can clear up the post-war mess.'

There is a grain of truth in such explanations, but no more than a grain. The main reason for the fruitlessness of efforts towards post-war reconstruction is different. The main reason is this: the bourgeoisie likes contemplating the future and making plans for the future when it's on the up. It does not like contemplating the future and making plans for it when it's on the slide. The British bourgeoisie is indeed sliding downhill, and rather quickly at that. Is it so surprising that it shies away from problems relating to the post-war order? Not at all. For, to judge by all the available signs, the future has nothing good in store for England's ruling elite.

What are these signs?

They are starkest in the 'imperial' sphere. A number of facts show that all is not well there. In early 1940, I happened to write that (at that moment) the Empire had successfully passed the test of war: all the dominions, excluding Ireland, and even many of the colonies had sided with the mother country without any hesitation and embarked on the broad mobilization of their resources to support the war. Today, two years later, the situation is very, very different. Here are the crucial facts.

Malaya and Singapore are lost. Burma is on the verge of being lost. Australia and New Zealand have been entrusted with a US military protectorate because the British government acknowledges its inability to render them effective assistance. The fate of India is presently in the balance: no matter how Cripps's mission ends, it is absolutely clear that the old India is lost to the English. Churchill admitted this unequivocally in his last conversation with me (16 March). South Africa has always maintained cold relations with the mother country – today this is especially obvious. It is enough to recall our talks with the South Africans on the procedure of appointing the consul-general to Pretoria. Canada is more loyal than South Africa, but it did not want the Canadian government to be named 'the Government of the Dominion of Canada' in the Soviet–Canadian agreement on the establishment of consular relations, and insisted that it should be named simply the 'Government of Canada' (which indeed is what was done). The catastrophe in Malaya and Burma cast the following question in sharp relief: are the foundations of British rule stronger in other colonies, especially in Africa? In South America, and particularly in Argentina, England is definitely losing out in economic terms to the USA.

What is the meaning of these and many other similar facts? The disintegration of the Empire?

For the time being I would hesitate to draw such a conclusion. The situation is unclear. The facts I enumerated may signify the beginning of the disintegration of the Empire, but they may also simply signify a transitional phase in the transformation of the Empire. All will depend on the English 'spirit', and primarily that of the ruling class. If the leaders fail to show the necessary flexibility and fail to make sufficient concessions in various parts of the Empire in good time, its disintegration as a result of the war will become inevitable. If, on the other hand, the leaders succeed in showing these qualities, the transformation of the Empire is possible. One example: India may become a dominion or even formally an independent state after the war, but if the British government succeeds in signing proper trade, political and military agreements with her in advance, as well as with Egypt, England will still be able to maintain a significant number of its advantages there. The same goes for other parts of the Empire.

In which of the two directions are events unfolding? My general impression is that events are advancing more in the second direction, i.e. that the leaders are making considerable efforts to save whatever can be saved of their position in the Empire and inside the country. The latest government reshuffle clearly testifies to this. So does Cripps's visit to India. And so does the heated debate under way in the press and in political quarters about the need for urgent and radical reforms in the colonial system of Great Britain.

So much for the imperial sphere. Curious symptoms are also discernible on the domestic front. One of these is the change in the office of the archbishop of Canterbury: the reactionary and anti-Soviet Dr Lang has retired on grounds of old age (78) and Dr Temple (60), a progressive *social reformer* and formerly the archbishop of York, has taken his place. Richard Acland, a left (and somewhat wild) Liberal, told me the other day about a speech he made recently in front of 200 priests in Liverpool on the subject 'Christianity and Politics'. Acland defended the argument, in the spirit of last year's ecclesiastical conference in Malvern, that private ownership of the means of production contradicts Christian doctrine. At the end Acland posed the question: which of those present were in favour of calling a conference that would make a clear and firm statement to this effect? Ninety per cent of the audience raised their hands. A few days ago, *The Times* published a letter signed by several of the City's largest magnates demanding that the government make better use of its right, granted back in the spring of 1940 for the duration of the war, to subordinate private interests to public ones. One could quote many similar facts.

If we add to the aforesaid the fact that along with Singapore there are Tobruk and Malta, that throughout the war the merchant seamen have given a fine example of modest but genuine heroism, and that in the difficult days of the *Battle of Britain* the entire British population displayed exceptional courage and resilience, then the possibility of a transformation of the British Empire as a result of war cannot be excluded. The possibility! For the speed of change plays a colossal role here, and when it comes to speed the English are not so good. The future alone can show whether the current pace of restructuring is fast enough to prevent the disintegration of the British Empire and to bring about its transformation.

Even if transformation does take place, what would its impact be, as seen from the point of view of the British ruling class?

At best, transformation would mean a drastic scaling down of exploitation and, as a consequence, a sharp decrease in profits. The financial and economic consequences of the colossal war expenditure should be added to this, as should the complete dislocation of the global market that will follow the war. It is perfectly clear that the English ruling class is heading toward impoverishment with all the ensuing consequences. It is sliding downhill fast. To some extent, its representatives are consciously aware of this; but they also sense it instinctively. That is why they are so reluctant to give any thought to the future. That is why, when drawing up plans for post-war reconstruction, they will only do as much as pressure from the lower classes and the USSR compels them to do. That is why Greenwood's work went so badly, and why his successor *Jowitt*,[i] who on top of being paymaster general is now in charge of matters relating to post-war reconstruction, will also have a rough time of it. Churchill may nurture a purely personal aversion to such problems, but in this instance subjective and objective attitudes are in perfect harmony: the prime minister's resistance is a good reflection of the spirit of his class.

---

[i] William Allen Jowitt, solicitor-general, 1940–42; paymaster general, 1942; minister without portfolio, 1942–44.

And the mood of this class is now very troubled and gloomy. Not long ago I attended a lunch arranged by Rothschild, the banker. There were 7–8 people from the City, including Sir Auckland Geddes.[i] I gently pushed the conversation in the direction of post-war prospects. It soon became apparent that I had touched a nerve. A sharp debate developed. The guests were divided into three groups: the first held that after the nightmare of the war everything would more or less revert to the old order, and the City would flourish once again; the second, including Geddes, argued the contrary: capitalism as people knew it before the war had died and would be replaced with 'planning' (though no one could specify what he meant by that term); the position of the third group lay somewhere between those of the first and second. The host closed the debate with a characteristic remark: 'To avoid sleepless nights my wife forbids me to think about the future.'

What a fine illustration of the current mental state of the representatives of the ruling class!

One further example: nearly three months have passed since I handed the British government and the other Allies our project for the reorganization of the 'Inter-Allied Committee on post-war raw materials and food' (the so-called Leith-Ross committee), a project which ought to make this committee more serious and business-like. No reply has come from the British government.

No, the English bourgeoisie does not want to think about the future!

6 April

Continuing the thoughts which I noted down yesterday, I arrive at the following conclusion.

What will the world look like at the end of the war? An end, of course, which we desire and are counting on.

Germany, Italy and Japan will be crushed and weakened for a long time. France will be in the process of a slow and painful recovery, having lost its status as a great power. The British Empire will be significantly weaker (I choose the optimum scenario for her: not disintegration, but transformation). China will be triumphant, but licking her wounds and regaining her strength with great difficulty.

Against this background, two powers will present a somewhat different picture – the USSR and the USA.

The USSR will also have to tend to its wounds, but, emerging from the war with a powerful army, a vast industry, mechanized agriculture and a wealth of

[i] Campbell Auckland Geddes, president of the Board of Trade, 1919–20; British ambassador to the USA, 1920–24; chairman of the Rio Tinto Company, 1925–47.

raw materials, it will be the mightiest international power. The socialist system will help the USSR to overcome the grave consequences of the war faster than other countries.

The USA, in its turn, will become the second largest power because it will, by all appearances, suffer least from the war and maintain its strength to a greater degree than anyone else. The American army will probably be ready for serious battle only once the war is over. Together with the mighty navy, air force and military industry, this army will make the USA very powerful.

The USSR and the USA will represent the two social and international poles of socialism and capitalism in the post-war period. For in the USA capitalism will have preserved infinitely more of its vital juices by the end of the war than in England. The USA will become the citadel of capitalism. That is why the post-war period will most probably be marked by a contest between the USSR and the USA rather than between England and the USA. That is also why it is not in our interest to go out of our way to strengthen the USA and in particular to allow the handover to it of Australia and New Zealand.

Today is the 6th of April. A year ago to the day Hitler attacked Yugoslavia. Almost on the same day two years ago (on the night of 8–9 April) he attacked Norway. All is calm for the time being. Obviously, the situation in 1942 is far more difficult and complicated for Hitler than in previous years.

I certainly do not rule out the possibility that Hitler may mark the month of April with novelties of one kind or another. But it is also possible that this will not happen. Everything depends on the conditions, on the speed with which Hitler manages to prepare for the spring offensive, on the weather on our front, especially the Ukrainian front. Time will tell. I, in any case, think it most probable that Hitler's aim this year will be to conquer the Caucasus, with all the ensuing consequences. It is on this region that his plans will focus, and he will use various methods to fulfil them, stopping at nothing. Might Hitler have some new military invention? Might he have some kind of gas which nobody else knows of?

As we approach the spring–summer campaign, what kind of shape are we in?

The winter offensive had major significance. It gave a big boost to the morale of the Red Army and of the entire Soviet population. It gave the Red Army very valuable experience of war. It returned to us a number of our territories. It deprived Hitler of the possibility of calmly waiting out the winter while preparing a tremendous reserve force for the spring. It compelled the Germans to fight through the whole winter, sustaining heavy losses. It consumed a significant quantity of the German reserves that were being kept for the spring. It demolished the myth of the 'invincibility' of the German hordes and dealt a heavy blow to their morale, as well as to that of the German population at home. It facilitated the growth of discontent and anti-German activity in the occupied countries.

These, of courses, are all pluses. But I am somewhat disappointed that our territorial gains have fallen short of my expectations. I had thought that by the end of winter we would at least have taken Smolensk, driven the Germans from Leningrad and liberated the Crimea. But it hasn't happened and there's nothing you can do about it now.

What are the prospects? It's hard to predict, especially in the absence of any kind of accurate information from the USSR. But this is what strikes me as probable (or, to put it more precisely, this is how I would go about devising a strategic plan were I to be assigned such a task).

Hitler has evidently recovered somewhat from the initial confusion sown in the German ranks by our December offensive. By February it was clear that it was too early to speak of the disintegration of the German army. The German troops did not retreat in disarray and panic. On the contrary, their stubbornness intensified as they fell back. Clearing the regions and cities seized by the Germans became a laborious and costly business. Our leaders must have decided that there was no point expending too many men and too much matériel on regaining territories in winter. They decided only to maintain *heavy pressure* along the whole front so as to deprive the Germans of the time and opportunity to prepare systematically for the spring offensive, to make sure they sustained heavy losses, and to undermine their morale. Of course, we recaptured this or that point, city or region whenever we could. The main aim, however, was not to win back some territories, but to destroy the German army's manpower and equipment.

Meanwhile, we got on with preparing the Red Army for the spring. Reserves were called up, extensive efforts were made to expand military production, and we imported as much as we could from abroad. We know that the Germans are preparing a spring offensive. What is the best way of confronting them? Evidently, by launching a counteroffensive before the enemy attacks himself. It seems to me that this is indeed our plan now. Using the men and matériel saved during the winter, and the reserves who have been mobilized over that time, we must strike hard before the Germans make their first move in spring. Perhaps it was to some extent intentional that we left in German hands the points which have long been 'ripe' for recapture, such as Rzhev, Vyazma, Orel, Kursk, Kharkov and the Crimea. It is possible that we will regain them within just a few weeks. And at the same time we may see muddle and confusion descend on Hitler's plans for the spring. Who knows?

We will find out soon.

[There are no further entries in the diary until mid-June, with the exception of an abbreviated record of a meeting with Beaverbrook on 7 May (not reproduced here) and the telegrams exchanged between Stalin and Churchill concerning Molotov's visits to London and Washington in May and early June. The tension that pervaded relations between Maisky and Molotov – tension which came bubbling to the surface a couple of times during and immediately after the latter's visit to London – and the uncertainty over the Kremlin's intentions in the period preceding the resumption of the German offensive probably account for Maisky's ominous silence. Those factors, which had a tremendous impact on the course of the war and its outcome, are somewhat misrepresented by scholars, but are an indispensable contextual background to the diary.

Eden had explained to Maisky that Churchill was seeking at least tacit American support for the treaty, given that there was 'relatively little' the British could do 'by way of military aid to Russia'.[70] An unintended consequence of the excuse was that it enabled Roosevelt to forestall the treaty by backing the Russian demands for the second front, thereby diverting the pressure onto Britain.[71] When he transmitted Churchill's messages to Welles, Halifax's attempt to scare the Americans further only made matters worse: he warned that a failure to sign an agreement might lead to a separate peace, followed by the rise to power of Cripps, under whom 'a frankly Communist, pro-Moscow policy would be pursued'. Infuriated by this obvious attempt at blackmail, Roosevelt declined even to meet the ambassador in person.[72] At the same time, he was puzzled by the Soviet démarche, which could be 'a manifestation of resentment' or 'an indication of Stalin's withdrawal in the face of America's objection'.

Inundated by intelligence reports on the state of 'anxiety, despondence, and pessimism' in Britain, Roosevelt wondered whether Churchill was losing his grip on the domestic scene. Neither the civilians nor the military, he was informed by Donovan, director of strategic services (predecessor of the CIA), 'seemed to know the aims for which they are sacrificing their lives and labor', and there was an overwhelming demand for 'stronger action at home and abroad'. The efficiency of Russia and Germany was often contrasted with British 'dilatory muddling'. People seemed to 'pin their faith on Russia almost entirely, the chaps who don't talk but keep on killing Huns'. What was desired above all was 'an offensive attitude on the part of the fighting forces instead of continual retreat and defense, efficient and strong leadership at home towards a real total war effort'.[73]

Since his visit to Moscow, Hopkins had been arguing with the president that there was nothing 'as important as getting some sort of a front this summer against Germany'. He urged Roosevelt to adopt General Marshall's carefully worked-out plans and impose them on Churchill. The pressing need to keep Russia at war had led Marshall to accept that Western Europe was the only theatre in which an effective offensive could be launched. Such a decision, he insisted to the president, had to be taken '*now*' to ensure that all necessary logistical and deployment preparations were completed in time for an operation at the beginning of April 1943. In the meantime, he presented a contingency plan for an offensive in September 1942, 'a sacrifice for the common good', were the Germans successful enough in their campaign to bring about an imminent collapse of Russian resistance.[74]

Marshall particularly loathed the indecisiveness of the British joint chiefs of staff over the cross-channel operation. He believed it was imperative to establish precisely where the first major offensive effort of the united powers should take place. This he discussed thoroughly with Roosevelt over lunch in the White House on 25 March. Stimson, the secretary of war, was 'disappointed … and staggered' to find the president still 'going off on the wildest kind of dispersion debauch', particularly being 'charmed' by the options presented in North Africa and the Middle East. Indeed, Hopkins had revealed to Halifax a day earlier that the president was opposed to 'frittering away' Allied strength, and favoured concentrating it either in Great Britain, for an attack on Europe, or in the Middle East – an option which seemed to the president more viable and attractive.[75]

However, in the face of Eisenhower's logical and water-proof memorandum in favour of a cross-channel attack, Marshall overcame his doubts and succeeded in shifting the emphasis onto the second-front option. Roosevelt, still wavering, wondered whether the plan should be submitted to the British chiefs of staff, but he was discouraged by Hopkins.[76] During a heavy drinking bout with Beaverbrook that same evening at the White House, the president made his case 'with great earnestness and force' against a political agreement with the Russians. However, he now 'seemed to come down pretty well on the side of an attack on France ... this year'.[77]

With growing anxiety, Stimson continued to watch the president 'failing as a war leader' in a crisis situation. 'We cannot make our offensive diversion this summer,' growled the war secretary, 'unless we have the courage, even the hardness of heart.' Fully backed by Hopkins and Marshall, he prodded Roosevelt to submit his plans to Churchill and then 'lean with all your strength on the ruthless rearrangement of shipping allotments and the preparation of landing gear for the ultimate invasion' not later than September.[78] On 1 April, Eisenhower's plans were approved by the president. They comprised three distinct operations, culminating in an invasion of Europe on 1 April 1943. The first was Operation *Bolero*, under which the Americans would deploy some 30 divisions in Britain, including six armoured divisions and around 3,250 aircraft. The follow-up Operation *Roundup* would see those forces backed by 18 British divisions landed on the stretch between Boulogne and Le Havre. *Sledgehammer* was an emergency operation aimed at establishing bridgeheads in a French seaport – either Brest or Cherbourg – during the early autumn of 1942, particularly if the Soviet Union was on the brink of collapse.[79] Mackenzie King, the Canadian prime minister, emerged from a meeting with Roosevelt convinced that, in advocating a second front, he was seeking ways of 'satisfying Stalin without the necessity of making agreement with him on frontiers' – a view which Churchill dismissed offhandedly as 'a very foolish' one. He was as shocked to find Roosevelt completely ignorant of the military state of affairs in Britain.[80]

Churchill's defiance, as well as growing domestic pressure, encouraged Roosevelt to approach Stalin direct. The president, Ambassador Davies[i] noted, 'had done this more or less to propitiate Stalin, at least in part, because of his opposition to the Curzon Line being included in the British Treaty'.[81] Churchill had justified the decision to conclude the political treaty by his failure to assist Russia on the battlefield. To steal a march on the British prime minister and forestall any agreement, Roosevelt resorted to the military card. He informed Stalin of the 'very important military proposal' he had for 'military action of our forces in a manner to relieve your critical western front'. He urged Stalin to send 'Molotov and a General' to Washington without delay to provide crucial advice before the Americans 'determine with finality' the common strategy and action.[82] He

[i] Joseph E. Davies, ambassador to the Soviet Union, 1936–38 and chairman of Roosevelt's War Relief Control Board from 1942–46.

then informed Churchill *en passant* that he was summoning two 'special representatives' from Moscow (though he failed to mention Molotov by name) to discuss the plan, which he hoped would be 'greet[ed] with enthusiasm'. Finally, conscious of Churchill's predicament at home, he rather maliciously reminded him that the plan was 'in full accord with trend of public opinion' in Great Britain and the United States, and he wished to label it 'The plan of the United Nations'.[83] In a telegram which crossed with that of the president, Churchill tried (alas unsuccessfully) to pre-empt Roosevelt, playing down the 'vast Russo German struggle'. He did not expect the renewed offensive before mid-May at the earliest, while in the meantime Stalin seemed to be 'pleased' with the supply and with Churchill's vow to treat any gas attack on Russian troops as if it were directed at Britain. Obviously disconcerted by the lead taken by Roosevelt, Churchill proposed 'to flip over' to Hyde Park (Roosevelt's estate in upstate New York) for a weekend as there was 'so much to settle that would go easily in talk'.[84]

On 8 April, Maisky was informed by Eden that, despite Roosevelt's reservations, the Cabinet was now prepared to negotiate[85] 'a treaty on the lines desired by M. Stalin', with only some minor modification to accommodate American sensibilities.[86] Amidst growing concern that there would be either a separate Soviet–German peace agreement or a successful Soviet offensive which would pave the Russians' way to Berlin, Eden was anxious for Molotov to come to London. A major bone of contention, however, remained Stalin's insistence on recognition of the Curzon Line as Russia's future border with Poland. Eden suggested, probably after consulting Maisky, that if Molotov was indisposed, the ambassador would be authorized to sign the agreement.[87] Molotov indeed did prefer that Maisky should stand in for him at the negotiations (ominously reminiscent of when, in May 1939, the ambassador replaced him as chairman of the League of Nations). Eden was told that, much as Molotov appreciated the invitation, he had been charged by Stalin 'with more important duties' which would not allow him to 'absent himself from Moscow during the next few critical months'.[88]

So far the Americans had adhered to the premises of the December 'Arcadia' conference, focusing on the long-term expansion of armament production and on the concentration and deployment of Allied troops in Britain, while remaining strategically defensive in all theatres.[89] However, Marshall and Stimson, the First World War veteran and experienced secretary of war, were increasingly disturbed by the British dithering. They believed it was psychologically right for the United States to 'press hard enough on the expeditionary force through Great Britain to make the Germans keep looking over their shoulder in the fight with Russia'. This would prove that the United States was totally committed to operations on the continent and was 'not going to let our strength be dissipated in any more side tracks'.[90] They were puzzled by the British view that it would be possible to urge upon the Russians 'the *indirect* advantages that will accrue to them from Allied operations in distant parts of the world'. Russia's problem was '*to sustain herself during the coming summer* and she must not be permitted to reach such a precarious position that she will accept a negotiated peace, no matter how unfavorable to herself, in preference to a continuation of the fight'.[91]

Their British counterparts were far from enthusiastic about a cross-channel operation in 1942. Insufficient resources, they argued, ruled out a landing in France once the Germans resumed their onslaught on Russia, anticipated for June. The furthest they were prepared to go involved short-term diversionary raids. But their objections emanated to a large extent from Churchill's determination not to slacken off on the North African campaign and to make sure that supplies earmarked for the Mediterranean theatre were not diverted to the eastern front. Within this context, the prime minister remained sceptical about the feasibility of a cross-channel attack even in 1943. The British hoped that if the constraints were properly explained to their American allies, it might encourage their 'participation in or assistance to the British defence of the Middle East in 1942'. No wonder, then, that in the initial British plans *Sledgehammer* was often perceived as a deception, to divert German attention from the main effort in North Africa.[92]

At his meeting with the British chiefs of staff in London on 12 and 13 April, Marshall dug in his heels, insisting that the Americans 'did not wish to see possible reverses and additional commitments in other theatres affecting the full execution of the plan, once accepted'.[93] Hopkins left Churchill in no doubt that the 'United States was prepared to take great risks to save the Russian front'. However Marshall, somewhat gullible, was beguiled by Churchill's portrayal of himself as an advocate of offensive action who was constrained by his own chief of staff, Alan Brooke. The latter, lacking 'Dill's brains', left 'an unfavourable impression' on him.[94] In subsequent conversations, the real Churchill emerged in clearly 'depressed spirits', complaining about the 'irresponsible youngsters' of the press and 'intellectuals who might more usefully be planting potatoes in their backyards', rather than pressing him to disregard the obstacles and 'take the initiative' or 'establish a second front'.[95] However, at a well-orchestrated meeting of the Defence Committee, to which Marshall and Hopkins were invited, Churchill resorted to flamboyant rhetoric, hailing the American plan, which ensured that 'the two nations would march ahead together in a noble brotherhood of arms'. The desultory debate cast doubt on the implementation of the plan, so long as Churchill continued to insist that 'it was essential to carry on the defence of India and the Middle East'. Britain could not 'entirely lay aside everything in furtherance of the main object proposed by General Marshall'.[96]

Marshall, however, returned to Washington believing that a 'complete agreement' had been achieved, at least on the need to launch a cross-channel offensive in 1943. Roosevelt was further assured, in a personal telegram from Churchill, of his intention to adopt the American proposals, though the message included a cryptic comment that 'an interim operation in certain contingencies this year met the difficulties and uncertainties in an absolutely sound manner'.[97] Churchill conceded, rather vaguely, that the execution of *Sledgehammer* was conditioned on the Allies being 'compelled to make a supreme effort ... if Russia is being defeated'. Alas, he knew that if such a situation were to arise in June, the Americans could at best deploy two and a half divisions not earlier than mid-September. Moreover, he had 'no illusions as to the chiselling and other efforts that will be made to slow us down and nullify our work'.[98]

It is hardly surprising, therefore, that when the joint British and American planners set out to define Allied strategy, they could hardly reconcile the short-term and long-term objectives. The urgent and undisputed necessity of keeping Russia fighting clashed with recognition of the meagre means to hand for a diversionary action in 1942, and exposed the conflicting strategic interests of the two countries. While they were supposedly unanimous about the primacy of the European theatre, the British peripheral strategy would hardly allow an offensive across the channel to become 'ripe' before May 1943.[99] Marshall and Hopkins left London with the impression that Churchill 'didn't much like having to consult Roosevelt about the war, which he would prefer to run by himself!' Indeed, the chiefs of staff did not envisage a full-scale engagement across the channel, but rather, as Admiral Pound confided to Halifax, 'something in the way of a landing in order to bring on an air battle' once the situation on the Russian front became perilous.[100] For the time being, Roosevelt sided with his advisers in accepting the Soviet view that, regardless of the obvious obstacles, the sacrifice was worthwhile, since 'one armored division of the allies operating in Western Europe in 1942 is more effective than five such divisions in 1943'.[101] While the Americans gave an impetus to the preparations for a second front, Churchill assured Cabinet that Britain was 'not committed to carry out such an operation this year'.[102]

No wonder Maisky was most alarmed to learn from Eden that although an agreement in principle had been reached in the Defence Committee during Marshall's visit, 'no precise' decision had yet been taken on the actual opening of the second front, which required close coordination with the Americans.[103] His vast experience allowed him to see through Churchill's manoeuvres. He was quick to discern that the declaration specified neither 'when nor where'. His evaluation was reinforced by Lloyd George, who thought that 'Winston's nerve was broken by the Dardanelles... He was afraid of another Dardanelles... I suppose man's nerve is not as good at 67 as it is at 40.'[104]

On 20 April, Stalin, pinning his hopes on the Americans, welcomed Roosevelt's invitation for Molotov to go to Washington and exchange ideas about the creation of a second front. He further announced that Molotov would stop over in London. The same day Clark Kerr, the new British ambassador in Moscow, who had successfully 'fraternised' with Stalin 'over pipes and ... each other's jokes' and who found the man in the Kremlin to be 'just my cup of tea', was informed by the Russians that they 'wished at once' to send to London a four-engine plane directly from Moscow without specifying who the passengers were. The messenger 'seemed to be fussed and begged for an immediate answer'.[105] Roosevelt's response was resolute, and he assured Litvinov the following day that the Americans were set on creating a second front 'now'. He hoped Molotov would stop off in London on the way back, where he could 'exert double pressure' on the British, speaking on behalf of the American president as well.[106]

A couple of days earlier, Eden had rejected the Soviet proposal to attach to the agreement a secret protocol on post-war collaboration which had been floated by Stalin in December.[107] Weighing up various options, Molotov persevered, criticizing the British for producing a draft agreement which, as he instructed Maisky, differed substantially from the original one which had been discussed in Moscow during Eden's visit.[108] Yet, with the renewed German offensive in the offing, Maisky was instructed to submit to the British a modified draft 'to save the Polish case and American susceptibilities'. Maisky, however, found Eden to be 'on the whole disappointed and distressed'. By now his initial crusade in favour of an agreement had given way to compliance with the firm views held by the prime minister and his subordinates at the Foreign Office that 'the settlement of Europe' was not an exclusive Anglo-Soviet affair, and that 'fundamentally it is more important to agree with the Americans, the Dominions and the Allies than with the Russians'. Eden surely was not amused to learn from Winant, back from Washington, that he was 'regarded as a Bolshevik in America!'[109] The difficulties in reconciling the British and the Russian expectations indeed raised 'rather formidable difficulties'. Cadogan found it curious that, of all people, Eden 'should have hopes of "appeasement"!!' He believed it was better 'not to crawl to the Russian over the dead bodies of *all* our principles'.[110]

Maintaining a similar position to the one he held in 1939, Molotov did not appear to be particularly enthusiastic about an agreement which was unlikely to address Soviet demands. His harsh, almost brutal, reaction to Maisky's reporting was that simultaneous signing of the treaty and the secret protocol was 'imperative and unconditional' for the Soviet government. He doubted the sincerity of the British and, rather than making 'more obsequious concessions' just to satisfy their desires, he would prefer to 'interrupt the negotiations ... and postpone them indefinitely'.[111] Maisky, too, found himself in a conundrum, reminiscent of the turbulent 1938–39 period. He desperately needed an agreement which would also ensure his continued precarious presence in London, if not his survival. Rather than allow the negotiations to lapse, he preferred to play down the difficulties, reducing them to 'one or two general observations ... about the background of the treaty'. Still trusting Eden, he preferred to make a personal appeal, underlining the fact that, after 16 months of fighting 'practically alone', Russia was about to face 'great trials'. The absence of a second front created 'a measure of resentment, even bitterness, in Moscow'. If the conditions for opening a second front were insurmountable 'then it seemed more than ever desirable to help her politically'. Eden, who had been advised by Winant about Roosevelt's objection to a treaty, was obviously reluctant to proceed with the negotiations, complaining that the Russians were invariably raising their price at every meeting.[112] Two days later, Eden called Maisky on the phone, only to be told that he was expecting no response from Moscow but was still hoping for a further communication from the British government. Informed that there 'was no likelihood of that', Maisky now feared that an 'agreement would not be possible'.[113]

Having lost all hope, Maisky was informed out of the blue that Molotov would be arriving in Scotland within days and wished to proceed to London by train – 'no flying in British aeroplanes in fact!' Mistrust had reached such a level that when an RAF plane carrying members of the Russian military mission had crashed a week earlier, Maisky was 'very disturbed and suspicious of sabotage'.[114] In his memoirs, Admiral Kharlamov, the head of the military mission, admits: 'My first thought was that it had been an act of subversion organised either by Nazi agents or by the opponents of British–Soviet cooperation.'[115] Everyone was left in suspense, as the Russians preferred to keep the date of Molotov's arrival secret. It seemed as if he might not come at all, particularly as intelligence reports indicated that the offensive had started in earnest and the Russians had been pushed back in the Crimea and Kerch. Cadogan and Maisky, who, on 10 May, went ahead by special train to greet Molotov in Scotland, spent four days touring Edinburgh, Balmoral and other sights before returning empty-handed to London.

There was no one of stature to greet Molotov when he finally arrived on 20 May, on board the highly sophisticated TB-7 Soviet bomber, of which there were only six in existence.[116] The plane, which could fly at 30,000 feet, beyond the reach of any German fighter, took off from Moscow on 19 May at 7.05 in the evening and, flying over enemy territory, arrived over a military airfield not far from Dundee the following morning at 5.15 London time – a mere 7 hours and 10 minutes later, a great aviation achievement for the time. The plane had undertaken a test flight to England four days earlier on the same route, carrying on board Stalin's personal interpreter and a number of Molotov's

100. Molotov in pilot's gear, arriving in Scotland, greeted by British RAF pilots and Pavlov (to his left).

aides. Pavlov[i] was charged with delivering to Maisky the latest revised Soviet draft agreement.[117] Soviet suspicion had reached such a state that the draft was sewn into his waistcoat and he was personally instructed to encrypt it in Moscow and decipher it at the embassy in London. Molotov's own well-rehearsed flight was uneventful, but communications with the British were established only on the approach to the British coast – 'The British are to be blamed', the pilot informed his superiors in Moscow. In the absence of proper landing lights at the airfield, the plane continued to circle for more than an hour, before touching down at seven in the morning. Molotov emerged from the plane wearing bizarre fur-lined aviation gear, which had kept him warm in the freezing conditions which prevailed during the flight.

By the time Cadogan and Eden boarded his train, not far out of London, he was already in 'cracking form, all smiles and in a smart brown suit – very different to the usual Molotov'. Maisky joined Molotov only half way to London, most likely after Pavlov had had ample time to harp on the foreign minister's disdain for the ambassador, giving him a disparaging account of his sojourn at the embassy. His testimony, as well as Litvinov's row with Molotov in Washington,[118] foreshadowed their removal from office a year later and therefore deserves to be quoted in full.[119] Pavlov recalled:

[i] Vladimir Nikolaevich Pavlov, recruited by Molotov in 1939, he served as first secretary in the Berlin embassy, 1939–41, and became interpreter for both Molotov and Stalin during the Second World War. Associated with the Ribbentrop–Molotov Pact, he was sidelined by Khrushchev to work at the Progress publishing house.

101. Molotov, Eden and Maisky: a semblance of harmony.

> I.I. Maisky suggested that I stay in his apartment in the embassy to await the arrival in England of V.M. Molotov. I endured one night, but was uncomfortable, as I felt that my presence had disrupted the English daily routine of my hosts. I therefore 'ran away' to A.E. Bogomolov, the ambassador for the governments in exile. He warmly welcomed me.[120]
>
> I was left with a particularly bad impression from a lunch at Maisky's home, to which the prominent members of the embassy were invited. The conversation at table focused on the difficult situation at the Soviet–German front in the summer of 1941. Spurred on by the conversation, and concerned about her husband's and her own fate, the wife of I.M. Maisky, Agniya Aleksandrovna, said to I.M. Maisky: 'Vanechka, I think that the English will take care of us in much the same way as they had looked after the Austrian ambassador to London following the German occupation of Austria in March 1938.' Maisky did not respond. These were the thoughts which were turning over in A.A. Maisky's head.

Maisky, according to his own admission, was able to warn Molotov only briefly that his draft treaty stood little chance of approval by the British. 'Manifestly displeased', Molotov dismissed him with a curt comment: 'We shall see.'

Litvinov, who had been rushed to England from Washington to brief Molotov about the mood in the US was eventually left out of the negotiations there. After the preliminary talks at the White House with the president, it was observed by the hosts that Molotov took a walk with Litvinov, during which he informed Litvinov that he would not be participating in the talks, 'to the Ambassador's obvious annoyance'.[121]

Maisky had toiled hard before Molotov's arrival in England to ensure his safety and to shield him from the press. When a journalist, friendly to the Russians, sought information from Maisky, he found the ambassador dismissive: 'Oh, those rumours have been going the rounds for a couple of months ... and he may never come.' For whatever reason – security, a desire to keep the visit out of the public eye (thereby leaving all options open), or simply because Molotov was reluctant to stay at the ambassador's residence in Kensington Palace Gardens – Maisky arranged, through Eden, for Molotov to be a guest of Churchill's at the prime minister's country house at Chequers. Though he hosted two dinners in honour of the visitors, Churchill himself chose to remain at his temporary lodgings in the War Rooms annex to 10, Downing Street. Though the British had been more or less 'bounced' by Maisky into issuing the invitation to Chequers, he represented it to Molotov as a sign of the respect they had for the foreign minister. Chequers was where Hopkins and other dignitaries had been hosted.[122] Churchill was astounded at the degree of Molotov's suspicion. Keys were provided reluctantly to the doors of the guests' rooms, which were guarded day and night by NKVD officers and special maids brought along from Moscow. Every piece of furniture in Molotov's room was thoroughly searched by his police officers, and at night 'a revolver was laid out beside his dressing-gown and his dispatch case'.

The negotiations came unstuck over the question of the Soviet demand for an immediate recognition of the Soviet–Polish frontier as had existed prior to the German invasion of Russia. On a personal level, Molotov hardly seemed to possess the diplomatic

102. A smoking break in the negotiations in the garden of 10, Downing Street (left to right: Cadogan, Attlee, Maisky, Molotov, Eden and Churchill).

virtues which Litvinov and Maisky could boast. He had, observed Cadogan, 'all the grace and conciliation of a totem pole'. This was in stark contrast to Maisky, whom Churchill found to be 'the best of interpreters, translating quickly and easily, and possessing a wide knowledge of affairs'.[123] Maisky had found out that Molotov's main task was to ensure the opening of a second front in 1942. Churchill, however, had been armed by the chiefs of staff with arguments to deflect any demands from 'Mr Cocktail'.[124] Following their advice, he tried to divert the negotiations on the second front in the direction of the generals, but Molotov insisted that it was a political decision. While committing himself in principle to a second front, from the outset Churchill expressed reservations, promising to launch the operation 'as soon as the adequate conditions existed', but dwelling at length on the constraints under which the government was acting. He also misled Molotov, who was eager to find out whether unanimity existed between the American and the British views, that they were fully coordinated. When pressed by Molotov, Churchill conceded that the operation would 'be possible only in 1943, or perhaps at the end of 1942'.[125]

Molotov, who had been reluctant to leave Moscow in the first place, emerged from the talks despondent. He was little taken by the personal attention bestowed on him by Churchill – the dinners and chats well into the small hours. What mattered to him was that, when it came to the two substantial issues, Churchill was 'manifestly unsympathetic'. Molotov gained the accurate impression that Churchill preferred to watch events unfold on the Russian front and 'was not in a hurry' to reach any agreement. Molotov no longer entertained any hopes for his forthcoming visit to Washington, but, he conceded to Stalin, 'obligations had to be honoured'. He certainly saw no point in stopping over in London and conducting a second set of futile talks on his way back to Moscow.[126]

Maisky's optimistic expectations, again dovetailing with his outlook in 1939, certainly did not conform to Molotov's. Once again they reflected his wishful thinking, perhaps an existentialist instinct, enhanced by a growing confidence in his own ability to manoeuvre the British. 'The popularity of the USSR is immense,' he confided to Kollontay. 'It feels somewhat strange and unusual to live in such a general atmosphere of friendship and empathy following many years of icy indifference and hostility.' He believed the Western Allies were now firmly committed to the second front, and he was confident that the answer to the crucial question of the timing of the attack was 'sometime this year'. His pressing task was 'to hasten its birth'.[127]

As the negotiations ground to a halt, the situation at the front, Stalin briefed Molotov, was deteriorating fast. Speaking to Roosevelt far more truthfully a few days later, Molotov conceded that Marshal Timoshenko's counteroffensive at Kharkov 'resulted unfavourably for the Russians', and 'The German easy success in the Crimea had rather surprised them.'[128] It had become crucial both to ensure the continued flow of supplies and to press for a second front. Since the gap between the Soviet and the British expectations appeared insurmountable, Eden had prepared an alternative draft of an agreement of a very general nature.[129] On the evening of 24 May, Molotov was unexpectedly instructed by Stalin to adopt the declarative treaty produced by Eden earlier that day. The treaty provided for a twenty-year alliance, reaffirmed mutual military assistance, and set vague general principles for post-war collaboration, while avoiding the contentious frontiers issue. Far from sharing Molotov's view of the treaty ('an empty declaration'), Stalin thought it was 'an important document' – a morale

103. Churchill and Maisky watch over Molotov and Eden signing the Treaty of Alliance.

booster at home and a display of Allied unity vis-à-vis Germany. More significantly (and here he revealed again the lingering suspicions among the Allies) it would forestall a potential Anglo-German separate peace – a fear alluded to by Molotov earlier on in the negotiations. Stalin further put Molotov's mind at rest by assuring him that (as Eden had dreaded) the failure to define the post-war borders would leave Russia with 'free hands' in the future.[130]

The minor alterations to Molotov's proposed brief title of the agreement, in Stalin's own handwriting (not reproduced in Rzheshevsky's collection), are most intriguing. Particularly the addition of 'Hitlerite' to Molotov's original title: 'A treaty on alliance and mutual assistance in the war against Germany'. This was in no way a slip of the pen. The 'Hitlerite' addition gave Stalin manoeuvrability in the event of a communist uprising (to which Maisky had often alluded) or any regime change. In Stalin's order of the day on 23 February, he had dismissed attempts to suggest that the Soviet aim was 'to exterminate the German people and to destroy the German nation' as 'senseless slander' and 'idiotic'. 'Past experience,' he remarked, showed that 'Hitlers come and go whereas the German people and German nation remain.'[131]

'It is desirable,' Stalin wound up his instructions to Molotov, 'to hastily conclude the treaty after which fly to America.' The trade-off he could expect from concluding the treaty was – as the American ambassador explained to Molotov at a nocturnal meeting urgently arranged by Maisky at the embassy – the backing of Roosevelt, who was an ardent supporter of a second front but who had vehemently opposed the earlier draft. Molotov responded rather cunningly – misleading the ambassador into believing that it was American intervention which had brought about the change – that in view 'of what you have said, and the message from the President, it is not the treaty we will sign. We will ... sign a treaty that will relieve the President of any possible embarrassment.' Winant later boasted to the president that it was due to his personal presentation of Roosevelt's objections to the treaty that Molotov had 'abandoned his position on frontiers and agreed to recommend to Stalin the draft Treaty'.[132] Consequently historians and politicians alike were led to believe, as Cadogan noted in his diary, that 'Winant twisted *their* tails last night'.[133] Molotov's apparent display of authority even misled Churchill into insisting to Roosevelt that Molotov was 'a statesman and has a freedom of action very different from what you and I saw with Litvinov'.[134]

The fresh agreement was hastily prepared and signed with pomp and ceremony on 26 May. Accompanied by Eden and Maisky, Molotov was received by the king, who found him to be 'a small quiet man with a feeble voice' but who was 'really a tyrant'. Noticing the 'twinkle in his eye & a sense of humour', he could only hope that the visit 'made him understand the meaning of personal contacts'. This hardly seems to have been the case, as Molotov left Beaverbrook with the impression of being 'a Crippen' and regretting that 'Litvinov was not the man with whom we had to deal'. Molotov himself was little impressed, dismissing the visit to the palace in a telegram to Stalin as 'nothing remarkable'. He was more flattered by succeeding in attracting the entire War Cabinet to a lunch at the embassy.[135] Molotov then left for the United States, preferring to be seen off at the railway station not by Maisky, but rather by Admiral Kharlamov, the head of the military mission.[136]

The gamble in adopting the American-approved treaty indeed seemed to pay off. 'Heavens,' exclaimed Welles, 'seem to have opened.'[137] Churchill, however, was bent on deterring Roosevelt from committing himself to a second front. Hardly had the Russians taken off for Washington than he hastened to send the president a telegram, attached to which was a record of his meeting with Molotov at which he had expounded the obstacles to mounting a second front. 'Dicky [Mountbatten],'[i] he added, 'will explain to you the difficulties of 1942 when he arrives.' He further tried to lure the president into dropping *Sledgehammer* in favour of a landing in northern Norway to secure the convoy route to Russia (a plan which the Russians rejected, as it would have required them to divert troops to the north). But as was Churchill's custom, the most important message appeared at the end: he was looking forward to 'the trial of strength' posed by Rommel's renewed offensive in Libya, for which fresh resources would have to be allocated. 'We must never let gymnast[138] pass from our mind,' he concluded, 'all other preparations would help if need be towards that.'[139]

The negotiations started in earnest on the evening of 29 May. Molotov went out of his way to court Roosevelt, but the president was ill at ease and 'it was pretty difficult to break the ice'. Roosevelt reasserted the need to assist Russia, but referred to the generals, who, 'being narrow specialists in their own fields, always see difficulties'. He personally was prepared to experience another Dunkerque, even if it meant sacrificing '100,000–120,000' people. But his proposal to deploy at best 8–10 divisions on the continent hardly satisfied Molotov, whose instructions were to seek the diversion of at

[i] Lord Louis Francis Albert Mountbatten, chief of combined operations, 1942–43; Supreme Allied Command, South-East Asia, 1943–46; viceroy of India, 1947.

least 40 German divisions from the eastern front.[140] Hopkins paid a nocturnal visit to Molotov's room to reaffirm Roosevelt's pledge to launch a second front. But he prodded the foreign minister 'to draw a gloomy picture' in his preliminary talks with the president the following day.[141]

Roosevelt seemed indeed to be touched. He became aware that unless there was a massive invasion of France in 1942, the Russians might need to retreat from Moscow and the Baku oil fields, thereby aggravating the situation for the Western Allies. 'We are willing to open the second front in 1942,' he concluded. 'This is our hope. This is our wish.' Reading between the lines, Roosevelt was obviously still wavering, sharing Marshall's doubts as to the feasibility of transferring American troops first to Great Britain, and then across the channel. According to the interpreter, Roosevelt asked Marshall whether he could tell Stalin that the Americans were 'preparing a second front'. The general replied in the affirmative. The president then 'authorized Mr Molotov to inform Mr Stalin that we expect the formation of a second front this year'. The subtleties were not lost on Molotov, who, summing up the conversation in a cable to Stalin, was most cautious, suggesting that 'nothing concrete' was achieved on the issue of the second front. He hoped to spend the following three days – needed to overhaul the plane's engines – in paying a visit to New York.[142]

Molotov, however, had succeeded in placing Roosevelt in an uncomfortable position, by harping on the fact that he had come to the United States at the president's invitation. While his visit to Britain had yielded a treaty, he was returning from Washington to London and Moscow empty-handed. Just as Molotov was touring New York, Roosevelt exchanged urgent messages with Churchill and conducted frenzied talks with Marshall, at the end of which Molotov was again invited to the White House and informed, still in guarded terms, that if the Russians agreed to give up on part of the supply effort, the shipping could then be used to expedite the opening of a second front in 1942.[143] Roosevelt's commitment was reaffirmed by Hopkins during a lunch at the Soviet embassy in his honour. The president, he claimed, was clearly in favour of a second front and regretted being 'vague' and unable to provide Molotov with a more specific answer. It all depended now on the British, who were expected to provide most of the troops for the offensive.[144] Indeed, Roosevelt passed the buck to Churchill, hoping that he would be able 'to bring to an end that part of the work which was left uncompleted'.[145] Hopkins came out of the talks convinced that the visit had gone 'extremely well', and that Roosevelt had 'got along famously' with Molotov. He was convinced that the second front 'was moving as well as could be expected', even if 'some of the British' were 'holding back a bit'.[146]

Molotov left the United States 'much happier than he had come, and was entirely satisfied'. He confided to Ambassador Davies that the second front had been 'settled and agreed upon'. He was much taken by Roosevelt, who had 'an extraordinary strategic and practical perspective on the immediate as well as the entire problems of the war … he was particularly impressed because of the vision, the broad humanitarianism and practical idealism' with which the president approached the current and post-war problems.[147] Molotov's and Maisky's optimism was not shared by Litvinov, who wrote to Maisky: 'I am, of course, depressed by the poor results of the London negotiations on the second front … I fear the military will delay this issue until it no longer will produce the desired effect.' Litvinov alerted the Kremlin that 'Great attention should be given to the role of the United States both during the war and its aftermath.' He believed that both Roosevelt's opposition to the treaty and his commitment to the second front were a result of his fear that the United States might find itself isolated at the end of the war, while Britain and the Soviet Union dictated the post-war world order. Roosevelt was eager to drive a wedge between the two by cooperating with Stalin on an anti-imperialist agenda. Litvinov was so disillusioned by the West and so out of tune with Moscow that he had decided, as he wrote to Maisky, 'to maintain silence until the day of victory, if it ever happens in the course of my own lifetime. As you can see, my mood is not very bright and cheerful. Somehow it is hard for me to see how an uninterrupted series of defeats can produce the total sum of a victory – a serious defeat for Hitler. But I do not wish to infect you with my pessimism.'[148] Isolated in Washington, Litvinov remained 'worried and bitter'. His scepticism – similar to the feeling he had had about British politics in 1938–39 – led him to the conclusion that 'for political and Empire reasons' Churchill was now set against a second front in 1942.[149]

Counting on Roosevelt's commitment to a cross-channel attack, which now hinged on British approval, Stalin pursued his divide-and-rule politics, instructing Molotov to 'exert pressure on Churchill to organize a second front and carry it out already in this year'. If the supplies to Russia deprived the Allies of material that was indispensable for such an operation, he was prepared to bow to Roosevelt's request and agree to strip those back to the bare minimum, despite the urgent needs of the Russian front.[150] Back at Downing Street, Molotov followed Stalin's instructions to the letter. He embarked on a lengthy diatribe concerning the opening of the second front. He did not hesitate to spill the beans about the content of his talks with Roosevelt, who he claimed was 'fully sympathetic to the idea of opening a second front' in 1942, and with Marshall, 'who held similar views'. He further referred to the communiqué on the talks in Washington which, *inter alia*, stated that 'full understanding was reached with regard to the urgent task of creating a second front in Europe in 1942'.

Familiar with what had transpired in Washington, on the eve of Molotov's return Churchill hastened to fend off the chiefs of staff's inclination to launch raids on the continent in 1942. He dismissed such endeavours as a response to a 'cri de coeur' from Russia, rather than 'the calm determination and common sense of professional advisers'. He, unlike Roosevelt (as he later told Molotov as well), did not approve of an operation which was bound to waste valuable lives and matériel, and would make 'ourselves and our capacity for making war ridiculous throughout the world'. Far from sharing the American and the Russian belief that *Sledgehammer* should be executed at whatever cost if Russia was in peril, Churchill would sanction it only if the Germans were demoralized by 'ill success' against Russia. For the time being, he objected to any 'substantial landing in France unless we are going to stay' and unless it was conditioned on Russian success in the battlefield. He therefore remained evasive during the talks with Molotov, stating that a decision 'would only be taken in the light of the situation prevailing when the moment came' – which in his book meant a Soviet success in the battlefield.[151] Despite the failure 'to come to grips' with the Russians on the second front, Churchill was satisfied with the relations, which had become 'much more intimate'. Absorbed in his own campaign against Rommel, he did 'not anticipate any smooth or rapid advance for the Germans into the Caucasus', as the Russians, 'though anxious', were 'in very good heart and the forces on either side seem well matched'.[152]

A short farewell party at Downing Street on the evening of 10 June concluded Molotov's visit. Churchill, 'in his rompers', produced a bottle of champagne to celebrate what he considered to be a successful visit. Though forced to adopt the American communiqué, he left Molotov in no doubt that he did not consider the date of the second front to be binding. Pledging to continue the preparations, Churchill's final aide-mémoire would make 'no promise in the matter'. The Russians departed for the military airfield at Cheddington in Buckinghamshire. Eden got to see them off after Maisky 'made no bones about indicating … that that was expected!' 'What savages' was Cadogan's final judgement.[153]

Against the background of growing alienation between Maisky and Narkomindel, the success of Molotov's visit was vital. The ambassador toiled behind the scenes to reduce the conflicts to a minimum, while ensuring that Molotov was given the royal treatment. As Negrín, his insightful and intimate friend, acknowledged, the success was due to his 'magnificent and relentless difficult work', as well as to his 'charming but Stormovich-like[154] personal intervention'. He was praised by leading British politicians for having made the Soviet embassy 'the centre of world affairs'.[155] Maisky had to manoeuvre cautiously. His success smacked of the power he had accumulated in London, his direct access to the top politicians, autonomy and growing public popularity. Generally an asset, in Stalin's authoritarian Russia this paradoxically heralded his downfall.[156]]

13 June

Visited Lloyd George in Churt. We talked about many things, in particular the Anglo-Soviet treaty. Lloyd George thanked me for my *suggestion* (which I had conveyed through Sylvester) that he should speak in parliament with regard to Eden's communication concerning the treaty and Molotov's visit. Lloyd George had not intended to speak on the matter, but after receiving my message he thought: 'Well, perhaps it would be worth saying a few words.'

And so he did. I complimented him on his performance. The old man was pleased.

Lloyd George then recalled his negotiations with Krasin in 1920–21. They were discussing the possibility of a trade agreement. The attitude of the British government was cool, to say the least. Many ministers were against it. Curzon, the foreign secretary, categorically refused to conduct the talks. But Lloyd George was not discouraged. He decided to carry out the negotiations on his own, with the help of Sir Robert Horne,[i] president of the Board of Trade.

When Krasin arrived in the spring of 1920, Lloyd George received him in his official residence at *10, Downing Street*. After a preliminary, semi-official exchange of opinions, they got down to official negotiations. They went reasonably well. Krasin made a good impression on Lloyd George: he

[i] Robert Stevenson Horne, president of the Board of Trade, 1920–21; chancellor of the exchequer, 1921–22.

seemed to be a clever, adaptable and business-like man, who was blessed with a good dose of common sense. Rapid success, however, was hindered by various attendant circumstances, such as the Polish–Soviet war, the arrival of Kamenev[i] and his propaganda among the workers, etc. Nevertheless, progress was made. When Curzon realized that despite his boycott the talks were advancing, he changed his tactics: he started attending the meetings without taking part in the negotiations. He just sat there in silence, stiff as a poker. The first meeting between Curzon and Krasin is etched in Lloyd George's memory. Curzon arrived first and instead of taking a seat at the table, he remained by the fireplace in the prime minister's office. He stood facing away from the hearth, his hands behind his back. Krasin came in and started shaking hands with all those present. Finally, Krasin approached Curzon and held out his hand. The foreign minister maintained his pose, with his hands clasped behind his back, and gazed straight past Krasin. Everyone was embarrassed. Lloyd George flared up and snapped: 'Curzon, be a gentleman!'

Curzon gave a start, came to his senses and reluctantly stretched out his hand to Krasin.

It was a good lesson. In the following meetings Curzon behaved better.

The Swedish ambassador Prytz told me a funny story.

Not long ago, he paid a visit to princess Helena Victoria and conveyed greetings to her from King Gustav. The king had recently had a bout of pneumonia, and the princess was very anxious to know how he was. Prytz, obviously forgetting whom he was talking to, answered very casually: 'Oh, the king feels just fine! *He is a remarkable old chap*!'

The princess was shaken and shocked.

'*Old chap*?' she echoed, half in surprise and half in reproach.

Only then did Prytz realize that he had committed a faux pas.

A few days later Prytz related this minor incident to the Dutch ambassador.

'Imagine,' Verduynen[ii] exclaimed, 'almost exactly the same thing happened to me!'

And the Dutch ambassador told him that just the other day he had gone to play a round of golf and met an English acquaintance, who asked after Wilhelmina's health: 'How is your remarkable old girl?'

Verduynen calmly answered that the queen was quite well. One of the Dutch courtiers was present at the scene and described it later to Wilhelmina. The old lady was indignant at such 'disrespect' towards her lofty title and reprimanded

[i] Lev Borisovich Kamenev was deputy chairman of the Council of People's Commissars, 1923–26 and member of the Politburo in the 1920s. A victim of the show trials, he was executed in 1936.
[ii] Edgar van Verduynen, Dutch ambassador to London, 1939–42; minister without portfolio, 1942–45.

Verduynen at the first opportunity: 'Does my ambassador not know that the queen is the queen, and not an *old girl*?'

Prytz fairly trilled with laughter as he told me all this. Yes, the era of royalty has passed! Kings and queens are living out their last days, yet they still put on airs and play at their trivial monarchic games.

19 June

Nice examples of political idiocy.

On 29 August of last year I arranged a grand 'Allied' lunch, to which I invited the prime ministers and foreign ministers of all governments in exile resident in London, along with the ambassadors of other Allied governments (USA, China). A few days earlier I decided to sound out the Dutch as to whether or not I should invite them. On the one hand, the Dutch were rather like allies; on the other, we have never had diplomatic relations with Holland. I didn't wish to offend them, but nor did I want to invite a refusal. I made a 'private' inquiry through Feonov, our *liaison man* on economic matters with the Dutch. The Dutch took the matter very seriously: they even discussed it at a government meeting! Their reply was: better not… lest the government's behaviour be 'misunderstood' both in Holland and the Dutch Indies and merely go to serve Goebbels' propaganda. So the Dutch thanked me through Feonov for the kind thought, but asked me to refrain from sending an invitation. That was stupid, but it was not for me to answer for the idiocy of the Dutch sages. They were not invited, and the lunch was held without them. At that time, though, Queen Wilhelmina still had the Dutch Indies…

At the end of February this year, the Dutch foreign minister, Van Kleffens,[i] went to America on an official visit. Singapore had fallen. The Dutch Indies had been lost. Queen Wilhelmina had been 'orphaned', having neither kingdom nor empire. Van Kleffens thought it an appropriate moment to probe the possibility of establishing diplomatic relations between Holland and the USSR. He came to Litvinov and proposed mutual recognition, but…

'Oh, not full recognition, of course,' Van Kleffens explained. 'We can't recognize you fully as yet… Our public is not quite ready for that… It's a complicated and difficult matter… With time, of course…'

In short, what Van Kleffens was suggesting as 'a first stage' was the exchange not of ambassadors but of diplomatic representatives. Litvinov responded to that, of course, with the diplomatic: 'Go to hell!'

Moscow later approved his stance.

---

[i] Eelco Nicolaas Van Kleffens, minister for foreign affairs of the Dutch government in exile, 1939–45.

Today I had a visit from the Dutch ambassador in London, who bears the elaborate name Van Verduynen.

On behalf of his government he proposed that diplomatic relations be established between Holland and the USSR. I asked, not without irony: 'Full relations? Including the exchange of ambassadors?'

Verduynen took the hint and hastened to assure me: 'Yes, of course.'

Then, without any encouragement on my behalf, Verduynen told me about Van Kleffens' talk with Litvinov and tried to explain his strange behaviour. His explanations were boring and uninteresting.

I reported the Dutch proposal to Moscow. I doubt we shall be in any particular hurry. Holland does not deserve it: it has been ignoring the existence of the USSR for 25 years and its behaviour today strongly suggests political cretinism. Let it wait.

21 June (Bovingdon)

A hot and oppressive sunny day, just like a year ago…

I can't help recalling the thoughts, feelings and sensations that engulfed me on the eve of the German attack on the USSR. Much has changed since then. The main change, it seems, is this.

A year ago the Germans were convinced they would win – the only question was: When? Now they have lost that belief. They don't yet perceive their defeat as inevitable, but its terrible spectre already troubles their minds. It is no accident that, to judge by the latest information, the main topic of conversation in Germany this summer is: How to avoid defeat? And not: What will we do once we win?

A year ago we still did not know what the war held in store for us. We had a profound faith that the USSR could not perish, that we would save our country one way or another. But how? By what means? Within our ranks there also prevailed a certain *inferiority complex*: the myth of the 'invincibility' of the German army had some impact in the USSR as well. 'Tank phobia' among the troops was also observed in the first months of the war. Today things are different. The experience of the past 12 months, and especially the experience of the winter offensive, has changed the entire mood of the country. The myth of the 'invincibility' of the fascist hordes has been destroyed. The *inferiority complex* has vanished. On the eve of the first anniversary of the war we know that we will prevail. We can even envisage, more or less, how this will happen. The only question is: When and at what price?

In essence Hitler has already lost the war. That much is clear today. But how much more blood and effort will be required to kill the mad beast!…

Contemplating the immediate prospects for the war, I recalled my recent conversation with Lloyd George. The old man's train of thought goes like this.

The nature of the war on the Soviet front this summer is not as it was last year, when German superiority was overwhelming, thanks to the surprise element in their attack, their numbers, better weapons and greater experience of waging 'total war'. As a result, they managed to gain a number of major and serious victories. True, they did not succeed in conducting a *Blitzkrieg* in the full sense of the word, and the Russian campaign was not completed in 10 weeks, as Hitler had planned. But still, this was a war that never stood still, and the Germans managed to seize vast territories at a relatively (only relatively, of course!) low cost and to approach the gates of Moscow and Leningrad.

The situation in 1942 is entirely different. The Germans have grown weaker over the winter, and the Russians have strengthened. Now the Russians boast numerical superiority over the Germans. Parity has almost been attained in terms of arms and aircraft. The Red Army has received its baptism of fire and learned the techniques of 'total war'. Consequently, the morale of the German army has fallen, while that of the Soviet army has risen. The myth of the 'invincibility' of the German army has been destroyed. At the same time, the front line has been reinforced on both sides, and every attempt at a breakthrough has entailed an extremely arduous and costly operation. The result is that the situation on the Soviet front this summer has come to bear some resemblance to the situation on the French front in 1914–18. The front has become less mobile, more static and fixed. Not quite what we saw in the west in the last war, but not entirely different either.

The Germans, of course, can scarcely fail to grasp the change. And, if that is so, then can all the talk about Hitler's 'big summer offensive' have any basis in reality? How can he launch an attack? All right, it is possible. But a general, crushing, decisive offensive to compare with that of last year?... No, most unlikely. Hitler doesn't have the guts anymore! Goebbels, of course, will be in favour of attacking, but Hitler... I doubt it. If that is the case, then what does Hitler's strategy amount to this year?

It seems to Lloyd George that Hitler will probably choose to remain on the defensive in the USSR (which of course does not exclude isolated offensive operations on a modest scale) and try to exploit the occupied territories to the utmost, first and foremost the Ukraine. The Ukraine, after all, is Hitler's long-cherished dream, and he now has almost all of it in his hands. The Ukraine cannot give him much this year, of course, but what about next year? In 1943, the Ukraine may well be able to render significant results in terms of food and industry... if the Germans manage to hold onto it, that is.

Will they? The answer to this question depends on the answer to another question: what are the Red Army's chances in 1942?

Lloyd George is not overly optimistic. Of course, there can no longer be any question of the Red Army being routed. That much is obvious to everyone. But, on the other hand, can one really expect the Red Army to crush the German army this summer? The old man thinks not. Since hostilities on the Soviet front increasingly assume the character of trench warfare, both sides would require an enormous numerical advantage (3:1 or at least 2:1) to execute a successful offensive. The Red Army cannot boast such superiority as yet. An effective second front in the west would be helpful here, but Lloyd George doubts that it will be created in 1942 (not a second front in general, but an effective one). So the offensive capabilities of the Red Army are also limited for the time being.

The conclusion that Lloyd George draws from all this is that the situation on the Soviet front in the summer of 1942 is very close to *stalemate*, making it possible that autumn will set in, and even winter, without the front undergoing any crucial changes to its current shape. So the old man does not consider 1942 to be the decisive year. The war will be protracted. One must put one's hopes on Germany's exhaustion, the sapping of morale at the front and at home, and Germany's internal disintegration. But this is a very lengthy process.

I demurred. We had a long dispute. Eventually, Lloyd George exclaimed: 'Please don't misunderstand me! The picture I am sketching may strike you as excessively pessimistic, but this is certainly not what I would like to see occur. This is what I'm afraid will actually occur. As for me, I dream of just one thing: a second front and victory in 1942. But will this happen? I doubt it.'

I keep turning this conversation over in my mind. Is Lloyd George right or wrong? Undoubtedly there is much truth in what the 'Old Wizard' says. But not the whole truth. What will actually happen?

Only events can tell us that.

24 June[157]

Last 'weekend' brought the anniversary of the German–Soviet war. England greeted it noisily, with fervour and enthusiasm… The England, I mean, of the masses, the workers, the ordinary citizens, the intellectual class. Not the England of the government or the City. The latter England expressed its cordial disposition and fellow-feeling, but 'without overdoing it'. The major newspapers, which take their lead from the government, did the same.

But the masses have spoken. A wave of big meetings dedicated to the anniversary and the Anglo-Soviet treaty swept across the country. Everyone in unusually high spirits. The idea of a second front in 1942 dominated proceedings.

I myself attended a 10,000-strong mass meeting in the Empress Hall, where Cripps was the main speaker. His speech was fairly decent on the whole. He drew most applause when he let it be understood that the British government was preparing a second front this year. Very energetic clapping also accompanied the moment when, to my embarrassment, Cripps showered me with praise. The English just can't do without compliments! Agniya and I were sitting on the dais in the front row and the audience gave us a real ovation. When Cripps finished his speech I reprimanded him for his indiscretion, but it was hard to get through to him.

'Just what was needed!' he replied innocently.

Then he asked me somewhat anxiously: 'Do you have the full text of my speech…for Moscow?'

I said I did not. He then pulled the original copy of his speech out of his pocket and gave it to me.

Leaving aside my personal involvement, I should say that the meeting was quite astonishing: the atmosphere, the speeches, the greetings and telegrams. Greetings arrived, incidentally, from Timoshenko, General MacArthur[i] and the archbishop of Canterbury. As they left the meeting, some of our comrades were saying: 'Almost as if we were in Moscow.'

An exaggeration, of course, but a revealing comment none the less.

Similar events were held in other cities. I sent Novikov to Birmingham, Graur to Manchester, and Zonov to Cambridge. The meeting in Birmingham, where Beaverbrook was the main speaker, was especially interesting. Held in the open air, it drew some 50,000 people. Spirits were high. Beaverbrook delivered a very good speech (he had consulted me about it two days before), posing the question of the second front in the sharpest terms. It was met with thunderous applause. The words of the lord mayor of Birmingham, Tiptaft,[ii] who chaired the meeting, were even more interesting. In his opening address, he remarked: 'Speaking of communism… Were we to hold a vote on this matter today, most of the country would probably turn out to be communist.'

The crowd responded with a vociferous 'Hear! Hear!' and drowned the lord mayor's voice in cheers.

Who'd have thought we would live to see this! Tiptaft's words may also contain some exaggeration, but still: to hear such statements from the lord mayor of Birmingham, that stronghold of metallurgy and lair of Chamberlainites… It speaks of great shifts in the country's mood!

The past 'weekend' has clearly shown the idea of a second front to be ripe among the masses. I'll bear it in mind. It's useful to know this in my negotiations

---

[i] Douglas MacArthur, general, commander-in-chief of Allied forces, South-West Pacific Area, 1942; commander-in-chief, US forces, Far East Command until 1951.

[ii] Norman Tiptaft, lord mayor of Birmingham, 1941–42.

on the matter with the British government. What about the British government, incidentally? I wonder what Churchill will bring back from America…

Yes, there are shifts in England, and big ones at that. National patriotism is mixed up with socio-political radicalism, and all this is clothed in fervent Sovietophilia. We shall see what comes next.

27 June

Citrine called on me, having just returned from the USA, where he went in the hope of turning the Anglo-Soviet trade union committee into an Anglo-American–Soviet committee. He failed in his mission. The executive committee of the American Federation of Labor did not want to work 'with communists'. For their part, they proposed setting up an Anglo-American federation in addition to the Anglo-Soviet Committee. The English will be in both, for *liaison* purposes. Citrine and the General Council like the idea, but they wish to consult Shvernik[i] before making a final decision. Citrine gave me a batch of letters and documents for the information of VTsSPS [All-Union Central Council of Trade Unions].

Then we spoke of British affairs. I asked Citrine why all industry *controls*, introduced by the government for the duration of the war and placed under the Ministry of Supply, are in the hands of the big owners of the corresponding branches of production? Why don't the trade unions and Labour demand some 'controls' for themselves, or at least their participation in the existing 'controls'.

Citrine replied: 'The "control" of industry is a complex and difficult business. We don't have men of sufficient competence.'

I expressed my doubts as to whether this was really the case. Citrine reluctantly agreed and added: 'Of course, it might be possible to find people among the trade union leaders who would be up to the task, but who would take it on? This is a temporary engagement for 2–3 years, and one would have to leave one's *life job* in the union. Who would agree to that? I for one have been offered various high positions in government, but I have always refused. For that same reason. My colleagues act in the same way.'

I expressed my amazement and asked why he considered 'control' work short term? Wouldn't many branches of industry be nationalized after the war?

Citrine said he was doubtful. It was possible, of course, that some branches (coal, the railway, etc.) would leave private hands, but would they be nationalized? Citrine is inclined to think not. The government will probably act in the same way as it did in the matter of the coal industry. In other words, the

[i] Nikolai Mikhailovich Shvernik, first secretary of the USSR's All-Union Central Council of Labour Unions, 1930–44.

usual 'English compromise'. Why? For the same reason, according to Citrine: because there are no men among the workers sufficiently qualified to run industrial enterprises. In general, this lack of expertise seems to weigh heavily on Citrine's mind.

'Fifteen years ago,' he concluded, 'I happened to give a speech in a summer school in Bristol. We were discussing the forms of transition from capitalism to socialism. Even then I was making the argument that it was senseless to go over to socialism while the working class still lacked leaders trained to manage socialized industry. And it is very difficult to obtain such training in a capitalist society. I see no reason to change the views I expressed at that time.'

What an astonishing *inferiority complex*! With such leaders it will take British workers a long time to eliminate capitalism.

29 June

The situation in Libya is now critical.[158] I saw Eden today and asked him to brief me about the situation. By way of a reply, Eden asked his secretary to bring in Auchinleck's[i] cipher messages of the last few days and gave them to me to read. Gloomy reading!

Mersa Matruh, which had been considered the main British stronghold in Egypt, fell in the course of some three days. Rommel outflanked it from the south. The British beat a hasty retreat to Fukah, where they are now engaged in desperate *delaying action* against the Germans. Further east, 60–70 miles from Alexandria, there is one more fortified position, El Alamein. Its advantage lies in the fact that here, between the coast and the Qattara Depression, there is a narrow 'neck' some 40 metres wide. It offers a relatively narrow front which is easier to defend. That's where the British intend to make a firm *stand*. Will they succeed?

I don't know. The British defeats on land (and they have already had plenty) render me sceptical. Particularly after learning the details. Among the cipher messages from Cairo there was one which truly appalled me. The commanders in Cairo gave their assessment of the situation and drew provisional plans for the immediate future – what a terrible document! Not a word about an attack or an offensive, nor even of their determination to hold one or other position at all costs! Quite the reverse: constant talk of evacuation, retreat, and the abandoning of positions… 'We shall defend El Alamein… If it proves impossible to hold on to El Alamein, we shall retreat in two columns: one towards Cairo and another towards Alexandria… We are forming special units for the defence of the Nile

[i] Sir Claude John Auchinleck, field marshal, commander-in-chief India, 1941 and 1943–47; commander-in-chief Middle East, 1941–42.

delta… If they fail to check Rommel we shall make a fighting retreat to the Suez Canal', etc. etc. That's more or less the spirit of the thing… The devil knows what! Sheer defeatism! And it's all set out so evenly, so calmly and methodically, as if these were the calculations of a land surveyor…

As I read the message I couldn't help recalling the Austrian General Weyrother in Tolstoy's *War and Peace*, who, on the eve of the Battle of Austerlitz, monotonously reads out his 'disposition' for the next day to the war council: 'Die erste Kolonne marschiert' … 'Die zweite Kolonne marschiert'… At least Weyrother was planning to march forwards; Auchinleck is planning to march back… Contemptible!

With the high command in this sort of mood, you're not likely to win!

That much is clear. Tobruk fell within 24 hours. What happened? The details are not yet known, but it is clear from the Cairo cipher messages that keeping Tobruk was part of the plan of the British command; that an entire South African division had been stationed there since the very beginning of hostilities; that it had plenty of supplies and munitions; and that the fortifications were all in order. The decision to hold on to Tobruk was not a local commander's sudden wheeze, thought up at the last minute. So what happened? There can be only one explanation: panic and cowardice. There are allusions to that effect in the cipher messages. But the general picture, it seems, is not yet entirely clear.

Eden added a revealing detail. This morning he received a telegram from Cairo with the request: 'What to do with the Egyptian government?' To where should it be evacuated, should the need arise?

I expressed my feelings in the frankest terms. Eden did not even try to defend Cairo (where, it should be said, there are some 160 British generals!). On the contrary, he set about assuring me that Churchill would deal a crushing blow to the defeatist attitudes of Auchinleck and Co. Eden also said that he had already sent a very sharp telegram in reply to the inquiry concerning the Egyptian government, making it clear that he refuses even to discuss the matter… So much the better!

But where does the root of the Libyan disaster lie? For, as far as I know, the forces on both sides were more or less even at the beginning of the battle; indeed, the British even had a certain preponderance over the Germans.

Among the cipher messages from Cairo, I found a quite interesting one which shed some light on the matter. It turns out that a few days ago the War Cabinet sent Auchinleck a detailed questionnaire about the events in Libya, and he submitted his replies. The documents are long and detailed. But in essence they boil down to the following: at the root of the disaster, according to Auchinleck, lie two critical elements – the 'greenness' of the British army and the inferiority of its arms.

On the first point, Auchinleck states quite plainly: 'Our army of amateurs is up against an army of professionals.' A valuable admission! And a justified one if it refers also to the lack of an 'offensive' spirit.

As for the second point, Auchinleck emphasizes in particular the weakness of British tanks (2-pound guns against German 88mm guns) and affirms unequivocally that the *Crusader*, *Stuart*, *Valentine*, and *Matilda* operating in North Africa are entirely useless. The American *Grant* is good, but there were few such tanks (just over a hundred) in Libya. Further on, Auchinleck states that although the British air force surpasses the German one in number, the technical characteristics of the *Messerschmitt 109* surpass those of the planes at the disposal of the English: the *Tomahawk*, *Kittyhawk* and even the *Hurricane*.

In short (this is my conclusion): it's the commanders, generals and senior officers who are to blame, as ever in the past.

I asked Eden: 'So what are the British government's plans?'

Eden shrugged his shoulders and replied: 'To hold El Alamein and defend Egypt. We are bringing up reinforcements. A fresh armoured division (350 tanks with 2-pound guns) has just arrived.'

I argued that the British government must revise its strategy: it must switch to active defence in the Near East and concentrate all its offensive energy in

104. Medals being presented to British *Hurricane* pilots in Russia.

Europe. We had a long talk on this subject. Eden agreed with me on the whole, but what about Churchill? At bottom, everything depends on him.

It seems unlikely that Churchill will agree. Today I asked Eden about the results of the Roosevelt–Churchill meeting, particularly on the issue of a second front. Eden said that everything was as it was, that is, as it was during Churchill's talks with Molotov on 9–10 June. Events in the Middle East do not affect the British government's plans for a second front in any way. The prime minister asked Eden specially to convey this to me.

I inquired: 'No date for opening a second front was set during Molotov's talks with Churchill. Are you able to tell me anything more definite in the wake of Churchill's visit to Washington?'

Eden could not and suggested that I should go and see the prime minister myself. I agreed. But this all sounds bad. I fear that a second front will not be opened in 1942 and that Churchill, together with Roosevelt, will try to make 1943 the 'decisive year'.

2 July

Spent two days sitting in parliament. The conduct of the war was being debated in connection with a resolution of no confidence submitted by a group of 21 MPs headed by Sir John Wardlaw-Milne.

Conclusions?

The main and essential conclusion is that the country is very alarmed and vexed about the disaster in Libya. The mood is close to that which followed Dunkerque. True, England has been astonishingly unsuccessful on land throughout this war. It's enough to recall Norway, France, Greece, Crete, Malaya, Singapore and Burma. But none of this made as strong an impression on the country as the current defeats. Why? Partly, of course, because at a certain stage quantity is expected to be translated into quality. But that's not the main point here. The main point is that in all previous cases there were always some 'extenuating' circumstances that cushioned the impact: either the English did not bear the brunt of the blame (in France, for example), or they were fully aware that they were not ready for the fight, but were forced into it for reasons beyond their control (Greece, Crete, Malaya, etc.). In Libya, there were no 'extenuating' circumstances. This was the best British front, the PM's very own '*darling*', which was never refused anything and was built up stubbornly and systematically over the last two years. Churchill spoke openly about this today: in the period in question, the British government dispatched to the Middle East 950,000 troops, 6,000 aircrafts, 4,500 tanks, 5,000 guns, 50,000 machine-guns, and so on. What more could have been done?

Yet it was on this very '*darling front*' that in the last few days the British suffered their most decisive defeat! They were defeated in spite of the fact that not only were they not at a numerical disadvantage at the beginning of the battle, but even had a certain superiority (100,000 British and 90,000 Germans, British superiority in the air, a 7:5 advantage in tanks and 8:5 in artillery). How to explain this?

It's hard to find any sort of adequate explanation. That is why the prevailing mood in the country and in parliament is anxiety, anger, agitation and the growing suspicion that there is an intrinsic defect in the British military machine, one fraught with the gravest of consequences. For if Rommel is not beaten now, or at least stopped dead in his tracks, the whole Middle East will be under threat, as will be both India and the British Empire in Africa.

Such are the circumstances under which the parliamentary debates were held.

The situation in parliament in itself, however, did not pose any danger to Churchill. Party discipline played its role here. So, too, did the MPs' fear of revealing any internal discord to the outside world (to the enemy, in particular) at such a trying time. Lastly, one should note the disparate and feeble character of the official opposition. Among these 21 could be found the most diverse elements – such as the diehard Wardlaw-Milne, the left Labourite A. Bevan, and the offended careerist Hore-Belisha. Even their speeches took off in different directions. Wardlaw-Milne demanded that the duke of Gloucester be appointed commander-in-chief, while Bevan demanded the appointment of political commissars in the army! What a wide spectrum! It was all too easy for a masterful parliamentary strategist and speaker such as Churchill to see off his opponents. And that's precisely what happened. The prime minister's closing speech was very forceful and imposing, and the voting went as follows: 476 for the government, 25 against, about 30 abstentions.

So, Churchill has won a brilliant victory in parliament. But he shouldn't get carried away. In fact, the overwhelming majority in the House is in a very anxious and critical mood, blaming the government for the long chain of military defeats that has ended, for now, in Libya. This feeling is yet stronger among the masses. I have the sense that the country would be ready to replace the government or to reshape it radically, but is stopped short by the baffling question: who would be any better? In particular, who would be better than Churchill as prime minister?

There is no satisfactory answer to this question. Personally, I consider Churchill, for all his failings, to be the best of all possible prime ministers today. That is why I take a 'pro-Churchill' line. However, it should be borne in mind that today's voting in no way relieves the prime minister of his enormous responsibility for how events unfold in the immediate future. After all, what is the meaning of today's vote? It is this: 'We are putting our trust in you once more, but you must *put your house in order*.'

What does this really mean? It means: hold on to Egypt and stop all the defeats.

How can such a result be achieved? These, in my view, are the minimum requirements: (a) establish a single general staff, (b) replace the secretary of state for war, (c) undertake a thorough purge of the senior officers and generals and boldly promote young cadres in the army irrespective of their social origin.

If Churchill does not follow this route, he will prove Bevan right for saying today: 'You win parliamentary debates, but lose battles.'[159]

Will Churchill implement the minimum programme indicated above? I don't know. I can't say I'm overly optimistic in this respect. But we shall see.

3 July

Today, at long last, I had the detailed conversation with Churchill that I have been hoping for ever since he returned from America. I've been wanting to learn what effect his meeting with Roosevelt had on the prospects for a second front. But Churchill isn't having much luck with his trips to the USA: as soon as he gets back, he is greeted by a domestic political storm. So it was in January and so it was in June. While he was engrossed in overcoming this most recent storm, it was difficult to reach him. But yesterday the storm was silenced – for the time being, at least. And today I went to see the prime minister.

He asked me to come at 12.45. When I arrived, the Cabinet was still in session. I was kept waiting in the reception room for some 20 minutes. Soon after one o'clock Churchill summoned me at last. He apologized for the delay, glanced at his watch, and said: 'You know what?… Let's have lunch together! I've kept you waiting so long. Are you free?'…

It was a bit awkward for me as I was meant to be seeing Vansittart, Lobkowicz[i] and others for lunch today, but when a prime minister invites you, you can hardly say no. Besides, I very much needed to talk to him. I called Agniya at home, told her I couldn't come to lunch with Vansittart, asked her to represent me there, and remained at *10, Downing Street*.

Before sitting down to lunch, I congratulated the prime minister on his victory in parliament yesterday. A smile of satisfaction crossed his face before he replied with emphatic modesty: 'Such victories are not the hardest things in our life.'

---

[i] Maximilian Lobkowicz, 1941–45, ambassador to London for the Czechoslovak government in exile.

Nonetheless Churchill willingly continued the conversation on the topic I had raised. He recalled with pleasure various details of yesterday's sitting of parliament, the speeches of various MPs, the adroit gestures and comments. In short, he was reliving and savouring a debate that had only just concluded. Churchill's countenance, the tone of his voice, and the glint in his eye made one feel what an *old, very old parliamentary hand* he is; that it's precisely in parliament that his soul and his life reside; that he sees the entire world and all its events primarily from the parliamentary point of view; and that he is interested first and foremost in how those events are reflected in parliament and in the reactions or attitudes they elicit there. I remember how I used to be astonished by Martov years ago: he saw everything in the world through the lines of a newspaper editorial. Churchill sees the world in terms of the effect of a parliamentary performance. And is it any surprise? Parliament is in the blood of every Englishman, and Churchill has been warming the benches of Westminster for more than 40 years.

The prime minister asked what impression the debates had made on me. I replied that the current opposition presented no danger to the government for the simple reason that it was such a motley crew. Thus, Wardlaw-Milne could propose that the duke of Gloucester be appointed commander-in-chief, while Bevan could demand that political commissars be appointed to the army. Such was the diversity of opinions among the members of the opposition!

Churchill liked my remark very much, and he exclaimed with a laugh of approval: 'Precisely!'

But then I added: 'Still, the situation is grave. In spite of your victory yesterday.'

The prime minister immediately turned red and frowned. Rising abruptly from his seat, he said: 'Let's go and find Mrs Churchill! She must be fed up with waiting for us.'

We found Mrs Churchill seated in the garden beneath the broad branches of a tree. She was writing something in pencil in a notebook. Her cousin was with her. The PM left us for a minute, and Mrs Churchill started talking to me about the recent events in parliament. She was most perturbed. Yesterday's vote was a victory for the government, of course, but…

'If the situation at the front does not improve,' Mrs Churchill continued, 'who knows what may happen?'

There were four of us at the table: Churchill, his wife, his wife's cousin and myself. Entering the dining room, the prime minister asked somewhat anxiously: 'And where is Mary?'

'Mary *is lunching out*,' answered Mrs Churchill.

The PM said nothing, but his disappointment was obvious: Churchill certainly loves his younger daughter!

The conversation over lunch was of a more general nature. Someone happened to mention Lady Astor. Churchill laughed and said that this lady voted in favour of the government yesterday.

I remarked that of late the Astor couple had been doing their best to represent the fifth column. She, in particular, is spreading anti-Soviet propaganda wherever she can.

'Where? When?' Churchill suddenly flared up.

I told them about the behaviour of the *Royal Institute for International Affairs* and about those of Lady Astor's speeches which were known to me. This made an impression.

Mrs Churchill backed me up and told us, in her turn, that an acquaintance of hers who worked at the *Royal Institute* had to leave as she couldn't bear the political atmosphere there.

'Excuse me!' Churchill suddenly roared. 'The government subsidizes the *Royal Institute* from the tax payer's pocket. It is a public, state institution, not a private one. We have the right to take an interest in its activity. Yes, we do!'

Then the prime minister turned to me and added: 'Send me a letter on this subject – I'll take the appropriate measures.'

I promised to carry out the PM's request.

Excellent! Let's sock it to the representatives of the English fifth column! I can fully understand Churchill's zeal: during the Chamberlain years, the Astors were a constant thorn in his side. Now he has a chance to settle his score with them.

Churchill turned to Stalin's proposal to send three Polish divisions, which are being formed in the USSR, to the Near East to assist the British.

'I'm very touched by Stalin's action,' he exclaimed. 'I'll write to him myself.'

Then the prime minister remembered about the convoy which recently left Iceland carrying a valuable cargo and which he feared might be attacked by the *Tirpitz*. In this connection I asked Churchill whether he had replied to Stalin's question, posed a fortnight ago, concerning the scale of England's possible participation in the so-called 'northern operation' (i.e. in northern Finland and Norway). It transpired that the prime minister had not yet replied. Somewhat embarrassed, he promised to send the reply in the next couple of days. In principle, the British government is ready to employ all three arms of its military in the northern operation – its naval, land and air forces.

I enquired about the British government's latest information concerning the quantity of Japanese forces in Manchuria. Churchill replied: 24 divisions and a relatively modest quantity of aircraft. Only six divisions are presently stationed in Japan itself.

After lunch Churchill and I retired to his office. And there our conversation started in earnest.

I asked Churchill what news he had brought back from America about the second front.

Churchill replied that he had none. Everything is as it was at the moment of Molotov's departure, i.e. as set out in the memorandum of 10 June.

This did not satisfy me, of course, and I tried to make the prime minister shift from his position. I reasoned in the following way.

After the collapse of France, when England was left to fight on her own, the *Middle East* naturally became her main front on land. As far as I know, the initial plan for Libya set far-reaching objectives. The intention was not only to secure Egypt, but also to capture all of Libya and reach Tripoli. Had it been executed successfully, the effect would have been considerable: the Mediterranean would have been opened for the Allies, French North Africa would probably have broken with Vichy, and a base would have been established to move the war over to Italy. Unfortunately, two years of immense effort failed to yield this outcome. The British government made three attempts to drive the Axis out of North Africa, and all of them came to nothing. I shall not set about analysing the causes for this failure now, but there's one thing I can say: Libya's remoteness from Britain, with all the ensuing problems of transportation, has played a very major role.

We must face the facts. It is absolutely clear that for the moment one must abandon all notion of the British government fulfilling its original, wide-ranging plans for North Africa. They are beyond its power for now. So those plans must be jettisoned and Britain must go on to the *defensive* – not static defence, of course, but active defence which does not exclude but, on the contrary, presupposes offensive operations on a more limited scale. For instance, to guarantee the security of Egypt it is essential to win back Mersa Matruh, or better still Sollum, from the Germans. It is also necessary to establish more effective control over the central part of the Mediterranean. On the whole, though, it would be advisable for the British in the Middle East *to dig in* and to reduce the quantity of troops and matériel sent out there accordingly. The forces and reserves currently available in the Middle East are quite sufficient for defensive operations (I am not speaking, of course, about the inevitable but limited reinforcements which will be needed in any case). This would immediately yield a great saving in the sphere of shipping.

Instead of large-scale plans in North Africa, it would be better to focus attention and efforts on major objectives closer to home – aims which would have a more direct and more decisive effect on the general course of the war than operations in Egypt and Libya. I consider a second front in Europe, and specifically in France, Belgium and Holland, to be just such an objective. It would hit the target directly and it would also yield many considerable advantages: *shipping difficulties* here would be minimal (the distance from England to the second front would be measured in dozens of marine miles instead of the many thousands separating her from the Middle East), commanding the front would be easier, frequent visits to the front from London would be possible, and the psychological effect in Britain would be massive. The country would immediately feel that it was really fighting.

'In a word,' I concluded, 'I believe Egypt must be defended now not in Egypt but in France.'

Churchill listened to me attentively, then set about making his case.

It is, of course, quite possible that Britain will have to curtail its operations in North Africa and *dig in*, but this has no direct bearing on a second front. Preparations for the latter are in full swing. Trial landing operations are being undertaken and will continue to be undertaken. But there is neither sense nor profit in plunging into an adventure that is doomed to failure.

Churchill spoke to Roosevelt a lot about a second front. Roosevelt is entirely in favour of it, but US troops in Britain still number less than 80,000, while US aircraft arrive only after great delays and in small quantities. Owing to the shipping situation, the more or less regular transfer of US troops to Britain can begin only in September, and even then in quantities of no more than 90,000 a month. Major air forces may be expected from the USA no sooner than in September–October. And the British deem it impossible to launch a second front without the Americans.

'I repeat once again,' Churchill added, 'that I'll do all I can to expedite the opening of a second front. Should the possibility present itself in any form, we shall open a second front in 1942, but I can't make you any firm promises. I told Molotov and I tell you once again: one has to deceive one's enemy, one can sometimes deceive the general public for its own good, but one must never deceive one's ally. I don't want to deceive you, and I don't want to mislead you. That is why I refuse to make pledges which I am unsure of being able to honour.'[160]

I indicated, in a somewhat veiled form, the psychological impact which the failure to open a second front in 1942 might have in the USSR, but the prime minister remained unmoved.

Then Churchill spoke of the *Middle East*. He immediately came to life. It was obvious that the Middle East is his '*darling*', that it dominates his mind. Churchill set about explaining to me in detail the strategic situation at El Alamein and the arrangement of the British and German forces. Large British reinforcements from Egypt and Palestine (up to 60,000) are on the way to El Alamein, as well as a brand-new armoured division that has just landed from England. Rommel has no more than 40–50,000 troops at present. The British will soon boast a significant numerical advantage, for the Germans do not appear to have sent any major reinforcements yet to Rommel. Nevertheless, Churchill is anxious: once bitten, twice shy.

'I constantly expect bad news from Egypt. I'm ready for it.'

I asked what the British government would do if the Nile Delta were lost.

'Fight, fight at all costs!' exclaimed Churchill.

Churchill pursued the theme further. The Nile Delta is all marshes and canals. Such terrain is not fit for tanks. The English have every chance of detaining the enemy there. But even if the Germans were to penetrate into the Delta, the British army would continue to loom over their right flank. The British fleet, having lost Alexandria, can operate from Haifa and Beirut: there haven't been any battleships in the Mediterranean for many months, while cruisers and other small ships can make do with the above-mentioned harbours. The British also have many aircraft, including American *Liberators*, with the help of which they will be able to control the Mediterranean quite effectively and to bomb harbours not only in North Africa, but also in Sicily and Italy.

'Yes, we shall fight,' Churchill continued. 'We shall fight for El Alamein, we shall fight in the Delta if need be, and beyond the Delta, in Sinai, Palestine, Arabia… We shall fight!'

Then the prime minister added emphatically: 'We shall protect your left flank at all costs! We are defending it now in Egypt. If necessary, we will defend it in Asia Minor and in the Middle East.'

I asked Churchill how he explains the British failures in Africa.

'The Germans wage war better than we do,' Churchill answered frankly. 'Especially tank wars… Also, we lack the "Russian spirit": die but don't surrender!'

I enquired about the circumstances leading to the fall of Tobruk. Churchill turned a deep shade of red, as always happens with him when he is very angry, and said that Tobruk was a shameful page in the history of the British military. In Tobruk there were sufficient troops, ammunition and supplies (enough for three months!). Tobruk could have resisted no worse than Sevastopol, but the Tobruk commander, the South African General Klopper, got cold feet and waved the white flag 24 hours after the German attack began.

'I'd have shot a general like that on the spot!' I blurted out.

'I'd have done the same,' Churchill responded. 'But just you try!'

I looked at the PM in bewilderment. He understood me and explained that Klopper was South African and that the South Africans (including Smuts) raise hell whenever anyone tries to call Klopper's action by its real name: 'Hands off the heroes of Tobruk!'

Churchill angrily snatched his customary cigar out of his mouth, as if he wanted to say: 'See how difficult it is to conduct a war!'

So what are my conclusions from my conversation with Churchill today?

Less than rosy. Churchill's visit to America has not yielded a favourable outcome with respect to a second front. If anything, the opposite is the case: Churchill has convinced Roosevelt not to be in too much of a hurry about this. At the same time, *the spell of the Middle East* still holds the PM in its grip. He still hopes for a sudden turn of events which will provide England with the opportunity to realize its initial ambitions in North Africa.

I met Churchill on this same day two years ago, on 3 July 1940, and we talked about the military situation. It was a tragic moment. France had just collapsed. Britain was left alone – without allies, without friends, without an army, and without weapons. In the immediate wake of Dunkerque there was only one well-equipped and trained division in the whole country. The spectre of a German invasion of the island pervaded the atmosphere. People were digging trenches, constructing anti-tank barriers on the roads, making ditches and stationing wrecked cars on clearings that could be used by German planes for landing. Government buildings in London were surrounded with barbed wire, and there was even an entire fort erected by the entrance to *10, Downing Street*.

It was at that moment that I had my conversation with the prime minister. I remember asking him: 'What fate awaits the French fleet?'

Churchill answered with a grin: 'The French fleet?… To use the diplomatic jargon, "*we are very much alive*" to the importance of this matter and are taking due measures.'

Churchill added nothing more to help me decipher these enigmatic words but, as it turned out later, it was during those very hours that British battleships were shelling French ships in Oran.

Yes, that episode in Oran will remain forever the highpoint of Churchill's career: there he showed himself to be a statesman of great resolve and great courage!

Then I asked the prime minister: 'What is your general strategy in this war?'

His face broke into an even broader grin and he uttered: 'My general strategy is to survive the next three months.'

How the situation has changed since then! There can be no comparison with England's present position – it has improved immensely. But even if we take a general overview of the war and compare the balance of forces between the fascist and anti-fascist camps, then, notwithstanding all our present problems, the future looks infinitely better and brighter than in 1940!

This is our source for hope in victory and confidence in the future.

[Eden felt uncomfortable concealing from Maisky the nature of Churchill's talks in Washington. He encouraged Maisky to approach the prime minister, though he claimed that nothing had changed since Molotov's departure.[161] Churchill, who came across as being frank, nonetheless deceived Maisky. Following Mountbatten's face-to-face talks in the White House, Churchill had become aware that Roosevelt's advocacy of a second front was due not only to his anxieties about the Russian front, but also to the fact that he was itching 'to get into the war and get his troops fighting'. It certainly was a wise move to send Admiral Mountbatten, the director of combined operations, to Washington in the wake of Molotov's visit. Mountbatten succeeded in raising 'unanswerable arguments ... about invading France this autumn', leading Roosevelt to 'desperately cast round for something else'. Mountbatten's suggestion was that the Americans should send six divisions, initially earmarked for the cross-channel invasion, to fight alongside British troops in North Africa. Churchill's blitz visit, within days of Molotov's return to Moscow, was motivated by a desire to counter the impact of the Soviet foreign minister's visit by shifting the emphasis from *Sledgehammer* to *Round-Up*, the preparations for a cross-channel invasion in 1943.[162] Overlooking Marshall's fierce and well-argued opposition, Roosevelt 'in his foxy way to forestall trouble that is now on the ocean coming towards us in the shape of a new British visitor' urged his War Cabinet 'to take up the case of *Gymnast* again'.[163]

As was to be expected, Churchill arrived in Washington 'full of discouragement and new proposals for diversions'. He was 'pessimistic regarding *Bolero* and interested in August *Gymnast*'. He flew straight away to Hyde Park to meet Roosevelt, to the manifest dismay of Stimson, the war secretary, who could not 'help feeling a little bit uneasy about the influence of the Prime Minister on the President'. And rightly so. Churchill later recalled how he was welcomed personally by Roosevelt, who insisted on driving him alone around his splendid estate and 'all the time we talked business ... we made more progress than we might have done in formal conference'. That evening, the president hastened to send Marshall a list of queries posed by Churchill. This practically wrote off operations on the continent in 1942, while introducing 'some other operation by which we may gain positions of advantage'. To make the proposal attractive to the Americans, it was presented as a move which would 'directly or indirectly take some of the weight off Russia'.[164]

Marshall held fast to his appraisal that dispersing the forces might jeopardize an invasion of the continent even in 1943. His defiant message to Churchill maintained that an operation on the continent in 1942 was the best and only way of assisting the Russians. He dismissed *Gymnast*, arguing that, even if successful, it would not result 'in removing one German soldier, tank, or plane from the Russian Front'. He shared the opinion of the operations department (whose advice Roosevelt sought as well) that if the Germans had 'a strangle hold upon the Russian Army' they were unlikely to be diverted 'from their murderous purpose by pin prick operations. The further any such pin prick operation is removed from the Nazi citadel, the less will be its effect.'[165] But this correspondence was superseded by the dramatic defeat of the British at Tobruk, of which Churchill and Roosevelt became aware on their return to Washington. It was, as Churchill later recalled, 'one of the heaviest blows' inflicted on him during the war.[166]

Inadvertently, however, the timing was most propitious. It allowed him to brilliantly overcome the stiff opposition of the American military to his efforts to forsake a second front in 1942 in favour of operations in the Middle East. Churchill wasted little time in launching 'a terrific attack on *Bolero*', in the presence of Marshall and Hopkins, and taking up *Gymnast*, 'knowing perfectly well that it was the President's great secret baby' and that the operation would have to be carried out by American troops. A compromise was eventually reached to pursue the preparations for *Bolero*, while *Gymnast* was revived, drawing on American forces initially earmarked for the second front. General Auchinleck was informed that 'he might expect a reinforcement of a highly trained American Armoured Division' equipped with Sherman tanks.[167] The war secretary, the architect of the second front, was summoned to the White House in the evening. There he found the president in a 'most irresponsible mood. He was talking of a most critical situation and in the presence of the head of another government with the frivolity and lack of responsibility of a child.' In the course of the conversation, it turned out that the president, whose mind was 'evidently tenaciously fixed to some kind of a diversion from Bolero', had proposed to Churchill to send a major force to sustain the denuded Middle Eastern front. No reference was made at all to the repercussions which a diversion might have on the Russian front – hardly a week after Molotov had left Washington convinced that the Americans were committed to a second front. Stimson was the only one to warn that if *Bolero* was 'delayed by diversions ... it would not be made in '43'.[168] Ironically, a somewhat complacent Molotov, driven by an antagonism to his predecessor, now ambassador in Washington, wrote to Litvinov on the same day: 'no one can deny that our relations with the USA have lately not worsened but improved'.[169]

Two days after meeting Maisky, Churchill addressed the chiefs of staff with incisive arguments against *Sledgehammer* 'as a desirable or even as a practicable operation in 1942'. He presented it as 'a premature action' likely to end in disaster and 'decisively injure the prospects of well-organised, large-scale action in 1943'. But such arguments were just a prelude to the reintroduction of Operation *Gymnast* as the main thrust for 1942, while for 'political and military' reasons the Russians could be compensated by Operation *Jupiter* – seizing the northern tip of Norway and thereby eliminating the danger to the Arctic convoys posed by the Luftwaffe. Particularly as Stalin had approached Churchill on this issue and been left without a response.[170] This operation never materialized. 'Second Front in Europe this year definitely off', noted Cadogan in his diary, after talking to Eden. 'President wants to do "Gymnast".'[171] In private, Churchill admitted that his policy was 'to bluff the Germans into believing we shall have second front this year and to conceal from Russians that we can't!'[172] Informing Roosevelt of his decision on 8 July, he presented *Gymnast* as the president's 'commanding idea' and as 'the true second front' for 1942.[173] An unequivocal presentation of his plan 'as clear as noonday' followed suit. *Sledgehammer* was discarded as 'impossible and disastrous', while Roosevelt was urged to 'do *Gymnast* as soon as possible', leaving the British and Russians to 'try for *Jupiter*' while preparations continued unhindered for *Round-Up* in 1943.[174] This plan, however, was misleading. The joint planning staff, which had been instructed to look into the repercussions of an invasion of North Africa, had come up with a warning that if *Gymnast* was carried out wholeheartedly 'indeed *Round Up* would have to be postponed until 1944'.[175] In a bitter telegram to Eisenhower, Marshall conceded that the demands of *Gymnast* would 'curtail, if not make impossible' an invasion of Europe in 1943.[176]]

9 July

I have drawn the following conclusion from my life experience: 'Never say never in politics.'

And another one: 'Hitler has victories but he has no victory', and that's all there is to it.

10 July

The history of Dutch political cretinism, of which I wrote not long ago, ended today with a reasonable step: Verduynen and I signed an agreement on the establishment of diplomatic relations between our countries. Verduynen was awfully pleased. He arrived dressed in a morning coat and accompanied by a 'retinue' of six people, speaking profusely about the 'historic' significance of the event. He made a big fuss of it.

Verduynen strikes me as a sensible and educated man, but his worldview is nevertheless confined by Dutch limits. Today's document is of course 'historic' for him – both as a representative of Holland and for Verduynen personally. I nurture considerable suspicion that he exploited Van Kleffens' departure for the USA (Van Kleffen was accompanying Wilhelmina) so as to inscribe the establishment of diplomatic relations between Holland and the USSR in his own personal history. Well, let him satisfy his ambitions. So long as it's good for us.

11 July

Sometimes I want to tear myself away from the blood-stained sea of the present and travel in thought to the distant future, when the brilliance of human genius will be expended not on the invention of the most sophisticated means of self-destruction, but on truly creative, constructive deeds…

Today I am in just such a mood. And this is what I have been thinking.

In the twenty-first or twenty-second century, when fully developed communism will be established everywhere, the problem of creating a unified humanity will come to the fore. It's not that national distinctions should be entirely eliminated – no, that would be difficult and even, perhaps, undesirable. Let there be diversity in the world. Let there be different characters, different faces, different songs, different tastes. Life would be very dull without this, and human progress would be hampered.

At the same time, it will be necessary to find a way of merging those motley national streams in a single, bursting river of humanity. It will be necessary to create forms of life whereby national distinctions enrich the common life of mankind instead of dividing it into mutually hostile elements. Communism, of course, will forge a solid economic foundation for the edifice of a unified humanity, yet 'vestiges of the past' may still persist in people's minds. Perhaps we will have to think of some special measures to accelerate the process of creating a unified humanity. What measures?

Measures aimed at mixing up the various nationalities more vigorously. For instance, why not send Russian children to study for a while in Spanish schools, and vice versa? Why not send Chinese students to study in English universities and English students in Chinese ones? Or how about setting up international high schools in appropriate locations, where young people of both sexes could enrol regardless of nationality? Why not arrange extensive population exchanges between countries (though not in the style of the Nazis)?

How distant is all this from the present day!

[Maisky's confidante, Beatrice Webb, had observed a few days earlier: '... he maintains a strangely aloof attitude towards dogmatic communism; he is no marxist, not bigoted, he does not idolise Lenin or Stalin'.[177]]

12 July (Bovingdon)

The Germans have finally launched their major summer offensive. Fierce fighting has been under way for two weeks already in Kursk–Kharkov region. It flared up right after the heroic fall of Sevastopol (what an unprecedented lesson in heroism this city has given us!). The German side has had indisputable success. They assembled huge quantities of tanks and aircraft (the figure of 8,000 tanks is mentioned, though this seems exaggerated to me), broke through our lines at Kursk and fought their way to Voronezh. They also captured Rossosh farther to the south. We had to evacuate Stary Oskol and retreat to Kantemirovka. The Germans are urgently trying to cross the Don, regardless of losses, and relatively small numbers of them have managed to do so here and there. But the Red Army is putting up very strong resistance, and the enemy has not yet succeeded in entrenching itself on the left bank of the Don. Nonetheless the general situation on this section of the front is exceptionally complicated, tense and unsafe. The Germans have also proved unable to encircle our large units (the Red Army has toughened up in this respect compared with last year), but on the other hand we have had to retreat and relinquish important positions. This is especially true of the Moscow–Rostov railway, which has been cut off at Rossosh and is almost cut off at Voronezh, although the city itself, despite Goebbels' premature communiqués, is still in our hands.

What next?

I am disinclined to think that the Germans will dare move further east from Voronezh. That would expose their flanks far too much. The Germans are more likely to try to 'straighten' the front line between Voronezh and the Azov Sea, shifting it some 100–150 miles to the east (the distance from Kursk to Voronezh is about 130 miles). This seems to follow from today's communication that the Germans have launched an attack at Lisichansk. A serious German offensive in the centre (against Moscow) or in the north (against Leningrad) is scarcely possible. It is no longer 1941, and a coordinated offensive along the entire length of the front is now beyond the Germans' strength. However, the experience of the past two weeks has shown that the Germans can still be very dangerous on individual sections of the front.

We shall certainly do our utmost to prevent the Germans from advancing. We are in a much better position to do so than we were a year ago. We shall exhaust and weaken the enemy with rear-guard actions, inflicting as many losses in men and matériel as possible. In all probability we shall follow the tactics of last summer and wait for more favourable conditions to present themselves for a counteroffensive. Perhaps this will happen in winter once again. Perhaps earlier. Everything suggests that we do not intend to deal the Germans a serious blow (i.e. try to break through their front line as they broke through ours) in the next 2–3 months. But this does not rule out counterattacks and limited offensives from our side, as an important method of active defence.

This policy has been forced on us by the general situation that has emerged this summer.

Indeed, were the Allies to establish an effective second front in the west this summer, we could risk a major strategic offensive in 1942 (or, to be more precise, in the summer of 1942) with the aim of breaking Hitler's backbone now and ending the war in Europe in 1943. Unfortunately, no effective second front is to be expected in the west either in summer or in early autumn. My conversation with Churchill on 3 July made this quite clear. From everything that I see, hear and read here, there seems little doubt that the British and the Americans have no serious intention of opening a second front before 1943. Why? For two main reasons.

First, because the ruling groups in both countries are banking on the exhaustion of both Germany and the USSR, which, each in her own way, threaten their dominant position. This feeling may be stronger in the USA than in England because the USA, fearing less for its existence than England, is freer to play big political games; but such sentiments are fairly strong in England, too. These ruling circles would be terribly put out if Germany were to be defeated by the Red Army this year, while the British–American forces were unwilling or still unable to take an active part in the operation. On the contrary, those ruling circles are very keen for Germany to be beaten by Anglo-

American forces. Then Britain and the USA would have the decisive say at the future peace conference, not the USSR. Then capitalism, not socialism, would have every chance of winning out in Europe. To secure such an outcome it is necessary to bleed the USSR white and to postpone the 'settling' of the war until 1943, when Anglo-American forces will be in a better position to launch serious operations on the European continent. That is why Churchill and Roosevelt are so reluctant to consider a second front in 1942.

The second reason is in much the same vein: the Anglo-American elite is terrified of the might of the German war machine. Their experience in this regard has been lamentable… Norway, France, Greece, Crete, Libya… When I raise the possibility of a second front with the prime minister, Eden, Pound, Brooke or others, they immediately become *uneasy*. They become afraid. They lose confidence in themselves. They reveal a genuine *inferiority complex*. 'Let this cup pass', they think, and if that is already impossible then they wish to delay its arrival for as long as possible. Hence their very pronounced psychological predisposition to drag things out, to put off the second front, to find thousands of obstacles for its realization, and to ensure, whatever happens, that such an operation is not launched before the Anglo-American army can claim manifest and significant preponderance over the enemy in the air and at sea – i.e. before the enemy has become a good deal weaker. And they're more than happy to allow us, the Soviet Union, to do the weakening and to perform all the dirty work necessary for victory.

One way or another, there are no grounds to expect an effective second front in 1942 (unless something entirely unexpected happens). Naturally, this imposes certain limitations on us.

Above all, we must save our resources. For the prospect of a much longer war than could have been anticipated now looms on the horizon. I have not yet lost all hope that 1942 will be the decisive year. But I must say frankly that this hope (now that the intentions of Britain and the USA concerning the second front have become clear) has become a good deal fainter than it was, say, in March, when I made a speech at an award ceremony for English pilots.

If the war is going to drag on, we cannot take too great a risk in the summer of 1942, fighting alone against the entire might of the German war machine. We must save our strength so as not to bleed ourselves dry, so as not to cross the finishing line in total exhaustion (as the Americans and the British would be so keen for us to do).

Hence the conclusion: we cannot risk a major offensive against Germany now. We have to remain in an essentially defensive position. This has its advantages: fewer losses in men (but not arms). It has its disadvantages, too: the initiative remains in the hands of the enemy and we have to lose ground and resources.

Is it in our interests to pursue these tactics? That all depends on how the advantages and disadvantages balance out. If our loss of life really is much lower than the enemy's while we remain on the defensive, then the tactics indicated are the right ones. If not, they are not.

It's difficult for me to assess this balance from London. It can be better judged from Moscow. If Moscow finds it necessary to remain on the defensive, then it must be advantageous for us to adhere to these tactics. Or perhaps we simply have no alternative for the time being.

13 July

Oliveira always struck me as the perfect embodiment of diplomatic emptiness. As doyen (1933–40), though, he behaved in a tactful and appropriate manner. He even displayed these qualities towards me, despite the absence of relations between the USSR and Brazil and despite the fact that the general spirit of Brazilian politics was, of course, anti-Soviet. Oliveira's wife, who grew up and was educated in Paris, was considered the *smartest lady* in the diplomatic corps and at the Court. She really did dress magnificently and with excellent taste. For all my indifference to ladies' apparel, I still haven't forgotten the light-blue mantilla in which she once appeared at the Palace.

14 July

Went to see Eden this morning. He told me that very unpleasant news had arrived from the north: Convoy No. 17 has been badly wrecked by the Germans. Out of 35 ships, 19 have been sunk (this is known for certain), four have made it to Arkhangelsk, five are in Novaya Zemlya, two in Iceland, and the fate of five is still unknown. This terrible experience puts in serious doubt the possibility of sending further convoys, at least until the nights draw in in the Arctic zone. The Admiralty, according to Eden, is against sending more convoys. But no decision has yet been taken.

I was greatly disturbed by this and asked Eden whether a meeting could be arranged before a decision was taken, to be attended by himself, Alexander, Pound, me, Kharlamov and Morozovsky. Eden agreed, and promised to speak with the people concerned about the date and time of the meeting. Eden, as if thinking aloud, observed that it wouldn't be a bad thing for Churchill to attend the meeting as well. I, of course, had no objections.

Eden also told me that the British government was ready to embark on more detailed negotiations concerning the preparations for the northern operation. I promised to inform Moscow.

I then asked Eden what he knew about the current arrangement of the Japanese forces, about Japan's intentions towards the USSR in general, and also about Germany's intentions to use gas on our front. Recently I received information suggesting that the Germans ceased their preparations for using gas in the east following Churchill's warning on 10 May. But they have now resumed their preparations. Was this true?

Eden was unable to give me a reply right away, but promised to make enquiries and then inform me.[178]

[To a great extent, the order given to convoy PQ 17 to disperse and then to scatter and its fatal repercussions were the result of a self-fulfilling prophecy. Admiral Pound, the first sea lord, had been predisposed to disperse the convoys. As early as March, he had voiced reservations concerning the northern convoys, outlining to the joint chiefs of staff the difficulties which were likely to increase, leading to 'heavy losses' in the future.[179] A month later, he pleaded with the Defence Committee to reduce the number of convoys, warning again that the losses of ships and their escorts may become so great 'as to render the running of these convoys uneconomical'.[180] On 20 April, the Admiralty demanded that 'convoys to North Russia should be suspended during months of continuous light unless the very high percentage of losses can be accepted or sufficient air protection can be provided'.[181] 'The German concentration of naval

105. Maisky presents a medal to Mrs Woodward, widow of a naval officer killed in action in the Arctic convoys, who is holding her five-month-old daughter.

force' north of Norway, moaned Stimson from Washington, 'has scared the bits out of the British admiralty and our Navy, and they are afraid that they cannot protect the Russian convoys'.[182] From London, Harriman confirmed that the cycle of convoys to Russia would have to be reduced and that there was 'no immediate prospect of an improvement in the position'.[183]

This information was gently conveyed to Stalin by Roosevelt on 25 April. He apologized for the restrictions which had to be imposed just as Russia was 'in need of larger and larger shipments of munitions'.[184] Though Roosevelt exerted tremendous pressure on Churchill to sail more than a hundred ships destined for Russia but stuck in American ports, the prime minister insisted that 'three convoys every two months with either 35 or 25 ships in each convoy ... represent extreme limit' of what Britain could handle. He justified his decision by rather cynically raising the competing demands of *Bolero*, the deployment of the American troops in Britain in preparation for a cross-channel attack, which he expected would absorb all the scarce shipping available. There was little Hopkins could do but relay the decision to Litvinov, attributing it to the British.[185]

It prompted an immediate telegram from Stalin, urging Churchill to allow the convoys to sail without delay, as the materials were vital for the forthcoming offensive. With Molotov on his way to London, Churchill avoided a straightforward rejection, but put the onus on the Russians for failing to give any appreciable air and naval assistance to protect the convoys.[186] But on 15 May, while Molotov was preparing to take off, Pound returned to the Chiefs of Staff Committee to demand that Stalin should be firmly told that the convoys would have to be suspended for six weeks until the ice receded and allowed them to sail a northern route, out of reach of the German air force. The chiefs of staff heeded his clairvoyant warning that future convoys would be subjected 'to such a heavy scale of attack that only a small proportion of the ships of the convoy will reach their destination'.

Churchill, however, was left with only a few cards to play in his encounter with Molotov. The proposed political agreement had been pared to the bone, while a second front in 1942 was ruled out. A postponement of the convoys on the eve of the major battle in the east, the Foreign Office warned, would have a devastating effect on Soviet morale. Bearing in mind Roosevelt's insistence on a second front 'now' and his demand that the flow of supplies to Russia should continue, Churchill had to concede that postponement of the convoys was bound to 'weaken our influence with both our major Allies'. Convoy PQ 16 was accordingly ordered to sail.[187]

Despite heavy attacks, it sustained relatively minor losses, which led the American naval commander in charge of the convoys to suggest that 'with present disposition and composition of covering and escort forces north Russian convoy is reasonably secure from surface and submarine attack'.[188] Even before PQ 17 set sail in June, Admiral Brind, whose command consisted of Home Fleet and Arctic Convoys, was convinced that the Germans had mastered the convoy routines and would now 'try conclusions against the convoy with surface vessels', the effect of which would be 'devastating'.[189] Churchill, however, never felt comfortable with Admiral Hamilton's[i] decision to withdraw the six

[i] L.H.K. Hamilton, rear admiral, in command of the cruiser squadron accompanying the Arctic Convoys.

destroyers from the convoy and then order it to scatter. He further played down the threat posed by the *Tirpitz* – most likely because he was prepared to pay the heavy toll involved in resuming the convoys in September, now that a decision had been taken to postpone the opening of the second front.[190]]

15 July

Events are developing faster than I could have anticipated. I thought I'd be able to sound out the British government's immediate intentions at the meeting I spoke about with Eden yesterday. Things turned out rather differently. Yesterday at about four in the afternoon I had a call from the prime minister's office inviting me and my wife for dinner that same evening. I accepted. We dined on the lower floor of *10, Downing Street.* Seated around the table were Churchill and his wife, I and my wife, and… Admiral Pound. I realized at once that matters had taken a serious turn. I was not mistaken. Eden arrived after dinner. But by then nothing remained to be discussed.

Churchill spoke first. He mentioned Convoy 17 and related those details about its fate which I had already heard from Eden in the morning.

'What shall we do now?' Churchill went on. 'The seamen advised us not to send Convoy 17. They took the view that the danger was too great. The War Cabinet disregarded their advice and ordered that the convoy depart. We thought that even if a mere half of the ships reached Arkhangelsk the game would be worth the candle. It came out worse than we had expected: three-quarters of the convoy perished; 400 tanks and 300 planes lie on the sea-bed!… My heart bleeds.'

The prime minister emitted an angry wheeze and banged his fist on the table. Then he continued: 'But all the same, what should we do? There's no sense in sending tanks and planes to certain ruin. We might just as well sink them in the Thames. It seems that we will have to stop sending convoys for the time being and wait for the nights to draw in in the Arctic… True, Arkhangelsk will be ice-bound in winter, while Murmansk is too close to German airfields and has suffered terribly from air strikes… Nonetheless…'

I strongly objected. What's that? Stop supplying the USSR? When? At the very moment when it is fighting for its life? When it needs arms more than even before? What effect would such a step have on the fate of the war? What impact would it have on the psychology of my country?… Stopping the convoys is out of the question. They must continue. But the protection of the convoys must be organized better. That can be done. The big ships should keep closer to the convoys than was the case with Convoy 17 (when they were 400 miles away), and they should be accompanied by an aircraft carrier. Then convoys would be feasible even now. Later, when the nights draw in, it will become even easier.'

At this point Pound butted in and asked with a superior air: 'Do you consider it possible to bet against *certainty?*'

'*Certainty*,' I replied, 'is a relative term. What may be deemed *certainty* under some conditions may not be so under others.'

'Well,' Pound continued with the same air of superiority, '*take it from me:* if we send Convoy 18, it will fare no better than its predecessor. Perhaps even worse. That is a *certainty.* Were I at the helm of the *Tirpitz*, not a single vessel would make it to Arkhangelsk. I guarantee it. The fact that we may have managed to get 16 convoys through in the past is simply a "miracle". The Germans did not yet know how to fight against convoys. Now they have learnt and we must reckon with that. We cannot risk our big ships. The situation at sea is now much too delicate. The loss of 2–3 big ships would be sufficient to tip the entire balance of the war at sea against us. We would not be able to maintain our superiority even in the Atlantic. We would not be able to transport the American army to Britain... And the threat to the major vessels in the region of northern Norway is very real – both from the German coastal air force and from the German submarines with which the Barents Sea is teeming.'

Scowling, Churchill came to Pound's support.

'That's right,' he said. 'It's all too easy to lose 2–3 major vessels, and what then? No amount of crying will bring them back.'

I began disagreeing once more. I said that the story of Convoy 17 had left me with many puzzling questions. Why, for instance, did the escort comprise, in the critical moment, only destroyers, corvettes and submarines, with no big ships anywhere in the vicinity? We know that two battleships, one aircraft carrier and 17 destroyers were cruising 400 miles from the site of the catastrophe. Why, once it became known that the *Tirpitz* had left the Norwegian fjords and was moving north, was the weak escort accompanying the convoy hastily withdrawn, to say nothing of the failure to send a powerful fleet to intercept the *Tirpitz*? Why was the slow-moving convoy ordered to scatter, when it was quite obvious that effective dispersal was no longer possible?[191] Why doesn't the Admiralty block the exits from the fjords where the *Tirpitz* and other German ships are moored with mines and submarines? Why doesn't the Admiralty carry out special reconnaissance expeditions while the convoy is on the move? Why aren't aircraft carriers deployed to accompany the convoys?... These and many other questions arise when one analyses the fate of Convoy 17. I, of course, am not a seaman and am prepared to admit that answers of one kind of another may exist to all these questions, but I'm convinced of one thing: that the protection of the convoys can be organized better than has been the case hitherto. One merely needs the will and requisite courage to do so.

Pound set about answering my objections once again. The problem, don't you see, is that the British have only one aircraft carrier in northern waters, and they cannot risk it. Besides, the carrier's planes are greatly inferior to those of the German coastal air force. The escort was withdrawn because it was no match for the *Tirpitz* and would have been sunk to no purpose. The major fleet was 400 miles away from the site of the catastrophe so as not to fall victim to German bombers. The order was given for the convoy to 'scatter', as otherwise the *Tirpitz* would have sunk every single vessel within an hour or so. As it happened, the submarines and aircraft needed at least two days to do their work and nearly a quarter of the convoy survived. The other explanations of the gallant admiral were in the same vein.

The PM supported Pound, though without much enthusiasm. Then, adopting a philosophical tone, Churchill said: 'Just think: the Germans assembled about 300 planes in the region of Nord Kapp and three or four divisions to guard them… As a result, they cut off communication between 130 million Americans and 47 million British on the one side and 180 million Russians on the other. This is what aviation means!'

As this philosophizing was leading nowhere, I asked the PM what, after all, was to happen with Convoy 18.

Churchill thought for a moment and then, as if making a concession, replied that he would ask the Americans about it. As more than 22 ships in Convoy 18 are to be American, let them decide: if they want to take the risk, the British government will provide the escort.

The situation was quite clear to me: Pound, of course, would give the Americans a good fright and that would be the end of Convoy 18.

'So,' I concluded, 'you are ceasing the delivery of military supplies at the most critical moment for us. In that case, the question of a second front becomes all the more urgent. What are the prospects here?'

Churchill replied that we were familiar with his position on this matter. It was stated in the memorandum of 10 June handed to Molotov. He reaffirmed it during our conversation on 3 July.

'I know this,' I rejoined, 'but the situation has dramatically changed not only since the 10th of June, but also since the 3rd of July. The last ten days have been of momentous significance. They have shown that Hitler has succeeded in assembling more forces for his offensive than had been anticipated. Also, our failures at the front were far greater than we had expected. The situation on the Soviet–German front is now perilous. The Red Army will of course fight heroically, as it has done throughout, but there is a limit to everything. Who knows what may happen? If the USSR does not receive prompt support from the west in the form of a second front, a retreat far to the east cannot be excluded. In that case the USSR will lose a vast and valuable territory with a large population, important communication lines, and major resources.

This fact, of course, would inevitably affect the morale of the population and the army. Eventually, the USSR would become weaker, and Germany would become stronger than she is today. What does this mean? It means that in the spring of 1943 Britain and the USA would have to face far greater German forces than today. And although Britain and the USA will feel stronger in 1943 than in 1942, they will gain nothing if the USSR weakens at the same time. As a result the quantity of divisions which you and Roosevelt are planning to prepare in order to invade the continent in the spring of 1943 would turn out to be insufficient. It would have to be doubled. Where will you get additional forces from?… My conclusion: better 25 divisions in 1942 than 50 divisions in 1943! It's just a simple, sober calculation.'

Churchill listened to me attentively. Then he said: 'Yes, I agree with you. I have already heard those arguments during Molotov's visit. It's quite possible that you'll have to retreat further to the east. It's quite possible that in the spring of 1943 we'll face on the continent not the 25 second-rate divisions that are presently protecting France and Belgium, but 50 or 60 first-line German divisions… I understand all of this… But what is to be done?… In 1942 we are simply in no condition to undertake serious operations in order to open a second front. There is no sense getting involved in an absurd adventure which is bound to end in disaster. This will help neither you nor us. Only the Germans will profit from it.'

Pound, grinning in self-satisfaction, hastened to take the prime minister's side. I took the greatest exception to him. This gouty 65-year-old, who has won not a single battle in his entire life but has proved very adept at winning high positions and decorations in ministerial quarters, had stretched my patience to the limit. Churchill intervened in our dispute and said: 'We are ready to assist you any way we can. For instance, we are ready to take part in the northern operation with every kind of weaponry at our disposal.'

'Including the army?' I asked. 'In what numbers?'

'Including the army,' Churchill affirmed. 'I ordered General McNaughton,[i] commander of the Canadian corps, to work out the plan in its entirety. He is a good man. We could allocate 3–4 divisions to this operation. Northern Norway must be cleared of German brigands. I'd go a long way to do it.'

Churchill took a sip of wine and continued: 'We'll spare no efforts to expand the transfer of arms to the USSR through Persia… If things go well in Egypt, I'm prepared to shift a large number of our aircraft to your southern front.'

Churchill went on to describe the situation in Egypt. Everything is turning out well: reinforcements are reaching Rommel at a trickle, the English are

[i] Andrew George McNaughton, general, commander-in-chief of the First Canadian Army, 1942–43.

outnumbering him again not only in infantry, but also in tanks and cannons, to say nothing of aircraft. Decisive developments are to be expected any day now.

'If we can't achieve a big success even now,' the PM concluded, 'then I don't know what to think of our army.'

As I listened to Churchill, my anxiety grew. How many times has the prime minister's optimism portended England's defeats on land! Won't it happen again now?…

I asked Churchill why big air raids on Germany had ceased in the last couple of weeks.

The PM replied that this was partly due to the weather and partly because of a change in the policy of the British government: air bombardments are now targeted first and foremost at submarine construction sites and bases. 'Submarines are the main thing,' Pound hastened to interject. 'The outcome of the war depends on them.'

'But don't you think, Admiral,' I retorted crossly, 'that the outcome of the war depends to a far greater extent on tanks?'

Churchill intervened and said in a conciliatory tone that British planes will bomb not just submarine bases but other targets as well. I am far from convinced, however, that this correction on the part of the PM will have any serious practical consequences.

Churchill then said: '*My worries* may be arranged in the following order. In the first place, the battle in Russia. That is the main thing. In the second place, the situation at sea. Then finally, after a significant, indeed a most significant interval, the battle in Egypt.'

After dinner we moved to a small, neighbouring room. We smoked. Pound puffed away haughtily at his cigar, releasing rings of smoke into the air. Eden arrived. He looked embarrassed. He asked Churchill: 'So, shall we discuss the convoys and the northern operation?'

'We already have,' Churchill muttered gloomily.

Conversation stalled. Mrs Churchill, who was not herself during the dinner, was striving heroically to keep the conversation alive. Poor Mrs Churchill! She was very upset and made several cautious attempts over dinner to support me. But the PM would roar and she would fall silent. Churchill himself was in a gloomy mood. He had to force the words out and spoke roughly, indistinctly, with obvious irritation – either at himself or at the circumstances that were forcing bad acts upon him.

Agniya asked Churchill: 'So how can you help us now?'

Churchill's reply was sullen and carefully measured: 'Unfortunately we can do very little, Mrs Maisky, very little.'

Then he added with sudden animation: 'But we shall still celebrate victory together!'

It was evident that the PM felt ill at ease.

Only Pound felt on top of the world – smoking, laughing, telling jokes. No wonder: he'd done his job!

It's people like Pound, these top bureaucrats tied by thousands of threads to the top bourgeoisie, who rule England, not the ministers who come and go! Yesterday's dinner was a fine illustration of this fact…

I returned home full of oppressive thoughts. I felt troubled and uneasy.

16 July

Since Churchill had told me on the evening of the 14th that he would talk with the Americans about Convoy 18, I decided to pay Winant and Harriman a visit on the morning of the 15th. I explained the situation to both of them and asked them not to call a halt to the convoys. Winant promised to help. Harriman was *noncommittal* and expressed his regret that the Soviet government insisted on the use of northern ports and did not pay sufficient attention to the Persian Gulf route. For all Winant's good intentions, I don't expect his intervention to lead to much because, as Harriman said, the British government has brought the matter to the attention of Roosevelt himself.

After lunch, I went to see Beaverbrook and talked to him, too, about the convoys.

Beaverbrook promised to make inquiries and do what he could. Then we talked about the second front and the general political situation. I acquainted Beaverbrook with the content of my conversation with the prime minister on the evening of the 14th and summed up my view of the second front as follows: better 25 divisions in 1942 than 50 in 1943. Beaverbrook remarked that, in his opinion, the operation could be embarked upon even with just ten divisions. He displayed great anxiety about the situation on our front ('I never expected the Germans to reach the Don valley by July') and, assuming a mysterious air, added that developments in the USSR could have major repercussions in England. Imitating his tone, I asked whether the rumours of his imminent return to the Cabinet were true.

'Churchill is asking me once again,' Beaverbrook replied with the same air of mystery. 'His invitations have been particularly persistent ever since Russia's luck began to change, but I don't want to return to the government … I think it is probably in the public interest for me to wait… The moment may come when I'll be able to do something, but it has not yet arrived.'

Beaverbrook's ploy is clear enough: he aspires to be prime minister and is waiting for Soviet failures, along with Churchill's reluctance to open a second front immediately, to create a situation in the country such that Churchill will have to go. Churchill's ploy is also obvious: he wants Beaverbrook in the government so as to tie his hands. Personal designs against the background of a global tragedy.

In the late afternoon I visited Cripps in his official lodgings (Tudor House, Whitehall). We talked about the convoys. Cripps defended Pound's and Churchill's position. I heard something from him which helped explain the prime minister's conduct. It turns out that the British government is seized by fear at present: the Germans have just finished work on the *Graf Zeppelin* aircraft carrier and are testing it in the Baltic Sea. The Germans are developing a programme: 500 submarines by the spring of 1943. What should be done? What will happen to Britain when the aircraft carrier and 500 submarines are launched? What will happen to Anglo-American naval communications?... Hence the conclusion: look after your big ships as if your life depended on it!

How the English have lost all semblance of fighting spirit! There's the *Tirpitz* in Norwegian fjords, yet instead of mustering all their energy to destroy or at least inflict some serious damage, the English discontinue the convoys. The Germans are preparing an aircraft carrier and a pack of submarines, yet instead of active resistance to the impending danger we see moaning, fear and lamentations.

We then spoke about the second front. Here, too, Cripps adheres to the official standpoint, emphasizing that there is still hope for a limited landing operation in 1942. The British government is preparing it...

By now I was at the end of my tether and I said not very politely: 'Oh yes, preparing... But when it comes to making the landing some pretext or other will be found to postpone the operation... I know your Pounds!'

Cripps just shrugged his shoulders in puzzlement.

19 July (Bovingdon)

A hard week!

The situation at the front is extremely grave. True, Voronezh is still in our hands, and we have even started putting the squeeze on the Germans there. This is very important. But the situation in the south looks ever more threatening. We've lost Kantemirovka, Boguchary and Millerovo. The Germans say they have also taken Voroshilovgrad (Lugansk). I don't know the truth of this. There has been no confirmation from our side. At any rate, the German offensive in the Don valley has made rapid and successful progress over the past week, and Rostov is clearly under threat. It is quite obvious that the Germans are headed for Stalingrad, with the aim of breaking through the Volga line and tearing the Caucasus from the rest of the USSR. If they were to succeed, the situation would become critical. Will they succeed? Some inner feeling tells me they will not. This inner feeling is reinforced, strange as it may seem at first glance, by the speed and ease of the German eastward advance. The general impression is that instead of putting up serious resistance we are merely conducting rear-guard actions in order to hold up the enemy. In the meantime, the main forces must be retreating according to plan. If this is so, it means we shall make a strong *stand* somewhere. And if we do, it will obviously be somewhere closer to Stalingrad, and in conditions that give hope of success. We shall see. But in the meantime we must acknowledge the fact that we stand before a deadly danger to our country, to the revolution, and to the entire future of humanity.

But it was not only at the front that this past week proved difficult. It was also hard here in London. My talks with Churchill, Eden, Cripps, Beaverbrook and others, and everything I heard, saw and read here, lead me to the following conclusions:

(1) There will be no second front in 1942.

(2) Supplies to the USSR from Britain and the USA will be reduced (because of the difficulty of continuing with the northern convoys).[192]

(3) Possibilities include: a northern operation (Petsamo, etc.), a landing across the channel, as discussed during Molotov's visit (though I would make no guarantee of its implementation), the intensification of air bombing over Germany and of raids on the French coast (provided we exert serious pressure), and the transfer of part of the British air force from the Middle East to our southern front (provided the situation in Egypt changes in favour of the British).

Translated into plain language, this means that we can only count on ourselves during this year's campaign. In other words, our allies have abandoned us to the mercy of fate at the most critical moment. This is a most unpleasant truth, but there is no point in closing our eyes to it. It must be taken into account in all our plans and calculations. And it must be remembered for the future.

[Maisky was spot on. Stimson and Marshall were infuriated by Churchill's determination to 'reverse the decision which was so laboriously accomplished' during his visit, thereby diverting the American 'strength into a channel in which we cannot effectively use it, namely the Middle East'.[193] Likewise the joint chiefs of staff, never certain of the president's inner thoughts, were strongly opposed to the shift, convinced that it would mean 'definitely no Bolero in 1942' and 'probably make the execution of Bolero in 1943 out of the question'. Their appraisal coincided with the views held by the joint planning staff in London that, even if Russia avoided defeat, Germany would still be able to withdraw sufficient troops to France 'to prohibit "Round-up" next spring'. A concerned General Dill pleaded with Churchill to avoid a showdown with the Americans. 'Marshall believes,' he alerted the prime minister, 'that your first love is "Gymnast" just as his is "Bolero", and that with the smallest provocation you always revert to your old love.'[194] General Eisenhower, who had just arrived in London, was astounded by the foregone conclusion to abandon *Sledgehammer.* Regardless of the risks involved, he thought the operation was preferable to *Gymnast*, which would open a new front 'unrelated to this theatre'.[195] If a diversion was indeed to be effected, the military pressed the president to revive the Pacific Ocean alternative.

To prevent Britain and the United States from drifting apart, Roosevelt sent Marshall and Hopkins to London to sort out the conflicting strategies within a week (rather than do it himself, he most likely preferred to have Churchill discourage them). Churchill's position, he instructed his delegation in London, did 'not wholly take me by surprise'. The priority he had given to an invasion in 1942 hardly stemmed from a desperate need to assist the Russians, but rather from domestic considerations – the need to see American troops engaged in battle 'at the earliest possible moment in 1942'. As important was the apprehension that the anticipated collapse of the Russian front might make it nigh impossible for Allied troops to face the entire might of the Wehrmacht on the western front in 1943.[196]

Churchill, as the president rightly anticipated, would not budge. In the notes he prepared for the meeting with the American guests, the prime minister discarded the second front altogether, shifting the entire weight to the operation in North Africa. Churchill successfully imposed his will on the War Cabinet, thereby burying once and for all the cross-channel operation for 1942. 'Just because the Americans can't have a massacre in France this year,' he commented in private, 'they want to sulk and bath in the Pacific!' In Washington, the secretary of war was shattered by the news. He felt in his 'soul that the going on with *Gymnast* would necessarily destroy *Bolero* even in 1943'. Roosevelt, he feared, 'was only giving lip service to *Bolero*', while he 'really was thinking *Gymnast*'. Cross-examined, the president admitted that the decision 'would certainly curtail and hold up *Bolero*'.[197] The American planners now visualized *Sledgehammer* 'blossoming into "Round Up" perhaps in 1944'.[198]]

21 July

I spent last weekend in Bovingdon contemplating a plan of action for the immediate future. One question plagued me: what else can I, the Soviet ambassador in England, do to help my country at this critical time? What can I do to rouse the ruling circles in England from their dangerous lethargy, to mobilize the forces stuck in this country, and to hasten the launching of a second front?

Turning these questions over in my mind, I strolled around the garden and lay down on the grass, gazing into the blue and distant sky and exposing my face, neck, arms and chest to the hot sun whose appearances in England are such a rarity. And I came up with the following plan:

(1) Stalin should confront Churchill with the matter of the convoys and the second front, stressing the fact that our people fail to understand Britain's passivity at a moment of such terrible danger for our country, and that if a second front is not opened in 1942 the war may be lost or, at the very least, the USSR will be weakened to such an extent that it will not be able to take an active part in the struggle.

(2) Once Stalin sends such a message to Churchill I shall speak in the same vein at an informal meeting of MPs and before the editors of the London newspapers (without referring to the message, of course).

I have suggested the plan to Moscow and am waiting for a reply.

My calculation: this plan could have a certain impact on the situation and help hasten a second front. At the very least, it could facilitate the implementation of secondary measures, such as the resumption of convoys, the intensification of air raids on Germany, etc.

Finally, *if the worst comes to the worst*, my plan will serve as a vindication of the Soviet government before our people and history in so far as it will show that the Soviet government did all that was humanly possible to rouse the British ruling circles from their lethargy, and that it was not our fault if this did not happen.

[This entry reveals the extent to which Maisky was still acting as he had done during the abortive 1939 negotiations: desperately plotting behind the scenes to bring about collaboration, but equally seeking 'vindication' for whatever the Kremlin might do – obviously including the possibility of a separate peace if the alliance failed to materialize.[199] Vyshinsky had indeed been telling diplomats in Kuibyshev that 'the time might come when they could not go on'. Both Maisky and Bogomolov, the ambassador to the governments in exile in London, were hinting in various conversations that 'Russian resistance might not be able to continue indefinitely', and that, if delayed for much longer, a second front 'would be too late'. Maisky produced a more subtle argument in advancing his case in London, warning that Stalin might adopt the strategy Kutuzov used in the war against Napoleon, by retreating until the Red Army was ready for battle.

Increasingly isolated, Maisky reverted to his old practice of initiating policy. On 16 July, he drew Molotov's attention to the fact that, as Churchill had avoided mentioning the second front in his message to Stalin, it was 'necessary to establish that we were in fact being left to the mercy of fate by our Allies in the most critical moment for us'. The scheme he concocted was for Stalin to harshly reproach Churchill and then seek reconciliation through a meeting of the two leaders.[200]]

23 July

Moscow has accepted my plan.

Late in the evening today I handed Stalin's message to Churchill. It is somewhat gentler than I had expected, but strong and resolute enough.[201] I wanted to hand the message to the prime minister in Eden's presence, but Eden had to deliver a major speech this evening in Nottingham, so he was out of town. As Churchill did not want to postpone receiving the reply to his message of 18 July until tomorrow, I came to *10, Downing Street* at 10.30 p.m. and handed over the document.

Churchill was in his *siren suit* and in a bad mood. As I was soon to learn, he had just received disheartening news from Egypt. The British attack, on which the PM had pinned so many hopes, came to nothing. True, Rommel was forced back a bit, but he was not crushed – and the aim was precisely to crush him! If the English fail to do this now, when the Germans have their hands full in the USSR and when it is extremely difficult for Rommel to obtain reinforcements, then what is to be expected in the future? In his distress, Churchill must have had a drop too much whisky. I could tell from his face, eyes and gestures. At times his head shook in a strange way, betraying the fact that in essence he is already an old man and that it won't be long before he starts sliding downhill fast. It is only by a terrific exertion of will and mind that Churchill remains fit for the fight.

Stalin's message produced the impression I had expected on the PM. He was depressed and offended at the same time. The PM's self-esteem was seriously wounded (especially by Stalin's charge that he had failed to fulfil his obligations) and the thought even seemed to flash through his mind that the USSR might withdraw from the war, because he said out of the blue: 'Well, we have been alone before… We still fought… It's a miracle that our little island survived… But…'

'Drop this nonsense!' I interrupted Churchill brusquely. 'The thought of laying down arms has not crossed the mind of any of us. Our path has been defined once and for all – *to the bitter end*. But the present situation must be taken into account: in 1942 we are, in all probability, stronger than we shall be in 1943. Neither we nor you should ignore this fact!'

Churchill calmed down, but he continued to argue for a good long while that he was doing all he could and that, as far as the matter of the second front was concerned, the memorandum of 10 June remained in force…

In conclusion the prime minister said that he would report Stalin's message to the War Cabinet and only then might he be in a position to say something.

In the course of the conversation, I took advantage of the impression which Stalin's message had produced on Churchill to raise the issue of the resumption of convoys and the intensification of the air bombardment of Germany. It proved a good ploy: Churchill was now ready to agree that Convoy 17 should not serve as a precedent for the future, for the Admiralty's actions may not have been the best in this instance, and he was inclining to the idea of sending the next convoy in September. I argued in favour of August, but to no avail. The reason is Malta: the British government must supply Malta with provisions and equipment in August, otherwise it might not hold out, and such an operation requires a tremendous concentration of forces. Since a convoy to Arkhangelsk also requires a great number of forces in the current circumstances, it is impossible to carry out both operations at the same time. Hence the conclusion:

Malta in August and Arkhangelsk in September. I had, I felt, come up against a brick wall.

Churchill was much more lavish with his promises when it came to the air bombardment of Germany. Since I had heard these same promises from him more than once (but without their subsequent complete fulfilment), I asked whether I might participate more closely in the elaboration and supervision of the bombing plans for August and September. These months are especially important from the point of view of the events unfolding in the USSR.

Churchill did not object and suggested that I speak to Air Marshal Sir Arthur Harris,[i] commander-in-chief of Bomber Command. I took good note of this.

24 July

On his return from Nottingham, Eden summoned me and said that he had acquainted himself with Stalin's message. Churchill is very *hurt* and in some distress about it. At the same time the prime minister is tormented by the thought that at this difficult hour there is so little he can do for his ally. The War Cabinet also feels wounded by Stalin's message. To avoid further exacerbation and further polemical exchanges, Eden thinks it better to leave Stalin's last message unanswered. Better to allow the passions to subside and the atmosphere to become calmer.

'After all,' Eden added, 'you expect a response from us not in words but in deeds. Let's wait for the deeds.'

Then he remarked with a faint smile: 'Two great men have clashed… They've had a tiff… You and I need to reconcile them… Too bad they've never met face to face!'

This all sounded fine. So far everything is going as I'd expected.

Churchill is hot-tempered, but he is easily appeased. After his initial emotional reaction, he begins to think and calculate like a statesman, and, even more so, a parliamentarian. And in the end he arrives at the necessary conclusions. The stronger the shock, the greater the chances that Churchill will do the right thing. I remember the case of Stalin's missive of 8 November last year. First Churchill flew into a rage – right in front of me. Then Eden and Beaverbrook tried to calm him down. Then he himself began to think and work things out. As a result, Churchill made the suggestion to Stalin of sending Eden to Moscow, and peace was restored. This led to Eden's visit in December 1941, talks in the Kremlin, Molotov's visit to London, and the signing of the Anglo-Soviet treaty.

---

[i] Sir Arthur Travers Harris, 'Bomber Harris', marshal of the Royal Air Force; deputy chief of air staff, 1940–41; commander-in-chief Bomber Command, 1942–45.

What will be the outcome this time? I don't know. My calculations, at any rate, have proved correct so far. We shall see.

I promised Eden my assistance in restoring 'peace' between the two great men and then turned to the convoys and the bombing of Germany, referring to my conversation yesterday with the prime minister. Eden responded positively. We agreed that a meeting would be held next week on the subject of the convoys, as would a meeting between myself and Harris.

At the same time, I'm taking steps to organize my speech to members of parliament.

[Seen from Moscow it was becoming increasingly apparent that the key politicians cultivated by Maisky over the years were deserting him at this crucial time. That applied not only to Churchill, but also to Eden, who was clearly speaking out of both sides of his mouth (strangely enough, not unlike Halifax in 1939). As Eden's private secretary despaired, the foreign secretary's relations with Churchill were those of 'son and heir' to 'father'. While unflinchingly supporting the prime minister's decision to shift from the second front to the North Africa campaign in Cabinet, he was also plotting with Maisky behind the scenes.

Maisky's relations with Lloyd George, now in the twilight of his parliamentary career, were no better. The elder statesman came especially to London to see a performance of Gilbert and Sullivan, rather than attend Maisky's crucial speech to MPs (still less to speak at that special gathering). After all, he told his private secretary, he was not 'just an ordinary Member of Parliament' but had 'a responsibility in the matter as one who conducted the last war'. In his meetings with Maisky he assumed the worst, convinced that Stalingrad would fall to the Germans. 'He uttered not one word of encouragement, appreciation or praise.'[202]

Maisky's plans were therefore only partially successful. He must have noticed, Eden told him, that Stalin's acrimonious message 'had had the opposite effect' to that expected: Churchill was sulking and preferred not to respond to the message at all. Strangely enough, Eden avoided any mention of a possible meeting between Stalin and Churchill in both his extensive report of the meeting and at the Cabinet meeting the following day. The Cabinet stood united behind the prime minister and sanctioned once again the switch from the second front to *Torch*.[203]]

26 July (Bovingdon)

Yet another hard week!

Our troops continue to retreat. The Germans continue to capture one region after another. Rostov has fallen. The enemy crossed the lower reaches of the Don near Tsimlyansk. The fascist hordes are drawing ever closer to Stalingrad. Ever closer to the Caucasus. Will we really prove unable to contain the Germans? Will they really cut us off from the Caucasus and gain a firm footing on the Volga? It seems like a nightmare from a horrifying fairy tale.

No! Both intuition and cold calculation tell me that this cannot happen. It seems increasingly certain that our retreat in the last two weeks was planned. It was, of course, a forced retreat, dictated by the enemy's superiority in numbers of tanks and planes, but there was no flight, no panic. The troops endured a hard and painful march, stubbornly fighting off the advancing enemy, but they were doing so in accordance with instructions worked out by the general staff. The moment must come when the retreat will end, when fresh reserves will be brought in, when we shall be able to move onto the offensive and attack an enemy weakened by losses and a long line of communication. This moment, to all appearances, is not far off.

I spent all Sunday at the typewriter, preparing my speech to MPs scheduled for 30 July.

28 July

The conference regarding the convoys was held today in Eden's office in parliament. Eden, Alexander and Pound participated on the British side; I, Kharlamov and Morozovsky on ours.

Eden (who was in the chair) made the opening remarks, suggesting that as we had gathered to discuss the question of the convoys, it would be desirable to hear Pound first. This appeal to Pound was quite typical. For throughout the conference it was only Pound who spoke and made decisions on behalf of the English. Eden and Alexander either kept silent, leaving everything to Pound, or permitted themselves brief comments while looking timidly into the admiral's eyes. It was as though Pound were the teacher and Eden and Alexander his pupils, who desired nothing more than to receive a good mark. A fine illustration of the theme: the relationship between ministers and *civil servants* in Great Britain! Alexander spoke only once. With a certain amount of ardour. But to what end? To defend Pound against my and Kharlamov's criticism. I'll come back to it later.

Before Pound had even managed to get a word out, however, I charged in: 'The question is: when can the next convoy be sent? It would be desirable to receive a reply from Admiral Pound to this question!'

This formulation was not to Pound's taste. So, playing for sympathy, he said that in his latest message to Stalin (of 18 July) the prime minister had proposed sending a top air force officer to Moscow to examine the possibility of protecting the convoys, but unfortunately Stalin left this point without reply. He simply ignored it. This point, however, is of exceptional importance since, according to Pound, the possibility of sending convoys depends entirely on the possibility of halting the operations of the *Tirpitz* in the Barents Sea. To achieve this, one must 'render the Barents Sea dangerous for the *Tirpitz*'. And to achieve that one must have strong air defences at Murmansk. The officer mentioned in the prime minister's missive was expected to come to Moscow, acquaint himself with the entire situation and report on the possibilities of organizing the necessary air cover. Only after that would it be possible to discuss the resumption of the convoys. Pound's conclusion was as follows: let us send an officer to Moscow and then we shall see.

The intentions of the honourable admiral were absolutely clear: he just wanted to delay a decision on the convoys question for many weeks, perhaps even months.

I replied that the method proposed by Pound did not suit me at all. We have to act quickly. There is no time to lose. So, seizing the bull by the horns, I suggested: 'Tell me now: how many planes and what sort of planes are needed, in your opinion, in order to make the Barents Sea dangerous for the *Tirpitz*. I'll send a telegram to the Soviet government and within 2–3 days we shall know whether the Soviet government is able to provide the necessary cover. Why drag it out?'

Pound did not like my proposal. He continued to insist on sending an officer to Moscow. In so doing, he mentioned the Air Ministry, saying that it was *very keen* to send its man to the USSR.

I replied that there is a British military mission stationed in Moscow, headed by Admiral Miles and with Air Vice-Marshal Collier on its staff. Why couldn't Pound delegate these men to get all the necessary information and documents? A telegram is all it would take; the reply would be in London within a few days.

But Pound did not like this suggestion either. He continued to insist that unless somebody was sent no progress would be made.

So then I made another *suggestion*. 'Well,' I said, 'send your man if you wish, but don't tie his mission to the sailing of the next convoy. As for the latter, let's use the telegraph – you use your channels and I'll use mine.'

But Pound dug his heels in, muttering something under his breath. I could stand it no longer and exclaimed with irritation: 'I implore you, Admiral, to tell me how many planes are needed in Murmansk? Or do you not know?'

This touched a nerve. The admiral, turning red, answered sulkily: 'Six bomber squadrons and four squadrons of torpedo carriers.'

'Very well,' I responded, 'I'll send a request to my government today and as soon as I receive the reply it will be possible to fix definitively the departure date of the next convoy. So as to pose the question as precisely as possible, I would like to know what share of the necessary air cover England could take upon herself?'

Pound frowned, shrugged his shoulders and finally said that the English could provide one squadron of torpedo carriers.

'Not a lot!' I noted ironically, but I didn't start pressing for more. This could wait until the entire matter had been agreed in principle.

Eden was in favour of the method I had suggested for clarifying the question, Alexander did not object, and Pound had to accept it, however grudgingly.

With this the meeting could have ended. Kharlamov, however, wanted to speak to Pound about the best way of navigating convoys through the dangerous zone. He set forth his considerations and naturally touched upon Convoy 17 and the reasons for its destruction.

Pound listened to Kharlamov with growing impatience, the colour rushing to his face. His entire appearance said: 'Don't teach a chicken how to lay eggs! Ha! Some Soviet admiral, still wet behind the ears, wishes to give advice to me, a British admiral! Impossible!'

When Kharlamov cautiously suggested that the order to detach the escort from the convoy and for the convoy itself to scatter may not have been the right one, Pound exploded: 'What do you mean, not the right one?' he very nearly screamed. 'I gave that order! That was me! What else should have been done?'

I objected that the order had been given in anticipation of an attack by the *Tirpitz* on the convoy, but in fact the *Tirpitz* made no such attack. However, the removal of the escort allowed the submarines and planes to sink our transport ships unhindered. The submarines were especially ferocious: they sank 16 out of 21 ships. Had the convoy scattered in groups, accompanied by the destroyers and corvettes, the vessels would at least have been protected from the submarines.

Pound became quite furious.

'I'm not a clairvoyant,' the admiral exclaimed angrily. 'I could not know what the *Tirpitz* was going to do!'

It was now Alexander's turn to intervene. He made a passionate speech in defence of Pound and the Admiralty. They are working superbly. They have saved England from hunger and continue to do so. They make it possible for British industry to function and for troops and supplies to be dispatched to the various theatres of war. They have rendered great services to their country, etc., etc.

I listened calmly to Alexander's flight of eloquence and said: 'Nobody denies the great services rendered by the Admiralty and the British fleet in this war, but does it follow from this that the Admiralty can never, in any circumstances, put a foot wrong?'

Eden set about trying to make peace between the parties and to cool everyone down. But Pound was still seething and snorting to himself. This provoked me and I said, with emphasis: 'Even British admirals err!'

Eden tapped me on the shoulder and said in a hurry: 'There's no use arguing! So, the ambassador will send a request to his government and then we shall see what can be done.'

Red stains continued to appear on Pound's face.

And here the meeting ended. Eden saw me off to my car. We walked for a good while along the corridors of parliament. I made no attempt to conceal my feelings.

'All your *civil servants* are like this! Arrogant, haughty, convinced that they know everything and that the ministers understand nothing.'

Eden tried to defend *civil servants*, insisting that they are excellent workers.

'I'm reminded,' I remarked, 'of Clemenceau's words: "War is much too serious a business to be entrusted to soldiers." Quite right. When you listen to the Pounds of this world, you begin to realize what a wise man Clemenceau was.'

Eden laughed and said: 'Clemenceau may not have been entirely wrong.'

[Drawing on the experience gained during the Russian Civil War, when Britain contemplated military intervention, Maisky appealed to his supporters, mostly on the left, to exert pressure through the formation of Anglo-Soviet committees in the various cities, and to organize vast public meetings to pass resolutions containing pledges to provide the Soviet Union with unstinting assistance. Churchill seemed far less concerned about Maisky's attempts to influence public opinion than about his plotting with Lloyd George and the opposition behind the prime minister's back.[204]]

29 July

Stukalov (naval attaché for air) and I, accompanied by Cadogan, went out of town to visit Air Marshal Harris. I had a long talk with him and came to an agreement about the plan for bombing Germany in August. If this plan is implemented, the effect will be quite decent. But will it be implemented?

I'm not entirely sure.

30 July

A hot day, and one fraught, perhaps, with far-reaching consequences!

At three in the afternoon, I delivered my speech in parliament (the text is appended). There were about 300 people present, and the 'old-timers' assure me that this is unprecedented in the history of such meetings. Sir Percy Harris (a Liberal) presided. There were quite a few big names: Elliot, Hore-Belisha, Mander, Aneurin Bevan, Erskine-Hill[i] (president of the notorious '1922

[i] Alexander Galloway Erskine-Hill, chairman of the Conservative 1922 Committee, 1940–44; Edinburgh North MP, 1935–45.

Committee'), the three 'chief whips', and others. The main thing, though, was that old Lloyd George was sitting in the presidium. At first he didn't wish to come: Sylvester, who had seen Lloyd George over the 'weekend', conveyed his master's blessing for my speech, but couldn't promise that he would appear. It seemed unlikely: I had the distinct impression that for whatever reason the old man wished to steer clear of the meeting. At the last moment, however, Lloyd George changed his mind and decided to attend. This caused a stir and 'set the mood', as Sylvester put it.

I was well received. Harris's *Introduction* was actually a statement to the effect that I did not need an *introduction*. These words from the chairman were met with loud applause. While I spoke you could have heard a pin drop, and the audience hung on every word – which was also an unusual thing at such meetings, if the elders are to be believed. I felt that my words were 'hitting home'. At times my speech was interrupted by loud applause – when, for instance, I said that what the Allies need above all is a joint strategy. The same thing happened when I noted that putting one's trust in the enormous quantities of potential Allied resources is one of the most dangerous forms of complacency. My figures and facts produced a very strong impression and even scared many listeners. When I mentioned that we first raised the question of a second front in July 1941, it was as if an electric current coursed through the audience. But when I suggested that the only remedy for saving the situation was to open a second front in 1942, there was not a single cheer. The chamber simply froze in tense silence.

My speech was followed by questions. Quite a lot of them, but hardly any were hostile. Only the Right Honourable Hopkins tried to ride his anti-Soviet hobby-horse, saying that the demand for a second front came from the communists. He was shouted down. Dozens of voices yelled: 'That's a lie!'

Hopkins had to beat a rapid retreat.

After the meeting, Lloyd George led me into his room in parliament. Megan dropped by. It was already 4.15 (the meeting had lasted just over an hour). Tea was served. We drank and talked. The old man said that among the many meetings he had attended throughout his long life in parliament he remembered few like today's, in terms of the numbers present, the attentiveness of the audience, and the impression made by the speaker.

'*Very powerful statement*,' was Lloyd George's assessment. '*Very powerful!* It's good you were *blunt*, nearly *brutal*. This had an effect. You were in a difficult position, but you coped with your task very skilfully: you went quite far but you didn't overstep diplomatic boundaries.'

'Though I was right at the edge,' I laughed.

'Perhaps so,' Lloyd George agreed. 'But the main thing is that the MPs understood and sensed the gravity of the situation. It's from you that they have learned the truth. The government, after all, feeds them with syrup.'

Lloyd George expressed his opinion that such a meeting cannot fail to exert some influence on the government.

'But what practical outcome can follow?' I asked, before adding: 'Of course I am pleased with the success of my speech, but oratorical skill is not the point here. The point is to push the British government towards concrete actions to help the USSR. Will this happen? Will the meeting hasten the opening of a second front?'

Lloyd George shrugged his shoulders. He himself understands perfectly well the significance of a second front in 1942. This is the Allies' sole chance of victory. But Churchill is displaying a strange, incomprehensible passivity. It seems to Lloyd George that Churchill currently finds himself in a mental state that precludes him from taking a major decision. This happens to Churchill now and then. It's a great shame.

'He has,' Lloyd George continued, 'some sort of *inferiority complex* when it comes to offensive operations. He was "bruised" already in the last war by the Dardanelles. He's not had much luck in this war either: Norway, Greece, Libya… Churchill fears offensive operations. He does not trust himself. Just think: to go to Greece, where it was clear from the very beginning that we had not a *dog's chance* of winning, and not to go to help Russia, where there is every possibility of routing Hitler!'

The old man shook his shoulders again. He's sceptical enough about a second front being opened in 1942, that's for sure!…

At 12.30 a.m. a call came from the prime minister's office. His secretary asked me to come to *10, Downing Street* right away. What's the matter? What's happened? All sorts of thoughts ran through my mind. An inner voice was telling me that this midnight invitation to see the prime minister was connected one way or another with today's meeting. But in what way? I had no doubt from the very beginning that my speech to the MPs, in which I demanded the opening of a second front, would cause displeasure and perhaps even irritation in the government, to Churchill in particular. I knew exactly what I was doing, believing that at moments like the present one should not be worrying about a prime minister's moods. Was the PM going to reprimand me for today's speech? And was this such an urgent matter as to require the summoning of an ambassador at midnight?

I admit that I racked my brains over this all the way to the PM's residence, without coming up with anything satisfactory.

Churchill's secretary met me in the corridor and we were joined by Bracken a few seconds later. The three of us sat in the reception room, chatting about various issues of the day. Eventually, Bracken said: 'I would like to hear your predictions for the future. You have often proved right. What do you expect to happen in the next two months?'

I had no time to answer him for at this very moment I was ushered in to see the prime minister. Churchill was sitting at the government's conference table. He was wearing his customary *siren suit* on top of which he had thrown a gay, black and grey dressing gown. Eden was sitting next to him in slippers and the green velvet jacket which he wears 'at home' in the evening. Both looked tired but excited. The prime minister was in one of those moods when his wit begins to sparkle with benevolent irony and when he becomes awfully charming.

'Take a look. Is it any use?' Churchill asked with a smile, passing me a sheet of paper.

It was the text of his message to Stalin. I quickly ran my eyes over the document.

'But of course! It's worth a great deal, a very great deal!' I responded after reading the message.

And how! A meeting between Churchill and Stalin could have very important consequences. I supported the prime minister's intention in every possible way. He smiled, drank whisky and puffed away at his irreplaceable cigar. I was looking at him and thinking: 'My calculations have been fully vindicated. Not a trace has remained of the irritation Churchill displayed upon receiving Stalin's message of 23 July. The PM has cooled down. Now he is preoccupied with thoughts about his trip to the USSR and his meeting with Stalin. So much the better.'

I inquired whether Churchill would come to Moscow should Stalin be unable to travel to the south, as Churchill requests? The PM dithered, and would not commit himself. He mentioned Tbilisi as a possible location a couple of times. Eventually, though, he let it be understood that he would be prepared to agree to Moscow in the last resort.

I was also satisfied with the decision to send the next convoy in early September. Ha, ha, ha, Sir Dudley Pound!

I promised to wire the news to Moscow right away. As Churchill was planning to fly overseas on 1 August, he asked for Stalin's reply to be handed to Eden in his absence.

Eden saw me to the door. On parting he said casually: 'It would be so good if you could go with the PM!'

I answered that I would very much like to go but that was for the Soviet government to decide.

As for today's meeting, neither Churchill nor Eden said a word about it.

Yet I was left with the vague feeling that Churchill's message was connected with the meeting in some way. But how?

I thought about this on my way back to the embassy, but could not come up with any definite conclusion. Time will tell.

31 July

Beaverbrook called early in the morning. He had already made his excuses on the eve of the parliament meeting, saying he wouldn't be able to attend (playing games!). Yesterday evening he called again to find out how the meeting went. I briefly described the events to him. Today Beaverbrook was most excited. 'There has never been such a meeting,' he yelled into the phone. 'All the MPs were *tremendously impressed*. I congratulate you on a major political success!'

It turned out that Beaverbrook was acquainted with the content of my speech down to the last detail, that the audience had been particularly struck by my information concerning our 5 million dead, the loss of half of our iron production and three-quarters of our aluminium output, and the possible weakening of our resistance in 1943, and much else besides.

I asked Beaverbrook what practical consequences could be expected to follow from my speech?

Beaverbrook shouted again: 'Major consequences! They have already begun!'

I wondered what he had in mind. Was Beaverbrook already in the know about my nocturnal meeting with Churchill and Eden?

Eden summoned me at 12.30. He expressed great satisfaction about the prime minister's decision to visit the USSR, although the PM would be flying off to Egypt before the reply was received – for a few days, possibly a week. The Air Ministry will have a plane at the ready for me.

I thanked Eden and said I had nothing to tell him as yet about the matter that interested him. Everything depends on Moscow.

Speaking about the prime minister's forthcoming visit, Eden expressed his hope that Churchill and Stalin would get on well and understand each other.

'It would be so good if you could be their interpreter! One must be able to translate not the words, but the spirit of a conversation! You have that gift! The prime minister was telling me that when you interpreted during our talks with Molotov he had the impression that the language barrier between him and Molotov had fallen, that it no longer existed.'

I repeated once again that the decision on this matter rested with Moscow…

[The diary for 1942 ends abruptly at this dramatic and fateful moment, most likely because Maisky's hopes of participating in the summit meeting and influencing the course of events failed to materialize, while the policies he had promoted proved to be all for naught. The idea of a meeting between Stalin and Churchill is often associated with Kerr's proposal made on 30 June, which Eden brought over to Churchill, who 'jumped at it', remaining 'fixed on the trip' despite futile attempts by Lord Moran, his doctor, and others to discourage him.[205] As we have seen, it was part of the subversive scheme plotted by Eden and Maisky. A day earlier, Cadogan had submitted to the prime minister a long minute attaching 'enormous importance to a Stalin–Churchill meeting'. Cadogan had spent a whole morning with Maisky, visiting Bomber Command, and had surely been exposed to the ambassador's initiative. Expecting things 'to go badly in Russia for some time', Cadogan advised Churchill that the moment may well come 'when the Russians are no longer attracted by "jam tomorrow"'. The British could either 'go out to turn up the cards', or risk a Russian disappointment, hoping that the prime minister might 'go out and comfort them if, in fact, they are disappointed. The former course is taking a gamble; the latter condemns the PM certainly to a most unpleasant trip.'[206] When Churchill, therefore, announced his intention of going to Egypt on 29 July, the possibility was already there that he might press on for Moscow.

Only a successful summit meeting could arrest Maisky's fast-declining influence in Moscow. He now staked the considerable power he had gained in mobilizing public opinion to exert pressure on Churchill. However, the resort to an unprecedented emotional appeal to the members of parliament, over the head of the government, seemed to some to be 'a speech of a man in a desperate position'. Never since Gondomar,[i] it was observed, 'have we allowed a foreign ambassador to interfere so much in our domestic affairs'. So far Maisky had successfully convinced Moscow that, despite his personal reservations and scepticism about the prime minister's military capability, Churchill was still 'the most likely premier to keep [Britain] in the war', while any successor might turn out to be 'a stopgap leading very shortly to appeasement and a separate peace'. Maisky's interest in a summit meeting coincided with that of Churchill, who 'had let it be understood' in conversations with the Russians that 'he would very much like to meet Stalin'.[207]

But the two were operating at cross-purposes. Maisky was gambling on Churchill's need to bolster his political standing at home through a display of unity with Stalin. He attributed the prime minister's offhand dismissal of the enormous public pressure for a second front as 'a Red stunt' to a genuine concern. He failed to realize that Churchill's overriding objective was to achieve a breathing space, during which he could pursue unhindered his preparations for the invasion of North Africa, while deflecting pressure for a second front and securing continued Russian resistance on the battlefield. Churchill believed he could achieve this with Stalin by resorting to his unrivalled power of persuasion and charm.[208]

So far Churchill had resisted with tenacity any attempt by his new Russian and American allies to alter his peripheral strategy. He had successfully imposed it on the reluctant chiefs of staff (though only after purging the top brass) as well as on Roosevelt, against the better judgement of the president's professional military advisers. This was a remarkable achievement, particularly against the backdrop of the horrific defeats he had suffered throughout 1941. Churchill had successfully exploited the rout in Tobruk to sway Roosevelt from the cross-channel attack (now scheduled for 1943, but conceded by the military to become feasible only in 1944) to Operation *Torch.* As much as he abhorred the idea of going to Moscow, Churchill assumed that a *tête a tête* meeting would convince Stalin of the insurmountable difficulties involved in launching a

---

[i] Diego Sarmiento de Acuña, count of Gondomar, Spanish ambassador to London from 1613–22, saw his embassy as an isle in a hostile land. He had, however, cultivated numerous powerful intimate friends at the Court of King James I through whom he exercised great influence on British politics. He was judged to be 'a cleverer man than any in England'.

cross-channel attack and would convert him to the Mediterranean campaign as the genuine second front. He hoped to assuage the Russian leader with vague promises to persevere in the preparations for Operation *Bolero* the following year. The concrete bait was an undertaking to resume the normal run of the convoys in September, while intensifying air raids on German towns.[209]

Numerous highly coloured and anecdotal descriptions of the dramatic twists during the stormy encounters in the Kremlin emanated mostly from Churchill's own highly distorted and tendentious narrative and from that of his immediate entourage, who were briefed by him. Churchill himself changed the narrative a couple of times while still in Moscow. In his final report to Attlee, his deputy, having at last established 'cordial and friendly' relations with Stalin, he ultimately produced a rosy report which discounted his 'too gloomy' earlier report.[210] This narrative continues to dominate the current historiography while avoiding the core issues, which Churchill was keen to conceal, and the Soviet point of view.

Maisky's hopes of enhancing his own position in the Kremlin as the go-between – a role he had successfully assumed during Eden's two earlier visits to Moscow and Molotov's London visit – were cruelly dashed. The bleak script for the conversations in Moscow was in the public domain even before Churchill set foot in Russia.[211] In seeking Eden's intervention to secure his own presence in Moscow, Maisky merely aggravated his position. On 4 August, the humiliated Soviet ambassador not only conceded to Eden that he would not be going to Moscow, but pleaded with him 'not to make further representations to his government in the matter'. To add insult to injury, Stalin had instead instructed Maisky's counsellor, Novikov, to join Churchill in Cairo and proceed with him to Moscow.[212] In his memoirs, Maisky prefers to deflect the reader's attention from the genuine reasons for his exclusion, attributing it to 'the Soviet Government's dissatisfaction with Britain's conduct' on the issue of the second front.[213] It was, however, a severe personal blow, which Maisky evidently associated with the reproaches over his supposedly defeatist outlook that was exposed during Molotov's visit. He found himself in a dismal situation, not dissimilar to that in 1939, desperately seeking to dissociate himself from Litvinov's brazen critical attitude of the Kremlin. Litvinov had been making no secret in Washington of his conviction that 'everything was over … Russia has been defeated and there is no hope left for us.' When Molotov was informed of this statement, he received the news with 'incredulity', attributing it to Litvinov 'feeling "homesick" in the midst of American prosperity'.[214] Maisky tried to absolve himself in the eyes of the Kremlin, using every possible channel to display his loyalty and commitment to the war effort. 'Our life revolves around the front,' he wrote to Kollontay in an unusually long letter – most likely intended for interception by various agents on its way to Stockholm – 'from one communiqué to the next one':

> We firmly believe in our final victory … we try to make a contribution, even if small, to our Soviet kitty. We have our successes but also our failures … I very much wished that I would have not been refused permission to travel with Churchill to Moscow.[215]

Likewise, in two untypically long letters to Litvinov within a space of two weeks, Maisky repeated that 'notwithstanding the difficulties and disappointments, I am all the same convinced of our eventual victory'.[216]

But he was not helped by Churchill's promotion of his case. Churchill, who in Moscow was frustrated by the language barrier, lamented to Attlee that Pavlov, 'the little interpreter, was a very poor substitute for Maisky'. In his final candid conversations with Stalin at his Kremlin apartment, Churchill was surprised to discover that Stalin was 'very critical of Maisky'. When Churchill commended Maisky as 'a good Ambassador', he seemed only to increase the host's suspicions as to where Maisky's loyalties lay. Stalin, reported Churchill, 'agreed, but said that he might be better; he spoke too much and could not keep his tongue between his teeth'.[217] Churchill returned to London convinced, as he told Cripps, that the Soviet government would recall Maisky, who 'talked too much', to join the Soviet Cabinet in Moscow, while the recently appointed counsellor of the embassy would replace him.[218]

Maisky nonetheless tried desperately to have an impact on the negotiations by 'taking the liberty' of addressing Stalin personally, in a long and detailed brief on Churchill's objectives. He gambled on his unparalleled familiarity with the prime minister to dare to submit to Stalin precise recommendations on how he should handle Churchill. Fearing the worst, it was now vital for him to dispel any illusions (which he himself had cultivated in the Kremlin) about the likelihood that Churchill would agree to a second front. Indeed, in a personal letter to Litvinov on the same day, Maisky stressed twice that he was 'not feeling particularly optimistic' and believed Churchill would postpone the second front to 1943. However, it was as important for him to try and overturn the ideologically oriented appraisal, prevalent in Moscow since Molotov's return from London and Washington, that Churchill and Roosevelt were deliberately avoiding a second front and seeking to weaken Russia. He knew that such thoughts, which he did not share, might lead to Soviet disengagement and further strategic retreat, or still worse to a separate peace.

He was right to be concerned. Just as the talks got under way in Moscow, the 32-year-old Andrei Gromyko (son of a peasant and a product of Molotov's new face of Narkomindel's 'yes men', loyal and submissive though poorly informed about the American scene) sent his master a long and devastating survey of the prospects for a 'second front'. Gromyko, counsellor at the Washington embassy, had been sent to Washington to keep a close watch on Ambassador Umansky, who had fallen out of favour with Stalin; he would soon seize the ambassadorial role from Litvinov.[219] Gromyko clearly tailored his memorandum to please Molotov and reinforce his entrenched suspicion of the West. Molotov read the document attentively, underlining with his thick black pencil large segments which conformed to his views. The gist of the argument was that the American government was not seriously considering and preparing for a cross-channel attack. Resorting to ideological rhetoric, Gromyko wrongly attributed the negative attitude to 'strong anti-Soviet moods among the American military' and particularly to Stimson (who, as we have seen, was the most ardent advocate of a second front). He went on to suggest that the generals had pinned their hopes (and continued to do so) on the destruction of both Hitlerite Germany and the Soviet Union. These hopes coincided with those of industrial circles which were aired publicly at the outbreak of war. They did not want to see Hitler victorious, but still less did they wish to see a Soviet victory.

He even suggested that a small but influential group among the generals continued to cherish hopes of an arrangement with Hitler. Likewise (and here Molotov added exclamation marks in the margins of the document), the mood of the naval commanders was 'dictated by their political and ideological point of view' and was 'hostile towards the Soviet Union'. The conclusion was therefore that appeasement led many to prefer Hitler's victory to a victory of the Soviet Union.[220]

Maisky would find it increasingly difficult to dent the new narrative which was taking firm hold in the Kremlin. While proposing to maintain the pressure in favour of a cross-channel attack, he advocated the 'more feasible' 'subsidiary demands', such as increased supplies and military assistance in the north and the Caucasus; but above all he advocated the forging of a long-term political and military association with Churchill.[221] Despite his personal dislike of Maisky, Stalin lent a guileful ear to his ambassador's advice. It was not the first time that Stalin had adopted the ideas of an opponent as his own, and then disposed of the draughtsman. However, he would certainly not share Maisky's optimism that the visit could 'serve as a starting point for forging a single allied strategy without which victory will be inconceivable'.[222]

The long-anticipated encounter between the two leaders took place on 12 August, in the evening, shortly after Churchill arrived in the Soviet capital. The impetuous prime minister rushed into the meeting without waiting for his political and military advisers, including the chief of staff, who were held up in Tehran for another day due to mechanical failure of their plane. Stalin's 'face crumpled up into a frown' a couple of times as Churchill conceded that there would be no second front in 1942. He was particularly upset about the breach of the promises made to Molotov, though Churchill insisted that he had endorsed those only with serious reservations. Stalin took heed of Maisky's advice, seeking to end the first round of the discussions by noting that, while he was not entitled to demand the second front, 'he was bound to say that he did not agree with Mr Churchill's arguments'.

Churchill now enthusiastically plunged into a protracted presentation of *Torch* as an alternative second front, which 'did not necessarily have to be embarked upon in Europe'. Waving a drawing of a crocodile that he had made while Stalin was talking, Churchill explained that it was his intention 'to attack the soft belly of the crocodile as [the Russians] attacked his hard snout'. Taking his leave, Churchill stopped by a globe in the middle of the room to expound the immense advantages of clearing the Germans out of the Mediterranean. He returned to Stalin's guest house in the woods convinced that he had succeeded in swaying Stalin. The British ambassador enthusiastically (but alas prematurely) informed Eden that Churchill's method of approach was 'masterly'. The bluntness with which he had demolished the prospects of the second front 'on which Stalin had set his heart made that which the Prime Minister now set before him appear all the more attractive'. The visit, he concluded, 'promises very well'.[223]

Churchill, still in euphoric mood, could hardly wait for the opportunity to discuss *Torch* further with Molotov the following morning. Oblivious both to the microphones installed in the dacha and the presence of the Russian staff, he was beside himself over lunch, describing Stalin 'as just a peasant' whom he 'knew exactly how to tackle'. Eventually relations between the two would be further marred when it became known in Moscow that on his way back to the dacha, when Stalin's name was mentioned, Churchill referred to him as 'that monstrosity'.[224] To his chagrin, Churchill found the Soviet foreign minister elusive and preferring to defer the topic for Churchill's meeting with Stalin that evening. All attempts to extract from Molotov a positive reaction to the talks so far elicited an ominous response which disclosed the suspicion prevailing in the

Kremlin that, as in 1939, the British were eager to see the Soviet Union and Germany scuffle in the east, and were perhaps even seeking a separate peace. 'It had obviously been decided not to create a second front in Europe in 1942,' Molotov summed things up succinctly, 'and there was no absolute certainly about the "Torch" operation taking place.' It was all shrouded in 'considerable ambiguity'.[225]

Arriving at the Kremlin, Churchill was confronted by Stalin with an acrimonious aide-mémoire remonstrating against the decision to scrap the second front operation in 1942, while paying no heed to Operation *Torch*. The absence of a second front, it warned, would have a calamitous impact on the morale of the Soviet population and the Red Army, the consequences of which were unpredictable. Lulled by a feeling that he had succeeded in masterly manner in diverting Stalin from the second front on the continent to the North African campaign, Churchill, who had emerged from the first meeting convinced that the rest of the talks would be 'plain sailing', was knocked off balance and was shattered by Stalin's callous dismissal of his case. But the Soviet leader did not leave it there.

To deflect Stalin from an ideologically oriented interpretation of Churchill's dithering, Maisky had produced for him a psychological profile of the prime minister. He attributed Churchill's dithering to the haunting memories of the crushing and costly defeats he had suffered in the Dardanelles in the First World War and in Norway, Crete, Singapore and France in the present one. Making full use of this, Stalin resorted to blunt and ironic language in castigating the prime minister, suggesting that the British should not be 'afraid of the Germans, if they fought against them they would find out they were not invincible, soldiers had to be blooded'. Moreover, he challenged the British intelligence estimates of the strength and location of the crack Wehrmacht units in the west, not missing the opportunity to remind Churchill of the failure of British intelligence in the Dardanelles in the First World War. A string of accusations followed. Stalin claimed that the only goods the Soviet Union was receiving from the West were those that it was only too happy to be rid of. It was proof of the 'underestimation of the significance of the Russian front for the allies, as the only front where the enemy was engaged on a massive scale'. Finally, though Stalin did not find disagreement between the Allies to be 'tragic', he vehemently objected to any suggestion that the operation in North Africa – even if it was 'right from the military point of view' – had any relevance for the Soviet Union. 'One had to remember,' agreed Air Chief Marshal Tedder,[i] that for Stalin the North African campaign 'appeared very much small beer – and rather flat beer at that!'[226] Churchill, who clearly was not accustomed to the 'almost brutal directness' with which Stalin could pose 'searching questions, each of them loaded like a revolver', was shattered.[227]

In his reports to Roosevelt and the Cabinet, Churchill described the 'most unpleasant discussion', during which Stalin said 'a great many insulting things' which Churchill claimed to have repulsed 'without taunts of any kind'. This was hardly the case. Churchill lost his composure, and his doctor, who accompanied him to the dacha, was surprised 'to find the violence and depth of resentment that he had worked up'. He looked 'like a bull in the ring maddened by the pricks of picadors'. While making much of his mistreatment at the Kremlin, he brilliantly concealed from his entourage – as well

[i] Arthur William Tedder (1st Baron Tedder), marshal of the RAF, commander of the Mediterranean Air Command.

as from the Cabinet and future historians – that his plan to convert Stalin to *Torch* had been quashed. The fear of the reaction at home was uppermost in his mind, particularly when he was confronted with the Russian draft communiqué summing up the talks, which avoided any mention of the desert offensive but announced the failure to reach an agreement on the cross-channel operation. To forestall the reopening of the strategic debate, he reassured Cabinet and Roosevelt that 'in his heart, so far as he has one, Stalin knows we are right' and his 'sure-footed and quick military judgment' made him 'a strong supporter of TORCH'. He conveniently adopted a rather ridiculous explanation which Harriman had concocted to account for Stalin's mood swings, attributing them to opposition within the Council of Commissars, which might have 'more power than we suppose', as well as to bad manners.[228]

Sulking, Churchill made up his mind to return to London first thing the following morning. Averell Harriman, Roosevelt's personal representative to the conference, who had been subjected to similar treatment a year earlier while accompanying Beaverbrook, persuaded Churchill that it was a 'poker' game or 'some sort of Slav technique'. It was left to the British ambassador to awaken Churchill 'from the intense, and alas, no longer very actual, family and natitude pride'. Clark Kerr left a bitter description of Churchill's demeanour, full of recriminations. 'I don't like to see a man in whose hands lies the fate of whole peoples,' he wrote in his diary, 'behave like a spoilt child. I don't like to have to shake a great leader of men out of whimsicalities or rather out of sheer folly.' In a most extraordinarily frank conversation, Clark Kerr convinced Churchill that he 'couldn't leave Russia in the lurch whatever Stalin had said to hurt his pride. He would have to swallow his pride if only to save young lives.'[229]

The third scene of the drama was about to unfold. Maisky had advised Stalin that the key to Churchill's heart was 'a purely private chat on varied themes', in the course of which it was possible to gain his confidence and establish a closer understanding. After about an hour of futile meetings at Stalin's office in the Kremlin, the Soviet leader made an unprecedented gesture, inviting Churchill to his private quarters for 'a drink'. Stalin had deliberately withheld his response to Churchill's request for a final meeting, but at the same time hastily set the scene at home, ordering an elaborate dinner and laying the table for three (Molotov was to join later), while requesting his daughter to be available to meet the prominent guest. The two strolled along the endless corridors of the Kremlin to Stalin's modest 'empty and depressing' apartment, from which all valuables and books had been transferred to Kuibyshev.

There, 'sitting with a heavily laden board between them: food of all kinds crowned by a suckling pig, and innumerable bottles', it all 'seemed to be as merry as a marriage bell'.[230] Stalin went out of his way throughout the intimate dinner (which went on until 3 a.m.) to charm his guest, avoiding the pitfall of the second front. He secured what Maisky had called the 'soft second line' assistance, but considering his ever-growing fear of a separate peace, perhaps more significant was an undertaking he extracted from Churchill that Prussian militarism would be smashed and Germany disarmed after the war.[231]

The prime minister returned to the dacha in euphoric mood, convinced that he had been 'taken into the family', having 'seen the daughter and drink, food and jokes'. Henceforth he was 'all for Uncle Joe', certain that he had 'established with Stalin a personal relationship of the same kind as he had already built up with President

Roosevelt'. Colonel Jacob,[i] a witness to the events, was not taken in by the theatricality of it all. Observing Stalin's 'complete self-possession and detachment' and reflecting on the course of history, he doubted 'whether any of the really great figures thrown up by times of turmoil have made friends to whom they would stick through thick and thin. They would not have reached the unchallenged position which they achieved if they had been governed by the ordinary human sentiment.'[232]

Churchill left Moscow boasting that the disappointing news concerning the second front could not have been imparted except by him 'personally without leading to really serious drifting apart'. More significant was the effort he invested in deluding both Cabinet and Roosevelt into believing that, once reconciled to the bad news, Stalin was 'entirely convinced of the great advantages of TORCH', which, Churchill added, he hoped was 'being driven forward with super-human energy on both sides of the ocean'.[233] It did not take long, however, for this version to be discredited. The demands for the second front resurfaced when Maisky explained to Eden that it was 'difficult to persuade the Russian people that any operations which we might undertake in Africa were of equivalent value to the creation of a second front in Europe'. Likewise, Litvinov continued to relay a grim prognosis for the war in the east if a second front failed to materialize. Maisky, to his dismay, gleaned from Eden that even a successful *Torch* did not guarantee a cross-channel attack in spring 1943.[234]

Though excluded from the talks, Maisky was hardly taken in by the joint communiqué, which, at Churchill's insistence, alluded to strategic decisions which in reality had not been agreed upon. Maisky kept spreading to the press 'pessimistic accounts' of Churchill's visit. He regarded the absence of a second front as a 'calamity' and, notwithstanding his 'great personal admiration for the Prime Minister', it 'would be remembered as the greatest mistake of his career'. In prophetic mood, he warned his British interlocutors that 'if we did not have a second front while Russia was still a fighting partner, we should never have one at this'.[235]

Nonetheless Maisky made a last-ditch attempt to convince Molotov that Churchill's visit, which he had contrived, was perceived in London as a great success. The excerpts from Churchill's telegrams which Eden had read to him extolled 'the real Stalin' he had come to know and the latter's 'profound understanding of military matters'. He had been assured by Eden that the amicable comradeship established in Moscow was bound to 'produce even better results in the future'. But Maisky's influence was fast waning. Molotov, who sensed that the ambassador was again bent on launching personal initiatives, as he had done in 1939, warned him in unequivocal terms that the idea he had raised on 'devising a unified strategy' had been deliberately left out of the talks in Moscow because, as long as Russia was fighting alone, it was absolutely 'unacceptable'. 'You should not,' he was reprimanded, 'put forward this idea to the British. You have never been given, you could not have been given, directions to that effect from us.'[236]

The disagreeable role he was now assigned was to diminish the impression projected by Churchill that the Moscow negotiations had been successful, while reviving the agitation for a second front. He resorted to 'seriatim' meetings with the editors of all leading London papers.[237] Inevitably this put him on a collision course with his allies in

[i] Sir Ian Claud Jacob, lieutenant general, a colonel at the time of *Bracelet*, he was Churchill's personal military assistant.

the British government. Over tea at the embassy, Maisky, who was 'more aggressively bitter than ever', told representatives of the American press that the cause of the failure to mount the second front was 'lack of will power'. The journalists gained the impression 'that the suspicion of the Russians has reached the point where it was in 1939'. Maisky regretted that the Americans, who had been in favour of a second front, had been talked out of it by Churchill, who told Stalin that he expected the war to last for five more years. 'On such an estimate,' Maisky caustically remarked, 'no considerations of urgency were involved.' He feared that 'the prospect of Anglo-Soviet cooperation after the war was imperilled'. The fact that Maisky was 'intriguing everywhere with the ignorant and disgruntled' drove Eden to file a complaint with Churchill that 'Maisky was overstepping bounds of an Ambassador's privilege' and demand that he be reprimanded.[238]

It is rather odd that Stalin should have chosen this moment to confer on Maisky the Order of Lenin (the highest order of the Soviet Union), ostensibly in recognition of 'outstanding services to the Soviet State' to mark 'the completion of the tenth year of his mission in London'. Although outwardly glowing with pride, Maisky, familiar with Stalin's cynical way of removing opponents, must have sensed that it carried with it an intimation that his mission was being wound up. By publicly demonstrating who had the power to bestow honours, Stalin was most likely reacting to Churchill's commendation of the ambassador. Both he and Molotov had come to doubt Maisky's loyalties. Maisky would indeed eventually be charged with treason, having been in London too long to recognize clearly whom he was serving. This official recognition of the ambassador further signalled to the British government that his reproaches were done not 'off his own bat but on the orders of his Govt.'.[239]

106. Maisky opening the exhibition 'Soviet Life' in London.

Meanwhile Maisky was swiftly losing his grip on the media and public opinion. The disastrous raid on Dieppe in late August turned out to be a deathblow to his campaign in favour of a second front – to the extent that a motion urging the government to promptly launch a second front was even defeated at the annual meeting of the Trades Union Congress. 'The workers,' noted Brendan Bracken, Churchill's confidant, were being 'very good ... not very responsive to Stalin's appeals for a second front.'[240]

Churchill tried in vain to place the onus for the failure of the second front on the Americans. He was, as Stimson wrote in his diary, 'evidently at his wits' end, particularly when realizing that the consequence of the diversion to North Africa would lead to the postponement of *Roundup* to 1944'. News he would have to break to Stalin before long. The postponement, noted the American secretary of war, 'was of course a direct result of his own action last August when Marshall went over to the London conference'.[241]

The successful Anglo-American landing in North Africa and the victory at El Alamein in early November literally brought to an end the 'Second Front Now' movement, so laboriously set up by Maisky, and on which he had staked his diplomatic career, if not indeed his survival.[242] The Soviet victory in Stalingrad gave Stalin a confidence boost and ironically further reduced the likelihood that a unified Allied strategy might ever be attained in the war. Maisky's assets were fast dwindling.

Churchill's dismissal of the persistent Soviet demands for a second front as mere 'propaganda', as well as his unconcealed predilection for the Poles, led Stalin to think that the British were 'back on the policy of cordon sanitaire'. Maisky disclosed to the ageing Webbs the intense suspicion in the Kremlin that the British generals and governing class were 'anxious that the German and Russian armies should exterminate each other' and thus enable Britain and the United States to dominate the peace-making process. Perhaps in a mirror image of the Soviet consideration of an arrangement with Germany earlier, he feared that the government 'might come to terms, not with Hitler and his Nazi Party, but with the German capitalists glad to resume control of Germany'. In Washington, Litvinov conveyed the Kremlin's view that Hess was being detained in Britain without trial to serve as a go-between in negotiations with Hitler's Germany or a post-war government in Germany which would be friendly to Great Britain 'after Russia had been bled white in defeating Hitler's Army'.[243]

Maisky's confrontation with the Kremlin placed him in an increasingly awkward situation in Britain, too, where he seemed to be 'behaving in a very odd and indeed alarming way'.[244] His relations with Eden, and particularly with Churchill, were undermined by Stalin's insistence that 'no operations *outside Europe* would count as a Second Front' and by various indiscretions to the press regarding Operation *Torch*, probably in the hope of forcing the British and Americans to revert to *Round-Up*. Those stood in sharp contrast to the way Churchill had construed the narrative of the relations he had established with Stalin in Moscow. The derogatory attitude of Stalin to his own ambassador now led the British to assume that his criticisms and outbursts were done 'off his own bat'.

Eden was 'bored' with Maisky, whom he found to be increasingly 'troublesome' and 'very difficult'. When Maisky expressed gratitude for assistance given to Russia, the foreign secretary was heard muttering: 'I have never known the little blighter say thank you for anything before.'[245] When Oxford University consulted the Foreign Office about the possibility of conferring an honorary doctorate on Maisky, Eden provided only a lukewarm recommendation.[246]

For Maisky, however, the intimacy he had established with Churchill remained vital for his political survival and continued stay in London – particularly in view of a new wave of rumours suggesting he was 'being moved to Stockholm'. It was he who had championed the prime minister in Moscow and vouched for his determination to pursue the war to its end. He now desperately clung to Churchill, corresponding with him privately and reminding him of their 'long and friendly association' which 'existed in the past, exists now and, I sincerely hope, will exist in the future'. This evoked a noncommittal polite response from the prime minister 'cordially reciprocating the sentiments'.

Rather alarmingly, Churchill, using flimsy excuses, declined an invitation to a star-studded celebration of the twenty-fifth anniversary of the Soviet Union. His absence was most conspicuous. Maisky persevered, however. On the occasion of Churchill's birthday, he wrote to him again at considerable length to express the hope of seeing Churchill representing Britain at the peace conference after the war 'among the leaders of that grand alliance of free peoples'. And he concluded: 'On this memorable anniversary I recall with great satisfaction my long and friendly associations with you in various circumstances on various occasions. Looking back on all these years I think I can say that they have served our common cause which unites us now in the common struggle against Hitlerism.'[247]

On 18 October, Maisky reported to Moscow that he had succeeded in foiling attempts by the British government to convince the public that Stalin had accepted Churchill's reasoning for abandoning the second front in 1942 and replacing it with operations in North Africa. The following day, Stalin rushed a telegram to his ambassador, expressing his view that Churchill's opposition to the second front clearly reflected a wish to see the Soviet Union defeated 'in order to then come to terms with the Germany of Hitler or Brüning[i] at the expense of Britain'. He also referred to Hess as a potential intermediary in the negotiations with Germany, an idea which was then splashed on the front page of various Soviet newspapers.[248]

After a couple of probably sleepless nights, Maisky cautiously addressed to Stalin a long and well-argued rebuttal, rejecting the idea that Churchill was seeking either Russia's destruction or negotiations with the Germans. Maisky might have been encouraged by Montgomery's[ii] offensive at El Alamein which opened on that day and led to victory over Rommel by 11 November. He challenged Stalin, insisting that Churchill could not possibly be craving the defeat of the USSR, which would 'inevitably mean the end of the British Empire' once Germany became the hegemonic power in Europe, if not in large parts of Asia and Africa. He argued that the reason why Churchill had not intensified the bombing of Berlin (as he had promised Stalin) was clear: he did not wish the Germans to resume the bombing of Britain. Likewise, the reason he did not put Hess on trial was to prevent Hitler from taking retaliatory measures against British prisoners of war.

---

[i] Heinrich Brüning, German chancellor in the waning days of the Weimar Republic.

[ii] Bernard Law Montgomery, field marshal, commander of the Eighth Army from July 1942 to 1943 in North Africa, during which he defeated the Germans and Italians at El Alamein in November 1942, and captured Tripoli and Tunisia in 1943. Commanded the invasion of Italy in September 1943.

Displaying an uncharacteristic temerity, Maisky told Stalin that he had drawn some 'practical conclusions' concerning Soviet 'policy and strategy', which he promised to impart in due course.[249] Stalin, however, put an end to the discussion, waving away the arguments. 'Being the champion of an easy war,' he instructed Maisky, 'Churchill is clearly under the influence of those who are interested in the defeat of the Soviet Union ... and a compromise with Germany.' Clairvoyantly, he dismissed the promises made to him by Churchill to launch the cross-channel attack in 1943, as he 'belonged to those political figures who easily make promises only to forget or break them as easily'.[250]

Just two days after the conclusion of Montgomery's successful offensive against Rommel and the launch of *Torch*, Maisky was obliged to remind Churchill that the operation did not constitute a second front, but was 'only a prelude or a trampoline for it'. The view in Moscow was that the British and Americans were exploiting the dire situation of the Wehrmacht in Stalingrad to mount their own offensive.[251] In early December, Churchill told Maisky that although he favoured the idea of a second front in 1943, he did not think the Americans would be able to complete their deployment in England by then. This was far from the truth. Over dinner at home with Halifax, General Marshall was highly critical of Churchill's strategy. He was against extending the war to Italy and favoured pouring American troops into Britain to prepare for a landing on the Brest Peninsula by April 1943. He was most reluctant to see Churchill in Washington or to launch a new set of talks in London which would rightly 'look too much like the dotted line for Stalin'.

Maisky, now in tune with his master in the Kremlin, reported his impression that the way the Americans and the British were throwing the ball to each other meant 'that both were embracing the same idea – the idea of an easy war for themselves'.[252] Indeed, the general strategic plans of the British for 1943 subordinated the cross-channel operations to the campaign in Italy, while the Balkans now emerged as a possible new theatre.[253] Rather than respond directly to Stalin's repeated queries about the likelihood of a second front in 1943, Churchill and Roosevelt proposed to discuss future strategy with him at a summit meeting. Aware, however, that all they wished was to impart the sombre news that the operations on the continent would have to be further postponed, Stalin preferred not to join Churchill and Roosevelt at their forthcoming summit meeting in Casablanca.[254]]

1943

1 January

1 January 1943. The old year has died, a new one is born.

We welcomed the New Year with good cheer. The mood was quite different to a year ago. The main difference is this: over the course of these 12 months we have tested ourselves against the enemy in every department, we have sensed his strength and we have sensed our own, we have compared our strength with his and are firmly convinced that ours is the greater. True, much time and effort will still be needed to crush the enemy, but the outcome is certain. The crucial thing now is to ensure that in the course of beating the enemy we do not overstrain ourselves and reach the finishing line in a state of complete exhaustion. For this, skilful tactical manoeuvring is required – on the battlefield and in the sphere of diplomacy. Will we succeed in this? I think we shall. Stalin has shown that he has a superb understanding of the art of the calculated manoeuvre.

My thoughts involuntarily run ahead.

First of all, when should we expect the war in Europe to end.

I stand by the opinion which I first expressed back in October that the end of the war in Europe can be expected no earlier than 1944. And even then only if things go well for the Allies, if, that is, there is no split between them, no frictions which might paralyse the effectiveness of their joint operations, and if a proper front is established in Europe in 1943. It is difficult to forecast precisely when in 1944 the end of the war may be expected, but I'm inclined to think it will be in the spring or summer of 1944.

And the prospects for 1943?

I hope that in the course of the winter we shall liberate the Volga, the Don, the northern Caucasus and perhaps the Donets Basin, and lift the Leningrad blockade. I also hope we shall recapture Rzhev, Vyazma and perhaps Smolensk. I'm not certain of the latter, though. I think the capture of northern Finland and Norway, jointly with the British, would be helpful, but will it happen? It seems unlikely. No more can be expected during the winter, and anyway it would be undesirable to set ourselves any greater tasks – considering the need for prudent manoeuvring mentioned above. What we intend to do this summer and autumn is not yet clear. To me, at least. Much will depend on the conduct of Britain and the USA.

What can be expected from our allies in 1943?

Here, all is still fuzzy. It seems as if Churchill and the British government are currently in favour of establishing a serious second front in France in the spring. Roosevelt and the American government are evidently not so keen on the idea at present.[1] It seems that London and Washington have swapped positions in comparison with 1942. As the British won't open a second front in France without the Americans, it would be risky to count on an effective second front being established this spring. It may be opened, and it may not. Of course, were the Red Army to start approaching Poland's borders this winter, the British and the Americans would positively race to open a second front in France. No extra encouragement would be needed from our side: after all, one can't allow the USSR to enter Berlin before England and the USA! But I doubt that the Red Army can get that far by spring.

If no second front is opened by May or June, what can be expected then?

Then, in all probability, the Allies will concentrate their attention on the Mediterranean, that is, on Italy or the Balkans. For now I believe that Italy, being nearer to the English and the Americans, is the likelier target. This is particularly true for the Americans. The Allies would head for the Balkans only if they were joined by Turkey. This can't be excluded, but everything seems to indicate that Turkey is disinclined to abandon its policy of 'sitting on the fence' so lightly. But time will tell.

In any case, if the Allies do indeed establish an effective second front in France this spring, it will be to our advantage to mount a general offensive in the east so as to finish Germany off and reach her borders, or perhaps even advance into her territory, by the end of the year. If the Allies fail to open an effective second front, but choose to undertake operations in Italy or in the Balkans, it would be more advantageous for us to postpone the general offensive and confine ourselves to limited offensive operations so as to retain the initiative, prevent a German offensive in 1943, and win back certain particularly important regions or sites from the Germans. This is what the principle of careful manoeuvring is telling me.

I wonder what will actually happen in 1943.

Now to politics. One must expect political issues to come ever more prominently to the fore in 1943. For two reasons. First, because the world increasingly recognizes that the tide is turning in the war, with the Allies' eventual victory becoming more and more obvious; so post-war problems are becoming a good deal more tangible. Second, because the outcome of the war for the Germans is less and less a question of warfare (they can't win by military means) and ever more one of politics (to avoid defeat by concluding a separate or compromise peace).

From the political point of view the most important thing is to consolidate the alliance between the USSR, Britain and the USA. I hope this objective will be achieved. However, there are dangers here, too. The weakest link is the USA.

I don't expect any serious complications in relations between the USSR and Britain at this stage. We have an alliance treaty and, which is yet more important, England is more dependent on us in matters of war and peace, while its bourgeoisie possesses enough experience and flexibility to recognize the need for cordial relations with the USSR. Churchill, as head of the British government, and Eden, as head of the Foreign Office, represent the embodiments of this tendency.

The USA is a different matter. This country is, to all appearances, entering a period of frenzied imperialist expansion. Lloyd George told me the other day that as a result of this war the USA hopes to seize (de facto or perhaps de jure) western and northern French Africa, the Dutch Indies and possibly Australia as well. In addition, the USA wants to play a major role in Europe. With this in mind, it is already preparing a political base for itself in Europe through various Conservative-Catholic elements. Hence we see Washington flirting with the Vichy government, extending patronage towards Franco and Salazar,[i] making a deal with Darlan, allowing Otto von Habsburg to form an Austrian legion in America, and lending a solicitous ear to Sikorski's complaints about the threat of 'Bolshevization' facing Poland from the USSR. The fact that the November elections to Congress weakened Roosevelt's position considerably[2] and that a Republican leader may well become US president in less than two years should also be taken into consideration. Willkie would not be so terrible, but what if it were to be Dewey?[ii] If one adds to this the USA's limited dependence on the USSR and Britain and the American bourgeoisie's inexperience and inflexibility in its conduct of international affairs, then one can easily concede the possibility of serious frictions arising between the USA and its allies this year and further down the line.

Take, for example, the war. The USA is still in the initial stages of its formation as a military power. It is particularly weak on land, having no experience, no training and no tradition. This explains (at least partially) the strange conduct of the Americans in North Africa. Moreover, there are reports that the USA is little inclined to open a second front in France (after the completion of operations in North Africa), preferring instead to pursue the Italian course.

---

[i] António de Oliveira Salazar, Portuguese prime minister, 1932–68; minister for foreign affairs, 1936–47.

[ii] Thomas Edmund Dewey, US special assistant attorney-general, 1934–45; governor of New York, 1942–54; Republican candidate for US presidency in 1944 and 1948.

Why? First, I think, because Italy is easier than France and, secondly, because the 'liberation' of Italy ties in well with notions of creating a conservative-Catholic bloc in Europe. Here the pope will also lend a helping hand, and some Italian Darlan is sure to be found.

And that's not all. I'm increasingly convinced that, contrary to the grandiloquent Atlantic Charters, the 'war aims' of the USA are to establish a Great American Empire in Africa and Asia. The more so since, as is well known, the Americans are very passionate when it comes to the struggle against Japan and very cool when it comes to the struggle against Germany. Roosevelt and Co. see things differently, but I'm referring here to the broad circles of the bourgeoisie, to the petty bourgeoisie, the workers and farmers. Why should the USA invest so much effort in the European war? Leave it the European powers, and the USSR in particular. This is advantageous for the Americans for another reason also: the 'Bolsheviks' may exhaust themselves and become weak.

This is the basis of tension and disagreements among the Allies, especially between the USA and the USSR.

At the same time there are areas of friction between the USA and Britain as well. In fact, the differences between these two powers are even more clear-cut at the current moment than those between the USA and us. I'll list the most important bones of contention: (1) North Africa: the Darlan affair in the political sphere and operations in Tunisia in the military sphere. (2) Djibouti: the British government favoured giving the colonies to de Gaulle, the US government was against. The British government pushed through its point of view. (3) Air bombardment of Rome: the British government is in favour, the US government against. The matter is still in the balance. (4) The merchant navy: the British receiving practically nothing from the American shipbuilding industry. (5) The military navy: the Americans flatly refuse to help the British in the Atlantic. They are sending all their new military vessels to the Pacific (60 destroyers, for example). Of course, all these disputes (there are others) are not serious enough to render cooperation impossible. Bridges are being found and will continue to be found to span the areas of tension. Nonetheless, we must keep a close eye on these disagreements. Moreover, we can even gain from them directly, since they hinder the formation of a solid Anglo-American bloc which under certain conditions (especially after the war) might turn against the USSR. But the same disagreements would become dangerous if they threatened the stability of the Anglo-Soviet–American coalition. It's a dialectical process.

As for the future peace conference (if there is going to be one at all), the USSR will come to it possessing the most powerful army in the world, provided we manage to pursue tactics to avoid total exhaustion. The reason for this is that the British army, despite being stronger, will still be a far less effective military machine than the Red Army, while the US army, despite its size and equipment, will be too 'green' and 'raw' to undertake serious, large-scale operations.

The prospect is not bad. But the key to it is skilful manoeuvring.

3 January (Bovingdon)

Victories on the fronts. We have achieved much during this six-week offensive. Stalingrad has been liberated, and 22 enemy divisions have been encircled and are slowly perishing near Stalingrad. Nearly the entire Don Bend has been regained. More than 100 miles of the Voronezh–Rostov railway are in our hands. We are advancing fast along the Stalingrad–Tikhoretskaya railway (the capture of Remontnaya 120 miles away from Stalingrad was announced today). In the Caucasus we have recaptured Mozdok and launched a successful offensive at Nalchik. On the central front we took Velikie Luki and have almost completely encircled Rzhev. Colossal losses in men and matériel have been inflicted on the Germans. Our human losses are relatively small, while the quantity of matériel increases. In the Don region, for instance, we seized more than 500 undamaged planes and 2,000 undamaged tanks from the Germans. We'll make the most of them.

Certainly, things are very, very different from how they were in summer and autumn, when the Germans were advancing and I had to record our failures every week with bitterness and a heavy heart. Stalin was right when he said that our turn for celebrating will come. Our turn has come, though this is just the beginning. There may be pauses and interruptions, but still: our turn has come. The crucial thing is that you sense in every fibre of your being that the scales of history are tipping in our favour – slowly but surely. It's quite clear: Hitler has already lost the war. Historically and in principle, the matter is already resolved. But his defeat in practice will take some time yet and demand many sacrifices.

Nonetheless, the first sunrays have broken through the dark heavy clouds on the horizon.

5 January

I've been thinking a great deal these past few days about my conversation with Cripps (on 30 December), and particularly about the future of Germany.[3] I've reached the following conclusions:

(1) Our aim is to prevent the renewal of German aggression. The guarantees for this may be either internal or external. Internal guarantees can be established only by means of a full-blooded and profound proletarian revolution as a result of the war and by the creation in Germany of a sustainable Soviet order. Poisoned by fascism, the psychology of the German masses must melt in the furnace of

such a revolution, while the present German ruling classes must be completely destroyed. We can't trust anything less than that. Soviet power on shaky legs will not do. Will such a revolution happen in Germany? I don't know. But I am full of doubts because I cannot yet see those forces and conditions which could lead to the birth of robust proletarian rule in Germany (the Communist party in particular is not strong enough). In the absence of internal guarantees, external guarantees of non-aggression are indispensable: in other words, the severe and long-lasting weakening of Germany, enough to render any act of aggression a physical impossibility.

(2) The major components of the external guarantees ought to be the following:

(a) The breaking up of Germany into several more or less independent states. This would lead, of course, as Cripps suggests, to the growth of a national movement among Germans for the unification of Germany, but at least it will raise colossal obstacles to any joint action by the German states for a long period of time. Besides, it will divert the Germans' national energy towards the struggle for unification rather than towards preparations for a new war. Comrade Stalin discussed the breaking up of Germany with Eden during their talks in December 1941.

(b) 'Economic decentralization' (as mentioned by Cripps): i.e. the industrial disarming of Germany. This is perhaps even more significant than military disarmament because without its military industry Germany would pose no threat even if the Anglo-Soviet–American coalition were to dissolve, something which is quite possible, even probable, soon after the war (history shows that wartime coalitions dissolve quickly and that their members can even start fighting one another).

(3) We shall, of course, demand reparations from Germany, but in what form? I heard from Comrade Stalin in December 1941: '40,000 machine-tools from Germany – these are our reparations!' Quite right. But how can we get these 40,000 machine-tools? Obviously either by ordering their manufacture at German plants after the war and then receiving them by instalments over several years, or by removing the machine-tools already available in German factories. Which is better? In my view, the latter. First, because we would gain time, second – and this is much more important – because we would thereby facilitate the liquidation of the German military industry. Should we order the machine-tools, we would lose time and contribute to the preservation of German machine-tool construction, which might be switched at any moment to the production of arms. In this way, 'economic decentralization' follows logically from Comrade Stalin's statement on reparations.

(4) I think we must demand one additional form of reparations – German labour. Let the Germans themselves restore what they have wrecked. The

significance of this would be considerable in practical terms and massive politically. Practically speaking, it would facilitate the restoration of innumerable ruined cities, villages, factories, plants, etc. Politically speaking, it would give immense moral satisfaction to our masses and would knock it into the heads of the German masses that aggression does not pay and that you must return all you have destroyed. This would also have a major effect in other countries, particularly the occupied countries. It would be useful to arrange it so that the Germans who participated, say, in the destruction of Stalingrad, were sent to rebuild this very city. German labour should be organized in a military way: the Germans should live in concentration camps and not be paid, or receive a negligible sum. Of course, reparation labour will not be terribly productive, but it can achieve much all the same, especially if a system of incentives is developed, etc. Reparations by labour, using prisoners of war, could be started before the war is even over.

6 January

Eden.

(1) The British government wants to bomb Rome. The American government objects. That is why the British government has decided for the time being to refrain from responding to the pope's démarche (that Rome should not be bombed on condition that Italian military institutions, etc., leave the city). They don't want their hands tied.

(2) The situation in Tunisia: the Axis has 55,000 men (two-thirds are Germans), 250 tanks and 190 aircraft (155 German). Reinforcements: 1,500 men daily (by sea and by air). Rommel is heading for Tunisia: 50,000 men, 340 aircraft, 100 tanks. Soon there may be some 100,000–120,000 in total. In Sicily and Sardinia: 1,100 aircraft (385 German). The English, Americans and French currently have four divisions in Tunisia, with another 2–3 arriving from Algeria. Aerodromes are being built. Rain. Mud. Delays. Eden doesn't anticipate the end of the campaign before March.

(3) Macmillan arrived in North America. Had a talk with Eisenhower. De Gaulle's meeting with Giraud[i] was a failure. De Gaulle's visit to Washington has been postponed at the request of the US government. Eden sighs: 'One must be careful with the French: it's easy to burn one's fingers.'

---

[i] Henri Honoré Giraud, general, commander of the 7th and 9th armies; escaped from France in a British submarine; commanded French forces in North Africa and served as high commissioner; temporarily shared with de Gaulle the chairmanship of the French Committee for National Liberation after the Casablanca Summit, but remained commander-in-chief until spring 1944, when the post was abolished.

(4) Monteiro told Eden that Jordana[i] has been to Portugal to discuss measures to protect the 'neutrality' of the Pyrenees. Franco is inclined to switch from 'non-belligerent' to 'neutral'. He is concerned about the course of the war. Hints that he is prepared to 'make peace' with 'communism'.

(5) Eden is concerned about the weakening of Roosevelt's position and growing isolationism in the USA. He says: 'It would be tragic if the history of the last war were to be repeated and isolationists were to gain power just at the moment when the position of the USA in world politics was becoming especially important. This makes cooperation between our two countries all the more valuable. This is our only hope, the only anchor for our countries, for Europe, for Asia.'

[Now that his campaign for a second front lay in ruins, Maisky's stay in London hinged on his ability to persuade the British to cooperate with the Russians in the organization of the post-war reconstruction. 'I think the most important thing for us,' he advised Vernon Bartlett, a leading journalist and MP, 'is not to bother too much about the past but to be concerned with the future.'[4] As was his habit, he attributed the initiative to Eden when reporting to Moscow. Exploiting the swing in the American by-elections towards the Republicans, Maisky, according to Eden, anxiously remarked that 'if America continued to be interested in Europe, so much the better; but we must face the possibility that her interest might fade'. That, he argued, made it 'more than ever necessary' that the two countries 'should work closely together'. 'I agreed,' noted Eden.[5] Maisky's continued remonstrations, however, eroded his relations with Churchill, who from Casablanca instructed Eden to inform Maisky that he was 'getting to the end of [his] tether with these repeated Russian naggings' and that it was 'not the slightest use trying to knock [him] about any more'.[6] The other distinct but related change in Maisky's orientation was a noticeable shift from the Conservatives, whom he had been instructed to cultivate when assigned to London, in favour of Labour, which he had avoided to a large extent. He now pinned great hopes on the role that Labour might play at the end of the war. He was enthusiastic about William Beveridge's[ii] report submitted to parliament, which laid the foundations for the welfare state in post-war Britain. At the same time, he remained suspicious of the official Labour leadership, and discouraged Morrison and Dalton from heading a Labour delegation to Moscow.[7]]

7 January

Churchill and Roosevelt are to meet very soon to discuss war plans for 1943. There are two alternatives: (1) to invade France in spring or in summer, and (2) to capture Sicily with subsequent landings in southern Italy.

---

[i] Francisco Gómez-Jordana Sousa (count of Jordana), general, Franco's prime minister, 1937–38 and foreign minister, 1942–44.

[ii] William Henry Beveridge, economist and social reformer. His report on Britain's social services focused on unemployment, health care and poverty and eventually became the blueprint for the 'welfare state' legislation of 1944 to 1948.

The question of operations in the Balkans is not yet on the table: it would be relevant only if Turkey were to join, but Turkey, by all appearances, is not about to change her position.

According to Eden, Churchill has a definite preference for the French option, while Roosevelt and his advisers seem inclined to gamble on Sicily and Italy.[8]

I fear the question will be resolved in favour of the second option, as it is easier from the military point of view; what's more, the British and Americans have various political reasons for postponing an effective second front in Europe.

8 January

K. Martin.[i] Arrived from the USA. His impressions:

(1) Roosevelt's position is weakening. The Democrats have a negligible majority in the new Congress. Taking into account the presence of conservative Democrats, Roosevelt may find himself in the minority. If Roosevelt had the time to deal with domestic policies, he might have been *OK* today and might even have got re-elected in 1944, but he has a war to run. His re-election is therefore doubtful. Assuming, that is, that there is no split among the Republicans. A split is possible. Willkie, who is not trusted by the Republican 'machine', which instead is backing the unremarkable Ohio governor Bricker[ii] (Dewey is too odious), may nonetheless run for president. Then Roosevelt would win. But all this is mere speculation.

(2) War aims. For Roosevelt and others: the Atlantic Charter. But the Republicans and a considerable section of the Democrats think differently: we've been drawn into the war and we must get something out it. More concretely:

(i) The Dutch Indies, West Africa and maybe North Africa should become American in one form or another ('Are we really fighting for the Dutch brokers to get a monopoly on rubber once again?' – 'The French were unable to defend their empire; so they don't deserve it.')

(ii) The Americans must be the main players in air and naval communications after the war.

(iii) The USA's food resources should contribute to the 'strengthening of American world influence' after the war.

(iv) When it comes to Europe there is a split: some are in favour of the introduction of an 'American order' in Europe, while others support the policy of 'keeping out of European quarrels and squabbles'.

---

[i] Kingsley Martin, editor of the *New Statesman*, 1930–60.

[ii] John William Bricker, US attorney-general, 1933–37; governor of Ohio, 1939–41, 1941–43 and 1943–45.

On the whole, Martin thinks that all manner of surprises are to be expected from the USA in the near future – mostly unpleasant ones.

11 January

Today I had a long talk with Eden on various current issues. Two are of particular significance.

First, the air bombardment of Berlin. I raised this matter once again and enquired about the reasons for the recent severe slackening of air raids on Germany? Why, in particular, is Berlin not being bombed? After all, Churchill promised Stalin he would do so. He promised back in September–October. Now it's January and still, *nothing doing*. What's wrong? Are Eden and the prime minister fully aware of the harm thus inflicted on relations between the Soviet Union and Britain in general, and on relations between Stalin and Churchill in particular?

Eden was embarrassed, blamed the weather, referred to the absence of American aid, and promised better things in the future. I simply shrugged my shoulders and remarked that promises were not enough for me. I have heard too many of those. The road to hell is paved with good intentions. I needed deeds, not words. Eden's embarrassment grew all the while and finally he said: 'I'll spare no efforts to fulfil your and Stalin's wish… Just wait a little more… I hope you won't have to wait long.'

We shall see. I have somehow lost all faith in English promises.

Second, Eden and I had a serious conversation about the convoys. It seemed we had only just settled that matter, but suddenly: stop, once again!

The December convoy (two groups of 16 and 14 ships) arrived safely in Murmansk and Arkhangelsk. True, there was a battle en route, near Medvezhy island, in which the British lost one destroyer, but the Germans also lost a destroyer and on top of that their heavy cruiser was damaged. Most importantly, not a single ship in the convoy was sunk. All reached their destination. A new convoy was scheduled to sail in January, also in two groups comprising up to 30 ships. Churchill made a definite promise to this effect in his message to Stalin of 30 December. And suddenly, barely a week later, everything has changed: the Admiralty has decided to send only one group in a convoy of 15 ships in January and attach the second group to the first group of the February convoy. Why? Because, you see, the Admiralty does not have enough ships to provide proper cover for two groups and can't include more than 15 ships in one group during the season of the long Arctic nights: the ships might get lost in the dark.

I learned all this on 8 January. I heard about it from Kharlamov, and a crooked version at that: Firebrace[i] had told Kharlamov that the second group of

[i] Roy Firebrace, British army officer, 1908–46; military attaché in Moscow until 1940.

the convoy could not set sail in time because the tanks and planes it was to carry were not yet ready. This struck Kharlamov and me as a peculiar explanation. I decided to check it and called Sinclair and Grigg, asking whether they really were unable to deliver the tanks and Hurricanes on time. Both made inquiries and replied that this was not the case: the tanks and planes were ready – the delay was nothing to do with the War Office and Air Ministry. Sinclair added: 'Talk to Alexander.'

I then called Alexander and discovered the truth as to why the dispatching of the second group had been postponed. I decided to appeal to Eden and phoned him at his country house (he was out of town). Eden confirmed the reasons given by Alexander. I protested resolutely and demanded the reversal of the Admiralty's decision, referring specifically to Churchill's promise of 30 December. Eden found himself in a tricky situation. He promised to contact the relevant offices and informed me on the phone from his country house on the morning of the 9th that the first group of the convoy would be enlarged to 20 ships (the absolute maximum to which the Admiralty could agree). Nothing more could be done at present. But a convoy of 30 ships would be sent in the first half of February. That would be our compensation. I expressed my displeasure with this solution over the phone and announced that I would discuss the matter in detail with Eden on Monday, 11 January.

That conversation took place today. We argued at length. Eden kept referring to the difficult position of the British navy. It loses one destroyer a week, but doesn't get a new one each week. The Americans are not assisting the English in the Atlantic. They have already sent out 60 new destroyers, but all to the Pacific. Meanwhile, the British navy's obligations are immense – in the Atlantic, the Mediterranean and the Indian Ocean. The submarine war is very intense. The British don't have sufficient forces for all this. That is why the convoys to the USSR are being delayed.

I objected that there was another side to the story: the USSR is locked in a desperate, essentially solitary fight with Germany and badly needs arms and raw materials. Can the Allies, who help the USSR so little on the field of battle, really refuse to help with supplies? We can't accept such a situation. England must find a way out of the current difficulties.

Eden again started repeating the same old story. I finally lost my patience and asked: 'If that really is the true state of affairs, then why did Churchill promise Stalin just a few days ago that he would send 30 ships in January?'

This hit the mark. Spreading out his arms, Eden replied: 'I fully agree with you here. The prime minister made a mistake in giving such a definite promise. You know what he's like: he often makes promises without thinking and weighing up the real possibilities. It ends up badly. That's the case now.

But the actual state of affairs is such that we can't send the second group of the convoy in January.'

I shrugged my shoulders and said that I hardly found Eden's explanations satisfactory.

In conclusion, Eden said that Churchill had sent a message to Stalin yesterday explaining why he was unable to fulfil his promise. Eden gave me a copy.[9]

15 January

Elmhirst,[i] who is just back from a long trip to Africa and the Middle East, paid me a visit. He had strange and revealing things to tell me about Egypt. He said: 'The Egyptians now have heaps of money... They are not fighting yet they are making money from our war, from the English and American troops stationed in Egypt.'

'What is this money spent on?' I asked.

'The peasants,' Elmhirst replied, 'who also have a lot of money, buy cattle and women. Egyptians are Muslim, as you know, and polygamy is permitted... Meanwhile, the wealthy class – all those landowners, merchants and industrialists – spends its money on three things: jewels, women and tombs...'

'Tombs?' I asked in bewilderment. 'I can understand the Egyptian upper crust spending a lot of money on jewels and women, but tombs? What does it mean?'

'I shall gladly explain,' Elmhirst responded. 'West of Cairo there is a big city called the City of the Dead. I'm not joking. When you enter it, your first impression is of an ordinary, well-planned and well-arranged city: beautiful houses, wide streets, little street signs on the walls, little lanterns above the house numbers... But this is a phantom city. Nobody lives in it. It is a city of ghosts, or rather a city of tombs. Every wealthy family in Egypt deems it essential to have its place in the City of the Dead: its own house in which to bury its dead. The richer the family, the bigger and better the house. In the very wealthiest and noblest families each member has an entire house for its tomb. Families one rung beneath them bury several members in one house, but each has a separate room. On the next rung down, two or three members are buried in a single room. House-tombs are now an essential attribute of social rank in Egypt. A man's status is judged by the dimensions and magnificence of the house. How much envy and jealousy surrounds these houses-tombs, how many fights and intrigues!'

---

[i] Leonard Knight Elmhirst, chairman of political and economic planning, 1939–53.

Elmhirst gave a cheerful laugh and was about to move on to another topic.

'But tell me,' I stopped him, 'what does a house-tomb look like? Have you been inside one?'

'Yes, I have,' he replied. 'What do they look like? They look just like ordinary houses… There are large ones, smaller ones, and ones that are very small indeed… Corresponding precisely to the various strata of the social pyramid… The first thing you see on entering such a house is a spacious reception room beautifully decked out with furniture, rugs, columns… Doors lead into adjoining rooms… Each room is equally well presented: furniture, rugs, divans… And in the middle of the room stands a tomb with a stone slab or an obelisk… The house is empty… No one lives in it… The family gathers there once a year to remember the deceased. That's all. But a lot of money is spent on these houses-tombs, as much as on women and jewels.'

A strange custom! The genuine Orient. Well actually, not so genuine. Tainted with the present day. Just like the pyramids of the ancient pharaohs, but clothed in the garb of democratic modernity: not only for pharaohs, but for all men with means.

When I asked Elmhirst what Cairo was like, he answered with a smile: 'A cross between Paris and Baghdad.'

* * *

A few days ago I met Sir William Dobbie,[i] former governor of Malta, at a lunch. He looks a total wreck; seeing him, one can hardly imagine how he led the heroic defence of the island for two years. Or perhaps it was the defence itself which turned him into a wreck?

Be that as it may, I learnt something interesting from Dobbie: apparently the people of Malta are direct descendants of the Phoenicians and Carthaginians. Their language is of Phoenician origin. There are some admixtures of course (Arabic, Italian, English), but basically it's the same language once spoken by Salammbô.

Carthage has risen in my esteem! The Maltese have fought heroically in this war. My enthusiasm for *Salammbô*[10] (which I reread with pleasure in Bovingdon three months ago), grows keener still…

16 January

My suggestions concerning North Africa:

(1) Establish a single administration for those parts of the French Empire lost by Vichy. Preferably with de Gaulle at its head and Giraud as commander-in-chief (state this in my private capacity).

---

[i] Sir William George Dobbie, general, governor of Malta, 1940–42.

(2) Cleanse the North African administration of Pétain's followers.

(3) Set up an interim representative body – maximize democracy – with the participation of all parties.

(4) Immediately free all political prisoners in North Africa, irrespective of party affiliation and nationality.

The purpose of all this is to create a more authoritative French centre that would be more independent vis-à-vis England and the USA.

Moscow doesn't want to be drawn into the generals' scheming. It doesn't recommend making any statements to the British government. But it prefers de Gaulle to Giraud.

17 January (Bovingdon)

Things are going well on the front! We have lived to see the day.

The 22 German divisions encircled at Stalingrad on 23 November are nearing their complete destruction. As a result of the fighting, hunger and cold their strength has been reduced by two-thirds and now stands at 70–80,000. On 8 January, our command delivered an ultimatum: either surrender on honourable terms (including repatriation after the war) or total destruction. The Germans refused to capitulate. Their liquidation is now taking place. Another week or two and it will all be over. Glorious Stalingrad will be liberated once and for all.

In the Caucasus, our troops continue to oust the Germans from their positions: during the last 2–3 weeks we have advanced from Nalchik and Mozdok to a point 30 miles beyond Mineralnye Vody along the railway line. All our spas have been liberated (Pyatigorsk, Zheleznovodsk, Essentuki, Kislovodsk). The column from Kalmykia is merging more and more with the column of Caucasian forces. Both are rapidly driving the Germans north and north-west.

On the Don the entire bend of the river has been liberated, as has the Voronezh–Rostov railway line as far as Millerovo (Germans still holding out there), the Stalingrad–Likhaya line (almost up to Likhaya), and the Stalingrad–Tikhoretskaya line almost as far as Manych. Our troops are quickly advancing on Rostov from three directions. At one point we are just 60 miles away.

On the central front we have taken Velikie Luki. Fighting has begun near Leningrad to lift the blockade (though these battles are not yet in full swing).

We have taken a huge haul of weaponry in the last two months and up to 170,000 prisoners, about half of whom are Germans and more than 60,000 Rumanians. Colossal quantities of matériel: more than 2,000 undamaged tanks, more than 800 undamaged planes, more than 20,000 undamaged lorries, etc. The Germans will soon become our main source of supplies from abroad. Just think: nearly 10 armoured divisions can be formed from the captured German tanks!

The large quantity of prisoners and spoils is a good sign: it bears witness not only to our growing mastery in the art of war, but also to growing disarray in the enemy's ranks. The Germans' refusal to capitulate at Stalingrad is a bad sign: it bears witness to the fact that the morale of the German army has not yet been sufficiently undermined.

However that may be, things are going well on the front. May we continue in the same spirit! May the offensive not pause! We must at all costs preserve the initiative that we have wrenched from the Germans!

We have a marvellous people, a marvellous army and a marvellous leader!

Yet a colossal task, great difficulties and heavy losses still lie ahead of us. The Germans have already lost the war, but we have not yet won it. To win the war as quickly and easily as possible, we need a second front, we need the English and the Americans.

* * *

Today, at around noon, Eden unexpectedly phoned me at Bovingdon.

He said: 'Do you remember asking me about a certain city the other day?'

'Yes, of course,' I responded quickly, understanding at once that he meant Berlin.

'Well, your wish has been fulfilled,' he continued. 'Last night it was visited by 380 fighting machines. Most effective. A great deal of destruction, and many fires. Amazingly, we lost just one plane!'

I thanked Eden for the news.

Eden added: 'The prime minister has sent a short message to this effect to your boss. And one other thing… a pleasant surprise for Mr Stalin! I'll tell you about it tomorrow.'

Hm! What could it be?… We shall see.

The Berlin raid is good news. But frequent repeats are required. We'll apply pressure.

* * *

Lloyd George is 80 today. The newspapers carry articles about him and photographs. Lord Winterton spoke about him over the radio (Lord Winterton is the eldest MP in terms of uninterrupted membership of the Commons – since 1904), Lloyd George was saluted in Welsh, and a concert of Welsh music was broadcast in the evening.

[Maisky, who had become reticent in his private correspondence, nonetheless sent Lloyd George an exceptionally warm letter expressing his life-long admiration, and stating 'without any flattery, that in my estimation you are probably the most outstanding statesman Great Britain has produced throughout this period'. This comment was not confined to Lloyd George's *de facto* recognition of the Soviet Union in 1921, but to the guidance, 'good advice and the valuable information' he had offered Maisky throughout his ambassadorship. It evoked an effusive response from 'the Welsh wizard', stating the 'privilege' he felt in having met Maisky and 'the highest opinion' he had formed of his 'capabilities and insight'. Lloyd George was swept away by the recent successes of the Soviet Red Army, which, he believed, might 'yet revolutionise the whole prospect of European democracy, and the influence may even extend to America'. This seemed to reinforce Maisky's fears that the British assumption that Soviet policy was revolutionary overlooked the realpolitik aspects of its foreign policy. He was quick, therefore, to correct Lloyd George. While sharing the hope that the Soviet Union would be able 'to exercise strong influence in shaping the coming peace', he had his doubts about whether it would 'revolutionise' the European scene.[11] Such views dovetailed with Stalin's outlook, as was shortly manifested by the dissolution of Comintern in May 1943, thus paving the way for collaboration on a post-war European order. Since his arrival in London, Maisky had consistently embraced a pragmatic vision of Anglo-Soviet relations, based on common strategic and economic interests. Such principles were indeed encapsulated in the memorandum on post-war reconstructions which he submitted to Stalin in 1944.[12]]

18 January

Those Americans are a strange lot!

Roosevelt has sent several messages to Stalin. They amount to the following: a promise of 200 transport aircraft (many thanks for that); the expression of his wish to transfer 100 bombers with American personnel to our Far East right now 'just in case' Japan should attack the USSR; and the statement that General Bradley[i] and a few other officers appointed by Roosevelt should start negotiations with Soviet representatives immediately, carry out a 'preliminary inspection' in the Far East and draw up plans together with our men. Roosevelt reports that in the very near future he intends to send General Marshall (the chief of staff) to Moscow to brief us about the state of affairs in Africa and about the military operations planned for 1943.

Stalin produced a good reply. He sent Roosevelt a message the other day in which he thanks him for the 200 transport planes, but expresses bewilderment at Roosevelt's intention to send a fleet of 100 bombers to the Far East. First, we have told the Americans more than once that we need machines, not pilots. Second, we require planes not in the Far East, where we are not at war, but on the Soviet–German front, where the need for aircraft is very acute.

---

[i] Omar Nelson Bradley, general, commanded II United States Corps in northern Tunisia and in Sicily, April–September 1943; commanded US troops in invasion of France, June 1944.

Next, Roosevelt's proposal that General Bradley inspect our military facilities in the Far East is hard to understand. Russian military facilities, obviously enough, may be inspected by Russian inspectors, just as American facilities may be inspected by Americans. 'In this sphere,' says Stalin, 'there can be no room for ambiguity.'

As for General Marshall's visit, Stalin would like to know first and foremost: what would be the objective of the general's mission?

In conclusion, Stalin asks Roosevelt to explain the reasons for such a protracted delay in operations in North Africa and says that his 'colleagues' are greatly confused by this circumstance.

Roosevelt will probably take offence. It can't be helped! The Americans need to be taught a lesson. They really do fancy themselves to be the salt of the earth and the mentors of the world.

19 January

I turn 59 today. Another year and I'll be celebrating my 60th.

I have mixed feelings. On the one hand, cold, sober reason tells me that the autumn of my life is upon me. On the other, my subjective sense of my physical and spiritual state does not register any twilight symptoms or moods. My health is *all right*, my capacity for work has not diminished, and my acuity of mind even seems to have grown (though the latter may be the result of accumulated experience).

My mind tells me: 'You're nearing old age.'

But my body replies: 'You are still far from old.'

Four years ago, when I turned 55, I wrote that, taking the average human span as my guide, I still had some 20 years ahead of me. It was then that I sketched a rough 'plan' for those 20 years: the first 10 years (till 65) would be devoted to active political work, and the next 10 (till 75) to bringing my life's journey to completion, that is, to summing things up and writing my memoirs. I also calculated that during my first, active decade a new world war would break out, which would clear the path for the construction of socialism in Europe.

This calculation proved correct, for this surely is a world war. Indeed, my prediction was fulfilled even sooner than I expected. Will socialism in Europe happen too? We shall see. In any case (since war was inevitable) I'm glad that the post-war period, when this issue comes to the fore, will still find me in full working order. I hope to make my small contribution to this great cause.

I'm not looking beyond 75. What for?

I know several outstanding people here older than 75:

Bernard Shaw and his wife – he's 87 and she must be about 89.

The Webbs – she's 85, he's 83 and a half.

Lloyd George is 80.

Looking at them, I have no desire to reach their age. Not to mention the fact that the general conditions of their existence have been more conducive to keeping healthy than those in my life – in the past and the probable future…

Yesterday evening it was announced over the wireless that the blockade of Leningrad has been lifted. What joy! And what a wonderful gift on my birthday!

* * *

On 17 and 18 January, Churchill informed Stalin by special telegram that the British air force has dropped 142 and 117 tons of explosives and 218 and 211 tons of incendiaries on Berlin. Ever keen to demonstrate Britain's activity.

On 19 January Stalin replied by telegram, thanking him for the information and adding: 'I wish the British air force success. Especially in bombing Berlin.'

21 January

I had two interesting conversations with Eden this week: one on the 18th and one today.

Churchill and Roosevelt have met: the two of them have been in Morocco, near Marrakesh, since the end of last week. It was Churchill's idea to meet there. The chiefs of staff and other senior army and navy men are with them. So far the results of the meeting are as follows:

(1) Military affairs in North Africa. The Eighth Army's campaign is coming to an end. Montgomery plans to reach Tripoli on 22 or 23 January. He has three British divisions in tow. Tunisia is next on the agenda. Churchill and Roosevelt have decided between themselves that this will basically change from being an American–English operation to an Anglo-American one. In concrete terms, this means that General Alexander becomes Eisenhower's deputy and assumes sole command of operations in Tunisia. Further, the English are providing 10 divisions for these operations (four from Algeria, which are already in position, and six from Tripoli, of which three are in position and three are soon to arrive), the Americans – two, and the French – one. Alexander believes he will be able to launch the Tunisian operation in earnest only at the end of February. He hopes to occupy Tunisia in March. We shall see. In essence, the Churchill–Roosevelt decisions on this matter represent recognition that the US army is still too 'green' to wage serious military operations and that the English influence in the Anglo-American combination has grown. Judging by the tone of Churchill's telegrams (Eden acquainted me with them), the prime minister is extremely pleased. He is particularly glad that General Alexander, whom he summoned to the conference from the front, made a good impression on the Americans and established good relations with Eisenhower.

107. A caricature by David Low.

(2) General strategy for 1943. It has been decided that immediately after the completion of the Tunisia campaign, the Allies will launch a military operation in Sicily. At the same time, it has been decided to start massing large forces on the British Isles immediately, with the aim of 'a return to the European continent' in the course of this year. But the following remains unclear from Churchill's telegrams: will the Allies proceed to Italy if they seize Sicily? When do they intend to make their 'return to the European continent' – concurrently with the operation in Sicily or after it? Where is this 'return to the European continent' expected to occur? With which forces? I sought a reply to these questions from Eden, but failed to receive one. Eden evidently does not yet know himself. I'll have to wait for the prime minister's return to learn more about the Anglo-American plans for Europe.

(3) The political situation in North Africa. On 17 January, Eden received a telegram from Churchill asking him to convey a message from the PM to de Gaulle, inviting de Gaulle to fly immediately to Morocco for a meeting with Giraud. It would be a tête-à-tête meeting between the French generals, without the participation of the British and the Americans. Churchill added, however, that if the French should find it necessary in the course of their talks to seek clarification on various questions from the American and British

governments, the presence of Roosevelt and himself could facilitate the prompt settling of many problems. Eden summoned de Gaulle and handed him the prime minister's message. De Gaulle regarded Churchill's proposal with strong suspicion. He thought that Churchill was laying a trap for him and that, once having arrived in Morocco, he would become a plaything in the hands of the English and the Americans. Eden spent all of the 17 January in lengthy and heated discussion with de Gaulle and Pleven[i] (de Gaulle's commissioner for foreign affairs), after which de Gaulle sent his refusal to Churchill. In his response, de Gaulle wrote that the fate of North Africa was a matter for the French, that it should be decided freely among the French, that the presence of foreigners (i.e. Roosevelt and Churchill) on French soil during the talks would not create a conducive atmosphere for success, and that, therefore, he did not find the present moment suitable for a meeting with Giraud. This reduced Eden to utter despair. He complained to me (on 18 January) that 'the French are a very difficult people, just like the Poles' and that French generals are 'just like ballet dancers': each considers himself 'unique and irreplaceable', sniffs at his rival and imposes impossible conditions for cooperation.

'Just think,' Eden exclaimed. 'The prime minister suggested in his telegram that de Gaulle might take Catroux[ii] with him to Morocco. De Gaulle would not so much as listen to the idea. He must have quarrelled with Catroux. The PM also said that Giraud would probably bring General Bergeret[iii] with him to the meeting. On hearing this, de Gaulle's expression changed completely and he declared that he had no wish to see Bergeret or to hold any talks with him.'

24 January (Bovingdon)

Good news from the front. Our troops took Armavir yesterday. Ha, ha, ha! I can just see those German financial barons, who received oil concessions from Hitler, skedaddling from Maikop. And all Hitler can do is exclaim in sadness: Farewell, Caucasian oil!...

Salsk, Konstantinovka and Valuiki have been taken. An iron semi-circle is being formed around Rostov, the various points of which are at a distance of between 60 and 100 miles from the city. No doubt, the Germans will put up a stubborn defence at Rostov, but will they hold it? I don't think so. There is something in the Red Army's movement in recent weeks which resembles rising water during a flood. Something spontaneous, irrepressible, inescapable.

---

[i] René Pleven, national commissioner for the economy, finance, the colonies and foreign affairs of the French Committee of National Liberation, 1941–44.

[ii] Georges Catroux, general, de Gaulle's representative in the Near East, 1940; commander-in-chief of the Free French troops in the Levant, 1941; governor-general of Algeria, 1943–44.

[iii] Jean Marie Bergeret, general, commander of the North African air force under General Giraud, 1940–43.

Valuiki is very significant. Not only does it interrupt one of the most important railway lines held by the Germans, but it also poses a threat, albeit a still distant one, to Kharkov.

Yet nothing excited and thrilled me more than the lifting of the blockade of Leningrad last week. It's as if one can breathe easier now. I've sent a warm congratulatory telegram to Voroshilov, who has played a major role in this success.

What will happen next?

Let's try to guess. The winter offensive still has 1.5–2 months to run. I think we shall manage to achieve the following over this period:

(1) Cleanse the entire northern Caucasus and Kuban of Germans, take Rostov, finish off the Germans on the Don, reach Kursk and restore the front line to its basic shape on the eve of the German offensive in the summer of 1942.

(2) Fully liberate Leningrad, re-establish its communications with Moscow via the Oktyabrskaya railway, and oust the Germans from Novgorod and the surrounding region.

This is, so to speak, the minimum programme. As an optimal scenario I envisage the capture of Kharkov and our advance to Estonia, but I am not so sure of this.

We shall see whether my forecasts come true. Suppose they do – what then? What should our strategy be?

A great deal depends on what happens before spring. Where will the front line be, say, in May? What will the German losses be over the course of the winter and will the Germans be in a position to contemplate a serious offensive this summer? What will our losses be and will it be in our interests to implement an *all-out* strategy this summer?

So, this is an equation that contains many unknowns. Not easy to solve. Nevertheless, the following thoughts occur to me:

(1) If the English and the Americans were to open an effective second front now in Western Europe, it would be in our interests to mount a general offensive as well, so as to deliver a mortal blow to Germany in 1943 and end the war in Europe in 1944.

(2) If the English and the Americans decide not to open an effective second front now, it will probably be to our advantage to save our forces during the spring and summer and confine ourselves to such operations as would prevent a German offensive on our front, before embarking on an all-out offensive in the winter of 1943/44 – this time with a view to approaching the German borders and perhaps even reaching Berlin. In this war we have been using a new method – winter offensives. They are proving successful and should be continued. In the past – in the Russo-Turkish wars, say, or in the war of 1914–

18 – winter usually brought a lull in fighting. The enemy dug in and made preparations for spring. Battles were waged in warmer seasons. The Bolsheviks turned this upside down – with decent results.

(3) If our losses in the current winter offensive were to prove tolerable, and if the German defence were to show signs of serious disarray, we could try to pursue the offensive in spring and summer without interruption and regardless of the actions of the English and Americans. Who knows, perhaps we would enter Berlin first? I doubt it, though. For if the Allies were to see that the Red Army had broken the back of the German war machine and that the denouement was approaching, they would rush to open a second front so as not to reach Berlin too late. And the Germans themselves might well assist them in this so as to prevent Germany being occupied by our troops alone. Some German Darlans would doubtless be found…

Well, time will tell.

[Stalin repeatedly stated in his telegrams that all he was interested in was finding out when and where the second front was to be established in Europe. He believed a promise had been made for an invasion in 1942, which had now been postponed to 1943. He saw no point in convening a summit conference, as it was his right 'to sit back and demand the fulfilment of the British and American pledges'. Churchill assumed that Roosevelt's conviction that Stalin would dislike the idea of Britain and the United States 'putting their heads together before bringing him into the discussion' was 'fallacious'. He thought it would be 'fatal' to arrive at the negotiating table with Stalin before a common strategy for 1943 had been devised. Once in Casablanca, General Marshall was 'most anxious not to become committed to interminable operations in the Mediterranean', while King criticized the British for not having 'definite ideas as to what the next operation should be' and for failing to have 'an overall plan for the conduct of the war'.[13] Churchill made sure that the military negotiations were protracted, like 'the dripping of water on a stone'. While they dragged on, he was able to sway the president his way, as he had done in Washington the previous May. Aware of the American suspicion of his Mediterranean ambitions, he rendered them less conspicuous by presenting a long list of operations, which his own military entourage warned was 'biting off more than we could chew'. The 'moderate scale' operation in northern France appeared at the bottom of the list, while priority continued to be given to operations in North Africa and to the invasion of Sicily, followed by that of Italy, which Churchill now termed 'the soft underbelly of Europe'. No real long-range plans to defeat the 'Axis' powers were worked out. The issue of the cross-channel and Far Eastern operations was simply left open 'pending new talks'. It was an open secret that 'only small forces' could be earmarked for cross-channel operations, even in 1943. There was nothing left for the American planners but to concede: 'We came, we saw, we were conquered.'[14] Though Stalin's shadow hovered over the conference, there was hardly any reference to the Russian front.[15]

Impatient as ever, Churchill wasted little time in exploiting his success. He embarked on an impromptu lightning visit of Turkey, straight from Casablanca (which is referred to later in the diary). Although Churchill presented the visit to Maisky as part of his efforts to assist the Russians, it fitted all too well into his grand strategy scheme. Turkey's entry into the war would pave the way for a Balkan campaign after the completion of Operation *Husky* (the landing in Sicily) and the likely invasion of Italy. The extension of the war into the Eastern Mediterranean would have significantly delayed the cross-channel attack. This explains why Churchill went a long way to placate Stalin in his message of 1 February, in which he stressed their common interest in British involvement in Turkey and the Balkans once the North African campaign was over. But an evasive short sentence, tucked neatly between the main body of the telegram and congratulations for the capitulation of Paulus's[i] 6th Army in Stalingrad, surely set alarm bells ringing with Stalin: 'I'll answer your quite reasonable questions concerning the second front before long.'[16]]

26 January

It had just struck half past seven. Eden's room was dimly lit. A bright flame blazed in the large fire-place.

'What do you make of Badoglio's[ii] appeal?' I asked Eden.

Eden had just told me that Badoglio was trying to get in touch with the British and even appeared to be ready to form an army of 'free Italians' from the Italian POWs held by the British.

'I don't take it too seriously,' Eden replied, 'but Badoglio's move is symptomatic all the same.'

I asked whether there had been any 'peace feelers' coming from the German side of late. Eden said there hadn't.

'We do receive reports that German morale is cracking fast,' Eden continued, 'but I don't know how far to trust them. What do you think?'

'I'm inclined to take such information with a pinch of salt,' I replied. 'I think that the time for a genuine collapse in morale has not yet arrived.'

'Why not?' Eden enquired.

'You see, Mr Eden,' I began, 'the question of "morale" is a complex one. It cannot be dealt with in generalities. One should differentiate between the various elements that make up Nazi Germany. First, the broad masses. What can be said about their morale? There is no doubt that it is being steadily undermined and corroded. The contrast between two key moments is of particular significance here. In October 1941, Hitler declared that the "Russian army" had been destroyed, that "Russia has ceased to exist as a military power". But in January 1943 that same "destroyed" Russian army destroys crack German

[i] Friedrich Wilhelm Ernst Paulus, commander during the forlorn Sixth Army's assault on Stalingrad in 1942.
[ii] Pietro Badoglio, general, as Italian prime minister in 1943–44, he brokered the armistice with the Allies.

troops at Stalingrad, forces that elite army to clear out of the Caucasus in due haste and drives back the rest of the German army all along the front, inflicting heavy losses. Moreover, the Germans attribute their recent failures to the "superior Russian forces". A glaring contradiction. Even the thickest German burgher can't help but be struck by it. The deeper this contradiction seeps into the consciousness of each and every German, the more fragile the "morale" of the German population will become.'

Eden nodded his approval. I went on: 'But we should be under no illusions: this process is still in its initial stage. The broad German masses know little about what is really going on at the front; they are subject to the unremitting impact from all sides of fascist propaganda, and so it seems premature to me to speak of the imminent collapse of the German population's morale. Nor do I believe that Hitler's own "morale" is truly shattered. Not yet. Hitler is none too happy, of course, but then he is a mystic maniac who probably still believes in his "star" and hopes to muddle through one way or another. Besides, he has no choice but to fight to the end.'

Eden nodded his approval once more.

'The men whose "morale" has really suffered as a result of recent events,' I continued, 'are the generals and all those connected to them. The generals know what is going on at the front and they do not share Hitler's mysticism. It must already be clear to them by now that Germany cannot win the war on the battlefield. That prospect no longer exists. Of course, it's too early to speak of Germany's defeat. It's quite possible that Germany may launch another offensive (despite Stalingrad!) and this summer may bring us some unpleasant surprises in this sphere. We shall see. But even if Germany has lost its ability to mount a serious offensive, her defensive capabilities are still vast. We should not deceive ourselves. Further colossal efforts and sacrifices will be required before Germany is finally beaten. That is why a second front in 1943 is so urgently needed. Nevertheless, the German generals can be in no doubt now that a purely military victory is out of the question.'

'You think the generals are aware of this?' Eden asked.

'Yes, I do,' I replied. 'And some information exists to this effect… I'll continue. So, if military victory is impossible, what is left for the generals? One thing only: to try to achieve a favourable peace deal for Germany. A separate peace would be best of all; next best is a general, compromise peace settlement. The sooner it happens, the better, as Germany still has many strong cards in her hand, but the tide has turned against her. From here on she will have fewer and fewer cards to play. Hitler himself, of course, is hardly a plus point in the light of such prospects. That is why I wouldn't be at all surprised if, waking up one fine morning, we were to read in the papers that Hitler had committed suicide or died in a "car accident". Hitler's days are numbered: 1943 may well be his last year, politically if not physically. Once Hitler disappears, the possibility of forming a new government will open before the generals. In essence, of course, this will be that same bloodthirsty German fascism in disguise, but who knows – maybe some elements in England and the USA will swallow the bait? Especially if the generals present it, as they are sure to do, as a dish entitled "Bolshevik scarecrow". I have no doubt that this scarecrow will be fetched from the pantry very soon. It may be all moth-eaten and bitten by mice, but who cares? The German bosses can't be choosers. Maybe some small fry in Britain and the USA will take the bait, even such a suspicious one as this.'

'I don't think so,' Eden protested. 'I know which elements you are referring to. I assure you that they are absolutely powerless now.'[17]

'So much the better!' I replied. 'Whatever happens, this is what we should expect in the next few months: first, persistent attempts on the part of the Germans to split the united front – the Allied front, and, second, equally stubborn attempts to test the ground for a compromise peace. Does the British government understand this? Is it prepared to nip all such attempts in the bud?'

Eden rose in agitation from his armchair and replied with uncharacteristic energy: 'As long as Churchill is prime minister and I am foreign secretary, there will be no compromise with Germany!'[18]

1 February

For all his seriousness, Churchill is a rather amusing man!

Eden called me over today late in the evening. He showed me a heap of ciphered messages from and to the prime minister, concerning the latter's visit to Turkey. They made for interesting reading. Churchill's mood is joyful, cheerful, almost boyish. In fact, boyish is just what it is. Flipping through the telegrams, it is sometime hard to believe that they were written by the leader of Great Britain in the heat of the greatest war in history.

First, the background to this visit. Churchill has long nurtured the idea of drawing Turkey over to our side. When he was in Casablanca, it got into his head that a meeting with İnönü would serve this purpose. Roosevelt gave his approval, but London started objecting because: (1) Churchill's prestige might be damaged should the Turks refuse to fight, and (2) London did not want to subject Churchill to unnecessary risk and fatigue.

'After all, the prime minister is 68!' exclaimed Eden, telling me of the Cabinet's reservations.

Mrs Churchill was also against the trip on the grounds of her husband's health. She even asked a few members of the government not to agree to his proposal.

But Churchill dug his heels in. And when he digs his heels in, nobody can budge him. It's obvious from his telegrams that he was desperate to go. Not only for reasons of state, but also, and perhaps even more so, because he was fed up with sitting in London and had a rush of blood. He wanted to stretch his limbs and travel the world a bit. In one of the telegrams the Cabinet objected to the trip under the pretext that parliament was eager to hear his report on the meeting in Casablanca. Getting into the plane, Churchill sent a humorous telegram in reply: I wish you fun shining the dusty benches in Westminster, while I gallivant around Africa and the Near East to my heart's content. Churchill yielded to the Cabinet on one point only: his meeting with İsmet [İnönü] took place not in Ankara, where an attempt upon the PM's life could easily have been made, but in Adana.

There, to judge by his messages, he was evidently *in high spirits*. İsmet, Saraçoğlu, Çakmak,[i] Menemencioğlu[ii] and others came to meet him. They had long and detailed talks on the current situation and the prospects for the future. Churchill put the gist of his statements down on paper and gave his notes to the Turks. For some odd reason, he refers to them in the ciphered messages as 'the morning thoughts' of a pious man! They are very detailed, these 'thoughts': three single-spaced typewritten pages. Their substance is simple. Clearly and even somewhat cynically, Churchill confronts the Turks with the question: we (Britain, the USSR and the USA) will win – do you wish to be on the side of the winners? If you do, give us assistance during the war. If you do not assist us you'll find yourself after the war in the position of a neutral, and not a very powerful neutral at that. It's your choice. You say you have no arms? All right, we'll give you some. Once this is done, think it over and decide.

Such are Churchill's 'morning thoughts'. How will the Turks act?

Churchill is clearly in a rather optimistic mood. It follows from his other telegrams that he hopes Turkey will take an active part in military operations this summer, or, at any rate, will be prepared to allow the Allies to use her bases and let Allied ships sail through the Straits. I don't know if this will work. I fear the Turks may take the arms but then refuse to help us.

The concrete results of the visit: Britain hands over five ships to Turkey which will transport the arms it needs (tanks, guns and a few aircraft), Britain builds airfields, etc. in Turkey, trains Turkish pilots and tank-men, opens its military schools to the Turks, carries out exchanges of officers with Turkey for purposes of liaison and study.

---

[i] Marshal Mustafa Fevzi Çakmak, Turkish chief of general staff.

[ii] Hüseyin Numan Menemencioğlu, Turkish foreign minister, 1942–44.

On his way back, Churchill stopped over in Cyprus. It's not quite clear why. Incidentally, a 'cipher catastrophe' very nearly occurred during the PM's stay in Cyprus. Churchill, who is rather careless about ciphering in general, was on the verge of sending a message for publication from Cyprus, which only had a rather primitive military code. Had the message been published, the code would have been cracked and the Axis would have been able to read all the secrets of the British military command in the Middle East. The FO's cipher department was in panic. But 'catastrophe' was averted at the last moment.

[The following entry was triggered by a high-society 'ladies' tea party' given in honour of Maisky's wife, Agniya. The conversation revolved around plans for 'rest and relaxation' after the war, not in ruinous Europe, but in places not affected by the war like Latin America. It put Maisky on guard, realizing suddenly that once the defeat of the Germans seemed certain after the battle of Stalingrad, the trend was to 'forget about the war … and return to conditions and habits of peace time'.[19] In a speech delivered on the Red Army's day he warned against the 'optimistic illusion' that the Germans were already on the run and that victory was 'just round the corner'. 'Nothing,' he said, 'is more dangerous than this mood. We cannot afford to live in a fool's paradise.'[20]]

5 February

What is Britain's reaction to our victories?

It is impossible to answer this question in a word or two. For England's reaction to the Red Army's successes is complex and contradictory. I'll try to sum up my impressions.

What strikes me first when I ask myself this question is the general amazement at the might of the USSR and the strength of the Red Army. Nobody expected us to be able to retain such fighting capability after the ordeals of last summer. It was assumed that the Red Army might be able to hold the front line, established in November, through the winter. It was anticipated that the Red Army would move on to the offensive in winter, as it had done last year, but this would be an offensive on a modest scale aimed at improving our position on some of the most important sections of the front. But what happened in reality surpassed the expectations of even the bravest optimists. That is why the paramount feeling which our victories elicit in England is universal amazement. The feeling is equally strong everywhere, from the top to the bottom of the social pyramid.

The second feeling, aroused by events unfolding in the USSR, is great admiration for the Soviet people, the Red Army and Comrade Stalin personally. But this feeling is less sweeping than the amazement described above. Among the masses it is unreserved and unrestrained. Here the prestige of the USSR has soared over the last three months. I heard about this, for example, from Kerr,

108. Maisky donating the Soviet embassy's iron railing to Britain's wartime scrap drive.

who visited many factories and plants during his holiday and mingled with thousands of workers. An endless number of other signs indicate the same. I shall just mention Stalin's popularity. His appearance on the screen always elicits loud cheers, much louder cheers than those given to Churchill or the king. Frank Owen[i] told me the other day (he is in the army now) that Stalin is the soldiers' idol and hope. If a soldier is dissatisfied with something, if he has been offended by the top brass, or if he resents some order or other from above, his reaction tends to be colourful and telling. Raising a menacing hand, he exclaims: 'Just you wait till Uncle Joe gets here! We'll even up with you then!'

This war has been a great object lesson for the entire world. All countries have been put through a severe historic examination. And it is already clear to the English masses that only the USSR has passed the test with flying colours, while Britain deserves no more than a C+. This correlation is grasped more by heart and instinct than by reasoning. But the masses have made their judgement, which is reflected in their infinite admiration for the Red Army and the USSR.

[i] Frank Owen, editor of the *Evening Standard*, 1938–41; lieutenant-colonel in the Royal Armoured Corps, 1942–43.

The higher the strata of the social pyramid, the more the sense of admiration is mixed up with other feelings, largely ones of a corrosive nature.

Take the intellectuals, for example – intellectuals of all stripes, including Labour and socialist. The reaction of this social stratum to our victories is bewilderment. The reasons are obvious. English intellectuals have been brought up to believe that bourgeois democracy is the best, most perfect and most effective system of government. To them it represents the pearl of creation and the crown of human wisdom.

And all of a sudden – by divine intervention – everything has been turned upside down! The great historical examination has shown that 'communist dictatorship', a form of government still regarded by English intellectuals with a mixture of resentment and contempt as a manifest symptom of the Soviet Union's political immaturity, supplies quite astonishing models of courage, heroism, foresight, organizational skill and governmental wisdom. Models that surpass everything which the bourgeois democracies of Great Britain and the United States have been able to demonstrate in this sphere so far. How come? Why?

For fully comprehensible reasons, the intellectual class cannot and will not get to the root of this 'incomprehensible' phenomenon. That is why they are currently in a state of alarmed bewilderment. This is particularly true of Labourite intellectual circles (including the Labour leaders), who fear that the Red Army's victories might eventually lead to a massive surge in communist rivalry among the working masses.

The reaction of Britain's ruling classes to our military successes is even more complicated.

On the one hand, they are glad: it's a very good thing that the Russians are smashing the Germans. It will make things easier for us. It will spare us losses and destruction. Once again we can implement our age-old policy of getting others to fight our battles.

On the other hand, the ruling classes are displeased or, rather, disquieted: won't the Bolsheviks get too strong? Won't the prestige of the USSR and the Red Army grow too much? Won't the likelihood of the 'Bolshevization of Europe' rise too high? The more success the Soviet military achieves, the deeper the concern in the hearts of the ruling elite.

These two contradictory feelings live side by side in the bosom of the British ruling class and find expression in the sentiments of its two main groupings, which may be called the Churchillian and Chamberlainian groups, for short. The first currently tends towards a sense of satisfaction about our victories; the second towards a sense of fear. Yet now the Red Army is still only in the vicinity of Rostov. It is difficult to say what the sentiments of even the Churchillian group will be when the Red Army finds itself in the vicinity of Berlin. I can't rule out some unpleasant surprises.

Although the Churchillian group is now, undoubtedly, the dominant one, English policy nevertheless tends to steer a middle course between the two trends just mentioned. The result? The British government seeks methods and means of continuing to have its war fought by others (i.e. us), while also securing for itself a leading role at the post-war peace conference. What specific forms is this process taking, and what forms may it take in the future?

There are two main problems here: (1) the problem of supplies, and (2) the problem of a second front in Europe.

As regards the problem of supplies, the British government may take advantage of this in order to 'restrain' our surge by 'regulating' the flow. Some symptoms of this are already apparent: the refusal to supply aluminium since 1 January, the growing difficulties in placing orders, the delay in shipping spare parts for the *Hurricanes*, the lack of punctuality in dispatching convoys, etc. These tendencies may intensify in the future.

However, the sabotaging of supplies cannot be particularly harmful for us now or in the future. This is not 1941. Our evacuated industry is back on its feet and produces more than before. In addition, we now have a new and rich source of supplies – the defeated German armies. Over the last three months we have seized from the Germans more than 1,000 aircraft, 4,000 tanks, 100,000 lorries, etc. This source promises to become ever more plentiful. Allied supplies never represented more than a small percentage of our requirements (10–15% at most, I believe), and this proportion will decrease further with time.

This means that in the sphere of supplies England (and the USA) can hardly have a serious impact on the pace of the Red Army's advance and the success of its operations.

The question of the second front is rather different. Once again, there is internal disagreement here among the ruling class. On the one hand, it would like to postpone the opening of a second front for as long as possible and wait for us to break Germany's backbone, so that the Anglo-American forces can make a 'comfortable' landing in France and march on Berlin with minimum losses. On the other hand, if the delay in opening a western front is too protracted, England (and the USA) may miss the boat and allow the Red Army to be the first to enter Berlin. The ruling class fears this greatly: the spectre of the 'Bolshevization of Europe' looms large in their imagination. So the timing for the opening of the second front is the major tactical question facing the British (and American) governments. They reckon this should be done not too early and not too late – *just in time*. But when exactly? This is what preoccupies Churchill, Eden, the War Cabinet and the entire ruling elite. No decision is visible as yet. Nor, it seems, was a precise decision arrived at in Casablanca. We shall see what Churchill has to say when he returns.

For now, my impression is the following: Britain and the USA will not open a second front by spring, while in summer and winter they will divert themselves with various secondary operations in the Mediterranean (Sicily, Crete, Dodecanese and other places). Perhaps they will cook up some Dieppe monstrosity or other in the north, but they are hardly likely to undertake a serious invasion of France.

It's unpleasant, but that's how it is. One has to face the facts. This inauspicious prospect may alter, I believe, only under one circumstance: if our successes assume such colossal dimensions that Germany's collapse and the Red Army's entry into Berlin in 1943 become real possibilities. Am I mistaken? Time will tell.

Azcárate told me the other day that he saw some Swedish officials at a lunch arranged by Prytz. They had just arrived from Stockholm. Azcárate asked them what impression the Soviet victories had produced in Sweden. They reply was very telling: 'We are glad, of course, but we are also afraid.'

Just like the English upper crust.

The same attitude is shared by the Poles (especially the Poles), the Yugoslavs, Greeks, Belgians and Dutch, less so the Norwegians and Czechs.

Kuh[i] told me that the people in the US embassy are not in the best of moods: 'Their faces lengthen every time they hear of your victories.'

A complex situation. We must steer a course between Scylla and Charybdis. Will we succeed? We will: Stalin will help us out.

[Maisky was spot on. In private, he expressed similar thoughts. 'The Casablanca decisions,' he wrote to Lloyd George, 'are in some respects still an enigma to me. Perhaps later on this enigma will resolve itself into something very hopeful. But bearing in mind the experiences of the last nineteen months, I reserve my judgement until more light is thrown on the impending actions of the Western Allies.'[21] Success on the battlefield, though, was for the moment limited. The Soviet winter offensive of 1943 was a logical outcome of the victory at Stalingrad. After regrouping its forces, the Red Army launched a series of offensives between December 1942 and February 1943 which cleared the German and Axis forces from the south bank of the Don River. Its forces further advanced westward into the Donbass and Kharkov regions, the objective of which was the liberation of Kursk. However, Field Marshal von Manstein[ii] manoeuvred his troops brilliantly, exploiting the overextended south-western front to successfully contain the Soviet 'winter offensive' by 6 March. By the end of the month, the *Stavka* had been forced to assume a defensive position in the Kursk bulge. The initial ambitious Soviet plans account for the confidence displayed by the Kremlin in the political dialogue

---

[i] Frederick Kuh, an American wartime diplomatic correspondent covering mostly Moscow and London.

[ii] Erich von Manstein, field marshal, commander of the 56th Panzer Corps, February 1941, and of the Eleventh Army in Operation *Barbarossa*; dismissed by Hitler in 1944 following his defeat in the battle of Kursk in 1943 and the Wehrmacht retreat from Russia.

with their Allies, as is indeed well reflected in Maisky's diary entries. It accounts for the somewhat premature raising of the post-war agendas and a temporary abandonment of the demands for a second front. Those were resumed as soon as the ferocious German offensive was launched in May, though for the first time since the beginning of the war in the east, the Germans failed to break through the Soviet defences, forcing Hitler to call the offensive off on 17 July 1943. The lessons gained from Stalingrad and the winter offensive dictated prudence, which was displayed by the moderate objective set by the Red Army of reaching the Dnepr River line. But, as Guderian and von Manstein recognized at the time, the Soviet offensive could no longer be halted, and Soviet troops would reach Berlin some two years later.[22] From Moscow, Clark Kerr wondered how 'horrible' it would be for his country's prestige if the Russians entered Berlin in tanks 'and we calmly travel to meet them on the train'.[23]]

6 February

Negrín enlightened me on Latin American practices.

The Mexican government has made good money out of the Spanish Republican immigrants. When the deal was agreed by Negrín and Cárdenas[i] in 1939, the Mexicans demanded that the Republicans set up cooperative, industrial, farming and other concerns where the immigrants could earn their living. Negrín agreed. Large sums of money were transferred to Mexico for this purpose, but the enterprises failed to appear. The money was pocketed by various Mexican high officials, starting with the president himself.

The same year Negrín helped a certain number of Republicans emigrate to San Domingo. At that time there was nowhere else to send them. It proved a profitable business for San Domingo, or, to be more precise, for its notables: the president of the republic had to be paid 5 million francs, while the San Domingo envoy in Paris took 1,500 francs (for himself!) from each Republican sent to San Domingo.

Now the suggestion has been floated of sending Republicans held in North African concentration camps to Mexico. Negrín spoke about it with the Mexican envoy in London. The first thing the envoy asked Negrín was: 'And how much will you pay us for this?'

What people! What morals!

7 February (Bovingdon)

I've not been to Bovingdon for two weeks.

During that time great progress has been made at the front. Greater than I expected. On 24 January, when I last mentioned our operations, we had just

[i] Lázaro Cárdenas, president of Mexico, 1934–40; governor of Michoacán, 1928–32.

taken Armavir. Today our troops are already outside Rostov. Maikop is in our hands. The remnants of the German armies have been pressed back to the Kerch Strait and the Sea of Azov. Some will probably escape, but some will be liquidated. Those armies will almost certainly leave us all their heavy weaponry. Another week or two and the Kuban will be liberated. Just in time: we shall still be able to sow and harvest this year. This is exceptionally important from the point of view of provisions.

At the other end of the active front, Golikov surged through the German lines at Voronezh and some ten days later was almost in Kursk. At one point, just north of Kursk, he cut the Orel–Kursk railway line and sent his vanguard to the west of Kursk. On the way, Golikov surrounded and destroyed German–Hungarian forces numbering up to 50,000.

The most remarkable and certainly dramatic event of the last two weeks was the definitive annihilation of Field Marshal Paulus's 6th German Army at Stalingrad. The 2nd of February is a date to remember.[24] Paulus and two dozen German and Rumanian generals were taken prisoner. Ninety thousand prisoners of war, mostly Germans, were captured between 10 January and 2 February, the period during which our forces launched the decisive offensive after Paulus had refused to surrender. Now Berlin radio asserts that transport planes managed to rescue 47,000 of the 6th Army's sick and wounded during the encirclement and fighting. The figure is clearly exaggerated. But let's assume for the moment that it is correct. Together with the prisoners of war that comes to 137,000, or even 150,000, since we also captured a certain number of prisoners before 10 January. Since we now know that in November the 6th Army numbered not 220,000, as we had thought, but 330,000, this means that the total number of dead reaches 180,000. Some hecatomb!

Stalingrad brought us enormous spoils: more than 700 aircraft, 1,500 tanks, 60,000 lorries, etc. The lorries are especially valuable: we are in dire need of them. The Americans deliver them in dribs and drabs. Everyone puts it down to a shortage of tonnage.

The moral and psychological significance of Stalingrad is colossal. Never before in military history has a powerful army, besieging a city, itself become a besieged stronghold that was then annihilated – down to the very last general, the very last soldier. Never before in military history has there been such a decisive and definitive victory. Even Napoleon never experienced a success quite like it. This is our retribution for Tannenberg, a twofold or threefold retribution. What a model of brilliant strategy and tactics! We've left the Germans trailing in the dust – yet they've always been considered first in the field, and not without reason. That's what Stalin's leadership means! That's what the strength of the great revolution means! Among the generals who developed and implemented the Stalingrad operation, Zhukov, Rokosovsky[i] and Voronov[ii] are evidently the most talented.

Yes, things are going well, and our offensive increasingly resembles a spontaneous, irresistible wave. And yet… how great is the task still before us! How many sacrifices and efforts will it still cost us to clear the entire German-occupied territory of the USSR! It can't be helped: we'll have to pay the inescapable price.

Ah, if only England and the USA could launch a real second front in the west this year! We shall see. In all honesty, I have no confidence that the Allies will do it. Too bad…

Or perhaps it's not so bad after all?

Recently the following comparison has been occurring to me every now and again.

In 1920 a decree granting concessions to foreign capitalists was published in our country. The economic situation of the RSFSR at that time was desperate. The national economy was at its lowest point. We were far from sure that we could cope with our problems, and time was pressing. Ilich, being a stern realist, decided to bring Western concessionaires into play. He would, of course, have to pay a heavy price, and not only in money, but what else could be done? There seemed to be no other way out. Had Western concessionaires accepted our offer, had they truly taken advantage of the opportunities the decree on concessions presented to them, a good many enterprises and even entire industries would probably have fallen into the hands of Western capitalists. This would not have altered the general line of revolutionary development, but it would have greatly hindered and complicated the process. It's enough to recall the troubles we had with those few concessions which were taken up. The Lena Goldfields, for one! What's more, the NEP period would have proved far more dangerous to the socialist economy…

But most Western capitalists responded reservedly or with overt hostility to the decree on concessions. They did not wish to make any compromises with the Soviet state as they nurtured hopes for its swift and total collapse. Only a modest number of concessions were taken up. They did not bring in large investments and had no great significance for our economy. At the time, we regretted this turn of events, but now? Now, looking back over the past 22 years, I'm inclined to think that the low effectiveness of the decree on

---

[i] Konstantin Rokosovsky, marshal, commander of the central front from February 1943, of the Belorussian front from October 1943; commanded major tank battles including Moscow, Stalingrad and Kursk.

[ii] Nikolai Voronov, general, member of the Soviet general staff; planner, together with Zhukov, of the Stalingrad campaign.

concessions was a *blessing in disguise* for the USSR. Temporarily, our problems were more painful and acute than they might otherwise have been, but the process of socialist development in our country continued more smoothly and swiftly than would have been the case if a great many capitalist concessions had been embedded in the structure of the national economy. In the long run, we have not lost; we have gained.

And now the second front… We would, of course, welcome a second front enthusiastically today. A second front would accelerate and facilitate the defeat of Germany, and our losses would be smaller. We regret the absence of a second front, we are indignant at the way England and the USA conduct themselves in this matter, we are and will be doing everything humanly possible to ensure the opening of a second front in Europe in 1943.

However, if in spite of all our efforts a second front were not to be opened, would this really be an unalloyed misfortune? I doubt it.

True, it would be bad in the short run: the war would drag on and our losses would be greater. But what about in the long run? Here, the balance might well be different. First, should the Allies refuse to play a major role on the field of battle, all the glory for defeating Germany would be ours. This would make for a massive rise in the prestige of the Soviet Union, the revolution and communism – not only now but also in the future. Second, England and the USA would emerge from the war with weak and inexperienced armies, while the Red Army would become the most powerful army in the world. This could not but tip the international balance of power in our favour. Third, in the absence of a second front in the west the Red Army would stand a good chance of entering Berlin first and thereby having a decisive influence on the terms of peace and on the situation in the post-war period.

So which course of events would be more advantageous for us in the final analysis?

Hard to say. At first glance, a second front would seem preferable. But is that really the case?

Time will tell.

9 February

On 7 February, Churchill finally returned to London. I was in Bovingdon and didn't go to see him. But then, I hadn't been informed of the date of his return.

When I saw Eden on the afternoon of the 8th, I told him I wanted to hand Churchill the message I had just received from Stalin concerning Turkey. Early in the evening, the PM's secretary notified me that Churchill would receive me at 10.30 p.m.

The meeting took place in the prime minister's private apartment. I was shown through to the study and asked to wait. There was a fire going. A bottle of whisky stood on the table with some soda water. For a few minutes there was nobody but me and I whiled away the time inspecting a large map of the USSR that was hanging on the wall. Finally, Eden walked in (I had asked for him to be present at the conversation).

'Our troops have taken Kursk,' I said, informing Eden of the latest news.

'Wonderful!' Eden responded heartily. 'Wait a sec, I'll just tell Beaverbrook. He's in the next room.'

Eden disappeared for a short while and exclaimed on his return: 'Max is utterly delighted!'

Churchill came in a moment later. He was wearing a dressing gown thrown over his customary *siren suit*. His eyes were not yet fully open. His hair was tousled. It was obvious that he had just got out of bed.

'Welcome home,' I greeted him.

He gave me a friendly smile and then immediately asked with a note of impatience: 'I believe you are bringing me a reply from Stalin?'

I confirmed this and proffered the envelope to the prime minister. As on previous occasions Churchill asked me before opening it: 'It won't upset me, will it?'[25]

I laughed and answered: 'No, I don't think so.'

Churchill opened the envelope and started reading the message aloud. Stalin's rebuke for the incomplete information about Adana irritated the prime minister, but not for long. Having reached the end, Churchill gave his brief summary: 'A good message!… Is it not?'

The question was addressed to Eden. Eden hastened to agree.

Churchill was in a good mood now and started to speak about his meeting with the Turks. He spoke with feeling, fervour and animation. It was obvious that he was terribly pleased with his Turkish escapade.

'The Turks are awfully afraid of you,' Churchill reported. 'Especially after your latest victories. They told me: how can we possibly get involved in the war? We'll lose 300,000 or 400,000 men, we'll become weak, and then what will happen? Russia will simply crush us in the palm of her hand. But I objected to this. Do you know what I said? I made four points:

(1) Soviet Russia never violates the agreements it has signed.

(2) After the end of the war Soviet Russia will for many years be engaged in the restoration of its devastated regions and the development of its internal resources in general. It will have no time for any complications in foreign policy.'

Here Churchill looked at the map on the wall and exclaimed: 'You have a veritable ocean of land! I can't believe you should want more!'

Then Churchill continued: 'The third point: after the war we shall set up a strong international institution to fight aggression, wherever it may come from. This should serve Turkey as a guarantee. And lastly, the fourth point. I told the Turks: if you are so apprehensive about your future, wouldn't it be more advantageous for you to be on the side of the victors at the end of the war? Just imagine: the war is over, the trial begins. On the judges' bench, the victors. On the benches of the accused, the defeated. In the hall, seated on chairs a little further off, the spectators, that is, the neutrals… Ha-ha-ha!… I'd like to be in the position of a spectator like that… And the victors will be us, the Allied nations! There can be no doubt about that! So what use is there in you, the Turks, keeping out of the fray?'

'And how did the Turks react?' I asked.

'I convinced them!' Churchill answered confidently. 'But naturally they won't risk entering the war straightaway. A transition stage is needed. My hope is that we'll be able to use Turkish bases this summer and bomb Rumanian oil fields from the air. I also hope we'll be able to start supplying you through your Black Sea ports in summer. In a word, let the Turks observe neutrality after the American model! Do you remember the time when the USA was not yet involved in the war, but served as the arsenal of democracy?'

Churchill paused for an instant, but only an instant. Then he continued: 'The main thing, though, is that the Turks should stop fearing you. They want very much to improve their relations with you. They all took turns to emphasize: "The Soviet ambassador has been attentive and amicable with us lately…" They want this! I have no doubts about it! If only Stalin could make some gesture! He is a great and wise leader, after all… You are an enormous and strong country. You can afford to be magnanimous and appreciative.'

I asked Churchill what specifically he had in mind.

The prime minister burst out laughing and exclaimed: 'Germany undertook to supply arms to Turkey. Not a great deal, but something nonetheless… The Germans are not fulfilling their obligations: partly because they need arms for themselves and partly because they don't know how Turkey would use them. You've seized a vast quantity of German arms. Why not supply Turkey with those German weapons which Germany fails to provide her with?… Now that would be a gesture! It would have colossal reverberations both in Turkey and outside.'

I laughed too and replied that Churchill's offer was highly original.

'However,' I continued, 'the experience of the past, and especially of the recent past, has taught us to be very cautious with respect to Turkey. You say the Turks want to improve relations with us and are just waiting for a hint from our side. But how then can one explain their conduct in connection with the assassination attempt on Papen?'

'That was earlier, when the Turks still feared the Germans,' parried Churchill. 'It's quite different now. The Turks are not afraid of the Germans anymore.'

I objected that some kind of statement from the Turks about their readiness to seek rapprochement with us is still needed. Stalin is absolutely right about that. Otherwise it will be difficult to get things going.

Churchill suddenly became agitated and declared: 'I'll send İsmet a telegram. I am on such close terms with him now that I can address him directly on any question.'

Eden advised sleeping on the idea, but Churchill couldn't wait.

'Why wait till tomorrow?' he exclaimed. 'Why not now? Go to the next room and jot down a draft of the message to İsmet.'

Eden obeyed, but without much enthusiasm. He returned in about 20 minutes with the draft and gave it to Churchill. Churchill ran his eyes down it and gave it to me to read.

'What do you think of this?' he asked.

The draft boiled down to the following: Churchill was notifying İsmet that he had informed Stalin of Turkey's desire to improve its relations with the USSR, that Stalin had notified Churchill of his readiness to reach agreement with Turkey if Turkey stated this desire, and that he, Churchill, recommends that İsmet should not waste time and should present the USSR with concrete proposals for the improvement of Soviet–Turkish relations.

I said that I had no objection to the message in principle, but there was one expression I did not like: the message seemed to suggest that Churchill had been 'authorized' by Stalin to inform İsmet, etc. I commented that no 'authorization' for Churchill to communicate this or that to İsmet was implicit in the message from Stalin that I had handed over today. Churchill agreed with me and the appropriate passage was amended.

Eden, however, clearly disliked all the haste. Having introduced the amendment I required, he proposed to finalize the wording the following morning. Churchill did not object. As a result, the sending of the message to Ankara was postponed until 9 February, and I do not know what form it eventually took.

Churchill then read me the speech he made at his first conference with the Turks. It was long but interesting. In his speech, Churchill, while not inviting the Turks directly to join the war, made it patently clear that they ought to do so. In the same speech, he promised to supply Turkey with arms. The conclusion to be drawn from this was unstated but unmistakable: once you receive a sufficient quantity of tanks and other arms, we expect Turkey to support the Allies openly against Germany.

'Those were my "Evening Thoughts",' Churchill said with a laugh, alluding to the 'Morning Thoughts' which Eden had told me of earlier.

Then Churchill exclaimed: 'I hope Moscow won't suspect that by giving weapons to Turkey I harbour designs against the USSR!… That would be ridiculous!… Russia is at least twice as strong as Turkey…'

Flicking ash from his eternal cigar, Churchill repeated emphatically: 'That would be simply ridiculous!'

All of this was most curious. But I was much more interested in the military plans adopted in Casablanca. I already knew a few things from my previous talks with Eden and from the Roosevelt–Churchill message to Stalin on this matter. However, there were some salient gaps in this information and I decided to try to get to the bottom of it all.

I asked Churchill what he could tell me about the Anglo-American military plans for 1943. The prime minister was evidently expecting this question. He asked for the relevant documents from the secretariat, and read to me his telegram to Roosevelt and Roosevelt's reply on the matter that interested me. Churchill's telegram included the outline of a draft reply to Stalin's message of 30 January. Roosevelt, in his telegram, offered some (insignificant) amendments to Churchill's proposals.

What does the plan amount to?

The main points are as follows:

(1) The operation in Tunisia is expected to be concluded by April at the latest.

(2) Next, approximately in June or July, comes the operation for the capture of Sicily, which is linked to the capture of Italy's 'boot'. After that, one of two things may happen. If the Italians' resistance proves weak or a pro-Allied coup happens in Italy by that time, the British and the Americans will make for the north of the Apennine Peninsula and from there head west to southern France and east to the Balkans. If the Italians, backed up by the Germans, put up serious resistance, or if a pro-Allied coup fails to materialize, the British and the Americans will move from Italy, Apulia and Calabria to Yugoslavia and Greece, that is, to the western part of the Balkans.

(3) Somewhat later an operation (of secondary importance) to seize the Dodecanese, possibly Crete.

(4) At some time in August or September, and independently of the operations in the Mediterranean, a landing operation will be carried out across the channel in France.

(5) Anglo-American forces will intensify the air offensive against Germany and Italy.

(6) Extremely vigorous anti-submarine warfare.

I asked Churchill which forces would be available to carry out the said operations in the south and in the north.

Churchill replied that after capturing Tunisia, the British and the Americans would be able to assign 300–400,000 men to other operations in the Mediterranean.

'As far as the cross-channel operation is concerned,' the PM continued, 'I honestly can't say anything definite for the moment. We, the English, would be able to assign 12–15 divisions for this purpose. But the Americans?…'

Here Churchill gave a bewildered shrug of his shoulders and exclaimed: 'Right now the Americans have only one division here!'

'How come only one?' I echoed in surprise. 'You told me in November that one American division was stationed in England… Has nothing been added since then?'

'That is so,' Churchill replied. 'The Americans have sent nothing since November.'

'How many American divisions do you expect by August?' I inquired.

'I wish I knew,' Churchill responded with comical despair. 'When I was in Moscow, I proceeded from the assumption that by spring 1943, the Americans would have dispatched 27 divisions to England, just as they promised. This was my assumption during my conversations with Stalin. But where are they, those 27 divisions? Now the Americans promise to send only 4–5 divisions by August!… If they keep their word, then the cross-channel operation will be carried out with 17–20 divisions.'[26]

'What if the Americans deceive you once again?' I asked.

Churchill thought for a moment before answering firmly: 'I'll carry out this operation whatever happens!'

The prime minister, however, did not specify what he would do if the American forces failed to arrive in due time.

Churchill suddenly burst out laughing as if he had recalled something funny and asked me: 'Do you know how many men there are in an American division?'

A little puzzled, I replied: 'I don't know for certain, but I expect about 18–19,000.'

'Right!' Churchill roared still louder. 'If you count the combatants alone… But 50,000 if you count the entire attending personnel!'

I gasped: 'How do you mean, 50,000?'

'I mean 50,000!' Churchill exclaimed once more, and then, with blatant sarcasm in his voice, started enumerating. 'What don't you have in an American division!… Of course, there's transport, medical staff, quartermaster service and so on. That's normal. But they also have two laundry battalions, one battalion of milk sterilizers, one battalion of hairdressers, one battalion of tailors, one battalion *for the uplift of the troops and what not*!… Ha-ha-ha!… We've sent nearly half a million combatants to North Africa… But it actually amounts to a mere 10–11 divisions.'

Churchill once again burst out laughing and added: 'We, the English, are poor in this respect, but the Americans are even worse.'

Our conversation jumped from one topic to another. Churchill's thoughts kept leaping this way and that. Some interesting examples: 'Stalin was very sharp with Roosevelt,' Churchill remarked half in derision, half in reproach. 'The president showed me Stalin's last message.'

Then, turning to Eden, he added with a laugh: 'Stalin hasn't always been gentle with me either… Do you remember?… But Roosevelt got it worse…'

'Roosevelt deserved it,' I rejoined. 'Are you familiar with the content of Roosevelt's message, to which Stalin replied with the message you cited?'

'What message was that?' asked Eden, who had clearly never heard about it.

'Oh, it's a remarkable message!' Churchill exclaimed with hilarity. 'I read it, too.'

Churchill then briefly related the content of Roosevelt's message to Stalin, in which Roosevelt suggesting sending 100 bombers to Vladivostok with American personnel 'just in case' and giving the American generals permission to 'inspect' our Far Eastern air and naval bases. Roosevelt also proposed to send General Marshall to Moscow to discuss the 1943 campaign.[27]

Eden's face was a picture of horror when he heard of the proposal to send 100 bombers. His reaction could be interpreted in the following way: 'How clumsy and naive the Americans are!'

'Well,' Churchill went on, 'Roosevelt was, frankly speaking, enraged by Stalin's message and wanted to send an abusive reply. But I managed to talk him out of it. I told him: Listen, who is really fighting today?… Stalin alone! And look how he's fighting! We must make allowances… The president eventually agreed and thought better of starting a row with Stalin.'

Churchill took a long drag on his cigar and said, staring at the tongues of flame playing in the fireplace: 'Roosevelt asked me what was the genuine reason for Stalin not attending the conference…'

'But you know the reason,' I interrupted, 'and so does the president.'

'Yes, of course.' Churchill responded. 'He is busy directing military operations and so on… That's right. But that is not all. I responded to Roosevelt's question as follows: Stalin is a realist. You can't catch him with words. Had Stalin come to Casablanca, the first thing he would have asked you and me would have been: "How many Germans did you kill in 1942? And how many do you intend to kill in 1943?" And what would the two of us have been able to say? We ourselves are not sure what we are going to do in 1943. This was clear to Stalin from the very beginning. So what would have been the point of him coming to the conference?… All the more so as he is accomplishing great things at home.'

But it seems that the 'tiff' between Stalin and Roosevelt is of real concern to Churchill. He explained to me at length how important it is for good relations and mutual understanding to exist between the leaders of the two governments – the USSR and the USA.

'It is important now, and it will be even more important after the war.'

Here Churchill's eyes suddenly became moist and he began speaking in a heartfelt, emotional tone: 'For me, personally, it's all the same… I'm an old man. I'm nearly 70. But the country, the people will remain… When peace arrives, the situation will become exceptionally difficult… I see no other salvation for mankind except close cooperation between the three of us – the USSR, the USA and England. It will be far from easy. The USA is a capitalist country and is moving fast to the right. The USSR is a socialist country. Britain will have to be the bridge between them. This is why any personal friction between Roosevelt and Stalin is extremely undesirable.'

Churchill grinned and continued: 'England and the USSR need each other too much – in Europe, in Asia and in various common matters. They will always reach an agreement in the end. With America it's different. The Americans think that since they are separated from you and from us by two oceans, they don't need you and us so very much… A gross error! But you know how naive and inexperienced the Americans are in politics. That is why I'm so worried about this conflict between Stalin and Roosevelt. It would be best if they could meet. I've been thinking about it for quite a while…'

Churchill puffed at his cigar again and, pulling a terribly cunning face, asked me slyly: 'Why do you think I made a stopover in Cyprus on my way back from Adana?'

I shrugged.

'The newspapers wrote,' Churchill went on, 'that a regiment I once served in is stationed in Cyprus, and so on. That's right: there is such regiment. But that's all balderdash! The real reason I stopped in Cyprus was different: I wanted to see whether it would be an appropriate place for a meeting between Stalin and Roosevelt in the future. And it's a jolly good thing I flew there. The island is perfect. Easily cut off from everywhere. Nobody will know a thing. It takes no more than five hours to fly from Tiflis to Cyprus. The president is ready to travel to Cyprus. After his first taste of flying, he's developed a liking for it. He'll get to Cyprus if needs must. I confess I've already given instructions for a few modest but comfortable buildings to be built on the island to accommodate three delegations.'

Churchill told me all this with manifest excitement, animated gestures and sparkles in his eyes. I could see how much he enjoys all that secrecy, all that romanticism. Truly, there is still something boyish about the prime minister of Great Britain, despite his 68 years.

Then he suddenly gave a start and exclaimed: 'Only please, don't tell a soul about it!'

I promised not to say a word.

A propos Churchill's boyishness. He described to me in great detail the measures he took to prevent an attempt on his life during the journey. He had everything you could think of: armoured cars, bullet-proof windows, automatic pistols and revolvers, secret buildings surrounded by armed guards, a sudden change of route, and much more besides. Sounded a bit like vaudeville. Of course, Churchill does have to take security measures. Yet, judging by the way he recounted his adventures, he got quite carried away by all this and approached it with quite boyish exaggeration. I asked him if the rumours were true that he had seen Franco somewhere on the way.

Churchill flared up and exclaimed indignantly: 'Utter nonsense!'

A minute later, however, it transpired that the reason for the prime minister's indignation had nothing to do with politics. Heaven forbid! No, Churchill flared up because his meeting with Franco could have taken place only in Gibraltar, and stopping in Gibraltar would have wreaked havoc with Churchill's carefully worked out 'system' of precautionary measures. Churchill did not stop in Gibraltar. He flew from Algeria straight to England.

Churchill mentioned de Gaulle and Giraud in the course of our conversation. The prime minister is highly irritated with de Gaulle and perhaps that is why he leans towards Giraud. I'm not surprised: Churchill has never liked de Gaulle, and that episode concerning his trip to Casablanca incensed the prime minister even more.

'I'm fed up with that Jeanne d'Arc in trousers!' Churchill snarled.[28]

Eden tried to mollify Churchill and calm him down, but without much success.

I fear that the entire de Gaulle movement may suffer as a result. We shall see.[29]

Churchill came back several times to our victories and the Red Army. He cannot speak about the Red Army without admiration and emotion. Even his eyes glisten… You can't help but recall 1920! How the wheel of history can turn![30]

'Taking all factors into account,' Churchill stated, 'the obvious conclusion presents itself that the Russia of today is five times stronger than the Russia of the last war.'

I teased him a little: 'And how do you explain this phenomenon?'

Churchill understood and replied in the same vein: 'If your system gives the people more happiness than ours, I'm all for it!… Not that I'm greatly interested in what happens after the war: communism, socialism, cataclysm… Isn't it all the same?… So long as the Huns are crushed!'

We shall see.

Churchill is definitely growing old. Yesterday he lost the thread of our conversation several times and, turning to Eden, asked with impatience: 'Remind me – what were we saying?'

I hope Churchill will last till the end of the war. It's very important. England needs him. We need him too.[31]

14 February (Bovingdon)

A good week! Our troops have taken Rostov, Kursk, Voroshilovgrad, Novocherkassk and Shakhty. They are on the approaches to Kharkov, some 12–20 miles from the city. The ring round the German armies in the Donbass is tightening. They have only a 60-mile corridor and a single railway line for their retreat. Will Stalingrad be repeated? The next few days will show.

New opportunities keep appearing on the horizon. What seemed an unrealizable dream just a few weeks ago is becoming a probable reality: the liberation of the Crimea, the capture of Dnepropetrovsk, and the advance into right-bank Ukraine.

What's most important, though, is the ever-increasing number of indications that the morale of the German army is on the wane, that it has lost all its confidence, that it can no longer put up serious resistance in its *hedgehogs* and on its fortified lines, that its retreat is gradually turning into a stampede. I am still scared to believe this, lest disappointment should follow. It seems to me that the German army, battered though it is, still has a lot of fight left in it – as will become especially apparent once the war reaches the borders of its homeland. But the tide has turned on our front, no doubt about that. The waves spread wider and stronger. Our advance assumes the likeness of an elemental, irresistible torrent. Could victory really come this year? Now that would be superb!

It seems that Moscow intended to end the winter campaign in mid-February. But events at the front are going so well (better than could have been expected) that this intention is unlikely to be realized. We shall advance further – not, of course, at the risk of exhaustion or of running into a powerful German counterattack, but advancing all the same. Perhaps until mid-March in the south and until mid-April in the north. Somewhere near Leningrad.

17 February

Today I handed Churchill Stalin's message, in which the latter insists on the swift opening of a second front in Europe. This message is Stalin's reply to Churchill's message of 9 February, which summarized all I had heard from the prime minister the previous evening.

I received the message in the afternoon and called Eden immediately to tell him I wanted to see Churchill in the evening in order to deliver Stalin's message. The appointment was set for ten in the evening. But when I arrived at the PM's apartment, Eden met me and said that Churchill was in bed with a high temperature. He'd been struggling with illness for a few days and now it had confined him to his bed. The nature of Churchill's illness is not yet entirely clear, but evidently it's some ailment of the bronchial tubes and of the respiratory passages in general.[32]

Eden accepted the message from me and took it to the bedroom, where the prime minister was lying. He returned some 20 minutes later and said that Churchill found Stalin's message quite in line with his expectations and that the prime minister would write a reply as soon as he was in a physical condition to do so.

I was about to leave when Eden poured me a whisky and soda, did the same for himself, and proposed that we sit down and have a little chat. This 'little chat' proved quite long.

At first we discussed Stalin's message and the Allies' military plans for the summer. I insisted on the necessity of exploiting the Germans' current confusion to the utmost and of the prompt opening of a second front in Europe. Moreover, I outlined the following concrete plan: to end the operation in Tunisia, postpone further operations in the Mediterranean (Sicily, Italy, etc.), and focus all attention on the cross-channel operations, transferring the Eighth Army to England for this purpose and appointing Alexander commander-in-chief of the entire offensive operation in France.

Eden liked my plan. He confessed that he had been in favour all along of a cross-channel operation, found operations in the Mediterranean (with the exception of Tunisia) inexpedient, and considered a direct attack on Germany through France to be undeniably preferable to indirect blows via Italy or the Balkans. Eden promised to bring up this topic with the prime minister the next morning and present my plan to him.

Then we touched upon Eden's forthcoming visit to the USA. He is going because he has not been to the USA since the beginning of the war. Besides, he said, it is very important to maintain contact with the American government, particularly now that the end of the war is already visible on the horizon (though it won't happen tomorrow). Specifically, Eden wishes to discuss the following issues with the Americans:

(1) the very prompt dispatch of American troops to Britain for the opening of a second front;

(2) post-war arrangements in Europe (borders, states, what to do with Germany, etc.). Eden wants to acquaint himself with the American views on all these matters;

(3) Anglo-Soviet relations, to explain to the Americans the meaning of our 20-year alliance and the importance of Soviet participation in the post-war construction of Europe;

(4) to enter into contact with leading Republican circles so as to sound out their feelings and exercise his influence insofar as he is able – particularly in view of the likelihood of the Republicans coming to power in 1945. Eden also hopes thereby to ease somewhat the position of Roosevelt;

(5) lend-and-lease issues, particularly the interpretation of Article 7 of the relevant Anglo-American agreement.

Eden thinks he will be away for 3–4 weeks. The prime minister will replace him during that period. While in the United States, Eden wishes to keep in close touch with M.M. Litvinov. He will give me a full 'report' upon his return home. So long as Churchill's illness doesn't hold him back!... From the USA, Eden will proceed to Canada.

Eden has no luck with America! In 1938, soon after quitting the Chamberlain government, he made a trip to the United States with his wife. He met all the notables there, starting with Roosevelt, but... he failed to make a good impression on the Americans. He failed to win their hearts.

On returning from Moscow at the end of 1941, Eden tried to arrange a visit to Washington, evidently in the interests of 'balance': he'd been to the Soviet Union, now... spend time in the United States as well. Even though Eden had long ago decided to place his stake on Anglo-Soviet relations, it was important for him as foreign secretary of Great Britain to maintain decent relations with the United States as well. However, though many of the preparations had been made, Eden failed to visit America last year, thanks mostly to sabotage on the part of Halifax (Halifax and Eden are, after all, 'great friends'!).

Ever since Eden was appointed leader of the House of Commons, which is seen by everyone here as preparation for the post of prime minister, visiting the USA has become imperative. It was essential for him if not to 'win' the hearts of Americans, then at least to 'make his peace' with them. Churchill decided to help Eden out when he went to Casablanca. While the PM was there, Eden told me anxiously one day that he had heard nothing from Churchill regarding this matter.

'Maybe he is too preoccupied with other matters?' Eden wondered. 'Or maybe Roosevelt gave him to understand that in view of his own precarious position as a result of the Republican victory at the elections, it would be better for me not to come for the time being?'

Eventually, however, the matter was settled. I learned about Eden's forthcoming visit to the USA a few days ago and asked him about it over the phone yesterday. Eden promised to fill me in with the details at our next meeting. He did so today.

We shall see what Eden's visit to America will bring. Will he be able to impress the Americans? Or, on the contrary, will the Americans succeed in influencing Eden? I don't know. The latter, I fear, is more likely: for all his merits, Eden is not a very strong person.

In our conversation today, Eden said, among other things: 'I've just had lunch with a group of MPs. They asked me about the prospects for Anglo-Soviet relations in the post-war period. Could the Anglo-Soviet alliance become a reality? Do you know what I replied?'

'What?' I asked.

'I told the MPs,' Eden continued, 'that this depends almost entirely on the role England plays in Hitler's defeat. If her role is substantial – on land as well – then the alliance will become a reality. Otherwise, no guarantees can be given.'

'Quite right,' I responded.

'That's why I am so strongly in favour of the opening of a second front in France,' Eden concluded.

[Eden's positive reaction is not to be found in his long report of the meeting, though it seems more than likely that the two were again plotting behind their leaders' backs. Considering the altered strategic circumstances following the successes of the Red Army on the battlefield, Maisky hoped it might still be possible to reverse the strategic decisions taken in Casablanca, and thus pave the way to conducive political dialogue on post-war Europe. Such dialogue would obviously have vindicated his continued stay in London. He pleaded with Eden, far more forcefully than the diary suggests, to reconsider the postponement of the second front and the launching of Operation *Husky*. It left the foreign secretary wondering whether Maisky would have been 'so emphatic if he had not received some guidance from Moscow'. Maisky's arguments that 'simultaneous pressure' on the battlefield from the east and west were bound to yield the best prospects for future collaboration certainly appealed to him.[33] They were reinforced by an even more candid and blunt conversation that Maisky had with Boothby, who, he knew, tended to have Eden's ear. Adhering to the line he had been advocating together with Litvinov since 1934, Maisky defined Russia's 'perfectly clear objectives' in eastern Europe, which boiled down to 'the strategic control of the Baltic & Black seas, the annexation of the Baltic States, the Curzon line in Poland, and "spheres of influence" further south'.[34] Litvinov conveyed the same ideas when he met Hopkins on 16 March.[35] Their ideas dovetailed with the appreciation of Cavendish-Bentinck, the chairman of the Joint Intelligence Committee. He stood fast against attempts in the Foreign Office to suggest that Maisky had some ulterior mischievous reasons for seeking the transfer of the American and British troops in North Africa to Britain 'for the express purpose of causing the Americans and ourselves to incur heavy casualties'. The Russians, he concluded, 'genuinely believe that a second front was the only operation which could bring them effective assistance'.[36]]

19 February

I've just spent three days (16–18 February) sitting in parliament. Beveridge's plan was being debated. A storm erupted, which nobody had anticipated, and which the government could have avoided, had it shown greater tactical skill. Churchill's illness may have contributed: he was unable to take an active part in the parliamentary debates. In essence, the Cabinet accepts 70% of the plan. The MPs might have raised this percentage to 80–85% by arguing and bargaining. Not so bad. By English standards, very good indeed. There seemed to be no reason for a storm. But it erupted nonetheless! Why?

Setting out the sequence of events may provide the answer.

Anderson spoke in the afternoon of the 16th. He is a quite useless parliamentarian. He has the air of an Indian bureaucratic administrator about him. The MPs don't like him. His manner of speech irritates the audience. This time he outdid himself: he would approve one point of Beveridge's plan and then immediately add two reservations. Another point, and another two reservations. And so on for the length of his entire speech. As a result, although Anderson approved 70% of Beveridge's plan, the chamber had the impression that the government was scheming, playing for time and trying to deceive the masses.

This immediately produced a strong effect on the Labourites. The British workers remember how the ruling classes 'inspired' them to fight in the previous war by promising them 'homes for heroes'. They also remember how the ruling classes repaid them with poverty and unemployment for millions of people. The workers do not want a repeat of that lesson after the current war. That is why they have grabbed with both hands the Beveridge plan, which they regard as a means of preventing a repeat of what happened after 1918. There is nothing lion-like about Labour MPs. They remind one sooner of those affectionate calves that suck on two mothers. So there must have been a very good reason for the quite uncharacteristic firmness and decisiveness which they displayed, as we shall see, during the debates. It means that the pressure from the masses is exceptionally strong.

After Anderson's speech, the Parliamentary Labour Party conferred and decided to enter a resolution expressing dissatisfaction with the British government's stand on the Beveridge plan.

An emergency session of the Parliamentary Labour Party was held on the morning of the 17th. All Labour members of the government were present. Bevin kept silent for the most part, but Attlee and Morrison spoke profusely, urging the MPs to withdraw the resolution of no confidence (for that, in essence, is what it was). But the eloquence of the Labour ministers met with a stony response: the resolution was not withdrawn.

Kingsley Wood spoke on behalf of the government on the afternoon of the 17th. The message of this diehard follower of Chamberlain was that the implementation of Beveridge's plan depended on the economic and financial state of the country and, since it was impossible to foresee the situation at the end of the war, this was not the right time for making any definitive decisions. Wood's speech added fuel to the flames. The Labourites were furious. 'Crisis' was in the air.

On the morning of the 18th, Labour held another emergency session: Attlee and Morrison spoke little, but Bevin was profuse and passionate. The minister of labour demanded not only the withdrawal of the resolution entered by the Parliamentary Labour Party, but also support for another resolution approving the British government's stand with regard to Beveridge's plan. Bevin threatened to resign if this was not done. His threats made little impression. Only seven members of the 130 present voted in favour of Bevin's proposal. Throughout the day Bevin tried to blackmail the faction. New rumours spread from his office every hour: 'Bevin has decided to resign'... 'Bevin is writing a letter of resignation to the PM'... 'Bevin is sending his letter of resignation to the prime minister', etc. This assault had no effect on the MPs: they stood firm, did not withdraw the resolution of no confidence, and actually voted unanimously in its favour. Even Morrison's speech, which closed the debate, achieved nothing! And this, undoubtedly, was a very clever and skilful speech, the best of all

109. Maisky with Britain's future Labour foreign secretary, Bevin.

the speeches on the part of the government. It was a curious scene during Morrison's speech: the Conservatives kept interrupting him with loud cheers, while the Labour benches maintained an icy silence. What is this? A blueprint for the future? A *pointer* showing where Morrison is headed and where he will end up?

The resolution of no confidence was rejected by a majority of 335 against 119, with 20 abstentions. This surely represents a moral defeat for the government, particularly its Labour ministers. There are 166 members in the Parliamentary Labour Party. Twenty were absent for valid reasons; 22 are members of the government; 20 abstained (i.e. they were essentially opposed to the government, but did not dare express this openly); and 101 voted against the government. So the entire Labour faction voted against the British government and against the Labour ministers in the government. The conclusion was surely clear: the Labour ministers had to resign… But no! The Labour ministers cling to their portfolios. They will not resign so easily. Even Bevin will not quit, for all his demagogy. They will think up some wheeze or other. They will find some boyar or other to plead with Godunov to remain on the throne. Such rumours are already circulating and I have no doubt they will be proved true.

So, the recent storm in parliament is unlikely to have any notable, direct consequences for now. But it is a stark symptom… And in the future, events may take a more serious turn.

21 February

The past week on the front was simply brilliant: we took Rostov, Kharkov, Lozovaya, Krasnograd and Pavlograd. Our troops are reaching the Dnepr line. Zaporozhe and Dnepropetrovsk are the next objectives.

Churchill congratulated Stalin warmly on the capture of Rostov, and Stalin sent him a warm reply.

What are the prospects? It's difficult to say. I'm inclined to think that our advance will slow down a little. First, the season of bad roads is almost upon us. Second, the Germans must make every effort to avoid a second Stalingrad in the Donbass or, worse still, on the Dnepr (which may happen if we take the Dnepr line before the Germans evacuate their troops positioned east of the Dnepr). Third, our troops need to rest and regroup. A three-month winter offensive is not child's play. We shall see.

Today the British government ceremoniously celebrated the twenty-fifth anniversary of the Red Army. A British government, that is, headed by Churchill, that same Churchill who led the crusade against the Bolsheviks during the Civil War! How times change! History has turned full circle within a quarter of a century.

I attended the event at the Albert Hall. It was all very ceremonious, even majestic. An intricate and beautiful performance was staged. Some details might be criticized from the purely artistic point of view, but that hardly matters very much. On the whole, the spectacle was very, very *impressive*. Especially the episode where a gigantic hammer-and-sickle flag was raised above the stage while, against this background, there rose the figure of a Red Army soldier in uniform and with a rifle.

Eden made a speech. His speech was quite *OK*. Stalin sent a congratulatory telegram (I saw to this beforehand).

Agniya, the Bogomolovs, Sobolev[i] and I sat in the Royal Box. Also present were Mrs Churchill, the Sinclairs, the Griggs, the Mountbattens and other notables. Our military men and diplomats sat in special boxes. Our whole colony was given special seats, all together.

Similar meetings, at which members of the government made speeches, took place in the major provincial cities (Birmingham, Manchester, Glasgow, Sheffield, Leeds, Bristol and others – 11 in all). I sent two representatives, one military and one civilian, to each meeting.

A characteristic detail: the war minister, Grigg, did not speak at any of the meetings, although he should have been the first to do so. It's hardly surprising: Grigg gets furious at the very mention of the Soviet Union. I talked with Eden about the arrangements a few days before the celebrations and asked in passing why Grigg would not be speak at any of the gatherings.

Eden professed ignorance, but promised to find out.

'In any case,' he added, 'there is nothing political in it.'

I grinned and replied: 'I do hope not.'

Eden has not clarified the reasons for Grigg's absence. There's no need anyway. It's all perfectly clear.

Oh, how crafty and clever is the English bourgeoisie!

Admiration for the Red Army in England is now unstinting. Everywhere – among the masses and in the army. To fight this wave would have been dangerous. So the government has decided to stand at its head – that is, to ride the wave. It makes it easier to smooth any rough edges. Or even to draw political profit. Hence today's festivities.

One can't help recalling once again the English saying: if you can't beat them, join them.

But this is good for us, too. Events like the one in the Albert Hall sanction interest in and admiration of the Red Army and, consequently, of all that is Soviet, throughout the machinery of state and public life in Britain. So much the better.

---

[i] Arkadii Aleksandrovich Sobolev, general secretary to the USSR People's Commissariat for Foreign Affairs, 1939–42; counsellor to the Soviet mission in Great Britain, 1942–45.

20 or 21 February [this was added by Maisky to his entry of 16 March]

At the official celebrations to mark the anniversary of the Red Army, which took place at the end of the week, Lyttelton represented the War Cabinet at Tyneside. Lord Ridley, the deputy mayor, gave a luncheon in his honour. In the course of the conversation over lunch, Lyttelton said that before the war we had suffered from excessive appeasement of Hitler; now, it seems, we are starting to appease Stalin excessively.

As the lunch was drawing to an end Lyttelton said it was absurd and ridiculous to send people like him to Tyneside to celebrate the achievements of people who had murdered the Russian imperial family.

The above is confirmed by a sympathetic individual who was present at the luncheon.

[To mark the twenty-fifth anniversary, Maisky held a reception at the embassy, which was 'an immense crush and literally hundreds of cars'. However, rather ominously Stalin's order of the day failed to mention the Allies, except for an indirect reference to the fact that the Red Army had borne the whole brunt of the war.[37] The Albert Hall salute to the Red Army was described by *The Times* as:

> a setting for a production in which pageantry, drama, verse, and music combined to pay tribute to the Red Army … M. Maisky and his compatriots in the audience must have felt that their country was being honoured in a way it could understand and appreciate … A huge, stylized view of a Russian city swept round in a great curve behind the tiered seats at the stage end of the all, and the producer used the arena in front of it as an artist uses a canvas. Lights from the roof and the galleries multiplied, criss-crossed, changed colour, and vanished, sometimes making the stage an impressionist design in cubism … Mr MacNeice[i] began with Alexander Nevsky (enacted by Lieutenant Laurence Olivier) and worked up to an over-delayed climax with the voice of Moscow Radio (Mr John Gielgud), symbolizing the resistance of the spirit of a people and its army to a destructive materialism, and, as the argument was every now and again interrupted by music and singing, so was the stage broken up by groups of men and women coming forward with their own contributions in praise of the Red Army.[38]]

24 February

Complacency and the wish to resume the norms and habits of peace time, wherever possible, are growing in step with our victories, and are even overtaking them. The Court, of course, is no exception to the general tendency. There had been no receptions at the Palace since July 1941, and that party was

---

[i] Frederick Louis MacNeice, Irish poet and playwright.

a very modest affair, with a small quantity of guests. We drank tea and talked about the Soviet–German war that had just begun. Now the Palace has decided to arrange three parties (*tea parties*, as it would still be awkward to have a genuine *court* reception), each attended by approximately 300 guests. The first of the three parties was held today. Agniya and I were invited to the Palace, together with the Bogomolovs and Kharlamovs.

I was summoned for a talk with the king. I began by thanking the king for his intention to present 'the sword of honour' to Stalingrad. Eden had told me that it was the king's own idea and I thought it would be a good thing to express my appreciation for the king's initiative.[39] All the more so as the idea really appeals to me.

The king was obviously flattered, but then, somewhat baffled and even, as it seemed to me, offended, he remarked that although Kalinin's telegram in reply to the king's congratulations of 23 February had been read over the radio and published in the press, he himself had not received it. Through whom, the king enquired, had the telegram been sent? Through me?... I replied in the negative and suggested that it had probably been sent to the British embassy in Moscow. I promised, in any case, to make the necessary inquiries and to inform the king.

Then the king asked me about the military situation, the condition of the German army, the internal situation in Germany, the probable line the Germans would try to hold, etc. Moving on to political matters, the king expressed satisfaction with the improvement of Anglo-Soviet relations and asked what, in my opinion, should be done to maintain close cooperation between our countries after the war.

I replied: 'The post-war future of Anglo-Soviet relations is currently being forged on the battlefield. We are conducting a common war against a common enemy. If both nations, the Soviet and the British, come out of this war confident that each has fulfilled its duty to the best of its ability, close alliance and mutual good feeling are guaranteed after the war. If either of the nations does not share this conviction, the outcome will be different. That is why it is so important to establish a second front. It is important from the military point of view, but it is also important from the political point of view.'

The king neither objected to nor approved my remarks. As always, he remained absolutely *noncommittal*. But I had expected nothing else.

26 February

Went to see Eden today. He did not go to the USA after all because of the prime minister's illness. Our talk was not particularly pleasant.

First, Eden told me that Churchill had decided to adhere after all to the military plans adopted in Casablanca. The morning after his evening conversation with me on the 17th, Eden conveyed my scheme to the prime minister. Churchill seemed interested and asked Eden to prepare a memorandum. Eden drafted the memorandum and Churchill passed it on to the general staff for consideration. The general staff presented its comments to the prime minister. Churchill thought over all the relevant details and reached the conclusion that my scheme was impractical. The main argument to this effect was that the troops wouldn't be able to arrive from North Africa to England in time for the cross-channel operation. Churchill thinks therefore that operations in the Mediterranean (Sicily, Dodecanese, etc.) should be continued after the occupation of Tunisia and that heroic measures should be taken simultaneously – irrespective of the Mediterranean – to prepare the cross-channel operation. Churchill is prepared to launch this operation even without the Americans, but will, of course, pull out all the stops in order to engage the Americans as early as possible. Eden imparted all this to me by way of preliminary information. Churchill wishes to see me as soon as he recovers and speak to me about it personally.

I don't like the sound of all this. Operations in Tunisia are dragging on because of the Americans' latest defeats and are hardly likely to be completed before April. So operations in the Mediterranean will begin no earlier than June or July. They won't be easy. They will probably drag on as well and I doubt they'll go smoothly. The British will have to concentrate their attention on the transfer of reinforcements to Sicily, the Dodecanese, or wherever. Transport ships will be loaded with supplies to be carried thousands of miles from England. As for the cross-channel operation, the British government will delay it, size it up, postpone it. I know them only too well!... The English can't do anything quickly. And here they face so many additional obstacles!... What will become of the second front? When will the Red Army get real help at last? No, I don't like this situation one bit.

The second issue I discussed with Eden was Simon's speech in the House of Lords on 23 February. Beaverbrook raised the question of the urgency of a second front. Strabolgi seconded him. Trenchard and Listowel[i] argued against debating this question. Simon was the last to speak on behalf of the British government and delivered a nasty, truly 'Simonean' speech, the essence of which was: no second front is needed as the British fleet, the air attacks on Germany, the supplies to the USSR and the operations in North Africa already constitute that second front.

Having cited the most 'criminal' passages in Simon's speech, I asked Eden who was telling the truth on behalf of the British government – those who promise the opening of a second front before long or those who believe that a second front already exists?

---

[i] William Francis Hare (5th earl of Listowel), Labour Party whip in House of Lords, 1941–44.

Eden replied that I should know the British government's point of view from my talks with him and with Churchill, as well as from the correspondence between Churchill and Stalin.

I objected that the talks and correspondence were known to only a few people, while Simon's speech was known to all. In order to avoid confusion and misunderstanding in the minds of the masses, it would be desirable to clarify the true position of the British government on the matter of a second front from a public platform.

Eden would not commit himself to anything, but promised to raise this matter with Churchill. It seemed to me he was not displeased by my démarche. Hardly surprising: there's no love lost between Eden and Simon!

Simon couldn't attend our reception on the 23rd as he was speaking in the Lords. He did, however, inform us an hour beforehand by telephone. Yesterday I also received a personal, handwritten letter from him in which he expresses his 'deep regret' at not being able to come, for he has a burning desire, don't you know, to express his admiration personally for 'the magnificent feats of the Red Army'... Simon! The real Simon![40]

I told Eden about my conversation with the king at the reception on 24 February. Eden was pleased and remarked: 'It's very good for the king to know the true state of affairs. It's useful.'

I also explained to Eden what had happened to Kalinin's telegram. It had been sent plaintext from Moscow and received at the London telegraph on 23 February at 2.40 in the morning. Our radio broadcast it on the same day at 6.00 in the morning. I don't know why the telegram was not delivered to the king until after lunch on the 24th. Eden promised to bring my explanation to the king's attention.

[Eden sympathized with the ideas raised by Maisky. Harvey, his private secretary, noted in his diary that 'a landing in France may be possible against diminished resistance this summer. Under the existing plan all our landing craft would be either wending their way beyond recall round the Cape or engaged in a big but not necessarily determining operation in Sicily.'[41] Considering Churchill's resolve to pursue *Husky*, it is most unlikely that Eden exerted any serious pressure on him to revisit British strategy, beyond recycling a censored version of his talk with Maisky to the Defence Committee. The committee, however, decided to defer the matter until Churchill recovered from his illness. Restive, Churchill quashed the idea at its incipience, instructing the committee from his sick bed: 'There can be no change of plan. I am going to telegraph to M. Stalin in a few days.'[42] In his memoirs,[43] Eden prefers to ignore the episode altogether, and to focus instead on what he calls the 'obstructive' attitude of the Russians, which led to the postponement of the convoys from March to November and the diversion of the supply ships to the Mediterranean area. The postponement was a double blow for Stalin. Breaking the news to him, Churchill dwelt on the insurmountable obstacles in running the convoys, but a single sentence disclosed an ulterior and decisive consideration in suspending them: 'Assuming HUSKY goes well we should hope to resume the convoys in early September.' In his talks with Hopkins in Washington a month later, Eden alluded approvingly to Maisky's most detailed survey of post-war Europe, which apparently was unfolded during the meeting on 26 February. Eden's only reservation concerned Maisky's opposition to his own vision of federated Europe, an arrangement which Maisky referred to as 'vegetarian – meaning, presumably, innocuous'.[44] Surely the wish to muzzle Soviet criticism and tie British hands accounts for the pressure exerted by Churchill on Eisenhower on 17 February to bring forward Operation *Husky* through swift conclusion of the campaign in Tunisia.[45]]

26 February

Kerr, having returned to Moscow, started to display almost feverish levels of activity.[46] On 20 February, he paid a visit to Molotov and declared that he was going to engage him in a series of discussions on post-war matters, since the British government considers it absolutely essential to reach agreement on these matters with the USA and the USSR before the end of the war. Then Kerr immediately handed Molotov the plan for a post-war clearing union prepared at the inter-allied financial conference in London (by Keynes, to be precise) and asked the Soviet government to study it and give its response. Kerr said the Americans had written their own plan and perhaps it would be expedient to develop a third version on the basis of these two.

Kerr then asked Molotov to explain to him the meaning of Stalin's statement, in his address of 6 November 1942, that the USSR is not planning to destroy the German state and the German military. These comments caused bewilderment in London. They seemed to contradict what Stalin told Eden in December 1941.

Molotov evaded Kerr's questions and told him that Stalin would be better placed to reply. Kerr clothed his questions in the form of a letter. On 24 February, Stalin received him and gave him a written reply, the essence of which was that there was no point engaging in general non-binding talks on post-war matters, and that it would be far more expedient for official representatives of the two states to meet, discuss these matters and sign a binding agreement on behalf of the two states. This is precisely the method Stalin proposed to Eden in December 1941, but Eden would not commit himself. If the British government now deems it necessary to arrange such a meeting and to conclude an agreement with the USSR concerning the fate of Germany or other states, we are prepared to play our part.

27 February

Agniya and I attended a football match between England and Wales at Wembley. There were 75,000 people at the stadium. It was a splendid day:

sunny and cloudless. We sat in the Royal Box together with the king, the queen, Mrs Churchill, Alexander, Attlee, Morrison, Leathers and other ministers. Tremendous *excitement*. Not for me, of course (I'm always calm on such occasions), but among this gigantic mass of people. The result: England beat Wales 5-3. Had it not been for the regular flow of *Spitfires* guarding the stadium, it would have seemed just like peace time. Yes, *complacency* is rapidly growing in England in parallel with our victories, and even outpaces them.

Mrs Churchill sat next to me. She is a very pleasant woman and we get along well. Mrs Churchill sometimes talks with me openly on various personal and family themes. Today she shared with me her fears and hopes concerning her husband's health. Churchill fell ill about a fortnight ago. It was only a mild form of pneumonia, but he had a fever. He is a terrible patient. He ignores what the doctors tell him. He refuses to rest. He thinks constantly about various governmental matters. He works. He worked even with a high fever. Now he feels better. His temperature is back to normal. The pneumonia has passed. But the prime minister's bedroom is dark and sunless. Mrs Churchill wants to take her husband to Chequers at the beginning of next week – for the fresh air and sunlight. He'll recover more speedily there and have a rest.

Mrs Churchill said all this quickly, hastily, swallowing her words and laughing infectiously. She always talks like that. Then she thought for a moment and uttered with deep confidence: 'He must get better! Nothing will happen to him: he is destined to lead his country in such times!'

110. A soft spot for Clementine, the prime minister's wife.

I thought to myself: 'Not bad!'

Mrs Churchill added with a note of bitterness: 'It's a pity the war should have happened now, when he is already 68. It would have been better had he been a bit younger. Well, it can't be helped.'

Yes, this woman believes in fate. There you have it, the bourgeois society of today!

I turned to Mrs Churchill and said: 'Some five or six years ago, long before the war, a friend of mine from Moscow asked me whether your husband had any chance of gaining power. Do you know what I told him?'

'What?' Mrs Churchill asked with the greatest interest.

'I told him: in ordinary circumstances – no, for the mediocrities in the Conservative Party would never let him come to power. They'd be afraid lest he hindered and squashed them. But in a moment of great danger for the country, Churchill would undoubtedly take the reins.'

Mrs Churchill exclaimed with fervour: 'How remarkable! I had exactly the same thoughts. I was always telling my husband: You will be in power when war breaks out.'

She paused and added: 'He was born for it, after all!… But what a pity he is already 68 years old!'

* * *

Easterman came to see me and told me two *stories* connected with my name:

(1) The Poles are telling everyone that representatives of the Allied nations met in London recently to discuss the terms of an armistice (already!). I am supposed to have attended the meeting. The most heated debate revolved around the question of which armed force or forces would occupy Germany. Various opinions were expressed, but the majority agreed that Germany should be occupied by an international police force. I am said to have maintained a stubborn silence throughout the discussion. When the discussions were over, I allegedly stood up, thrust my hands into my pockets and scornfully declared: 'All your talks and schemes are just so much hot air. Germany will be occupied by the Red Army.'

Then I supposedly turned round and left the room without saying another word.

Ha-ha-ha!… Perhaps Germany will be occupied by the Red Army one day, but the strange thing is that no Allied meeting concerning the terms of an armistice has been held, and I have never said any of the things which the Poles attribute to me. The Poles' objective is clear: to scare the British with the communist bogey.

(2) If the first story is a fact, then the second is indeed an anecdote. It is called: 'Low's unpublished cartoon'. The cartoon allegedly depicts a railway

station in London. The entire diplomatic corps is at the station. They are seeing off the Anglo-American troops bound for North Africa. I am shaking hands with the commander-in-chief and at the same time pointing at the poster on the wall: '*Is your journey really necessary*?' (Such posters may currently be found at all railway stations.)

(3) One more *story*, not related by Easterman, but also connected with me. According to this story, which is doing the rounds among Allied government people in London, the following conversation took place not long ago between an 'ally' and an FO official:

Ally: 'When will the second front be opened at last?'

FO official: 'We are ready. Everything now depends on Maisky. It's his fault that a second front has not yet been opened.'

Ally: 'Why? Is Maisky against the opening of a second front?'

FO official: 'No, of course he is not against it. But he still can't give us the exact date of the Red Army's arrival in England so as to open a second front in France.'

(4) Finally, the last *story*, at least for today. Speaking to one of the Allies the other day Masaryk said: 'The British have found their Alexander, but I can't say whether he'll prove to be a Nevsky.' He was referring to General Alexander, commander-in-chief of the British forces in Africa.

Most such *stories* come from Allied circles. No wonder. The Allies have nothing to do. They are most dissatisfied with Britain and the USA, but don't dare protest openly, so they find an outlet for their feelings by inventing numerous political jokes. They're not short of wits. Masaryk, for one!

28 February (Bovingdon)

The past week has not brought us any major achievements at the front. On the contrary, the difficulties have multiplied. The Germans have brought up large reinforcements and are attacking frantically in the Donbass and the Dnepr region. Just as I expected. But this is not so terrible. The Kotelnikov episode is evidently being repeated. When Paulus's army was encircled at Stalingrad, von Manstein and his eight divisions tried to free it by attacking Kotelnikov. Von Manstein temporarily pushed our forces back and occupied several stations and villages along the railway line leading to Stalingrad. But he was defeated and beat a disorderly retreat. Paulus's fate was sealed. The threat to the German forces in the Donbass and east of the Dnepr is even greater today. Naturally enough, the German command has to apply maximum effort in order to prevent a catastrophe that might be even more dreadful than the catastrophe at Stalingrad. Hence the events of the past few days. I hope we shall manage to defeat the Germans this time too, with all the ensuing consequences. There

111. Attending one of Myra Hess's famous wartime concerts.

are certain 'buts' of course: our troops are tired after three months of incessant fighting, the Germans have moved in more than eight divisions, the roads will soon be barely passable… Still, I remain hopeful! Well, we shall see.

It's good we have liberated Kuban in time for sowing: as far as food is concerned, next winter will be better.

3 March

That was an original way to spend an evening.

The Crippses invited us a while ago to dine with them and then listen to the music of Myra Hess.[i] We arranged to meet this evening. We met them at a French restaurant on *Charlotte Street*. Cripps's daughter, who accompanied her father to Moscow, then worked at the British mission in Tehran, and now has a job at the Ministry of Information, came along, too.

We had hardly sat down to dinner than the sirens began to wail. A rare event nowadays! It will soon be two years since the air raids on London ceased. Today

[i] Dame Myra Hess, British pianist who organized and performed in a series of daily chamber music concerts at the National Gallery in London during the Blitz and throughout the war. Her concerts were attended by over three-quarters of a million people.

112. Maisky hosting the Afro-American singer and advocate of civil rights, Paul Robeson, at the embassy.

was a special occasion: on the night of the 1st to the 2nd March, 700 four-engine English bombers raided Berlin and obviously did a great deal of damage. Göring, of course, could not remain indifferent, and this evening 40 German bombers made a 'retaliatory' raid. Forty! Only forty!... Such is the extent to which the Germans have weakened (although if it came to it they could still muster 100–150 machines for a sortie on London in a single night). Only a few of these 40 'Germans' reached London. The effect of the attack, of course, was negligible. But the anti-aircraft barrage from the ground was astonishing. Not at all what it was like in those memorable days of the 'big Blitz' of 1940. It was the barrage fire that kept us in the restaurant until nearly ten o'clock.

But we made our way to Myra Hess's place nonetheless. I liked her apartment very much: two grand pianos, bookcases with a huge musical library, simple but somehow intelligent furniture, portraits of great performers and composers, a fine statuette of Beethoven on the table... All exuding high culture, the peaks of the human spirit...

Myra played us Beethoven's 'Appassionata'. A wonderful interpretation!

I told Myra Hess that this was Ilich's favourite piece. Myra was greatly impressed by this fact, and the Crippses even more so.

Myra, by the way, resembles Pichuzhka very much, only she is somewhat fuller and taller. Seeing Myra at the piano in that dimly lit room, I couldn't help wondering: 'Isn't that Pichuzhka playing?'

Memories of the distant past surfaced in my mind.[47]

113. Sharing a musical moment with Henry Wood, creator of the BBC 'Proms' concerts.

4 March

The Poles are behaving quite idiotically. Not long ago the Polish government and the Polish 'National Council' adopted an official resolution, later made public, stating that they stand firmly by the basis of the 1939 borders.

We responded with a sharp TASS communiqué. In addition, Korneichuk[i] published a brilliant article in *Pravda*, in which he declared that the Ukrainians would never again submit themselves to the rule of the Polish pans. I think the exchange of pleasantries may end with that, unless the Poles concoct further provocations. I think it would be inexpedient to take it further: why add grist to Goebbels' mill? He is already doing all he can to foment discord in our coalition.

The Poles are a peculiar nation! Throughout their history they have vividly demonstrated a total lack of talent for serious state building (in foreign and domestic policy). Two things played an especially important role here:

(1) In the sphere of foreign policy, Poland more than once set itself objectives which were clearly beyond its real economic, political and military capabilities (e.g. the conquest of Moscow in the early seventeenth century). They ended in fiascos and heavy defeats.

---

[i] Aleksandr Evdokimovich Korneichuk, a Soviet Ukrainian playwright and literary critic.

(2) On the domestic front, Poland never displayed that minimal national discipline, that minimal subordination of the private and the personal to the common good without which a strong state cannot be built. The *liberum veto* was the shining example of this.

It is difficult to escape the conclusion that Poland is generally incapable of prolonged and sustained existence as a fully independent and sovereign national organism. The fate of Poland in the period between the two wars and the conduct of Sikorski and Co. in the last 20 months are perfect illustrations of this. Well, we shall see what the future holds in store. One thing is already clear: the Polish question will be one of the hardest 'nuts' to crack at the end of the war.

The Finns are another strange nation. In recent weeks there has been a lot of noise about Finland in the press and in political circles here and in America. Assertions have been flying around that the Finns want to withdraw from the war and are merely seeking an appropriate route of retreat. Particular emphasis has been placed on Tanner's and Fagerholm's[i] visit to Stockholm. Prytz was summoned to Sweden on the same matter some three weeks ago. Ostensibly he went to attend his daughter's wedding, but in fact he was there to seek some kind of compromise with the Finns and to try to get Britain involved. Before departing, Prytz visited Eden to find out the British position on this matter. Eden replied quite reasonably: if Finland wants peace (which in itself, of course, is desirable), it should speak directly with the USSR. Britain does not wish to act as go-between.

Prytz was disappointed and began to view his mission in an even more pessimistic light than before (he had never been an optimist on this matter). For Prytz himself (as I heard from Gu Weijun) considered a separate Soviet–Finnish peace possible only on roughly the following basis:

(1) The borders of Finland will be definitively fixed after the war; in the meantime a temporary demarcation line corresponding to the borders of 1941 should be established.

(2) Only *token forces* remain on either side of the demarcation line.

(3) The Germans stationed in Finland are evacuated.

(4) The Allied nations promise to meet Finland's minimal provisional requirements.

Prytz, however, seriously doubts that the Finns would accept this basis. He doubts this even more than he doubts the Germans' readiness to evacuate their troops. In Prytz's opinion, the Germans could be 'persuaded' to withdraw their

[i] Karl-August Fagerholm, Finnish minister for social affairs, 1937–43 and three times prime minister of Finland, 1948–50, 1956–57 and 1958.

eight divisions from Finland: they are 'shortening' their front line in any case and those divisions might come in handy somewhere else.

Prytz complained to a Swedish journalist before his departure: 'I don't understand those Finns! After all, the issue at hand is: will Finland be independent or won't she?… But there they are clinging to scraps of territory and borders!'

Prytz is right. The Finns, as represented by their ruling classes, are pursuing an absolutely idiotic policy. It was so in the past, and it is so now.

When I was ambassador to Finland, I told her leaders (including Tanner and Ryti) more than once: 'Remember, there are two indisputable and immutable facts: one, that Finland borders the USSR, and two, that Finland has a population of 3.5 million people while the USSR has a population of 170 million. You should construct your policy on the basis of these two facts. I believe that the only correct policy for you would be one of friendship with the USSR. This is entirely possible. The USSR has no aggressive intentions in respect to Finland. It is prepared to pursue a policy of friendship with Finland. But the prerequisite for this is the same policy on your part, with all the ensuing consequences.'

What was the response of the Finnish 'statesmen' (I can hardly call them by this name without using marks of quotation)?

Those 'statesmen' encouraged the Karelian Academic Union, which distributed maps of the future 'Great Finland' to foreign diplomats, on which Leningrad was marked as a Finnish domain. Sheer idiocy!

And those very same 'statesmen' have now brought Finland to the edge of ruin!

The doubt inevitably arises as to whether Finland is at all capable of pursuing a fully independent existence. The last 25 years would seem to suggest that she isn't.

This is hardly surprising: Finland was part of Sweden for 600 years, then she was part of Russia for more than 100 years, and has been an independent state only for the last 25 years. Her experience of independence proved unsuccessful. If this problem only concerned the Finns, we would have no need to rack our brains over it. Unfortunately, the USSR is vitally concerned with what is happening in Finland. The present war is the best illustration of this. That is why we can't leave this problem solely to the discretion of the Finns. We should take a most active part in its solution. In what form? It's still difficult to say. One thing is clear: the danger to our borders from Finland must be eliminated once and for all. From this point of view, the stubborn adherence of Tanner and Co. to their absurd policy might turn out to be not so bad for us after all. We shall see.

7 March (Bovingdon)

A good week on the front! True, there is a temporary stalemate in the Donets basin (it even seems that the Germans may have pressed us back a little – they say the Germans have assembled 22 divisions there) and there is a lull at Novorossiisk. But significant events are taking place in the north, where it is still winter. Rzhev, Demyansk and Gzhatsk were captured last week and the westward advance continues. Rzhev is especially important. This was a German 'super-hedgehog'[48] threatening Moscow which we had vainly been trying to take all year long. Now Rzhev has fallen. The threat to Moscow has been completely eliminated and, figuratively speaking, the gates to Germany are now open, although the road to Germany is of course still long.

Between 2 and 7 March, Churchill sent Stalin three telegrams informing him of the raids on Berlin, Hamburg and other cities (700–900 bombs were dropped on each city in one night). Stalin replied with two telegrams thanking Churchill and encouraging the British air force.

9 March

On 6 March the rank of Marshal of the Soviet Union was conferred on Stalin. Excellent. He fully deserves this, the highest military honour – more than anybody else not just in our time but throughout the long history of our country.

What rare happiness has fallen the way of the Soviet people: to have had two such leaders as Lenin and Stalin over the course of the last twenty-five years, the most decisive period in our development and that of humanity in general! This is yet further proof of the untapped reserves of talent and energy that lie concealed in the midst of our people. Our people will, without doubt, play a very great role in the destiny of humanity.

11 March

Eden flew off to America today. He plans to be away for 3–4 weeks. We'll have to manage without him. This is somewhat unfortunate: we have established good relations and he tells me a lot. We have also learned to catch one another's drift. This makes our work easier. Still, it can't be helped. I'll have to adjust to the situation.

Yesterday I had a talk with Eden before his departure. An interesting talk.

'Well, what farewell wishes do you have for me?' Eden asked when I had made myself comfortable in the chair opposite him.

'What wishes do I have?' I echoed. 'One wish above all others: don't commit yourself in the USA to any issue which concerns us as well. If you bind yourself with obligations in Washington, you might find yourself in a difficult position with respect to us afterwards… This happened, for instance, during your visit to Moscow in December 1941.'

'You may rest assured in this regard,' Eden said with confidence. 'I won't undertake any obligations in America. We have an alliance with you. We must reach an agreement with you first before arranging tripartite negotiations. But before reaching such agreements, I would like to have a general idea of what the Americans think about a number of issues that concern us. That is the purpose of my visit to the USA. Nothing else.'

I expressed my approval of Eden's line.

Conversation then turned to the main European problems. Before leaving for America, Eden wanted to run over our views on these matters in their general outline. I warned Eden that in view of the latest talks in Moscow (between Kerr, Stalin and Molotov) I could discuss the issues he was interested in only in my private capacity and express only my personal opinion. Eden was satisfied with this.

The first question concerned Germany. What should its future be after our collective victory?

This was straightforward enough. We recalled the Moscow talks on this matter (December 1941) and further statements made by Stalin and other Soviet representatives. The final conclusion was: Germany must be weakened for a long time after the war to prevent her from even dreaming of any fresh act of aggression. The means for that are disarmament, partition (perhaps in the form of a federation of several German states), and various economic measures, including reparations in kind. Eden fully agreed with this conclusion.

The second question related to Poland. What would its future be? What should be done with it?

'I won't hazard any guesses on this,' I said, 'but one thing at least is already clear to me now: Western Ukraine and Western Belorussia will become part of the Soviet Union. It is out of the question that they might fall under Polish rule again. The British government, as it happens, is essentially of the same opinion: the Curzon line generally corresponds to our 1941 borders.'

'But you, it seems, demand more than the Curzon line – Lvov for instance,' Eden warily retorted.

'Yes, we demand Lvov because it is a Ukrainian, not a Polish city,' I answered. 'However, Lvov is just a minor deviation from the Curzon line, while we accept the Curzon line only "in general" …There is scope for agreement here.'

Eden began complaining that a worsening of relations between the Polish and Soviet governments had been observed of late and even that we appear to have been blaming the British government for the Poles' present stance.

'I can assure you,' Eden went on, 'that from our side we are doing all we can to neutralize the current trends in the Polish government.... But it is not easily influenced.'

I did not fully agree with Eden: the British government allows the Polish press in England to publish articles which poison Polish–Soviet relations. Why does the British government do this? By doing so, it assumes a share of responsibility for the conduct of the Poles.

Eden objected: 'But you are familiar with our attitude to the press, not only Polish, but British as well. We have freedom of the press. We can't forbid opinions from being expressed.'

'Mr Eden,' I rejoined. 'I am perfectly familiar with your ways of doing things. And my conclusion is that if the British government really wanted to prevent the Polish press from printing stupidities, it would find ways and means of doing so. Are you really unable to demand from the Poles, who are your guests, that they should behave decently or, at any rate, should not spoil your relations with other countries? I can't believe it.'

But Eden would not agree. He told me that Sikorski and Raczyński had paid him a visit not long ago and asked him to take measures against the 'oppositional' Polish press. The problem, though, is that the 'oppositional' press – leaflets, to be more exact – is printed in secret and catching its authors is not easy.

I laughed: 'Has Scotland Yard become so decrepit? Five weeks have passed and they have not been able to find the culprits in the assault on the Lenin monument. Now I hear that they are also unable to find Polish underground publishers. Poor Scotland Yard!'

Eden hastened to change the topic and expressed his concern for the future of Poland. I shared his anxiety. I said that the future of post-war Poland was genuinely unclear to me. Eden knows our opinion on this matter. I stated it plainly at the very beginning of our talks about a mutual assistance pact with the Poles in 1941. We stand for an independent and free Poland, but within its ethnographic boundaries. We shall willingly help such a Poland; we shall be able to maintain friendly relations with it. We do not intend to interfere in Poland's internal affairs. Let them arrange things as they wish. And as Eden also knows, we are not against bringing East Prussia into the future Poland – with an exchange of population. Once again, that is, we are talking about Poland within its ethnographic boundaries.

'The trouble,' I continued, 'is that the Polish government in London has quite different ideas... It is full of imperialist ambitions!... This is very much in the spirit of Polish history down the ages. The Poles have never been able to create a stable and systematically developing state. Why? The reason is clear. The essence of statesmanlike wisdom consists in setting yourself political goals commensurate with the resources and means you have available. The Poles have never acted in accordance with this principle. On the contrary: they have nearly always been chasing the unattainable. To quote a Russian proverb, they've had one kopeck of ammunition for every rouble of ambition. It's enough to recall their attempt at conquering Russia in the seventeenth century. How absurd!... As a result, the Poles have never managed to build a strong and viable state.'

Eden interrupted me: 'There is much truth in what you say. You remember Bismarck's words: "Politics is the art of the possible"?'

'Quite right,' I agreed, 'but does the London Polish government understand this? No, it does not. Otherwise it would not pursue such an absurd line. It is patently clear that the USSR will be the decisive force in Eastern Europe after the war, so what sense is there in the Polish government quarrelling with the USSR? All the more so as it would be perfectly possible not to quarrel. Would it not be better for the Polish government and also for the future of Poland to make every effort to seek friendship and mutual understanding with the USSR? Such should be the sensible, statesman-like policy of the Polish government. But what does it do? It does exactly the opposite. Frankly, it is hard for me to imagine good relations between the USSR and Poland if the future Polish government should resemble the present Polish government in London. Don't get me wrong: even in this case we shall be in favour of an independent Poland, but our relations with it will be far from ideal.'

'And what kind of government would you like to see in the future Poland?' Eden interposed.

'And what kind of government would you like to see?' I parried his question. 'What kind of governments would you like to see in general in the countries liberated from German occupation – in Belgium, Holland, Czechoslovakia, Yugoslavia, France, etc.?'

Eden thought for a moment and replied: 'What governments?... If possible, governments which are not dictatorial, which rely on elected representatives, and which are based on the broadest possible social foundation... Of course, such governments would have different political colourings in different countries.'

'Should I understand you as saying that you would like to see popular front governments in the liberated countries?' I specified. 'What matters is, of course, not the label (for the term "popular front" is associated with certain memories and concepts), but the essence.'

Eden reflected again and then replied: 'Perhaps!... But I would prefer to say national front governments.'

'I repeat, the label is not the issue,' I remarked. 'You would like national front governments on the broadest possible social foundation... Well, I'm ready to agree with that. So, if in the future Poland were to have a popular front or, if you prefer, a broad national front government, I'm sure we would be able to establish genuine friendly relations with it. But will that happen? Time will tell. At any rate, Sikorski and Co. are doing all they can to hamper its emergence.'

'I must say you are most sceptical about the London Polish government,' Eden objected.

'Alas! The experience of the last 20 months is to blame.'

From Poland we moved on to the Baltic States.

'When talking with the Americans,' I said, 'let them understand that it's high time to drop all those *monkey tricks* concerning the Baltic question. The fate of the Baltic States has been decided for us once and for all. This question, as far as we are concerned, is simply not up for discussion. If the Americans pose it all the same, nothing will come of it except *bad blood* between the USA and the USSR. Who needs that? The Baltic States will remain part of the USSR whatever happens.'

Eden replied that for him personally the Baltic question had been resolved. He will sound out the Americans' attitudes to this issue during his visit. Then Eden asked: 'And what about Finland?'

I replied that Eden was well acquainted with our point of view from our correspondence and negotiations. We want to reinstate the terms of the Soviet–Finnish peace agreement of 1940, plus Petsamo, plus a mutual assistance pact. We can't accept any less than that. The threat to our state from Finland must be eliminated once and for all. It's our duty towards future generations.

Eden neither objected nor agreed. His attitude, it seemed to me, could be summed up as follows: 'As you like, just so long as it doesn't lead to any complications with the Americans.'

I added: 'And if the Americans raise the issue of a separate peace between the USSR and Finland, you should remember that, as far as Moscow's attitude is known to me on this question, we are not prepared to pay dearly for such a peace.'

'I know that,' Eden replied. 'Yes, and why should you pay dearly? I see no reason for that.'

Eden was evidently disappointed, but he refrained from making any comments.

Moving on to federations, I observed that all those combinations of small powers hardly struck me as very viable. It is usually maintained that their existence would raise the level of security in Europe. I don't believe that. First, the real power of such federations would be fragile (particularly on account of inevitable, chronic internal frictions, such as, for instance, in the Balkans); they simply would not be able to serve as a serious barrier to aggression from a major power. Such federations would be more likely to turn into an arena for all sorts of intrigues on the part of major powers seeking territorial gains. Second, the preservation and maintenance of peace in post-war Europe is conceivable only within the framework of a general European organization (political and military) headed by the USSR and Britain. I don't know whether it will prove possible to create such an organization, but in any case it is the sole realistic path. Playing with local federations of small states will only distract attention from the main task. If a general European organization is created, every small state will find in its structure its appropriate place.

My considerations produced a noticeable impression on Eden. He nodded approvingly several times while I was speaking and eventually said: 'I fully agree that peace can be secured only by a general European organization in which our countries will serve as the two pillars. It is possible that the question of federations of small states will fall away or, at any rate, will look different. We shall see.'

'In conclusion,' I said, 'may I ask you to let the Americans understand that the worst way of improving relations between the USA and the USSR is fatherly back-slapping. Henry Wallace's[i] last speech was very culpable in this respect, although he may have had the very best intentions.'

I cited a few passages from Wallace's speech which could be interpreted as follows: 'We, the Americans, are a kind and generous people. We wish you, the Russians, all the best. But you must remember: everything depends on you. If you behave well, we shall display our benevolence. If you behave badly, World War Three will become inevitable.'

Eden said in reply: 'I did not like Wallace's speech either, or, rather, it did not quite satisfy me. First, he is unjust to Britain. True, former British governments bear great responsibility for this war. But what about the United States? Haven't they also borne great responsibility from 1920 onwards? Second, Wallace's remarks concerning Russia were unfortunate. They can hardly facilitate the strengthening of bonds between our three countries. Well, we shall see. Now I'm off to America and I'll see for myself how things are there.'

I continued: 'There is a school of thought in America (I don't say Wallace belongs to it, but its spirit is not perhaps entirely alien to him) that asserts that the twentieth century will be the "American century". I find such slogans to be mistaken in general. Yet, if we have to speak in these terms, I think one would be more justified in saying that the twentieth century will be the "Russian century".'

'Why do you think so?' Eden asked with interest.

'For the following reasons,' I answered. 'If you try to imagine the general, major vectors of historical processes, then what is happening in the world today? It is quite obvious that the era of capitalist civilization is giving way to

[i] Henry Agard Wallace, vice-president of the United States, 1941–45.

that of socialist civilization. This began in 1917. I don't know how much time the process of change will take, but there can be no doubt about its basic line. What will the world look like, say, in the twenty-first century? It will, of course, be a socialist world. So the twentieth century will, by all appearances, prove to be a century of transition from capitalism to socialism. It becomes quite clear, from a broad historical perspective, that the USSR represents the rising sun, and the USA the setting sun, a fact which does not exclude the possibility of the relatively lengthy continued existence of the USA as a mighty capitalist power. So isn't it obvious that there are far better grounds for naming the twentieth century the "Russian" rather than "American" century?'

Eden smiled and said: 'There is much that is interesting and perhaps correct in what you say… Now, if the USA is a setting sun, then what do we, Britain, represent?'

'You?' I said, 'You, as always, are trying to find a middle course of compromise between two extremes. Will you find it? I don't know. That is your concern. To judge by the response to Beveridge's report, you still don't quite comprehend the meaning of the radical historical changes which our age is fraught with.'

I don't know whether Eden understood me or not, or whether I succeeded in convincing him with my arguments, but one thing was certain: my thoughts interested him deeply and gave him food for his own reflections.

Eden told me on parting: 'I'm truly grateful to you for this conversation. It will help me a great deal with my talks in America and in general…'

'I wish you every success!' I replied.

We shall see what will come of it. To be sure, Eden has many good intentions and I have no reason to question his sincerity with regard to the Anglo-Soviet alliance. But he is not a very strong or firm man, and I'm rather afraid that the American surroundings may have a negative influence on him. That is why it seemed like a good idea to strengthen Eden's 'backbone' a little before his departure. In essence, I did not tell him anything new. I had articulated the same thoughts to him, piece by piece, many times before on this or that issue. However, repetition (especially in a more comprehensive and finished form) can sometimes prove helpful, if the moment is right. This seemed to be the right moment.

[Maisky's report to Molotov was rather laconic, insisting that he was only a listener – 'at no time did I engage in conversation'.[49] Eden's official report of the meeting dovetails with Maisky's diary entry, though Eden appears to have been entirely passive, while Maisky does all the talking.[50] In his memoirs, Eden reduced the report to a skeleton, removing any trace of his compliance with the gist of Maisky's ideas. However, while in Washington Eden told Sumner Welles that 'Mr Maisky had called upon him and had given him in complete detail the position of the Soviet Union.' Eden recapitulated the position in minute detail, adding that, although he was not coming to Washington as 'Russian Ambassador', he believed that 'the views expressed to him by Mr Maisky could be of value to us'. In his memoirs, over which the Cold War cast a cloud, Eden preferred to dissociate himself from those ideas, concluding with a brief judgemental sentence: 'Most of this was stubbornly negative.'[51] On this occasion, Maisky's *modus operandi* worked to perfection. Eden, on his return to London, described to Maisky in detail the negotiations in Washington and the president's adherence to most of the ideas which, unbeknownst to Moscow, had in fact originated with Maisky himself. Stalin and Molotov displayed great interest in them, allowing Maisky to formulate them at the great length of a 23-page telegram on the possibility of creating a common political platform on post-war Europe.[52] However, the crisis over the Katyn massacre[53] which erupted a couple of days later shuffled the cards and, following the Soviet triumph in the battle of Kursk, the negotiations resumed in Moscow in a completely different atmosphere when the foreign ministers met in the autumn. By then Maisky had already been recalled.

While progress was achieved on the political front, the differences on strategy remained unresolved. On the day of Eden's meeting with Maisky, Churchill, who was convalescing, responded to Stalin's queries concerning the strategic plans for 1943 formulated in Casablanca. After dwelling on the progress of the operation in Tunisia and future plans for the campaign in Sicily, in the Dodecanese, and perhaps even on mainland Greece, Churchill turned to the preparations undertaken in Britain for a cross-channel attack. Although it was 'the earnest wish' of the president and himself to see the troops in battle in Europe, he regretted that the need to sustain the campaign in North Africa had cut supplies to Britain 'to the bone', and the second front could be mounted only if Germany weakened sufficiently. A premature attack 'would merely lead to a bloody repulse'. Churchill therefore reserved for himself the 'freedom of decision' nearer the summer.[54]

The attitude towards Russia in London was clearly fluctuating. The enthusiasm for a second front receded considerably after the British victories in the desert war – certainly among diehard Conservatives in parliament. Sir Cuthbert Headlam, prominent among these, complained in his diary that the Russians were refusing to admit that the North African campaign was 'clearly becoming "a second front" for Hitler'; 'I see that that little swine Maisky is still suggesting that we are not doing all we can to help his people – I distrust this man greatly: from all I hear of him he is a real danger in this country politically.'[55] Roosevelt, too, was getting impatient with Litvinov's 'second front zeal'. He asked Harriman to call him to order 'even to the point of saying we might ask for his recall'.[56]]

14 March (Bovingdon)

The situation on the front has worsened in the past week.

On the one hand, we have further successes in the centre: we took Vyazma and continue to advance westward. In recent weeks the Germans have lost three important 'hedgehogs': Rzhev, Gzhatsk and Vyazma. The road to Smolensk grows ever wider.

But on the other hand, the Germans had a number of major successes in the south: they have not only checked our progress towards the Dnepr but have even pressed us back considerably in the Donbass and at Kharkov. We evacuated Pavlograd, Krasnograd, Krasnoarmeisk, Kramatorsk, Barvenkovo and other centres. The Germans have reached the Donets again, but have failed to cross it as yet. The Germans have also broken through to Kharkov and are fighting on the approaches to the city and, if the Germans are to believed, inside the city too.

If we compare gains and losses over the past two weeks, they will most likely turn out even. Nonetheless, our failures in the south are a great disappointment. They derive from the fact that the Germans have succeeded in assembling a huge force in the south – 25 divisions (including 12 mechanized divisions), which were transferred from Western Europe (12 divisions), Germany and other sectors of the front. Evidently carried away by the relatively easy victories, we pushed on from Kharkov with smallish forces, overlooking the concentration of German forces. In the end we suffered a major failure.

Such is life: war is a good teacher. And the present failure will certainly prove a good lesson for us. But it is unpleasant all the same. And another thing: anger towards the English and the Americans grows all the while. Had they opened a second front, the whole situation would be different.[57]

16 March

Today I handed Churchill the message from Stalin concerning the American offer of mediation between the USSR and Finland.

Churchill's reaction was quick and spontaneous.

'This is entirely your own business,' he exclaimed. 'Finland did not attack either us or the Americans. Finland attacked you. So, it is for you to decide when and how to conclude peace with her. I'm not going to exert any pressure on you in this matter, not even indirectly. Remember just one thing: the Americans are very touchy. You should be careful with them.'

Churchill is sceptical about the possibility of concluding a separate peace with Finland at present: Finland is not yet 'ripe' for that. It's hard for the Finns to free themselves from Germany's clutches.

'At any rate,' Churchill concluded, 'I don't see why you should have to pay a high price for peace with Finland. The war situation is such that it is not you who should be courting Finland, but Finland who should be courting you. If the Finns want peace, they must address you themselves.'

In connection with Finland, Churchill recalled the Baltic States. With a sly twinkle in his eye, he muttered: 'Once your troops occupy the Baltics, the whole matter will be resolved.'

Churchill has just one piece of advice to give us to 'soften the hearts' of the Americans: allow those Baltic people who do not want to live in the USSR to emigrate with all their belongings.

I shook my head in reply and said that as far as we were concerned, the Baltic question had been decided once and for all. To myself I thought: 'But it is worth remembering his advice. Maybe it will come in handy one day.'

We moved on to the topic of Tunisia. I was dumbfounded to learn from Churchill that the Anglo-American troops will evidently need a further 60–70 days to complete their operations. That means dragging things out until mid-May! Disgusting!

Churchill hastened to console me with the news that the Sicilian operation would be carried out a month earlier, in June. As for the cross-channel operation, the plans have not changed: it will take place in August at the earliest. Churchill blames the Americans: they're not sending their divisions to Europe. When you ask why, the reply is always the same: *shipping*. It's a kind of black magic. Churchill, incidentally, says that the first half of March was most unfortunate for the Allies at sea: they lost 300,000 tons, as against 250,000 and 300,000 during the entire previous two months, January and March. I could not agree with Churchill. We argued at length. Churchill, however, stuck to his guns. Bad.

Then Churchill started complaining about our reluctance to receive 750 pilots in Murmansk.

'What harm could they do to you?' he asked in bewilderment. 'We need them badly to guard the convoys. We shall run into enormous difficulties without them. All the more so now that we have information about the concentration of the *Tirpitz*, *Scharnhorst*, *Lutzow* and other ships in Narvik.'

I replied that 750 British airmen would certainly do us no harm, but the problem was that Murmansk had been burned down by German bombers and there was simply nowhere to billet them.

22 March

Prytz came to see me. Just back from Stockholm (gave his daughter in marriage).

Brought a letter from Kollontay. Spoke with her on the phone. Her condition has improved, she is writing much (letters in many foreign languages); has a secretary in the sanatorium. Prospects? Another stroke is possible.

Finnish–Soviet relations are predominant in Sweden today. (My question: Do the Finns really want peace?) The mood of the Finns (Prytz spoke with the Finnish ambassador in Stockholm Vaasenshentno…): they want peace, but don't know how to get it. They are afraid that approaching the Soviet government again = a break with Germany (consequences, food). That is, subjecting themselves to the mercy of the USSR. What'll happen? They wish to know our terms. They turned to the Swedes – 'We don't know'. Turned to the USA – 'We don't know'. The trip made by the US ambassador in Finland, Schoenfeld,[i] to the USA in December was related to this. So the Finns are marking time. They no longer believe that Germany will win, but haven't lost hope of a 'compromise peace' – what's more, they might 'slip through' somehow. They're counting on a split among the Allies. In Prytz's opinion: 'The Finns are not yet *ripe* for peace; one more change of the Finnish government is required (expects it before long). Tanner is particularly harmful.' Prytz sounded me out as to our terms. I evaded the topic. I merely said: for us the question of Finland is the question of the security of Leningrad and our north-western borders. The friendlier Finland is to us, the fewer physical guarantees (territories, bases, etc.) we can demand from it. And *vice versa*. Finland must never forget two constant factors: (1) they are our neighbours, and (2) there are 193 million of us and 3.5 million of them. This should be the basis on which they construct their policy. I spoke in this vein more than once with Tanner, Ryti and others when I was ambassador to Finland – but what has come of it? Prytz fully agreed with my arguments, but asked whether it might not be worth the Soviet government making a statement about its attitude to Finland. I replied: we shall not pay a high price for peace with Finland.

Other issues. (1) Fear of Germany (Hitler), of an invasion of Sweden has passed. The [abbreviation indecipherable] that Sweden granted to Germany (passage of troops, etc.) may soon be cancelled. Nobody believes that Hitler will win, but they are not entirely sure that the Allies will gain a decisive victory either – owing to the conduct of Britain and the USA. They don't rule out a 'compromise' or 'anaemic' victory for the Allies. There is a small group (around the Court) which fears Soviet victory, but not the masses.

(2) Germany's internal situation remains stable. There are no signs of a *crack*. Difficulties with oil. The ongoing mobilization supplies the military with poor material. Hitler will (probably) revert to the defensive, seeking to stabilize the east and trying to drive a wedge between the Allies.

(3) The Swedes gave the British government their consent for two Norwegian vessels to leave Göteborg – the Germans retaliated by barring the passage of Swedish ships from the USA. Sweden is deprived of supplies from across the ocean.

25 March

About Eden's trip.

Not much news from Eden. He will give a detailed report upon his return. Cadogan reads excerpts from Eden's telegram.

---

[i] Hans Frederick Schoenfeld, US ambassador to Finland, 1937–42.

Lunches with Roosevelt and Hopkins – general exchange of opinions. *Compare notes.*

Meetings – more official – with Hull, Sumner Welles, Knox,[i] Wallace and others. *Compare notes.* Disputes.

So far – *in flux* – possibly something more substantial closer to the end. Roosevelt's idea.

Specific issues:

(1) Shipping – a committee headed by Hopkins – the result is not yet clear.

(2) Germany – Roosevelt is for dismembering (Summer Welles particularly *emphatic*!), full disarmament, protracted occupation.

(3) Poland – must accept whatever the Big Three agree on. Nothing about the Baltic States.

(4) Only the Big Three to possess heavy weapons, the others – rifles (Roosevelt's idea). Eden pointed out the difficulty of implementing such a plan.

(5) Conversations about the Balkans, Yugoslavia, Giraud, de Gaulle, etc. No conclusions as yet.

(6) Meeting with Stalin – in July.

29 March

Went to see Churchill. On instructions from Moscow, I informed him of our reply to the Americans on the question of Finland.

Molotov gave Standley to understand that he has little faith in the possibility of concluding a separate peace with Finland now on terms acceptable to us. However, in view of the interest displayed by the American government in this matter, he was ready to formulate for their information our minimum conditions for a separate peace. Here they are:

(1) The Finns break with the Germans immediately and German troops are withdrawn from Finnish territory.

(2) The reinstatement of the 1940 Soviet–Finnish peace treaty in its entirety, with all the ensuing consequences.

(3) The Finnish army should be demobilized and placed on a peace footing.

(4) Compensation for the damage (half, at least) caused to the Soviet Union as a result of Finland's attack on the USSR.

Molotov noted that, considering the violation of the 1940 peace treaty by Finland and her attack on the USSR, we actually have the right to demand more, such as complete disarmament or 100% reparations. The USSR does not wish to take vengeance on Finland, however, and would be satisfied with the aforesaid.

[i] Frank Knox, US secretary of the navy, 1940–44.

Churchill listened to me with interest but little emotion. He said right away (once again) that he is not counting on the possibility of peace with Finland at the present time: Finland is not 'ripe' for that yet.

As for our conditions, Churchill had no objection to the first three points. It even seemed to me that he was surprised at how modest our territorial claims were. But Churchill did not like the fourth point at all. He said Finland was a poor country and would not be able to pay anything, that the experience with reparations in the last war was unsuccessful, and that in general it was pointless to raise such a question at this stage in the war.

I replied that I failed to understand Churchill's attitude. Does he really think that the aggressor need not pay for the damage he has caused? We think he must. This is a matter of principle. We have adhered to it and will do so in the future. Next, why does Churchill think that Finland is not in a position to pay us for the damage she has inflicted on us? We don't mean Finnish marks, of course, we mean payment in kind – with timber, paper, etc. Besides, we do not demand compensation in full, only half. This would seem magnanimous and realistic.

'Well, if it's payment in kind,' Churchill reacted, 'then that's better.'

But it was evident nonetheless that he hadn't fully accepted the fourth point.

'Germany is another matter,' Churchill continued. 'When it comes to settling scores, I'll be all in favour of removing factories and plants from Germany in order to restore your industry, which the Germans destroyed. But Finland… Finland is different.'[58]

When we had exhausted the Finnish question, I asked Churchill why the March convoy has been delayed. The ships were loaded five days ago but still no progress.

Churchill suddenly frowned and became gloomy.

'There are some complications with the convoy,' said the prime minister.

'Nothing serious, I hope?' I asked, anticipating bad news.

'I can't tell you anything today,' Churchill answered sullenly. 'I'll inform you of the final decision tomorrow. I'm waiting for a reply from Roosevelt.'

I made another attempt to find out what the matter was, but Churchill was unbending.

Well, I'll have to wait till tomorrow. But I don't like this one bit. I fear things will go badly with the convoys.

30 March

Alas, my fears have materialized, and in an even worse form than I had expected.

This evening Cadogan invited me to the Foreign Office and handed me a copy of Churchill's message to Stalin, which was sent to Moscow in the morning. It notifies Stalin that in view of the concentration of large surface ships in Narvik (the *Tirpitz, Scharnhorst, Lutzow* and others) the British government deems it impossible to send the next convoy to the north; that in view of the forthcoming operations in the Mediterranean it will not be able to send any convoys to Arkhangelsk and Murmansk from May onwards; and that the convoys may be resumed no earlier than in September, provided the disposition of German naval forces and the state of the sea war in the Atlantic permit this.[59] By way of consolation, the message promises to increase deliveries to the USSR through Vladivostok and the Persian Gulf, claiming that in August the traffic capacity of the Iranian route will increase to 240,000 tons a month. Of course, all this is sweetened with kind words and sorrowful exclamations, but what's the use of them? The main point is that we shan't be getting arms and raw materials from Britain and the USA for six months at least! For Vladivostok and Iran can't compensate us for the loss of the northern convoys.

Very bad. This will be a heavy blow to our people in Moscow. Especially at such a critical moment – on the eve of Germany's spring offensive.

[To soothe Maisky, Churchill had resorted to rhetoric in a personal message he sent him shortly after the Cabinet meeting had sanctioned the suspension of the convoys:

> My dear Ambassador
> I am very much obliged to you for sending me your new film 'Stalingrad', and I shall be glad if you would convey my most cordial thanks to Marshal Stalin.
>
> I have just seen the film and I must tell you that I think it is a worthy portrayal of the great feat of arms of the Red Army. I hope that it will be shown widely in this country so that all may have a chance of paying tribute once again to the immortal defenders of Stalingrad.
>
> Yrs. Sincerely
> Winston S. Churchill[60]

At Maisky's instigation, the Soviet government chose this moment to decorate members of the Royal Navy and Merchant Navy for valour and courage shown in sailing the Arctic convoys in appalling conditions. Maisky used the occasion on which Admiral Pound and other dignitaries were present to state that it was not only 'an expression of gratitude for past services' but also 'an encouragement to the services of the future'. The Soviet people were expecting that 'in the military campaigns of this year the Western Allies will pull their full weight in the common struggle against our common enemy'.[61]]

31 March

I went to see Churchill again today.

First, I had to deliver Stalin's message, which arrived yesterday. Secondly, I thought it necessary to have a serious talk with him about the convoys.

Churchill met me looking gloomy and beetle-browed. He probably thought I was bringing with me Stalin's reply to yesterday's message concerning the convoys and was expecting something unpleasant. I handed him the envelope. He slowly pulled out the sheet of paper, slowly put on his glasses and slowly began to read. Suddenly the PM's face brightened up. No wonder! Stalin was congratulating Churchill on the successes in Tunisia, expressing his hope that the British mechanized troops would give the retreating enemy vigorous chase, allowing him no respite.

Churchill jumped up from his chair, walked around the long table at which the Cabinet held its meetings, and walked up to the map hanging on the wall. There he began describing to me with fervour and great expressiveness his strategic plan: in about two weeks' time the Germans and Italians would be pressed into the north-eastern corner of Tunisia within a radius of 50 miles from Bizerta, showered with bombs from the air and cut off from the sea by the British fleet.

'It's not enough to drive the enemy out of Tunisia,' Churchill exclaimed. 'The enemy must be annihilated! This must be our Stalingrad!'

I listened to him and thought: 'We shall see. How many times have Churchill's sweeping declarations been frustrated by reality!'

Churchill then returned to his place and continued to read the message, where Stalin informed him that the previous evening he had watched the film *Desert Victory*, which Churchill had sent him. Stalin liked the film very much. And that wasn't all. Stalin wrote that the film superbly portrays how Britain fights while at the same time exposing those 'rascals (there are some in our country too) who claim that Britain does not fight at all but remains on the side-lines'. In conclusion, Stalin informed Churchill that *Desert Victory* would be widely shown to the Red Army at the front and to the masses at home.

I carefully observed Churchill's expression. When he got to the phrase about 'rascals', something strange happened to him. The prime minister's face was convulsed by a spasm, he shut his eyes for a moment, and when he opened them I could see tears. Churchill was so excited that he couldn't remain in his seat. He jumped up from his chair again, walked to the fireplace and exclaimed with feeling: 'The deepest thanks to Stalin!… You have never brought me such a wonderful message before.'

Was all this genuine? Or was it an act? There was a bit of both, it seems to me, in Churchill's behaviour. The phrase about 'rascals' must have touched the prime minister deeply. He must have perceived in it longed-for recognition of his war efforts of these past three years. And from whose lips?… From Stalin's! This could and must have moved Churchill deeply and brought tears to his eyes. The prime minister has an emotional-artistic temperament. Sudden bursts of feeling overwhelm him like inspiration overwhelms a poet. At such moments, Churchill somewhat loses control of himself and is capable of giving promises which later, when he is in a more normal and sober mood, he fails to fulfil. But Churchill is also an actor. During his years in opposition he memorized his speeches to parliament in front of a mirror. That is why at certain moments Churchill, like a good actor, gives vent to his emotional temperament and does not prevent genuine tears from watering his eyes.

Having regained control of himself, Churchill lavished praise on *Stalingrad*, which I had sent to him a few days ago on Stalin's instructions.

I took the opportunity to tell him: 'Please ask your censors not to cut out the *grim spots* from *Stalingrad*. There are some. It is important that your public should see such things.'

'But of course!' Churchill responded promptly. 'Let them see it! Let them know what the Nazis are like!'

And thus the inviolability of *Stalingrad* was secured.

The first topic on the agenda was exhausted. I moved on to the second.

I spoke about Churchill's message of 30 March and said that it had left me simply astounded. After all, what does it mean? That there will definitely be no convoys until September. And I doubt that the convoys will be resumed even then, for there are too many tricky and elastic 'ifs' concerning their resumption. It would seem that the convoys are effectively being suspended until darkness sets in once more, i.e. November–December. This means that for the next eight or nine months we shouldn't count on receiving remotely sufficient supplies. We can't accept this situation at all.

'And what effect,' I continued, 'will it have on the mood of the Red Army and among the population at large?… Put yourself in their shoes. This is the third summer that they are waiting for a second front from their Western Allies. Will there be a second front now or won't there?… You know better than I do. My personal impression is that nothing definite can be said – maybe there will, maybe there won't. And that is the best that can be said today about the opening of a second front… So, summer will come, the Germans will start their offensive and we shall once again have to survive difficult weeks and months, and what's more – without a second front and without supplies! What will the mood of our people be? Don't you see that they will start exclaiming with indignation: Where are our allies? And do you call these allies?… Who will profit from such feelings?'

The more I spoke, the more excited Churchill was becoming. Eventually he could no longer restrain himself. 'Yes, I know,' he exclaimed, 'that this is a heavy blow for you… It's terrible! I fear that the cessation of convoys will have a serious impact on our relations…'

Tears once again appeared in his eyes. He stood up and began pacing the room in agitation.

'But what could I do?'… Churchill continued with great emotion. 'I had no alternative!… Please understand, I have no right to jeopardize the entire course of the war, not even for the sake of your supplies!… I can't do it! I can't!… It seems strange, but our entire naval supremacy is based on the availability of a handful of first-class combat units. Your people may not understand this, but your government must!'

Churchill made another round of the room and added: 'I considered it my duty to tell Stalin the whole truth. You mustn't deceive an ally. Stalin should know the real situation. One should face even the most unpleasant news with courage. And Stalin is a man of courage.'

It was clear that the thought of the inevitable suspension of the convoys had engulfed Churchill entirely. I know from experience that he cannot be budged at such moments. It is useless and even harmful to try. So I began thinking about some practical alternatives which I might suggest to Churchill in order to mitigate the consequences of the suspension of the convoys. But before I had uttered a word, Churchill came up very close to me and, looking straight into my eyes, asked hurriedly: 'Tell me honestly, what do you personally think about this situation?… Will it mean a split with Stalin or won't it?'

'I don't deem it possible to speak for Stalin,' I replied. 'He will speak for himself. I know one thing for sure, though: your decision will arouse very strong feelings in Stalin.'

Churchill moved away from me a little. His disappointment was obvious. He sighed, walked round the table once again, and said quickly: 'Anything but a split! I don't want a split. I don't! I want to work with Stalin, and I feel that I can work with him!… If I'm destined to live longer, I can be very useful to you… In settling your relations with America. That is very important. It is exceptionally important. Whatever happens we, the three great powers – the USSR, the USA and Great Britain – should maintain our friendship and work together after the war. Otherwise the world will perish.

Then, as if recalling something amusing, Churchill added more calmly: 'In America they took offence at my failure to mention China as the fourth member of a possible combination when I was speaking about the post-war future in my recent radio broadcast (21 March). Hm!… How could I do it?… I like and respect the Chinese people. They are wonderful people. Just read what Pearl Buck writes about them… I wish China well. But all the same, is it possible to compare China with the USA, Britain or Russia?… No comparison is possible! To make one would be an insult to our intelligence. It's good they have Jiang Jieshi there now. He keeps a grip on things. Just imagine Jiang Jieshi disappearing tomorrow, dying, leaving the stage – what would happen then? Sheer chaos!… No, I'm too old to lie just for the sake of cheap applause from the gallery!'

Churchill fell silent for a moment and paused. With a sudden grimace, he nodded at the message he had just received from me and exclaimed bitterly: 'What a shame that my message about the cessation of convoys should overlap with the message you brought me from Stalin today!… But what could I do?'

I took advantage of the pause following these words to make two practical proposals:

(1) To redirect the March convoy, already loaded but not sent to the north, to the Persian Gulf.

(2) To set up a special committee chaired by Eden as soon as he returns (he will be back in a few days) which would devise ways to compensate us for the suspension of the northern convoys.

Churchill eagerly accepted both proposals. He made only one alteration: there was no need to wait for Eden to come back; the committee I mentioned can start working tomorrow with Lyttelton in the chair, and I can take part in it together with my experts.

With this we parted.

2 April

Yesterday Lyttelton's committee was convened, with myself, Kharlamov and Morozovsky in attendance. I raised the matter of 'compensation' and asked the committee to seek corresponding measures. Leathers, Cadogan and other members of the committee took part in the debate. They outlined various paths towards the solution of the problem.

Today I handed Churchill Stalin's reply to his message concerning the cessation of convoys (of 30 March). Considering the general situation, I had imagined that Stalin's reply might not be especially sharp, but it turned out to be far milder than I had expected. Stalin acted most wisely: he expressed neither indignation nor irritation. He merely noted the decision by Roosevelt and Churchill to suspend the convoys and pointed out that such a decision could not but affect the position of Soviet troops in the forthcoming summer campaign.

Churchill was staggered by this. He had been very gloomy and tense when I arrived. I could feel that he was expecting a sharp, abusive response. He put on his glasses and slowly, reluctantly unfolded the message, as if trying to postpone the moment when he would have to swallow the bitter pill. And then this!

He could not remain seated. He leapt out of his armchair in a state of extreme excitement and started rapidly pacing the room.

'Tell Stalin,' Churchill finally said, continuing to pace out the distance around the Cabinet table, 'that this is a magnanimous and courageous reply. He has simply crushed me with his response.[62] Such a reply makes me feel doubly obliged to do absolutely all that is humanly possible to compensate him. I'll be working like a horse! And I'll find some solutions.'

Churchill made two more tours of the table, then spoke again: 'With this response, Stalin has shown once again how great and wise a man he is… I want to work with him without fail! When the war ends I'll spare no effort to help Russia heal its wounds as quickly as possible… We shall also help the world get to its feet as quickly as possible… Stalin *is a man of great size*, Roosevelt *is also a man of great size*… Yes, the three of us can achieve much!'

4 April (Bovingdon)

We haven't been to Bovingdon for three weeks. I caught a cold in the middle of March and spent two weeks in a strange condition: neither sick nor well. My temperature was normal, but there was something wrong with my voice and nose, especially my nose. I didn't want any complications – at such a time I can't permit myself the luxury of being unwell and out of action for long – so I stayed at home. My health only began to improve last week, and now here we are in Bovingdon again.

There is a lull on our front. We've lost Kharkov, but have held the Donets and Kursk. The season of bad roads is upon us. Military actions on both sides have practically ceased, but preparations for the spring and summer are in full swing. The atmosphere is very tense. What does the future hold in store?

The keynote of British press reports from Moscow today (especially the one by Alexander Werth in the *Sunday Times*): we expect a fresh German offensive in spring on a major scale in the Orel–Belgorod area, i.e. against Moscow and the central front in general. Werth writes that Moscow is apprehensive of developments in the coming months. It is thought that this summer might be as *grim* as the last one. Who knows? Time will tell.

I'll try myself to make sense of the future. First of all, what should any possible conjectures and predictions be based on? The following:

(1) The total mobilization being carried out by Hitler in Germany at the moment basically covers his losses in the USSR last winter – in quantity, but not quality.

(2) If so, then by mid-summer Hitler will probably have the same number of troops as he had in the summer of 1942, but of poorer quality and with somewhat lower morale.

(3) As the front line in the USSR has shortened considerably during the winter (from 2,300 to 1,200 miles, excluding the front north of Leningrad), Hitler will have strategic reserves of about 100 divisions (my calculation: 232 divisions occupy the 2,300-mile front line, meaning roughly one division every 10 miles).

(4) A serious second front in the west is not to be expected in spring or summer, but some operations will be undertaken in the Mediterranean. A serious air offensive against Germany will be undertaken as well. Hitler, however, does not know about the small likelihood of a serious second front and so he has to guess.

What conclusions can be drawn from these premises? Here they are:

(1) The above-mentioned 100 divisions represent Hitler's last reserves. That is why he has to deploy them very carefully. In other words, he can use them either

(a) to bring the war to a definitive end, that is, to crush the USSR completely, or

(b) to gain positions which, even though they would not bring the war to an end immediately, would offer him a good chance of doing so in the more distant future. This, at any rate, is how any sensible commander-in-chief would reason.

(2) I doubt that after nearly two years' experience of war with the USSR Hitler (and especially his generals) could be counting on the final defeat of the USSR with the help of his 100 divisions.

(3) As concerns point (b), only the Caucasus and Baku could represent critically important targets, providing Hitler with oil and wide-ranging possibilities in the Middle East, India and Africa. The stubbornness with which Hitler is clinging on to the Taman peninsula evidently indicates that he entertains such thoughts. However, in the opinion of all the military specialists I have spoken to, an isolated operation in the direction of the Northern Caucasus through Rostov and Taman is strategically unthinkable because our entire army would be concentrated on its left flank and communications on such a narrow section of the front would mean that only a relatively small number of forces could be supported (about 30 divisions at most). If the aim is to advance to the Caucasus, it is necessary to return to the Volga first and establish a rather broad and defensible front there. But it seems unlikely that the Germans would head back to the Volga after Stalingrad.

(4) So, if points (a) and (b) seem to fall away, what can be expected? A number of military specialists believe that the Germans will try to stabilize their front in the USSR roughly along its current line, deploying 120–150 divisions, and either (a) remain on the defensive everywhere this year, leaving the Allies to bang their heads against the walls of the 'European fortress' or (b) mount an

easier and more promising offensive in another direction, say, in the direction of Spain, Italy or Turkey.

(5) Quite weighty arguments can be adduced in favour of the first hypothesis. The Germans must understand now that they are unable to win the war by military means alone. The best they can hope for is a more or less advantageous compromise peace. The precondition for such a peace is a split in our coalition, or at least disagreements. In the event of a split hopes could be pinned on a separate peace (which would be ideal from the German point of view). Disagreements would raise hopes for a general compromise peace (which would be worse from the German point of view but still acceptable). But time is needed for the process of disintegration to develop within any coalition. That is why it would seem advantageous for Hitler to spend the year 1943 on the defensive, keeping his 100 reserve divisions as an important card in future peace negotiations.

(6) Solid arguments can likewise be advanced in favour of the second supposition. After two years of losses, failures, indecisive battles, etc. on the eastern front, Germany badly needs some brilliant and rapid victories to lift her spirits. The ebbing morale of Italy also needs to be boosted, which can be done only by achieving large successes in the Mediterranean. Hitler's encroachment into North Africa (through Spain) would present him with broad opportunities for new conquests, new sources of raw materials and manpower, and new naval and air bases for the sea war with the Allies.

(7) Yet there are a number of serious counterarguments to the arguments raised in points (5) and (6). First, according to German military doctrine, attack is the best form of defence. The German army has been brought up in that spirit. That is why it is difficult to imagine Hitler remaining solely on the defensive everywhere in 1943. Secondly, Hitler has committed himself too much in the east to retreat from there (unless he is forced to retreat, but such a situation has not yet occurred). Thirdly, Hitler must be expecting a summer offensive from us. This excludes the possibility of the eastern front being stabilized. If that is the case, he will prefer to attack himself. Fourthly and lastly, Hitler, unconvinced by the likelihood of an effective second front being opened against him this summer, may think that one more German offensive in the USSR in the absence of a second front in the west will prove the best means of splitting, or at least weakening, the hostile coalition.

So what do we have in the final analysis?

I think Hitler will launch an offensive in summer, most probably in the USSR. Where exactly? It's difficult to say. Maybe on the central front, as they now suppose in Moscow. Since there is little hope for an effective second front in the west, we must obviously seek to forestall Hitler's offensive by launching a counteroffensive. I see no other solution.

9 April

An unexpected summons from Churchill. What was behind it? The convoys? Or the message from Comrade Stalin that I had forwarded to him this morning? Or some other matter?

My frantic guesswork failed to hit on the real reason for the invitation.

When I entered the prime minister's office, I immediately noticed that Churchill was in a foul mood. We shook hands in silence. Then Churchill snapped and exclaimed in fury: 'Here, see what your correspondents write! You could have left this dirty work to Goebbels!'

Saying this, he thrust into my hand a sheet of paper containing some twenty typewritten lines.

Somewhat taken aback by this welcome, I swiftly ran my eye over the text. It was an excerpt from a BBC report. It conveyed the content of a telegram from the TASS correspondent in Algeria. The author of the telegram, reporting the Eighth Army's seizure of a large quantity of war material, added in passing that these include many outdated tanks and guns (including 1917 Škoda guns) which the Germans dare not use on the Soviet front.

'Well, what do you make of it?' Churchill fumed. 'Here's Stalin sending me wonderful messages (the PM nodded at the message on the table which I had forwarded to him this morning) and attributing the very greatest significance to our victories in Tunisia, and now the TASS correspondent in Algeria wants to sully all this with dirt!'

I was about to answer Churchill, but he beat me to it, exclaiming with a new rush of anger: 'Bracken is here in my residence. He is just waiting for the word to bring an end to this disgrace, to deprive the TASS correspondents of all their *facilities*! Both in Algeria, and in London…'

'But why in London?' I barely managed to ask.

'What do you mean, why?' responded Churchill abruptly. 'The TASS office in London copied and sent this telegram.'

Sensing that Churchill, in his fury, might start breaking things any moment, I hastened to interrupt him and calm him down.

'First of all,' I began, 'permit me to ask you not to draw any hasty conclusions. We need to find out what this is all about. I, for one, know nothing about it. Give me time to get to the bottom of it and then we will see what we should do. For now, I can say just one thing: I seriously doubt that the London TASS office was involved in this affair.'

My calm tone evidently had an effect on Churchill. He began to cool off and revert to a more normal state of mind.

'All right,' he replied, 'make your investigations. But make sure you inform Moscow of the incident. I am so delighted with Stalin's recent messages. I feel as if he were my brother-in-arms. And I don't want some TASS correspondent to poison the atmosphere between us and obstruct friendly cooperation between myself and Stalin!'

Then, having fully composed himself, Churchill concluded: 'I don't know whether what the TASS correspondent says is true or not. But even if it is true, you'd better inform your government by cipher. What's the point of shouting about it to the entire world?'

Once Churchill had finished with the Algerian correspondent, I asked him what news there was on the matter of the convoys.

'I've been working like a horse every day,' Churchill answered, 'and seem to have come up with something…'

'May I know what exactly?' I inquired.

Churchill suddenly made a terribly cunning face, similar to the one he had made when telling me of his visit to Cyprus, and said: 'No, I won't tell you now! I want to inform Stalin about it myself!'

But I could tell from various hints dropped by Churchill that it concerned the transfer to the USSR by air of those American and British fighters which had got stuck in England.

I asked when the ten British ships from the postponed March convoy would be sent to the Persian Gulf.

Churchill answered that it made no sense to send them around Africa on the eve of the capture of Tunisia. It would be better to wait another 2–3 weeks and send the ships through the Mediterranean. The cargoes of those ten ships would need to be reloaded onto other, faster ships.

'You must understand, however,' Churchill said, 'that the convoy sailing to the Persian Gulf should carry only the most valuable cargo, such as tanks, planes, explosives, critical military raw materials, the cargoes sent by my wife, the cargoes sent by your wife… For the carrying capacity of the Persian route is still modest. But I'll do it and inform Stalin about everything in a few days.'

We shall see what will come of Churchill's promises. I am not very optimistic.

'By the way,' Churchill added, 'my experts assert that the main transit difficulties through Persia lie in your zone of occupation: the railway, the ports, the shipping facilities in the Caspian Sea… Could you provide me with the relevant information?'

I said I would ask Moscow.

In conclusion, I acquainted Churchill with the upshot of Comrade Molotov's talks with the Turkish ambassador in the USSR. It is very meagre. The Turks proposed publishing a joint communiqué confirming the existence of cordial relations between the USSR and Turkey over the past 25 years and presently.

Comrade Molotov rejected this proposal, arguing that it would serve merely to devalue the Soviet–Turkish agreements currently regulating relations between the two countries. The Turks agreed with Comrade Molotov but had nothing else to offer. Comrade Molotov finally stated that the Turks were evidently not yet ready to take a real step towards improving relations between the two countries. Therefore, the Soviet government would rather wait until the Turks come up with some fresh proposals. So far, then, nothing has come of the attempt, initiated by Churchill, to bolster Soviet–Turkish friendship – and the fault is not ours.

Churchill listened to me with great interest and then replied that he considered our position to be absolutely correct, while the Turks had not moved far enough towards the Allies.

'Just wait a little,' Churchill added. 'As soon as we finish with Tunisia and give the Turks some of the arms we promised, I'll put pressure on them. I'll demand that they interpret their neutrality in the "American sense"... Do you remember how the Americans conducted themselves even before they entered the war? The Turks should let us use their bases and airfields for air attacks on Rumania and the Dodecanese. Or allow us to ship munitions and raw materials to you through their territory or through the Straits. Roosevelt has promised me his assistance in exerting pressure on Turkey. I hope Stalin won't refuse me either.'

'You'll have to ask Stalin yourself,' I remarked.

'Of course, of course!' Churchill assured me. 'And then I'll give the Turks a choice: their aid to the Allies, their place at the victors' table, and guarantees of Turkey's inviolability or, if they refuse to help us, the status of "neutral" after the war and no guarantees of Turkey's inviolability. We shall see what Turkey chooses.'

Back home I asked Teplov[i] (first secretary) to make the necessary inquiries and headed off to give a speech at the Bombardment Training Station, some 90 miles from London. When I returned home late in the evening the picture was clear. The London TASS office did not, of course, send the telegram which so enraged Churchill. Rather, the TASS correspondent in Algeria sent it directly to Moscow. Moscow radio broadcast it on 8 April at 9.30 p.m. The Algerian correspondent's report was long, unbiased and unobjectionable. The ill-fated phrase came at the very end of his communication. But, after all, the whole report must have been cleared by the Algerian military censor!

I reported the incident to Moscow.

---

[i] Leonid Fedorovich Teplov, recruited to NKID in 1941; first secretary at the Soviet embassy in London, 1943–44.

11 April (Bovingdon)

All quiet on our front. Local battles on the Donets and the steady, but slow ousting of the Germans from the Novorossiisk area and the Taman peninsula. The sooner this latter operation is completed the better! I worry about the Kuban. What's more, the atmosphere is tense. One can feel that both sides are hastily preparing for the spring. Who will overtake whom? Who will be the first to launch an offensive?… Time will tell.

Matters seem to be reaching a conclusion in Tunisia. Yesterday the British captured Sfax. The Anglo-American–French troops are approaching Kairouan and Bizerta. Tunis is not far off. It's time! High time! Tunisia has been a great disappointment. Its capture was supposed to be a matter of some 2–3 weeks, but the fighting has dragged on for five months! So much valuable time has been lost! And as a result so many strategic opportunities have been missed! Even though the end there is near, I look ahead without any great enthusiasm. I don't see any prospect of a real second front in 1943, not at any rate this spring or summer, when it will be most needed.[63]

[Maisky's well-informed 'guess' was right. As he was making his way back to London from Bovingdon, the chiefs of staff were impressing on an ostensibly surprised Churchill that the transfer to North Africa of landing craft (indispensable for executing Operation *Husky* and exploiting its success for an operation in Italy) excluded the possibility of launching a cross-channel attack in 1943. 'We must recognize,' Churchill conceded to his senior advisers, 'that no important Cross-Channel enterprise is possible this year.' Although he continued to sanction the build-up of troops in Britain for a 1944 operation, he remained aloof and made its execution conditional on the existence of circumstances which might allow 'taking advantage of any collapse on the part of the enemy'. He specifically noted that he wished Stalin not to be informed of the decision.[64]]

18 April (Bovingdon)

Wonderful weather: warm, bright sun, blue skies streaked with light, fleecy clouds. At night, everything is bathed in soft moonlight. Just like summer.

And together with this summer weather, which set in last week, summer thoughts creep into my mind… not the summer thoughts once so familiar in those distant times of peace, but the summer thoughts that have become an integral part of our psychological processes since the beginning of the war.

The picture of what we can <u>really</u> count on from Britain and the USA this year becomes ever more clear:

(1) a serious and intensifying air offensive against Germany and Italy,

(2) offensive operations in Sicily, Sardinia, southern Italy, and a bit later in the Dodecanese and the Balkans.

This is realistic. In addition, a few possibilities:

(3) air bombardment of Rumania and its oil fields, provided Churchill succeeds in fulfilling his plans vis-à-vis Turkey.

(4) offensive operations across the Channel, in France, towards the end of the year.

All this, of course, is not the second front we need, but still, what effect will the above-named developments have in the east?

The following, as it seems to me:

(1) Germany's position in the air on the Soviet front will be considerably weakened.

(2) Italy will quit the scene as Germany's auxiliary force in the east.

(3) The supplies to the German armies in the USSR will be reduced due to the destruction of Essen, Pilsen and other centres of military production.

(4) The morale of the German population will decline somewhat as a result of defeats in Africa and, even more so, as a result of the Anglo-American air offensive.

All this, of course, is better than nothing. But can it prevent a German offensive in the USSR this spring?

I don't think so, unless the Red Army forestalls the German offensive by attacking first.

20 April

Moscow displayed great interest in Eden's reports about his conversations in America. They asked me to convey to Eden the gratitude of the Soviet government for his information, and I was asked to prepare a detailed record of the talks. Our people are also prepared to discuss matters relating to air communications after the war and have declared that they will participate in the international organization of these communications.

21 April

Two days ago Churchill asked Stalin (for information has come in that the Germans are planning to use gas on the Soviet front): should he not repeat the warning concerning possible gas reprisals by Britain against Germany which he first gave last May?

Stalin replied favourably and added that we, too, have information about German intentions to use gas in battles this spring and summer.

Iris called Churchill's secretary this morning and asked her to arrange a meeting for me with the prime minister, as I had an important *message* for him.

Churchill's secretary said in reply that the prime minister would like me to proceed immediately to parliament, where the Cabinet was in session.

I entered the prime minister's office in the House of Commons at about twelve o'clock. The secretary asked me to wait a minute and went into the next room, from where I could hear muffled conversation, to report my arrival.

Suddenly the door was flung open and Churchill rushed out – looking a bit dishevelled, agitated and impatient.

The secretaries went out, leaving Churchill and me alone. The PM asked tersely: 'You have Stalin's reply about the gas?'

'Yes,' I answered and gave him the envelope.

'I knew it,' the prime minister said cheerfully.

Then he rummaged frantically in his pockets for his glasses. They weren't there: he had left them in the conference room. So I said: 'Allow me to read the message.'

'Please do,' Churchill replied, giving me the sheet of paper he had just removed from the envelope.

I read the message from beginning to end. Churchill listened attentively. Then he exclaimed: 'I shall do it without fail!'

'When?' I asked. 'Time is short. The ground in the USSR is drying quickly and military operations may begin very soon.'

Churchill replied: 'I shan't dither! The Cabinet is meeting and I'll raise the matter immediately.'

'May I count on the fact that you will publish the warning tomorrow? This would be good.'

'Agreed!' Churchill paused, before adding: 'Last year I gave the warning in my radio broadcast… This time I'll publish it on behalf of the British government, from 10, Downing Street. It will be strongly worded.'

'Permit me to request one thing,' I began, and reminded the prime minister that in last year's warning he had threatened the Germans with reprisals in the event of 'the unprovoked use of gas' in the east. The word 'unprovoked' made a very bad impression in Moscow at the time. It was as if Churchill was admitting the possibility of the Soviet government's initiative in the use of gas. I expressed my hope that Churchill would omit the word 'unprovoked' in his warning this time.

'All right,' Churchill replied. 'I'll bear your suggestion in mind.'

He paused for a moment and said, shaking my hand: 'Well, we are a great deal closer to each other today than a year ago.'

[The partition of Poland in 1939 had ended with a large number of Polish prisoners of war being interned by the Russians. Most of the prisoners were released in the wake of the Soviet–Polish agreement brokered by Maisky and Sikorsky in July 1941. Close to 20,000 officers, however, remained unaccounted for. Stalin went a long way, as the diary shows, to conceal the cold-blooded massacre of those officers, condoned by the Politburo in March 1940. No historian has come up with a conclusive and convincing explanation for the motives behind the massacre. The Germans, who had stumbled across the graves during their campaign, made full use of the affair to sow discord among the Allies. On 12 April, they publicized their report, inviting the Poles to investigate the findings jointly with the Red Cross. The Katyn affair became a serious source of embarrassment for Stalin. Had the truth about the fate of the prisoners been unearthed, it could have jeopardized the delicate fabric of the precarious alliance, just as the purges had crippled Soviet diplomacy and undermined negotiations with the West in 1939. Stalin therefore reacted violently to any accusations and conducted an aggressive cover-up operation, which even included a misleading post-mortem of the bodies dug from the grave, once the Katyn area was liberated by the Red Army.[65]]

23 April

Stalin's message arrived before lunch. It concerns Poland. Stalin informed Churchill that in view of the entirely abnormal relations between the USSR and Poland, an abnormality caused by the conduct of the Polish government, and in particular by its stance in connection with the recent German provocation (the 'discovery' of the bodies of 10,000 Polish officers near Smolensk), the

114. Happier days: Maisky with General Sikorski and Eden a couple of days before the revelations of the Katyn massacre.

Soviet government has been compelled to 'break off' relations with Sikorski's government. The message further expressed the conviction that an agreement on this matter exists between Sikorski's and Hitler's governments: the campaign about the 'discovery' of the bodies began concurrently in the German and Polish press. Stalin expressed his hope that the British government would understand the inevitability of such a move, which was imposed on the Soviet government by the political line pursued by Sikorski's government. Stalin sent a similar message to Roosevelt.[66]

Today is 'Good Friday', and it immediately occurred to me that the prime minister was probably out of town. I called his secretary myself. I was quite right: yesterday evening Churchill went to spend Easter at his small country estate, Chartwell (30 miles south of London). I had to choose: either to go to Chartwell myself or to forward the message via the prime minister's secretariat. Considering the importance of the matter, I chose the first. The secretary called Churchill and told me the prime minister would expect me for dinner in Chartwell and would send a car for me.

I left the embassy at around 7 p.m. and by 8 p.m. I was already there. Although the car was from the PM's garage and an army driver was at the wheel, we were stopped at the entrance to the estate by military guards. Several fully armed young soldiers shouted 'Halt!', manifesting great zeal and even pointing their bayonets at us. I couldn't help smiling to myself. Later Churchill said with a chuckle: 'I don't need them (the soldiers), but the War Office insists…'

He waved his hand, as if to say: 'Let them amuse themselves. I couldn't care less.'

The main building at Churchill's country estate, where he lived in the years before the war and where I visited him more than once, was closed. Only a small wing close to the main building remained inhabited. Churchill had built it himself (he is a mason, after all!) on the site of the old stables. I remember Churchill proudly showing me his creation (in 1938, if I am not mistaken). Then it served him as his study and studio for painting (for Churchill is also an artist!). Now it houses Churchill's main apartment, where he stays when he occasionally visits his estate.

I was met by one of Churchill's secretaries, who immediately offered me a glass of sherry.

'The prime minister is changing,' the secretary said. 'He will be back soon.'

I couldn't help wondering: 'Has the process of "normalization" really reached the point of Churchill wearing black tie for dinner?'

I asked the secretary whether there was anyone else at home besides the prime minister. The secretary said that Mrs Churchill was at the seaside and the daughters in London. However, Bracken had come to spend the weekend with the prime minister.

115. Maisky with Churchill's intimate, Brendan Bracken.

'The minister of information is taking a bath,' smiled the secretary. 'He too will be down soon.'

As if in confirmation of this, I heard the sound of water draining from a bathtub somewhere close behind the wall.

'And here is the prime minister!' the secretary suddenly exclaimed, rising from his seat and walking towards the door.

In walked Churchill. My fears proved mistaken! The prime minister was wearing his habitual *siren suit*. He greeted me heartily with a firm handshake.

The secretary left and I presented Churchill with Stalin's message. He began reading it, and the further he read the darker his face became. Bracken entered the room just when Churchill had finished reading… The minister of information was in a dinner-jacket! What the devil!

Churchill passed the message to Bracken without a murmur and then, turning to me, asked: 'What does it mean: breaking off relations?'

I replied that it meant the breaking off of relations *de facto*, without any public statements and without any official documents being handed to the Polish government. Those, at least, were the instructions we had received here in London. For now. As for the future, I had no idea. Much would depend on the conduct of the Polish government.

'It is necessary at any rate to take steps to prevent the decision taken by the Soviet government being publicized,' Churchill continued. 'Publicity would be most unfortunate. Only the Germans would stand to gain by it.'

I said that as far as I could gather from our correspondence, the Soviet government does not currently intend to publish anything concerning the severance of relations. Churchill calmed down a little and asked Bracken to see to it that nothing of the kind should appear in the British press.

Then Churchill said: 'I can't believe Sikorski was in cahoots with Hitler. It's impossible. Accusing Sikorski of having concluded an agreement with Hitler merely means that Moscow is very angry with the Poles.'

'But how then,' I objected, 'do you explain the touching coincidence in the course followed by the Polish government and Hitler?'

'It's very simple,' Churchill replied. 'The Poles are poor politicians in general, and now they're in exile they've lost their heads completely. The Germans set a trap and the Poles fell into it.'

Bracken hastened to back up Churchill.

'This conflict must be resolved at all costs,' Churchill spoke again. 'Whose interests does it serve? Only the Germans'. The disintegration of our coalition is precisely what they're after – disagreements among the Allies, a split… So our task is clear.'

At that moment the butler entered the room and announced that dinner was served. We dined in a small room at a small table. There were five of us (Churchill, Bracken, myself, the secretary and the housekeeper) and I can't say there was much space around the table. The menu was almost spartan: milk soup (edible!), a piece of fried salmon and a bit of asparagus from Churchill's 'own plots'. Afterwards we drank coffee and smoked. Churchill, of course, sucked at his habitual cigar.

During dinner the secretary reported to Churchill that his order had been carried out, and the content of the message had been conveyed to Eden by telephone.

'Eden is very *upset*!' the secretary added.

When dinner was over, the housekeeper and secretary left. The three of us remained, Churchill, Bracken and I. We resumed our conversation about the message.

Churchill said he had just finished writing his message to Stalin today – on the same Polish question! Had I not come, he would have sent it tonight. Now, in the light of Stalin's message, Churchill deemed it necessary to amend his own, or perhaps to write a new one. The prime minister rang his secretary and asked him to bring the text of the unsent document. He gave it to me, saying half-jokingly: 'There you are, if you wish read it. But then forget all about it, for this message no longer exists.'

I laughed, took the message from Churchill and quickly ran my eyes over it. Churchill informed Stalin that the worsening of Polish–Soviet relations which had recently been observed was a great worry to the British government; that a series of measures undertaken by the Soviet government (the closure of the Polish aid organization in the USSR, the declaration that all Poles who find themselves in the USSR are Soviet citizens, the refusal to let out the families of Polish soldiers evacuated from the USSR, etc.) causes great distress among Polish units in the Middle East; that while Polish émigrés in Britain and the USA did undoubtedly conduct themselves in a provocative manner, it would be desirable in the interests of the unity of the Allied front to improve Polish–Soviet relations, to which end it would be good to allow the families of the Polish soldiers stationed in the Middle East, as well as the 40,000 Poles fit for military service who are still in the USSR, to leave the Soviet Union.

'A good thing you haven't sent this document,' I remarked, summing up my impression of Churchill's message. 'It would have met with ill-feeling in Moscow.'

'Why?' Churchill asked.

'Simply because the thread running throughout the message is that it is the Soviet side which is most to blame for the deterioration of Polish–Soviet relations. Meanwhile, reality suggests the exact opposite.'

I explained to Churchill in detail why Polish–Soviet relations have worsened recently. I listed a number of facts: the espionage activities of the aid organization, the anti-Soviet propaganda of the Polish press in Britain, the official decision of the Polish government to claim the 1939 borders, and so on.

'By the way,' I continued, addressing Bracken in particular, 'you bear special responsibility for what has happened. Why did you allow the Polish press to behave so outrageously all this time? Last year I drew Eden's attention to these outrages more than once, but to no avail.'

Bracken began to defend himself, arguing that the law does not give him the right to close down newspapers on the grounds of their political content.

'But you supply them with paper!' I parried. 'Cannot paper be an excellent instrument for influencing the Polish press?'

Bracken started describing to me in detail how paper is distributed and how the censorship system functions, suggesting that the Ministry of Information can do nothing about the disgraceful behaviour of the Polish press.

'How come?' Churchill interrupted Bracken. 'Does this mean that the Poles can spread anti-Soviet propaganda from our territory and poison our relations with our ally, and we are powerless to stop them? No, it's not on! We must find means to call them to order.'

The prime minister's intervention confused Bracken. He began to give ground and argue that some measures against the outrageous Polish press had been taken, but it was no easy task. Bracken suggested a 'radical' solution of the problem: to give all the paper allocated to the Poles to the Polish government and let them distribute it between the various organs. The responsibility for the conduct of the press would then rest with the Polish government.

'What if this system does not help either?' I asked. 'What then?'

Bracken spread his arms and replied: 'Then it will be for Eden to decide. If Eden recognizes that a certain Polish organ is harmful to the strengthening of relations between the Allies, then we shall close it down.'

So, it is possible to close down a newspaper after all!

I then touched upon the Polish government's conduct in connection with Goebbels' latest provocation and noted that it has exceeded all bounds. The Soviet government is aware of the significance of maintaining unity among the Allies no less than the British government. In view of this, the Soviet government has been demonstrating exceptional patience for more than a year with respect to the Polish government and Polish émigrés. But there is a limit to everything. This limit has been reached, and the Soviet government has been forced to react sharply.

Churchill asked Bracken to tell him the particulars of the recent affair. When Bracken mentioned the Polish–German plan of 'investigating' the circumstances of the crime through the Red Cross, the prime minister exclaimed in irritation: 'What nonsense! What kind of investigation can there be under German occupation?'

Then, with a cunning smile, Churchill added: 'Let the Germans first withdraw their troops from that region and then we shall carry out an investigation!… Only I doubt that Hitler would show the necessary altruism!'

I said that the entire plan of 'investigating' should be 'killed' at the outset. Yet the British government and the British press keep silent, creating the impression that while they may not necessarily favour the project, they at least have nothing against it.

'Bracken!' uttered Churchill. 'This whole idiotic venture must be "killed" at once. Take the necessary measures.'

Bracken promised to fulfil the prime minister's instruction as a matter of urgency.

Churchill continued: 'Nonetheless, the conflict between you and the Poles is an utterly unpleasant affair. It should be resolved as soon as possible. If you were to agree to let the families of Polish soldiers and the 40,000 Poles fit for military service leave the USSR, peace could be restored. We, on our side, would take measures to pacify the Poles and make them change their behaviour… What the hell do you need those Polish women and children for? They are just a burden to you. Meanwhile, the Polish soldiers in the Middle East are on the verge of mutiny because of them. There are 80,000 of them there and they are well armed now. We could use them with profit in the forthcoming offensive on Europe. But what do we have instead? General Anders, their commander, told Sikorski recently: "Relieve me of my command, please, and let me command a regiment. It would be better. I've had as much as I can take." That's no good at all. I asked Sikorski to go himself to the Middle East and exert his influence on the troops. But I don't know what will come of it…'

Then Churchill, with occasional interruptions and interventions from Bracken, began telling me that Sikorski now finds himself in a critical position. The 'extremists' are waging a vehement campaign against him, accusing him of weakness and servility to the Bolsheviks. It's not clear whether Sikorski will manage to hold on. If not, who will come to power? Those very 'extremists' will take charge of the government. This has led Churchill to the conclusion that the present Polish government should be treated with care.

Bracken, in his turn, gave a vivid description of the 'American danger': Roosevelt's position is very delicate: there are many Poles in the United States, they represent a substantial electorate, and Catholics, of whom there are 33 million in the United States, may easily choose to support them. The election is at hand. Roosevelt cannot ignore the mood of the Catholics in general and of the Poles in particular. All this may tie the president's hands and lead to the deterioration of relations between the USA and the USSR. Bracken's conclusion was as follows: the Soviet government should let the Polish families plus the 40,000 Poles fit for military service leave the USSR, and everything will settle down. Meanwhile, the British government's propaganda machine will exploit this fact to the full here and in America in the interests of the USSR and of all the Allies.

Churchill seconded Bracken and added that he had talked with Anders in Egypt on his way home from Moscow last year. Anders asked him, among other things, to exert his influence on Moscow on the question of the Polish families.

'At the time,' Churchill went on, 'I told Anders that I was in no position to do so. I had no victories. All I had were failures. Only once I won a major victory would I be able to address Stalin on this matter.'

I objected, saying that the Poles themselves were to blame for what had happened to their families, and I briefly outlined the current situation. In general, the Poles follow an absurd, simply suicidal, line. There are two facts which nobody can change under any circumstances, namely: (1) the Poles are our neighbours and (2) the Poles number 20 million, while we number nearly 200 million. Proceeding from these circumstances, it would seem only reasonable for the Poles to strive to maintain good relations with the USSR. This would be quite possible, and even straightforward, should the Poles pursue a sensible policy, as we mean no harm to the Polish people, we want to maintain friendly relations with them, and we are in favour of a strong and independent Poland – within its ethnographic borders. We have never concealed this. I said this directly to Sikorski and Zaleski when we opened negotiations on a mutual aid pact in 1941. But what do we see in reality? In reality we see on the part of the Polish government only malevolence, slander, anti-Soviet intrigues and outrageous aspirations. And the result? The result was contained in the message from Comrade Stalin which I had brought with me.

'And I should say frankly,' I continued, 'that the British government bears its share of responsibility for the said result. Its tolerance of Polish outrages encouraged all sorts of Polish "extremists", who have thrown aside all restraint.'

Churchill objected, saying that the Poles have many good qualities, that they are very brave, staunch, etc.

I replied that nobody was questioning the Poles' bravery and valour, but, regrettably, they have not a grain of statesmanlike wisdom.

'Take, by way of contrast, the Czechs,' I continued. 'Our former relations with the Czechs have left a bad legacy… You surely know this.'

'Oh, yes, I am quite aware of it,' Churchill laughed.

'Nonetheless,' I concluded, 'We have very good relations with the Czechs today. Why? Because the Czechs don't get above themselves and know how to pursue a wise policy. They took a friendly line towards us several years before the war began, and they have shown how to behave during the war. They formed their army in the USSR, went to the front, fought bravely at Kharkov, and won the hearts of our people. A number of Czech soldiers were awarded Soviet medals, and one Czech was made a Hero of the Soviet Union. As a result, we are forgetting the past and Soviet–Czech friendship is growing and strengthening… This is what I call wise policy. And the Poles?'

Churchill kept silent and sucked slowly at his cigar. From time to time he took a sip of whisky and soda from the glass placed in front of him. Finally, he said: 'This Polish issue needs our full attention… In the next few days. I'll talk with Eden. And I'll send another message to Stalin. I'll need to think it over.'

I stayed with Churchill until almost midnight. We spoke a lot, discussing many issues. Quite a number of matters were raised besides Poland. Too many to remember. I shall note a few moments of particular interest.

Churchill stressed that of course he does not believe the German lies about the murder of 10,000 Polish officers… But is this so? At one point during our conversation, Churchill dropped the following remark: 'Even if the German statements were to prove true, my attitude towards you would not change. You are a brave people, Stalin is a great warrior, and at the moment I approach everything primarily as a soldier who is interested in defeating the common enemy as quickly as possible.'

At a different point in the conversation, Churchill told me that a couple of days earlier he had been informed by Sikorski of several thousand Polish officers 'missing' in the USSR. Sikorski asked Stalin about their fate in December 1941, but 'did not receive a clear answer'.

On a third occasion, Churchill suddenly started expounding the thought that 'everything can happen in war' and that lower-rank commanders acting on their own initiative are sometimes capable of 'doing terrible things'.[67]

I criticized Churchill firmly for his half-suspicions. He hastened to assure me that he harboured no suspicions whatsoever. But the impression remained that Churchill had some '*mental reservations*' concerning our innocence in the murder of the Polish officers.

Churchill recalled his meeting with Stalin with great pleasure. He said, among other things, that he had put the following question to Stalin: 'Tell me, what has been more difficult for you – this war or the collectivization of the peasants?'

Stalin, according to Churchill, said that collectivization was more difficult because he had to deal with tens of millions of stubborn people who failed to understand or see the advantages of the new system. Taking a somewhat philosophical tone, Churchill added: 'Collectivization cost you the lives of several hundred thousand people, possibly even millions, in one generation. But the next generations will derive great benefit from it without any further losses. We would not have acted like you did. We attach too much value to each individual life. We would probably have tried to stretch out the process for many years, in order to avoid such a concentration of losses in a short space of time. Consequently our next generations would also have had to pay a 'blood tax' for the restructuring of the system. Which method is better? I don't know. It could even be that yours is better. But I am quite sure that it can't be applied in our country.'

Churchill is highly impressed not only by Stalin's military prowess, but also by his military rank. There is even a degree of envy. Churchill told me today: 'I no longer call Stalin premier, I call him marshal! Of course, he is marshal and commander-in-chief!'

Then, turning to Bracken, he added with a laugh: 'Maybe I should be marshal, too?'

Bracken encouraged Churchill, but the latter retorted: 'No, I can't be marshal… We have no such title. Captain general, perhaps?'

Churchill burst into laughter again, but I could see that the idea of having a high military rank holds him in thrall. Then, addressing me in a more serious tone, he remarked: 'Basically, I am commander-in-chief here. Naturally enough, I can't always carry out what I want, but I can always prevent that which I don't want.'

Churchill asked me: 'How to explain the very poor performance of your army in the Finnish war? Göring even advanced a whole theory about this: that you did it on purpose to mislead Germany...'

'What nonsense!' I rejoined. 'To believe Göring, we deliberately provoked Germany to attack us, to devastate the Ukraine, Belorussia, the Caucasus... Who could believe such a thing?'

'I certainly don't,' Churchill said. 'Yet I fail to understand why your superb army performed so badly during the Finnish campaign. Why?'

'First,' I argued, 'we experienced failure only in the first half of the Finnish war. The Red Army fought very well in the second half and had big successes. It is enough to recall the breach of the Mannerheim Line. Second, why did things go rather badly for us in the first half of the war? The answer is simple. We had underestimated the enemy and had not prepared properly for the war. We had to rectify this mistake as we fought.'

Churchill concluded: 'Your explanation sounds convincing... Yet I must say that the Finnish campaign did you more harm than good. It created the impression in Germany and elsewhere, particularly among military experts, that the Red Army was weak. Had this not been so, Germany would probably not have risked attacking you...'

I asked Churchill: 'You were a member of the government during the last war and had dealings with the tsarist government. Now you are head of the government during this war and have dealings with the Soviet government. Tell me, do you perceive any difference between the two governments and if so, what is it?'

Churchill replied: 'Of course I do. The main thing is that the Soviet government is immeasurably stronger than the tsarist government was.'

He added: 'But what exists for me above all is Russia... Russia... Its people, its fields, its forests, its culture, music, dances... They never change... I deal with Russia, I wage war with Russia, and I want to build the future with Russia...'

And yet in his attitude to communism, Churchill is implacable. At one point he uttered: 'I don't want communism! It goes against our nature, our history, our view of life... If anyone came here wishing to establish communism in our country, I would fight him just as ferociously as I'm fighting the Nazis now!'

Churchill's voice resounded like a trumpet and his eyes burned with a hostile, angry flame.

It was past one in the morning when I returned home.

One last thing. During our talk, Churchill exclaimed: 'I hate Hitler and I want to destroy him! Not politically, but physically! Not in the gallows, nor against the wall – those are all forms of death that may help create legends around Hitler's name. After all, so many truly great people ended their lives in this way in the past and were later poeticized by posterity... No, I want Hitler to die in the electric chair like a criminal. Such a death cannot be poeticized! You can't build legends from a death like that!'

25 April

Our people know how to express themselves! Not very diplomatically perhaps, if they are to be judged by the standards of old diplomacy, but colourfully and robustly. 'The devil and his grandmother' (from Stalin's message to Churchill about Darlan) made a powerful impression on governmental and political circles in England. Here is another example.

In early April, Kerr informed Molotov by letter that the Rumanians were spreading rumours in one neutral country suggesting that Germany would soon be compelled to sue for peace with the USSR, conceding Eastern Europe and the Balkans to her as 'spheres of influence'. Comrade Molotov recently responded, also by letter, thanking the British ambassador for his communication and adding that nobody had yet approached us with an offer of peace and that if anyone (the Rumanians, the Japanese, etc.) so much as 'poked their noses in' with such a proposal on behalf of the Germans, we would 'send them to the devil'.

27 April

Yesterday I was summoned urgently from Bovingdon, where Agniya and I were spending Easter.

A new message from Stalin had arrived, which I was to deliver promptly to Churchill. It turned out that, after I had left, Churchill sent Stalin a new message on 24 April concerning the Polish question, in which he asked him not to aggravate the situation, adducing the 'American menace' as his cardinal argument. But his message contained nothing more specific than that.

Stalin replied that the matter of the 'severance' of ties with the Polish government had already been settled and that Molotov had presented Romer[i] (the Polish ambassador in Moscow) with a note in this vein on 25 April. Moreover: our note to Romer would be published in the Moscow evening press on 26 April.

So, the situation becomes more serious. Our objective, as it seems to me, is to explode Sikorski's government and clear the way for the creation of a more democratic and friendly Polish government by the time or at the time when the Red Army enters Polish territory. This course is correct: over the last year

[i] Tadeusz Romer, Polish ambassador to the Soviet Union, 1942–43; minister of foreign affairs, 1943–44.

and a half I have reached the conclusion that the London émigrés, including Sikorski's government, are quite hopeless. However, pursuing this line will bring us up against certain difficulties – from the British side and even more so from the side of the USA. Well, we shall have to overcome them. Perhaps some sort of acceptable compromise will emerge along the way. Time will tell.

I draw the following conclusion from our note: on the eve of the military events of the forthcoming summer campaign, the Soviet government feels very confident and deems this an appropriate moment to inform Britain and the USA through its actions: 'When it comes to Eastern Europe, we are the masters!'

This is pleasing.

28 April

Masaryk told me the following *story*.

Berlin. 1950. A stranger enters a large pub and takes a seat at a table where a German is drinking beer. The stranger also buys a jug of beer. After a while they strike up a conversation. The stranger asks: 'You don't happen to know what became of that strange, loud man, do you? The one with the little moustache?'

'With the little moustache?' the German repeats. 'Ah, perhaps you mean Hitler?'

'Yes, Hitler, Hitler,' nods the stranger.

'But of course I know!' the German replies. 'He's taken up his true occupation again: he's a decorator in Australia.'

The stranger takes two gulps of beer and asks another question: 'And do you know what happened to that big, fat chap?… The one who liked to cover himself with badges and medals whenever he went anywhere?'

'Who? Perhaps you mean Göring?' guesses the German.

'That's right, Göring! Now I remember!' replies the stranger.

'Göring?' repeats the German. 'Oh, Göring's doing all right for himself: he's a pilot for a private airline in South America.'

After another two gulps of beer, the stranger asks again: 'And what about that small, darkish, ugly one with the squeaky voice and the lame leg, where did he end up?'

'Squeaky voice and a lame leg?' asks the German, scratching his head. 'Oh, you mean Goebbels?'

'But of course, Goebbels! How could I forget?'

'Goebbels is just fine,' the German says. 'He edits a newspaper in West Africa.'

For a minute or two neither of them says anything. Eventually, the German addresses the stranger with a question: 'And why are you so interested in all this? Who would you be?'

'Me? I'm Lord Hess,' replies the stranger in perfect German, but with a slight English accent.

29 April

The Polish events are developing apace.

After delivering Stalin's message of 26 April to Churchill, I decided to take a 'wait-and-see' stance. In Polish–British circles, however, there was a flurry of activity. A series of meetings was held between Churchill and Eden on the one side and Sikorski and Raczyński on the other. The main issue concerned how the Polish government should respond to Molotov's note of 25 April. The Poles were on their high horses and the English were holding them back. The draft of the Polish communiqué was returned to the Polish government twice for revision. It was said that Churchill had given the Poles an earful for their behaviour. I don't know how true that is. One way or another, the long-awaited and repeatedly re-drafted Polish communiqué finally appeared in the evening of the 28th. Rothstein[i] read the text to me over the phone. It was worse than might have been expected.

At around eleven o'clock in the evening I received an unexpected call from Eden.

'Your *Soviet War News* is a good newspaper,' he said, 'but why does it attack Sikorski and his government so fiercely? "Hitler's agents"... "The fascists' helpers"... Are such expressions admissible? Whatever your attitude to Sikorski, you should remember that we, the British government, recognize the Polish government and treat it as an Allied government. The Cabinet has just resolved to take measures against the excesses of the Polish press, but if the *SWN* continues its attacks on the Polish government, I'm afraid it will be impossible to prevent the Polish press from retaliating. What good can all these rows do? We need to establish a calm atmosphere as soon as possible. It would make it easier to solve the problems at hand... I would be very grateful to you if you could give instructions to the *SWN* to show more restraint and civility.'

I asked Eden which specific *SWN* issues or articles he was referring to. It turned out that he was speaking about reprints of articles on the Polish question from *Pravda* and *Izvestiya*. Playing for time, I told Eden that I had not yet seen that particular issue and must first acquaint myself with it before returning to the matter he had raised. As a preliminary step, though, I said that the severity of *Pravda* and *Izvestiya* pale in comparison with the unbridled licence of the Polish press with respect to the USSR. If the British government has tolerated

[i] Andrew Rothstein, an active founding member of the British Communist Party and a close associate of Maisky; a correspondent for TASS in London, he became president of the Foreign Press Association, 1943–50.

this unruliness for over a year, why is Eden now so worked up about some editorial in a Moscow paper?

When this part of the discussion was over, Eden asked: 'Have you read the Polish communiqué that has just been released?... The PM and I really sweated over it!'

'No, I haven't read it, but I heard it over the phone,' I replied.

'And what was your impression?'

'Negative,' I snapped back.

'Negative?' Eden cried in disappointment. 'But why?'

'I would prefer not to comment until I have read the communiqué myself,' I replied.

And that was the end of our telephone conversation.

This morning I got an urgent call from Eden to come over and see him. It was our first meeting since I had visited Churchill in *Chartwell*. Eden did not keep me posted during the Polish–British talks of 27 and 28 April; I learned bits and pieces from other sources. Now Eden had evidently decided to carry out his duty 'as an ally' and inform me officially.

First, Eden acquainted me with Churchill's three messages to Stalin on the Polish question (25 and 25 April). Then he told me that in accordance with the prime minister's wishes, he had met Sikorski on the 24th and obtained a number of large concessions from him – concessions which made it possible to avoid a severance of relations. Churchill informed Stalin of these developments immediately by telegraph, but...

'Unfortunately, the prime minister's message arrived too late. Ties had already been severed. In Moscow Kerr went to see Molotov and tried to prevent the break-off, but he also met with failure.'

Eden looked genuinely distressed.

'In recent weeks,' he continued, 'everything had been going so well. Our relations with you were better than ever before. The prime minister was very satisfied. And all of a sudden such a blow!... I fear that this ill-starred Polish question may complicate relations between our countries. For my part, I'll do all I can for this not to happen, of course, but who knows?... I'd like to ask you, for your part, to help me keep Anglo-Soviet relations on the same friendly course as before.'

I replied that Eden should have no doubts about my help, but that I did not think my assistance was at all necessary. Entirely reasonable people are sitting there in Moscow and they, for their part, will do all they can to localize the complication that had arisen. I'm not so sure the same can be said of England. Eden's active assistance would be very useful here.

Eden assured me once more that he would do his bit.

I then moved on to the matter of the *SWN*. I said I had familiarized myself with the issue number which Eden had complained to me about yesterday and confessed that I had found nothing particularly vicious there.

'Just compare it with what is written in the Polish press!'

'But that was all in the past!' Eden reacted. 'Now we are taking steps to bring the Polish press into line. And we shall do so!'

Then, as if frightened by the categorical nature of his own words, Eden hastened to play safe: 'Provided, of course, that the Moscow press does not declare Sikorski a traitor day in day out.'

I replied that the Moscow press had the same right to express its opinion as the London press. And as for Eden's promise to restrain the Polish press, frankly speaking, I had to take it with a grain of salt. Past experience had taught me caution in this respect.

'No, now everything will be different!' Eden retorted. 'Give me some time. Remain calm for a while. And you will see the results.'

I said I would bear this request in mind.

'By the way,' Eden continued, 'that woman writer of yours back home… What's her name again?'

He rubbed his forehead, but couldn't remember.

I tried to help him. 'Wanda Wasilewska, perhaps?'

'Yes, that's it,' he said with relief. 'Wanda Wasilewska, exactly! A very dangerous woman!'

I laughed and replied: 'A brilliant writer!'

'And all the more dangerous for it!' Eden responded.

I couldn't help laughing. 'Just you wait. Wasilewska's novel *The Rainbow* is to be published in English translation soon. I'll send you a copy.'

'Very good,' Eden replied. 'In the meantime, let us arrange a truce in the press regarding the Polish issue.'

I said once more that I'd take his wish into consideration.

Then I referred to the communiqué. I said I had managed to read it and form a clear impression of this document. My opinion had not changed. I wouldn't start discussing the main points of communiqué. I just wanted to ask Eden one question: 'The "integrity of the Polish Republic" is underlined several times in the communiqué. Translated into plain language, this means the borders of 1939. Yesterday evening you told me that you and the prime minister had sweated over the communiqué. That seems to imply that you and Churchill are its co-authors. Should I deduce from this that the British government has recognized the 1939 Polish borders? It is important for me to know this before I advise my government on how it should interpret the meaning and significance of the communiqué.'

Eden was almost dumbfounded. Evidently it hadn't occurred to him that the events of the last two days might give rise to such an interpretation.

'Nothing of the kind!' Eden exclaimed with uncharacteristic fervour. 'The British government's stance on the matter of the Polish borders has not changed one bit. Everything remains as it was. It's wrong to name the prime minister and me as co-authors of the communiqué. Wrong! We told Sikorski bluntly: "This is your, Polish, communiqué! We are not responsible for it!" The prime minister and I made a few improvements to the initial Polish draft. That's all. Do you know what was in it? Just Smolensk graves and nothing else. The prime minister told Sikorski: "Stop thinking about the dead. You can't help them anyway! Think about the living, about what you can do for them!" The Poles yielded to our pressure. What has been published is the best that could have been achieved. But neither the prime minister nor I are co-authors.'

I let Eden finish and then said: 'Your distinction between what represents co-authorship and what doesn't is so subtle as to lie beyond my comprehension. But that is not the main point now. The main point is this: what can I tell my government about the British position regarding the Polish borders?'

'Tell your government,' Eden answered heatedly, 'that the British government, as before, does not in any way guarantee the Polish borders of 1939!'

30 April

Today, at five in the morning, Beatrice Webb died!

She had been unwell for the past ten days, lay unconscious for several days, and finally left this world.

What a bitter loss! Beatrice Webb was over 85, of course, but what of that?... She was her usual self just a few weeks ago when we visited *Liphook* – lively, talkative, deeply interested in all that surrounded her. She paid particular attention to the USSR, and to all the developments on the 'Russian front'.

What a sad blow! I had just been planning to visit the Webbs, to see them and talk to them...

So, Beatrice was the first to go of the glorious 'four'. Such a surprise. I did not think she would be the first.

['We both had a feeling for her,' Maisky wrote to H.G. Wells, 'which it is very difficult to describe, but which contained the elements of admiration, sympathy and warm friendship in the highest degree.'[68]]

30 April

I received an unexpected summons from Churchill today at about 5 p.m. He asked me to come immediately. On my way there I speculated as to why the prime minister needed me so urgently, and, after racking my brains and recalling his invitation on 9 April, I decided that the matter in question must be the *Soviet War News.*

I was not mistaken. But first Churchill declared that he wanted to inform me of a passage to be added to his message to Stalin of 28 April and to be sent to Moscow post factum following a special decision of the Cabinet. In this passage Churchill expressed his regret at Comrade Stalin's hasty actions in terminating ties with the Polish government, so hasty that Churchill was unable even to complete his 'conciliatory' efforts. Having read the passage, Churchill added: 'The Cabinet finds that I leaned too far in your direction and wishes to restore the balance with this addition.'

I couldn't restrain a snigger.

However, all this was a mere prelude. The main drama followed immediately afterwards. Today's issue of the *SWN* lay on Churchill's table. It carried Wanda Wasilewska's latest article published in *Izvestiya* (abridged and toned down). Poking his finger at the article and becoming increasingly heated as he spoke, Churchill roared: 'I don't want any more arguments about this matter! It merely poisons the atmosphere! I won't let the Poles attack you anymore, but I also can't allow you to attack the Poles – at least not here in London. In fact, it would be better if you were to stop attacking the Poles so much in Moscow as well. We simply have to seek ways of settling this conflict.'

Churchill continued in the same vein for a few more minutes. He became increasingly worked up, he almost started shouting, and his eyes were rolling wildly. The more the prime minister fumed, the calmer I became. When Churchill finally stopped, I said with a faint smile: 'Mr Churchill, in the first place, it is best not to get so excited. What is the point? We're better off speaking calmly and amicably. I'm sure we shall come to an understanding quicker that way. Secondly, you are indignant about Wanda Wasilewska's claim that Sikorski's government does not represent the Polish people. But is this really untrue? Whom does the Polish government in London actually represent?'

Churchill gestured vaguely with his hand and remarked: 'You know, if we were to start applying this criterion to all governments-in-exile, who knows where we'd end up… Just try defining who represents whom.'

'But you wouldn't claim,' I went on, 'that Sikorski's government was formed according to the letter of the British constitution, would you?'

The link between Sikorski and the British constitution amused Churchill so much that he laughed out loud and added more amiably: 'Be warned: if you try to attack Sikorski in the *Soviet War News* again, I'll publish an article in his defence in the *Britansky Soyuznik*.'

I replied: 'Thirdly, Mr Churchill, if you object to the publication of articles directed against Sikorski in our organ, I shall take your wishes into consideration. But on one condition: that the Polish press in London radically changes its behaviour. From now on I shall be watching it closely and acting accordingly.'

'No, no!' said Churchill. 'Rest assured: I shan't let the Poles behave outrageously! If you notice anything untoward in the Polish press, tell Eden or Cadogan.'

Saying this, Churchill nodded in the direction of Cadogan, who was sitting beside him (Eden was off on his 'weekend'!).

Assuming that the matter was settled, I rose to say goodbye. At that moment Cadogan bent forward to Churchill and whispered something in his ear.

'Yes, and by the way,' the prime minister began again, 'it seems that you are intending to set up a parallel Polish government in Moscow?... Bear in mind that we, the British government, will support Sikorski as before. And the Americans, as far as I know, will do the same.'

Churchill was getting worked up once again and raising his voice. Once again, I answered calmly: 'You shouldn't believe everything you hear! Germans spread false rumours, Poles pick them up, and good-natured Englishmen believe them. It's all complete nonsense. We don't intend to set up any kind of parallel government in Moscow.'

'Really?' Churchill and Cadogan exclaimed, as if they could not believe their ears. They both cheered up immediately.

'Yes, really!' I reassured them. 'I can say this with absolute certainty.'

Just a few hours before my meeting with Churchill I had received a message to that effect from Moscow, asking me to refute the rumours spread by the Germans.

'However,' I continued, 'we shall not be restoring ties with the present Polish government.'

Churchill's and Cadogan's spirits sank at once.

'But why not?' asked Churchill.

'How do you mean, why not?' I answered in surprise. 'Has not Sikorski's government revealed its true face through its behaviour? It is hostile, or at best semi-hostile, to the USSR. We could restore ties only with a Polish government that found ways of establishing cordial relations with us.'

Cadogan intervened and immediately sought to address the question from a practical point of view.

'Tell me, is the present Polish government unacceptable to you in its entirety? Or do you make exceptions? Sikorski, for instance?'

I replied that the composition of the Polish government was a matter for the Poles. I would not care to interfere. As for Sikorski personally, he appears to me to be a man who understands the importance of good relations with the USSR, but unfortunately he is too weak.

'Wait a month or two and you'll see changes!' exclaimed Churchill.

On parting, he remarked with admiration: 'Stalin is a wise man!'

Shaking my hand, he added: 'Now I'll leave for the weekend in a calmer state of mind.'

The weekend! Oh, that sacred British institution!

[Although convinced that a massacre had taken place, the British had been (as rightly established by the historian P.M.H. Bell) 'consciously engaged in deception, or in later jargon, a "cover-up"'.[69] Great care was taken not to damage Anglo-Russian relations. The Poles were urged to withdraw their demand for an inquiry, and the Ministry of Information was instructed to ensure that the British press 'did not canvass the Russo-Polish quarrel'. Although Maisky, too, was asked to exercise restraint, he appeared to be far more fearful of Stalin than of Churchill. The Soviet embassy's *Soviet War News* printed foul attacks on the Polish government, depicting the Poles as 'accomplices of the cannibal Hitler'. This provoked a strong reaction from both Eden and Churchill. The severity of the reproach is missing both from Maisky's diary and from his reports to Moscow. Cadogan, however, who was present, testifies that Maisky was accused of 'disseminating poison'. 'We kicked Maisky all round the room,' he entered in his diary with manifest delight, 'and it went v. well.' Maisky, commented Churchill, 'took all this quite well – as I am inclined to think Russians do take plain speaking'.[70]]

1 May

A surprise visit. Inspector Wilkinson of Scotland Yard (the very same inspector who guarded Molotov in London last year) came on behalf of the head of the Metropolitan Police, *Sir Philip Game*, to offer me special protection in view of the threats to have me killed that, according to reports at Scotland Yard's disposal, are spreading among circles of 'irresponsible Poles'.

I took a sceptical view of these reports. But Wilkinson insisted. Eventually I consented to there being more policemen on our street, around the embassy (Sikorski's HQ, opposite our embassy, does rather concern me), but I rejected the suggestion that I should be constantly escorted by a police car during my travels about town.

Note, 6 May

I informed Moscow of Wilkinson's visit and my reaction to it. I received instructions from Moscow to agree to a car escort. I shall have to do so, although I will find it inhibiting. I am not fond of being surrounded by 'pomp' (even police 'pomp').

2 May

The clock ticks, and the old near their end…

This thought struck me with particular insistence when Agniya and I went to see the Shaws a few days ago. We hadn't seen them for several months. We had heard from the Webbs that the Shaws were having a hard time of it: sick, down in the dumps, lonely. That they had some *troubles* or other with ration cards, petrol, servants. We'd been meaning to visit the old couple for some time – and now here we were.

Not much fun! Mrs Shaw is bed-bound. Agniya went into her room and spoke with her. Mrs Shaw is in a bad way: she has severe curvature of the spine and was all twisted. She's become very small and crooked. Complains of losing her memory: reads all the time and can't remember a word of it. Even forgets the names and faces of friends. She told Agniya that when she was 16 she fell off a horse and injured her spine. Then it passed. Mrs Shaw hurt her back on a few more occasions. While she was still in good health, she barely noticed a thing, but now nature has recalled her old sins and is taking its revenge.

'I can feel that I'm dying,' Mrs Shaw was saying. 'Inch by inch…'

Mrs Shaw is nearly 90, of course, but still…what a shame!

Shaw himself is better. After all, he's only 87! He looks much as he always has done: tall, slim, with a big grey beard and bushy, unruly white brows. His eyes are alive, restless, expressive. Only his complexion has become somehow paler, and a suspicious bluishness has begun to appear around the eyes, beneath the lids. As if his body were short of blood.

His passion for paradox and wit is intact.

'I made a discovery recently,' Shaw exclaimed, with a great sweeping gesture. 'Stalin is the most important Fabian in history!'

'How's that?' I replied with a laugh.

'Because Stalin took the socialism that the Fabians merely dreamed and nattered about and turned it into reality.'

I roared with laughter. Shaw hasn't changed.

Then Shaw launched into a furious diatribe against [Ivan] Pavlov. He's not fond of our great scholar. It's probably because Pavlov cut up dogs and rabbits, and Shaw, as we all know, is an anti-vivisectionist! Shaw won't say this openly, of course, so he tries to smear Pavlov in various roundabout ways. That's why Shaw started trying to convince me that 'Pavlov's so-called discoveries about the conditioned reflex and other such nonsense' are, first of all, not discoveries, and secondly, had been made long before Pavlov…by Shaw himself!

I roared once more.

Shaw hasn't stopped writing. At the moment he is busy compiling a 'Guide' for today's politicians and public figures. He's been working on it for two years now. He complains that the work is moving more slowly than he would like, but at least it is moving. I can just imagine the final result! If I am to believe what Shaw told me about the contents of the 'Guide' (although Shaw's accounts of his own writing are not always to be trusted), it will be a very witty text, dominated by irrepressible paradox. Poor Pavlov gets it in the neck here as well.

Then Shaw fell to reminiscing. Talked at length about his May Day – in 1889! I read about it all a few days later on the pages of *Reynolds News*.

How much longer will this couple hold out? I have a bad feeling about it all.

We thought we should visit the Webbs in the next few days.[71] We gave them our word that we would see the Shaws and distract them a little. That promise has been fulfilled. Now we can get together with the Webbs and have a good chat. Yesterday I heard that Mrs Webb is poorly. So we will have to wait a little.

Two couples. Our contemporaries. Comrades in their vision of the world, comrades in the struggle. Friends. Both world-famous. Both of similar age. In both, life's candle is burning right to the end…

Sad.

Agniya and I have been in England for so long now! When we arrived in 1932, the Shaws and the Webbs were still so vigorous, active, energetic. Every winter the Shaws would undertake some big *cruise* or other around the globe, during the course of which he would write a new work, while the Webbs were still working hard at their *Soviet Communism* and travelling to the USSR to gather new impressions and material. The Webbs' last trip abroad was in the spring of 1936, for a holiday after the publication of their monumental opus about the USSR. On that occasion, they visited the Balearic Islands. I saw them off at the station. They returned on the very eve of the war in Spain. How symbolic! It was then that Europe set foot on the 'path to war'. Never again has the old couple left England.

3 May

Just back from Beatrice Webb's funeral. A private affair. Only members of her extensive family were present, including Stafford Cripps and his wife. An exception was made only for Agniya and me: our friendship with the deceased was extremely close. The body was cremated in Woking. The crematorium is a quiet, solemn place: a modestly sized, handsome building in an enormous park with old, mighty trees. A service preceded the cremation, but it was very short – about five minutes long. The priest read some parting prayers, said some parting words. Then the coffin vanished in the wall, behind which lies the furnace…

The funeral was attended by more than 60 mostly ageing or even elderly people. Lots of grey hair, lots of wrinkles. After the funeral Beatrice's sister –

116. Chivalrous treatment of Agniya, who, together with Ivan Maisky, is a guest of Stafford Cripps, minister of aircraft production (second to the left of Maisky).

the youngest of the nine Potter sisters and the only one still alive – came up to us. A truly ancient woman! And in appearance nothing like majestic, inspired Beatrice.

Sidney Webb was also there. With his well-made black suit and fine black hat he exuded exceptional solemnity. His grey hair and grey beard stood out sharply against his dark attire. I was struck by Sidney's complexion: bright pink, unusually healthy... Healthy? Perhaps this was some trick of nature? Such things happen. But his eyes! They scared me: wide open, lids swollen, filled with pain. When Sidney saw us, they glistened with tears and became even scarier. Even so, he held himself together and didn't give in to his emotions. And in fact, according to Barbara Drake (Beatrice's niece), who was at *Passfield Corner* throughout Beatrice's final days, Sidney showed unexpected reserves of resilience, courage and restraint at this difficult time.

Returning home from Woking, Agniya and I experienced profound sadness. Gone forever was a great person, a strong spirit, a heartfelt friend of the USSR, our own close personal friend, the only one, perhaps, of all our English acquaintances that we truly loved.

[Maisky learnt of Litvinov's recall (which heralded his own) a couple of days before he attended Beatrice Webb's funeral, visiting the terminally ill Mrs Shaw, as well as H.G. Wells and Lloyd George.[72] His meetings with his long-standing close friends betrayed a strong sense – perhaps a mirror image – of his own ageing and fragility, if not of finality. Having emerged from the funeral, Maisky composed and deposited with Agniya his own political will.[73] That his testament, which focuses mainly on the fate of his diary, is linked to those events is evident in the concluding words of his long personal tribute to Beatrice Webb in *The Times* on 3 May: 'My only consolation is that her testament on the friendship between the British and Soviet peoples will become a living and lasting reality in the days to come.']

6 May

I found the following communication in today's 'Monitor':

> GERMANY'S FUTURE
> The following is taken from a speech given by M.B. Mitin, director of the Marx–Engels–Lenin Institute, on Moscow Radio, 5 May 1943, on the subject 'Karl Marx in the Struggle against German Reaction' on the occasion of the 125th anniversary of Marx's birth. M.B. Mitin noted the need for the German people to endure a period of great tribulation in order, among other objectives, to destroy German militarism once and for all, to incinerate the Nazi mob and all its satellites. 'This must be done in order for the German people to be given a chance to take their place in the global community of free democratic nations…'

Quite right. Matches my own thoughts. A useful *pointer* from Moscow.

12 May

The French communist Grenier called by. He arrived in London a few months ago to work with de Gaulle, in his capacity as representative of the Central Committee of the French party. I cannot say that they have made good use of Grenier: he currently serves as an 'adviser' in de Gaulle's Information Ministry, which is headed by the Christian socialist André Philip. Philip and Grenier do not get on, by all accounts, so he has no real job to do.

Grenier spoke a great deal about France's internal situation. Two conclusions follow from his description: (1) In France, the wave of 'Jacobin patriotism' is rising ever higher – Grenier particularly stressed the term 'Jacobin'; (2) the only organization that currently exists on a 'national' scale in France is the Communist Party. It is the CP, without doubt, that is leading the resistance movement against Germany.

Grenier drew a further conclusion from this: post-war France will be a leftist France, and the communists and elements close to them ought to play the leading role in France's Constituent Assembly of the future.

I asked Grenier what he thought the economic system of post-war France would look like.

Grenier replied that, in all likelihood, the big industries would be nationalized.

'Actually nationalized?' I queried.

Grenier hesitated. Then he said: 'At the very least, they will be placed under public control. The same goes for the banks.'

'And the peasantry?' I went on. 'Do you foresee any serious changes in this sphere as well? Something along the lines of rudimentary collectivization, the broad application of the cooperative principle?'

Grenier's face was a picture of horror.

'What are you saying?' he cried. 'The French peasant is incorrigible! He will never give up his private property, that's for sure. I don't see any major changes in this sphere.'

How revealing! Especially if one bears in mind that Grenier is a member of the French Central Committee.

* * *

H.G. Wells came for lunch.[74] There were three of us – me, Agniya and our guest.

Wells has aged terribly. His hands shake, he can barely walk. Just one flight of steps to the first floor and he is completely out of breath. Occasionally you can see in his eyes the sparkle of the author of *War of the Worlds* and *The Time Machine*, but for the most part they are clouded by a deathly film. Wells is 76 now and looking at him, I thought: 'Is it worth living to such an age?'

Nevertheless, Wells is still writing. And still writing well. It's enough to read his obituary for Beatrice Webb. It touched me deeply, and I wrote to Wells to say so. He was extremely flattered.

A young man's organism is filled to bursting with vital energy. He has enough of it for everything: writing talented novels, studying foreign languages, playing sports and preserving a radiant complexion. The closer one gets to old age, the more limited are those reserves of vital energy and the more prudently they need to be spent: no more sports, no more foreign languages, no more radiant complexion. Whatever energy remains has to be focused on that one, most important, most essential thing – writing. This is the stage at which Wells currently finds himself. Whatever energy he still has is expended entirely on writing. He is helped, of course, by his immense experience as a writer, by his refined literary technique, by the habits and inertia of a long literary life…

We spoke at length about this and that – chiefly, about humanity's future after the war. Wells kept emphasizing that modern technology is turning the world into one single system, while the old psychology is breaking it up into dozens of nationally isolated entities. Unless this contradiction is resolved, humanity will perish. Will it be resolved?

Wells is not entirely confident it will. He said: 'Either the world will advance through rapid leaps, or it will become a desert. There is no alternative.'

Wells pins his hopes on the USSR, but feels that his soul contains 'reserves' of some kind. I am not surprised. The muddle in Wells' head is quite something. The contradiction he speaks of is real. The very fact that he articulates it indicates the presence of some logical thought. But when it comes to the question of how this contradiction can be resolved, all hell breaks loose in Wells' mind and he suddenly declares: 'We must create a "Fifth International"!'

I'm not joking. At the start of our war Wells submitted an article to *Soviet War News*, in which he tried to prove the necessity of forming a 'Fifth International'. Poor [S.N.] Rostovsky came to me in a state of complete desperation: what should he do? I advised him to send the article back to the author with a note to the effect that *SWN* is not a newspaper and it only publishes material received from Moscow.

Wells also said this today: 'What a giant that Lenin was!'

And then, alluding to his meeting with him in 1920, added: 'He was right then, and I was wrong!'

Thank you for acknowledging the fact! Just a shame that Wells has needed almost a quarter of a century and a second world war to see the error of his ways. A high price!

Then the subject turned to Stalin and Wells remarked: 'I like "Uncle Joe" very much… He's a great man. I'm not even sure who's greater: Lenin or Stalin. It would be truer to say that each is No. 1 in his own way.'

Well, that's progress: Wells is acknowledging Stalin's greatness now, without waiting for 23 years to elapse.

16 May (Bovingdon)

Three weeks since I was last at Bovingdon. A lovely day: heat, sun, blue sky, flowers all around.

I keep thinking about the future. All quiet on our front. It has been like that for almost two months. But this, one feels, is just the calm before the storm. When will the storm erupt? And where? Each new day receives my intense scrutiny. But no clarity as yet.

On 13 May operations ceased in Tunisia. Complete victory: 175,000 men have been captured along with 19 generals (including German Commander-in-Chief von Arnim).[i] More than 1,000 weapons seized, as well as 250 tanks and

[i] Hans-Jürgen von Arnim, general, replaced Rommel as commander of the Army Group Africa in December 1942.

about 500 planes. It is clear that in the final phase of the struggle the Germans simply 'cracked'. There is no other way of explaining what happened. Hence the modest losses on the British side. A good sign. The 'invincible' army with its 'invincible' morale is beginning to show weakness. First at Stalingrad, now in Tunisia. Churchill's personal contribution to the liberation of N[orth] Africa from the 'Axis' is very great indeed. Were it not for him, nothing would have happened. I can say this with confidence, having observed at close quarters all the ups and downs of Great Britain's three-year African campaign.

What next?

Soon the British and Americans will strike against S[outhern] Italy and its islands. Will Hitler strike in the east before that happens?

There are currently two theories in play. One states that Hitler will wait it out and refrain from a large offensive in the USSR until the true intentions of the British and Americans have become clear. If these intentions turn out to be sufficiently dangerous from his point of view, he may rule out offensive operations in the east altogether. The other theory states that Hitler will strike in the east any day now and will make one final, definitive attempt to destroy the Red Army or, at any rate, weaken it to such an extent that it will cease to be an active factor in the subsequent course of the war.

Who is right?

For my part, I believe that Hitler will soon strike in the east.

20 May

The ironies of protocol: at this thanksgiving I ended up being placed next to Sikorski. A matter of diplomatic seniority? The Polish ambassador comes after me, and the seating of émigré governments is meant to follow the same principles of seniority as are applied to the corresponding ambassadors in the Court of St James's. Sikorski greeted both me and Agniya. Raczyński and his wife 'walked straight past'!

The fact that Sikorski and I sat next to each other has, of course, been noticed by all today's newspapers.

26 May

The first anniversary of the Anglo-Soviet treaty. Duly celebrated in Moscow and London.

Aside from an exchange of telegrams between Kalinin and the king, and between Molotov and Eden, aside from corresponding articles in both countries' press, and aside from corresponding statements on the BBC and Radio Moscow, there have been two ceremonial lunches.

In Moscow, Molotov invited the personnel of the British embassy and the British military mission plus Standley and Joseph Davies (the latter just happened to be in the USSR at the time). Our side was represented by Molotov, Mikoyan, Litvinov (who had just arrived in Moscow), Vyshinsky, Dekanozov and others. There were speeches. Kerr, incidentally, rose to eloquence, drawing a comparison between the Anglo-Soviet treaty and an infant hero requiring attentive care.

It was all rather different in London. Eden also organized a lunch, but the invitees on the British side were members of the War Cabinet (Eden, Anderson, Lyttelton, Attlee, Bevin; neither Morrison nor Churchill could attend, as the former was busy in parliament and the latter was in Washington), *service ministers* (Alexander, Grigg, Sinclair), deputy chiefs of staff (the chiefs themselves are in Washington), Cripps and Cadogan. Our side was represented by myself, Sobolev, Zinchenko, Kharlamov, Sklyarov, Borisenko and Dragun. Good food, but no speeches. There were, however, toasts, accompanied by 'a few words' – depending on the toast. Eden raised a glass first for the king and Kalinin, then for Stalin. I responded with a toast for Churchill. Then Eden proposed a toast for me, and I proposed one for him. And that was that.

To mark the first anniversary, the Ministry of Foreign Affairs and Ministry of Information have commissioned a large painting from Salisbury that depicts the signing of the treaty. The picture is ready and will be dispatched to the USSR any day now. Its artistic quality is not high, but as a historical document it has its uses. It reproduces the office of the minister of foreign affairs. Seated at the table, in a variety of poses, are (from right to left): Sinclair, Cadogan, Attlee, Churchill, Eden, Molotov, me and Sobolev. Behind are two secretaries (the British one is not known to me; ours is Kozyrev).

At today's lunch my neighbour to my right was Anderson (Eden was to my left). He couldn't contain his delight about British successes at sea. During the month of May, 25 German submarines have been destroyed, i.e. more than Germany produces during the same period of time. I asked whether the current month was a welcome exception, or whether it represents a turning point in the naval war in the Allies' favour. Anderson replied that the May successes are no whim of fate, but the result of a complex web of initiatives undertaken by the British government.

'Yes,' Anderson declared. 'In the war at sea, as in the war on land, there has been a turn in the desired direction.'

Next I asked Anderson (who is closely linked to all manner of academic research in matters related to the war) whether the British had any information or even merely indirect evidence that this year the Germans have some new, unprecedented, secret and powerful weapon at their disposal against which no antidote has yet been devised and which they can deploy on the Soviet (or some other) front.

Anderson replied that, although such surprises can never be ruled out in theory, in reality the British have not yet received any reports or even indirect hints about German possession of new and secret types of weapons, including gas weapons.

If that is the case, Germany has no way out. It cannot avoid being destroyed. It is just a matter of time.

Eden spoke with great empathy about the dissolution of the Comintern: 'This is a very wise step, whose effect will be very considerable, especially in America.'

* * *

The British give the following statistics about the deployment of front-line German aircraft at the current time: 1,800 in the USSR, 1,600 in the west, including Norway, 900 in the Mediterranean. The total quantity, therefore, is 4,300.

27 May

Yesterday Agniya and I went to see Lloyd George at *Churt*.

The old man is becoming more and more decrepit. Age has really caught up with him in the last 5–6 months. This is not the Lloyd George I used to know. How long will he last?...

We drank tea. Chatted. Lloyd George is in an irritable, carping mood. Especially when it comes to Churchill. Lloyd George finds something dark and sinister in whatever Churchill does. Might it be because the old man has been twiddling his thumbs during this war, and now he is taking it out on Churchill?

Churchill's statement to the press in Washington has prompted gloomy thoughts in Lloyd George. Lloyd George is convinced that a decision has been taken to divide the Allied forces equally between the west and the F. East. I objected, citing Eden. But Lloyd George does not believe Eden and claims that from now on the USA will only really be fighting with Japan; in Europe, it will limit itself to a 'symbolic' operational role. From this Lloyd George drew the conclusion that the war will drag on and require gigantic losses; there can be no question of the war in Europe ending in 1944.

We also spoke about Poland. Lloyd George supports our position and criticizes the Poles. He recalled how many *troubles* the Poles caused in the last war.

'There wasn't one sensible man among them!' Lloyd George exclaimed. 'All dreamers, megalomaniacs, impudent aggressors!… The best of the bunch was Paderewski,[i] but he was clueless when it came to politics and weak in character. Egged on by Clemenceau, the Poles lost all restraint and refused to listen to me or Wilson. The consequences are now plain to see.'

Lloyd George believes that the USSR would be best off ignoring the Polish government and putting off its 'reorganization', since it would be impossible to make up a satisfactory government in any case: there are no such people outside Poland. When the Red Army restores the 1941 borders, everything will fall into place by itself.

I think Lloyd George is right about this. My thoughts have often leaned in the same direction.

Over tea, Lloyd George suddenly asked me: 'Have you ever looked closely at Hitler's signature?'

I looked at Lloyd George in bewilderment and simply replied: 'No!'

Lloyd George got up from his chair, hobbled somewhat towards his desk and, returning with a piece of paper, gave me a demonstration of Hitler's signature. As he did so, the last two letters in Hitler's surname dropped sharply. Pointing to them, Lloyd George said with a very meaningful air: 'Now pay attention to this. There's a reason behind it.'

Again I looked at him in bewilderment and asked: 'And what is it supposed to mean?'

Lloyd George hesitated for a moment before replying, with a very particular grin: 'Who knows? A great deal, perhaps… The signature of the late leader of the Conservative Party, Bonar Law, was distinguished by the very same characteristic.'

I still did not understand what Lloyd George was getting at. Then he condescended to my 'ignorance' and gave the following explanation: when, during the last war, Asquith hit rock bottom and the question of the next prime minister arose, the first candidate earmarked for the role was Bonar Law. Everything was agreed, every group and authority had given its blessing. But at the very last moment Bonar Law chose to behave like [Gogol's] Podkolesin:[75] he got cold feet and rejected the post. As a result, Lloyd George became prime minister. Now the old man is thinking: mightn't the same thing happen with Hitler? Mightn't he get cold feet at the last minute and fail?…

I listened to these deliberations and couldn't help recalling the pitiful cry of Taras Bulba: 'Oh, old age! Old age!'

---

[i] Ignacy Jan Paderewski, Polish prime minister and foreign minister in 1919, representing Poland at the Paris Peace Conference in 1919.

* * *

Today I had a long conversation with Eden about Britain's post-war prospects and Anglo-Soviet relations.

28 May

I can't help thinking back to my first meeting with the old queen. On 8 November 1932, I presented my credentials to the king. The next day, 9 November, Agniya presented herself to Queen Mary (at the time George V was king). I accompanied Agniya.

Queen Mary received us in her boudoir. It was obviously costing her a great effort to do the 'Bolsheviks' this honour. And she was hardly concealing her feelings. The entire audience lasted no longer than five minutes. The queen asked Agniya when she arrived and whether she had visited England before. She kept her eyes fixed above our heads, staring straight at the wall. She sighed with relief when we took our leave.

Nevertheless, the queen received Agniya immediately after I presented my credentials. She did not receive Sokolnikova [wife of the previous ambassador, G.Y. Sokolnikov] for almost a month and a half after her husband presented his credentials and only did so after Kagan made the corresponding démarche in the FO.

That is what the English call progress!

29 May

A week has passed since the Comintern was dissolved. The upshot?

First and foremost: this is a very important milestone in the development not only of the USSR but of the entire world. It means that we are not counting on revolution after the war. Needless to say, the war can and will result in all manner of disturbances, strikes, uprisings and so on in various countries, but that is something different. A real, full-blooded proletarian revolution is clearly not anticipated. Which is no surprise to me after the conversations I had in Moscow in December 1941.

But if not a proletarian revolution, then what? This still remains vague, and it cannot be otherwise. Time will tell. But I certainly do not rule out the appearance after the war of a new International – not a second and not a third, but some other kind.

Next: why was the Comintern dissolved? The reasons are clear: fundamentally, the Comintern has been dead for a long time, but its ghost created major difficulties in relations between the USSR and other powers, and also in relations between local communist parties and other workers' parties and organizations in various countries. Now, when the most essential task is to consolidate a united front of all forces to destroy Hitler's Germany, this ghost has had to be liquidated.

Thirdly: what was the reaction of the outside world to the dissolution of the Comintern? Most favourable. On the one side, Goebbels is livid (he has been deprived of his most effective propaganda scarecrow), on the other, the average American has sighed with relief (no more scary 'Reds' under his bed). In England, the Conservatives couldn't be happier. Churchill, when asked by a journalist in Washington what he thought of the dissolution of the Comintern, gave a brief but telling reply: '*I like it.*' And Eden told me just the other day: 'This is a very wise step, one which will have extremely favourable consequences – especially in the USA.' The Tory press (in particular, *The Times*) warmly welcomed Moscow's decision. Only the *Telegraph* said nothing, but that, too, is understandable. Camrose[i] is unsympathetic to the notion of an Anglo-Soviet union being preserved after the war. Camrose and Kemsley (*Sunday Times* and others) have not forgotten Chamberlain.

In Labour circles, by contrast, the dissolution of the Comintern has elicited mixed feelings. On the one hand, the Labourites are pleased, because they understand how important this is from the foreign policy and military point of view. But on the other hand, they are displeased, because they understand that the dissolution of the Comintern has greatly complicated their situation, from the point of view of internal politics. And one can see why: it has deprived them of a crucial weapon against the communists. The Labour leaders, needless to say, will find some other way of excluding the Communist Party from its ranks, but all the same its position vis-à-vis the communists has been weakened, while the position of the communists vis-à-vis the Labour Party has been strengthened. Attlee and Co. were confident that the Communist Party's request for *affiliation* would meet with swift rejection at the forthcoming Labour Party conference, on 11 June, but now – who knows? Rejection, I expect, is still guaranteed, but will it be swift? Time will tell. Besides, even if the Communist Party remains outside the Labour Party, as before, its appeal will undoubtedly increase, thanks to the dissolution of the Comintern. So Labour will have a more dangerous competitor than in the past. That is also unpleasant.

In order to get out of this situation, Labour has put out a slogan: if the Communist Party is sincere in its concern for the unity of the workers' movement, then it should follow the example of the Comintern and dissolve itself. They must think we are stupid!

---

[i] William Ewart Berry (1st Viscount Camrose) and his brother Viscount Kemsley (see below) were the owners and chief editors of numerous papers, among them the *Sunday Times* (1915–37), *The Telegraph*, *The War Illustrated* and the *Financial Times*.

Bevin came for lunch the other day. In the course of conversation, he asked: 'Tell me, has the Comintern really, properly been dissolved?'

I looked at Bevin in astonishment and replied: 'Why, do you think we are just fooling around?'

Bevin was embarrassed and beat a quick retreat. We moved on to another topic. After a short while Bevin asked again, as if in passing: 'But do you not think that the dissolution of the Comintern may be followed by the dissolution of the CPSU?'

Once again I looked at Bevin in astonishment and asked in my turn: 'And what will take the place of the CPSU?'

Bevin thought about it and replied without much confidence: 'I don't know, military dictatorship... or something of the kind.'

I laughed at Bevin, but the train of his thoughts was entirely clear to me. After all, wouldn't it be wonderful if the CPSU dissolved itself and in its place there arose a Russian version of the Labour Party! How easy it would be then to do away with all the communist parties in the world, especially the English one!

The intellectual subtlety of the Labour leaders does not bear thinking about!

It is hard to predict the future, but it seems to me that right now, after the dissolution of the Comintern, the Brit[ish] Communist Party actually has a fighting chance – providing, of course, it can capitalize on this opportunity. Can it? I don't know. Time will tell.

The reasons for this opportunity are as follows. A revolution in England would be possible, even inevitable, only in the event of its Empire being lost. It is already clear now, however, that England will come out of the war having not just retained, but even augmented its Empire, if only in an indirect form. Its ruling class, therefore, will be able to get by without fascism and to continue governing nation and empire with velvet gloves. One of the probable consequences of this course of events will be a split in the Labour Party after the war. There will be a repeat, more or less, of what happened in 1931, when MacDonald, Snowden, Thomas and others defected to the Conservatives – only on a much larger scale. In such circumstances, the Communist Party could play a major role in the fate of the British workers' movement. But will it? We will see.

[The Comintern had been a millstone around the neck of Soviet diplomacy since the late 1920s. In the midst of his desperate attempts to appease Germany in mid-1941, Stalin was resolved to free himself from the ideological shackles which limited his political manoeuvrability by taking initial steps to dissolve it.[76] The formal dissolution in May 1943 served the same purpose, but now paved the way for a post-war arrangement with the Allies. Maisky went on to explain to his interlocutors in the Foreign Office that in reality the Comintern had been 'moribund for years' and its dispersal was a natural result of 'Stalin's policy of nationalism … Lenin thought the Russian revolution could only survive if there were world revolution; Stalin thought Russia big enough to make the experiment alone and if she succeeded that would be the best propaganda for communism.'[77] Maisky vehemently rejected Lloyd George's suggestion that communism was bound to triumph in Germany once Nazism collapsed. Russia's wish, he insisted, was 'not to make Communistic revolutions for other countries, but to secure frontiers and generally to secure the restoration of [Russia]'.[78]]

30 May (Bovingdon)

Still quiet on our front. True, resistance remains stubborn near Novorossiisk, and there are quite serious local skirmishes near Lisichansk, Sevsk and so on. But that's not the same thing. I was expecting a big German offensive in mid-May. Our press also warned the army and citizenry about the likelihood of major developments in May. But May has passed and calm continues to reign over the Soviet–German front. This is, needless to say, the calm before the storm, but still: however one looks at it, we have gained three weeks. Last year the Germans began their offensive – in the Crimea – on 8 May. Today is 30 May, and there is no sign of an offensive. Well, even three weeks is not to be sniffed at!

1 June

Eden has flown to Algiers. For the following reasons.

From Washington, Churchill went to N. Africa by aeroplane, as Eden told me last week. He surmised that this was related to preparations for operations against Italy. On Saturday, 29 May, I arranged a meeting with Eden for Monday, 31 May, at 4.30 p.m. But yesterday, at about 3 p.m., Eden's secretary called and informed Iris that unfortunately Eden would not be able to see me that day. At my instruction, Iris requested another time for my visit. Eden's secretary fixed an appointment for today. But this morning Harvey (Eden's private secretary) called me directly and proposed a meeting with Cadogan rather than Eden. I asked him what this was all about. Harvey replied that he would like to see me and discuss the matter. As it happens, I was about to go to parliament for the debate on the future of civil aviation. We agreed that Harvey would come to parliament as well. He did indeed arrive and informed me that Churchill had summoned Eden to Algiers as a matter of urgency, and that Eden had flown there yesterday.

At 4 p.m. I called on Cadogan and enquired about the reasons behind such an unexpected turn of events. Cadogan replied that he did not know the full story himself.[79] On Sunday, 30 May, a telegram addressed to Eden came through from Churchill in which the prime minister said that, if the situation in parliament permitted, it would be a good thing for Eden to fly to Algiers forthwith. 'Much is happening here,' Churchill added, 'that requires your presence.' Churchill did not clarify what he meant by 'much'. Eden was already on his way to the airfield when a second telegram arrived in which Churchill mainly touched on French affairs, adding: 'Here we are expecting the marriage of groom (i.e. de Gaulle) and bride (i.e. Giraud). It would be useful if you could be present in the capacity of best man.' Still, according to Cadogan, the second telegram was formulated in such a way that it remained not entirely clear whether Churchill wanted to see Eden only on account of the French or for other reasons as well. In any case, Eden is now in Algiers. Cadogan is expecting his return later in the week.

I also talked to Cadogan about the new convoy across the Mediterranean Sea, about our provision of Mosquito aeroplanes, and other things.

2 June

Butler came for lunch. We spoke a great deal about England's post-war prospects (aside from being nat[ional] education minister,[80] Butler is also chair of the Conservative Party's Committee on Post-War Problems). Butler anticipates that Britain's future development will take the following paths:

(1) A mixed type of economy, i.e. some sectors (electricity, the railways, possibly coal) will be nationalized, some (road and sea transport, civil aviation, etc.) will come under *public control*, and the rest will remain in the hands of individual entrepreneurs.

(2) The 'constitutional factory' will gradually emerge, i.e. factories in which workers' representatives will participate in the management of the business. Among the supporters of this idea is Butler's father-in-law Courtauld (artificial silk).

(3) The education system should be democratized, i.e. almost all *public schools* should be abolished (though Butler would like to keep two or three of them) and the number of state bursaries in secondary schools should be greatly increased.

I asked Butler: 'So you want England to develop along Fabian lines?'

Butler replied: 'Call it what you will. We English, you know, can do revolutionary things, so long as they are done under the old names.'

Fabianism, of course, is not revolution. But for the Conservatives it might as well be. Butler (who undoubtedly reflects the mood of the ruling Tory elite) is clearly thinking of Fabianism, though he doesn't want to name it.

Then Butler spoke at length about the need for friendship and collaboration between our countries after the war, before asking: 'If England develops along what you call Fabian lines, will this, do you imagine, help to strengthen relations between us?'

'I think it will,' I replied.

Butler was visibly impressed by my reply.

[Butler informed Eden of the 'long entre tien' with Maisky. He thought that 'Psychologically his general approach is not at all uninteresting and I have never taken the view that he is either quite uninformed of his country's views or without influence.' The candid conversation very much revealed the strength and consistency of Maisky's belief that Anglo-Soviet interests coincided and that at present both were facing the danger of the United States 'entering upon a period of Imperialism'. The Americans, he maintained, 'had always been pushing towards a frontier, and now their frontier would be the world, and they would stretch out their tentacles as far as they could'. With the end of his mission looming on the horizon, Maisky allowed himself to be in an exceptionally expansive mood. He seemed to be, noted Butler, 'in a more carefree, philosophical and historical frame of mind than usual'. Digressing into history, he argued that the French Revolution had marked 'the bridge between Feudalism and Capitalism', while the Russian Revolution could mark 'the bridge between Capitalism and Economic Democracy'. In clairvoyant fashion, he argued that economic controls would have to be removed on the international scene. He went on to 'praise the genius of Marshal Stalin' who knew how to time strategic and political moves accurately. The move to disband the Comintern was 'an indication that the Soviet Union were looking ahead to real international collaboration, both in Asia and in Europe'.[81]]

3 June

Morrison came for lunch. It so happened that our conversation also revolved for the most part around the subject of post-war problems. Morrison expounded on ideas with which I was already familiar from his speeches, published a few days ago in the small collection *Prospects and Policies*. The more Morrison spoke, the more I was struck by the convergence of his views with those of Butler. Of course, there are certain differences of nuance and emphasis between the two men, but essentially they share the same fundamental platform. Astonishing! Listening to Morrison, I thought how easy it will be after the war for the Conservatives to reach agreement with Labour on matters of internal reconstruction in England, assuming, of course, that the proletariat will allow the likes of Morrison to continue playing their game… I fear they will!

Morrison said that he is still undecided in his own mind about the question of whether or not to continue the coalition with the Conservatives after the war. He even asked my advice. But I side-stepped the role of counsellor.

My general impression is that, in the absence of any utterly exceptional circumstances, Morrison will eventually decide in favour of a coalition.

4 June

Agniya and I went to see Webb.

The house we know so well is still there. But approaching it on this occasion, we were not met, as in the past, by a tall, beautiful old woman with lively eyes and a profoundly spiritual face…

Inside, the house is just as it was. Clean, cosy, tidy. A faint smell of carbolic acid. The same two elderly Scottish women who, in the capacities of cook and maid, served the Webbs for so many, many years. They still look after the old man. There is also the *Nurse*.

We went through to the *drawing room*, where we were such frequent guests in the past. We sat in the armchairs, as in the past. Once again, the lady of the house was not to be seen in her usual place – the low step by the fireplace. But on the bookcase nearby was a large white urn – with the ashes of she who was never to return.

'I've found a spot in the woods,' said Webb, slowly, 'which is just right for this urn, but it takes so long for orders to be processed at the moment and I am still waiting for the bronze slab with the inscription…'

Then, after a period of silence, the old man added: 'That's where I will end up, too.'

Webb is clearly unable to shake off thoughts of his own approaching death. I picked up several other signs of this. No wonder: he is 83, five years ago he experienced a stroke from which he has still not fully recovered, and his companion of half a century, with whom he formed a single physical and spiritual whole, has just gone for good.

'I feel very lonely,' he said in passing.

Before adding: 'I can no longer write, I find it difficult to walk, I'm losing my memory… I can still read, but I get nothing out of it…'

Agniya said what a marvellous woman Beatrice was and described the conversation we had with Lloyd George about her a few days ago. Lloyd George also considers Beatrice an utterly exceptional phenomenon in English history. Together we had gone through a list of other great daughters of England and come to the conclusion that the only one who can compare with Beatrice in stature is Queen Elizabeth. All this evidently pleased the old man. You could see that he often thinks about such things himself. At a certain point he asked pensively: 'And Florence Nightingale?'

It would seem, then, that it is precisely Florence, that wonderful woman, whom the old man considers most comparable to Beatrice.

Webb, however, has not lost all interest in the present day. I told him about my recent talks with Butler and Morrison. Webb listened attentively, then said: 'That isn't surprising. It would not be the first time in our history that the Tories have taken their opponents' agenda and made it a reality. It is perfectly possible that the socialization of England – along Fabian lines – will be carried out by the new breed of Conservatives. That would be entirely in the English spirit.'

The old man told me that almost all the books put out by the Webbs were written by him. The idea for the book, the outline, the gathering of material and so on would all be done jointly. But the actual process of writing was Webb's responsibility. Usually, Beatrice would just cast a critical eye over the text, make corrections and additions – after joint discussion, of course. Webb always wrote evenly, assiduously and quickly – by hand. He just couldn't get used to typewriters. An example: the book *Soviet Communism* (more than 1,000 pages long) was written over two years. 'Written' in the narrowest sense of the word. The gathering of material, the thinking, etcetera, took another two and a half years or so.

Webb's account surprised me a little. I already knew that, in this marvellous 'union of two', spiritual primacy belonged to Beatrice. I had observed this in practice on numerous occasions. I also knew that most of the drafting was carried out by Sidney, that Beatrice usually provided the thoughts, the idea, the general outline and plan for the book, which Sidney filled in with figures and facts. I had imagined that Sidney usually wrote most of their books, with Beatrice contributing only the crucial, summarizing chapters. But I had never thought that practically all of the writing fell to Sidney.

Webb said that after his death their entire home, with all its books, manuscripts and materials, would be handed over to the *London School of Economics*. As for Beatrice's memoirs (which went up to 1911) and her diaries (which she kept almost until her death), their fate would be determined by the five *Trustees* she had chosen during her life: Barbara Drake, Harold Laski, Margaret Cole, [John] Parker (secretary of the Fabian Society) and Saunders (director of the *School of Economics*).

As we were leaving, the Scottish women started complaining to Agniya about food shortages: the old man needs apples and fruit, but there are hardly any to be found. Agniya promised to take action.

5 June

On 1 June, I spent almost the entire day in parliament, attending the debate on civil aviation. I listened closely to all the speeches, all the arguments, fears and hopes…

My personal view is that the first practical steps towards solving the problem of civil aviation after the war might be roughly as follows:

(1) The USSR, the Brit[ish] Empire and the USA – each should have its own civil air fleet, operating within the confines of each. These three chunks of the

world are so large (while also possessing sizeable aviation industries) that they can each lay claim to their own independent, 'national' air fleet.

(2) In Europe (i.e. in the geographical space between England and the USSR) an international community for civil aviation should be formed. It will include all European countries, including the USSR and England. Taken individually, the European countries are too small in territorial terms, and too weak in aircraft construction, for any plans to be viable.

(3) In Asia (i.e. in the geographical space between the USSR, the Brit[ish] Empire and the USA) a similar type of international community should be formed as in Europe. It will include the USSR, China, Holland, the Brit[ish] Empire, the USA, Siam.

(4) France and its empire could, I suppose, be a member of two schemes – that of the British Empire (since France's possessions are geographically mixed up with Britain's) and that of the European community.

(5) Turkey, Iran, Afghanistan, Egypt, Arabia, Abyssinia – the *Middle East* in general – could all be joined either to the European, or to the British, or to the Soviet scheme.

(6) Southern and Central America would, naturally, enter the American scheme.

(7) It would make most sense to put air traffic across the Atlantic and Pacific oceans in the hands of the European and Asian schemes.

(8) Germany, Italy and Japan should be deprived of the right to participate in any such civil aviation scheme.

(9) There should be agreement between all the separate schemes that passengers can travel without impediment along all the global air routes. Formalities should be reduced to a minimum. Timetables should be precisely aligned. At the head of each of the schemes there should be a worldwide council to regulate all matters of global air communication.

(10) The right to fly over the territory of the USSR should belong, as a rule, only to Soviet aviation, over the territory of the USA – to American aviation, over the territory of Britain and its larger possessions – to British aviation. The right to fly over other territories (Europe, Asia, the oceans) should be granted to a mixture of aircraft industries in accordance with special agreements.

These are the fundamental principles on which, it seems to me, civil aviation can be based in the initial post-war period. This, of course, is merely a sketch. Each of the aforementioned points requires further thought and refinement. It is possible, indeed certain, that adjustments will have to be made to the plan I have outlined. But what matters most here is the fundamental idea. A higher level of internationalization in the nearest future is not, in my view, practicable.

6 June (Bovingdon)

Still quiet on our front – at least, on the ground. The major German offensive that was expected this summer has still not materialized, and General Dietmar (the main German radio commentator) has even started claiming that it is now in Germany's interests to take up defensive positions. Some German newspapers go so far as to say that Germany must have a year of relative calm in order to prepare for the next phase of the war. All of this sounds most suspicious. More like disinformation. Let's see.

In the skies, however, the battle becomes ever fiercer, and today's communications from Moscow make one think that, alongside the uncertainty surrounding the second front, the relative weakness of the Germans in the air is another reason for the postponement of the offensive. Indeed, within the space of a single day – 2 June – the Germans lost 243 aeroplanes, 162 of them over Kursk. It is unsurprising that, having lost the dominance in the air to which they are accustomed, and instead coming face to face with the aerial dominance of the enemy, they should be so hesitant about the offensive. After all, the Germans are down to their last reserves. If these reserves are eliminated without yielding a resolution to the war, at least on the eastern front, then Germany is ruined. It has no choice but to exercise caution, to think twice before it acts.

Nevertheless, I still do not think there are grounds for excluding the possibility of a major German offensive this summer.

* * *

In Bovingdon today, Negrín received a visit from [Jules] Moch, the French socialist, a former minister in several French governments, and a man close to Blum. He fled France and arrived in England about two months ago. Now he is quite an important figure in de Gaulle's fleet and wears the *Croix de Lorraine* on his chest.

I asked Moch about the mood in France and the probable political post-war prospects. In contrast to Grenier, Moch is of the view that the events of the past three and a half years have not brought about any radical change in France's political configuration. Loathing for the Germans is universal, of course, but people's loyalties to political parties have changed relatively little. Thus, if elections were to be held in France tomorrow, the new chamber would not look radically different to how it did before the war.

This is a very important statement. I do not know how accurate it is, but it should be remembered. Perhaps the truth lies somewhere between Grenier and Moch.

As for the attitude of the average Frenchman to the USSR, Moch says even now: 'Oh, it goes without saying that he's filled with admiration for the heroism of the Red Army and the Soviet people. He is aware of the fact that the USSR is fighting for the freedom of all subjugated nations, for the freedom of France… But there's one comment that comes up again and again: if only the Soviets had signed a treaty with England and France instead of Germany, there would have been no war.'

Another important statement that must not be forgotten.

7 June

Saw Eden. He has returned from Algeria refreshed and very tanned. He ascribes his summons to North Africa chiefly to the fact that Churchill felt exhausted after Washington and wanted to have one of the senior members of the War Cabinet at his side, to carry most of the burden of the work, meetings, etc. – all the more so because Churchill was sure that the Giraud–de Gaulle negotiations would place a great strain on him. In reality, everything went much more smoothly than could have been expected. Eisenhower and Alexander had done so much preparatory work in the military sphere that Churchill was left with no real decisions to make. All he had to do was inspect. And this is what Churchill and Eden were mainly doing. Both went to Tunis. Both gave speeches in the dilapidated stadium of ancient Carthage. According to Eden, the stadium's acoustics are remarkable: there were more than 4,000 people there but you could speak effortlessly, in an ordinary voice, and every word would carry to the last row.

'I'm jealous!' I joked. 'You've visited the grave of my heroine, Salammbô!'

Eden provided me with vital information about the military operations under preparation in the region of the Mediterranean Sea and added that Alexander takes an optimistic view of the Allies' prospects, certainly as regards the first phase of the operation. I am wary of this British military optimism! It has proved misplaced so many times already. Let's see.

There also turned out to be much less work regarding French matters than Eden had expected. In the end, he didn't even intervene in the de Gaulle–Giraud negotiations. Where such intervention was required, it was carried out by Macmillan. And the results are not bad. A unified French Committee has been created. True, we don't know what will happen next. Eden is inclined to take a cautious view of the committee's prospects, but he still said that the Brit. Gov. would, in all probability, gradually transfer to it all the rights and obligations which formerly belonged to de Gaulle. Eden asked me to clarify the position of the Soviet government vis-à-vis the Algerian committee. He is clarifying the position of the American government. I promised to ask Moscow.

Eden told me a few interesting things. Peyrouton, realizing that his time was up, decided to have his revenge, and perhaps postpone his fall, by setting the two generals against each other. It was for this reason that he wrote to de Gaulle to inform him of his resignation. Without breathing a word to Giraud, de Gaulle immediately sent his reply, accepting Peyrouton's resignation and moving him to the army. Not only that, de Gaulle even appointed Peyrouton's successor as governor-general of Algeria. Also without consulting Giraud. Peyrouton has thus proved himself a good psychologist, laying a clever trap into which de Gaulle duly fell.

After de Gaulle had committed himself beyond the point of no return, Peyrouton sent a similar letter of resignation to Giraud. The latter, learning of de Gaulle's actions, was furious. An argument ensued. The generals exchanged sharp letters. Peyrouton exulted. The fate of the treaty was up in the air. And this is when Macmillan intervened. He invited de Gaulle for a conversation and pointed out the incorrectness of his actions – particularly since, at the time of the events just described, the committee had not yet been formed and, therefore de Gaulle had no right at all to accept Peyrouton's resignation. De Gaulle reacted to Macmillan's words with the cry: 'Haven't I always told you that Peyrouton is a scoundrel? Well, here's your proof.'

Eventually, Macmillan succeeded in calming things down and bringing the feuding generals together. The committee was established. On the day of their departure from Algiers (4 June) Churchill and Eden took part in a 'friendly' lunch, organized to mark the birth of the committee. All the French notables were present, as well as all the Allied military and political leaders. The atmosphere was warm. The speeches (incl. those by Churchill and Eden) appeared to leave no doubt about the desire of all the participants to work together in the task of fighting the enemy and restoring France. The next day Macmillan – so Massigli claims – even reported back to London that at the end of a long session 'de Gaulle and Giraud embraced'. Aren't these Frenchmen a funny lot!

Even so, the future is unclear. My personal view is that the current arrangement, whereby Giraud and de Gaulle are co-chairmen with equal rights, is unlikely to last. It is simply too artificial. Besides, the committee's political composition is too right-wing and does not correspond to the mood of the masses in France. After all, it includes four generals (de Gaulle, Giraud, Catroux, Georges[i]), of whom just one, de Gaulle, can be considered relatively progressive, and even then only with major reservations. Other members of the committee include one representative of the '200 families' – Monnet,[ii] one

---

[i] Alphonse Joseph Georges, general, was commander of the French field armies at the outbreak of the Second World War. Churchill was vetoed by Roosevelt when he wanted to make him commander of the French forces in North Africa in early 1942.

[ii] Jean Monnet, the disillusioned deputy secretary general of the League of Nations went on to pursue business interests in Asia during the 1930s, only to re-emerge as a leading economic planner during the war.

representative of the 'conciliatory' diplomacy of the pre-war period – Massigli, and one representative of the 'resistance front' in France itself – the Christian socialist André Philip (i.e. in reality the representative of only a small section of this front). The committee contains not a single communist, not a single socialist, not a single genuine Democrat with republican leanings. And all this at a time when the foundation of the 'resistance front' in France is provided by communists and, to a lesser extent, socialists. In such circumstances, how can the Algerian committee count on a lengthy and effective existence?

I shared these thoughts quite openly with Eden. At the end I said: 'Post-war Europe, which is what we need to be thinking about now, will be a democratic Europe that leans notably to the left…'

Eden objected: 'Democratic?… Yes!… But I am far from certain that it will lean to the left.'

'Time will tell,' I answered.

As for the special Algerian committee, Eden acknowledged that there was much truth in my remarks, but consoled himself with the fact that the current arrangement is temporary and that a great deal may yet change for the better.

12 June

Dejan came to say goodbye. He used to be a professional diplomat. The first secretary, if I am not mistaken, of the French embassy in Berlin. Went over to de Gaulle a long time ago. For a considerable period he was his 'commissar for foreign affairs' and had dealings with me in this capacity, especially when relations were being established between ourselves and de Gaulle (end of 1941). Then de Gaulle removed him from his post, apparently because he was too weak towards the British. For a time he was more or less unemployed. Eventually, following the arrival of Massigli and the latter's appointment to the post of commissar for FA in de Gaulle's 'National Committee', Dejan was made Massigli's deputy. Now that the united Committee of National Liberation has been formed in Algiers, Dejan is following de Gaulle over there. I asked: 'And what are your plans?'

'I myself am not yet sure,' Dejan replied. 'For now, I am going to Algiers. Then I hope to do a tour of South America and arrange a few things there… That's to say, I want to establish relations between the Committee and various S[outh] American states, and also inject some clarity and order into the minds of the Frenchmen living in S[outh] America, including French diplomats… Confusion reigns in the minds of my compatriots in America – some support Vichy, some de Gaulle, some Giraud, many are unsure… And of course, if you are going to S[outh] America, you must first pass through Washington: that is where the key to S[outh] America is to be found. But these are just plans. How everything will work out in reality I cannot say. My wife will remain in London for now.'

And then, in a rather different tone, Dejan added: 'You know, I have the sense that it would be good to fade into the background of French affairs for a while… There is so much fighting in our ranks at the moment, so much squabbling between the generals… So many personal feelings involved… It would be better to do something useful somewhere on the margins and wait it out.'

Dejan may be right. He is not a major figure, but he is not stupid and he is decent enough. Quite well disposed to the USSR. Understands contemporary politics. Could be useful in the future. It's clear that he doesn't want to overcommit himself to any side.

Dejan told me that in Algeria alone there are 183 French generals, 27 admirals and 65 air force generals, yet there are only 40 French planes! What an extraordinary picture! The vast majority of the generals are old men who have had their day, but they hang on to their ranks and decorations for dear life and are in no hurry to die. This is why the atmosphere in Algeria and N. Africa is so pervaded by intrigues of every kind among the generals.

* * *

Laski told me a perfectly Chekhovian story today.

In the Labour Party's head office there is a certain Gillies, the Labour Party's secretary for foreign affairs. A fool, an ignoramus and a rabid enemy of the USSR whose loathing for the 'Bolsheviks' sometimes takes on a pathological character.

Over the course of two years Cudlipp, editor of the *Daily Herald*, did all he could to avoid having anything to do with Gillies. Gillies eventually caused a fuss and as a result Cudlipp had to invite Gillies for lunch. Over lunch, Cudlipp offered Gillies a glass of sherry. He drank it. Cudlipp offered another – Gillies refused. Cudlipp asked why. Gillies replied that his heath forbade it, then confessed that he suffers terribly from constipation.

'You know,' Gillies continued, 'I've been having this nightmare for two years now… I keep imagining that, as a result of the war, production of cascara will cease, but cascara is what I live on. So every time I walk past a chemist, I always drop in and buy a bottle of cascara. I have enough to fill a larder.'

Cudlipp, who is far from stupid and sometimes cutting, remarked: 'As it happens, I know a chemist who makes cascara.'

Gillies's face lit up and he could barely contain his excitement: 'Really?'

Cudlipp confirmed that this was so and that, if Gillies wished, he could help him acquire the necessary quantity of cascara.

The next morning Cudlipp received a letter from Gillies, with a cheque attached, asking to be supplied with twelve dozen bottles of cascara!

13 June

Another week has passed. Still quiet on our front – at least, on land. No serious fighting even in the Kuban region. Only in the air do we continue to show great activity, bombing the enemy's fortifications, railways and lines of communication, as well as aerodromes. Our raids become ever more massive – 500, 600, 700 machines. We are managing to destroy many of the enemy's planes on the ground. Our own losses are very small. In sum: it is plain that we are dominating the Germans in the air. Will we be able to maintain this superiority in the future? We will see.

So: the Germans have already lost five spring/summer weeks in comparison with last year. We, by contrast, have gained five. And for the time being there are no signs of an imminent and large-scale German offensive on our front. Why not? One's thoughts keep returning to this question ever more often and insistently. Only history, of course, will supply a full and accurate answer, but now, on 13 June 1943, in the light of everything I know at this moment in time, it seems to me that the reasons for German inactivity are as follows:

(1) The collapse of Axis resistance in Tunisia some three months earlier than the German general staff had reckoned on. Citing the captured General von Arnim, who was in charge in Tunisia, Eden told me that Berlin had reckoned on holding out in Tunisia until August. Berlin had also assumed that the Allies would need another two months or so after the fall of Tunis to prepare for their offensive against Italy. In other words, Hitler was not expecting that offensive to occur before October and was even hoping that bad weather in the Mediterranean Sea in October would cause further delay. Thus, concentrating his divisions on the Soviet front in March and April, Hitler calculated that he had at least five months at his disposal (May–September) for operations in the USSR before the threat of an Anglo-American attack to the west or the south became serious. In reality, things turned out differently: by that same German calculation, Hitler ended up with not five but only two months at his disposal for the 'east'. The entire strategic plan, as previously drawn up, was in tatters. There was no choice but to adapt to a completely new and unexpected situation. Deployment plans, in particular, had to be changed, first and foremost in the air, and secondarily on the ground. Hence the delays, hesitations, temporizing: it is exceptionally dangerous to commit yourself in the east until you can at least gain an approximate notion of the size of the threat coming from the opposite direction.

(2) The dominance of Soviet over German aircraft that has become so patent in recent weeks all along the eastern front. This dominance is explained on the one hand by the sharp growth of our air power over the course of the winter, and on the other by the diversion of significant German air forces in the

direction of the Mediterranean Sea and the west. Our dominance has been a surprise for Hitler, too. As a result, he has once again been compelled to change previous plans, for without adequate air cover not a single army (least of all the German one) can now undertake a successful offensive in summer conditions.

(3) The heavy aerial attacks against Germany from the west that have been observed during the past two months. Everything would suggest that the strength and concentration of these attacks, as well as their systematic nature, have also caught Hitler by surprise and forced him to reassess previous plans. On the one hand, he has had to concentrate far more people, anti-aircraft guns and aeroplanes to defend the Ruhr and other regions than had been anticipated; on the other hand, the damage caused by the Allied air offensive to German military production and German morale has proved more significant than was first calculated. But without a guaranteed flow of supplies in adequate quantities, no serious offensive is possible.

(4) The more effective work done by partisans behind German lines in the USSR. This stems on the one hand from the improved organization of the partisan movement in 1943 when compared to 1941 or even 1942, and on the other from its improved morale as a result of the general swing towards the Allies on every front.

But can a large German offensive in the USSR in the course of this year be discounted? No, that would be premature. A large German offensive is still possible, and we must be ready for it.

14 June

A few days ago (9 June) Air Chief Marshal *Sir Arthur Harris*, the head of RAF Bomber Command, came with his wife for lunch. Harris is a striking representative of the camp that believes that the war can be won from the air. I asked Harris whether he continues to hold that view.

'Of course I do!' Harris cried. 'Now more than ever. Everything depends on the number of bombers you are able to deploy. I assure you quite categorically that if I had the capacity to send a thousand heavy bombers to Germany every night that we fly, Germany would surrender within three months at most. And then the entire army of occupation could consist of just three policemen – American, English and Soviet, who would take Berlin not only without meeting resistance, but with the enthusiasm of the local population.

According to Harris, current navigation technology means that about twenty days each month are suitable for carrying out air raids on Germany. That is the average. In certain periods the number is higher. But this only applies to night flights. By day the situation is different and the Americans, for example, who specialize in precision bombing by day, are, for now, only able to fly 5–6 days a month. The weather does not permit any more: the air is not clear enough for them to take aim from a height of 20–25,000 feet. It is possible, however, that the situation may yet improve.

Harris's comments deserve serious attention. After all, his school of thought is currently enjoying great popularity. Three weeks or so ago, Bevin told me that aerial warfare is the most economical form of war, at least as regards the loss of human life. The capture of Pantelleria and Lampedusa by aerial assault alone provides the Harris school with a very effective (albeit far from wholly convincing) weapon. It's certainly true that in the last 2–3 days the British press has been playing endless variations on this theme: look, we have taken a stronghold with a garrison of 15,000 men at the cost of 20 planes and 40 pilots! How incredibly cheap!

15 June

Jules Moch told me the following story:

In autumn 1942, not long before his escape to Algiers, Giraud did a tour of the garrisons of the towns in unoccupied France and gave speeches at officer meetings. He gave the same speech wherever he went. It was composed of two parts. In the first, Giraud appealed, in extravagant French style, to his audience's patriotism; in the second, he gave practical answers to certain political questions. This second part is particularly interesting.

'Who is our enemy?' Giraud would ask, before immediately replying: 'Germany.'

'Who is our friend?' Giraud would continue, before immediately replying: 'Our Friend No. 1 is the USA. There have never been wars or major conflicts between France and the USA. They are natural allies. They have been and ought to remain sincere friends.' (Needless to say, the names of La Fayette, Pershing and others were very prominent in this part of the speech.)

'Who else is our friend?' Giraud continued, and replied: 'Our Friend No. 2 is England. It is true that in the past there have been quite a few difficult episodes between England and France – Trafalgar, Fashoda, Oran. Moreover, the English are sly and they are only out for themselves. But in the current circumstances, England must be viewed as Friend No. 2.'

'There is one other state,' Giraud went on, 'that is also waging war with Germany, but the less said about it, the better. This state is the enemy of religion, the family, civilization. Of course, the Russians are killing plenty of Germans, while the Germans are killing plenty of Russians – and a good thing, too. France will only gain from it.'

'Who will come out on top from the current struggle?' Giraud finally asked, before replying: 'Probably the Allies, while Germany, in all likelihood, will be destroyed. The conclusion? The "National Revolution" headed by Pétain has been good for France, but if France remains with Germany, then the "National Revolution" will also perish under the ruins of a vanquished Germany.'

For these reasons Giraud would like to convince France to break away from Germany in time and cross to the Anglo-American camp. Then the 'National Revolution' would be saved.

While the events just described were taking place, Moch was in France, playing an active part in the internal 'resistance front'. Moch had received reports about Giraud's speeches from three towns, and all three reports converged on the fundamental points.

That's Giraud for you. But perhaps he has undergone 're-education' over the past six months? I doubt it. French generals are not prone to mental revolutions at the age of 64, and in any case all the reports from N. Africa confirm that, deep down, Giraud has not changed. All his 'democratic' gestures (which are mainly confined to internal politics) are dictated by the Americans and especially the English. The political nudity of the Americans' chosen one was truly repulsive. It was all very awkward. The Anglo-Americans will have to find a way round this.

And how typical of Giraud that the USSR is nowhere to be seen in any of his public speeches! Either he does not mention us at all or, when he cannot avoid doing so, he mentions us hurriedly, in passing, so that 'no one notices'. Moch's account explains why this should be so.

Giraud is a nasty piece of work. De Gaulle is also far from ideal, but he is infinitely more tolerable. At the current stage, at least.

16 June

Went to see Eden. At first we spoke about various matters of the day: about our supplies of Mosquito planes, about the imminent organization of a second convoy to the Persian Gulf, and about the shipment of a larger quantity of petrol to us in Abadan.

Then Eden informed me that [General] Alexander, who was in England just a few days ago, has been instructed to expedite 'Husky' by every means. It is possible, therefore, that the operation will begin earlier than planned. I wouldn't object, but I doubt it will happen. We'll see. Then Eden said that an agreement has been reached with the Americans about the bombing of Rome's railways (half a year ago, Washington was opposed to any bombing of Rome).

I asked about Turkey. Eden was unable say anything reassuring. The Turks are still 'sitting on the fence'. In recent days they have been emphasizing their neutrality more strongly than ever. Two vessels (of a promised five), dispatched by the British specifically to carry weapons, have been employed by the Turks for sabotage that has nothing to do with the war. The British government became angry and decided not to supply the other three boats. Churchill was on the point of making a scene with the Turks, but Eden restrained him and advised laying off them until the operations against Italy began in earnest. In the meantime, Rear Admiral John Cunningham (cousin of Andrew Cunningham, commander-in-chief of the Mediterranean fleet) has been sent to Turkey. He is meant to exert a certain mental pressure on the Turk. Gov. and military circles and thus pave the way for Churchill's démarche.

Next I asked about Argentina. Eden replied that Ramírez's[i] new government is an improvement on the previous one but that sensational developments are not to be expected in the nearest future. After all, this is still a military government with all the ensuing consequences. Having said that, the FA minister (an admiral) is pro-Allies. Eden is of the view that, after a while, Argentina will probably break with the Axis.

We also spoke about French affairs. Eden showed me a series of Macmillan's telegrams. From them the following emerges: on 9 June, de Gaulle submitted his proposals for army reforms to the committee. They boil down to two points: (1) much younger officers, i.e. most of the old generals should retire (there are currently 176 army generals gathered in Algiers, 63 air force generals – though the French air fleet has just 40 aeroplanes – and 27 admirals); (2) restructuring of command, i.e. the commander-in-chief should not be a member and president of the committee, but stand outside and beneath it, while all military affairs should be managed by a minister of war – a member of the committee and, if necessary, its president. The minister of war de Gaulle has in mind is, of course, de Gaulle.

De Gaulle's proposals enraged Giraud, who made a gigantic scene. Then, on 10 June, de Gaulle sent a letter to the committee tendering his resignation. Turmoil ensued. Many committee members asked de Gaulle to retract his letter. Macmillan had a conversation with him to the same effect. Meetings are still ongoing in Algiers. Conciliatory phrases are being sought, letters and notes exchanged. A solution has yet to be found.

[The diary entry on the meeting with Eden (and the subsequent silence) avoids mentioning the bitter clash between Churchill and Stalin which triggered the recall of Maisky from London. Following the final defeat of the Axis forces in North Africa, Churchill felt confident enough to openly adhere to his peripheral strategy. He now envisaged a post-war world based on the special and equal relationship with the Americans. His impatience with Stalin impacted on Maisky's standing. Even before setting off for Washington for his fifth summit meeting with Roosevelt, he warned Eden

---

[i] Pedro Pablo Ramirez Machuca, admiral, founder of Argentina's fascist militia, was the Argentinian president in 1943–44 and maintained Argentina's neutrality during the war.

that 'it would be a great pity to establish the principle that Ambassador Maisky should receive copies of all telegrams other than operational which I send to Marshal Stalin. I should object very strongly to this.'[82]

Churchill left for the US on 5 May, on board the *Queen Mary*, with an entourage of 150 advisers, including the chiefs of staff. 'It is an amusing form of megalomania on Winston's part,' jotted down Halifax in his diary, 'but he would no doubt feel the war would gravely suffer if he did not move so attended.'[83] Churchill believed he could convert Roosevelt once again to his strategic and political vision, the implication of which was a definite postponement of the second front to spring 1944, at the earliest, and the introduction of various diversions in the Mediterranean, as well as in the Far East. He hoped also to dissuade the president from ending the war with an international structure which included the Soviet Union and perhaps China as equal partners. The former American ambassador to Moscow, Joseph Davies, was indeed busy conducting clandestine talks in the Kremlin to secure a bilateral meeting between the two leaders.[84] Eager to gain the president's support for an invasion of Italy, Churchill continued to dwell on the unresolved difficulties involved in landing on the continent – an operation which could only be undertaken once 'a plan offering reasonable prospects of success could be made'. The turbulent summit ended with *Avalanche*, the plan for the Italian campaign, finally confirmed, while the invasion of France was now set for spring 1944.[85] Both Admiral Pound and General Dill complained to Halifax about Churchill's indecisiveness, while Brooke, the chief of staff, grumbled that Churchill was thinking 'one thing at one moment and another at another moment. At times the war may be won by bombing and all must be sacrificed to it. At others it becomes essential for us to bleed ourselves dry on the Continent because Russia is doing the same. At others our main effort must be in the Mediterranean, directed against Italy or Balkans alternatively, with sporadic desires to invade Norway and "roll up the map in the opposite directions simultaneously irrespective of shortages of shipping!"'[86]

'Isn't he a sly rogue?' was Maisky's reaction to information coming out of Washington. 'Not only does he want to preserve control over the Mediterranean for Britain and not to allow the Americans to look in there, he intends to do it at the expense of US forces and resources.'[87] Indeed, when Maisky met Churchill as soon as he returned to London, his fears that the prime minister now considered the Italian campaign, combined with the air offensive, to be a substitute for the cross-channel campaign were confirmed. Churchill remained deliberately noncommittal when the possibility of bringing the war to a conclusion in Europe in 1944 was raised by the ambassador.[88]

Having gleaned from Maisky what had transpired in Washington and Algiers, Stalin bitterly remonstrated with Roosevelt about the exclusion of the Soviet Union from the strategic discussions while she was facing 'single-handed a still very strong and dangerous enemy'. His indictment of the Allies (a copy of which was transmitted to Churchill on 11 June) warned of the grave consequences that the decision would have on 'the people and the army of the Soviet Union'. With *Avalanche* now firmly secured, Churchill reminded Stalin of his determination to 'never authorize any cross-Channel attack which … would lead only to useless massacre'. He could hardly see 'how a great British defeat and slaughter would aid the Soviet Armies'. Stalin retorted with accusations of perfidy on the part of his Western Allies, again referring to the 'colossal sacrifices' made by the Red Army. On 26 June, Churchill, maintaining that his 'own

117. Just recalled to Moscow, a sad Maisky entertains members of the 'Old Vic' theatre.

long-suffering patience [was] not inexhaustible', removed the gloves: he recalled that, as a result of the Ribbentrop–Molotov Pact, Britain had been 'left alone to face the worst that Nazi Germany could do to us', and that presently 'a more hopeful and fruitful strategic policy' had opened up 'in another theatre'.[89]

In a frenzy, Maisky found it difficult to reach Eden, who had been advised by Churchill 'not to have anything to do with him'. When he finally did get through, it was to break the news of his recall to Moscow.[90] However, even at such a dramatic moment, Maisky had not given up on his persistent efforts to defuse the tension between the two leaders. He appealed to Beaverbrook at the eleventh hour to intervene with the prime minister.[91] Finally, he secured a meeting with the prime minister on the eve of his departure. According to Churchill, the ambassador was 'extremely civil', repeatedly assuring him that he 'ought not to attach importance to the tone of Stalin's messages'. On the thorny issue of the second front, it quickly transpired that Churchill clung on to his belief that the Mediterranean strategy was 'gaining Russia valuable breathing-space to regather her strength'. Depicting the 'great sufferings and losses of Russia', Maisky explained that although Stalin was harsh in scolding the prime minister, there was nothing sinister in his messages. Eager not to return to Moscow empty-handed, he succeeded in extracting from Churchill an undertaking to continue working with Stalin. He wished to ensure that the failure to embark on joint strategy would not impair the negotiations now taking place on the post-war order. Here he was partially successful, encouraging Churchill to send Eden to Moscow, thereby paving the way for the Moscow summit meeting of the Allied foreign ministers in the autumn.[92]]

17 June

The contours of our post-war politics are gradually emerging.

Over the course of the last few months, the British (especially Kerr in Moscow) have been informing us of various 'amicable soundings' on the part of official and unofficial Hungarians, and every so often they have asked our opinion. On 7 June, Molotov responded to Kerr with a letter setting out our point of view on a whole host of post-war matters. The main points of the letter boil down to the following:

(1) Responsibility for the war and wartime atrocities is borne not just by the Hungarian government but by Hungarian society as well (I interpret this formulation to mean that various ruling elements are intended, including the intelligentsia, the kulak class, etc.)

(2) The obligatory conditions that we would set Hungary (and other satellite countries) are:

(a) Unconditional surrender.

(b) The return of captured territories.

(c) Compensation of losses occasioned by the war.

(d) Punishment of war culprits.

(3) The arbitrary award of 30 August 1940 transferring northern Transylvania to Hungary cannot be considered fully justified. Reappraisal cannot be discounted.

(4) Negotiations and contact with oppositional elements in Hungary (and also, obviously, in other satellite countries) are possible, but in the course of the negotiations no promises should be given that contradict the conditions listed above under points (2) and (3). The negotiations should be conducted after the exchange of preliminary information.

(5) On the question of plans for a federation of Poland, Czechoslovakia, Yugoslavia, Greece, Hungary, Austria, our view is that:

(a) Now is certainly not the time to commit ourselves.

(b) Hungary and Austria, at any rate, should not be members of such a federation.

All this is very important and interesting. It sets the line.

There is also an indication, later on, of our position in relation to de Gaulle and Giraud. We support de Gaulle for two reasons:

(a) de Gaulle takes a completely uncompromising position in relation to Germany and demands its complete destruction; the same cannot be said of Giraud.

(b) de Gaulle supports the restoration of the Republican-democratic order in France and will not compromise with Vichy; the same cannot be said of Giraud.

Quite right. I have held fast to this line since last November. Now it has been confirmed in Moscow. A good thing too.

19 June

Coates said that at the Labour conference he has seen Petrov (in the capacity of 'guest') with his wife and two children. Petrov looks very old: his face is deeply furrowed with wrinkles, his hair is white and he has lost all his teeth. His wife looks even worse…

A distant scene surfaces unbidden in my mind. London. 1913. 1 May. Bright sun. Blue sky. A small May Day demonstration progresses along the city's sooty, sultry streets, in the direction of Hyde Park. Two to three thousand people. Dozens of red flags flutter in the air. The sound of singing… of socialist and revolutionary songs. And, though the procession is not large and the singing not especially loud, everyone is in the most wonderful spirits. Cheerful, animated, full of joy. Everyone is living for the future, and this future seems so bright, broad, so full of promise. Another year, it seems, another five, another ten at the very most – and everything these people are thinking, dreaming, talking and singing about will become reality. Socialism will triumph!

I, too, am walking in the ranks of the May Day procession and my heart, too, is jumping for joy. How magnificent the world is! How wonderful the prospects opening up before us! Forward! Forward! Quick! Quick! To victory!…

At my side walks Petrov, and at his side – a young, blooming girl of 23. This is a German social democrat recently arrived in London, a pleasant, cheerful, intelligent creature. Petrov is *Peter Petroff*, the legislator, leader and dictator of the *Kentish Town Branch of the British Socialist Party*. He is about 30. Tanned, black-haired, with sharp facial features and a booming voice, Petrov speaks well (the London type of *street corner speaker*) and within his own party his popularity keeps rising. He is being taken seriously in the party; a big political future is predicted for him. Petrov met the girl who is now walking alongside him by chance, met her and immediately fell in love. Petrov's love affair is progressing at a gallop, although it has not yet reached its logical conclusion. It is clear, though, that Petrov and the German girl will soon marry. At this May Day demonstration, they cling very close to one another, exchange glances and smiles, like people who share a special language inaccessible to anyone else. They are having fun. They are bursting with enthusiasm. Their personal emotions merge so well with the general mood of the procession. And both of them feel that life is unveiling before them a long and broad path, filled with joy, splendour, success…

Yes, 30 years have passed since that day.

How cruelly life has deceived Petrov!

He arrived in Russia in 1918 or 1919. He received a magnificent welcome: at that time his old London friends – Chicherin, Litvinov, Rothstein and others – held leading posts in the Soviet administration. Petrov even got to see Lenin. His prospects, evidently, were brilliant. But alas.

By nature, Petrov is almost an anarchist. Accustomed to being a dictator on the scale of *Kentish Town*, he did not manage to become a useful link in a large machine on the scale of the USSR. Petrov kept having clashes, squabbles and rows with his work comrades and with the leaders of party and state. He almost always turned out to be in the wrong. His star began to fall. On my way from Moscow to London in 1925, I met Petrov outside the Berlin embassy. He was working at the time for our trade mission in Germany (as an economist, if I'm not mistaken) and looked rather ragged. He was in a bad mood. He was annoyed with everything and everyone. Then I lost sight of him. The years passed. Every now and again I heard rumours that Petrov was acting oddly, that there was something wrong with him, that he was switching to the anti-Soviet side…

And then a few years ago, out of the blue, Petrov suddenly showed up in England again – already an old man, a wreck, and an undisguised enemy of the USSR. Gillies, needless to say, took him under his wing. For a while Petrov campaigned furiously against the Soviet Union – especially after 23 August 1939 – and I even had to take some countermeasures. Then, when Germany attacked the USSR, all this died down. Petrov vanished completely. I didn't even know whether he was alive or dead. And now Coates has reminded me of him once more.

The life cycle of Petrov and his wife is complete, or almost complete. What a bitter, stupid, vile fate!

20 June (Bovingdon)

Still quiet on our front. The Germans are spreading rumours via foreign correspondents in Berlin that the major offensive against the USSR has been postponed indefinitely, since the fundamental task this summer, allegedly, is the safeguarding of the borders of the stronghold – Europe. Sounds suspicious. Whatever the truth, another week has been gained.

It is cold and windy; grey clouds sweep across the sky. I have caught a cold. There is a hum in my left ear.

2 July

Tomorrow I am flying to Moscow.

About a week ago, I received a telegram summoning me to Moscow for consultations on post-war matters. Very good. I'm glad of the chance to see my people and 'touch native soil' once more.

I think, however, that there is more to this than consultations. My recall, it seems to me, may also be a way of expressing our dissatisfaction with the British government for failing to keep its word on the second front. This is precisely how Eden interpreted the announcement of my departure. He was greatly alarmed and exclaimed: 'What? You are leaving London at such a moment?'

'What particular moment?' I retorted. 'After all, there won't be a second front now. So there is no reason why I should not fly to Moscow for a period of time.'

It took a week to arrange the flight. The British are putting a plane at my disposal in which they will also be sending out some employees bound for their embassy in Moscow. One of our military men, who is returning to the USSR, is flying with me. The route is interesting: Gibraltar–Cairo–Habbaniya–Kuibyshev–Moscow. I've never been to Egypt – I'll see the pyramids!

Bon voyage!

118 & 119. A sad farewell to Britain, 15 September 1943.

End of an Era: Maisky's Recall

Maisky's departure for Moscow on 3 July via Cairo started off inauspiciously. His brief stopover in Gibraltar gave rise to a conspiracy theory which continued to haunt him for years and which was revived in the wake of Poland's regained independence. It suggests that the crash of Sikorski's plane shortly after take-off in the early hours of the following morning (the plane had been parked on the tarmac next to Maisky's) was a result of Soviet sabotage. This theory feeds on an earlier attempt on Sikorski's life (when an incendiary device was found and defused by the pilot who was flying him to the United States) and the fact that Kim Philby, the notorious Soviet mole at MI6, happened to be in Spain at the time of the crash. The earlier attempt on Sikorski's life was, however, attributed to Sikorski's opponents, who were resentful of the Polish–Soviet agreement he had signed with Maisky in July 1941. An exhaustive investigation by the British security services established that the pilot had faked the incident simply to draw attention to himself.[1] Suspicion of Maisky's complicity in the fatal crash lingers on, despite an official investigation, carried out in 1943, which blamed the crash on a technical malfunction. In its most extreme version, the conspiracy suggests that the murder had been ordered by Churchill, who then tried to implicate Maisky and the Russians.[2]

Maisky was met in Gibraltar by the governor, General Mason-MacFarlane, who, until recently, had been the British military attaché in Moscow. Bound by 'the laws of wartime hospitality', Mason-MacFarlane reluctantly invited him to the official residence in the fortress. Embarrassingly, Mason-MacFarlane had already extended an invitation for Sikorski (who was due from Cairo a few hours earlier) to spend the night at his palace. The governor arranged with the Foreign Office that Maisky's arrival would be delayed until breakfast. As soon as Sikorski arrived, Mason-MacFarlane informed him of the mishap and begged him to ensure that none of his party left their rooms until he waved a white handkerchief to signal that Maisky had departed and that the coast was clear. He further took special precautions to have two sentries present by the locked plane and an NCO inside. Maisky apparently heard of the plane crash that claimed the life of Sikorski over breakfast in the Cairo residence of Lord Killearn shortly after his landing in Cairo the following morning. Only then did it dawn on him 'why MacFarlane was in such a frightful hurry to get [him] off the Rock'.[3]

Both Litvinov and Maisky chose to present their recall to Moscow as a remonstration against the decision to postpone the second front, rather than as a personal rebuff in the protracted struggle between the old school of Soviet diplomacy and Stalin's now fully erected authoritarian edifice. They were most anxious to impress on their interlocutors in the West that their promotion to the position of deputy foreign minister within the ministry reflected their personal appreciation by the Kremlin and their continued relevance. Maisky's confidants, notably Lord Beaverbrook, echoed him in attributing the recall to Stalin's deepening suspicion of British intentions, the fault for which 'lay entirely with the Prime Minister who was fundamentally anti-Russian and who was too old now to change'.[4] Litvinov left Under Secretary of State Welles with the impression that it was he who had insisted on returning to Moscow to directly influence Stalin's foreign policy. And yet, in the same breath, he complained of being completely 'bereft of any information as to the policy or plans of his own Government'.[5] Bruce Lockhart, an old Russia hand, describes how Maisky was most anxious to figure out how public opinion in Britain reacted to his recall. When he learned that there were two conflicting schools of thought – one attributing it to Stalin's dismay of British inaction and the other suggesting that Stalin 'would benefit from the presence in Moscow of so great a connoisseur of England as himself' – his 'eyes twinkled' as he admitted that 'in Moscow there were also two interpretations'.[6] The third option, of being out of favour, was thus avoided.

Once in Moscow, the unrelenting Maisky was quick to brief the British press about his new 'elevated' position and the fact that he, as they put it, was 'held in high regard by Joe'.[7] *The Times* reported that Stalin wished him 'to remain at his right hand, with M. Molotov', while Russia was preparing her post-war policy, considering his 'direct knowledge and understanding of Great Britain', as well as his rare and shrewd views on 'Germany, France, and other countries'.[8] The bleaker reality, more accurately surmised by *Time* Magazine, was that 'Little Maisky' would 'get lost in the bureaucratic maze of the Narkomindel (signifying that his tireless bouncing around London had displeased his superiors)'.[9] Ironically, it was Maisky who had had a similar observation about Vansittart's 'promotion' in 1938: 'the new appointment will have to be regarded as a demotion or, more precisely, as a retirement ticket, only with uniform, decorations and a pension'.[10]

Stalin and Molotov had been seeking the removal of Maisky and Litvinov from London and Washington, which the two ambassadors considered to be their 'personal territory'.[11] Neither returned to Moscow willingly. The memory of the horrifying fate of their colleagues who had been summoned to Moscow was still painfully fresh. Averell Harriman remembered Litvinov being 'ebullient' up to the moment of his recall: 'I have never seen a man collapse so completely. His attitude showed that he was in a rather tenuous position with Stalin and he must have feared for his life in the event that his Washington mission ended in disgrace.' Litvinov's wife Ivy, who for a while stayed behind in Washington, confided to friends that she feared she might never see her husband again.[12] In her unpublished memoirs, she describes emphatically how her husband 'went nearly mad … he wanted to stay … he started what he longed for more than anything else [writing his memoirs] because he did not want to go back to Russia'. She goes on to describe how he 'did nothing but quarrel with Stalin at that time – unappeasably quarrel with Stalin … he could do nothing but quarrel with everybody … with Molotov … with everybody, and nothing they could do was right'.[13] Back in Moscow, Ivy cast 'a heedful eye on every side. She begged her friends not to send books to Litvinov nor to come and see them, that was "safer for both".'[14]

The presentation of the recall as a protest against the West has led historians down a false track. The decision to withdraw Litvinov, it should be remembered, had been taken earlier, in late April, prior to the eruption of the major conflict between the Allies.[15] It signalled to Maisky that his days in Britain were numbered. As soon as the news from Washington came through, he wasted little time in depositing a political will with his wife:

> Dear Agniya,
>
> My instructions for whatever happens:
>
> (1) My notes (the diary, or my Old Lady, as I like to call her), should be sent to Comrade Stalin. They are in my two little suitcases.
>
> (2) You yourself should go through all my papers and sort them out into those which are of public and those which are of personal nature. Those which are of public interest should be given to Comrade Molotov. All these materials are in my personal safe, in the iron cupboard next to the safe, in the small suitcases, as well as in other places in our apartment.
>
> (3) I should like my childhood memoir to be published.[16]

In his memoirs, Gromyko, who at the time was very much under Molotov's spell, describes how Maisky's appointment to the post in London had 'shocked many': how could someone who had served in the Menshevik government in Saratov during the Civil War assume such a prominent diplomatic position and for such a long period? His activities in London, he claims, 'were always assessed with some reserve ... the political past of this man prevailed over all appraisals of his work'. As the war dragged on, his 'unjustified' long telegrams, describing in detail his meetings with British politicians 'drowned in his own description of the situation', had become 'irritating to the leadership'. Gromyko finally recalls a conversation with Molotov, when the latter and Stalin decided that 'Maisky had to be replaced.'[17]

Stalin did not, however, shy away from drawing on the unrivalled connections and familiarity with the West of Litvinov and Maisky, though under close surveillance and within limited scope. Maisky was nominally put in charge of the commission on reparation, but was kept at arm's length. His request that the commission should 'enjoy sufficient authority and independence' and that he personally should be 'directly subordinated' to Molotov was not heeded.[18] Litvinov fared slightly better. He met Stalin five times during 1943, and his expert advice was welcome in the impending meeting of the Allied foreign ministers and at the following summit meeting in Tehran. Maisky was denied access to the Kremlin. 'I asked Stalin to receive me, in order to report to him direct on the British situation and all the problems connected with it,' he remembers, 'but he did not find it necessary to talk with me.'[19] Keeping Litvinov and Maisky in the wings was a typical method used by Stalin for his divide-and-rule tactics – asserting his power and curtailing Molotov's increasing influence in the formulation of foreign policy.[20] A good indicator of Maisky's perilous position was his desperate effort to avoid Kerr, the British ambassador in Moscow, who was most eager to get him, Litvinov and the American ambassador 'to come and dine for a no fig-leaf kind of talk'. The ambassador, reported Kerr, 'had so many conferences, that he didn't know what to do', while later on he was 'in the country and would let me know when he got back'. Maisky met him finally only on the official turf of Narkomindel, confessing that he did not yet know what his tasks would be. His plans, however, to return to England for a short while made it clear to Kerr 'that there [was] no hurry about his taking up his new job in Moscow'.[21]

Neither Stalin nor Molotov could watch with equanimity the popular cult of Maisky in London, which reached dimensions second only to the cult of Stalin himself.[22] Maisky had always been heedful of being seduced by the bourgeois environment, an inescapable consequence of the nature of the diplomatic profession. The high esteem in which he was held, especially after Molotov's visit in May 1942, could quickly turn against him – an unresolved paradox of which he had been fully aware from the outset of his ambassadorship.[23] While flattered by the cult evolving around him, Maisky was anxious to keep it on the back burner. He was quick to turn down an invitation by the sculptor Epstein to attend the private viewing of his works at Leicester Galleries, using the flimsy excuse that he did 'not think it would be appropriate for me to be present as the bust of my own head will be shown there'.[24] A similar source of discomfort was the publication of his biography, shortly after the recall, by the Russian-born journalist Bilainkin, who had always been welcome at his ambassadorial residence. Not only did Maisky dissociate himself from the author, but he appeared extremely anxious to find out from his trusted colleagues at the embassy whether it contained any incriminating information. He likewise declined an offer by Birmingham University to bestow on him an honorary doctorate a few days before he was called back to Moscow.[25]

When the Treaty of Alliance was signed in London, following Molotov's visit in May 1942, Lord Cecil and other speakers in the House of Lords went out of their way to praise Maisky for his 'valuable contribution to Anglo-Russian understanding ... over a long period of years'. They paid tribute to his 'patient and exceedingly difficult work ... undertaken for many years past'. In the Commons debate, Eden paid similar tribute to the 'valuable contribution to Anglo-Russian understanding' made by Maisky 'over a long period of years'. Only passing references were made to either Stalin or Molotov.[26] Likewise, a week later, during a formidable rally at the Albert Hall in support of a second front, Cripps mentioned Molotov *en passant*, before going on to say: 'I could not omit in mentioning ... a very special reference to one other Soviet statesman. We regard him more generally as a diplomat but I can assure you that he is a statesman too, Soviet Ambassador, M. Maisky.' Maisky tried in vain to play down such an homage. 'One has to understand,' he explained to his friends, 'that in all these events the first and foremost honour belongs to our great people and to our brilliant leadership.'[27] Even after his departure from London, farewell letters from ministers kept streaming in and surely would have raised an eyebrow or two in the Kremlin. 'I need not say,' wrote Noel-Baker in one such typical letter, 'and I am sure hundreds of other people have already written to you similarly – how ever sorry we all are that you and your wife are leaving London; how very much you will be missed; and how long and how gratefully your memory will be kept alive here. As I am sure the Government have said to you officially, we all feel an immense debt of gratitude for your services in bringing our countries closer together.'[28] Under any normal circumstances, such recognition would have endeared an ambassador at home, but in the Kremlin it would have confirmed the independent position Maisky had assumed, certainly not the servile diplomat now characterizing Molotov's Narkomindel.

One of the worse consequences of the uncalled-for cult of personality was a most powerful portrait of Maisky, done by the famous Austrian painter Oskar Kokoschka shortly before his withdrawal. The whole experience was far from pleasant for both. Unusually for him, Maisky was uneasy. He 'read *The Times* throughout the sittings', grumbled Kokoschka in his memoirs. 'I could not get him to talk: perhaps he regarded a portrait as some new form of brainwashing. Finally, after hours of sitting, I suggested he reverse the paper behind which he was hiding, for I had finished reading the part turned to me. At length he became a little more talkative, and told me about his student days in Vienna and Munich.'[29] However, the worst was yet to come. A benefactor was found, who agreed to contribute the sum of the purchase to a Stalingrad Hospital Fund, stipulating, though, that it would care for both German and Russian wounded soldiers. As embarrassing for Maisky was the artist's wish for the painting to be given to the Museum of Contemporary Art in Moscow. The idea of 'a small token of Anglo-Russian goodwill' was raised with Eden, who passed it on to Maisky as soon as he returned to England to wind up his affairs before his final departure.[30]

The intermediary, Beddington-Behrens, a patron of the arts, was urgently invited to the Soviet embassy. He left a most disturbing description of Maisky's state of mind at the time of his recall:

> As I waited outside, a little peephole in the door was opened, from which I saw two eyes peering at me. When at last I was admitted to the Embassy I was followed into the waiting-room by two men, who remained there but did not speak a word to me. Finally, I was shown into the ambassador's room, where I also found Madame Maisky. To my astonishment, the first thing Mr Maisky did was to take the precaution of locking the three doors leading into the room. Then he asked me not to press for the picture by Kokoschka to be sent to the Moscow Art Gallery … He also asked me to omit any mention of the proposed gift of the portrait in any official communications to the Embassy concerning the generous donation of the money. His wife begged me to do as he wished, and I suddenly realised that Maisky was probably a victim of one of Stalin's ruthless purges. Both of them appeared to be very nervous, and I was quite moved by Madame Maisky's obvious devoted love for her husband, and her anxiety to shield him in any way that lay in her power.[31]

Maisky's fears proved justified when Kokoschka went ahead with his offer, only to be flatly rebuffed by the Soviet government. The painting was then donated to the Tate Gallery.

Always torn between fear and conceit, Maisky faced a similar conundrum when Epstein offered him a bronze copy of the bust he had made of him three years earlier. The correspondence concerning the gift was conducted with the embassy after Maisky's departure and seems to have embarrassed him, considering the negative impact his popularity in London was having on his relations with the Kremlin. While, in his customary way, he was making meticulous arrangements for the safe shipping of the bust, he tried to persuade his successor that the sculpture was done 'not of my own will, but at [Epstein's] own initiative'.[32] Distressed by the Kokoschka affair, Maisky went on to excuse himself for not taking appropriate precautions concerning Epstein's possible use of the bust, as he had considered him to be 'generally of a progressive leaning and unlikely to misuse it'. He claimed that there was no way of refusing to accept the bust done by 'the most famous contemporary sculptor in England and on top of that a person with much sympathy towards us'.[33]

Notwithstanding his extreme cautiousness, Maisky found it increasingly difficult to conform to the new role assigned to him as a passive ambassador in London. It is hardly a surprise that he was incensed at being involved in fighting a losing battle over the attempts by Molotov to reduce diplomats to pure messengers.[34] The attitude in the Kremlin to the ambassadors, considered to be the vestige of the 'old guard', evinced contempt and resentment. Pavlov (the personal interpreter of Stalin and Molotov) left an account of Maisky's recall. Significantly, his narrative is bound together with his earlier devastating critique of the ambassador and his wife at the time of Molotov's visit to London in May 1942.[35] The institutionalization of diplomacy, through the imposition of military order and hierarchy, symbolically deprived diplomats of their individuality and segregated them from their foreign colleagues. The new style was perhaps an allusion to Peter the Great's 'table of ranks', which had militarized the civil service and secured loyalty to the tsar, service to whom became the only criterion for advancement. The whole drift, seemingly innocuous in itself, signalled the emasculation of Soviet diplomats abroad and their growing dependence on Moscow.

Shortly before learning of his recall, Maisky addressed Molotov with a personal rebuff, of the sort the commissar was hardly accustomed to:

120. In uniform, with a marshal's shoulder straps.

Dear Vyacheslav Mikhailovich,

Rumours travel faster than light, and it has reached my ears that a decision concerning uniforms to be worn by diplomats has been reached in Narkomindel – moreover, that the uniform has already been designed and, if one is to believe the rumours, it even includes … a dagger! Is it true, a dagger?[36] I understand that if a sailor carries a dagger it symbolizes to a degree his military profession. But what is the relevance of a dagger to diplomacy? And what is it supposed to symbolize in this case? As far as I can recall, neither English diplomats nor the French, nor the vast majority of diplomats of other nations, carry daggers.[37]

Such an unprecedented and blunt criticism of Molotov hardly endeared him to Moscow and must have further contributed to the decision to recall him – which saved him from wearing the uniform in London, but not in Moscow. In November, now nominally in a high position at Narkomindel, he was given his new uniform. A strange blend of estrangement and suppressed vanity emerges in his diary:

The uniform is better, more comfortable and more handsome than I had expected. But I feel awkward in it just the same. I haven't worn any kind of uniform for 40 years, ever since my expulsion from St Petersburg University in 1902. I've been in civilian clothes all my life. Now, nearly 60, I find myself wearing uniform once more. It's only natural that it should feel a bit strange. I'll have to get used to it. And another thing: I have a high rank and Marshal shoulder-straps, which attract the attention of passers-by. The military salute me. This also feels novel and awkward.[38]

The diplomatic correspondent of *The Times*, who visited Maisky at the 'shabby old ministry of foreign affairs', commented on how odd it was to see the face of the 'old revolutionary' looking out at him 'from between the glistering, Tsarist-style epaulettes on the uniforms – greyish fawn'.[39]

Assuming the withdrawal of the ambassadors to be mainly an expression of protest, the Foreign Office failed to see the significance of the metamorphosis of Narkomindel. Embracing Maisky (as they did at this point) did little but intensify the Kremlin's mistrust of him, and the suspicion that his loyalties no longer lay with Moscow. Indeed such accusations figured prominently in his trial in 1955.[40] Kerr disputed openly with Molotov the wisdom of withdrawing Maisky from London, even if his services were urgently needed in Moscow. Maisky was, Kerr tried to impress on him, enjoying in London 'a position which no ambassador has had ever before'. It was a 'unique position in every sense'. He was 'loved in England by all from the left to the right, for all he [was] trustworthy'. Listening politely, Molotov did not even blink, but proceeded to ask an *agrément* for the new ambassador. Kerr did not give up. Although the Soviet Union had 180 million inhabitants, he argued, it would 'be difficult to find among them a successor for Maisky'. 'Eden,' he now resorted to the heavy guns, would 'certainly be sorry to see Maisky go.' When Kerr referred to the love engulfing Maisky in London, Molotov cynically replied that 'we in Moscow also like Maisky'. He mentioned how, during his visit to London, he was able to appreciate the extensive contacts Maisky had forged – a compliment for any ambassador, but not in Stalin's Russia. Kerr was misled to inform Eden in his brief report of Molotov's 'warm praise of Maisky', which he took at face value. In a follow-up telegram, he criticized Eden for 'reading too much into the appointment' of a new ambassador. He wrongly assumed that as a result of the purges there were 'only a handful of men of the calibre required' in Moscow and Maisky's presence was imperative.[41]

The decision of the Foreign Office 'to make a bid … to retain him in London' would also have an adverse effect on Maisky. Eden instructed Kerr to tell Molotov 'how much we appreciated M. Maisky's services in the cause of Anglo-Soviet co-operation and how greatly we regret the departure of such an old and trusted friend'. In conversations with the Soviet chargé d'affaires, Eden 'noted with regret' the withdrawal of Maisky. He even went so far as to question whether 'it was really more important to be one of six Assistant Commissars than to be an Ambassador in one of the principal capitals'.[42] Unlike Eden, many were misguided enough to assume that Maisky was indeed being promoted. Sir Charles Trevelyan, the radical Labour MP, for instance, congratulated him on the 'great advancement to the very responsible place … which will make your advice effective in the critical decisions of the next few years. Like many others I have formed the highest opinion of your judgment. What we lose in England by your leaving us the world will gain from Moscow.'[43] The remonstrations were becoming a source of personal and political embarrassment to Maisky, who brought them to an end in a formal, and hardly sincere, message (most likely dictated to him) to Eden:

> We appreciate your feeling but I am sure you will understand how happy I am after so many years abroad to live again in my country and to work at Narkomindel. I will tell you more about it when I will come to London to say good-bye. I hope that you will establish best relations with my successor.[44]

The choice of Fedor Tarasovich Gusev as the new ambassador, despite his apparent lack of experience, was a well thought-out move. He was the antidote to Maisky, just as Gromyko was to Litvinov in Washington. His appointment signalled what the new profile of Soviet diplomacy would be – a signal lost on the Foreign Office. They opted to ignore Stalin's and Molotov's statements to Kerr that plenipotentiaries were there 'to sign agreements rather than exchanges of views'. Gusev, a loyal party member, had studied law and had worked in various institutes in Leningrad. He was recruited to the ministry during the purges. Following Molotov's takeover, he was put in charge of its West European department. His British interlocutors in Moscow had a poor opinion of his 'abilities & character' and thought he was 'rather uncouth'. His English was 'sparse and peculiar … he took no initiative and had the appearance of having come from a collective farm after a short course of GPU training.' When approached, he would refuse to say anything except for 'I will refer the matter to my superiors.' In a nutshell, Kerr summed up, he was a man 'without grace, and his appearance is distressing'. When General Brooke met Gusev for the first time, at a luncheon given in the ambassador's honour at the end of October, he was not at all taken by '"frogface" Gousev, a former butcher', who was 'certainly not as impressive as that ruffian Maisky was!' Few in London entertained any illusions concerning Gusev's appointment. They anticipated that it would 'certainly make any kind of free exchange of views in London virtually impossible'. Slowly it sank in that rather than being promoted, Maisky was 'being demoted, being placed under Molotov in the Moscow Foreign Office', while being succeeded in London by a diplomat who was 'quite unable to replace him for the purpose of any serious political discussions'. Maisky's warnings that a failure on post-war Europe might encourage the Russians 'to plough a lonely furrow' seemed to be materializing.[45]

Until his recall, Maisky had succeeded in masterly fashion at navigating the stormy turns of his career – a career in which diplomatic achievements and personal survival were tightly intertwined. Now the moment of truth had come. The recall threatened to wipe out, at a stroke, his political assets, while compromising his standing at home and in Britain. Ostensibly the recall was a result of the Russians' grievances over their exclusion from Casablanca, Churchill's unannounced visit to Washington and the decision to postpone the offensive across the Channel until spring 1944 without consulting the Soviet Union. Maisky genuinely feared the 'grave' consequences of the lack of a strategic and political dialogue, which was bound to 'endanger our relations not only in the closing stages of the war but in the post-war settlement'. A successful Soviet winter offensive could bring the Russians to the German border and enhance the feeling in Moscow that the Allies had played only a minor part in the victory, thus leading to unilateral arrangements and Soviet isolation. His professional future in Moscow hinged on sustaining the collaboration which he hoped to foster, should he be allowed to return briefly to London.[46]

In a series of personal letters and telephone conversations with Molotov (reminiscent in style of his pleadings with Litvinov in the 1920s),[47] Maisky resorted to mundane reasons for seeking permission to return to London: he was concerned about Agniya, who had been left behind and could hardly face a journey back alone in the hazardous wartime conditions, about her 'ear condition' which made it hard for her to fly, about her 'susceptibility to sea-sickness', and about the 'vast amount of luggage (I have many books and other things)' which he wished to ship to Russia. His presence in London – he threw the bait to Molotov – could save the government money, as the British were bound to put at his disposal the appropriate means of transport. Molotov was decisively against, arguing that it would nullify the protest which the recall evoked. But Maisky persevered. He was certain that the British government, which had 'become accustomed to linking [his] name with the idea of Anglo-Soviet cooperation' would have perceived his departure 'as a symptom of our displeasure at British policy, as a symptom of the fact that some cracks have grown in the Anglo-Soviet relationship'. His sojourn in London, which he promised would be 'a careful farewell', could further help 'prepare the ground a little' for Gusev, his successor. True to himself, however, Maisky perceived his recall as a personal setback. His wish to return to England was genuinely motivated by the need (as he wrote in a draft letter to Molotov and then crossed out) to ensure that the 'Soviet government's discontent with the policy of the British government would not appear to foreigners, and still less to our Soviet people, to indicate discontent with the Soviet government's ambassador in London (if, of course, such dissatisfaction actually does not exist)'. In his memoirs, published during the de-Stalinization period, he describes how he looked 'meaningfully' at Molotov, telling him that 'above all' he wished to go to London to prevent the spreading gossip concerning his recall. He goes on to explain that:

> In the years of the great man cult there were many cases when Soviet Ambassadors were unexpectedly recalled to Moscow and then vanished without a trace – either into the grave or behind the bars of some camp. Therefore in the West there had been created the impression that, once a Soviet Ambassador was recalled to Moscow, some unpleasantness or other was awaiting him at home. I wanted to protect myself against this kind of interpretation and suspicion.[48]

Molotov, who could see through Maisky, was determined to remove the final stumbling block to his complete control of the ministry. After almost a month of beseeching, Maisky was granted merely five days to wind up his eleven-year sojourn in London, rendering it impractical for him to engage in extensive political conversations. Placed in a straitjacket, Maisky found it most embarrassing to concede to his British friends the restrictive terms of his return. Former acquaintances who came to bid farewell found him 'sad and depressed' and 'in a subdued mood'. There was 'a queer distant look in his Mongolian eyes which seemed to indicate that he was sad to leave London'.[49] Short of time, he had to resort to flimsy excuses in turning down numerous invitations – even an invitation from Churchill's wife, Clementine, to attend an Allied rally.[50]

Maisky's intentions were, just as they had been in 1939,[51] to return to Moscow with tangible political achievements concerning post-war collaboration and the definition of European borders. In a last-ditch attempt to mollify his masters in Moscow, and to exhibit his new formal status to London, Maisky exploited his short sojourn in London to embark upon a series of lightning unauthorized negotiations with Churchill and Eden. He once again plotted with Eden, who was concerned about the way Churchill was becoming 'dangerously Anti-Russian'.[52] The two met on almost a daily basis, at one point three times a day. Maisky was most candid with Eden, expressing his own private views 'off record'. Eden, though, found it difficult to decide whether Maisky's words 'expressed only his own opinion, and to what degree it had reflected the opinion of his chiefs'.[53] Maisky sought a quick agreement – before the military reality on the battlefield dictated the political outcome of the war – leading to the establishment of an indivisible Europe, where both British and Russian interests were taken into account. Personally, he told Eden, he was 'fundamentally opposed to any Russian domination in Central Europe and has always dreaded Pan-Slavism almost as much as he hates Pan-Germanism'. He remained faithful to his enduring belief that no conflict of interests existed between Britain and the Soviet Union on spheres of influence. He visualized the establishment of consensual independent democracies in Europe, expecting them to be centre-left in their orientation. Like Litvinov, he rejected any idea of setting up revolutionary regimes in the liberated countries. Russia's sphere of interests, according to his scheme, went only slightly beyond Russia's 1941 borders, extending into the Balkans and the Black Sea littoral.

Having witnessed at close quarters the extent of the devastation in Russia and the high price paid on the battlefield, Maisky hoped he could help dispel the growing suspicion in Moscow that both Churchill and Roosevelt were interested in prolonging the war. Although he had not been authorized to pursue the matter with Eden, he knew that Stalin and Molotov attached great importance to an imminent convening of the Allied foreign ministers and the setting up of a permanent commission in Sicily to coordinate the strategic conduct of the war. He still favoured a second front in France (this would be Maisky's last appeal in the relentless campaign he had pursued over the previous two years), but he now advocated such a front 'anywhere, including the Balkans', provided it drew away from the Russian front a sufficient number of divisions and brought the war to a quick conclusion. It is worth noting that Eden gained the right impression that Maisky 'seemed to wish to attend' the projected conference, which he hoped would be convened in London. Stalin, however, fully backed by Roosevelt (to Churchill's manifest dismay and Maisky's disappointment), was determined to hold it in Moscow.[54] Maisky also met Churchill on 9 September to transmit Stalin's response to Churchill's report on his American trip, but alas no record of their last meeting has survived.

Maisky obviously found it difficult to reconcile himself to the fact that he was no longer the serving ambassador in Britain and reckoned that a diplomatic coup might make it possible for him to extend his stay in London. The reaction from Moscow, however, was chillingly cynical advice from Molotov not to 'waste his strength and endanger his health in vain'. He was encouraged to return promptly to Moscow.[55] At the same time, the young Soviet chargé d'affaires, Arkadii Aleksandrovich Sobolev (one of Molotov's new recruits) was praised for his harsh uncooperative dealings with Eden. This did not prevent him from writing to Maisky a year later that Gusev was 'no good' and was 'undoing' all the good work done by the former ambassador.[56] Understandably, Maisky was eager to keep a low public profile. 'The less that was said in public by either of us,' he pleaded with Eden, 'the better.' He was relieved by Eden's assurances that there were to be no public speeches at a farewell luncheon. Yet it was as important for him to display in Moscow his powerful standing in London, which could secure for him a favourable role as an influential go-between. The farewell lunch at the fashionable Dorchester Hotel, attended by Halifax, Lloyd George, Bevin, Brooke, Cripps and many other prominent British politicians, certainly served that end.[57] But the double-edged strategy could not be received with equanimity in Moscow, particularly not by Molotov, who surely resented newspaper headlines such as 'Eden, Maisky Open Wide Talks Today', exalting Maisky's new role in the ministry:

> Foreign Secretary Anthony Eden will meet Ivan M. Maisky, Vice Foreign Commissar and former Ambassador to London, tomorrow for the first of a series of discussions that, it is hoped in diplomatic circles, will lead to a conference attend by Vyacheslaff M. Molotoff, Russian vice premier and foreign Commissar; Cordell Hull, United States Secretary of State, and the British Foreign Secretary sometime this autumn. Tomorrow's meeting and those that follow should help to dispel rumors of a serious break between the western allies and Russia.[58]

The eagerness to present his return to Moscow as a promotion, and his absence as merely a brief interlude, is evident in the dozens of letters Maisky wrote to prominent politicians of his acquaintance during the short time he spent in London. He assured Butler, after informing him of his departure and new appointment that, 'although now we part we shall meet again in the future, as the world is a very small place, and there is always an opportunity to meet at one place or another'.[59] In a letter to Vansittart, Maisky announced in great pomp and circumstance his departure 'to take up my new duties at the Foreign Commissariat in Moscow'.[60]

Although most of the letters were almost identical, each of them included a specific personal tribute to endear him to the addressee. Bernard Pares, the renowned British historian of Russia, for instance, was captivated by Maisky's recognition of his 'important work ... getting the Russian people understood by the British people', and his 'excellent' translation of Krylov's fables. He considered the letter to be 'among those which I value highest'.[61] Some letters aimed at securing the friendship he had forged with outstanding intellectuals and writers over decades of acquaintance. 'I shall always remember our talks on various occasions,' he sought to impress Bernard Shaw, 'for the pleasure your wit, your eloquence, your erudition and your creative vision gave me ... it was a joy to follow the brilliant pulsations of your mind. After all life would be a terribly dull affair without a certain spiritual draught to disperse the fumes of petty-fogginess and the tuppenny-halfpenny sagacity of everyday traditionalism, and you are just the man to dispense this.'[62] On the morning of his departure, Maisky flipped through the pages of *The Times*, as was his daily habit, and his heart sank on seeing the death notice of Bernard Shaw's wife, whom he and Agniya had visited only recently. He followed up with a second letter of condolence, revealing the warm relations that had existed between the two for over 25 years: 'This year has brought us the loss of two very dear friends – your wife and Beatrice Webb. I wish I could have seen you before leaving to express the sympathy I feel for you in person.'[63]

121. Maisky takes stock of his treasures in Baghdad.

Maisky arrived in Cairo with seven trunks full of personal belongings and some 70 pieces of heavy luggage, which required six three-ton trucks for the long drive from Cairo to southern Russia, via Palestine, Iraq and Iran. All attempts to separate Maisky from his luggage, in spite of the long slow journey ahead at 15 miles per hour, were stubbornly rejected. The security arrangements, testified the British intelligence officer in charge of the convoy, were 'out of all proportion for a retiring ambassador'. He could see no reason why anyone would be interested in assassinating him or 'why a grave situation should arise if he was killed'. The convoy consisted of 11 cars. Once in Cairo, Maisky decided to send ahead to Tehran the three Soviet diplomatic couriers assigned to accompany him. 'Obviously a suspicious man,' thought Major Sansom, 'presumably he did not trust them either.' When any of the vehicles broke down, Maisky insisted on stopping the whole convoy while he 'watched the repairs unblinkingly from start to finish'.[64] The British minister in Damascus, General Spears, was flabbergasted by the enormous quantity of books and documents which were taken out from the trucks in bundles to Maisky's room, while there were 'always two men involved in each journey, as it was so arranged that never was a single man left in charge of a consignment. And the men looked terrified. I do not suppose I will ever have to describe a line of men in a queue on the steps to the guillotine. If I had to, I would only have to recall the expressions of these Russian couriers.'[65]

Having achieved remarkable progress in defusing the crisis in Anglo-Soviet relations and securing Eden's visit to Moscow, Maisky intended to exploit his presence in the Middle East to make a bold move aimed at drawing the Zionist *Yishuv* into the Soviet orbit. His initiative was prompted by information he had gleaned from Chaim Weizmann, the president of the World Zionist Organization, on the eve of his departure,

122. Maisky in 'colonial' attire visiting General Spears (right), British minister to Syria and the Lebanon.

concerning Anglo-American plans for the settlement of the Jewish–Arab conflict which left Russia out in the cold. Maisky's confidence seems to have been bolstered by the positive reaction in the Soviet capital to the establishment of diplomatic relations with Egypt, which he had brought about during his July visit to the Middle East. 'When I received a telegram recalling me to Moscow,' he later reminisced, 'the idea immediately flashed through my mind: "Aha! When I pass through Cairo I will try and come to an agreement about diplomatic relations directly with Prime Minister Nahas Pasha."'[66] Having already prepared the ground in London, Maisky arrived in Cairo, according to the British ambassador, 'with all his ideas nicely taped: exactly what he wanted to do and when … As I had expected one of the first items on his agenda was to see our local Prime Minister … the result was a foregone conclusion, the elimination of all points of difficulty in the way of the immediate opening of relations between Cairo and Moscow.'[67]

On his way home in October, Maisky spent three crucial days in Palestine, which gave him a unique opportunity to gain a first-hand impression of the viability of the Zionist movement in Palestine and of the ability of the country to absorb a considerable Jewish immigration. Defying the British high commissioner, Maisky spent time visiting the old religious Jewish quarters in Jerusalem and touring the modern part of the city. He further met Ben-Gurion, Golda Meirson (Meir) and other leaders of the Jewish *Yishuv* in the exemplary kibbutzim of Ma'ale HaHamisha and Kiryat Anavim. Despite his lifelong deliberate effort to distance himself from his Jewish origins, the visit appears to have 'captivated him'. Agniya was 'intensively involved; she wanted to know what everything was called in Hebrew'. The affinity was undoubtedly enhanced by the sense of familiarity Maisky must have felt in Palestine. Most of his interlocutors spoke fluent

123. Maisky (front row, third from left) confers with Ben-Gurion (on his left) at a kibbutz near Jerusalem.

Russian, displayed confidence in the efficacy of the Zionist movement as a political force, once the British left Palestine, and embraced genuine socialist ideas.[68]

As part of his desperate attempts to play up his own status, Maisky misled Ben-Gurion (and subsequent historians) into believing that he was conveying his government's views. He was now, so he boasted, 'number three in foreign affairs', after Stalin and Molotov, and as the expert on Europe it was 'up to him' to deal with the future of the region.[69] Oblivious to Maisky's precarious standing at home, the Zionist leaders later maintained that a direct link existed between Maisky's visit to Palestine and the surprising Soviet decision in November 1947 to support partition, paving the way to the creation of the State of Israel.[70] Though apparently Maisky did prepare a glowing report for Stalin, on his return he found the doors to the Kremlin bolted, while he was pretty much incarcerated in the Ministry for Foreign Affairs, his activities confined to research work on reparations and post-war plans.[71] It is little known that in spring 1947, Stalin in fact instructed the Soviet delegation to the United Nations to advocate the creation of 'a single, independent and democratic Palestine', where the Jews would have been a minority. His dramatic volte-face in support of partition into two states had little to do with the Arab–Zionist conflict as such, but was a result of the emerging Cold War and of Western attempts to exclude him from the arrangements concerning the Middle East.[72]

After two days in Tehran, Maisky set off on his arduous but ostensibly adventurous trip, finally reaching Tabriz, where he boarded a train to Moscow.

There was little, however, to genuinely boost Maisky's standing in Moscow on his return. Although his persistence might have contributed to the convening of the summit meetings, he had failed to ensure any concrete Western commitment. Rather than pledging a cross-channel attack in 1945, the British prime minister was determined to follow a 'sound strategy' so long as he could not rule out 'a startling [German] comeback'.[73]

Maisky arrived in the Soviet capital too late to take part in the conference, which he had laboured so hard to assemble. Within days, his assignments were defined: he was to work together with Litvinov on post-war issues, while 'gathering ammunition for future peace talks'.[74] He was manifestly disappointed to be entrusted with the issue of reparations, while Litvinov was granted the major commission dealing with post-war issues. He instructed Gusev, his successor in London, to publicize the fact that both were engaged in work on the peace agreement, but Gusev was specifically told to avoid mentioning the nature of the work assigned to each.[75] Maisky tried in vain to establish warm and personal relations with Molotov. On the occasion of his own sixtieth birthday, Maisky presented Molotov with his youth memoirs. 'It is said,' he wrote to him, 'that writing memoirs is a sign of old age.' Boasting that he still possessed 'enough gunpowder in the cannon', he vowed to continue active work in the service of the party and the nation.[76]

It was just as important for him to impress on his successor and colleagues in London, who in a flash had cut him out, that he was engaged 'up to the neck' in work on reparations, enjoying the support of the teamwork within Narkomindel,[77] and also to maintain the special relations he believed he had forged in London. He sent his memoirs to Churchill as 'one man of letters to another quite apart from our official positions … reminiscences of a man with whom you were so closely associated in the darkest days of our great struggle against the common foe'.[78] The book to Eden arrived with a short letter highlighting his 'important and interesting job' on post-war problems, which kept him 'fully engaged in planning the future'.[79] All to no avail. He must have felt deeply humiliated when, a year later, he was instructed by Molotov to publish in the newspapers highly critical articles on British politics which were hardly congruent with his own views.[80]

Regardless of the dramatic twist in his political fortunes, Maisky did not budge, as he told Eden, from his old belief in the 'similarity' of the historical development of Britain and Russia 'and the complementary nature of our national interests. We were both on the fringes of Europe. Neither of us wished to dominate Europe, but neither of us would tolerate any other Power doing so.' But this was the sober swan song of the old school of Soviet diplomacy. It was a generation, he wrote to the aged Lloyd George, when presenting him with his memoirs, 'which so much contributed to the building of the modern Russia – the USSR', but which had vanished.[81] His and Litvinov's removal from London and Washington left unchecked the triumphant march of Stalin's authoritarian foreign policy, just as the clouds of the Cold War were gathering on the horizon.[82]

The Price of Fame: A Late Repression

Sequestered in the back rooms of Narkomindel while the anti-cosmopolitan campaign and the drift towards confrontation with the West raged on, Maisky was destined for oblivion – particularly as he was anxious to steer clear of his British acquaintances. When one of them turned up unannounced at his apartment in Moscow, 'Maisky refused to let him in, whispering in urgent tones, "You will only endanger me if you try to see me."'[1] His correspondence with his friends on the British political scene was reduced to brief, infrequent and predictable messages. Churchill's greetings for the new year of 1945 were acknowledged, for example, in a single sentence: 'Sincere thanks for your kind greetings and good wishes for 1945, which we both reciprocate.'[2] When Maisky and Litvinov were visited by the diplomatic correspondent of *The Times*, Litvinov did not hide his frustration: 'You've come to see me to learn about Soviet foreign policy? Why me? What do I know about it? Does my government ever consult me? Oh dear me no. I am only Litvinov. I am only the man who was charged with the conduct of foreign

124. On the move, the cosmopolitan leaving Paris for Geneva.

policy for many years, who knows America, who knows Britain. They don't need *my* advice, thank you very much.'[3] The return to Moscow also entailed previously unknown economic hardship. It necessitated coming to terms with an entirely different lifestyle. When Maisky was away at the Yalta conference, Agniya spent his entire salary on new cutlery (as it was becoming 'embarrassing to use the old stuff'); she hesitated to tell him how much it cost, lest he accuse her of thoughtlessness.[4]

The Yalta summit was going to be Maisky's last glorious moment on the international scene. He could be observed by Churchill, Eden and Roosevelt seated next to Stalin (though mostly as an interpreter). While his expertise on reparations won him great plaudits (admittedly exclusively from the Western side), his apparent prominence was deceptive.[5] In a letter to Agniya, he suggested that the work 'was proceeding better than expected', but he added cautiously that 'one should not count one's chickens before they are hatched'. Being accommodated in 'dull and primitive' lodgings with no bath, he knew where he stood.[6] Molotov, apparently deliberately kept him away from the conference until he was urgently summoned by Stalin to replace Pavlov, whose interpreting was manifestly unsatisfactory. Stalin's rude treatment of Maisky, despite his excellent performance, perhaps best epitomized their relationship. According to Maisky, Stalin turned to him angrily and asked: '"Why didn't you turn up for the first session?" I replied that I had not been told that I was needed in that session. Stalin continued in a rage: "You weren't informed? What do you mean by – you weren't informed? You're simply undisciplined. Following your own will. Your oversight has cost us several lend-leases."'[7]

125. The swan song: interpreting for Stalin at the Yalta conference (Roosevelt is to the right, at the top of the table, while Churchill is seated in the front to the left, his back to the camera).

Maisky still made a brief appearance at the Potsdam summit, but Churchill's defeat in the elections and the 'surprising appearance' of Attlee and Bevin, with whom he had a rather distant (if not hostile) relationship, further underlined his irrelevance. Rather paradoxically, it had been Maisky's high standing with the Conservatives which gained him Stalin's respect, while his relations with the members of the Labour government could now prove a pitfall. Those in power in the Kremlin (Kollontay explained to Kerr before he left Moscow to take up the Washington embassy) 'could not forget that [Bevin] was a man of the "old International" which had been against the Bolsheviks in 1917', and it would 'take a long time to live this down'. In the new circumstances, Maisky no longer proved an asset, particularly as Soviet mistrust of Labour would rekindle similar suspicions concerning Maisky's own Menshevik past.[8]

Back from Potsdam, Maisky was kept at arm's length in the ministry. Relieved of his position as head of the reparations committee, he was given no new assignment. He could not even secure an audience with Molotov. He was finally received by the foreign minister, after repeated pleas, in March 1946 – only to be castigated for 'passivity in writing and lack of involvement in the everyday working of the People's Commissariat' and for the work on reparations, which was 'weak'. He was further humiliated, assigned to a large team which was collectively preparing a Soviet diplomatic dictionary. He surely found the work – a highly censored monument to Molotov's transformation of the ministry – humiliating.[9]

Maisky's survival instincts now led him to reinvigorate his status in the less hazardous, yet prestigious, sphere of the Russian Academy of Sciences. Sensing earlier that his career at the ministry was drawing to an end, Maisky was quick to take charge of his own destiny. He resorted to flattery, congratulating Stalin personally on being made a 'Hero of the Soviet Union':

> ... my heart is full of joy. I can remember no other occasion than this when the reward so well matched the effort. It is difficult for me to imagine what would have happened to our people, to our party, to all of us if you had not throughout these years, and in particular these terrible last four years, been the leader of the Soviet Union.
>
> And one more thing: what a marvellous speech it was you made at the last reception in the Kremlin! It was deep and very timely.
>
> Yours with deep respect
> I. Maisky[10]

Maisky now made a bold personal appeal to Stalin, arguing that his literary and research skills could be better employed at the Academy of Sciences – an appeal accompanied by two expensive British pipes from a leading manufacturer. At 62, he wrote to Stalin, it was 'right to think of a more serious move to the academic and literary environment'. 'If you have no objection to my plan,' he suggested, 'I would be most grateful to you were it to be implemented. It so happens that the Academy is committed to reinvigorate its ranks through the recruiting of fresh forces ... candidates' names need to be put forward no later than 24 June.' It did not require much persuasion on the part of Stalin to ensure that a month later Maisky was unanimously voted into the Academy.[11] Though he was brilliantly qualified for such a position – boasting an extensive bibliography of close to 250 publications and vast experience as a penetrating analyst of contemporary history – the circumstances of his appointment nonetheless raised an eyebrow or two. Endorsing the appointment, Stalin went on amusing himself by offering membership of the Academy to politicians he no longer trusted. While Vyshinsky accepted, both Litvinov and Molotov declined the honour.[12]

The transition was timely: in January 1947, Maisky was relieved of his work at the ministry, and by a unanimous vote was stripped of his candidate membership of the Central Committee of the Communist Party. The stifling atmosphere of the terror, which resumed to some extent in the early 1950s, hampered any serious work at the Academy. The projects he was entrusted with hardly lifted his spirits. As the nephew of Tarle (the famous Russian historian who stood by the Maiskys during his arrest and trial) observed: 'Maisky had turned from a careful but very self-confident diplomat into a know-nothing academician working on some kind of problems of Spanish history that only he knew about and even he didn't care about.'[13]

Maisky's cohort of colleagues from the 'Chicherin–Litvinov school of diplomacy' had thinned, through purges, natural causes – and often through 'diversions to other work'. One could still run into a gloomy Litvinov, somewhere in the House on the Embankment. Sensitive acquaintances, who had once adored the grand Maisky couple, quickly vanished 'and the inseparable childless couple were left on their own, fearfully waiting'. The anti-cosmopolitanism campaign deplored the 'worship of foreign things' with which Maisky was associated. How sad it was to see the fragile, ageing and sick Kollontay obliged to remove from her walls the portraits of Swedish King Gustaf Adolf and his son, which were given to her as an appreciative souvenir for her services in Stockholm.[14] Over dinner at a friend's dacha, Maisky, 'an avowed story-teller who had been accustomed to assume centre stage, was now dull and passive, while Agniya bloomed like a rose when she felt like an ambassador's wife, but suddenly stopped when she remembered who she really was now'. It was 'hard to shake a sense of fear coming from them'.[15]

The year 1952 saw the death of Litvinov, Surits and Kollontay, the last survivors of the old 'Narkomindel'. A critical appraisal of Maisky's work in October at the Academy of Sciences was a premonition of things to come. By the end of the year, his relations with Molotov had deteriorated to the point that the latter told Khrushchev he suspected Maisky of being 'an English spy'.[16] It was no surprise, therefore, when on 19 February 1953, Maisky was indeed arrested and accused of 'high treason'. The arrest followed the new wave of purges triggered by the 'doctors' plot' of January 1953, when the Kremlin doctors (mostly Jews) were accused of plotting to murder Soviet leaders. Maisky was quick to 'confess' that he had been recruited as a British spy by Churchill. He was, however, saved by the bell when Stalin died on 5 March, but the amnesty which followed was not extended to him.[17]

Maisky, who was interned in a cell at the basement of the Lubyanka, was subjected to 36 interrogations prior to Stalin's death. It must have been devastating for the 70-year-old revered diplomat who had so resourcefully steered clear of the worst phases of the repressions in the 1930s.[18] The trauma of finding himself in jail on his seventieth birthday was movingly expressed in a poem he wrote to his wife. In tone it echoes Beethoven's *Fidelio*, alluding to Florestan's cry of solitude from prison, as he longed for his lover and for freedom:[19]

… Today I am seventy years old!
Movements, revolutions, wars, openings-up
Of our world have I seen over these years!
In another time this would be enough for three centuries…
I absorbed all of this
With the proud thought of a man
Who knows that it is the course of history that leads him to the place
Where the banner of communism will shine brightly,
I spent my life under the banner of work,
I spent my life believing in the study of optimism …
I brightly lived, and brightly fought and suffered,
I did not spare my strength for the battle,
I lived life in a major key …
And now my star has flickered out in a dark sky,
And the way forward is hidden in a dark shroud,
And I meet this day behind a stone wall;
… My darling! Today, on this cherished day,
From my half-dark room
I call my greetings to you
And in my mind hug you to my bosom.
Thank you so much, my dearest,
For all the happiness you gave me,
For the love which, shining and playing,
Has given me so much warmth and delight
In times of struggle, in times of toil, in times of thought …[20]

The arrest crushed Agniya. Acquaintances recall how all her pretentiousness and self-importance vanished without trace: 'From an English-style lady in trousers she became a downtrodden old lady begging for meetings and trying to find out how he was doing "there".'[21] His image was further tarnished when he was officially declared 'an enemy of the people' by the Institute of General History, while each of his students was called upon to publicly denounce him.[22]

The need to regain his party membership and be fully rehabilitated led Maisky to blot out the short-lived association he had formed with Beria at the time. 'As I have long noted,' commented his student and confidant, the prominent historian Aleksandr Nekrich, 'I.M. does not like to be questioned about that topic.'[23] His prolific literary output categorically avoided commenting on the period following his return to Moscow in 1943, and particularly his arrest and trial. His friends realized that it was a 'bleak period' in his life and that there were 'considerations on that account which he did not intend to share with [them]'. On the rare occasions he referred to the association with Beria, Maisky maintained that throughout his life he had only met him twice – at official luncheons at the Kremlin during the war. All he was prepared to volunteer was that 'facing the threat of harsh physical torture' after his arrest, he had 'entered on the road of self-slander … in a moment of weakness'.[24] He went a long way to impress on his student Nekrich that he had been personally tortured by Beria – though when he expounded the events in a letter to Khrushchev, he claimed to have met Beria for the first time only after Stalin's death and in far more convivial circumstances. Likewise he apparently told Valentin Berezhkov, Stalin's interpreter and later a senior Soviet diplomat, that he had been personally interrogated by Beria and 'hit with a chain and a lash' to force him to confess his spying activities. The interrogation led him to believe that 'Beria was trying to get at Molotov'. Indeed some of his few subordinates in London who had survived the repressions were also arrested and expected to substantiate Stalin's wild theory that when Molotov had a *tête á tête* with Eden on board the train taking him to London from the airport in 1942 he was recruited to British intelligence.[25] Unwillingly Maisky once again found himself on a collision course with Molotov. What Maisky admitted to only a few close friends was that being perceived as Jewish also contributed to his arrest, which happened shortly after the episode of the 'murderers in white gowns'.[26] After all, it was Maisky who had been trying to reconcile Stalin with Zionism.[27]

Though his life was spared, the arrest and trial took an ominous turn, haunting him for the rest of his life. Later, trying to seek his rehabilitation, Maisky concocted a story that on 13 May 1953, once he heard of Stalin's death, and on his own initiative, he sought an interview with his interrogator, Lieutenant General Fedotov, and demanded to recant his earlier false confessions. The interview with the head of counter-intelligence at the Ministry of the Interior was cut short by a personal call from Beria, demanding to see Maisky 'at once'. Maisky insists that this was the only occasion on which he met Beria after his arrest. What exactly happened at this meeting – by no means an interrogation – has been shrouded in mystery. New archival material makes it now possible to reconstruct more faithfully the course of events. It explains why throughout the rest of his life Maisky made a supreme effort to conceal the unfortunate association with Beria. Not only did it cost him two more years of incarceration, but it reinforced the suspicion and hostility towards him due to his Menshevik past, which he would never succeed in discarding.

What is indisputable is that between 15 May and 5 August, the period roughly coinciding with Beria's alleged bid for power, there was, to quote Maisky himself, an inexplicable 'break in the interrogations'. Sergio Beria claims in his memoirs that while his father had a poor opinion of Litvinov (whom he considered 'weak, yielding to pressure from above'), he 'particularly esteemed' Maisky, whom he regarded as 'more quick witted than Litvinov ... a real diplomat who loved his job'. There is no reason to question the testimony of Beria's son concerning Maisky's relations with his father, particularly as Sergio was not particularly fond of the 'agile little Jew who resembled a mouse'. Beria, according to his son, would have preferred to see Maisky replace Litvinov as foreign minister already in 1939, but he was not yet in a position to make his voice heard. He further claims that during Maisky's sojourn in England, his father 'kept up close relations with him – more frequently than with other diplomats' and Maisky 'used to visit us'. Beria's high esteem of Maisky would fit only too well with his admiration of Britain, his support of the triple alliance in 1939, and his impressive library at home boasting scores of books on British history and culture. After Stalin's death, Beria encountered strong opposition from Molotov over his plans to relax the Soviet grip on Eastern Europe and to seek accommodation with the West. 'Seeing how stupidly obstinate' Molotov was, Beria even proposed that he should be replaced by Maisky. He even clashed openly with Molotov over the conduct of foreign affairs, telling him bluntly: 'If you don't agree, you can resign.' Beria further saw to it that Molotov's power in the ministry was curtailed, insisting that major issues of foreign policy should be dealt with by the Presidium of the Council of Ministers.[28] In his memoirs, Molotov indeed claims that in 1953 Beria intended 'to appoint Maisky as minister of foreign affairs' to replace him. He even recalls their 'sharp clash' during the week following Stalin's death. No wonder Molotov returned to his office from that meeting 'in a highly excited state'.[29]

Maisky had in fact learnt of Stalin's death and had an adequate knowledge of the political realignment of forces at the Kremlin much earlier than he would like us to believe. On 31 March he addressed Georgii Malenkov, the newly elected chairman of the Council of Ministers, with a handwritten letter admitting his guilt in betraying the motherland and expressing 'a burning desire to do something that could at least to a small degree atone for the evil' he had inflicted on the USSR. He was prepared 'to accept any form of redemption which will be decided by the relevant "instantsiya"'. Aware of Maisky's wide net of contacts in Britain, which could be conducive for implementing his grand design of a thaw in relations with the West, Beria withheld the letter.

On 7 May, Maisky, contrary to his later version, was summoned by Fedotov for an interrogation where, fearing a provocation, he continued to admit his guilt. Four days later, he sought a second meeting. Far from recanting, as he later suggested, he wished to supplement his initial statement. The third interrogation on the evening of 13 May was interrupted by the phone call from Beria, summoning him to his office right away. As he entered the room, Beria at once told him: 'you have spun your testimony', letting him understand from the tone of the conversation 'that he believed my testimony had been untrue'. 'By so doing,' admitted Maisky to his interrogators, 'Beria encouraged me, if not explicitly told me, to file an official statement renouncing my previous statement.' Beria promised to rehabilitate him, and proposed placing him in charge of work with the intelligence in Britain under the auspices of the Ministry of the Interior. Subsequently, within a day, Maisky indeed handed in his written recantation. To facilitate his work, he was to be elected chairman of the Society for Cultural Relations with Foreign Countries. Insisting that he had not 'the slightest shadow of suspicion' concerning Beria's plans for a coup d'état, Maisky happily obliged, submitting to Beria a detailed outline for action shortly before the latter's arrest at the end of June.[30] It is, of course, inconceivable that such plans were prepared by Maisky in his cell. Berezhkov recalls Maisky telling him that he was escorted from the prison cell to Beria's office, where the table was laid with fruit and a bottle of Georgian wine. He was given back his clothes and personal belongings and allowed to go home.[31] There is a grain of truth in this recollection, but the far more likely scenario is that provided by Lieutenant General Pavel Sudoplatov, in charge of counter-intelligence and special operations at the Ministry of the Interior. The essence of this version was confirmed by the interrogation of Beria after his arrest. Sudoplatov was entrusted with Maisky by Beria, described as 'the ideal man to present to the West' the new Soviet foreign policy.[32] Maisky, however, could not be released right away. He had been implicated by slanderous testimony forced out of the leaders of the Jewish Anti-Fascist Committee before they were executed. Their case still had to be fully reviewed. The solution found for the interregnum was to keep Maisky 'in hiding', residing with his wife in comfortable conditions in the rooms adjacent to General Fedotov's office. Agniya told her friends that the conditions 'there' were now excellent and he had even started writing his memoirs. This, alas, was where the ill-disposed Molotov and Malenkov found him when Beria was arrested.[33]

The insurrection of 16 June in East Germany provided Khrushchev with a pretext to rally opposition against Beria and halt his reforms. Beria was arrested on 26 June and placed in military custody to prevent the domestic security forces from coming to his aid. In presenting the case against Beria before a special plenary session of the Central Committee, both Molotov and Khrushchev blamed him for the events in Germany, which they attributed to his attempts to liberalize relations with the West. Beria was accused of 'getting cues from the chiefs of foreign intelligence'.[34] Once Beria was detained, Khrushchev and Molotov, fearing a backlash from the Ministry of the Interior, were quick to intern his associates, too. Given Molotov's deep-seated distaste for Maisky, who, he claimed, had 'given his consent to Beria' to replace him, it is hardly surprising that (as Molotov put it laconically) 'Maisky was checked out too.' Although most documents relating to Maisky's arrest are under lock and key, the little evidence available suggests that Maisky was rearrested as soon as Beria was taken into custody, and unsurprisingly, he suffered a nervous breakdown.[35] This course of events is confirmed in Ivy Litvinov's unpublished draft autobiography. Apparently she remained Agniya's 'only friend at that time, nobody went to see her, she was absolutely lonely'. From Agniya she learned that 'the reason Maisky got into trouble after Stalin's death was because of Beria, because he was friendly with him'. She gleaned from Agniya that during the agonizing moments of his arrest, 'Maisky had appealed to Beria. He didn't know what he was doing.' This hardly surprised Ivy, who knew that paradoxically 'Maisky couldn't fail to be arrested – because he was friendly with everybody.' Keeping in step with her husband, Agniya later changed her story, arguing that after Stalin's death absurd charges were pressed against Maisky for 'embezzling Government funds'.[36]

The indictment of Beria was based on an alleged plan 'of creating the type of bourgeois order which would be useful to the Eisenhowers, Churchills, and Titos'. 'Skilfully, like a spy,' it continued, Beria 'wove a web of all-manner of intrigues', aiming at placing his own people in key administrative positions. The sentence of the Supreme Court of the USSR, handed down on 24 December 1953, specifically mentioned Beria's 'criminal-treasonous activity' in establishing 'secret ties with foreign espionage'. Seen from this perspective, Maisky, placed by Beria in charge of such activities in Britain, and presumably destined to be foreign minister, implicated him in the eyes of the insurgents, particularly Molotov, his lifelong adversary.[37] Though he was not specifically mentioned in Beria's sentence, Maisky's assumed complicity became public knowledge following a letter that was sent to all party organizations. It suggested that it had been Beria's intention to release 'the British spy' Maisky from imprisonment and install him as his own minister of foreign affairs. It further included excerpts from Maisky's earlier forced confessions that 'having spent so many years working abroad, he had lost the feeling of belonging to his homeland'. When Agniya saw the letter, she turned 'crazy with worry', assuming it implied Maisky's guilt. She was further humiliated by her own party cell, required to produce an account of her relations with her husband. Others who had placed their bets on Beria, including Dekanozov and Merkulov, former head of foreign intelligence, with whom Maisky was now associated, were executed by firing squad. Foreign policy returned to the hands of Molotov.[38]

The interrogation of Maisky resumed on 5 August, when he was placed in the custody of the state procurator, rather than the Ministry of the Interior. He was now charged – according to article 58/1,10 and 11 of the penal code – with 'counter-revolutionary' activities, aimed at the overthrow, subversion or weakening of the Soviet state. In one of the few references ever made by Maisky to his arrest, he summed up the grave accusation in the single word 'treason', thereby relating it to the absurd accusations of espionage which had been levelled against him by Stalin's henchmen. However, the new accusations were, as he himself was quick to recognize at the time, an attempt 'to implicate me in the Beria case'. The most serious accusation levelled at Beria, himself under investigation at the time before his execution in December, was that 'right up to his arrest' he had 'cultivated secret contacts with foreign intelligence services' in preparing his coup d'état. The basis for such accusations was Beria's decision to close Maisky's file and put him in charge of communication with Churchill and intelligence circles in England.[39] Maisky was now removed from the Lubyanka to Butyrka prison, where, apparently fearing provocations through inmates, he demanded to remain in solitary confinement. He successfully resisted the attempts of ten interrogators to extract a confession from him, which would have been used in the ongoing proceedings against Beria. The punitive response was the removal of all books from his cell, while he was denied the use of pen and paper for the next two years of his detention.

The abortive protracted interrogations, throughout the summer of 1954 and early 1955, were accompanied by Maisky's repeated pleas to Khrushchev and Voroshilov to drop the accusations and fully rehabilitate him. He remained in jail for another year before charges were formally brought against him. In mid-May 1955, he was finally given the 39-page indictment – and a pencil. Having refused a defence counsellor, he was allowed to use the reverse of the document to prepare his case personally. After Beria's execution, the interrogators had made futile attempts to frame Maisky through confessions which had been extracted from his colleagues in the embassy following their arrest in 1937. They also forced G.A. Deborin, a professor at the Military Academy, to dig into Maisky's confiscated papers and come up with incriminating material concerning his ambassadorship in London.

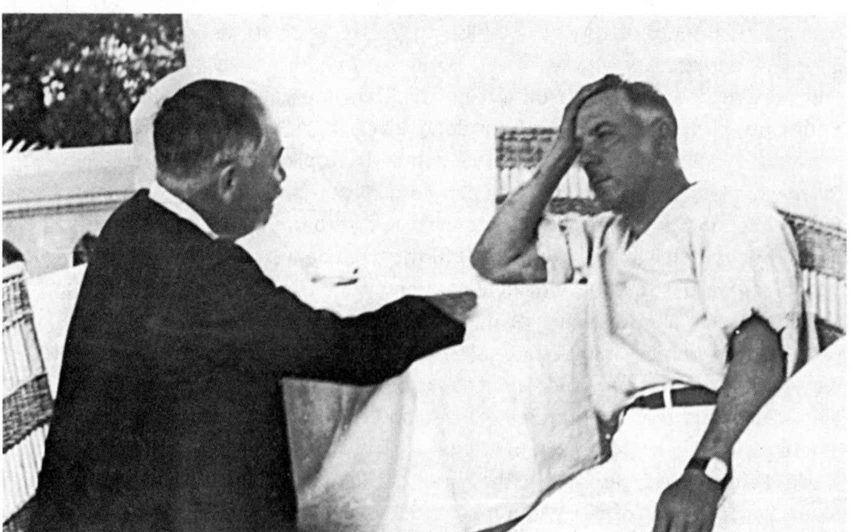

126. Voroshilov and Maisky had seen better days in Sochi in 1934.

When Maisky set off for London in 1932, he had been tipped off by Litvinov that his achievements 'would be measured in Moscow by the close personal relations he would forge in London'. His outstanding success, however, now proved his downfall. Once the accusations of espionage and complicity with Beria were dropped, the main corpus of the indictment was based on information which was retrieved from his confiscated diary, allegedly exposing excessive intimacy in his relations with Churchill and Eden, as well as initiatives which he had concealed from his government. Moreover, he was accused of withholding from it vital information, sending disinformation, and providing wrong advice concerning the triple negotiations and the campaign for a second front. Though generally absurd, there was a grain of truth in the accusations. Maisky successfully exposed the falsity of what he described as 'Arabian nights fairy tales', but he found it difficult to convince the court that the intimacy he had established with the British elite was only motivated by 'alter ego' reasons. The inept handling of the case by the procurator, culminating in slanderous and unsubstantiated accusations of treason, could no longer secure indictment in the post-Stalinist period. The more so as no hard evidence was produced, while the historical context of the accusations was never properly explored.

The procurator did finally stumble on a delicate matter which proved to be a source of embarrassment for Maisky. The new indictment, and eventual conviction according to article 109 of the penal code, cited abuse of his power, 'having allegedly hidden from the Soviet government a microfilm of the British White Paper of 1939 on the triple negotiations between the Soviet Union, Britain and France'. Maisky belittled the significance of the White Paper. He contended that it had been an attempt to discredit the Soviet Union, and was eventually scrapped, as it would also have revealed the conflict between the French and the British concerning the conclusion of a triple alliance. Moreover, he claimed that it was in the second part of July 1941, after the conclusion of the Anglo-Soviet treaty, that he received from 'some English friends of the Soviet Union' a microfilm of the White Paper. It being wartime, the courier service was disrupted and it was difficult to pass it on to Moscow. Moreover, he wished to ascertain further that the documents and the commentary had not been falsified. However, because of the burden of work at the time, he set it aside among his papers and forgot about the documents, which he 'did not even read'. His vast archives, he reminded them, contained some 80 large boxes, which were pretty much in a chaotic state. The microfilm, 'the size of a small match box, disappeared like a needle in a haystack'. Only during the investigation, he asserted, 'turning over in his head every small detail', did he 'suddenly remember the microfilm' and informed his investigators, of his own volition, of its location. Rather than a deliberate action, it was 'forgetfulness'; rather than 'a crime', it was 'negligence ... a lapse'.[40] He contended that, had he not revealed the existence of the microfilm, it would never have seen the light of day, as 'no one in the London embassy or in Moscow' knew of its existence. But this fevered argument only served to emphasize the significance he had attached to it in the first place, its compromising nature and the secrecy which involved its procurement, most likely already back in 1940.[41] In a draft letter to Khrushchev concerning the incident, shortly after his release from prison, Maisky carefully crossed out argumentative sentences which might have sounded apologetic, but which nonetheless revealed his true state of mind.[42] The narrative concocted in court was repeated in his personal appeal to Khrushchev for full rehabilitation four years later.[43] It was accepted – with great scepticism – when a final decision on his rehabilitation was approved at the end of 1960. By then, however, the struggle for power within the party had been decided, Molotov had been sidelined, and the issue had lost all its political relevance.[44]

In facing the Supreme Military Court, Maisky apparently conducted his defence brilliantly. The testimony of former subordinates at the embassy – Kharlamov, the naval attaché, and Zinchenko, the first secretary – was 'somehow toothless' and even supportive of his case. According to Maisky, the virulent Deborin was 'torn to pieces' by him. Exposed as 'a liar and a scoundrel he became confused, lost his composure' and responded to the counter-interrogation with 'complete silence'. Maisky was aware that the political atmosphere was changing when, before being returned to prison, he was offered 'coffee and waffles'.[45]

The summing up of the defence was scheduled for 2 June, but the meeting was postponed. Maisky rightly assumed that the court was 'seeking instructions from the Central Committee which failed to arrive'. Following a second appeal to Voroshilov, he was finally summoned on 12 June to be sentenced. The charge of abuse of power and privileges while at his ambassadorial post carried with it six years of internal exile. This appears to have been a compromise reached between Molotov and Khrushchev who, as *primus inter pares*, had established himself firmly in the saddle. These developments unexpectedly played to Maisky's advantage. Maisky was hastily pardoned by the Presidium of the Supreme Soviet, spared punishment and allowed to return home. And yet, a special decree had been issued the day before, specifically excluding Maisky from the amnesty of 27 March 1953, which would have led to his full rehabilitation.

The decision to release Maisky seems to have been motivated by Khrushchev's clash with Molotov over the course of Soviet foreign policy. In July 1955, Khrushchev was due to attend a summit meeting in Geneva. Keeping Maisky in prison would have been most embarrassing when he met Anthony Eden (the newly elected prime minister, who was heading the British delegation), who had enjoyed such an intense and close relationship with the former ambassador in London. Full rehabilitation, though, came only in 1960, once Khrushchev had succeeded in consolidating his grip on the Party and overcoming the challenges posed to him by Molotov.[46]

Convicted of an administrative rather than a political crime, Maisky was now, at his request, provided with a desk, paper and stationery. He now felt confident enough to complain to the director of the prison that the desk he had been given had 'legs of different lengths and the surface wobbles, and there is no space for me to put my legs as I write. The desk is also too low. Would it not be possible to bring me even the simplest kitchen table, which would at least give me somewhere to put my legs when I write?'[47] His first action was to scribble a plea for clemency to Voroshilov. This was followed two days later by a detailed critique of the verdict, introducing some 60 corrections to the protocol of the trial.[48] These were accepted by the court and, 'after protracted haggling', he was granted permission to include in the protocol his defence speech and a poem which he had addressed to the judges at the end of the trial:

Beneath a stony vault, on a prison bunk,
I lie abandoned, forgotten, alone…
Confined… By whom?… Not enemies, no!

Confined by friends under lock and key!
    Oh, such madness! Am I really a foe?
And is this how enemies behave?
Thirty long years we have walked the same road,
Shoulder to shoulder, keeping in step!
    We walked and we struggled, and higher
And higher the victory banner was hoisted.
Many of us died… Yet Communism's flames
Flickered from afar to those who remained.
    Then sudden confusion!… Into the dungeon
I am hurled, cast out, named an enemy.
And why? For what? For which terrible deeds?
By whom am I slandered? And who is rejoicing?
… Oh citizen judges, look with eyes open
At the living truth, as duty commands!
Before you today there stands not a criminal
But an honest Soviet fighter and patriot![49]

Maisky devoted the rest of his time in jail to penning an allegoric novel he had composed in his head during the two years of prison, *Close and Far Away* (*Blizko-Daleko*). On 22 July, the Presidium of the Supreme Council of the USSR granted the plea for

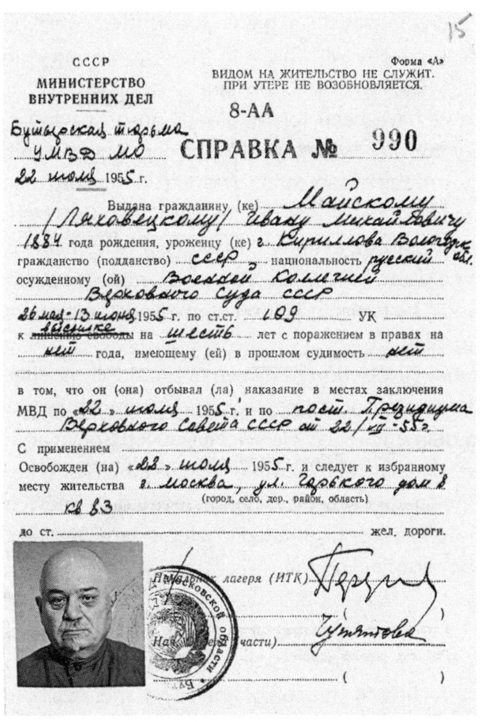

15

СССР
МИНИСТЕРСТВО
ВНУТРЕННИХ ДЕЛ

Форма «А»
ВИДОМ НА ЖИТЕЛЬСТВО НЕ СЛУЖИТ.
ПРИ УТЕРЕ НЕ ВОЗОБНОВЛЯЕТСЯ.

8-АА

Бутырская тюрьма
УМВД МО

СПРАВКА № 990

22 июля 1955 г.

Выдана гражданину (ке) Майскому /Ляховецкому/ Ивану Михайловичу
1884 года рождения, уроженцу (ке) г. Кириллова Вологодск. обл.
гражданство (подданство) СССР, национальность русский
осужденному (ой) Военной Коллегией Верховного Суда СССР
26 мая–13 июня 1955 г. по ст.ст. 109 УК
к ~~лишению свободы~~ ссылке на шесть лет с поражением в правах на нет года, имеющему (ей) в прошлом судимость нет

в том, что он (она) отбывал (ла) наказание в местах заключения МВД по «22» июля 1955 г. и по пост. Президиума Верховного Совета СССР от 22/VII-55 г.
С применением
Освобожден (на) «22» июля 1955 г. и следует к избранному месту жительства г. Москва, ул. Горького дом 8 кв. 83
(город, село, дер., район, область)
до ст. жел. дороги.

Начальник лагеря (ИТК) ( )
Нач. части) ( )
( )

127. The decree on Maisky's release from prison, 22 July 1955.

clemency. Maisky was driven home right away from the Butyrka prison by the officer who had brought the clemency certificate to the prison.

Back at the Academy of Sciences, deprived of many of his rights – including his salary – Maisky was sidelined to work on Spanish history. Only after his full rehabilitation and re-admittance to the party in 1960 (and increasingly after the creation of the Institute of General History) was he able to again steer his career in the direction he had set for himself – writing his memoirs, though always remaining attuned to the winds blowing from the Kremlin.[50] The outpouring of his prolific writings was barely affected by a severe stroke he suffered at the age of 81. His convalescence was, however, set back by severe criticism of his work following Khrushchev's fall. A ground-breaking book by his disciple, A.M. Nekrich, *June 22, 1941*, was publicly denounced and the author expelled from the Party. The English version of Maisky's own memoirs, which included criticism of Stalin's conduct on the eve of the German invasion of Russia, was condemned as 'subjective'.[51] In an unusual move, the ever-cautious Maisky signed a petition, together with the human rights activist Andrei Sakharov and others, protesting against attempts to rehabilitate Stalin.[52]

Confined to his dacha outside Moscow, shielded and pampered by Agniya, he remained lucid and continued to write his memoirs until his death on 3 September 1975. Despite his distinguished position at the Academy of Sciences, Maisky remained a solitary figure. He never again rode the crest of the Soviet political and cultural elite, and was forced to dissociate himself from the powerful and close friends he had made in London. Coveting his glory days in London, Maisky appeared envious of his friend, the radical lawyer Pritt, who was still a 'great globetrotter', while his own life was 'more sedentary', spent in the dacha with his wife 'busy gardening', while he continued to write his memoirs.[53]

How tragic it must have been for Maisky to go on paying a heavy price for his survival until his very last day, forced to atone for his 'ancient' mistakes – forgiven but not forgotten. Only a fragmentary draft was left of his last manuscript, *Memoirs of Churchill, his Circle and his Times*. It was rejected, and then lost, by his publishers, Nauka. 'The blow struck by the publishing house,' Maisky wrote to them, 'is all the more painful as I am now 91 years old and have been working on my book for the last five years, and had hoped that it would be the culmination of my work (I realize that I am now not that far from the end of my life).'[54]

Maisky's long sojourn in London remained undoubtedly his 'finest hour'. The last 20 years of his life at the Russian Academy of Sciences were entirely devoted to recording those formative and dramatic years. 'He sincerely loved Britain and the British,' attested the head of the military mission at the embassy during the war. '[He] spoke fluent English, admittedly, with a noticeable accent … [and] seemed to know every connotation of every word.'[55] His nostalgia is encapsulated in a letter he sent shortly before his death to the then Soviet ambassador in London:

> … We spent 11 years in London, and there has been nothing like that! … and I also spent five years there (1912–1917) as an émigré from tsarist Russia. Naturally, I got attached to this town, and more specifically to particular sites, buildings and monuments … I find myself even now sometimes wondering: How did he set up his study? And what does their dining room look like? And

128. The inseparable couple: with Agniya in old age.

> are there any remnants around from the time of the blitz in the Second World War?[56] … We keep remembering the friendships we forged with the Webbs and Bernard Shaw. Of course, the London of your days will be very different from the London of our time …[57]

Visiting Maisky shortly before his death, his loyal student, the renowned historian Nekrich, found him

> 'moving', literally, pushing a straw chair in front of him and leaning on it, taking heavy steps with one leg and then the other. If it hadn't been for his legs you would never have imagined that I.M. was pushing 90: his dark eyes were mobile, gleaming with thought, and although he spoke slowly and, I would say, slightly falteringly, his speech was entirely coherent and logical and it was clear that he had an excellent command of his memory.

Asked by Nekrich how he had managed to survive, being on the brink of catastrophe so often, Maisky looked at him, 'smiled slightly, and said, "I always kept a cool head on my shoulders." And I thought: Had Stalin lived just a month or two longer, nothing would have helped Ivan Mikhailovich.'[58]

Notes to Volume 3

1941

1. Maisky told Eden that 'he had himself never doubted our ability to resist'; TNA FO 371 29262 N104/50/59, 6 Jan. 1941.

2. 'We howl with laughter at each other but get nowhere'; Pimlott, *Second World War Diary of Hugh Dalton*, p. 148.

3. The Central Zionist Archives (CZA) J89/26, N. Goldmann (Washington) to the Jewish Agency, Sept. 1940.

4. Inspired probably by Wells' meeting with Maisky on 17 January. Michael J. Cohan (ed.), *The Letters and Papers of Chaim Weizmann* (Jerusalem, 1979), XX/A, Weizmann to Wells, 25 Jan. 1941, doc. 102.

5. AVP RF f.059 op.1 p.352 d.2404 ll.158-9, Maisky to Molotov, 2 Sep. 1941.

6. Ben-Gurion Archives, record of a meeting with Maisky, 9 Oct. 1941.

7. AVP RF f.0129 op.26 p.2 d.143, Litvinov on meeting with Weizmann, 2 March 1942.

8. See the chapter on Maisky's recall.

9. RAN f.1702 op.4 d.1194 l.1, 4 Oct. 1940; J. Epstein, *An Autobiography* (London, 1955). p. 123.

10. RAN f.1702 op.4 d.1194 l.2 & 3, 27 & 31 Jan. 1941, exchange of letters with Epstein.

11. *Hansard*, HC Deb 9 April 1946, vol. 421, col.1791; A.J.P. Taylor, *Beaverbrook* (London, 1972), p. 558.

12. TNA PREM, 3/395/16, 22 Feb. 1941; A. Eden, *The Eden Memoirs: The Reckoning* (London, 1965), p. 190.

13. G. Gorodetsky, *Stafford Cripps in Moscow, 1940–1942: Diaries and papers* (London, 2007), pp. 91–6; Eden, *The Reckoning*, pp. 224–5.

14. Cripps returned to Moscow from Ankara firmly convinced, as he intimated to the press and fellow ambassadors, that Russia and Germany would be at war 'before summer'. He cast doubt on Dill's insistence that Hitler would not commence a war on two fronts and predicted that he would attack Russia 'not later than the end of June'; see NA, State Department, 740.0011 EW/39/8919, telegram from Steinhardt, 7 March 1941; V. Assarasson, *I Skuggan av Stalin* (Stockholm, 1963), p. 56; G. Gafencu, *Prelude to the Russian Campaign* (London, 1945), p. 198; W. Duranty, *The Kremlin and the People* (New York, 1942), pp. 151–2; and A. Werth, *Moscow '41* (London, 1942), p. 133. Maisky told the Webbs that 'Eden was friendly, the British Foreign Office was obdurate and Churchill supported the Foreign

Office. Stafford had *apparently* agreed with his government's policy – at any rate he had not succeeded in altering it'; Webb, diary, p. 7036, 3 March 1941.

15. RAN f.1702 op.4 d.848 l.10, 28 Feb. 1941.

16. I. Banac (ed.), *The Diary of Georgi Dimitrov, 1933–1949* (New Haven, 2003), pp. 148–50, 20 Feb., confirms the acute analysis of the *New York Times* and *The Times*, 22 Feb. 1941.

17. *DVP*, 1941, XXIII/1, doc. 707. Cadogan used the occasion to comment acidly in his diary that he rather liked Maisky 'although – or perhaps because – he's such a crook'; Dilks (ed.), *Diaries of Sir Alexander Cadogan*, p. 363.

18. TNA FO 418/87 N1257/3/38 & FO 954/1 BS/41/3.

19. TNA FO 371 29465 N1658/3/38. Eden, who suspected Novikov of being an NKVD agent, recalled to Bruce Lockhart that Maisky 'was very uncomfortable' and 'must have been under suspicion at that time'; Young, *Diaries of Sir Robert Bruce Lockhart*, p. 510.

20. Butler, *The Art of the Possible*, p. 90.

21. See diary entry for 13 June 1941.

22. Russian Military Archives, op.7237, report by Golikov, 16 April 1941. Razvedupravleniya GSH RKKA, *Iz razvedyvatel'noi svodki po zapadu*, 4, 20 April 1941. For detailed discussion of Soviet intelligence, see Gorodetsky, *Grand Delusion*, pp. 130–6, 179–89 and 243–5.

23. The most revealing and authoritative account of the games is in M.V. Zakharov, *General'nyi shtab v predvoennye gody: voennye memuary* (Moscow, 1989), pp. 239–51. See also Presidential Archives, t.8115 op.8 d.44 l.3, Stalin and Molotov to the CC of the CPSU, 21 Jan. 1941.

24. Presidential Archives, f.45 op.1 d.404 ll.91–101.

25. *DGFP*, XII, 537, Schulenburg to Foreign Ministry, 13 April 1941. A detailed discussion of these dramatic events based on Serbian, Russian and British archival material is in Gorodetsky, *Grand Delusion*, ch. 7, 9 and 10.

26. Refers to Vansittart's *Black Record: Germans past and present*, published in 1941, in which he suggested that German history had always been marked by militarism and aggression, of which Nazism was only the latest phase. He advocated the harsh treatment of Germany after the war.

27. F.H. Hinsley, *British Intelligence in the Second World War* (London, 1979), ch. 14.

28. See G. Gorodetsky, 'Churchill warning to Stalin: A reappraisal', *The Historical Journal*, 29/4 (1986). Churchill's version is in W.S. Churchill, *The Second World War: The Grand Alliance* (London, 1950), pp. 317–23, and a somewhat watered down version is in M. Gilbert, *Winston S. Churchill: Finest Hour, 1939–1941* (London, 1983), pp. 1050–1.

29. G.K. Zhukov, *Vospominaniya i razmyshleniya* (Moscow, 1990), I, pp. 368, 371 & 373; TNA FO 371 29465 N1828/3/38; and AVP RF f.069 op.25 d.36 p.73 l.53–61, reports by Eden and Maisky of the meeting, 16 April 1941; Eden, *The Reckoning*, p. 265.

30. AVP RF f.059 op.1 d.2401 l.130 & f.069 op.25 d.6 l.58–9, Maisky to Narkomindel, 9 & 30 April 1941.

31. Maisky is quoting from Pushkin's *Eugene Onegin*. I am grateful to Dr Oliver Ready for pointing this out.

32. Maisky probably means *Gleichschaltung* – 'forcible-coordination', a Nazi term used for establishing their authoritarian rule in occupied territories.

33. An association of the Polish and Lithuanian land nobility which had enjoyed institutional and economic privileges since the fifteenth century.

34. The proverb 'The wish is father to the thought' derives from Shakespeare's *Henry IV Part 2*, but it has become much more common in the German language – to the extent that Maisky, who uses it often throughout the diary, assumes it to be German.

35. Monckton papers, Trustees 5/20-21, Cripps to Monckton, 3 May; TNA FO 371 29465 N1658/3/38, 16 April 1941.

36. Hilger and Meyer, *Incompatible Allies*, p. 328. His memorandum, referred to also by Ribbentrop and Weizsäcker (*DGFP*, XII, 661), has never been recovered.

37. *DGFP*, XII, 666–9.

38. Dekanozov's report of a meeting with Schulenburg, 5 May 1941, reproduced facsimile in *Vestnik ministerstva inostrannykh del SSSR*, 20, 1990. The records of the meetings were preserved in a 'special collection' and not in the Foreign Ministry archives and have, therefore, come to light only since the collapse of the Soviet Union. See also V.A. Voyushin and S.A. Gorlov, 'Fashistskaya agressiya: O chem soobshchali diplomaty', *Vizh*, 6 (1991), pp. 22–3; Hilger and Meyer, *Incompatible Allies*, fn. 39, p. 331.

39. TNA FO 371 29481 N2418178/38, Cripps to FO, 15 May 1941.

40. *DGFP*, XII, 730, 7 May 1941.

41. This provides the long-sought explanation for the issue of the infamous Soviet communiqué of 13 June denying the rumours of an impending war.

42. A memorandum by Dekanozov on his meeting with Schulenburg addressed personally to Molotov in only two copies, reproduced in *Diplomaticheskii vestnik*, 11–12 (June 1993), pp. 75–7.

43. L. Hill, *Weizsäcker-Papiere, 1933–1950* (Berlin, 1996), fn. 38, 16 Feb. 1941, p. 238; and *DGFP*, XII, 734–5, 7 May.

44. J. von Ribbentrop, *The Ribbentrop Memoirs* (London, 1954), fn. 33, p. 152; E. von Weizsäcker, *Memoirs of Ernst von Weizsäcker* (London, 1951), fn. 30, pp. 253–4; and Hill, *Weizsäcker-Papiere*, 1 May 1941, fn. 38, pp. 252–3.

45. The record of the meeting is reproduced in *Diplomaticheskii vestnik*, 11–12 June 1993, pp. 77–8.

46. *DGFP*, XII, 750–1.

47. On this bizarre and intriguing episode, see David Stafford (ed.), *Flight from Reality: Rudolf Hess and His Mission to Scotland, 1941* (London, 2002); R.F. Schmidt, *Rudolf Hess: 'Botengang eines Toren?': der Flug nach Grossbritannien vom 10. Mai 1941* (Duesseldorf, 1997); L. Picknett, C. Prince and S. Prior, *Double Standards: The Rudolf Hess cover-up* (London, 2001); and G. Gorodetsky, 'The Hess affair and Anglo-Soviet relations on the eve of "Barbarossa"', *English Historical Review*, 101/399 (1986).

48. AVP RF, f.059 op.1 p.361 d.2401 ll.133–4, Maisky to Narkomindel, 10 April 1941, and see his diary entries for 1 March, 10 April and 5 May 1941.

49. Alexander papers, AVAR 5/8, 1 April 1941.

50. Maisky was spot on. Churchill instructed Eden that the Russians 'knew perfectly well their dangers and also that we need their aid. You will get much more out of them by letting these forces work than by frantic efforts to assure them of your love'; TNA FO 371 29465 N1725/3/38, 28 April 1941.

51. In Maisky's memoirs, with obvious hindsight, he uses the tale to depict a heroic Churchill who stood firm against all odds. But the impression he and Prytz had at the time was entirely different. Maisky, *Memoirs of a Soviet Ambassador*, pp. 144–5.

52. This metaphor was used by Churchill in his famous radio speech on the day Germany attacked Russia; see diary entry for 22 June 1941.

53. See, for instance, AVP RF f.059 op.1 d.2401 l.283, telegram to Narkomindel, 13 May 1941. For the Soviet reaction to the Hess affair, see Gorodetsky, *Grand Delusion*, ch. 12.

54. TNA FO 371 29501 N2227/122/38; AVP RF f.069 op.25 d.71 ll.72–4 & f.059 op.1 d.352 ll.12–14, 14 and 15 May 1941.

55. AVP RF f.069 op.25 d.6 ll.75–7, Maisky to Molotov, 16 & 21 May 1941; TsA FSB RF f.376 d.28889 t.1 l.47, the NKVD residency in London to the Centre, 14 May 1941. Philby's reports from London dovetailed with those of Maisky, TsA FSB RF f.338 d.20566 l.163, minute of the 1st Dept. of the NKVD, 3 June 1941.

56. Candid talk with the Webbs, diary, p. 7079.

57. Stamford papers, diary, conversations with Maisky, 30 July 1941.

58. Radio direction finder.

59. TNA FO 371 29465 N2570/3/38 & 954/24 SU/41/12&13, Eden's report of conversation, 2 June, and FO's minutes, 31 May–2 June 1941.

60. Dawson papers, diary, Box 45, 11 June 1941.

61. TNA PRO FO 800/279 SU/41/1, departmental minutes, 30 April 1941 & FO 371 29466 N2628/3/38, Eden's report of meeting Maisky, 5 June 1941; Monckton papers, Trustees 5/96, Maisky conversation with Monckton on 5 June.

62. *Pravda*, 14 June 1941.

63. Regardless of the tone of his entry, Maisky was most embarrassed by the incident. Upon returning to the embassy, he hastened to send Eden 'warm greetings' for his birthday and wished him 'many happy returns'. 'May the coming years,' he concluded, 'bring you good health and luck; and the faculty to find the right way in the very complicated circumstances of our time.' RAN f.1702 op.4 d.940 l.20.

64. Maisky, *Memoirs of a Soviet Ambassador*, pp. 149 ff. This episode, so central to any understanding of the events on the eve of war, was omitted from the later Russian version, *Vospominaniya sovetskogo diplomata* (Moscow, 1987). Just as misleading is his desperate attempt to show that he had been constantly warning Moscow before the war.

65. That this was not merely a slip of the pen is evident from the prominent place the incident occupies in another of Maisky's publications, 'The British and I', *Atlas World Press Review*, 11 (1966). Maisky's report to Moscow of his conversation with Cadogan on 16 June is in *DVP*, 1941, XXIII/1, doc. 864; Dilks, *Diaries of Sir Alexander Cadogan*, p. 388.

66. Stamford papers, diary, conversations with Maisky on 30 July 1940.

67. Enigma first revealed on 9 June that significant military and air units were being transferred by Germany to the eastern front in haste. Further corroborating information

emerged on 12 June; TNA CAB 65/22/24 WM(41)58. See also Hinsley, *British Intelligence in the Second World War*, I, pp. 465–83.

68. Dawson papers, diary, Box 45, 16 June 1941, report by McDonald on conversations with Maisky.

69. TNA FO 371 29482 N2793/78/38; AVP RF f.059 op.1 d.2402 ll.203–6, 13 June 1941. Eden gave a detailed report of his warning to the Americans, see *FRUS*, 1941, I, pp. 170–3. On Maisky's analysis of the intelligence, see, for example, I. McDonald (ed.), *The History of the Times*, V: *Struggle in War and Peace: 1939–1966* (London, 1984), p. 84.

70. TNA FO 371 29483 N3047/78/38, minute by Cadogan and Cavendish Bentinck on intelligence transmitted to Maisky, 15 June.

71. Maisky, *Memoirs of a Soviet Ambassador*, pp. 149, 165–71; Dilks, *Diaries of Sir Alexander Cadogan*, p. 388.

72. TNA FO 371 29466 N3099/3/38, memorandum by Cripps, 19 June 1941.

73. *The Times* archives, Dawson to Halifax, 22 June 1941.

74. On 18 June and again on 20 June, Enigma revealed specific instructions given to the German air force in the north for the offensive. Hinsley, *British Intelligence in the Second World*, p. 479. On Cripps's conviction, see also Dawson papers, diary, Box 45, 19 June 1941.

75. TNA FO 371 29466 N3099/3/38.

76. TNA FO 371 29466 N3232/3/38.

77. Library of Congress, Davies papers, Box 11. See also Halifax papers, diary, A7.8.19, 11 Dec. 1941.

78. TNA FO 371 29560 N3056/3014/38. Maisky's report is much more detailed in G.P. Kynin, P.P. Sevostianov and V.P. Suslov, *Sovetsko-angliiskie otnosheniya vo vremya Velikoi Otechestvennoi voiny, 1941–1945* (Moscow, 1983) (hereafter *SAO*), I, no. 2; Eden, *The Reckoning*, pp. 270–1.

79. TNA FO 37124852 N6029/24/38, memorandum by Sargent, 17 July 1940.

80. TNA CAB 79/12 COS(41)21O, 14 June; JIC in FO 371 29484 N3047/78/38, 15 June; CAB 84/31, 32 and JP(41)429, 451, 13 & 14 June 1941. At the end of April, Bruce Lockhart was asked by Alan Brooke, following consultations at the Foreign Office, to form a nucleus of loyal Russians in London, in the event of Germany 'walking through Russia like butter'. Alan Brooke, however, declined as he did not believe it was possible to do anything 'without Maisky knowing'; Bruce Lockhart Papers, diary, LOC/37-41, 30 April 1941.

81. Amery papers, diary, AMEL 7/35, 22 June 1941.

82. TNA FO 371 29483 N2904 & 29484 N3040/78/38, memoranda, 13 & 17 June; Harvey Papers, Ms. 53697, diary, 18 June 1941. When news of the attack reached Churchill, he castigated communism saying that 'the Russians were barbarians … that not even the slenderest thread connected Communists to the very basest type of humanity'; Colville, *Fringes of Power*, p. 405.

83. FO 371 29560 N3056/3014/38, Eden to Baggallay, Moscow, 22 June 1941; Maisky, *Memoirs of a Soviet Ambassador*, p. 160.

84. TNA WO 193/666, 29 June; TNA CAB 84/32 JP(41)478, 482, 485 & 500, 23, 24, 25 & 30 June; TNA CAB 79/12 COS(41)221 & 222, 23 & 24 June 1941. On the consistent 'wear down' element in Churchill's strategy rather than an offensive outlook, see B.P. Farrell,

'Yes, Prime Minister: Barbarossa, Whipcord, and the basis of British grand strategy, Autumn 1941', *Journal of Military History*, 57/4 (1993), and G. Gorodetsky, 'Geopolitical factors in Stalin's strategy and politics in the wake of the outbreak of World War Two', in S. Pons and A. Romano (eds), *Russia in the Age of Wars, 1914–1945* (Milan, 2000).

85. TNA CAB 84/3 JP(41)78, 465 & 482, 16, 19 & 24 June; and COS(41)218, 19 June 1941; E. Butler, *Mason-Mac: The life of Lieutenant-General Sir Noel Mason-MacFarlane* (London, 1972), pp. 133–4.

86. Illuminating evidence on Soviet priorities is in the British records of the COS meeting with the Soviet military mission, in TNA CAB 69/2 DO(41)45, 3 July & FO 37129466 N3304/3/38, telegram from Eden to Cripps, 30 June 1941. See also Molotov's talk with the British military mission on 30 June, in *SAO*, I, pp. 54–62, 83–4; N. Kharlamov, *Difficult Mission: War memoirs of a Soviet admiral in Great Britain during the Second World War* (London, 1986), pp. 33–6; and F.I. Golikov, 'Sovetskaya voennaya missiya v Anglii i SShA v 1941 g.', *Novaya i noveishaya istoriya*, 2 (2004).

87. TNA FO 371 29486 N3524/78/38; AVP RF f.059 p.423 d.3789 l.5 & p.415 d.3728 ll.15–16. Maisky spoke in the same vein to Butler a day earlier, TNA FO 371 29466 N3304/3/38, and Butler papers, RAB G13/111. See also TNA FO 954/31 W191/41/45, Eden's note to Churchill, 4 July.

88. Passfield papers, 2/4/M, 22 July 1941; RAN f.1702 op.4 d.143 l.71, 21 Sep. 1941.

89. AVP RF f.059 p.1 op.352, d.2402, ll.316–20, 26 June 1941. Much in the same vein, see a report of Maisky's meeting with Beaverbrook, *SAO*, I, no. 5, 28 June 1941.

90. TNA FO 371 29467 N3529/3/38, telegram from Cripps, 8 July; Cripps papers, diary, 9 July 1941.

91. *SAO*, I, pp. 47–8.

92. TNA FO 371 29466 N3304/3/38.

93. Webb, diary, p. 7121, 10 July 1941.

94. Dilks, *Diaries of Sir Alexander Cadogan*, p. 392.

95. Kharlamov, *Difficult Mission*, p. 37; F.I. Golikov, *On a Military Mission to Great Britain and the USA* (Moscow, 1987), pp. 42–6.

96. TNA CAB 69/2 DO(41)45, 3 July; CAB 79/13 COS(41)234, 5 July; WO 193/645A, 10 July 1941.

97. TNA FO 954/24 SU/41/36, Eden to Churchill, 16 July 1941; J. Harvey (ed.), *The War Diaries of Oliver Harvey, 1941–45* (London, 1978), p. 20.

98. Kharlamov, *Difficult Mission*, p. 45; Churchill, *Grand Alliance*, p. 343.

99. Tchaikovsky's '1812 Overture'.

100. Noel-Baker papers, NBKR 4/645, 14 July 1941. See also P.M.H. Bell, *John Bull and the Bear: British public opinion, foreign policy, and the Soviet Union, 1941–1945* (London, 1990), pp. 38–9. The government was criticized in the Commons, *Hansard*, HC Deb 24 July 1941, vol. 373 cols 1160.

101. Maisky's more synthesized report of the meeting is in *SAO*, I, no. 24.

102. The original house on the site was built in the twelfth century, but the present mansion dates back to the sixteenth century.

103. Taylor, *Beaverbrook*, ch. 19.

104. Beaverbrook papers, BBK\D\92, 1 July 1941.

105. E. Barker, *Churchill and Eden at War* (London, 1978), pp. 20–1; D. Carlton, *Anthony Eden: A biography* (London, 1981), pp. 168–70; S. Aster, *Anthony Eden* (London, 1976), pp. 17–19.

106. TNA FO 371 29467 N3607/3/38, exchanges between Churchill and Eden, 9 July 1941; Harvey, *War Diaries of Oliver Harvey*, pp. 17–19, 24. His commitment was reflected in his conversation with Maisky on 30 June 1941, reported in *SAO*, I, no. 7.

107. Nicolson, *Diaries*, 22 Oct. 1941, pp. 188–9.

108. TNA CAB 65/19 72(41)2, 3, 5 & 74(41)2, 21 & 24 July; CAB 79/13 COS(41) 259 & 264, 23 & 28 July 1941. See also W.A. Harriman and Elie Abel, *Special Envoy to Churchill and Stalin, 1941–1946* (New York, 1975), p. 72.

109. Churchill's telegrams of 25, 28 & 31 July 1941 are in TNA PREM 3/170/1. An account of the visit and Cripps's draft telegram to Stalin are in Hopkins papers, Box 306, 30 and 31 July, and in Cripps papers, diary, 1 & 2 Aug. See also Roosevelt papers, Box 2987, Cripps to Roosevelt, 1 Aug. 1941. Hopkins' mission is analysed in Gorodetsky, *Stafford Cripps' Mission in Moscow*, pp. 193–204. On the shift in the American position, see Jacob papers, diary, JACB 1/9, p. 46.

110. AVP RF f.059 op.1 p.412 d.3707 ll.14–22, 22 Aug. 1941.

111. 'Who,' Colville thought, 'looked down, rather disapprovingly' at the proceedings; Colville, *Fringes of Power*, p. 422.

112. Retinger, too, remarked that 'Churchill looked tired, and he was deeply and visibly moved. There were quivers in his voice, and tears in his eyes'; J. Retinger, *Memoirs of an Eminence Grise* (London, 1972), p. 120.

113. AVP RF f.059 p.415 d.3728 ll.1–4; detailed reports of the negotiations are in TNA FO 418/87 C7865/3226/55, FO 371 26755 C7865/3226/55 & 26756 C8028/3226/55; Dilks, *Diaries of Sir Alexander Cadogan*, p. 391. Beneš had arranged without a hitch an agreement with Maisky regulating the relations between Czechoslovakia and the Soviet Union; see E. Beneš, *The Fall and Rise of a Nation: Czechoslovakia, 1938–1941* (New York, 2004), pp. 128–9. See also A.M. Cienciala, 'Detective work: Researching Soviet World War II policy on Poland in Russian archives', *Cahiers du Monde Russe*, 40/1–2 (1999), pp. 256–60. Molotov's disparaging attitude to the Poles is evident in his correspondence with Maisky, for instance in AVP RF f.059 p.422 d.3778 ll.137–8, 23 July 1941.

114. TNA FO 371 26755 C7423/3226/55; see also Retinger, *Memoirs*, pp. 111–20. On Katyn, see diary entry for 23 April 1943.

115. Maisky was informed by Strang on 29 July that Sikorski had assured Eden that he did 'not intend to make a speech at the time of the signature of the agreement'; RAN f.1702 op.4 d.1596 l.5.

116. The word, obviously not a complimentary one, is deliberately omitted in the original manuscript.

117. Word left out in the original.

118. Britain had long had an interest in Iran, due to its vast oil fields and its strategic position safeguarding the gateways to India and the Orient. When the German armies invaded Russia and approached the Caucasus, fears arose that the Germans might turn

southwards towards Iran, thus threatening the entire British position in the area. To counter such a threat, a joint Anglo-Russian invasion of the country was launched on 25 August. The stated objectives of the operation, to counter German 'Fifth Columnists' in the country and to open a supply line to Russia, thinly veiled the genuine sole objective of forcing a division of Persia on the 1907 Anglo-Russian partition lines. Churchill told his son Randolph that the 'questionable' operation was 'like taking a leaf out of the German book', while Colville, his private secretary, referred to it as 'an aggressive and not really warranted act'. Eden, according to his private secretary, was 'ashamed of himself', and like the PM, regarded the invasion as England's 'first act of "naked aggression"'. M. Gilbert (ed.), *The Churchill War Papers* (New York and London, 2001), III, pp. 1132–3; Colville, *Fringes of Power*, p. 430; Harvey, *War Diaries of Oliver Harvey*, p. 36. Molotov briefed Maisky that the Soviet Union had no territorial claims, but wished to develop a transport route through the country to facilitate the transfer of British supplies to Russia. AVP RF f.059 p.422 d.3778 l.152 and TNA FO 954/24 SU/41/53, 26 and 28 July 1941.

119. Maisky's harsh report 'left a very strong impression on Eden', visibly embarrassing him. He made a 'faint effort to defend the British Government though one felt that he did so without conviction and out of duty'; TNA FO 954/24 SU/41/72 & 74, Eden on meeting Maisky, and Maisky reports in AVP RF f.059 op.1 p.412 d.3729 l.50, ll.62–3, ll.87, 96 & 102, 21, 22 & 26 Aug. 1941. See also Kharlamov, *Difficult Mission*, pp. 64–5.

120. The abbreviation is for *instantsiya*, which in Russian connotes *vlast* – the power or authority. In earlier days, instructions from the Central Committee of the CPSU were handed down under this title, before it was appropriated by Stalin. It was most unusual for Stalin to communicate directly with an ambassador, and it clearly flattered Maisky, whose stock had sunk low in the previous two years. Maisky pretty much produces the telegram in its entirety; AVP RF f.059 p.422 d.3779 l.58. Stalin's mistrust was evident in the way he scrutinized each of the public speeches made by Eden and Churchill, which were translated for him. See, for instance, Eden's speech in Coventry from that day in RGASPI, Stalin papers, f.558 op.11 d.280 l.41–2.

121. On 6 September, Maisky reported that Moore-Brabazon, the minister of aircraft production, had told representatives of the Trades Union Congress in Edinburgh over breakfast: 'Let Germany and the USSR weaken each other … at the end of the war England, with its powerful aviation, will command the mastery of Europe'; AVP RF f.059 p.415 d.3729 l.197, 6 Sep. 1941.

122. Maisky is referring to the successful measures taken by the retreating Red Army in 1941 to dynamite the most strategically important dam and electric power plant as part of their scorched-earth strategy.

123. The following two entries were most likely written after the entry for 7th. They were in abbreviated form and have here been expanded.

124. TNA PRO CAB 120/678, 5 Sept. 1941; see also Dilks, *Diaries of Sir Alexander Cadogan*, p. 405.

125. TNA PRO FO 371 29490 N5105/78/38, tel. to Cripps, 5 Sept. 1941. Typically, Churchill, *The Grand Alliance*, pp. 409–11, fails to mention Cripps's *coup*. A detailed account

of the events as seen from Churchill's vantage point is to be found in Gilbert, *Finest Hour*, pp. 1182–6.

126. See Gorodetsky, *Stafford Cripps in Moscow*, pp. 5–18.

127. J. Erickson, *The Road to Stalingrad* (New York, 1975), pp. 196–210.

128. Stalin presented a grave view of the situation on the front, ending with a plea: '... to open, already in this year, a second front in the Balkans or in France, which would draw 30–40 German divisions from the eastern front, as well as to provide for the delivery to the USSR of 30,000 tons of aluminium and minimum 400 planes and 500 tanks monthly by October. Without these two kinds of aid, the Soviet Union may either suffer a debacle or be weakened to such an extent that it would not be able to give active support to its allies in their struggle against Hitlerism for a long period of time. I am afraid my present message may disappoint Your Excellency. It cannot be helped. Experience taught me to look realities straight in the face, no matter how unpleasant they are, and fear not to tell the truth, no matter whether it is wished to be heard or not.' For Stalin's telegrams see V.O. Pechatnov and E.E. Magadeev, *Perepiska I.V. Stalina s F. Ruzvel'tom i U. Cherchillem v gody Velikoi Otechestvennoi voiny* (Moscow, 2015), I, Nos. 10–15.

129. Maisky is using the ammunition provided to him by Lloyd George in his tirade against Churchill in their conversation on 16 August.

130. Maisky's report in *SAO*, I, no. 39, and Eden in TNA FO 371 29490 N5096/78/38, 5 Sep. 1941; Dilks, *Diaries of Sir Alexander Cadogan*, pp. 404–5. See also AVP RF f.069 op.25 d.7 p.71 ll.28–9, a report by Zinchenko, second secretary at the embassy, of a meeting with McDonald, *The Times* foreign correspondent, on 4 Sept. 1941.

131. Eden gained the wrong impression that Maisky 'had at the finish a clearer perception of our weakness and limitations'. Eden, *The Reckoning*, p. 276; Maisky's report is in AVP RF f.059 p.423 d.3789 ll.167–8.

132. To 'celebrate' the successful conclusion of this round of exchanges, Churchill insisted on dragging Eden and Beaverbrook to the Ritz for a dinner of 'oysters, partridge etc.' and launched a tirade against Lloyd George, suggesting that if he had played his cards right with the Tory Party, he would have been the prime minister in the First World War. Eden, *The Reckoning*, pp. 276–7.

133. The message was prompted by Eden, who told Maisky on 10 September that Churchill was expecting a response to his own message; TNA FO 371 29468 N5291/3/38.

134. Maisky was determined to convince Stalin of Churchill's good faith. His telegraphed version of the conversation states more emphatically Churchill's satisfaction with Stalin and their common strategic goals; AVP RF f.059 p.423 d.3789 ll.180–4.

135. Beaverbrook initiated the 'Tanks for Russia Week' propagated by his *Daily Express*. Maisky launched the event at a factory in Birmingham, where Agniya 'pulled a string to release the red flag that covered a part of the tank', revealing the name given to this first offering (by Maisky in advance) – 'Stalin'. In his speech, shown on newsreels all over the country, Maisky castigated the British government, suggesting that 'These good machines will not rust in idleness. They will go into the battle line against the Nazis.' *New York Times*, 22 September; Bell, *John Bull and the Bear*, pp. 54–5. The soaring sympathy towards the

Soviet Union is manifest, for instance, in a letter from Harold Nicolson: 'You should know how deeply we all feel for you at this moment. It must be irritating for you to receive so many expressions of sympathy and so few tanks'; RAN f.1702 op.4 d.1495 l.7, 13 Oct. 1941.

136. Maisky repeated Stalin's request for British divisions to be deployed on the Russian front. On 21 September, he complained to Eden that 'unwillingly one gets the impression that Churchill wishes to silence and freeze Stalin's proposal'. When Eden explained that the troops were indispensable for the offensive in Libya, Maisky retorted that Libya was 'a minor matter', while the Soviet front would 'decide the fate of the war'; AVP f.059 p.423 d.3789 ll.194–197.

137. Stalin personally went through and corrected Maisky's speech to the Inter-Allied Conference. The speech so impressed Amery that he 'scribbled down a little Russian poem about the burning of Moscow and Borodino' which he had learnt in Russian before going to Harrow; RGASPI, Stalin papers, f.558 op.11 d.211 ll.1–5; Amery papers, diary, AMEL 7/35, 24 Sep. 1941.

138. It was a propitious moment to recognize de Gaulle in the hope that he would join the Russian demand for a second front; TNA FO 371 28568 Z8308/5538/17. On Maisky's ambivalent attitude to de Gaulle, see Kharlamov, *Difficult Mission*, pp. 84–6.

139. Beaverbrook papers, D90, Cripps to Beaverbrook, 22 Sept. 1941.

140. AVP RF f.059 p.415 d.3750 ll.91–2, Maisky report on meeting Eden, 29 Sep. 1941.

141. Beaverbrook papers, D100, report of the conference, 1 Oct. 1941.

142. The detailed but incomplete Soviet minutes of the conference convey more forcefully the strain in the negotiations and confirm Cripps's account of the events in his diary; *SAO*, I, pp. 132–40; Harriman and Abel, *Special Envoy to Churchill and Stalin*, p. 92; RAN f.1702 op.4 d.982 l.3, Maisky to Laski, 18 Oct. 1941.

143. Cripps papers, diary, 1 Oct. 1941.

144. See three versions of the conversation: Beaverbrook papers, D100, report, 1 Oct.; Hopkins papers, Box 306, memo by Harriman, 30 Sept. 1941; and Harriman and Abel, *Special Envoy to Churchill and Stalin*, p. 94. Agniya had earned herself a notorious reputation as a tireless chatterbox.

145. Young, *Diaries of Sir Robert Bruce Lockhart*, p. 123; Bruce Lockhart, *Comes the Reckoning*, pp. 139–40.

146. Anglo-Russian Parliamentary Committee.

147. The diary of A. Polyakov, under the title *With a Soviet Unit through the Nazi Lines*, was published by Hutchinson, with a preface by Maisky.

148. *The Times* described the event on 18 August 1941: 'The glass eyes of the slightly moth-eaten stuffed bear on the staircase of London's St James's Club should have bugged out last week. The ghost of suavely arrogant, egg-domed ex-Member George Nathaniel, Marquess Curzon of Kedleston and British Foreign Secretary of the 1920s, must have shivered in its shroud. Founded in 1757, St James's is famed for its claret, its caricatures by Sir Joshua Reynolds and the exclusiveness of its membership, mostly confined to diplomats from the topmost social drawer. A Tsarist prince once lost £10,000 in its card rooms. Last week's tradition-shattering new member was short, thick, athletic Ivan Mikhailovich Maisky,

57, Soviet Ambassador to the Court of St James's, whose moon face, chuckling dark eyes and ragged imperial whiskers make him look like a small-time conjurer of the old school.'

149. The treaty between Iran, Britain and the Soviet Union (signed in Tehran on 29 January 1942), which facilitated the transfer of supplies to Russia via Persia; TNA FO 371 27234 E6629/3444/34.

150. The topic of the intimate conversation was triggered by Maisky's complaints about a statement made by Halifax in Washington that he did not expect Britain 'to attack on the continent of Europe'; TNA FO 371 26144 A8293/2/45.

151. Maisky continues to misconstrue the narrative of the meeting in his attempt to exonerate the Soviet Union from the blame of signing the Ribbentrop–Molotov Pact. See entry in diary of 12 June 1939 and the following commentary.

152. Probably *Blithe Spirit.*

153. Best description is in R. Braithwaite, *Moscow 1941: A city and its people at war* (New York, 2006), Pt. 3. See also Gorodetsky, *Stafford Cripps' Mission to Moscow*, ch. 7.

154. General Tōjō, who became Japanese prime minister, told his cabinet that 'The attack must take place at a time when the Soviet Union is ready to fall to the ground like a ripe persimmon ...' See A.A. Koshkin, *Krakh strategii 'speloi khurmy'* (Moscow, 1989), pp. 139–40. Maisky told Eden on 16 October that 'Japan's waiting game is now at an end', but thought that 'General Winter' was fiercer in the Far East than in Europe and therefore expected Japan to strike in the south; TNA FO 371 27884 F10915/12/23 and *SAO*, I, no. 56.

155. Maisky's report to Eden in TNA FO 371 29492 N6040/78/38, 17 Oct. 1941.

156. An incomplete opera by Mussorgsky, based on a short story by Gogol.

157. Bevan was not as blunt, calling for the government 'to be wholly reconstructed'; *Hansard*, HC Deb 23 October 1941, vol. 374, col. 1982.

158. The 'family' feared that Beaverbrook was plotting against Churchill and might push Lloyd George aside, were Churchill to be ousted; Sylvester papers, diary, A50, 23 Oct. 1941. Frances, Lloyd George's secretary and lover, told Sylvester that Lloyd George did not want to join the government, as 'he was really anxious to see Winston get into a mess, even lose the war, in order that he might be brought in to conduct the peace negotiations'. He would ignore invitations coming from all over the constituency to speak 'even on the same platform as M. Maisky', as he was 'so angry when Russia came into the war ... because this gave this Govt another chance to win'; Sylvester papers, diary, A50, 30 Sep. & 2 Oct. 1941. Despite Churchill's warning that the result of his continued association with Lloyd George 'would be rough reaction and recrimination', Maisky continued to seek guidance from Lloyd George. 'Let me say quite frankly,' he wrote to him in September 1941, 'how much I owe to you in my work here. Your opinions, your judgement, your talks and advice in the course of these ten years greatly helped me to see things as they really are, and to steer the proper course'; Eden, *The Reckoning*, p. 276; Lloyd George Papers, LG/G/14/1/21, 29 Sep. 1941.

159. Added later in handwriting.

160. See, for example, a letter of invitation from E.H. Carr to Maisky, RAN f.1702 op.4 d.1371 l.5, 22 Sep.; RAN f.1702 op.4 d.1267 l.15, Vansittart to Maisky, 26 June. In September, Maisky wrote to Beatrice Webb: 'Since June 22nd we have found many new friends – too

many – but I am always glad to see that the turn of events has brought recognition and popularity to the people who were our friends before that date'; RAN f.1702 op.4 d.878 ll.20–1.

161. Like Beatrice Webb and others who met Maisky at the time Cecil gained the impression, as he reported to Eden, that Maisky was 'very deeply in earnest himself, and very conscious of the tremendous sufferings that are being endured by his fellow-countrymen'. From those conversations it could not be ruled out that Russia might find herself out of the war if immediate help was not forthcoming from Britain; TNA FO 371 29470 N6385/3/38, 31 Oct. 1941.

162. Gorodetsky, *Stafford Cripps' Mission to Moscow*, pp. 256–61. See also Young, *Diaries of Sir Robert Bruce Lockhart*, 3 Nov. 1941, p. 129.

163. This was not the case, though Maisky was instructed not to broach political-strategic issues in his meetings with Eden and Churchill, so as not to spoil the achievements made and to project a sense of success; AVP RF f.059 p.422 d.3779 l.125 & l.128, 5 Oct. 1941. Alluding to Molotov's telegrams, Maisky confirmed Eden's impression, in their meeting on 6 October, that the mission had been 'very satisfactory'; TNA FO 371 29577 N5817/3084/38.

164. TNA CAB 66/20 WP(41)272, telegrams from Cripps, 21 Oct. to 15 Nov. 1941.

165. Harvey, *War Diaries of Oliver Harvey*, p. 57; Dilks, *Diaries of Sir Alexander Cadogan*, p.370.

166. TNA CAB 69/2 DO(41)69, 27 Oct. 1941; CAB 79/55 COS(41)34 and minute by Churchill, 28 Oct. 1941.

167. TNA FO 37129471 N6583/3/38, 28 Oct. 1941.

168. TNA PREM 3 403/7, Churchill to Beaverbrook and Eden to Churchill, 14 Oct.; Beaverbrook papers, D93, Churchill to Eden and Beaverbrook, 1 Nov. 1941. See also Taylor, *Beaverbrook*, pp. 408–9.

169. TNA CAB 79/55 COS(41)34, minute by Churchill, 28 Oct.; CAB 84/37, 79/16, 84/3 & 84/38, JP(41)1016, COS(41)404, JP(41)164, 1025, 29 Nov., 1 & 2 Dec. 1941. The nature of the substantial differences of opinion between Dill and Churchill is presented in masterly fashion in A. Danchev's severe but sound critique of Churchill's history, '"Dilly-Dally", or having the last word: Field Marshal Sir John Dill and Prime Minister Winston Churchill', *Journal of Contemporary History*, 22/1 (1987).

170. TNA CAB 120/681, 24 Oct. 1941.

171. Cripps papers, diary, 26 July, 26 Sept. & 2 Oct. 1941.

172. Cripps papers, diary, 4–13 Nov. 1941; *FRUS*, 1941, I, pp. 852–3.

173. Churchill had informed Stalin on 4 November of the government's decision not to declare war on Finland and Hungary, whose troops were fighting the Russians. Stalin was also bitter about Churchill's failure to respond to his request for British troops to be deployed on the Russian front and his decision to send General Wavell to Russia, most probably to make further excuses. He further complained about the lack of trust between the two countries, which he ascribed to a failure to discuss a common military strategy or post-war cooperation. The harsh tone of Stalin's message may have been sparked by a letter which Maisky received from H.G. Wells, whom Stalin had met in 1934 and admired. Referring to the 'second front', Wells suggested: 'If Russia asks very plainly "when are you going to raid"

you will get these raids. If you don't you won't … 80% of the country is on your side. But if you do not express your wishes plainly the Government here will have the excuse: "Oh the Russians never asked for that'"; RAN f.1702 op.4 d.1628 ll.26–9.

174. Beaverbrook, under fierce attack for having concealed from Cabinet the rancorous side of his dealings with Stalin, was trying to pin the blame for Stalin's telegram on the Cabinet's handling of the Finnish issue. His own political interests required the tension to be relieved and for reconciliation with Eden by encouraging him to proceed to Moscow.

175. Eden was instructed by Churchill 'to be fairly stiff with Maisky'; Dilks, *Diaries of Sir Alexander Cadogan*, p. 412.

176. According to Eden, Maisky hinted that he realized Stalin's message 'was unfortunate' and asked for an 'off the record' conversation, begging Eden not to divulge its contents. Maisky favoured the holding of political and strategic negotiations in London (obviously through him), and was not yet aware of Eden's decision to proceed to Moscow. In his history of the war, Churchill seized upon the exceptionally biting telegram from Stalin which he claimed epitomized the Soviet leader's ungrateful attitude to the West. At the time, even the Foreign Office was forced to admit, after a thorough study of Britain's assistance to Russia since June 1941, that Stalin's criticism was justified, despite its grating tone. Churchill, *The Grand Alliance*, pp. 469–70; TNA FO 371 29470 N6288/3/38 & 29471 N6654/3/38, minutes, 18, 19 & 21 Nov. Likewise Cripps quickly grasped the artificial nature of the crisis; TNA FO 418/87, 15 Nov. 1941. Churchill, however, had put on the show of anger to justify postponing a response to Stalin until the middle of the month, when the long due Operation *Crusader* was launched in Libya, thus achieving a *fait accompli* of giving priority to the Middle Eastern strategy; see Harvey, *War Diaries of Oliver Harvey*, pp. 62–3, and Eden, *The Reckoning*, pp. 280–1.

177. Ismay had been forbidden by Beaverbrook from presenting the offer in Moscow.

178. E. Mawdsley, *Thunder in the East: The Nazi–Soviet War 1941–1945* (London, 2005), pp. 105–7.

179. AVP RF f.059 p.423 d.3789 l.344, Maisky to Molotov, 21 Nov. 1941.

180. TNA FO 800/300, Cadogan to Clark Kerr, 1 May 1942.

181. AVP RF f.059 p.399 d.3614 ll.45–6 & p.423 d.3789 l.369, exchange between Molotov and Maisky, 27 Nov. & 1 Dec. 1941.

182. Eden, *The Reckoning*, p. 280; Harvey, *War Diaries of Oliver Harvey*, pp. 58, 60–3.

183. TNA FO 954/24, telegram to Cripps, 20 Nov. 1941.

184. TNA FO 37129472 N6835/3/38, minutes, 21, 24 & 26 Nov. 1941.

185. TNA CAB 84/38 JP(41)1037, 1038 & 1066, 4 & 5 Dec.; CAB 79/86 COS(41)43, 4 Dec. 1941.

186. AVP RF f.059 p.423 d.3789 ll.375–7, Maisky to Molotov on a meeting with Churchill, 6 Dec. 1941.

187. Eden, *The Reckoning*, pp. 285–303.

188. TNA CAB 66/20 WP(24)8, 5 Jan. 1942, and the Russian version is produced in O.A. Rzheshevsky, *War and Diplomacy: The making of the Grand Alliance - documents from Stalin's archives* (London, 1996). The mission is vividly described by many of the participants, notably by Eden, *The Reckoning*, pp. 283–303; Maisky, *Memoirs of a Soviet Ambassador*,

pp. 217–42; Gorodetsky, *Stafford Cripps in Moscow*, ch. 9; Dilks, *Diaries of Sir Alexander Cadogan*, pp. 417–25; and Harvey, *War Diaries of Oliver Harvey*, pp. 65–81.

1942

1. Beaverbrook papers, BBK\C\238, exchange of letters with Maisky, 28 & 30 Jan. 1942; RAN f.1702 op.4 d.1438 l.1 & d.1127 l.26 with John Dayson (the Lord Mayor) and Benjamin Tillott, 29 Jan. & 2 Feb. 1942.

2. AVP RF f.059 op.1 d.3850 p.429 l.28, 11 Jan. 1942; *FRUS*, 1942, III, pp. 491–3, 512–21. The Polish government in exile gained the same impression of Eden's talks in Moscow; see General Sikorski Historical Institute (ed.), *Documents on Polish–Soviet Relations 1939–1945* (London, 1961), (hereafter *DPSR*), I, Doc. 183.

3. Webb, diary, 26 Jan. 1942, p. 7257.

4. TNA FO371 32905 N885/30/38, memo by Sargent, 5 Feb. 1942. A senior Foreign Office official told the Swedish ambassador: 'I hope to God that the Germans won't suddenly collapse now, precisely at the moment when the Russians would be top dog at the peace conference, having done more to beat the Germans than the British and much more than the Americans'; W.P. Crozier, *Off the Record: Political interviews, 1933–1943* (London, 1973), p. 271.

5. TNA CAB 66/21 WP(42)48, 28 Jan. 1942.

6. TNA PREM 3/399/1–2, 31 Jan. 1942.

7. TNA CAB 65/29 16 & 17(42)5; TNA CAB 66/22 WP (42)71, 6 Feb. 1942.

8. NA, State Department, London Embassy Box 218, 16 Feb. 1942.

9. TNA FO 371 32875 N846/1/38, 12 Feb. 1942.

10. See commentary following diary entry for 13 March 1942.

11. TNA FO 371 32876 N1113/5/38 & CAB 65/25 24(42)2; Roosevelt papers, PSF 4: Great Britain, Aide Memoire submitted by Eden to Winant, 25 Feb. 1942; TNA FO 371 32876 N1027/3/98, Halifax to Eden, 20 Feb.; AVP RF f.059 op.1 d.3832 p.427 l.178, Litvinov to Molotov; TNA FO 371 32876 N1115/5/38; *SAO*, I, no. 87, Eden's conversation with Maisky, 26 Feb. 1942.

12. RAN f.1702 op.4 d.111 l.25 & d.143 l.73, 27 & 28 Feb. 1942.

13. A number of entries, written in haste and abbreviated, are expanded here to facilitate reading.

14. Maisky became aware of Moscow's attempts to drive a wedge between London and Washington through an extremely flattering TASS communiqué on 31 January hailing the progressive policies of the 'courageous and resolute' American president on the occasion of Roosevelt's sixtieth birthday. This was followed by personal greetings in the same vein from Kalinin, the president of the Soviet Union, which left an impact; TNA FO 371 32896 N711/21/38; Roosevelt papers, OF 220, 7 Feb. 1942.

15. The copy of the letter to Litvinov is included in the diary under this date.

16. Webb, diary, 26 Jan. and 3 Feb. 1942, pp. 7255–8; P. Addison, *The Road to 1945: British politics and the Second World War* (London, 1975), ch. 7; Harvey, *War Diaries of Oliver Harvey*, pp. 101–2.

17. Sylvester papers, diary, B70, letter to Lloyd George, 9 Feb. 1942.

18. NA State Department (hereafter SD) 841.00/1548, 20 Feb. 1942. A thorough survey prepared for Beaverbrook by the chief editor of the *Daily Express* conceded that 'no one thought of you as a potential Prime Minister … the country thought of you as a go-getter, a man of vigour and dispatch, but not as the nation's leader'. Cripps was perceived as the likely contender, were Churchill to encounter further disasters. Beaverbrook papers, BBK\H\111, early February, Arthur Christiansen to Beaverbrook.

19. RAN f.1702 op.4 d.973 l.4, 20 Feb. 1941.

20. Crozier, *Off the Record*, p. 284; Halifax papers, diary, A7.8.10, 25 March 1942.

21. Churchill admitted it over lunch with Lloyd George, begging him: 'Do not repeat that'; Sylvester papers, diary, A52, 28 April 1942. See also Clarke, *The Cripps Version* and R.J. Moore, *Churchill, Cripps and India, 1939–1945* (Oxford, 1979), pp. 63–83, 122–32.

22. Addison, *The Road to 1945*, pp. 206–9; C.H. King, *With Malice toward None: A war diary by Cecil H. King* (London, 1970), pp. 182, 189–90; W.S. Churchill, *The Second World War: The Hinge of Fate* (London, 1950), pp. 202–3.

23. The reasons for his resignation.

24. Bruce Lockhart papers, diary, LOC 42, 17 March 1942.

25. TNA PREM 3/399/8, 17 March 1942.

26. Harvey, *War Diaries of Oliver Harvey*, 14 March 1942, p. 108.

27. Roosevelt papers, Map Room Papers, Winant to Roosevelt, 19 Feb. 1942; Halifax papers, diary, A7.8.19, 21 Feb. 1942.

28. On the intricacies of Iranian politics under occupation, see M.G. Majd, *August 1941: The Anglo-Russian occupation of Iran and change of shahs* (Lanham, MD, 2012).

29. TNA PREM 3/395/12.

30. Harriman and Abel, *Special Envoy to Churchill and Stalin*, p. 135.

31. TNA FO 371 32906 N1256/30/38, minutes by Lockhart and Sargent, 1 & 2 March; Bruce Lockhart papers, diary, LOC 42/43, 9 & 10 March 1942.

32. Halifax papers, diary, A7.8.19, 8 March 1942; telegram quoted in M. Gilbert, *Winston S. Churchill: Road to Victory, 1941–1945* (London, 1986), p. 67.

33. Harvey, *War Diaries of Oliver Harvey*, 17 March 1942, pp. 109–10; Gilbert, *Road to Victory*, p. 76.

34. TNA FO 371 32876 N1024 & N1025/5/38, 21 Feb. 1941, Halifax to Eden.

35. Stimson papers, diary, 5 March 1942. This policy was only challenged by Admiral King in a long memorandum he sent Roosevelt that same day; Roosevelt papers, Collection PSF, Box 5, 5 March 1942.

36. Stimson papers, diary, 6 March 1942.

37. NA Military Archives (hereafter RG) 165, ABC 371 3-5-42, 7 March; Roosevelt papers, Map Room Papers, Roosevelt to Churchill, 9 March 1942.

38. Roosevelt papers, Collection Morgenthau, Presidential Diaries, Vol. 5, p. 1075, Roosevelt to Morgenthau, 11 March 1942.

39. AVP RF f.059 op.1 d.3832 p.427 ll.233–7. Significantly the last sentence is missing from the Russian official publication, in *SAO*, I, pp. 155–7.

40. Roosevelt papers, Map Room Papers, 18 March 1942.

41. Bruce Lockhart papers, diary, LOC 42/43, 13, 14 & 15 March 1942; Harvey, *War Diaries of Oliver Harvey*, 15 March 1942, p. 109.

42. The evasive nature of the response was succinctly described by Cadogan: 'P.M. sending a good telegram to Stalin about maintaining quotas [of supply] – nothing else for the moment. We *are* going to study possibility of a "second front" in West!'; Dilks, *Diaries of Sir Alexander Cadogan*, p. 440. In drafting his message to Stalin, Churchill agreed with Eden that it was 'better not to give this bitter medicine to Russia at this juncture', though he wondered whether they had not 'found out for themselves what is going on'; TNA CAB 120/678, minute by Churchill, 4 March 1942.

43. Liddell Hart, *The Liddell Hart Memoirs*, p. 200; Pimlott, *Second World War Diary of Hugh Dalton*, pp. 389–90; Harvey, *War Diaries of Oliver Harvey*, 14 March 1942, p. 109.

44. Crozier, *Off the Record*, pp. 271–9.

45. AVP RF f.059 op.1427 d.3832 l.185, 20 Feb. 1942; Davies papers, Box 11, 'History of Cross Channel Second Front Operations', 15 April 1946.

46. AVP RF f.059 op.1 d.3920 p.438 l.103, 26 Feb. 1942.

47. Indeed it was perceived as such by the Foreign Office; TNA FO 371 32906 N1138/30/38, 2 March 1942. Maisky informed Litvinov that his speech was given considerable space in the British media; RAN f.1702 op.4 d.143 l.73. On the extent of the agitation for a second front, see Davies papers, diary, Box 11, 3 March 1942.

48. AVP RF f.059 op.1 d.3920 p.438 ll.110–12 & 115–16; Roosevelt papers, PSF 5, Litvinov to Hopkins, 4 March 1942.

49. Standley papers, 6-10/17, 17 March 1942.

50. AVP RF f.059 op.1 d.3832 p.427 l.243, 18 March 1942.

51. First raised in earnest by V. Mastny, 'Stalin and the prospects of a separate peace in World War II', *American Historical Review*, 77 (1972), though he focused mostly on summer 1943, as did I. Fleischhauer, *Die Chance des Sonderfriedens* (Berlin, 1986).

52. TNA CAB 66/23 WP(42)156, draft treaty submitted to Cabinet, 10 April 1942.

53. TNA FO 371 32876 N1156/5/38, 27 Feb. 1942.

54. NA SD, 740.0011 European War 1939/20007 Johnson to State Department, 7 March 1942; Moscow Embassy Box 5, 2 March 1942; TNA CAB 122/100, Halifax to FO, 19 March 1942.

55. Davies papers, diary, Box 11, 10 April 1942.

56. The supposedly declassified document was published by a veteran military-intelligence officer V. Karpov, *Generalissimus* (Moscow, 2012), I, pp. 458–62. I have been shown the document independently, with maps of the proposed settlement attached to it; alas outside the archives and in conditions which made it hard to establish its authenticity.

57. AVP RF f.059 op.1 d.3920 p.438 ll.117–20, Molotov to Litvinov, 3 March 1942. It is indeed most telling that this document is not included in the official publication of the Soviet documents and that there is an ominous gap in the exchanges with Litvinov between 18 Feb. and 12 March.

58. RAN f.1702 op.4 d.111 ll.26–7, Maisky to Kollontay, 2 April 1942.

59. Maisky, *Memoirs of a Soviet Ambassador*, pp. 253–6, 323.

60. Churchill papers, CHAR 20/72/44–5, 20 March; AVP RF f.059 g.1942 op.8 d.5574 p.2 l.39, 16 March 1942.

61. TNA FO 371 32877 N1413/5/38, 17 March 1942; AVP RF f.059 op.1 d.5574 p.2 ll.43–4, Maisky to Molotov, 17 March 1942.

62. AVP RF f.059 op.1 d.3852 p.429 l.156, 20 March 1942.

63. TNA FO 371 32864 N1947/1/38 & Air 19/290, 30 March & 7 April 1942.

64. French fascist organization in the 1930s.

65. Churchill told Hopkins that he was disappointed and 'bitter' about de Gaulle, who considered himself 'a modern Joan of Arc' but that he felt it difficult to 'eliminate' him, as he saw no substitute, while his name had become the symbol of resistance in France; NA SD 740.0011 European War 1939/20906, 9 April 1942.

66. AVP RF f.059 op.1 d.3833 p.427 ll.9–10, Litvinov to Molotov, 27 March 1942. Typically missing from the official published Soviet documents.

67. AVP RF f.059 op.1 d.3941 p.440 l.57 & d.3852 p.429 l.166, exchanges between Molotov and Maisky, 23 March 1942.

68. *Time*, 6 April 1942; *The Times*, 26 March 1942; Kharlamov, *Difficult Mission*, p. 99.

69. TNA FO 371 32864 N1947/1/38.

70. TNA FO 371 32878 N1526/5/38, 30 March 1942.

71. TNA CAB 65/29 37(42), 25 March; TNA FO 371 32878 N1670/5/38; AVP RF f.059 op.1 d.3852 p.429 l.185, reports on Eden's meeting with Maisky, 27 March 1942.

72. *FRUS*, 1942, III, pp. 536–8, minutes by Welles on meeting Halifax, 30 March and 1 April 1942.

73. Roosevelt papers, PSF 164/7 & 8, Donovan to Roosevelt, 10 & 23 March 1942, and Roosevelt papers, PSF 154: Great Britain, Memo by Hopkins on meeting Winant, 11 March 1942. Useful on the strategic debate, though on the whole only partially dealing with the Soviet side, are: M. Stoler, *The Politics of the Second Front* (Connecticut, 1977); M. Stoler, *Allies and Adversaries* (Chapel Hill, 2000); R.W. Steele, *The First Offensive 1942* (Bloomington, 1973); and the refreshing approach in F. Costigliola, *Roosevelt's Lost Alliances: How personal politics helped start the Cold War* (Princeton, 2012), ch. 4 & 5.

74. Roosevelt papers, PSF 152: Hopkins, 14 March; Truscott papers, Box 9/14, 1 April 1941. Winant, who had been thoroughly briefed by Maisky, arrived in Washington too late to make any impact on the political agreement, but was 'most heartily in favour' of the idea of a second front; Stimson papers, diary, 16 March 1942. Maisky remained sceptical about whether the Allies would do 'their *utmost* to win the war by sacrifice of men and wealth to the common cause'; Webb, diary, 13 April 1942.

75. Halifax papers, diary, A7.8.19, 25 March 1942. Taking leave of Roosevelt on 17 March, Admiral Standley, the new American ambassador to Moscow, noted the president's ambiguity and aloofness in regard to the second front issue and his desire to meet Stalin in person, while there was 'no mention of the British in this regard'; Standley papers, 6-10/17, 17 March 1942.

76. NA RG 218, CCS 334, 2-9-42, JCS 7/7, 23 March; NA RG 165, OPD 381 *Bolero* 1942, 25 March; Stimson papers, diary, 25 March 1942. See also A. Roberts, *Masters and Commanders: How Roosevelt, Churchill and Alanbrooke won the war in the west* (London, 2008), p. 128.

77. Halifax told Beaverbrook that this was 'very dangerous' and that 'neither the President nor Winston will be able to get very far without staff participation'; Halifax papers, diary, A7.8.19, 26 March 1942.

78. Stimson papers, diary, 27 March 1942 and copy of a letter to Roosevelt.

79. Truscott papers, Box 9/14, 1 April 1942; Roberts, *Masters and Commanders*, pp. 129–30.

80. TNA FO 371 32907 N2000/30/38, 17 April 1942.

81. Davies papers, diary, Box 11, 11 April 1942.

82. Roosevelt papers, Map Room papers, 31 March; Davies papers, diary, Box 11, 6 & 7 April 1942; Berle papers, diary, Box 218, 4 April 1942.

83. Roosevelt papers, Map Room papers, 1 April 1942.

84. Roosevelt papers, Map Room papers, Churchill to Roosevelt, 1 April 1942.

85. According to Maisky's cable home, Eden said 'to conclude' an agreement.

86. 'We're going to have trouble in America over our Russian agreement,' jotted Cadogan in his diary, 'but I warned A[nthony] of *that!*'; Dilks, *Diaries of Sir Alexander Cadogan*, 14 April 1942.

87. AVP RF f.059 op.1 d.3853 p.430 l.6; TNA FO 371 32878 N1861/5/38; Harvey, *War Diaries of Oliver Harvey*, pp. 41–5; Eden, *The Reckoning*, p. 324.

88. AVP RF f.059 op.1 d.3941 p.440 l.127, 11 April 1942; D. Watson, 'Molotov, the Grand Alliance and the second front', *Europe-Asia Studies*, 54/1 (2002), p. 61.

89. NA RG 218, CCS 381, 2-2-42, JPS 4A, 14 Feb. 1942.

90. Stimson papers, diary, 24 Feb. 1942.

91. NA RG 165, ABC 381 9-25-41 CPS 28/1, 8 April 1942.

92. TNA CAB 84/43 JP(42)289, 17 March 1942.

93. Unless otherwise stated, the account of the Marshall–Hopkins mission is mostly based on NA RG 218, CCS 334, 2-9-42, JCS 6/4, Dill to Marshall, 16 March; JPS 24.3 and JCS, 25 March, U.S.P.(42)3, 14 March; Marshall to McNarney, 14 April; Marshall to Roosevelt, 4 May 1942.

94. Hopkins papers, Box 308: Hopkins in London, April, 8 April; Roosevelt papers, Map Room Papers, Hopkins to Roosevelt, 9 April; Davies papers, Box 11, note by Ambassador Davies on conversations with Hopkins, 8 April 1942.

95. NA SD, 740.0011 European War 1939/20906, Hopkins's secretary to the Secretary of State, 9 April 1942.

96. TNA CAB 69/4 DO(42)10, 14 April 1942.

97. Hopkins papers, Box 308: Hopkins in London, April, telegram to Roosevelt, 15 April; Roosevelt papers, Map Room Papers, Churchill to Roosevelt, 12 April. Hopkins' confidence is attested in Stimson papers, diary, 20 April 1942.

98. NA RG 165, Exec. 1/4, 12 April 1942; Stimson papers, diary, 13 April 1942.

99. NA, RG 165, ABC 381 9-25-41(1) JPS 12th/3, 11 April 1942; Hopkins papers, Box 308: Hopkins in London, April, 11 April 1942.

100. Halifax papers, diary, A7.8.19, 21 & 24 April 1942. The planners of the joint chiefs of staff envisaged three different scenarios for a Soviet collapse, see TNA CAB 119/56 JP(42)421(S), 19 April 1942.

101. Roosevelt papers, PSF 5: Marshall, 28 April 1942, Roosevelt memo to Marshall.

102. TNA CAB 65/30 WM(42)54, 29 April 1942.

103. AVP RF f.059 op.8 d.5574 l.67, 17 April 1942.

104. Sylvester papers, diary, A52, 29 April 1942.

105. TNA FO 800/300, Clark Kerr to Cripps, 26 April; TNA FO 371 32879 N2060/5/38.

106. AVP RF f.059 op.1 d.3833 p.427 l.64.

107. AVP RF f.059 op.1 d.3853 p.430 l.78, 17 April 1942. 'This makes me laugh,' wrote Harvey in his diary. 'It was the Bolsheviks who in 1917 published all the secret treaties of the last war and put the democracies to shame. So much so that H.M.G. at least learnt their lesson and will never have another secret treaty, not even to please Stalin'; Harvey, *War Diaries of Oliver Harvey*, 2 May 1942, p. 120.

108. AVP RF f.059 op.1 d.3941 p.440 l.160, 18 April 1942.

109. AVP RF f.059 op.1 d.5574 p.2 ll.73–5, Maisky to Molotov, 1 May; TNA FO 371 32880 N2221 & N2336/5/38, 1, 3 & 15 May 1942; Harvey, *War Diaries of Oliver Harvey*, 2 May 1942, p. 120.

110. TNA FO 371 32881 N2498/5/38, minute of 3 May; Dilks, *Diaries of Sir Alexander Cadogan*, 3 May 1942, p. 449.

111. AVP RF f.059 op.1 d.3942 p.440 l.51, Molotov to Maisky, 2 May 1942.

112. TNA FO 371 32880 N2385/5/38; AVP RF f.059 op.1 d.5574 p.2 ll.82–91, Maisky and Eden reports, 5 May 1942.

113. TNA FO 371 32880 N2422/5/38.

114. Harvey, *War Diaries of Oliver Harvey*, 7 & 11 May, pp. 122–3; Dilks, *Diaries of Sir Alexander Cadogan*, pp. 451–3; *FRUS*, 1942, III, pp. 552–3.

115. Kharlamov, *Difficult Mission*, p. 104.

116. Dilks, *Diaries of Sir Alexander Cadogan*, pp. 451–2; Bruce Lockhart papers, diary, LOC Esco/42, 15 May 1942. Unless otherwise indicated, the report of his visit is based on AVP RF f.06 op.4 d.55 l.6, 20 May 1942; Sokolov, '"Avtobiograficheskie zametki" V.N. Pavlova', pp. 107–8; Harvey, *War Diaries of Oliver Harvey*, 21 May 1942, p. 125; Churchill, *Hinge of Fate*, pp. 300–1. For a colourful description of Molotov's arrival, see also Watson, 'Molotov, the Grand Alliance and the Second Front', p. 63; Watson, *Molotov*, pp. 199–203; and Maisky, *Memoirs of a Soviet Ambassador*, p. 265.

117. The instructions and the draft treaty are in RGASPI, Stalin papers, f.558 op.11 d.280 ll.53–66.

118. See commentary following diary entry for 28 April 1939.

119. It is doubtful whether Molotov, who was openly hostile to Litvinov, was more benign towards Maisky, as is argued in Roberts, *Molotov*, p. 61. Maisky, however, succeeded in continuing to make himself indispensable.

120. There certainly was tension between him and Maisky. Eden jotted in his diary that Bogomolov was 'an unhelpful creature, to all appearances a poor substitute for Maisky'; Eden, *The Reckoning*, p. 330.

121. *FRUS*, 1942, III, p. 568.

122. On this, see AVP RF f.45 op.1 ed.xr.232 l.1–2, Molotov to Stalin, 21 May 1942.

123. Maisky, *Memoirs of a Soviet Diplomat*, pp. 266–7; Dilks, *Diaries of Sir Alexander Cadogan*, p. 454.

124. TNA PREM 3/333/8, 21 May 1942.

125. AVP RF f.45 op.1 ed.xr.232 ll.12, 22–24, 28–39, 51–9, 66 & ll.3–21, reports of conversations with Churchill and Eden and exchange of telegrams between Molotov and Stalin, 22 & 23 May 1942; AVP RF f.45 op.1 ed.xr.232 ll.111–15; *FRUS*, 1942, III, pp. 558–63. Most of the documents related to Molotov's visits to London and Washington, emanating from the Presidential Archives, were produced in English by Rzheshevsky, *War and Diplomacy*. The author refers to the complete original set, which differs in places.

126. AVP RF f.45 op.1 ed.xr.232 ll.68–9.

127. Despite its cardinal significance, Maisky almost glosses over Molotov's mission in his memoirs. Nor is it covered by his diary; Maisky, *Memoirs of a Soviet Ambassador*, pp. 280–3; RAN f.1702 op.4 d.111 ll.28–29, Maisky to Kollontay, 20 May 1942. See also Pimlott, *Second World War Diary of Hugh Dalton*, p. 452–3.

128. Hopkins papers, Box 309: Molotov's visit, record by Prof. Cross (professor of Russian at Harvard, who acted as the interpreter), 29 May 1942. The British were well aware of the situation, see NA RG 165, G-2 Reg. Russia, 6910, 21 May 1942.

129. TNA FO 371 32881 N2500/5/38, 9 May 1942.

130. Harvey, Eden's secretary, rightly observed in his diary: 'If I were America, I would be more shocked by this new treaty than by the other'; Harvey, *War Diaries of Oliver Harvey*, 25 May 1942, p. 129.

131. On this, see Kuh papers, diary, 11 Oct. 1942.

132. AVP RF f.45 op.1 ed.xr.232 ll.65, 97, 98, 120 & 122, Stalin to Molotov, 23, 24 & 26 May 1942 & f.06 op.4 d.48 ll.13–16, report of conversations with Beneš, who had similar views on Germany, 9 June 1942. The British records are in TNA CAB 66 24/50 WP(42)220. Roosevelt papers, PSF 9: Winant, 3 June. See also Winant's conversations with Davies, in Davies papers, diary, Box 11, 24 Feb. 1943.

133. Dilks, *Diaries of Sir Alexander Cadogan*, 25 May 1942, p. 455. See also Eden's memo to Cabinet, TNA CAB 65/30, WM(42)66, 25 May 1942; the entries in his diary quoted in *The Reckoning*, pp. 328–9; and TNA PREM 3 399/8, 2 June 1942, Churchill to Roosevelt. Secretary of State Hull wrote to Roosevelt: 'it would seem that out of deference to our protest they have omitted the troublesome territorial question from the Treaty'; Roosevelt papers, PSF 68: Russia 1942–43, 26 May 1942. Watson, 'Molotov, the Grand Alliance and the Second Front', is the most meticulous in researching the visit, but he, too, gets the chronology wrong.

134. Roosevelt papers, Map Room Papers, 27 May 1942.

135. AVP RF f.45 op.1 ed.xr 232.158. King George VI to Queen Mary, quoted in J.W. Wheeler-Bennett, *King George VI: His life and reign* (London, 1958), pp. 539–40; Bruce

Lockhart papers, diary, LOC 42/43, 23 May; TNA FO 800/876 file 23, FO summary report of the visit, 11 June 1942.

136. Kharlamov, *Difficult Mission*, pp. 106–7.

137. Halifax papers, diary, A7.8.19, 29 May 1942.

138. Operation *Gymnast*, eventually renamed *Torch*, was the British plan for the invasion of French North Africa in 1942.

139. Roosevelt papers, Map Room Papers, 28 May 1942; AVP RF f.059 d.3943 p.440 l.136, Molotov to Maisky, 15 July 1942.

140. AVP RF f.45 op.1 ed.xr.232 ll.33–7, this is a vital source, as the amateur American interpreter, Prof. Cross from Harvard, did not take notes and produced a most selective record from memory; *FRUS*, 1942, III, p. 571.

141. AVP RF f.45 op.1 ed.xr.232 ll.67–70.

142. Davies papers, Box 11, memo on Molotov's visit. Marshall in fact thought that the reference to the second front in the communiqué was 'too strong' and urged that there should be no reference to 1942, but he was overruled by Roosevelt; Hopkins papers, Box 311: Molotov Visit, 3 June 1942; AVP RF f.45 op.1 ed.xr.232 ll.41–9, 30 May 1942; *FRUS*, 1942, III, p. 576–7.

143. AVP RF f.45 op.1 ed.xr.232 ll.58–66 & 72–5.

144. AVP RF f.45 op.1 ed.xr.232 ll.67–70. See also Roosevelt papers, PSF 194: Molotov, record of a meeting between Roosevelt, Marshall, King and Hopkins, 31 May 1942.

145. TNA CAB 66/25 WP (42) 232, 31 May 1942.

146. Roosevelt papers, Collection Hopkins, Box 311, Hopkins to Winant, 12 June 1942.

147. Davies papers, Box 11, diary, retrospective survey of the negotiations entered under 29 May 1942. On Molotov's optimism and turning into 'a new man' in the wake of the mission, see *FRUS*, 1941, III, pp. 598–9. On the personal relationship established between Molotov and Roosevelt, see F. Costigliola, *Roosevelt's Lost Alliances*, pp. 165–73.

148. AVP RF f.059 op.1 d.3838 p.427 ll.200–4. See also Molotov to Stalin in AVP RF f.45 op.1 ed.xr.233, ll.3–4; RAN f.1702 op.4 d.546 ll.68–9, 25 June 1942.

149. Davies papers, Box 11, diary, 17 June 1942.

150. AVP RF f.059 op.1 d.3808 p.425 l.15, 7 June 1942.

151. TNA PREM 3/333/19, Churchill's instructions to the COS, and record of their meeting, COS(51), 8 June; TNA CAB 66/25, Record of the meetings with Molotov; AVP RF f.45 op.1 ed.xr. 233 ll.69–80, Meeting with Molotov, 9 June 1942.

152. TNA PREM 3/395/18, 11 June 1942, Churchill to Lyttelton.

153. AVP RF f.45 op.1 ed.xr.233, ll.101–8; TNA PREM 3/333/8, 10 June 1942; Dilks, *Diaries of Sir Alexander Cadogan*, p. 457.

154. A state of the art Soviet dive-bomber.

155. RAN f.1702 op.4 d.1491 l.9, 12 June 1942; RAN f.1702 op.4 d.1260 ll.14–15, Boothby to Maisky. Eden made a similar contribution in his farewell speech, as well as in parliament. On this, see the chapter 'End of an Era'.

156. For instance, the honour he was given of carrying the Soviet flag at a ceremonial parade celebrating the Grand Alliance at Buckingham Palace in the presence of the king; RAN f.1702 op.4 d.1029 l.8, Maisky to Monck, 12 June 1942.

157. The essence of this entry was relayed in a telegram to Molotov, *SAO*, I, no. 118.

158. The most illuminating rendition of the North African campaign is in M. Kitchen, *Rommel's Desert War: Waging World War II in North Africa, 1941–1943* (Cambridge, 2009).

159. Bevan was more eloquent than Maisky suggests: '…the country is now more concerned with the Prime Minister winning the war than with his winning a Debate in the House of Commons. The Prime Minister wins Debate after Debate and loses battle after battle. The country is beginning to say that he fights Debates like a war and the war like a Debate'; *Hansard*, HC Deb 2 July 1942, vol. 381, col. 528.

160. Eden was more truthful, though, telling Bruce Lockhart: 'We are in a jam over this second front business. We have to try to "bluff" the Germans; to do so we must deceive our friends at the same time'; Bruce Lockhart papers, diary, LOC 42/43, 15 July 1942.

161. AVP RF f.059 op.1 d.5574 p.2 l.156, Maisky to Molotov, 30 June 1942.

162. Halifax papers, secret diary, A7.8.19, 14 June; Roosevelt papers, PSF 194: Mountbatten, Mountbatten to Roosevelt, 15 June 1942 & Map Room Papers, Churchill to Roosevelt, 13 June 1942. Gilbert, *Road to Victory*, ch. 7.

163. Stimson papers, diary, and Marshall papers, Pentagon, 'Gymnast Operations', 17 June 1942.

164. Stimson papers, diary, 19 & 20 June; Churchill, *Hinge of Fate*, pp. 338–9; Marshall papers, Pentagon, Box 80/33, Marshall to Roosevelt, 19 June 1942.

165. TNA CAB 88/1 CCS 28, 20 June; NA RG 165, ABC 381 9-25-41(7), 'Notes on the Letter of the Prime Minister to the President', 20 June 1942; NA RG 165, Exec. 1/10, OPD to COS, 20 & 21 June 1942.

166. Gilbert, *Road to Victory*, p. 128.

167. Stimson papers, diary, 21 & 25 June; record of the meeting is in TNA CAB 120/33. Marshall's opposition to the operation is in Marshall papers, Pentagon, Box 80/33, 'American Forces in Middle East', 23 June 1942 and in TNA CAB 88/6 CCS 83/1.

168. Stimson papers, diary, 22 June 1942; for a discussion of the context of the debate, see Stoler, *Allies and Adversaries*, pp. 71–9 and *The Politics of the Second Front*, ch. 3.

169. AVP RF f.059 op.1 d.3921 p.438 l.159.

170. TNA PREM 3/257/5; the War Cabinet approved the new strategy on 7 July, TNA CAB 65/31 WM(42)87.

171. Dilks, *Diaries of Sir Alexander Cadogan*, p. 469, 8 July 1942.

172. Young, *Diaries of Sir Robert Bruce Lockhart*, II, p. 182.

173. Roosevelt papers, Map Room Papers.

174. TNA PREM 3/333/19, 14 July 1942, Churchill's draft telegram to Roosevelt.

175. TNA CAB 79/22 JP(42)670, 14 July 1942.

176. Quoted in Stoler, *Allies and Adversaries*, p. 82.

177. Webb, diary, 27 June 1942, pp. 7341–2.

178. Maisky's objective was to impress on Eden the 'very grave' situation on the Russian front. Russian manpower, he warned 'was not inexhaustible'. He was bitter about the withdrawal of the British promise to launch the second front and warned that the effect of

a suspension of convoys 'on Russian resistance at this time must be very serious'; TNA FO 371 32910 N3692/30/38. Maisky was completely distraught at an urgent meeting he sought with Winant two days later, after his meeting with Churchill, at which he still hoped the Americans might force the British hand; *FRUS*, 1942, III, pp. 714–15.

179. NA RG 218, CCS 334, 3-10-42, CCS 11th, 10 March 1942.

180. TNA CAB 69/4 DO(42)37, 8 April 1942.

181. TNA PREM 3/324/17, C.S. 18 to Admiralty, CIC Home Fleet.

182. Stimson papers, diary, 25 April 1942; see also TNA PREM 3/393/2, Churchill to Hopkins, 25 April 1942.

183. Roosevelt papers, Map Room 13/1, 25 April 1942.

184. Roosevelt papers, PSF 7: Russia.

185. TNA PREM 3/393/2; Roosevelt papers, Map Room Papers, draft letter to Churchill, 2 May; AVP RF f.059 op.1 d.3833 p.427 l.95, Litvinov to Molotov, 3 May 1942.

186. TNA PREM 3/393/1&2, 6 & 9 May; TNA ADM 205/21, Pound to Churchill, 9 May 1942.

187. TNA PREM 3/392/2, 17 May; COS(42)151 & 152, 15 May 1942; TNA FO 371 32984 N2591/1214/38, FO's minutes.

188. Roosevelt papers, Map Room Papers, 121, 2 June 1942.

189. NA RG 218, CCS 334, CCS 045.4, 7-9-42, Winant conversation with Rear-Admiral Brind, 13 June 1942.

190. TNA CAB 69/4 DO(42)14; TNA PREM 3/393/14, Churchill to Alexander, 24 July 1942. The entry in the diary of Fairbanks from 4 July 1942 well reflects what many felt: 'We try and tell ourselves that there must have been good reasons for us to have avoided further action as none of us are ones to evade a battle … We hate leaving PQ17 behind. It looks so helpless now since the order to disperse has been circulated. The ships are going around in circles, turning this way and that, like so many frightened chicks. Some can hardly go at all. If only our men knew the details they would not feel so badly about it … Morale throughout the ship is very low. The men feel ashamed and resentful.'

191. The convoy was first ordered to disperse and then to scatter.

192. Churchill informed Stalin on 15 July that the convoys would be suspended.

193. Stimson papers, diary, 10 July 1942.

194. NA RG 218, CCS 381, 3-23-42(3/2), JCS to Roosevelt, 10 July; TNA CAB 79/22 JP (42) 679, 17 July 1942; on Dill, CAB 120/689.

195. NA RG 165, OPD 381 ETO/I, Eisenhower to Marshall, 11 July 1942.

196. NA RG 218, CCS 381, 3-23-42(3/2); Stimson papers, diary, 12 & 23 July 1942.

197. Roosevelt papers, PSF 4; Hopkins papers, Box 308: Draft and final instructions by Roosevelt to Marshall; Marshall papers, Verifax 2428, minutes by Hopkins, 15 July; Halifax papers, diary, A7.8.19, 15 July; TNA PREM 3/333/9, Churchill notes, 20 July 1942; TNA CAB 65/31 WM(42)94, Conclusions, 22 July; Stimson papers, diary, 24 & 25 July 1942.

198. Truscott papers, Box 9/1, 26 July 1942.

199. This part of the entry, otherwise fully quoted in *Memoirs of a Soviet Ambassador*, pp. 291–2, is typically omitted.

200. AVP RF f.059 op.1 d.5574 p.2 ll.202–3; TNA FO 371 32910 N3706 & 37077/30/38, 17 July; Sylvester papers, diary, A52, 24 July 1942.

201. Stalin's brief message contested the reasoning of the British naval experts for suspending the convoys and expressed his opinion 'frankly and honestly … in the most emphatic manner' that in view of the critical situation at the front his government could not 'acquiesce in the postponement of a second front in Europe until 1943'; TNA PREM 3/393/3, 23 July 1942.

202. Sylvester papers, diary, A52, 24 July & 8 Sep. 1942.

203. TNA FO 371 32870 N3846/1/38; CAB 65/31/7 WM(42)95. See also Harvey, *War Diaries of Oliver Harvey*, pp. 41–5. See also Bell, *John Bull and the Bear*, pp. 76–81, 104–5.

204. See, for instance, RAN f.1702 op.4 d.1532 ll.17–18, Pritt to Maisky, 15 Sep. 1941 and extensive correspondence with Gollancz on the activities of the Anglo-Soviet Public Relations Committee, Gollanz papers, MSS 151/3/ASP/1/6–17.

205. Dilks, *Diaries of Sir Alexander Cadogan*, pp. 464–5; Eden, *The Reckoning*, p. 338; RGASPI, Stalin papers, f.558 op.11 d.282 ll.4–5, Vyshinsky meeting with Kerr. But the telegram only put a seal on the idea floated by both Maisky and Eden throughout the preceding week; TNA FO 800/300A, Eden to Kerr, 5 Aug. 1942.

206. TNA PREM/3/26A/1, Note by Cadogan transmitted to Churchill, 29 July 1942.

207. Maisky, *Memoirs of a Soviet Ambassador*, p. 297; Bell, *John Bull and the Bear*, pp. 104–5.

208. King, *With Malice toward None*, pp. 185–7; Sylvester papers, diary, A52, 30 July 1942.

209. TNA PREM 3/393/14, Churchill to Alexander, 24 July 1942.

210. TNA PREM 3/76A/9, 15 Aug. 1942; Churchill, *Hinge of Fate*, ch. XXVI–XXVIII. On the misleading narratives, uncritically embraced by historiography, see comments made by Lord Moran in C.M.W. Moran, *Churchill: Taken from the diaries of Lord Moran* (London, 1966), pp. 70–1, as well as D. Reynolds, *In Command of History: Churchill fighting and writing the Second World War* (London, 2005), ch. 21. The accounts include TNA FO 800/300, Reed (British embassy), letter-diary, 19 Aug. 1942; Dilks, *Diaries of Sir Alexander Cadogan*, pp. 469–74; G. Pawle, *The War and Colonel Warden: Based on the recollections of Commander C.R. Thompson, personal assistant to the prime minister, 1940–1945* (London, 1963), ch. 21; Lord Tedder, *With Prejudice: The war memoirs of Marshal of the Royal Air Force, Lord Tedder* (London, 1966), pp. 320–32, and a colourful report in TNA CAB 120/69, 17 Aug. 1942; Harriman and Abel, *Special Envoy to Churchill and Stalin*, ch. 7. The only exception, which rightly attributes the change of heart to Churchill's failure to convince Stalin that *Torch* was the real second front, is sounded by Admiral William Standley, the rather ineffectual American ambassador to Moscow, in *Admiral Ambassador to Russia* (Chicago, 1955), pp. 204–18. For recent works perpetuating the trend, see Costigliola, *Roosevelt's Lost Alliances*, pp. 173–8; J. Fenby, *Alliance: The inside story of how Roosevelt, Stalin and Churchill won one war and began another* (London, 2007), ch. 9; Gilbert, *Road to Victory*, ch. 11; M. Folly, 'Seeking comradeship in the "ogre's den": Winston Churchill's quest for a warrior alliance and his mission to Stalin, August 1942', *Brunel University Research Papers*,

6/2 (2007), pp. 276–303; and G. Ross, 'Operation Bracelet: Churchill in Moscow, 1942', in David Dilks (ed.), *Retreat from Power* (London, 1981), II, pp. 101–19. M. Kitchen, *British Policy towards the Soviet Union during the Second World War* (London, 1986), pp. 132–40, produces a more thorough contextual narrative.

211. King, *With Malice toward None*, p. 185.

212. Churchill papers, CHAR 20/87/7 and TNA PREM3/76/4, exchanges between Churchill and Eden, 4 Aug. 1942; RGASPI, Stalin papers, f.558 op.11 d.282 ll.14–15, Clark Kerr to Molotov, 8 Aug. 1942.

213. Maisky, *Memoirs of a Soviet Ambassador*, p. 297.

214. Roosevelt papers, PSF 68: Russia 1942–43, Welles to Roosevelt on conversations with the Mexican ambassador, 12 Aug.; TNA FO 371 32884 N5029/5/38, Clark Kerr on conversations with Molotov, 30 Sept. 1942.

215. RAN f.1702 op.4 d.111 l.31, 31 Aug. 1942.

216. RAN f.1702 op.4 d.143 l.77 & 79–80, 7 Aug. & 18 Sept. 1942.

217. TNA PREM 3/76A/12, record of Churchill's meeting with Stalin on 15 Aug.; *DPSR*, I, Doc. 262, record of Churchill's conversations with Sikorski, 30 Aug. 1942.

218. Webb, diary, 26 Oct. 1942, p. 7426.

219. Gromyko, *Memoirs*, pp. 26–37.

220. AVP RF f.0129 op.26 d.6 p.143 ll.14–23.

221. AVP RF f.059 op.1 d.2530 p.372 ll.195a-I; RAN f.1702 op.4 d.143 l.77, 7 Aug. 1942.

222. See Resis, *Molotov Remembers*, pp. 45–6, and the following account of the meeting.

223. A detailed record of the first meeting by Clark Kerr is in TNA FO 800/300, 12 Aug., and an almost identical Russian version is in AVP RF f.048 op.24 d.3 p.35 ll.96–99 & d.2 p.23 l.263.

224. On this, see TNA FO 800/300, Clark Kerr to Cadogan; TNA PREM 3/395/18, Churchill's minutes, 21 Oct. 1942.

225. TNA FO 800/300, handwritten notes by Harriman, 13 Aug. 1942.

226. The memorandum is in RGASPI, Stalin papers, f.558 op.11 d.282 ll.35–6 & ll.48–52; AVP RF f.048 op.24 d.2 p.23 l.263; Tedder, *With Prejudice*, pp. 328, 330–1.

227. B. Ellsworth, *Wendell Willkie, Fighter for Freedom* (Michigan, 1966), p. 263.

228. TNA PREM 3/76A/11, 14 Aug. 1942; Moran, *Churchill*, pp. 66–7.

229. TNA FO 800/300, Clark Kerr diary, 15 Aug.; TNA FO 800/300, Reed (British embassy), letter-diary; Churchill acknowledged the 'wise advice' he had received in a letter to the ambassador, TNA CAB 120/67, 19 Aug. 1942.

230. TNA FO 1093/247, Cadogan to Halifax, 29 Aug. 1942; the reference is to Byron's 'The Eve of Waterloo'.

231. RGASPI, Stalin papers, f.558 op.11 d.282 ll.58–61, 16 Aug. 1942; S. Alliluyeva, *Twenty Letters to a Friend* (New York, 1967), pp. 170–1.

232. Harriman papers, Box 164, personal diary of the mission; Jacob papers, diary, JACB 1/15–1/17, 15 Aug. 1942. Berezhkov, Stalin's young interpreter, made a similar observation: 'Stalin was so gracious and courteous that at first Churchill was stunned. But pretty soon he joined his Kremlin host in the game of "friendship"'; V.M. Berezhkov, *At Stalin's Side: His*

interpreter's memoirs from the October Revolution to the fall of the dictator's empire (Secaucus, NJ, 1994), p. 298.

233. TNA PREM 3/76A/11, Churchill to Attlee, 16 Aug. & to Roosevelt, 18 Aug. 1942.

234. TNA FO 371 32884 N4590/5/38, 4 Sep. 1942.

235. N. West (ed.), *Guy Liddell Diaries* (London, 2005), I, p. 258; TNA FO 800/872, Bruce Lockhart on meeting Maisky, and Bruce Lockhart papers, diary, LOC 42/43, 17 Aug. 1942.

236. AVP RF f.059 op.8 d.7 p.2 ll.256–7 & op.1 d.2542 p.374 ll.97–101, exchanges between Maisky and Molotov, 20 Aug. 1942. Maisky intimated to Eden that rumours he had heard from Moscow 'had made him anxious'; TNA FO 954/25B, 20 Aug. 1942.

237. TNA FO 371 32884 N4767/5/35, minutes, 1–3 Sept. 1942; Beaverbrook papers, BBK\H\111; AVP RF f.059 d.5574 p.2 l.286 & d.385 p.430 ll.30 & 40, Maisky's conversations with Eden and report to Molotov, 18 Oct. 1942.

238. TNA FO 371 32914 N4868 & 4819/30/38, 16 & 18 Sept.; Dilks, *Diaries of Sir Alexander Cadogan*, p. 477; Eden, *The Reckoning*, p. 340; McDonald, *A Man of the Times*, pp. 78–80; NA RG 226/21957, OSS report from London, 7 Oct. 1942.

239. TNA FO 371 33021 N5446/3178/38; *The Times*, 28 Sept.; Sylvester papers, diary, A52, 22 Sep.; Garvin papers, letter from Maisky, 1 Oct. 1942. Stalin spoke in the same vein to the Associated Press, reiterating the significance attached by the Russians to the second front, making a direct appeal to public sentiment in Britain and the United States over the head of the government; *FRUS*, 1942, III, p. 460, Harriman to Roosevelt, 5 Oct.; TNA FO 371 32914 N5197/30/38, Philip Kerr to FO, 9 Oct. 1942.

240. Bruce Lockhart papers, diary, LOC 42/43, 5 Oct. 1942.

241. TNA CAB 84/47 JP(42)849; COS 100, 3 Oct.; Stimson papers, diary, 23 Sept. 1942.

242. Bell, *John Bull and the Bear*, pp. 76–82.

243. Bruce Lockhart papers, diary, LOC 42/43, 4 Oct. 1942; Webb, diary, 15 Oct. 1942, p. 7413; Davies papers, Box 12, conversations with Litvinov, 3 & 15 Oct. 1942.

244. Harvey, *War Diaries of Oliver Harvey*, p. 168; TNA FO 954/25B, Maisky's luncheon to journalists, 21 Oct. 1942.

245. Bruce Lockhart papers, diary, LOC 42/43, 27 & 28 Oct. 1942; Eden, *The Reckoning*, p. 344; Harvey, *War Diaries of Oliver Harvey*, pp. 168–9; Dilks, *Diaries of Sir Alexander Cadogan*, pp. 483–4; Pimlott, *Second World War Diary of Hugh Dalton*, p. 502.

246. TNA FO 371 33021 N5718/3178/38 & N5446/3178/38, 2 & 19 Nov. 1942.

247. RAN f.1702 op.4 d.1175 l.14 & ll.16–17; Churchill papers, CHAR 20/54B/139 & 180, correspondence between Maisky and Churchill, 13, 14, 30 Oct. & 30 Nov. 1942. Description of the reception in Sylvester papers, diary, A52, 7 Nov. 1942.

248. AVP RF f.059 d.385 p.430 ll.30–40; *SAO*, I, no. 147.

249. AVP RF f.059a op.7 d.5 p.13 ll.175–89.

250. AVP RF f.059 op.1 d.2543 p.374 ll.38–43, 28 Oct. 1942.

251. AVP RF f.059 op.1 d.3856 p.430 ll.180–6, 10 Nov. 1942.

252. AVP RF f.059 op1. d.3858 p.430 l.19, 6 Dec. 1942. On Marshall's critical views, see Halifax papers, diary, A7.8.19, 15 Dec. 1942; NA RG 218, CCS 334, 11-10-42, JCS 47/9,11, 22 Dec. 1942.

253. TNA CAB 84/51 JP(42)1017 & CAB 119/56 COS(42)452, 27 & 31 Dec. 1942.

254. Pechatnov and Magadeev, *Perepiska I.V. Stalina*, I, doc. 150.

1943

1. The hopelessly optimistic Maisky looked ahead to 1943, convinced that Britain and the Soviet Union had become 'ever closer "allies"'. He was misled by Churchill, as well as by Stalin, into believing that the Americans were the genuine obstacle to a cross-channel attack. However, aware of the 'potholes' on the road ahead, he set out to galvanize into action his own allies in the government, in order to ensure closer collaboration; RAN f.1702 op.4 d.111 l.34, Maisky to Kollontay, 28 Dec. 1942; see, for instance, RAN f.1702 op.4 d.940 l.36 & d.854 l.31, letters to Eden and Beaverbrook, 1 Jan. 1943.

2. The Republicans won nine additional seats in the Senate and 47 in the House of Representatives in the mid-term congressional elections of November 1942. Roosevelt nonetheless won the 1944 presidential elections. The Russians, as is clear from Maisky's conversations with Beaverbrook, acted on the premature assumption that 'power has already passed from the President to the Congress'; Beaverbrook papers, BBK\D\140, report on a meeting with Maisky, 7 Jan. 1943.

3. Following their talk, Cripps wrote to his aunt, Beatrice Webb, that he was 'in complete accord' with Maisky 'about the conditions of the Peace which should be made after we had won the war'. Maisky's ideas were not, as he suggests, sparked by the meeting, but rather, as in his talk with Eden on the 5th, were floated by him; Webb, diary, 4 Jan. 1943, p. 7462.

4. RAN f.1702 op.4 d.847 l.4, 7 Jan. 1943.

5. TNA FO 371 36954 N119/66/38, 5 Jan. 1943.

6. TNA FO 954/3/22, 8 Jan. 1943.

7. Webb, diary, 14 Jan. 1943, pp. 7464–5. Maisky also restored relations with his old socialist friends, such as Brailsford; see RAN f.1702 op.4 d.1248 ll.23–30, Brailsford to Maisky, & d.1325 l.5, Dalton to Maisky, 16 Jan. 1943.

8. The opposite was true, as may be seen throughout the commentaries; also W.F. Kimball (ed.), *Churchill and Roosevelt: The complete correspondence* (Princeton, 1984), II, p. 121.

9. According to Eden, Maisky appeared on the whole 'to understand the position, though he said that it was difficult to explain our point of view to the authorities in Moscow'; TNA FO 954/3 Cosu 43/8-10, 11 Jan. 1943.

10. A historical novel by Gustave Flaubert set in Carthage during the 3rd century BC.

11. Lloyd George papers, LG/G/14/1/27, 28 & 29, 16 & 26 Jan. & 3 Feb. 1943.

12. G. Roberts, *Stalin's Wars: From World War to Cold War, 1939–1953* (London, 2007), p. 232.

13. Those quotes are taken from a thorough and lively coverage of the conference by J. Fenby, *Alliance: The inside story*, pp. 164–79.

14. A.C. Wedemeyer, *Wedemeyer Reports* (New York, 1958), ch. XIV. On the capricious emergence of the Dodecanese Islands as a jumping board for an invasion of Greece and a campaign in the Balkans, see E. Roosevelt, *As He Saw It* (New York, 1946), pp. 84–7, 93–4.

15. Jacob papers, Casablanca diary, JACB 1/17–18; Kimball, *Churchill and Roosevelt.* See also the still authoritative works by M. Matloff and E.M. Snell, *Strategic Planning for Coalition Warfare, 1941–42* (Washington, DC, 1953), pp. 372–82; G.A. Harrison, *Cross-Channel Attack* (Washington, DC, 1951), pp. 33–45; A.F. Wilt, 'The significance of the Casablanca Decisions, January 1943', *Journal of Military History,* 55 (1991).

16. Maisky reproduced the copies of the telegrams exchanged between Churchill and Stalin in his original diary. The quotes here are from his version, unless otherwise stated. The telegrams were published by the Soviet Foreign Ministry, *Correspondence between the Chairman of the Council of Ministers of the USSR and the Presidents of the USA and the Prime Ministers of Great Britain during the Great Patriotic War of 1941–1945* (Moscow, 1957), I, nos. 109–12.

17. On 20 July 1944, an unsuccessful attempt was indeed made to assassinate Hitler by Claus von Stauffenberg and other conspirators from the military and Foreign Ministry, inside his Wolf's Lair field headquarters near Rastenburg, East Prussia.

18. Included are the content of messages exchanged between Roosevelt, Churchill and Stalin on 26 January 1943, informing Stalin of the decision taken at Casablanca. The underlying assumption was that the 'mighty advance' of the Red Army might force Germany to its knees already in 1943. In other words, it removed the urgency for opening a second front. The message reaffirmed the Western Allies' intention of pursuing their peripheral strategy. Lip service was paid to the need to intensify the efforts to defeat Germany and attain victory in Europe and as much attention was drawn to the need to exert pressure on Japan, keep the initiative in the Pacific and the Far East, support China, and prevent the expansion of Japanese aggression to other theatres. The immediate objectives were to liquidate the Axis in North Africa and to undertake a large-scale amphibious operation in Sicily and Italy. At the same time, the concentration of troops in Britain for landing on the European continent was to continue and the operation was to be executed 'as soon as this becomes feasible'. The message from Churchill ended with the customary expression of admiration for the marvellous feats of the Soviet armies. It evoked a succinct and bitter message from Stalin on 30 January 1943, asking for information about the 'concrete planned operations and their timing'.

19. Maisky, *Memoirs of a Soviet Ambassador*, pp. 345–6.

20. *The Times*, 24 Feb. 1943.

21. RAN f.1702 op.4 d.994 l.26 & d.1192 l.16, 3 & 6 Feb. 1943.

22. D.M. Glantz, *From the Don to the Dnepr: Soviet offensive operations, December 1942–August 1943* (London, 1991), and D.M. Glantz, 'Prelude to Kursk: Soviet strategic operations, February–March 1943', *The Journal of Slavic Military Studies*, 8/1 (1995). See also E. Mawdsley, *Thunder in the East: The Nazi–Soviet War 1941–1945* (London, 2005), ch. 9; and Roberts, *Stalin's Wars*, ch. 5.

23. Pimlott, *Second World War Diary of Hugh Dalton*, p. 551.

24. Speaking to journalists in Cairo on the day of the surrender, Churchill hailed the 'tremendous feat of arms performed by our Russian Ally under the general command and direction of Premier Stalin, a great warrior, and a name which will rank with those most

honoured and most lasting in the history of the Russian people'; Churchill papers, CHAR 9/161, 1 Feb. 1943.

25. In a message from Casablanca to the Cabinet, Churchill conceded that 'Nothing in the world will be accepted by Stalin as an alternative to our placing 50 to 60 Divisions in France by the spring of this year. I think he will be disappointed and furious with the joint message'; Churchill papers, CHAR 20/127, 26 Jan. 1943.

26. In his *Memoirs of a Soviet Ambassador*, pp. 352–3, Maisky suggests that the conversation with Churchill convinced him that 'it was no use reckoning on a second front in Northern France in the spring of 1943'. As we have seen, he had given up on a second front earlier, and even saw in its failure an advantage for the Soviet Union. Stalin, however, returned to the topic later in the month, when he realized that the Soviet offensive would be slower than he had anticipated.

27. Maisky had told Harriman that Stalin saw in the request a desire to embroil Russia in a war with Japan, at a time when there was no indication of any imminent prospect of a Japanese attack; Harriman and Abel, *Special Envoy to Churchill and Stalin*, p. 198.

28. Making the same allusion in Casablanca, Churchill added: 'and we are looking for some bishops to burn him'; quoted by Fenby, *Alliance: The inside story*, p. 179.

29. Questioning Churchill's attitude, in a letter to H.G. Wells, Maisky argued that de Gaulle was not 'less acceptable' than a good many other members of the Alliance. Notwithstanding his political opinions, he had 'demonstrated great courage and determination' in his attitude to Nazi Germany when France collapsed, and for two years had been and remained 'the only visible standard bearer of French independence'; RAN f.1702 op.4 d.1141 ll.67–8, 7 Jan. 1943; Pimlott, *Second World War Diary of Hugh Dalton*, p. 549. See also F. Lévêque, 'La place de la France dans la strategie Soviétique de la fin de la guerre en Europe (fin 1942-fin 1945), *Matériaux pour l'Histoire de Notre Temps*, 36 (1994).

30. Churchill was referring to Tukhachevsky's victory over the Polish army, which brought the Russians to the gates of Warsaw. General Józef Piłsudski, however, exploited the extended Soviet line and the logistic disarray to repel the Red Army behind the Neman river.

31. Maisky sent Molotov a detailed and fairly accurate report of the conversation, emphasizing, though, Churchill's supposed concern about the rift between Roosevelt and Stalin; AVP RF, f.059 op.10 d.64 ll.23–6.

32. Earlier in the day, Churchill had been diagnosed with acute pneumonia. He reluctantly submitted to the doctors' orders to stay in bed and reduce his workload to a minimum, after being told that the illness was called 'the old man's friend'. 'Why?' he had asked. 'Because it takes them off so quietly'; quoted in Gilbert, *Road to Victory*, p. 340. Stalin pressed again for a second front when he realized that the Soviet offensive, successful as it was, had been contained by General von Manstein, about to be promoted to marshal for his masterly manoeuvring; Mawdsley, *Thunder in the East*, p. 261.

33. TNA FO 954/32A.

34. TNA FO 954/26 SU/43/17/A, Boothby to Eden, 25 Feb. 1943.

35. Quoted in R.E. Sherwood, *Roosevelt and Hopkins: An intimate history* (New York, 1948), p. 713.

36. TNA FO 954/32 W(g)/43/22, 24 Feb. 1943.

37. Bruce Lockhart papers, diary, LOC/45-49, 23 Feb. 1943.

38. *The Times*, 21 Feb. 1943.

39. The double-edged two-handed Sword of Stalingrad was a bejewelled ceremonial longsword specially produced by command of George VI of the United Kingdom as a homage to the Soviet defenders of the city. It was presented by Churchill to Stalin during the Tehran Summit Conference on 29 November 1943. *Sword of Honour* was the title chosen by Evelyn Waugh for his brilliant trilogy on the Second World War, very much based on his own experiences in the war. The episode left a strong enough impression on him, symbolizing the cynical nature of alliances at war and the absence of any morality at their foundation.

40. Simon expressed his 'apologies and regrets' for failing to attend the reception: 'I particularly wanted to do so, to pay my personal tribute to the amazing and glorious achievements of your heroic fellow countrymen'; RAN f.1702 op.4 d.1561 ll.6–7, 26 Feb. 1943. Maisky told Boothby that Simon's speech was a terrible blow to Moscow and 'had undone all the good of last Sunday's Red Army demonstrations'; TNA FO 954/26 SU/43/17/A, 25 Feb. 1943. See also a minute in the same vein by Warner, head of the northern department, TNA FO 371 36971 N1136/172/38, 2 March 1943. Maisky's self-censored report of the conversation, trying to minimize the damage caused by Simon but avoiding the cardinal issues, is in *SAO*, I, no. 191.

41. Harvey, *War Diaries of Oliver Harvey*, 22 Feb. 1943, p. 222.

42. TNA PREM3/393/14, memo by Ismay and a note by Churchill, 24 & 25 Feb. 1943.

43. Eden, *The Reckoning*, pp. 368–9.

44. Sherwood, *Roosevelt and Hopkins*, p. 714.

45. Gilbert, *Road to Victory*, pp. 340–2; Reynolds, *In Command of History*, pp. 316–18.

46. This was a bad omen for Maisky. Stalin, who got on well with Philip Kerr, preferred henceforth to conduct negotiations directly through him in Moscow, leaving Maisky in the lurch until his recall. Molotov's report of the meetings in Moscow, which Maisky recapitulates in his diary, was merely informative and did not call for any response or action on his behalf; AVP RF f.059 p.10 d.174 ll.53–6, 24 Feb. 1943.

47. Further reminiscences of that evening are in Maisky, *Memoirs of a Soviet Ambassador*, pp. 330–1.

48. A surrounded stronghold, left unconquered by an advancing offensive, which nonetheless continues to fight.

49. *SAO*, I, no. 195.

50. TNA FO 954/19 Pol/43/4.

51. Eden, *The Reckoning*, p. 371; *FRUS*, 1943, III, pp. 19–24.

52. AVP RF f.06 op.5 p.16 d.154 ll.2–25, 7 & 13 April 1943. There are no relevant entries in the diary for the meetings with Eden. For the Soviet interest in his report, see Maisky's entry of 22 April.

53. See diary entry for 23 April and the preceding commentary.

54. Churchill papers, CHAR 20/107.

55. S. Ball (ed.), *Parliament and Politics in the Age of Churchill and Attlee: The Headlam Diaries 1935–1951* (London, 2000), p. 362.

56. Harriman and Abel, *Special Envoy to Churchill and Stalin*, p. 199.

57. Included in the entry is Stalin's telegram to Churchill from 15 March reminding him of his firm commitment to a second front in spring of 1943 and ending with a stern warning on 'how dangerous a further delay of a second front could be for our common cause'.

58. The Cabinet, which met shortly after the meeting, found the Russian terms 'not unreasonable'; TNA CAB 65/37/14.

59. That the suspension was dictated not merely by the threat posed by the big ships, but more likely by British shipping and supply requirements for the operations in Tunisia and Sicily, is attested by Admiral Pound's disclosure to Churchill, during the Cabinet meeting of the previous evening, that the 'latest information was that the statement … in the draft telegram to Premier Stalin, as to the German naval concentration at Narvik, was no longer accurate. It was known that most of these ships had left Narvik Fjord' and that it would take a couple of days to establish their new location; TNA CAB 65/37/14.

60. Churchill papers, CHAR 20/93A/12.

61. TNA FO 371 36989 N2497/408/38, 23 April 1943.

62. Churchill, replacing Eden at the Foreign Office during his trip to the United States, cabled the ambassador in Moscow: 'Let me know what you think of Joe's reply about the convoy business. My own feeling is that they took it like men.' To which Kerr responded: 'I have been prepared for a very tart reply and was surprised by Joe's moderation. I share your feeling, but it should be remembered that he believes in your good faith'; TNA FO 954/3 Cosu 43/73 & 78.

63. On 1 April, Maisky wrote to Kollontay: 'Unfortunately, I am not very optimistic about the *contribution* of our Allies this coming summer'; RAN f.1702 op.4 d.111 ll.35–6.

64. Quoted in Gilbert, *Road to Victory*, pp. 382–4. See also A. Danchev and D. Todman (eds), *Alanbrooke: War diaries* (London, 2002), p. 393.

65. Natalia Lebedeva was the first brave voice in Russia to expose the massacre. Her exemplary work culminated in the teamwork of A. Cienciala, N. Lebedeva and Wojciech Materski (eds), *Katyn: A crime without punishment* (New Haven, 2008). On the impact which a revelation might have had on the alliance, see G. Sanford, 'The Katyn Massacre and Polish–Soviet relations, 1941–1943', *Journal of Contemporary History*, 41/1 (2006), and his book *Katyn and the Soviet Massacre of 1940: Truth, justice and memory* (London, 2005). See also Roberts, *Stalin's Wars*, pp. 172–3.

66. Stalin's behaviour throughout the crisis was chillingly cynical, as becomes obvious from his correspondence with Churchill on the subject. The Soviet cover-up of the 1940 massacres persisted unabated until, in 1990, Gorbachev handed General Jaruzelski a list of the Polish officers murdered by the NKVD at Katyn. Beria's proposal that the interned Polish officers who were defined as unreformed enemies of the Soviet Union should be executed without trial was approved by the Politburo on 5 March 1940.

67. Churchill may have had a soft spot for Sikorski, but less so for the Polish government in exile. Earlier in the month, he had expressed in private his impatience with the Poles in language similar to that used by Maisky: 'We see all those elements of instability which have led to the ruin of Poland through so many centuries in spite of the individual qualities and virtues of the Poles.' When he met Sikorski to discuss the allegations, Churchill

conceded that 'the German revelations are probably true. The Bolsheviks can be very cruel'; Dilks (ed.), *Cadogan Diaries*, pp. 520–1; see also Gilbert, *Road to Victory*, p. 376. But his uppermost interest was to suppress the horrific story rather than forgo his alliance with Stalin. Particularly at the moment that he had suspended the Arctic convoys and postponed indefinitely the second front. 'Grim things happen in war,' he simply told Maisky. 'This affair of the missing Polish Officers was indeed grim. But if they were dead they could not be resurrected to life. It was the case of the living Poles in Russia that required attention'; TNA FO 954/19 Pol/43/12, 23 April 1943. Churchill held to the same view during the Tehran summit meeting, at the end of the year, telling Stalin that 'nothing was more important than the security of the Russian Western frontier'. As Anita Prazmowska has shown convincingly, during 1943 the Polish government 'had become increasingly irrelevant in British and United States politics, in spite of its increased military contribution to the war'; *Britain and Poland, 1939–1943: The betrayed ally* (Cambridge, 1995), pp. 191–2.

68. RAN f.1702 op.4 d.1141 l.73, 5 May 1943.

69. Bell, *John Bull and the Bear*, pp. 116–22.

70. Dilks, *Diaries of Sir Alexander Cadogan*, p. 525; Churchill's report in TNA FO 371 35474 C5136/258/55.

71. Beatrice Webb died on 30 April. Maisky is writing two days later about the visit to the Shaws which had taken place a couple of days before her death. It has to be assumed that he is describing the thoughts that went through his head while at the Shaws.

72. See entry of 27 May 1943.

73. See the chapter 'End of an Era'.

74. Maisky invited Wells for lunch after reading his obituary of Beatrice Webb in the *Manchester Guardian*, which he thought 'transcends the small happenings of every-day life' evoking the 'admiration, sympathy and warm friendship in the highest degree' which he himself felt for her; RAN f.1702 op.4 d.1141 l.73, Maisky to Wells, 5 May 1943.

75. Maisky refers to Gogol's comedy *The Marriage*, where Podkolesin mirrors Gogol's (a lifelong bachelor) ambivalent attitude to the institution of marriage.

76. See a detailed account of the dissolution in 1941, in Gorodetsky, *Grand Delusion*, pp. 199–201.

77. Harvey, *War Diaries of Oliver Harvey*, p. 261. Maisky used similar words speaking to the American ambassador in London; *FRUS*, 1943, III, pp. 532–4. See also Roberts, *Stalin's Wars*, pp. 168–70.

78. Sylvester papers, diary, A54, 7 Sep. 1943.

79. Maisky, according to Cadogan, was 'frightfully inquisitive about A's trip. Told him *all* I (and A[Anthony Eden] knew), which wasn't much, and M. was not satisfied'; Cadogan papers, diary, ACAD 1/11, 1 June 1943.

80. Actually president of the Board of Education at this time.

81. TNA FO 371 36983 N3547/315/38, Butler to Eden, 2 June 1943.

82. TNA FO 954/26 SU/43/46, 5 May 1943.

83. Halifax papers, diary, A7.8.19, 6 May 1943.

84. Fenby, *Alliance: The inside story*, pp. 187–94.

85. Gilbert, *Road to Victory*, ch. 23. Halifax papers, diary, A7.8.19, 16 May 1943.

86. Halifax papers, diary, A7.8.19, 16 May 1943; Danchev and Todman, *Alanbrooke*, p. 405.

87. Kharlamov, *Difficult Mission*, p. 157.

88. TNA FO 954/26 SU/43/52-4-5; *SAO*, I, no. 224, 9 June is Maisky's report of the meeting which he sent to Moscow; see also Churchill papers, CHAR 20/93B/174, Churchill to Maisky, 13 June 1943.

89. Based on Gilbert, *Road to Victory*, ch. 25.

90. 'I don't like this', was Cadogan's brief but perceptive observation in his diary; Dilks, *Diaries of Sir Alexander Cadogan*, p. 539. Halifax and Hopkins reacted similarly: Halifax papers, diary, A7.8.19, 1 July 1943.

91. Beaverbrook papers, BBK\D\140, record of meeting with Maisky, 30 June 1943.

92. TNA FO 954/26 SU/43/65, 2 July 1943.

End of an Era: Maisky's Recall

1. On this episode, see TNA KV 3/275, and Halifax papers, diary, A7.8.19, 5 May 1942.

2. D. Irving, *Accident: The death of General Sikorski* (London, 1967). The net is swarming with 'information' about the crash. A good example is J. Kazimierz Kubit, 'Was General Sikorski a victim of the Katyn massacre?', at www.polishnews.com/historia-history/historia-polskipolish-history/537-was-general-sikorski-a-victim-of-the-katyn-massacre.

3. Maisky, *Memoirs of a Soviet Ambassador*, p. 369; Irving, *Accident*, pp. 51–2, 166–7.

4. Beaverbrook papers, BBK\D\140, 30 June 1943; Young, *Diaries of Sir Robert Bruce Lockhart*, II, 3–4 July 1943.

5. *FRUS*, 1943, III, pp. 522–3.

6. TNA FO 800/872, memo on a meeting with Maisky, 2 Sep. 1943.

7. G. Bilainkin, *Second Diary of a Diplomatic Correspondent* (London, 1947), p. 106.

8. *The Times*, 18 July & 26 Aug. 1943. See also Ambassador Standley falling into this 'trap', *FRUS*, 1943, III, pp. 567–8.

9. *Time* Magazine, 26 August 1943.

10. See diary entry for 4 January 1938.

11. V. Zubok and C. Pleshakov, *Inside the Kremlin's Cold War: From Stalin to Khrushchev* (Boston, 1996), pp. 28–33. Uldricks, 'Impact of the Great Purges', pp. 193–5, had convincingly argued, even before Soviet archives were open, that the recall marked the completion of the process of the transformation of the revolutionary Narkomindel into a Stalinist Foreign Ministry. He further argued that the 'promotion' of Maisky and Litvinov to the position of 'deputy foreign minister' in fact deprived them of the power they had exercised.

12. Harriman and Abel, *Special Envoy to Churchill and Stalin*, p. 199.

13. Ivy Litvinov papers, Box 10/3.

14. Young, *Diaries of Sir Robert Bruce Lockhart*, II, pp. 348–9.

15. G. Roberts, 'Litvinov's lost peace, 1941–1946', *Journal of Cold War Studies*, 4/2 (2002).

16. From the private archives of Voskresensky's family, quoted in Myasnikov, *Maiskii: Izbrannaya perepiska*, II, p.126.

17. Gromyko, *Pamyatnoe*, I, pp. 416–18. Not in the English edition.

18. AVP RF f.06 op.6 p.62 d.834 ll.97–8, 22 July 1943.

19. *Istoricheskii Arkhiv*, 4 (1998), and Maisky, *Memoirs of a Soviet Ambassador*, p. 378.

20. V. Mastny in 'Reconsiderations: The Cassandra in the Foreign Commissariat – Maxim Litvinov and the Cold War', *Foreign Affairs*, 54 (1986), overplays the importance of Litvinov after his return to Moscow.

21. TNA FO 371 36956 N5158/66/38, 10 Aug. 1943.

22. Foster, 'The Beaverbrook press and appeasement', p. 15.

23. See the chapter 'Making of a Soviet Diplomat'.

24. RAN f.1702 op.4 d.1194 l.4, 14 July 1943.

25. TNA FO 371 33021 N3178/3178/38, FO minutes and correspondence, 24–26 June 1943; Sylvester papers, diary, A54, 31 May 1943 & B74, letter to Lloyd George, 3 June 1943; RAN f.1702 op.4 d.79 l.12, Maisky to Zinchenko, 21 April 1944.

26. *Hansard*, HL Deb 11 June 1942, vol. 123, cols 359–64 & *Hansard*, HC Deb 11 June 1942, vol. 380, cols 1347–54.

27. The speech is reproduced in full in the Maisky diary entry of 20 June 1942 but is omitted from this edition. Letter to Negrín, RAN f.1702 op.4 d.1040 l.4, 20 June 1942.

28. Noel-Baker papers, NBKR 4/639, 15 Sep. 1943. See also similar examples in RAN f.1702 op.4 d.1267 l.26, d.1399 l.11, Vansittart and Cranborne to Maisky, 13 Sep. 1943.

29. O. Kokoschka, *My Life* (London, 1971), p. 34.

30. I am grateful for information given to me by Beatrice von Bormann, a thoughtful curator of Kokoschka's portrait exhibitions, and Anna Müller-Härlin, an art historian who is pursuing research on Kokoschka; see also Richard Calvocoressi's Kokoschka Catalogue (Tate Gallery, 1986).

31. E. Beddington-Behrens, *Look Back Look Forward* (London, 1963), pp. 165–6.

32. This was only partially true. It was very much manipulated by Agniya (see the commentary following the diary entry for 14 February 1941). Maisky later expressed to Epstein his 'debt of gratitude' for the 'fine piece of work' and 'appreciated very much your wish to do it'; RAN f.1702 op.4 d.1194 ll.8–9, 21 March 1944.

33. RAN f.1702 op.4 d.1194 ll.6–7, Maisky to Gusev, 25 Dec. 1943.

34. See the commentary following the diary entry for 4 April 1940.

35. See the commentary following the diary entry for 6 April 1942.

36. May well be an allusion to Macbeth's famous line: 'Is this a dagger which I see before me?'

37. Voskresensky's private archives, quoted by Myasnikov, *Maiskii: Izbrannaya perepiska*, II, p. 126, 28 May 1943.

38. Maisky, diary entry for 5 November 1943, written in Moscow after his return to the Soviet Union.

39. McDonald, *A Man of the Times*, p. 93.

40. See the chapter 'The Price of Fame'.

41. For Molotov's most detailed report of the meeting, see AVP RF f.06 op.5 p.17 d.159 ll.74–81, and Kerr's brief one in TNA FO 371 36925 N4253/22/38 and a follow-up in TNA FO 371 36925 N4375/22/38, 7 Aug. 1943.

42. TNA FO 371 36925 N4323/22/38; *SAO*, I, no. 238, 29 July 1943.

43. RAN f.1702 op.4 d.1616 l.41, 5 Aug. 1943.

44. TNA FO 954/26 SU/43/75, Kerr to Eden, 8 Aug. 1943.

45. TNA FO 371 36925 N4253/22/38 & TNA FO 371 36925 N4375/22/38, minutes by Warner, Sargent, Cadogan and Eden, 27–28 July & 4–7 Aug. 1943. Danchev and Todman, *Alanbrooke*, p. 464.

46. Maisky shared his candid outlook with General Spears, the British minister in Damascus, with whom he had fostered close relations even during the difficult early days of his ambassadorship. See TNA FO 954/26A, Spears' report to Eden, 6 Oct. 1943. On the very special relations between Spears and Maisky, see Spears papers, SPRS 1/221, letter to Maisky, 5 April 1945.

47. See the chapter 'Making of a Soviet Diplomat'.

48. A letter to Molotov and a draft letter from the private archives of Voskresensky's family, quoted in Myasnikov, *Maiskii: Izbrannaya perepiska*, II, pp. 128–9; Maisky, *Memoirs of a Soviet Ambassador*, pp. 380–2. A year later, Eden made a similar observation, following a most frustrating meeting with Gusev, Maisky's successor: 'Tried to impress upon him the difficulties Russian methods make for us. He appeared to understand, but God knows whether he did. One misses Maisky very much, for it was always possible to have a heart to heart with him. Which is perhaps the reason why Mr Maisky did not stay with us'; Eden, *The Reckoning*, p. 450.

49. Bruce Lockhart papers, special diary/45, 9 Sep. 1943; Bruce Lockhart, *Comes the Reckoning*, p. 256.

50. RAN f.1702 op.4 d.1172 l.2, 7 Aug. 1943.

51. See the commentary following the diary entry for 28 April 1939.

52. Harvey, *War Diaries of Oliver Harvey*, pp. 41–5.

53. On this see *DPSR*, II, Doc. 32, record of conversation between Raczyński and Eden, 3 Sep. 1943.

54. TNA FO 371 36956 N4977/66/38, 31 Aug., FO 954/26A & FO 371 36956 N5232/66/38, Eden's meetings with Maisky, 31 Aug., 3 Sep. & 9 Sep.; TNA FO 800/872, Lockhart's memo on a meeting with Maisky, 2 Sep. 1943; Eden, *The Reckoning*, pp. 404–5. See also S. Kudryashov, 'Stalin and the Allies: Who deceived whom?' *History Today*, 45/5 (1995).

55. Sokolov, '"Avtobiograficheskie zametki"'.

56. See a representative uncritical article by V. Shustov, 'A.A. Sobolev: A portrait of excellence', *International Affairs*, 50/3 (2004); Young, *Diaries of Sir Robert Bruce Lockhart*, II, p. 348.

57. TNA FO 954/13B, 7 Sep. 1943; Danchev and Todman, *Alanbrooke*, p. 451; Lloyd George papers, LG/G/14/1, 8 Sep. 1943.

58. *New York Times*, 28 July 1943; see also *The Times*, 6 Sep. 1943.

59. RAN f.1702 op.4 d.848 l.23, 2 Sep. 1943. See also letters in the same vein: RAN f.1702 op.4 d.1192 l.19, to Walter Elliot, 2 Sep.; d.1132 l.29, to Charles Philips Trevelyan, 3 Sep.; d.946 l.13, to Cadogan, 11 Sep.; d.953 l.7, to Keynes, 11 Sep.; d.869 l.11, to Brendan Bracken, 11 Sep. 1943; Greenwood papers, box 128, letter to Greenwood, 11 Sep. 1943; Garvin papers, letter to Garvin, 4 Sep. 1943.

60. RAN f.1702 op.4 d.876 l.19, 8 Sep. 1943.

61. RAN f.1702 op.4 d.1074 l.13, 12 Sep. 1943. See also B. Pares, *The New Russia* (London, 1931), pp. 362–3.

62. RAN f.1702 op.4 d.1184 l.25, 12 Sep. 1943.

63. RAN f.1702 op.4 d.1184 l.26, 14 Sep. 1943. On their close friendship, see Maisky, 'Bernard Shou'.

64. A.W. Sansom, *I Spied Spies* (London, 1965), pp. 152–9.

65. Spears, *Fulfilment of a Mission*, pp. 285–6.

66. Maisky, *Memoirs of a Soviet Ambassador*, p. 372. On his earlier meeting with Weizmann, see the diary entry for 3 February 1941.

67. TNA FO 371/35589, Miles to Eden, 15 July 1943. See also Rami Ginat, *The Soviet Union and Egypt, 1945–1955* (London, 1994).

68. See J. Ben-Tov, 'Contacts between Soviet Ambassador Maisky and Zionist leaders during World War II', *Soviet Jewish Affairs*, 8/1 (1978); B. Pinkus, *The Soviet Government and the Jews, 1948–1967* (Cambridge, 2008); and N. Levin, *The Jews in the Soviet Union from 1917 to the Present* (New York, 1991), pp. 395–7.

69. CZA S100/40, Ben-Gurion's report to the meeting of the Jewish Agency Executive, 4 Oct. 1943.

70. AVP RF f.017 op.1 p.4 d.39 ll.58–9, Ben-Gurion to Maisky, 8 Aug. 1943; AVP RF f.0118 op.7 p.4 d.4 l.1, A. Sultanov's reports on a meeting with M. Shertok in Cairo, 4 Oct. 1943. Ben-Gurion continued to provide Maisky with information about the ability of the country to absorb a large number of Jews in Palestine, unaware of the changing fortunes of the deputy foreign minister; see AVP RF f.017 op.1 p.4 d.39 ll.58–9, 8 Aug. 1944.

71. See information gleaned by Sulzberger and reported in the *New York Times*, 30 October 1943.

72. G. Gorodetsky, 'The Soviet Union's role in the creation of the State of Israel', *Israeli Studies*, 22/1 (2003).

73. TNA FO 954/3B, Churchill to Eden, 18 Oct. 1943.

74. RAN f.1702 op.4 d.79 ll.4–5, Maisky to Zinchenko, 25 Nov. 1943.

75. RAN f.1702 op.4 d.52 l.1, 26 Nov. 1943.

76. From the private archives of Voskresensky's family, quoted in Myasnikov, *Maiskii: Izbrannaya perepiska*, II, p. 137.

77. RAN f.1702 op.4 d.52 l.3 & d.79 l.7, letters to Gusev and Zinchenko, 27 Jan. 1944.

78. Churchill papers, CHAR 20/144A/36, 20 March 1944.

79. RAN f.1702 op.4 d.940 ll.42–3, 20 March 1944.

80. See, for example, Voskresensky's family archives, Maisky to Molotov, 6 April 1944, quoted in Myasnikov, *Maiskii: Izbrannaya perepiska*, II, p. 143.

81. Lloyd George papers, LG/G/14/1/35, 21 March 1944. See also a letter to Cripps in the same vein, RAN f.1702 op.4 d.973 l.14, 21 March 1944.

82. TNA FO 954/26A, Eden on meeting Maisky, 3 Sep. 1943.

The Price of Fame: A Late Repression

1. Beddington-Behrens, *Look Back Look Forward*, p. 166.

2. RAN f.1702 op.4 d.1677 ll.23–4, 7 Jan. 1945. In *Men of Influence*, pp. 281–4, Dullin analyses most competently the political and administrative workings of Narkomindel, acutely identifying the waning influence of the 'old guard' of Soviet diplomacy.

3. McDonald, *A Man of the Times*, p. 93.

4. RAN f.1702 op.4 d.565 ll.41–2, Agniya to Maisky, 6 Feb. 1945.

5. The record of the conference and Maisky's role in it is described in TNA CAB/66/63/12 P(45)157, 12 March 1945.

6. RAN f.1702 op.4 d.155 l.50, 7 Feb. 1945.

7. RAN f.1702 op.2 d.79 ll.66–7, Maisky's interview with P.T. Komarev, deputy chairman of the Control Committee of the CPSU, Feb. 1957.

8. Inverchapel papers, Box 61, Kerr to Bevin, 29 Jan. 1946.

9. Myasnikov, *Maiskii: Izbrannaya perepiska*, II, pp. 532–3.

10. Voskresensky's family archives, quoted in Myasnikov, *Maiskii: Izbrannaya perepiska*, II, p. 164, 7 June 1945.

11. RAN f.1702 op.3 d.418 ll.1–2 & op.2 d.157 l.4, 3 May & 20 June 1946.

12. Sheinis, *Litvinov*, p. 343.

13. L. Yakovlev, 'Ivan Mikhailovich Maiskii s suprugoyu svoeyu Agnei Aleksandrovnoi', *Shtrikhi k portretam i nemnogo lichnykh vospominanii* (Kharkov, 2005).

14. Sheinis, *Litvinov*, p. 347.

15. Yakovlev, 'Ivan Mikhailovich Maiskii'.

16. A. de Baets, *Censorship of Historical Thought* (London, 2002), p. 487; A. Nekrich, *Forsake Fear: Memoirs of an historian* (London, 1991), p. 57.

17. Stanford archives, Nekrich interview with Maisky, July 1973.

18. Unless otherwise stated, the story of Maisky's arrest (19 February 1953 to 22 July 1955) is based on his own 14-page narrative, attached to an appeal for rehabilitation sent to the Military Court; RAN f.1702 op.2 d.76 ll.1–14.

19. Translation by Oliver Ready.

20. RAN f.1702 op.1 d.820 ll.41–5, 19 Jan. 1954. As Maisky was forbidden to have any contact with the outside world, he composed poems in his head and wrote them down only after his release. Some 57 such poems were written, but only a few have survived.

21. Yakovlev, 'Ivan Mikhailovich Maiskii'.

22. Nekrich, *Forsake Fear*, pp. 69–70.

23. Stanford archives, Nekrich interview with Maisky, 7 Aug. 1973.

24. RAN f.1702 op.2 d.79 ll.9–13, Maisky's description of the nature of his relations with Beria in a letter to Voroshilov, 5 Aug. 1955.

25. On Molotov's visit see the commentary following the diary entry for 6 April 1942.

26. The doctors' plot.

27. V.M. Berezhkov, *At Stalin Side*, p. 340. On the Jewish aspect, see B. Efimov and V. Fradkin, 'Slozhnaya sud'ba diplomata', in B. Efimov and V. Fradkin, *O vremenakh i lyudyakh* (Moscow, 2000), and J. Ben-Tov, 'Contacts', p. 54. See the chapter 'End of an Era' and the diary entry for 3 February 1941.

28. S. Beria, *Beria My Father: Inside Stalin's Kremlin* (Bristol, 2003), pp. 47–8; Watson, *Molotov*, p. 244.

29. Resis, *Molotov Remembers*, pp. 341–2.

30. RAN f.1702 op.2 d.79 ll.9–13, Maisky description of the nature of his relations with Beria in a letter to Voroshilov, 5 Aug. 1955. Much of the information revealed here is derived

from the report on Beria's interrogation on 20 August 1953, and segments of the reports of Maisky's interrogation a day earlier with which he was confronted, RGASPI f.17. op.171. d.466. ll.201–10.

31. Berezhkov, *At Stalin's Side*, pp. 340–1.

32. P. Sudoplatov, *Special Tasks: The memoirs of an unwanted witness – a Soviet spymaster* (London, 1994), p. 344.

33. Sudoplatov, *Special Tasks*, pp. 344–5; Yakovlev, 'Ivan Mikhailovich Maiskii'. See also Berezhkov, *At Stalin's Side*, pp. 340–1; Efimov, *O vremenakh i lyudyakh.*

34. Zubok and Pleshakov, *Inside the Kremlin's Cold War*, pp. 163–4. According to A.I. Mikoyan, *Tak bylo: razmyshleniya o minuvshem* (Moscow, 1999), ch. 47, Beria did not wait long after Stalin's death to signal that he was 'preparing the ground' for seizing power. A. Knight, *Beria, Stalin's First Lieutenant* (Princeton, 1993). See also *The Telegraph*, 28 July 2001; and R. Service writing in *The Guardian*, 30 June 2001.

35. Resis, *Molotov Remembers*, pp. 341–2, 264; Gromyko, *Memoirs*, p. 322; Sudoplatov, *Special Tasks*, p. 345.

36. Draft memoirs of Ivy Litvinov, Stanford University.

37. D.M. Stickle (ed.), *The Beria Affair: The secret transcripts of the meetings signalling the end of Stalinism* (New York, 1992), pp. 158, 195–7; Nekrich's report of an interview with Maisky in Stanford and *Forsake Fear*, pp. 84–6; Sudoplatov, *Special Tasks*, p. 372.

38. RAN f.1702 op.2 d.73 ll.128–9, Draft letter to Malenkov, 1 July & ll.159–60, letter to Molotov, 8 July 1954; Nekrich, 'The arrest and trial of I.M. Maisky', pp. 317–18.

39. S. Dorril, *MI6: Inside the covert world of Her Majesty's Secret Intelligence Service* (London, 2002), p. 506; Sudoplatov, *Special Tasks*, ch. 12.

40. Forty-six pages of the draft defence prepared by Maisky are in RAN f.1702 op.2 d.75 ll.1–46. Maisky never tired of trying to persuade the court, and subsequently politicians, that holding back the microfilm was a mere 'slip-up' and was therefore a result of 'forgetfulness and the extreme pressure of work during the war period'. See, for instance, RAN f.411 op.3 d.349 ll.64–6, letter to president of the Academy of Sciences & f.1702 op.2 d.79 ll.40–8, and speech to the Party Control Committee.

41. RAN f.1702 op.2 d.76 ll.24–8, Maisky to Gorkin, president of the Supreme Court, 7 May 1956. See Maisky's diary entry of 8 January 1940, where he admits to having learned of the contents of the White Paper, the exposure of which at the time would have seriously jeopardized his position.

42. RAN op.2 d.79 ll.32–3, 25 Oct. 1956. See also the speech to the Party Control Committee in RAN f.1702 op.2 d.79 ll.40–8.

43. RAN f.1702 op.2 d.76 ll.38–9, 21 April 1960.

44. RAN f.1702 op.2 d.76 ll.47–8, Maisky's response to queries by Khrushchev, 14 July 1960.

45. RAN f.1702 op.2 d.75 l.57, 18 June 1955.

46. O. Troyanovskii, *Cherez gody i rasstoyaniya* (Moscow, 1997), p. 173. On the background to the struggle, see the excellent survey by Y. Gorlizki and O. Khlevniuk, *Cold Peace: Stalin and the Soviet ruling circle, 1945–53* (Oxford, 2004). See also Watson, *Molotov*,

p. 251, and V.V. Sokolov, 'Molotov Vyacheslav Mikhailovich', *Diplomaticheskii vestnik* (July, 2002).

47. RAN f.1702 op.2 d.75 l.57, 18 June 1955.

48. RAN f.1702 op.2 d.76 ll.38–9, appeal for rehabilitation by Maisky to Khrushchev, 21 April 1960.

49. RAN f.1702 op.2 d.75 l.47, 13 June 1955.

50. See the 'Introduction'.

51. *Sovetskaya Kultura*, April 1966.

52. *The Times*, 17 March 1966.

53. RAN f.1702 op.4 l.27, 5 May 1962.

54. RAN f.1702 op.3 d.541 ll.13–16.

55. Kharlamov, *Difficult Mission*, p. 53.

56. The tremendous concrete shelter installed in the gardens of the embassy (see commentary following 12 October 1940) proved far too expensive to remove, and is still a monumental feature of the grounds.

57. RAN f.1702 op.4 d.240 ll.2–3, Letter to M.N. Smirnovsky, 3 July 1971.

58. Nekrich papers, report of his interview with Maisky, and *Forsake Fear*, p. 87.

Select Bibliography

The bibliography is not a comprehensive list of works on the topic; it includes only those books and articles which are referred to in the commentary and notes.

The major state archives researched by the editor and their abbreviations are:

- Archives of the Russian Foreign Ministry (AVP RF)
- Archives of the Russian Security Services (TsA FSB RF)
- Russian State Archive of Socio-Political History (RGASPI): Papers of Maisky, Stalin, Litvinov and Molotov
- Archives of the Russian Academy of Sciences (RAN)
- The National Archives, London (TNA): Archives of the Foreign Office (FO), Prime Minister's Office (PREM), Joint Intelligence Committee (JIC), Chiefs of Staff (COS), Joint Planning Staff (JP), Ministry of Economic Warfare (MEW), War Office (WO), Cabinet Offices (CAB), Defence Committee (DO), Cipher and Signal Department (KV)
- The National Archives, Washington, DC (NA): State Department (SD), Military Archives (RG)

The following abbreviations are used in the endnotes for the volumes of published documents:

DDF – P. Renouvin and J.B. Duroselle (eds.), *Documents diplomatiques francais*, vols. for 1932–1939

DGFP – *Documents on German Foreign Policy* (London, 1956), Series D (1937–1945)

DPSR – General Sikorski Historical Institute (ed.), *Documents on Polish–Soviet Relations 1939–1945* (London, 1961)

DVP – *Dokumenty vneshnei politiki SSSR* (Moscow 1958–2000)

FRUS – *Foreign Relations of the United States*, vols. 184–221 (1937–1943)

God Krizisa – Russian Foreign Ministry, *God krizisa: 1938–1939: dokumenty i materialy* (Moscow, 1990), 2 vols.

SAO – G.P. Kynin, P.P. Sevostianov and V.P. Suslov, *Sovetsko-angliiskie otnosheniya vo vremya Velikoi Otechestvennoi voiny, 1941–1945* (Moscow, 1983), 2 vols.

SPE – A. Gromyko et al. (eds.), *Soviet Peace Efforts on the Eve of World War II (September 1938–August 1939)* (Moscow, 1973)

VSD – I.M. Maisky, *Vospominaniya sovetskogo diplomata, 1925–1945 gg.* (Moscow, 1987)

* * *

The following collections of private papers were consulted and used by the editor in writing the commentary for these volumes:

Russia

I.M. Maisky papers, Russian Academy of Sciences, Moscow.

Great Britain

A.V. Alexander, Churchill Archives, Churchill College, Cambridge.

L.C. Amery, Churchill Archives, Churchill College, Cambridge.

N. Astor, Reading University Library.

C.R. Attlee, Bodleian Library, Special Collections and Western Manuscripts, Oxford University.

A.W. Beaverbrook, House of Lords Record Office: The Parliamentary Archives.

R. Bruce Lockhart, House of Lords Record Office: The Parliamentary Archives.

R.A. Butler, Trinity College Library, Cambridge University.

A. Cadogan, Churchill Archives, Churchill College, Cambridge.

A.N. Chamberlain, Birmingham University, Special Collections Department.

W. Churchill, Churchill Archives Centre, Churchill College, Cambridge.

R.S. Cripps, Bodleian Library, Special Collections and Western Manuscripts, Oxford University.

P. Cunliffe-Lister, Churchill Archives Centre, Churchill College, Cambridge.

H.J. Dalton, London School of Economics Library, Archives Division.

G.G. Dawson, Bodleian Library, Special Collections and Western Manuscripts, Oxford University.

C. Eade, Churchill Archives Centre, Churchill College, Cambridge.

J.L. Garvin, Harry Ransom Humanities Research Center Library, University of Texas at Austin.

V. Gollancz, Modern Records Centre, Warwick University.

Lord Inverchapel, Bodleian Library, Special Collections and Western Manuscripts, Oxford University.

Lord Halifax, Manuscript Department, University of York.

B. Hamilton, House of Lords Record Office: The Parliamentary Archives.

O. Harvey, Manuscript Department, the British Museum.

L. Hore-Belisha, Churchill Archives, Churchill College, Cambridge.

T.W.H. Inskip, Churchill Archives Centre, Churchill College, Cambridge.

E.I.C. Jacob, Churchill Archives Centre, Churchill College, Cambridge.

J.M. Keynes, King's College, Archive Centre, Cambridge University.

B.H. Liddell Hart, Liddell Hart Centre for Military Archives, King's College, University of London.

D. Lloyd George, Department of Collection, National Library of Wales, Aberystwyth, and House of Lords Record Office: The Parliamentary Archives.

H.D. Margesson, Churchill Archives Centre, Churchill College, Cambridge.

G.C. Marshall, Marshall Museum, Lexington, Virginia.

W.T. Monckton, Bodleian Library, Special Collections and Western Manuscripts, Oxford University.

I. Montagu, People's History Museum, Manchester.

G. Murray, Bodleian Library, Special Collections and Western Manuscripts, Oxford University.

P.J. Noel-Baker, Churchill Archives, Churchill College, Cambridge.

Lord Passfield, London School of Economics Library, Archives Division.

H.L. Samuel, House of Lords Record Office: The Parliamentary Archives.

W. Seeds, papers with his granddaughter, Corinna Seeds, Hydra, Greece.

E.L. Spears, Churchill Archives Centre, Churchill College, Cambridge.

Lord Stamford papers, accessed by courtesy of his family.

A.J. Sylvester, diary and papers, Department of Collection, National Library of Wales, Aberystwyth, and House of Lords Record Office: The Parliamentary Archives.

R.G. Vansittart, Churchill Archives Centre, Churchill College, Cambridge.

B. Webb, London School of Economics Library, Archives Division.

United States

A.A. Berle papers, Franklin D. Roosevelt Library, Hyde Park, NY.

J.E. Davies papers, Washington, Library of Congress.

H.L. Hopkins papers, Franklin D. Roosevelt Library, Hyde Park, NY.

F. Kuh papers, Special Collections Research Center, George Washington University.

I. Litvinov papers, Stanford, Hoover Institution Archives.

G. Marshall papers, Marshall Research Library, Virginia.

A. Nekrich papers, Stanford, Hoover Institution Archives.

F.D. Roosevelt papers, Franklin D. Roosevelt Library, Hyde Park, NY.

W.H. Standley papers and diary, University of Southern California, Los Angeles.

H. Stimson, Manuscripts and Archives, Yale University Library, New Haven, Connecticut.

L. Truscott Papers, US Army Military History Institute, Carlisle, Pennsylvania.

Other

Ada Nilsson papers, Göteborgs universitetsbibliote, Sweden.

D. Ben-Gurion papers, Central Zionist Archives, Jerusalem.

Diaries, Memoirs and Biographies

Alliluyeva, S., *Twenty Letters to a Friend* (New York, 1967)

Amery, L.S., *My Political Life* (London, 1955)

Assarasson, V., *I Skuggan av Stalin* (Stockholm, 1963)

Aster, S., *Anthony Eden* (London, 1976)

Atholl, K.S., *Working Partnership* (London, 1958)

Ball, S. (ed.), *Parliament and Politics in the Age of Churchill and Attlee: The Headlam diaries 1935–1951* (London, 2000)

Banac, I. (ed.), *The Diary of Georgi Dimitrov, 1933–1949* (New Haven, CT, 2003)
Bardens, D., *Portrait of a Statesman* (London, 1955)
Barnes, J. and D. Nicholson (eds.), *The Empire at Bay: The Leo Amery diaries* (London, 1988)
Bartlett, V., *I Know What I Liked* (London, 1974)
Beddington-Behrens, E., *Look Back Look Forward* (London, 1963)
Beneš, E., *Memoirs of Dr Eduard Beneš* (London, 1954)
Beneš, E., *The Fall and Rise of a Nation: Czechoslovakia, 1938–1941* (New York, 2004)
Berezhkov, V.M., *At Stalin's Side: His interpreter's memoirs from the October Revolution to the fall of the dictator's empire* (Secaucus, NJ, 1994)
Beria, S., *Beria My Father: Inside Stalin's Kremlin* (Bristol, 2003)
Bilainkin, G., *Diary of a Diplomatic Correspondent* (London, 1942)
Bilainkin, G., *Maisky: Ten years ambassador* (London, 1944)
Bilainkin, G., *Second Diary of a Diplomatic Correspondent* (London, 1947)
Boothby, R., *Recollections of a Rebel* (London, 1978)
Bullard, J. and M. Bullard (eds.), *Inside Stalin's Russia: The diaries of Reader Bullard, 1930–1934* (Charlbury, 2000)
Butler, E., *Mason-Mac: The life of Lieutenant-General Sir Noel Mason-MacFarlane* (London, 1972)
Butler, R., *The Art of the Possible* (London, 1970)
Carlton, D., *Anthony Eden: A biography* (London, 1981)
Carswell, J., *The Exile: Life of Ivy Litvinov* (London, 1983)
Churchill, W.S., *The Second World War: The gathering storm* (London, 1948)
Churchill, W.S., *The Second World War: Their finest hour* (London, 1949)
Churchill, W.S., *The Second World War: The grand alliance* (London, 1950)
Churchill, W.S., *The Second World War: The hinge of fate* (London, 1950)
Citrine, W., *Men and Work: An autobiography* (London, 1964)
Clarke, P., *The Cripps Version: The life of Sir Stafford Cripps 1889–1952* (London, 2002)
Cohan, M.J. (ed.), *The Letters and Papers of Chaim Weizmann* (Jerusalem, 1979)
Colville, J., *The Fringes of Power: 10 Downing Street diaries 1939–1955* (London, 1985)
Crozier, W.P., *Off the Record: Political interviews, 1933–1943* (London, 1973)
Dalton, H., *The Fateful Years* (London, 1957)
Danchev, A. and D. Todman (eds.), *Alanbrooke: War diaries* (London, 2002)
Delpha, F. (ed.), *Les papiers secrets du Général Doumenc, un autre regard sur 1939–1940* (Paris, 1992)
Dilks, D. (ed.), *The Diaries of Sir Alexander Cadogan 1938–1945* (London, 1971)
Duranty, W., *The Kremlin and the People* (New York, 1942)
Dutton, D., *Neville Chamberlain* (London, 2001)
Eden, A., *The Eden Memoirs: Facing the dictators* (London, 1962)
Eden, A., *The Eden Memoirs: The reckoning* (London, 1965)
Ellsworth, B., *Wendell Willkie, Fighter for Freedom* (Michigan, 1966)
Epstein, J., *An Autobiography* (London, 1955)
Fischer, L., *Men and Politics: An autobiography* (London, 1941)

Gafencu, G., *Prelude to the Russian Campaign* (London, 1945)
Gilbert, M., *Winston S. Churchill*, Companion Vol. V, Part 3, *The Coming of War, 1936–1939* (London, 1982)
Gilbert, M., *Winston S. Churchill: Finest hour, 1939–1941* (London, 1983)
Gilbert, M., *Winston S. Churchill: Road to victory, 1941–1945* (London, 1986)
Gilbert, M. (ed.), *Winston Churchill and Emery Reves, Correspondence, 1937–1964* (London, 1997)
Gilbert, M. (ed.), *The Churchill War Papers* (New York and London, 2001)
Gilbert, M., *Winston S. Churchill: The prophet of truth, 1922–1939* (London, 2009)
Gleasor, J., *War at the Top: Based on the experiences of General Sir Leslie Hollis* (London, 1959)
Gnedin, E.A., *Vykhod iz labirinta* (Moscow, 1994)
Golikov, F.I., *On a Military Mission to Great Britain and the USA* (Moscow, 1987)
Golikov, F.I., 'Sovetskaya voennaya missiya v Anglii i SShA v 1941 g.', *Novaya i noveishaya istoriya*, 2 (2004)
Gollancz, V., *Reminiscences of Affection* (London, 1968)
Gorodetsky, G., *Stafford Cripps in Moscow, 1940–1942: Diaries and papers* (London, 2007)
Gromyko, A., *Memoirs* (London, 1989)
Gromyko, *Pamyatnoe* (Moscow, 1990)
Harriman, W.A. and E. Abel, *Special Envoy to Churchill and Stalin, 1941–1946* (New York, 1975)
Harvey, J. (ed.), *The Diplomatic Diaries of Oliver Harvey 1937–1940* (London, 1970)
Harvey, J. (ed.), *The War Diaries of Oliver Harvey, 1941–45* (London, 1978)
Hilger, G. and A. Meyer, *The Incompatible Allies: A memoir-history of German–Soviet relations, 1918–1941* (New York, 1950)
Hill, L., *Weizsäcker-Papiere, 1933–1950* (Berlin, 1996)
James, R.R., *Bob Boothby: A portrait* (London, 1991)
Karpov, V., *Generalissimus* (Moscow, 2012)
Kershaw, I., *Making Friends with Hitler: Lord Londonderry and the British road to war* (London, 2004)
Kessler, H., *The Diaries of a Cosmopolitan, 1917–37* (London, 1971)
Kharlamov, N., *Difficult Mission: War memoirs of a Soviet admiral in Great Britain during the Second World War* (London, 1986)
Khlevniuk, O. et al. (eds.), *Stalin i Kaganovich perepiska, 1931–1936 gg.* (Moscow, 2001)
Kimball, W.F. (ed.), *Churchill and Roosevelt: The complete correspondence* (Princeton, 1984)
Kitchen, M., *Speer: Hitler's architect* (London, 2015)
Knight, A., *Beria, Stalin's First Lieutenant* (Princeton, 1993)
Kokoschka, O., *My Life* (London, 1971)
Kollontay, A.M., *Diplomaticheskie dnevniki, 1922–1940* (Moscow, 2001)
Korotkov, A.V. and A.A. Chernobaev (eds.), 'Posetiteli kabineta Stalina: 1938–1939', *Istoricheskii Arkhiv*, 5–6 (1996)
Kotkin S., *Stalin: Paradoxes of power, 1878–1928* (London, 2014)

Kvashonkin, A.V. *Sovetskoe rukovodstvo: perepiska, 1928–1941* (Moscow, 1999)
Liddell Hart, B.H., *The Liddell Hart Memoirs* (London, 1965)
Lockhart, B., *Comes the Reckoning* (London, 1947)
MacKenzie, N. and J. MacKenzie (eds.), *The Diary of Beatrice Webb* (London, 1985)
Maclean, F., *Fitzroy Maclean* (London, 1992)
Maisky, I.M., *Sovremennaya Mongoliya* (Irkutsk, 1921)
Maisky, I.M., *Before the Storm* (London, 1943)
Maisky, I.M., 'Bernard Shou – Vstrechi i razgovory', *Novy Mir*, 1 (1961)
Maisky, I.M., *Journey into the Past* (London, 1962)
Maisky, I.M., *Who Helped Hitler?* (London, 1964)
Maisky, I.M., 'V Londone' in Ya.I. Koritskii, S.M. Melnik-Tukhachevskaya and B.N. Chistov (eds.), *Marshal Tukhachevskii: vospominaniya druzei i soratnikov* (Moscow, 1965)
Maisky, I.M., 'The British and I', *Atlas World Press Review*, 11 (1966)
Maisky, I.M. *Spanish Notebooks* (London, 1966)
Maisky, I.M., *Memoirs of a Soviet Ambassador: The war, 1939–43* (London, 1967)
Maisky, I.M., *B. Shou i drugie: Vospominaniya* (Moscow, 1967)
Maisky, I.M., *The Munich Drama* (Moscow, 1972)
Maisky, I.M., *Vospominaniya sovetskogo posla v Anglii* (Moscow, 1960)
Maisky, I.M., *Vospominaniya sovetskogo diplomata* (Moscow, 1987)
Mal'tsev, V. et al. (eds.), *Dokumenty po istorii myunkhenskogo sgovora 1937–1939* (Moscow, 1979)
Martin, K., *Editor* (London, 1968)
Martov, Y., 'Vospominaniya renegata', *Sotsialisticheskii vestnik*, 9 December 1922
McDonald, I., *A Man of the Times* (London, 1976)
Merekalov, A.F., 'Missiya polpreda Merekalova', *Voenno-istoricheskii zhurnal*, 12 (2002)
Mikoyan, A.I., *Tak bylo: Razmyshleniya o minuvshem* (Moscow, 1999)
Minney, R.J. (ed.), *The Private Papers of Hore-Belisha* (New York, 1961)
Montefiore, S., *Stalin: The court of the Red Tsar* (London, 2003)
Moran, Lord, *Churchill: Taken from the diaries of Lord Moran* (London, 1966)
Morrison, H., *An Autobiography by Lord Morrison of Lambeth* (London, 1960)
Myasnikov, V.S. (ed.), *Ivan Mikhailovich Maiskii: Izbrannaya perepiska s rossiiskimi korrespondentami* (Moscow, 2005)
Myasnikov, V.S. et al., *Ivan Mikhailovich Maiskii: Dnevnik diplomata, London, 1934–43* (Moscow, 2006)
Nekrich, A., *Forsake Fear: Memoirs of an historian* (London, 1991)
Nicolson, N., (ed.), *Harold Nicolson: Diaries and letters, 1939–1945* (London, 1967)
Novikov, N.V., *Vospominaniya diplomata: Zapiski 1938–1947* (Moscow, 1989)
Pares, B., *A Wandering Student: The story of a purpose* (London, 1948)
Sokolov, V.V., '"Avtobiograficheskie zametki" Pavlova – perevodchika I.V. Stalina', *Novaya i noveishaya istoriya*, 4 (2000)
Pawle, G., *The War and Colonel Warden: Based on the recollections of Commander Thompson, personal assistant to the prime minister, 1940–1945* (London, 1963)

Pechatnov, V.O. and E.E. Magadeev, *Perepiska I.V. Stalina s F. Ruzvel'tom i U. Cherchillem v gody Velikoi Otechestvennoi voiny* (Moscow, 2015)
Pimlott, B. (ed.), *The Political Diary of Hugh Dalton* (London, 1986)
Pimlott, B. (ed.), *The Second World War Diary of Hugh Dalton, 1940–45* (London, 1986)
Pritt, D.N., *The Autobiography of D.N. Pritt* (London, 1965)
Resis, A. (ed.), *Molotov Remembers: Inside Kremlin politics, conversations with Felix Chuev* (Chicago, 1993)
Retinger, J., *Memoirs of an Eminence Grise* (London, 1972)
Rhodes, R., (ed.), *Chips, the Diaries of Sir Henry Channon* (London, 1967)
Ribbentrop, J. von, *The Ribbentrop Memoirs* (London, 1954)
Roberts, A., *'The Holy Fox': A biography of Lord Halifax* (London, 1991)
Roberts, G., *Molotov: Stalin's cold warrior* (Washington, DC, 2011)
Roosevelt, E., *As He Saw It* (New York, 1946)
Roosevelt, E. (ed.), *F.D.R. His personal letters, 1928–1945* (New York, 1950)
Rose, N. (ed.), *Baffy: The diaries of Blanche Dugdale, 1936–1947* (London, 1973)
Rose, N., *Vansittart: Study of a diplomat* (London, 1978)
Rothenstein, J., *Brave Day Hideous Night, The Tate Gallery Years, 1939–1965* (London, 1966)
Rzheshevsky, O.A., *War and Diplomacy: The making of the Grand Alliance – documents from Stalin's archives* (London, 1996)
Sansom, A.W., *I Spied Spies* (London, 1965)
Self, R. (ed.), *The Neville Chamberlain Diary Letters: The heir apparent, 1928–33* (London, 2002)
Self, R. (ed.), *The Neville Chamberlain Diary Letters: The Downing Street years, 1934–40* (London, 2005)
Sheean, V., *Between the Thunder and the Sun* (London, 1943)
Sheinis, Z., *Maxim Litvinov* (Moscow, 1990)
Shustov, V. 'A.A. Sobolev: A portrait of excellence', *International Affairs*, 50/3 (2004)
Smart N., (ed.), *The Diaries and Letters of Robert Bernays, 1932–1939: An insider's account of the House of Commons* (London, 1996)
Smith, A. (ed.), *Hostage to Fortune: The letters of Joseph P. Kennedy* (New York, 2001)
Sokolov, V.V. (ed.), '"Avtobiograficheskie zametki" V.N. Pavlova – perevodchika I.V. Stalina', *Novaya i noveishaya istoriya*, 4 (2000)
Soviet Foreign Ministry, *Correspondence between the Chairman of the Council of Ministers of the USSR and the Presidents of the USA and the Prime Ministers of Great Britain during the Great Patriotic War of 1941–1945* (Moscow, 1957)
Spears, E., *Fulfilment of a Mission: The Spears mission to Syria and Lebanon, 1941–1944* (London, 1977)
Standley, W., *Admiral Ambassador to Russia* (Chicago, 1955)
Sudoplatov, P., *Special Tasks: The memoirs of an unwanted witness – a Soviet spymaster* (London, 1994)
Sylvester, A.J., *Life with Lloyd George: The diary of A.J. Sylvester, 1931–1945* (London, 1975)
Taylor, A.J.P. (ed.), *Lloyd George: A diary by Frances Stevenson* (London, 1971)

Taylor, A.J.P., *Beaverbrook* (London, 1972)

Tedder, Lord, *With Prejudice: The war memoirs of Marshal of the Royal Air Force, Lord Tedder* (London, 1966)

Trotsky, L., *The Revolution Betrayed* (London, 2004)

Troyanovskii, O., *Cherez gody i rasstoyaniya* (Moscow, 1997)

Utley, F., *Odyssey of a Liberal: Memoirs* (Washington, 1970)

Watson, D. *Molotov: A biography* (London, 2005)

Wearing J.P. (ed.), *Bernard Shaw and Nancy Astor* (Toronto, 2005)

Wedemeyer, A.C., *Wedemeyer Reports* (New York, 1958)

Weizsäcker, E. von, *Memoirs of Ernst von Weizsäcker* (London, 1951)

Werth, A., *Moscow '41* (London, 1942)

West, N., (ed.), *Guy Liddell Diaries* (London, 2005)

Wheeler-Bennett, J.W., *King George VI: His life and reign* (London, 1958)

Williams, F., *Nothing So Strange: An autobiography* (London, 1970)

Woodward, E.L. and R. Butler (eds.), *Documents on British Foreign Policy* (London, 1947–48)

Yakovlev, L., 'Ivan Mikhailovich Maiskii s suprugoyu svoeyu Agnei Aleksandrovnoi', *Shtrikhi k portretam i nemnogo lichnykh vospominanii* (Kharkov, 2005)

Young K., (ed.), *The Diaries of Sir Robert Bruce Lockhart* (London, 1980)

Zhukov, G.K., *Vospominaniya i razmyshleniya* (Moscow, 1990)

Secondary Sources

Addison, P., *The Road to 1945: British politics and the Second World War* (London, 1975)

Anderson, P. and A.O. Chubaryan (eds.), *Komintern i vtoraya mirovaya voina* (Moscow, 1994)

Andrew, C. and V. Mitrokhin, *The Mitrokhin Archive: The KGB in Europe and the West* (London, 1999)

Aster, S. 'Ivan Maisky and parliamentary anti-appeasement 1938–1939', in A.J.P. Taylor (ed.), *Lloyd George: Twelve essays* (London, 1971)

Aster, S., *1939: Making of the Second World War* (London, 1973)

Aster, S., 'Sir William Seeds: The diplomat as scapegoat?', in B.P. Farrell (ed.), *Leadership and Responsibility in the Second World War* (Montreal, 2004)

Aster, S., 'Appeasement: Before and after revisionism', *Diplomacy and Statecraft*, 19/3 (2008)

Aster, S. and T. Coates, *Dealing with Josef Stalin: The Moscow White Book, 1939* (London, 2009)

Baets, A. de, *Censorship of Historical Thought* (London, 2002)

Barker, E., *Churchill and Eden at War* (London, 1978)

Barros, J. and R. Gregor, *Double Deception: Stalin, Hitler, and the invasion of Russia* (Chicago, 1995)

Beck, P., 'Searching for peace in Munich, not Geneva: The British government, the League of Nations, and the Sudetenland question', *Diplomacy and Statecraft*, 10/2–3 (1999)

Beck, P., 'Searching for peace in Munich, not Geneva: The British government, the League of Nations and the Sudetenland question', in I. Lukes and E. Goldstein (eds.), *The Munich Crisis, 1938: Prelude to World War II* (London, 1999)

Beck, R.J. 'Munich's lessons reconsidered', *International Security*, 14/2 (1989)

Beevor, A., *The Battle for Spain: The Spanish Civil War, 1936–1939* (London, 2006)

Bell, P.M.H., *The Origins of the Second World War in Europe* (London, 1987)

Bell, P.M.H., *John Bull and the Bear: British public opinion, foreign policy, and the Soviet Union, 1941–1945* (London, 1990)

Ben-Tov, J., 'Contacts between Soviet Ambassador Maisky and Zionist leaders during World War II', *Soviet Jewish Affairs*, 8/1 (1978)

Bezymenskii, L., 'Al'ternativy 1939 goda: vokrug Sovetsko-Germankogo pakta 1939', in *Arkhivy raskryvayut tainy* (Moscow, 1991)

Bezymenskii, L., 'Dvenadtsat' minut iz zhizni posla Merekalova', *Novoe Vremya*, 7 (1996)

Bezymenskii, L., 'Sovetsko-germanskie dogovory 1939 g.', *Novaya i noveishaya istoriya*, 3 (1998)

Bezymenskii, L., *Gitler i Stalin pered skhvatkoi* (Moscow, 2009)

Bialer, U., 'Telling the truth to the people: Britain's decision to publish the diplomatic papers of the inter-war period', *The Historical Journal*, 26/2 (1983)

Bilainkin, G., 'Mr Maisky sees it through', *Contemporary Review*, 162 (1942)

Bilainkin, G., 'The Ivan Maisky legend', *Contemporary Review*, 211 (1967)

Bourette-Knowles, S., 'The Global Micawber: Sir Robert Vansittart, the Treasury and the global balance of power 1933–35', *Diplomacy and Statecraft*, 6/ 1 (1995)

Braithwaite, R., *Moscow 1941: A city and its people at war* (New York, 2006)

Brovkin, V.N., *The Mensheviks after October* (Ithaca, NY, 1987)

Carley, M.J., 'End of the "low, dishonest decade": Failure of the Anglo-Franco-Soviet alliance in 1939', *Europe-Asia Studies*, 45/2 (1993)

Carley, M.J., 'Down a blind-alley: Anglo-Franco-Soviet Relations, 1920–39', *Canadian Journal of History*, 29/1 (1994)

Carley, M.J., 'Generals, statesmen, and international politics in Europe, 1898–1945', *Canadian Journal of History*, XXX (1995)

Carley, M.J., 'Prelude to defeat: Franco-Soviet relations, 1919–39', *Historical Reflections*, 22/1 (1996)

Carley, M.J., '"A fearful concatenation of circumstances": The Anglo-Soviet rapprochement, 1934–6', *Contemporary European History*, 5 (1996)

Carley, M.J., *1939: The alliance that never was and the coming of World War II* (Chicago, 1999)

Carley, M.J., '"A situation of delicacy and danger": Anglo-Soviet relations, August 1939–March 1940', *Contemporary European History*, 8/2 (1999)

Carley, M.J., 'Soviet foreign policy in the West, 1936–1941: A review article', *Europe-Asia Studies*, 56/7 (2004)

Carley, M.J., 'A Soviet Eye on France from the Rue de Grenelle in Paris, 1924–1940, *Diplomacy and Statecraft*, 17 (2006)

Carley, M.J., 'Caught in a cleft stick: Soviet diplomacy and the Spanish Civil War', in Gaynor Johnson (ed.), *The International Context of the Spanish Civil War* (Newcastle upon Tyne, UK, 2009)

Carley, M.J., '"Only the USSR has … clean hands": The Soviet perspective on the failure of collective security and the collapse of Czechoslovakia, 1934–1938', *Diplomacy and Statecraft*, 21/3 (2010)

Carley, M.J., *Silent Conflict: A hidden history of early Soviet–Western relations* (London, 2014)

Charbonnières, G. de, *La plus evitable de toutes les guerres* (Paris, 1985)

Cienciala, A.M., 'Detective work: Researching Soviet World War II policy on Poland in Russian archives', *Cahiers du Monde Russe*, 40/1–2 (1999)

Cienciala, A.M., N.S. Lebedeva and W. Materski (eds.), *Katyn: A crime without punishment* (New Haven, CT, 2008)

Cocket, R., *Twilight of Truth: Chamberlain, appeasement, and the manipulation of the press* (New York, 1989)

Colvin, I., *Vansittart in Office* (London, 1965)

Colvin, I., *The Chamberlain Cabinet: How the meetings in 10 Downing Street, 1937–1939, led to the Second World War* (London, 1971)

Costigliola, F., *Roosevelt's Lost Alliances: How personal politics helped start the Cold War* (Princeton, 2012)

Crowson, N.J., *Facing Fascism: The Conservative Party and the European dictators, 1935–1940* (London, 1997)

Curtis, M. (ed.), *Documents on International Affairs. 1938*, Vol. 1 (London, 1939)

Danchev A., '"Dilly-Dally", or having the last word: Field Marshal Sir John Dill and Prime Minister Winston Churchill', *Journal of Contemporary History*, 22/1 (1987)

David-Fox, M., 'Stalinist Westernizer? Aleksandr Arosev's literary and political depictions of Europe', *Slavic Review*, 62/4 (2003)

David-Fox, M., *Showcasing the Great Experiment: Cultural diplomacy and Western visitors to the Soviet Union, 1921–1941* (Oxford, 2011)

Dorril, S., *MI6: Inside the covert world of Her Majesty's Secret Intelligence Service* (London, 2002)

Duggan, S., *A Professor at Large* (London, 1943)

Dullin, S., 'Litvinov and the People's Commissariat of Foreign Affairs: The fate of an administration under Stalin, 1930–39', in S. Pons and A. Romano (eds.), *Russia in the Age of Wars, 1914–1945* (Milan, 2000)

Dullin, S., *Des Hommes d'Influences: Les ambassadeurs de Staline en Europe, 1930–1939* (Paris, 2001)

Dullin, S., 'L'Union soviétique et la France à un tournant: conjoncture extérieure et évolution interne en 1936–1937', *Matériaux pour l'Histoire de Notre Temps*, 65–6 (2002)

Dullin, S., *Men of Influence: Stalin's diplomats in Europe, 1930–1939* (Edinburgh, 2008)

Dunn, D., 'Maksim Litvinov: Commissar of contradiction', *Journal of Contemporary History*, 23/2 (1988)

Duroselle, J.B., *Politique etrangere de la France. La decadence 1932–1939* (Paris, 1979)

Efimov, B. and V. Fradkin, *O vremenakh i lyudyakh* (Moscow, 2000)

Erickson, J., *The Road to Stalingrad* (New York, 1975)

Farnsworth, B., 'Conversing with Stalin, surviving the Terror: the diaries of Aleksandra Kollontai and the internal life of politics', *Slavic Review*, 69/4 (2010)

Farrell, B.P., 'Yes, Prime Minister: Barbarossa, Whipcord, and the basis of British grand strategy, Autumn 1941', *Journal of Military History*, 57/4 (1993)

Fenby, J., *Alliance: The inside story of how Roosevelt, Stalin and Churchill won one war and began another* (London, 2007)

Ferris, J.R., '"Indulged in all too little?"': Vansittart, intelligence and appeasement', *Diplomacy and Statecraft*, 6/1 (1995)

Fleischhauer, I., *Die Chance des Sonderfriedens* (Berlin, 1986)

Fleischhauer, I., *Der Pakt, Hitler, Stalin und die Initiative der Deutschen Diplomatie 1938–1939* (Berlin, 1990)

Folly, M., 'Seeking comradeship in the "ogre's den": Winston Churchill's quest for a warrior alliance and his mission to Stalin, August 1942', *Brunel University Research Papers*, 6/2 (2007)

Foster, A., 'The Beaverbrook press and appeasement: The second phase', *European History Quarterly*, 21/5 (1991)

Fry, 'Agents and structures: The dominions and the Czechoslovak Crisis, September 1938', *Diplomacy and Statecraft*, 10/2–3 (1999)

Gafencu, G., *Prelude to the Russian Campaign* (London, 1945)

Getty, J.A. and O.V. Naumov, *The Road to Terror: Stalin and the self-destruction of the Bolsheviks, 1932–1939* (New Haven, CT, 1999)

Ginat, R., *The Soviet Union and Egypt, 1945–1955* (London, 1994)

Glantz, D.M., *From the Don to the Dnepr: Soviet offensive operations, December 1942–August 1943* (London, 1991)

Glantz, D.M., 'Prelude to Kursk: Soviet strategic operations, February–March 1943', *The Journal of Slavic Military Studies*, 8/1 (1995)

Gorlizki, Y. and O. Khlevniuk, *Cold Peace: Stalin and the Soviet ruling circle, 1945–53* (Oxford, 2004)

Gorodetsky, G., *Stafford Cripps' Mission to Moscow, 1940–42* (Oxford, 1984)

Gorodetsky, G., 'Churchill warning to Stalin: A reappraisal', *The Historical Journal*, 29/4 (1986)

Gorodetsky, G., 'The Hess affair and Anglo-Soviet relations on the eve of "Barbarossa"', *English Historical Review*, 101/399 (1986)

Gorodetsky, G., *Grand Delusion: Stalin and the German invasion of Russia* (New Haven, CT, 1999)

Gorodetsky, G., 'Geopolitical factors in Stalin's strategy and politics in the wake of the outbreak of World War Two', in S. Pons and A. Romano (eds.), *Russia in the Age of Wars, 1914–1945* (Milan, 2000)

Gorodetsky, G., 'The Soviet Union's role in the creation of the State of Israel', *Israeli Studies*, 22/1 (2003)

Gorodetsky, G., *Stafford Cripps in Moscow, 1940–1942: Diaries and papers* (London, 2007)

Gorodetsky, G., *The Precarious Truce: Anglo-Soviet Relations, 1924–27* (Cambridge, UK, 2008)

Grayson, R.S., *Liberals, International Relations, and Appeasement: The Liberal Party, 1919–1939* (Abingdon, UK, 2001)

Harris, J., 'Encircled by enemies: Stalin's perceptions of the capitalist world, 1918–1941', *Journal of Strategic Studies*, 30/3 (2007)

Harrison, G.A., *Cross-Channel Attack* (Washington, DC, 1951)

Haslam, J., 'The Soviet Union and the Czechoslovakian Crisis of 1938', *Journal of Contemporary History*, 14/3 (1979)

Haslam J., *The Soviet Union and the Struggle for Collective Security in Europe, 1933–39* (New York, 1984)

Haslam, J., 'Soviet–German relations and the origins of the Second World War: The jury is still out', *Journal of Modern History*, 69/4 (1997)

Haslam, J., 'Stalin and the German invasion of Russia 1941: A failure of reasons of state?' *International Affairs*, 76/1 (2000)

Hellbek, J., *Revolution on my Mind: Writing a diary under Stalin* (Cambridge, MA, 2009)

Hinsley, F.H., *British Intelligence in the Second World War* (London, 1979)

Hochman, J., *The Soviet Union and the Failure of Collective Security, 1934–1938* (Ithaca, NY, 1984)

Hucker, D., 'The unending debate: Appeasement, Chamberlain and the origins of the Second World', *Intelligence and National Security*, 23/4 (2008)

Imlay, T., 'A reassessment of Anglo-French strategy during the phony war, 1939–40', *English Historical Review*, cxix, April (2004)

Irving, D., *Accident: The death of General Sikorski* (London, 1967)

Ivanov, I. et al. (eds.), *Essays on the History of the Russian Ministry of Foreign Affairs* (Moscow, 2002)

Jukes, J., 'The Red Army and the Munich Crisis', *Journal of Contemporary History*, 26/2 (1991)

Kennedy, P., *Strategy and Diplomacy, 1870–1945* (London, 1983)

Khaustov, V.N., V.P. Naumov and N.S. Plotnikov (eds.), *Lubyanka: Stalin i NKVD-NKGB-GUKR 'Smersh', 1939–1946* (Moscow, 2006)

Khlevniuk, O. 'The reasons for the "Great Terror": The foreign-political aspect', in S. Pons and A. Romano (eds.), *Russia in the Age of Wars, 1914–1945* (Milan, 2000)

Khlevniuk, O., *Master of the House* (New Haven, CT, 2009)

Kikuoka, M.T., *The Changkufeng Incident: A study in Soviet–Japanese conflict, 1938* (Lanham, MD, 1988)

King, C.H., *With Malice toward None: A war diary by Cecil H. King* (London, 1970)

Kitchen, M., *British Policy towards the Soviet Union during the Second World War* (London, 1986)

Kitchen, M. 'Winston Churchill and the Soviet Union during the Second World War', *The Historical Journal*, 30/2 (1987)

Kitchen, M., *Rommel's Desert War: Waging World War II in North Africa, 1941–1943* (Cambridge, UK, 2009)

Knight, A., *Who Killed Kirov? The Kremlin's greatest mystery* (New York, 1999)

Kocho-Williams, A., 'The Soviet diplomatic corps and Stalin's purges', *Slavonic and East European Review*, 86/1 (2008)

Koshkin, A.A., *Krakh strategii 'speloi khurmy'* (Moscow, 1989)

Kudryashov, S., 'Stalin and the Allies: Who deceived whom?' *History Today*, 45/5 (1995)

Lamb, R., *The Drift to War 1922–1939* (New York, 1991)

Lentin, A., *Lloyd George and the Lost Peace: From Versailles to Hitler, 1919–1940* (London, 2001)

Lévêque, F., 'La place de la France dans la strategie Soviétique de la fin de la guerre en Europe (fin 1942-fin 1945), *Matériaux pour l'Histoire de Notre Temps*, 36 (1994)

Levin, N., *The Jews in the Soviet Union from 1917 to the Present* (New York, 1991)

Liebich, A., 'Diverging paths: Menshevik itineraries in the aftermath of revolution', *Revolutionary Russia*, 4/1 (1991)

Lough, D., *No More Champagne: Churchill and his money* (London, 2015)

Lukacs, J., *June 1941: Hitler and Stalin* (New Haven, CT, 2006)

Lukes, I., *Czechoslovakia between Stalin and Hitler: The diplomacy of Edvard Beneš in the 1930s* (Oxford, 1996)

Lukes, I., *The Munich Crisis, 1938: Prelude to World War II* (London, 1999)

Lukes, I., 'Stalin and Czechoslovakia in 1938–39: An autopsy of a myth', *Diplomacy and Statecraft*, 10/2–3 (1999)

Maisky, I.M., 'Mirovaya ekonomicheskaya konferentsiya, 1933g. v Londone', in *Voprosy istorii*, 5 (1961)

Majd, M.G., *August 1941: The Anglo-Russian occupation of Iran and change of shahs* (Lanham, MD, 2012)

Mallett, R., 'Fascist foreign policy and official Italian views of Anthony Eden in the 1930s', *The Historical Journal*, 43/1 (2000)

Manne, R., 'The British decision for alliance with Russia, May 1939', *Journal of Contemporary History*, 9/3 (1974)

Manne, R., 'The Foreign Office and the failure of Anglo-Soviet rapprochement', *Journal of Contemporary History*, 16/4 (1981)

Martel, G. (ed.), *The Times and Appeasement: The journals of A.L. Kennedy, 1932–1939* (Cambridge, UK, 2000)

Mastny, V., 'Stalin and the prospects of a separate peace in World War II', *American Historical Review*, 77 (1972)

Mastny V., 'Reconsiderations: The Cassandra in the Foreign Commissariat – Maxim Litvinov and the Cold War', *Foreign Affairs*, 54 (1986)

Matloff M. and E.M. Snell, *Strategic Planning for Coalition Warfare, 1941–42* (Washington, DC, 1953)

Mawdsley, E., *The Russian Civil War* (London, 2001)

Mawdsley, E., *Thunder in the East: The Nazi-Soviet War 1941–1945* (London, 2005)

May, E.R., *Strange Victory: Hitler's conquest of France* (New York, 2000)

McDonald, I. (ed.), *The History of the Times*, V: *Struggle in war and peace: 1939–1966* (London, 1984)

McKercher, B.J.C., 'The last old diplomat: Sir Robert Vansittart and the verities of British foreign policy, 1903–30', *Diplomacy and Statecraft*, 6/1 (1995)

Moore, R.J., *Churchill, Cripps and India, 1939–1945* (Oxford, 1979)

Morgan, K.O., 'Lloyd George and Germany', *The Historical Journal*, 39/3 (1996)

Morrell, G.W., *Britain Confronts the Stalin Revolution: Anglo-Soviet relations and the Metro-Vickers crisis* (Ontario, 1995)

Murray, W., *Strategy for Defeat: The Luftwaffe 1935–1945* (Princeton, 2002)

Naveh, S., *In Pursuit of Military Excellence: The evolution of operational theory* (London, 1997)

Neilson, K., '"Pursued by a bear": British estimates of Soviet military strength and Anglo-Soviet relations, 1922', *Canadian Journal of History*, 28 (1993)

Neilson, K., *Britain, Soviet Russia and the Collapse of the Versailles Order, 1919–1939* (Cambridge, UK, 2006)

Nekrich, A., 'The arrest and trial of I.M. Maisky', *Survey*, 22/3–4 (1976)

Neville, P., 'Sir Alexander Cadogan and Lord Halifax's "Damascus Road" conversion over the Godesberg Terms 1938', *Diplomacy and Statecraft*, 11/3 (2000)

Neville, P., 'Lord Vansittart, Sir Walford Selby and the debate about Treasury interference in the conduct of British foreign policy in the 1930s', *Journal of Contemporary History*, 36/4 (2001)

Newton, S., *Profits of Peace: The political economy of Anglo-German appeasement* (Oxford, 1996)

Overy, R., *The Road to War* (London, 1999)

Overy, R., *The Battle of Britain: The myth and the reality* (London, 2002)

Overy, R.J. *The Dictators: Hitler's Germany and Stalin's Russia* (New York, 2004)

Owen, G.L., 'The Metro-Vickers crisis: Anglo-Soviet relations between trade agreements, 1932–1934', *Slavonic and East European Review*, 49/114 (1971)

Padover, S. (ed.), *On Education, Women, and Children* (New York, 1975)

Pares, B., *The New Russia* (London, 1931)

Pares, B., *Russia and the Peace* (London, 1944)

Parker, R.A.C., *Chamberlain and Appeasement: British policy and the coming of the Second World War* (London, 1993)

Peters, A.R., *Anthony Eden at the Foreign Office, 1931–1938* (Aldershot, 1986)

Phillips, H.D., *Between the Revolution and the West* (Boulder, CO, 1992)

Picknett, L., C. Prince and S. Prior, *Double Standards: The Rudolf Hess cover-up* (London, 2001)

Pinkus, B., *The Soviet Government and the Jews, 1948–1967* (Cambridge, UK, 2008)

Pons, S., *Stalin and the Inevitable War: 1936–1941* (London, 2002)

Prazmowska, A., *Britain, Poland and the Eastern Front, 1939* (Cambridge, UK, 1987)

Prazmowska, A., *Britain and Poland, 1939–1943: The betrayed ally* (Cambridge, UK, 1995)

Pritt, D.N. (ed.), *Soviet Peace Policy: Four speeches by V. Molotov* (London, 1941)

Radosh, R., M.R. Habeck and G. Sevostianov, *Spain Betrayed: The Soviet Union in the Spanish Civil War* (New Haven, CT, 2001)

Ragsdale, H., 'Soviet military preparations and policy in the Munich Crisis: New evidence', *Jahrbücher für Geschichte Osteuropas*, 47/2 (1999)

Ragsdale, H., *The Soviets, the Munich Crisis, and the Coming of World War II* (Cambridge, UK, 2004)

Resis, A., 'The fall of Litvinov: Harbinger of the German–Soviet non-aggression pact', *Europe-Asia Studies*, 52/1 (2000)

Reynolds, D., *The Creation of the Anglo-American Alliance 1937–1941: A study in competitive cooperation* (Chapel Hill, 1982)

Reynolds, D., 'Churchill's writing of history: Appeasement, Autobiography and *The Gathering Storm*', *Transactions of the Royal Historical Society*, 11 (2001)

Reynolds, D., *In Command of History: Churchill fighting and writing the Second World War* (London, 2005)

Roberts, G., 'The Soviet decision for a pact with Nazi Germany', *Soviet Studies*, 44/1 (1992)

Roberts, G., 'The fall of Litvinov: A revisionist view', *Journal of Contemporary History*, 27/4 (1992)

Roberts, G. 'Infamous encounter? The Merekalov–Weizsäcker meeting of 17 April 1939', *The Historical Journal*, 35/4 (1992)

Roberts, G., 'On Soviet–German relations: The debate continues', *Europe-Asia Studies*, 50/8 (1998)

Roberts, G., 'The fascist war threat and Soviet politics in the 1930s', in S. Pons and A. Romano (eds.), *Russia in the Age of Wars, 1914–1945* (Milan, 2000)

Roberts, G., 'Litvinov's lost peace, 1941–1946', *Journal of Cold War Studies*, 4/2 (2002)

Roberts, G., *Stalin's Wars: From World War to Cold War, 1939–1953* (London, 2007)

Roberts, G., *Masters and Commanders: How Roosevelt, Churchill and Alanbrooke won the war in the West* (London, 2008)

Roberts, G., 'Stalin, the pact with Nazi Germany, and the origins of postwar Soviet diplomatic historiography', *Journal of Cold War Studies*, 4/4 (2002)

Roi, M.L., 'From the Stresa Front to the Triple Entente: Sir Robert Vansittart, the Abyssinian crisis and the containment of Germany', *Diplomacy and Statecraft*, 6/1 (1995)

Roi, M.L., *Alternative to Appeasement: Sir Robert Vansittart and alliance diplomacy*, 1934–1937 (Westport, CT, 1997)

Roshchin, A., 'People's Commissariat for Foreign Affairs before World War II', *International Affairs* (May 1988)

Ross, G., 'Operation Bracelet: Churchill in Moscow, 1942', in David Dilks (ed.), *Retreat from Power* (London, 1981)

Rzheshevsky, O.A. (ed.), *1939. Uroki istorii* (Moscow, 1990)

Salmon, P., 'Great Britain, the Soviet Union and Finland at the beginning of the Second World War', in J. Hiden and T. Lane (eds.), *The Baltic and the Outbreak of the Second World War* (Cambridge, UK, 1992)

Samsonov, A.M. (ed.), *K 100-letiyu so dnya rozhdeniya akademika I.M. Maiskogo* (Moscow, 1984)

Sanford, G., *Katyn and the Soviet Massacre of 1940: Truth, justice and memory* (London, 2005)

Sanford, G., 'The Katyn Massacre and Polish–Soviet relations, 1941–1943', *Journal of Contemporary History*, 41/1 (2006)

Schellenberg, W., *Invasion 1940: The Nazi invasion plan for Britain* (London, 2000)

Schmidt, R.F., *Rudolf Hess: 'Botengang eines Toren?': der Flug nach Grossbritannien vom 10. Mai 1941* (Duesseldorf, 1997)

Service, R., *Trotsky: A Biography* (London, 2009)

Shaw, L.G., *The British Political Elite and the Soviet Union, 1937–1939* (London, 2003)

Sheinis, Z., 'Sud'ba diplomata, shtrikhi k portretu Borisa Shteina', in *Arkhivy raskryvayut tainy* (Moscow, 1991)

Sherwood, R.E., *Roosevelt and Hopkins: An intimate history* (New York, 1948)

Shukman, H. and A.O. Chubarian, *Stalin and the Soviet-Finnish War, 1939–1940* (London, 2002)

Sipols, V.Ya, *Vneshnaya politika Sovetskogo Soyuza 1936–1939* (Moscow, 1987)

Smele, J.D., *Civil War in Siberia: The anti-Bolshevik government* (Cambridge, UK, 1997)

Smith, D.C., *The Correspondence of H.G. Wells* (London, 1996)

Smith, S.B., *Captives of Revolution: The socialist revolutionaries and the Bolshevik dictatorship, 1918–1923* (Pittsburgh, 2011)

Smyth, D., 'The politics of asylum, Juan Negrín in 1940', in R. Langhorne (ed.), *Diplomacy and Intelligence during the Second World War* (Cambridge, UK, 1985)

Snyder, T., *Bloodlands: Europe between Hitler and Stalin* (New York, 2010)

Sokolov, V.V., 'Narkomindel Vyacheslav Molotov', *Mezhdunarodnaya zhizn'*, 5 (1991)

Sokolov, V.V., 'Tragicheskaya sud'ba diplomata G.A. Astakhova', *Novaya i noveishaya istoriya*, 1 (1997)

Sokolov, V.V., 'Dve vstrechi Sun Fo s I.V. Stalinym v 1938–1939gg.', *Novaya i noveishaya istoriya*, 6 (1999)

Sokolov, V.V., 'Molotov Vyacheslav Mikhailovich', *Diplomaticheskii vestnik* (July 2002)

Stafford, D. (ed.), *Flight from Reality: Rudolf Hess and his mission to Scotland, 1941* (London, 2002)

Stafford, P. 'Political autobiography and the art of the possible: R.A. Butler at the Foreign Office, 1938–1939', *The Historical Journal*, 28/4 (1985)

Steele, R.W., *The First Offensive 1942* (Bloomington, 1973)

Stegnii, P. 'Ivan Maisky's diary on the Molotov-Ribbentrop Pact', *International Affairs*, 6 (2009)

Stegnii, P. and V. Sokolov, 'Eyewitness testimony (Ivan Maiskii on the origins of World War II)', *International Affairs*, 154 (1999)

Steiner, Z., 'The Soviet Commissariat of Foreign Affairs and the Czechoslovakian Crisis in 1938: New material from the Soviet archives', *The Historical Journal*, 42/3 (1999)

Steiner, Z., *The Triumph of the Dark: European international history, 1933–1939* (Oxford, 2011)

Stickle, D.M. (ed.), *The Beria Affair: The secret transcripts of the meetings signalling the end of Stalinism* (New York, 1992)

Stoler, M., *The Politics of the Second Front* (Westport, CT, 1977)

Stoler, M., *Allies and Adversaries* (Chapel Hill, 2000)

Thomas, M., 'France and the Czechoslovak crisis', *Diplomacy and Statecraft*, 10/2–3 (1999)

Trubnikov, V.I., 'Sovetskaya diplomatiya nakanune Velikoi Otechestvennoi voiny: usiliya po protivodeistviyu fashistskoi agressii', *Voenno-istoricheskii zhurnal*, 7 (2001)

Uldricks, T., 'The impact of the Great Purges on the People's Commissariat of Foreign Affairs', *Slavic Review*, 6/2 (1977)

Uldricks, T., 'Soviet security policy in the 1930s', in G. Gorodetsky, *Soviet Foreign Policy, 1917–1991* (London, 1994)

Voyushin, V.A. and S.A. Gorlov, 'Fashistskaya agressiya: O chem soobshchali diplomaty', *Vizh*, 6 (1991)

Wark, W., 'Something very stern: British political intelligence, moralism and grand strategy in 1939', *Intelligence and National Security*, 5/1 (1990)

Watson, D., 'Molotov, the Grand Alliance and the second front', *Europe-Asia Studies*, 54/1 (2002)

Watt, D.C., 'Sir Nevile Henderson reappraised', *Contemporary Review*, March (1962)

Watt, D.C., *How War Came: The immediate origins of the Second World War 1938–1939* (London, 1989)

Wilt, A.F., 'The significance of the Casablanca decisions, January 1943', *Journal of Military History*, 55 (1991)

Zakharov, M.V., *General'nyi shtab v predvoennye gody: voennye memuary* (Moscow, 1989)

Zubok V. and C. Pleshakov, *Inside the Kremlin's Cold War: From Stalin to Khrushchev* (Boston, 1996)

Illustration Credits

Photographs from Agniya Maisky's album are published with the permission of the Voskressenski family, owners of the copyright and Ivan Maisky's heirs.

The following illustrations are from the private photo albums of Ivan and Agniya Maisky, deposited in the archives of the Russian Academy of Sciences and reproduced here by courtesy of the Scheffer-Voskressenski family, the copyright owners: numbers 1, 3–17, 20–24, 29–42, 44–54, 57–59, 61–62, 64–80, 82–106, 108–128. Numbers 18–19 and 25–28 are reproduced by courtesy of the Russian Foreign Ministry. I would like to thank Corinna Seeds for the rare photo (55) of her father, Sir William Seeds. The David Low cartoons, figures 43, 56, 60, 63 and 107, are published by permission of the *London Evening Standard*. Figure 81 is reproduced by courtesy of the late Lady Anne Theresa Ricketts (Cripps).

Index of Names and Places

Page numbers in *italics* indicate photographs. For longer entries, **boldface** bracketed numbers indicate years. As the thread of the narrative of the entire diary is the relations between the Soviet Union, Britain and France, and the reader will encounter them on almost every page of the diary, the references to these countries were excluded from the index.